Financial Reporting and Statement Analysis

A Strategic Perspective

FOURTH EDITION

Clyde P. Stickney Paul R. Brown

FINANCIAL REPORTING AND STATEMENT ANALYSIS

A Strategic Perspective

FOURTH EDITION

CLYDE P. STICKNEY
Amos Tuck School of Business Administration
Dartmouth College

PAUL R. BROWN
Leonard N. Stern School of Business
New York University

THE DRYDEN PRESS
HARCOURT BRACE COLLEGE PUBLISHERS
Fort Worth   Philadelphia   San Diego   New York   Orlando   Austin   San Antonio
Toronto   Montreal   London   Sydney   Tokyo

Publisher:	GEORGE PROVOL
Executive Editor:	MIKE REYNOLDS
Product Manager:	DEBBIE ANDERSON
Developmental Editor:	JESSICA FIORILLO
Project Editor:	JIM PATTERSON
Art Director:	BURL DEAN SLOAN
Production Manager:	EDDIE DAWSON

Cover Photographer: Hiroshi Sakuramoto with Photonica

ISBN: 0-03-023811-0
Library of Congress Catalog Card Number: 98-70563

Address for orders:
The Dryden Press
6277 Sea Harbor Drive
Orlando, FL 32887-6777
1-800-782-4479

Address for editorial correspondence:
The Dryden Press
301 Commerce Street, Suite 3700
Fort Worth, TX 76102

Web site address:
http://www.hbcollege.com

The Dryden Press, Dryden, and the Dryden Press logo are registered trademarks of Harcourt Brace & Company.

Printed in the United States of America

8 9 0 1 2 3 4 5 6 7   039   9 8 7 6 5 4 3 2 1

The Dryden Press
Harcourt Brace College Publishers

For our students,
with thanks for permitting us to take the journey with you

THE DRYDEN PRESS SERIES IN ACCOUNTING

The effective analysis of a set of financial statements requires an understanding of (1) the economic characteristics and current conditions of a firm's businesses, (2) the particular strategies the firm selects to compete in each of these businesses, and (3) the accounting principles and procedures underlying the firm's financial statements. Equipped with these three essential building blocks, the analyst can assess the success of the strategies as measured by profitability, relative to the level of risk involved. The analyst can then use this information to project the firm's future earnings and cash flows as a basis for valuation. This three-fold approach to financial statement analysis elevates it from one involving the mechanical calculation of a long list of financial statement ratios to one where the analyst has an opportunity to integrate concepts from economics, business strategy, accounting, and other business disciplines. This synthesizing experience rewards the student both intellectually and practically.

The premise of this book is that students learn financial statement analysis most effectively by performing the analysis on actual companies. The text portion of the book sets forth the important concepts and analytical tools and demonstrates their application using the financial statements of The Coca- Cola Company. Each chapter contains a set of problems and/or cases based for the most part on financial data of actual companies. A financial statement analysis package (FSAP) that runs on a PC computer with Excel is available to aid in the analytical tasks.

OVERVIEW OF TEXT

This section describes briefly the content of each chapter, indicating the major changes made since the previous edition.

Chapter 1 introduces five key interrelated sequential steps in financial statement analysis that serve as an organization structure for the book: (1) identifying economic characteristics of a firm's businesses; (2) identifying the strategies a firm follows to compete in its industries; (3) understanding and cleansing the financial statements; (4) performing profitability and risk analyses; and (5) valuing a firm or using the analysis for some other purpose. Chapter 1 presents several frameworks for assessing the industry economics and business strategies of a firm. It also reviews the purpose and content of each of the three principal financial statements, including those of non-U.S. companies appearing in a different format. End-of-chapter material includes three new "ratio detective" problems as well as an integrated review case involving Nike.

Chapter 2 reviews the statement of cash flows and presents a model for relating the cash flows from operating, investing, and financing activities to a firm's position in its product life cycle. The chapter demonstrates procedures for preparing the statement of cash flows when a firm provides no cash flow information. Several new interpretative problems, as well as a new "ratio detective" problem involving the statement of cash flows appears at the end of the chapter.

Chapter 3 introduces analytical tools for assessing profitability and risk. Our experience in using previous editions is that profitability and risk analysis serves as a useful framework for studying the effects of alternative accounting principles discussed in Chapters 4 through 7. Thus, Chapter 3 introduces the analytical tools. Chapters 8 and 9 explore in greater depth the economic and strategic factors affecting the interpretation of the financial statement ratios. Chapter 3 contains new or updated problem and case material using companies such as Jumbosports, Hasbro, Lands' End, Microsoft, Wal-Mart, The Gap and The Limited that are of high interest to students.

Chapter 4 discusses the concept of the quality of earnings, with the associated concepts of earnings sustainability, earnings measurement, and earnings management. It describes and illustrates earnings quality issues that the analyst should address before embarking on a financial statement analysis, including nonrecurring income items (restructuring charges, asset impairments, discontinued operations, extraordinary items, changes in accounting principles, changes in estimates), the use of originally reported versus restated data (related to acquisitions and divestitures), the effect of alternative accounting principles, and the impact of different reporting periods. The chapter includes substantial new material on the nature and analytical treatment of nonrecurring income items because of their increasing prevalence in corporate annual reports. It contains three new problems and an updated case study of International Paper Company related to nonrecurring income items. The chapter also summarizes alternative accounting principles in major industrialized countries and contains problems or cases involving firms in the United Kingdom, Italy, and Japan.

Chapter 5 introduces the concept of the quality of financial position, the balance sheet counterpart to the quality of earnings. The chapter discusses alternative accounting principles that primarily affect the analysis of profitability, including income recognition, inventory cost-flow assumption, and accounting for depreciable and intangible assets. Appendix 5.1 contains a discussion of accounting for the effects of changing prices. This topic is important as developing countries play an increasing role in international markets. Updated problem materials involve Deere (income recognition), USX (inventory cost-flow and depreciation method), and chemical companies (depreciation method). Problems or cases new to the last edition but which have worked well include Chiron (research and development arrangements), Chilgener (Chilean firm involving changing prices) and Corporacion Industrial Sanluis (Mexican firm involving changing prices). Case 5.4 is a new case examining the capitalization of subscriber acquisition costs by American Online. The Arizona Land Development case (Case 5.1) continues to be a rich illustration of the effect of alternative income recognition methods.

Chapter 6 continues the discussion of the quality of financial position by examining topics that primarily affect the assessment of risk, including off-balance sheet financing arrangements, derivative financial instruments, leases, pension and other retirement benefits, income taxes, and reserves. The chapter incorporates new reporting standards on derivative securities and other financial instruments, and pensions and other retirement benefits. The problem material at the end of the chapter emphasizes the interpretation of disclosures related to these reporting issues taken from annual reports of publicly held companies. Case 6.1 analyzes the effect of operating leases and underfunded pension and health care obligations on the risk assessments of American Airlines and United Airlines. Case 6.2 interprets the income tax position of Sun Microsystems. Case 6.3 illustrates the use of reserves by CIFRA, a Mexican company, to shift earnings between accounting periods.

Chapter 7 explores accounting principles that affect many accounts on the financial statements, including corporate acquisitions, investments in securities, foreign currency translation, and segment reporting. The chapter incorporates the new reporting standard on segment reporting. Case 7.1 (Fisher Corporation) illustrates the effects of accounting, tax, and financing decisions on the structure of a corporate acquisition and the related financial statement impact. Case 7.2 (Clark Equipment Company) analyzes the effect on the financial statements of alternative ways of accounting for a joint venture. Case 7.3 (Loucks Corporation) illustrates the choice of a functional currency and the financial statement impact of alternative methods of foreign currency translation.

Chapter 8 discusses economic factors (degree of capital intensity, regulation, and other barriers to entry, stage in the product life cycle, and commodity nature of products) and strategic factors (product differentiation versus low cost leadership) that affect the interpretation of the rate of return on assets and the rate of return on common shareholders' equity. The chapter also describes techniques for analyzing the profitability of high technology, service, capital-intensive, and retailing firms. This chapter and Chapters 9 to 12 now includes both problem and case materials at the end of the chapter, whereas the previous edition included only cases. New problems involve the analysis of Kelly Services, La Quinta Inns, Prime Hospitality, Brinker International, Wendy's, Wells Fargo, J.P. Morgan, AT&T, British Telecommunications, and Nippon Telephone & Telegraph. Three new problems ask students to suggest economic and strategic reasons for differences in the rates of return of segments of various industries or over time for particular industries. Case 8.1 analyzes Hewlett-Packard and Sun Microsystems, competitors in the engineering workstation computer market. Case 8.2 is a new case involving the three leading firms in the cellular phone industry, Ericsson (Sweden), Motorola (U.S.), and Nokia (Finland). These cases serve as excellent synthesizing experiences for students of the material covered in the first eight chapters of the book. The cases contain the necessary information for students to adjust the financial statements for nonrecurring income items, operating leases, and similar factors. The financial statement analysis package (FSAP) available with the text contains data files for the companies used in the cases.

Chapter 9 explores risk analysis in greater depth than the introduction in Chapter 3. The emphasis is on the prediction of financial distress. The chapter includes an expanded discussion of the analysis of credit risk. It also incorporates research on bankruptcy prediction and presents both discriminant and logit prediction models. Case 9.1 (Massachusetts Stove Company) involves a credit lending decision to a small, privately held wood stove company in an industry experiencing downsizing. Case 9.2 (Fly-By-Night International Group) involves bankruptcy prediction and raises ethical questions about dealings between a firm and its chief executive officer who is also its majority shareholder. Case 9.3 (Millenial Technologies) is a new case that asks students to detect signals of potential fraudulent reporting and to analyze both credit and bankruptcy risk. Case 9.4 (Kroger) studies the effect of a special dividend to fight a hostile takeover on the firm's risk.

Chapter 10 describes and illustrates the procedures for preparing pro forma financial statements. This material plays an important role in the valuation of companies discussed in Chapters 11 and 12. Appendix 10.1 includes a detailed description of the procedure for preparing an Excel spreadsheet for pro forma financial statements for Coke. Short problems illustrate techniques for determining the cost structure of a firm and dealing with irregular changes in accounts. Longer problems require the preparation of pro forma financial statements for cases discussed in earlier chapters involving Wal-Mart (Case 3.1), The Gap and The Limited (Case 3.2), and Massachusetts Stove Company (Case 9.1). Case 10.1 illustrates the preparation of pro forma financial statements for McDonald's under two scenarios: one involving greater use of franchising and one involving decreased use of franchising. Case 10.2 is a follow-up case to Case 9.1 in which pro forma financial statements are prepared to assist in a decision to add gas stove to the firm's wood stove line. The problems and cases in this chapter specify the pro forma assumptions students are to use to illustrate the preparation procedure. The cases in Chapters 11 and 12 require students to make their own pro forma assumptions.

Chapters 11 and 12 include an expanded discussion of valuation. Chapter 11 explores cash-based approaches to valuation, with emphasis on the present value of future cash flows. The chapter considers various issues in applying this valuation model, including the appropriate measure of cash flows, the measurement of the terminal value, and the nature of the discount rate. New problem material explores the effect of residual values on valuation, the calculation of the cost of capital, and the valuation of leveraged buyout candidates. Case 11.1 (Holmes Corporation) involves a leveraged buyout and serves as an excellent introduction to valuation because the company is not particularly complex. It includes sufficient information to value the firm using both cash-based approaches (Chapter 11) and earnings-based approaches (Chapter 12). Case 11.2 (Rodriguez Home Center) involves the valuation of the equity of a retail store using both cash-based and earnings-based approaches.

Chapter 12 discusses the use of price-earnings ratios and market value to book value of shareholders' equity to value companies. This chapter explores recent research that attempts to link earnings and book values with stock prices. The research underlying the material in this chapter is still evolving. New problem material involves the application of the theoretical price-earnings and market value to book value models to firms in retailing, consumer products, and pharmaceutical industries. Case 12.1 (Revco) involves valuation in a fraudulent conveyance case. Case 12.2 (Kleen Cleaners) relates to pricing an initial public offering of a rapidly growing company.

Appendix A includes the financial statements and notes for Coke. The text makes frequent references to these financial statements. Appendix B includes Coke's management discussion of its operations and financial position, as well as a description of the firm's business strategy. We incorporate material from Appendix B in the interpretations of Coke's profitability and risk throughout the text. Appendix C includes a printout of the FSAP, the financial statement analysis package available with the text, for Coke.

Significant Changes in this Edition

The preceding section discussed the major changes in this edition, which are summarized below.

1. Chapter 1 sets forth five interrelated sequential steps in financial statement analysis that provide the organization structure for the entire text. Chapter 1 also introduces frameworks for understanding the economic attributes of a business, including Porter's five forces, value chain analysis and economic value added, and an economic attributes framework.
2. Chapter 4 includes an extensive discussion of the concept of the quality of earnings and Chapter 5 includes a discussion of the quality of financial position. We use the concepts as an integrative theme throughout the discussion of various generally accepted accounting principles in Chapters 5 to 7.
3. Chapter 8 includes new material on analyzing the profitability of firms in technology, service, retailing, and capital-intensive industries.
4. Chapter 9 includes an expanded discussion of the analysis of credit risk.
5. Appendix 10.1 describes the procedure for preparing an Excel spreadsheet for pro forma financial statements.
6. Chapters 11 and 12 include an expanded discussion of cash-based and earnings-based approaches to valuation, incorporating recent research linking accounting data and stock prices.
7. The chapters contain substantially new assignment material, with 82 new problems and 11 new cases. Chapters 8 to 12 now contain problems as well as cases. The problems and cases use more companies of high interest to students, including Sun Microsystems, Lands' End, Microsoft, Nike, McDonald's, Wal-Mart, Nokia, America Online, and others.

Overview of the Ancillary Package

A financial statement analysis package (FSAP) is available free to all adopters of the text. The package performs various analytical tasks (common size and trend statements, ratio computations) and displays the results both numerically and graphically. By altering data files for the companies in the cases (also included), students can study the impact of the capitalization of operating leases, the conversion from LIFO to FIFO, the elimination of nonrecurring income items, and similar adjustments of reported data. Using FSAP to perform the tedious number crunching frees time and energy that the analyst can devote to the important interpretive task.

An Instructor's Manual is also available to adopters. It contains suggestions for using the textbook, solutions to problems, and teaching notes to cases.

ACKNOWLEDGMENTS

Many individuals provided invaluable assistance in the preparation of this book and we wish to acknowledge their help in a formal manner here.

The following professional colleagues have assisted in the development of this edition by reviewing or providing helpful comments on the previous edition:

Rick Antle, Yale University

M.D. Beneish, Indiana University

Howard Bunsiss, Southern Methodist Univeristy

James Largay, Lehigh University

Krish Menon, Boston University

Stephen Penman, University of California at Berkeley

Tom Selling, American Graduate School of International Management

Virginia Soybel, Babson College

Steve Sung, Dartmouth College

Gary Waters, Auburn University

We want to thank Jessica Fiorillo of The Dryden Press for her guidance and enthusiasm as developmental editor and Jim Patterson of The Dryden Press for his patience and level-headedness as project editor. The following individuals at The Dryden Press also contributed to the development, production, and marketing of this edition: Mike Reynolds, Debbie Anderson, Burl Sloan, Eddie Dawson, Linda Blundell, and Kimberly Powell.

Pat Peat did a superb job of copyediting the manuscript. Sarah Leonard wrote the software for the Financial Statement Analysis Package included with the text and assisted, along with David Shelton of The Dryden Press, in preparing a Web page with the software. Thanks also to Horngjun (Tony) Shieh of New York University, who checked the solutions to all of the problems and cases.

We owe a particular debt of gratitude to Tammy Stebbins, whose organizational skills, perseverance, and patience have kept us going. Thanks, Tammy.

Finally, we wish to acknowledge the role played by former students in our financial accounting and financial statement analysis courses at The Amos Tuck School of Business Administration, Dartmouth College, and the Leonard N. Stern School of Business, New York University. Learning is a mutual endeavor, and you have certainly been challenging and encouraging partners. This book is dedicated to each of you with thanks.

Clyde P. Stickney
Paul R. Brown

ABOUT THE AUTHORS

CLYDE P. STICKNEY is the Signal Companies Professor of Management at the Amos Tuck School of Business Administration, Dartmouth College. He received his doctoral degree from Florida State University and served on the faculties of the University of Chicago and the University of North Carolina at Chapel Hill before joining the faculty of the Tuck School in 1977. He has also taught at the International University of Japan, Swinburne Institute of Technology, and Helsinki School of Economics and Business Administration.

Professor Stickney's teaching and research interests center around the interpretation and analysis of financial statements. Recent research has examined the impact of different accounting principles on U.S. versus Japanese price-earnings ratios, the use of financial statement ratios to infer the content, and to evaluate the success, of corporate-level strategies. He has authored and co-authored books on financial accounting, managerial accounting, and financial statement analysis. Professor Stickney is a member of the American Accounting Association.

PAUL R. BROWN, Ph.D., CPA is Chairman of the Department of Accounting, Taxation and Business Law of the Leonard N. Stern School of Business, New York University. He received his doctoral degree from the University of Texas at Austin and has served on the faculties of the Yale School of Organization and Management and INSEAD. He is the founding editor-in-chief of *The Journal of Financial Statement Analysis*. The journal is published by Institutional Investor with the objective of enhancing the understanding and interpretation of an firm's activities in the context of financial statements.

Professor Brown has published extensively in both *The Journal of Financial Statement Analysis* and a wide range of other academic and professional publications. Recent research has examined regulatory issues related to auditor independence, and the importance of industry-specific factors when assessing firms in the biotechnology and high technology industries. Prior to entering academe, he worked as an auditor for Arthur Andersen & Co., and as a staff member of the Financial Accounting Standards Board. Professor Brown is a member of both the American Institute of Certified Public Accountants and the American Accounting Association.

BRIEF CONTENTS

Contents

PART I

FOUNDATION FOR EFFECTIVE FINANCIAL STATEMENT ANALYSIS

INTERRELATED SEQUENTIAL STEPS IN FINANCIAL STATEMENT ANALYSIS

1. Identify Economic Characteristics

2. Identify Company Strategies

3. Understand and Cleanse the Financial Statements

4. Analyze Profitability and Risk

5. Value the Firm

Part I provides a broad overview of each of the five, interrelated sequential steps in financial statement analysis. This part places particular emphasis on the first and second steps to underscore the importance of industry knowledge to effective financial statement analysis. Cash flows are discussed in this part in the context of industry analysis as well.

Financial analysts study financial statements to understand a firm's success in the past and to project its likely future performance. A study of a firm's financial reports is not undertaken in a vacuum, however. Rather, the analysis is attached to a study of the industry in which the firm operates and the strategies pursued by the firm to compete within its industry. Armed with an understanding of (1) the industry, (2) firm strategies, and (3) rules employed by the firm to prepare its financial statements, analysts assess the firm's profitability or risk. Often times the culmination of the analysts' work is firm valuation.

Part I, chapters 1 to 3, describes and illustrates a comprehensive approach to effective analysis of financial statements. A model for assessing a firm's cash flows, as well as its profitability and risk, is presented in these chapters and is explored in greater depth in subsequent parts of the book. Part I examines the following:

CHAPTER 1 OVERVIEW OF FINANCIAL REPORTING AND FINANCIAL STATEMENT ANALYSIS

Framework for Effective Financial Statement Analysis; Industry Economics and Firm Strategies; Principal Financial Statements and Notes; Sources of Financial Information.

CHAPTER 2 INCOME FLOWS VERSUS CASH FLOWS: KEY RELATIONSHIPS IN UNDERSTANDING THE DYNAMICS OF A BUSINESS

Preparation of the Statement of Cash Flows; Net Income and Cash Flows from Operations; Understanding Cash Flow Patterns of Various Industries; Cash Flows and Firm Life Cycles.

CHAPTER 3 INTRODUCTION TO PROFITABILITY AND RISK ANALYSIS

Operating Profitability; Assessing Return to the Common Shareholders; Short-term Liquidity Risk; Long-term Solvency Risk; Earnings Per Common Share.

CHAPTER 1

OVERVIEW OF FINANCIAL REPORTING AND FINANCIAL STATEMENT ANALYSIS

Learning Objectives

1. Understand the links among the economic characteristics and strategies of a business, its financial statements and notes, assessments of its profitability and risk, and its market valuation.
2. Review the purpose, underlying concepts, and format of the balance sheet, income statement, and statement of cash flows.
3. Learn the sources of financial information about publicly held firms.

Financial statements portray the operating performance and financial health of a business firm for periods such as three months (quarterly reports) or a year (annual reports). Financial analysts study financial statements both to evaluate the organization's past success in conducting its activities and to project its likely future performance.

Common reasons for performing financial statement analysis include:

1. Making an investment in a firm's common or preferred stock.
2. Extending credit, either for a short-term period (for example, a bank loan used to finance accounts receivable or inventories) or for a longer-term period (for example, a bank loan or public bond issue used to finance the acquisition of property, plant, or equipment).

3. Assessing the operating performance and financial health of a supplier, customer, or competitor.
4. Valuing a firm in settings such as the initial public offering of its common stock, as an acquisition candidate, in court-directed bankruptcy hearings, or in liquidation actions.
5. Forming a judgment about damages sustained in a lawsuit.
6. Forming an opinion on a client's financial statements with respect to whether the client is a "going concern."
7. Assessing whether combinations in an industry might generate unreasonable (monopoly) returns, thus prompting antitrust action by government regulators.

OVERVIEW OF FINANCIAL STATEMENT ANALYSIS

The effective analysis of financial statements requires five interrelated, sequential steps, as depicted in Exhibit 1.1:

1. **Identify the economic characteristics of the particular industry.** For example, does the industry include a large number of firms selling similar products, such as grocery stores, or is it characterized by a smaller number of competitors selling unique products, such as pharmaceutical companies? Does technological change play an important role in a firm's maintaining a competitive advantage, as in computer software? Are industry sales growing rapidly, as in Internet services, or is demand growing slowly, as with lumber products?
2. **Identify the strategies that a particular firm pursues to gain competitive advantage.** Are its products designed to meet the needs of specific market segments, such as ethnic or health foods, or are they intended for a broader consumer market, such as cafeterias and family restaurants? Has the firm integrated backward into the growing or manufacturing of raw materials for its products, such as a steel company that owns iron mines? Has the firm integrated forward into retailing to final consumers, such as an athletic footwear manufacturer that operates retail stores to sell its products? Is the firm diversified across several geographic markets or industries?
3. **Understand the financial statements of the particular firm and cleanse them of nonrecurring and unusual items.** Has the firm prepared its financial statements in accordance with generally accepted accounting principles (GAAP) of the United States, Japan, Brazil, or some other country, or are finan-

---

EXHIBIT 1.1

Interrelated Sequential Steps in Financial Statement Analysis

1. Identify Economic Characteristics	2. Identify Company Strategies	3. Understand and Cleanse the Financial Statements	4. Analyze Profitability and Risk	5. Value the Firm

cial statements prepared in accordance with GAAP of the International Accounting Standards Committee (IASC)? Do earnings include nonrecurring gains and losses, such as a writedown of an obsolete plant, that the analyst should either disregard or weigh less heavily than recurring components of earnings? Has the firm structured transactions or selected accounting principles that make it appear more profitable or less risky than economic conditions otherwise suggest?

4. **Assess the profitability and risk of the firm using information in the financial statements.** Most financial analysts assess the profitability of a firm relative to the risks involved. Assessments of most recent profitability provide a basis for projecting likely future profitability and thus the likely future returns from investing in the company. Assessments of a firm's ability to deal with risks, particularly those elements of risk with measurable financial consequences, permit the analyst to estimate the likelihood that the firm will experience financial difficulties in the future.

5. **Value the particular firm.** Perhaps the most frequent application of financial statement analysis is to value companies. Financial analysts issue buy, sell, and hold recommendations on companies when they think the stock price is too low, too high, or about right. Investment banking firms that underwrite initial public offerings of a firm's common stock must set the initial offering price. Translating information from financial statements into "appropriate" stock prices is perhaps as much art or psychology as it is science, but it is the principal activity of security analysts.

These five steps describe the subject matter of this book, and this chapter explores each of the steps briefly. Throughout the book we use financial statements, notes, and other information provided by The Coca-Cola Company (Coke) to illustrate the various topics discussed.

Appendix A at the end of the book provides the financial statements and notes for Coke for a recent year, as well as independent auditor and management opinions regarding the financial statements. Appendix B includes a financial review provided by management that discusses Coke's business strategy and offers explanations for changes in its profitability and risk over time. Appendix C presents the output of a software analysis package showing Coke's profitability and risk ratios for five years.

IDENTIFY THE INDUSTRY ECONOMIC CHARACTERISTICS

The economic characteristics of an industry play a key role in dictating the sorts of financial relationships the analyst might expect to see in a set of financial statements. Consider, for example, the data for firms in four different industries in Exhibit 1.2. This exhibit expresses all items on the balance sheet and income statement as a percentage of sales revenue.

EXHIBIT 1.2

Common Size Financial Statement Data for Four Firms

	Grocery Store Chain	Pharmaceutical Company	Electric Utility	Commercial Bank
Balance Sheet at End of Year				
Cash and Marketable Securities	0.7%	11.0%	1.5%	261.9%
Accounts and Notes Receivable	0.7	18.0	7.8	733.5
Inventories	8.7	17.0	4.5	—
Property, Plant, and Equipment (net)	22.2	28.7	159.0	18.1
Other Assets	1.9	72.8	29.2	122.6
Total Assets	34.2%	147.5%	202.0%	1,136.1%
Current Liabilities.	7.7%	30.8%	14.9%	936.9%
Long-Term Debt	7.6	12.7	130.8	71.5
Other Noncurrent Liabilities.	2.6	24.6	1.8	27.2
Shareholders' Equity	16.3	79.4	54.5	100.5
Total Equities	34.2%	147.5%	202.0%	1,136.1%
Income Statement for Year				
Sales Revenue	100.0%	100.0%	100.0%	100.0%
Cost of Goods Sold	(74.1)	(31.6)	(79.7)	—
Operating Expenses.	(19.7)	(37.1)	—	(41.8)
Research and Development.	—	(10.1)	—	—
Interest	(0.5)	(3.1)	(4.6)	(36.6)
Income Taxes	(2.2)	(6.0)	(5.2)	(8.6)
Net Income.	3.5%	12.1%	10.5%	13.0%

The economic characteristics of these industries affect their financial statement relationships in a variety of ways.

Grocery Store. The products of a particular grocery store chain are very similar to the products of other grocery store chains. There are also low barriers to entry in the grocery store industry; an entrant needs merely retail space and access to food product distributors. Thus, in this industry, extensive competition and non-differentiated products result in a relatively low net income to sales percentage, or profit margin (3.5 percent in this case).

Grocery stores, however, need relatively few assets in order to generate sales (34.2 cents in assets for each dollar of sales in this case). The assets are described as turning over 2.9 times (= 100.0%/34.2%) per year. Each time the assets of this grocery store chain turn over, a profit of 3.5 cents is generated for each dollar of assets. Thus, during a one-year period, the grocery chain earns 10.15 cents (= 3.5% × 2.9) for each dollar invested in assets.

Pharmaceutical Company.   In the pharmaceutical industry, the barriers to entry are higher than they are for grocery stores. Pharmaceutical firms must invest considerable amounts in research and development to create new drugs. Only after a lengthy government approval process does a firm receive a patent for a new drug. Then the patent gives the firm exclusive rights to manufacture and sell the product for a long time. These high entry barriers permit pharmaceutical firms to realize higher profit margins than grocery stores.

Pharmaceutical firms, however, face unique product liability risks as well as the risk that competitors will develop superior drugs that make one firm's drug offerings obsolete. Because of these business risks, pharmaceutical firms tend to take on relatively small amounts of debt financing.

Electric Utility.   The principal assets of an electric utility are its capital-intensive generating plants. Thus, property, plant, and equipment dominate a utility's balance sheet.

Because of the large investments required in such assets, electric utility firms have traditionally required a monopoly position in a particular locale. Regulators permit this monopoly position, but set the rates that utilities charge customers for electric services. Thus, electric utilities have traditionally realized relatively high profit margins (10.5% in this example) to offset their relatively low total asset turnover (.495 = 100%/202% in this case). A utility's monopoly position and regulatory protection served to reduce the risk of financial failure and permitted electric utilities to take on relatively high proportions of debt.

The economic characteristics of electric utilities have changed dramatically in recent years, with a strong push for deregulation. The elimination of monopoly positions and the setting of rates as market conditions dictate have reduced profit margins considerably.

Commercial Bank.   The principal assets of commercial banks are investments in short-term financial securities and loans to businesses and consumers. Their financing comes from customers' deposits and short-term borrowing. Because customers can generally withdraw deposits at any time, commercial banks invest in short-term liquid securities that they can turn into cash quickly.

The lending of money is a commodity business: Money borrowed from one bank is just like money borrowed from another bank. Thus, one would expect a commercial bank to realize a small excess margin on the price it earns from lending (interest revenue) over the price it pays for funds (interest expense).

The profit margins on lending are indeed relatively small. The 13.0 percent margin for the commercial bank shown in Exhibit 1.2 in fact reflects the much higher profit margins it generates from offering fee-based financial services, such as arranging mergers and acquisitions, structuring financing packages for businesses, and guaranteeing financial commitments of business customers. Note that the assets of this commercial bank turn over just .09 (=100.0%/1,136.1%) times per year, reflecting the net effect of interest revenues from investments and loans of six to eight percent per year and fee-based revenues which require relatively few assets.

TOOLS FOR STUDYING INDUSTRY ECONOMICS

Three tools for studying the economic characteristics of an industry are (1) value chain analysis, (2) Porter's five forces classification, and (3) an economic attributes framework.

VALUE CHAIN ANALYSIS

A value chain for an industry isolates the various activities involved in the creation, manufacture, and distribution of its products and services. Exhibit 1.3 demonstrates a value chain for the pharmaceutical industry.

Pharmaceutical companies invest in research and development to discover and develop new drugs. Once promising drugs emerge, a lengthy drug approval process begins. Recent estimates suggest that it takes 12 years and $250 million to discover and obtain approval for a new drug. To expedite the approval process, reduce costs, and permit their scientists to devote energies to the more creative drug discovery phase, pharmaceutical companies have begun to contract with clinical research firms to conduct tests and shepherd new drugs through the approval process.

The manufacture of drugs involves the combining of various chemicals and other ingredients. For quality control and product purity reasons, the manufacturing process is heavily mechanized.

Pharmaceutical companies employ sales forces to market drugs to doctors and hospitals. In an effort to create demand, the companies increasingly advertise new products on television, suggesting that consumers ask their doctors about the drug. Drug distribution is typically through pharmacies, although bulk mail order purchases are increasingly common (and encouraged by health insurers).

To the extent that prices are available for products or services at any of the stages in a value chain, the analyst can see where value gets added within an industry. For example, to ascertain the value of the drug discovery phase, the analyst can look at the prices paid to acquire firms with promising or newly discovered drugs. The prices that clinical research firms charge to test and obtain approval of new drugs provide a signal of the value added by this activity. The higher the value-added from any activity, the more profitable it should be to engage in that phase.

EXHIBIT 1.3

Value Chain for the Pharmaceutical Industry

| Research to Discover Drugs | Approval of Drugs by Government Regulators | Manufacture of Drugs | Creation of Demand for Drugs | Distribution to Consumers |

EXHIBIT 1.4

Value Chain for the Beverage Industry

| Creation of Beverage Product | Manufacture of Concentrate | Mixing of Concentrate, Water, Sweetener to Produce Beverage or Syrup | Containerizing Beverage or Syrup in Bottles, Cans or Other Container | Distribution to Retail Outlets |

The analyst can also use the value chain to identify the strategic positioning of a particular firm within the industry. Pharmaceutical firms have traditionally maintained a presence in the research discovery, manufacturing, and demand creation phases, leaving distribution to consumers to pharmacies, and increasingly contracting out the drug testing and approval phase.

Exhibit 1.4 sets forth a value chain for the beverage industry. Appendix B contains information about Coke, including the company's description of its business and its involvement along the value chain.

Although the classic Coke drink has not changed for many years, the company is always engaged in new product development. Once a product appears to have commercial feasibility, Coke combines raw materials into a concentrate or beverage base. The ingredients and their mixes are highly secret. Coke then ships this concentrate to its bottlers, which combine it with water and sweeteners to produce the finished beverage or syrup used in fountain drinks.

Coke uses independent bottlers for 40 percent of its worldwide case volume, noncontrolled affiliates for 45 percent, and controlled subsidiaries for 15 percent. Thus, Coke primarily contracts out the bottling operation (we discuss the rationale for this arrangement in the strategy section later in the chapter). The bottlers are responsible for transporting beverages and syrups to retail establishments.

Because the analyst can obtain separate financial statements for Coke and for the bottlers, it is possible to see where along the value chain value gets added. (We examine the profitability of Coke and its bottlers in Chapters 3 and 7.)

PORTER'S FIVE FORCES CLASSIFICATION

Porter suggests that five forces influence the average profitability of an industry.[1]

1. **Buyer Power.** Are consumers sensitive to product prices? If products are similar to those offered by competitors, consumers may switch to the lowest-priced offering. If consumers view a particular firm's products as unique, however, they will likely be less sensitive to price differentials. Another dimension of price sensitivity is the relative cost of a product. We are less sensitive to prices

---

[1]Michael E. Porter, *Competitive Strategy* (New York: The Free Press), 1980.

of products that represent a small portion of our income, such as soft drinks, than we are to higher-priced products, such as automobiles.

Buyer power also relates to relative bargaining power. If there are many sellers of a product and a small number of buyers, such as in the case of military equipment and weapons systems bought by governments, the buyer can exert significant downward pressure on prices and thus constrain the profitability of suppliers. If there are few sellers and many buyers, as with soft drinks, it is the sellers who have more bargaining power. Brand loyalty, control of distribution channels, low price, and a small number of suppliers result in low buyer power in the soft drink industry.

2. **Supplier Power.** A similar set of factors apply on the input side as well. Soft drink companies purchase the raw materials that make up their concentrate. Although Coke does not disclose every ingredient, it is unlikely that it is dependent on one or only a few suppliers for any of its raw materials. It is also unlikely that any of these ingredients are so unique that the suppliers could exert much power over Coke. Given Coke's size, the power more likely resides with Coke than with its suppliers.

3. **Rivalry Among Firms.** Coke and Pepsi dominate the soft drink industry in the United States. Because some consumers view their products as similar, intense competition based on price could develop. Also, the soft drink market in the United States is mature (that is, not growing rapidly), so price could become a weapon to gain market share.

   While intense rivalries have a tendency to reduce profitability in an industry, in this case Coke and Pepsi, the only two major players, can tacitly minimize competition based on price and compete instead on image or other attributes. Growth opportunities do exist in other countries, which these companies are pursuing aggressively. Thus, we might characterize industry rivalry as moderate.

4. **Threat of New Entrants.** How easily can new firms enter a market? Are there entry barriers such as large capital investment, technological expertise, or regulation that inhibit new entrants? If so, firms in an industry will likely generate higher earnings than if new entrants could easily enter the market and compete away the profitability.

   Entry barriers in the soft drink industry are high. Brand recognition by Coke and Pepsi serves as one entry barrier. Another barrier is domination of the distribution channels by these two firms. Most restaurant chains sign exclusive contracts to serve the soft drinks of one or the other. Coke and Pepsi also dominate shelf space in grocery stores.

5. **Threat of Substitutes.** How easily can customers switch to substitute products? How likely are they to switch? When there are close substitutes in a market, as in the case of grocery stores and most airlines, profitability is dampened. Unique products with few substitutes, such as certain prescription medications, enhance profitability. Fruit juices, bottled waters, and sports drinks for many people serve a similar function to soft drinks. Consumer buying habits, brand loyalty, and channel availability, however, minimize the threat of substitutes in the soft drink industry.

Thus, the soft drink industry rates low on buyer power, supplier power, threat of new entrants, and threat of substitutes, and moderate on rivalry within the industry. Unless either Coke or Pepsi decides to compete on the basis of low price, the analyst might expect these firms to continue to report relatively high profitability.

ECONOMIC ATTRIBUTES FRAMEWORK

An economic attributes framework is useful in studying the economic characteristics of a business, in part because it ties in with items reported in the financial statements.

1. **Demand**
   - Are customers highly sensitive to price, as in the case of automobiles, or are they relatively insensitive, as in the case of soft drinks?
   - Is demand growing rapidly, as in the case of Internet software, or is the industry relatively mature, as in the case of grocery stores?
   - Does demand move with the economic cycle, as in the case of construction of new homes and offices, or is it insensitive to business cycles, as in the case of the demand for food products or medical care?
   - Does demand vary with the seasons of a year, as in the case of toys or ski equipment, or is it relatively stable throughout the year?
2. **Supply**
   - Are there many suppliers offering similar products, or few suppliers offering unique products?
   - Are there high barriers to entry, or can new entrants gain easy access?
3. **Manufacturing**
   - Is the manufacturing process capital-intensive, as in the case of electric power generation, labor-intensive, as in the case of advertising and professional services, or a combination of the two, as in the case of automobile manufacturing or airline transportation?
   - Is the manufacturing process complex with low tolerance for error, as for heart pacemakers, or relatively simple with ranges of acceptable-quality products, such as for nonmechanized toys?
4. **Marketing**
   - Is the product promoted to other businesses, where a sales staff plays a key role, or is it promoted to consumers, where advertising and coupons serve as the principal promotion mechanisms?
   - Does steady demand pull products through distribution channels, or must firms continually create demand?
5. **Financing**
   - Are the assets of firms in the industry relatively short term, as in the case of commercial banks, which require assets to match their short-term sources of funds? Or, are assets relatively long term, as in the case of electric utilities, requiring primarily long-term financing?

EXHIBIT 1.5

Economic Characteristics of Soft Drink Industry

Demand
- Relatively insensitive to price.
- Growth of 2% to 3% a year in the United States but more rapid growth opportunities in other countries.
- Demand is not cyclical.
- Demand is higher during warmer weather.

Supply
- Two principal suppliers selling branded products.
- Branded products and domination of distribution channels by two principal suppliers create high barriers to entry.

Manufacturing
- Manufacturing process is relatively capital intensive.
- Manufacturing process is simple (essentially a mixing operation) with some tolerance for quality variation.

Marketing
- Brand recognition and established demand pull products through distribution channels but advertising can stimulate demand to some extent.

Financing
- Bottling operations and transportation of products to retailers require long-term financing.
- Profitability is relatively high and growth is slow in the United States, leading to excess cash flow generation. Growth markets in other countries require financing from internal domestic cash flow or from external sources.

- Is there relatively little risk in the assets of firms in the industry so firms can carry high proportions of debt financing, as in the case of consumer finance companies? Alternatively, are there high risks resulting from short product life cycles or product liability concerns that dictate low debt and high owners' equity financing?
- Is the industry relatively profitable and mature, generating more cash flow from operations than is needed for acquisitions of property, plant, and equipment? Or, is the industry growing rapidly and in need of external financing?

Exhibit 1.5 summarizes the economic characteristics of the soft drink industry.

IDENTIFY THE COMPANY STRATEGY

Firms establish business strategies in an attempt to differentiate themselves from competitors, but an industry's economic characteristics affect the flexibility that firms have in designing these strategies. In some cases, firms can create sustainable competitive advantages. Coke's size and brand name give it a sustainable competitive advantage, although Pepsi can boast similar advantages. Its reputation for family entertainment provides Disney with a sustainable advantage.

In many industries, however, products and ideas get quickly copied. Consider, for example, computer software and hardware; chicken, pizza, and hamburger restaurant chains; and financial services. In some of these instances, firms may achieve competitive advantage by being the first to introduce new concepts or ideas (referred to as *first mover advantage*) or by constantly investing in product development to remain on the leading edge of change within an industry.

FRAMEWORK FOR STRATEGY ANALYSIS

The set of strategic choices confronting a particular firm varies across industries. A framework dealing with product and firm characteristics helps in structuring the choice set.

1. **Nature of Product or Service.** Is a firm attempting to create unique products or services for particular market niches and thereby achieve relatively high profit margins (referred to as a *product differentiation strategy*), or is it offering nondifferentiated products at low prices, accepting a lower profit margin in return for a higher total asset turnover (referred to as a *low-cost leadership strategy*)? Is it possible for the firm to achieve both objectives by creating brand loyalty and maintaining control over costs?

2. **Degree of Integration within Value Chain.** Will the firm pursue a vertical integration strategy, participating in all phases of the value chain, or will it select only certain phases within the chain? With respect to manufacturing, will the firm conduct all manufacturing operations itself (as usually occurs in steel manufacturing); outsource all manufacturing (common in athletic shoes); or outsource the manufacturing of components but conduct the assembly operation in-house (common in automobile and computer hardware manufacturing)?

   With respect to distribution, will the firm maintain control over the distribution function, or will it outsource it? Wendy's, for example, owns most of its restaurants (maintains control); McDonalds depends on independent franchisees to operate most of its restaurants (outsources). Computer hardware firms have recently shifted from selling through their own sales staffs to using various indirect sellers, such as value-added resellers and systems integrators, in effect shifting from insourcing to outsourcing of the distribution function.

3. **Degree of Geographical Diversification.** Is the firm targeting its products to its domestic market or integrating horizontally across many countries? Operating in other countries creates opportunities for growth, although it exposes firms to risks from exchange rate changes, political uncertainties, and additional competitors.

4. **Degree of Industry Diversification.** Will the firm operate in a single industry, or will it diversify across multiple industries? Operating in multiple industries permits firms to diversify and moderate the product, cyclical, regulatory, and other risks that it encounters when operating in a single industry, but it requires managers to understand and manage multiple and different businesses effectively.

APPLICATION OF STRATEGY FRAMEWORK TO COKE

To apply this strategy framework to Coke, we rely on the description by Coke's management found in Appendix B. Most U.S. firms include this information in the "Business" section of their Form 10-K filings with the Securities and Exchange Commission.

1. **Nature of Product or Service.** Coke competes broadly in the beverage industry, with offerings in soft drinks, fruit juices, tonic waters, and sports drinks, but its principal product is soft drinks. Although we could debate whether its products differ from similar products offered by its competitors, brand recognition and domination of distribution channels permit it to sell a somewhat differentiated product.

2. **Degree of Integration within Value Chain.** We have indicated that Coke engages in new product development, manufactures its concentrates, and promotes its products, while it allows its bottlers to manufacture and distribute the soft drink products. Assuming that maintaining product quality and efficient and effective distribution channels are critical to Coke's success, one wonders why Coke would primarily outsource these functions.

   The narrative by Coke in Appendix B emphasizes the important role that the bottlers play as well as the oversight role that the company plays to insure their financial strength and efficient operation. Thus, there is a close operational relationship between Coke and the bottlers.

   The likely reason for this arrangement is that Coke perceives its principal value-added is in access to the secret formula that makes up the concentrate and in promotion of its product to maintain its brand name and brand loyalty. A bottling operation is relatively simple and not particularly value-enhancing. Bottling operations are also capital-intensive and require long-term, typically debt, financing. By not owning the bottling and distribution operations, Coke reports less debt on its balance sheet and appears less risky.

   Because of its heavy influence (seller power) over its bottlers, Coke is able to price its concentrate sales to these bottlers to garner a significant portion of the profit margin for itself. The bottlers are willing to accept a smaller margin because Coke gives them monopoly power in a particular locale, and there is a strong demand for Coke products. (We will consider Coke's strategy with respect to its bottlers when we assess the company's profitability, quality of earnings, and risk.)

3. **Degree of Geographical Diversification.** Note 16 to Coke's financial statements discloses the geographical distribution of its operations. During Year 7, Coke derived 67 percent of its revenues and 79 percent of its operating income from outside North America. Central Europe and the Middle East and Far East are responsible for 54 percent of its revenues and 58 percent of its operating income. Sales in North America grew at a compound annual growth rate of 6.6 percent during the last three years, while sales outside North America grew at a 7.2 percent rate. Thus, Coke is operating in diverse geographic locations, and tending increasingly to do so.

4. **Degree of Industry Diversification.** Coke operates almost exclusively in the beverage industry. Although Coke indicates that its product line includes orange juice (Minute Maid), fruit juices (Hi-C), iced tea (Nestea), and sports drinks (POWERaDE), its principal products are soft drinks (Coke, Barq's Root Beer, Sprite, Fanta).

PRINCIPAL FINANCIAL STATEMENTS AND NOTES

Business firms typically prepare three principal financial statements to report the results of their activities: (1) balance sheet, (2) income statement, and (3) statement of cash flows. Firms also include a set of notes that elaborate on the items included in these statements. We review the purpose and content of each of these three financial statements using the financial statements and notes for Coke in Appendix A as examples.

Generally accepted accounting principles, or GAAP, determine the valuation and measurement methods used in preparing the financial statements. Official rule making bodies set these principles. The Securities and Exchange Commission (SEC), an agency of the federal government, has the legal authority to specify acceptable accounting principles in the United States. The SEC has, for the most part, delegated the responsibility for establishing GAAP to the Financial Accounting Standards Board (FASB), a private-sector body within the accounting profession. The FASB specifies acceptable accounting principles only after receiving extensive comments on proposed accounting standards from various preparers and users of financial statements.

The process followed in other countries varies widely. In some countries, the amounts reported for financial reporting and tax reporting closely conform. In these cases, legislative arms of the government play a major role in setting acceptable accounting principles. Other countries employ a model similar to that in the United States, where financial and tax-reporting methods differ, and the accounting profession plays a major role in establishing GAAP.

The International Accounting Standards Committee, or IASC, is an independent entity comprised of representatives from over 70 countries. The IASC strives to mitigate divergence in accounting principles across countries and to encourage greater standardization. Its pronouncements, however, have no enforceability of their own. Rather, the representatives to the IASC pledge their best efforts in establishing the pronouncements of the IASC as GAAP within their countries.

BALANCE SHEET—MEASURING FINANCIAL POSITION

The balance sheet, or statement of financial position, presents a snapshot of the resources of a firm (assets) and the claims on those resources (liabilities and shareholders' equity) as of a specific time. The assets portion of the balance sheet reports the effects of a firm's investing decisions.

Refer to the balance sheet for Coke on December 31, Year 6 and Year 7, in Exhibit 1.6. Coke's principal assets are trade accounts receivable (allowing customers

EXHIBIT 1.6

The Coca-Cola Company and Subsidiaries
Consolidated Balance Sheets
(Dollars in millions except per share data)

December 31,	Year 6	Year 7
Assets		
Current		
Cash and cash equivalents.........................	$ 1,167	$ 1,433
Marketable securities...............................	148	225
	1,315	1,658
Trade accounts receivable, less allowances of $34 in Year 6 and $30 in Year 7	1,695	1,641
Inventories..	1,117	952
Prepaid expenses and other assets	1,323	1,659
Total Current Assets	5,450	5,910
Investments and Other Assets		
Equity method investments		
Coca-Cola Enterprises Inc.	556	547
Coca-Cola Amatil Limited	682	881
Other, principally bottling companies	1,157	2,004
Cost method investments, principally bottling companies .	319	737
Marketable securities and other assets................	1,597	1,779
	4,311	5,948
Property, Plant, and Equipment		
Land	233	204
Buildings and improvements	1,944	1,528
Machinery and equipment..........................	4,135	3,649
Containers.......................................	345	200
	6,657	5,581
Less allowances for depreciation	2,321	2,031
	4,336	3,550
Goodwill and Other Intangible Assets	944	753
	$15,041	$16,161

to delay their cash payments to Coke represents an implicit investment of cash in these customers by Coke); investments in the equity securities of bottlers; and investments in land, buildings, machinery, and equipment.

The liabilities and shareholders' equity portion of the balance sheet reports the effects of a firm's financing decisions. Coke obtains financing from suppliers of goods and services (reported as accounts payable and accrued expenses); bank loans (reported as loans and notes payable); long-term debt; and shareholders' equity.

The balance sheet derives its name from the fact that it shows a balance or equality:

EXHIBIT 1.6		

continued

December 31,	Year 6	Year 7
Liabilities and Share-Owners' Equity		
Current		
Accounts payable and accrued expenses	$ 3,103	$ 2,972
Loans and notes payable	2,371	3,388
Current maturities of long-term debt.	552	9
Accrued income taxes	1,322	1,037
Total Current Liabilities	7,348	7,406
Long-Term Debt	1,141	1,116
Other Liabilities.	966	1,182
Deferred Income Taxes	194	301
Share-Owners' Equity		
Common stock, $.25 par value—		
Authorized: 5,600,000,000 shares;		
Issued: 3,423,678,994 shares in Year 6;		
3,432,956,518 shares in Year 7	856	858
Capital surplus	863	1,058
Reinvested earnings.	12,882	15,127
Unearned compensation related to outstanding		
restricted stock.	(68)	(61)
Foreign currency translation adjustment	(424)	(662)
Unrealized gain on securities available for sale	82	156
	14,191	16,476
Less treasury stock, at cost (919,081,326 shares in Year 6;		
951,963,574 common shares in Year 7)	8,799	10,320
	5,392	6,156
	$15,041	$16,161

See Notes to Consolidated Financial Statements.

$$\text{Assets} = \text{Liabilities} + \text{Shareholders' Equity}$$

That is, a firm's assets or resources are in balance with, or equal to, the claims on those assets by creditors (liabilities) and owners (shareholders' equity).

The balance sheet views resources from two perspectives: a list of the specific forms in which a firm holds the resources (cash, inventory, equipment), and a list of the persons or entities that provided the funds to obtain the assets and therefore have claims on them (suppliers, employees, governments, shareholders). Thus, the balance sheet portrays the equality of investing and financing.

Formats of balance sheets in some countries differ from the format in the United States. In Germany and France, for example, property, plant, and equipment and other noncurrent assets appear first, followed by current assets. On the financing side, shareholders' equity appears first, followed by noncurrent liabilities and then current liabilities. This format maintains the balance between investing and financing, but the accounts are presented in the opposite sequence to that common in the United States.

In the United Kingdom, the balance sheet equation takes the form:

$$\text{Noncurrent Assets} + [\text{Current Assets} - \text{Current Liabilities}]$$
$$- \text{Noncurrent Liabilities} = \text{Shareholders' Equity}$$

This format takes the perspective of shareholders by reporting the assets available for shareholders after subtracting claims by creditors. Financial analysts can rearrange the components of published balance sheets in whatever format they consider most informative, although ambiguity may exist for some balance sheet categories.

Assets—Recognition, Valuation, and Classification.

Which of its resources does a firm recognize as assets? At what amount does the firm report these assets? How does it classify them within the assets portion of the balance sheet? GAAP determines responses to these questions.

Assets are resources that have the potential for providing a firm with future economic benefits: the ability to generate future cash inflows (as with accounts receivable and inventories) or to reduce future cash outflows (as with prepayments). A firm recognizes as assets those resources (1) to whose future use it has acquired rights as a result of a past transaction or exchange, and (2) whose future benefits the firm can measure, or quantify, with a reasonable degree of precision.[2] Resources that firms do not normally recognize as assets because they fail to meet one or both of these criteria include purchase orders received from customers, employment contracts with corporate officers, and a quality reputation with employees, customers, or citizens of the community.

Perhaps the most valuable resource Coke has is its brand name. The Coke symbol is one of the most widely recognized in the world. Coke has created this brand name through past expenditures on advertising, event sponsorships, and quality control. Yet, it is too uncertain to define the portion of these expenditures that creates sustainable future benefits and the portion that simply stimulates sales during the current period to justify recognition of this resource as an asset. The amounts that Coke does report for goodwill and other intangible assets result from Coke's acquisition of other companies.

Assets on the balance sheet are either *monetary* or *nonmonetary*. Monetary assets include cash and claims to a fixed amount of cash receivable in the future. Coke's monetary assets include cash and investments in the debt (not equity) securities of other firms. The balance sheet reports monetary assets at the amount of cash the firm expects to receive in the future. If the date or dates of receipt extend

---

[2]Financial Accounting Standards Board, *Statement of Financial Accounting Concepts No. 6*, "Elements of Financial Statements," 1985, para. 25.

beyond one year, the firm reports the monetary asset at the present value of the future cash flows (using a discount rate that reflects the underlying uncertainty of collecting the cash as assessed at the time the claim initially arose).

Nonmonetary assets include inventories, buildings, equipment, and other assets that do not represent a claim to a fixed amount of cash. Firms can report nonmonetary assets at the amounts initially paid to acquire them (historical cost); the amount required currently to acquire them (current replacement cost); the amount for which the firm could currently sell the asset (current net realizable value); or the present value of the amount the firm expects to receive in the future from selling or using the asset (present value of future cash flows). GAAP generally requires the reporting of nonmonetary assets on the balance sheet at their historical cost amount, because this valuation is usually more objective and verifiable than other possible valuation bases. GAAP in some countries, such as the United Kingdom and the Netherlands, permits periodic revaluation of property, plant, and equipment to current values. Chapter 5 discusses alternative valuation methods and their implications for measuring earnings.

The classification of assets on the balance sheet varies widely in published annual reports. The principal asset categories are as follows:

Current Assets.   Current assets include cash and other assets that a firm expects to sell or consume during the normal operating cycle of a business, usually one year. Cash, marketable securities, accounts receivable, inventories, and prepayments appear as current assets for Coke.

Investments.   This category includes long-term investments in the debt and equity securities of other entities. If a firm makes such investments for short-term purposes, it classifies them under current assets. One of Coke's principal assets is investments in its bottlers (Coca-Cola Enterprises, Coca-Cola Amatil, and other bottlers). Note 2 to Coke's financial statements indicates that it owns less than 50 percent of the common stock of these bottlers. Coke therefore does not prepare consolidated financial statements with these bottlers; it instead reports the investments on the balance sheet using the equity method (discussed in Chapter 7).[3]

Property, Plant, and Equipment.   This category includes the tangible, long-lived assets that a firm uses in operations over a period of years. Coke includes land, buildings and improvements, machinery, equipment, and containers in this category. It reports property, plant, and equipment at historical cost and then subtracts the accumulated depreciation recognized on these assets since acquisition (which it labels as allowances for depreciation).

---

[3]As this book goes to press, the Financial Accounting Standards Board is reconsidering the criteria for preparing consolidated financial statements. The proposed standard would require consolidation whenever one company effectively controls another entity, regardless of the percentage of ownership. Given the relationship between Coke and its bottlers, effective control may be present in these circumstances.

Intangibles.   Intangibles include the rights established by law or contract to the future use of property. Patents, trademarks, and franchises are intangible assets. The most troublesome asset recognition questions revolve around which rights satisfy the criteria for an asset. As the discussion in Chapter 5 makes more clear, firms generally recognize as assets intangibles acquired in external market transactions with other entities (as is the case for goodwill and other intangible assets on Coke's balance sheet), but do not recognize as assets intangibles developed internally by the firm (Coke's brand name, for example).

Liabilities—Recognition, Valuation, and Classification.

A liability represents a firm's obligation to make payments of cash, goods, or services in a reasonably definite amount at a reasonable definite future time for benefits or services received in the past.[4] Liabilities for Coke include obligations to suppliers of goods and services (accounts payable and accrued expenses); banks (loans and notes payable); governments (accrued income taxes); and lenders (long-term debt).

Most troublesome questions regarding liability recognition relate to executory contracts. GAAP does not recognize labor contracts, purchase order commitments, and some lease agreements as liabilities because firms will receive the benefits from these items in the future; they have not received them in the past. Notes to the financial statements disclose material, executory contracts and other contingent claims. Chapter 6 discusses these claims more fully.

Most liabilities are monetary, requiring payments of fixed amounts of cash. GAAP reports those due within one year at the amount of cash the firm expects to pay to discharge the obligation. If the payment dates extend beyond one year, GAAP states the liability at the present value of the required future cash flows (discounted at an interest rate that reflects the future uncertainty of paying the cash as assessed at the time the obligation initially arose). Some liabilities, such as warranties, require the delivery of goods or services instead of the payment of cash. The balance sheet states these liabilities at the expected future cost of providing the goods and services.

Published balance sheets classify liabilities in various ways. Virtually all firms use a current liabilities category, which includes obligations that a firm expects to settle within one year. Balance sheets report the remaining liabilities in a section labeled noncurrent liabilities or long-term debt. Coke uses three noncurrent liability categories: long-term debt, other liabilities, and deferred income taxes. Chapter 6 discusses deferred income taxes.

Shareholders' Equity Valuation and Disclosure.

The shareholders' equity in a firm is a residual interest or claim. That is, the owners have a claim on all assets not required to meet the claims of creditors. The valuation of assets and liabilities in the balance sheet therefore determines the valuation of total shareholders' equity.[5]

---

[4]Financial Accounting Standards Board, op. cit., para. 35.

[5]The issuance of bonds with equity characteristics, such as convertible bonds, and of preferred stock with debt characteristics, such as redeemable preferred stock, clouds the distinction between liabilities and shareholders' equity.

Balance sheets separate total shareholders' equity into (1) amounts initially contributed by shareholders for an interest in a firm (Coke uses the accounts common stock and capital surplus); (2) cumulative net income in excess of dividends declared (Coke's account is reinvested earnings); (3) equity effects of the recognition or valuation of certain assets or liabilities (Coke includes items related to unearned compensation, foreign currency translation, and valuation of marketable securities); and (4) treasury stock (Coke shares that are repurchased by Coke).

Assessing the Quality of the Balance Sheet.   Analysts frequently examine relationships among items in the balance sheet when they assess a firm's risk. For example, an excess of current assets over current liabilities suggests that a firm has sufficient liquid resources to pay short-term creditors. A relatively low percentage of long-term debt to shareholders' equity suggests that a firm has sufficient permanent shareholders' capital in place to reduce the risk that it will be unable to repay the long-term debt at maturity.

An analyst using the balance sheet for these purposes must recognize that:

1. Certain valuable resources of a firm that generate future cash flows, such as a patent for a pharmaceutical firm or a brand name for a consumer products firm, do not appear as assets.
2. Nonmonetary assets appear at historical cost, even though their current market values might exceed their recorded amounts. An example is the market value versus recorded value of land on the balance sheets of railroads and many urban department stores.
3. Certain claims against a firm may not appear as liabilities. We will not see, for example, the commitments by airlines to make lease payments on their aircraft or commitments by steel, tire, and automobile companies under labor union contracts.
4. Noncurrent liabilities appear at the present value of expected cash flows discounted at an interest rate determined at the time the liability initially arose, not at a current market interest rate.

These factors mean that the balance sheet reports incomplete or inaccurate measures of a firm's economic position. The analyst should consider making adjustments for items that impact balance sheet quality in this way. Chapters 5 through 7 discuss these issues more fully.

INCOME STATEMENT—MEASURING OPERATING PERFORMANCE

The total assets of a firm change over time because of a firm's investing and financing activities. For example, a firm may issue common stock for cash, acquire a building by assuming a mortgage for part of the purchase price, or issue common stock in exchange for convertible bonds. These investing and financing activities affect the amount and structure of a firm's assets and equities.

The assets of a firm also change over time because of operating activities. A firm sells goods or services to customers for more than it cost the firm to acquire or produce the goods and services. Creditors and owners provide capital to a firm with the expectation that the firm will use it to generate a profit and provide them an adequate return for the level of risk involved in supplying the capital.

The second principal financial statement, the income statement, provides information about the operating profitability of a firm for some particular time period. Exhibit 1.7 presents an income statement for Coke for Year 5, Year 6, and Year 7.

Net income equals revenues and gains minus expenses and losses. Revenues measure the inflows of net assets from selling goods and providing services (that is, assets minus liabilities). Expenses measure the outflows of net assets that a firm uses, or consumes, in the process of generating revenues. As measures of operating performance, revenues reflect the services rendered by a firm, and expenses indicate the efforts required or expended.

Coke generates revenues from selling concentrate to its bottlers. Because Coke prepares consolidated financial statements with bottlers who sell 15 percent of its worldwide volume, revenues also include sales of finished Coke products to retailers by these consolidated bottlers (see Appendix B). Revenues also include interest income from investments in debt instruments and equity income from investments in affiliated but noncontrolled bottlers.

EXHIBIT 1.7			
The Coca-Cola Company and Subsidiaries **Consolidated Statements of Income** **(Dollars in millions except per share data)**			
Year Ended December 31,	**Year 5**	**Year 6**	**Year 7**
Net Operating Revenues	$16,181	$18,018	$18,546
Cost of goods sold	6,168	6,940	6,738
Gross Profit	10,013	11,078	11,808
Selling, administrative and general expenses . .	6,376	7,052	7,893
Operating Income	3,637	4,026	3,915
Interest income	181	245	238
Interest expense	199	272	286
Equity income	134	169	211
Other income (deductions)—net	(25)	86	87
Gain on issuance of stock by equity investees. .	—	74	431
Income before Income Taxes	3,728	4,328	4,596
Income taxes	1,174	1,342	1,104
Net Income.	$2,554	$2,986	$3,492
Net Income per Share	$ .99	$1.18	$ 1.40
Average Shares Outstanding	2,580	2,525	2,494

See Notes to Consolidated Financial Statements.

Expenses include the cost of manufacturing concentrate sold to noncontrolled bottlers and the cost of converting concentrate into finished Coke products by controlled bottlers. Expenses also include advertising and other promotion costs (included in selling expenses), information systems, product development, administrators' compensation (included in administrative and general expenses), and interest expense on short- and long-term borrowing.

Gains and losses arise from sales of assets or settlements of liabilities that relate only peripherally to a firm's primary operating activities (for example, the sale of a building, or the repayment of long-term debt prior to maturity). These gains and losses arise when a firm receives or pays a different amount from the amount at which the accounting records state the asset or liability. Coke, for example, reports a gain on issuance of stock by equity investees. Such sales do not relate directly to Coke's ongoing beverage business and therefore do not appear as part of operating revenues. Note that gains and losses appear as net amounts on the income statement; we do not see the selling price as a revenue and the book value of the items sold as an expense.

Accrual Basis of Accounting.   Exhibit 1.8 depicts the operating, or earnings, cycle for a manufacturing firm. Net income from this series of activities equals the amount of cash received from customers minus the amount of cash paid for raw materials, labor, and the services of production facilities. If the entire operating cycle occurred within one accounting period, it wouldn't be too hard to measure operating performance. Net income would equal cash inflows minus cash outflows related to these operating activities. In fact, of course, firms acquire raw materials in one accounting period and use them in several future accounting periods. They acquire buildings and equipment in one accounting period and use them during many future accounting periods. A firm often sells goods or services in a period before the period it receives cash from customers.

Under the cash basis of accounting, a firm recognizes revenues when it receives cash from customers and recognizes expenses when it pays cash to suppliers, employees, and other providers of goods and services. Because a firm's operating cycle usually extends over several accounting periods, the cash basis of accounting provides a poor measure of operating performance for specific periods of time. To

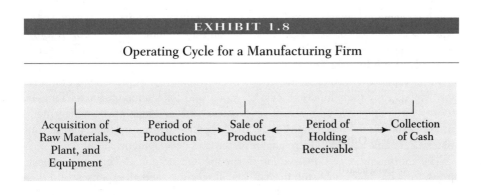

EXHIBIT 1.8

Operating Cycle for a Manufacturing Firm

overcome this deficiency of the cash basis, GAAP generally requires that firms use the accrual basis of accounting to measure operating performance.

Under the accrual basis, a firm recognizes revenue when it performs all, or a substantial portion, of the services it expects to perform, and receives either cash or a receivable whose cash-equivalent amount the firm can measure objectively. Most firms recognize revenue at the time they sell goods or render services. They match expenses with the associated revenues.

Consider the accrual basis of accounting applied to a manufacturing firm. The cost of manufacturing a product remains on the balance sheet as an asset (inventory) until the time of sale. At the time of sale, the firm recognizes revenue in the amount of cash it expects to collect. It recognizes the cost of manufacturing the product as a matching expense. When a firm cannot easily link costs (the salary of the chief executive officer, for example) to a particular revenue, it recognizes an expense in the period when it consumes services in operations.

Note that a firm need not delay revenue recognition until it receives cash from customers, as long as the firm can estimate fairly accurately the amount of cash it will ultimately receive. The amount will appear in accounts receivable prior to the receipt of cash. The accrual basis provides a better measure of operating performance than the cash basis because it matches inputs with outputs more accurately.

Classification and Format within the Income Statement.   The future earnings stream of an asset or collection of assets is often the basis for placing a value on the assets. Analysts form predictions of the future earnings, or net income, of a firm by studying the past trend of earnings. Inaccurate projections from past data can occur if net income includes unusual or nonrecurring amounts. To provide more useful information for prediction, GAAP requires that the income statement include some or all of certain sections or categories, depending on the nature of the firm's income for a period:

1. Income from continuing operations.
2. Income, gains, and losses from discontinued operations.
3. Extraordinary gains and losses.
4. Adjustments for changes in accounting principles.

The first section, Income from Continuing Operations, reports the revenues and expenses of activities in which a firm anticipates an ongoing involvement. If a firm does not have any of the other three categories of income in a particular year, it will probably not use the continuing operation label as such.

Firms report their expenses in various ways. Most firms in the United States report expenses by their function: cost of goods sold for manufacturing; selling expenses for marketing; administrative expenses for administrative management; interest expense for financing. Other firms report expenses by their nature: raw materials, compensation, advertising, research and development.

The continuing operations section of the income statement frequently appears in two formats. The single-step format lists all revenues and all expenses, and then derives net income in a single mathematical step as the difference between the two. The multiple-step format generally lists revenues from selling a firm's goods and services, then shows subtractions for the costs of goods and services sold and the costs of selling and administrative services, and finally reports a subtotal for operating income. The multiple-step format derives its name from the various subtotals that generally appear before the disclosure of net income. Coke uses this multiple-step format, but there are many variations in income statement format in corporate annual reports.

The income statement will then report nonoperating revenues (interest income, equity income), nonoperating expenses (interest expense), and nonoperating gains and losses (gain on issuances of stock by equity investees).

A firm that intends to remain in a line of business but decides to sell or close down some portion of that line of business would report any income, gain, or loss from such an action under continuing operations. Coke would continue its soft drink business, for example, but might close a particular consolidated bottling operation. If a firm decides to terminate its involvement in a line of business, however, it would report the income, gain, or loss in the second section of the income statement labeled Income, Gains, and Losses from Discontinued Operations.

Extraordinary gains and losses arise from events that are (1) unusual, given the nature of a firm's activities, (2) nonrecurring, and (3) material in amount. Corporate annual reports rarely disclose such items (except for gains and losses on early debt retirements, which GAAP requires firms to report as extraordinary items).

Many firms in recent years have reported restructuring charges and impairment losses in their income statements. Such items reflect the writedown of assets or the recognition of liabilities arising from changes in economic conditions and corporate strategies. Because restructuring charges and impairment losses do not usually satisfy the criteria for discontinued operations or extraordinary items, firms report them in the continuing operations section of the income statement. If the amounts are material, they will appear on a separate line to distinguish them from recurring income items. Coke discloses in Note 14 that it recognized impairment losses in Year 6 and Year 7 and included them in selling, administrative, and general expenses.

When firms change their methods of accounting, GAAP generally requires them to report the cumulative difference between the income reported under the old method and the new method in a separate section of the income statement. Note 1 indicates that Coke adopted new accounting methods during Year 7, but that the effect was not sufficiently material to require the disclosure in a separate section of the income statement.

All four categories of income items appear in the income statement net of any income tax effects. The majority of published income statements include only the first section because discontinued operations, extraordinary gains and losses, and changes in accounting principles occur infrequently.

Comprehensive Income. The recognition and valuation of assets and liabilities usually give rise to an adjustment to some other account. This other account is often a revenue or expense account. For example, a firm might sell inventory for cash. Cash increases by the amount of the selling price, and revenues, a component of retained earnings, increase. Inventory decreases by the amount of the acquisition cost of the inventory item sold, and expenses, a negative component of retained earnings, increase.

Some changes in the recognition and valuation of assets and liabilities do not immediately affect net income and retained earnings but will likely affect them in future periods. Chapter 7 discusses, for example, the effect of exchange rate changes on the valuation of assets and liabilities of a foreign subsidiary of a U.S. company. Any gain or loss from exchange rate changes is unrealized until the foreign unit makes a currency conversion from its currency into U.S. dollars or vice versa. These unrealized "gains" and "losses" appear in a separate shareholders' equity account.

Look at the balance sheet for Coke in Appendix A. It reports two items that relate to the valuation of assets and liabilities: (1) foreign currency translation adjustment, and (2) unrealized gain on securities available for sale. Chapter 7 discusses the accounting for each of these items.

The Financial Accounting Standards Board is aware that users of financial statements might overlook items of this nature that might affect the market value of firms but that do not yet appear in net income. It therefore requires firms to report an amount in one of its financial statements that the FASB refers to as *comprehensive income*.[6]

Comprehensive income equals net income for a period plus or minus the changes in shareholders' equity accounts other than changes from net income and transactions with owners. Comprehensive income for Coke for Year 7 is as follows (in millions):

Net Income	$3,492
Change in Foreign Currency Translation Adjustment ($662 − $424)	(238)
Change in Unrealized Gain on Securities Available for Sale ($156 − $82) .	74
Comprehensive Income	$3,328

Firms have considerable flexibility as to where they report comprehensive income in the financial statements. It may appear in the income statement, in a separate statement of comprehensive income, or as part of the analysis of changes in shareholders' equity accounts. Exhibit 1.9 presents a partial statement of changes in shareholders' equity for Coke in one possible format.

Firms also have flexibility as to how they label disclosures related to comprehensive income. That is, firms need not use the term "comprehensive income," but instead may label the amount, for example, as net income plus or minus changes in other non-owner equity accounts. The balance sheet disclosure might use the term "accumulated other comprehensive income" for the portions of comprehensive net income not related to reported earnings, or use a term such as "accumulated non-owner equity account changes."

---

[6]Financial Accounting Standards Board, *Statement of Financial Accounting Standards Statement No. 130,* "Reporting Comprehensive Income," 1997.

EXHIBIT 1.9

Partial Statement of Changes in Shareholders' Equity for Coke
(amounts in millions)

	Reinvested Earnings	Accumulated Other Comprehensive Income	Compre-hensive Income	Other Equity Accounts	Total
Balance December 31, Year 6	$12,882	$(342)[a]		$(7,148)[b]	$5,392
Net Income	3,492		$3,492		3,492
Translation Adjustments.		(238)	(238)		(238)
Net Change in Unrealized Gain on Securities, net of Deferred Taxes . .		74	74		74
Comprehensive Income			$3,328		
Other Changes in Shareholders' Equity Accounts	(1,247)			(1,317)[d]	(2,564)
Balance, December 31, Year 7	$15,127	$(506)[c]		$(8,465)	$6,156

[a]($424) + $82 = ($342).
[b]$856 + $863 − $68 − $8,799 = ($7,148).
[c]($662) + $156 = ($506).
[d]$2 + $122 + $63 + $10 + $7 − $1,521 = ($1,317).

There was a lot of contentiousness attached to enactment of the reporting standard on comprehensive income. Business firms argued that the reporting of both net income and comprehensive income would confuse statement users. The FASB therefore gave business firms considerable flexibility as to how they report comprehensive income. When we consider various elements of comprehensive income in future chapters, we will discuss how the analyst might treat them in assessments of a firm's profitability.

Assessing the Quality of Earnings. Because earnings figures are frequently used in management compensation contracts and in the valuation of firms (witness, for example, frequent references to the price-earnings ratio in the financial press), the analyst needs to be alert to the possibility that the reported earnings for a particular period may not be a good predictor of ongoing profitability. For example, net income may include restructuring or impairment charges; income, gains, and losses from discontinued operations; extraordinary gains or losses; or adjustments for changes in accounting principles. Coke, for example, reports in Note 14 that it recognized charges to streamline operations, recognize impairment losses, and redesign information systems. The analyst may wish to eliminate the effects of nonrecurring items when assessing operating performance.

Management can also use more subtle means to "manage" earnings. The firm might cut back on advertising or research and development expenditures or delay maintenance expenditures in order to increase earnings in a particular period.

Chapter 4 discusses adjustments that the analyst might make to improve the quality of earnings.

STATEMENT OF CASH FLOWS

The third principal financial statement is the statement of cash flows. Exhibit 1.10 presents the statement of cash flows for Coke for Year 5, Year 6, and Year 7. This

---

EXHIBIT 1.10

The Coca-Cola Company and Subsidiaries
Consolidated Statements of Cash Flows
(Dollar amounts in millions)

Year Ended December 31,	Year 5	Year 6	Year 7
Operating Activities			
Net income.	$ 2,554	$ 2,986	$ 3,492
Depreciation and amortization	411	454	479
Deferred income taxes	58	157	(145)
Equity income, net of dividends	(4)	(25)	(89)
Foreign currency adjustments.	(6)	(23)	(60)
Gains on issuances of stock by equity investees	—	(74)	(431)
Other noncash items	41	45	181
Net change in operating assets and liabilities	307	(192)	36
Net cash provided by operating activities	3,361	3,328	3,463
Investing Activities			
Acquisitions and investments, principally bottling companies.	(311)	(338)	(645)
Purchases of investments and other assets	(379)	(403)	(623)
Proceeds from disposals of investments and other assets	299	580	1,302
Purchases of property, plant and equipment.	(878)	(937)	(990)
Proceeds from disposals of property, plant, and equipment	109	44	81
Other investing activities	(55)	(172)	(175)
Net cash used in investing activities	(1,215)	(1,226)	(1,050)
Net cash provided by operations after reinvestment	2,146	2,102	2,413
Financing Activities			
Issuances of debt	491	754	1,122
Payments of debt	(154)	(212)	(580)
Issuances of stock.	69	86	124
Purchases of stock for treasury.	(1,192)	(1,796)	(1,521)
Dividends	(1,006)	(1,110)	(1,247)
Net cash used in financing activities.	(1,792)	(2,278)	(2,102)
Effect of Exchange Rate Changes on Cash and Cash Equivalents	34	(43)	(45)
Cash and Cash Equivalents			
Net increase (decrease) during the year	388	(219)	266
Balance at beginning of year.	998	1,386	1,167
Balance at end of year.	$ 1,386	$ 1,167	$ 1,433

See Notes to Consolidated Financial Statements.

statement reports for a period of time the net cash flows (inflows minus outflows) from three principal business activities: operating, investing, and financing.

Rationale for the Statement of Cash Flows. Profitable firms, especially those growing rapidly, sometimes find themselves strapped for cash and unable to pay suppliers, employees, and other creditors. This occurs for two principal reasons:

1. The timing of cash receipts from customers does not necessarily coincide with the recognition of revenue, and the timing of cash expenditures does not necessarily coincide with the recognition of expenses under the accrual basis of accounting. In the usual case, cash expenditures precede the recognition of expenses, and cash receipts occur after the recognition of revenue. Thus, a firm might have positive net income for a period, but its cash outflow for operations could exceed the cash inflow.
2. The firm may acquire new property, plant, and equipment, retire outstanding debt, or reacquire shares of its common stock when there is insufficient cash available.

In many cases, a profitable firm finding itself short of cash can obtain the needed funds from either short- or long-term creditors or owners. The firm must repay with interest the funds it borrows from creditors. Owners may require that the firm pay periodic dividends as an inducement to invest in the firm. Eventually, the firm must generate sufficient cash from operations if it is to survive.

Cash flows are the connecting link among operating, investing, and financing activities. They permit each of these three principal business activities to continue functioning smoothly and effectively. An examination of the statement of cash flows for Coke reveals that cash flow from operations exceeded the net cash outflow for investing activities in each of the three years. Coke used the excess cash flow to pay dividends to shareholders and to repurchase shares of its common stock.

Classification of Cash Flows. The statement of cash flows classifies cash flows as relating to either operating, investing, or financing activities.

Operating. Selling goods and providing services represent the most important ways that a financially healthy company generates cash. When cash flow from operations is assessed over several years, it indicates the extent to which operating activities have provided the necessary cash to maintain operating capabilities and the extent to which firms have had to rely on other sources of cash.

Investing. The acquisition of noncurrent assets, particularly property, plant, and equipment, usually represents a major ongoing use of cash. Firms must replace such assets as they wear out as well as acquire additional noncurrent assets if they are to grow. Firms can obtain a portion of the cash needed to acquire noncurrent assets from sales of existing noncurrent assets, but such cash inflows are seldom sufficient to cover the cost of new acquisitions.

Financing. A firm obtains cash from short- and long-term borrowing and from issuing preferred and common stock. It uses cash to repay short- and long-term borrowing, to pay dividends, and to reacquire shares of outstanding preferred and common stock.

Firms sometimes engage in investing and financing transactions that do not directly involve cash. For example, a firm might acquire a building by assuming a mortgage obligation. It might issue common stock upon conversion of long-term debt. Firms disclose these transactions in a supplementary schedule or note to the statement of cash flows in a way that clearly indicates that they are investing and financing transactions that do not affect cash. Coke does not disclose any such transactions.

The statement of cash flows is not a required financial statement in some countries. Chapter 2 describes and illustrates analytical procedures for preparing a statement of cash flows.

SUMMARY OF FINANCIAL STATEMENTS AND NOTES

Exhibit 1.11 summarizes the principal activities of a business and the three principal financial statements. An environmental factors assessment includes consideration of the economic characteristics of an industry and the strategies of competitors. Corporate goals and strategies address how a particular firm intends to compete within the industry to gain competitive advantage. The balance sheet reflects the results of a firm's investing and financing activities. The income statement reports the results of a firm's operating activities. Firms prepare their balance sheets and income statements using the accrual basis of accounting. The statement of cash flows reports the cash effects of operating, investing, and financing activities.

PROFITABILITY AND RISK ANALYSIS

Armed with three key building blocks: (1) an understanding of the economics of the industry in which a firm competes; (2) an understanding of the particular strategies that the firm has chosen to compete in its industry; and (3) an understanding of the financial statements and notes that report the results of a firm's operating, investing, and financing activities, the analyst is ready to conduct a financial statement analysis.

Most financial statement analyses aim to assess some aspect of a firm's *profitability* or its *risk*. This two-fold focus stems from the emphasis of investment decisions on returns and risk. Investors acquire shares of common stock in a company because of the return they expect from such investments. This return includes any dividends received plus the change in the market price of the shares of stock while the investor holds them. An investor will not be indifferent between two investments that are expected to yield, say, 20 percent, if there are differences in the uncertainty, or risk, of earning 20 percent. The investor will likely demand a higher expected return from higher-risk investments to compensate for the additional risk assumed.

Summary of Principal Business Activities and Financial Statements

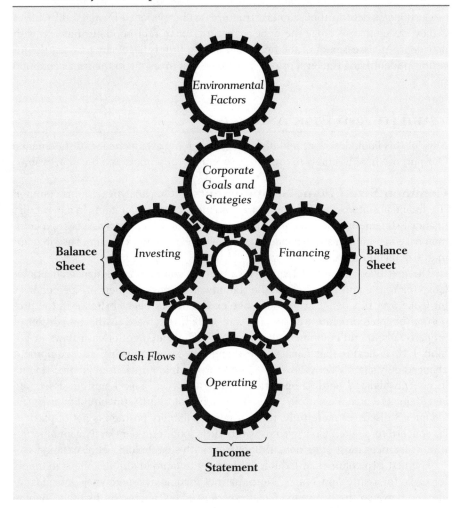

The income statement reports a firm's net income during the current and prior years. An assessment of the profitability of the firm during these periods, after adjusting as appropriate for nonrecurring items, is necessary before the analyst can gauge the likely future profitability of the firm. Empirical research has shown an association between earnings and market rates on return on common stock.[7] Thus, assessments of profitability are related to stock pricing. Chapter 12 discusses these links more fully, but a later section will introduce the valuation models.

---

[7]The classic study is by Ray Ball and Philip Brown, "An Evaluation of Accounting Income Numbers," *Journal of Accounting Research,* Autumn 1968, pp. 159–178.

Financial statements are also useful for assessing the risk of a firm. Firms that are unable to generate cash flow from operations for several periods will likely encounter financial difficulties and perhaps even bankruptcy. Firms that have high proportions of debt in their capital structures will experience financial difficulties if they are unable to repay the debt at maturity or to replace maturing debt with new debt. An assessment of the financial risk of a firm is necessary to assist the investor in identifying the level of risk incurred when investing in the firm's common stock.

TOOLS OF PROFITABILITY AND RISK ANALYSIS

Most of this book describes and illustrates tools for analyzing financial statements. Our purpose here is simply to introduce several of these tools as a broad overview.

Common Size Financial Statements.   One analytical tool is common size financial statements. Common size statements express all items in a particular financial statement as a percentage of some common base. Total assets are a common base in common size balance sheets. Sales revenue is a common base in common size income statements.

The first two columns of Exhibit 1.12 present common size balance sheets for Coke for Year 6 and Year 7. Note the stability of various common size percentages for Coke over this two-year period. Coke experienced a slight increase in the proportion of intercorporate investments and a slight decrease in the proportion of property, plant, and equipment during Year 7. The statement of cash flows in Exhibit 1.10 indicates that Coke's investments in property, plant, and equipment changed only slightly between Year 6 and Year 7, while it increased its investments in nonconsolidated bottling operations during the year. Coke's current assets are less than its current liabilities, usually a signal of short-term liquidity risk. (As Chapter 3 discusses more fully, this net current liability position is not of particular concern for Coke.) Coke also uses very little long-term debt in its capital structure. It finances most of its noncurrent assets with shareholders' equity capital.

The first two columns of Exhibit 1.13 present common size income statements for Coke for Year 6 and Year 7. Note that net income as a percentage of sales increased between the two years. Coke experienced an increase in its other income percentage and reductions in its cost of goods sold to sales and income tax expense to sales percentages, but these changes were offset by an increase in its selling, administrative, and general expense percentage. Management's discussion and analysis of operations presented in Appendix B provides explanations for some of these changes. The task of the financial analyst is to delve into the reasons behind such changes, taking into consideration industry economics, company strategies, management's explanations, and the operating results for competitors.

The analyst must interpret common size financial statements carefully. The amount of any one item in these statements is not independent of all other items. The dollar amount for an item might increase between two periods, but its relative percentage in the common size statement would decrease if the item increased at a lower rate than other items. Common size percentages provide a general

	EXHIBIT 1.12

Common Size and Percentage Change Balance Sheets for Coke

	Common Size		Percentage Change	
				Five-Year Compound Annual
	Year 6	Year 7	Year 7	Growth Rate
Assets				
Cash and Marketable Securities	8.7%	10.3%	26.1%	8.2%
Accounts Receivable.	11.3	10.2	(3.2%)	11.1%
Inventories	7.4	5.9	(14.8%)	(.7%)
Other Current Assets	8.8	10.2	25.4%	9.2%
Total Current Assets	36.2%	36.5%	8.4%	7.4%
Investments	28.7	36.8	38.0%	16.8%
Property, Plant, and Equipment	28.9	21.9	(18.1%)	4.2%
Intangible and Other Assets	6.3	4.7	(20.2%)	13.7%
Total Assets.	100.0%	100.0%	7.4%	9.7%
Liabilities and Shareholders' Equity				
Accounts Payable	20.6%	18.4%	(4.2%)	9.2%
Short-Term Borrowing	19.5	21.0	16.2%	21.2%
Other Current Liabilities	8.8	6.4	(21.6%)	2.9%
Total Current Liabilities	48.9%	45.8%	.8%	12.5%
Long-Term Debt.	7.6	6.9	(2.2%)	2.5%
Other Noncurrent Liabilities	7.7	9.2	27.8%	8.5%
Total Liabilities.	64.2%	61.9%	3.7%	10.4%
Common Stock.	11.4%	11.8%	11.5%	15.1%
Retained Earnings	85.7	94.2	18.0%	16.5%
Cumulative Translation Adjustment	(2.8)	(4.1)	56.1%	165.7%
Treasury Stock	(58.5)	(63.8)	17.3%	21.2%
Total Shareholders' Equity	35.8%	38.1%	14.2%	8.6%
Total Liabilities and Shareholders' Equity.	100.0%	100.0%	7.4%	9.7%

overview of financial position and operating performance, but the analyst must supplement them with other analytical tools.

Percentage Change Statements. Another analytical tool is percentage change statements. These statements present the percentage change in the amount of an item from its amount in the previous period or the average change over several prior periods. The last two columns in Exhibit 1.12 present changes in balance sheet items between Years 6 and 7 and the compound annual growth rates between Year 2 and Year 7. Coke has increased its investments in bottlers at a faster rate than it has increased property, plant, and equipment during the

---

EXHIBIT 1.13

Common Size and Percentage Change Income Statements for Coke

	Common Size		Percentage Change	
	Year 6	Year 7	Year 7	Five-Year Compound Annual Growth Rate
Sales	100.0%	100.0%	2.9%	9.1%
Other Revenues	3.2	5.2	68.5%	30.5%
Cost of Goods Sold	(38.5)	(36.3)	(2.9%)	7.4%
Selling and Administrative Expenses	(39.1)	(42.6)	11.9%	10.7%
Interest Expense	(1.5)	(1.5)	5.1%	13.7%
Income Before Income Taxes	24.1%	24.8%	(5.7%)	14.1%
Income Tax Expense	(7.5)	(6.0)	(17.7%)	7.6%
Net Income	16.6%	18.8%	16.9%	16.7%

---

previous five years. Thus, it appears that Coke has shifted more operating responsibility to its nonconsolidated bottlers.

The analyst must exercise particular caution in interpreting percentage change balance sheets for any particular year. If the amount for the preceding year that serves as the base is relatively small, then even a small change in dollar amount can result in a large percentage change. Note in Exhibit 1.12, for example, that the percentage change in the cumulative translation adjustment for Year 7 is 56.1 percent. This change reflects an increase from $424 million in Year 6 to $662 million in Year 7. Note, however, that the cumulative translation adjustment account constitutes only 2.8 percent of total liabilities plus shareholders' equity at the end of Year 6. A large percentage change in an account that represents only a small portion of total financing is not as meaningful as a smaller percentage change in an account that makes up a larger portion of total assets or total financing.

The third and fourth columns of Exhibit 1.13 present percentage change income statement amounts for Coke. Note that for the five-year period, net income for Coke increased faster than sales. Cost of goods sold increased at a slower rate than sales, suggesting either improved manufacturing efficiencies or a higher proportion of sales from higher-margin activities. Selling and administrative expenses increased at a faster rate than sales, perhaps because of expansion into other countries as well as increased competition from Pepsi and other beverages in the domestic market.

Financial Statement Ratios.   Perhaps the most useful analytical tools for assessing profitability and risk are financial statement ratios. Financial ratios express relationships between various items from the three financial statements that researchers and practitioners find serve as effective indicators of some dimension of profitability or risk. Chapter 3 discusses these financial ratios in depth. The discussion here merely introduces several of them.

Profitability Ratios.   Perhaps the most commonly encountered financial ratio is earnings per common share (EPS). EPS equals net income allocable to the common shareholders divided by the weighted average number of common shares outstanding. Firms typically report earnings per share in their income statements, and financial analysts often use a multiple of EPS to derive what they consider an appropriate price for a firm's common stock. For Year 7, EPS for Coke (see Exhibit 1.7) is $1.40 (= $3,492/2,494).

Another profitability measure is the rate of return on common shareholders' equity (ROCE). ROCE equals net income allocable to the common shareholders divided by average common shareholders' equity for the year. ROCE for Coke for Year 7 is 60.5 percent [= $3,492/0.5($5,392 + $6,156)]. This ROCE is extremely large relative to most other firms. The average ROCE for soft drink firms for the actual equivalent of Year 7 was 19.5 percent.[8] The average ROCE for industrial firms in the United States during the last thirty years is approximately 13 percent.[9]

Risk Ratios.   To assess the ability of firms to repay short-term obligations, analysts frequently calculate the current ratio, which equals current assets divided by current liabilities. The ratio for Coke at the end of Year 7 is 0.8 (= $5,910/$7,406). The average current ratio for all soft drink firms for that year-end is 0.9. Most firms have current ratios that exceed 1.0, so Coke would appear to have considerable short-term risk. Another short-term risk ratio is cash flow from operations divided by average current liabilities. This ratio for Coke for Year 7 equals 46.9 percent [= $3,463/0.5($7,348 + $7,406)]. As Chapter 3 discusses, a ratio above 40 percent is common for a financially healthy firm. Thus, Coke's low current ratio does not suggest inordinate short-term risk.

To assess the ability of firms to continue operating for the longer term (that is, avoid bankruptcy), the analyst looks at the amount of long-term debt in the capital structure. The ratio of long-term debt to shareholders' equity for Coke at the end of Year 7 is 18.1 percent (=$1,116/$6,156). This percentage has steadily declined for Coke in recent years. The average long-term debt to shareholders' equity ratio for soft drink firms for this year-end was 68.4 percent. Thus, Coke would appear to have low debt levels. Given Coke's level of profitability and low debt levels, bankruptcy risk is very low.

This section merely introduces a few tools for analyzing financial statements to provide a flavor for the material to be covered in later chapters.

---

[8]Leo Troy, *Almanac of Business and Industrial Financial Ratios,* 28th Edition (Englewood Cliffs, NJ: Prentice-Hall), 1997.

[9]Stephen H. Penman, "An Evaluation of Accounting Rates-of-Return," *Journal of Accounting, Auditing and Finance,* Spring 1991, pp. 233–255.

VALUATION OF FIRMS

One of the most frequent uses of financial statement analysis is to value firms. Analysts use measures of a firm's past and current profitability and risk to predict future returns and risk. Chapters 11 and 12 discuss various approaches to valuation. Here we describe two of these valuation methods briefly.

PRICE-EARNINGS RATIO

One valuation method relates earnings to the market price of the common stock. Given a market price of $52.63 at the end of Year 7, the price-earnings ratio for Coke is 37.6 (= $52.63/$1.40). A useful approach for analysts is to compare this price-earnings ratio to those of Coke's competitors. Pepsi's price-earnings ratio at this time, for example, was 25.3.

Another approach applies the theoretical model for the price-earnings ratio as follows:

$$\frac{\text{Price-Earnings}}{\text{Ratio}} = \frac{1 + \text{Growth Rate in Earnings}}{\text{Desired Rate of Return by Equity Investors} - \text{Growth Rate in Earnings}}$$

Appendix C indicates that net income to common shareholders grew at a compound annual growth rate of 16.7 percent during the five years preceding Year 7. For purposes of illustration, let's assume that Coke's earnings will continue to grow at this rate in future years. Equity investors' desired rate of return is a concept known in finance as the *cost of equity capital*. Chapter 11 illustrates how to compute this rate. Again for purposes of illustration, assume that a return of 20 percent is necessary to induce investors to purchase and hold shares in Coke. The theoretical price-earnings ratio is 35.4 [= (1 + 0.167)/(0.20 − 0.167)]. Thus, Coke's actual price-earnings ratio of 37.6 suggests a slight overvaluation.

MARKET-TO-BOOK-VALUE RATIO

A second approach to valuation relates a firm's market value to the book value of common shareholders' equity. The book value per common share for Coke at the end of Year 7 is $2.48 [= $6,156/(3,433 shares issued − 952 shares held as treasury stock)]. The actual market-to-book-value ratio is 21.2 (= $52.63/$2.48). The corresponding ratio for Pepsi is 6.9.

Chapter 12 develops the theoretical model for the market-to-book-value ratio. We merely introduce it here. The model presumes that a firm's value should equal the current book value of common shareholders' equity plus the present value of its ability to earn in the future a rate of return on common shareholders' capital in excess of the cost of that equity capital. Thus:

$$\frac{\text{Market-to-}}{\text{Book-Value}} = \frac{\text{Current Book}}{\text{Value of Common}} + \frac{\text{Expected ROCE} - \text{Cost of Equity Capital}}{\text{Cost of Equity Capital} -}$$
$$\text{Ratio} \qquad \text{Shareholders'} \qquad \text{Growth Rate in Common Shareholders' Equity}$$
$$\text{Equity}$$

Coke generated an ROCE of 60.5 percent during Year 7. For purposes of illustration, assume that Coke will continue to earn this level of ROCE in the future.[10] Appendix C indicates that Coke's common shareholders' equity grew at a compound annual rate of 8.6 percent during the preceding five years. We assume that this growth rate will continue in the future. The cost of equity capital is, as above, 20 percent. The theoretical market-to-book-value ratio is 4.6 [$= 1 + (0.605 - 0.20)/(0.20 - 0.086)$].

According to the theoretical model, Coke appears significantly overvalued by the market. It is premature, however, to jump to this conclusion. Coke's market price in fact reflects the value of its relationships with its bottlers, and only a small portion of these relationships are accounted for in Coke's consolidated financial statements. Also, Coke has expensed the cost of developing and maintaining its brand name over the years, thereby reducing retained earnings and common shareholders' equity. Finally, Coke has repurchased significant amounts of its common stock in recent years. These three factors tend to reduce the book value of Coke's common shareholders' equity and inflate its actual market-to-book-value ratio.

ROLE OF FINANCIAL STATEMENT ANALYSIS IN AN EFFICIENT CAPITAL MARKET

There are differing views as to the benefits of analyzing a set of financial statements. One view is that the stock market is efficient in reacting to published information about a firm. That is, market participants react intelligently and quickly to information they receive, so that market prices continually reflect underlying economic values. One implication of an efficient capital market is that financial statement users cannot routinely analyze financial statements to find "undervalued" or "overvalued" securities. The market quickly impounds new information into security prices.

Opposing views include the following:

1. Even if markets are perfectly efficient, someone must do the analysis to bring about the appropriate prices. Financial analysts, with their expertise and access to information about firms, can do the analysis quickly and engage in the trading necessary to achieve efficient pricing.
2. Research on capital market efficiency aggregates financial data for individual firms and studies the average reaction of the market to earnings and other financial statement information. A finding that the market is efficient on average does not mean that individual firms' shares cannot be mispriced.[11] A principal task of the financial analyst is to identify mispriced securities of particular firms and to take actions to bring about appropriate pricing.

---

[10]Coke will not likely continue to earn an ROCE of 60.5 percent forever. Chapter 12 develops the theoretical model for the market-to-book value ratio that allows for a reversal of ROCE over time to a level equal to the cost of equity capital.

[11]For an elaboration on the role of financial statement analysis in an efficient capital market and on the insights provided by academic research into this process, see Clyde P. Stickney, "The Academic's Approach to Securities Research: Is It Relevant to the Analyst?" *Journal of Financial Statement Analysis,* Summer 1997, pp. 52–60.

3. Research has shown that equity markets are not perfectly efficient. Anomalies include the tendency for market prices to adjust with a lag to new information, systematic underreaction to the information in earnings announcements, and the ability of a combination of financial ratios to detect under- and overpriced securities.[12]

4. Managers have incentives related to their job security and compensation to report as favorable a picture as possible in the financial statements while still following GAAP. Financial statements may therefore be biased indicators of the economic performance and financial position of firms. Financial analysts must cleanse the financial statements of such biases if market prices are to reflect underlying economic values.

5. There are numerous settings outside the capital equity markets where financial statement analysis is valuable (for example, credit analysis by a bank to support corporate lending, competitor analysis to identify competitive advantages, merger and acquisition analysis to identify buyout candidates).

SOURCES OF FINANCIAL STATEMENT INFORMATION

Firms in the United States whose bonds or capital stock trade in public markets typically make available the following information:

1. **Annual Report to Shareholders.** The widely distributed annual report includes balance sheets for the most recent two years and income statements and statements of cash flows for the most recent three years, along with various notes and supporting schedules. The annual report also includes a letter from the chairperson of the board of directors and the chief executive officer summarizing the activities of the most recent year. There is also a discussion and analysis by management of the firm's operating performance, financial position, and liquidity. Firms vary with respect to the information they provide in their Management Discussion and Analysis of operations. Some firms, such as Coke, as shown in Appendix B, give helpful information about the firm's strategy and reasons for the changes in profitability, financial position, and risk. Other firms merely repeat amounts presented in the financial statements without providing any expanded explanations for operating results.

2. **Form 10-K Annual Report.** The Form 10-K annual report filed with the Securities and Exchange Commission (SEC) includes the same financial statements and notes as the corporate annual report plus additional supporting schedules required by the SEC. For example, the 10-K includes more detailed information than the corporate annual report on changes in the allowance for uncollectible accounts and other valuation accounts.

3. **Form 10-Q Quarterly Report.** The Form 10-Q quarterly report filed with the SEC includes condensed balance sheet and income statement information for the most recent three months, as well as comparative data for earlier quarters.

---

[12]For a summary of the issues and related research, see Ray Ball, "The Theory of Stock Market Efficiency: Accomplishments and Limitations," *Journal of Applied Corporate Finance*, Spring 1995, pp. 4–17.

4. **Prospectus or Registration Statement.** Firms intending to issue new bonds or capital stock file a prospectus with the SEC that describes the offering (including amount and intended uses of proceeds). The prospectus includes much of the financial information found in the 10-K annual report.
5. **Form 20-F Annual Report.** Non-U.S. firms whose bonds or capital stock trade in capital markets in the United States must file annual reports with the SEC. The Form 20-F annual report is similar to the 10-K except that it includes schedules to reconcile net income and shareholders' equity according to GAAP of the domicile of the non-U.S. firm with GAAP in the United States.

Most firms will send single copies of their corporate annual reports to anyone requesting them. An increasing number of firms include all or a portion of their annual reports on a Web site home page. Firms are now required to file reports electronically with the SEC. These filings for recent years are available at the Web site for the SEC (http://www.sec.gov) by searching the Edgar data base. There are also numerous commercial on-line and CD-ROM services that provide financial statement information (Disclosure, Bloomberg, Lotus One Source, Standard & Poor's, Moody's, and others).

SUMMARY

The purpose of this chapter has been to provide a broad overview of five interconnected activities related to financial statement analysis:

1. Identification of the economic characteristics of the industry in which a firm operates.
2. Identification of the corporate strategy that a firm pursues to compete within its industry.
3. Understanding the principal financial statements and the need to cleanse them of unusual, nonrecurring items and of biases injected by management in an effort to look better.
4. Analysis and interpretation of the profitability and risk of a firm, assessing performance and the strength of the firm's financial position.
5. Valuation of the firm or use of financial statement analysis in a decision to extend credit, evaluate the performance of a competitor, identify a merger candidate, or some other purpose.

You should not expect to understand any of these five steps fully at this stage. Future chapters discuss each in greater depth. Chapter 2 explores the preparation and interpretation of the statement of cash flows for firms in various industries at various stages in their growth. Chapter 3 describes common financial statement ratios for assessing profitability and risk and illustrates their calculation and interpretation for Coke. Chapters 4 through 7 examine GAAP for various financial statement items and address concerns that affect the quality of earnings and financial position. Chapters 8 and 9 build on Chapter 3 by delving more deeply into profitability and risk analysis. In those chapters we consider industry economics and business strategy factors more fully and explore analytical approaches for particular industries.

Chapters 10 to 12 shift the focus to valuation. Chapter 10 demonstrates the preparation of pro forma financial statements. Chapter 11 examines valuation models based on cash flows and Chapter 12 presents valuation models based on earnings and book values.

PROBLEMS AND CASES

1.1 EFFECT OF INDUSTRY CHARACTERISTICS ON FINANCIAL STATEMENT RELATION-SHIPS. Effective financial statement analysis requires an understanding of a firm's economic characteristics. The relationships among various financial statement items provide evidence of

---

EXHIBIT 1.14

Common Size Financial Statement Data for Firms in 12 Industries
(Problem 1.1)

	(1)	(2)	(3)	(4)
Balance Sheet at End of Year				
Cash and Marketable Securities	1.9%	8.3%	8.7%	.9%
Receivables	16.8	.8	18.5	20.2
Inventories	—	12.7	16.7	19.8
Property, Plant, and Equipment Cost	4.9	15.8	26.5	53.1
Accumulated Depreciation	(2.0)	(6.5)	(12.1)	(18.4)
Net	2.9	9.3	14.4	34.7
Other Assets	3.8	2.7	13.8	8.2
Total Assets	25.4%	33.8%	72.1%	83.8%
Current Liabilities	9.8%	13.0%	27.6%	16.0%
Long-Term Debt	—	—	6.7	32.1
Other Noncurrent Liabilities	—	.9	2.8	5.2
Owners' Equity	15.6	19.9	35.0	30.5
Total Equities	25.4%	33.8%	72.1%	83.8%
Income Statement for Year				
Operating Revenues	100.0%	100.0%	100.0%	100.0%
Cost of Goods Sold (excluding				
depreciation) or Operating Expenses[a]	(81.4)	(54.5)	(63.0)	(68.9)
Depreciation	(.8)	(1.2)	(3.4)	(3.1)
Selling and Administrative	(14.1)	(36.7)	(16.9)	(15.8)
Interest	—	—	(.9)	(2.3)
Research and Development	—	—	(7.1)	—
Income Taxes	(1.5)	(3.1)	(2.9)	(4.0)
All Other Items (net)	—	.1	.9	.3
Total Expenses	97.8%	95.4%	93.3%	93.8%
Net Income	2.2%	4.6%	6.7%	6.2%
Cash Flow from Operations/Capital Expenditures	3.4	6.6	1.6	2.0

[a]See the problem narrative for items included in operating expenses.

many of these economic characteristics. Exhibit 1.14 presents common size condensed balance sheets and income statements for 12 firms in different industries. These common size balance sheets and income statements express various items as a percentage of operating revenues (that is, the statement divides all amounts by operating revenues for the year). The last line of Exhibit 1.14 also shows the cash flow from operations to capital expenditures ratio.

Absence of a particular item percentage does not necessarily mean that the amount is zero. It merely indicates that the amount is not sufficiently large for the firm to disclose it. The 12 companies and a brief description of their activities are:

1. **AK Steel**: Manufactures and sells a broad line of steel products.
2. **Allstate Insurance**: Sells property and casualty insurance, primarily on buildings and automobiles. Operating revenues include (a) insurance premiums collected or due from customers

EXHIBIT 1.14

continued

(5)	(6)	(7)	(8)	(9)	(10)	(11)	(12)
8.2%	.9%	11.8%	20.7%	3.1%	25.8%	240.0%	49.8%
11.3	28.1	3.4	114.2	5.4	3.7	11.1	479.3
15.7	14.0	1.7	—	.7	24.5	—	—
69.2	47.0	123.4	24.0	90.4	266.7	5.3	18.7
(24.0)	(20.6)	(51.8)	(11.4)	(44.7)	(97.2)	(2.4)	(11.7)
45.2	26.4	71.6	12.6	45.6	169.5	2.9	7.0
6.2	38.2	21.2	48.6	145.6	47.3	52.6	48.9
86.6%	107.6%	109.7%	196.1%	200.4%	270.8%	306.6%	585.0%
15.7%	30.3%	11.0%	131.6%	20.0%	29.2%	219.7%	226.8%
14.1	15.4	28.6	14.3	82.9	76.1	8.8	292.6
26.1	15.3	3.9	13.4	15.9	18.2	22.7	—
30.7	46.6	66.2	36.8	81.6	147.3	55.4	65.6
86.6%	107.6%	109.7%	196.1%	200.4%	270.8%	306.6%	585.0%
100.0%	100.0%	100.0%	100.0%	100.0%	100.0%	100.0%	100.0%
(80.5)	(34.1)	(51.2)	(55.3)	(50.7)	(62.0)	(79.1)	(19.4)
(3.3)	(3.9)	(5.0)	(3.7)	(6.9)	(16.2)	—	(4.8)
(5.0)	(40.9)	(30.2)	(29.1)	(17.4)	(6.3)	(9.1)	(29.4)
(1.7)	(.8)	(.4)	(1.7)	(3.2)	(5.7)	(.3)	(30.1)
—	—	—	—	—	(7.6)	—	—
(4.0)	(7.4)	(5.2)	(6.2)	(7.1)	(2.5)	(2.7)	(5.6)
(.8)	.3	—	4.4	—	11.4	—	—
93.7%	87.4%	92.0%	91.6%	85.3%	88.9%	91.2%	89.3%
6.3%	12.6%	8.0%	8.4%	14.7%	11.1%	8.8%	10.7%
.6	1.2	.6	3.1	1.0	.6	24.1	16.7

and (b) revenues earned from investments made with cash received from customers before Allstate must pay customers' claims. Operating expenses include amounts actually paid or expected to be paid in the future on insurance coverage outstanding during the year.

3. Gillette: Manufactures and sells a variety of consumer personal care and household products. Gillette has acquired several branded consumer products companies in recent years.

4. Hewlett-Packard: Develops, manufactures, and sells computer hardware. The firm outsources many of its computer components.

5. Household International: Lends money to consumers for periods ranging from several months to several years. Operating expenses represent estimated uncollectible loans.

6. Interpublic Group: Creates advertising copy for clients. Purchases advertising time and space from various media for sale to clients. Operating revenues represent the commission or fee earned by Interpublic for advertising copy created and media time and space sold. Operating expenses include compensation paid to employees. Interpublic has acquired other marketing services firms in recent years.

7. Kelly Services: Provides temporary office services to business and other firms. Operating revenues represent amounts billed to customers for temporary help services, and operating expenses include amounts paid to Kelly temporary help employees.

8. Lands' End: Sells apparel through catalogs, primarily through third-party credit cards.

9. May Department Stores: Operates several department store chains nationwide. Offers its own credit card.

10. McDonald's: Operates fast food restaurants worldwide. A large percentage of McDonald's restaurants are owned and operated by franchisees. McDonald's frequently owns the restaurant buildings of franchisees and leases them to franchisees under long-term leases.

11. Newmont Mining: Mines for gold and other minerals. Research and development expense includes exploration costs for Newmont.

12. Wendy's: Operates fast food restaurants worldwide. Wendy's owns a large percentage of its restaurants.

Required

Use whatever clues you can to match the companies in Exhibit 1.14 with the 12 firms listed above.

1.2 **EFFECT OF INDUSTRY CHARACTERISTICS ON FINANCIAL STATEMENT RELATIONSHIPS.** Effective financial statement analysis requires an understanding of a firm's economic characteristics. The relationships among various financial statement items provide evidence of many of these economic characteristics. Exhibit 1.15 presents common size condensed financial statement information for firms in 12 industries. These common size balance sheets and income statements express various items as a percentage of operating revenues (that is, the statements divide all amounts by operating revenues for the year). The last line of Exhibit 1.15 also shows the cash flow from operations to capital expenditures ratio for the year.

Absence of a particular item percentage does not necessarily mean the amount is zero for a particular firm. It merely indicates that the amount is not sufficiently large for the firm to disclose it. The 12 companies and a brief description of their activities are:

1. AT&T: Provides telecommunication services. AT&T has made major acquisitions of other companies in recent years.

2. Brown Forman: Distills hard liquors, which requires aging, and manufactures tonic waters.

3. Champion: Harvests timber and processes pulp into various paper products.

4. Citibank: Lends money to businesses and consumers and provides financial consulting services. Operating expenses for Citibank include compensation expense and estimated losses from uncollectible loans.

5. Commonwealth Edison: Generates and sells electricity to businesses and households. Currently operates under regulatory authority that sets electric rates but will transition into more competitive, less regulated environment in the years ahead.
6. Delta: Provides airline transportation services.
7. Eli Lilly: Develops, manufactures, and markets prescription drugs.
8. Kellogg: Manufactures and markets breakfast cereals.
9. Marriott: Manages hotels owned by others.
10. Microsoft: Designs, manufactures, and markets computer software.
11. Nike: Designs and markets athletic footwear and apparel. Nike outsources the manufacturing to firms in East Asia and outsources the retailing to retail and specialty stores.
12. USLife: Provides life insurance services. During the lag between collecting insurance premiums from policyholders and paying out benefits, USLife invests the cash in various financial securities. Operating expenses include the current year's portion of the amount USLife expects ultimately to pay to policyholders.

Required

Use whatever clues you can to match the companies in Exhibit 1.15 with the 12 firms listed above.

1.3 VALUE CHAIN ANALYSIS AND FINANCIAL STATEMENT RELATIONSHIPS. Exhibit 1.16 presents common size income statements and balance sheets for seven firms that operate at various stages in the value chain for the pharmaceutical industry. These common size statements express all amounts as a percentage of sales revenue. The last line of Exhibit 1.16 also shows the cash flow from operations to capital expenditures ratios for each firm.

Absence of a particular financial statement item percentage does not necessarily mean that the amount is zero. It merely indicates that the amount is not sufficiently large for the firm to disclose it. The seven companies and a brief description of their activities are:

1. Pfizer: Develops, manufactures, and sells ethical drugs (that is, drugs requiring a prescription). Pfizer's drugs primarily represent mixtures of chemical compounds. Ethical drug companies must obtain approval of new drugs from the Food and Drug Administration (FDA). Patents protect such drugs from competition until other drug companies develop more effective substitutes or the patent expires.
2. Amgen: Develops, manufactures, and sells drugs based on biotechnology research. Biotechnology drugs require approval from the FDA and enjoy patent protection similar to that for chemical-based drugs. The biotechnology segment is less mature than the ethical drug industry, with relatively few products having received FDA approval.
3. Mylan Laboratories: Develops, manufactures, and sells generic drugs. Generic drugs have the same chemical composition as drugs that were once protected by patent but for which the patent has now expired. Generic drug companies have benefited in recent years from patent expiration of several major ethical drugs. The major ethical drug companies, however, increasingly offer generic versions of their ethical drugs to compete with the generic drug companies.
4. Johnson & Johnson: Develops, manufactures, and sells over-the-counter health care products. Such products do not require a prescription and often benefit from brand recognition.
5. Quintiles: Offers laboratory testing services and facilitation of the FDA drug approval process for ethical drug companies that have discovered new drugs. Cost of goods sold for this company represents the salaries of personnel conducting the laboratory testing and drug approval services.

	EXHIBIT 1.15			
	Common Size Financial Statement Data for Firms in 12 Industries (Problem 1.2)			
	(1)	**(2)**	**(3)**	**(4)**
Balance Sheet at End of Year				
Cash and Marketable Securities	2.6%	4.0%	3.7%	3.5%
Current Receivables	7.4	20.8	8.9	16.6
Inventories..................................	1.7	14.4	6.4	28.0
Property, Plant, and Equipment Cost	22.7	17.1	73.2	38.5
Accumulated Depreciation	(4.1)	(7.2)	(29.3)	(20.3)
Net.......................................	18.6	9.9	43.9	18.2
Other Assets	19.6	11.9	12.7	23.1
Total Assets	49.9%	61.0%	75.6%	89.4%
Current Liabilities............................	17.3%	22.7%	32.9%	19.6%
Long-Term Debt	9.9	.2	10.9	13.7
Other Noncurrent Liabilities....................	10.3	.6	12.6	15.0
Owners' Equity	12.4	37.5	19.2	41.1
Total Equities	49.9%	61.0%	75.6%	89.4%
Income Statement for Year				
Operating Revenues.........................	100.0%	100.0%	100.0%	100.0%
Cost of Goods Sold (excluding depreciation) or Operating Expenses[a]............	(92.3)	(60.4)	(43.0)	(40.6)
Depreciation	(1.5)	(1.5)	(3.8)	(2.4)
Selling and Administrative......................	(.8)	(23.1)	(36.8)	(39.2)
Interest	(.8)	(.6)	(1.0)	(1.3)
Research and Development.....................	—	—	—	—
Income Taxes	(1.9)	(5.3)	(5.6)	(6.3)
All Other Items (net).........................	.3	(.6)	(.5)	.2
Total Expenses.............................	97.0%	91.5%	90.7%	89.6%
Net Income................................	3.0%	8.5%	9.3%	10.4%
Cash Flow from Operations/ Capital Expenditures	1.8	1.5	2.3	2.9

[a]See the problem narrative for items included in operating expenses.

6. Cardinal Health: Distributes drugs as a wholesaler to drugstores, hospitals, and mass merchandisers. Also offers pharmaceutical benefit management services in which it provides customized data bases designed to help customers order more efficiently, contain costs, and monitor their purchases. Cost of goods sold for Cardinal Health includes the cost of drugs sold plus the salaries of personnel providing pharmaceutical benefit management services.

7. Walgreen: Operates a chain of drug stores nationwide. The data in Exhibit 1.16 for Walgreen include the recognition of operating lease commitments for retail space.

EXHIBIT 1.15

continued

(5)	(6)	(7)	(8)	(9)	(10)	(11)	(12)
.3%	80.0%	13.3%	3.0%	13.0%	.4%	364.8%	271.9%
17.2	7.4	7.8	9.9	20.1	9.5	22.2	518.7
—	—	.6	7.8	12.0	6.7	—	—
75.7	22.1	213.8	198.3	96.6	414.0	2.5	26.0
(37.8)	(11.8)	(96.2)	(62.0)	(38.0)	(165.5)	(1.9)	(11.7)
37.9	15.3	117.6	136.3	58.6	248.5	.6	14.3
51.1	13.7	21.9	10.1	91.0	69.7	48.7	57.0
106.5%	116.4%	161.2%	167.0%	194.7%	334.8%	436.3%	861.9%
31.3%	28.0%	29.2%	16.1%	57.5%	28.1%	348.4%	740.5%
15.1	—	80.5	52.5	34.2	92.8	16.6	57.8
21.2	—	31.1	34.4	20.0	113.4	3.6	—
38.9	88.4	20.4	64.0	83.0	100.5	67.7	63.6
106.5%	116.4%	161.2%	167.0%	194.7%	334.8%	436.3%	861.9%
100.0%	100.0%	100.0%	100.0%	100.0%	100.0%	100.0%	100.0%
(49.5)	(11.7)	(60.6)	(80.4)	(25.9)	(61.3)	(70.7)	(19.2)
(5.3)	(5.5)	(5.1)	(6.9)	(7.4)	(13.7)	(.6)	(2.2)
(28.3)	(30.8)	(17.9)	(6.2)	(24.3)	—	(19.9)	(21.9)
(.6)	—	(8.0)	(3.8)	(3.9)	(7.3)	(2.4)	(38.1)
—	(16.5)	—	—	(14.5)	—	—	—
(6.2)	(13.7)	(3.3)	(1.1)	(6.9)	(6.7)	(2.2)	(7.0)
.6	3.5	.5	.8	3.6	—	—	—
89.3%	74.7%	94.4%	92.6%	79.3%	89.0%	95.8%	88.4%
10.7%	25.3%	5.6%	2.4%	20.7%	11.0%	4.2%	11.6%
1.4	5.7	1.5	.8	4.5	1.7	53.0	6.4

Required

Use whatever clues you can to match the seven companies above with the seven companies in Exhibit 1.16.

1.4 RECASTING THE FINANCIAL STATEMENTS OF A U.K. COMPANY ACCORDING TO U.S. FORMAT, TERMINOLOGY, AND ACCOUNTING PRINCIPLES. WPP Group, headquartered in the United Kingdom, is one of the largest marketing services firms in the world. It offers advertising, market research, public relations, and other marketing services through a worldwide network of offices. The financial statements of WPP Group

EXHIBIT 1.16

Common Size Financial Statement Data for Seven Firms in the Pharmaceutical Industry
(Problem 1.3)

	1	2	3	4	5	6	7
Income Statement							
Sales..............................	100.0%	100.0%	100.0%	100.0%	100.0%	100.0%	100.0%
Cost of Goods Sold	(50.3)	(13.6)	(19.2)	(55.3)	(32.5)	(72.3)	(91.9)
Selling and Administrative	(14.3)	(22.5)	(38.6)	(34.9)	(38.8)	(20.8)	(4.9)
Research and Development	(9.9)	(25.3)	(14.9)	—	(8.8)	—	—
Interest..........................	—	(.3)	(1.0)	(1.8)	(.6)	(1.8)	(.3)
Income Taxes....................	(10.0)	(13.5)	(7.7)	(3.2)	(5.3)	(2.0)	(1.3)
Other	4.2	7.8	(1.5)	1.3	(.4)	.1	.2
Net Income	19.7%	32.6%	17.1%	6.1%	13.6%	3.2%	1.8%
Balance Sheet							
Cash.............................	48.2%	51.6%	14.5%	18.5%	9.9%	.1%	3.9%
Receivables......................	18.3	10.8	19.9	33.2	15.0	2.4	6.4
Inventories......................	25.6	4.7	14.1	—	11.6	13.9	14.0
Other Current	4.4	4.9	8.7	2.4	6.9	.8	1.1
Intercorporate Investments	—	5.2	10.3	—	—	—	—
Property, Plant, and Equipment (net)..	31.0	43.6	34.0	23.1	26.1	35.4	1.7
Other Noncurrent Assets	41.9	11.6	28.2	19.2	23.1	1.3	3.2
Total Assets	169.4%	132.4%	129.7%	96.4%	92.6%	53.9%	30.3%
Current Liabilities	12.4%	30.8%	49.9%	36.2%	24.0%	10.0%	15.6%
Long-Term Debt.................	—	2.8	6.1	31.4	6.5	23.1	3.0
Other Noncurrent Liabilities	6.9	7.5	11.8	1.9	12.0	3.5	1.2
Shareholders' Equity	150.1	91.3	61.9	26.9	50.1	17.3	10.5
Total Equities....................	169.4%	132.4%	129.7%	96.4%	92.6%	53.9%	30.3%
Cash Flow from Operations/ Capital Expenditures	2.4	3.1	2.7	.7	2.8	1.1	1.7

for Year 6 and Year 7 appear in Exhibit 1.17 (balance sheet), Exhibit 1.18 (profit and loss account), and Exhibit 1.19 (cash flow statement). These financial statements reflect reporting formats, terminology, and accounting principles employed in the United Kingdom.

Required

Recast the financial statements of WPP Group according to the reporting format, terminology, and accounting principles customarily used in the United States. Include a separate analysis of the changes in retained earnings.

1.5 RECASTING THE FINANCIAL STATEMENTS OF A GERMAN COMPANY ACCORDING TO U.S. FORMATS AND TERMINOLOGY. Volkswagen Group manufactures automobiles and provides financing for its customers' purchases. Exhibit 1.20 presents a balance sheet at the end of Year 4 and Year 5, and Exhibit 1.21 presents an income statement for Year 4 and Year 5 for Volkswagen.

Required

a. Prepare a balance sheet for Volkswagen as of December 31 Year 4 and Year 5 using reporting formats and terminology commonly encountered in the United States.

b. Prepare an income statement for Volkswagen for Year 4 and Year 5 using terminology commonly encountered in the United States. Separate operating revenues and expenses from nonoperating revenues and expenses.

EXHIBIT 1.17

WPP Group
Consolidated Balance Sheet
(amounts in millions of pounds)
(Problem 1.4)

	December 31	
	Year 6	**Year 7**
Fixed Assets		
Intangible Assets (Note 1)	£ 350	£ 350
Tangible Assets.	139	139
Investments	36	46
Total Fixed Assets	£ 525	£ 535
Current Assets		
Stocks.	£ 93	£ 94
Debtors (Note 2)	888	854
Investments	34	37
Cash at Bank and In Hand	342	375
	£ 1,357	£ 1,360
Creditors: Amounts Falling Due Within One Year (Note 3) .	(1,522)	(1,508)
Net Current Liabilities	£ (165)	£ (148)
Total Assets Less Current Liabilities.	£ 360	£ 387
Creditors: Amounts Falling Due After One Year.	(329)	(282)
Provisions for Liabilities and Charges (Note 4).	(89)	(78)
Net Liabilities.	£ (58)	£ 27
Capital and Reserves		
Called Up Share Capital.	£ 74	£ 74
Share Premium Account.	409	416
Goodwill Write-Off Reserve (Note 5)	(1,040)	(1,069)
Other Reserves (Note 6).	97	118
Profit and Loss	398	483
Share Owners' Funds	£ (62)	£ 22
Minority Interests.	4	5
Total Capital Employed	£ 58	£ 27

NOTES TO EXHIBIT 1.17

Note 1: Intangible assets represent the portion of the purchase price of marketing services agencies acquired that WPP allocated to the brand names of these agencies.

Note 2: Debtors include the following:

	December 31	
	Year 6	Year 7
Trade Debtors.	£ 690	£ 723
Other Debtors.	155	90
Prepayments	43	41
Total	£ 888	£ 854

Note 3: Creditors falling due within one year include the following:

	December 31	
	Year 6	Year 7
Bank Loans.	£ 73	£ 86
Trade Creditors.	1,009	953
Taxation	84	97
Other Creditors and Accruals	356	372
Total	£1,522	£1,508

Note 4: Provisions include the following:

	December 31	
	Year 6	Year 7
Deferred Taxation	£ 7	£ 10
Pensions	50	46
Other	32	22
Total	£ 89	£ 78

Note 5: GAAP in the UK allows firms to write off goodwill in the year of an acquisition against share owners' equity.

Note 6: Other reserves include the following amounts:

	December 31	
	Year 6	Year 7
Cumulative Translation Adjustment . . .	£ 14	£ 41
Revaluation of Tangible Fixed Assets . .	83	77
Total	£ 97	£ 118

EXHIBIT 1.18

WPP Group
Consolidated Profit and Loss Account
(amounts in millions of pounds)
(Problem 1.4)

	Year 6	Year 7
Turnover	£1,555	£1,691
Gross Profit	£1,328	£1,436
Other Operating Expenses	1,178	1,254
Operating Profit	£ 150	£ 182
Interest Receivable	11	10
Interest Payable	(47)	(39)
Profit on Ordinary Activities Before Taxation	£ 114	£ 153
Tax on Profit on Ordinary Activities	(43)	(50)
Profit/(Loss) on Ordinary Activities After Taxation	£ 71	£ 103
Minority Interest	(2)	(3)
Profit/(Loss) for the Financial Year	£ 69	£ 100
Ordinary Dividends	(10)	(15)
Retained Profit/(Loss) For The Year	£ 59	£ 85

EXHIBIT 1.19

WPP Group
Consolidated Cash Flow Statement
(amounts in millions of pounds)
(Problem 1.4)

	December 31	
	Year 6	**Year 7**
Operating Activities		
Operating Profit....................................	£150	£182
Depreciation Charge	26	28
(Increase) Decrease in Stocks	13	(9)
(Increase) Decrease in Debtors	(108)	(13)
Increase (Decrease) in Trade Creditors	154	69
Increase in Provisions	11	9
Other Adjustments................................	(10)	(28)
Net Cash Flow from Operating Activities...............	£236	£238
Returns on Investments and Servicing of Finance		
Interest and Dividends Received	£ 10	£ 12
Interest Paid	(48)	(39)
Dividend Paid	(10)	(11)
Net Cash Flow from Investments and Servicing of Finance..	£ (48)	£ (38)
Taxation..	£ (29)	£ (39)
Investing Activities		
Purchase of Tangible Fixed Assets.....................	£ (35)	£ (36)
Proceeds from Sale of Tangible Fixed Assets	2	2
Other Investing Activities...........................	(19)	(18)
Net Cash Outflow from Investing Activities..............	£ (52)	£ (52)
Financing Activities		
Proceeds from Issue of Share Capital	—	£ 3
Increase (Decrease) in Bank Loans	£ (39)	£ (34)
Net Cash Flow from Financing Activities................	£ (39)	£ (31)
Effect of Exchange Rate Changes on Cash and Cash Equivalents	£ (4)	£ (45)
Cash and Cash Equivalents—Beginning of Year	£278	£342
Cash and Cash Equivalents—End of Year	£342	£375

EXHIBIT 1.20

Balance Sheet for Volkswagen Group
(in millions of deutsche mark)
(Problem 1.5)

	December 31	
	Year 4	Year 5
Assets		
Fixed Assets		
Intangible Assets (Note 1)	DM 91	DM 120
Tangible Assets (net)	28,568	32,749
Financial Assets.	3,198	3,274
Total Fixed Assets.	DM 31,857	DM 36,143
Current Assets		
Inventories.	DM 9,392	DM 10,368
Receivables	27,248	31,205
Securities.	2,156	3,499
Cash on Hand	13,174	13,080
Total Current Assets.	DM 51,970	DM 58,152
Prepaid and Deferred Charges (Note 2).	DM 250	DM 273
Balance Sheet Total.	DM 84,077	DM 94,568
Shareholders' Equity and Liabilities		
Shareholders' Equity		
Subscribed Capital: Ordinary Shares	DM 1,388	DM 1,388
Preferred Shares.	326	437
Capital Reserve	4,557	4,946
Revenue Reserves (Note 3)	4,038	4,378
Net Earnings Available for Distribution	209	318
Minority Interests (Note 4)	472	468
Total Shareholders' Equity	DM 10,990	DM 11,935
Special Items with an Equity Portion (Note 5) . . .	1,664	1,385
Provisions (Note 6)	31,742	36,026
Liabilities (Note 7)	37,823	41,996
Deferred Income	1,858	3,226
Balance Sheet Total.	DM 84,077	DM 94,568

EXHIBIT 1.21

Income Statement for Volkswagen Group
(in millions of deutsche mark)
(Problem 1.5)

	Year Ended December 31	
	Year 4	**Year 5**
Sales.....................................	DM 88,119	DM 100,123
Cost of Sales............................	(80,699)	(90,504)
Gross Profit.............................	DM 7,420	DM 9,619
Selling and Distribution Expenses............	(7,089)	(8,301)
General and Administrative Expenses.........	(2,368)	(2,660)
Other Operating Income (Note 8)............	6,811	7,487
Other Operating Expenses (Note 9)..........	(4,659)	(5,760)
Results from Participations (Note 10).........	229	509
Interest Results (Note 11).................	979	1,209
Write-down of Securities Classified as Current Assets (Note 12)	(210)	(131)
Income Before Taxation	DM 1,113	DM 1,972
Taxes on Income.........................	(777)	(1,294)
Net Earnings............................	DM 336	DM 678

NOTES TO EXHIBITS 1.20 AND 1.21

Note 1: Intangible assets consist of license rights.

Note 2: Prepaid and deferred charges consist of the following:

	December 31	
	Year 4	**Year 5**
Prepaid Operating Costs	DM 160	DM 199
Deferred Bond Issue Costs	90	74
Total	DM 250	DM 273

Note 3: Revenue reserves represent earnings not officially designated by the board of directors as available for dividends.

Note 4: Minority interests represent the ownership interests of entities outside of the Volkswagen Group in a consolidated entity within the Group.

Note 5: Special items with an equity portion represent the income taxes saved because taxing authorities allowed firms to revalue certain assets to market value for purposes of calculating depreciation for tax purposes. Volkswagen has no obligation to repay these income taxes at a later date.

Note 6: Provisions include the following:

	December 31	
	Year 4	**Year 5**
Pensions	DM 11,571	DM 13,651
Warranties................	5,200	5,600
Restructuring	5,902	6,388
Other Provisions	9,109	10,387
Total	DM 31,742	DM 36,026

Note 7: Liabilities consist of the following:

	December 31	
	Year 4	**Year 5**
Bonds	DM 3,044	DM 3,019
Bank Loans	19,150	20,253
Advances from Customers....	674	969
Trade Payables	6,038	7,626
Other Operating Liabilities ...	8,917	10,129
Total	DM 37,823	DM 41,996

Note 8: Other operating income consists of the elimination of provisions made in prior years.

Note 9: Other operating expenses consist primarily of the effects of exchange rate changes.

Note 10: Results from participation represent Volkswagen Group's share in the earnings of less than majority owned entities.

Note 11: Interest results consist of the following:

	December 31	
	Year 4	**Year 5**
Interest Income............	DM 3,323	DM 3,655
Interest Expense	(2,344)	(2,446)
Total	DM 979	DM 1,209

Note 12: The write-down of securities would appear in a separate shareholders' equity account in the United States, instead of a charge against earnings. Assume that cumulative write-downs of such securities were DM 430 on January 1, Year 4. Also assume that there is no income tax effect to the writedown.

NIKE: SOMEWHERE BETWEEN A SWOOSH AND A SLAM DUNK

Nike boasts the largest worldwide market share in the athletic footwear industry and a leading market share in sports and athletic apparel. Nike, Reebok, and Adidas combined hold approximately a 67 percent market share in the athletic footwear industry in the United States. This case uses the financial statements for Nike and excerpts from its notes to review important concepts underlying the three principal financial statements (balance sheet, income statement, and statement of cash flows) and relationships among them. The case also introduces tools for analyzing financial statements, comparing amounts for Nike (Year 8 sales of $6.5 billion) to those of Reebok (Year 8 sales of $3.5 billion) and Adidas (Year 8 sales of $2.4 billion). Nike and Reebok are U.S.-based companies, and Adidas is headquartered in Germany.

INDUSTRY ECONOMICS

PRODUCT LINES

Industry analysts debate whether the athletic footwear industry is a performance-driven athletic footwear industry or a fashion-driven sneaker industry. Proponents of the performance view point to Nike's dominant market position, which results in part from ongoing innovation in product development. Proponents of the fashion view point to the difficulty of protecting technological improvements from competitor imitation (for example, most companies market shoes with an inner air system); the large portion of total expenses dedicated to advertising; the role of sports and other personalities in promoting athletic shoes; and the fact that only 20 percent of athletic footwear consumers use the footwear for its intended purpose (that is, basketball or running, say).

GROWTH

Growth opportunities for footwear in the United States have slowed considerably in recent years. There is doubt about both volume increases (the number of pairs of athletic shoes that consumers will tolerate in their closets) and price increases (whether consumers will continue to pay prices for newly innovated athletic shoes that are often twice as expensive as other footwear).

Athletic footwear companies have diversified their revenue sources in two directions in recent years. One direction involves increased emphasis on international sales. As dress standards become more casual in Europe and East Asia, and as interest in American sports such as basketball and football becomes more widespread, industry analysts look to international markets as the major growth markets during the next several years. Increased emphasis on soccer in the U.S. will also help companies such as Adidas with reputations for quality soccer footwear.

The second direction for diversification is sportswear and athletic apparel. The three leading athletic footwear companies are capitalizing on their brand name recognition and distribution channels to create lines of sportswear that coordinate with their footwear. Team uniforms and matching apparel for coaching staffs have become a major growth avenue recently.

PRODUCTION

Nearly 99 percent of athletic footwear and over 50 percent of apparel products come from factories in East Asia, primarily South Korea, China, Taiwan, Thailand, Indonesia, and Malaysia. The footwear companies do not own any of these manufacturing facilities. They typically hire manufacturing representatives to source and oversee the manufacturing process, helping to insure quality control and serving as a link between the design and the manufacture of products. The manufacturing process is labor-intensive; sewing machines are the primary equipment. Footwear companies typically price their purchases from these factories in U.S. dollars. This production strategy subjects the footwear companies to political risk (the "most favored nation" trading status of China is a perennial political football), as well as import tariffs.

MARKETING

Athletic footwear and sportswear companies sell their products through various independent department, specialty, and discount stores. Their sales forces function to educate retailers on new product innovations, store display design, and similar activities. The dominant market shares of Nike, Reebok, and Adidas, limits on retailers' shelf space, and slowing growth in sales all make it increasingly difficult for the remaining athletic footwear companies to gain market share.

Nike, Reebok, and Adidas have typically used independent distributors to market their products in other countries. With increasing brand recognition and anticipated growth in international sales, these companies are acquiring an increasing number of their distributors to capture more of the profits generated in other countries and to maintain better control of international marketing.

FINANCE

Compared to other apparel firms, the athletic footwear firms generate higher profit margins and rates of return. They use cash flow generated from this superior profitability to finance needed working capital investments (receivables and inventories). Long-term debt tends to be minimal, reflecting the absence of significant investments in manufacturing facilities.

NIKE

Nike targets the serious athlete with its performance-driven footwear. Phil Knight, Chairman, CEO, and major shareholder, sums up the company's philosophy and the driving force behind Nike's success by saying: "We have the edge because we are not shoe makers; we're athletes who make shoes." Although generally only 20 percent of athletic footwear sold is used for its intended purpose, among Nike customers the rate is 40 percent. The company is a major supplier of footwear and uniforms to high school, college, and professional sports teams.

To maintain its technological edge, Nike engages in extensive research at its research facilities in Beaverton, Oregon. It alters its product line constantly to introduce new footwear and evolutionary improvements in existing products.

Nike has a reputation for timely delivery of footwear products to its customers, primarily as a result of its Futures program. Under this program, retailers book orders five to six months in advance. Nike guarantees 90 percent delivery of the order within 15 days of the promised date at the agreed-upon price at the time of ordering. Approximately 88 percent of footwear orders received by Nike during Year 8 came though its Futures program. This program allows the company to improve production scheduling, thereby reducing inventory risk. It also locks in prices and increases Nike's risk of change in raw materials and labor costs, however. Nike is currently implementing a similar Futures program for its apparel products.

Independent contractors manufacture virtually all of Nike's products. Nike sources all of its footwear from other countries and approximately 50 percent of its apparel.

Six exhibits present information for Nike, Reebok, and Adidas:

Exhibit 1.22: Consolidated balance sheet for Nike for Year 7 and Year 8.

EXHIBIT 1.22

Consolidated Balance Sheet for NIKE
(amounts in millions)
(Case 1.1)

May 31:	Year 7	Year 8
Assets		
Cash and Cash Equivalents	$ 216	$ 262
Accounts Receivable, less Allowance for Doubtful		
Accounts of $33 and $43	1,053	1,346
Inventories.	630	931
Deferred Income Taxes	73	93
Prepayments	74	95
Total Current Assets	$ 2,046	$ 2,727
Property, Plant, and Equipment net of Accumulated		
Depreciation of $336 and $404	555	643
Identifiable Intangible Assets and Goodwill	496	475
Deferred Income Taxes and Other Assets	46	107
Total Assets	$ 3,143	$ 3,952
Liabilities and Shareholders' Equity		
Accounts Payable.	$ 298	$ 455
Notes Payable	397	445
Current Portion of Long-Term Debt	32	7
Other Current Liabilities	381	560
Total Current Liabilities.	$ 1,108	$ 1,467
Long-term Debt.	11	10
Deferred Income Taxes	18	2
Other Liabilities.	42	41
Total Liabilities	$ 1,179	$ 1,520
Common Stock	$ 125	$ 158
Foreign Currency Translation	1	(16)
Retained Earnings	1,838	2,290
Total Shareholders' Equity.	$ 1,964	$ 2,432
Total Liabilities and Shareholders' Equity	$ 3,143	$ 3,952

EXHIBIT 1.23

Consolidated Income Statement for NIKE
(amounts in millions)
(Case 1.1)

Year Ended May 31:	Year 6	Year 7	Year 8
Sales Revenue..........................	$ 3,790	$ 4,761	$ 6,471
Cost of Goods Sold.....................	(2,301)	(2,865)	(3,907)
Selling and Administrative................	(974)	(1,210)	(1,589)
Interest................................	(15)	(24)	(39)
Other Income Expense, Net..............	(9)	(12)	(37)
Income Before Income Taxes.............	$ 491	$ 650	$ 899
Income Taxes.........................	(192)	(250)	(346)
Net Income...........................	$ 299	$ 400	$ 553

Exhibit 1.23: Consolidated income statement for Nike for Year 6, Year 7, and Year 8.

Exhibit 1.24: Consolidated statement of cash flows for Nike for Year 6, Year 7, and Year 8.

Exhibit 1.25: Excerpts from Notes to Nike's financial statements.

Exhibit 1.26: Common size and percentage change income statements for Nike, Reebok, and Adidas.

Exhibit 1.27: Common size and percentage change balance sheets for Nike, Reebok, and Adidas.

Required
Study the financial statements and notes for Nike, and then respond to all the questions below.

INCOME STATEMENT

a. Identify the time at which Nike recognizes revenues. Does this timing of revenue recognition seem appropriate? Explain.

b. Identify the cost-flow assumptions that Nike uses to measure cost of goods sold. Does Nike's choice of cost flow assumptions seem appropriate? Explain.

c. Nike reports property, plant, and equipment on its balance sheet, and discloses the amount of depreciation for each year in its statement of cash flows. Why doesn't depreciation expense appear among its expenses on the income statement?

d. Identify the portion of Nike's income tax expense of $346 million for Year 8 that is currently payable to governmental entities and the portion that is deferred to future years. Why do governmental entities permit firms to defer payment of their income taxes to future years?

EXHIBIT 1.24

Consolidated Statement of Cash Flows for NIKE
(amounts in millions)
(Case 1.1)

Year Ended May 31:	Year 6	Year 7	Year 8
Operations			
Net Income..............................	$299	$ 400	$ 553
Depreciation	65	71	97
Deferred Income Taxes	(24)	(25)	(72)
Other	8	19	33
(Increase) Decrease in Accounts Receivable	24	(302)	(293)
(Increase) Decrease in Inventories	161	(70)	(301)
(Increase) Decrease in Other Current Assets ...	9	(10)	(21)
Increase (Decrease) in Accounts Payable	75	87	157
Increase (Decrease) in Other Current Liabilities.	(41)	85	177
Cash Flow from Operations...............	$576	$ 255	$ 330
Investing			
Additions to Property, Plant, and Equipment ...	$ (95)	$(154)	$(216)
Disposals of Property, Plant, and Equipment ...	13	9	12
Additions to Other Assets	(5)	(6)	(26)
Acquisitions of Subsidiaries.................	(4)	(430)	—
Cash Flow from Investing	$ (91)	$(581)	$(230)
Financing			
Additions to Long-Term Debt	$ 6	$ 3	$ 5
Reductions in Long-Term Debt..............	(57)	(40)	(30)
Increase (Decrease) in Notes Payable	(3)	264	48
Proceeds from Exercise of Stock Options	4	6	21
Repurchase of Common Stock	(140)	(143)	(19)
Dividends	(60)	(65)	(79)
Other	(7)	(2)	—
Cash Flow from Financing	$(257)	$ 23	$ (54)
Change in Cash.........................	$228	$(303)	$ 46
Cash—Beginning of Year	291	519	216
Cash—End of Year	$519	$ 216	$ 262

EXHIBIT 1.25

Excerpts from Notes to Consolidated Financial Statements for NIKE
(amounts in millions)
(Case 1.1)

Summary of Significant Accounting Policies

Recognition of Revenues: NIKE recognizes revenue at time of sale to its customers
and as it earns fees on sales by licensees.

Inventory Valuation: Inventories appear at lower of cost or market. NIKE
determines cost using the last-in, first out (LIFO) method for substantially all
U.S. inventories and the first-in, first-out (FIFO) method for international
inventories. The excess of replacement cost over LIFO cost was $20 million on
May 31, Year 7 and $16 million on May 31, Year 8.

Property, Plant, and Equipment and Depreciation: Property, plant, and equipment
appear at acquisition cost. NIKE computes depreciation using the straight-line
method for buildings and leasehold improvements and a declining balance
method for machinery and equipment, based on estimated useful lives ranging
from three to thirty-two years.

Identifiable Intangible Assets and Goodwill: This account represents the excess of
the purchase price of acquired businesses over the market values of identifiable
net assets, net of amortization to date.

Corporate Acquisition: NIKE acquired Bauer, Inc., the world's largest hockey
equipment manufacturer, in the third quarter of Year 7 for $409 million and
used the purchase method of accounting. NIKE allocated $73 to tangible net
assets and $336 to identifiable intangible assets and goodwill.

Income Taxes: NIKE provides deferred income taxes for temporary differences
between income before taxes for financial reporting and tax reporting. Income
tax expense includes the following:

	Year 6	Year 7	Year 8
Currently Payable	$210	$283	$418
Deferred	(18)	(33)	(72)
Income Tax Expense	$192	$250	$346

Stock Repurchases: NIKE repurchases outstanding shares of its common stock
each year and retires them. Any difference between the price paid and the book
value of the shares appears as an adjustment of retained earnings.

EXHIBIT 1.26

Common Size and Percentage Change Income Statements
for NIKE, Reebok, and Adidas
(Case 1.1)

NIKE	Common Size Income Statements Fiscal Year Ended May 31:			Percentage Change Income Statements Fiscal Year Ended May 31:		
	Year 6	Year 7	Year 8	Year 6	Year 7	Year 8
Sales Revenues	100.0%	100.0%	100.0%	(3.6%)	25.6%	35.9%
Other Revenues	.5	.5	.2	24.0%	36.9%	(38.4%)
Cost of Goods Sold	(60.7)	(60.2)	(60.4)	(3.6%)	24.5%	36.3%
Selling and Administrative Expenses .	(26.4)	(26.2)	(25.4)	6.6%	24.6%	31.6%
Interest Expense	(.4)	(.5)	(.6)	(40.6%)	58.4%	63.2%
Income Before Taxes	13.0%	13.6%	13.8%	(17.5%)	32.5%	38.4%
Income Taxes	(5.1)	(5.2)	(5.3)	(16.4%)	30.4%	38.2%
Net Income	7.9%	8.4%	8.5%	(18.1%)	33.8%	38.4%

	Common Size Income Statements Calendar Year Ended December 31:				Percentage Change Income Statements Calendar Year Ended December 31:	
	Year 7	Year 8	Year 7	Year 8	Year 8	Year 8
	Reebok		Adidas		Reebok	Adidas
Sales Revenues	100.0%	100.0%	100.0%	100.0%	6.1%	9.3%
Other Revenues	.4	.3	.2	.3	(24.4%)	27.0%
Cost of Goods Sold	(59.9)	(60.7)	(63.7)	(60.1)	7.5%	3.1%
Selling and Administrative Expenses .	(27.3)	(28.8)	(30.8)	(30.7)	12.3%	8.8%
Interest Expense	(.5)	(.7)	(1.2)	(1.3)	55.8%	23.9%
Special Charge	—	(2.1)	—	—	—	—
Minority Interest	(.3)	(.3)	(.1)	(.2)	28.4%	82.2%
Income Before Taxes	12.4%	7.7%	4.4%	8.0%	(35.2%)	94.5%
Income Taxes	(4.6)	(3.0)	(.8)	(1.2)	(35.2%)	40.0%
Net Income	7.8%	4.7%	3.6%	6.8%	(35.2%)	108.8%

EXHIBIT 1.27

Common Size and Percentage Change Balance Sheets for NIKE, Reebok, and Adidas (Case 1.1)

	Percentage Change Balance Sheets NIKE		Common Size Balance Sheets NIKE			Reebok	Adidas
	Year 7	Year 8	Year 6	Year 7	Year 8	Year 8	Year 8
Assets							
Cash	(58.4%)	21.3%	20.2%	6.4%	6.2%	4.6%	2.2%
Accounts Receivable	49.7%	27.8%	27.3	31.0	31.7	28.7	24.9
Inventories	34.0%	47.9%	18.3	18.5	22.0	36.0	45.3
Prepayments	88.5%	27.7%	3.0	4.3	4.4	6.8	5.4
Total Current Assets	15.6%	33.3%	68.8%	60.2%	64.3%	76.1%	77.8%
Property, Plant, and Equipment	34.3%	14.7%	23.6	23.9	22.0	17.0	15.1
Other Noncurrent Assets	174.3%	7.3%	7.6	15.9	13.7	6.9	7.1
Total Assets	32.2%	24.7%	100.0%	100.0%	100.0%	100.0%	100.0%
Liabilities and Shareholders' Equity							
Accounts Payable	41.4%	52.9%	8.2%	8.7%	10.7%	9.4%	19.3%
Notes Payable	211.7%	12.1%	4.9	11.7	10.5	3.8	23.0
Current Portion of Long-term Debt	728.2%	(77.1%)	.1	.9	.2	.1	—
Other Current Liabilities	73.0%	47.0%	8.6	11.3	13.2	11.2	17.0
Total Current Liabilities	97.1%	32.5%	21.8%	32.6%	34.6%	24.5%	59.3%
Long-term Debt	26.8%	11.0%	8.3	7.9	7.1	20.5	5.5
Deferred Income Taxes	(2.4%)	(89.4%)	.7	.5	—	.3	.1
Other Noncurrent Liabilities	4.7%	(1.1%)	1.6	1.3	1.0	—	2.9
Minority Interest	—	—	—	—	—	1.7	1.2
Total Liabilities	72.5%	25.9%	32.4%	42.3%	42.7%	47.0%	69.0%
Common Stock	(.3%)	.1%	.1%	.1%	.1%	.1%	12.2%
Additional Paid-in Capital	13.1%	26.5%	4.2	3.6	3.7	2.2	.8
Retained Earnings	11.7%	24.6%	63.9	54.0	54.0	84.2	18.0
Foreign Currency Translation	(110.5%)	(1,141.1%)	(.6)	—	(.5)	.7	—
Treasury Stock	—	—	—	—	—	(34.2)	—
Total Shareholders' Equity	12.9%	23.8%	67.6%	57.7%	57.3%	53.0%	31.0%
Total Liabilities and Shareholders' Equity	32.2%	24.7%	100.0%	100.0%	100.0%	100.0%	100.0%

BALANCE SHEET

    a. Why do accounts receivable appear net of allowance for doubtful accounts? Identify the events or transactions that cause the allowance account to increase or decrease.

    b. Refer to Exhibit 1.25. Why do firms like Nike that use a LIFO cost flow assumption report the excess of replacement cost over LIFO cost for inventories? What are the likely reasons for the relatively small amount for Nike?

    c. Identify the depreciation methods that Nike uses for its buildings and equipment. Does Nike's choice of depreciation methods seem appropriate?

    d. Nike includes identifiable intangible assets and goodwill on its balance sheet as an asset. Does this account include the value of the Nike name and the "swoosh" trademark? Explain.

    e. Nike includes deferred income taxes in three places: under current assets, noncurrent assets, and noncurrent liabilities. Under what circumstances will deferred income taxes give rise to an asset? To a liability?

STATEMENT OF CASH FLOWS

    a. Why does the amount of net income differ from the amount of cash flow from operations?

    b. Why does Nike report depreciation as an addition to net income in calculating cash flow from operations?

    c. Why does Nike report deferred income taxes as a subtraction from net income when it calculates cash flow from operation?

    d. Why does Nike subtract increases in accounts receivable from net income when it calculates cash flow from operations for Year 8?

    e. Why does Nike subtract increases in inventory from net income when it calculates cash flow from operations for Year 8?

    f. Why does Nike add increases in accounts payable and other current liabilities to net income when it calculates cash flow from operations for Year 8?

    g. Given that firms often sell property, plant, and equipment at a gain or loss, why does Nike include the proceeds of disposal of these assets as an investing activity instead of as an operating activity?

    h. Given that notes payable appear on the balance sheet as a current liability, why does Nike include changes in this liability as a financing activity instead of an operating activity?

RELATIONSHIPS AMONG FINANCIAL STATEMENT ITEMS

    a. Compute the amount of cash collected from customers during Year 8.

    b. Compute the amount of cost of goods sold for Year 8, assuming that Nike uses a FIFO cost flow assumption for all of its inventories and cost of goods sold.

    c. Compute the amount of cash payments made to suppliers of merchandise during Year 8.

    d. Prepare an analysis that accounts for the change in the property, plant, and equipment account and the accumulated depreciation account during Year 8. Calculate the gain or loss that Nike recognized on the disposal of property, plant, and equipment during Year 8.

    e. Prepare an analysis that accounts for the change in the current portion of long-term debt and the long-term debt accounts during Year 8.

    f. Identify the reasons for the change in retained earnings during Year 8.

INTERPRETING FINANCIAL STATEMENT RELATIONSHIPS

a. Exhibit 1.26 presents common size and percentage change income statements for Nike for Year 6, Year 7, and Year 8. Exhibit 1.26 also presents similar information for Reebok and Adidas, Nike's two principal competitors. What are the likely reasons for the increased net income/sales revenue percentages for Nike during the last three years?

b. What are the likely reasons for the increased income taxes/sales revenue percentages for Nike during the last three years?

c. What does the relation between the percentage change in sales and the percentage change in cost of goods sold for Nike during the three years suggest about the behavior of this expense item?

d. The three companies report cost of goods sold/sales percentages between 60 percent and 61 percent during Year 8. Why might these percentages be so similar? (Hint: Consider how these firms likely set purchase and selling prices for their products.)

e. Nike experienced the highest net income/sales percentage of the three companies during Year 7 and Year 8. What is the apparent source of its competitive advantage?

f. Exhibit 1.27 presents common size and percentage change balance sheets for Nike at the end of Year 6, Year 7, and Year 8. Exhibit 1.27 also presents common size balance sheets for Reebok and Adidas at the end of Year 7 and Year 8. The amounts in Exhibit 1.27 reflect the capitalization of commitments under operating leases (increase property, plant, and equipment and long-term debt) and therefore differ from the amounts in the published balance sheets. What is the likely explanation for the relatively small percentages for property, plant, and equipment for these three companies?

g. What is the likely explanation for the relatively small percentages for long-term debt for these three companies?

h. What is the likely explanation for the increase in the percentage for other noncurrent assets for Nike for Year 7?

i. The proportion of total assets constituting accounts receivable and inventories increased steadily during the three years for Nike. Do these increasing percentages suggest an unreasonable buildup of receivables and inventories? Explain.

j. The proportion of total financing for accounts payable and other operating current liabilities increased steadily during the three years for Nike. Do these increasing percentages suggest an unreasonable stretching of creditors? Explain.

k. Which of the three firms appears to be the most risky from a financial structure perspective? Explain your reasoning.

l. Look at the statement of cash flows for Nike in Exhibit 1.24. Net income increased between Year 6 and Year 7, but cash flow from operations decreased. What is the likely reason for the different direction of these changes?

m. Nike's net income and cash flow from operations both increased between Year 7 and Year 8. Why does this pattern of changes differ from that between Year 6 and Year 7?

n. Nike's cash flow from operations exceeded net income during Year 6 but was less than net income during Year 7 and Year 8. Why do these relations differ between these years?

o. How has Nike primarily financed its acquisitions of property, plant, and equipment during the three years?

p. How did Nike apparently finance its acquisition of Bauer, Inc. during Year 7?

q. What are the likely reasons for Nike's repurchases of common stock during the three years?

Learning Objectives

1. Understand the relation between net income and cash flow from operations for firms in various industries.
2. Understand the relation between cash flows from operating, investing, and financing activities for firms in various stages of their life cycles.
3. Prepare a statement of cash flows from balance sheet and income statement data.

The income statement reports the revenues and expenses of a firm, for a particular period of time, stated according to the accrual basis of accounting. The objective of preparing an income statement is to obtain a measure of operating performance that matches a firm's outputs (revenues) with the associated inputs (expenses).

In Chapter 1 we pointed out that a firm's cash flows will not precisely track, or mirror, its income flows for several reasons: (1) cash receipts from customers do not necessarily occur in the same period when a firm recognizes revenues, (2) cash payments to employees, suppliers and governments do not necessarily occur in the same period when a firm recognizes expenses, and (3) cash inflows and outflows occur relating to investing and financing activities that do not flow directly through the income statement.[1] Thus, although the accrual basis of accounting properly measures operating performance each period, its application does not reveal the critical variable for remaining in business: cash flows.

The statement of cash flows reports the relation between income flows and cash flows from operations. It also reports the cash flow effects of investing and financing activities. An understanding of the relation between income flows and cash flows is essential for analyzing both the profitability and financial health of a business.

This chapter explores the statement of cash flows. We look at the relation between income flows and cash flow from operations for various types of businesses, and we also look at the relationships among the cash flows from operating, investing, and financing activities for firms in various stages of their life cycles. We describe and illustrate procedures for preparing the statement of cash flows using information from the balance sheet and income statement.[2]

INCOME FLOWS, CASH FLOWS, AND LIFE CYCLE RELATIONS

Interpreting the statement of cash flows requires an understanding of two relations:

1. The relation between net income and cash flow from operations.
2. The relation among the net cash flows from operating, investing, and financing activities.

NET INCOME AND CASH FLOW FROM OPERATIONS

The first section of the statement of cash flows reports the amount of cash flow from operations: the cash received from selling goods and services to customers, net of the cash paid to suppliers, employees, governments, and other providers of goods and services. Firms present cash flow from operations using one of two formats: the *direct method* and the *indirect method.* Under the direct method, firms list the cash inflows from selling goods and services, and then subtract the cash outflows to providers of goods and services. The top panel of Exhibit 2.1 shows the calculation of cash flow from operations for Forest City Enterprises, a real estate development company, using the direct method.

Under the indirect method, firms begin the calculation of cash flow from operations with net income for the period. They then adjust net income for noncash

---

[1]This chapter uses income flows to mean net income and not revenues.

[2]Financial Accounting Standards Board *Statement No. 95* defines cash flows in terms of their effect on cash and cash equivalents. Cash equivalents include highly liquid investments that are both readily convertible into cash and so near to maturity that changes in interest rates present an insignificant risk to their market value. Cash equivalents usually include Treasury bills, commercial paper and money market funds. Throughout this book, we use the term cash to mean cash and cash equivalents.

EXHIBIT 2.1

Cash Flow from Operations Presented in Direct and Indirect Methods for Forest City Enterprises
(amounts in millions)

	Year Ended January 31		
	Year 5	Year 6	Year 7
Direct Method			
Rents and Other Revenues Received...........................	$ 480	$ 508	$ 531
Proceeds from Land Sales..	42	45	44
Land Development Expenditures	(33)	(24)	(26)
Operating Expenditures	(238)	(324)	(352)
Interest Paid	(119)	(132)	(135)
Cash Flow from Operations....................................	$ 132	$ 73	$ 62
Indirect Method			
Net Income (Loss)	$ (49)	$ 6	$ 7
Depreciation and Amortization	66	66	66
Deferred Income Taxes	24	11	10
Writedown of Real Estate to Market Value	10	10	12
(Gain) Loss on Disposition of Properties......................	31	1	(18)
Working Capital from Operations	$ 82	$ 94	$ 77
(Increase) Decrease in Accounts and Notes Receivable	1	29	(41)
(Increase) Decrease in Land Held for Development......	19	—	(12)
Increase (Decrease) in Accounts Payable.....................	37	(29)	40
Increase (Decrease) in Other Current Liabilities	(7)	(21)	(2)
Cash Flow from Operations	$ 132	$ 73	$ 62

revenues and expenses to obtain cash flow from operations. The lower panel of Exhibit 2.1 illustrates the indirect method of presentation.

The vast majority of firms use the indirect method, because it reconciles the level of earnings for a period with the net amount of cash received or paid. Critics of the indirect method, however, suggest that it is hard for less sophisticated users to understand the rationale for some of the reconciling items. We use the indirect method throughout this text.

The calculation of cash flow from operations under the indirect method involves two types of adjustments: (1) changes in nonworking capital accounts and (2) changes in operating working capital accounts (for example, accounts receivable, inventories, accounts payable).

Changes in Nonworking Capital Accounts. Certain revenues and expenses relate to changes in noncurrent asset or noncurrent liability accounts, and have cash flow effects that differ from their income effects. For example, depreciation expense reduces net property, plant, and equipment and net income.

Yet depreciation expense does not require an *operating* cash outflow in the period of the expense (on the contrary, firms classify the cash outflow to acquire depreciable assets as an *investing* activity in the year of acquisition). The addback of depreciation expense to net income (see Exhibit 2.1) offsets the effect of the subtraction of depreciation expense (that is, nets its effect to zero) in the computation of cash flow for operations.

Firms that sell an item of property, plant, or equipment report the full cash proceeds as an investing activity.[3] Because net income includes the gain or loss on the sale (that is, sales proceeds minus the book value of the item sold), the operating section of the statement of cash flows shows an addback for a loss and a subtraction for a gain to offset their inclusion in net income. Forest City Enterprises reports adjustments for gains and losses on disposition of properties in computing cash flow from operations (see Exhibit 2.1). These properties are buildings that Forest City Enterprises had previously rented to others and has now sold.

Chapter 7 points out that a firm holding an investment of 20 percent to 50 percent in another entity uses the equity method to account for the investment (a noncurrent asset). The investor recognizes its share of the investee's earnings each period, increasing the investment account and net income. It reduces the investment account for dividends received. Thus, net income reflects the investor's share of earnings, not the cash received. The statement of cash flows usually shows a subtraction from net income for the excess of the investor's share of the investee's earnings over dividends received (see Coke's statement of cash flows in Appendix A).

Other examples of revenues and expenses that relate to changes in noncurrent asset or noncurrent liability accounts include: amortization of intangible assets; the deferred portion of income tax expense; minority interests in the earnings of consolidated subsidiaries; and some restructuring charges and adjustments for changes in accounting principles. (Later chapters discuss each of these items more fully.) Published statements of cash flows sometimes report a subtotal after adjusting net income for these particular items, and label the subtotal "working capital from operations." Firms with high proportions of noncurrent assets on the balance sheet—such as capital-intensive manufacturing and transportation companies—will find that net income and working capital from operations will likely differ by a substantial amount. Firms with high proportions of current assets, such as retailers that rent their retail space and banks that rent their office space, will find that net income and working capital from operations are similar in amount.

Changes in Operating Working Capital Accounts. The second type of adjustment to reconcile net income to cash flow from operations involves changes in operating current asset and current liability accounts. For example, an increase in accounts receivable indicates that a firm did not collect as much cash from customers as the amount of sales revenue for the period. A subtraction from net income for the increase in accounts receivable converts sales revenue on an

---

[3]The sale of land by a land development company, such as Forest City Enterprises in Exhibit 2.1, represents an operating activity since land is "inventory" to such a business.

accrual basis to cash received from customers. An increase in current operating liabilities means that a firm did not use as much cash for operating expenses as the amount appearing on the income statement. An addition to net income for the increase in current operating liabilities converts operating expenses on an accrual basis to cash paid to suppliers of various goods and services. Similar adjustments for changes in inventories, prepayments, and accounts payable convert accrual basis income amounts to their associated cash flow amounts.

Firms that are mature and not growing rapidly will report relatively small amounts for changes in operating current asset and current liability accounts as compared to the amount of working capital from operations. Thus, their cash flow from operations will not differ substantially from working capital from operations. Firms that grow rapidly will report more substantial adjustments for changes in accounts receivable, inventories, and operating current liabilities. If a firm uses current operating liabilities to finance the increases in accounts receivable and inventories, then the adjustments for changes in working capital will net to a relatively small amount, and working capital from operations will approximately equal cash flow from operations. Accounts receivable and inventories for most growing firms, however, grow more rapidly than the firm's current operating liabilities so that cash flow from operations is typically less than both net income and working capital from operations.

Another factor that may cause cash flow from operations to differ from working capital from operations is the length of a firm's operating cycle (see Exhibit 1.8 in Chapter 1 for a graphic depiction). The operating cycle encompasses the time when a firm begins to manufacture its products until it receives cash from customers when it sells the products. Firms such as construction companies and aerospace manufacturers with relatively long operating cycles will often experience a lag between the time they expend cash for raw materials and employee services and the time they receive cash from customers. Unless such firms receive cash advances from their customers prior to completion and delivery of the products, or unless they delay payments to their suppliers, cash flow from operations will be less than working capital from operations. The longer the operating cycle and the more rapid the growth of a firm, the more the difference between these two amounts. Firms with short operating cycles, such as restaurants and service firms, will experience less of a lag between the creation and delivery of their products and the collection of cash from customers. Thus, cash flow from operations will not differ substantially from working capital from operations.

A study of the relationships of net income, working capital from operations, and cash flow from operations reveals: (1) a high correlation between net income and working capital from operations and (2) a low correlation between net income and cash flow from operations and between working capital from operations and cash flow from operations.[4] The primary difference between net income and working capital from operations for most firms is the addback for depreciation expense. If a firm's income growth tracks its additions to property, plant, and equipment, one would expect a high correlation between net income and working

---

[4]Robert M. Bowen, David Burgstahler and Lane A. Daley, "Evidence on the Relationship Between Earnings and Various Measures of Cash Flow," *Accounting Review* (October, 1986), pp. 713–725.

capital flow from operations. The low correlation between these two measures and cash flow from operations suggests that changes in operating working capital accounts do not track changes in net income.

RELATIONSHIPS OF CASH FLOWS FROM OPERATING, INVESTING, AND FINANCING ACTIVITIES

The product life cycle concept provides a helpful framework for understanding the relationship of income flows and cash flows. It is a concept that comes out of marketing and microeconomics. Individual products (goods or services) move through four general phases—introduction, growth, maturity, and decline—as the top panel of Exhibit 2.2 depicts. The length of the phases and the steepness of the revenue curve vary by the type of product. Although it is hard to pinpoint the precise location of a product on its life cycle curve at any particular time, it is usually possible to identify the phase and whether the product is in the earlier or later portion of that phase.

The middle panel of Exhibit 2.2 shows the trend of net income over the product life cycle. Net losses usually occur in the introduction and early growth phases when revenues do not cover the cost of designing and launching new products. Net income peaks during the maturity phase, and then begins to decline.

The bottom panel of Exhibit 2.2 shows the cash flows from operating, investing, and financing activities during the four life cycle phases. During the introduction and early growth phases, there is a negative cash flow from operations, because of the cash outflows needed to launch the product. Negative cash flow from investing activities also occurs during these early phases, as the firm builds productive capacity. The level of this negative cash flow for investing activities depends on the degree of capital intensity of the business. Firms must obtain the cash needed for operating and investing activities during these early phases from external sources (debt and shareholders' equity).

As the growth phase accelerates, operations become profitable and begin to generate cash. Firms use this cash, however, to finance accounts receivable and build inventories for expected higher sales levels in the future. Thus, net income usually turns positive earlier than cash flow from operations. The extent of the negative cash flow from investing activities depends on a firm's rate of growth and its degree of capital intensity. As in the introduction phase, firms obtain most of the cash needed during the growth phase from external sources. A multiproduct firm has other options; it can use cash generated from products in the maturity phase of their life cycle to finance other products that are in their introduction and growth phases and therefore avoid seeking as much external financing.

As products move through the maturity phase, the cash flow pattern changes dramatically. Operations become a net provider of cash, both because of market acceptance of the product and a leveling off of working capital needs. Also, with revenues leveling off, firms invest to maintain rather than increase productive capacity. During the later stages of the maturity phase, net cash flows from investing activities may even turn positive as cash inflows from sales of unneeded plant assets exceed new investments. Firms can use the excess cash flow from operations

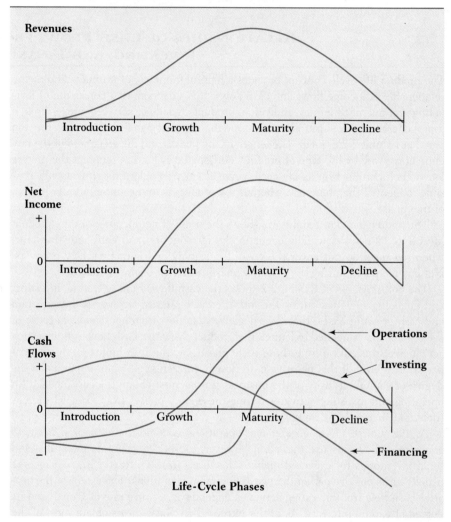

EXHIBIT 2.2

Relation of Income Flows and Cash Flows from Operations, Investing, and Financing at Various Stages of Product Life Cycle

(and to a lesser extent from the sale of investments) to repay debt incurred during the introduction and growth phases and to pay dividends.

During the decline phase, cash flow from operations and investing activities tails off as sales decrease. Firms repay their remaining debt.

The product life cycle model provides helpful insights about the relationships among sales, net income, and cash flows from operating, investing, and financing activities for a single product. Few business firms, however, rely on a single product; most have a range of products at different stages of their life cycles. Furthermore, the statement of cash flows reports amounts for a firm as a whole and not for each product. If the life cycle concept is to assist in interpreting published statements of cash flows, the analyst needs a multiproduct view.

The way to obtain such a multiproduct view is to aggregate the position of each of a firm's products, in their respective life cycles, into a reading on the average life cycle position of the firm. For example, the average firm in technology-driven industries, such as biotechnology, is probably in the growth phase. Although such firms will have some products fresh off the drawing board and other products in their decline phase as new technologies emerge, most of these firms' products are in their high growth phase. Most consumer foods companies are in the maturity phase. Branded consumer foods products can remain in the maturity phase for many years with proper product quality control and promotion (consider, for example, Coke and Pepsi). Such companies are always bringing new products to the market and eliminating products that do not meet consumer acceptance, but their average position is probably in the maturity phase. Certain industries in the United States, such as textiles and steel, are probably in the early decline phase because of foreign competition and outdated technology. Some companies in these industries have built technologically advanced production facilities to compete more effectively on a worldwide basis and essentially reentered the maturity phase. Other firms have diversified into more growth-oriented industries.

ILLUSTRATIONS OF CASH FLOW RELATIONS

Look at the statement of cash flows for Coke in Appendix A. It shows an excess of cash inflows from operations over cash outflows for investing, which is typical of mature firms. Coke labels this excess amount "Net cash provided by operations after reinvestment" on its statement of cash flows. In its glossary of terms at the end of Appendix B, Coke describes this excess as *free cash flows*, indicating that the excess along with borrowing is available to pay dividends and make share repurchases.[5] Most security analysts interpret free cash flows even more broadly—as a resource that firms can use to repay debt, make acquisitions, or increase investment in research and development, among other uses. Coke primarily used its excess cash flow to pay dividends and repurchase shares of its common stock in recent years.

Exhibits 2.3 through 2.7 present statements of cash flows for firms in five different industries to illustrate how a firm's phase in its aggregate product life cycle affects the interpretation of its statement of cash flows.

Netscape Communications. Exhibit 2.3 shows a statement of cash flows for Netscape Communications, a provider of Internet software. Netscape commenced operations in Year 4 and is in the rapid growth phase of its life cycle. The firm operated at a net loss in Year 4, but its operating performance improved over the three years. Cash flow from operations is negative in Year 4 because expenses exceeded revenues. Netscape received cash from its customers before it provided services, however (these advances are in "other current liabilities"), so

---

[5]Financial analysts and the financial press define free cash flows in various ways. Some mean cash flow from operations net of expenditures on property, plant, and equipment. Others mean cash flow from operations net of cash flow from investing activities and changes in short- and long-term borrowing. One encounters other definitions as well. Thus, the reader should ascertain the particular definition used.

	EXHIBIT 2.3		

Netscape Communications Corporation
Statement of Cash Flows
(amounts in thousands)

	Year 4	Year 5	Year 6
Operations			
Net Income (Loss)...................	$(13,830)	$ (6,613)	$ 20,908
Depreciation	345	3,853	16,320
Other Addbacks...................	0	2,553	2,456
Other Subtractions	0	0	(23,747)
Working Capital Provided by Operations..	$(13,485)	$ (207)	$ 15,937
(Increase) Decrease in Receivables	(1,688)	(24,929)	(83,525)
(Increase) Decrease in Other Current Assets.........................	(298)	(5,989)	(10,473)
Increase (Decrease) in Accounts Payable..	1,506	6,696	18,951
Increase (Decrease) in Other Current Liabilities......................	6,845	36,437	74,197
Cash Flow from Operations..........	$ (7,120)	$ 12,008	$ 15,087
Investing			
Fixed Assets Acquired	$ (3,175)	$ (20,522)	$ (81,931)
Change in Marketable Securities........	—	(116,367)	(87,120)
Other Investing Transactions..........	(1,089)	(2,891)	(5,363)
Cash Flow from Investing	$ (4,264)	$(139,780)	$ (174,414)
Financing			
Increase in Long-Term Borrowing.......	0	$ 2,200	0
Issue of Capital Stock	$ 17,852	171,059	$ 192,182
Decrease in Long-Term Borrowing	(504)	(401)	(601)
Cash Flow from Financing...........	$ 17,348	$ 172,858	$ 191,581
Change in Cash....................	$ 5,964	$ 45,086	$ 32,254
Cash—Beginning of Year.............	4,226	10,190	55,276
Cash—End of Year	$ 10,190	$ 55,276	$ 87,530
Growth in Revenues from Previous Year ..	—	1,963.5%	305.4%

cash flow from operations is not as negative as net income. Sales grew rapidly between Year 4 and Year 5, but Netscape still operated at a loss. Its cash flow from operations turns positive because of substantial advances from customers. Continued growth in sales in Year 6 then led to positive net income and cash flow from operations. Although accounts receivable grew rapidly during Year 6, Netscape stretched its creditors and received additional advances from customers. Thus, the net change in its operating working capital accounts is small.

Under investing, the rapid increase reported to acquire fixed assets indicates Netscape was building manufacturing and communications capacity to support its increasing levels of sales. In none of the three years is cash flow from operations sufficient to finance these capital expenditures. Under financing, we see that Netscape obtained cash primarily by issuing capital stock. The short product life cycle for computer software is likely the motivation for using equity financing instead of long-term debt. Netscape did not use all of the cash obtained for capital expenditures immediately; it invested the temporarily excess cash in marketable securities.

Wal-Mart Stores.　Exhibit 2.4 presents a statement of cash flows for Wal-Mart Stores, a rapidly growing discount store, warehouse club, and grocery store chain. Working capital provided by operations exceeds net income each year

EXHIBIT 2.4					
Wal-Mart **Statement of Cash Flows** **(amounts in millions)**					
	Year 5	**Year 6**	**Year 7**	**Year 8**	**Year 9**
Operations					
Net Income	$ 1,995	$ 2,333	$ 2,681	$ 2,740	$ 3,056
Depreciation	649	849	1,070	1,304	1,463
Other Addbacks	13	0	0	0	0
Other Subtractions	0	(75)	(118)	(227)	0
Working Capital Provided by Operations	$ 2,657	$ 3,107	$ 3,633	$ 3,817	$ 4,519
(Increase) Decrease in Receivables	(106)	(165)	(84)	(61)	(58)
(Increase) Decrease in Inventories	(1,884)	(1,324)	(3,053)	(1,850)	99
(Increase) Decrease in Other Current Assets	(20)	(1)	(147)	(77)	38
Increase (Decrease) in Accounts Payable	420	230	1,914	448	1,208
Increase (Decrease) in Other Current 　Liabilities	211	349	643	106	124
Cash Flow from Operations	$ 1,278	$ 2,196	$ 2,906	$ 2,383	$ 5,930
Investing					
Fixed Assets Acquired	$(3,366)	$(3,644)	$(3,734)	$(3,566)	$(2,643)
Other Investing Transactions	(140)	(842)	(58)	234	575
Cash Flow from Investing	$(3,506)	$(4,486)	$(3,792)	$(3,332)	$(2,068)
Financing					
Increase in Short-Term Borrowing	$ 1,135	0	$ 220	$ 660	0
Increase in Long-Term Borrowing	1,367	$ 3,108	1,250	1,004	$ 632
Issue of Capital Stock	16	10	0	0	0
Decrease in Short-Term Borrowing	0	(14)	0	0	(2,458)
Decrease in Long-Term Borrowing	(67)	(456)	(107)	(207)	(615)
Acquisition of Capital Stock	0	0	0	0	0
Dividends	(241)	(299)	(391)	(458)	(481)
Other Financing Transactions	0	(51)	(61)	(12)	(140)
Cash Flow from Financing	$ 2,210	$ 2,298	$ 911	$ 987	$(3,062)
Change in Cash	$ (18)	$ 8	$ 25	$ 38	$ 800
Cash—Beginning of Year	$ 30	12	20	45	83
Cash—End of Year	$ 12	$ 20	$ 45	$ 83	$ 883
Growth Rate in Revenues	26.4%	21.4%	22.5%	13.6%	12.0%

because of the addback for depreciation expense. Cash flow from operations is less than working capital from operations in all years, except Year 9, because of the need to acquire merchandise for higher future sales. Accounts payable to suppliers increase less than the increase in inventories, indicating that Wal-Mart was using its suppliers to finance only a portion of the inventory buildup. Wal-Mart slowed the growth in inventories during Year 9 but stretched its suppliers, resulting in more cash flow from operations than working capital from operations. Wal-Mart sells either for cash or uses bank credit cards, so it does not need to carry heavy investments in receivables.

Except for Year 9, Wal-Mart's positive cash flow from operations is not sufficient to completely finance its rapid expansion of stores and buildup of fixed assets. (Note that the acquisition of fixed assets exceeds depreciation expense each year, an indication of growth in property, plant, and equipment.) Wal-Mart relied primarily on long-term borrowing to complete the funding of fixed assets. There are a variety of reasons Wal-Mart used debt as opposed to equity financing, including the predictable cash flows of a large retailer, the collateral value of its stores and store equipment, and the lower cost of debt financing.

Note that Wal-Mart's sales growth slowed considerably beginning in Year 8 and Year 9. It decreased its capital expenditures and its inventory buildup and used excess cash flow to repay short-term borrowing.

Merck.   Exhibit 2.5 shows the statement of cash flows for Merck, a pharmaceutical company. During Year 4 and Year 5 net income, working capital provided by operations, and cash flow from operations were similar in amount. Merck is not heavily capital-intensive, as indicated by the relatively small percentage of depreciation and amortization expense to net income. Changes in its current operating liabilities approximately match changes in its current operating assets. Merck used the cash flow from operations to finance capital expenditures, pay dividends, and repurchase capital stock.

It also used the excess cash flow in Year 5 to make a major acquisition, reported in "other investing transactions." The acquisition had several effects on its cash flow statement in subsequent years. First, Merck recognized goodwill on its balance sheet because it paid more for the acquired company than the market value of the net assets acquired. Merck amortizes this goodwill beginning in Year 6, which increases the addback for depreciation and amortization. Second, the rapid growth in revenues during Year 6 results from including the acquired firm's revenues with the Merck revenues for Year 6; Year 5's revenues include primarily only Merck's. Note, though, that net income remained relatively flat between Year 5 and Year 7.

Merck's cash flow from operations in Year 6 through Year 8 continued to exceed its capital expenditures. Merck used the excess cash flow to pay dividends and repurchase its common stock. The repurchase of common stock reduced the proportion of equity and increased the proportion of debt in the capital structure, thereby increasing the degree of financial leverage. (We discuss the benefits of financial leverage in Chapter 3). The increase in capital stock in Year 7 represents the issue of preferred stock. Merck also sold off some operations during Year 7 (reported

EXHIBIT 2.5

Merck & Co.
Statement of Cash Flows
(amounts in millions)

	Year 4	Year 5	Year 6	Year 7	Year 8
Operations					
Net Income	$ 2,446	$ 2,941	$ 2,997	$ 2,827	$ 3,881
Depreciation and Amortization	321	386	682	667	731
Other Addbacks	0	0	8	455	175
Other Subtractions	(92)	(230)	(11)	0	0
Working Capital Provided by Operations . . .	$ 2,675	$ 3,097	$ 3,676	$ 3,949	$ 4,787
(Increase) Decrease in Receivables	(298)	(263)	(265)	(244)	(225)
(Increase) Decrease in Inventories	(177)	(47)	(26)	(272)	(268)
Increase (Decrease) in Accounts Payable	101	(123)	291	383	414
Increase (Decrease) in Other Current Liabilities	203	384	464	(872)	720
Cash Flow from Operations	$ 2,504	$ 3,048	$ 4,140	$ 2,944	$ 5,428
Investing					
Fixed Assets Acquired	$(1,067)	$(1,013)	$(1,009)	$(1,006)	$(1,197)
Change in Marketable Securities	(273)	342	269	(1,342)	(640)
Other Investing Transactions	(12)	(1,917)	772	1,026	(142)
Cash Flow from Investing	$(1,352)	$(2,588)	$ (32)	$(1,322)	$(1,979)
Financing					
Increase in Short-Term Borrowing	$ 480	$ 911	0	$ 40	0
Increase in Long-Term Borrowing	141	354	$ 337	550	$ 328
Issue of Capital Stock	52	83	139	1,284	442
Decrease in Short-Term Borrowing	0	0	(1,580)	0	(7)
Decrease in Long-Term Borrowing	(121)	(39)	(152)	(108)	(342)
Acquisition of Capital Stock	(863)	(371)	(705)	(1,571)	(2,493)
Dividends	(1,064)	(1,174)	(1,434)	(1,540)	(1,729)
Other Financing Trans	0	30	62	(34)	(143)
Cash Flow from Financing	$(1,375)	$ (206)	$(3,333)	$ 1,379	$(3,944)
Change in Cash	$ (223)	$ 254	$ 775	$ 243	$ 495
Cash—Beginning of Year	798	575	829	1,604	1,847
Cash—End of Year	$ 575	$ 829	$ 1,604	$ 1,847	$ 1,352
Growth in Revenues	12.3%	8.6%	42.6%	11.4%	18.9%

under "other investing transactions") and invested the proceeds in marketable securities (reported as an investing activity).

American Airlines. Exhibit 2.6 presents a statement of cash flows for American Airlines. Cash flow from operations significantly exceeds net income or net loss in each year because of the large addback of depreciation expense.

EXHIBIT 2.6

American Airlines
Statement of Cash Flows
(amounts in millions)

	Year 4	Year 5	Year 6	Year 7	Year 8
Operations					
Net Income...........................	$ (475)	$ (110)	$ 228	$ 167	$ 1,016
Depreciation and Amortization.............	1,041	1,223	1,250	1,259	1,204
Other Addbacks	165	196	488	624	605
Other Subtractions......................	(101)	(30)	0	0	(497)
Working Capital Provided by Operations	$ 630	$ 1,279	$ 1,966	$ 2,050	$ 2,328
(Increase) Decrease in Receivables..........	(144)	37	(135)	(109)	(225)
(Increase) Decrease in Inventories	(85)	(27)	(19)	(11)	(66)
(Increase) Decrease in Other Current Assets ..	244	(128)	49	(37)	(150)
Increase (Decrease) in Accounts Payable	(53)	(27)	(1)	(103)	251
Increase (Decrease) in Other Current Liabilities..	251	243	(251)	395	581
Cash Flow from Operations	$ 843	$ 1,377	$ 1,609	$ 2,185	$ 2,716
Investing					
Fixed Assets Sold	0	0	0	0	0
Fixed Assets Acquired....................	$(3,299)	$(2,080)	$(1,114)	$ (928)	$ (547)
Investments Acquired....................	0	0	(239)	(65)	(924)
Other Investing Transactions	345	326	(110)	68	257
Cash Flow from Investing	$(2,954)	$(1,754)	$(1,463)	$ (925)	$ (1,214)
Financing					
Increase in Short-Term Borrowing	$ 122	0	0	0	0
Increase in Long-Term Borrowing	2,397	$ 1,811	$ 426	$ 184	0
Issue of Capital Stock...................	454	0	0	0	$ 589
Decrease in Short-Term Borrowing.........	(153)	(380)			
Decrease in Long-Term Borrowing	(779)	(1,069)	(549)	(1,401)	(2,130)
Acquisition of Capital Stock	0	0	0	0	0
Dividends	0	(49)	(66)	(5)	0
Other Financing Transactions	21	82	3	21	25
Cash Flow from Financing	$ 2,062	$ 395	$ (186)	$ (1,201)	$ (1,516)
Change in Cash	$ (49)	$ 18	$ (40)	$ 59	$ (14)
Cash—Beginning of Year	94	45	63	23	82
Cash—End of Year......................	$ 45	$ 63	$ 23	$ 82	$ 68
Growth in Revenues	11.7%	9.9%	2.0%	4.7%	4.6%

Depreciation is an expense that does not use cash; the cash outflows occur at the time the company acquires its fixed assets.

The relation between net income and cash flow from operations for American is typical of capital-intensive firms. Although American experiences a positive cash flow from operations each year, this cash flow is not sufficient to finance capital expenditures during Year 4 and Year 5. American uses long-term debt to finance these acquisitions. Debt is usually a less costly source of capital than equity. The assets acquired serve as collateral for the borrowing.

American's cash flow pattern changes substantially beginning in Year 6. Net losses during Year 4 and Year 5 result in low retained earnings and a high proportion of debt relative to equity in the company's capital structure. American was probably close to violating covenants in its borrowing contracts that preclude taking on too much additional debt.

The reduced amounts shown for acquisitions of fixed assets beginning in Year 6 suggest that American stopped growing its fleet of aircraft. It chose instead to acquire new airplanes by leasing. Most of these leases are in the form of operating leases. Because the signing of an operating lease does not involve an immediate exchange of cash, the obligation does not appear on the statement of cash flows. American used the cash generated from operations (resulting from increased net income) in excess of the reduced level of capital expenditures to repay long-term debt. The increased profitability coupled with decreased long-term debt then reduced the proportion of debt in its capital structure.[6]

Interpublic Group.   Finally, Exhibit 2.7 presents a statement of cash flows for Interpublic Group, an advertising agency. Depreciation represents a less significant addback for Interpublic, a service firm, than for American. The primary source of variation between its net income and cash flow from operations is management of working capital, particularly accounts receivable and accounts payable. An advertising agency serves as a conduit between clients placing advertisements (giving rise to an account receivable for the agency) and the various media in which the agency places the advertisements (giving rise to an account payable). Interpublic manages its position so that the receivables and payables do not completely offset each year, resulting in a varying relationship between net income and cash flow from operations. Because advertising agencies are not capital-intensive, cash flow from operations is more than sufficient to finance Interpublic's capital expenditures. Cash flow from operations was also sufficient to finance acquisitions of other advertising agencies (included in "other investing transactions"). Interpublic uses the excess cash to pay dividends and repurchase its common stock.

These five statements of cash flows present typical patterns for firms in different types of industries and in different stages of their product life cycles. They also illustrate some of the interpretations that an analyst can make about the economic characteristics and performance of an entity by studying its statement of cash flows.

---

[6]Although American properly follows generally accepted accounting principles with respect to its leases, we suggest in Chapter 6 that the analyst should routinely include the present value of operating lease commitments in property, plant, and equipment and in long-term debt. This procedure attempts to reflect the economic substance of most operating leases instead of the "window-dressing" evident from the reporting by American and other airlines.

Interpublic Group
Statement of Cash Flows
(amounts in millions)

	Year 4	Year 5	Year 6	Year 7	Year 8
Operations					
Net Income	$ 112	$ 126	$ 93	$ 130	$ 205
Depreciation and Amortization	40	43	46	50	60
Other Addbacks	45	49	80	91	65
Other Subtractions	(11)	(9)	(21)	(34)	(54)
Working Capital Provided by Operations	$ 186	$ 209	$ 198	$ 237	$ 276
(Increase) Decrease in Receivables	24	(66)	(114)	(243)	(244)
(Increase) Decrease in Inventories	0	0	0	0	0
(Increase) Decrease in Other Current Assets	(17)	(13)	1	(32)	(49)
Increase (Decrease) in Accounts Payable	(16)	59	193	183	264
Increase (Decrease) in Other Current Liabilities	11	14	7	19	2
Cash Flow from Operations	$ 188	$ 203	$ 285	$ 164	$ 249
Investing					
Fixed Assets Sold	$ 3	$ 1	$ 34	$ 2	$ 39
Fixed Assets Acquired	(37)	(79)	(56)	(70)	(79)
Investments Acquired	(2)	0	0	0	0
Other Investing Transactions	(20)	(83)	(50)	(87)	(33)
Cash Flow from Investing	$ (56)	$(161)	$ (72)	$(155)	$ (73)
Financing					
Increase in Short-Term Borrowing	0	$ 35	0	$ 18	0
Increase in Long-Term Borrowing	$ 113	42	$ 33	68	$ 76
Issue of Capital Stock	11	19	13	31	20
Decrease in Short-Term Borrowing	(70)	0	(44)	0	(25)
Decrease in Long-Term Borrowing	(69)	(15)	(24)	(15)	(52)
Acquisition of Capital Stock	(52)	(37)	(44)	(70)	(87)
Dividends	(32)	(36)	(40)	(46)	(52)
Other Financing Transactions	(17)	(14)	15	9	(6)
Cash Flow from Financing	$(116)	$ (6)	$ (91)	$ (5)	$(126)
Change in Cash	$ 16	$ 36	$ 122	$ 4	$ 50
Cash—Beginning of Year	240	256	292	414	418
Cash—End of Year	$ 256	$ 292	$ 414	$ 418	$ 468
Growth in Revenues	10.6%	−3.3%	10.6%	9.9%	16.1%

PREPARING THE STATEMENT OF CASH FLOWS

Publicly held firms in the United States must include a statement of cash flows in their published financial statements each period.[7] Smaller, privately held firms often prepare just a balance sheet and an income statement. Firms outside the United States also usually include a statement of cash flows in their published statements, although some provide only a balance sheet and an income statement.

We describe here a way to prepare a statement of cash flows using information from the balance sheet and income statement. While the resulting statement merely approximates the amounts that would be reported if the analyst had full access to a firm's accounting records, the estimated amounts should approximate the actual amounts well enough for the analyst to make meaningful interpretations.

ALGEBRAIC FORMULATION

We know from the accounting equation that:

$$\text{Assets} = \text{Liabilities} + \text{Shareholders' Equity}$$

This equality holds for balance sheets at the beginning and end of each period. If we subtract the amounts on the balance sheet at the beginning of the period from the corresponding amounts on the balance sheet at the end of the period, we obtain an equality for changes (Δ) in balance sheet amounts:

$$\Delta \text{ Assets} = \Delta \text{ Liabilities} + \Delta \text{ Shareholders' Equity}$$

We can now expand the change in assets term as follows:

$$\Delta \text{ Cash} + \Delta \text{ Noncash Assets} = \Delta \text{ Liabilities} + \Delta \text{ Shareholders' Equity}$$

Rearranging terms:

$$\Delta \text{ Cash} = \Delta \text{ Liabilities} + \Delta \text{ Shareholders' Equity} - \Delta \text{ Noncash Assets}$$

The statement of cash flows explains the reasons for the change in cash during a period. We can see that the change in cash equals the change in all other (noncash) balance sheet amounts.

---

[7]Financial Accounting Standards Board, *Statement of Financial Accounting Standards No. 95,* "Statement of Cash Flows," 1987.

Look at Exhibit 2.8, which shows the comparative balance sheet of Logue Shoe Store for the years ending December 31, Year 5, Year 6, and Year 7. The balance sheets at the end of Year 5 and Year 6 report these equalities:

	Cash	+	Noncash Assets	=	Liabilities	+	Shareholders' Equity
Year 5	$13,698	+	$132,136	=	$105,394	+	$40,440
Year 6	$12,595	+	$129,511	=	$ 85,032	+	$57,074

EXHIBIT 2.8

Logue Shoe Store
Balance Sheet

	December 31, Year 5	December 31, Year 6	December 31, Year 7
Assets			
Cash	$ 13,698	$ 12,595	$ 5,815
Accounts Receivable	1,876	1,978	1,816
Inventories.....................	98,824	106,022	123,636
Other Current Assets.............	3,591	—	1,560
Total Current Assets............	$117,989	$ 120,595	$132,827
Property, Plant and Equipment (cost) .	$ 63,634	$ 65,285	$ 64,455
Less Accumulated Depreciation.....	(37,973)	(45,958)	(54,617)
Net Property, Plant and Equipment..	$ 25,661	$ 19,327	$ 9,838
Other Assets	2,184	2,184	2,184
Total Assets	$145,834	$ 142,106	$144,849
Liabilities and Shareholders' Equity			
Accounts Payable................	$ 21,768	$ 15,642	$ 13,954
Notes Payable	—	—	10,814
Current Portion of Long-Term Debt .	18,256	10,997	7,288
Other Current Liabilities	4,353	6,912	5,489
Total Current Liabilities.........	$ 44,377	$ 33,551	$ 37,545
Long-Term Debt	61,017	51,481	43,788
Total Liabilities	$105,394	$ 85,032	$ 81,333
Common Stock	$ 1,000	$ 1,000	$ 1,000
Additional Paid-in Capital	124,000	124,000	124,000
Retained Earnings	(84,560)	(67,926)	(61,484)
Total Shareholders' Equity........	$ 40,440	$ 57,074	$ 63,516
Total Liabilities and Shareholders' Equity.....................	$145,834	$ 142,106	$144,849

Subtracting the amounts at the end of Year 5 from the amounts at the end of Year 6, we obtain:

$$\Delta \text{ Cash} + \Delta \text{ Noncash Assets} = \Delta \text{ Liabilities} + \Delta \text{ Shareholders' Equity}$$

$$-\$1,103 + \quad (-\$2,625) \quad = \quad -\$20,362 + \qquad \$16,634$$

Rearranging terms:

$$\Delta \text{ Cash} = \Delta \text{ Liabilities} + \Delta \text{ Shareholders' Equity} - \Delta \text{ Noncash Assets}$$

$$-\$1,103 = \quad -\$20,362 + \qquad \$16,634 \qquad - \qquad (-\$2,625)$$

CLASSIFYING CHANGES IN BALANCE SHEET ACCOUNTS

The statement of cash flows classifies the reasons for the change in cash as either an operating, investing, or financing activity. The remaining task then is to classify the change in each noncash balance sheet account (right-hand side of the equation above) into one of these three categories.

For some of the changes in balance sheet accounts, there is no ambiguity about the correct category (a change in common stock is a financing transaction, for example). Other balance sheet changes, however (retained earnings, for example), result from the netting of several changes, some of them relating to operations (net income) and some of them relating to investing or financing (dividends). The analyst should use whatever information the financial statements and notes provide about changes in balance sheet accounts to classify the net change each period.[8]

Exhibit 2.9 classifies the changes in the noncash balance sheet accounts, and we discuss each account in turn.

Accounts Receivable.   Cash collections from customers during a period equal sales for the period plus accounts receivable at the beginning of the period minus accounts receivable at the end of the period. Thus, the change in accounts receivable clearly relates to operations. Line (18) of Exhibit 2.9 shows net income as a source of cash from operations. Net income includes sales revenue. The amount for sales revenue included in the amount on line (18) plus or minus the change in accounts receivable in line (1) results in the amount of cash received from customers.

Marketable Securities.   Firms typically acquire marketable securities when they temporarily have excess cash; they sell these securities when they need cash. The holding of marketable securities for a relatively short period might make purchase and sale transactions look like operating activities. In fact, the

---

[8]The change in balance sheet accounts of publicly traded companies will not always equal the amount reported on their statement of cash flows related to these accounts. The usual explanation is that the firm made an acquisition or disposition of a business during the period and classified the change in the balance sheet accounts (for example, accounts receivable) partially as an operating activity (cash collections from customers exceeded or fell short of sales) and partially as an investing activity (accounts receivable of the acquired or disposed business).

EXHIBIT 2.9

Worksheet for Preparation of Statement of Cash Flows

	Balance Sheet Changes	Operations	Investing	Financing
(Increase) Decrease in Assets				
(1) Accounts Receivable		x		
(2) Marketable Securities			x	
(3) Inventories		x		
(4) Other Current Assets		x		
(5) Investments in Securities			x	
(6) Property, Plant, and Equipment Cost ..			x	
(7) Accumulated Depreciation		x		
(8) Other Assets		x	x	
Increase (Decrease) in Liabilities and Shareholders' Equities				
(9) Accounts Payable		x		
(10) Notes Payable				x
(11) Current Portion of Long-Term Debt ...				x
(12) Other Current Liabilities		x		
(13) Long-Term Debt				x
(14) Deferred Income Taxes		x		
(15) Other Noncurrent Liabilities				x
(16) Common Stock				x
(17) Additional Paid-in Capital				x
(18) Retained Earnings		x (net income)		x (dividends)
(19) Treasury Stock				x
(20) Cash				

temporarily excess cash could result from selling fixed assets or issuing bonds or common stock, as well as from operating activities. Likewise, firms might use the cash inflow from the sale of marketable securities to purchase fixed assets, retire debt, and repurchase common or preferred stock, as well as finance operating activities.

GAAP in the United States ignores the *reason* for the excess cash (with which firms purchase marketable securities) and the *use* of the cash proceeds (from the sale of marketable securities) and simply classifies the cash flows associated with purchases and sales of marketable securities as investing activities. Because net income includes these gains or losses on sales of marketable securities, the analyst must subtract the gains and add back the losses to net income to derive cash flow from operations. Failure to offset the gains or losses included in earnings will result in reporting too much cash flow from operations (sales of marketable securities at a gain) or too little cash flow from operations (sales of marketable securities at a loss). None of the cash flows associated with sales of marketable securities should be included in cash flow from operations; these transactions are investing activities.

Inventories.   Inventory purchases during a period equal cost of goods sold for the period plus inventories at the end of the period minus inventories at the beginning of the period. Line (18) includes cost of goods sold as an expense in measuring net income. The change in inventories in line (3) coupled with cost of goods sold included in the amount in line (18) results in the amount of purchases for the period.

The presumption at this point is that the firm made a cash outflow equal to the amount of purchases. If the firm does not pay cash for all of its inventories purchases, then accounts payable changes. We adjust for the change in accounts payable in line (9), as discussed below.

Other Current Assets.   This balance sheet account typically includes prepayments for various operating costs. Unless the financial statements and notes present information to the contrary, the presumption is that the change in other current assets relates to operations.

Investments in Securities.   The investments in securities account can change for several possible reasons:

Source of Change	Classification in Statement of Cash Flows
Acquisition of New Investments	Investing (outflow)
Recognition of Income or Loss Using Equity Method	Operations (subtraction or addition)
Receipt of Dividends from Investee	Operations (inflow)
Sale of Investments	Investing (inflow)

If the balance sheet, income statement, or notes provide information that permits the net change in investments in securities to be identified with one or another of these components, the analyst can make the appropriate classifications. Without such information, we classify the change in the account as an investing activity.

Property, Plant, and Equipment.   We classify the cash flows related to purchases and sales of fixed assets—property, plant, and equipment—as investing activities. Because net income includes any gains or losses from sales of fixed assets, we offset their effect on earnings by adding back losses and subtracting gains from net income when we compute cash flow from operations.

Accumulated Depreciation.   The amount of depreciation recognized each period reduces net income but does not use cash. Thus, we classify depreciation as an operating item with a positive sign in line (7). When we add the amount for depreciation included under operations in line (7) to depreciation expense included as a negative element in net income in line (18), we get rid of the effect of depreciation in the operations column. This treatment is appropriate because depreciation is not a cash flow (ignoring income tax consequences).

Other Assets.   Other assets on the balance sheet include patents, copyrights, goodwill, and similar assets. A portion of the change in these accounts represents amortization, which requires an addback to net income in order to compute cash flow from operations. Unless the financial statements and notes provide contrary information, the presumption is that the remaining change in these accounts is an investing activity.

Accounts Payable.   The cash outflow for purchases equals purchases during the period plus accounts payable at the beginning of the period minus accounts payable at the end of the period. We derive the amount for purchases in the period as part of the calculations in line (3) for inventories. The adjustment in line (9) for the change in accounts payable converts purchases to cash payments on purchases and, like inventories, is an operating transaction.

Notes Payable.   Notes payable is the account generally used to describe a firm's short-term borrowing from a bank or other financial institution. GAAP in the United States classifies such borrowing as a financing activity on the statement of cash flows, even though the firm might use the proceeds to finance accounts receivable, inventories, or other working capital needs. The presumption underlying the classification of bank borrowing as a financing activity is that firms derive operating cash inflows from their customers, not by borrowing from banks.

Current Portion of Long-Term Debt.   The change in the current portion of long-term debt during a period equals (1) the reclassification of long-term debt from a noncurrent liability to a current liability (that is, debt that the firm expects to repay within one year as of the end-of-the-period balance sheet) minus (2) long-term debt actually repaid during the period. The latter amount represents the cash outflow from this financing transaction. We consider the amount arising from the reclassification in connection with the long-term debt item below.

Other Current Liabilities.   Firms generally use this account for obligations related to goods and services used in operations other than purchases of inventories. Thus, changes in other current liabilities appear as operating activities.

Long-Term Debt.   This account changes for a variety of reasons, including:

Issuance of new long-term debt
Reclassification of long-term debt from a noncurrent to a current liability
Early retirement of long-term debt
Conversion of long-term debt to preferred or common stock

These items are clearly financing transactions but they do not all affect cash. The issuance of new debt and the early retirement of old debt do affect cash flows. The reclassification of long-term debt included in the amount in line (13) offsets the corresponding amount included in the change in line (11), and these calculations effectively cancel each other. This is appropriate because the reclassification does not affect cash flow.

Likewise, any portion of the change in long-term debt in line (13) that is due to a conversion of debt into capital stock offsets a similar change in line (16). The analyst enters reclassifications and conversions of debt, such as those described above, on the *worksheet* for the preparation of a statement of cash flows since such transactions help explain changes in balance sheet accounts. These transactions do not appear on the formal statement of cash flows, however, because they do not involve actual cash flows.

Deferred Income Taxes. Income taxes currently payable equal income tax expense (included in line (18) as a negative element of net income) plus or minus the change in deferred taxes during the period. Thus, changes in deferred income taxes appear as an operating activity.

Other Noncurrent Liabilities. This account includes unfunded pension or retirement benefit obligations, long-term deposits received, and other miscellaneous long-term liabilities. Changes in pension and retirement benefit obligations are operating activities. Absent information to the contrary, however, we classify the changes in other noncurrent liability accounts as financing activities.

Common Stock and Additional Paid-in Capital. These two accounts change when a firm issues new stock or repurchases and retires outstanding stock. The transactions appear as financing activities.

Retained Earnings. Retained earnings increase by the amount of net income and decrease with the payment of dividends in each period. Net income is an operating activity, and dividends are a financing activity.

Treasury Stock. Repurchases of a firm's outstanding capital stock are classified as a financing activity.

ILLUSTRATION OF PROCEDURE FOR PREPARING CASH FLOW STATEMENT

We illustrate the procedure for preparing the statement of cash flows using the data for Logue Shoe Store in Exhibit 2.8. Net income is $16,634 for Year 6 and $6,442 for Year 7.

Exhibit 2.10 presents the worksheet for Year 6. The first column shows the change in each noncash balance sheet account that nets to the $1,103 decrease in cash for the period. We have to be particularly careful with the direction of the change.

EXHIBIT 2.10

Logue Shoe Store
Worksheet for Statement of Cash Flows
Year 6

	Balance Sheet Changes	Operations	Investing	Financing
(Increase) Decrease in Assets				
Accounts Receivable...................	$ (102)	$ (102)		
Inventories	(7,198)	(7,198)		
Other Current Assets	3,591	3,591		
Property, Plant, and Equipment	(1,651)		$ (1,651)	
Accumulated Depreciation	7,985	7,985		
Other Assets.........................	—			
Increase (Decrease) in Liabilities and Shareholders' Equities				
Accounts Payable	$ (6,126)	$ (6,126)		
Notes Payable.......................	—			—
Current Portion of Long-Term Debt........	(7,259)			$ (7,259)
Other Current Liabilities	2,559	2,559		
Long-Term Debt......................	(9,536)			(9,536)
Common Stock.......................	—			—
Additional Paid-in Capital...............	—		—	—
Retained Earnings....................	16,634	16,634		
Cash..............................	$ (1,103)	$17,343	$ (1,651)	$(16,795)

Recall from the earlier equation:

$$\Delta \text{Cash} = \Delta \text{Liabilities} + \Delta \text{Shareholders' Equity} - \Delta \text{Noncash Assets}$$

Increase	=	Increase		
Decrease	=	Decrease		
Increase	=		Increase	
Decrease	=		Decrease	
Increase	=			Increase
Decrease	=			Decrease

Thus, changes in liabilities and shareholders' equity have the same directional effect on cash, while changes in noncash assets have just the opposite directional effect.

We classify the change in each account as an operating, investing, or financing activity. Observe the following for Year 6:

1. Operating activities are a net source of cash for the period. The firm used the cash derived from operations to repay long-term debt.

2. Inventories increase substantially during the period, while accounts payable decrease. The two events reduce operating cash flows. Most firms report increases in accounts payable in amounts approximately equal to the increase in inventories.
3. Compared to the level of depreciation during the year, capital expenditures on new property, plant, and equipment are small.

Exhibit 2.11 presents a worksheet for Year 7. The preparation procedure is identical to that used in Exhibit 2.10. Note in this case that operations are a net user of cash. The increase in accounts payable does not match the substantial increase in inventories. Long-term debt is again redeemed in Year 7, but it appears that the firm used short-term bank borrowing to finance the redemption. The negative cash flow from operations coupled with the use of short-term debt to redeem long-term debt suggests an increase in short-term liquidity risk.

Exhibit 2.12 presents the statement of cash flows for Logue Shoe Store for Year 6 and Year 7 using the amounts taken from the worksheets in Exhibits 2.10 and 2.11.

EXHIBIT 2.11

Logue Shoe Store
Worksheet for Statement of Cash Flows
Year 7

	Balance Sheet Changes	Operations	Investing	Financing
(Increase) Decrease in Assets				
Accounts Receivable....................	$ 162	$ 162		
Inventories	(17,614)	(17,614)		
Other Current Assets	(1,560)	(1,560)		
Property, Plant, and Equipment	830		$830	
Accumulated Depreciation	8,659	8,659		
Other Assets	—			
Incease (Decrease) in Liabilities and Shareholders' Equities				
Accounts Payable	$ (1,688)	$ (1,688)		
Notes Payable........................	10,814			$10,814
Current Portion of Long-Term Debt........	(3,709)			(3,709)
Other Current Liabilities	(1,423)	(1,423)		
Long-Term Debt.......................	(7,693)			(7,693)
Common Stock........................	—			—
Additional Paid-in Capital................	—		—	—
Retained Earnings.....................	6,442	6,442	—	—
Cash................................	$ (6,780)	$ (7,022)	$830	$ (588)

	EXHIBIT 2.12	

Logue Shoe Store
Statement of Cash Flows

	Year 6	Year 7
Operations		
Net Income	$ 16,634	$ 6,442
Depreciation	7,985	8,659
(Increase) Decrease in Accounts Receivable	(102)	162
(Increase) Decrease in Inventories	(7,198)	(17,614)
(Increase) Decrease in Other Current Assets	3,591	(1,560)
Increase (Decrease) in Accounts Payable	(6,126)	(1,688)
Increase (Decrease) in Other Current Liabilities	2,559	(1,423)
Cash Flow from Operations	$ 17,343	$ (7,022)
Investing		
Sale (Acquisition) of Property, Plant and Equipment . . .	$ (1,651)	$ 830
Financing		
Increase in Notes Payable	—	$ 10,814
Repayment of Long-Term Debt	$ (16,795)	$ (11,402)
Cash Flow from Financing	$ (16,795)	$ (588)
Net Change in Cash	$ (1,103)	$ (6,780)

SUMMARY

Compared to the balance sheet and income statement, the statement of cash flows is a relatively new statement. The Financial Accounting Standards Board issued its most recent comprehensive standard on the statement of cash flows in 1987, although GAAP in the United States has required some form of "funds flow" statement since the late 1960s.

The statement of cash flows will continue its usefulness in the future for a variety of reasons:

1. Analysts will understand better the types of information that this statement presents and the kinds of interpretations that are appropriate as they become more familiar with it over time.
2. Analysts increasingly recognize that cash flows do not necessarily track income flows. A firm with a healthy income statement is not necessarily financially healthy. Cash requirements to service debt, for example, may outstrip the ability of a firm's operations to generate cash.
3. Differences in accounting principles have less of an impact on the statement of cash flows than on the balance sheet and income statement. Such differences in accounting principles between countries are a major issue as capital markets become more integrated across countries.

PROBLEMS AND CASES

2.1   INTERPRETING THE STATEMENT OF CASH FLOWS. The Procter & Gamble Company manufactures and markets a wide variety of branded consumer products. Exhibit 2.13 presents a statement of cash flows for Procter & Gamble for Year 7 through Year 11.

EXHIBIT 2.13

Procter & Gamble Company
Statement of Cash Flows
(amounts in millions)
(Problem 2.1)

	Year 7	Year 8	Year 9	Year 10	Year 11
Operating					
Net Income	$ 1,872	$ 2,027	$ 2,211	$ 2,645	$ 3,046
Depreciation	1,051	1,140	1,134	1,253	1,358
Other Addbacks	77	79	501	327	460
Other Subtractions	(203)	(118)	0	0	0
Working Capital from Operations	$ 2,797	$ 3,128	$ 3,846	$ 4,225	$ 4,864
(Increase) Decrease in Accounts Receivable	23	(9)	40	(225)	17
(Increase) Decrease in Inventories	160	97	25	(401)	202
(Increase) Decrease in Prepayments	(1)	79	(7)	(309)	(115)
Increase (Decrease) in Accounts Payable	278	(54)	335	287	(366)
Increase (Decrease) in Other Current Liabilities	(232)	97	(590)	(9)	(444)
Cash Flow from Operations	$ 3,025	$ 3,338	$ 3,649	$ 3,568	$ 4,158
Investing					
Fixed Assets Acquired	$(1,911)	$(1,911)	$(1,841)	$(2,146)	$ (2,179)
Change in Marketable Securities	0	(306)	23	96	(331)
Other Investing Transactions	(949)	587	(190)	(313)	44
Cash Flow from Investing	$(2,860)	$(1,630)	$(2,008)	$(2,363)	$ (2,466)
Financing					
Increase in Short-Term Borrowing	0	0	0	0	$ 242
Increase in Long-Term Borrowing	$ 1,608	$ 1,001	$ 414	$ 449	339
Issue of Capital Stock	71	77	36	66	89
Decrease in Short-Term Borrowing	(156)	(277)	(281)	(429)	0
Decrease in Long-Term Borrowing	(433)	(939)	(797)	(510)	(619)
Acquisition of Capital Stock	(49)	(55)	(14)	(114)	(432)
Dividends	(788)	(850)	(949)	(1,062)	(1,202)
Other	(26)	(119)	1	50	(63)
Cash Flow from Financing	$ 227	$(1,162)	$(1,590)	$(1,550)	$ (1,646)
Change in Cash	$ 392	$ 546	$ 51	$ (345)	$ 46
Cash—Beginning of Year	1,384	1,776	2,322	2,373	2,028
Cash—End of Year	$ 1,776	$ 2,322	$ 2,373	$ 2,028	$ 2,074
Change in Sales from Previous Year	+ 8.6%	+ 3.8%	− .4%	+ 10.2%	+ 5.4%

Required

Discuss the relationships among net income, working capital from operations, and cash flow from operations and among cash flows from operating, investing, and financing activities for P&G over the five-year period.

2.2 INTERPRETING THE STATEMENT OF CASH FLOWS. Texas Instruments primarily develops and manufactures semiconductors for use in a variety of technology-based products for various industries. The manufacturing process is capital-intensive. Because of overcapacity in the industry, semiconductor prices collapsed during Year 11. Exhibit 2.14 presents a statement of cash flows for Texas Instruments for Year 7 through Year 11.

Required

Discuss the relationships among net income, working capital from operations, and cash flows from operations and among cash flows from operating, investing, and financing activities for TI over the five-year period.

2.3 INTERPRETING THE STATEMENT OF CASH FLOWS. Champion International grows and harvests timber and processes the timber into various paper products in capital-intensive plants. Sales of paper products vary with conditions in the economy and the amount of available paper processing capacity that becomes available in a particular year. Forest products companies have shifted the location of some of their paper mills in recent years and have constructed technologically more sophisticated processing plants. Exhibit 2.15 presents the statement of cash flows for Champion International for Year 7 through Year 11.

Required

Discuss the relationships among net income, working capital from operations, and cash flow from operations and among cash flows from operating, investing, and financing activities for Champion over the five-year period.

2.4 INTERPRETING THE STATEMENT OF CASH FLOWS. Montgomery Ward operates a retail department store chain. It filed for bankruptcy during the first quarter of Year 12. Exhibit 2.16 presents a statement of cash flows for Montgomery Ward for Year 7 through Year 11. The firm acquired Lechmere, a discount retailer of sporting goods and electronic products, during Year 9. It acquired Amoco Enterprises, an automobile club, during Year 11. During Year 10 it issued a new series of preferred stock and used the cash proceeds in part to repurchase a series of outstanding preferred stock. The "other subtractions" in the operating section for Year 10 and Year 11 represent reversals of deferred tax liabilities.

Required

Discuss the relationships among net income, working capital from operations, and cash flow from operations and among cash flows from operating, investing, and financing activities for Montgomery Ward over the five-year period. Identify signals of the firm's difficulties that may have led to its filing for bankruptcy.

2.5 INTERPRETING THE STATEMENT OF CASH FLOWS. Ciprico develops and manufactures disk arrays used in visual computing markets. It designs its products to meet the complex image processing needs of film, video, graphic, photographic, animation, and special effects applications. It sells its products to computer manufacturers such as Hewlett-Packard, Sun Microsystems, Silicon Graphics, and IBM. Exhibit 2.17 presents a statement

EXHIBIT 2.14

Texas Instruments
Statement of Cash Flows
(amounts in millions)
(Problem 2.2)

	Year 7	Year 8	Year 9	Year 10	Year 11
Operating					
Net Income	$ 247	$ 476	$ 691	$ 1,088	$ (46)
Depreciation	610	617	665	756	904
Other Addbacks	49	91	88	25	177
Other Subtractions	(93)	(59)	(20)	(48)	(51)
Working Capital from Operations	$ 813	$1,125	$ 1,424	$ 1,821	$ 984
(Increase) Decrease in Accounts Receivable	(111)	(258)	(197)	(870)	250
(Increase) Decrease in Inventories	50	(88)	(60)	(253)	245
(Increase) Decrease in Prepayments	1	(3)	(9)	9	9
Increase (Decrease) in Accounts Payable	(16)	37	330	677	(404)
Increase (Decrease) in Other Current Liabilities	64	121	44	283	(286)
Cash Flow from Operations	$ 801	$ 934	$ 1,532	$ 1,667	$ 798
Investing					
Fixed Assets Acquired	$(429)	$ (730)	$(1,076)	$(1,439)	$(2,063)
Change in Marketable Securities	(354)	19	(47)	343	175
Other Investing Transactions	48	0	0	0	(163)
Cash Flow from Investing	$(735)	$ (711)	$(1,123)	$(1,096)	$(2,051)
Financing					
Increase in Short-Term Borrowing	$ 92	$ 35	$ 40	$ 12	$ 288
Increase in Long-Term Borrowing	150	14	1	24	871
Issue of Capital Stock	25	100	110	111	35
Decrease in Short-Term Borrowing	(61)	(72)	(41)	0	(2)
Decrease in Long-Term Borrowing	(117)	(15)	(88)	(12)	(199)
Acquisition of Capital Stock	(146)	(150)	0	0	0
Dividends	(98)	(86)	(79)	(111)	(129)
Other	(7)	(1)	4	9	(17)
Cash Flow from Financing	$(162)	$ (175)	$ (53)	$ 33	$ 847
Change in Cash	$ (96)	$ 48	$ 356	$ 604	$ (406)
Cash—Beginning of Year	452	356	404	760	1,364
Cash—End of Year	$ 356	$ 404	$ 760	$ 1,364	$ 958
Change in Sales from Previous Year	+ 9.7%	+ 14.6%	+ 21.0 %	+ 27.3%	− 12.9%

of cash flows for Ciprico for Year 7 through Year 11. Year 8 was a year of recessionary conditions in the U.S. economy.

Required

Discuss the relationships among net income, working capital from operations, and cash flow from operations and among cash flows from operating, investing, and financing activities for Ciprico over the five-year period.

EXHIBIT 2.15

Champion International Corporation
Statement of Cash Flows
(amounts in millions)
(Problem 2.3)

	Year 7	Year 8	Year 9	Year 10	Year 11
Operating					
Net Income	$ 14	$ (156)	$ 63	$ 772	$ 141
Depreciation	411	443	459	471	502
Other Addbacks	0	38	66	244	16
Other Subtractions	(142)	(37)	(45)	(57)	(93)
Working Capital from Operations	$ 283	$ 288	$ 543	$1,430	$ 566
(Increase) Decrease in Accounts Receivable	(11)	(28)	(71)	(78)	65
(Increase) Decrease in Inventories	(5)	(14)	22	(73)	(34)
(Increase) Decrease in Prepayments	5	(3)	(1)	(6)	(5)
Increase (Decrease) in Accounts Payable	(10)	(61)	5	118	(38)
Increase (Decrease) in Other Current Liabilities	(4)	19	30	62	(116)
Cash Flow from Operations	$ 258	$ 201	$ 528	$1,453	$ 438
Investing					
Fixed Assets Sold	$ 174	$ 305	$ 39	$ 181	$ 43
Fixed Assets Acquired	(718)	(606)	(329)	(624)	(582)
Change in Marketable Securities	(58)	107	33	(98)	98
Other Investing Transactions	(9)	(18)	0	(10)	(113)
Cash Flow from Investing	$(611)	$ (212)	$(257)	$ (551)	$ (554)
Financing					
Increase in Short-Term Borrowing	0	0	0	0	0
Increase in Long-Term Borrowing	$ 770	$ 1,383	$ 425	$ 826	$ 834
Issue of Capital Stock	0	0	0	0	0
Decrease in Short-Term Borrowing	0	0	0	0	0
Decrease in Long-Term Borrowing	(440)	(1,308)	(622)	(951)	(645)
Acquisition of Capital Stock	0	0	0	(550)	(199)
Dividends	(46)	(46)	(46)	(32)	(19)
Other	(7)	1	7	31	3
Cash Flow from Financing	$ 277	$ 30	$(236)	$ (676)	$ (26)
Change in Cash	$ (76)	$ 19	$ 35	$ 226	$ (142)
Cash—Beginning of Year	113	37	56	91	317
Cash—End of Year	$ 37	$ 56	$ 91	$ 317	$ 175
Change in Sales from Previous Year	+ 2.9%	+ 2.9%	+ 4.9%	+ 31.1%	− 15.7%

EXHIBIT 2.16

Montgomery Ward
Statement of Cash Flows
(amounts in millions)
(Problem 2.4)

	Year 7	Year 8	Year 9	Year 10	Year 11
Operating					
Net Income	$ 100	$ 101	$ 109	$ (9)	$ (237)
Depreciation	97	98	109	115	122
Other Addbacks	32	25	24	8	13
Other Subtractions	0	0	(29)	(119)	(197)
Working Capital from Operations	$ 229	$ 224	$ 213	$ (5)	$ (299)
(Increase) Decrease in Accounts Receivable	9	(9)	(38)	(54)	(32)
(Increase) Decrease in Inventories	(38)	(204)	(229)	(112)	225
(Increase) Decrease in Prepayments	36	(58)	(39)	(32)	27
Increase (Decrease) in Accounts Payable	(17)	148	291	85	(222)
Increase (Decrease) in Other Current Liabilities	(64)	28	(45)	(64)	(55)
Cash Flow from Operations	$ 155	$ 129	$ 153	$(182)	$ (356)
Investing					
Fixed Assets Acquired	$(146)	$(142)	$ (184)	$(122)	$ (75)
Change in Marketable Securities	137	(27)	(4)	(14)	20
Other Investing Transactions	9	6	(113)	27	(93)
Cash Flow from Investing	$ 0	$(163)	$ (301)	$(109)	$ (148)
Financing					
Increase in Short-Term Borrowing	0	0	$ 144	$ 16	$ 588
Increase in Long-Term Borrowing	0	$ 100	168	205	0
Issue of Capital Stock	$ 1	1	78	193	3
Decrease in Short-Term Borrowing	0	0	0	0	0
Decrease in Long-Term Borrowing	(403)	(18)	(275)	(17)	(63)
Acquisition of Capital Stock	(97)	(11)	(9)	(98)	(20)
Dividends	(19)	(23)	(24)	(4)	(9)
Other	2	2	1	0	0
Cash Flow from Financing	$(516)	$ 51	$ 83	$ 295	$ 499
Change in Cash	$(361)	$ 17	$ (65)	$ 4	$ (5)
Cash—Beginning of Year	442	81	98	33	37
Cash—End of Year	$ 81	$ 98	$ 33	$ 37	$ 32
Change in Sales from Previous Year	+ 2.0%	+ 3.7%	+ 17.2%	− .5%	− 10.0%

EXHIBIT 2.17

Ciprico, Inc.
Statement of Cash Flows
(amounts in thousands)
(Problem 2.5)

	Year 7	Year 8	Year 9	Year 10	Year 11
Operating					
Net Income	$ 427	$(1,778)	$ (320)	$ 396	$ 3,444
Depreciation	626	725	691	712	841
Other Addbacks	134	358	399	415	402
Other Subtractions	0	0	(1)	(32)	0
Working Capital from Operations	$ 1,187	$ (695)	$ 769	$1,491	$ 4,687
(Increase) Decrease in Accounts Receivable	(138)	83	(1,077)	(894)	(1,440)
(Increase) Decrease in Inventories	(561)	663	51	(742)	(1,912)
(Increase) Decrease in Prepayments	(5)	10	(43)	47	(146)
Increase (Decrease) in Accounts Payable	(7)	39	813	866	627
Increase (Decrease) in Other Current Liabilities .	172	(44)	52	237	1,665
Cash Flow from Operations	$ 648	$ 56	$ 565	$1,005	$ 3,481
Investing					
Fixed Assets Acquired	$ (656)	$ (719)	$ (612)	$ (683)	$ (1,997)
Change in Marketable Securities	(102)	70	107	97	(22,591)
Other Investing Transactions	(421)	39	264	143	8
Cash Flow from Investing	$(1,179)	$ (610)	$ (241)	$ (443)	$(24,580)
Financing					
Increase in Short-Term Borrowing	0	0	0	0	$ 0
Increase in Long-Term Borrowing	0	0	0	0	0
Issue of Capital Stock	$ 83	$ 44	$ 38	$ 707	$ 31,100
Decrease in Short-Term Borrowing	0	0	0	0	0
Decrease in Long-Term Borrowing	(28)	(5)	(12)	(20)	(28)
Acquisition of Capital Stock	0	0	0	0	0
Dividends	0	0	0	0	0
Other	0	0	0	0	0
Cash Flow from Financing	$ 55	$ 39	$ 26	$ 687	$ 31,072
Change in Cash	$ (476)	$ (515)	$ 350	$1,249	$ 9,973
Cash—Beginning of Year	2,817	2,341	1,826	2,176	3,425
Cash—End of Year	$ 2,341	$ 1,826	$ 2,176	$3,425	$ 13,398
Change in Sales from Previous Year	+ 25.7%	− 31.3%	+ 42.4%	+ 21.7%	+ 71.7%

2.6   IDENTIFYING INDUSTRY DIFFERENCES IN STATEMENTS OF CASH FLOWS. Exhibit 2.18 presents common size statements of cash flows for eight firms in various industries. All amounts in the common size statements of cash flows are expressed as a percentage of cash flow from operations. To construct the common size percentages for each firm, reported amounts for each firm for three consecutive years were summed, and the common size percentages are based on the summed amounts. This procedure reduces the effects of a nonrecurring item in a particular year, such as a major debt or common stock issue. Exhibit 2.18 also shows in the last line the compound annual rate of growth in revenues over the three-year period.

The eight companies are as follows:

1. Biogen: Creates and manufactures biotechnology drugs. Many drugs are still in the development phase in this high-growth, relatively young industry. Research and manufacturing facilities are capital-intensive, although the research process requires skilled scientists.
2. Chevron: Explores, extracts, refines, and markets petroleum products. Extraction and refining activities are capital-intensive. Petroleum products are in the mature phase of the product life cycle.
3. H.J. Heinz: Manufactures and markets branded consumer food products. Heinz has acquired several other branded food products companies in recent years.
4. Home Depot: Retails home improvement products. Home Depot competes in a new retail category known as "killer category" stores. Such stores offer a wide selection of products in a particular product category (for example, books, pet products, office products). These stores have taken significant market share away from the more diversified department and discount stores in recent years.
5. Inland Steel: Manufactures steel products. Steel plants are capital-intensive and use unionized workers to process iron into steel products. Demand for steel products follows cyclical trends in the economy. Steel manufacturing in the U.S. is in the mature phase of its life cycle.
6. Pacific Gas & Electric: Provides electric and gas utility services. The electric utility industry in the U.S. has excess capacity. Increased competition from less regulated, more open markets has forced down prices and led some utilities to reduce capacity.
7. Servicemaster: Provides home cleaning and restoration services. Servicemaster has recently acquired firms offering cleaning services for healthcare facilities and broadened its home services to include termite protection, garden care, and other services. Servicemaster operates as a partnership. Partnerships do not pay income taxes on their earnings each year. Instead, partners (owners) include their share of the earnings of Servicemaster in their taxable income.
8. Sun Microsystems: Creates, manufactures, and markets computers, primarily to the scientific and engineering markets and to network applications. Sun follows an assembly strategy in manufacturing computers, outsourcing components from various other firms worldwide. Sun has been rumored to be a takeover target by larger technology companies in recent years.

Required

Use whatever clues you can to match the companies in Exhibit 2.18 with the eight companies described. Discuss the reasoning for your selection in each case.

2.7   PREPARING A STATEMENT OF CASH FLOWS FROM BALANCE SHEETS AND INCOME STATEMENTS. Fuso Pharmaceutical Industries develops, manufactures, and markets pharmaceutical products in Japan. Exhibit 2.19 presents the firm's balance sheets for the years

EXHIBIT 2.18

Common Size Statements of Cash Flows for Selected Companies
(Problem 2.6)

	1	2	3	4	5	6	7	8
Operations								
Net Income	34.9%	38.6%	40.9%	45.4%	61.2%	62.4%	76.5%	97.6%
Depreciation	47.9	55.2	62.9	37.7	46.0	22.3	38.0	23.3
Other	3.1	24.3	5.1	(5.0)	9.4	11.6	2.3	3.9
Working Capital from Operations	85.9%	118.1%	108.9%	78.1%	116.6%	96.3%	116.8%	124.8%
(Increase) Decrease in Accounts Receivable	6.5	(4.8)	(.6)	(12.4)	(34.2)	(7.8)	(6.8)	(8.5)
(Increase) Decrease in Inventories	1.5	(15.1)	(1.2)	(14.4)	(11.9)	(3.1)	(7.4)	(58.4)
Increase (Decrease) in Accounts Payable	1.5	3.1	(5.6)	12.4	3.0	2.9	12.6	39.9
Increase (Decrease) in Other Current Liabilities	4.6	(1.3)	(1.5)	36.3	26.5	11.7	(15.2)	2.2
Cash Flow from Operations	100.0%	100.0%	100.0%	100.0%	100.0%	100.0%	100.0%	100.0%
Investing								
Fixed Assets Acquired	(37.1)%	(64.0)%	(81.1)%	(165.7)%	(44.7)%	(13.4)%	(39.3)%	(153.4)%
Change in Marketable Securities	—	—	(2.8)	(75.1)	(14.8)	(3.5)	5.9	(17.5)
Other Investing Transactions	(7.7)	8.5	16.4	(28.4)	(15.9)	(17.3)	(40.6)	23.2
Cash Flow from Investing	(44.8)%	(55.5)%	(67.5)%	(269.2)%	(75.4)%	(34.2)%	(74.0)%	(147.7)%
Financing								
Change in Short-Term Debt	(.6)%	0	(7.4)%		(2.4)%	—	7.9%	—
Increase in Long-Term Debt	19.5	41.4%	8.4	75.7%	—	33.1%	24.0	46.9%
Issue of Capital Stock	11.2	9.9	0	82.5	17.7	1.7	6.7	13.5
Decrease in Long-Term Debt	(36.0)	(85.0)	(9.1)	(2.7)	(7.0)	(27.6)	(3.1)	(1.2)
Repurchase of Capital Stock	(18.9)	(1.5)	(.1)	—	(50.7)	(21.4)	(26.9)	—
Dividends	(29.5)	(10.9)	(29.9)	—	—	(46.1)	(43.5)	(11.5)
Other Financing Transactions	—	—	(.2)	—	—	.6	9.8	1.9
Cash Flow from Financing	(54.3)%	(46.1)%	(38.3)%	155.5%	(42.4)%	(59.7)%	(25.1)%	49.6%
Net Change in Cash	.9%	(1.6)%	(5.8)%	13.7%	(17.8)%	6.1%	.9%	1.9%
Growth in Revenues	(3.6)%	5.7%	5.7%	23.0%	18.2%	7.7%	8.6%	28.3%

EXHIBIT 2.19

Fuso Pharmaceutical Industries
Balance Sheets
(amounts in millions of yen)
(Problem 2.7)

March 31:	Year 8	Year 9	Year 10	Year 11
Assets				
Cash	¥ 2,820	¥ 3,205	¥ 2,258	¥ 1,645
Marketable Securities	8,496	7,867	7,702	7,514
Accounts and Notes Receivable—Trade	20,668	20,029	18,710	18,121
Inventories	6,550	7,433	7,533	8,110
Prepayments	166	139	452	524
Total Current Assets	¥ 38,700	¥ 38,673	¥ 36,655	¥ 35,914
Investments	5,058	4,900	5,088	4,738
Property, Plant, and Equipment	43,381	49,224	56,243	61,659
Less Accumulated Depreciation	(19,153)	(20,786)	(22,744)	(24,964)
Other Assets	2,243	1,978	1,971	1,926
Total Assets	¥ 70,229	¥ 73,989	¥ 77,213	¥ 79,273
Liabilities and Shareholders' Equity				
Accounts and Notes Payable—Trade	¥ 12,307	¥ 12,548	¥ 11,256	¥ 10,206
Notes Payable to Banks	4,776	5,000	6,479	8,067
Current Portion of Long-Term Debt	395	402	362	1,119
Other Current Liabilities	8,432	10,190	9,663	8,310
Total Current Liabilities	¥ 25,910	¥ 28,140	¥ 27,760	¥ 27,702
Long-Term Debt	2,640	3,236	6,449	8,530
Employee Retirement Benefits	1,883	2,307	2,336	2,305
Total Liabilities	¥ 30,433	¥ 33,683	¥ 36,545	¥ 38,537
Common Stock	¥ 10,757	¥ 10,758	¥ 10,758	¥ 10,758
Additional Paid-in Capital	15,011	15,012	15,012	15,012
Retained Earnings	14,028	14,536	14,898	14,966
Total Shareholders' Equity	¥ 39,796	¥ 40,306	¥ 40,668	¥ 40,736
Total Liabilities and Shareholders' Equity ..	¥ 70,229	¥ 73,989	¥ 77,213	¥ 79,273

ending March 31, Year 8 through Year 11, and Exhibit 2.20 presents the firm's income statements for the years ending March 31, Year 9 through Year 11.

Required

a. Prepare a worksheet in order to develop a statement of cash flows for Fuso Pharmaceutical Industries for each of the years ending March 31, Year 9 through Year 11. Follow the format of Exhibit 2.9 in the chapter body. Notes to the financial statements indicate the following:
   (1) The changes in the Investments in Securities account represent purchases and sales of marketable securities held as long-term investments.
   (2) There were no sales of property, plant, and equipment during the three-year period.
   (3) The changes in the Other Noncurrent Assets account represent investing transactions.

EXHIBIT 2.20

Fuso Pharmaceutical Industries
Income Statements
(amounts in millions of yen)
(Problem 2.7)

Year Ended March 31:	Year 9	Year 10	Year 11
Sales	¥ 42,845	¥ 40,915	¥ 40,025
Other Revenues	1,052	504	954
Total Revenues	¥ 43,897	¥ 41,419	¥ 40,979
Cost of Goods Sold	(26,159)	(24,991)	(25,165)
Selling and Administrative Expenses	(13,114)	(12,941)	(13,065)
Interest Expense	(634)	(679)	(636)
Income Tax Expense	(2,513)	(1,473)	(1,074)
Net Income	¥ 1,477	¥ 1,335	¥ 1,039

---

(4) The changes in the Employee Retirement Benefits account relate to provisions made for retirement benefits net of payments made to retired employees, both of which the statement of cash flows classifies as operating activities.

b. Discuss the relationship between net income and cash flow from operations and the patterns of cash flows from operating, investing, and financing transactions for Year 9, Year 10, and Year 11.

2.8 PREPARING A STATEMENT OF CASH FLOWS FROM BALANCE SHEETS AND INCOME STATEMENTS. Flight Training Corporation is a privately held firm that provides fighter pilot training under contract to the U.S. Air Force and the U.S. Navy. The firm owns approximately 100 Lear jets that it equips with radar jammers and other sophisticated electronic devices to mimic enemy aircraft. The company recently experienced cash shortages to pay its bills. The owner and manager of Flight Training Corporation stated: "I was just dumbfounded. I never had an inkling that there was a problem with cash."

Exhibit 2.21 presents comparative balance sheets for Flight Training Corporation on December 31, Year 1 through Year 4, and Exhibit 2.22 presents income statements for Year 2 through Year 4.

Required

a. Prepare a worksheet in order to develop a statement of cash flows for Flight Training Corporation for each of the years ending December 31, Year 2 through Year 4. Follow the format in Exhibit 2.9 in the chapter body. Notes to the financial statements indicate the following:

(1) The firm did not sell any aircraft during the three-year period.
(2) Changes in Other Noncurrent Assets are investing transactions.
(3) Changes in Deferred Income Taxes are operating transactions.
(4) Changes in Treasury Stock are financing transactions.

EXHIBIT 2.21

Flight Training Corporation
Balance Sheets
(amounts in thousands)
(Problem 2.8)

December 31:	Year 1	Year 2	Year 3	Year 4
Current Assets				
Cash	$ 142	$ 313	$ 583	$ 159
Accounts Receivable	2,490	2,675	4,874	6,545
Inventories	602	1,552	2,514	5,106
Prepayments................	57	469	829	665
Total Current Assets	$ 3,291	$ 5,009	$ 8,800	$ 12,475
Property, Plant, and Equipment..	$17,809	$24,039	$ 76,975	$106,529
Less Accumulated Depreciation..	(4,288)	(5,713)	(8,843)	(17,231)
Net......................	$13,521	$18,326	$ 68,132	$ 89,298
Other Assets	$ 1,112	$ 641	$ 665	$ 470
Total Assets..............	$17,924	$23,976	$ 77,597	$102,243
Current Liabilities				
Accounts Payable	$ 939	$ 993	$ 6,279	$ 12,428
Notes Payable...............	1,021	140	945	—
Current Portion of Long-Term Debt	1,104	1,789	7,018	60,590
Other Current Liabilities	1,310	2,423	12,124	12,903
Total Current Liabilities	$ 4,374	$ 5,345	$ 26,366	$ 85,921
Noncurrent Liabilities				
Long-Term Debt.............	6,738	9,804	41,021	—
Deferred Income Taxes........	—	803	900	—
Other Noncurrent Liabilities....	—	226	—	—
Total Liabilities	$11,112	$16,178	$ 68,287	$ 85,921
Shareholders' Equity				
Common Stock..............	$ 20	$ 21	$ 22	$ 34
Additional Paid-in Capital......	4,323	4,569	5,685	16,516
Retained Earnings............	2,469	3,208	3,802	(29)
Treasury Stock	—	—	(199)	(199)
Total Shareholders' Equity	$ 6,812	$ 7,798	$ 9,310	$ 16,322
Total Liabilities and Shareholders' Equity	$17,924	$23,976	$ 77,597	$102,243

EXHIBIT 2.22

Flight Training Corporation
Comparative Income Statement for the Year Ended December 31
(amounts in thousands)
(Problem 2.8)

Year Ended December 31:	Year 2	Year 3	Year 4
Continuing Operations			
Sales..............................	$20,758	$36,597	$54,988
Expenses			
Cost of Services	14,247	29,594	47,997
Selling and Administrative	3,868	2,972	5,881
Interest.............................	1,101	3,058	5,841
Income Taxes	803	379	(900)
Total Expenses	$20,019	$36,003	$58,819
Net Income..........................	$ 739	$ 594	$ (3,831)

(5) The firm violated covenants in its borrowing agreements during Year 4. The lenders can therefore require Flight Training Corporation to repay its long-term debt immediately. Although the banks have not yet demanded payment, the firm reclassified its long-term debt as a current liability.

b. Prepare a comparative statement of cash flows for Flight Training Corporation for each of the years ending December 31, Year 2 through Year 4.

c. Comment on the relationship between net income and cash flow from operations and the pattern of cash flows from operating, investing, and financing activities for each of the three years.

d. Describe the likely reasons for Flight Training Corporation's cash flow difficulties.

2.9   PREPARING A STATEMENT OF CASH FLOWS FROM BALANCE SHEETS AND INCOME STATEMENTS. GTI, Inc. manufactures parts, components, and processing equipment for electronics and semiconductor applications in the communications, computer, automotive, and appliance industries. Its sales tend to vary with changes in the business cycle, because the sales of most of its customers are cyclical. Exhibit 2.23 presents balance sheets for GTI as of December 31, Year 7 through Year 9, and Exhibit 2.24 presents income statements for Year 8 and Year 9.

Required

a. Prepare a worksheet to develop a statement of cash flows for GTI, Inc. for Year 8 and Year 9. Follow the format in Exhibit 2.9 in the chapter body. Notes to the firm's financial statements reveal the following (amounts in thousands):

   (1) Depreciation expense was $641 in Year 8 and $625 in Year 9.

   (2) Other Assets represent patents. Patent amortization was $25 in Year 8 and $40 in Year 9.

   (3) Changes in Deferred Income Taxes are operating transactions.

b. Discuss the relationship between net income and cash flow from operations and the pattern of cash flows from operating, investing, and financing activities.

EXHIBIT 2.23

GTI, Inc.
Balance Sheets
(amounts in thousands)
(Problem 2.9)

December 31:	Year 7	Year 8	Year 9
Assets			
Cash..................................	$ 430	$ 475	$ 367
Accounts Receivable...................	3,768	3,936	2,545
Inventories	2,334	2,966	2,094
Prepayments.........................	116	270	122
Total Current Assets	$ 6,648	$ 7,647	$ 5,128
Property, Plant, and Equipment (net).......	3,806	4,598	4,027
Other Assets..........................	193	559	456
Total Assets........................	$10,647	$12,804	$ 9,611
Liabilities and Shareholders' Equity			
Accounts Payable	$ 1,578	$ 809	$ 796
Notes Payable to Banks	11	231	2,413
Other Current Liabilities	1,076	777	695
Total Current Liabilities	$ 2,665	$ 1,817	$ 3,904
Long-Term Debt.......................	2,353	4,692	2,084
Deferred Income Taxes.................	126	89	113
Total Liabilities......................	$ 5,144	$ 6,598	$ 6,101
Preferred Stock........................	$ —	$ 289	$ 289
Common Stock.........................	83	85	85
Additional Paid-in Capital...............	4,385	4,392	4,395
Retained Earnings	1,035	1,440	(1,259)
Total Shareholders' Equity	$ 5,503	$ 6,206	$ 3,510
Total Liabilities and Shareholders' Equity..	$10,647	$12,804	$ 9,611

EXHIBIT 2.24

GTI, Inc.
Income Statements
(amounts in thousands)
(Problem 2.9)

	Year 8	Year 9
Sales	$ 22,833	$ 11,960
Cost of Goods Sold	(16,518)	(11,031)
Selling and Administrative Expenses	(4,849)	(3,496)
Interest Expense	(459)	(452)
Income Tax Expense	(590)	328
Net Income................................	$ 417	$ (2,691)
Dividends on Preferred Stock	(12)	(8)
Net Income Available to Common..............	$ 405	$ (2,699)

W.T. GRANT CO.*

At the time that it filed for bankruptcy in October 1975, W.T. Grant was the 17th largest retailer in the U.S.; it had almost 1,200 stores, over 82,000 employees, and sales of $1.7 billion. It had paid dividends consistently since 1906. Grant's collapse came largely as a surprise to the capital markets, and particularly to the banks that had provided it short-term working capital loans. Grant had altered its business strategy in the mid-sixties to transform itself from an urban discount chain to a suburban household goods chain. Its failure serves as a classic study of poor implementation of what seemed like a sound business strategy. What happened to Grant and why are questions that, with some analysis, we can answer. At the same time, why the symptoms of Grant's prolonged illness were not diagnosed and treated earlier is difficult to understand.

THE STRATEGIC SHIFT

Prior to the mid-sixties, Grant had built its reputation on sales of low-priced soft goods (clothing, linens, sewing fabrics). It placed its stores in large, urban locations and appealed primarily to lower-income consumers. The mid-sixties, however, marked the beginning of urban unrest and a large movement to the suburbs. To service the needs of these new homeowners, suburban shopping centers sprung up.

Sears led the way in the shopping center movement, establishing itself as the anchor store in many of the more upscale locations. Montgomery Ward and JC Penney followed suit. At the time, Sears held a dominant market share in the middle-income consumer market. It soon saw an opportunity to provide a more upscale product line to compete with the established department stores (Macy's, Marshall Field), which had not yet begun their movement to the suburbs. To implement this new strategy, Sears introduced its Sears Best line of products.

The population movement to the suburbs and increased competition from growing discount chains such as Kmart caused Grant to alter its strategy as well. One aspect of its strategic shift was rapid expansion of new stores into suburban shopping centers. Between 1963 and 1973, Grant opened 612 new stores and expanded 91 others. Most of its expansion was concentrated in the 1969–1973 period, when it opened 369 new stores, 15 of them on the same day. Because Grant's reputation had been built on sales to lower-income consumers, it was often unable to locate its new stores in the choicest shopping centers.

Louis C. Lustenberger, President of Grant from 1959 to 1968, started the expansion program, although later, as a director, he became concerned over dimensions of the growth and the problems it generated. After Mr. Lustenberger stepped down, the pace of expansion accelerated under the leadership of Chairman Edward Staley and President Richard W. Mayer.

A second aspect of Grant's strategy involved a change in its product line. Grant perceived a vacuum in the middle-income consumer market when Sears moved more upscale. Grant introduced a higher-quality, medium-priced line of products in its new shopping center stores to fill this vacuum. It also added furniture and private-brand appliances to its product line and implemented a credit card system. As much of the movement to the sub-

---

*This case was coauthored with Professor James A. Largay.

urbs was by middle-income consumers, Grant attempted to position itself as a primary supplier to outfit the new homes being constructed.

To implement its expansion strategy, Grant chose a decentralized organizational structure. Each store manager controlled credit extension and credit terms. At most stores, Grant gave customers 36 months to pay for their purchases; the minimum monthly payment was $1, regardless of total purchase amount. Bad debt expenses averaged 1.2 percent of sales each year until fiscal 1975, when a provision for bad debts of $155.7 million was made.

Local store managers also made inventory and pricing decisions. Merchandise was either acquired from regional Grant warehouses or ordered directly from the manufacturer. There was no information system in place that permitted one store to check the availability of a needed product at another store. Compensation of employees was considered among the most generous in the industry; most employees owned Grant's common stock acquired under employee stock option plans. Compensation of store managers included salary plus stated percentages of the store's sales and profits.

To finance the expansion of receivables and inventory, Grant used commercial paper, bank loans, and trade credit. To finance the expansion of store space, it entered into leasing arrangements. Because the company was liquidated before the Financial Accounting Standards Board issued *Statement of Financial Accounting Standards No. 13,* which requires the capitalization of capital leases on the balance sheet and the disclosure of information on operating leases in the notes to the financial statements, Grant's did not need to (and did not) disclose its long-term leasing arrangements. Property, plant, and equipment reported on its balance sheet consisted mostly of store fixtures. Grant's long-term debt included debentures totaling $200 million issued in 1971 and 1973. Based on per square foot rental rates at the time, Grant's disclosures of total square footage of space, and an 8 percent discount rate, the estimated present values of Grant's leases are as follows (in thousands):

January 31	Present Value of Lease Commitments	January 31	Present Value of Lease Commitments
1966	$394,291	1971	$496,041
1967	400,090	1972	626,052
1968	393,566	1973	708,666
1969	457,111	1974	805,785
1970	486,837	1975	821,565

ADVANCE AND RETREAT— THE ATTEMPT TO SAVE GRANT

By 1974, it became clear that Grant's problems were not of a short-term operating nature. In the spring of 1974, both Moody's and Standard & Poor's eliminated their credit rating for Grant's commercial paper (that is, they no longer gave Grant's commercial paper a credit rating). Banks entered the picture in a big way in the summer of that year. To provide financing, a group of 143 banks agreed to offer lines of credit totaling $525 million. Grant obtained a short-term loan of $600 million in September 1974, with three New York money center banks absorbing approximately $230 million of the total. These three banks also lent $50 million out of a total of $100 million provided to Grant's finance subsidiary.

Support of the banks during the summer of 1974 was accompanied by a top management change. Messrs. Staley and Mayer stepped down in the spring and were replaced in August 1974 by James G. Kendrick, brought in from Zeller's Ltd., Grant's Canadian subsidiary. As Chief Executive Officer, Mr. Kendrick moved to cut Grant's losses. He slashed payroll significantly, closed 126 unprofitable stores, and phased out the big-ticket furniture and appliance lines. New store space added in 1975 was 75 percent less than in 1974.

The positive effects of these moves could not overcome the disastrous events of early 1975, however. In January, Grant defaulted on about $75 million in interest payments. When results of operations for the year ended January 31, 1975, were released in February, Grant reported a loss of $177 million, with substantial losses from credit operations accounting for 60 percent of the total.

When Robert H. Anderson, at the time a Sears Vice President, was offered a lucrative $2.5 million contract, he decided to accept the challenge to turn the company around, and joined Grant as its new president in April 1975. Mr. Kendrick remained as Chairman of the Board. The banks now assumed a more active role in what was becoming a struggle to save the company. The banks holding 90 percent of Grant's debt extended their loans from June 2, 1975, to March 31, 1976. The balance of about $56 million was repaid on June 2.

A major problem confronting Mr. Anderson was to maintain the continued flow of merchandise into Grant stores. Suppliers became skeptical of Grant's ability to pay for merchandise, and, in August 1975, the banks agreed to subordinate $300 million of debt to suppliers' claims for merchandise shipped. With the approach of the Christmas shopping season, the need for merchandise became critical. Despite the banks' subordination of their claims to those of suppliers and the intensive cultivation of suppliers by Mr. Anderson, Grant did not receive sufficient quantities of merchandise in the stores.

During this period, Grant reported a $111.3 million net loss for the six months ended on July 31, 1975. Sales had declined 15 percent from the comparable period in 1974. Mr. Kendrick observed that a return to profitability before the fourth quarter was unlikely.

On October 2, 1975, Grant filed a Chapter XI bankruptcy petition. The rehabilitation effort was formally under way, and the protection provided by Chapter XI permitted a continuation of the reorganization and rehabilitation activities for the next four months. On February 6, 1976, after store closings and liquidations of inventories had generated $320 million in cash, the creditors' committee overseeing the bankruptcy voted for liquidation, and W.T. Grant ceased to exist.

FINANCIAL STATEMENTS FOR GRANT

Two changes in accounting principles affect Grant's financial statements. Prior to fiscal 1970, Grant accounted for the investment in its wholly owned finance subsidiary using the equity method. Beginning with the year ending January 31, 1970, Grant consolidated the finance subsidiary.

Prior to fiscal 1975, Grant recorded the total finance charge on credit sales as income in the year of the sale. Accounts receivable therefore included the full amount to be received from customers, not the present value of such amount. Beginning with the fiscal year ending January 31, 1975, Grant recognized finance changes on credit sales over the life of the installment contract.

Exhibit 2.25 presents comparative balance sheets, and Exhibit 2.26 presents statements of income and retained earnings for Grant, based on the amounts as originally reported for each year. Exhibits 2.27, 2.28, and 2.29 present balance sheets, income statements, and statements of cash flow based on revised amounts reflecting retroactive restatement for the two changes in accounting principles discussed above. These latter statements consolidate the finance subsidiary for all years. Grant provided the necessary data to restate for the change in income recognition of finance charges for the 1971 to 1975 fiscal years only. Exhibit 2.30 presents selected other data for Grant, the variety chain store industry, and the aggregate economy.

Required

Using the narrative information and the financial data provided in Exhibits 2.25 through 2.30, your mission is to apply tools of financial analysis to determine the major causes of Grant's financial problems. If you had been performing this analysis at the time that various publicly reported information about the firm was released, when would you have become skeptical of Grant's ability to continue as a viable going concern?

To help you in this analysis, Exhibits 2.31 through 2.33 present selected ratio and growth rate information based on assumptions as follows:

Exhibit 2.31: Based on the amounts as originally reported for each year (Exhibits 2.25 and 2.26).

Exhibit 2.32: Based on the amounts as retroactively restated for changes in accounting principles (Exhibits 2.27, 2.28, and 2.29).

Exhibit 2.33: Same as Exhibit 2.32, except assets and liabilities reflect the capitalization of leases using the amounts presented in the case.

EXHIBIT 2.25

W.T. Grant Company
Comparative Balance Sheets
(as originally reported)
(Case 2.1)

January 31:	1966	1967	1968	1969
Assets				
Cash and Marketable Securities	$ 22,559	$ 37,507	$ 25,047	$ 28,460
Accounts Receivable[c]	110,943	110,305	133,406	154,829
Inventories	151,365	174,631	183,722	208,623
Other Current Assets	—	—	—	—
Total Current Assets	$284,867	$ 322,443	$342,175	$391,912
Investments	38,419	40,800	56,609	62,854
Property, Plant, and Equipment (net)	40,367	48,071	47,572	49,213
Other Assets	1,222	1,664	1,980	2,157
Total Assets	$364,875	$ 412,978	$448,336	$506,136
Equities				
Short-Term Debt.	$ —	$ —	$ 300	$ 180
Accounts Payable—Trade	58,252	75,885	79,673	102,080
Current Deferred Taxes	37,590	47,248	57,518	64,113
Total Current Liabilities	$ 95,842	$ 123,133	$137,491	$166,373
Long-Term Debt	70,000	70,000	62,622	43,251
Noncurrent Deferred Taxes.	6,269	7,034	7,551	7,941
Other Long-Term Liabilities	4,784	4,949	4,858	5,519
Total Liabilities	$176,895	$ 205,116	$212,522	$223,084
Preferred Stock.	$ 15,000	$ 15,000	$ 14,750	$ 13,250
Common Stock.	15,375	15,636	16,191	17,318
Additional Paid-in Capital.	25,543	27,977	37,428	59,945
Retained Earnings.	132,062	149,249	167,445	192,539
Total	$187,980	$ 207,862	$235,814	$283,052
Less Cost of Treasury Stock	—	—	—	—
Total Stockholders' Equity.	$187,980	$ 207,862	$235,814	$283,052
Total Equities	$364,875	$ 412,978	$448,336	$506,136

[a]In the year ending January 31, 1970, W.T. Grant changed its consolidation policy and commenced consolidating its wholly-owned finance subsidiary.
[b]In the year ending January 31, 1975, W.T. Grant changed its method of recognizing finance income on installment sales. In prior years, Grant recognized all finance income in the year of the sale. Beginning in the 1975 fiscal period, it recognized finance income over the time the installment receivable was outstanding.
[c]Accounts receivable comprises the following:

Customer Installment Receivables.	$ 114,470	$ 114,928	$ 140,507	$ 162,219
Less Allowances for Uncollectible Accounts	(7,065)	(9,383)	(11,307)	(13,074)
Unearned Credit Insurance	—	—	—	—
Unearned Finance Income.	—	—	—	—
Net	$ 107,405	$ 105,545	$ 129,200	$ 149,145
Other Receivables	3,538	4,760	4,206	5,684
Total Receivables.	$ 110,943	$ 110,305	$ 133,406	$ 154,829

EXHIBIT 2.25

continued

1970[a]	1971	1972	1973	1974	1975[b]
$ 32,977	$ 34,009	$ 49,851	$ 30,943	$ 45,951	$ 79,642
368,267	419,731	477,324	542,751	598,799	431,201
222,128	260,492	298,676	399,533	450,637	407,357
5,037	5,246	5,378	6,649	7,299	6,581
$628,409	$719,478	$ 831,229	$ 979,876	$1,102,686	$ 924,781
20,694	23,936	32,367	35,581	44,251	49,764
55,311	61,832	77,173	91,420	100,984	101,932
2,381	2,678	3,901	3,821	5,063	5,790
$706,795	$807,924	$ 944,670	$1,110,698	$1,252,984	$1,082,267
$182,132	$246,420	$ 237,741	$ 390,034	$ 453,097	$ 600,695
104,144	118,091	124,990	112,896	104,883	147,211
80,443	94,785	112,846	130,137	132,085	2,000
$366,719	$459,296	$ 475,577	$ 633,067	$ 690,065	$ 749,906
35,402	32,301	128,432	126,672	220,336	216,341
8,286	8,518	9,664	11,926	14,649	—
5,700	5,773	5,252	4,694	4,196	2,183
$416,107	$505,888	$ 618,925	$ 776,359	$ 929,246	$ 968,430
$ 11,450	$ 9,600	$ 9,053	$ 8,600	$ 7,465	$ 7,465
17,883	18,180	18,529	18,588	18,599	18,599
71,555	78,116	85,195	86,146	85,909	83,914
211,679	230,435	244,508	261,154	248,461	37,674
$312,567	$336,331	$ 357,285	$ 374,488	$ 360,434	$ 147,652
(21,879)	(34,295)	(31,540)	(40,149)	(36,696)	(33,815)
$290,688	$302,036	$ 325,745	$ 334,339	$ 323,738	$ 113,837
$706,795	$807,924	$ 944,670	$1,110,698	$1,252,984	$1,082,267
$ 381,757	$ 433,730	$ 493,859	$ 556,091	$ 602,305	$ 518,387
(15,270)	(15,527)	(15,750)	(15,770)	(18,067)	(79,510)
(5,774)	(9,553)	(12,413)	(8,768)	(4,923)	(1,386)
—	—	—	—	—	(37,523)
$ 360,713	$ 408,650	$ 465,696	$ 531,553	$ 579,315	$ 399,968
7,554	11,081	11,628	11,198	19,484	31,233
$ 368,267	$ 419,731	$ 477,324	$ 542,751	$ 598,799	$ 431,201

EXHIBIT 2.26

W.T. Grant Company
Statements of Income and Retained Earnings
(as originally reported)
(Case 2.1)

Year Ended January 31	1967	1968	1969
Sales..	$920,797	$979,458	$1,096,152
Concessions...................................	2,249	2,786	3,425
Equity in Earnings	2,072	2,987	3,537
Finance Charges.................................	—	—	—
Other Income...................................	1,049	2,010	2,205
Total Revenues............................	$926,167	$987,241	$1,105,319
Cost of Goods Sold.............................	$631,585	$669,560	$ 741,181
Selling, General & Administration	233,134	253,561	287,883
Interest.......................................	4,970	4,907	4,360
Taxes: Current	13,541	17,530	25,600
Deferred	11,659	9,120	8,400
Total Expenses............................	$894,889	$954,678	$1,067,424
Net Income	$ 31,278	$ 32,563	$ 37,895
Dividends.....................................	$ (14,091)	$ (14,367)	$ (17,686)
Change in Accounting Principles:			
Consolidation of Finance Subsidiary...............	—	—	4,885
Recognition of Financing Changes	$ —	$ —	$ —
Change in Retained Earnings......................	$ 17,187	$ 18,196	$ 25,094
Retained Earnings—Beginning of Period	132,062	149,249	167,445
Retained Earnings—End of Period..................	$149,249	$167,445	$ 192,539

EXHIBIT 2.26

continued

1970	1971	1972	1973	1974	1975
$1,210,918	$1,254,131	$1,374,811	$1,644,747	$1,849,802	$1,761,952
3,748	4,986	3,439	3,753	3,971	4,238
2,084	2,777	2,383	5,116	4,651	3,086
—	—	—	—	—	91,141
2,864	2,874	3,102	1,188	3,063	3,376
$1,219,614	$1,264,768	$1,383,735	$1,654,804	$1,861,487	$1,863,793
$ 817,671	$ 843,192	$ 931,237	$1,125,261	$1,282,945	$1,303,267
307,215	330,325	374,334	444,879	491,287	769,253
14,919	18,874	16,452	21,127	78,040	86,079
24,900	21,140	13,487	9,588	(6,021)	(19,439)
13,100	11,660	13,013	16,162	6,807	(98,027)
$1,177,805	$1,225,191	$1,348,523	$1,617,017	$1,853,058	$2,041,133
$ 41,809	$ 39,577	$ 35,212	$ 37,787	$ 8,429	$ (177,340)
$ (19,737)	$ (20,821)	$ (21,139)	$ (21,141)	$ (21,122)	$ (4,457)
(2,932)	—	—	—	—	—
$ —	$ —	$ —	$ —	$ —	$ (28,990)
$ 19,140	$ 18,756	$ 14,073	$ 16,646	$ (12,693)	$ (210,787)
192,539	211,679	230,435	244,508	261,154	248,461
$ 211,679	$ 230,435	$ 244,508	$ 261,154	$ 248,461	$ 37,674

EXHIBIT 2.27

W.T. Grant Company
Comparative Balance Sheets
(as retroactively reported for changes in accounting principles)
(Case 2.1)

January 31:	1966	1967	1968
Assets			
Cash and Marketable Securities	$ 22,638	$ 39,040	$ 25,141
Accounts Receivable[c]	172,706	230,427	272,450
Inventories	151,365	174,631	183,722
Other Current Assets	3,630	4,079	3,982
Total Current Assets	$ 350,339	$ 448,177	$ 485,295
Investments	13,405	14,791	16,754
Property, Plant, and Equipment (net)	40,372	48,076	47,578
Other Assets	1,222	1,664	1,980
Total Assets	$ 405,338	$ 512,708	$ 551,607
Equities			
Short-Term Debt	$ 37,314	$ 97,647	$ 99,230
Accounts Payable	58,252	75,885	79,673
Current Deferred Taxes	36,574	44,667	56,545
Total Current Liabilities	$ 132,140	$ 218,199	$ 235,448
Long-Term Debt	70,000	70,000	62,622
Noncurrent Deferred Taxes	6,269	7,034	7,551
Other Long-Term Liabilities	4,785	5,159	5,288
Total Liabilities	$ 213,194	$ 300,392	$ 310,909
Preferred Stock	$ 15,000	$ 15,000	$ 14,750
Common Stock	15,375	15,636	16,191
Additional Paid-in Capital	25,543	27,977	37,428
Retained Earnings	136,226	153,703	172,329
Total	$ 192,144	$ 212,316	$ 240,698
Less Cost of Treasury Stock	—	—	—
Total Stockholders' Equity	$ 192,144	$ 212,316	$ 240,698
Total Equities	$ 405,338	$ 512,708	$ 551,607

---

[a]See Note a to Exhibit 2.25.

[b]See Note b to Exhibit 2.25.

[c]Accounts receivable comprises the following:

Customer Installment Receivables			
Less Allowances for Uncollectible Accounts	NOT DISCLOSED ON A FULLY		
Unearned Credit Insurance	CONSOLIDATED BASIS		
Unearned Finance Income			
Net	WITH FINANCE SUBSIDIARY		
Other Receivables			
Total Receivables	$ 172,706	$ 230,427	$ 272,450

EXHIBIT 2.27

continued

1969	1970[a]	1971	1972	1973	1974	1975[b]
$ 25,639	$ 32,977	$ 34,009	$ 49,851	$ 30,943	$ 45,951	$ 79,642
312,776	368,267	358,428	408,301	468,582	540,802	431,201
208,623	222,128	260,492	298,676	399,533	450,637	407,357
4,402	5,037	5,246	5,378	6,649	7,299	6,581
$551,440	$628,409	$658,175	$762,206	$ 905,707	$1,044,689	$ 924,781
18,581	20,694	23,936	32,367	35,581	44,251	49,764
49,931	55,311	61,832	77,173	91,420	100,984	101,932
2,157	2,381	2,678	3,901	3,821	5,063	5,790
$622,109	$706,795	$746,621	$875,647	$1,036,529	$1,194,987	$1,082,267
$118,125	$182,132	$246,420	$237,741	$ 390,034	$ 453,097	$ 600,695
102,080	104,144	118,091	124,990	112,896	104,883	147,211
65,073	80,443	58,536	72,464	87,431	103,078	2,000
$285,278	$366,719	$423,047	$435,195	$ 590,361	$ 661,058	$ 749,906
43,251	35,402	32,301	128,432	126,672	220,336	216,341
7,941	8,286	8,518	9,664	11,926	14,649	—
5,519	5,700	5,773	5,252	4,694	4,196	2,183
$341,989	$416,107	$469,639	$578,543	$ 733,653	$ 900,239	$ 968,430
$ 13,250	$ 11,450	$ 9,600	$ 9,053	$ 8,600	$ 7,465	$ 7,465
17,318	17,883	18,180	18,529	18,588	18,599	18,599
59,945	71,555	78,116	85,195	86,146	85,909	83,914
189,607	211,679	205,381	215,867	229,691	219,471	37,674
$280,120	$312,567	$311,277	$328,644	$ 343,025	$ 331,444	$ 147,652
—	(21,879)	(34,295)	(31,540)	(40,149)	(36,696)	(33,815)
$280,120	$290,688	$276,982	$297,104	$ 302,876	$ 294,748	$ 113,837
$622,109	$706,795	$746,621	$875,647	$1,036,529	$1,194,987	$1,082,267
	$ 381,757	$ 433,740	$ 493,859	$ 556,091	$ 602,305	$ 518,387
	(15,270)	(15,527)	(15,750)	(15,770)	(18,067)	(79,510)
	(5,774)	(9,553)	(12,413)	(8,768)	(4,923)	(1,386)
	—	(61,303)	(69,023)	(74,169)	(57,997)	(37,523)
	$ 360,713	$ 347,347	$ 396,073	$ 457,384	$ 521,318	$ 399,968
	7,554	11,081	11,628	11,198	19,484	31,233
$ 312,776	$ 368,267	$ 358,428	$ 408,301	$ 468,582	$ 540,802	$ 431,201

W.T. Grant Company
Statements of Income and Retained Earnings
(as retroactively revised for changes in accounting principles)
(Case 2.1)

Year Ended January 31	1967	1968	1969
Sales	$920,797	$979,458	$1,096,152
Concessions	2,249	2,786	3,425
Equity in Earnings	1,073	1,503	1,761
Finance Charges	—	—	—
Other Income	1,315	2,038	2,525
Total Revenues	$925,434	$985,785	$1,103,311
Cost of Goods Sold	$631,585	$669,560	$ 741,181
Selling, General & Administration	229,130	247,093	278,031
Interest	7,319	8,549	9,636
Taxes: Current	14,463	18,470	27,880
Deferred	11,369	9,120	8,400
Total Expenses	$893,866	$952,792	$1,065,128
Net Income	$ 31,568	$ 32,993	$ 38,183
Dividends	$ (14,091)	$ (14,367)	$ (17,686)
Change in Accounting Principles:			
Consolidation of Finance Subsidiary	—	—	(3,219)
Recognition of Financing Changes	$ —	$ —	$ —
Change in Retained Earnings	$ 17,477	$ 18,626	$ 17,278
Retained Earnings—Beginning of Period	136,226	153,703	172,329
Retained Earnings—End of Period	$153,703	$172,329	$ 189,607

EXHIBIT 2.28

continued

1970	1971	1972	1973	1974	1975
$1,210,918	$1,254,131	$1,374,812	$1,644,747	$1,849,802	$1,761,952
3,748	4,986	3,439	3,753	3,971	4,238
2,084	2,777	2,383	5,116	4,651	3,086
—	63,194	66,567	84,817	114,920	91,141
2,864	2,874	3,102	1,188	3,063	3,376
$1,219,614	$1,327,962	$1,450,303	$1,739,621	$1,976,407	$1,863,793
$ 817,671	$ 843,192	$ 931,237	$1,125,261	$1,282,945	$1,303,267
307,215	396,877	445,244	532,604	601,231	769,253
14,919	18,874	16,452	21,127	78,040	86,079
24,900	22,866	13,579	11,256	(6,021)	(19,439)
13,100	9,738	12,166	14,408	9,310	(98,027)
$1,177,805	$1,291,547	$1,418,678	$1,704,656	$1,965,505	$2,041,133
$ 41,809	$ 36,415	$ 31,625	$ 34,965	$ 10,902	$ (177,340)
$ (19,737)	$ (20,821)	$ (21,139)	$ (21,141)	$ (21,122)	$ (4,457)
—	—	—	—	—	—
$ —	$ (21,892)	$ —	$ —	$ —	$ —
$ 22,072	$ (6,298)	$ 10,486	$ 13,824	$ (10,220)	$ (181,797)
189,607	211,679	205,381	215,867	229,691	219,471
$ 211,679	$ 205,381	$ 215,867	$ 229,691	$ 219,471	$ 37,674

EXHIBIT 2.29

W.T. Grant Company
Statement of Cash Flows
(as retroactively revised for changes in accounting principles)
(Case 2.1)

	1967	1968	1969
Operations			
Net Income.	$ 31,568	$ 32,993	$ 38,183
Depreciation	7,524	8,203	8,388
Other	66	(856)	(1,140)
(Increase) Decrease in Receivables	(57,721)	(42,023)	(40,326)
(Increase) Decrease in Inventories	(23,266)	(9,091)	(24,901)
(Increase) Decrease in Prepayments	(449)	97	(420)
Increase (Decrease) in Accounts Payable	17,633	3,788	22,407
Increase (Decrease) in Other Current Liabilities	8,093	11,878	8,528
Cash Flow from Operations	$ (16,552)	$ 4,989	$ 10,719
Investing			
Acquisition of Property, Plant, and Equipment	$ (15,257)	$ (7,763)	$ (10,626)
Acquisition of Investments	(269)	(418)	(35)
Cash Flow from Investing	$ (15,526)	$ (8,181)	$ (10,661)
Financing			
Increase (Decrease) in Short-Term Borrowing	$ 60,333	$ 1,583	$ 18,895
Increase (Decrease) in Long-Term Borrowing.	—	(1,500)	(1,500)
Increase (Decrease) in Capital Stock	2,695	3,958	844
Dividends	(14,091)	(14,367)	(17,686)
Cash Flow from Financing	$ 48,937	$ (10,326)	$ 553
Other	$ (457)	$ (381)	$ (113)
Change in Cash	$ 16,402	$ (13,899)	$ 498

EXHIBIT 2.29

continued

1970	1971	1972	1973	1974	1975
$ 41,809	$ 36,415	$ 31,625	$ 34,965	$ 10,902	$(177,340)
8,972	9,619	10,577	12,004	13,579	14,587
(1,559)	(2,470)	(1,758)	(1,699)	(1,345)	(16,993)
(55,491)	(11,981)	(49,873)	(60,281)	(72,220)	109,601
(13,505)	(38,364)	(38,184)	(100,857)	(51,104)	43,280
(635)	(209)	(132)	(1,271)	(650)	718
2,064	13,947	6,899	(12,094)	(8,013)	42,328
15,370	(21,907)	13,928	14,967	15,647	(101,078)
$ (2,975)	$(14,950)	$(26,918)	$(114,266)	$(93,204)	$ (84,897)
$(14,352)	$(16,141)	$(25,918)	$ (26,251)	$(23,143)	$ (15,535)
—	(436)	(5,951)	(2,216)	(5,700)	(5,282)
$(14,352)	$(16,577)	$(31,869)	$ (28,467)	$(28,843)	$ (20,817)
$ 64,007	$ 64,288	$ (8,679)	$ 152,293	$ 63,063	$ 147,598
(1,687)	(1,538)	98,385	(1,584)	93,926	(3,995)
(17,860)	(8,954)	7,407	(8,227)	1,833	886
(19,737)	(20,821)	(21,139)	(21,141)	(21,122)	(4,457)
$ 24,723	$ 32,975	$ 75,974	$ 121,341	$137,700	$ 140,032
$ (58)	$ (416)	$ (1,345)	$ 2,484	$ (645)	$ (627)
$ 7,338	$ 1,032	$ 15,842	$ (18,908)	$ 15,008	$ 33,691

EXHIBIT 2.30

W.T. Grant Company
Other Data
(Case 2.1)

December 31:	1965	1966	1967	1968
W.T. Grant Co.				
Sales (millions of dollars)[a]	$ 839.7	$ 920.8	$ 975.5	$ 1,096.1
Number of Stores.	1,088	1,104	1,086	1,092
Store Area (thousands of square feet)[a]				
	———————DATA NOT AVAILABLE———————			
Dividends per Share[a]	$ .80	$ 1.10	$ 1.10	$ 1.30
Stock Price—High	$ 31⅛	$ 35⅛	$ 37⅜	$ 45⅛
—Low.	$ 18	$ 20½	$ 20¾	$ 30
—Close (12/31)	$ 31⅛	$ 20¾	$ 34⅜	$ 42⅝
Variety Chain Store Industry				
Sales (millions of dollars)	$ 5,320.0	$ 5,727.0	$ 6,078.0	$ 6,152.0
Standard & Poor's Variety Chain Stock Price				
Index—High.	31.0	31.2	38.4	53.6
—Low.	24.3	22.4	22.3	34.7
—Close (12/31)	31.0	22.4	37.8	50.5
Aggregate Economy				
Gross National Product (billions of dollars)	$ 684.9	$ 747.6	$ 789.7	$ 865.7
Average Bank Short-Term Lending Rate. . .	4.99%	5.69%	5.99%	6.68%
Standard & Poor's 500 Stock Price				
Index—High.	92.6	94.1	97.6	108.4
—Low.	81.6	73.2	80.4	87.7
—Close (12/31)	92.4	80.3	96.5	103.9

[a]These amounts are for the fiscal year ending January 31 of year after the year indicated in the column. For example, sales for W.T. Grant of $839.7 in the 1965 column are for the fiscal year ending January 31, 1966.

EXHIBIT 2.30

continued

1969	1970	1971	1972	1973	1974
$ 1,210.9	$ 1,254.1	$ 1,374.8	$ 1,644.7	$ 1,849.8	$ 1,762.0
1,095	1,116	1,168	1,208	1,189	1,152
—	38,157	44,718	50,619	53,719	54,770
$ 1.40	$ 1.40	$ 1.50	$ 1.50	$ 1.50	$ .30
$ 59	$ 52	$ 70⅝	$ 48¾	$ 44⅜	$ 12
$ 39¼	$ 26⅞	$ 41⅞	$ 38¾	$ 9⅞	$ 1½
$ 47	$ 47⅛	$ 47¾	$ 43⅞	$ 10⅞	$ 1⅞
$ 6,426.0	$ 6,959.0	$ 6,972.0	$ 7,498.0	$ 8,212.0	$ 8,714.0
66.1	61.4	92.2	107.4	107.3	73.7
48.8	40.9	60.2	82.1	60.0	39.0
59.6	60.4	88.0	106.8	66.2	41.9
$ 932.1	$ 1,075.3	$ 1,107.5	$ 1,171.1	$ 1,233.4	$ 1,210.0
8.21%	8.48%	6.32%	5.82%	8.30%	11.28%
106.2	93.5	104.8	119.1	120.2	99.8
89.2	69.3	90.2	101.7	92.2	62.3
92.1	92.2	102.1	118.1	97.6	68.6

EXHIBIT 2.31

W.T. Grant Company
Financial Ratios and Growth Rates for W.T. Grant Based on Amounts as Originally Reported
(Case 2.1)

Financial Ratios	1967	1968	1969
Profitability Analysis			
Profit Margin.	3.7%	3.6%	3.7%
Assets Turnover.	2.4	2.3	2.3
Return on Assets	8.7%	8.2%	8.4%
Return on Common Shareholders' Equity	16.8%	15.5%	15.2%
Operating Performance			
Cost of Goods Sold/Sales.	68.6%	68.4%	67.6%
Sell. & Admin. Exp./Sales	25.3%	25.9%	26.3%
Asset Turnovers			
Accounts Receivable	8.3	8.0	7.6
Inventory.	3.9	3.7	3.8
Fixed Asset	20.8	20.5	22.7
Short-Term Liquidity Risk			
Current Ratio	2.62	2.49	2.36
Quick Ratio.	1.20	1.15	1.10
Days Receivables.	44	45	48
Days Inventory.	94	98	97
Days Payables	37	42	43
Operating Cash Flow/Current Liabilities	(15.1%)	3.8%	7.1%
Long-Term Solvency Risk			
Liabilities/Assets	49.7%	47.4%	44.1%
Long-Term Debt/Assets	17.0%	14.0%	8.5%
Operating Cash Flow/Liabilities.	(8.7%)	2.4%	4.9%
Interest Coverage.	12.4	13.1	17.5

Growth Rates		1968	1969
Accounts Receivable		20.9%	16.1%
Inventories.		5.2%	13.6%
Fixed Assets.		(1.0%)	3.4%
Total Assets		8.6%	12.9%
Accounts Payable.		5.0%	28.1%
Bank Loans		—	(40.0%)
Long-Term Debt		(10.5%)	(30.9%)
Shareholders' Equity		13.4%	20.0%
Sales		6.4%	11.9%
Cost of Goods Sold		6.0%	10.7%
Sell. & Admin. Expense		8.8%	13.5%
Net Income		4.1%	16.4%

EXHIBIT 2.31

continued

1970	1971	1972	1973	1974	1975
4.1%	3.9%	3.2%	3.0%	2.6%	(7.5%)
2.0	1.7	1.6	1.6	1.6	1.5
8.2%	6.5%	5.0%	4.7%	4.1%	(11.4%)
15.1%	13.7%	11.4%	11.7%	2.5%	(84.1%)
67.5%	67.2%	67.7%	68.4%	69.4%	74.0%
25.4%	26.3%	27.2%	27.0%	26.6%	43.7%
4.6	3.2	3.1	3.2	3.2	3.4
3.8	3.5	3.3	3.2	3.0	3.0
23.2	21.4	19.8	19.5	19.2	17.4
1.71	1.57	1.75	1.55	1.60	1.23
1.09	.99	1.11	.91	.93	.68
79	115	119	113	113	107
96	104	110	113	121	120
45	46	46	35	30	37
(1.1%)	(3.6%)	(5.8%)	(20.6%)	(14.1%)	(11.8%)
58.9%	62.6%	65.5%	69.9%	74.2%	85.9%
5.0%	4.0%	13.6%	11.4%	17.6%	20.0%
(.9%)	(3.2%)	(4.8%)	(16.4%)	(10.9%)	(9.0%)
6.4	4.8	4.8	4.0	1.1	(2.4)

1970	1971	1972	1973	1974	1975
137.9%	14.0%	13.7%	13.7%	10.3%	(28.0%)
6.5%	17.3%	14.7%	33.8%	12.8%	(9.6%)
12.4%	11.8%	24.8%	18.5%	10.5%	.9%
39.6%	14.3%	17.0%	17.6%	12.8%	(13.6%)
2.0%	13.4%	5.8%	(9.7%)	(7.1%)	40.4%
N/A	35.3%	(3.5%)	64.1%	16.2%	32.6%
(18.1)%	(8.8%)	297.6%	(1.4%)	73.9%	(1.8%)
2.7%	3.9%	7.8%	2.6%	(3.2%)	(64.8%)
10.5%	3.6%	9.6%	19.6%	12.5%	(4.7%)
10.3%	3.1%	10.4%	20.8%	14.0%	1.6%
6.7%	7.5%	13.3%	18.8%	10.4%	56.6%
10.3%	(5.3%)	(11.0%)	7.3%	(77.7%)	(2203.9%)

EXHIBIT 2.32

W.T. Grant Company
Financial Ratios and Growth Rates for W.T. Grant Based on Amounts Retroactively Restated for Changes in Accounting Principles (Leases Not Capitalized)
(Case 2.1)

Financial Ratios	1967	1968	1969
Profitability Analysis			
Profit Margin	3.8%	3.8%	3.9%
Assets Turnover	2.0	1.8	1.9
Return on Assets	7.7%	7.0%	7.4%
Return on Common Shareholders' Equity	16.6%	15.3%	15.3%
Operating Performance			
Cost of Goods Sold/Sales	68.6%	68.4%	67.6%
Sell. & Admin. Exp./Sales	24.9%	25.2%	25.4%
Asset Turnovers			
Accounts Receivable	4.6	3.9	3.7
Inventory	3.9	3.7	3.8
Fixed Asset	20.8	20.5	22.5
Short-Term Liquidity Risk			
Current Ratio	2.05	2.06	1.93
Quick Ratio	1.23	1.26	1.19
Days Receivables	80	94	97
Days Inventory	94	98	97
Days Payables	37	42	43
Operating Cash Flow/Current Liabilities	(9.4%)	2.2%	4.1%
Long-Term Solvency Risk			
Liabilities/Assets	58.6%	56.4%	55.0%
Long-Term Debt/Assets	13.7%	11.4%	7.0%
Operating Cash Flow/Liabilities	(6.4%)	1.6%	3.3%
Interest Coverage	8.8	8.1	8.7

Growth Rates		1968	1969
Accounts Receivable		18.2%	14.8%
Inventories		5.2%	13.6%
Fixed Assets		(1.0%)	4.9%
Total Assets		7.6%	12.8%
Accounts Payable		5.0%	28.1%
Bank Loans		1.6%	19.0%
Long-Term Debt		(10.5%)	(30.9%)
Shareholders' Equity		13.4%	16.4%
Sales		6.4%	11.9%
Cost of Goods Sold		6.0%	10.7%
Sell. & Admin. Expense		7.8%	12.5%
Net Income		4.5%	15.7%

EXHIBIT 2.32

continued

1970	1971	1972	1973	1974	1975
4.1%	3.7%	2.9%	2.8%	2.8%	(7.5%)
1.8	1.7	1.7	1.7	1.7	1.5
7.5%	6.4%	5.0%	4.8%	4.6%	(11.6%)
15.1%	13.2%	11.3%	11.9%	3.6%	(90.2%)
67.5%	67.2%	67.7%	68.4%	69.4%	74.0%
25.4%	31.6%	32.4%	32.4%	32.5%	43.7%
3.6	3.5	3.6	3.8	3.7	3.6
3.8	3.5	3.3	3.2	3.0	3.0
23.0	21.4	19.8	19.5	19.2	17.4
1.71	1.56	1.75	1.53	1.58	1.23
1.09	.93	1.05	.85	.89	.68
103	106	102	97	100	101
96	104	110	113	121	120
45	46	46	35	30	37
(.9%)	(3.8%)	(6.3%)	(22.3%)	(14.9%)	(12.0%)
58.9%	62.9%	66.1%	70.8%	75.3%	89.5%
5.0%	4.3%	14.7%	12.2%	18.4%	20.0%
(.8%)	(3.4%)	(5.1%)	(17.4%)	(11.4%)	(9.1%)
6.4	4.7	4.5	3.9	1.2	(2.4)

1970	1971	1972	1973	1974	1975
17.7%	(2.7%)	13.9%	14.8%	15.4%	(20.3%)
6.5%	17.3%	14.7%	33.8%	12.8%	(9.6%)
10.8%	11.8%	24.8%	18.5%	10.5%	.9%
13.6%	5.6%	17.3%	18.4%	15.3%	(9.4%)
2.0%	13.4%	5.8%	(9.7%)	(7.1%)	40.4%
54.2%	35.3%	(3.5%)	64.1%	16.2%	32.6%
(18.1%)	(8.8%)	297.6%	(1.4%)	73.9%	(1.8%)
3.8%	(4.7%)	7.3%	1.9%	(2.7%)	(61.4%)
10.5%	3.6%	9.6%	19.6%	12.5%	(4.7%)
10.3%	3.1%	10.4%	20.8%	14.0%	1.6%
10.5%	29.2%	12.2%	19.6%	12.9%	27.9%
9.5%	(12.9%)	(13.2%)	10.6%	(68.8%)	(1726.7%)

W.T. Grant Company
Financial Ratios and Growth Rates for W.T. Grant Based on Amounts Retroactively Restated for Changes in Accounting Principles (Leases Capitalized)
(Case 2.1)

Financial Ratios	1967	1968	1969
Profitability Analysis			
Profit Margin	3.8%	3.8%	3.9%
Assets Turnover	1.1	1.1	1.1
Return on Assets	4.1%	4.0%	4.3%
Return on Common Shareholders' Equity	16.6%	15.3%	15.3%
Operating Performance			
Cost of Goods Sold/Sales	68.6%	68.4%	67.6%
Sell. & Admin. Exp./Sales	24.9%	25.2%	25.4%
Asset Turnovers			
Accounts Receivable	4.6	3.9	3.7
Inventory	3.9	3.7	3.8
Fixed Asset	2.1	2.2	2.3
Short-Term Liquidity Risk			
Current Ratio	2.05	2.06	1.93
Quick Ratio	1.23	1.26	1.19
Days Receivables	80	94	97
Days Inventory	94	98	97
Days Payables	37	42	43
Operating Cash Flow/Current Liabilities	(9.4%)	2.2%	4.1%
Long-Term Solvency Risk			
Liabilities/Assets	76.7%	74.5%	74.0%
Long-Term Debt/Assets	51.5%	48.3%	46.4%
Operating Cash Flow/Liabilities	(2.5%)	.7%	1.4%
Interest Coverage	8.8	8.1	8.7

Growth Rates		1968	1969
Accounts Receivable		18.2%	14.8%
Inventories		5.2%	13.6%
Fixed Assets		1.6%	14.9%
Total Assets		3.5%	14.2%
Accounts Payable		5.0%	28.1%
Bank Loans		1.6%	19.0%
Long-Term Debt		(3.0%)	9.7%
Shareholders' Equity		13.4%	16.4%
Sales		6.4%	11.9%
Cost of Goods Sold		6.0%	10.7%
Sell. & Admin. Expense		7.8%	12.5%
Net Income		4.5%	15.7%

EXHIBIT 2.33

continued

1970	1971	1972	1973	1974	1975
4.1%	3.7%	2.9%	2.8%	2.8%	(7.5%)
1.1	1.0	1.0	1.0	1.0	.9
4.4%	3.8%	2.9%	2.8%	2.7%	(6.8%)
15.1%	13.2%	11.3%	11.9%	3.6%	(90.2%)
67.5%	67.2%	67.7%	68.4%	69.4%	74.0%
25.4%	31.6%	32.4%	32.4%	32.5%	43.7%
3.6	3.5	3.6	3.8	3.7	3.6
3.8	3.5	3.3	3.2	3.0	3.0
2.3	2.3	2.2	2.2	2.2	1.9
1.71	1.56	1.75	1.53	1.58	1.23
1.09	.93	1.05	.85	.89	.68
103	106	102	97	100	101
96	104	110	113	121	120
45	46	46	35	30	37
(.9%)	(3.8%)	(6.3%)	(22.3%)	(14.9%)	(12.0%)
75.6%	77.7%	80.2%	82.6%	85.3%	94.0%
43.8%	42.5%	50.2%	47.9%	51.3%	54.5%
(.3%)	(1.6%)	(2.5%)	(8.6%)	(5.9%)	(4.9%)
6.4	4.7	4.5	3.9	1.2	(2.4)

1970	1971	1972	1973	1974	1975
17.7%	(2.7%)	13.9%	14.8%	15.4%	(20.3%)
6.5%	17.3%	14.7%	33.8%	12.8%	(9.6%)
6.9%	2.9%	26.1%	13.8%	13.3%	1.8%
10.6%	4.1%	20.8%	16.2%	14.6%	(4.8%)
2.0%	13.4%	5.8%	(9.7%)	(7.1%)	40.4%
54.2%	35.3%	(3.5%)	64.1%	16.2%	32.6%
4.4%	1.2%	42.8%	10.7%	22.8%	1.1%
3.8%	(4.7%)	7.3%	1.9%	(2.7%)	(61.4%)
10.5%	3.6%	9.6%	19.6%	12.5%	(4.7%)
10.3%	3.1%	10.4%	20.8%	14.0%	1.6%
10.5%	29.2%	12.2%	19.6%	12.9%	27.9%
9.5%	(12.9%)	(13.2%)	10.6	(68.8%)	(1726.7%)

Learning Objectives

1. Analyze and interpret changes in the operating profitability of a firm using the rate of return on assets and its components: profit margin and total assets turnover.
2. Analyze and interpret changes in the rate of return on common shareholders' equity, including identifying when a firm uses financial leverage to increase the return to its common shareholders.
3. Understand the importance of effective working capital management, and apply analytical tools for assessing short-term liquidity risk.
4. Understand the benefits and risks of financial leverage, and apply analytical tools for assessing long-term solvency risk.
5. Calculate earnings per common share, and understand the strengths and weaknesses of this financial ratio as a measure of return to common shareholders.

Most financial statement analysis examines some aspect of a firm's *profitability* or a firm's *risk*. Assessments of profitability permit the analyst to study a firm's past operating performance and to project its likely future profitability. Evaluations of risk involve judgments about how successful a firm has been in coping with various dimensions of risk in the past and how apt it is to continue operating as a going concern.

This chapter describes several commonly used financial statement ratios for assessing profitability and risk and illustrates their application to the financial statements of Coke. We introduce these financial statement ratios now to provide an analytical framework for the discussion of alternative accounting principles and other data issues in Chapters 4 through 7. Chapters 8 and 9 explore the rationale and the usefulness of each of these financial statement ratios in greater depth. Although we make some preliminary interpretations of Coke's results in this chapter, a more comprehensive understanding requires consideration of data issues relating to Coke's financial statements and of the effect of economic and strategic factors on the behavior of the financial statement ratios.

Our analysis examines changes in the financial ratios for Coke over time, a process referred to as *time series analysis*. Is Coke becoming more or less profitable over time? Is it becoming more or less risky? Are changes in Coke's strategy, economic conditions, competition, or other factors causing its profitability and risk to change? Time series analysis attempts to answer these questions. An alternative approach examines the financial ratios for Coke relative to those of its competitors, a process referred to as *cross-sectional analysis*. We explore cross-sectional analysis more fully in problems at the end of this chapter and in Chapter 8.

Coke's principal competitor is Pepsi. The revision of this book took place at the time when Pepsi spun off its restaurant businesses (Taco Bell, Pizza Hut, and KFC) into a separate entity and distributed the shares of common stock of the new entity to its shareholders. At the time of this writing, Pepsi had not provided financial statements for its beverage and snack food business separate from its restaurant businesses that would have permitted us to use Pepsi as a meaningful comparison company for Coke.

An alternative basis for comparison for most industries is information on average industry financial ratios published by Robert Morris Associates, Dun & Bradstreet, and others (discussed later in the chapter). In this case, Coke and Pepsi dominate the beverage industry, and their financial ratios essentially *are* the average beverage industry ratios.

PROFITABILITY ANALYSIS

First we discuss and relate two measures of profitability: (1) the rate of return on assets (ROA), and (2) the rate of return on common shareholders' equity (ROCE).

RATE OF RETURN ON ASSETS

The rate of return on assets measures a firm's success in using assets to generate earnings, independent of the financing of those assets. Look at Exhibit 3.1. ROA takes the particular set of environmental factors and strategic choices that a firm makes as a given, and focuses on the profitability of its operations relative to the investments (assets) in place. ROA ignores, however, the means of financing these investments (that is, the proportion of debt versus equity financing). The ROA measure thus separates financing activities from operating and investing activities.

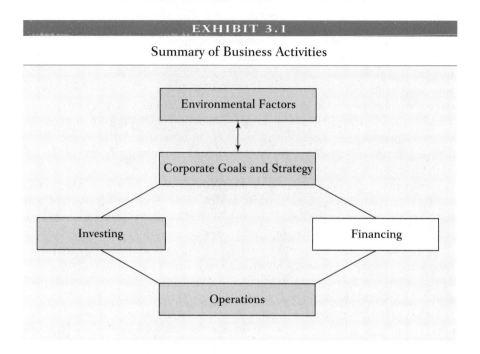

EXHIBIT 3.1

Summary of Business Activities

The analyst calculates ROA as follows:

$$\text{ROA} = \frac{\text{Net Income} + (1 - \text{Tax Rate})(\text{Interest Expense}) + \text{Minority Interest in Earnings}}{\text{Average Total Assets}}$$

The numerator in the fraction measures operating income after income taxes, excluding any financing costs. To calculate the numerator, it is usually easiest to start with net income, and then adjust that number to eliminate financing costs.[1] Because accountants subtract interest expense in computing net income, the analyst must add it back. When they calculate their taxable income, however, firms can deduct interest expense. The *incremental* effect of interest expense on net income therefore equals one minus the marginal (not average) tax rate times interest expense.[2] That is, the analyst adds back the full amount of interest expense to net income and then subtracts, or eliminates, the tax savings from that interest expense. Because accountants do not subtract dividends on preferred and common

---

[1] The analyst should use income from continuing operations, or possibly some other measure, instead of net income if the objective is to assess a firm's profitability as a going concern. Chapter 4 discusses this issue more fully.

[2] The marginal tax rate is the statutory tax appropriate to a particular type of income or expense. The income tax note will disclose the statutory, or marginal, tax rate each year. The income tax note will also show a reconciliation between the statutory tax rate and the effective, or average, tax rate. The latter rate is equal to income tax expense divided by book income before taxes (see the discussion in Chapter 6). Revenues and expenses that are included in the calculation of book income but do not impact income tax expense (for example, interest on state and municipal securities, goodwill amortization) cause the effective tax rate to differ from the statutory tax rate.

stocks in measuring net income, calculating the numerator of ROA requires no adjustment for dividends.[3]

We add back the minority interest in earnings to attain consistency between the numerator and the denominator of ROA. The denominator of ROA includes all assets of the consolidated entity, not just the parent's share. Net income in the numerator, however, represents the parent's earnings plus the parent's share of the earnings of consolidated subsidiaries. The accountant subtracts the minority interest's claim on the earnings of a consolidated subsidiary in measuring net income. If all the assets of the consolidated entity are included in the denominator of ROA, the numerator must include all the earnings of the consolidated entity. The addback of the minority interest in earnings accomplishes this objective.

Most publicly traded corporations do not disclose the minority interest in earnings because its amount is usually immaterial. Thus, the analyst makes this adjustment only for significant minority interests.

Because operating income in the numerator of ROA reports the results for a period of time, the denominator uses a measure of average assets in use during that same period. For a nonseasonal business, an average of assets at the beginning and the end of the year is usually satisfactory. For a seasonal business, the analyst should use an average of assets as of the end of each quarter.

Look at the financial statements for Coke in Appendix A. The calculation of ROA for Year 7 is as follows:

$$\text{ROA} = \frac{\text{Net Income} + (1 - \text{Tax Rate})(\text{Interest Expense}) + \text{Minority Interest in Earnings}}{\text{Average Total Assets}}$$

$$23.6\% = \frac{\$3,492 + (1 - .35)(\$286) + \$0}{.5(\$15,041 + \$16,161)} = \frac{\$3,677.9}{\$15,606.0}$$

Coke's ROA was 20.7 percent in Year 5 and 21.9 percent in Year 6. Thus, Coke experienced a continually increasing ROA over the three years.

DISAGGREGATING ROA

The analyst obtains further insight into the behavior of ROA by disaggregating it into components of profit margin and total assets turnover (hereafter referred to as assets turnover) as follows:

$$\textbf{ROA} = \textbf{Profit Margin} \times \textbf{Assets Turnover}$$

$$\frac{\text{Net Income} + \text{Interest Expense (net of taxes)} + \text{Minority Interest in Earnings}}{\text{Average Total Assets}} = \frac{\text{Net Income} + \text{Interest Expense (net of taxes)} + \text{Minority Interest in Earnings}}{\text{Sales}} \times \frac{\text{Sales}}{\text{Average Total Assets}}$$

---

[3]One could argue that the analyst should exclude returns from short-term investments of excess cash (that is, interest revenue) from the numerator of ROA under the view that such investments are really negative financings. We make no such adjustment in this book.

EXHIBIT 3.2			
ROAs, Profit Margins, and Assets Turnovers for Coke—Year 5 to Year 7			
	Year 5	**Year 6**	**Year 7**
ROA	20.7%	21.9%	23.6%
Profit Margin	16.6%	17.6%	19.8%
Assets Turnover	1.2	1.2	1.2

The profit margin is a measure of the ability of a firm to generate operating income from a particular level of sales.[4] The assets turnover is a measure of a firm's ability to manage its level of investment in assets for a particular level of sales, or, to put it another way, its ability to generate sales from a particular investment in assets.

The disaggregation of ROA for Coke for Year 7 is as follows:

$$\textbf{ROA} \quad = \textbf{Profit Margin} \times \textbf{Assets Turnover}$$

$$\frac{\$3,667.9}{\$15,606.0} = \frac{\$3,667.9}{\$18,546} \times \frac{\$18,546}{\$15,606}$$

$$23.6\% \quad = \quad 19.8\% \quad \times \quad 1.2$$

Exhibit 3.2 summarizes ROA, profit margin, and assets turnover for Coke for Year 5, Year 6, and Year 7. Coke's profit margin steadily increased, while its assets turnover remained stable.

ANALYZING THE PROFIT MARGIN

The analyst can identify the reasons for differences in the profit margin percentage by studying the relation between individual expenses and sales. Exhibit 3.3 presents these expense percentages for Coke.

The task for the financial analyst is to identify likely reasons for the changes in these expense percentages. As Chapter 1 indicates, the annual report to shareholders and the Form 10-K report to the SEC include a narrative discussing management's reasons for changes in a firm's profitability and risk. Appendix B provides that management discussion for Coke.

Firms vary in the informativeness of these discussions. Some firms, like Coke, give specific reasons for changes in various financial ratios. Other firms simply indicate the rate of increase or decrease, without providing any explanation of the changes. Even when firms do provide explanation, the analyst needs to assess how reasonable the explanations are in light of conditions in the economy and in the industry, and in light of results for the firms' competitors.

---

[4]One might argue that the analyst should use total revenues, not just sales, in the denominator because assets generate returns in forms other than sales (for example, interest revenue, equity in earnings of affiliates). Interpretations of various expense ratios (which we discuss later in the chapter) are usually easier when we use sales in the denominator, however.

EXHIBIT 3.3			
Analysis of the Profit Margins for Coke—Year 5 to Year 7			
	Year 5	**Year 6**	**Year 7**
Sales	100.0%	100.0%	100.0
Other Revenues	1.8	3.2	5.2
Cost of Goods Sold	(38.1)	(38.5)	(36.3)
Selling and Admin.	(39.4)	(39.1)	(42.6)
Income Taxes	(7.7)	(8.0)	(6.5)
Profit Margin	16.6%	17.6%	19.8%

Other Revenues.   A principal reason for Coke's increasing profit margin is an increase in the other revenues to sales percentage. This account includes (1) interest revenue from investments in cash, cash equivalents, and marketable securities; (2) equity income from investments in bottlers; and (3) gains from the issuance of stock by equity method investees.

Interest revenue increased between Year 5 and Year 6, and then decreased slightly during Year 7. The balance sheet for Coke in Appendix A indicates that cash, cash equivalents, and marketable securities (the latter including amounts in current assets and in investments) increased between Year 6 and Year 7. These accounts increased for the most part during the three-year period.

Not all of the cash in Coke's bank accounts likely earns interest, so it is difficult to tell with any certainty that Coke should have a generally upward trend in its interest income. Also, interest rates declined somewhat over this three-year period. Interest income as a percentage of the average balance in cash, cash equivalents, marketable securities (current asset), and marketable securities and other assets (noncurrent asset) is 7.5 percent [= $238/.5($1,315 + $1,597 + $1,658 + $1,779)] during Year 7. Thus, the upward trend in interest income results from increasing amounts invested in interest yielding investments.

The income statement reports that equity income increased steadily during the three-year period. Recall from Chapter 1 that Coke maintains less than controlling interests in many of its bottlers. We explain in Chapter 7 that firms (investors) owning between 20 percent and 50 percent of the outstanding common stock of another company (the investee) must generally use the equity method to account for the investment. Thus, Coke accounts for its bottling investments using the equity method, which requires it to recognize its share of the earnings of investees each year. Note 2 to Coke's financial statements in Appendix A sets forth condensed financial statements for these investments.

The net income of these bottlers increased steadily during the three years. Although Coke's ownership percentages in these bottlers changed somewhat during these years, an increasing amount of equity method income is consistent with the increasing earnings of the investees.

The third element of other revenues relates to gains recognized when equity method investees issue stock. Understanding this transaction requires knowledge of the equity method, discussed in Chapter 7, but a brief overview of the transaction at this time may prove helpful.

Coke reports its investments in equity method bottlers on the balance sheet at the amount originally paid to acquire the investments, plus Coke's share of the earnings of investees each year, minus dividends received from the investees. The book value per share of Coke's investments in these bottlers equals the amount shown on Coke's balance sheet divided by the number of common shares owned in these investees. If an equity method investee issues common stock to the public at an amount per share that exceeds the book value per share of Coke's investment in the investee, Coke reports a gain. Although Coke's ownership interest in the investee declines with the issuance of additional common stock, Coke's claim per share on the net assets, or shareholders' equity, of the investee increases as a result of the infusion of cash at a higher price per share than the book value of Coke's investment.

The rationale for reporting a gain is perhaps more evident if we assume that Coke sold some of the shares it owns in the investee directly on the market instead of having the investee issue additional shares. Coke's ownership interest would decline, just as when the investee issues additional shares. Coke would recognize a gain equal to the difference between the selling price and the book value of the shares sold, again similar to the gain that it recognizes when the investee issues the shares.

There is considerable disagreement currently as to whether gains and losses on the sale of stock by equity method investees represent legitimate earnings. Opponents argue that these stock issues represent capital transactions, much the same as if Coke were to issue its own common shares on the market. Opponents further point out that Coke receives no cash from the investee's stock issuance. Proponents resort to the analogy we use above about Coke selling a portion of the shares it owns in the investee versus having the investee sell shares on the market. Coke is obviously aware that most of its increased net income during Year 7 is attributable to a large gain on the issuance of stock by its bottling investees and it is aware as well of the debatable nature of this type of earnings. Management states (see Appendix B):

> We continue our well-established strategy of strengthening our distribution system by investing in, and subsequently reselling, ownership positions in bottling operations. This strategy provides our Company with yet another value stream resulting from gains on the sale of these investments.

Directing equity method investees to sell additional shares reduces Coke's ownership much the same as if Coke were to sell its shares directly. The sale of shares directly gives rise to taxable gains, while the issuance of additional stock by investees does not give rise to taxable income immediately (Coke will recognize taxable gains when it ultimately sells its shares).

Coke implies that this source of revenues will continue into the future. The firm reported such gains for two out of the last three years. The analyst must assess whether (1) such gains represent legitimate earnings, (2) such gains will recur, and (3) the large gain during Year 7 represents a recurring level of such gains or a one-time level.

In Chapter 4 we discuss assessments of the quality of earnings and the treatment of nonrecurring income items. At this point, we simply point out that the increased profit margin during Year 7 results in part from this controversial gain.

Cost of Goods Sold. Exhibit 3.3 indicates that the cost of goods sold to sales percentage increased between Year 5 and Year 6, and then decreased between Year 6 and Year 7. Management's discussion of the results of operations in Appendix B indicates that the increased percentage between Year 5 and Year 6 resulted from an increase in the cost of raw materials, such as sweeteners and packaging. The analyst can evaluate this explanation by examining changes in the cost of goods sold to sales percentages for Coke's competitors, since such firms purchase similar raw materials. The analyst might also examine price changes in general for sugar and packaging materials during the year.

Coke attributes the decrease in the cost of goods sold to sales percentage between Year 6 and Year 7 in part to the sale of previously consolidated subsidiaries in Germany, France, and Belgium. Recall from Chapter 1 that Coke sells concentrate to its bottlers, and the bottlers in turn sell finished Coke products to retail outlets. The price that Coke charges its bottlers for the concentrate determines the margins on concentrate sales versus sales of finished products. Coke's cost of goods sold to sales percentage during Year 7 was 36.3 percent. Note 2 to Coke's financial statements indicates that the cost of goods sold to sales percentage for Year 7 was 61.8 percent (= $4,896/$7,921) for Coca-Cola Enterprises; 59.8 percent (= $1,737/$2,905) for Coca-Cola Amatil; and 69.0 percent (= $8,028/$11,640) for other investees.

Thus, Coke generates most of its gross margin from selling concentrate as opposed to bottling. When Coke sells a previously consolidated bottler, as it did during Year 7, it removes the lower margin bottling operation and its gross margin increases (the cost of goods sold decreases). Thus, Coke can manage its cost of goods sold to sales percentage over time by acquiring and reselling investment positions in its bottlers. Such transactions affect both other revenues (gains on sales of stock) and cost of goods sold.

Coke also indicates in management's discussion of operations that the cost of goods sold to sales percentage decreased during Year 7 because of a change in product mix. Coke provides sales and operating income data for its geographical segments (discussed later in this chapter), but does not provide any information about individual products (soft drinks, juices, sports drinks, and so on). Thus, the analyst cannot evaluate this explanation further.

Interpreting changes in the cost of goods sold to sales percentage is often difficult because explanations could relate to sales revenue only, to cost of goods sold only, or to common factors affecting both the numerator and the denominator.

Consider, for example, these several possible explanations for a decrease in the cost of goods sold to sales percentage for a firm:

1. An increase in demand for products in excess of available capacity in an industry will likely result in an increase in selling prices. Even though the cost of manufacturing the product does not change, the cost of goods sold percentage will drop.
2. As a result of effective advertising, a firm's market share for its product increases. The firm allocates the fixed cost of manufacturing the product over a larger volume of production, thereby lowering its per unit cost. Even though selling prices do not change, the cost of goods sold to sales percentage will drop.
3. A firm lowers the price for its product in order to gain a larger market share. It reduces its manufacturing cost per unit by purchasing raw materials in larger quantities to take advantage of quantity discounts. The cost of goods sold per unit declines more than the selling price per unit, causing the cost of goods sold to sales percentage to drop.
4. A firm sells multiple products with different costs of goods sold to sales percentages. The product mix shifts toward higher-margin products, thereby reducing the overall cost of goods sold to sales percentage.

Thus, the analyst must consider changes in both selling prices and manufacturing costs when interpreting changes in the cost of goods sold percentage.

Selling and Administrative Expenses. Most firms combine selling and administrative expenses on their income statements. This practice is unfortunate from an analysis perspective, because different factors tend to drive these two expenses. Selling expenses include sales commissions and advertising and promotion materials, and usually vary with the level of sales. Administrative expenses include top management's salaries and the cost of operating staff departments such as information systems, legal services, and research and development, costs that tend not to vary with the level of sales.

Coke's selling and administrative expense to sales percentage dropped slightly between Year 5 and Year 6 and then rose significantly between Year 6 and Year 7. The management discussion of operations in Appendix B discloses the amounts for selling expenses separately from administrative expenses. These disclosures indicate that selling expenses as a percentage of sales increased from 30.0 percent (= $5,399/$18,018) in Year 6 to 31.8 percent (= $5,891/$18,546) in Year 7. Management indicates simply that higher marketing expenditures to support higher volumes of sales are the explanation for the increased selling expense percentage.

Note 1 to Coke's financial statements discloses advertising expenses for each year. Advertising expenses as a percentage of sales were 7.2 percent (= $1,292/$18,018) in Year 6 and 7.7 percent (= $1,437/$18,546) in Year 7. Thus, 0.5 of the 1.8 percentage point increase in the selling expense to sales percentage was due to increased advertising.

A portion of the remainder of the increased selling expense percentage relates to the sale of some of its bottlers (see discussion under the cost of goods sold percentage). Coke conducts promotion activities on behalf of its bottlers. These promotion costs continue, even when Coke no longer owns a majority of the common stock of a bottler. Thus, selling expenses include these promotion costs, but sales revenue does not include the sales of these bottlers. The selling expense to sales percentage will therefore rise. Thus, Coke's strategy of selling investments in bottling operations has the effect of decreasing the cost of goods sold percentage, but increasing the selling expense percentage.

The administrative expense to sales percentage steadily increased during the three-year period from 8.9 percent (= $1,445/$16,181) in Year 5, to 9.2 percent (= $1,653/$18,018) in Year 6, and to 10.8 percent (= $2,002/$18,546) in Year 7. Thus, most of the change occurred during Year 7. Management's discussion of the results of operations in Appendix B indicates that the Year 7 amount includes "certain nonrecurring provisions," as follows (in millions):

Streamlining of Operations, principally in Europe and Latin America	$130.0
Impairment Charges in The Minute Maid Company Operations	146.0
Impairment Charges Related to Information Systems	80.0
Contribution to Coca-Cola Foundation	28.5
Total	$384.5

These charges total 2.1 percent of sales and more than account for the change in the administrative expense to sales percentage for Year 7. Chapter 4 indicates that the analyst must assess whether such charges are indeed nonrecurring. Management's discussion of operations for Year 6 indicates that it took an $86 million charge in that year to "increase efficiencies in the Company's operations in North American and Europe." The Year 5 annual report discloses a $63 million provision related to "increasing efficiencies in European, domestic and corporate operations." Thus, the charge during Year 7 to "streamline operations" appears to be a recurring charge.

The impairment charge related to the Minute Maid orange juice operation results from a decision to close certain manufacturing facilities. Coke entered into alliances and joint ventures with other companies during Year 7, and intends to have these companies conduct a portion of the manufacturing operations in the future. Coke's provision results from specific decisions made during Year 7 to outsource production. Thus, one might view the charge as nonrecurring. At the same time, it is unclear how much of the charges in recent years to "increase efficiencies" and "streamline operations" relate to similar plant closings.

Coke describes the impairment charge related to information systems as "a strategic initiative, Project Infinity, to redesign and enhance information systems and communications capabilities." Given rapid changes in technology, one suspects that Coke will continue to invest in information and communications systems. It is also likely that Coke will make ongoing contributions to its charitable foundation.

The principal message of this discussion of administrative expenses is that we should not automatically take management's word for it that certain expenses (or revenues) are nonrecurring. The analyst must consider the nature of the expenses, whether similar charges occurred in prior years, and whether such charges will likely occur in the future. Chapter 4 discusses such quality of earnings issues more fully.

Income Taxes.   Income taxes as a percentage of sales increased between Year 5 and Year 6 and decreased significantly between Year 6 and Year 7. These changes in the income tax percentage do not necessarily mean that Coke's income tax burden is changing. Income taxes are imposed on income (that is, revenues minus expenses), not on sales. A more appropriate measure of the income tax burden, referred to as the *effective tax rate*, relates income tax expense to net income before income taxes. By this measure, Coke had a slightly lower effective tax rate in Year 6 but a much lower effective tax rate in Year 7, as Exhibit 3.4 shows.

As Chapter 6 discusses, firms must disclose in notes to the financial statements the reasons why their effective tax rates differ from the statutory tax rate. Note 13 to Coke's financial statements in Appendix A indicates that a tax settlement during Year 7 reduced its effective tax rate seven percentage points below the statutory tax rate. The note indicates that the settlement relates to U.S. taxes on Coke's operations in Puerto Rico for years prior to Year 7.

No such reconciling adjustments appear for Year 5 or Year 6. Thus, the adjustment seems nonrecurring. Furthermore, the settlement relates to income taxes recognized in computing net income for prior years. The reduction in income tax expense during Year 7 represents an offsetting adjustment for income tax expense of earlier years.

EXHIBIT 3.4			
Calculation of Effective Tax Rate on Operating Income **(Amounts Taken from Exhibit 3.3)**			
	Year 5	**Year 6**	**Year 7**
Numerator			
(1) Income Taxes	7.7%	8.0%	6.5%
Denominator			
(2) Profit Margin	16.6%	17.6%	19.8%
(3) Income Taxes	7.7	8.0	6.5
(4) Profit Margin Before Income Taxes	24.3%	25.6%	26.3%
(5) Effective Tax Rate on Operations (1) ÷ (4) ..	31.7%	31.3%	24.7%

The analyst should probably eliminate the effects of the tax settlement when assessing operating performance for Year 7. The adjustment involves increasing income tax expense and decreasing net income for Year 7 by the $320 million settlement amount. The analyst should preferably adjust income tax expense and net income of previous years for the same $320 million amount. Unfortunately, Coke does not indicate the specific years and the specific amounts to which the $320 million settlement applies. Adjusting for the settlement results in an effective tax rate for Year 7 of approximately 31 percent, the same as in Year 5 and Year 6.

Summary of Profit Margin Analysis. We noted at the beginning of this section that Coke's profit margin increased steadily between Year 5 and Year 7. Most of the increased profit margin between Year 5 and Year 6 relates to increases in other revenues. Two items explain a large portion of the increased profit margin between Year 6 and Year 7: (1) the gain on issuance of stock by equity investees of $431 million pretax and $246 after taxes (see note 3 to Coke's financial statements), and (2) a $320 million tax settlement. Excluding these two items results in a profit margin for Year 7 of 16.8 percent [= ($3,492 + 0.65($286) − $246 − $320)/$18,546]. Thus, excluding these two items, Coke's profit margin declined between Year 6 and Year 7.

ANALYZING ASSETS TURNOVER

We can gain greater insight into changes in the total assets turnover by examining turnover ratios for particular assets. Analysts frequently calculate three turnover ratios: accounts receivable turnover, inventory turnover, and fixed asset turnover. The management discussion and analysis of operations usually does not include explanations for changes in asset turnovers, so the analyst will need to search for possible clues.

Accounts Receivable Turnover. The rate at which accounts receivable turn over gives an indication of how soon sales will be converted into cash. The analyst calculates the accounts receivable turnover by dividing net sales on account by average accounts receivable.

Most sales transactions between businesses are on account instead of for cash. Except in the case of retailers who deal directly with consumers, the assumption that business sales are on account is usually reasonable. The calculation of the accounts receivable turnover for Year 7 for Coke, assuming that it makes all sales on account, is as follows:

$$\frac{\text{Accounts Receivable}}{\text{Turnover}} = \frac{\text{Net Sales on Account}}{\text{Average Accounts Receivable}}$$

$$11.1 = \frac{\$18,546}{.5(\$1,695 + \$1,641)}$$

Coke's accounts receivable turnover was 11.7 in Year 5 and 11.2 in Year 6. Thus, Coke's accounts receivable turnover decreased steadily during the three years.

The analyst often expresses the accounts receivable turnover in terms of the average number of days that receivables are outstanding before their conversion into cash. The calculation divides 365 days by the accounts receivable turnover. The average number of days that accounts receivable were outstanding for Coke is 31.2 days (= 365/11.7) for Year 5, 32.6 days (= 365/11.2) for Year 6, and 32.9 days (= 365/11.1) for Year 7. Thus, even though the accounts receivable turnover declined, the turnover rate is high enough that it does not drastically change the number of days receivables were outstanding.

Interpretation of the average collection period depends on the terms of sale. If customers must pay within 30 days, then it appears that most of Coke's customers pay within the required period. If the terms of sales are, say, 15 days, then Coke does not collect on average within the required period. Most firms specify terms of 30 days. Thus, it appears that Coke does not have a major problem collecting its accounts receivable.

Interpretation of changes in the accounts receivable turnover and average collection period also relates to a firm's credit extension polices. Firms will often use credit terms as a means of stimulating sales. A garden equipment shop might permit customers to delay making payments on purchases of lawn mowers until the end of the summer; a snow machine dealer might extend payment for a snowmobile until the end of the winter—both in an effort to stimulate sales. Such policies would produce a decrease in the accounts receivable turnover and an increase in the days receivables are outstanding. The changes in these accounts receivable ratios should not necessarily signal negative news if the increase in profit margin on the additional sales exceeds the cost of carrying accounts receivable for the extra time.

Retailing firms, particularly department store chains such as Sears and JCPenney, offer their own credit cards to customers. They use credit cards both to stimulate sales and to earn interest revenue from delayed payments by customers. Interpreting an increase in the number of days accounts receivable are outstanding in this case involves two conflicting signals. The lengthening of payment period might suggest greater risk of uncollectibility, but it also would provide additional interest revenues. Some firms price their products to obtain a relatively low gross margin from the sale and depend on interest revenues as their principal source of earnings. Thus, the analyst must consider a firm's credit strategy and policies when interpreting the accounts receivable turnover and days receivable outstanding ratios.

Inventory Turnover.   The rate at which inventories turn over gives an indication of how soon they will be sold. The analyst calculates the inventory turnover by dividing cost of goods sold by the average inventory during the period. The calculation of inventory turnover for Coke for Year 7 is as follows:

$$\frac{\text{Inventory}}{\text{Turnover}} = \frac{\text{Cost of Goods Sold}}{\text{Average Inventories}}$$

$$6.5 = \frac{\$6,738}{.5(\$1,117 + \$952)}$$

Thus, Coke's inventory was on hand for 56.2 days (=365/6.5) on average during Year 7. Coke's inventory turnover was 5.9 (61.9 days) in Year 5 and 6.4 (57.0 days) in Year 6.

The increasing inventory turnover over the three years might be a result of more effective inventory control systems. The trend these days is toward just-in-time inventory systems. Firms plan to make products with a minimum amount of raw materials and finished goods inventories on hand. Raw materials arrive just in time to be input into production, and finished goods are transferred immediately to customers. The movement toward just-in-time systems will increase the inventory turnover ratio. Coke's average days inventory of approximately two months, however, does not suggest that it uses just-in-time systems.

The increasing inventory turnover for Coke might also reflect a decrease in the number of consolidated bottlers, who carry beverages in inventory until needed by retailers. The two-month holding period, however, seems too long a period for bottled beverages.

The interpretation of the inventory turnover figure involves two opposing considerations. A firm would like to sell as many goods as possible with a minimum of capital tied up in inventories. An increase in the rate of inventory turnover between periods would seem to indicate more profitable use of an investment in inventory. On the other hand, a firm does not want to have so little inventory on hand that shortages result, and the firm must turn away customers. An increase in the rate of inventory turnover in this case may mean a loss of customers and thereby offset any advantage gained by a decreased investment in inventory. Firms must make trade-offs in deciding the optimum level of inventory and thus the desirable rate of inventory turnover.

The analyst often gains insights into changes in the inventory turnover by examining how it changes with changes in the cost of goods sold to sales percentage. There can be a variety of scenarios and possible interpretations:

1. **Increasing cost of goods sold to sales percentage, coupled with an increasing inventory turnover.** Firm lowers prices to sell inventory more quickly. Firm shifts its product mix toward lower-margin, faster-moving products. Firm outsources the production of a higher proportion of its products, requiring the firm to share profit margin with the outsourcer but at the same time reducing the amount of raw materials and work in process inventories.
2. **Decreasing cost of goods sold to sales percentage coupled with a decreasing inventory turnover.** Firm raises prices to increase its gross margin,

but inventory sells more slowly. Firm shifts its product mix toward higher-margin, slower-moving products. Firm produces a higher proportion of its products instead of outsourcing, thereby capturing more of the gross margin but at the same time requiring the firm to carry raw materials and work in process inventories.

3. **Increasing cost of goods sold to sales percentage coupled with a decreasing inventory turnover.** Weak economic conditions lead to reduced demand for a firm's products, necessitating price reductions to move goods. Despite price reductions, inventory builds up.

4. **Decreasing cost of goods sold to sales percentage, coupled with an increasing inventory turnover.** Strong economic conditions lead to increased demand for a firm's products, allowing price increases. The inability to replace inventory as fast as the firm sells it leads to an increased inventory turnover.

Some analysts calculate the inventory turnover ratio by dividing sales, rather than cost of goods sold, by the average inventory. As long as there is a reasonably constant relation between selling prices and cost of goods sold, the analyst can identify changes in the trend of the inventory turnover using either measure. It is inappropriate to use sales in the numerator if the analyst wants to use the inventory turnover ratio to calculate the average number of days inventory is on hand until sale.

Fixed Asset Turnover.   The fixed asset turnover ratio measures the relation between sales and the investment in property, plant, and equipment. The analyst calculates the fixed asset turnover by dividing sales by average fixed assets (net) during the year. The fixed asset turnover ratio for Coke for Year 7 is as follows:

$$\frac{\text{Fixed Asset}}{\text{Turnover}} = \frac{\text{Sales}}{\text{Average Fixed Assets}}$$

$$4.7 = \frac{\$18,546}{.5(\$4,336 + \$3,550)}$$

The fixed asset turnover for Coke was 4.1 in Year 5 and 4.3 in Year 6. Thus, Coke's fixed asset turnover steadily increased during the three-year period. As in the case of the inventory turnover, an increase in the fixed asset turnover is consistent with a decrease in the number of consolidated bottlers. A bottling and distributing operation is more capital-intensive than the making of concentrate.

The analyst must interpret changes in the fixed asset turnover ratio carefully. Firms make investments in fixed assets in anticipation of higher sales in future periods. Thus a low or decreasing rate of fixed asset turnover may be an indication of an expanding firm that is preparing for future growth. On the other hand, a firm may cut back its capital expenditures if the near-term outlook for its products is poor. Such an action could lead to an increase in the fixed asset turnover ratio.

Many firms in recent years have increased the proportion of production outsourced to other manufacturers. This lets firms achieve the same (or increasing) sales levels with fewer fixed assets, thereby increasing the fixed asset turnover.

Coke's reduction in the number of consolidated bottlers results from increased outsourcing. Our discussion of administrative expenses earlier indicated that Coke entered into strategic alliances and joint ventures during Year 7 that will shift production of orange juice to these other entities. Coke therefore plans to curtail some of its manufacturing capacity. Thus, one would expect a continuing increase in Coke's fixed asset turnover.

Summary of Assets Turnover Analysis.   To summarize, Coke's stable total assets turnover (see Exhibit 3.2) results from the offsetting effects of a slower accounts receivable turnover and higher inventory and fixed asset turnovers. Changes in cash, marketable securities, and intercorporate investments also impact the total assets turnover. These accounts increase the denominator of the total assets turnover but do not affect the numerator. If the numerator included not only sales revenue but also interest revenue and equity in earnings, then the buildup of these financial assets would not have such a dampening effect on the assets turnover ratio.

Even with this modification, increasing proportions of financial assets tend to decrease the total assets turnover. These financial assets generate returns of approximately 6 percent to 12 percent each year. Thus, their turnover ratios (that is, interest and equity method revenues divided by average cash, marketable securities, and investments) are approximately 0.06 to 0.12 per year, considerably lower than the typical total asset turnover above 1.0 (Coke's is 1.2).

Many firms, particularly in high technology industries, have experienced a buildup of cash and marketable securities on their balance sheets in recent years. The buildups occur either because of extremely profitable operations or the issuance of common stock to finance growth. Earnings on cash and marketable securities are typically less than the profit margins on products sold, so the overall profit margin declines. Assets turnover also declines with the higher proportion of financial assets. Thus, overall ROAs tend to decline.[5]

Summary of ROA Analysis.   Our analysis of operating profitability thus far involves three levels of depth:

Level 1: ROA for the firm as a whole.

Level 2: Disaggregation of ROA into profit margin and assets turnover for the firm as a whole.

Level 3a: Disaggregation of profit margin into expense ratios for various cost items.

Level 3b: Disaggregation of assets turnover into turnovers for individual assets.

Exhibit 3.5 summarizes this analysis in a format that we use throughout the book.

---

[5]Such firms often use the excess cash to repurchase their common stock. Not only does using the cash reduce the dampening effects of financial assets on ROAs, profit margins, and asset turnovers, but it tends to increase the market price of the firm's stock (making both shareholders and management happier) and provide for greater benefits from financial leverage (discussed later in this chapter).

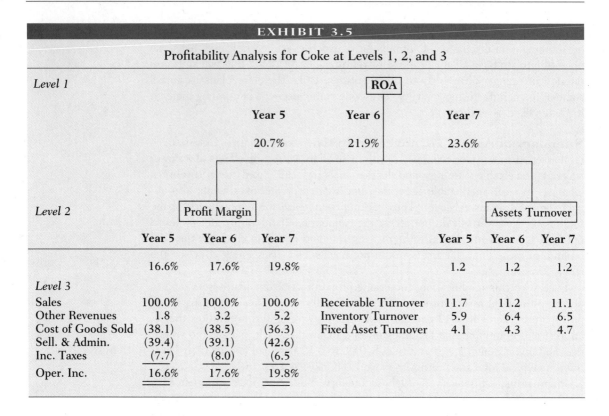

EXHIBIT 3.5

Profitability Analysis for Coke at Levels 1, 2, and 3

Level 1

ROA

	Year 5	Year 6	Year 7
	20.7%	21.9%	23.6%

Level 2

Profit Margin — **Assets Turnover**

	Year 5	Year 6	Year 7		Year 5	Year 6	Year 7
	16.6%	17.6%	19.8%		1.2	1.2	1.2
Level 3							
Sales	100.0%	100.0%	100.0%	Receivable Turnover	11.7	11.2	11.1
Other Revenues	1.8	3.2	5.2	Inventory Turnover	5.9	6.4	6.5
Cost of Goods Sold	(38.1)	(38.5)	(36.3)	Fixed Asset Turnover	4.1	4.3	4.7
Sell. & Admin.	(39.4)	(39.1)	(42.6)				
Inc. Taxes	(7.7)	(8.0)	(6.5				
Oper. Inc.	16.6%	17.6%	19.8%				

ANALYSIS OF SEGMENT DATA

Most firms in the United States provide profitability data for product and geographic segments. Note 16 to Coke's financial statements presents segment data for each of its geographic segments. Coke indicates that it operates in a single product segment—beverages—and therefore it does not provide segment data for soft drinks, juices, sports drinks, or other products.

Firms report segment sales, operating income, assets, capital expenditures, and depreciation and amortization for each segment of their businesses. The segment disclosures permit the analyst to examine ROA, profit margin, and assets turnover at an additional level (Level 4) of depth.

Unfortunately, firms do not report cost of goods sold and selling and administrative expenses for each segment, so we cannot reconcile changes in segment profit margins with changes in the overall levels of these two expense percentages. Chapter 7 discusses the accounting issues in preparing segment profitability data.

Exhibit 3.6 presents ROAs, profit margins, and assets turnovers for each of Coke's geographic segments. Firms report segment income amounts on a pre-tax basis, so the segment ROAs and profit margins in Exhibit 3.6 exceed those presented in Exhibit 3.5.

The geographic sales mix for Coke changed very little during the three-year period. Coke derived approximately one-third of its sales from North America, one-

---

EXHIBIT 3.6

Geographical Segment Profitability Analysis for Coke

ROA

	Year 5	Year 6	Year 7
North America	29.7%	24.6%	24.9%
Africa	48.9%	58.9%	36.2%
Europe	28.5%	29.2%	44.1%
Latin America	61.0%	61.7%	58.0%
Middle & Far East	85.6%	96.5%	92.8%

	Profit Margin			Assets Turnover		
	Year 5	Year 6	Year 7	Year 5	Year 6	Year 7
North America	17.2%	15.5%	15.7%	1.7	1.6	1.6
Africa	33.3%	34.5%	24.8%	1.5	1.7	1.5
Europe	22.4%	20.9%	21.5%	1.3	1.4	2.1
Latin America	36.8%	41.6%	40.9%	1.7	1.5	1.4
Middle & Far East	34.5%	35.4%	33.7%	2.5	2.7	2.8

third from Europe, 21 percent from the Middle and Far East, 10 percent from Latin America, and 3 percent from Africa.

Exhibit 3.6 indicates considerable variability across time and across geographic segments in ROA, profit margins, and assets turnovers. We observe the following:

1. Profitability in North America declined between Year 5 and Year 6 and remained stable in Year 7, probably reflecting the maturity of this market. The level of the profit margin in North America compared to the other geographic segments further indicates the maturity of this market and competition from Pepsi.

2. The ROA in Europe increased substantially between Year 6 and Year 7, largely the result of an increased assets turnover. Recall that Coke sold a portion of its investments in bottlers in Germany, France, and Belgium during Year 7. This action reduced segment assets for Europe. At the same time, it increased the profit margin because Coke's margin on concentrate sales exceeds that on bottling operations.

3. Profitability in the Middle and Far East segment generally increased during the three-year period, driven largely by increasing assets turnover. This segment encompasses many rapidly growing economies. The high profit margins in this segment (and in Latin America) suggest almost monopoly power. The high assets turnovers suggest either heavy use of independent bottlers or monopoly pricing.

Thus, the segment data reinforce the earlier conclusion that converting consolidated bottlers into equity method investments explains part of Coke's improved profitability. The segment data provide new insights into profitability of the Middle East, Far East, and Latin America segments, geographic areas that are today experiencing the fastest growth in the world.

RATE OF RETURN ON COMMON SHAREHOLDERS' EQUITY

The rate of return on common shareholders' equity (ROCE) measures the return to common shareholders after subtracting from revenues not only operating expenses (such as cost of goods sold, selling and administrative expenses, income taxes) but also the costs of financing debt and equity securities that are senior to the common stock. The latter costs include interest expense on debt and dividends on preferred stock (if any). Thus, ROCE expresses the results of a firm's operating, investing, and financing decisions altogether.

The analyst calculates ROCE as follows:

$$\text{ROCE} = \frac{\text{Net Income} - \text{Preferred Stock Dividends}}{\text{Average Common Shareholders' Equity}}$$

The numerator of the fraction measures the amount of income for the period allocable to the common shareholders after all amounts allocable to senior claimants are subtracted. The accountant subtracts interest expense on debt in measuring net income, so calculation of the numerator of ROCE requires no adjustment for creditors' claims on earnings. The analyst must subtract dividends paid or payable on preferred stock from net income to obtain income attributable to the common shareholders.

The denominator of ROCE measures the average amount of common shareholders' equity in use during the period. An average of the total amount of common shareholders' equity at the beginning and the end of the year is appropriate unless a firm made a significant new common stock issue or buyback during the year. If the latter occurred, the analyst should use instead an average of the common shareholders' equity as of the end of each quarter.

Common shareholders' equity equals total shareholders' equity minus the par value of preferred stock. Firms seldom issue preferred stock significantly above par value, so the analyst can assume that any amount in the Additional Paid-in Capital account relates to common stock. Because net income to common shareholders in the numerator reflects a subtraction for the minority interest in earnings of consolidated subsidiaries, the denominator should also exclude a firm's minority interest in net assets (if any).

The calculation of the ROCE of Coke for Year 7 is as follows:

$$\text{ROCE} = \frac{\text{Net Income} - \text{Preferred Stock Dividends}}{\text{Average Common Shareholders' Equity}}$$

$$60.5\% = \frac{\$3,492 - \$0}{.5(\$5,392 + \$6,156)}$$

Coke's ROCEs were 52.0 percent in Year 5 and 56.2 percent in Year 6, reflecting an increase over the three-year period.

Relating ROA to ROCE.   Return on assets measures operating performance independent of financing, while return on common equity explicitly considers the amount and the cost of debt and preferred stock financing. The relation between ROA and ROCE is as follows:[6]

Return on Assets		**Return on Creditors**	**Return to Preferred Shareholders**	**Return on Common Shareholders**
$\dfrac{\text{Net Income} + \text{Interest Expense Net of Taxes}}{\text{Average Total Assets}}$	$\rightarrow$ $\rightarrow$	$\dfrac{\text{Interest Expense Net of Taxes}}{\text{Average Total Liabilities}}$	$\dfrac{\text{Preferred Dividends}}{\text{Average Preferred Shareholders' Equity}}$	$\dfrac{\text{Net Income to Common}}{\text{Average Common Shareholders' Equity}}$

The analyst allocates each dollar of return generated from using assets to the various providers of capital. Creditors receive their return in the form of interest. The cost of this capital is interest expense net of the income tax benefit derived from deducting interest in calculating taxable income. Many liabilities, such as accounts payable and salaries payable, entail no explicit cost.

Preferred stock carries a cost equal to the preferred dividend rate. Firms historically could not deduct preferred dividends in calculating taxable income. More recently, they have been successful in structuring preferred stock issues so that preferred stock dividends paid qualify as tax deductible outlays. In this case, the cost of preferred dividends may be after taxes.

The income from operations (that is, the numerator of ROA) that is not allocated to creditors or preferred shareholders belongs to the common shareholders as the residual claimants. Likewise, the portion of a firm's assets not financed with capital that has been provided by creditors or preferred shareholders represents the capital provided by the common shareholders.[7]

Consider now the relation between ROA and ROCE. Under what circumstances will ROCE exceed ROA? Under what circumstances will ROCE be less than ROA?

ROCE will exceed ROA whenever ROA exceeds the cost of capital provided by creditors and preferred shareholders. If a firm can generate more earnings on capital provided by creditors and preferred shareholders than that capital costs, the excess return belongs to the common shareholders.

To illustrate, recall that Coke generated an ROA of 23.6 percent during Year 7. The after-tax cost of capital provided by creditors during Year 7 was 1.9 percent

---

[6]Note that the relation does not appear as an equation. We use an arrow instead of an equal sign to indicate that the return on assets gets allocated to the various suppliers of capital. To express the relation as an equality requires that we weight each rate by the proportion of each type of capital in the capital structure.

[7]If a firm does not own 100 percent of the common stock of a consolidated subsidiary, the accountant must allocate a portion of the ROA to the minority shareholders. Thus, a fourth term appears on the right-hand side of the arrow: minority interest in earnings/average minority interest in net assets.

[= (1 − .35)($286)/.5($9,649 + $10,005)].[8] The difference between the 1.9 percent cost of creditor capital and the 23.6 percent ROA generated from using this capital belongs to the common shareholders. The common shareholders also have a full claim on the 23.6 percent ROA generated on the capital that they provided. Thus, Coke's ROCE for Year 7 comprises the following (calculations use rates taken to more decimal points than the three decimal points shown):

Excess Return on Capital Provided by Creditors:	
[.236 − .019][.5($9,649 + $10,005)]	$2,130.8
Return on Capital Provided by Common Shareholders:	
[.236][.5($5,392 + $6,156)]	1,361.2
Total Return to Common Shareholders	$3,492.0
ROCE: $3,492.0/.5($5,392 + $6,156)	60.5%

The practice of using lower-cost creditor and preferred stock capital to increase the return to common shareholders is commonly referred to as *financial leverage*. Financial leverage worked to the advantage of Coke's shareholders in Year 5, Year 6, and Year 7.

Disaggregating ROCE. We can disaggregate ROCE into several components to aid in interpretation of it, much as we did earlier with ROA. The components of ROCE are ROA, common earnings leverage, and capital structure leverage.

ROCE	=	ROA	Common Earnings Leverage	Capital Structure Leverage
$\dfrac{\text{Net Income to Common}}{\text{Average Common Shareholders' Equity}}$	=	$\dfrac{\text{Net Income + Interest Expense (net of taxes)}}{\text{Average Total Assets}}$ ×	$\dfrac{\text{Net Income to Common}}{\text{Net Income + Interest Expense (net of taxes)}}$ ×	$\dfrac{\text{Average Total Assets}}{\text{Average Common Shareholders' Equity}}$

ROA, as you know, indicates the return from operations independent of financing.

The common earnings leverage (CEL) ratio indicates the proportion of operating income (that is, net income before financing costs and related tax effects) that is allocable to the common shareholders. The difference between the numerator and the denominator of CEL is interest cost on debt and dividends on preferred

---

[8]The amounts in the denominator for Coke equal total assets minus total shareholders' equity, or total liabilities. The after-tax cost of creditor capital seems low, but recall that many liabilities do not carry an explicit interest cost.

EXHIBIT 3.7

Disaggregation of ROCE of Coke for Year 5 to Year 7

	ROCE	=	ROA	×	Common Earnings Leverage	×	Capital Structure Leverage
Year 5	52.0%	=	20.7%	×	.95	×	2.6
Year 6	56.2%	=	21.9%	×	.94	×	2.7
Year 7	60.5%	=	23.6%	×	.95	×	2.7

stock. The higher the cost of these sources of capital, the less income will remain for the common shareholders, and the smaller the CEL ratio will be.

The capital structure leverage (CSL) ratio measures the degree to which a firm uses common shareholders' funds to finance assets. The difference between the numerator and the denominator of CSL is the amount of the liabilities and pre-ferred shareholders' equity in the capital structure. The more capital obtained from these senior sources, the less capital obtained from common shareholders, and thus the higher the CSL ratio.

CEL and CSL demonstrate that there is a multiplier effect on ROA of using debt and preferred stock financing to increase the return to the common share-holders. CEL focuses on the cost of this capital, and CSL focuses on the propor-tion of such capital in the capital structure. Chapter 8 discusses these two components of financial leverage more fully.

The disaggregation of ROCE for Coke for Year 7 appears as follows:

$$
\begin{array}{ccccccc}
\textbf{ROCE} & = & \textbf{ROA} & \times & \begin{array}{c}\textbf{Common}\\\textbf{Earnings}\\\textbf{Leverage}\end{array} & \times & \begin{array}{c}\textbf{Capital}\\\textbf{Structure}\\\textbf{Leverage}\end{array}
\end{array}
$$

$$
\frac{\$3{,}492 - \$0}{.5(\$5{,}392 + \$6{,}156)} = \frac{\$3{,}492 + (1-.35)(\$286)}{.5(\$15{,}041 + \$16{,}161)} \times \frac{\$3{,}492 - \$0}{\$3{,}492 + (1-.35)(\$286)} \times \frac{.5(\$15{,}041 + \$16{,}161)}{.5(\$5{,}392 + \$6{,}156)}
$$

$$
60.5\% = 23.6\% \times .95 \times 2.7
$$

Exhibit 3.7 presents the disaggregation of Coke's ROCE for Year 5 through Year 7. The increasing ROCE results from an increasing ROA and a slightly increased CSL. The latter results primarily from repurchases of common stock. The CEL ratio remains approximately the same.

RISK ANALYSIS

The sources and types of risk that a firm faces are numerous and often interre-lated. They include:

Source	Type or Nature
International	Host government regulations and attitudes
	Political unrest
	Exchange rate changes
Domestic	Recession
	Inflation or deflation
	Interest rate changes
	Demographic changes
	Political changes
Industry	Technology
	Competition
	Regulation
	Availability of raw materials
	Unionization
Firm-Specific	Management competence
	Strategic direction
	Lawsuits

Although a firm must constantly monitor all these sources of risk, we will concentrate on the financial consequences of the elements of risk using data from the financial statements. Each type of risk ultimately affects net income and cash flows. Bankruptcy will be the result if a firm is unable either to generate sufficient cash internally or to obtain needed cash from external sources to sustain operating, investing, and financing activities. The statement of cash flows, which reports the net amount of cash generated or used by operating, investing, and financing activities, is an important source of information for studying risk, as we discussed in Chapter 2.

Exhibit 3.8 relates the factors affecting a firm's ability to generate cash to its need to use cash. Most risk analysis focuses on a comparison of the supply of cash and the demand for cash. Risk analysis using financial statement data typically ex-

EXHIBIT 3.8

Structure for Financial Statement Analysis of Risk

Activity	Ability to Generate Cash	Need to Use Cash	Financial Statement Analysis Performed
Operations	Profitability of goods and services sold	Working capital requirements	Short-term liquidity risk
Investing	Sales of existing plant assets or investments	Plant capacity requirements	Long-term liquidity (solvency) risk
Financing	Borrowing capacity	Debt service requirements	

amines (1) an entity's near-term ability to generate cash to service working capital needs and debt service requirements, and (2) its longer-term ability to generate cash internally or from external sources to satisfy plant capacity and debt repayment needs. We therefore structure our discussion of the analytical tools for assessing risk around short-term *liquidity* risk and long-term *solvency* risk.

SHORT-TERM LIQUIDITY RISK

The analysis of short-term liquidity risk requires an understanding of the operating cycle of a firm, which we introduced in Chapter 2. Consider a typical manufacturing firm. It acquires raw materials on account, promising to pay suppliers within 30 to 60 days. The firm then combines the raw materials, labor services, and other factor inputs to produce a product. It pays for some of these costs at the time it receives the product or service, and it delays payment of other costs. At some point, the firm sells the product to a customer, probably on account. It then collects the customer's account and pays suppliers and others for purchases it made on account.

If a firm (1) delays all cash outflows to suppliers, employees, and others until it receives cash from customers, and (2) receives more cash than it must disburse, it is not likely that the firm will face short-term liquidity problems. Most firms, however, cannot time their cash inflows and outflows this precisely. Employees may be paid weekly or semimonthly, while customers may delay payments for 30 days or more. Firms may experience rapid growth and need to produce more units of product during a period than they sell. Even if perfectly timed, cash outflows to support the higher level of production can exceed cash inflows from customers at the current level of sales. Firms that operate at a net loss for a period often find that by the end of the operating cycle they have experienced a net cash outflow instead of a net cash inflow.

Short-term liquidity problems may also be the result of longer-term solvency difficulties. For example, a firm may assume a relatively high percentage of debt in its capital structure, as many firms did in the leveraged buyout movement in the late 1980s. Debt usually requires periodic interest payments and may require repayments of principal as well. For some firms, interest expense is their largest single cost. An operating cycle must not only generate sufficient cash to supply operating working capital needs but also provide cash to service debt.

Financially healthy firms frequently close any cash flow gap in their operating cycles with short-term borrowing. They may issue commercial paper on the market or obtain three- to six-month bank loans. Most such firms maintain a line of credit with their banks so they can obtain cash quickly for working capital needs. The notes to the financial statements usually disclose the amount of the line of credit and the level of borrowing used on that line during the year.

We discuss here six financial statement ratios for assessing short-term liquidity risk. Three ratios relate the level of resources available to meet short-term commitments to the level of those commitments: (1) the current ratio, (2) the quick ratio, and (3) the operating cash flow to current liabilities ratio. Three ratios relate the amount of working capital required to the level of sales generated: (4) the accounts receivable turnover, (5) the inventory turnover, and (6) the accounts payable turnover.

Current Ratio.   The current ratio equals current assets divided by current liabilities. It indicates the amount of cash available at the balance sheet date plus the amount of current assets that the firm expects to turn into cash within one year of the balance sheet date (from collection of receivables and sale of inventory) relative to obligations coming due during that period. The current ratio for Coke on December 31, Year 7, is:

$$\text{Current Ratio} = \frac{\text{Current Assets}}{\text{Current Liabilities}}$$

$$.80 = \$5,910/\$7,406$$

The current ratio for Coke was 0.84 at the end of Year 5 and 0.74 at the end of Year 6.

Prior to the 1980s, the average current ratios for most industries exceeded 2.0. As interest rates increased in the early 1980s, firms attempted to stretch their accounts payable and permit suppliers to finance a greater portion of their working capital needs (receivables and inventories). As a consequence, current ratios began moving in the direction of 1.0. Current ratios hovering around this level are now not uncommon.

Although this trend suggests a general increase in short-term liquidity risk, this level of risk is not necessarily intolerable. Recall that accountants report inventories—a major component of current assets for many firms—at acquisition cost. The cash that firms expect to generate from inventories is more than the amount used in calculating the current ratio.

Coke's current ratios are less than 1.0. Although this level of current ratio is low from a historical perspective, note that 28 percent (= $1,658/$5,910) of current assets for Coke at the end of Year 7 are in the form of cash and readily marketable securities. Recall also from the discussion earlier in this chapter that Coke realizes gross margins (that is, sales minus cost of goods sold) of just over 60 percent. Thus, inventories have selling prices of 2.5 (= 1.00/0.40) times the amount appearing on the balance sheet. Also, Coke reports in Note 6 that it has a $0.9 billion unused line of credit at the end of Year 7. Thus, a current ratio lower than 1.0 is not a major concern for Coke.

There are several additional problems that can arise with interpretation of the current ratio:

1. An increase of equal amount in both current assets and current liabilities (for example, purchasing inventory on account) results in a decrease in the current ratio when the ratio is higher than 1.0 before the transaction but an increase in the current ratio if it is less than 1.0 before the transaction. Similar difficulties with interpretation arise when current assets and current liabilities decrease by an equal amount. With current ratios for many firms now in the neighborhood of 1.0, this concern with the current ratio gains greater significance.

2. A very high current ratio may accompany unsatisfactory business conditions, while a falling ratio may accompany profitable operations. In a recessionary period, businesses contract, firms pay current liabilities, and, even though current assets reach a low point, the current ratio can increase to very high levels. In a boom period, just the reverse can occur.

3. The current ratio is susceptible to "window dressing"; that is, management can take deliberate steps at the balance sheet date to produce a better current ratio than the normal or average ratio for the period. For instance, toward the end of the period a firm may accelerate normal purchases on account (current ratio is less than 1.0) or delay such purchases (current ratio is greater than 1.0) in an effort to improve the current ratio. Alternatively, a firm may collect loans to officers, classified as noncurrent assets, and use the proceeds to reduce current liabilities.

Given these interpretation problems, the analyst may find widespread use of the current ratio as a measure of short-term liquidity risk surprising. The explanation lies partially in the fact that it is easy to calculate. Furthermore, empirical studies of bond default, bankruptcy, and other conditions of financial distress have found the current ratio to have strong predictive power. Chapter 9 discusses this empirical research more fully.

Quick Ratio. A variation of the current ratio is the quick ratio, or acid test ratio. The analyst computes the quick ratio by including in the numerator only those current assets that the firm could convert quickly into cash. The numerator customarily includes cash, marketable securities, and receivables. Analysts should study the facts in each case before deciding whether to include receivables and to exclude inventories. Some businesses can convert their inventory of merchandise into cash rather quickly (like a retail chain such as Wal-Mart), but it would take more time for other businesses to collect their receivables (such as an automobile manufacturer like Ford that provides financing for its customers' purchases).

Assuming that we include accounts receivable but exclude inventories, Coke's quick ratio at the end of Year 7 is:

$$\text{Quick Ratio} = \frac{\text{Cash} + \text{Marketable Securities} + \text{Receivables}}{\text{Current Liabilities}}$$

$$.45 = \frac{\$1,433 + \$225 + \$1,641}{\$7,406}$$

The quick ratio for Coke was .49 at the end of Year 5 and .41 at the end of Year 6. In general, the trends in the quick ratio and the current ratio are highly correlated. That is, the analyst obtains the same information about improving or deteriorating short-term liquidity by examining either ratio. Note that the current and quick ratios for Coke follow similar trends. With current ratios recently trending toward 1.0, quick ratios have trended toward .5.

Operating Cash Flow to Current Liabilities Ratio.   It is possible to overcome the deficiencies associated with using current assets as an indicator of a firm's ability to generate cash in the near term by using cash flow from operations instead. Cash flow from operations, reported on the statement of cash flows, indicates the excess amount of cash that the firm has derived from operations after funding working capital needs. Because the numerator of this ratio uses amounts over a period of time, the denominator uses an average of current liabilities for the period. This ratio for Coke for Year 7 is:

$$\text{Operating Cash Flow to Current Liabilities Ratio} = \frac{\text{Cash Flow from Operations}}{\text{Average Current Liabilities}}$$

$$.47 = \frac{\$3,463}{.5(\$7,348 + \$7,406)}$$

The ratio was .56 in Year 5 and .49 in Year 6. Thus, the ratio declined during the three-year period. An empirical study using the operating cash flow to current liabilities ratio finds that a ratio of .40 or higher is common for a healthy manufacturing or retailing firm.[9] Coke consistently has an operating cash flow to current liabilities ratio in excess of 40 percent. Thus, even though the current and quick ratios appear somewhat low, Coke does not display much short-term liquidity risk.

Working Capital Activity Ratios.   The analyst uses three measures of the rate of activity in working capital accounts to study the cash-generating ability of operations and the short-term liquidity risk of a firm:

$$\text{Accounts Receivable Turnover} = \frac{\text{Sales}}{\text{Average Accounts Receivable}}$$

$$\text{Inventory Turnover} = \frac{\text{Cost of Goods Sold}}{\text{Average Inventories}}$$

$$\text{Accounts Payable Turnover} = \frac{\text{Purchases}}{\text{Average Accounts Payable}}$$

At the beginning of the chapter we discussed the first two of these ratios, the accounts receivable and inventory turnovers, components of the total assets turnover. We use these ratios here as measures of how fast firms turn accounts receivable into cash and sell inventories.

The accounts payable turnover indicates how quickly a firm pays for purchases on account. Purchases is not an amount that the financial statements typically disclose, but the analyst can approximate purchases as follows:

$$\text{Purchases} = \text{Cost of Goods Sold} + \text{Ending Inventory} - \text{Beginning Inventory}$$

---

[9]Cornelius Casey and Norman Bartzcak, "Cash Flow—It's Not the Bottom Line," *Harvard Business Review* (July–August 1984), pp. 61–66.

EXHIBIT 3.9		
Working Capital Activity Ratios for Coke for Year 7		

Accounts Receivable Turnover		Days Receivables Outstanding
$\dfrac{\$18,546}{.5(\$1,695 + \$1,641)}$	$= 11.1$ times per year	$\dfrac{365}{11.1} = 33$ days

Inventory Turnover		Days Inventory Held
$\dfrac{\$6,738}{.5(\$1,117 + \$952)}$	$= 6.5$ times per year	$\dfrac{365}{6.5} = 56$ days

Accounts Payable Turnover		Days Accounts Payable Outstanding
$\dfrac{(\$6,738 + \$952 - \$1,117)}{.5(\$3,103 + \$2,972)}$	$= 2.2$ times per year	$\dfrac{365}{2.2} = 169$ days

The analyst often expresses all three of these ratios in terms of the number of days each balance sheet item (that is, receivables, inventories, accounts payable) is outstanding. This is done by dividing 365 days by the three turnover amounts.

Exhibit 3.9 presents calculation of these three turnover ratios for Coke for Year 7. The accounts payable turnover ratio appears quite small relative to the accounts receivable and inventory turnover ratios. The principal explanation lies in Coke's disclosure practice of combining accounts payable and other accrued expenses.

Note 4 to Coke's financial statement provides additional detail on this account. Using the amounts in Note 4 yields an accounts payable turnover of 3.3 [= ($1,117 + $6,738 − $952)/0.5($2,074 + $2,055)] and days accounts payable of 109 days (= 365/3.3). These amounts still overstate the days accounts payable for Coke because Coke lumps some other accrued expenses with accounts payable.

Summary of Short-Term Liquidity Risk.   The short-term liquidity risk ratios suggest that Coke has relatively little short-term liquidity risk. Although the current and quick ratios are on the low side, the operating cash flow to current liabilities ratio exceeds 40 percent in all years. Coke has an established brand name and along with Pepsi dominates the soft drink industry. All the analysis in this chapter of Coke's profitability suggests a healthy picture; it could obtain short-term financing if needed. Coke's established line of credit provides a cushion if short-term liquidity should become a problem.

LONG-TERM SOLVENCY RISK

Analysts use measures of long-term liquidity, or solvency, risk to examine a firm's ability to meet interest and principal payments on long-term debt and to fulfill similar obligations as they come due. If the firm cannot make payments on time, it becomes insolvent and may require reorganization or liquidation.

Perhaps the best indicator for assessing long-term solvency risk is a firm's ability to generate earnings over a period of years. Profitable firms either generate sufficient cash from operations or obtain needed cash from creditors or owners. The measures of profitability we have discussed in this chapter therefore apply for this purpose as well. Four other measures used in examining long-term solvency risk are (1) debt ratios, (2) the interest coverage ratio, (3) the operating cash flow to total liabilities ratio, and (4) the operating cash flow to capital expenditures ratio.

Debt Ratios.   Analysts use debt ratios to measure the amount of liabilities, particularly long-term debt, in a firm's capital structure. The higher this proportion, the greater the long-term solvency risk. Several variations in debt ratios exist. Three commonly encountered measures are:

$$\text{Long-Term Debt Ratio} = \frac{\text{Long-Term Debt}}{\text{Long-Term Debt} + \text{Shareholders' Equity}}$$

$$\text{Debt/Equity Ratio} = \frac{\text{Long-Term Debt}}{\text{Shareholders' Equity}}$$

$$\text{Liabilities/Assets Ratio} = \frac{\text{Total Liabilities}}{\text{Total Assets}}$$

The debt ratios for Coke at the end of Year 7 are as follows:

$$\text{Long-Term Debt Ratio} = \frac{\$1,116}{\$1,116 + \$6,156} = 15.3\%$$

$$\text{Debt/Equity Ratio} = \frac{\$1,116}{\$6,156} = 18.1\%$$

$$\text{Liabilities to Assets Ratio} = \frac{\$16,161 - \$6,156}{\$16,161} = 61.9\%$$

Exhibit 3.10 shows the debt ratios for Coke as of the end of the last three years. The debt ratios using long-term debt decline over the three-year period. Although Coke issued additional long-term debt during the period, its shareholders' equity increased even more because of the retention of earnings in excess of dividends and common stock repurchases. The total liabilities to total assets ratio is relatively stable during the period studied, suggesting that other liabilities (current and non-current) increased more than long-term debt.

Note the high correlation between changes in the two long-term debt ratios over time. This result is not surprising, since the ratios use the same financial statement data. The analyst can generally select one of these ratios and use it consistently over time. Because there are several different debt ratios, the analyst should use caution when reading financial periodicals and discussing debt ratios with others to be sure which specific expression of the debt ratio is being used. A

EXHIBIT 3.10			
Debt Ratios for Coke at the End of Year 5 to Year 7			
	Year 5	**Year 6**	**Year 7**
Long-Term Debt Ratio	21.4%	17.5%	15.3%
Debt/Equity Ratio	27.2%	21.2%	18.1%
Liabilities to Assets	62.3%	64.2%	61.9%

debt/equity ratio higher than 1.0 (that is, more long-term debt than shareholders' equity) is not unusual, but a long-term debt ratio or liabilities to assets ratio higher than 1.0 is highly unusual (requiring a negative shareholders' equity).

In an effort to appear less risky and to reduce their cost of financing, firms often attempt to structure financing so as to keep debt off the balance sheet. Chapter 6 discusses some of the avenues available under generally accepted accounting principles to minimize reported long-term debt. The analyst interpreting debt ratios needs to recognize that a firm may resort to such actions and therefore show less debt that it actually has.

Interest Coverage Ratio.   The interest coverage ratio indicates the number of times that net income before interest expense and income taxes exceeds interest expense. The interest coverage ratio for Coke for Year 7 is:

$$\text{Interest Coverage Ratio}[10] = \frac{\substack{\text{Net Income} + \text{Interest Expense} \\ + \text{ Income Tax Expense} + \text{Minority Interest in Earnings}}}{\text{Interest Expense}}$$

$$17.1 = \frac{\$3,492 + \$286 + \$1,104 + \$0}{\$286}$$

Coke's interest coverage ratio was 19.7 in Year 5 and 16.9 in Year 6. Analysts typically view coverage ratios of less than approximately 2.0 as risky situations. Thus Coke does not exhibit long-term solvency risk by this measure.

If a firm must make other required periodic payments (for example, pensions, leases), the analyst could include these amounts in the calculation as well. If so, the analyst refers to the ratio as the fixed charges coverage ratio.

One criticism of the interest or fixed charges coverage ratios as measures of long-term solvency risk is that they use earnings rather than cash flows in the numerator. Firms pay interest and other fixed charges with cash, not with earnings.

---

[10]Increased precision suggests that the denominator include total interest cost for the year, not just the amount recognized as interest expense. If a firm self-constructs fixed assets, it must capitalize a portion of its interest cost each year and add it to the cost of the self-constructed assets. The analyst should probably apply this refinement of the interest coverage ratio only to electric utilities, which engage in heavy borrowing to construct their capital intensive plants.

When the value of the ratio is relatively low (that is, less than approximately 2.0), the analyst should use cash flow from operations before interest and income taxes in the numerator to calculate coverage ratios.

To illustrate, cash flow from operations for Coke for Year 7 is $3,463 million. Note 6 indicates that cash payments for interest total $315 million. Note 13 indicates that the cash payment for income taxes totals $1,242 million. The calculation of the interest coverage ratio using cash flows is as follows:

$$\frac{\text{Interest Coverage Ratio}}{\text{Based on Cash Flows}} = \frac{\text{Cash Flow from Operations} + \text{Payments for Interest and Income Taxes}}{\text{Cash Payments for Interest}}$$

$$15.9 = \frac{\$3,463 + \$315 + \$1,242}{\$315}$$

Operating Cash Flow to Total Liabilities Ratio.   The debt and interest coverage ratios give no recognition to the ability of a firm to generate cash flow from operations to service debt. The ratio of cash flow from operations to total liabilities overcomes this deficiency. This cash flow ratio is similar to the one used in assessing short-term liquidity, but here the denominator includes all liabilities (current and noncurrent).

Coke's operating cash flow to total liabilities ratio for Year 7 is as follows:

$$\frac{\text{Operating Cash Flow}}{\text{to Total Liabilities Ratio}} = \frac{\text{Cash Flow from Continuing Operations}}{\text{Average Total Liabilities}}$$

$$.35 = \frac{\$3,463}{.5(\$15,041 - \$5,392 + \$16,161 - \$6,156)}$$

The ratio for Coke was .40 in Year 5 and .36 in Year 6. A ratio of .20 or more is common for a financially healthy company.[11] Thus, Coke appears to have low long-term solvency risk by this measure.

Operating Cash Flow to Capital Expenditures Ratio.   A final ratio for assessing long-term solvency risk is the operating cash flow to capital expenditures ratio. This ratio provides information about the ability of a firm to generate cash flow from operations in excess of the capital expenditures needed to maintain and build plant capacity. The firm can use any excess cash flow to service debt. The analyst calculates this ratio as follows:

$$\frac{\text{Operating Cash Flow to}}{\text{Capital Expenditures Ratio}} = \frac{\text{Cash Flow from Continuing Operations}}{\text{Capital Expenditures}}$$

$$3.5 = \frac{\$3,463}{\$990}$$

---

[11]Casey and Bartzcak, *op. cit.*

The corresponding ratios are 3.6 for both Year 5 and Year 6. Thus, Coke generated more than enough cash from operations to finance capital expenditures and to have amounts remaining to service debt. Recall that consumer foods products are in the maturity stage of their product life cycles, and thus the analyst should expect a ratio higher than 1.0.

The operating cash flow to capital expenditures ratio indicates the ability to service debt but does not explicitly consider the future level of debt that a firm must repay. Moreover, managers have discretion in making capital expenditures each year, and a change in expenditure levels will affect this ratio. A firm experiencing poor profitability may cut back its capital expenditures sufficiently to induce an increase in the ratio in such a year. Thus, the analyst should interpret trends in the ratio cautiously.

Summary of Long-Term Solvency Risk Analysis.   The debt, interest coverage, and cash flow ratios indicate that Coke has low long-term solvency risk. Coke is profitable and generates the needed cash flow to service its debt.

INTERPRETING FINANCIAL STATEMENT RATIOS

One way for an analyst to evaluate firm performance is to compare financial ratios of a particular firm to its ratios for earlier periods (time series analysis), as we do in this chapter for Coke. Another way is to compare a firm's financial ratios to those of other firms for the same period (cross-sectional analysis). This section discusses some of the issues involved in making such comparisons.

COMPARISONS WITH CORRESPONDING RATIOS OF EARLIER PERIODS

A time series analysis of a particular firm's financial statement ratios lets us track historical trends of ratios and variability in the ratios over time. The analyst can study the impact of economic conditions (recession, inflation), industry conditions (shift in regulatory status, new technology), and firm-specific conditions (shift in corporate strategy, new management) on the time series pattern of these ratios.

Some of the questions that the analyst should raise before using ratios of past financial statement data as a basis for interpreting ratios for the current period include:

1. Has the firm made a significant change in its product, geographic, or customer mix that would affect the comparability of financial statement ratios over time?
2. Has the firm made a major acquisition or divestiture?
3. Has the firm changed its methods of accounting over time? For example, does the firm now consolidate a previously unconsolidated entity?

One concern with using past performance as a basis for comparison is that a firm's earlier performance may have been unsatisfactory in a variety of ways. Any improvement during the current year might still leave the firm at an undesirable level. An improved profitability ratio may mean little if a firm ranks last in its industry in terms of profitability in all years.

Another concern involves interpreting the rate of change in a ratio over time. The analyst would certainly interpret a 10 percent increase in profit margin differently, depending on whether other firms in the industry experienced a 15 percent or a 5 percent increase.

Comparing a particular firm's ratios with those of similar firms should serve to lessen these concerns, however.

COMPARISONS WITH CORRESPONDING RATIOS OF OTHER FIRMS

The major issue in performing a cross-sectional analysis is to identify the firms to use for comparison. The objective is to select firms with similar products and strategies and similar size and age. Few firms may meet these criteria. Pepsi, for example, is a logical comparison firm for Coke. The drawback here is that Pepsi's financial statements for the period include significant restaurant operations. The economic characteristics of restaurant businesses differ substantially from the characteristics of beverage companies. For example, restaurants carry virtually no accounts receivable, and their inventories turn over more rapidly than beverage company inventories.

An alternative approach uses average industry ratios, such as those published by Dun & Bradstreet and Robert Morris Associates or those we can derive from computerized data bases. Exhibit 3.11 summarizes the information provided in two of

---

EXHIBIT 3.11

Description of Published Industry Ratios

Robert Morris Associates, *Annual Statement Studies*

1. Presents common size balance sheets and income statements and 16 financial statement ratios by four-digit standard industrial classification (SIC) code.
2. Provides data for firms within each four-digit industry code for each of the last five years. Only firms with assets less than $250 million are included in the data.
3. Provides data for the most recent year only by size of firm, using both assets and sales as the size variables.
4. Common size statements represent the average for each industry category (not clear whether this is a simple or a weighted average).
5. The summaries present the median and upper and lower quartiles for each ratio.

Dun and Bradstreet, *Industry Norms and Key Financial Ratios*

1. Presents dollar-based and common-size balance sheets and income statements and 14 financial statement ratios by four-digit SIC code.
2. Presents data for the most recent year only.
3. Gives no breakdown by size of company.
4. Common size statements constructed for the industry using total assets (balance sheet) and sales (income statement) as the base. The common size percentages represent simple averages of the common size percentages of all firms in the industry. The dollar-based financial statements result from multiplying the average common size percentages times the median level of assets and sales for the firms in the industry.
5. The summaries present the median and upper and lower quartiles for each ratio.

these published surveys. These published ratios provide an overview of the performance of an industry.

Analysts should consider a number of issues when they use industry ratios:

1. **Definition of the industry.** Publishers of average industry ratios generally classify diversified firms according to the industry of their major product. Until recently, Pepsi, for example, appeared as a beverage company, even though it has generated over one-third of its sales from restaurants. Similarly, Pepsi had owned three of the largest restaurant chains in the United States (Pizza Hut, Taco Bell, KFC), but the restaurant category in standard industry publications had not included amounts for Pepsi's restaurants. The traditional practice, moreover, is not to include privately held and foreign firms in an industry classification. If foreign or privately held firms are significant in a particular industry, the analyst should recognize the possible impact of their exclusion from the published data.

2. **Calculation of industry average.** Is the published ratio a simple (unweighted) average of the ratios of the included firms, or is it weighted by size of firm? Is the weighting based on sales, assets, market value, or some other factor? Is the median of the distribution used instead of the mean?

3. **Distribution of ratios around the mean.** To interpret divergence of a particular firm's ratio from the industry average requires information on the distribution around the mean. The analyst should interpret a ratio that is 10 percent higher than the industry mean differently, depending on whether the standard deviation is 5 percent or 15 percent higher or lower than the mean. The published sources of industry ratios give either the quartiles or the range of the distribution.

4. **Definition of financial statement ratios.** The analyst should examine the definition of each published ratio to ensure that it is consistent with the definition the analyst is using to make the calculations. For instance, is the rate of return on common shareholders' equity based on average or beginning-of-the-period common shareholders' equity? Does the debt/equity ratio include all liabilities or just long-term debt?

Average industry ratios serve as a useful basis of comparison as long as the analyst recognizes their possible limitations.

SUMMARY

This chapter presents various financial statement ratios that are useful for the assessment of a firm's profitability and risk. While the number of financial ratios we have covered may seem overwhelming right now, using and interpreting them for a time will enhance your understanding. Memorizing them does not help much.

Exhibit 3.12 summarizes all the financial ratios discussed. Profitability analysis can be described according to four levels of depth. At Level 1 we measure prof-

EXHIBIT 3.12

Summary of Profitability and Risk Ratios

Profitability Ratios

Level 1   Rate of Return on Assets ——————→ Rate of Return on   +   Rate of Return on
                                              Liabilities and   Common Stock Equity
                                              Preferred Shareholders

Level 2   Profit Margin   Total Assets   Return on   Common   Capital
           Percentage   Turnover Ratio   Assets   Earnings   Structure
                                                                                     Leverage   Leverage

Level 3   Various   Accounts Receivable
           Expense-to-Sales   Turnover: Inventory
           Percentages   Turnover: Fixed Assets
                              Turnover

Level 4   ROA, Profit Margin and Assets
           Turnover for Product and Geographical
           Segments

Risk Analysis
Short-Term Liquidity Risk   **Ability**   **Needs**

Current Ratio	Current Assets	Current Liabilities
Quick Ratio	Quick Assets	Current Liabilities
Operating Cash Flow to Current Liabilities Ratio	Cash Flow from Operations	Current Liabilities
Working Capital Activity Ratios	Accounts Receivable and Inventory Turnovers	Accounts Payable Turnover

Risk Analysis
Long-Term Solvency Risk

Debt Ratios	—	Debt Service
Interest Coverage Ratio	Income before Interest, Taxes, and Minority Interest	Interest Expense
Operating Cash Flow to Total Liabilities Ratio	Cash Flow from Operations	Total Liabilities
Operating Cash Flow to Capital Expenditures Ratio	Cash Flow from Operations	Capital Expenditures

itability for a firm as a whole: the rate of return on assets and the rate of return on common shareholders' equity. Level 2 disaggregates ROA and ROCE into important components. ROA is broken into profit margin and assets turnover components. ROCE is broken into return on assets and leverage components. Level 3 breaks the profit margin into various expense to sales percentages and the assets turnover into individual asset turnovers. Level 4 uses product and geographic segment data to study ROA, profit margin, and assets turnover more fully.

Risk analysis requires analysts to compare (1) a firm's ability to generate or obtain cash with (2) its need for cash to pay obligations as they come due. This matching must occur with respect to both the amount and the timing of cash flows. All the risk ratios discussed in this chapter (except for the debt ratios) relate ability to needs, as the lower portion of Exhibit 3.12 shows. Because the ability to generate cash and the need for cash can differ depending on the time horizon, the analyst assesses both short-term liquidity risk and long-term solvency risk.

EARNINGS PER COMMON SHARE

Another financial statement ratio common equity investors use to assess profitability is earnings per common share (EPS). As Chapter 12 discusses more fully, analysts and investors frequently use EPS to value firms. EPS is the only financial ratio covered by the opinion of the independent auditor. This appendix briefly describes the calculation of EPS and discusses some of its uses and limitations.[12]

CALCULATING EPS

Firms that do not have (1) outstanding convertible bonds or convertible preferred stock that holders can exchange for shares of common stock or (2) options or warrants that holders can use to acquire common stock have simple capital structures. For such firms, the accountant calculates basic EPS as follows:

$$\text{Basic EPS (Simple Capital Structure)} = \frac{\text{Net Income} - \text{Preferred Stock Dividends}}{\text{Weighted Average Number of Common Shares Outstanding}}$$

The numerator of basic EPS for a simple capital structure is identical to the numerator of the ROCE calculation. The denominator is a daily weighted average of common shares outstanding during the period, reflecting new stock issues, treasury stock acquisitions, and similar transactions.

EXAMPLE 1

Brown Corporation had the capital structure described below during its most recent year.

	January 1	December 31
Preferred Stock, $20 par Value, 500 Shares Issued and Outstanding............	$10,000	$10,000
Common Stock, $10 par Value, 4,000 Shares Issued.............................	40,000	40,000
Additional Paid-in Capital	50,000	50,000
Retained Earnings	80,000	85,600
Treasury Shares—Common (1,000 shares)	—	(30,000)
Total Shareholders' Equity...................	$180,000	$155,600

---

[12]Financial Accounting Standards Board, *Statement of Financial Accounting Standards No. 128,* "Earnings per Share," 1997.

Retained earnings changed during the year as follows:

Retained Earnings, January 1..................	$80,000
Plus Net Income	7,500
Less Dividends:	
Preferred Stock	(500)
Common Stock	(1,400)
Retained Earnings, December 31...............	$85,600

The preferred stock is not convertible into common stock. The firm acquired the treasury stock on July 1. There are no stock options or warrants outstanding. Basic earnings per share for Brown Corporation is calculated as follows:

$$\frac{\text{Basic}}{\text{EPS}} = \frac{\$7,500 - \$500}{(.5 \times 4,000) + (.5 \times 3,000)} = \frac{\$7,000}{3,500} = \$2.00 \text{ per share}$$

Firms that have either convertible securities or stock options or warrants outstanding have complex capital structures. Such firms must present two EPS amounts: the basic EPS we have described, plus diluted EPS. Diluted EPS reflects the potential of convertible securities, options, and warrants to dilute the shareholders' ownership rights. "Dilution" is the word used to describe the reduction in basic EPS that would result if holders of convertible securities were to exchange them for shares of common stock or holders of stock options or warrants were to exercise them.

Accountants calculate diluted EPS as follows:

$$\begin{array}{l} \text{Diluted EPS} \\ \text{(Complex Capital} \\ \text{Structure)} \end{array} = \frac{\begin{array}{l}\text{Net Income-Preferred}\\\text{Stock Dividends}\end{array} + \begin{array}{l}\text{Adjustments for Dilutive}\\\text{Securities}\end{array}}{\begin{array}{l}\text{Weighted Average}\\\text{No. of Common}\\\text{Shares Outstanding}\end{array} + \begin{array}{l}\text{Weighted Average Number}\\\text{of Shares Issuable from}\\\text{Dilutive Securities}\end{array}}$$

To calculate diluted EPS only, the accountant assumes that convertible bonds and convertible preferred stock will be converted and stock options and warrants will be exercised. This requires adding back any interest expense (net of taxes) on convertible bonds and dividends on convertible preferred stock that the firm subtracted in computing net income to common. Also added back to the numerator is any amount recognized as compensation expense on stock options.

The additional common shares issuable upon the conversion of bonds and preferred stock and the exercise of stock options and warrants are added to the denominator. Calculation of the additional shares to be issued upon the exercise of stock options assumes that the firm would use any cash proceeds from such exercise to repurchase its common shares on the open market. Only the net incremental shares issued (shares issued under options minus assumed shares repurchased) enter the computation of diluted EPS.

EXAMPLE 2

Assume the preferred stock of Brown Corporation is convertible into 1,000 shares of common stock. Also assume that Brown Corporation has stock options outstanding that holders can currently exchange for 300 incremental shares of common stock. Brown Corporation recognized $600 of compensation expense (net of taxes) related to these stock options during the current year. The calculation of diluted EPS is as follows:

$$\text{Diluted EPS} = \frac{\$7,500 - \$500 + \$500 + \$600}{(.5 \times 4,000) + (.5 \times 3,000) + (1.0 \times 1,000) + (1.0 \times 300)} = \frac{\$8,100}{4,800}$$

$$= \$1.69 \text{ per share}$$

The calculation assumes conversion of the convertible preferred stock into common stock as of January 1. If conversion took place, the firm would not have paid preferred dividends during the year. Thus, the analyst adds back to the numerator of fully diluted earnings per share the $500 preferred dividends that the accountant subtracted in computing net income available to common stock. The weighted average number of shares in the denominator increases for the 1,000 common shares that the firm would issue upon conversion of the preferred stock.

The accountant likewise adds back to net income the after-tax cost of stock options initially recognized as expense in computing net income. The weighted average number of shares in the denominator increases for the incremental shares issuable.

The accountant makes these adjustments to EPS for complex capital structures only if their effect is dilutive (that is, if the adjustments reduce basic EPS). Both EPS amounts appear on the income statement.

Look at Coke's income statements and notes on its accounting policies. Coke shows only a single EPS amount. Note 6 indicates that it has no convertible debt outstanding. Note 11 indicates that it does have stock options outstanding. Yet in Note 1 to its financial statements, Coke reports that its EPS uses the weighted average number of common shares outstanding in the denominator, implying that the dilutive effect of options is either immaterial or antidilutive.

CRITICISMS OF EPS

Critics of EPS as a measure of profitability point out that it does not consider the *amount of* assets or capital required to generate a particular level of earnings. Two firms with the same earnings and earnings per share are not equally profitable if one firm requires twice the amount of assets or capital to generate those earnings than the other firm does.

Also, a firm's number of shares of common stock outstanding serves as a poor measure of the amount of capital in use. The number of shares outstanding usually relates to a firm's attempts to achieve a desirable trading range for its common stock. For example, suppose the aggregate market value of a firm's common shares is $10 million. If the firm has 500,000 shares outstanding, the stock will sell for $20 per share. If the firm has 1,000,000 shares outstanding, the stock will sell for $10 per share. The amount of capital in place is the same in both instances; only the number of shares outstanding, and therefore EPS, is different.

These differences all explain why analysts cannot compare EPS amounts across firms. Two firms can have identical earnings, common shareholders' equity, and ROCEs, but their EPS will differ if they have different numbers of shares outstanding.

Another reason EPS is an ambiguous measure of profitability is that it reflects (1) operating performance in the numerator, and (2) capital structure decisions in the denominator. For example, a firm could experience reduced earnings during the year, yet report a higher EPS than the previous year if it has repurchased sufficient shares during the period. An analyst assessing earnings performance must separate the impact of these two factors on EPS.

PROBLEMS AND CASES

3.1 ANALYZING OPERATING PROFITABILITY. Exhibit 3.13 presents selected operating data for three retailers for a recent year. Wal-Mart sells a wide variety of household, personal, and grocery products following an everyday low-price strategy. It locates its stores in both urban and rural areas. Home Depot sells products for the home improvement industry, ranging from riding lawnmowers to lighting fixtures to kitchen countertops. It locates its stores in suburban locations. May Department Stores operates several different chains selling products ranging from clothing to china, cosmetics to bedding. It locates its stores in urban and suburban areas.

Required
 a. Compute the rate of return on assets for each firm. Disaggregate the rate of return on assets into profit margin and assets turnover components. The income tax rate is 35 percent.
 b. Describe the likely reasons for the differences in the profit margins and asset turnovers of the three companies. You may wish to use the other data presented in Exhibit 3.13 in your interpretations.

3.2 CALCULATING AND INTERPRETING OPERATING PROFITABILITY RATIOS. Sony Corporation, a Japanese company, manufactures and markets consumer electronics products (video and audio equipment, televisions), produces and distributes entertainment products (music, motion pictures), and provides life insurance and financing services. Exhibit 3.14 presents a partial income statement for Sony Corporation for Year 6, Year 7, and Year 8. Exhibit 3.15 presents selected product and geographic segment data.

| | EXHIBIT 3.13 | | |

Selected Data for Three Retailers
(in millions)
(Problem 3.1)

	Wal-Mart Stores	Home Depot	May Department Stores
Sales....................	$106,146	$19,536	$11,650
Cost of Goods Sold..........	83,663	14,101	8,226
Interest Expense............	1,053	168	300
Net Income...............	3,056	938	749
Average Inventory...........	15,943	2,194	2,257
Average Fixed Assets.........	22,201	6,846	4,238
Average Total Assets.........	41,164	10,245	10,376

Required

a. Prepare a common size income statement for Sony Corporation for Year 5, Year 6, and Year 7, with sales equal to 100 percent.

b. Suggest likely reasons for changes in Sony's profitability during this three-year period. The statutory tax rate in Japan is 51 percent for each year involved.

3.3 CALCULATING AND INTERPRETING OPERATING PROFITABILITY RATIOS. Champion International Corporation and Kimberly Clark Company are forest products companies. Champion derives the majority of its revenues from the sale of printing paper and newsprint for a variety of business and publishing needs. Kimberly derives the majority of its revenues from the sale of tissues, diapers, and other personal care products. Champion derives 85

| | EXHIBIT 3.14 | |

Sony Corporation
Partial Income Statement
(amounts in billions of yen)
(Problem 3.2)

	Year 6	Year 7	Year 8
Sales	¥ 3,965	¥ 4,571	¥ 5,636
Other Revenues.....................	25	22	27
Cost of Goods Sold	(3,049)	(3,439)	(4,161)
Selling and Administrative Expenses	(843)	(918)	(1,132)
Operating Income before Income Taxes	¥ 98	¥ 236	¥ 370
Income Tax Expense on Operating Income	(55)	(132)	(194)
Operating Income	¥ 43	¥ 104	¥ 176

EXHIBIT 3.15

Sony Corporation
Segment Data
(Problem 3.2)

	Sales Mix			Profit Margin		
	Year 6	Year 7	Year 8	Year 6	Year 7	Year 8
Electronics	77%	77%	78%	4.0%	5.4%	6.9%
Entertainment...........	19	18	18	(1.0%)	6.6%	6.5%
Insurance	4	5	4	4.3%	3.6%	8.4%
	100%	100%	100%			
Japan..................	28%	30%	28%	5.1%	8.3%	12.7%
United States............	29	27	29	(2.7%)	2.6%	1.8%
Europe	23	23	23	6.0%	5.5%	6.4%
Other..................	20	20	20	8.3%	8.1%	8.3%
	100%	100%	100%			

percent of its revenues from sales within the United States. Kimberly derives 67 percent of its revenues from sales within the United States. Data for these companies for Year 3, Year 4, and Year 5 appear in Exhibit 3.16.

Required

a. Calculate the accounts receivable turnover ratios for Champion and Kimberly for Year 3, Year 4, and Year 5.

b. Suggest possible reasons for the differences in the accounts receivable turnovers for the two firms during the three-year period.

c. Suggest possible reasons for the increase in the accounts receivable turnover for both firms between Year 3 and Year 4 and the decrease in the accounts receivable turnover for both firms between Year 4 and Year 5.

EXHIBIT 3.16

Selected Data for Champion International and Kimberly Clark
(amounts in millions)
(Problem 3.3)

	Year 3	Year 4	Year 5
Champion			
Sales	$ 5,318	$ 6,972	$ 5,880
Average Accounts Receivable.........	528	610	839
Change in Sales from Previous Year ...	+4.9%	+31.1%	−15.7%
Kimberly Clark			
Sales	$11,628	$13,373	$13,149
Average Accounts Receivable.........	1,385	1,573	1,669
Change in Sales from Previous Year ...	+2.9%	+15.0%	−1.7%

EXHIBIT 3.17

Selected Data for Eli Lilly and Merck
(amounts in millions)
(Problem 3.4)

	Year 5	Year 6	Year 7
Eli Lilly			
Cost of Goods Sold................	$1,680	$1,836	$2,118
Average Inventories	1,036	904	861
Change in Sales from Previous Year	+9.9%	+18.4%	+8.6%
Merck			
Cost of Goods Sold................	$5,962	$7,456	$9,319
Average Inventories	1,651	1,767	2,011
Change in Sales from Previous Year	+14.7%	+11.4%	+18.9%

3.4 CALCULATING AND INTERPRETING INVENTORY TURNOVER RATIOS. Eli Lilly and Merck develop, manufacture, and market prescription drugs worldwide. Merck also provides managed prescription drug programs for various businesses, purchasing drugs in bulk quantities for distribution to health care providers and monitoring usage patterns, costs, effectiveness, and other factors. Lilly derives approximately 56 percent of its revenues from sales within the United States. The comparable percentage for Merck is 30 percent. Both firms use the same cost flow assumptions for inventories and cost of goods sold. Selected data for each firm for Year 5, Year 6, and Year 7 appear in Exhibit 3.17.

Required
   a. Calculate the inventory turnover ratio for each firm for Year 5, Year 6, and Year 7.
   b. Suggest reasons for the differences in the inventory turnover ratios of the two firms.
   c. Suggest reasons for the changes in the inventory turnover ratios of the two firms during the three-year period.

3.5 CALCULATING AND INTERPRETING ACCOUNTS RECEIVABLE AND INVENTORY TURNOVER RATIOS. AK Steel and Nucor are steel manufacturers. AK Steel is an integrated steel producer, transforming ferrous metals into rolled steel and then into various steel products for the automobile, appliance, construction, and other industries. Its steel falls on the high end in terms of quality. Nucor produces steel in mini-mills. Mini-mills transform scrap ferrous metals into standard sizes of rolled steel, which Nucor then sells to steel service centers and distributors. Its steel falls on the low end in terms of quality. Exhibit 3.18 sets forth various data for these two companies for Year 7, Year 8, and Year 9.

Required
   a. Calculate the accounts receivable turnovers for AK Steel and Nucor for Year 7, Year 8, and Year 9.
   b. Describe the likely reasons for the differences in the accounts receivable turnovers for the two firms.

EXHIBIT 3.18

Selected Data for AK Steel and Nucor
(amounts in millions)
(Problem 3.5)

	Year 7	Year 8	Year 9
AK Steel			
Sales................................	$2,017	$2,257	$2,302
Cost of Goods Sold...............	1,645	1,768	1,852
Average Accounts Receivable........	193	233	239
Average Inventories	311	350	359
Change in Sales from Previous Year...	+26.4%	+11.9%	+2.0%
Nucor			
Sales................................	$2,976	$3,462	$3,647
Cost of Goods Sold...............	2,492	2,900	3,139
Average Accounts Receivable........	230	271	288
Average Inventories	303	363	430
Change in Sales from Previous Year...	+32.0%	+16.3%	+5.3%

c. Describe the likely reasons for the trend of the accounts receivable turnovers of the two firms over the three-year period.
d. Calculate the inventory turnovers for AK Steel and Nucor for Year 7, Year 8, and Year 9.
e. Describe the likely reasons for the differences in the inventory turnovers of the two firms.
f. Describe the likely reasons for the trend in the inventory turnovers of the two firms over the three-year period.

3.6 CALCULATING AND INTERPRETING FIXED ASSET TURNOVER RATIOS. Hewlett-Packard Corporation and Sun Microsystems manufacture computer hardware products designed for engineers, architects, and others requiring high-resolution graphic capabilities. H-P is an integrated manufacturer, producing most of the components for its products and then assembling them into finished products. Sun subcontracts out most of its component manufacturing, and then assembles the final product in its factories. Exhibit 3.19 presents selected data for H-P and Sun for Year 8, Year 9, and Year 10.

Required
a. Compute the fixed asset turnover for each firm for Year 8, Year 9, and Year 10.
b. Suggest reasons for the difference in the fixed asset turnovers of H-P and Sun.
c. Suggest reasons for the changes in the fixed asset turnovers of H-P and Sun during the three-year period.

3.7 CALCULATING AND INTERPRETING THE RATE OF RETURN ON COMMON SHARE-HOLDERS' EQUITY AND ITS COMPONENTS. Jumbosports operates a chain of retail stores emphasizing sports equipment and apparel. Exhibit 3.20 presents selected data for Jumbosports for Year 4, Year 5, and Year 6.

EXHIBIT 3.19

Selected Data for Hewlett-Packard and Sun Microsystems
(amounts in millions)
(Problem 3.6)

	Year 8	Year 9	Year 10
Hewlett-Packard			
Sales	$24,991	$31,519	$38,420
Capital Expenditures	1,257	1,601	2,201
Average Fixed Assets	4,811	5,046	5,734
Sun Microsystems			
Sales	$ 4,690	$ 5,902	$ 7,095
Capital Expenditures	213	242	296
Average Fixed Assets	619	653	731

Required

a. Calculate the rate of return on common shareholders' equity for Jumbosports for Year 4, Year 5, and Year 6. Disaggregate ROCE into rate of return on assets (ROA), common earnings leverage (CEL), and capital structure leverage (CSL) components.

b. Suggest reasons for the changes in ROCE over the three years.

c. Did financial leverage work to the advantage of the common shareholders in each of the three years? Explain.

3.8 INTERPRETING THE RATE OF RETURN ON COMMON SHAREHOLDERS' EQUITY AND ITS COMPONENTS. Selected financial data for AMR, parent company of American Airlines, appear in Exhibit 3.21.

EXHIBIT 3.20

Selected Data for Jumbosports
(amounts in thousands)
(Problem 3.7)

	Year Ended January 31:		
	Year 4	Year 5	Year 6
Net Income (Loss)	$15,714	$ 6,996	$(30,544)
Interest Expense................	4,815	11,254	19,840
Income Tax Rate................	35%	35%	35%

	January 31			
	Year 3	Year 4	Year 5	Year 6
Total Assets	$233,220	$389,852	$484,843	$525,586
Total Common Shareholders' Equity...................	$117,379	$180,122	$187,530	$159,624

EXHIBIT 3.21

Selected Data for AMR Corporation
(Problem 3.8)

	Year 3	Year 4	Year 5	Year 6	Year 7
Rate of Return on Common Shareholders' Equity	(13.3%)	(4.8%)	5.3%	4.7%	21.8%
Rate of Return on Assets	(.6%)	1.6%	3.2%	3.1%	6.7%
Common Earnings Leverage	424.1%	(51.1%)	27.4%	27.1%	75.8%
Capital Structure Leverage	4.9	5.8	6.0	5.6	4.3
Growth Rate in Sales	11.2%	9.9%	2.0%	4.8%	5.0%
Growth Rate in Assets	15.4%	3.3%	.8%	.4%	4.8%

Required

a. In which years did financial leverage work to the advantage of AMR's common share-holders, and in which years did it work to their disadvantage? Explain.

b. Identify possible reasons for the changes in AMR's capital structure leverage ratio during the five-year period.

c. Identify possible reasons for the changes in AMR's common earnings leverage ratio during the five-year period. Consider the interpretation of the common earnings leverage ratio in excess of 100 percent during Year 3 and the negative ratio during Year 4.

3.9 CALCULATING AND INTERPRETING THE RATE OF RETURN ON COMMON SHARE-HOLDERS' EQUITY AND EARNINGS PER COMMON SHARE. Selected data for General Mills for Year 2, Year 3, and Year 4 appear below (amounts in millions):

	Year 2	Year 3	Year 4
Net Income.	$472.7	$ 505.6	$ 506.1
Weighted Average Number of Common Shares Outstanding	164.5	165.7	163.1
Average Common Shareholders' Equity	$961.6	$1,242.2	$1,294.7

a. Compute the rate of return on common shareholders' equity (ROCE) for General Mills for Year 2, Year 3, and Year 4.

b. Compute basic earnings per common share (EPS) for Year 2, Year 3, and Year 4.

c. Interpret the changes in ROCE versus EPS over the three-year period.

3.10 CALCULATING AND INTERPRETING SHORT-TERM LIQUIDITY RATIOS. Hewlett Packard manufactures and markets electronic products and services for a wide range of business, government, and consumer needs. Net income and cash flow from operations for three recent years appear below (amounts in millions):

	Year 5	Year 6	Year 7
Sales	$14,494	$16,410	$20,317
Cost of Goods Sold	$7,858	$9,158	$12,123
Net Income	$755	$881	$1,177
Cash Flow from Operations.............	$1,552	$1,288	$1,142

Exhibit 3.22 presents partial balance sheets for Hewlett Packard on December 31 for Year 4, Year 5, Year 6, and Year 7.

    a. Compute the following short-term liquidity ratios for Hewlett-Packard for Year 5, Year 6, and Year 7:

       1. Current Ratio (year end).

       2. Quick Ratio (year-end).

       3. Cash Flow from Operations to Average Current Liabilities Ratio.

       4. Days Accounts Receivable.

       5. Days Inventory.

       6. Days Accounts Payable.

    b. Assess the changes in the short-term liquidity risk of Hewlett-Packard over the three-year period.

3.11 CALCULATING AND INTERPRETING PROFITABILITY AND RISK RATIOS. Hasbro is a leading firm in the toy, games, and amusements industry. Among its promoted brands are Batman®, Nerf®, and Easy Bake® Oven products. Its games and puzzles group includes

---

EXHIBIT 3.22

Partial Balance Sheet for Hewlett Packard Corporation
(amounts in millions)
(Problem 3.10)

	December 31			
	Year 4	Year 5	Year 6	Year 7
Current Assets				
Cash.......................	$1,077	$ 625	$ 641	$ 889
Marketable Securities.........	—	495	394	755
Accounts Receivable..........	2,883	2,976	3,497	4,208
Inventories	2,092	2,273	2,605	3,691
Prepayments.................	458	347	542	693
Total Current Assets	$6,510	$6,716	$7,679	$10,236
Current Liabilities				
Accounts Payable	$ 660	$ 686	$ 925	$ 1,223
Bank Loans.................	1,896	1,201	1,384	2,190
Other Current Liabilities	1,887	2,176	2,785	3,455
Total Current Liabilities	$4,443	$4,063	$5,094	$ 6,868

Monopoly®, Scrabble®, Barney®, G.I. Joe®, Tinkertoys®, and Play-Doh® products. Hasbro invested in the development of CD-ROM-based interactive versions of several of its games during Year 4. Interest rates declined during the three-year period we are looking at.

   Exhibit 3.23 presents the balance sheets for Hasbro for the years ending December 31, Year 2 through Year 5. Exhibit 3.24 presents the income statement, and Exhibit 3.25 presents the statement of cash flows, for Year 3 through Year 5. Exhibit 3.26 presents geographic segment data.

EXHIBIT 3.23

Hasbro
Balance Sheets
(amounts in millions)
(Problem 3.11)

	December 31			
	Year 2	**Year 3**	**Year 4**	**Year 5**
Assets				
Cash	$ 186	$ 137	$ 161	$ 219
Accounts Receivable	721	718	791	807
Inventories	250	244	316	274
Prepayments	144	153	158	187
Total Current Assets	$1,301	$1,252	$1,426	$1,487
Property, Plant, and Equipment (net)	280	309	313	314
Other Assets	712	817	877	901
Total Assets	$2,293	$2,378	$2,616	$2,702
Liabilities and Shareholders' Equity				
Accounts Payable	$ 174	$ 165	$ 198	$ 174
Short-Term Borrowing	62	82	120	121
Other Current Liabilities	512	517	552	536
Total Current Liabilities	$ 748	$ 764	$ 870	$ 831
Long-Term Debt	200	150	150	150
Other Noncurrent Liabilities	68	69	71	69
Total Liabilities	$1,016	$ 983	$1,091	$1,050
Common Stock	$ 44	$ 44	$ 44	$ 66
Additional Paid-in Capital	297	282	279	283
Retained Earnings[a]	921	1,071	1,201	1,363
Foreign Currency Translation Adjustment	15	15	23	21
Treasury Stock	0	(17)	(22)	(81)
Total Shareholders' Equity	$1,277	$1,395	$1,525	$1,652
Total Liabilities and Shareholders' Equity	$2,293	$2,378	$2,616	$2,702

---

[a]The change in retained earnings does not equal net income (Exhibit 3.24) minus dividends (Exhibit 3.25) because of adjustments to net income for nonrecurring items discussed in later chapters.

EXHIBIT 3.24

Hasbro
Income Statements
(amounts in millions)
(Problem 3.11)

	For the Year Ended December 31		
	Year 3	Year 4	Year 5
Sales	$ 2,670	$ 2,858	$ 3,002
Other Revenues (principally interest)	26	17	6
Cost of Goods Sold	(1,161)	(1,237)	(1,329)
Selling and Administrative Expenses:			
Advertising.	(397)	(418)	(418)
Research and Development			
and Royalties	(273)	(305)	(320)
Amortization of Intangibles	(37)	(38)	(40)
Other Selling and Administrative.	(494)	(555)	(563)
Interest Expense	(31)	(38)	(31)
Income Tax Expense	(116)	(108)	(107)
Net Income.	$ 187	$ 176	$ 200

EXHIBIT 3.25

Hasbro
Statements of Cash Flows
(amounts in millions)
(Problem 3.11)

	For the Year Ended January 31		
	Year 3	Year 4	Year 5
Operations			
Net Income	$ 187	$ 176	$ 200
Depreciation and Amortization	122	130	138
Addbacks and Subtractions—Net	(39)	(17)	(8)
(Increase) Decrease in Accounts Receivable . .	10	(67)	(22)
(Increase) Decrease in Inventories.	29	(65)	43
(Increase) Decrease in Prepayments	(3)	(2)	(37)
Increase (Decrease) in Accounts Payable			
and Other Current Liabilities.	(22)	72	(34)
Cash Flow from Operations	$ 284	$ 227	$ 280
Investing			
Property, Plant, and Equipment Acquired	$(111)	$(101)	$(102)
Other Investing Transactions.	(133)	(108)	(25)
Cash Flow from Investing	$(244)	$(209)	$(127)

	For the Year Ended January 31		
Exh. 3.25—Continued	**Year 3**	**Year 4**	**Year 5**
Financing			
Increase in Short-Term Borrowing..........	$ 19	$ 21	0
Increase in Long-Term Borrowing..........	0	434	$ 265
Increase in Common Stock	0	0	0
Decrease in Short-Term Borrowing	0	0	(6)
Decrease in Long-Term Borrowing	(54)	(417)	(256)
Acquisition of Common Stock.............	(26)	(15)	(84)
Dividends.............................	(24)	(27)	(33)
Other Financing Transactions	(4)	10	19
Cash Flow from Financing..............	$ (89)	$ 6	$ (95)
Change in Cash........................	$ (49)	$ 24	$ 58
Cash—Beginning of Year.................	186	137	161
Cash—End of Year	$ 137	$ 161	$ 219

EXHIBIT 3.26

Hasbro
Segment Data
(Problem 3.11)

	Year 3	**Year 4**	**Year 5**
Sales Mix			
United States	57%	54%	55%
Other Countries...................	43	46	45
	100%	100%	100%
	Year 3	**Year 4**	**Year 5**
Rate of Return on Assets			
United States	10.5%	8.2%	11.2%
Other Countries...................	16.4%	15.2%	14.4%
	Year 3	**Year 4**	**Year 5**
Profit Margin			
United States	11.1%	9.5%	12.3%
Other Countries...................	11.0%	9.7%	9.6%
	Year 3	**Year 4**	**Year 5**
Assets Turnover			
United States	.95	.87	.92
Other Countries...................	1.49	1.56	1.49

Required

    a. Exhibit 3.27 presents profitability and risk ratios for Hasbro for Year 3 and Year 4. Calculate these financial ratios for Year 5. The income tax rate is 35 percent.

    b. Assess the changes in Hasbro's profitability over the three-year period, and suggest reasons for the changes observed.

    c. Assess Hasbro's short-term liquidity and long-term solvency risk.

3.12 **CALCULATING AND INTERPRETING PROFITABILITY AND RISK RATIOS.** Lands' End Corporation sells men's, women's, and children's clothing through catalogs. Financial statements for Lands' End for fiscal years ending January 31, Year 5, Year 6, and Year 7 appear in Exhibit 3.28 (balance sheet), Exhibit 3.29 (income statement), and Exhibit 3.30 (statement of cash flows). Exhibit 3.31 presents financial statement ratios for Year 5 and Year 6.

    Sales increased 14.0 percent between Year 4 and Year 5, 4.0 percent between Year 5 and Year 6, and 8.5 percent between Year 6 and Year 7. Because of industry capacity shortages, paper prices rose significantly during Lands' End's year ending January 31, Year 6, but declined in Year 7. Lands' End shipped 88 percent of orders at the time that cus-

---

EXHIBIT 3.27

Hasbro
Financial Statement Ratio Analysis
(Problem 3.11)

	Year 3	Year 4	Year 5
Profit Margin for Rate of Return on Assets	7.8%	7.0%	
Assets Turnover.	1.1	1.1	
Rate of Return on Assets	8.9%	8.0%	
Common Earnings Leverage	90.3%	87.7%	
Capital Structure Leverage	1.7	1.7	
Rate of Return on Common Shareholders'			
Equity	14.0%	12.1%	
Cost of Goods Sold ÷ Sales.	(43.5)	(43.3)	
Selling and Administrative Expense ÷ Sales	(45.0)	(46.0)	
Income Tax Expense (excluding tax effects of			
interest expense) ÷ Sales.	(4.8)	(4.2)	
Accounts Receivable Turnover.	3.7	3.8	
Inventory Turnover	4.7	4.4	
Fixed Asset Turnover.	9.1	9.2	
Current Ratio	1.6	1.6	
Quick Ratio	1.1	1.1	
Operating Cash Flow ÷ Average Current			
Liabilities.	37.6%	27.8%	
Days Accounts Receivable	98	96	
Days Inventory.	78	83	
Days Accounts Payable	54	51	
Long-Term Debt Ratio.	9.7%	8.9%	
Debt-Equity Ratio	10.8%	9.8%	
Liabilities ÷ Total Assets.	41.3%	41.7%	
Operating Cash Flow ÷ Average Total Liabilities .	28.4%	21.9%	
Interest Coverage Ratio	10.8	8.5	
Operating Cash Flow ÷ Capital Expenditures	2.6	2.3	

EXHIBIT 3.28

Lands' End
Balance Sheets
(amounts in thousands)
(Problem 3.12)

	January 31			
	Year 4	Year 5	Year 6	Year 7
Assets				
Cash..............................	$ 21,569	$ 5,426	$ 17,176	$ 92,827
Accounts Receivable....................	3,644	4,459	8,064	8,739
Inventories	149,688	168,652	164,816	142,445
Prepayments.........................	17,375	19,631	32,033	28,028
Total Current Assets....................	$192,276	$198,168	$222,089	$ 272,039
Property, Plant, and Equipment (net).........	79,691	96,991	98,985	103,684
Other Assets..........................	1,863	2,453	2,423	2,322
Total Assets	$273,830	$297,612	$323,497	$ 378,045
Liabilities and Shareholders' Equity				
Accounts Payable......................	$ 54,855	$ 52,762	$ 62,380	$ 76,585
Short-Term Borrowing	0	7,579	9,319	11,195
Current Portion of Long-Term Debt.........	40	0	0	0
Other Current Liabilities	36,154	42,369	43,045	57,786
Total Current Liabilities	$ 91,049	$102,710	$114,744	$ 145,566
Long-Term Debt.......................	40	0	0	0
Other Noncurrent Liabilities	5,456	5,774	7,561	9,474
Total Liabilities.......................	$ 96,545	$108,484	$122,305	$ 155,040
Common Stock........................	$ 201	$ 402	$ 402	$ 402
Additional Paid-in Capital	33,288	34,217	34,565	34,630
Retained Earnings	191,705	228,417	259,276	310,069
Treasury Stock	(47,909)	(23,908)	(93,051)	(122,096)
Total Shareholders' Equity	$177,285	$189,128	$201,192	$ 223,005
Total Liabilities and Shareholders' Equity....	$273,830	$297,612	$323,497	$ 378,045

tomers placed their orders during Year 5, 90 percent during Year 6, and 86 percent during Year 7.

Required

a. Calculate the ratios in Exhibit 3.31 for Year 7. The income tax rate is 35 percent.
b. Assess the changes in the profitability of Lands' End during the three-year period, suggesting possible reasons for the changes observed.
c. Assess the short-term liquidity risk and the long-term solvency risk of Lands' End.

3.13 INTERPRETING PROFITABILITY AND RISK RATIOS. Microsoft Corporation is one of the largest and fastest-growing software development firms in the world. It sells operating systems for computers and applications software for word processing, graphics, numerical analysis, and communications. Microsoft launched its Windows 95 operating system near

	EXHIBIT 3.29		

Lands' End
Income Statements
(amounts in thousands)
(Problem 3.12)

	For the Year Ended January 31		
	Year 5	**Year 6**	**Year 7**
Sales......................	$ 992,106	$1,031,548	$1,118,743
Cost of Goods Sold............	(571,265)	(588,017)	(609,168)
Selling and Administrative			
Expenses..................	(357,516)	(392,484)	(424,390)
Interest Expense..............	(1,769)	(2,771)	(510)
Other Income (Expense)........	(1,893)	2,649	244
Income Tax Expense...........	(23,567)	(20,370)	(33,967)
Net Income	$ 36,096	$ 30,555	$ 50,952

the end of Year 8. Exhibit 3.32 presents financial statement ratios for Microsoft for Year 7, Year 8, and Year 9.

Required
  a. What are the likely reasons for the decrease in Microsoft's profit margin for ROA between Year 7 and Year 8?
  b. What are the likely reasons for the decrease in the total assets turnover between Year 7 and Year 8?
  c. What are the likely reasons for the increase in the profit margin for ROA between Year 8 and Year 9?
  d. What is the likely explanation for the decreases in the current and quick ratios during the three-year period?

3.14 INTERPRETING PROFITABILITY AND RISK RATIOS. H.J. Heinz manufactures and markets consumer food products worldwide. It derived 57 percent of its revenues from within the U.S. and 43 percent from other countries during Year 4, Year 5, and Year 6. Exhibit 3.33 presents financial statement ratios for Heinz.

Required
  a. What are the likely reasons for Heinz's decreasing common earnings leverage ratio during the three-year period?
  b. What are the likely reasons for the decrease in the current ratio between Year 4 and Year 5?
  c. What are the likely reasons for the decreases in the operating cash flow to current liabilities and operating cash flow to total liabilities ratios during the three-year period?
  d. What are the likely reasons for the decreases in the interest coverage ratios during the three-year period?
  e. The profit margin for ROA increased between Year 5 and Year 6, but the profit margin in both the U.S. and in other countries decreased between these two years. Explain this apparent paradox.

EXHIBIT 3.30

Lands' End
Statements of Cash Flows
(amounts in thousands)
(Problem 3.12)

	For the Year Ended January 31		
	Year 5	Year 6	Year 7
Operations			
Net Income	$ 36,096	$ 30,555	$ 50,952
Depreciation and Amortization	10,311	12,456	13,558
Addbacks and Subtractions—Net	(987)	1,140	2,030
(Increase) Decrease in Accounts			
Receivable	(264)	(4,888)	(675)
(Increase) Decrease in Inventories	(16,544)	1,423	22,371
(Increase) Decrease in Prepayments	597	(9,929)	4,613
Increase (Decrease) in Accounts Payable .	(2,093)	9,618	14,205
Increase (Decrease) in Other Current			
Liabilities	7,345	1,017	14,741
Cash Flow from Operations	$ 34,461	$ 41,392	$121,795
Investing			
Property, Plant, and Equipment			
Acquired	$(32,102)	$(13,904)	$(18,481)
Other Investing Transactions	0	1,665	0
Cash Flow from Investing	$(32,102)	$(12,239)	$(18,481)
Financing			
Increase in Short-Term Borrowing	$ 7,539	$ 1,780	$ 1,876
Increase in Common Stock	1,978	858	604
Decrease in Short-Term Borrowing	0	0	0
Decrease in Long-Term Borrowing	(40)	(40)	0
Decrease in Common Stock	(27,979)	(20,001)	(30,143)
Dividends	0	0	0
Other Financing Transactions	0	0	0
Cash Flow from Financing	$(18,502)	$(17,403)	$(27,663)
Change in Cash	$(16,143)	$ 11,750	$ 75,651
Cash—Beginning of Year	21,569	5,426	17,176
Cash—End of Year	$ 5,426	$ 17,176	$ 92,827

EXHIBIT 3.31

Lands' End
Financial Statement Ratio Analysis
(Problem 3.12)

	Year 5	Year 6	Year 7
Profit Margin for Rate of Return on			
Assets	3.8%	3.1%	
Assets Turnover	3.5	3.3	
Rate of Return on Assets	13.0%	10.4%	
Common Earnings Leverage	96.9%	94.4%	
Capital Structure Leverage	1.6	1.6	
Rate of Return on Common			
Shareholders' Equity	19.7%	15.7%	
Cost of Goods Sold ÷ Sales	57.6%	57.0%	
Selling and Administrative			
Expense ÷ Sales	36.0%	38.0%	
Income Tax Expense (excluding tax			
effects of interest expense) ÷ Sales	2.4%	2.1%	
Accounts Receivable Turnover	244.9	164.7	
Inventory Turnover	3.6	3.5	
Fixed Asset Turnover	11.2	10.5	
Current Ratio	1.9	1.9	
Quick Ratio	.1	.2	
Days Accounts Receivable	1	2	
Days Inventory	102	103	
Days Accounts Payable	33	36	
Operating Cash Flow ÷ Average			
Current Liabilities	35.6%	38.1%	
Total Liabilities ÷ Total Assets	36.5%	37.8%	
Long-Term Debt Ratio	0	0	
Debt-Equity Ratio	0	0	
Operating Cash Flow ÷ Average Total			
Liabilities	33.6%	35.9%	
Interest Coverage Ratio	34.7	19.4	
Operating Cash Flow ÷			
Capital Expenditures	1.1	3.0	

EXHIBIT 3.32			

Microsoft Corporation
Financial Statement Ratio Analysis
(Problem 3.13)

	Year 7	Year 8	Year 9
Profit Margin for Rate of Return on			
Assets	24.7%	24.5%	25.3%
Assets Turnover	1.0	.9	1.0
Rate of Return on Assets	25.0%	23.1%	25.4%
Common Earnings Leverage	1.0	1.0	1.0
Capital Structure Leverage	1.2	1.3	1.4
Rate of Return on Common Share-			
holders' Equity	29.8%	29.7%	35.9%
Other Revenues (principally interest)			
÷ Sales	2.2%	3.2%	3.7%
Cost of Goods Sold ÷ Sales	16.4%	14.8%	13.7%
Selling and Administrative Expense			
÷ Sales	35.6%	37.5%	34.5%
Research and Development Expense			
÷ Sales	13.1%	14.5%	16.5%
Income Tax Expense (excluding			
tax effects of interest expense)			
÷ Sales	12.4%	12.0%	13.7%
Accounts Receivable Turnover	11.4	11.2	14.2
Inventory Turnover	6.7	8.3	10.3
Fixed Asset Turnover	5.2	5.6	6.9
Current Ratio	4.7	4.2	3.2
Quick Ratio	4.5	4.0	3.1
Operating Cash Flow Average			
÷ Current Liabilities	215.9%	176.1%	197.2%
Days Accounts Receivable	32	32	26
Days Inventory	55	44	35
Days Accounts Payable	139	183	209
Long-Term Debt Ratio	—	—	—
Debt-Equity Ratio	—	—	—
Liabilities ÷ Total Assets	17.0%	26.0%	31.6%
Operating Cash Flow ÷ Average			
Total Liabilities	215.9%	142.7%	146.9%
Interest Coverage Ratio	—	—	—
Operating Cash Flow ÷ Capital			
Expenditures	5.7	4.0	7.5
Sales (Year 6 = 100)	123.9	158.2	231.0
Sales—United States (Year 6 = 100)	130.8	169.3	249.1
Sales—Europe (Year 6 = 100)	108.7	122.2	173.9
Sales—Other International			
(Year 6 = 100)	94.9	141.3	244.3

(continued)

Exh. 3.32—Continued	Year 7	Year 8	Year 9
Sales Mix			
Operating Systems	40%	40%	47%
Applications and Products	60	60	53
	100%	100%	100%
Sales Mix			
United States	66%	68%	67%
Europe	27	24	23
Other International	7	8	10
	100%	100%	100%
Rate of Return on Assets			
United States	31.7%	29.2%	29.4%
Europe	25.3%	22.8%	29.8%
Other International	7.3%	13.2%	36.1%
Profit Margin			
United States	40.1%	38.0%	36.4%
Europe	24.7%	26.2%	30.3%
Other International	8.3%	16.3%	39.0%
Assets Turnover			
United States	.8	.8	.8
Europe	1.0	.9	1.0
Other International	.9	.8	.9

EXHIBIT 3.33

H.J. Heinz Company
Financial Statement Ratio Analysis
(Problem 3.14)

	Year 4	Year 5	Year 6
Profit Margin for Rate of Return on			
Assets	8.8%	9.0%	9.2%
Assets Turnover	1.1	1.1	1.1
Rate of Return on Assets	9.3%	10.0%	10.0%
Common Earnings Leverage	84.3%	81.2%	78.5%
Capital Structure Leverage	2.8	3.0	3.3
Rate of Return on Common Share-			
holders' Equity	22.3%	24.6%	25.5%
Cost of Goods Sold ÷ Sales	62.2%	63.3%	63.4%
Selling and Administrative			
Expense ÷ Sales	24.5%	22.4%	22.5%
Income Tax Expense (excluding			
tax effects of interest expense)			
÷ Sales	4.7%	5.2%	5.1%
Accounts Receivable Turnover	7.9	8.8	8.1
Inventory Turnover	3.8	4.1	4.0

Exh. 3.33—Continued	Year 4	Year 5	Year 6
Fixed Asset Turnover	3.3	3.4	3.5
Current Ratio	1.4	1.1	1.1
Quick Ratio	.6	.5	.5
Operating Cash Flow Average			
÷ Current Liabilities	40.9%	35.3%	27.9%
Days Accounts Receivable	46	42	45
Days Inventory	97	90	91
Days Accounts Payable	47	44	49
Long-Term Debt Ratio	42.5%	48.5%	45.7%
Debt-Equity Ratio	73.8%	94.1%	84.3%
Liabilities ÷ Assets	63.3%	70.0%	68.6%
Operating Cash Flow ÷ Average			
Total Liabilities	21.8%	15.3%	12.6%
Interest Coverage Ratio	6.3	5.5	4.5
Operating Cash Flow ÷ Capital			
Expenditures	3.4	2.2	2.2
Growth in Sales from Previous Year	(.8%)	14.8%	12.7%
Rate of Return on Assets			
United States	14.7%	13.7%	15.4%
Non–U.S.	19.6%	14.5%	14.3%
Profit Margin			
United States	13.3%	14.2%	14.1%
Non–U.S.	17.6%	14.4%	14.1%
Assets Turnover			
United States	1.10	.96	1.09
Non–U.S.	1.11	1.01	1.01

PROFITABILITY AND RISK ANALYSIS OF WAL-MART STORES

Wal-Mart Stores is the largest retailer in the U.S. It follows an "everyday-low-price" strategy and operates through three principal store concepts:

1. **Wal-Mart Stores:** Discount department stores that offer clothing, housewares, electronic equipment, pharmaceuticals, health and beauty products, sporting goods, and similar items. During its Year 7, these stores derived 25 percent of sales from soft goods, 25 percent from hard goods, 11 percent from stationery and candy, 10 percent from pharmaceuticals, 9 percent from electronic products, 8 percent from sporting goods and toys, 8 percent from health and beauty products, and 2 percent each from shoes and jewelry. These mix percentages have not changed significantly in recent years. The number of Wal-Mart Stores grew at a compound annual rate of .8 percent, and square footage grew at a compound annual rate of 3.6 percent, during the last three years. The average size of a Wal-Mart Store was 92,600 square feet at the end of fiscal Year 7.

2. **Sam's Clubs:** Members only warehouse stores that offer large quantities of food and household products as well as automotive, electronic, sporting goods, and similar products at wholesale prices. Compound annual growth rates during the last three years for Sam's Clubs are 1.5 percent in the number of stores and 1.6 percent in square footage. The average size of a Sam's Club store was 121,200 square feet at the end of fiscal Year 7. Sales of Sam's Clubs constituted 18.9 percent of Wal-Mart's total sales in fiscal Year 7, compared to 20.4 percent in fiscal Year 6 and 22.9 percent in fiscal Year 5.

3. **Wal-Mart Supercenters:** A full-line supermarket combined with a discount department store. Supercenters represent for Wal-Mart a movement to grocery products. The combination of grocery products with Wal-Mart's traditional discount department store offerings attempts to capitalize on the consumer draw of one-stop shopping and to take advantage of efficiencies in product distribution, stocking, and advertising. Compound annual growth rates during the last three years for Wal-Mart Supercenters are 68.4 percent in the number of stores and 70.8 percent in square footage. A portion of the growth in Wal-Mart Supercenters represents conversions of previous Wal-Mart Stores. The average size of a Wal-Mart Supercenter was 183,300 square feet at the end of fiscal Year 7.

Exhibit 3.34 sets out various operating data for Wal-Mart for its most recent four years.

In addition to domestic operations, Wal-Mart has expanded into Canada and Central and South America in recent years. In fiscal Year 5, Wal-Mart acquired 122 Woolco department stores in Canada and converted them into Wal-Mart Stores. Wal-Mart has also expanded into Mexico, Puerto Rico, Brazil, Argentina, Indonesia, and China. At the end of fiscal Year 7, Wal-Mart operated 262 stores with 26.8 million square feet outside the U.S. 136 of these stores were located in Canada, and 41 stores were located in Mexico.

Wal-Mart uses centralized purchasing through its home office for substantially all its merchandise. It distributes products to its Wal-Mart Stores and Wal-Mart Supercenters through 34 regional distribution centers. Sam's Clubs receive the majority of their merchandise directly from suppliers rather than through Wal-Mart's distribution centers.

Exhibit 3.35 presents comparative balance sheets; Exhibit 3.36 presents comparative income statements; and Exhibit 3.37 presents comparative statements of cash flows for Wal-Mart for its fiscal Year 5, Year 6, and Year. Exhibit 3.38 presents selected financial statement ratios for Year 5 and Year 6. The income tax rate is 35 percent.

a. Compute the amounts of the ratios listed in Exhibit 3.38 for the Year 7 fiscal year.
b. What are the likely reasons for the changes in Wal-Mart's rate of return on assets during the three-year period? Analyze the financial ratios to the maximum depth possible.
c. What are the likely reasons for the changes in Wal-Mart's rate of return on common shareholders' equity during the three-year period?
d. How has Wal-Mart's short-term liquidity risk changed during the three-year period?
e. How has its long-term liquidity risk changed during the three-year period?

EXHIBIT 3.34

Operating Data for Wal-Mart Stores
(Case 3.1)

	Fiscal Year Ended January 31:			
	Year 4	**Year 5**	**Year 6**	**Year 7**
Wal-Mart Stores				
Number	1,950	1,985	1,995	1,960
Square Footage (millions) ..	163.6	173.7	181.9	181.7
Sam's Clubs				
Number	417	426	433	436
Square Footage (millions) ..	50.4	51.7	52.5	52.7
Wal-Mart Supercenters				
Number	72	147	239	344
Square Footage (millions) ..	12.7	26.8	43.6	63.3
Total Stores				
Number	2,439	2,558	2,667	2,740
Square Footage (millions) ..	226.7	252.2	278.0	297.7
Sales per Square Foot	$299.89	$330.73	$340.82	$356.55
Comparable Store Sales				
Increase	6%	7%	4%	5%
Employees				
(full and part-time)	528,000	622,000	675,000	728,000

EXHIBIT 3.35

Wal-Mart Stores, Inc.
Comparative Balance Sheets
(amounts in millions)
(Case 3.1)

	January 31:			
	Year 4	**Year 5**	**Year 6**	**Year 7**
Assets				
Cash	$ 20	$ 45	$ 83	$ 883
Accounts Receivable	690	900	853	845
Inventories	11,014	14,064	15,989	15,897
Prepayments	391	329	406	368
Total Current Assets	$12,115	$15,338	$17,331	$17,993
Property, Plant, and Equipment (net)	15,675	18,485	21,497	22,904
Other Assets	1,151	1,607	1,316	1,287
Total Assets	$28,941	$35,430	$40,144	$42,184
Liabilities and Shareholders' Equity				
Accounts Payable	$ 4,104	$ 5,907	$ 6,442	$ 7,628
Notes Payable	1,646	1,882	2,798	618
Other Current Liabilities	1,656	2,184	2,214	2,711
Total Current Liabilities	$ 7,406	$ 9,973	$11,454	$10,957
Long-Term Debt	10,460	12,320	13,203	12,596
Other Noncurrent Liabilities	322	411	731	1,488
Total Liabilities	$18,188	$22,704	$25,388	$25,041
Common Stock	$ 230	$ 230	$ 229	$ 228
Additional Paid-in Capital	536	539	545	547
Retained Earnings	9,987	11,957	13,982	16,368
Total Shareholders' Equity	$10,753	$12,726	$14,756	$17,143
Total Liabilities and Shareholders' Equity	$28,941	$35,430	$40,144	$42,184

EXHIBIT 3.36

Wal-Mart Stores, Inc.
Comparative Income Statements
(amounts in millions)
(Case 3.1)

| | Year Ended January 31: | | |
	Year 5	Year 6	Year 7
Sales Revenue	$83,412	$94,749	$106,146
Expenses:			
Cost of Goods Sold	65,586	74,564	83,663
Marketing and Administrative	12,858	14,951	16,788
Interest	706	888	845
Income Taxes	1,581	1,606	1,794
Total Expenses	$80,731	$92,009	$103,090
Net Income	$ 2,681	$ 2,740	$ 3,056

EXHIBIT 3.37

Wal-Mart Stores, Inc.
Comparative Statements of Cash Flows
(amounts in millions)
(Case 3.1)

| | Year Ended January 31: | | |
	Year 5	Year 6	Year 7
Operations			
Net Income	$ 2,681	$ 2,740	$ 3,056
Depreciation	1,070	1,304	1,463
Other	21	0	0
(Increase) in Accounts Receivable	(84)	(61)	(58)
(Increase) in Inventories	(3,053)	(1,850)	99
(Increase) in Prepayments	(139)	(80)	38
Increase in Accounts Payable	1,914	448	1,208
Increase in Other Current Liabilities	496	(118)	124
Cash Flow from Operations	$ 2,906	$ 2,383	$ 5,930
Investing			
Acquisition of Property, Plant, and			
Equipment	$(3,734)	$(3,566)	$(2,643)
Other	(58)	234	575
Cash Flow from Investing	$(3,792)	$(3,332)	$(2,068)

(continued)

Exh. 3.37—Continued	Year Ended January 31:		
	Year 5	Year 6	Year 7
Financing			
Increase (Decrease) in Short-Term Borrowing	$ 220	$ 660	$(2,458)
Increase in Long-Term Borrowing	1,250	1,004	632
Increase in Common Stock	0	0	0
Decrease in Long-Term Borrowing	(107)	(207)	(615)
Acquisition of Common Stock	0	0	0
Dividends	(391)	(458)	(481)
Other	(61)	(12)	(140)
Cash Flow from Financing	$ 911	$ 987	$(3,062)
Change in Cash	$ 25	$ 38	$ 800
Cash—Beginning of Year	20	45	83
Cash—End of Year	$ 45	$ 83	$ 883

EXHIBIT 3.38

Wal-Mart Stores, Inc.
Financial Ratio Analysis
(Case 3.1)

	Year 5	Year 6	Year 7
Rate of Return on Assets	9.8%	8.8%	
Profit Margin for Rate of Return on Assets	3.8%	3.5%	
Total Assets Turnover	2.6	2.5	
Cost of Goods Sold/Sales	78.6%	78.7%	
Marketing and Administrative Expense/Sales	15.4%	15.8%	
Interest Expense/Sales	.8%	.9%	
Income Tax Expense/Sales	1.9%	1.7%	
Accounts Receivable Turnover Ratio	104.9	108.1	
Inventory Turnover Ratio	5.2	5.0	
Plant Assets Turnover Ratio	4.9	4.7	
Rate of Return on Common Shareholders' Equity	22.8%	19.9%	
Common Earnings Leverage Ratio	85.4%	82.6%	
Capital Structure Leverage Ratio	2.7	2.7	
Current Ratio	1.54	1.51	
Quick Ratio	.09	.08	
Cash Flow from Operations to Current Liabilities Ratio	33.4%	22.2%	

Exh. 3.38—Continued	Year 5	Year 6	Year 7
Accounts Payable Turnover Ratio	13.71	12.39	
Long-Term Debt Ratio	49.2%	47.2%	
Debt-Equity Ratio	96.8%	89.5%	
Cash Flow from Operations to Total Liabilities Ratio	14.2%	9.9%	
Interest Coverage Ratio	7.0	5.9	

CASE 3.2

SPECIALTY RETAILING INDUSTRY ANALYSIS: THE GAP AND THE LIMITED

The Gap and The Limited compete in the specialty retailing segment of the retail industry. This segment experienced its most significant growth during the 1980s. During the decades before that, traditional department stores had held the leadership position in retailing. Department stores offered the advantage of one-stop shopping by carrying broad lines of clothing, household, furniture, and other products. The size and the product line diversity of department stores provided them with certain economies of scale (such as in purchasing, storage, transportation).

The two main drawbacks of the department store approach became the competitive weapons of specialty retailers: both breadth and depth of a specialty product line, and expertise in services offered in support of that product line. Specialty retailers tended to locate in shopping centers anchored by established department stores, benefiting from shopping center traffic without incurring much of the promotion cost to attract customers.

The 1990s witnessed a change in the economics of specialty retailing. Competition among specialty retailers increased significantly as their numbers reached the saturation point in many locales. Moreover, many department stores adopted a "mini-boutique" strategy, offering a collection of specialty retail shops under one roof. A second factor affecting specialty retailing was the movement toward at-home shopping. This movement is part of a complex change related to consumers' perceived lack of time for shopping and also to concerns about personal safety (catalogs and home shopping television networks are both responses to this need).

The Gap and The Limited initially entered the specialty retailing market with clothing designed for teenagers and young working women. The Gap subsequently expanded its product line to include men's and children's apparel.

The Gap's product line includes basic clothing (such as jeans and shirts), which it sells in a variety of sizes and colors to customers of all ages. It operates stores under the names of The Gap, Gap Kids, Banana Republic, and Old Navy Clothing. The Gap has recently significantly expanded the number of its Old Navy Clothing Co. Stores, retailers of casual basic clothing at a lower price point than the other Gap retail chains.

The Limited subsequently expanded its product line to include men's, women's, and children's apparel as well as personal care products. It operates stores under four brand groups: women's (Limited Stores, Express, Lerner New York, Lane Bryant, and Henri Bendel), intimate (Victoria's Secret, Bath & Body Works, Cacique), emerging (Structure, Limited Too, Galyan's Trading), and Abercrombie & Fitch. Its clothing products tend to be more glitzy than those of The Gap. The Limited gives the managers of each of its chains considerable freedom to make strategic and operating decisions.

Both firms source the majority of their products in East Asia, and price their purchases in U.S. dollars. Both firms locate the majority of their stores in shopping malls. The Gap grew the number of its stores 10.9 percent annually between Year 5 and Year 7, with much of the growth in non-mall locations. The average size of Old Navy Clothing Stores is approximately twice the square footage of other Gap stores. The Limited has adopted the strategy of locating stores from several of its chains in the same shopping mall. This strategy provides The Limited with bargaining power on lease terms and with possible economies of scale in transportation, information processing, and other support services. The Limited also offers some of its products through catalogs. The Limited increased the number of its stores 7.6 percent annually between Year 5 and Year 7. Both firms lease the space in their stores, primarily under operating lease arrangements.

The Gap relies on print promotions (that is, local newspapers) to stimulate demand and attract customers to its stores. The Limited relies more on in-store promotions, with two-for-one discounts and special daily price reductions.

Exhibit 3.39 presents selected data for The Gap and The Limited. Exhibits 3.40 through 3.42 present the financial statements of The Gap for Year 5 through Year 7, and Exhibits 3.43 through 3.45 present the financial statements for The Limited for these same years. These financial statements reflect the capitalization of lease commitments for store space. Exhibits 3.46 and 3.47 present segment data for each company.

Required

    a. Exhibits 3.48 and 3.49 present financial ratios for The Gap and The Limited for Year 5 and Year 6. Calculate these financial ratios for each company for their Year 7 fiscal years. The income tax rate is 35 percent.

    b. Assess the changes in the profitability and risk of The Gap during the three-year period, offering possible reasons for the changes observed.

    c. Repeat part b. for The Limited.

    d. Compare the profitability and risk of The Gap versus The Limited during the three-year period, suggesting possible reasons for the differences observed.

EXHIBIT 3.39

Selected Data for The GAP and The Limited
(Case 3.2)

	The GAP			The Limited		
	Year 5	Year 6	Year 7	Year 5	Year 6	Year 7
For the Year Ended January 31:						
Number of Stores	1,508	1,680	1,854	4,867	5,298	5,633
Total Square Footage (000s)	9,166	11,100	12,645	25,627	27,403	28,405
Sales per Ave. Square Foot	$444	$425	$441	$270	$272	$285
Fixed Assets per Square Foot	$283	$276	$268	$218	$213	$206
Sales per Employee (000s)	$68	$73	$80	$69	$76	$70
Total Sales Growth	13%	18%	20%	1%	8%	10%
Comparable Store Sales Growth	1%	0%	5%	(3%)	(2%)	2%

EXHIBIT 3.40

The GAP
Balance Sheets
(amounts in millions)
(Case 3.2)

	January 31			
	Year 4	Year 5	Year 6	Year 7
Assets				
Cash	$ 460	$ 414	$ 579	$ 485
Marketable Securities	84	174	90	136
Accounts Receivable	15	18	21	24
Inventories	331	371	483	579
Prepayments	66	79	107	105
Total Current Assets	$ 956	$1,056	$1,280	$ 1,329
Property, Plant, and Equipment				
(net)	2,464	2,592	3,065	3,390
Other Assets	66	119	105	162
Total Assets	$3,486	$ 3,767	$4,450	$ 4,881

(continued)

	January 31			
Exh. 3.40—Continued	Year 4	Year 5	Year 6	Year 7
Liabilities and Shareholders' Equity				
Accounts Payable	$ 214	$ 264	$ 283	$ 352
Short-Term Borrowing	8	2	22	40
Current Portion of Long-Term Debt	0	0	0	0
Other Current Liabilities	240	234	247	383
Total Current Liabilities	$ 462	$ 500	$ 552	$ 775
Long-Term Debt	1,798	1,763	2,107	2,254
Other Noncurrent Liabilities ...	99	129	151	197
Total Liabilities	$2,359	$2,392	$2,810	$ 3,226
Common Stock	$ 8	$ 8	$ 16	$ 16
Additional Paid-in Capital	240	298	335	442
Retained Earnings	971	1,220	1,511	1,886
Treasury Stock	(92)	(151)	(222)	(689)
Total Shareholders' Equity ...	$1,127	$1,375	$1,640	$ 1,655
Total Liabilities and Shareholders' Equity	$3,486	$3,768	$4,450	$ 4,881

EXHIBIT 3.41

The GAP
Income Statements
(amounts in millions)
(Case 3.2)

	For the Year Ended January 31		
	Year 5	Year 6	Year 7
Sales	$ 3,723	$ 4,395	$ 5,284
Other Revenues	12	15	20
Cost of Goods Sold	(2,210)	(2,680)	(3,074)
Selling and Administrative Expenses	(854)	(1,004)	(1,270)
Interest Expense	(142)	(141)	(211)
Income Tax Expense	(209)	(231)	(296)
Net Income	$ 320	$ 354	$ 453

EXHIBIT 3.42

The GAP
Statements of Cash Flows
(amounts in millions)
(Case 3.2)

	For the Year Ended January 31		
	Year 5	Year 6	Year 7
Operations			
Net Income	$ 320	$ 354	$ 453
Depreciation	168	197	215
Addbacks and Subtractions—Net	(5)	9	18
(Increase) Decrease in Accounts Receivable	(3)	(3)	(3)
(Increase) Decrease in Inventories	(40)	(113)	(94)
(Increase) Decrease in Prepayments	(8)	(12)	(13)
Increase (Decrease) in Accounts Payable	46	1	89
Increase (Decrease) in Other Current Liabilities . .	26	56	170
Cash Flow from Operations	$ 504	$ 489	$ 835
Investing			
Property, Plant, and Equipment Acquired	$(233)	$(302)	$(372)
Investments Sold (Acquired)	(122)	86	(52)
Other Investing Transactions	(5)	(7)	(12)
Cash Flow from Investing	$(360)	$(223)	$(436)
Financing			
Increase in Short-Term Borrowing	0	$ 21	$ 19
Increase in Long-Term Borrowing	0	0	0
Increase in Common Stock	$ 13	17	37
Decrease in Short-Term Borrowing	(4)	0	0
Decrease in Long-Term Borrowing	(75)	0	0
Decrease in Common Stock	(58)	(71)	(467)
Dividends	(66)	(67)	(84)
Other Financing Transactions	0	(1)	2
Cash Flow from Financing	$(190)	$(101)	$(493)
Change in Cash	$ (46)	$ 165	$ (94)
Cash—Beginning of Year	460	414	579
Cash—End of Year	$ 414	$ 579	$ 485

EXHIBIT 3.43

The Limited
Balance Sheets
(amounts in millions)
(Case 3.2)

	January 31			
	Year 4	Year 5	Year 6	Year 7
Assets				
Cash	$ 320	$ 242	$1,645	$ 312
Marketable Securities	0	0	0	0
Accounts Receivable	1,057	1,292	77[a]	69
Inventories	734	871	959	1,007
Prepayments	110	143	119	157
Total Current Assets	$2,221	$2,548	$2,800	$ 1,545
Property, Plant, and Equipment				
(net)	5,346	5,595	5,844	5,853
Other Assets	248	330	725	746
Total Assets	$7,815	$8,473	$9,369	$ 8,144
Liabilities and Shareholders' Equity				
Accounts Payable	$ 250	$ 275	$ 281	$ 308
Short-Term Borrowing	16	25	0	0
Current Portion of Long-Term				
Debt	0	0	0	0
Other Current Liabilities	441	497	435	599
Total Current Liabilities	$ 707	$ 797	$ 716	$ 907
Long-Term Debt	4,330	4,553	4,753	4,674
Other Noncurrent Liabilities . . .	336	361	654	573
Minority Interest in Subsidiary . .	0	0	45	67
Total Liabilities	$5,373	$5,711	$6,168	$ 6,221
Common Stock	$ 190	$ 190	$ 180	$ 180
Additional Paid-in Capital	129	133	137	143
Retained Earnings	2,397	2,717	3,200	3,526
Treasury Stock	(274)	(278)	(316)	(1,926)
Total Shareholders' Equity . . .	$2,442	$2,762	$3,201	$ 1,923
Total Liabilities and				
Shareholders' Equity	$7,815	$8,473	$9,369	$ 8,144

[a]The Limited sold a 60 percent interest in its previously wholly-owned credit card subsidiary to an investment firm during the last quarter of fiscal Year 6.

EXHIBIT 3.44

The Limited
Income Statements
(amounts in millions)
(Case 3.2)

	For the Year Ended January 31		
	Year 5	Year 6	Year 7
Sales	$ 7,321	$ 7,882	$ 8,645
Other Revenues	11	22	42
Cost of Goods Sold	(4,913)	(5,481)	(5,738)
Selling and Administrative Expenses	(1,315)	(1,475)	(1,849)
Interest Expense	(360)	(390)	(485)
Income Tax Expense	(296)	(223)	(241)
Minority Interest in Subsidiary	0	(22)	(46)
Net Income	$ 448	$ 313	$ 328

EXHIBIT 3.45

The Limited
Statements of Cash Flows
(amounts in millions)
(Case 3.2)

	For the Year Ended January 31		
	Year 5	Year 6	Year 7
Operations			
Net Income	$ 448	$ 313	$ 328
Depreciation	268	286	290
Addbacks and Subtractions—Net	0	15	22
(Increase) Decrease in Accounts Receivable	(235)	(104)	8
(Increase) Decrease in Inventories	(137)	(71)	(48)
(Increase) Decrease in Prepayments	(33)	25	38
Increase (Decrease) in Accounts Payable	25	6	27
Increase (Decrease) in Other Current Liabilities	25	(113)	47
Cash Flow from Operations	$ 361	$ 357	$ 712
Investing			
Property, Plant, and Equipment Acquired	$(320)	$ (374)	$ (410)
Investments Acquired	0	0	0
Other Investing Transactions	0	842	(41)
Cash Flow from Investing	$(320)	$ 468	$ (451)

(continued)

	For the Year Ended January 31		
Exh. 3.45—Continued	Year 5	Year 6	Year 7
Financing			
Increase in Short-Term Borrowing	$ 10	$ 250	$ 150
Increase in Long-Term Borrowing	0	0	0
Increase in Common Stock	12	801	129
Decrease in Short-Term Borrowing	0	(275)	(150)
Decrease in Long-Term Borrowing.	0	0	0
Decrease in Common Stock	(12)	(55)	(1,615)
Dividends	(129)	(143)	(108)
Other Financing Transactions	0	0	0
Cash Flow from Financing	$(119)	$ 578	$(1,594)
Change in Cash	$ (78)	$1,403	$(1,333)
Cash—Beginning of Year	320	242	1,645
Cash—End of Year.	$ 242	$1,645	$ 312

EXHIBIT 3.46

The GAP
Segment Data
(Case 3.2)

	Year 5	Year 6	Year 7
Number of Stores			
GAP	1,261	1,339	1,443
Banana Republic.	188	210	218
Old Navy Stores	59	131	193
Total	1,508	1,680	1,854
Square Footage (000s)			
GAP	not	not	8,445
Banana Republic.	disclosed	disclosed	1,300
Old Navy Stores			2,900
Total	9,166	11,100	12,645

EXHIBIT 3.47

The Limited
Segment Data
(Case 3.2)

	Year 5	Year 6	Year 7
Number of Stores			
Women's Brands..................	3,087	3,093	3,038
Emerging Brands	676	812	859
Intimate Brands	1,037	1,293	1,609
Abercrombie & Fitch	67	100	127
	4,867	5,298	5,633
Square Footage (000s)			
Women's Brands..................	19,247	19,235	18,780
Emerging Brands	2,420	3,146	3,572
Intimate Brands	3,419	4,230	5,047
Abercrombie & Fitch	541	792	1,006
	25,627	27,403	28,405
Sales per Square Foot			
Women's Brands..................	$ 224	$ 223	$ 225
Emerging Brands	$ 332	$ 288	$ 306
Intimate Brands	$ 486	$ 482	$ 494
Abercrombie & Fitch	$ 350	$ 354	$ 373
Percentage of Sales			
Women's Brands..................	59%	54%	49%
Emerging Brands	10	11	12
Intimate Brands	29	32	35
Abercrombie & Fitch	2	3	4
	100%	100%	100%
Percentage of Operating Income			
Women's Brands..................	31%	9%	10%
Emerging Brands	25	24	11
Intimate Brands	42	63	72
Abercrombie & Fitch	2	4	7
	100%	100%	100%

EXHIBIT 3.48			
The GAP Ratio Analysis (Case 3.2)			
	Year 5	**Year 6**	**Year 7**
Profit Margin for ROA	11.1%	10.1%	
Assets Turnover	1.0	1.1	
Rate of Return on Assets	11.4%	10.8%	
Common Earnings Leverage Ratio	77.6%	79.4%	
Capital Structure Leverage Ratio	2.9	2.7	
Rate of Return on Common Shareholders' Equity	25.6%	23.5%	
Cost of Goods Sold ÷ Sales	59.4%	61.0%	
Selling and Administrative Expense ÷ Sales	22.9%	22.8%	
Income Tax Expense ÷ Sales[a]	6.9%	6.4%	
Accounts Receivable Turnover	225.6	225.4	
Inventory Turnover	6.3	6.3	
Plant Asset Turnover	1.5	1.6	
Current Ratio	2.1	2.3	
Quick Ratio	1.2	1.3	
Cash Flow from Operations ÷ Current Liabilities	104.8%	93.0%	
Days Accounts Receivable	2	2	
Days Inventory	58	58	
Days Accounts Payable	39	36	
Long-Term Debt Ratio	56.2%	56.2%	
Debt-Equity Ratio	128.2%	128.5%	
Cash Flow from Operations ÷ Total Liabilities	21.2%	18.8%	
Interest Coverage Ratio	4.7	5.2	
Cash Flow from Operations Capital Expenditures	2.2	1.6	

[a]Excluding tax effects of interest expense.

EXHIBIT 3.49

The Limited
Ratio Analysis
(Case 3.2)

	Year 5	Year 6	Year 7
Profit Margin for ROA.	9.3%	7.5%	
Assets Turnover.	.9	.9	
Rate of Return on Assets	8.4%	6.6%	
Common Earnings Leverage Ratio.	65.7%	53.2%	
Capital Structure Leverage Ratio.	3.1	3.0	
Rate of Return on Common Shareholders'			
Equity	17.2%	10.5%	
Cost of Goods Sold ÷ Sales.	67.1%	69.5%	
Selling and Administrative Expense ÷ Sales	18.0%	18.7%	
Income Tax Expense ÷ Sales[a]	5.8%	4.6%	
Accounts Receivable Turnover.	6.2	11.5	
Inventory Turnover	6.1	6.0	
Plant Asset Turnover	1.3	1.4	
Current Ratio	3.2	3.9	
Quick Ratio.	1.9	2.4	
Cash Flow from Operations ÷ Current			
Liabilities.	48.0%	47.2%	
Days Accounts Receivable	59	32	
Days Inventory.	60	61	
Days Accounts Payable	19	18	
Long-Term Debt Ratio.	62.2%	59.8%	
Debt-Equity Ratio	164.8%	148.5%	
Cash Flow from Operations Total ÷ Liabilities . . .	6.5%	6.0%	
Interest Coverage Ratio	3.1	2.4	
Cash Flow from Operations ÷ Capital			
Expenditures	1.1	1.0	

[a]Excluding tax effects of interest expense.

PART II

IMPACT OF GENERALLY ACCEPTED ACCOUNTING PRINCIPLES ON PROFITABILITY AND RISK ANALYSIS

FINANCIAL STATEMENT ANALYSIS

1. Identify Economic Characteristics

2. Identify Company Strategies

3. Understand and Cleanse the Financial Statements

4. Analyze Profitability and Risk

5. Value the Firm

Part II emphasizes the third step in the five interrelated sequential steps in financial statement analysis. Effective analysis of financial statements requires a close scrutiny of how the statements are prepared. This entails obtaining both a thorough understanding of how the financial statements are constructed and, in some cases, cleansing the statements for comparability and management biases.

Generally accepted accounting principles, or GAAP, stipulate the manner in which firms measure financial position, earnings, and cash flows. GAAP, however, provides firms with considerable flexibility in choosing and applying their accounting methods. Firms may have incentives to report as favorable a picture as possible of their profitability or risk. The financial analyst must be alert to intentional actions taken by management to portray the firm in a favorable light.

Part II, Chapters 4 to 7, describe and illustrate important choices firms must make in preparing their financial statements and the impact of their choices on the quality of earnings and financial position. These chapters also discuss adjustments that the analyst might make to cleanse reported data of reporting games played by management. Part II examines the following:

CHAPTER 4 RELEVANT FINANCIAL STATEMENT DATA FOR ANALYSIS

Concept of the Quality of Earnings; Reporting Recurring and Nonrecurring Income Items; Restating Accounting Data; Alternative Accounting Principles across Countries.

CHAPTER 5 GENERALLY ACCEPTED ACCOUNTING PRINCIPLES: INCOME RECOGNITION AND ASSET VALUATION

Revenue Recognition; Inventory and Cost of Goods Sold; Fixed Assets and Depreciation; Intangible Assets and Amortization; Changing Prices.

CHAPTER 6 GENERALLY ACCEPTED ACCOUNTING PRINCIPLES: LIABILITY RECOGNITION AND RELATED EXPENSES

Off-Balance Sheet Financing; Leases, Pensions and Other Retirement Benefits; Income Taxes; Reserves.

CHAPTER 7 GENERALLY ACCEPTED ACCOUNTING PRINCIPLES: INTERCORPORATE ENTITIES

Corporate Acquisitions; Intercorporate Investments in Securities; Foreign Currency Translation; Segment Reporting

CHAPTER 4

RELEVANT FINANCIAL STATEMENT DATA FOR ANALYSIS

Learning Objectives

1. Understand the importance of working with comparable financial statement data both across time and across firms so that the analyst can identify economic, strategic, and other important differences.
2. Review reasons why financial data may not be comparable, stressing that analysts must often adjust raw financial statement information before using it in analysis.
3. Develop an understanding of the concept of "earnings quality," with emphasis on the sustainability, measurement, and manageability of reported earnings.
4. Master the ability to decide when and how to adjust reported income in order to use it as a component for predicting future earnings of a firm.
5. Obtain an overview of differences in reporting systems across major industrialized countries, and highlight comparability concerns unique to the worldwide reporting environment.

In Chapters 8 and 9 we expand upon the framework provided in Chapter 3 for analyzing financial statements. That more comprehensive discussion of financial analysis, however, requires first a thorough understanding of (1) the data issues that analysts must consider in order to conduct effective financial analysis, and (2) the accounting principles and procedures that a firm uses in preparing its financial statements. This chapter explores that first component: issues having to do with the data from financial statements that are appropriate inputs to financial analysis. Chapters 5 through 7 then describe the more important accounting principles and procedures that a financial analyst is likely to encounter.

THE RAW DATA OF FINANCIAL STATEMENTS

For many reasons that will be discussed in this chapter, the *raw* financial statement data a firm reports often differ from the data used to calculate the ratios discussed in Chapter 3, and from the information used for performing other types of financial analysis. Adjustments to the information are necessary because the raw data often are not comparable across time and across firms. The goal is to achieve comparability in the data to the extent possible so that the analyst can identify economic, strategic, and other importance differences.

Data that are not comparable can hinder the effectiveness of both time series and cross-sectional analyses. Time series analysis is the comparison of an individual firm's financial data over several time periods. Cross-sectional analysis is the comparison of two or more firms' financial data in the same time period and/or across time periods. Financial data may not be comparable for a variety of reasons:

1. The sustainability, measurement, or manageability of the reported earnings number keep it from reflecting economic value-added of a firm.[1]
2. Financial statements of previous years are restated in the current year.
3. Financial statement items are classified in different ways across firms.
4. Financial statements are prepared for different time periods across firms.
5. Financial reporting systems employed for measuring and reporting financial data for firms headquartered in different countries may differ because of different accounting principles in those countries.

---

[1]Beginning with annual reports released in 1999, financial reporting requires firms to disclose an additional income figure that the FASB labels *comprehensive income* (Financial Accounting Standards Board, *Statement of Financial Accounting Standards No. 130,* "Reporting Comprehensive Income," 1997). Comprehensive income is reported earnings (net income as reported on the income statement) plus direct charges and credits to shareholders' equity that bypass the income statement but that are related to operating activities of a firm. Examples of such charges and credits include foreign currency translation adjustments and gains and losses on securities classified as available for sale (both discussed in Chapter 7). Although firms have the option of reporting these direct charges and credits below net income on their income statements, most firms will likely continue to report them in a revised and expanded Statement of Changes in Shareholders' Equity (that is, not as adjustments to net income on their Statements of Income). In this book, the term "reported earnings" denotes net income exclusive of any of these direct charges and credits to shareholders' equity. Most analysts define reported earnings in this way as well because (1) comprehensive income is a relatively new disclosure requirement, (2) the difference between reported earnings and comprehensive income is small for most companies (Coke's comprehensive income for Years 5 through 7 differs on average by only 5 percent from reported earnings), and (3) most valuation models incorporate reported earnings exclusive of these income-related charges or credits to shareholders' equity.

Of these five categories, adjusting for the first and the last is the most difficult and calls for the most judgment on the part of the analyst. Many of these comparability concerns are of course not unique to the reporting system in the United States. We discuss reporting systems employed outside the United States in order to highlight comparability concerns unique to the worldwide reporting environment.

We discuss each of these five reasons financial statement data may lack comparability and illustrate the way to adjust financial data to achieve comparability. Additional illustrations are provided throughout the remainder of the book.

REPORTED EARNINGS AND ECONOMIC VALUE-ADDED

Net income (or reported earnings) serves as (1) a measure of the past and current operating profitability of a firm, and (2) a principal variable in valuing a firm's common stock. In Chapter 3 we illustrated the analysis of profitability using ROA, profit margin, ROCE, and other financial statement ratios based on earnings. Chapter 12 discusses the use of earnings multiples for making judgments about the appropriate price of a firm's common stock. Underlying the use of reported earnings for these purposes is the assumption that it represents a reasonably accurate measure of the economic value-added by a firm during a particular reporting period and the economic value likely to be added in future periods.[2]

If earnings do not capture economic value-added in one or more reporting periods, then economic significance and comparability are lacking across time for any particular firm, and probably across firms as well. The difficult issue is determining when the link is missing between reported earnings and economic value-added.

A connection between reported earnings and economic value-added may be missing for any of a variety of reasons:

1. Inclusion in reported earnings of revenues, expenses, gains, and losses not expected to recur in the future (the "sustainable earnings" issue).
2. Inadequacy of accounting systems to measure the economic value-added by a firm's operating activities accurately and reliably during a reporting period (the "earnings measurement" issue).[3]
3. The opportunity for management to manage, or perhaps manipulate, the level or trend of reported earnings to its advantage (the "earnings management" issue).

Assessing reported earnings for the presence of one or more of these concerns is often referred to as evaluating the "quality of earnings." Similar concerns are used

---

[2]Given the articulation between the income statement and the balance sheet, any discussion of reported earnings and economic value-added leads inevitably to a consideration of assets and liabilities and their economic value-added as well. The discussion here, however, emphasizes reported earnings and economic value-added because, between the income statement and balance sheet, the income statement is the primary focus of most analysis.

[3]For a discussion of this point in the context of financial statement limitations, see Paul R. Brown, "The Substance of Financial Statements," *Journal of Financial Statement Analysis,* Fall 1995, pp. 83–86.

EXHIBIT 4.1

Elements of Earnings Quality

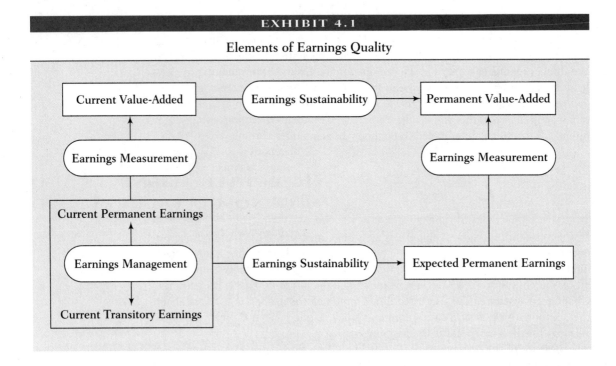

to judge the "quality of financial position," although this term is used much less than quality of earnings.[4]

Exhibit 4.1 depicts these three dimensions to earnings quality. Two additional concepts are introduced in Exhibit 4.1 as well—permanent and transitory earnings. Permanent earnings are defined as those that a firm can sustain over time; transitory earnings are those generated by "one-shot," "one-time," or nonrecurring events. These terms relate to both the sustainability and manageability of reporting earnings.[5]

The reported earnings number is important when it both accurately measures current economic value-added and is a good predictor of the economic value likely to be added in the future. As Exhibit 4.1 depicts, it is necessary to assess the sustainability of reported earnings (that is, assess whether there is economic value-

---

[4]For example, when American Online decided to write off almost $400 million in deferred subscriber acquisition costs, the effect was to eliminate a previously reported asset from the balance sheet. Prior to the writeoff, America Online capitalized subscriber marketing costs and amortized them over 24 months, rather than expensing them immediately. Some analysts argue that America Online's "quality of financial position" improved as a result of this decision. In analyst's parlance, it is labeled "cleaning up the balance sheet," that is, removing assets from the balance sheet that have questionable future value.

[5]Although practitioners use the terms "transitory" and "permanent" earnings infrequently, the terms are used extensively by accounting researchers. For example, a discussion of their use in the context of sales growth and order backlog can be found in Chi-Chun Liu, Joshua Livnat, and Stephen G. Ryan, "Forward-Looking Financial Information: The Order Backlog as a Predictor of Future Sales," *Journal of Financial Statement Analysis*, Fall 1996, pp. 89–99. Our discussion of earnings-based valuation approaches in Chapter 12 also addresses the importance of assessing whether current earnings include a transitory component.

added captured in current earnings) before concluding that it is relevant for predicting future value-added. If reported earnings are deemed sustainable, then the odds are high that reported earnings are a good predictor of expected permanent earnings. Alternatively, if reported earnings capture events that are not expected to recur in the future, then the measure is a poor predictor of expected permanent earnings.

Exhibit 4.1 also points out that assessing whether reported earnings is a relevant input for predicting future value-added depends on whether earnings are managed. If corporate officials can manage the levels or trends of reported earnings in any significant way, it is not unlikely that some transitory earnings are embedded in the reported number. The task for the analyst is to puzzle out current permanent earnings from the earnings reported as a result of management's tendency to present operations in the most favorable light. This is difficult because there are a number of different motivations that prompt managers to choose one or another reporting strategy to manipulate earnings.

Finally, Exhibit 4.1 shows that the ability to *measure* economic value-added accurately and reliably is an essential dimension to judging earnings quality. Both current value-added and permanent value-added are affected by the ability of financial reporting systems to capture a firm's activities in a meaningful way.

EARNINGS SUSTAINABILITY

Whether the reported earnings measure is a good predictor of future sustainable earnings depends on many factors. The overriding concern is the recurring nature, or permanent nature, of the amount reported. Making an assessment of this sort calls for a considerable amount of judgment. It requires the analyst to have knowledge about the industry, about the practices of the particular firm under scrutiny, and about the relevant financial disclosures.

Fortunately, financial reporting often requires firms to provide specific disclosures in certain areas that help analysts to judge the sustainability of earnings—although adjusting the financial data even using these disclosures to achieve comparability is not always easy. Financial disclosures in eight specific categories are prime candidates for judging the sustainability of current earnings:

1. Discontinued operations.
2. Extraordinary gains and losses.
3. Changes in accounting principles.
4. Impairment losses on long-lived assets.
5. Restructuring charges.
6. Changes in estimates.
7. Gains and losses from peripheral activities.
8. Management's analysis of operations.

Of these eight categories, financial disclosures related to the first four are the most comprehensive and consistent across firms because the FASB has issued specific pronouncements on the topics. We discuss disclosure and adjustment issues related to each of these categories in turn.

DISCONTINUED OPERATIONS

When a firm decides to exit a particular segment of its business, it classifies that business as a *discontinued business*. Financial reporting stipulates that a discontinued business must be separable, or distinguishable, both physically and operationally.[6] That is, a firm must be able to identify the particular assets of the discontinued business and the discontinued business must not be integrated operationally with ongoing businesses.

The degree to which a particular divested business is operationally integrated with ongoing businesses will likely vary across firms depending on their organizational structures and operating policies. Thus, the gain or loss from the sale of a business might appear in income from continued operations for one firm (that is, the divested business is operationally integrated) and in discontinued operations for another firm (that is, the divested business is not operationally integrated).

Two dates are important in measuring the income effects of discontinued operations. The *measurement date* is the date on which a firm commits itself to a formal plan to dispose of a segment. The *disposal date* is the date of closing the sale, if the firm intends to sell the segment, or the date that operations cease, if the firm intends to abandon the segment.

A firm reports net income or loss of the discontinued segment prior to the measurement date as a separate item in the discontinued operations section of the income statement. Firms report the gain or loss net of tax effects in a section of the income statement often labeled, "Income, Gains, and Loss from Discontinued Operations." Most U.S. firms include three years of income statement information in their income statements. A firm that decides during the current year to divest a business will include the net income or loss of this business in discontinued operations not only for the current year but also in comparative income statements for the preceding two years, even though the firm had previously reported the latter income in continuing operations in the income statements originally prepared for those two years.

At the measurement date, the firm estimates (1) the net income or loss it expects the discontinued business to generate between the measurement date and the disposal date, and (2) the gain or loss it expects from the sale or abandonment of the segment. The firm then nets these two amounts. If the net amount is an estimated *loss*, the firm recognizes the loss in the year that includes the measurement date. It simultaneously increases an account, Estimated Losses from Discontinued Operations, which appears among liabilities on the balance sheet. Realized losses (or gains) subsequent to the measurement date from either (1) or (2) above reduce (increase) this account instead of appearing in the income statements of those years.

---

[6]Accounting Principles Board, *Opinion No. 30*, "Reporting the Results of Operations," 1973.

If the amount from netting (1) and (2) above is a *gain,* the firm recognizes the income and gains only when realized in subsequent years. These provisions rest on the conservatism convention of recognizing losses as soon as they become evident but postponing the recognition of gains until realization occurs.

Example 1. Recently, Harley-Davidson decided to discontinue the "Transportation Vehicles" segment of its operations. The company wants to concentrate on its core motorcycle business rather than the recreational vehicles, commercial vehicles, and other products that constituted this segment. Harley-Davidson received $105 million from the sale of this segment, approximately $100 million of it in cash and $5 million in notes and preferred stock.

Exhibit 4.2 presents the disclosures provided by Harley-Davidson. The company shows in its income statement (1) the gain on the disposition of the segment in Year 6, and (2) the income from operations of the segment in both Year 4 and Year 5. Note that the income statement reports all amounts net of applicable income taxes.

EXHIBIT 4.2

Harley-Davidson, Inc.
Consolidated Statement of Operations
and Notes to Consolidated Financial Statements
(in thousands)

	Year 4	Year 5	Year 6
Income from continuing operations	$ 96,221	$111,050	$143,409
Discontinued operations:			
Income from operations, net of applicable income taxes	$ 8,051	$ 1,430	$ —
Gain on disposition of discontinued operations, net of applicable income taxes			$ 22,619
Net Income	$104,272	$112,480	$166,028

Notes to Consolidation Financial Statements:

On January 22, Year 6, the Company announced its strategic decision to discontinue the operations of the Transportation Vehicles segment in order to concentrate its financial and human resources on its core motorcycle business. The condensed statement of operations related to the discontinued operations is presented below:

(in thousands) Years ended December 31,	Year 4	Year 5
Net sales	$382,805	$443,950
Costs and expenses	377,176	441,388
Income before income taxes	$ 5,629	$ 2,562
Provision (benefit) for income taxes	(2,422)	1,132
Net Income	$ 8,051	$ 1,430

Exhibit 4.2 also presents the note disclosure provided by Harley-Davidson. The note details the components of the income reported in both Year 4 and Year 5. The income amounts reported in the note for each year, $8,051 (Year 4) and $1,430 (Year 5), correspond to the amounts reported in the income statement.

Example 2.   Black & Decker currently operates in two business segments: Consumer and Home Improvement Products, and Commercial and Industrial Products. In Year 9, the company sold the last remaining operating unit of a former segment—Information Technology and Services—for $425.0 million. Black & Decker's income statement reported earnings from this segment of $37.5 million for Year 6, $38.4 million for Year 7, and $70.4 million for Year 8.

Note 2 of Black & Decker's annual report provides more disclosures on the decision to discontinue operations in the Information Technology and Services segment. Exhibit 4.3 provides excerpts from that note. Unlike Harley-Davidson, Black & Decker reports the earnings and the gain on the sale of the segment as a combined number on the income statement.

The analyst must decide whether to include or exclude income from discontinued operations when estimating sustainable earnings and assessing profitability.

EXHIBIT 4.3

Black & Decker Corporation
Note 2: Discontinued Operations

Earnings from the discontinued Information Technology and Services segment amounted to $37.5 million in Year 6, $38.4 million in Year 7, and $70.4 million in Year 8, net of applicable income taxes of $4.0 million, $8.7 million, and $55.6 million, respectively. The results of the discontinued segment do not reflect any expense for interest allocated by or management fees charged by the Corporation.

On February 16, Year 8, the Corporation completed the sale of the last business in the discontinued segment, for $425.0 million. Earnings from discontinued operations in Year 8 consisted primarily of the gain on the sale of this business, net of selling expenses and applicable income taxes. Revenue and operating income of the business for the period from January 1, Year 8, through the date of sale were not significant. The terms of the sale of the business provided for an adjustment to the sales price, expected to be finalized in Year 9, based upon the changes in the net assets of the segment through February 16, Year 8.

The Corporation sold two businesses in Year 7 for proceeds of $60.0 million and $35.5 million, respectively. The aggregate gain on the sale of $2.5 million, net of applicable taxes of $5.5 million, is included in earnings from discontinued operations for Year 7.

Revenue of the discontinued segment were $883.1 million in Year 6 and $800.1 million in Year 7. These revenues are not included in sales as reported in the Consolidated Statement of Earnings.

Net assets of the discontinued segment as of December 31, Year 7, consisted principally of accounts receivable, goodwill, and other assets less accounts payable and other liabilities.

Using the concepts introduced in Exhibit 4.1, the analyst must assess whether income from discontinued operations can be sustained in the future, or whether it is transitory in nature.

The corporate strategy of some firms is to buy and sell businesses continuously. For such firms, income from discontinued operations is an ongoing source of profitability, and the analyst might decide to include this income in assessments of profitability. For most firms, however, income from discontinued operations represents a nonrecurring source of earnings. Remember that the definition of a discontinued operation assumes a firm is exiting from a major area of business, rather than divesting a portion of an ongoing business, such as a plant or a geographic division. Most firms do not change the major areas of business they are involved in often enough that the market can justify considering income from discontinued operations as a recurring source of profitability.

A second argument for excluding income from discontinued operations relates to its measurement. Recall that at the measurement date, the firm estimates (1) the net income or loss it expects the discontinued business to generate between the measurement date and the disposal date, and (2) the gain or loss it expects from the sale or abandonment of the segment. The amount the firm reports as income from discontinued operations for a particular year may represent either an estimated amount applicable to the current and future years, if the netting of (1) and (2) above at the measurement date is an estimated loss, or an actual, or realized, amount applicable to the current year only if the netting of (1) and (2) above at the measurement date is an estimated gain. These measurement and reporting procedures cloud the interpretation of the time series behavior of income from discontinued operations.

Thus, in most cases the analyst should exclude income from discontinued operations in order to estimate sustainable earnings. Then, in order to achieve consistency with the income statement, the analyst should eliminate the assets of the discontinued operations from the total assets. Some firms disclose the net assets of discontinued businesses on a separate line in the balance sheet. It is easy in this case for the analyst to achieve consistency by excluding these net assets from the balance sheets. Many firms, however, do not disclose these assets separately.

Cash flow from operations in the statement of cash flows includes the cash flows related to operating, as opposed to selling, a discontinued business. Consistency with the income statement suggests eliminating this source of operating cash flows if firms disclose the necessary information. The proceeds from the sale of a discontinued business appear as an investing activity. The analyst can either eliminate or deemphasize this source of cash when assessing the ongoing cash generating ability of a firm.

The analyst will likely encounter difficulties preparing an articulated set of financial statements that fully exclude discontinued operations. The desirable approach is to exclude the effects of discontinued operations to the extent that firms provide the necessary information, but keep the lack of articulation in mind when making interpretations.

EXTRAORDINARY ITEMS

The income statement can include extraordinary gains and losses. An income item classified as extraordinary must meet all three of certain criteria. It must be:[7]

1. Unusual in nature.
2. Infrequent in occurrence.
3. Material in amount.

A firm applies these criteria as they relate to its own operations and to similar firms in the same industry, taking into consideration the environment in which the entities operate. Thus, an item might be extraordinary for some firms but not for others.

Income items that meet all three of these criteria are rarely found in corporate annual reports in the United States. The most frequently encountered item classified as "extraordinary" is a gain or loss on the retirement of debt prior to maturity. As interest rates fluctuate, it is not unusual for a firm to issue new debt and use the proceeds to retire its old debt prior to maturity. Firms may not engage in such a transaction every year, but they often do so on a recurring basis. Thus, this item does not appear to satisfy the criteria for an extraordinary item.

Accounting policymakers, however, want to alert the user of financial statements to the existence of these gains and losses.[8] Including them among extraordinary items instead of in income from continuing operations increases the likelihood that they will not be overlooked.

Example 3. Black & Decker, in addition to reporting income from discontinued operations of $38.4 million in Year 7 (Exhibit 4.3), reports a loss from early extinguishment of debt for the same year. The income statement for the company reveals the following (in millions):

	Year 7
Earnings before extraordinary item	$254.9
Extraordinary loss from early extinguishment of debt (net of income tax benefit of $2.6)	(30.9)
Net earnings	$224.0

The question for the analyst is whether to include or exclude gains and losses from early retirement of debt when estimating sustainable earnings and assessing

---

[7]Ibid.

[8]Financial Accounting Standards Board, *Statement of Financial Accounting Standards No. 4,* "Reporting Gains and Losses from Extinguishment of Debt," 1975.

profitability. The answer depends on whether these gains and losses are recurring or nonrecurring for a particular firm. A firm that reports such gains in, say, two out of three years will likely continue to engage in early debt retirements. In this case, the analyst might consider including such gains and losses in earnings when assessing profitability. On the other hand, a firm that reports such items in, say, one out of five years will not likely engage in early debt retirements on a recurring basis.

In the case of Black & Decker, the analyst probably should exclude the extraordinary loss on the extinguishment of debt because Year 7 is the only year in the last three that the company reported such a gain or loss. The cash outflow to retire debt appears as a financing transaction on the statement of cash flows. The operations section of the statement of cash flows will show an addback (subtraction) for an extraordinary loss (gain) that does not use operating cash flows.

CHANGES IN ACCOUNTING PRINCIPLES

Changes in accounting principles are highlighted as a separate line item on the income statement. Firms may voluntarily change their accounting principles. They might shift, for example, from a first-in, first-out (FIFO) to a last-in, first-out (LIFO) cost flow assumption for inventories, or from an accelerated depreciation method to the straight-line depreciation method. More frequently, new FASB pronouncements will mandate a change in accounting principles. For example, a spate of pronouncements by the FASB in the early 1990s required the reporting of changes in accounting principles for health care benefits for retired employees,[9] income taxes,[10] and postemployment benefits.[11]

Firms that change their accounting principles must calculate, as of the *beginning* of the year of the change, the cumulative difference between net income under the accounting principle used previously and net income under the new accounting principle. The firm reports this cumulative difference (net of taxes) in a separate section of the income statement.[12]

Example 4. For many companies, the cumulative effect of the mandated accounting change for health care benefits for retired employers (*Statement No. 106*) results in especially large charges on the income statement. Exhibit 4.4 illustrates the case for Ford in Year 12.

The $7.5 billion charge related to *Statement No. 106* represents the obligation (net of taxes) as of the beginning of Year 12 to provide health care benefits to employees during retirement. Prior to *Statement No. 106*, firms recognized an expense

---

[9]Financial Accounting Standards Board, *Statement of Financial Accounting Standards No. 106*, "Employers' Accounting for Postretirement Benefits Other Than Pensions," 1990.

[10]Financial Accounting Standards Board, *Statement of Financial Accounting Standards No. 109*, "Accounting or Income Taxes," 1992.

[11]Financial Accounting Standards Board, *Statement of Financial Accounting Standards No. 112*, "Employers' Accounting for Postemployment Benefits," 1992.

[12]Accounting Principles Board, *Opinion No. 20*, "Accounting Changes," 1971.

EXHIBIT 4.4			
Ford Motor Company **Consolidated Statement of Earnings** **(in millions)**			
Ford	**Year 10**	**Year 11**	**Year 12**
Income from Continuing Operations	$860.1	$(2,258.0)	$ (501.8)
Cumulative Effect of Changes in Accounting Principles:			
Adoption of FASB Statement No. 106 .	—	—	(7,540.2)
Adoption of FASB Statement No. 109 .	—	—	657.0
Net Income (loss)	$860.1	$(2,258.0)	$(7,385.0)

each year as they paid health insurance premiums on behalf of retired employees, a so-called pay as you go system. *Statement No. 106,* however, requires firms to recognize an expense each year *during the employees' working years* for a portion of the present value of the health insurance premiums expected to be paid during the employees' retirement years.

The adoption of *Statement No. 106* results in an immediate obligation for health care benefits already earned by employees but not previously recognized as either an expense or a liability by the employer. This reporting standard gives firms the option of either recognizing the full amount of the health care obligation immediately, as Ford did, or recognizing it piecemeal over the remaining working lives of employees.[13]

The case for excluding the effect of adopting *Statement No. 106*—and the effects of similar mandated accounting changes—from net income in the year of adoption relies on several conditions: (1) the charge comes about because the firm did not recognize health care benefits expenses in prior years; one might thus view the charge as a correction of cumulative misstatements of previously reported expenses; (2) a charge of this magnitude is nonrecurring; and (3) the amount of the obligation and the timing of its recognition will vary across firms, depending on the reporting option selected.

In Ford's case, excluding the charge from net income in the year of adoption but allowing it to flow through to retained earnings results in (1) a reduction in retained earnings and (2) a recognition of an unfunded health care obligation and a deferred tax asset on the balance sheet at the beginning of the year of

---

[13]A examination of the motivation for firms' decisions to recognize the full amount of the obligation immediately or recognizing it piecemeal over the remaining working lives of employees can be found in Eli Amir and Joshua Livnat, "Adoption Choices of SFAS No. 106: Implications for Financial Analysis," *Journal of Financial Statement Analaysis,* Winter 1997, pp. 51–60. The authors also examine the effect of the different implementation methods on the financial statements.

adoption. The amounts taken from Ford's financial statements are as follows (in millions):

Health Care Benefits Liability	$12,040
Deferred Tax Asset Related to Above	(4,500)
Cumulative Effect of Change in Accounting Principle	$ 7,540

The analyst obtains a consistent comparative balance sheet at the beginning and the end of the year of adoption of *Statement No. 106* by reflecting this obligation on the balance sheet as of the end of the year preceding the year of adoption (that is, Year 11 for Ford). The journal entry to reflect this health care obligation on Ford's balance sheet at the end of Year 11 is:

December 31, Year 11

Deferred Tax Asset	$4,500	
Retained Earnings	7,540	
Health Care Liabilities		12,040

The debit of $7,540 million to retained earnings reflects the cumulative reduction in retained earnings that would have occurred if Ford had applied *Statement No. 106* in all years prior to Year 12.

Income from continuing operations for Year 12 will include an expense for the increase in the present value of the health care benefits obligation as a result of employees working an additional year and perhaps generating increased health care benefits. The amount reported in the notes to Ford's financial statements for Year 12 is $723 million pretax and $455 million after taxes. Charges of this nature will continue in future years as employees render services, so including the $455 million after-tax amount in income related to continuing operations seems appropriate.

The inclusion of the $455 million expense in net income for Year 12 creates an inconsistency with prior years, however. The analyst needs to know the expense *actually* recognized on a pay-as-you-go basis in each prior year analyzed compared to the amount that the firm would have recognized if it had applied *Statement No. 106* each year. Firms do not disclose this information.

Thus, the adjustment for adoption of *Statement No. 106* involves: (1) eliminating the cumulative effect of the change in accounting principles from net income in the year of adoption, and (2) reflecting the health care benefits obligation on the balance sheet at the end of the year preceding the year of adoption. The analyst should consider the effects of omitting the health care obligation from financial statements of earlier years when making interpretations of profitability and risk ratios.

Exhibit 4.4. also reports a mandated accounting change for Ford related to income taxes. The rationale for excluding the effect of this change from income and for adjusting the financial statements is the same as for recognition of health care benefits.

Example 5.   Prior to Year 5, Fruit of the Loom deferred preoperating costs associated with the start-up of significant new productions facilities and amortized these costs over three years. Then, on January 1, Year 5, the company recorded the cumulative effect of a change in accounting principle when it decided to expense preoperating costs as incurred. According to Fruit of the Loom, the reason for changing is conservatism.

The income statement for Year 5 of Fruit of the Loom includes the following (in thousands):

Cumulative effect of change in accounting for preoperating costs	$(5,200)

The note addressing this change indicates that the $5,200 is an after-tax charge, and that the effect of the change is not material to the reported results of operations for Year 5 or Year 4.

Although the charge is relatively small when compared to Fruit of the Loom's Year 5 earnings before the charge, the analyst would make financial statement adjustments similar to those described above for Ford.

Example 6.   Knight-Ridder is a communications company engaged in newspaper publishing, news and information services, electronic retrieval services, and graphic and photo services. Approximately 65 percent of its revenues are generated from newspaper advertising.

Knight-Ridder is headquartered in Miami, and recently pledged land it owns to the city for the location of a new arts center. The firm made the pledge in Year 8, although the actual transfer of the land will take place some time in the future. Knight-Ridder's income statement for Year 8 includes the following (in thousands):

Cumulative effect of change in accounting principle for contributions . . .	$(7,320)

The charge is necessary because financial reporting requires that firms recognize unconditional promises, including multiyear promises such as land pledges, as expenses in the year the promise is made.[14] Knight-Ridder reports that the $7.3 million charge is net of tax effects.

Summary of Adjustments for Changes in Accounting Principles.   The FASB continues to issue new reporting standards that require recog-

---

[14]Financial Accounting Standards Board, *Statement of Financial Accounting Standards No. 116,* "Accounting for Contributions Received and Contributions Made," 1993. Prior to *Statement No. 116,* firms recorded "contribution promises made" as expenses in the year firms made good on the promises, which might not have been the same year that the promises were made.

nition on the income statement as a change in accounting principle.[15] Firms periodically change reporting principles on a voluntary basis as well. Analysts need to examine carefully any voluntary changes that firms make in accounting principles. Such changes may reflect management's attempts to manage earnings upward or downward to accomplish some particular purpose and may therefore signal something regarding management's expectations about the future. (This issue of earnings management is discussed in depth later in the chapter.)

The nature of any adjustments depends on the particular reporting item but follows the general procedures discussed in the health care benefit example above.

IMPAIRMENT LOSSES ON LONG-LIVED ASSETS

When a firm acquires assets such as property, plant, and equipment, or intangible assets, we naturally assume and the firm assumes that future benefits will accrue to it through the use of those assets. This is not always the case, however. The development of new technologies by competitors, changes in government regulations, changes in demographic trends, and other factors external to a firm may all reduce the future benefits originally anticipated from particular assets. Financial reporting requires firms to assess whether the carrying amounts of long-lived assets are recoverable, and, if they are not, to writedown the assets to their market values and recognize an impairment loss in income from continuing operations.[16]

It is impractical to expect firms to evaluate every asset each reporting period, so financial reporting requires testing for asset impairment only when events or circumstances indicate that the carrying amounts of assets may be not recovered. Nurnberg and Dittmar suggest particular events or circumstances as examples that may signal recoverability problems:

1. A significant decrease in the market value of an asset.
2. A significant change in the extent or manner in which an asset is used, or a significant physical change in an asset.

---

[15]The FASB also issues new standards periodically that require changes in reporting *disclosures* but do not involve numerical recognition in any of the three principal financial statements. The rules for reporting a change in accounting principle do not apply to this type of new standard. For example, *Statement of Financial Accounting Standards No. 123,* "Accounting for Stock-Based Compensation" (1995), requires firms to *disclose* the economic sacrifice or cost to the firms of giving employees the right to purchase shares of stock at a price less than the market price for the same stock. Interestingly, the FASB originally proposed to require firms to record this cost as compensation expense on the income statement, but the business community lobbied various congressional interests and others so vigorously that the FASB withdrew the proposal.

Appendix A illustrates Coke's compliance with *Statement No. 123.* Note 11 of the annual report reports that had compensation cost for its various stock options plans been determined according to the fair value at the grant date for awards under the plan, the firm's net income and net income per share would have been reduced. The note reports pro forma net income and net income per share amounts.

[16]Financial Accounting Standards Board, *Statement of Financial Accounting Standards No. 121,* "Accounting for the Impairment of Long-Lived Assets and for Long-Lived Assets to be Disposed of," 1995.

3. A significant adverse change in legal factors or in the business climate that affects the value of an asset, or an adverse action or assessment by a regulator.
4. An accumulation of costs significantly in excess of the amount originally anticipated to acquire or construct an asset.
5. A current-period operating or cash flow loss combined with a history of operating or cash flow losses, or a projection or forecast that demonstrates continuing losses associated with an asset used for the purpose of producing revenue.
6. Insufficient rental demand for a rental project currently under construction.
7. Writedowns by competitors and other industry leaders.[17]

What is particularly noteworthy about this list (and about *Statement No. 121*) is that a firm, in effect, must disclose when it anticipates that assets previously acquired will no longer provide future benefits. This is a valuable disclosure for the analyst attempting to assess a past strategic decision by a firm.

Example 7. The Great Atlantic & Pacific Tea Company (A&P), a grocery store chain, expanded by acquiring a chain of stores in Canada. At the time of the acquisition, A&P reported fixed assets and goodwill, along with other assets and liabilities, on its consolidated balance sheet.[18] Analysis of *Statement No. 121* disclosures made by A&P in a subsequent year, however, makes it clear that the decision to expand into Canada was not a successful business strategy for the firm. A&P reports a $127 million writedown of goodwill and fixed assets of its Canadian stores in a recent year when its pretax loss from continuing operations is almost $130 million. A&P states that the writedown is necessary because the revised cash flow projections based on the Canadian store operations indicate that the fixed asset and goodwill balances are not recoverable.

A firm will test to see whether an actual writedown is necessary when it concludes that recoverability of long-lived assets may be a problem. The test entails estimating future cash flows expected from use of the assets. Asset impairment has occurred if the carrying amount of the assets under consideration exceeds the undiscounted future cash flows. At the time the firm judges that an impairment has occurred, the firm writes down the carrying value of the assets to their then-current fair value. The firm measures fair value by either the market value of the assets (if determinable), or the expected net present value of the future cash flows.

Use of future cash flows to estimate asset impairment is particularly sensitive to slight changes in underlying assumptions. The analyst needs to scrutinize closely

---

[17]Hugo Nurnberg and Nelson Dittmar, "Reporting Impairments of Long-Lived Assets: New Rules and Disclosures," *Journal of Financial Statement Analysis,* Winter 1997, pp. 37–50. The article includes examples of how these impairment indicators are applied by firms in the oil and gas, restaurant, retail food, and service-related industries.

[18]Accounting for fixed assets and goodwill is discussed in Chapters 5 and 7, respectively. In the case of goodwill, *Statement No. 121* addresses the writedown of only that goodwill related to the asset group deemed impaired. The necessity to writedown goodwill *unrelated* to the assets deemed impaired is addressed by *Accounting Principles Board Opinion No. 17,* "Intangible Assets," 1970. Generally, *Opinion No. 17* requires that firms writedown goodwill if the carrying amount exceeds the future benefits.

how firms may or may not recognize impairments based on slight changes in future cash flow estimates. Nurnberg and Dittmar provide an example of how a small increase or decrease in future cash flow estimates can dramatically affect the reported results:

> Suppose a group of assets has a carrying amount of $10.0 million and a fair value of $6.0 million. If cash flows are estimated at $10.1 million, an impairment loss would *not* be recognized because the undiscounted cash flows exceed the carrying amount of the assets. If the cash flows are estimated at $9.9 million, however, an impairment loss of $4.0 million would be recognized. Thus, a $200,000 difference in the cash flow estimate, which could be based on a fairly subjective cash flow forecast for many years, would result in recognizing a $4.0 million loss.[19]

Statement No. 121 requires that firms include impairment losses in income before taxes from continuing operations. Although impairments do not warrant special treatment such as that for discontinued operations or extraordinary gains or losses that we have discussed earlier in this chapter, there are alternative methods for disclosing the losses. These include a separate line item on the income statement, or a detailed note that describes what line item on the income statement includes the impairment losses.

Example 8.   PepsiCo. reports impairment charges of $681 million in Year 6 ($520 million in Year 5) and provides a detailed note on how it calculates the charges. Exhibit 4.5 presents the pertinent excerpts from that note. Pepsi provides this information in the note:

1. A schedule of *Statement No. 121* charges applicable to each segment in which PepsiCo. operates.
2. How the charges are reported and included in income before taxes from continuing operations.
3. The circumstances that led to the impairment losses and how the recorded amount is calculated.

The task for the analyst is to assess whether impairment losses should be excluded from reported earnings to estimate sustainable earnings for the period. In most cases, they are eliminated, net of any related tax effect, because the assumption is that the losses are nonrecurring. Elimination of the impairment losses lets the analyst establish a comparable trend line of past and current sustainable earnings that provides a relevant basis for estimating sustainable future earnings. Although it is probably not possible to adjust the balance sheet for impaired assets, it is debatable whether an adjustment is even appropriate, because these are still productive assets, even though not at the level the firm originally anticipated.

---

[19]Nurnberg and Dittmar, "Reporting Impairments of Long-Lived Assets: New Rules and Disclosures," p. 40.

EXHIBIT 4.5

PepsiCo. Inc.
Note 4—Impairment of Long-Lived Assets

Impairment charges of $681 million ($396 million after-tax or $.025 per share) in Year 6 and $520 million ($384 million after-tax or $0.24 per share) in Year 5 included in the Consolidated Statement of Income are set forth below:

	Year 5	Year 6
International beverages		
Investment in unconsolidated affiliates	$ —	$ 210
Concentrate-related assets	—	110
Non-core assets	—	53
	$ —	$ 373
Non-core U.S. restaurant businesses	$ —	246
Initial adoption of SFAS 121	520	—
Unusual charges	$ 520	$ 619
Restaurants-recurring SFAS 121 charges	—	62
	$ 520	$ 681

The unusual charges and the recurring restaurant charges are included in unusual impairment, disposal and other charges and selling, general and administrative expenses, respectively, in the Consolidated Statement of Income.

The impairment charges represented a reduction of the carrying amounts of impaired assets to their estimated fair market value. For assets to be held and used in the business, estimated fair market value was generally determined by using discounted estimated future cash flows. The estimated fair market value for assets to be disposed of was determined by using estimated selling prices based primarily upon the opinion of an investment banking firm, less costs to sell. Considerable management judgment is necessary to estimate fair market value. Accordingly, actual results could vary significantly from such estimates.

The international beverages assets were deemed impaired due to a reduction in forecasted cash flows that was attributable to increased competitive activity and weakened macroeconomic factors in various geographic regions and an estimate of the fair market value, less costs to sell, of certain non-core businesses PepsiCo. decided to dispose of.

The charges for PepsiCo.'s non-core U.S. restaurant businesses were a result of a decision made by PepsiCo. to dispose of its non-core U.S. restaurant businesses.

The recurring SFAS 121 restaurant charge results from the semi-annual impairment evaluations of all restaurants that either initially met the "two-year history of operating losses" impairment indicator that PepsiCo. uses to identify potentially impaired restaurants or were previously evaluated for impairment and, due to changes in circumstances, a current forecast of future cash flows would be expected to be significantly lower than the forecast used in the prior evaluation.

In the A&P example above, the pretax $127 million asset impairment loss is added back to the $130 pretax loss from continuing operations that A&P reported. In the case of PepsiCo., for Year 6 (Year 5) the $681 million ($520 million) impairment charge is added back to income before taxes of $2,047 million ($2,432). For PepsiCo., however, an argument could be made that a portion of the impairment charges is recurring and should not be adjusted for. If the impairment charge is eliminated, the analyst measures the related tax effects by (1) multiplying the statutory tax rate times the impairment charge and (2) increasing income tax expense by the result.

RESTRUCTURING CHARGES

The fact that the FASB has issued specific pronouncements on each of the four disclosure topics discussed to this point—discontinued operations, extraordinary gains and losses, changes in accounting principles, and impairment losses on long-lived assets—helps the analyst in the task of assessing the sustainability of current earnings. Disclosures for restructuring charges, for changes in estimates, for gains and losses from peripheral activities, and for management's analysis of operations are not as consistent across firms and not as comprehensive, because FASB rulings on the topic either do not exist or are more general in nature.

Firms will frequently stay in a particular area of business, but decide to make major changes in the strategic direction or level of operations of that business.[20] In many of these cases, firms record a restructuring charge against earnings for the estimated cost of implementing the decision. The treatment of restructuring charges in estimating sustainable earnings and assessing profitability is important for several reasons:

1. Recessionary conditions often induce firms to include restructuring charges in their reported earnings.
2. The Financial Accounting Standards Board has not issued a specific pronouncement regarding how firms should measure restructuring charges and when firms should include such charges in measuring income.

Interpreting a particular firm's restructuring charge is difficult because firms vary in their treatment of these items:

1. Some firms apply their accounting principles conservatively. They may, for example, use relatively short lives for depreciable assets, immediately expense expenditures for repairs of equipment, or use relatively short amortization lives for intangible assets. Such firms will have smaller amounts to write off as restructuring charges than firms that apply their accounting principles less conservatively.
2. Some firms attempt to minimize the amount of the restructuring charge each year so as not to penalize reported earnings too much. These firms often must take restructuring charges for several years in order to provide adequately for restructuring costs. An example is Digital Equipment Corporation in Example 9 on the next page.
3. Some firms attempt to maximize the amount of the restructuring charge in a particular year. This approach communicates the "bad news" all at once (it is

---

[20]If the firm decides to abandon a business altogether, the reporting policies discussed earlier for discontinued operations would apply. In many cases, however, firms are not abandoning current areas of business, but "restructuring" them to improve profitability.

called the "big bath" approach), and reduces or eliminates the need for additional restructuring charges in the future. If the restructuring charge later turns out to have been too large, income from continuing operations in a later period will include a restructuring credit that increases reported earnings (such as Hershey Foods in Example 15).

Example 9. Income from continuing operations of Digital Equipment Corporation (DEC) for three years includes restructuring charges of $550 million, $1,100 million, and $1,500 million. DEC reports that these charges relate to plant closings and employee separations. DEC downsized its computer operations in the face of recessionary conditions and a maturing of the computer industry worldwide. Because DEC remained in the computer business, these restructuring charges appear in income from continuing operations.

Example 10. Look at Coke's financial statements in Appendix A. Note 14, "Nonrecurring Items," identifies particular income items as peripheral to ongoing activities of the company for Year 7 (amounts in millions):

Streamlining of Operations, principally in Europe and Latin America	$130.0
Impairment Charges in the Minute Maid Company Operations	146.0
Impairment Charges Related to Information Systems	80.0
Contribution to Coca-Cola Foundation	28.5

Chapter 3 provides a detailed analysis of these items, which are reported as selling and administrative expenses on Coke's income statement. The bulk of the charges appear to be recurring, even though Coke labels them as "Nonrecurring Items." With the possible exception of the first two, however, the amounts involved for these items are relatively small when compared to Coke's income before income taxes of $4,596 million in Year 7.

Example 11. McCormick & Company is the largest spice company in the world. The company is the leader in the manufacture, marketing, and distribution of spices, seasonings, flavors, and other food products to the food industry—retail, food service, and food processors.

McCormick's chairman of the board is Charles P. McCormick, Jr. In the first paragraph of his letter to shareholders, McCormick captures McCormick's theme for the year:

> This year was approached as a turnaround year and turnaround it was. Our first-half performance, as expected, was sub-par. The second half returned to growth, and we are again pointed in the right direction.

"Pointed in the right direction" entails McCormick's recording of a pretax restructuring charge of $58,095 thousand in Year 6, as detailed in the note disclosure in

EXHIBIT 4.6

McCormick & Company
Note 2. Business Restructuring
(in thousands)

In the third quarter of Year 6, the Company began implementation of a restructuring plan and recorded a restructuring change of $58,095 in Year 6. This charge reduced net income by $39,582 or $.49 per share. In addition, there are approximately $1,915 of additional charges ($.02 per share) directly related to the restructuring plan which could not be accrued but will be expensed as the plan is implemented.

Major components of the restructuring charge include: severance and personnel costs of $9,983; a $44,562 writedown to net realizable value of assets and businesses identified for disposal; and other exit costs of $3,550. The $1,915 of additional charges which will be expensed during the implementation are principally costs to move equipment and personnel. These actions are expected to be completed in Year 7 and will require net cash outflows of approximately $12,000.

The components of the restructuring charge and remaining liability, are as follows:

	Restructuring Charge for Year 6	11/30/Year 6 Remaining Amount
Severance and personnel costs	$ 9,983	$ 2,628
Writedown of assets and businesses	44,562	23,378
Other exit costs	3,550	1.415
	$58,095	$27,421
Additional costs to be expensed		$ 1,915

Exhibit 4.6. The charge is included in income from continuing operations before taxes.

Example 12. The Nine West Group, a leading designer and manufacturer of women's footware and accessories, includes this item in Year 7's income statement (in thousands):

Business restructuring and integration expenses	$51,900

Nine West did not report any restructuring charges in Year 6 or Year 5. The company's Note 4 indicates that the expense is primarily related to integrating into Nine West a major company acquired during the year, which includes five categories of costs (in thousands):

1. Severance and termination benefits of $7,650.
2. Writedown of assets, principally leasehold improvements, of $14,620.

3. Accruals for lease and other contract terminations of $7,046.
4. Inventory valuation adjustments of $10,423.
5. Other integration and consolidation costs of $12,151.

Analysis. The task for the analyst in each of these four examples is to assess whether the restructuring charge adequately provides for the costs of the restructuring, or whether future charges will become necessary. If the latter is the case, estimates of future sustainable earnings must take this into account.

This task is made more difficult because firms follow different reporting strategies with respect to restructuring charges. As we have noted, some firms make restructuring charges for several years in a row, attempting perhaps to minimize the negative news by making smaller charges than are appropriate. This appears to be the case for DEC. Other firms make a single, presumably larger, restructuring charge in an effort to put the bad news behind them. This appears to be the case for McCormick. And still others report restructuring charges as a result of a substantive business decision, as with Nine West's acquisition of another large company in the same industry.

It is also possible that firms use the restructuring charge as an opportunity to writedown assets that do not even relate directly to the restructuring action, a phenomenon known as "taking a bath." This is always possible, given the lack of specific reporting guidance in the area by policymakers. The firm may hope that the stock market will view a restructuring charge as nonrecurring, and exclude it from estimates of sustainable earnings. Writing down assets now relieves future periods of depreciation and similar charges and increases reported earnings of those periods. Thus, restructuring charges may signal "earnings management," a topic discussed later in the chapter. The analyst must carefully examine the rationale for the amount and the time pattern of restructuring charges when estimating sustainable earnings.

Although it might appear desirable to eliminate the effect of a restructuring charge from all three financial statements—when, in fact, the analyst decides to adjust for the item—firms seldom provide the necessary information. The analyst can make certain assumptions to accomplish the articulation among the three statements, but the inaccuracy and level of bias injected into the resulting measures might be intolerably high. Eliminating the effect on income from continuing operations, by simply adding back the amount and adjusting for its related tax effect, at least removes it from the principal measure used to estimate sustainable earnings and to assess ongoing profitability. If the restructuring charge is eliminated, the analyst measures the related tax effect by (1) multiplying the statutory tax rate by the restructuring charge and (2) increasing income tax expense by the result.

CHANGES IN ESTIMATES

Application of generally accepted accounting principles sometimes requires firms to make estimates. Examples include the uncollectible rate for accounts receivable; the depreciable lives for fixed assets; the amortization period for intangibles;

the return rate for warranties; and interest, compensation, and inflation rates for pensions, health care, and other retirement benefits. Example 13 provides additional examples.

Firms periodically make changes in these estimates. The amounts reported in prior years for various revenues and expenses will then be misstated, given the new estimates. Firms might conceivably (1) retroactively restate prior years' revenues and expenses to reflect the new estimates, (2) include the cumulative effect of the change in estimate in income in the year of the change (similar to a change in accounting principle), or (3) spread the effect of the prior years' misstatement over the current and future years.

Financial reporting requires firms to follow the third procedure.[21] Policymakers view the making of estimates and the revising of those estimates as an integral and ongoing part of applying accounting principles. Financial statements would hardly be credibile if firms were to revise their financial statements each time they changed an accounting estimate. Policymakers are also concerned that users of the financial statements will overlook a change in an estimate if its effect does not appear in the income statement of the current and future years.

Example 13. Jostens Inc. is known for its school-related products and services—class rings, yearbooks, graduation products, student photography packages, and service and achievement awards. Jostens' financial statements include the introductory note:

> **Use of Estimates.** The preparation of financial statements in conformity with generally accepted accounting principles requires management to make estimates and assumptions that affect the amounts reported in the financial statements and accompanying notes. Actual results could differ from those estimates. The most significant areas that require the use of management's estimates relate to the allowance for uncollectible receivables, inventory reserves, sales returns, warranty costs, environmental accruals and deferred income tax valuations.

The first two sentences in the note are "boilerplate" statements in that most companies make these statements as a form of protection against lawsuits. The last sentence is more specific to Jostens in that the areas of significant estimates identified are discussed in greater detail in later notes to the financial statements.

Here is one of those disclosures:

> **Changes in Accounting Estimates.** As a result of certain changes in business conditions, the company conducted a review that concluded at the end of the third quarter of fiscal Year 9. That review led the company to increase reserves for inventories, receivables and overdrafts from independent sales representatives to reflect amounts estimated not to be recoverable, based upon current facts and circumstances. The revised estimates reduced pre-tax income for Year 9 by $16.9 million ($10.1 million after tax), or 22 cents per share.

---

[21]Accounting Principles Board, *Opinion No. 20.*

Example 14. Jostens identifies "environmental accruals" as a significant area that requires the use of management's estimates (Example 13). Compliance with environmental laws is of particular importance to Sherwin-Williams, a manufacturer, distributor, and retailer of paints and related products. Exhibit 4.7 provides the note from a recent annual report of the company that addresses the area—and highlights the fact that changes in estimates over time are inevitable. As a result of a ruling on environmental liabilities by the American Institute of Certified Public Accountants, in Year 8 Sherwin-Williams revised its estimate of cleanup and other costs. As stated in the note, the newly calculated costs are treated as a change in accounting estimate—as opposed to reporting the change as a change in accounting principle.

Example 15. We have noted that if, subsequently, a restructuring charge is deemed too high an estimate, income from continuing operations in a later period will include a restructuring credit—in effect, increasing reported earnings in the later period. In a recent year, Hershey Foods reported a reversal of a previous year's restructuring charge and attributed it to a change in estimates. The company states:

> As of December 31, Year 5, $81.1 million of restructuring reserves had been utilized and $16.7 million had been reversed to reflect revisions and changes in estimates to the original restructuring program.

Given the difficulty of estimating the cost of restructuring programs prior to their implementation, such a disclosure is not surprising. Unless a reversal is large com-

---

EXHIBIT 4.7

The Sherwin-Williams Company
Note 1—Significant Accounting Policies

Environmental matters.   Capital expenditures for ongoing environmental compliance measures are recorded in the consolidated balance sheets and related expenses are included in the normal operating expenses of conducting business. The Company is involved with environmental compliance and remediation activities at some of its current and former sites and at a number of third-party sites. The company accrues for certain environmental remediation-related activities for which commitments or clean-up plans have been developed or for which costs or minimum costs can be reasonably estimated. All accrued amounts are recorded on an undiscounted basis. In Year 8, the Company adopted American Institute of Certified Public Accountants Statement of Position (SOP) 96–1, "Environmental Remediation Liabilities." SOP 96–1 proscribes that accrued environmental remediation-related expenses include direct costs of remediation and indirect costs related to the remediation effort. Although the Company previously accrued for direct costs of remediation and certain indirect costs, additional indirect costs were required to be accrued by the Company at the time of adopting SOP 96–1 such as compensation and benefits for employees directly involved in the remediation activities and fees paid to outside engineering, consulting and law firms. The effect of initially applying the provisions of SOP 96–1 has been treated as a change in accounting estimate.

pared to the original estimate (Hershey Foods' restructuring charge originally was estimated at $106.1 million), most analysts are not distrustful of this type of disclosure.

The analyst needs to address a set of issues when evaluating changes in estimates. How reasonable are management's stated explanations for the change? Sherwin-Williams changed estimates partially in response to a ruling by policymakers, something beyond a company's control. Have economic conditions changed to justify an estimate change? A change in the economy was undoubtedly the situation that led Jostens to reestimate the portion of its receivables that will go uncollected. Has technology changed, necessitating shorter useful lives for depreciable assets, lower warranty reserve levels, or shorter periods before obsolescence takes place? Are the firm's new estimates in line with those of its competitors?

As we discuss more fully later, a company's need to make estimates increases the potential for earnings management. Does it appear that the firm changed estimates in order to increase reported earnings? That is, management may anticipate several periods of otherwise reduced earnings in the future. Or, does it appear that the firm changed estimates in order to *decrease* earnings? In this case, perhaps the firm is subject to government antitrust actions because of perceived monopoly profit making. The point is that the analyst looking at changes in estimates needs to evaluate whether management is signaling something about future expectations. In fact, the signals might warrant revisions by the analyst to sustainable earnings estimates.

GAINS AND LOSSES FROM PERIPHERAL ACTIVITIES

To develop, manufacture, and market products, firms generally need to invest in assets such as building and equipment that provide the capacity to carry out business activities. The sale of such "peripheral" assets usually results in a gain or loss. Like restructuring charges, gains and losses from activities peripheral to the primary activities of a firm are included in income from continuing operations. The analyst should seek out such nonrecurring items and decide whether to exclude them when estimating sustainable earnings and assessing profitability.

Example 16. Tandem Computers (a subsidiary of Compaq Computer Corporation) designs, develops, manufactures, markets, and supports a full range of computer systems and services. It also provides software and networking solutions to its customers. In a Tandem annual report published prior to its merger with Compaq, the firm reveals the following in its income statement (in thousands):

Gain on sale of subsidiaries and investments $9,297

The gain is included in income from continuing operations, located on the income statement below operating income and grouped with interest income and interest expense. Tandem provides a brief explanation for the gain in the notes: "One of the Company's equity investees entered into an agreement to sell its assets. Accordingly, the Company received $12.3 million in proceeds from the transaction, for a gain of $9.3 million."

Example 17.   Income from continuing operations of Delta Air Lines for three years includes gains from the disposition of flight equipment of $18 million, $17 million, and $35 million. Such gains relate, although indirectly, to providing transportation services. Clearly, Delta Air Lines needs to replenish its aircraft inventory periodically to carry out its business activities.

Example 18.   H.J. Heinz, a consumer foods company, regularly acquires and disposes of branded food products companies as it shifts its product line to high-growth markets. Gains and losses from divestitures appear in "other income" in the income from continuing operations section of the income statement, and are generally not material in amount. In Year 4, however, Heinz sold its investment in a cornstarch business at a pretax gain of $221 million, which represents 22 percent of income before taxes from continuing operations. Although divestitures can be recurring, a divestiture of this size has not occurred for Heinz for several years.

Example 19.   Look at Coke's financial statements in Appendix A. Income from continuing operations includes the following (in millions):

	Year 5	Year 6	Year 7
Gain on issuance of stock by equity investees	—	$74	$431

Notes 1 and 3 in Appendix A describe Coke's policy of accounting for gains on issuance of stock by equity investees. A closer inspection of Note 3 reveals that the gain in Year 7 consists of the following amounts (in millions):

Sale of Coca-Cola Erfischungsgetranke Gmb.H stock	$283
Sale of Coca-Cola Amatil stock	130
Sale of Coca-Cola FEMSA de Buenos Aires, S.A. stock	18
Total	$431

In each of these sales, the international equity investee sold additional shares to third parties. As a result, Coke's percentage ownership interest in the investee decreases. Since the selling price per share is higher than Coke's average carrying amount per share, the company recognizes a noncash gain on the issuance. Coke reports the gain in the period when the change of ownership interest occurs.

The task for the analyst in each of these four examples is to assess whether peripheral gains and losses should be removed from income from continuing operations. In each example, the firm makes some statement as to the inherent nature of the gain relative to the activities of the firm.[22] In most cases, even though the gains and losses do not relate to the sale of the firm's principal products and services, such gains and losses recur, and should enter into estimates of sustainable earnings. Of course, firms that rely heavily on such gains and losses for their earnings will not likely survive for long. Thus, a large percentage of reported earnings constituting gains and losses from peripheral activities might signal the need to revise estimates of sustainable earnings downward.

Like impairment and restructuring charges, peripheral gains and losses are reported on a *pretax* basis. Income tax expense includes the tax effects of the gain or loss. If the analyst decides to eliminate the gain or loss from income from continuing operations, the related tax effect must also be eliminated from income tax expense using the statutory rate as described for restructuring charges above.

MANAGEMENT'S ANALYSIS OF OPERATIONS

This final disclosure topic is one of the most difficult for an analyst to evaluate when estimating sustainable earnings. For the categories discussed so far, overt disclosures alert the financial statement reader to *potential* one-shot, one-time, or nonrecurring events that may influence future sustainable earnings. In fact, firms usually disclose the impact of each of a variety of potential nonrecurring items on earnings. Yet it still may be possible for earnings of the current period to be a poor predictor of future earnings, and for less evident reasons than the nonrecurring items. Often management's analysis of operations is an important source of meaningful disclosures.

Example 20.   Appendix B includes a section from Coke's annual report that the company labels, "Financial Review Incorporating Management's Discussion and Analysis." The section is typical of what is found in either the annual report or Form 10-K filing of all publicly held companies. Coke emphasizes:

1. The mission of the company.
2. The investments that the company emphasizes, including bottling operations, capital expenditures, marketing activities, and human capital.

---

[22]For example, Appendix B includes this following statement by Coke related to its analysis of operations:

> **Bottling Operations.** We continue our well-established strategy of strengthening our distribution system by investing in, and subsequently selling, ownership positions in bottling operations. This strategy provided our Company with yet another value stream resulting from the gains on the sales of these investments.
>
> Since some have criticized Coke for managing earnings through the use of gains on the sale of stock by equity investees, it is not surprising that this strategy is so forcefully stated. In his closely followed *Wall Street Journal* column, "Intrinsic Value," Roger Lowenstein details the controversy that surrounds Coke's, and analysts', treatment of these gains (May 1, 1997).

3. The financial strategies of the company.

4. The basis for judging the performance of the company.

5. An SEC-mandated section titled, "Management's Discussion and Analysis," that addresses the firm's operations, liquidity and capital resources, and financial position.

This portion of the annual report is extensive. It essentially recaps the recent past and provides a game plan as to Coke's future expectations related to its shareholders, customers, and employees. Coke's management carefully chooses the forward-looking disclosures in this section because any benchmarks presented will be used subsequently to evaluate the company's actual performance.

Example 21.   Sara Lee Corporation describes itself as a "global manufacturer and marketer of high-quality, brand-name products for consumers throughout the world." The management of Sara Lee Corporation provides a comprehensive discussion of its business and operations in a recent Form 10-K filing. Although similar discussions are provided by Sara Lee in its annual report, the Form 10-K filing is also an important disclosure medium because the SEC regulates its contents and format. Sara Lee analyzes its business and operations in sections of the Form 10-K filing titled:

1. General Development of Business.

2. Financial Information about Industry Segments.

3. Narrative Description of Business.

4. Financial Information about Foreign and Domestic Operations and Export Sales.

5. Management's Discussion and Analysis of Financial Condition and Results of Operations.

Analysis of Management's Analysis of Operations.   The analyst needs to discern whether corporate goals, trends in revenues or expenses, and competitor comments, among many other possible disclosures by management in the analysis of operations, signal whether some portion of earnings is not sustainable. The "Management's Discussion and Analysis" report is particularly recommended for scrutiny because of the SEC's increased reliance on this form of disclosure in recent years.

SUMMARY OF EARNINGS SUSTAINABILITY

We have discussed the reporting of various types of disclosures related to earnings. There are many factors that may affect the quality of current earnings as a predictor of future sustainable earnings. Understanding the nature and the extent of adjustments that need to be made to current earnings in order to use earnings as a predictor requires knowledge of (1) the industry, (2) the firm and its strategy, and (3) the required financial reporting. The process is more art than science. It will always require considerable judgment on the part of the analyst.

EARNINGS MEASUREMENT AND MANAGEMENT

Exhibit 4.1 points out that assessing earnings quality depends on two additional concerns besides earnings sustainability:

1. The ability of accounting systems to *measure* accurately and reliably the economic value-added by a firm's operating activities during a reporting period.
2. The opportunity for management to *manage* the level or trend of reporting earnings to its advantage.

EARNINGS MEASUREMENT

The reporting of a single earnings number and a single earnings per share ratio rounded to the nearest penny may lead the user of financial statements to think of the measurement of earnings as a precise exercise. When the major television networks report the annual earnings of Coke each January, for example, listeners may have the impression that earnings and earnings per share are the result of an objective and exact process that Coke follows in calculating the numbers. Some people would be surprised to hear that Coke has the ability to report a wide range of numbers for any one quarter or year, and that a company has "absolute control over near-term results," a position taken by Roy Burry of Oppenheimer & Co.[23]

In designing an earnings measurement system, policymakers often must make trade-offs between accurately measuring the economic value-added of operating activities, which is usually the most *relevant* measure of performance (but also difficult to observe, much less measure), and obtaining *reliable* earnings measurements. There is always some amount of distortion in the earnings measurement process as a result of this trade-off between economic accuracy and measurement objectivity. Chapters 5 through 7 discuss the most important earnings measurement issues.

EARNINGS MANAGEMENT

Choices, judgments, and estimates—by both management and analysts—are an inevitable consequence of not being able to observe, measure, and communicate economic value-added accurately and reliably. Yet the wider the range of choices, the more *opportunity* open to management to manage, or manipulate, reported earnings to its advantage.

The distinction between earnings management and management fraud is often a thin line. Earnings management here refers to choices made by management within the bounds of generally accepted accounting principles to influence earnings in a systematic direction. Management fraud refers to actions taken that are outside the bounds of generally accepted accounting principles to influence earnings. When there is substantial disagreement as to what is within versus outside

---

[23]Roger Lowenstein reported this comment by Roy Burry in his "Intrinsic Value" column.

the bounds of acceptable reporting, often ultimate resolution is achieved only through shareholder class action lawsuits brought against managers.

The Case for Earnings Management.   Suggested reasons *for* earnings management by a firm and its managers include:

1. Managers whose compensation is based on reported earnings have an incentive to maximize reported earnings.
2. Managers have job security incentives to maximize the reporting of "good" earnings news and minimize the reporting of "bad" earnings news. Earnings management often results in transforming mediocre earnings into "good" earnings, and transforming "bad" earnings into "acceptable" earnings.
3. Firms use earnings management to smooth changes in earnings over time, thereby reducing the perceived risk of the firm and its cost of capital.[24]
4. Firms might have incentives to minimize reported earnings to circumvent government antitrust actions against the firm.

The Case against Earnings Management.   Suggested reasons *against* earnings management by a firm and its managers include:

1. Earnings and cash flows ultimately coincide, so firms cannot manage earnings forever. Eventually, earnings aggressively reported in early years must be offset by lower earnings or even losses in later years to compensate.
2. Capital markets penalize firms identified as flagrant earnings managers.

Whether analysts of financial reports can detect earnings management and whether they can make appropriate adjustments to reported amounts in making investment decisions have been the subject of extensive but inconclusive research in recent years.[25] In general, managers have three primary means to manage earnings:[26]

> *Selection of Accounting Principles from Among Those Within the Bounds of Generally Accepted Accounting Principles.*   Firms have a choice as to the cost flow assumption for inventories and the depreciation method for long-lived assets, for example. Leases and corporate acquisitions can be ac-

---

[24]For a summary of the principal concepts underlying income smoothing, see Joshua Ronen and S. Sadan, *Smoothing Income Numbers: Objectives, Means and Implications* (Reading, MA: Addison-Wesley), 1981.

[25]See, for example, Katherine Schipper, "Commentary on Earnings Management," *Accounting Horizons,* December 1989, pp. 91–102; Harry DeAngelo, Linda DeAngelo, and Douglas J. Skinner, "Accounting Choice in Troubled Companies," *Journal of Accounting and Economics,* January 1994, pp. 113–143; and Patricia M. Dechow, Richard G. Sloan, and Amy P. Sweeney, "Detecting Earnings Management," *Accounting Review,* April 1995, pp. 193–225.

[26]Additionally, firms might attempt to manage earnings *per share* (rather than the earnings number) by actions that change the number of shares outstanding, such as repurchasing shares of the firm's common stock. See Linda J. Zucca, "The Use of Changes in Outstanding Common Shares to Smooth Earnings per Share," *Journal of Financial Statement Analysis,* Fall 1996, pp. 49–59.

counted for differently, depending on how the transactions are structured. These alternative accounting principles, together with others, are discussed more fully in later chapters.

Application of Accounting Principles Within the Bounds of Generally Accepted Accounting Principles. Determining the appropriate level of loan loss reserves by commercial banks and establishing warranty accruals by automobile manufacturers are examples of reporting areas that involve a great degree of subjectivity. Often the estimates necessary to apply a particular accounting principle are subject to substantial interpretation, and often estimates change over time as illustrated in the previous section on earnings sustainability. Subsequent chapters illustrate the reporting techniques that involve the highest degree of subjectivity in their application.

Timing of Asset Acquisitions and Dispositions. The sale of corporate assets can result in gains and losses reported on the income statement. The actual date of the sale often is negotiable, so a portion of earnings for any one period is under the control of management.[27] The peripheral gains and losses illustrated in the previous section typically involve asset acquisitions and dispositions.

Boundaries of Earnings Management. It is important to note that earnings management has some boundaries. Securities regulators and stock exchanges require annual audits by independent accountants. Auditors can monitor particularly aggressive actions that management may take to influence earnings, although their power to prevent actions taken within the bounds of generally accepted accounting principles is limited. The ongoing scrutiny of financial analysts also serves as a check on earnings management. Securities analysts typically follow several firms within an industry and have a sense of the corporate reporting "personalities" of various firms. The frequency, timeliness, and quality of management's communications with shareholders and analysts all serve as signals of the forthrightness of management and of the likelihood of earnings being highly managed.[28]

The task for the analyst is to identify the conditions that are conducive to earnings management and the avenues managers might take in those particular circumstances to carry out earnings management. To do this, analysts must understand the generally accepted accounting principles that adapt to earnings management so that they can separate economic value-added from "cosmetic" (that is, earnings managed) value-added. Thus, one of the objectives of the discussion of selected accounting principles in Chapters 5, 6, and 7 is to illustrate how the principles can be used to manage earnings.

---

[27]A discussion of whether firms use the sale of a segment or division to manage earnings can be found in Dov Fried, Haim A. Mozes, Donna Rapaccioli, and Allen I. Schiff, "Earnings Manipulation and the Sales of a Business Segment," *Journal of Financial Statement Analysis*, Spring 1996, pp. 25–33.

[28]See Mark H. Lang and Russell J. Lundholm, "Corporate Disclosure Policy and Analyst Behavior," *Accounting Review*, October 1996, pp. 467–492.

RESTATED FINANCIAL STATEMENT DATA

In several situations, financial reporting requires firms to restate retroactively the financial statements of prior years when the current year's annual report includes prior years' financial statements for comparative purposes:

1. A firm that decides during the current year to discontinue its involvement in a particular line of business must reclassify the income of that business for prior years as a discontinued operation, even though the firm included this income in continuing operations in income statements originally prepared for these years. The firm may also reclassify the net assets of the discontinued business as of the end of the preceding year to a single line—net assets of discontinued business—even though these net assets appeared among individual assets and liabilities in the balance sheet originally prepared for the preceding year.
2. If a firm merges with another firm in a transaction accounted for as a pooling of interests (discussed in Chapter 7), it must restate prior years' financial statements to reflect the results for the two entities combined.
3. Certain changes in accounting principles require the restatement of prior years' financial statements to reflect the new method. Examples are a change from a LIFO cost flow assumption for inventories to any other cost flow assumption and a change in the method of income recognition on long-term contracts, both discussed in Chapter 5.

The analyst must decide whether to use the financial statement data as originally reported for each year or as restated to reflect the new conditions. Because the objective of most financial statement analysis is to evaluate the past as a guide for projecting the future, the logical decision is to use the restated data.

There are difficulties in using restated data, however. Most companies include balance sheets for two years and income statements and statements of cash flows for three years in their annual reports. Analysts can calculate ratios and perform other analysis based on balance sheet data (for example, current assets/current liabilities, long-term debt/shareholders' equity) for only two years at most on a consistent basis. They can calculate ratios based on data from the income statement (for example, cost of goods sold/sales) or from the statement of cash flows (for example, cash flow from operations/capital expenditures) for three years at most on a consistent basis.

Many other important ratios and other analyses rely on data from both the balance sheet and either the income statement or the statement of cash flows. For example, the rate of return on common shareholders' equity equals net income to common stock divided by average common shareholders' equity. The denominator of this ratio requires two years of balance sheet data. Thus, it is possible to calculate ratios based on average data from the balance sheet and one of the other two financial statements for only one year under the new conditions. The analyst could obtain balance sheet amounts for prior years from earlier annual reports, but this results in comparing restated income statement or statement of cash flow data for those earlier years with nonrestated balance sheet data.

Example 22. Look at the financial statements of General Mills in Exhibits 4.8 (income statement) and 4.9 (balance sheet). The notes to Mills' financial statements indicate that Mills decided in Year 5 to dispose of its toy and fashion segments and the nonapparel retailing businesses within its specialty retailing segment. It reported a loss of $188.3 million from these discontinued operations in its income statement for Year 5 (see first column of Exhibit 4.8). In its comparative income statements for Year 4 and Year 3 (second and third columns), the income from these discontinued operations appears on the line, discontinued operations after tax. Exhibit 4.8 also shows the amounts as originally reported for Year 4 and

EXHIBIT 4.8				
General Mills, Inc. and Subsidiaries **Consolidated Statement of Earnings** (amounts in millions, except per share data)				
	Fiscal Year Ended			**As Originally Reported**
	May 26, Year 5 (52 Weeks)	May 27, Year 4 (52 Weeks)	May 29, Year 3 (52 Weeks)	May 27 Year 4 (52 Weeks)	May 29, Year 3 (52 Weeks)
Continuing Operations					
Sales	$4,285.2	$4,118.4	$4,082.3	$5,600.8	$5,550.8
Costs and Expenses: Cost of sales, exclusive of items below	2,474.8	2,432.8	2,394.8	3,165.9	3,123.3
Selling, general and administrative expenses	1,368.1	1,251.5	1,288.3	1,849.4	1,831.6
Depreciation and amortization expenses	110.4	99.0	94.2	133.1	127.5
Interest expense	60.2	31.5	39.5	61.4	58.7
Total Costs and Expenses	4,013.5	3,814.8	3,816.8	5,209.8	5,141.1
Earnings from Continuing Operations—Pretax	271.7	303.6	265.5	391.0	409.7
Gain (Loss) from Redeployments ...	(75.8)	53.0	2.7	7.7	—
Earnings from Continuing Operations after Redeployments—Pretax	195.9	356.6	268.2	398.7	409.7
Income Taxes	80.5	153.9	106.1	165.3	164.6
Earnings from Continuing Operations after Redeployments	115.4	202.7	162.1	233.4	245.1
Earnings per Share—Continuing Operations after Redeployments ..	$ 2.58	$ 4.32	$ 3.24	$ 4.98	$ 4.89
Discontinued Operations after Tax ..	(188.3)	30.7	83.0	—	—
Net Earnings (Loss)	$ (72.9)	$ 233.4	$ 245.1	$ 233.4	$ 245.1
Net Earnings (Loss) per Share	$ (1.63)	$ 4.98	$ 4.89	$ 4.98	$ 4.89
Average Number of Common Shares .	44.7	46.9	50.1	46.9	50.1

EXHIBIT 4.9

General Mills, Inc., and Subsidiaries
Consolidated Balance Sheets
(in millions)

	Fiscal Year Ended	
	May 26, Year 5	May 27, Year 4
Assets		
Current Assets		
Cash and Short-Term Investments	$ 66.8	$ 66.0
Receivables, Less Allowance for Doubtful Accounts		
of $4.0 in Yr. 5 and $18.8 in Yr. 4	284.5	550.6
Inventories	377.7	661.7
Investments in Tax Leases	—	49.6
Prepaid Expenses	40.1	43.6
Net Assets of Discontinued Operations and Redeployments	517.5	18.4
Total Current Assets	1,286.6	1,389.9
Land, Buildings and Equipment at Cost		
Land	93.3	125.9
Buildings	524.4	668.6
Equipment	788.1	904.7
Construction in Progress	80.2	130.0
Total Land, Buildings and Equipment	1,486.0	1,829.2
Less Accumulated Depreciation	(530.0)	(599.8)
Net Land, Buildings and Equipment	956.0	1,229.4
Other Assets		
Net Noncurrent Assets of Businesses To Be Spun Off	$ 206.5	$ —
Intangible Assets, Principally Goodwill	50.8	146.0
Investments and Miscellaneous Assets	162.7	92.8
Total Other Assets	420.0	238.8
Total Assets	$2,662.6	$2,858.1
Liabilities and Stockholders' Equity		
Current Liabilities		
Accounts Payable	$ 360.8	$ 477.8
Current Portion of Long-Term Debt	59.4	60.3
Notes Payable	379.8	251.0
Accrued Taxes	1.4	74.3
Accrued Payroll	91.8	119.1
Other Current Liabilities	164.0	162.9
Total Current Liabilities	1,057.2	1,145.4
Long-Term Debt	449.5	362.6
Deferred Income Taxes	29.8	76.5
Deferred Income Taxes—Tax Leases	60.8	—
Other Liabilities and Deferred Credits	42.0	49.0
Total Liabilities	1,639.3	1,633.5

	Fiscal Year Ended	
Exh. 4.9—Continued	**May 26, Year 5**	**May 27, Year 4**
Stockholders' Equity		
Common stock	$ 213.7	$ 215.4
Retained earnings	1,201.7	1,375.0
Less common stock in treasury, at cost	(333.9)	(291.8)
Cumulative foreign currency adjustment	(58.2)	(74.0)
Total Stockholders' Equity	1,023.3	1,224.6
Total Liabilities and Stockholders' Equity	$2,662.6	$2,858.1

Year 3 (columns four and five) in which Mills included the revenues and expenses from these operations in continuing operations.

Exhibit 4.9 shows the comparative balance sheets for Year 5 and Year 4. Note that the net assets of these discontinued businesses appear on a separate line in the Year 5 balance sheet. The amounts for these discontinued activities, however, are included in the individual asset and liability accounts in the Year 4 balance sheet. Thus, Mills provides three years of income statements in which the operations of these discontinued businesses are set out separately, but only one balance sheet. The analyst cannot calculate ratios using income statement and average balance sheet data for even one year on a consistent basis in this case.

When a firm provides sufficient information to restate prior years' financial statements without requiring an unreasonable number of assumptions, the analyst should use retroactively restated financial statement data. When the firm does not provide sufficient information to do these restatements, the analyst should use the amounts as originally reported for each year. Then, to interpret the resulting ratios, the analyst attempts to assess how much of the change in the ratios results from the new reporting condition and how much relates to other factors.

ACCOUNT CLASSIFICATION DIFFERENCES

Firms frequently classify items in their financial statements in different ways. The goal when comparing two or more companies is to obtain comparable data sets. A scan of the financial statements should permit the analyst to identify significant differences that might affect the analysis and interpretations.

Example 23. Exhibit 4.10 shows the disclosure of operating expenses for three leading manufacturers of cellular phones: Ericsson (Swedish), Motorola (U.S.), and Nokia (Finnish). Ericsson and Motorola report depreciation separately, while Nokia includes it in cost of goods sold and selling and administra-

EXHIBIT 4.10

Disclosure of Operating Expenses by Cellular Phone Companies
(in millions)

	Ericsson	Motorola	Nokia
Sales	SEK 124,266	$ 27,973	FIM 39,321
Cost of Goods Sold	(70,106)	(18,990)	(28,029)
Selling and Administrative . .	(40,803)	(4,715)	(3,512)
Depreciation	(4,216)	(2,308)	—
Research and Development . .	—	—	(3,514)
Operating Income	SEK 9,141	$ 1,960	FIM 4,266

tive expenses. Nokia reports research and development (R&D) expense separately; Ericsson and Motorola include it in selling and administrative expenses. There is no way to directly compare financial statement ratios across these three firms.

To deal with the depreciation differences, the analyst must either allocate the depreciation amount for Ericsson and Motorola to cost of goods sold and selling and administrative expenses or extract from cost of goods sold and selling and administrative expenses the depreciation amount of Nokia (Nokia reports total depreciation expense as an addback to net income in computing cash flow from operations). Both of these approaches require the analyst to make assumptions about the proportion of depreciation applicable to manufacturing versus selling and administrative expenses.

The classification differences for R&D expense are easier to fix. Ericsson and Motorola report the amount of R&D expense in their notes. Thus, the analyst can subtract the amounts from selling and administrative expenses.

When the analyst can easily and unambiguously reclassify accounts, the reclassified data should serve as the basis for analysis. If the reclassifications require numerous assumptions, then it is probably better not to make them. The analyst should make note of the differences in account classification for further reference when interpreting the financial statement analysis.

REPORTING PERIOD DIFFERENCES

Although the majority of publicly held corporations in the United States use a December year-end, there are several industries in which the principal competitors use different year-ends. To what extent should the analyst place firms on a comparable reporting period before performing financial statement analysis?

Example 24. Consider these year-ends for major firms in the consumer foods industry:

Company	Year-End
Campbell Soup	August
General Mills	May
Heinz	April
Kellogg	December
Quaker Oats	June

Whether the analyst should make an adjustment for different year-ends depends on (1) the length of the time period by which the year-ends differ, and (2) any events during the particular time period that make reasonable comparisons between companies difficult. If the year-ends differ by three months or less, then the analyst generally need not make adjustments. If the year-ends differ by more than three months, and the industry is either cyclical or subject to major strikes, raw materials shortages, or similar problems in the intervening period, then the analyst should examine the impact of different year-ends. Note that the analyst need not make adjustments when sales are seasonal (as opposed to cyclical), because the fiscal year for each firm will include a full set of seasonal and nonseasonal quarters.

The source for the data needed to make adjustments for different year-ends is quarterly reports. Publicly held firms provide certain income statement and balance sheet data quarterly, although they do not need to present a full set of financial statements. (Also, quarterly financial statements are typically not audited by independent accountants.) The annual report usually includes summary information from these quarterly reports.

Example 25. Exhibit 4.11 presents quarterly information from a recent annual report for Campbell Soup Company. Campbell shows various income statement items for each of the quarters of the last two fiscal years. With this information, the analyst can compute sales or earnings for various periods as follows (in millions):

Year Ended May, Year 8
Sales ($998.8 + $1,179.1 + $1,336.1 + $1,207.4) = $4,721.4
Net Earnings ($70.1 + $94.9 + $84.6 + $22.4)   =   272.0

Year Ended February, Year 8
Sales ($1,128.3 + $998.8 + $1,179.1 + $1,336.1) = $4,642.3
Net Earnings ($48.1 + $70.1 + $94.9 + $84.6)   =   297.7

Year Ended November, Year 7
Sales ($1,248.6 + $1,128.3 + $998.8 + $1,179.1) = $4,554.8
Net Earnings ($70.4 + $48.1 + $70.1 + $94.9)   =   283.5

Because each of these time periods represents the end of a quarter in Campbell's fiscal year, the quarterly report will include the balance sheet for that period end. Thus, the analyst would use the May data to compare Campbell and General

---

EXHIBIT 4.11

Campbell Soup Company
Quarterly Data
(amounts in millions)

	Year 7			
	First	**Second**	**Third**	**Fourth**
Net sales	$1,114.6	$1,248.6	$1,128.3	$ 998.8
Cost of products sold	798.7	872.8	812.0	697.0
Net earnings	58.7	70.4	48.1	70.1
Per share				
Net earnings	.45	.54	.37	.54
Dividends	.165	.18	.18	.18
Market price				
High	33.25	31.88	35.38	34.88
Low	26.38	28.00	29.44	30.13

	Year 8			
	First	**Second**	**Third**	**Fourth**
Net sales	$1,179.1	$1,336.1	$1,207.4	$ 1,146.3
Cost of products sold	830.7	920.3	857.8	784.0
Earnings before cumulative effect of accounting change	62.4	84.6	22.4	72.2
Cumulative effect of change in accounting for income taxes	32.5			
Net earnings	94.9	84.6	22.4	72.2
Per share				
Earnings before cumulative effect of accounting change	.48	.65	.17	.56
Cumulative effect of change in accounting for income taxes	.25			
Net earnings	.73	.65	.17	.56
Dividends	.18	.21	.21	.21
Market price				
High	34.19	30.00	31.25	26.88
Low	22.75	24.38	25.75	23.88

Mills. The November year-end data can be used to compare Campbell with Kellogg, because the year-ends are close enough.

FINANCIAL REPORTING WORLDWIDE

We have identified many reasons why historical data may not be comparable across time and across firms. The premise is that when past data are lacking in comparability because one or more years' data are highly managed, are subject to significant measurement error, or cover different reporting periods, for example, then adjustments to the raw data might be necessary. Many of the comparability concerns discussed in the chapter apply equally to firms that follow reporting systems used outside the United States. There are important additional concerns to take into account when comparing financial data for firms that operate in different countries. Analysis of multinational firms entails a two-step approach:

1. Achieve comparability of the reporting methods, or accounting principles, employed by the firms under scrutiny.
2. Understand corporate strategies, institutional structures, and cultural practices unique to the countries in which the firms operate.

Ideally, financial reporting would be the same worldwide. That has not happened to date, however, and differences in accounting principles worldwide may severely affect both time series and cross-sectional comparisons of data reported by multinational firms.[29]

Exhibit 4.12 compares and contrasts a set of acceptable accounting principles in the United States with those in five major industrialized countries. The analyst needs to thoroughly understand the reporting system that the firm under scrutiny uses in order to decide what data adjustments are necessary.[30]

Firms headquartered outside the United States whose debt or equity securities are traded in U.S. capital markets are required to file a Form 20-F report with the SEC annually. The Form 20-F report must include a reconciliation of shareholders' equity and net income as reported under GAAP of the firm's local country with GAAP in the U.S. With this information, the analyst can convert the financial statements of a non-U.S. firm to achieve comparable accounting principles with U.S. firms.

---

[29]The International Accounting Standards Committee (IASC) has as its objective to improve and harmonize standards of financial reporting worldwide. The members of the IASC are professional accountancy bodies throughout the world. The standards issued by the Committee are the result of the work of representatives from thirteen countries. A comprehensive description of the IASC and its activities can be found in *Understanding IAS: Analysis and Interpretation,*" Coopers & Lybrand, 1996.

[30]An extensive summary of accounting principle differences around the world is available in Frederick D. S. Choi, *International Accounting and Finance Handbook,* Second Edition, New York: John Wiley & Sons, Inc., 1997. The largest public accounting firms also prepare comprehensive guides of financial reporting practices worldwide.

EXHIBIT 4.12

Summary of Generally Accepted Accounting Principles for Major Industrialized Countries

	United States	Canada	France	Japan	Great Britain	Germany
Marketable Securities (current asset)	Market value method	Lower of cost or market	Lower of cost or market	Cost (unless price declines considered permanent)	Lower of cost or market	Lower of cost or market
Bad Debts	Allowance method	Allowance method	Allowance method for identifiable uncollectible accounts	Allowance method	Allowance method	Allowance method for identifiable uncollectible accounts
Inventories—Valuation	Lower of cost or market	Lower of cost or market	Lower of cost or market	Lower of cost or market	Lower of cost or market	Lower of cost or market
—Cost Flow Assumption	FIFO, LIFO, average	FIFO, average	FIFO, average	FIFO, LIFO average	FIFO, average	Average (unless physical flow is FIFO or LIFO)
Fixed Assets—Valuation	Acquisition cost less depreciation	Acquisition cost less depreciation	Acquisition cost less depreciation[a]	Acquisition cost less depreciation	Acquisition cost less depreciation[b]	Acquisition cost less depreciation
—Depreciation	Straight-line, declining balance, sum-of-the-years'-digits	Straight-line, accelerated	Straight-line, accelerated	Straight-line, declining balance, sum-of-the-years'-digits	Straight-line, declining balance, sum-of-the-years'-digits	Straight-line, accelerated
Research and Development	Expensed when incurred	Expensed when incurred	Generally expensed when incurred, but may be capitalized and amortized	Expensed when incurred or capitalized and amortized	Expensed when incurred	Expensed when incurred
Leases	Operating and capital lease methods	Operating and capital lease methods	Operating and capital lease methods	Operating and capital lease methods	Operating and capital lease methods	Operating and capital lease methods
Deferred Taxes	Deferred tax accounting required	Deferred tax accounting required	Book/tax conformity generally required so deferred tax accounting not an issue	Book/tax conformity generally required so deferred tax accounting not an issue	Deferred tax accounting required based on probability that liability or asset will crystallize	Book/tax conformity generally required so deferred tax accounting not an issue

Investments in Securities						
0%–20%	Market value method	Cost (unless price declines considered permanent)	Lower of cost or market[a]	Cost (unless price declines considered permanent)	Lower of cost or market	Cost (unless price declines considered permanent)
20%–50%	Equity method	Equity method	Equity method	Cost (unless price declines considered permanent)	Equity method	Cost (unless price declines considered permanent)
Greater than 50%	Consolidation required	Consolidation generally required	Consolidation required	Consolidation not required (except in certain filings with the Ministry of Finance)	Both parent company and group (consolidated) financial statements presented	Consolidation required
Corporate Acquisitions Accounting Method	Purchase and pooling of interests methods	Purchase method[c]	Purchase method	Purchase method	Purchase and pooling of interests methods	Purchase method
Amortization of Goodwill	Amortized over maximum of 40 years	Amortized over maximum of 40 years	Amortization required	Amortized over maximum of 5 years	Goodwill either written off immediately against a retained earnings reserve or capitalized and amortized over its expected useful life.	Amortized over period of 5 to 15 years

[a]Generally accepted accounting principles in France permit periodic revaluations of tangible fixed assets and investments to current market values. However, the book/tax conformity requirement in France results in immediate taxation of unrealized gains. As a consequence, revaluations are unusual.

[b]Generally accepted accounting principles in Great Britain permit periodic revaluations of land, buildings, and certain intangibles to current market values. The firm credits a revaluation reserve account, a component of shareholders' equity.

[c]Generally accepted accounting principles in Canada permit the pooling of interests method when the accountant cannot identify which firm is the acquiror and which firm is the acquiree.

EXHIBIT 4.13

Form 20-F Reconciliations for Ericsson
(in millions)

	Year 4	Year 5	Year 6
Adjustments to Shareholders' Equity			
Reported Shareholders' Equity	SEK 23,302	SEK 34,263	SEK 40,456
Capitalization of Software	3,916	5,158	6,100
Capitalization of Interest Expense	310	325	349
Pensions	406	588	746
Revaluation of Fixed Assets	(729)	(608)	(500)
Deferred Taxes	(1,510)	(1,848)	(2,230)
Approximate Equity According to U.S. GAAP	SEK 25,695	SEK 37,878	SEK 44,921
Adjustments to Net Income			
Reported Net Income	SEK 3,949	SEK 5,439	SEK 7,110
Depreciation of Revalued Fixed Assets	—	121	108
Capitalization of Software Development Costs	1,004	1,242	942
Capitalization of Interest Expenses	16	15	24
Pensions	112	182	158
Deferred Income Taxes	(190)	(338)	(382)
Approximate Net Income According to U.S. GAAP	SEK 4,891	SEK 6,661	SEK 7,960

Example 26. Exhibit 4.13 presents the reconciliations for Ericsson, a Swedish manufacturer of cellular telephones, for three recent years. (We study the particular accounting principles requiring adjustment in later chapters and will therefore not discuss them at this time.) Note, however, that net income under U.S. GAAP significantly exceeds that under Swedish GAAP, primarily because of differences in the treatment of software development costs.

Achieving comparability in reporting is important to the analysis of multinational firms, but the data always need to be carefully interpreted. Analysis of multinational firms is complicated by the fact that the environments in which the firms operate may be very different in different countries. Operational strategies may pertain in one firm's base country that are not common in another's. Institutional arrangements, such as significant alliances with banks and extensive intercorporate holdings, may be common in one country and not in another. Cultural characteristics will affect how firms do business in one country—and those same characteristics will be foreign to other business settings.

In a study addressing comparability of Japanese and U.S. financial reporting, Herrmann, Inoue, and Thomas identify several environmental characteristics that may influence interpretation of the data:

1. Profitability ratios often are more conservative in Japan, largely because in Japan there is a close link between tax and financial reporting systems. (As Exhibit 4.12 illustrates, tax and book conformity is also common in France and Germany.)

2. Japanese companies often have higher debt ratios. High debt ratios sometimes are considered a sign of financial strength because debt is the primary source of capital.

3. The corporate group is different in Japan in that Japanese groups are often based on bank dependence, intercompany loans, mutual shareholding, preferred business transactions, and multiple personal ties.[31]

Herrmann, Inoue, and Thomas stress that environmental factors unique to Japan may influence the financial data reported by Japanese firms so that it is next to impossible to make the data comparable to data reported by U.S. firms. That is, even once the analyst makes the necessary adjustments, the data can be effectively interpreted only by taking these unique factors into consideration.

Other countries have their own unique environmental and business practices. Analysts looking at multinational firms needs to incorporate these factors into their interpretation of the data. It is essential to understand that, although the data may be comparable from a measurement perspective, they may not be comparable on other dimensions.

SUMMARY

Corporate financial statement data may not be comparable for a variety of reasons:

1. The sustainability, or the measurement, or the manageability of the reported earnings number do not allow it to reflect the economic value-added of a firm.

2. Financial statements of prior years are partially, but not fully, restated in the current year.

3. Financial statement items are classified in different ways across firms.

4. Financial statements are prepared for different time periods across firms.

5. Financial reporting systems employed for measuring and reporting financial data differ across firms because there are different reporting systems in different countries.

All five of these categories are discussed in this chapter, and many illustrations of how to adjust the data are provided.

The notion of "earnings quality," particularly as it relates to category (1), is a theme that continues in Chapters 5 through 7. These subsequent chapters explore important financial reporting issues in greater depth, and assess how they might impact the sustainability, measurement, and manageability of reporting earnings. In this regard, Chapters 4 through 7 represent a unit that addresses what are the relevant financial data for analysis. Chapter 5 focuses on asset valuation and income measurement. Chapter 6 examines the recognition and valuation of liabilities. Chapter 7 explores topics that have pervasive effects on all three principal financial statements, including corporate acquisitions, intercorporate investments, and foreign currency translation.

---

[31]Don Herrmann, Tatsuo Inoue, and Wayne Thomas, "Are There Benefits to Restating Japanese Financial Statements According to U.S. GAAP?" *Journal of Financial Statement Analysis,* Fall 1996, pp. 61–73.

PROBLEMS AND CASES

4.1 ADJUSTING FOR UNUSUAL INCOME STATEMENT ITEMS. Cirrus Logic is a leading manufacturer of advanced integrated circuits for the desktop and portable computing, telecommunications, industrial, and consumer electronics markets. Exhibit 4.14 presents Cirrus Logic's income statements for Year 5, Year 6, and Year 7. The notes to its financial statements reveal this information:

1. *Restructuring costs.* In Year 7, Cirrus Logic reorganized into four market divisions and outsourced certain of its production testing. The result was a $21 million pretax restructuring charge. In Year 6, Cirrus Logic took certain steps to bring operating expenses and capacity in line with demand, which resulted in a pretax charge of approximately $12 million.
2. *Gain on sale of assets.* In Year 7, Cirrus Logic sold assets related to two product lines for a gain of $19 million. The firm concluded that the breadth of its programs was diverting engineering and management resources from products for the firm's core markets. The firm also concluded that assessments of this type will be made on an ongoing basis.
3. *Nonrecurring costs.* In Year 5 and Year 6, Cirrus Logic recorded costs associated with forming joint ventures. The firm periodically enters into agreements with other industry leaders for developing and acquiring technology, and for marketing rights related to niche products. The costs involved include one-time charges for financial advisory services, and legal and accounting fees associated with establishing the ventures.

EXHIBIT 4.14

Cirrus Logic, Inc.
Income Statement
(amounts in millions)
(Problem 4.1)

	Year 5	Year 6	Year 7
Net Sales	$ 895	$1,147	$ 917
Cost of Sales	(513)	(774)	(599)
Research and Development	(166)	(239)	(231)
Selling and Administrative	(127)	(165)	(127)
Restructuring Costs	—	(12)	(21)
Gain on Sale of Assets	—	—	19
Nonrecurring Costs	(6)	(2)	0
Interest Expense	(2)	(5)	(19)
Interest Income	9	8	9
Income (Loss) Before Income Taxes	$ 90	$ (42)	$ (52)
Income Taxes (Benefit)	(29)	6	6
Net Income (Loss)	$ 61	$ (36)	$ (46)

Required

    a. Discuss the appropriate treatment of (1) restructuring costs, (2) nonrecurring costs, and (3) gain on sale of assets in an assessment of the profitability of Cirrus Logic.

    b. Assume now that you have decided to eliminate each of the items in part a. Indicate the adjustments to the income statement of Cirrus Logic to eliminate each of the items in part a. The income tax rate was 35 percent in Year 5, Year 6, and Year 7.

4.2   ADJUSTING FOR UNUSUAL INCOME STATEMENT ITEMS. H.J. Heinz Company is in the processed food products business. Exhibit 4.15 presents an income statement for Heinz for Year 2, Year 3, and Year 4. Notes to the financial statements reveal this information:

1. ***Gain on Sale of Corn Starch Business.*** In Year 2, Heinz sold the Hubinger Company, a major worldwide producer of cornstarches, for $325 million. Other Year 2 sales did not materially affect earnings.

2. ***Gain on Sale of Confectionery and Specialty Rice Businesses.*** In Year 4, Heinz sold its Near East specialty rice business for $80 million. Also in Year 4, Heinz sold its confectionery business in Italy for $133 million. These sales include trademarks, brand names, inventory, and fixed assets.

3. ***Restructuring Charges.*** Heinz provided restructuring charges of $88 million in Year 2 for consolidation of functions, staff reductions, organizational reform, and plant modernizations and closures. Heinz includes $66 million of this charge in cost of goods sold and $22 million in selling and administrative expenses. Heinz provided restructuring charges of $192 million ($143 million in cost of goods sold and $49 million in selling and administrative expenses) in Year 3 relating to employee severance and relocation costs and facilities consolidation and closure costs. These charges resulted from a decision to reduce employment levels by 3,000. As of the end of Year 4, Heinz had reduced employment levels by 2,000 and anticipates completion of the reductions in Year 5.

EXHIBIT 4.15

Income Statement
H.J. Heinz Company
(amounts in millions)
(Problem 4.2)

	Year 2	Year 3	Year 4
Sales	$ 6,582	$ 7,103	$ 7,047
Gain on Sale of Corn Starch Business	221		
Gain on Sale of Confectionery and Specialty Rice Businesses			127
Other Income	13	1	3
Cost of Goods Sold	(4,103)	(4,530)	(4,382)
Selling and Administrative Expenses	(1,594)	(1,712)	(1,724)
Interest Expense	(135)	(146)	(149)
Income Before Income Taxes	$ 984	$ 716	$ 922
Income Tax Expense	(346)	(186)	(319)
Net Income	$ 638	$ 530	$ 603

4. The statutory income tax rate was 34 percent in Year 2 and Year 3 and 35 percent in Year 4.

Required

a. Discuss whether you would eliminate any of these items when you are assessing Heinz's operating profitability:
   1. Gain on sale of cornstarch business.
   2. Gain on sale of confectionery and specialty rice businesses.
   3. Restructuring charges.
b. Indicate the adjustment you would make to net income to eliminate each of the items in part a.
c. Prepare a common size income statement for Year 2, Year 3, and Year 4 using the amounts in Exhibit 4.15. Set sales equal to 100 percent.
d. Repeat part c using amounts that exclude the effects of the items in part a.
e. Assess the changes in the profitability of Heinz during the three-year period.

4.3 ADJUSTING FOR UNUSUAL ITEMS AND ASSET IMPAIRMENTS. Sizzler International operates midscale restaurants. The restaurants feature a selection of steak, chicken, and seafood entrees offered in a family dining environment. Sizzler restaurants are typically free-standing buildings at an average size of 5,000 to 6,000 square feet, with seating for 150 to 200. Exhibit 4.16 presents an income statement for Sizzler International for Year 7, Year 8, and Year 9. The notes to the financial statements reveal this additional information:

1. *Nonrecurring Items.* In Year 8, Sizzler recorded a pretax restructuring charge of $109 million. The restructuring costs included predominantly non-cash write-offs of assets

---

EXHIBIT 4.16

Sizzler International, Inc.
Income Statement
(amounts in millions)
(Problem 4.3)

	Year 7	Year 8	Year 9
Restaurant Revenues	$ 448	$ 424	$ 290
Other Revenues	16	13	11
Cost of Sales	(163)	(159)	(111)
Labor and Related Expenses	(133)	(132)	(85)
Other Operating Expenses	(96)	(98)	(66)
Depreciation and Amortization	(28)	(26)	(16)
Nonrecurring Items	—	(109)	—
Impairment of Long-Lived Assets	—	(13)	—
General and Administrative Expenses	(30)	(32)	(22)
Interest Expense (Loss)	(1)	(2)	(7)
Income (Loss) Before Income Taxes	$ 13	$(134)	$ (6)
Income Tax (Expense) Benefit	(4)	(5)	7
Net Income (Loss)	$ 9	$(139)	$ 1

and related disposition costs associated with the closure of 130 restaurants in the United States. Specifically, restructuring expenses were incurred for market and restaurant closures ($92 million), closure of regional offices and reduction of corporate headquarters ($9 million), guarantee of co-op advertising obligations ($4 million), and severance and other costs ($4 million).

2. **Impairment of Long-Lived Assets.** Sizzler periodically reviews its long-lived assets for impairment whenever events or changes in circumstances indicate that the carrying amount of an asset or a group of assets may not be recoverable. The firm considers a history of operating losses to be its primary indicator of potential impairment. Sizzler considers an asset to be impaired if a forecast of undiscounted future operating cash flows directly related to the asset, including disposal value, if any, is less than the carrying amount of the asset. If any asset is determined to be impaired, the loss is measured as the amount by which the carrying amount of the asset exceeds fair value. For Year 8, Sizzler reported an impairment loss of $13 million.

Required

a. Discuss the appropriate treatment of (1) nonrecurring items, and (2) impairment of long-lived assets in an assessment of the profitability of Sizzler International.

b. Indicate the adjustments to the income statement of Sizzler to eliminate the items in part a. The income tax rate was 35 percent in Year 7, Year 8, and Year 9.

c. Sizzler's statement of cash flows shows an addback to net income for "nonrecurring items and asset writedown" of $122 million in Year 8. What is your interpretation of this addback?

4.4 ADJUSTMENTS FOR IMPAIRMENT OF LONG-LIFED ASSETS AND OTHER UNUSUAL ITEMS. Toys "R" Us operates 1,372 stores in 27 countries. The firm operates stores under the name of Toys "R" Us, Kids "R" Us, and Babies "R" Us. In Year 5, the firm undertook a

---

EXHIBIT 4.17

Toys "R" Us, Inc.
Income Statement
(amounts in millions)
(Problem 4.4)

	Year 4	Year 5	Year 6
Net Sales	$ 8,746	$ 9,427	$ 9,932
Cost of Sales	(6,008)	(6,592)	(6,893)
Selling, Advertising, General and Administration	(1,664)	(1,895)	(2,019)
Depreciation and Amortization	(161)	(192)	(206)
Other Charges	—	(397)	(60)
Interest Expense	(84)	(103)	(99)
Interest and Other Income	17	17	17
Income Before Income Taxes	$ 846	$ 265	$ 672
Income Taxes	(312)	(118)	(246)
Net Income	$ 534	$ 147	$ 426

worldwide restructuring program to streamline operations and to adopt (early) *Statement No. 121*, "Accounting for the Impairment of Long-Lived Assets and for Long-Lived Assets to be Disposed of." The total charge of $397 million, reported in Year 5 in Exhibit 4.17 as "Other Charges," consists of: (1) $185 million for strategic inventory repositioning, (2) $84 million for the closing or franchising of stores, (3) $72 million for the consolidation of three distribution centers, (4) $24 million for early adoption of *Statement No. 121*, and (5) $32 million of other costs. The $24 million for early adoption of *Statement No. 121* relates primarily to the writedown of certain store assets to fair value. The firm has not engaged in a restructuring program of this magnitude in the 20 years since it became a public company. Toys "R" Us also reported "Other Charges" of $60 million in the subsequent year (Year 6). This amount represents settlement of a licensing dispute that involved toy stores operated in the Middle East over a decade earlier.

Required

a. Discuss whether you would eliminate any of the five items that constitute the $397 million "Other Charges" for Year 5 to assess the operating profitability of Toys "R" Us. Discuss whether you would eliminate the "Other Charges" of $60 million for Year 6 to assess the operating profitability of the firm.

b. Discuss the events or circumstances that may have signaled asset recoverability problems to Toys "R" Us and led the firm to adopt *Statement No. 121* early.

c. Indicate the adjustments to the income statement of Toys "R" Us to eliminate each of the items in part a. The income tax rate was 35 percent in Year 4, Year 5, and Year 6.

d. The statement of cash flows for Toys "R" Us shows an addback to net income for "Other Charges" in Year 5 of $397 million, but no addback in Year 6 for "Other Charges." What is your interpretation of these two disclosures?

e. Assess the changes in the profitability of Toys "R" Us during the three-year period.

4.5   ADJUSTING FOR UNUSUAL ITEMS. Borden, Inc., derives approximately 75 percent of its revenues from branded food products and 25 percent from packaging and industrial products. The geographic sales mix comprises approximately 67 percent in the United States and 33 percent in other countries, although, interestingly, the firm's manufacturing and processing facilities are equally split between the United States and other countries. In Year 14 and Year 15, Borden was acquired by a firm that specializes in takeovers and buyouts of established firms. As a result, the firm experienced substantial business realignments and financial restructuring during the period. Exhibit 4.18 presents an income statement and Exhibit 4.19 presents a statement of cash flow for Borden for Year 14, Year 15, and Year 16. The notes to the financial statements reveal this additional information:

1. *Restructuring Charges and Discontinued Operations.* For years, Borden reported continually increasing sales while maintaining a profit margin of approximately 4 percent. Borden regularly purchased branded food products companies and other businesses with the cash flows generated by its mature food products business. Sales and earnings started declining in Year 10, however, as a result of deteriorating market positions in certain branded food products segments as well as difficulties in managing the diverse set of businesses in which Borden was competing. Borden consequently embarked on a major restructuring program in Year 10. The restructuring program involved both organizational changes and divestiture of its North American snacks, seafood, jams and jellies, and other businesses. Four years later, Borden went through another restructuring brought on by factors similar to those identified in Year 10. (The firm reported no restructuring charges in Year 11, Year 12, or Year 13.) The restructuring charges and

EXHIBIT 4.18

Borden, Inc.
Income Statement
(amounts in millions)
(Problem 4.5)

	Year 14	Year 15	Year 16
Continuing Operations			
Sales	$ 6,226	$ 6,261	$ 5,944
Other Income (Expense)—Net	35	(138)	(18)
Cost of Goods Sold	(4,083)	(4,240)	(4,136)
Selling and Administrative	(2,045)	(1,963)	(1,809)
Restructing Expense	(115)	(15)	11
(Loss) Gain on Divestitures	15	59	(245)
Impairment Losses	0	(293)	(8)
Interest	(140)	(143)	(140)
Minority Interest	(41)	(41)	(16)
Income Taxes	51	(53)	(24)
Income (Loss) from Continuing Operations ...	$ (97)	$ (566)	$ (441)
Discontinued Operations			
Income (Loss) from Operations	$ (26)	$ (27)	$ 9
Loss on Disposal	490	(59)	67
Income (Loss) from Discontinued Operations ..	$ (516)	$ (32)	$ 76
Accounting Changes			
Postretirement Benefits Other than Pensions ..	(18)	—	—
Net Income (Loss)	$ (631)	$ (598)	$ (366)

credits in Year 14, Year 15, and Year 16 relate to streamlining operations. The charges involve employee severances and relocations and plant closings, part of which Borden includes in continuing operations, and part of which it includes in income from discontinued operations. The loss on disposal recognized in Year 14 represents a pretax charge of $637 million ($490 million after taxes) to provide for the expected future disposal of the North American businesses described above. The charges and credits in Year 15 and Year 16 relate to these businesses as well.

2. *Loss/Gain on Divestitures.* In Year 16, Borden redesigned its operating structure and made the decision to divest additional businesses. The firm recorded a $245 million charge related to the estimated losses on the disposal or consolidation of these businesses. The firm indicates that a large portion of the charge relates to the excess of net book values over expected proceeds.

3. *Impairment Losses.* In Year 15, Borden wrote down goodwill, plant, and equipment totaling $293 million. The firm concluded that ongoing and projected operating losses reported by the businesses represented by these assets indicated that the carrying values of the assets were not expected to be recovered by their future cash flows. Borden states that the future cash flow projections were measured at the business level at which the business is managed. A similar writedown of $8 million was recorded in Year 16.

EXHIBIT 4.19			

Borden, Inc.
Statement of Cash Flows
(amounts in millions)
(Problem 4.5)

	Year 14	Year 15	Year 16
Operations			
Net Income	$(631)	$(598)	$(366)
Depreciation and Amortization	224	193	157
Loss on Disposal—Discontinued Operations	637	95	245
Restructuring	53	(57)	(53)
Impairment Losses	—	293	8
(Increase) Decrease in Accounts Receivable	61	(41)	7
(Increase) Decrease in Inventories	30	(44)	10
Increase (Decrease) in Accounts Payable	3	50	(27)
Increase (Decrease) in Current and Deferred Taxes	(242)	(24)	9
Other Changes in Working Capital Accounts	17	(7)	92
Cash Flow from Operations	$ 152	$ (92)	$ 82
Investing			
Capital Expenditures	$(177)	$(150)	$(203)
Divestiture of Businesses and Sale of Securities ...	53	409	289
Purchase of Businesses	(9)	—	(6)
Cash Flow from Investing	$(133)	$ 259	$ 80
Financing			
Increase (Decrease) in Short-Term Debt	$(536)	$ (85)	$(192)
Increase in Long-Term Debt	275	616	3
Issuance of Capital Stock	12	6	998
Reduction in Long-Term Debt	(129)	(493)	(436)
Dividends	(127)	(36)	(43)
Other	400	(150)	(472)
Cash Flow from Financing	$(105)	$(142)	$(142)
Change in Cash	(86)	25	20
Cash—Beginning of Year	186	100	125
Cash—End of Year	$ 100	$ 125	$ 145

Required

    a. Why do the amounts for restructuring charges in the income statement in Exhibit 4.18 differ from the amounts for restructuring charges reported in the operations section of the statement of cash flows in Exhibit 4.19?

    b. Why does the amount for loss on disposal of discontinued operations in the income statement in Exhibit 4.18 in Year 14 differ from the amount reported in the operations section of the statement of cash flows in Exhibit 4.19?

   c. Discuss whether you would eliminate any of these items when you are assessing the operating profitability of Borden: (1) restructuring charges, (2) discontinued operations, (3) loss or gain on divestitures, and (4) impairment losses.

   d. Assume now that you have decided to eliminate each of the four items in part c, plus the adjustment for the accounting change. Indicate the change in net income as a result of such eliminations. The income tax rate is 35 percent for Year 14, Year 15, and Year 16.

   e. Prepare a common size income statement for Borden after eliminating the items in part d. Set sales equal to 100 percent.

   f. Assess the changes in the profitability of Borden during the three-year period.

4.6   USING ORIGINALLY REPORTED VERSUS RESTATED DATA. Prior to Year 8, General Dynamics Corporation was involved in a wide variety of industries, including weapons manufacturing under government contracts, information technologies, commercial aircraft manufacturing, missile systems, coal mining, material service, and ship management and ship financing. During Year 8, General Dynamics sold its information technologies business. During Year 9, it sold its commercial aircraft manufacturing business. During Year 9, it also announced its intention to sell its missile systems, coal mining, material service, and ship management and financing businesses. These strategic moves would leave General Dynamics with only its weapons manufacturing business.

Financial statements for General Dynamics for Year 8 as originally reported, Year 8 as restated in the Year 9 annual report for discontinued operations, and Year 9 as originally reported appear in Exhibit 4.20 (balance sheet), Exhibit 4.21 (income statement), and Exhibit 4.22 (statement of cash flows).

Required

   a. Look at the balance sheets of General Dynamics in Exhibit 4.20. Why does the restated amount for total assets for Year 8 of $4,672 million differ from the originally reported amount of $6,207 million?

   b. Look at the income statement for General Dynamics in Exhibit 4.21. Why are the originally reported and restated net income amounts for Year 8 the same (that is, $505 million) when all the individual revenues and expenses decreased upon restatement?

   c. Look at the statement of cash flows for General Dynamics in Exhibit 4.22. Why is the restated amount of cash flow from operations for Year 8 of $609 million less than the originally reported amount of $673 million?

   d. If an analyst wanted to analyze changes in the structure of assets and equities between Year 8 and Year 9, which columns and amounts in Exhibit 4.20 would the analyst use? Explain.

   e. If an analyst wanted to analyze changes in the operating profitability between Year 8 and Year 9, which columns and amounts in Exhibit 4.21 would the analyst use? Explain.

   f. If an analyst wanted to use cash flow ratios to assess short-term liquidity and long-term solvency risk, which columns and amounts in Exhibit 4.22 would the analyst use? Explain.

4.7   USING ORIGINALLY REPORTED VERSUS RESTATED DATA. INTERCO is a manufacturer and retailer of a broad line of consumer products, including London Fog, Florsheim Shoes, Converse, Ethan Allen Furniture, and Lane Furniture. During Year 9, INTERCO

EXHIBIT 4.20

General Dynamics Corporation
Balance Sheet
(amounts in millions)
(Problem 4.6)

	Year 8 as Originally Reported	Year 8 as Restated in Year 9 Annual Report	Year 9 as Reported
Assets			
Cash and Cash Equivalents	$ 513	$ 507	$ 513
Marketable Securities	307	307	432
Accounts Receivable	444	99	64
Contracts in Process	2,606	1,474	1,550
Net Assets of Discontinued Businesses	—	1,468	767
Current Assets	449	145	329
Total Current Assets	$4,319	$4,000	$3,655
Property, Plant, and Equipment (net)	1,029	372	322
Other Assets	859	300	245
Total Assets	$6,207	$4,672	$4,222
Liabilities and Shareholders' Equity			
Accounts Payable and Accruals	$2,593	$ 642	$ 553
Current Portion of Long-term Debt	516	450	145
Other Current Liabilities	—	1,174	1,250
Total Current Liabilities	$3,109	$2,266	$1,948
Long-term Debt	365	163	38
Other Noncurrent Liabilities	753	263	362
Total Liabilities	$4,227	$2,692	$2,348
Common Stock	$ 55	$ 55	$ 42
Additional Paid-in Capital	25	25	—
Retained Earnings	2,651	2,651	2,474
Treasury Stock	(751)	(751)	(642)
Total Shareholders' Equity	$1,980	$1,980	$1,874
Total Liabilities and Shareholders' Equity	$6,207	$4,672	$4,222

became the target of an unfriendly takeover attempt. In an effort to defend itself against the takeover, INTERCO declared a special dividend of $1.4 billion. It financed the dividend by issuing long-term debt and preferred stock. INTERCO planned to dispose of certain businesses to repay a portion of this debt.

Exhibits 4.23, 4.24, and 4.25 present balance sheets, income statements, and statements of cash flows for INTERCO. The first column of each exhibit shows the amounts as originally reported for Year 8. The second column shows the restated amounts for Year 8 to reflect the decision to dispose of certain businesses that INTERCO had previously included in continuing operations. The third column shows the amounts reported for Year 9.

EXHIBIT 4.21

General Dynamics Corporation
Income Statement
(amounts in millions)
(Problem 4.6)

	Year 8 as Originally Reported	Year 8 as Restated in Year 9 Annual Report	Year 9 as Reported
Continuing Operations			
Sales	$ 8,751	$ 3,322	$ 3,472
Operating Costs and Expenses	(8,359)	(3,207)	(3,297)
Interest Income (Expense), net	(34)	4	25
Other Expense, net	(27)	(27)	27
Earnings Before Income Taxes	$ 331	$ 92	$ 227
Income Tax Credit	43	114	21
Income from Continuing Operations	$ 374	$ 206	$ 248
Discontinued Operations			
Earnings from Operations	$ 131	$ 299	$ 193
Gain on Disposal	—	—	374
Net Income	$ 505	$ 505	$ 815

EXHIBIT 4.22

General Dynamics Corporation
Statement of Cash Flows
(amounts in millions)
(Problem 4.6)

	Year 8 as Originally Reported	Year 8 as Restated in Year 9 Annual Report	Year 9 as Reported
Operations			
Income from Continuing Operations	$ 374	$ 206	$ 248
Depreciation and Amortization	303	140	56
(Increase) Decrease in Accounts Receivable ...	(91)	4	35
(Increase) Decrease in Contracts in Process ...	237	(83)	(76)
(Increase) Decrease in Other Current Assets ..	13	8	(6)
Increase (Decrease) in Accounts Payable and Accruals	262	51	(66)
Increase (Decrease) in Other Current Liabilities	(469)	(41)	11
Cash Flow from Continuing Operations	$ 629	$ 285	$ 202
Cash Flow from Discontinued Operations	44	324	288
Cash Flow from Operations	$ 673	$ 609	$ 490

(continued)

Exh. 4.22—Continued	Year 8 as Originally Reported	Year 8 as Restated in Year 9 Annual Report	Year 9 as Reported
Investing			
Proceeds from Sale of Discontinued Operations . .	$ 184	$ 184	$ 1,039
Capital Expenditures	(82)	(29)	(18)
Purchase of Marketable Securities	(307)	(307)	(125)
Other	56	3	32
Cash Flow from Investing	$(149)	$(149)	$ 928
Financing			
Issue of Common Stock	—	—	$ 57
Repayment of Debt	$ (61)	$ (11)	(454)
Purchase of Common Stock	—	—	(960)
Dividends	(42)	(42)	(55)
Other	(17)	—	—
Cash Flow from Financing	$(120)	$ (53)	$(1,412)
Change in Cash	$ 404	$ 407	$ 6
Cash—Beginning of Year	109	100	507
Cash—End of Year	$ 513	$ 507	$ 513

EXHIBIT 4.23

INTERCO
Balance Sheet
(amounts in thousands)
(Problem 4.7)

	Year 8 as Originally Reported	Year 8 as Restated in Year 9 Annual Report	Year 9 as Originally Reported
Cash and Marketable Securities	$ 31,882	$ 23,299	$ 77,625
Receivables	486,657	310,053	329,299
Inventories	805,095	514,193	490,967
Prepayments	35,665	24,984	41,625
Net Assets of Discontinued Businesses	—	521,644	346,372
Total Current Assets	$ 1,359,299	$1,394,173	$ 1,285,888
Property, Plant, and Equipment (net)	479,499	317,238	327,070
Other Assets	146,788	118,989	162,344
Total Assets	$ 1,985,586	$1,830,400	$ 1,775,302

Exh. 4.23—Continued	Year 8 as Originally Reported	Year 8 as Restated in Year 9 Annual Report	Year 9 as Originally Reported
Current Liabilities	$ 373,343	$ 269,315	$ 736,268
Long-Term Debt	299,140	266,191	1,986,837
Other Noncurrent Liabilities	61,766	43,557	57,947
Total Liabilities	$ 734,249	$ 579,063	$ 2,781,052
Contributed Capital	$ 256,740	$ 256,740	$ 339,656
Retained Earnings	1,179,964	1,179,964	(1,208,250)
Treasury Stock	(185,367)	(185,367)	(137,156)
Total Shareholders' Equity	$1,251,337	$1,251,337	$(1,005,750)
Total Liabilities and Shareholders' Equity	$1,985,586	$1,830,400	$ 1,775,302

EXHIBIT 4.24

INTERCO
Income Statement
(amounts in thousands)
(Problem 4.7)

	Year 8 as Originally Reported	Year 8 as Restated in Year 9 Annual Report	Year 9 as Originally Reported
Sales	$3,341,423	$1,995,974	$2,011,962
Other Income	29,237	13,714	18,943
Total Revenues	$3,370,660	$2,009,688	$2,030,905
Cost of Goods Sold	$2,284,640	$1,288,748	$1,335,678
Selling and Administrative	799,025	493,015	537,797
Interest	33,535	29,188	141,735
Income Taxes	108,457	85,303	19,977
Total Expenses	$3,225,657	$1,896,254	$2,035,187
Income from Continuing Operations	$ 145,003	$ 113,434	$ (4,282)
Income from Discontinued Operations	—	31,569	74,432
Net Income	$ 145,003	$ 145,003	$ 70,150

Required

a. Look at the balance sheets of INTERCO in Exhibit 4.23. Why is the restated amount for total assets for Year 8 of $1,830,400 different from the originally reported amount for total assets of $1,985,586?

b. Look at the income statement of INTERCO in Exhibit 4.24. Why are the originally reported and restated net income the same ($145,003) when each of the Company's individual revenues and expenses decrease upon restatement?

c. Look at the statement of cash flows for INTERCO in Exhibit 4.25. Why is the restated amount of cash flow from operations for Year 8 of $94,447 less than the originally reported amount of $117,774?

EXHIBIT 4.25

INTERCO
Statements of Cash Flows
(amounts in thousands)
(Problem 4.7)

	Year 8 as Originally Reported	Year 8 as Restated in Year 9 Annual Report	Year 9 as Originally Reported
Operations			
Income (Loss) from Continuing Operations	$ 145,003	$ 113,434	$ (4,282)
Depreciation	62,772	40,570	40,037
Other Addbacks (Subtractions)	13,957	8,750	(24,230)
Change in Operating Working Capital Accounts	(103,958)	(96,271)	29,015
Cash Flow from Continuing Operations	$ 117,774	$ 66,483	$ 40,540
Cash Flow from Discontinued Operations	—	27,964	249,704
Cash Flow from Operations	$ 117,774	$ 94,447	$ 290,244
Investing			
Sale of Fixed Assets	$ 8,102	$ 1,145	$ 4,134
Acquisition of Fixed Assets	(65,880)	(45,925)	(50,966)
Cash Flow from Investing	$ (57,778)	$ (44,780)	$ (46,832)
Financing			
Increase in Short-Term Borrowing	$ 1,677	$ 1,677	$ —
Increase in Long-Term Borrowing	205,673	205,533	1,967,500
Increase in Capital Stock	4,606	4,606	19,994
Decrease in Long-Term Borrowing	(95,841)	(85,570)	(617,401)
Decrease in Capital Stock	(160,442)	(160,442)	(102,341)
Dividends	(64,219)	(64,219)	(1,456,162)
Other	54	252	(676)
Cash Flow from Financing	$(108,492)	$ (98,163)	$ (189,086)
Net Change in Cash	$ (48,496)	$ (48,496)	$ 54,326

d. If an analyst wanted to analyze changes in the structure of assets and equities between Year 8 and Year 9, which columns and which amounts in Exhibit 4.23 would the analyst use? Explain.

e. If an analyst wanted to compare the change in operating performance between Year 8 and Year 9, which columns and which amounts in Exhibit 4.24 would the analyst use? Explain.

f. Describe briefly how INTERCO's actions during Year 9 might serve to thwart an unfriendly takeover attempt.

4.8 ADJUSTING FINANCIAL STATEMENTS FOR DIFFERENT ACCOUNTING PRINCIPLES. In Year 6, Glaxo Holdings acquired Wellcome, maintaining its position as the largest pharmaceutical company in the United Kingdom. Glaxo prepares financial statements in accordance with generally accepted accounting principles (GAAP) in the U.K. The statements prepared by Glaxo prior to the acquisition of Wellcome appear in Exhibit 4.26 (balance sheet), Exhibit 4.27 (income statement), and Exhibit 4.28 (statement of cash flows). Exhibit 4.29 presents a reconciliation of shareholders' equity and net income from U.K. accounting principles to U.S. accounting principles. A description of the reconciling items appears below.

Deferred Taxation. U.K. GAAP requires the recognition of deferred taxes only when it is probable that deferred tax benefits or liabilities will be realized. U.S. GAAP requires the recognition of deferred taxes for all temporary differences between financial and tax reporting.

Post-retirement Benefits Other Than Pensions. U.K. GAAP allows recognition of postretirement benefits other than pensions on a cash basis. U.S. GAAP requires recognition of this benefit obligation on an accrual basis. The postretirements benefit obligation was £26 million on July 1, Year 3.

Goodwill. U.K. GAAP allows firms to write off goodwill against retained earnings. U.S. GAAP requires firms to capitalize and amortize goodwill over a maximum period of 40 years.

Dividends. U.K. GAAP provides for the recognition of a liability when a board of directors recommends a dividend to shareholders for their approval. U.S. GAAP does not recognize a dividend until it is declared by a board of directors, which occurs in the U.K. after shareholders' approval.

Required

a. Indicate the adjustments to the balance sheet, income statement, and statement of cash flows of Glaxo to convert its financial statements from U.K. GAAP to U.S. GAAP. Glaxo includes the dividend recommended to shareholders in other current liabilities.

b. Compute the rate of return on common shareholders' equity using the reported amounts (U.K. GAAP) and the adjusted amounts (U.S. GAAP). Disaggregate ROCE into ROA, common earnings leverage, and capital structure leverage components. The income tax rate is 33 percent.

c. Why are ROCE and ROA higher and the capital structure leverage ratio lower using the reported amounts (U.K. GAAP) than using the adjusted amounts (U.S. GAAP)?

4.9 ADJUSTING FINANCIAL STATEMENTS FOR DIFFERENT ACCOUNTING PRINCIPLES. Benetton, headquartered in Italy, operates women's retail apparel stores worldwide. Financial statements for Benetton prepared in accordance with generally accepted accounting principles (GAAP) in Italy appear in Exhibit 4.30 (balance sheet), Exhibit 4.31 (income statement), and Exhibit 4.32 (statement of cash flows). Exhibit 4.33 presents a reconciliation of shareholders' equity and net income from Italian accounting principles to U.S. accounting principles. A description of the reconciling items appears on the next page.

EXHIBIT 4.26

Glaxo
Balance Sheet
(amounts in millions)
(Problem 4.8)

	June 30		
	Year 2	Year 3	Year 4
Assets			
Cash	£ 225	£ 390	£ 119
Marketable Securities	1,524	2,107	2,644
Accounts Receivable	720	916	908
Inventories	475	595	575
Other Current Assets	211	234	234
Total Current Assets	£3,155	£4,242	£4,480
Investments in Securities	32	61	55
Property, Plant, and Equipment (net)	2,341	2,959	3,184
Other Assets	154	196	168
Total Assets	£5,682	£7,458	£7,887
Liabilities and Shareholders' Equity			
Accounts Payable	£ 162	£ 178	£ 188
Short-Term Debt	366	597	400
Other Current Liabilities	1,040	1,425	1,542
Total Current Liabilities	£1,568	£2,200	£2,130
Long-Term Debt	137	243	298
Deferred Income Taxes	179	193	139
Other Noncurrent Liabilities	159	165	154
Total Liabilities	£2,043	£2,801	£2,721
Minority Interests in Subsidiaries	£ 67	£ 111	£ 123
Common Stock	£ 753	£ 758	£ 762
Additional Paid-in Capital	77	151	229
Retained Earnings	2,742	3,637	4,052
Total Shareholders' Equity	£3,572	£4,546	£5,043
Total Liabilities and Shareholders' Equity . . .	£5,682	£7,458	£7,887

Revaluation of Fixed Assets. Prior to Year 4, Italian law permitted firms to revalue fixed assets to market values, increasing a shareholders' equity account for the writeup. Depreciation on the revalued amounts appears in depreciation expense in subsequent years.

Goodwill Writeoff. Italian GAAP allows firms to write off goodwill from corporate acquisitions against retained earnings in the year of acquisition. U.S. GAAP requires the capitalization and subsequent amortization of goodwill.

Deferred Taxes. The reconciling items for deferred taxes represent the deferred income tax effects of other reconciling adjustments.

EXHIBIT 4.27

Glaxo
Income Statement
(amounts in millions)
(Problem 4.8)

	Year Ended June 30	
	Year 3	**Year 4**
Sales	£ 4,930	£ 5,656
Other Revenues	206	65
Cost of Goods Sold	(871)	(1,007)
Selling and Administrative	(1,795)	(1,972)
Research and Development	(739)	(858)
Interest	(56)	(44)
Income Taxes	(461)	(525)
Minority Interest in Net Income	(7)	(12)
Net Income	£ 1,207	£ 1,303

EXHIBIT 4.28

Glaxo
Statement of Cash Flows
(amounts in millions)
(Problem 4.8)

	Year Ended June 30	
	Year 3	**Year 4**
Operations		
Net Income	£ 1,207	£ 1,303
Depreciation and Amortization	225	282
Other Addbacks	86	120
Other Subtractions	(29)	(11)
	£ 1,489	£ 1,694
(Increase) Decrease in Accounts Receivable	(196)	8
(Increase) Decrease in Inventories	29	5
(Increase) Decrease in Other Current Assets	102	0
Increase (Decrease) in Accounts Payable	16	10
Increase (Decrease) in Other Current Liabilities	30	41
Cash Flow from Operations	£ 1,470	£ 1,758

(continued)

	Year Ended June 30	
Exh. 4.28—Continued	**Year 3**	**Year 4**
Investing		
Property, Plant, and Equipment Sold	£ 84	£ 22
Property, Plant, and Equipment Acquired	(608)	(575)
Investments Acquired	(337)	(814)
Other Investing Transactions	3	4
Cash Flow from Investing	£ (858)	£(1,363)
Financing		
Increase (Decrease) in Short-Term Borrowing	£ 27	£ (12)
Issue of Common Stock	69	51
Dividends	(543)	(705)
Cash Flow from Financing	£ (447)	£ (666)
Change in Cash	£ 165	£ (271)
Cash—Beginning of Year	225	390
Cash—End of Year	£ 390	£ 119

EXHIBIT 4.29

Glaxo
Reconciliation of U.K. and U.S. GAAP
(amounts in millions)
(Problem 4.8)

	June 30		
	Year 2	**Year 3**	**Year 4**
Shareholders' Equity, U.K. GAAP	£3,572	£4,546	£5,043
Deferred Taxation	(218)	(279)	(307)
Post-retirement Benefits Other Than			
Pensions	—	—	(26)
Goodwill	23	27	35
Dividends	330	455	549
Shareholders' Equity, U.S. GAAP	£3,707	£4,749	£5,294

	Year Ended June 30	
	Year 3	**Year 4**
Net Income, U.K. GAAP	£1,207	£1,303
Deferred Taxation	(61)	(28)
Post-retirement Benefits Other than Pensions	—	(26)
Goodwill Amortization	(1)	(1)
Net Income, U.S. GAAP	£1,145	£1,248

EXHIBIT 4.30

Benetton
Balance Sheet
(amounts in millions of Italian Lire)
(Problem 4.9)

	Year 8	Year 9
Assets		
Cash	L 643,275	L 875,944
Marketable Securities	50,937	80,891
Accounts Receivable	1,401,541	1,404,810
Inventories	489,970	506,363
Other Current Assets	57,960	53,030
Total Current Assets	L 2,643,683	L 2,921,038
Investments in Securities	228,756	223,368
Property, Plant, and Equipment (net)	593,598	618,017
Other Assets	71,128	74,656
Total Assets	L 3,537,165	L 3,837,079
Liabilities and Shareholders' Equity		
Accounts Payable	L 500,414	L 517,298
Short-Term Debt	482,501	730,024
Other Current Liabilities	233,371	252,229
Total Current Liabilities	L 1,216,286	L 1,499,551
Long-Term Debt	630,661	483,896
Deferred Income Taxes	73,564	68,010
Other Noncurrent Liabilities	68,594	89,801
Total Liabilities	L 1,989,105	L 2,141,258
Minority Interests in Subsidiaries	L 43,904	L 38,863
Common Stock	L 87,277	L 87,277
Additional Paid-in Capital	472,661	472,661
Surplus from Revaluation of Assets	45,116	45,028
Retained Earnings	899,102	1,051,992
Total Shareholders' Equity	L 1,504,156	L 1,656,958
Total Liabilities and Shareholders' Equity	L 3,537,165	L 3,837,079

Required

a. Indicate the effect on the balance sheet, income statement, and statement of cash flows of adjusting the financial statements of Benetton to U.S. GAAP.

b. Compute rate of return on common shareholders' equity of Benetton using the reported amounts (Italian GAAP) and the restated amounts (U.S. GAAP). Disaggregate ROCE into ROA, common earnings leverage, and capital structure leverage components. The income tax rate is 36 percent. Use end-of-year balances in the calculations.

c. Discuss the effect of the restatements to U.S. GAAP on your assessments of the profitability of Benetton.

EXHIBIT 4.31

Benetton
Income Statement
(amounts in millions of Italian Lire)
(Problem 4.9)

	Year Ended December 31	
	Year 8	Year 9
Sales	L 2,787,672	L 2,939,134
Other Revenues	580,276	581,770
Cost of Goods Sold	(1,638,151)	(1,704,101)
Selling and Administrative	(818,880)	(812,700)
Interest	(553,174)	(593,008)
Income Taxes	(150,554)	(188,659)
Minority Interest in Net (Income) Loss	3,031	(2,181)
Net Income	L 210,220	L 220,255

EXHIBIT 4.32

Benetton
Statement of Cash Flows
(amounts in millions of Italian Lire)
(Problem 4.9)

	Year Ended December 31	
	Year 8	Year 9
Operations		
Net Income	L 210,220	L 220,255
Depreciation and Amortization	95,612	100,989
Other Addbacks	239,502	314,582
Other Subtractions	(19,702)	(21,505)
	L 525,632	L 614,321
(Increase) Decrease in Accounts Receivable	(100,768)	(106,688)
(Increase) Decrease in Inventories	(47,988)	(17,202)
(Increase) Decrease in Other Current Assets	(69,621)	28,301
Increase (Decrease) in Accounts Payable	(18,338)	13,670
Increase (Decrease) in Other Current Liabilities	(213,357)	(163,559)
Cash Flow from Operations	L 75,560	L 368,843

	Year Ended December 31	
Exh. 4.32—Continued	**Year 8**	**Year 9**

Investing

Property, Plant, and Equipment Sold	L 26,098	L 26,031
Investments Sold	24,463	7,793
Property, Plant, and Equipment Acquired	(141,532)	(136,673)
Investments Acquired	(51,672)	(37,581)
Other Investing Transactions	(9,126)	196
Cash Flow from Investing	L (151,769)	L(140,234)

Financing

Increase (Decrease) in Short-Term Borrowing	L (158,270)	L 99,378
Increase (Decrease) in Long-Term Borrowing	(91,510)	(23,234)
Sale of stock	300,767	—
Dividends	(80,200)	(75,719)
Other Financing Transactions	(62,835)	12,163
Cash Flow from Financing	L (92,048)	L 12,788
Effect of Translation Adjustment	L (1,533)	L (8,728)
Change in Cash	L (169,790)	L 232,669
Cash—Beginning of Year	813,065	643,275
Cash—End of Year	L 643,275	L 875,944

EXHIBIT 4.33

Reconciliation of Italian and U.S. GAAP for Benetton
(amounts in millions of Italian lire)
(Problem 4.9)

	Year 8	Year 9
Shareholders' Equity, Italian GAAP	L1,504,156	L1,656,958
Elimination of Revaluations of Fixed Assets		
Net of Depreciation	(8,625)	(8,150)
Reinstatement of Goodwill Previously		
Written Off	4,991	3,002
Deferred Taxes	(46,793)	(27,700)
Shareholders' Equity, U.S. GAAP	L1,453,729	L1,624,110

	Year Ended June 30	
	Year 8	**Year 9**
Net Income, Italian GAAP	L210,220	L220,255
Reduction in Depreciation on Revalued Fixed		
Assets	5,160	475
Amortization of Goodwill	(1,052)	(1,989)
Deferred Taxes	12,642	19,740
Net Income, U.S. GAAP	L226,970	L238,481

CASE 4.1

INTERNATIONAL PAPER: A RECURRING DILEMMA

International Paper Company is the largest forest products company in the world. It operates in five segments of the forest products industry:

1. **Printing Paper**. Uncoated and coated papers used for reprographic and printing, envelopes, writing tablets, file folders, and magazines.
2. **Packaging**. Liner board used for corrugated boxes and bleached packaging board used for food, pharmaceutical, cosmetic, and other consumer products.
3. **Distribution**. Sale of printing, graphic, packaging, and similar products through wholesale and retail outlets. Sales of these outlets comprise approximately 20 percent of International Paper's products and 80 percent of other manufacturers' products.
4. **Specialty Products**. Film, door facings, wood siding, fabrics, and chemicals used for adhesives and paints.
5. **Forest Products**. Logs, lumber, plywood, and wood panels. International Paper has the largest timber holdings of any private sector entity in the United States.

Exhibit 4.34 presents product segment data for International Paper for Year 7 through Year 10. The proportion of sales generated within the United States decreased from 79 percent in Year 7 to 71 percent in Year 10. The proportion generated within Europe fluctuated between 17 and 19 percent during the four-year period. The proportion from the rest of the world, primarily East Asia, increased from 3 percent in Year 7 to 12 percent in Year 10.

The financial statements for International Paper for Year 7 through Year 10 appear in Exhibit 4.35 (income statement), Exhibit 4.36 (balance sheet), and Exhibit 4.37 (statement of cash flows). Exhibit 4.38 presents financial ratios for International Paper based on the reported amounts.

The notes to the financial statements reveal this additional information:

1. **Change in Accounting Principle**. Effective January 1, Year 8, International Paper changed its method of accounting for start-up costs on major projects to expensing these costs as incurred. Prior to Year 8, the firm capitalized these costs as part of property, plant, and equipment and amortized them over a five-year period. The firm made the change to increase the focus on controlling costs associated with facility start-ups. International Paper recorded a pretax charge of $125 million ($75 million after taxes) as the cumulative effect of an accounting change in Year 8.
2. **Gain on Sale of Partnership Interest**. On March 29, Year 10, International Paper sold its general partnership interest in a partnership that owned 300,000 acres of forest lands located in Oregon and Washington. Included in the partnership were forest lands, roads, and $750 million of long-term debt. As a result of this transaction, International Paper recognized a pretax gain of $592 million ($336 million after taxes). International Paper maintains general partnership interests in several partnerships created by the firm as a means of raising capital from outside investors. International Paper consolidates the financial statements of these partnerships with its own financial statements, and shows the interest of the remaining partners (limited partners) as a minority interest.
3. **Restructuring and Asset Impairment Charges**. During the first quarter of Year 10, the firm's board of directors authorized a series of management actions to restructure

EXHIBIT 4.34

International Paper
Product Line Segment Profitability Analysis
(Case 4.1)

	Year 7	Year 8	Year 9	Year 10
Sales Mix				
Printing Papers	27%	28%	29%	26%
Packaging	22	22	21	23
Distribution	22	22	24	22
Specialty Products	17	17	16	16
Forest Products	12	11	10	13
	100%	100%	100%	100%
Rate of Return on Assets				
Printing Papers	(1.9%)	.3%	15.3%	2.1%
Packaging	6.2%	9.5%	17.9%	6.9%
Distribution	5.3%	6.1%	7.3%	8.1%
Specialty Products	10.1%	9.6%	5.7%	(1.4%)
Forest Products	30.4%	27.3%	8.7%	17.2%
Profit Margin				
Printing Papers	(3.1%)	.5%	17.7%	3.3%
Packaging	6.1%	8.7%	16.8%	8.5%
Distribution	1.8%	2.1%	2.1%	2.3%
Specialty Products	10.7%	10.3%	6.3%	(1.5%)
Forest Products	28.7%	24.4%	18.5%	34.7%
Assets Turnover				
Printing Papers	.60	.66	.87	.65
Packaging	1.03	1.09	1.07	.81
Distribution	2.89	2.86	3.46	3.47
Specialty Products	.94	.93	.91	.96
Forest Products	1.06	1.12	.47	.50

and strengthen existing businesses that resulted in a pretax charge of $515 million ($362 million after taxes). The charge included $305 million for the writeoff of certain assets, $100 million for asset impairments, $80 million in associated severance costs and $30 million in other expenses, including the cancellation of leases.

During the fourth quarter of Year 10, International Paper recorded a $165 million pretax charge ($105 million after taxes) for the writedown of its investments in a company that markets digital communications products and to record its share of a restructuring charge announced by that investee.

These restructuring charges were the first recognized by International Paper since Year 6. In November of Year 6, the firm recorded a pretax charge of $398 million ($263 million after taxes) to establish a productivity improvement reserve. Over 80 percent of this charge represented asset writedowns for facility closings or realignments and related

EXHIBIT 4.35

International Paper
Income Statements
(amounts in millions)
(Case 4.1)

	Year Ended December 31			
	Year 7	Year 8	Year 9	Year 10
Sales	$ 13,685	$ 14,966	$ 19,797	$ 20,143
Gain on Sale of Partnership Interest	—	—	—	592
Cost of Goods Sold	(11,051)	(11,977)	(14,927)	(16,095)
Selling and Administrative Expenses	(1,786)	(1,925)	(2,349)	(2,628)
Restructuring and Asset Impairment Charges	—	—	—	(680)
Interest Expense	(310)	(349)	(493)	(530)
Income Taxes	(213)	(236)	(719)	(330)
Minority Interest in Earnings	(36)	(47)	(156)	(169)
Income from Continuing Operations	$ 289	$ 432	$ 1,153	$ 303
Changes in Accounting Principles	—	(75)	—	—
Net Income	$ 289	$ 357	$ 1,153	$ 303

severance and relocation costs. The balance covers one-time costs of environmental cleanup, remediation, and legal costs. In December of Year 5, the firm recorded a $60 million ($37 million after taxes) reduction in work force charge to cover severance costs associated with the elimination of more than 1,000 positions from its worldwide work force. In December of Year 4, International Paper completed a review of operations in the context of its ongoing programs to emphasize value-added products in growing markets and improve the efficiency of its facilities. As a result, the firm recorded a pretax charge of $212 million ($137 million after taxes), principally related to the planned sale or closure of certain wood products and converting facilities, the estimated costs of environmental remediation, and severance and other personnel expenses associated with the business improvement program.

On July 9, Year 11, International Paper announced a plan to restructure or eliminate certain production operations and cut 9,000 jobs, more than 10 percent of its work force. It recognized a restructuring charge of $385 million pretax. It also recognized a $93 million charge related to pending litigation.

Required

a. In each of the three categories of income items described above for Year 7 through Year 10, discuss (1) whether you would eliminate the item when assessing the profitability of International Paper, and, if so, (2) the adjustments you would make to the income statement, balance sheet, and statement of cash flows.

b. Taking into consideration the adjustments from part a, analyze and interpret the changes in the profitability and risk of International Paper during this four-year period. The statutory tax rate is 35 percent in each year.

EXHIBIT 4.36

International Paper
Balance Sheets
(amounts in millions)
(Case 4.1)

	December 31				
	Year 6	Year 7	Year 8	Year 9	Year 10
Assets					
Cash	$ 225	$ 242	$ 270	$ 312	$ 352
Accounts Receivable	1,861	1,856	2,241	2,571	2,553
Inventories	1,938	2,024	2,075	2,784	2,840
Prepayments	342	279	244	206	253
Total Current Assets	$ 4,366	$ 4,401	$ 4,830	$ 5,873	$ 5,998
Investments in Securities	599	631	1,032	1,420	1,178
Property, Plant, and Equipment (net)	9,643	9,658	9,941	13,800	16,559
Other Assets	1,851	1,941	2,033	2,884	4,517
Total Assets	$16,459	$16,631	$17,836	$23,977	$28,252
Liabilities and Shareholders' Equity					
Accounts Payable	$ 1,259	$ 1,089	$ 1,204	$ 1,464	$ 1,426
Notes Payable	2,356	2,089	2,083	2,283	3,296
Other Current Liabilities	916	831	747	1,116	1,172
Total Current Liabilities	$ 4,531	$ 4,009	$ 4,034	$ 4,863	$ 5,894
Long-Term Debt	3,096	3,601	4,464	6,396	7,141
Deferred Income Taxes	1,417	1,614	1,612	1,974	2,768
Other Noncurrent Liabilities	1,226	1,182	870	980	1,240
Total Liabilities	$10,270	$10,406	$10,980	$14,213	$17,043
Minority Interest in Subsidiaries	—	—	$ 342	$ 1,967	$ 1,865
Common Stock	$ 127	$ 127	$ 256	$ 263	$ 301
Additional Paid-in Capital	1,792	1,704	1,658	1,963	3,426
Retained Earnings	4,472	4,553	4,711	5,627	5,639
Treasury Stock	(202)	(159)	(111)	(56)	(22)
Total Shareholders' Equity	$ 6,189	$ 6,225	$ 6,514	$ 7,797	$ 9,344
Total Liabilities and Shareholders' Equity	$16,459	$16,631	$17,836	$23,977	$28,252

EXHIBIT 4.37

International Paper
Statements of Cash Flows
(amounts in millions)
(Case 4.1)

| | Year Ended December 31 | | | |
	Year 7	Year 8	Year 9	Year 10
Operations				
Net Income	$ 289	$ 357	$ 1,153	$ 303
Depreciation	898	885	1,031	1,194
Restructuring and Asset Impairment Charges	—	—	—	680
Changes in Accounting Principles	—	75	—	—
Gain on Sale of Partnership Interest	—	—	—	(592)
Other Addbacks and Subtractions	32	8	54	240
	$ 1,219	$ 1,325	$ 2,238	$ 1,825
(Increase) Decrease in Accounts Rec	78	(339)	45	192
(Increase) Decrease in Inventories	(93)	8	(320)	174
(Increase) Decrease in Prepayments	63	(35)	38	(47)
Increase (Decrease) in Accounts Payable	(170)	115	260	(38)
Increase (Decrease) in Other Current Liabilities	(168)	169	(13)	(367)
Cash Flow from Operations	$ 929	$ 1,243	$ 2,248	$ 1,739
Investing				
Capital Expenditures	$ (971)	$(1,114)	$(1,518)	$(1,394)
Investments Acquired (net)	(151)	(396)	(1,038)	(1,586)
Cash Flow from Investing	$(1,122)	$(1,510)	$(2,556)	$(2,980)
Financing				
Increase in Short-Term Borrowing	—	—	$ 57	—
Decrease in Short-Term Borrowing	—	$ (115)	—	$ (23)
Increase in Long-Term Borrowing	$ 1,276	1,059	1,505	1,909
Issue of Common Stock	225	67	66	100
Decrease in Long-Term Borrowing	(1,016)	(275)	(950)	(375)
Dividends	(208)	(210)	(237)	(291)
Other Financing Transactions	(67)	(231)	(91)	(39)
Cash Flow from Financing	$ 210	$ 295	$ 350	$ 1,281
Change in Cash	$ 17	$ 28	$ 42	$ 40
Cash—Beginning of Year	225	242	270	312
Cash—End of Year	$ 242	$ 270	$ 312	$ 352

EXHIBIT 4.38

International Paper
Financial Statement Ratios
(Case 4.1)

	Year 7	Year 8	Year 9	Year 10
Profit Margin for ROA	3.8%	4.2%	8.2%	4.1%
Assets Turnover	.8	.9	.9	.8
Rate of Return on Assets	3.2%	3.7%	7.8%	3.1%
Common Earnings Leverage	54.9%	56.6%	70.8%	37.1%
Capital Structure Leverage	2.7	2.9	2.9	3.0
Rate of Return on Common Shareholders' Equity	4.7%	5.6%	16.1%	3.5%
Cost of Goods Sold ÷ Sales	80.8%	80.0%	75.4%	79.9%
Selling and Administrative Expense ÷ Sales	13.1%	12.9%	11.9%	13.0%
Interest Expense ÷ Sales	2.3%	2.3%	2.5%	2.6%
Income Tax Expense ÷ Sales	1.5%	1.6%	3.6%	1.7%
Accounts Receivable Turnover	7.4	7.3	8.2	7.9
Inventory Turnover	5.6	5.8	6.1	5.7
Fixed Asset Turnover	1.4	1.5	1.7	1.3
Current Ratio	1.1	1.2	1.2	1.0
Quick Ratio	.5	.6	.6	.5
Cash Flow from Operations ÷ Average Current Liabilities	21.8%	30.9%	50.5%	32.3%
Days Accounts Receivable	50	50	44	46
Days Inventory	65	62	59	64
Days Accounts Payable	38	35	31	33
Liabilities ÷ Assets	62.6%	61.6%	59.3%	60.3%
Long-Term Debt Ratio	36.6%	40.7%	45.1%	43.3%
Long-Term Debt ÷ Shareholders' Equity	57.8%	68.5%	82.0%	76.4%
Cash Flow from Operations ÷ Average Total Liabilities	9.0%	11.4%	16.3%	9.9%
Interest Coverage Ratio	2.7	3.1	5.1	2.5
Cash Flow from Operations ÷ Capital Expenditures	1.0	1.1	1.5	1.3

CASE 4.2

TANAGUCHI CORPORATION—PART A*

Dave Ando and Yoshi Yashima, recent business school graduates, work as security research analysts for a mutual fund specializing in international equity investments. Following several strategy meetings, senior managers of the fund decided to invest in the machine tool industry. One international company under consideration is Tanaguchi Corporation, a Japanese manufacturer of machine tools. As staff analysts assigned to perform fundamental analysis on all new investment options, Ando and Yashima obtain a copy of Tanaguchi Corporation's unconsolidated financial statements and notes (Appendix 4.1) and set out to calculate their usual spreadsheet of financial statement ratios. Exhibit 4.39 presents the results

---

*This case appeared in *Issues in Accounting Education* (Spring 1992), pp. 57–59, and is reproduced with permission of the American Accounting Association.

EXHIBIT 4.39

Comparative Financial Ratio Analysis for Tanaguchi Corporation and U.S. Machine Tool Companies
(Case 4.2)

	Tanaguchi Corporation	Median Ratio for U.S. Machine Tool Companies[a]
Profitability Ratios		
Operating Margin After Taxes (before interest expense and related tax effects)	2.8%	3.3%
× Total Assets Turnover	1.5	1.8
= Return on Assets	4.2%	5.9%
× Common Earnings Leverage Ratio	.83	.91
× Capital Structure Leverage	3.8	2.6
= Return on Common Equity	13.3%[b]	13.9%[b]
Operating Margin Analysis		
Sales	100.0%	100.0%
Other Revenue/Sales	.4	—
Cost of Goods Sold/Sales	(73.2)	(69.3)
Selling and Administrative/Sales	(21.0)	(25.8)
Income Taxes/Sales	(3.4)	(1.6)
Operating Margin (excluding interest and related tax effects)	2.8%	3.3%
Asset Turnover Analysis		
Receivable Turnover	5.1	6.9
Inventory Turnover	6.3	5.2
Fixed Asset Turnover	7.5	7.0
Risk Analysis		
Current Ratio	1.1	1.6
Quick Ratio	.7	.9
Total Liabilities/Total Assets	73.8%	61.1%
Long-Term Debt/Total Assets	4.7%	16.1%
Long-Term Debt/Stockholders' Equity	17.9%	43.2%
Times Interest Covered	5.8	3.1
Market Price Ratios (per common share)		
Market Price/Net Income	45.0	9.0
Market Price/Stockholders' Equity	5.7	1.2

[a]Source: Robert Morris Associates, *Annual Statement Studies* (except price-earnings ratio).

[b]The amounts for return on common equity may not precisely equal the product of return on assets, common earnings leverage, and capital structure leverage due to rounding.

of their efforts. As a basis for comparison, Exhibit 4.39 also presents the median ratios for U.S. machine tool companies for a comparable year. The following conversation ensues.

Dave: Tanaguchi Corporation does not appear to be as profitable as comparable U.S. firms. Its operating margin and rate of return on assets are significantly lower than the median rates for U.S. machine tool operators. Its rate of return on common equity is only slightly lower than its U.S. counterparts, but this is at the expense of assuming much more financial leverage and therefore risk. Most of this leverage is in the form of short-term borrowing. You can see this in its higher total liabilities to total assets ratio combined with its lower long-term debt ratio. This short-term borrowing and higher risk are also evidenced by the lower current and quick ratios. Finally, Tanaguchi Corporation's shares are selling at a higher multiple of net income and stockholders' equity than U.S. machine tool companies. I can't see how we can justify paying more for a company that is less profitable and more risky than comparable U.S. companies. It doesn't seem to me that it is worth exploring this investment possibility any further.

Yoshi: You may be right, Dave. However, I wonder if we are not comparing apples and oranges. As a Japanese company, Tanaguchi Corporation operates in an entirely different institutional and cultural environment from U.S. machine tool companies. Furthermore, it prepares its financial statements in accordance with Japanese generally accepted accounting principles (GAAP), which differ from those in the U.S.

Dave: Well, I think we need to explore this further. I recall seeing a report on an associate's desk comparing U.S. and Japanese accounting principles. I will get a copy for us (Appendix 4.2).

Required

Using the report comparing U.S. and Japanese accounting principles (Appendix 4.2) and Tanaguchi Corporation's financial statements and notes (Appendix 4.1), identify the most important differences between U.S. and Japanese GAAP. Consider both the differences in acceptable methods and in the methods commonly used. For each major difference, indicate the likely effect (increase, decrease, or no effect) of converting Tanaguchi's financial statements to U.S. GAAP (1) on net income, (2) on total assets, and (3) on the ratio of liabilities divided by stockholders' equity.

APPENDIX 4.1 (CASE 4.2)

UNCONSOLIDATED FINANCIAL STATEMENTS FOR TANAGUCHI CORPORATION

Tanaguchi Corporation Balance Sheet
(in billions of yen)
(Case 4.2)

	March 31:	
	Year 4	**Year 5**
Assets		
Current Assets		
Cash	¥ 30	¥ 27
Marketable Securities (Note 1)	20	25
Notes and Accounts Receivable (Note 2)		
Trade Notes and Accounts	200	210
Affiliated Company	30	45
Less: Allowance for Doubtful Accounts	(5)	(7)
Inventories (Note 3)	130	150
Other Current Assets	25	30
Total Current Assets	¥430	¥480
Investments		
Investment in and Loans to Affiliated		
Companies (Note 4)	¥110	¥140
Investments in Other Companies (Note 5)	60	60
Total Investments	¥170	¥200
Property, Plant, and Equipment (Note 6)		
Land	¥ 25	¥ 25
Buildings	110	130
Machinery and Equipment	155	180
Less: Depreciation to Date	(140)	(165)
Total Property, Plant and Equipment	¥150	¥170
Total Assets	¥750	¥850
Liabilities and Stockholders' Equity		
Current Liabilities		
Short-Term Bank Loans	¥185	¥200
Notes and Accounts Payable		
Trade Notes and Accounts	140	164
Affiliated Company	25	20
Other Current Liabilities	40	50
Total Current Liabilities	¥390	¥434

	March 31:	
	Year 4	Year 5
Long-Term Liabilities		
Bonds Payable (Note 7)	¥ 20	¥ 20
Convertible Debt	20	20
Retirement and Severance Allowance		
(Note 8)	122	153
Total Long-Term Liabilities	¥162	¥193
Stockholders' Equity		
Common Stock, 10 par value	¥ 15	¥ 15
Capital Surplus	40	40
Legal Reserve (Note 9)	16	17
Retained Earnings (Note 9)	127	151
Total Stockholders' Equity	¥198	¥223
Total Liabilities and Stockholders' Equity	¥750	¥850

Tanaguchi Corporation
Statement of Income and
Retained Earnings for Fiscal Year 5
(in billions of yen)
(Case 4.2)

Revenues	
Sales (Note 10)	¥1,200
Interest and Dividends (Note 11)	5
Total Revenues	¥1,205
Expenses	
Cost of Goods Sold	¥ 878
Selling and Administrative	252
Interest	13
Total Expenses	¥1,143
Income before Income Taxes	¥ 62
Income Taxes (Note 12)	(34)
Net Income	¥ 28
Retained Earnings	
Balance, Beginning of Fiscal Year 5	¥ 127
Net Income	28
Deductions:	
Cash Dividends	(3)
Transfer to Legal Reserve (Note 9)	(1)
Balance, End of Fiscal Year 5	¥ 151

NOTE 1: Marketable Securities Marketable securities appear on the balance sheet at acquisition cost.

TANAGUCHI CORPORATION
NOTES TO FINANCIAL STATEMENTS

NOTE 2: Accounts Receivable Accounts and notes receivable are noninterest bearing. Within 15 days of sales on open account, customers typically sign noninterest-bearing, single-payment notes. Customers usually pay these notes within 60 to 180 days after signing. When Tanaguchi Corporation needs cash, it discounts these notes with Menji Bank. Tanaguchi Corporation remains contingently liable in the event customers do not pay these notes at maturity. Receivables from (and payables to) affiliated companies are with Takahashi Corporation (see Note 4) and are noninterest bearing.

NOTE 3: Inventories Inventories appear on the balance sheet at lower of cost or market. The measurement of acquisition cost uses a weighted average cost flow assumption.

NOTE 4: Investments and Loans to Affiliated Companies Intercorporate investments appear on the balance sheet at acquisition cost. The balances in this account at the end of Year 4 and Year 5 are:

	Year 4	Year 5
Investments in Tanaka Corporation (25%)	¥ 15	¥ 15
Investment in Takahashi Corporation (80%)	70	70
Loans to Takahashi Corporation	25	55
	¥110	¥140

NOTE 5: Investments in Other Companies Other investments represent ownership shares of less than 20 percent and appear at acquisition cost.

NOTE 6: Property, Plant, and Equipment Fixed assets appear on the balance sheet at acquisition cost. The firm capitalizes expenditures that increase the service lives of fixed assets, but expenses immediately expenditures that maintain the originally expected useful lives. It computes depreciation using the declining balance method. Depreciable lives for buildings are 30 to 40 years; depreciable lives for machinery and equipment are 6 to 10 years.

NOTE 7: Bonds Payable Bonds payable represent two bond issues as follows:

	Year 4	Year 5
12% semiannual, ¥10 billion face value bonds, with interest payable on March 31 and September 30 and the principal payable at maturity on March 31, Year 20; the bonds were were initially priced on the market to yield 10%, compounded semiannually	¥11.50	¥11.45
8% semiannual, ¥10 billion face value bonds, with interest payable on March 31 and September 30 and the principal payable at maturity on March 31, Year 22; the bonds were initially priced on the market to yield 10%, compounded semiannually	¥ 8.50	¥ 8.55
	¥20.00	¥20.00

NOTE 8: *Retirement and Severance Allowance*   The firm provides amounts as a charge against income each year for estimated retirement and severance benefits, but does not fund these amounts until it makes actual payments to former employees.

NOTE 9: *Legal Reserve and Retained Earnings*   The firm reduces retained earnings and increases the legal reserve account for a specified percentage of dividends paid during the year. A plan for appropriation of retained earnings was approved by shareholders at the annual meeting held on June 29, Year 5, as follows:

Transfer to Legal Reserve	¥(1)
Cash Dividend	(3)
Directors' and Statutory Auditors' Bonuses	(1)
Elimination of Special Tax Reserve Relating to Sale of Equipment	1

NOTE 10: *Sales Revenue*   The firm recognizes revenues from sales of machine tools at the time of delivery. Reported sales for Year 5 are net of a provision for doubtful accounts of ¥50 billion.

NOTE 11: *Interest and Dividend Revenue*   Interest and dividend revenue includes ¥1.5 billion from loans to Takahashi Corporation, an unconsolidated subsidiary.

NOTE 12: *Income Tax Expense*   The firm computes income taxes according to a statutory tax rate of 55 percent for Year 5. Deferred tax accounting is not a common practice in Japan.

APPENDIX 4.2 (CASE 4.2)

COMPARISON OF U.S. AND JAPANESE GAAP

1. STANDARD SETTING PROCESS

U.S.

The U.S. Congress has the legal authority to prescribe acceptable accounting principles, but it has delegated that authority to the Securities and Exchange Commission (SEC). The SEC has stated that it will recognize pronouncements of the Financial Accounting Standards Board (FASB), a private sector entity, as the primary vehicle for specifying generally accepted accounting standards.

Japan

The Japanese Diet has the legal authority to prescribe acceptable accounting principles. All Japanese corporations (both publicly and privately held) must issue periodic financial statements to their stockholders following provisions of the Japanese Commercial Code. This Code is promulgated by the Diet. The financial statements follow strict legal entity concepts.

Publicly listed corporations in Japan must also file financial statements with the Securities Division of the Ministry of Finance following accounting principles promulgated by the Diet in the Securities and Exchange Law. The Diet, through the Ministry of Finance, obtains advice on accounting principles from the Business Advisory Deliberations Council (BADC), a body composed of representatives from business, the accounting profession, and

Sources: The Japanese Institute of Certified Public Accountants, *Corporate Disclosure in Japan* (July 1987); KPMG Peat Marwick, *Comparison of Japanese and U.S. Reporting and Financial Practices* (1989); Price Waterhouse, *Doing Business in Japan* (1993).

the Ministry of Finance. The BADC has no authority on its own to set acceptable accounting principles. The financial statements filed with the Securities Division of the Ministry of Finance tend to follow economic entity concepts, with intercorporate investments either accounted for using the equity method or consolidated.

All Japanese corporations file income tax returns with the Taxation Division of the Ministry of Finance. The accounting principles followed in preparing tax returns closely mirror those used in preparing financial statements for stockholders under the Japanese Commercial Code. The Ministry of Finance will sometimes need to reconcile conflicting preferences of the Securities Division (which wants financial information better reflecting economic reality) and the Taxation Division (which wants to raise adequate tax revenues to run the government).

2. PRINCIPAL FINANCIAL STATEMENTS

U.S.   Balance sheet, income statement, statement of cash flows.

Japan   Balance sheet, income statement, proposal for appropriation of profit or disposition of loss. The financial statements filed with the Ministry of Finance include some supplemental information on cash flows.

3. INCOME STATEMENT

U.S.   Accrual basis.

Japan   Accrual basis.

4. REVENUE RECOGNITION

U.S.   Generally at time of sale; percentage-of-completion method usually required on long-term contracts; installment and cost-recovery-first methods permitted when there is high uncertainty regarding cash collectibility.

Japan   Generally at time of sale; percentage-of-completion method permitted on long-term contracts; installment method common when collection period exceeds two years, regardless of degree of uncertainty of cash collectibility.

5. UNCOLLECTIBLE ACCOUNTS

U.S.   Allowance method.

Japan   Allowance method.

6. INVENTORIES AND COST OF GOODS SOLD

U.S.   Inventories valued at lower of cost or market. Cost determined by FIFO, LIFO, weighted average, or standard cost. Most firms use LIFO for domestic inventories and FIFO for nondomestic inventories.

Inventories valued at lower of cost or market. Cost determined by specific identification, FIFO, LIFO, weighted average, or standard cost. Most firms use weighted average or specific identification.   *Japan*

7. FIXED ASSETS AND DEPRECIATION EXPENSE

Fixed assets valued at acquisition cost. Depreciation computed using straight-line, declining balance, and sum-of-the-years'-digits methods. Permanent declines in value are recognized. Most firms use straight-line for financial reporting and an accelerated method for tax reporting.   *U.S.*

Fixed assets valued at acquisition cost. Depreciation computed using straight-line, declining balance, and sum-of-the-years'-digits methods. Permanent declines in value are recognized. Most firms use a declining balance method for financial and tax reporting.   *Japan*

8. INTANGIBLE ASSETS AND AMORTIZATION EXPENSE

Internally developed intangibles expensed when expenditures are made. Externally purchased intangibles capitalized as assets and amortized over expected useful life (not to exceed 40 years). Goodwill cannot be amortized for tax purposes.   *U.S.*

The cost of intangibles (both internally developed and externally purchased) can be expensed when incurred or capitalized and amortized over the period allowed for tax purposes (generally 5 to 20 years). Goodwill is amortized over 5 years. Some intangibles (e.g., property rights) are not amortized.   *Japan*

9. LIABILITIES RELATED TO ESTIMATED EXPENSES (WARRANTIES, VACATION PAY, EMPLOYEE BONUSES)

Estimated amount recognized as an expense and as a liability. Actual expenditures are charged against the liability.   *U.S.*

Estimated amount recognized as an expense and as a liability. Actual expenditures are charged against the liability. Annual bonuses paid to members of the Board of Directors and to the Commercial Code auditors are not considered expenses, but instead a distribution of profits. Consequently, such bonuses are charged against retained earnings.   *Japan*

10. LIABILITIES RELATED TO EMPLOYEE RETIREMENT AND SEVERANCE BENEFITS

Liability recognized for unfunded accumulated benefits.   *U.S.*

Severance benefits more common than pension benefits. An estimated amount is recognized each period as an expense and as a liability for financial reporting. The maximum liability recognized equals 40 percent of the amount payable if all eligible employees were terminated currently. There is wide variability in the amount recognized. Benefits are deducted for tax purposes only when actual payments are made to severed employees. Such benefits are seldom funded beforehand.   *Japan*

11. LIABILITIES RELATED TO INCOME TAXES

U.S.   Income tax expense based on book income amounts. Deferred tax expense and deferred tax asset or liability recognized for temporary (timing) differences between book and taxable income.

Japan   Income tax expense based on taxable income amounts. Deferred tax accounting not practiced. In consolidated statements submitted to the Ministry of Finance by listed companies (see No. 18), deferred tax accounting is permitted.

12. NONINTEREST-BEARING NOTES

U.S.   Notes stated at present value of future cash flows and interest recognized over term of the note.

Japan   Notes stated at face amount and no interest recognized over term of the note. Commonly used as a substitute for Accounts Payable.

13. BOND DISCOUNT OR PREMIUM

U.S.   Subtracted from or added to the face value of the bond and reported among liabilities on the balance sheet. Amortized over the life of the bond as an adjustment to interest expense.

Japan   Bond discount usually included among intangible assets and amortized over the life of the bonds. Bond discount and premium may also be subtracted from or added to face value of bonds on the balance sheet and amortized as an adjustment of interest expense over the life of the bonds.

14. LEASES

U.S.   Distinction made between operating leases (not capitalized) and capital leases (capitalized).

Japan   All leases treated as operating leases.

15. LEGAL RESERVE (PART OF SHAREHOLDERS' EQUITY)

U.S.   Not applicable

Japan   When dividends are declared and paid, unappropriated retained earnings and cash are reduced by the amount of the dividend. In addition, unappropriated retained earnings are reduced, and the legal reserve account is increased by a percentage of this dividend, usually 10 percent, until such time as the legal reserve equals 25 percent of stated capital. The effect of the latter entry is to capitalize a portion of retained earnings to make it part of permanent capital.

16. APPROPRIATIONS OF RETAINED EARNINGS

U.S.   Not a common practice in the U.S. Appropriations have no legal status when they do appear.

Stockholders must approve each year the "proposal for appropriation of profit or disposition of loss." Four items commonly appear: dividend declarations, annual bonuses for directors and Commercial Code auditors, transfers to legal reserves, and changes in reserves.

Japan

The income tax law permits certain costs to be deducted earlier for tax than for financial reporting, and permits certain gains to be recognized later for tax than for financial reporting. To obtain these tax benefits, the tax law requires that these items "be reflected on the company's books." The *pretax effect* of these timing differences *does not appear* on the income statement. Instead, an entry is made decreasing unappropriated retained earnings and increasing special retained earnings reserves (a form of appropriated retained earnings). When the timing difference reverses, this entry is reversed. The *tax effects* of these timing differences *do appear* on the income statement, however. In the year when the timing difference originates, income tax expense and income tax payable are reduced by the tax effect of the timing difference. When the timing difference reverses, income tax expense and income tax payable are increased by a corresponding amount.

17. TREASURY STOCK

Shown at acquisition cost as a subtraction from total shareholders' equity. No income recognized from treasury stock transactions.

U.S.

Reacquired shares are either canceled immediately or shown as a current asset on the balance sheet.

Japan

18. INVESTMENTS IN SECURITIES

A. Marketable Securities (Current Asset).

Market value method.

U.S.

Reported at acquisition cost, unless price declines are considered permanent, in which case reported at lower of cost or market.

Japan

B. Investments (Noncurrent Asset)

Accounting depends on ownership: Less than 20%, market value method; 20% to 50%, equity method; greater than 50%, consolidated.

U.S.

The principal financial statements are those of the parent company only (that is, unconsolidated statements). Intercorporate investments are carried at acquisition cost. Listed companies must provide consolidated financial statements as supplements to the principal statements in filings to the Ministry of Finance. The accounting for investments in securities in these supplementary statements is essentially the same as in the U.S.

Japan

19. CORPORATE ACQUISITIONS

Purchase method or pooling of interests method.

U.S.

Purchase method.

Japan

20. FOREIGN CURRENCY TRANSLATION

U.S.   The translation method depends on whether the foreign unit operates as a self-contained entity (all-current method) or as an extension of the U.S. parent (monetary/nonmonetary method).

Japan   For branches, the monetary/nonmonetary translation method is used, with any translation adjustment flowing through income. For subsidiaries, current monetary items are translated using the current rate; other balance sheet items use the historical rate; and the translation adjustment is part of shareholders' equity.

21. SEGMENT REPORTING

U.S.   Segment information (sales, operating income, assets) disclosed by industry segment, geographic location, and type of customer.

Japan   Sales data by segment (industry, geographic location).

CASE 4.3

TANAGUCHI CORPORATION—PART B*

Dave Ando and Yoshi Yashima spent the next several days converting the financial statements of Tanaguchi Corporation from Japanese to U.S. GAAP. Although their conversions required them to make several estimates, Dave and Yoshi felt comfortable that they had largely filtered out the effects of different accounting principles. Exhibit 4.40 of this case presents the profitability and risk ratios for Tanaguchi Corporation based on Japanese GAAP (column 1) and as restated to U.S. GAAP (column 2). Column 3 shows the median ratios for U.S. machine tool companies (the same as those reported in Exhibit 4.39).

After the analysts study the financial statement ratios in Exhibit 4.40, this conversation ensues:

Dave: The operating profitability of Tanaguchi Corporation, as evidenced by the rate of return on assets, is still lower than comparable U.S. firms, even after adjusting for differences in accounting principles. Although Tanaguchi's rate of return on common equity is now higher than that of its U.S. counterparts, the higher return occurs at the expense of taking on substantially more debt and therefore more risk. A significant portion of the differences in price-earnings ratios between Tanaguchi Corporation and U.S. companies results from differences in accounting principles, but there are still large differences. I'm still not convinced that investing in Tanaguchi Corporation makes sense. Yoshi, am I on track with my interpretations, or am I missing something?

Yoshi: I'm not sure we are yet to the point where we can make a recommendation regarding an investment in the shares of Tanaguchi Corporation. We need to develop a better understanding of why the restated financial ratios for Tanaguchi Corporation still differ so much from those for U.S. machine tool companies.

---

*Refer to Case 4.2, Tanaguchi Corporation: Part A, for background for this case.

EXHIBIT 4.40

Comparative Financial Ratio Analysis for Tanaguchi Corporation and U.S. Machine Tool Companies
(Case 4.3)

	Tanaguchi Corp. (Japanese GAAP) (1)	Tanaguchi Corp. (U.S. GAAP) (2)	Median Ratio for U.S. Machine Tool Cos.[a] (3)
Profitability Ratios			
Operating Margin After Taxes (before interest expense and related tax effects) . .	2.8%	2.9%	3.3%
× Total Assets Turnover	1.5	1.5	1.8
= Return on Assets	4.2%	4.5%	5.9%
× Common Earnings Leverage Ratio	.83	.83	.91
× Capital Structure Leverage	3.8	4.0	2.6
= Return on Common Equity	13.3%[b]	14.8%	13.9%[b]
Operating Margin Analysis			
Sales	100.0%	100.0%	100.0%
Other Revenue/Sales	.4	.4	—
Cost of Goods Sold/Sales	(73.2)	(73.4)	(69.3)
Selling and Administrative/Sales	(21.0)	(20.6)	(25.8)
Income Taxes/Sales	(3.4)	(3.5)	(1.6)
Operating Margin (excluding interest and related tax effects)	2.8%	2.9%	3.3%
Asset Turnover Analysis			
Receivable Turnover	5.1	5.0	6.9
Inventory Turnover	6.3	6.5	5.2
Fixed Asset Turnover	7.5	7.2	7.0
Risk Analysis			
Current Ratio	1.1	1.0	1.6
Quick Ratio	.7	.7	.9
Total Liabilities/Total Assets	73.8%	74.5%	61.1%
Long-Term Debt/Total Assets	4.7%	5.1%	16.1%
Long-Term Debt/Stockholders' Equity	17.9%	18.3%	43.2%
Times Interest Covered	5.8	5.7	3.1
Market Price Ratios (per common share)			
Market Price/Net Income	45.0	30.9	9.0
Market Price/Stockholders' Equity	5.7	4.6	1.2

[a]Source: Robert Morris Associates, *Annual Statement Studies* (except price-earnings ratio).

[b]The amounts for return on common equity may not precisely equal to the product of return on assets, common earnings leverage, and capital structure leverage due to rounding.

One possible explanation might relate to the practice of many Japanese companies to operate in corporate groups, which the Japanese call *keiretsu*s. Tanaguchi Corporation is a member of the Menji *keiretsu*. Each *keiretsu* typically comprises firms in eight or ten different industries (for example, one *keiretsu* might include firms in the steel, chemicals, forest products, retailing, insurance, and banking industries). The companies usually hold stock in each other; investments in the 25 percent to 30 percent range are common. These investments are not made for the purpose of controlling or even significantly influencing other members of the corporate group. Rather, they serve as a mechanism for providing operating links among the entities. It is common for one corporation in the *keiretsu* to source many of its raw materials from another group member and to sell a substantial portion of its products to entities within the group. Each *keiretsu* includes a bank that provides needed funds to group members. It is rare that the bank would allow a member of the group to experience significant operating problems or to go bankrupt for a lack of funds.

A second, but related, institutional difference between the U.S. and Japan concerns stock ownership patterns. Roughly one-third of Japanese company shares are held by members of its *keiretsu* and another one-third are held by financial institutions, typically banks and insurance companies not affiliated with the *keiretsu*. This leaves only one-third of the shares held by individuals.

This large percentage of intercorporate stock holdings has historically lessened the concern about keeping investors happy by paying large dividends or reporting ever-increasing earnings per share, as seems to be the case in the U.S. The emphasis of Japanese companies is instead on serving new or growing markets, increasing market share, and strengthening the members of the *keiretsu*. The Japanese economy has grown more rapidly than the U.S. economy during the last several decades. As Japanese companies have built their export markets and added operations abroad, their strategic emphasis has been on gaining market dominance in this growth environment, and not on attaining particular levels of profit margin, rates of return, or earnings per share.

Finally, stock price changes in Japan appear related more to changes in real estate values than to the operating performance of individual companies. Real estate values and stock prices moved dramatically upward during the eighties, although significant decreases have occurred recently. The increasing stock prices appeared to keep investors happy, leading them to deemphasize the kinds of profitability performance evaluation common in the U.S.

Required

After studying the financial statements and notes for Tanaguchi Corporation, develop explanations for the differences in the profitability and risk ratios for Tanaguchi Corporation reported in column 2 of Exhibit 4.40 as compared to those reported in column 3 for U.S. machine tool companies.

CHAPTER 5

GENERALLY ACCEPTED ACCOUNTING PRINCIPLES: INCOME RECOGNITION AND ASSET VALUATION

Learning Objectives

1. Review the criteria for recognizing income and expenses under the accrual basis of accounting, and apply these criteria to various types of business.
2. Calculate the income statement, balance sheet, and statement of cash flow effects of recognizing income prior to the point of sale, at the time of sale, and subsequent to sale.
3. Analyze and interpret the effects of FIFO versus LIFO on financial statements, and convert the statements of a firm from a LIFO to a FIFO basis.
4. Use financial statement disclosures for depreciable assets to calculate the average depreciable lives and the age of such assets, and convert the financial statements of a firm from a straight-line to an accelerated depreciation basis.
5. Understand the alternative ways that firms account for intangible assets (highlighting research and development expenditures, software development expenditures, and goodwill) and the difficulties that these alternatives present for the analysis of high technology firms.
6. Understand the distinction between changes in the general purchasing power of the monetary unit and changes in the prices of specific assets and liabilities, and understand furthermore the accounting methods designed to adjust financial statements for these two types of changing prices.

This chapter and the next two describe alternative methods of accounting for assets, liabilities, revenues, and expenses commonly encountered in corporate annual reports. These chapters emphasize the methods that have the greatest effect on the income statement and balance sheet.

Chapter 5 examines income recognition, inventory cost flow assumptions, and depreciable and intangible asset accounting. The focus is on acceptable reporting methods in the United States, although we note differences between the United States and other countries. For firms operating in countries that have experienced high inflation, Appendix 5.1 illustrates how significant changes in the general purchasing power of the reporting unit affect traditional performance and risk analysis.

Although the chapter's primary focus is on the impact of selected reporting principles on the financial statements, another objective is to show how a firm's choice of accounting principles and the way it implements them affect its *quality of earnings* and *quality of financial position*. Thus, this chapter explores key financial reporting issues in detail, and assesses how they might impact the sustainability, measurement, and manageability of reporting earnings—concepts introduced and discussed in the previous chapter. In this regard, Chapters 4 through 7 represent a unit. The chapters together address understanding corporate financial data and determining the relevant financial data for analysis.

INCOME RECOGNITION

Earnings from any operating activity undertaken by a firm are ultimately the difference between the cash received from customers and the cash paid to suppliers, employees, and other providers of goods and services. Economic value-added is the difference between the present value of these cash inflows and cash outflows.

Exhibit 5.1 depicts these cash inflows and outflows for a typical manufacturing firm. Most manufacturers use significant amounts of cash to acquire manufacturing facilities, raw materials, and labor services for producing their products. The products are then sold and delivered to customers. A few customers pay for the products immediately in cash, but in most cases the manufacturer holds an account receivable for some period of time before receiving the cash. For successful

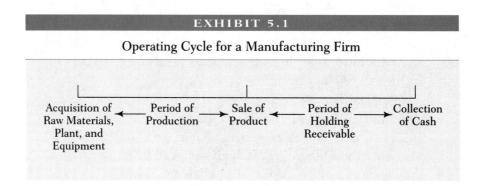

EXHIBIT 5.1

Operating Cycle for a Manufacturing Firm

Acquisition of Raw Materials, Plant, and Equipment — Period of Production → Sale of Product ← Period of Holding Receivable → Collection of Cash

manufacturers, this operating cycle continually repeats, allowing the firm to grow and expand.

The total *amount* of income for the manufacturer is the difference between its cash inflows and outflows. The manufacturer may receive the cash for any one sale in a different accounting period from the period in which it pays out the cash to produce the product it sold. Policymakers have decided that measuring earnings as the difference between the cash inflows and outflows *during any discrete accounting period* often results in a poor measure of value-added, because the effort, or the inputs, expended in one period are matched with the accomplishments, or the outputs, of another period. To address this problem, earnings as reported on the income statement are measured on the *accrual* basis of accounting.

Under the accrual basis of accounting, firms apply a set of specific criteria for revenue recognition to select the point in the operating cycle illustrated in Exhibit 5.1 when they will recognize revenue. After calculating revenue, firms attempt to match against this revenue all costs they incurred to generate that revenue. Following this procedure, inputs are matched with the resulting outputs. Policymakers have concluded that calculating *reported earnings* this way produces a more accurate measure of the value-added during the period.

Accepting the accrual basis, however, does not settle the question of *when* firms recognize revenues and matching expenses. Options for recognizing revenues include (1) during the period of production; (2) at the completion of production; (3) at the time of sale; (4) during the period while receivables are outstanding; or (5) at the time of cash collection. We provide in this chapter examples of applying the accrual basis of accounting at these various revenue recognition points.

INCOME RECOGNITION AND EARNINGS MANAGEMENT

We have said that the point when a firm recognizes revenue may not coincide with the time when it receives cash from customers. In fact, this is usually the case when the discrete accounting period is defined by a quarter, or even a year. The longer the time between (1) the recognition of revenue and the receipt of cash from customers, and (2) the payment of cash to providers of goods and services and the recognition of expenses, the more opportunity management has to manage reported earnings. The length of time between (1) and (2) often varies depending on whether the firm sells goods or services, and on the type of goods and services that are sold.

Consider, for example, the opportunities of a manufacturing firm and an advertising firm to manage earnings. A manufacturing firm acquires factory buildings that provide productive services for perhaps ten or twenty years, as well as equipment that the firm can use to manufacture products for five or more years. The production cycle may take a few days or many months, depending on the product. After completion and delivery of the product, the firm might not receive cash for months or even years. Thus, the firm must decide how to allocate the cost of buildings and equipment to the many years of their use. Given the homogeneity of most manufactured products, it must also decide whether goods sold during the current period came from inventory on hand at the beginning of the period (and therefore carry manufacturing costs of last period) or from goods manufactured this period (and therefore carry manufacturing costs of the current period). Because the manufacturer does not know definitely whether it will receive cash equal to the revenue recognized for the period, it must estimate the amount of the uncollectible accounts to match against the revenues. Thus, the time line illustrated in Exhibit 5.1 tends to be a relatively long one for a manufacturing firm, allowing considerable opportunity for earnings management.

An advertising firm is quite different. Most advertising firms rent office space, paying rent monthly as they use the physical facilities in providing advertising services. They pay employees weekly or monthly for creating advertising campaigns. An advertising firm bills its clients for advertising services performed, receiving cash soon thereafter. In this case, the time line illustrated in Exhibit 5.1 is more compressed for an advertising firm than for a manufacturing firm, and there is thus less opportunity to manage earnings.

We discuss the opportunity to manage earnings through the use of alternative accounting principles throughout the chapter. A useful exercise at this point is to consider the operating cycle of a particular firm or industry of interest, and assess the opportunity for earnings management. Draw a time line for the firm or industry similar to that in Exhibit 5.1, and identify where leads or lags occur between (1) revenues and cash receipts, and between (2) expenses and cash expenditures. Then identify the particular reporting principles employed at the lead or lag points for measuring the revenues and expenses. The resulting list of reporting principles should be carefully scrutinized, as the choices represent candidates for actual earnings management.

CRITERIA FOR REVENUE RECOGNITION

Financial reporting requires the recognition of revenue under the accrual basis of accounting when a firm:

1. Has provided all, or a substantial portion, of the services to be performed.
2. Has received either cash, a receivable, or some other asset whose cash-equivalent amount can be measured with reasonable precision.

Revenue Recognition Principles.   Most firms recognize revenue at the time of sale (delivery) of goods or services. At this point, the firm has completed production of the goods or creation of the services, so that the first criterion is satisfied. The firm has either already incurred or can estimate the amount of total cash outflow related to the production and sale of the goods or services. Such measurement of total costs permits an appropriate matching of expenses with revenues.

The benefit that a firm obtains from providing goods or services is the cash or other consideration that the firm expects to receive. If the customer promises to pay cash in the future, the firm examines the credit standing of the customer and assesses the likelihood of receiving the cash. The second criterion is satisfied so long as the firm can reasonably predict the amount of cash it will collect.

Sustainability of Earnings Problems. The recognition of revenue at the time of sale (delivery) is so common that analysts may neglect to assess at the outset whether this timing is appropriate for a particular firm. Firms may attempt to report as favorable a picture of themselves as possible either by accelerating the timing of revenues or by estimating the amounts too aggressively. If so, the quality of reported earnings suffers, because earings are managed and probably not sustainable.

Three signals that revenue recognition at the time of sale may be too early are large and volatile amounts of (1) uncollectible accounts receivable, (2) returned goods, and (3) warranty expenditures. These are all sales-related expenses that should bear a reasonably stable relationship to revenues over time. Large percentages of these expenses as a percentage of sales, or widely varying percentages from year to year, should raise questions about the appropriateness of revenue recognition at the time of sale.

Another possible signal related to accounts receivable is an increase in receivable days outstanding (Chapter 3 discusses how to calculate receivable days outstanding). Evidence that customers are taking longer to pay for their purchases may suggest that revenues and earnings are overstated. Note that the analyst should assess the receivables days outstanding and the stability of bad debt expense to revenue together, because either ratio by itself may provide a misleading signal. A firm that adequately provides for an increasing proportion of uncollectible sales will likely show a stable accounts receivable turnover, because providing for estimated uncollectible accounts has the same effect on accounts receivable as collecting the accounts in cash; it reduces them. Thus, examination of just the accounts receivable turnover is not enough to signal an increasing proportion of uncollectible accounts. A firm that does not adequately provide for an increasing proportion of uncollectible sales will experience a buildup of accounts receivable relative to sales and therefore higher accounts receivable days outstanding. Examining the ratio of bad debt expense to sales alone does not provide evidence of the slow rate at which customers are paying.

Recognizing revenues at the *time of sale* suffers from an even more fundamental problem at times: What is the definition of *sale*? Does the receipt of firm customer orders for goods held in inventory constitute a sale, or is physical delivery of the product to the customer necessary? Is completion of the production of custom-ordered goods sufficient to recognize revenue, or is physical delivery necessary? In an effort to achieve sales targets for a period, firms will sometimes record sales earlier than physical delivery. Audits should identify and correct abuses of the definition of *time of sale*, although cases where audits have been ineffective for this purpose periodically appear in the financial press. Exhibit 5.2 illustrates an egregious violation of revenue recognition by a firm in the information technology industry and its devastating consequences.

Some firms hungry for sales revenue even record sales based on merely an indication of a customer's *possible* interest in a product. Inevitably in these situations it is pressure placed on sales personnel, either by themselves or by senior managers, that leads to this violation of the revenue recognition rules. A related ploy is to accelerate the recognition of revenues, and then hide sales returns by customers. Firms store the returned goods in a remote or independently owned warehouse, hoping that the independent auditor will not detect them.

EXHIBIT 5.2

Centennial Technologies
Excerpts from *The Wall Street Journal*, June 13, 1997
By Jon G. Auerback, Staff *Reporter*

Centennial Technologies Inc. disclosed losses totaling $28.1 million for the 14 quarters through the end of Year 6, in a restatement of results stemming from allegations of securities fraud against the company's former chief executive.

The restatement, covering three fiscal years and the six months ended December 31 of last year, showed that Centennial, a maker of computer-memory cards, never had a profitable quarter during a period in which it often reported record earnings growth. Its stock was the top-performing issue on the New York Stock Exchange last year.

The corrected financials resulted from a four-month audit following the dismissal and arrest of the company's founder and ex-CEO, for alleged securities fraud. Although Centennial had previously disclosed it expected to find that its profits were ephemeral, it hadn't discussed the extent of losses.

The $28.1 million loss reported for the restated period through last December compares with aggregate net income of $12.1 million the company had previously reported for the 42-month period. Sales in the period totaled $67.5 million, sharply below the $109.6 million that had been reported. The Wilmington, Mass, company attributed the overstatements to its ex-CEO, awaiting trial in jail. According to the charges filed, the ex-CEO used personal funds to pay for phony sales, "sold" non-existent goods to friends' companies, and inflated inventories. The ex-CEO has denied all wrongdoing.

Centennial also reported a $6.4 million loss on $10.9 million in sales in the quarter ended March 31, compared with a loss of $1.2 million on $8.8 million in sales in the restated year-earlier period. Centennial's stock was delisted by the Big Board, and although it trades over-the-counter, no per-share amounts were given for the latest period.

Chapter 4 points out that the distinction between earnings management and management fraud is often a thin line. In this behavior, however, it appears that management crosses the line. The actions appear fraudulent because they are outside the bounds of generally accepted accounting principles, and management seemed to take these actions to mislead statement users intentionally.[1]

The analyst cannot be too vigilant in assessing whether sales are managed for one simple reason: Sales are at the core of a firm's ability to grow and prosper. A firm experiencing declining sales growth, particularly compared to other firms in its industry, is the type of firm most likely to be tempted to manage earnings by stretching the revenue recognition rules. Although this type of earnings management eventually catches up with a firm, it is precisely in these situations when a firm's sustainable earnings are likely to be declining. The analyst needs to take this into account when estimating future earnings.

---

[1]A summary of celebrated cases in which management abused the reporting system appears in Chapter 3 of Martin S. Fridson, *Financial Statement Analysis: A Practitioner's Guide*, Second Edition, New York: John Wiley & Sons, Inc., 1996; and Chapters 3 through 10 of Kathryn F. Staley, *The Art of Short Selling*, New York: John Wiley & Sons, Inc., 1997.

CRITERIA FOR EXPENSE RECOGNITION

Financial reporting requires the recognition of expenses under the accrual basis of accounting as follows:

1. Costs directly associated with revenues become expenses in the period when a firm recognizes the revenues.
2. Costs not directly associated with revenues become expenses in the period when a firm consumes the services or benefits of the costs in operations.

Most of the costs of manufacturing and selling a product closely relate to particular revenues. The firm matches expense recognition with revenue recognition for such costs, referred to as *product* costs. Other costs—such as insurance and property taxes on administrative facilities, salaries of corporate officers, and depreciation on computer equipment, for example—bear only an indirect relation to revenues generated during the period. Such costs become expenses in the period in which the firm consumes the benefits of the insurance, governmental, administrative, and computer services. Accountants refer to such costs as *period* expenses.

Since a large proportion of the expenses reported in the income statement are directly associated with revenue recognized, assessing the sustainability and manageability of expenses and the sustainablity and management of revenues are closely related tasks. Certain period expenses, however, are more susceptible to management than others. Analysts should carefully monitor advertising, research and development, and maintenance expenditures, for example, in order to discern whether there are substantive reasons for changes in the levels of these expenditures, or whether changes are the result of managed earnings. Expenditures that are somewhat discretionary in nature and that are reported on the income statement as period costs are prime candidates for managing earnings.

APPLICATION OF REVENUE AND EXPENSE RECOGNITION CRITERIA

Applying the revenue recognition and matching principles to actual business settings is not always as straightforward as the criteria might appear. The reporting system currently employed in the United States is strewn with measurement problems and inherent subjectivities. Couple these limitations with the complexities of many businesses today, and it is no wonder that appropriate application of these criteria is not always obvious. To demonstrate, we illustrate application of the revenue and expense criteria for four industries.

Example 1.   Paramount Communications is a subsidiary of Viacom, Inc., that produces motion pictures. It incurs production costs in filming the movies, advertising and exploitation costs in promoting the films, and royalty costs for the principal actors and actresses, producers, directors, and others. Paramount generates revenues from movie theaters depending on the number of tickets sold. It may also generate revenues from video sales and the sale of residual rights to the movies to television or cable networks or to foreign licensees. The amount of revenues generated from video sales and the sale of residual movie rights depends in part on the success of the films in their initial theater run.

Paramount can easily measure the amount of revenues from theater ticket sales and recognize it as sales occur. The amount of revenues that a film will generate from video sales and the sale of residual rights is highly uncertain as of the time of the movie's initial release. The criteria for the recognition of revenue are therefore not met until sales of videos and residual rights occur in later periods. The movie studio can easily match royalty expense with revenues in all periods, because the royalty amount is usually a percentage of the revenues.

The principal income recognition issue for movie studios is: How much of the costs of filming and promoting the movie should the studio match with theater ticket revenues, and how much should it leave on the balance sheet as an asset and match with revenues from video sales and residual rights in later periods? The revenue pattern of previous movies may provide a basis for projecting the likely total revenues from new releases. Also, one would expect a movie studio to consider revenue projections in establishing its cost budget for movies. When examining the financial statements of a movie studio, the analyst should carefully study the profit margin on movies reported in the income statement and the amount of deferred production costs remaining on the balance sheet.[2]

Example 2.   Columbia Records has been owned by several different organizations over the years. Currently, it is a division of the Sony Music Entertainment Group, a segment of Sony Corporation. The Sony Music Entertainment Group runs periodic promotions to enlist subscribers into its compact disc-of-the-month programs. For a nominal fee, new subscribers receive a set of compact discs and promise to purchase a certain minimum number of discs over some future period of time. The firm sends out cards each month with the list of compact discs available for that month. Subscribers return the cards if they wish to purchase one of the selections. Similar arrangements apply to book-of-the-month or craft-of-the-month programs.

The principal income measurement issue in these settings is the timing of revenue recognition. Should these firms recognize the revenues from selling the minimum number of required compact discs when customers commit to such purchases upon subscription? Or should they recognize a portion of the revenues each month when they send out the cards? The return rate from customers desiring to purchase the compact disc selection is relatively low each month. If the return rate were highly predictable, such as 20 percent or 30 percent, then the firms could simply recognize revenue for that portion of customer orders. The return rate, however, is not only low but also unpredictable. The selection in one month

---

[2]Film industry reporting is currently addressed by Financial Accounting Standards Board, *Statement of Financial Accounting Standards No. 53*, "Financial Reporting by Producers and Distributors of Motion Picture Films," 1981. In recent years, however, the industry has been criticized for abusing application of *Statement No. 53*, and possible changes to the statement may occur in the future. David J. Londoner provides a discussion of the difficulties in implementing *Statement No. 53* and its possible manipulation by managment in "What's the Problem with Film Industry Reporting?" *Journal of Financial Statement Analysis*, Spring 1996, pp. 6–12.

may have a 10 percent customer order rate, while the next month's selection may experience a 20 percent customer demand rate. Furthermore, several months might elapse before the size of customer orders becomes clear.

These firms do not meet the criteria for revenue recognition either at the time customers subscribe or at the time the firm sends out cards each month, because the amount of cash that the firm will ultimately receive and its date of receipt are not measurable with sufficient precision. Such firms should delay revenue recognition until they ship products to customers.

Additional income recognition issues arise with respect to the initial promotional offer. Should the firm recognize the costs of the compact discs as an expense in the period when the customer subscribes to the program, or should it spread such costs over the future periods when customers purchase the additional items required by the program? Firms that defer such costs report a deferred asset, such as deferred subscription costs, on their balance sheets.

Example 3.   Automotive and appliance manufacturers typically provide warranty or maintenance services for products sold. Some companies include such services automatically in the sale of their products; the selling price includes a charge for the automobile or appliance and its related warranty. Other companies provide a very limited warranty with the product, and sell a more comprehensive warranty or maintenance agreement separately. Customers can decide whether or not to purchase the extended protection. This protection may cover a period of three to five years.

These firms typically receive cash for both the product sold and any related warranty at the time they sell the main product. Thus, there is little uncertainty regarding the amount of revenue. The principal income recognition issue regards the amount of expense to match against the revenue. These firms must provide future services, whose cost the firms will not know with certainty for several years.

If the firm will perform only minimal future services or can predict the costs of such services with a reasonably high degree of precision, it can recognize the warranty revenue in the period when it sells the main product. It would also recognize an estimated warranty expense to match against such revenues. A warranty liability account appears on the balance sheet to reflect the expected costs of future warranty claims. If the firm must provide substantial future services, or if the cost of the future services is highly uncertain, then the firm should delay the recognition of warranty revenue. A warranty advances account in this case appears among liabilities for such firms. These firms recognize warranty revenue and warranty expense each period as time passes and customers make warranty claims.

Example 4.   Metropolitan Life Insurance Company sells life insurance policies to customers. The firm receives premium payments each year, and invests the cash in stocks, bonds, real estate, and other income-producing assets. The premiums received from customers plus the income from investments over the life of insured individuals provide the funds to pay the required death benefits.

Life insurance companies receive cash from premiums and from investments each period. They invest in readily marketable securities for the most part, so it is not hard to measure the changes in the market value of their investments. Nor does measuring the amount of revenue each period while the life insurance policy is outstanding present difficulties. The only issue on the revenue side is whether life insurance companies should recognize as revenue the unrealized gains and losses from changes in the market value of investments. Common practice in the insurance industry is to recognize such gains and losses each year in computing net income.[3]

There is usually little question about the total expense on a life insurance policy. Other than selling commissions and administrative costs, the only expense is the face value of the policy. The income recognition issue is how much of this total cost life insurance companies should recognize as an expense each year to match against premium and investment revenues. The objective is to spread these costs over the life of the insured. Determining the length of this period and the pattern of expense recognition requires actuarial calculations of expected life, investment returns, and similar factors. Note that allocating an equal portion of the total cost to each year of expected life will not necessarily provide an appropriate matching of revenues and expenses.

Although insurance premiums typically remain level over the contract period, investment revenues increase over time as premiums and investment returns accumulate. Life insurance companies increase a liability each period, often called policyholder reserves, for the amount of expense recognized. They reduce this account when they pay insurance claims. An analyst examining the financial statements of a life insurance company should be particularly aware of the amount shown for policyholder reserves and the change in this account each year. An evaluation of this account provides information about both the adequacy of investments to cover potential claims and the amount of net income each period.

Summary.   These four examples illustrate that firms in certain industries do not necessarily meet the criteria for revenue and expense recognition at the time of sale. An underlying theme in each instance is uncertainty: uncertainty about the amount of cash that the firm will ultimately receive, and uncertainty about the amount of cash it will ultimately disburse. Uncertainty results in a significant degree of estimation in future cash flows, which in turn gives rise to the potential for earnings management. The healthy skepticism that all analysts should bring to the analysis of reported financial data must be ratcheted up one notch when analysts review activities of firms or industries that involve the level of uncertainty and subjectivity present in these four illustrations.

We explore more fully the impact of recognizing income either earlier than the time of sale (a common practice among long-term contractors) or later than the time of sale (a common practice when firms sell goods on an installment payment basis and experience high uncertainty regarding the collectibility of cash).

---

[3]Chapter 7 provides a discussion of how firms other than life insurance companies account for investments in readily marketable debt and equity securities.

INCOME RECOGNITION FOR LONG-TERM CONTRACTORS

Long-term contractors such as building contractors, aerospace manufacturers, or shipbuilders are different from manufacturers that produce standard components or production items. The operating cycle for long-term contractors likewise differs from the typical manufacturing firm operating cycle depicted in Exhibit 5.1 in three important respects:

1. The period of production (or construction) for a long-term contractor may span several accounting periods.
2. Contractors identify customers and agree upon a contract price in advance (or at least in the early stages of construction).
3. Customers often make periodic payments on the contract price as work progresses.

The operating activities of long-term contractors often satisfy the criteria for the recognition of revenue during the period of construction. The presence of a contract indicates that the contractor has identified a buyer and agreed upon a price. The contractor either collects cash in advance or concludes, based on an assessment of the customer's credit standing, that it will receive cash equal to the contract price after completion of construction. Although the contract may obligate the contractor to perform substantial future services, the contractor should be able to estimate the cost of these services with reasonable precision. In agreeing to a contract price, the firm must have some confidence in its estimates of the total costs it will incur on the contract.

Percentage-of-Completion Method. When contractors meet the criteria for revenue recognition as construction progresses, they usually recognize revenue during the period of construction using the percentage-of-completion method. Under this method, contractors recognize a portion of the total contract price, depending on the degree of completion of the work during a period, as revenue for that period. They base this proportion either on engineers' or architects' estimates of the degree of completion or on the ratio of costs incurred to date to the total expected costs for the contract.

The actual schedule of cash collections is *not* a determining factor in measuring the amount of revenue recognized each period under the percentage-of-completion method. Even if a contractor expects to collect the entire contract price at the completion of construction, it would still use the percentage-of-completion method as long as it can make reasonable estimates as construction progresses of the amount of cash it will collect and of the costs it will incur.

As contractors recognize portions of the contract price as revenues, they recognize corresponding proportions of the total estimated costs of the contract as expenses. The percentage-of-completion method, following the principles of the accrual basis of accounting, matches expenses with related revenues.

Example 5. To illustrate the percentage-of-completion method, we assume that a firm agrees to construct a bridge for $5 million. Estimated costs are as follows: Year 1, $1.5 million; Year 2, $2 million; and Year 3, $0.5 million. Thus, the expected gross margin from the contract is $1,000,000 (= $5,000,000 − $1,500,000 − $2,000,000 − $500,000).

Assuming that the contractor bases the degree of completion on the percentage of total costs incurred to date, and that it incurs actual costs as anticipated, revenue and expense from the contract are as follows:

Year	Degree of Completion	Revenue	Expense	Gross Margin
1	$1,500,000/$4,000,000 = 37.5%	$1,875,000	$1,500,000	$ 375,000
2	$2,000,000/$4,000,000 = 50.0%	2,500,000	2,000,000	500,000
3	$500,000/$4,000,000 = 12.5%	625,000	500,000	125,000
		$5,000,000	$4,000,000	$1,000,000

Actual costs on contracts seldom coincide precisely with expectations. As new information on expected total costs becomes available, contractors must adjust reported income on the contract. They make these adjustments to reported income during the current and future periods rather than retroactively restating income of prior periods.

Example 6.   Look at Example 5 again. Assume now that actual costs incurred in Year 2 for the contract were $2.2 million instead of $2 million and that total expected costs on the contract are now $4.2 million. Revenue, expense, and gross margin from the contract are as follows:

Year	Cumulative Degree of Completion	Revenue	Expense	Margin
1	$1,500,000/$4,000,000 = 37.5%	$1,875,000	$1,500,000	$375,000
2	$3,700,000/$4,200,000 = 88.1%	2,530,000[a]	2,200,000	330,000
3	$4,200,000/$4,200,000 = 100%	595,000[b]	500,000	95,000
		$5,000,000	$4,200,000	$800,000

[a] (0.881 × $5,000,000) − $1,875,000 = $2,530,000
[b] $5,000,000 − $1,875,000 − $2,530,000 = $595,000

Example 7.   If it appears that the contractor will ultimately realize a loss upon completion of a contract, the contractor must recognize the loss in full as soon as it becomes evident. For example, if at the end of Year 2 the contractor expects to realize a loss of $200,000 on the contract, it must recognize a loss of $575,000 in Year 2. The $575,000 amount offsets the income of $375,000 recognized in Year 1 plus a loss of $200,000 anticipated on the overall contract.

Contractors report actual contract costs on the balance sheet in a contracts in process account. This account includes not only accumulated costs to date but

EXHIBIT 5.3			
Calculation of Balance in Contracts in Process Account Using the Percentage-of-Completion Method			

	Accumulated Costs	Accumulated Income	Amount in Contracts in Process Account
Example 5 (Profit = $1,000,000)			
During Year 1	$ 1,500,000	$ 375,000	$ 1,875,000
Balance, December 31, Year 1	$ 1,500,000	$ 375,000	$ 1,875,000
During Year 2	2,000,000	500,000	2,500,000
Balance, December 31, Year 2	$ 3,500,000	$ 875,000	$ 4,375,000
During Year 3	500,000	125,000	625,000
Completion of Contract during Year 3	(4,000,000)	(1,000,000)	(5,000,000)
Balance, December 31, Year 3	$ 0	$ 0	0
Example 6 (Profit = $800,000)			
During Year 1	$ 1,500,000	$ 375,000	$ 1,875,000
Balance, December 31, Year 1	$ 1,500,000	$ 375,000	$ 1,875,000
During Year 2	2,200,000	330,000	2,530,000
Balance, December 31, Year 2	$ 3,700,000	$ 705,000	$ 4,405,000
During Year 3	500,000	95,000	595,000
Completion of Contract during Year 3	(4,200,000)	(800,000)	(5,000,000)
Balance, December 31, Year 3	$ 0	$ 0	$ 0
Example 7 (Loss = $200,000)			
During Year 1	$ 1,500,000	$ 375,000	$ 1,875,000
Balance, December 31, Year 1	$ 1,500,000	$ 375,000	$ 1,875,000
During Year 2	2,200,000	(575,000)	1,625,000
Balance, December 31, Year 2 . . . . : . . .	$ 3,700,000	$ (200,000)	$ 3,500,000
During Year 3	1,500,000	—	1,500,000
Completion of Contract during Year 3	(5,200,000)	200,000	(5,000,000)
Balance, December 31, Year 3	$ 0	$ 0	$ 0

also any income or loss recognized on the contract. Exhibit 5.3 shows the contracts in process account for Examples 5 through 7. If the contractor periodically bills the customer for portions of the contract price, it would report the amount billed in accounts receivable and as a subtraction from the amount in the contracts in process account.

Completed-Contract Method. Some long-term contractors postpone the recognition of revenue until they complete the construction project. Such firms use the completed-contract method of recognizing revenue. This, in effect, is the "time of sale" method of recognizing revenue. If the firm in Example 6 had used the completed-contract method, it would have recognized no revenue or expense from the contract during Year 1 or Year 2. It would recognize contract revenue of $5 million and contract expenses of $4.2 million in Year 3. Note that total gross margin is $800,000 under both the percentage-of-completion and completed-contract methods, equal to cash inflows of $5 million less cash outflows of $4.2 million. If the contractor anticipates a loss on a contract, it recognizes the loss as soon as the loss becomes evident, even if the contract is incomplete.

The contracts in process account under the completed-contract method shows a balance of $1.5 million on December 31, Year 1, the accumulated costs to date. This account shows a balance on December 31, Year 2, of $3.5 million under Example 5; $3.7 million under Example 6; and $3.5 million under Example 7. These amounts reflect accumulated cost to date minus, in Example 7, the estimated loss on the contract.

These amounts are less than the amounts shown in the contracts in process account for Examples 5 and 6 under the percentage-of-completion method by the amount of accumulated income recognized under the latter method. Accelerating the recognition of income under the percentage-of-completion method increases both assets and net income (part of retained earnings). Thus, income recognition and asset valuation closely interrelate.

Choice of Reporting Method by Long-Term Contractors.   The primary reason that a contractor would not use the percentage-of-completion method when a contract exists is that there is substantial uncertainty regarding the total costs it will incur in completing the project. If the contractor cannot estimate the total costs, it will be unable to estimate the percentage of total costs incurred as of a given date and thereby the percentage of services it has already rendered. It will also be unable to estimate the total income from the contract.

In some cases, contractors use the completed-contract method because the contracts are of such short duration (such as a few months) that earnings reported with the percentage-of-completion method and the completed-contract method are not significantly different. In this case, the lower costs of implementing the completed-contract method explain its use. Contractors also use the completed-contract method when they have not obtained a specific buyer during the construction phase, as is sometimes the case in the construction of residential housing that may require future selling efforts. There could be substantial uncertainty regarding the ultimate contract price and the amount of cash that the contractor will receive.

Contractors must use the percentage-of-completion method for income tax purposes. Although most firms would prefer to use the completed-contract method for tax purposes, thereby delaying the recognition of income and payment of income taxes, the Internal Revenue Code does not permit it.

A statement of the International Accounting Standards Committee (IASC) requires the percentage-of-completion method except when the contractor cannot reliably estimate the total expected revenues and costs of a contract; in this case, the contractor recognizes revenue only to the extent of costs incurred.[4] There is

---

[4]International Accounting Standards Committee, *International Accounting Standard No. 11*, "Construction Contracts," 1993.

wide variation among member countries, however, with respect to implementing this IASC standard. For example, Canada, France, Germany, Japan, and the United States permit both methods; the United Kingdom and the Netherlands allow only the percentage-of-completion method; and Austria allows only the completed-contract method.

Examples 5 through 7 illustrate the degree of estimation and uncertainty involved with income recognition for long-term contractors. Sometimes a project can take up to five years to complete. In some cases, contractors are working with hundreds of subcontractors. Contract renegotiations several times during the course of a large contract are not unusual. Estimating future sustainable earnings using historical data for firms that construct (and sell) long-term products must take factors like this into consideration. Other firm-specific factors that can exacerbate uncertainty include the volume of projects underway at one time, a firm's success in completing projects on time and within budget, the duration of typical projects, and the types of projects undertaken.

Long-term contractors usually address many of these factors in the analysis of operations in their annual reports and Form 10-K filings. Yet the potential for earnings management in these environments is high for at least two reasons: (1) the time period between cash inflows and outflows for these firms is so long, and (2) there is a great deal of estimation needed to measure revenues and expenses. The analyst evaluating firms in the residential construction, aircraft, and defense-related industries must be particularly sensitive to these conditions.

REVENUE RECOGNITION WHEN CASH COLLECTIBILITY IS UNCERTAIN

Occasionally, estimating the amount of cash or cash-equivalent value of other assets that a firm will receive from customers is difficult. This may occur because the customer's future financial condition is highly uncertain, or because the customer may have the right to return the items purchased and thereby avoid the obligation to make cash payments. This uncertainty regarding future cash inflows may prevent the selling firm from measuring—at the time of sale—the present value of the cash it expects to receive. The firm will therefore recognize revenue at the time it collects cash using either the installment method or the cost-recovery-first method.

Unlike the cash method of accounting, these revenue recognition methods follow accrual principles by matching expenses with associated revenues. Without the installment and cost-recovery-first methods, applying the time of sale method to situations with high uncertainty as to cash inflows could result in widespread earnings management. When cash inflows are difficult to measure, managers are subject to a great deal of temptation to manage earnings. The uncertainty of future cash flows also affects the sustainability of earnings. The task for the analyst is to judge whether a firm that uses the time of sale method to recognize revenue ought instead to be using one of these two, more conservative, methods, which might reduce the level of uncertainty introduced into the reporting system.

Installment Method.   Under the installment method, a firm recognizes revenue as it collects portions of the selling price in cash. At the same time, it recognizes corresponding portions of the cost of the good or service sold as an expense. For example, assume that a firm sells for $100 merchandise that costs $60. The buyer agrees to pay (ignoring interest) $20 each month for five months. The firm recognizes revenue of $20 each month as it receives the cash. Likewise, it recognizes a cost of goods sold of $12 (=$20/$100 × $60) each month. By the end of five months, the firm recognizes total income of $40 [= 5 × ($20 − $12)].

Land development companies, which typically sell undeveloped land and promise to develop it over several future years, sometimes use the installment method. The buyer makes a nominal down payment and agrees to pay the remainder of the purchase price in installments over 10, 20, or more years. For a developer, future development of the land is a significant aspect of the earnings process. Also, substantial uncertainty often exists as to the ultimate collectibility of the installment notes, particularly those not due until many years in the future. The customer can always elect to stop making payments, losing the right to own the land.

Cost-Recovery-First Method. When firms experience substantial uncertainty about cash collection, they can also use the cost-recovery-first method of income recognition. The cost-recovery-first method matches the costs of generating revenues dollar for dollar with cash receipts until the firm recovers all such costs. Revenues equal expenses in each period until full cost recovery occurs. Only when cumulative cash receipts exceed total costs will a firm show a profit (that is, revenue without any matching expenses) in the income statement.

To illustrate the cost-recovery-first method, we can use the example relating to the sale of merchandise for $100. During the first three months, the firm would recognize revenue of $20 and expense of $20. By the end of the third month, cumulative cash receipts of $60 exactly equal the cost of the merchandise sold. During the fourth and fifth months, the firm would recognize revenue of $20 each month but without an offsetting expense. For the five months as a whole, total income is again $40 (equal to cash inflow of $100 less cash outflow of $60), but the income recognition pattern differs from that of the installment method.

Comprehensive Illustration of Income Recognition Methods for Installment Sales. Digital Electronics Corporation (DEC) sold a computer costing $16 million to the City of Boston for $20 million on January 1, Year 10. The City of Boston agreed to make annual payments of $5,548,195 on December 31, Year 10, through December 31, Year 14 (five payments in total).

The top panel of Exhibit 5.4 shows an amortization table for the note receivable underlying this transaction. The five payments of $5,548,195 each when discounted at 12 percent have a present value equal to the $20 million selling price. Thus, 12 percent is the interest rate implicit in the note. Column (2) shows the interest revenue that DEC recognizes each year from providing financing services to the City of Boston (that is, permitting the city to delay payment of the $20 million selling price).

The next panel of Exhibit 5.4 shows the revenue and expense that DEC recognizes under three income recognition methods. Columns (6) and (7) assume DEC recognizes income from the sale of the computer at the time of sale. Such immediate recognition rests on the premise that there is a high probability that the City of Boston will pay the amounts due under the note.

If substantial uncertainty exists regarding cash collectibility of the notes, then DEC should use either the installment or cost-recovery-first methods. Columns (8) and (9) show the amounts for the installment method. Revenues in column (8) represent collections of the $20 million principal amount of the note (that is, the portion of each cash payment made by the city that does not represent interest). Column (9) shows the expense each year, which represents 80 percent (= $16,000,000/$20,000,000) of the revenue recognized. Columns (10) and (11) show the amounts for the cost-recovery-first method. Note that DEC recognizes no income until Year 5, when cumulative cash receipts exceed the $16 million cost of manufacturing the computer.

Note that total cash inflows of $27,740,973 (column 3) equal total revenue, sales revenue (columns 6, 8, and 10) and interest revenue (column 12). Total cash outflows of $16 million equal total expense (columns 7, 9, and 11).

The last panel of Exhibit 5.4 shows the amounts that DEC reports on its balance sheet for each of the three income recognition methods. Recognizing income at the time of sale results in the largest cumulative income through the first four years and thus the greatest amount of assets. Recognizing income using the installment method results in the next-largest cumulative income and the next-greatest assets. The cost-recovery-first method results in the smallest cumulative income and the least amount of assets. The differences between the asset amounts equal the differences in cumulative income recognized.

Thus, we see again that asset valuation closely relates to income recognition. Note also that at the end of five years, cumulative income and assets are identical for all three income recognition methods.

Choice of Installment and Cost-Recovery-First Methods.

Financial reporting permits firms to use the installment method and the cost-recovery-first method only when substantial uncertainty exists about cash collection. For most sales of goods and services, a firm's past experience and its assessment of the credit standing of its customers provide a sufficient basis for estimating the amount of cash the firm will receive. In these cases, firms do not use the installment method and the cost-recovery-first method. These firms must generally recognize revenue at the time of sale.

Income tax laws allow the installment method for income tax reporting under some circumstances, even when no uncertainty exists regarding cash collections. Manufacturing firms selling on extended payment plans often use the installment method for income tax reporting (while recognizing revenue at the time of sale for financial reporting). Firms seldom use the cost-recovery-first method for tax reporting.

DISCLOSURE OF REVENUE RECOGNITION METHOD

Usually the first note to the financial statements discusses the accounting policies that a firm follows. If a firm recognizes a significant amount of revenue at times other than the time of sale, this note reports the methods followed.

EXHIBIT 5.4

Illustration of Income Recognition Methods from Installment Sales

Amortization Schedule for Note Receivable

Year	Note Receivable, January 1: (1)	Interest Revenue at 12 Percent (2)	Cash Payment Received (3)	Repayment of Principal (4)	Note Receivable, December 31: (5)
1	$ 20,000,000	$2,400,000	$ 5,548,195	$ 3,148,195	$16,851,865
2	16,851,865	2,022,217	5,548,195	3,525,978	13,325,827
3	13,325,827	1,599,099	5,548,195	3,949,096	9,376,731
4	9,376,731	1,125,208	5,548,195	4,422,987	4,953,744
5	4,953,744	594,449	5,548,193	4,953,744	0
		$7,740,973	$27,740,973	$20,000,000	

Column (2) = .12 × Column (1)

Column (3) = Given

Column (4) = Column (3) − Column (2)

Column (5) = Column (1) − Column (4)

Income Recognition from Sale of Computer

Year	Time of Sale Revenue (6)	Time of Sale Expense (7)	Installment Method Revenue (8)	Installment Method Expense (9)	Cost-Recovery-First Method Revenue (10)	Cost-Recovery-First Method Expense (11)	All Three Methods Interest Revenue (12)
1	$20,000,000	$16,000,000	$ 3,148,195	$ 2,518,556	$ 3,148,195	$ 3,148,195	$2,400,000
2	—	—	3,525,978	2,820,782	3,525,978	3,525,978	2,022,217
3	—	—	3,949,096	3,159,277	3,949,096	3,949,096	1,599,099
4	—	—	4,422,987	3,538,390	4,422,987	4,422,987	1,125,208
5	—	—	4,953,744	3,962,995	4,953,744	953,744	594,449
	$20,000,000	$16,000,000	$20,000,000	$16,000,000	$20,000,000	$ 16,000,000	$7,740,973

Column (8) = Column (4)

Column (9) = .80 × Column (8)

Column (10) = Column (4)

Column (11) = Column (10) until Cumulative Revenues = $16,000,000

Column (12) = Column (2)

Exh. 5.4—Continued

Time of Sale	Installment Method				Cost-Recovery-First Method		
Notes Receivable (13)	Notes Receivable (14)	Less Deferred Gross Margin (15)	Notes Receivable Net (16)	Notes Receivable (17)	Less Deferred Gross Margin (18)	Notes Receivable Net (19)

Notes Receivable-Net Reported on Balance Sheet

Income Recognition

	(13)	(14)	(15)	(16)	(17)	(18)	(19)
January 1, Year 1	$20,000,000	$20,000,000	$4,000,000	$16,000,000	$20,000,000	$4,000,000	$16,000,000
December 31, Year 1	16,851,865	16,851,865	3,370,361	13,481,504	16,851,865	4,000,000	12,851,865
December 31, Year 2	13,325,827	13,325,827	2,665,165	10,660,662	13,325,827	4,000,000	9,325,827
December 31, Year 3	9,376,731	9,376,731	1,875,346	7,501,385	9,376,731	4,000,000	5,376,731
December 31, Year 4	4,953,744	4,953,744	990,749	3,962,995	4,953,744	4,000,000	953,744
December 31, Year 5	—	—	—	—	—	—	—

Column (13), Column (14), Column (17) = Column (1)

Column (15) = $4,000,000 minus cumulative income recognized = Column (8) − Column (9) for the current and prior years. For example, $3,370,361 = $4,000,000 − ($3,148,195 − $2,518,556).

Column (16) = Column (14) − Column (15)

Column (18) = $4,000,000 minus cumulative income recognized = Column (10) − Column (11) for the current and prior years.

Column (19) = Column (17) − Column (18).

Example 8. The first note of Coke's financial statements (Appendix A) does not include information on how the company recognizes revenue on the sale of its beverages, implying that it uses the time of sale method. As we discussed in Chapter 4 (Example 19), however, Coke recognizes peripheral gains and losses when equity investees sell additional shares of stock to third parties. Coke states in Note 1 that "in the event the selling price per share is more or less than our average carrying amount per share, we recognize a noncash gain or loss on the issuance."

Example 9. Intel, the world's largest producer of microprocessors, generally recognizes revenue at the time of sale. For sales of its products to distributors, however, the introductory note to the financial statements discloses the following:

> **Deferred income on shipment to distributors.** Certain of the Company's sales are made to distributors under agreements allowing price protection and/or rights of return on merchandise unsold by the distributors. Because of frequent sales price reductions and rapid technological obsolescence in the industry, Intel defers recognition of such sales until the merchandise is sold by the distributors.

INVENTORY COST FLOW ASSUMPTION

Firms selling relatively high dollar value items, such as automobiles, trailers, and real estate, can ascertain from their accounting records the specific cost of the items sold. They recognize this amount as an expense—the cost of goods sold—and match it against sales revenue in measuring net income.

In most cases, however, firms cannot identify the cost of the specific items sold. Inventory items are sufficiently similar, and their unit costs sufficiently small, that firms cannot justify the cost of designing an accounting system to keep track of specific unit costs. To measure the cost of goods sold in these cases, firms must make some assumption about the *flow of costs* (not the flow of units, since firms usually sell the oldest goods first).

Once again, making cost flow assumptions raises the potential of earnings management and has implications for the degree of earnings quality. To analyze earnings quality in the context of inventory accounting, the analyst must understand the reporting options available to management.

Financial reporting permits three cost flow assumptions:

1. First-in, first-out (FIFO).
2. Last-in, first-out (LIFO).
3. Weighted average.

FIFO assigns the cost of the earliest purchases to the units sold and the cost of the most recent purchases to ending inventory. LIFO assigns the cost of the most recent purchases to the cost of goods sold and the earliest purchases to inventory. Weighted average assigns the average cost of all units available for sale during the period (units in beginning inventory plus units purchased) to both units sold and units in ending inventory.

Exhibit 5.5 depicts these relationships in schematic form, assuming that a firm purchases units evenly over the year.

FIFO

FIFO results in balance sheet amounts for ending inventory that are closest to current replacement cost. The cost of goods sold tends to be somewhat out of date, however, because FIFO charges to expense the earlier prices of beginning inven-

EXHIBIT 5.5

Cost Flow Assumptions

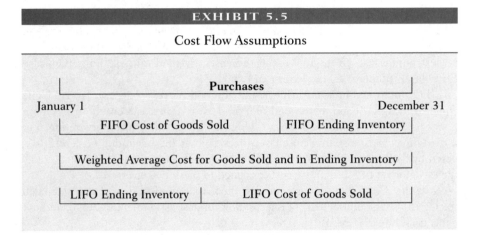

tory and the earliest purchases during the year. When prices are rising, FIFO leads to the highest reported net income (the lowest cost of goods sold) of the three methods, and when prices fall it leads to the smallest net income.

LIFO

LIFO results in amounts for cost of goods sold that closely approximate current replacement costs. Balance sheet amounts, however, can include the cost of acquisitions made many years previously. Consider the diagram in Exhibit 5.6. which shows purchases, LIFO ending inventory, and LIFO cost of goods sold over several periods for a firm.

EXHIBIT 5.6

Illustration of LIFO Ending Inventory Layers

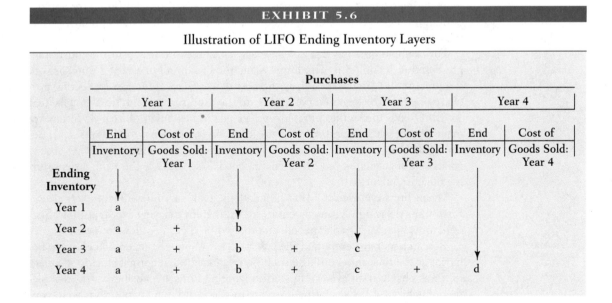

During each of the four periods shown, the firm purchases more units than it sells. Thus, the number of physical units in ending inventory grows each year. The firm assigns costs to the units in inventory at the end of Year 1 on the basis of the earliest purchases in Year 1. We call the costs assigned to these units the "base LIFO layer" (denoted by the letter a in Exhibit 5.6).

LIFO prices the units in inventory at the end of Year 2 in two layers. Units equal to those on hand at the end of Year 1 carry unit costs based on purchase prices paid at the beginning of Year 1. Units *added* to ending inventory during Year 2 carry unit costs based on purchase prices paid at the beginning of Year 2 (denoted by the letter b in Exhibit 5.6). The balance sheet at the end of Year 2 states the inventory at the sum of the costs assigned to these two layers.

Note that LIFO does not assume that the actual physical flow of units sold will track a LIFO assumption. LIFO is a *cost flow*, or cost assignment, method, and not a means of tracking the physical movement of goods.

As the quantity of units in ending inventory continues to increase in Year 3 and Year 4, the firm adds new LIFO layers. At the end of Year 4, LIFO assigns costs to ending inventory on the basis of purchases made at the beginning of Year 1, Year 2, Year 3, and Year 4. Thus, the longer a firm remains on LIFO, the more its ending inventory valuation will differ from current replacement costs.

During periods of rising prices, LIFO generally results in the highest cost of goods sold and the lowest net income of the three cost flow assumptions. It is for this reason that firms usually prefer LIFO for income tax purposes. If a firm chooses a LIFO cost flow assumption for tax purposes, the income tax law requires the firm to use LIFO for financial reporting to shareholders.

LIFO Liquidation.   One exception to the generalization that LIFO produces the lowest net income during periods of rising prices occurs when a firm sells more units during a period than it purchases. This is referred to as a LIFO layer liquidation. In this case, LIFO assigns the cost of all of the current period's purchases plus the costs assigned to the most recent LIFO layers to the cost of goods sold.

For example, assume that sales exceed purchases in Year 5 in the illustration presented in Exhibit 5.6. The firm assigns the cost of all of Year 5's purchases to the units sold. LIFO then assigns the cost of Year 4's LIFO layer (reflecting purchase prices at the beginning of Year 4) to the excess units sold, then assigns Year 3's LIFO layer (reflecting purchase prices at the beginning of Year 3) to any remaining excess units, and so on, until it has assigned a cost to all units sold. Because LIFO assigns older, lower costs to a portion of the units sold, LIFO cost of goods sold may not exceed FIFO cost of goods sold, despite the rising prices during the current period.

When firms experience LIFO liquidations, two cash flow effects likely occur. First, firms delay purchasing inventory items, thereby delaying a cash outflow. Second, firms increase taxable income and the required cash outflow for taxes.

Researchers have examined the effect of LIFO liquidations on stock price behavior at the time firms disclose such liquidations. No abnormal stock price reaction was observed on average in studies ignoring firms' tax positions (for example, the availability of net operating loss carryforwards). When tax positions were considered, low tax-paying firms had a higher abnormal price reaction to a LIFO liquidation than other firms.[5]

Characteristics of LIFO Adopters. Researchers have examined the characteristics of firms that do and do not adopt LIFO. Although these research studies do not always show consistent results, particular factors appear related to the decision to adopt LIFO:[6]

Direction and Rate of Factor Price Changes for Inventory Items. Firms experiencing rapidly increasing factor prices for raw materials, labor, or other product costs obtain greater tax benefits from LIFO than firms that experience smaller factor price increases or that experience price decreases.

Variability in the Rate of Inventory Growth. LIFO adopters show more variable rates of inventory growth before adopting LIFO than firms that remain on FIFO. The variability of inventory growth is reduced after the adoption of LIFO. Because LIFO tends to match more recent inventory costs with sales than do FIFO or weighted average (these methods use costs that are 6 to 15 months-old compared to current replacement costs), LIFO tends to result in less variability in the gross margin percentage over the business cycle. Firms with variable rates of inventory growth (perhaps because of cyclicality in their industry) can more easily accomplish an income smoothing reporting objective using LIFO than if they use FIFO or average cost.

Tax Savings Opportunities. LIFO adopters tend not to have tax loss carryforwards available to offset future taxable income. These firms instead adopt LIFO to provide future tax savings. LIFO adopters also realize larger tax savings in the year of adoption than in the years before or after, suggesting that the decision is in part motivated by tax rather than financial reporting considerations.

Industry Membership. Firms in certain industries are more likely to adopt LIFO than firms in other industries. Since firms in an industry face similar factor price changes and variability in their inventory growth rates, one would expect similar choices of cost flow assumptions.

Asset Size. Larger firms are more likely to adopt LIFO than smaller firms. LIFO increases recordkeeping costs, relative to FIFO, both in the year of adoption and in subsequent years. Larger firms realize larger amounts of tax savings than smaller firms to absorb the adoption and ongoing recordkeeping costs of LIFO.

---

[5]Thomas L. Stober, "The Incremental Information Content of Financial Statement Disclosures: The Case of LIFO Inventory Liquidations," *Journal of Accounting Research*, Supplement 1986, pp. 138–160, and Sen Yo Tse, "LIFO Liquidations," *Journal of Accounting Research*, Spring 1990, pp. 229–238.

[6]For a review of these studies, see Frederick W. Lindahl, "Dynamic Analysis of Inventory Accounting Choice," *Journal of Accounting Research*, Autumn 1989, pp. 201–226, and Nicholas Dopuch and Morton Pincus, "Evidence on the Choice of Inventory Accounting Methods: LIFO versus FIFO," *Journal of Accounting Research*, Spring 1988, pp. 28–59.

One hypothesis examined in the LIFO decision research is the relation between LIFO adoption and managerial compensation. Because LIFO usually results in lower earnings, one would expect that managerial compensation of LIFO adopters would either be less than compensation of non-LIFO adopters or else include a lower component of compensation based on earnings. Studies have found no difference in managerial compensation of LIFO and non-LIFO adopters, although it is true that managers in LIFO adopters are found to have a smaller earnings component to their compensation.

WEIGHTED AVERAGE

The weighted average cost flow assumption falls between the other two assumptions in its effect on the income statement. It is, however, much more like FIFO than like LIFO in its effects on the balance sheet. When inventory turns over rapidly, purchases during the current period receive a heavy weight in the weighted average unit cost. The weighted average assumption therefore reflects current prices almost as much as FIFO.

CONVERSION FROM LIFO TO FIFO

No cost flow assumption based on historical cost can allow the simultaneously reporting of current cost data on both the income statement and the balance sheet. If a firm reports current costs on the income statement under LIFO, its balance sheet amount for ending inventory includes some very old costs. The out-of-date LIFO inventory valuation provides potentially misleading information to users of financial statements. Consequently, the Securities and Exchange Commission requires firms using LIFO to disclose in notes to their financial statements the amounts by which LIFO inventories are less than if the firm had reported inventories at FIFO or current cost. Analysts sometimes refer to the difference in ending inventory valuation between LIFO and FIFO or current cost as the "LIFO reserve." From this disclosure, it is possible to restate a LIFO firm's income to a FIFO basis. The analyst can thus place firms using LIFO on a basis more comparable to firms using FIFO.

Example 10.   Note 1 to PepsiCo.'s financial statements indicates that it uses a combination of FIFO, LIFO, and average cost flow assumptions for inventories and cost of goods sold. A subsequent note also indicates that the current cost of inventories exceeds the LIFO amounts by $11 million at the end of Year 7 and $8 million at the end of Year 8. Exhibit 5.7 shows the conversion of PepsiCo.'s inventories and cost of goods sold from a combination of three cost flow assumptions to a combination of FIFO and average cost.

Because reporting standards do not require the disclosure of the excess of current cost over average cost of inventories, it is not possible to fully restate inventories and cost of goods sold on a FIFO basis. PepsiCo. does not report the liquidation of a LIFO layer during Year 8. Thus, the quantity of inventory items under LIFO likely increased. Yet, the excess of current cost over LIFO cost decreased during the period, suggesting that the acquisition costs of inventory items

	EXHIBIT 5.7		

Restatement of PepsiCo.'s Inventories and Cost of Goods Sold for Differences in Cost Flow Assumptions (in millions)

	FIFO/LIFO/ Average Cost	Excess of Current Cost Over LIFO Cost	FIFO/ Average
Cost			
Beginning Inventory	$ 1,051[a]	$11[c]	$ 1,062[d]
Purchases	15,370		15,370
Available	$16,421		$16,432
Less Ending Inventory. . .	1,038[a]	8[c]	1,046[e]
Cost of Goods Sold	$15,383[b]	$ 3	$15,386[b]

[a] As reported in Pepsi's balance sheet.

[b] As reported in Pepsi's income statement.

[c] As reported in Pepsi's note on inventories.

[d] $1,062 = $1,051 + $11.

[e] $1,046 = $1,038 + $8.

valued under LIFO dropped during the year. As one would expect during a period of decreasing prices, the cost of goods sold on a FIFO or average cost basis is higher than when a firm uses LIFO for a portion of its inventories. In this case, PepsiCo.'s use of a combination of the FIFO, LIFO, and average cost methods has virtually no effect on measures of its operating profitability.

Example 11. In Year 11, Bethlehem Steel Company changed its method of valuing inventories from the LIFO method to the FIFO method.[7] An annual report of Bethlehem Steel issued prior to the change provides substantial information on its inventories, as illustrated in Exhibit 5.8. Exhibit 5.9 shows the conversion calculations.

The gross margin percentage under LIFO is 16.2 percent [= ($5,250.9 − $4,399.1) ÷ $5,250.9], and under FIFO it is 16.8 percent [= ($5,250.9 − $4,366.7) ÷ $5,250.9]. The lower gross margin value under LIFO suggests that the manufacturing costs of steel increased during Year 9.

The inventory turnover ratio, a measure that indicates the efficiency with which a firm manages its inventory, is calculated as:

$$\text{LIFO: } \$4,399.1 \div 0.5(\$369.0 + \$410.3) = 11.3$$

$$\text{FIFO: } \$4,366.7 \div 0.5(\$899.1 + \$972.8) = 4.7$$

---

[7]The change is reported as a "change in accounting principle" as discussed in Chapter 4. However, a firm *restates* prior years' financial statements to reflect the change, a financial reporting requirement specific to a change from the LIFO to FIFO inventory cost flow assumption.

EXHIBIT 5.8

Bethlehem Steel Company
Annual Report Excerpts
(in millions)

	December 31	
	Year 8	Year 9
Inventories at FIFO Cost	$ 899.1	$ 972.8
Excess of FIFO Cost Over LIFO Cost	(530.1)	(562.5)
Inventories at LIFO Cost	$ 369.0	$ 410.3
Current Assets (LIFO)	$1,439.8	$1,435.2
Current Liabilities	870.1	838.0
	For Year 9	
Sales	$5,250.9	
Cost of Goods Sold (LIFO)	4,399.1	
Net Income	245.7	
Income Tax Rate	35%	

The dramatic difference in the inventory turnover ratios under LIFO and FIFO reflects the many years that have elapsed since Bethlehem Steel Company adopted LIFO. The current (FIFO) cost of its inventory is more than twice as high as its book (LIFO) value.

The inventory turnover ratio based on LIFO amounts gives a poor indication of the actual physical turnover of inventory items, because it divides a cost of goods sold amount reflecting current costs by an average inventory amount reflecting very old costs. The inventory turnover ratio under FIFO provides a better indication of the physical turnover of inventory items, because it divides a cost of goods

---

EXHIBIT 5.9

Conversion of Bethlehem Steel Company from LIFO to FIFO
(in millions)

	LIFO	Excess of FIFO Cost Over LIFO Cost	FIFO
Beginning Inventory	$ 369.0	$ 530.1	$ 899.1
Purchases	4,440.4		4,440.4
Available	$4,809.4	$ 530.1	$5,339.5
Less Ending Inventory	(410.3)	(562.5)	(972.8)
Cost of Goods Sold	$4,399.1	$ (32.4)	$4,366.7

sold reflecting only slightly out-of-date costs by an average inventory reflecting relatively recent costs.

Although the *trend* in the inventory turnover ratio for a particular firm is likely to be similar under LIFO and FIFO, cross-sectional comparisons are inappropriate if one firm uses LIFO and another uses FIFO. Also, the LIFO measure of the inventory turnover ratio does not accurately portray the number of days that inventories are held.

The inventory cost flow assumption also affects the current ratio, a measure commonly used to assess short-term liquidity risk (introduced in Chapter 3). Bethlehem Steel's conversion from LIFO to FIFO raises inventory values at the end of Year 9 by $562.5 million, increasing the current ratio. *Cumulative* pretax income and taxable income would also have been $562.5 million higher under FIFO. Income tax laws do not permit a firm to use LIFO for taxes if it uses FIFO for financial reporting. Thus, Bethlehem Steel Company would have paid $196.9 million (= 0.35 × $562.5) more in income taxes under FIFO than under LIFO. The income taxes saved by adopting LIFO are now partly in cash and partly in other assets (inventories or equipment, for example).

Assuming that the $196.9 million reduces cash on the December 31, Year 9, balance sheet, the current ratios under LIFO and FIFO are calculated as follows:

LIFO: $1,435.2 ÷ $838.0 . . . . 1.71

FIFO: $1,435.2 + (1 − 0.35)($562.5) ÷ $838 . . . . 2.15

The current ratios also differ significantly. The assumption that the extra income taxes paid under FIFO reduce cash only and not other assets moderates the difference, however. The current ratio on December 31, Year 9, under FIFO would likely exceed 2.15.

Conversion of the financial statements of Bethlehem Steel Company from LIFO to FIFO requires these adjustments:

	December 31	
	Year 8	Year 9
Balance Sheet		
Cash:		
0.35 × $530.1; 0.35 × $562.5	$ −185.5	$ −196.9
Inventories	+530.1	+562.5
Retained Earnings:		
0.65 × $530.1; 0.65 × $562.5	$ +344.6	$ +365.6

	For Year 9
Income Statement	
Cost of Goods Sold	$ −32.4
Income Tax Expense: 0.35 × $32.4	+11.3
Net Income: 0.65 × $32.4	$ +21.1

	For Year 9
Statement of Cash Flows	
Net Income	$ +21.1
Increase in Inventories:	
($410.3 − $369.0) − ($972.8 − $899.1)	(+32.4)
Cash Flow From Operations	$ −11.3

Cash flow from operations decreases for the extra income taxes paid under FIFO.

Users of financial statements find the conversion procedure illustrated in Exhibits 5.7 and 5.9 especially useful for comparing U.S. and non-U.S. firms. Most industrialized countries do not permit the use of LIFO for financial reporting. One important exception is Japan, but even in Japan most firms use specific identification or average costs rather than LIFO. Thus, the analyst should restate inventories and cost of goods sold for U.S. firms using LIFO to make them more comparable to cost flow assumptions used outside the U.S.

STOCK PRICE REACTION TO CHANGES IN INVENTORY COST FLOW ASSUMPTION

The required conformity of tax and financial reporting for firms choosing a LIFO cost flow assumption provides fertile ground for researchers studying the efficiency of capital markets. LIFO saves taxes, and therefore increases cash. A switch to LIFO should result in a positive stock price reaction if capital markets react intelligently to information about the switch. The switch also results in lower reported earnings to shareholders. A negative stock price reaction would suggest an inefficient stock market that fails to examine the underlying economic effects of accounting principles decisions.

Numerous research studies have examined this question, some observing positive price reactions and others observing negative price reaction at the time of the switch.[8] Refinements to the research methodology to provide for different earnings expectation models, tax positions, and other factors have not yet resulted in a definitive answer to the question about the intelligence of the market's reaction. Research studies have examined the characteristics of firms that remain on FIFO versus firms that switch to LIFO in an attempt to sort out these conflicting results.

EARNINGS SUSTAINABILITY AND THE COST FLOW ASSUMPTION

For most firms, cost of goods sold represents the largest expense on the income statement. Inventory represents one of the most active accounts on the balance sheet because the creation and selling of goods and services is the central activity of most firms. Thus, monitoring the cost of goods sold and inventory for their effects on the quality of financial reporting is critical. To do this, the analyst considers:

---

[8]For a summary of this research, see Dopuch and Pincus, "Evidence on the Choice of Inventory Accounting Methods: LIFO versus FIFO," *op. cit.*

1. The inventory cost flow assumption chosen by management.
2. Price variation and the speed at which inventory turns over.
3. Any liquidation of LIFO inventory layers.
4. Any inventory physical deterioration or obsolescence.
5. The financing of inventory acquisitions.

Choice of Cost Flow Assumption. Because LIFO generally matches the most recent acquisition costs against revenues in measuring earnings, LIFO-based earnings generally provide the best measure of economic value-added and of sustainable earnings. A firm must replace goods sold if it is to continue operating, and the most recent cost of the items purchased serves as the best predictor of their replacement costs. A FIFO cost flow assumption matches older acquisition costs with current revenues, and a weighted average cost flow assumption provides results between LIFO and FIFO. Researchers examining the relation between market returns for a firm's equity securities and earnings based on LIFO versus FIFO cost of goods sold have found that earnings based on LIFO explain more of the cross-sectional returns across firms than FIFO.[9]

Although LIFO generally provides higher-quality earnings measures, FIFO generally provides better *quality of financial position* valuations. This is because the inventory values under LIFO can be considerably less than current market values, which FIFO values often approximate. (Exceptions are discussed below.)

A firm cannot use LIFO for measuring cost of goods sold on the income statement and FIFO for measuring inventory on the balance sheet. All is not lost, however, because, as Examples 10 and 11 revealed, firms using LIFO must disclose the difference between the FIFO cost and LIFO cost of inventories. With this information, the analyst can convert inventory on the balance sheet to an amount more closely approximating current economic value.

Rapid Inventory Turnover and Price Stability. The preference for LIFO as the best indicator of economic value-added is tempered significantly when (1) inventory turns over quickly, or (2) acquisition costs of inventory items do not vary much. LIFO, FIFO, and weighted average cost flow assumptions all yield approximately the same amounts for cost of goods sold if inventory turns over roughly four or more times each year.

For some firms, inventory does not turn over quickly, but prices are so stable that the choice of the cost flow assumption is of little consequence. This is an unusual situation, however, and probably should cause the analyst to question the demand for the firm's products.

Liquidation of LIFO Inventory Layers. When firms dip into LIFO layers, they must report the amount by which cost of goods sold is reduced (the usual case) and earnings are increased. This is a good example of lower quality of

---

[9]Ross Jennings, Paul J. Simko, and Robert B. Thompson II, "Does LIFO Inventory Accounting Improve the Income Statement at the Expense of the Balance Sheet?" *Journal of Accounting Research*, Spring 1996, pp. 85–109.

earnings despite higher reported profits. When using earnings of the current period to estimate sustainable earnings, the analyst should eliminate the effect of the dip into old LIFO layers from the current period's earnings. The analyst should also ascertain from management the reason why inventory levels were depleted.

Obsolete or Damaged Inventory.   When the current value of inventories declines below acquisition cost because of obsolescence or physical deterioration, firms must write down their inventories to reflect the decline in value. The analyst needs to rely on management and the auditors to determine when inventory is overvalued, but a good gauge is whether competitors are taking writedowns too. Another signal comes from industrywide publications addressing the demand for the firm's products. In certain cases, it is reasonable for the analyst to independently estimate the economic value of inventory and adjust the reported values accordingly.

Inventory Financing Arrangements.   As Exhibit 5.1 illustrates, substantial amounts of cash are needed by a firm early in its operating cycle for the purchase of raw materials. Many such purchases are financed through short-term borrowing agreements with suppliers, which appear on the balance sheet as accounts payable. Some firms, however, may obtain financing for their inventories in a manner that avoids reporting the liability on the balance sheet. For example, a firm might create a legal trust for the sole purpose of purchasing raw materials that the firm needs in its operations. The trust would purchase the raw materials on account from various suppliers. The firm then purchases the needed raw materials from the trust at agreed-upon prices and reimburses the trust for the cost of carrying the raw materials until needed by the firm. The supplier is willing to sell to the trust on account because of the firm's purchase commitment.

The economic substance of this arrangement is that the firm has purchased raw material on account, and yet no accounts payable amount appears in the financial statements of the firm. Current financial reporting rules allow the firm to leave both the inventory and the accounts payable off the balance sheet, thereby lowering its debt levels and increasing inventory and accounts payable turnover ratios. The analyst should examine the notes to the financial statements for significant purchase commitments and consider adding them to inventories and accounts payable.

ACCOUNTING FOR FIXED ASSETS

Virtually all firms report some amount of property, plant, and equipment (sometimes collectively referred to as long-lived fixed assets) on their balance sheets. The greater the capital intensity of a firm, the higher will be the proportion of total assets represented by property, plant, and equipment. Among the questions analysts should raise about property, plant, and equipment are the following:

1. At what amount does the balance sheet report gross property, plant, and equipment?
2. Over what useful lives does the firm depreciate its plant and equipment?

3. What depreciation method does the firm use to write off the cost of property, plant, and equipment?

4. Are the carrying amounts of the fixed assets recoverable through productive use of the assets?

We consider each of these questions in turn.

ASSET VALUATION

Generally accepted accounting principles in the United States and virtually all other countries require the valuation of fixed assets at acquisition costs. Exceptions include Great Britain and the Netherlands, where financial reporting permits periodic revaluations to current replacement cost. (Appendix 5.1 discusses the accounting for such revaluations.)

The use of acquisition cost valuations rests on the presumption that such amounts are more objectively measurable than the current market values of fixed assets. Difficulties encountered in determining current market values include (1) the absence of active markets for many used fixed assets, particularly those specific to a particular firm's needs, (2) the need to identify comparable assets currently available in the market to value assets in place, and (3) the need to make assumptions about the effect of technological and other improvements when using the prices of new assets currently available on the market in the valuation process.

The disclosures of property, plant, and equipment on the balance sheet or in the notes permit the analyst to estimate the relative age of depreciable assets and to get some sense of the extent to which acquisition costs reflect outdated valuations. Appendix A discloses this information for Coke at the end of Year 7 (in millions):

Depreciable Assets (excluding land)	$5,377
Accumulated Depreciation	(2,031)
Net Depreciable Assets	$3,346
Depreciation and Amortization Expense	$ 479

Coke also discloses in Appendix A that it uses the straight-line depreciation method (discussed later in this section). At the end of Year 7, Coke's depreciable assets were approximately 4.2 years old on average (= $2,031 ÷ $479).[10] Given relatively low inflation rates in the United States in recent years, the historical cost values shown on Coke's balance sheet are probably not significantly out of date.

A second issue related to the amount shown for the gross amount of fixed assets is the treatment of expenditures to add to or improve existing plant and

---

[10]The average age of Coke's depreciable assets is slightly more than 4.2 years because the $479 million includes both depreciation expense and amortization of intangible assets.

equipment. Financial reporting stipulates that firms should capitalize (that is, add to the asset's cost) expenditures that increase the service potential (either in quantity or quality) of an asset beyond that originally anticipated. Firms should expense immediately those expenditures that merely maintain the originally expected service potential.

A firm's capitalization versus expense policy with respect to such expenditures affects its reported earnings and provides management with some potential to manage earnings. Unfortunately, firms do not provide sufficient information to permit the analyst to assess the quality of earnings with respect to such expenditures.

Example 12.   American Airlines, one of the largest airlines in the world, follows a rigorous maintenance program for all its aircraft. In a recent annual report, the firm provides the following very limited information about its maintenance and repair costs:

> *Maintenance and Repair Costs.* Maintenance and repair costs for owned and leased flight equipment are charged to operating expense as incurred, except engine overhaul costs.

American Airlines charges substantial costs to income for these operating expenses, and yet provides essentially no detail as to the amounts over time. Analysts often inquire as to the levels of spending by management, however.

DEPRECIABLE LIFE

Depreciation is a process of allocating the historical cost of depreciable assets to the periods of their use in a reasonably systematic manner. One factor in this depreciation process is the expected useful life of the asset. Both physical wear and tear and technological obsolescence affect this life. Firms make estimates of this expected total life, a process that again offers management an opportunity to manage reported earnings.

The disclosures firms make about depreciable lives are usually not very helpful to the analyst who wants to assess a firm's aggressiveness in lengthening depreciable lives to manage earnings. The problem often is the aggregated nature of the disclosures.

Example 13.   American, Delta, and United Airlines are dominant players in the airline industry worldwide, and account for a large percentage of domestic travel in the United States. Leased and owned aircraft of these firms, along with other fixed assets integral to operating airlines, are depreciated following the policies detailed in Exhibit 5.10.

The range of depreciable lives that the three airlines have chosen is large. In addition, note that depreciable lives for *leased* aircraft are often determined by the durations of the leases, which are not necessarily the same as the useful lives of the aircraft. (Chapter 6 discusses accounting for capital leases by the lessee.)

EXHIBIT 5.10

American, Delta and United Airlines
Note Disclosure Policies—Depreciable Lives

American Airlines

Equipment and Property. The provision for depreciation of operating equipment and property is computed on the straight-line method applied to each unit of property, except that spare assemblies are depreciated on a group basis. The depreciable lives and residual values used for the principal depreciable asset classifications are:

	Depreciable Life	Residual Value
Boeing 727–200 (Stage II)	3 years	None
Boeing 727–300 (to be converted to Stage III)	9 years	None
DC-10–10/DC-10–30	26 years	None
Other jet aircraft	20 years	5%
Regional aircraft and engines	15–17 years	10%
Major rotable parts, avionics and assemblies	Life of equipment to which applicable	0–10%
Improvements to leased flight equipment	Term of lease	None
Buildings and improvements (principally on leased land)	10–30 years or term of lease	None
Other equipment	3–20 years	None

Delta Airlines

Depreciation and Amortization. Flight equipment is depreciated on a straight-line basis to residual values (5% of cost) over a 20-year period from the dates placed in service (unless earlier retirement of the aircraft is planned). Flight equipment under capital leases is amortized on a straight-line basis over the term of the respective leases, which range from 6 to 12 years. Ground property and equipment are depreciated on a straight-line basis over their estimated service lives, which range from 3 to 30 years.

United Airlines

Depreciation and amortization of owned depreciable assets is based on the straight-line method over their estimated service lives. Leasehold improvements are amortized over the remaining period of the lease or the estimated service life of the related asset, which ever is less. Aircraft are depreciated to estimated salvage values, generally over lives of 10 to 30 years; buildings are depreciated over lives of 25 to 45 years; and other property and equipment are depreciated over lives of 3 to 15 years.

Properties under capital leases are amortized on the straight-line method over the life of the lease, or in the case of certain aircraft, over their estimated service lives. Lease terms are 10 to 30 years for aircraft and flight simulators and 25 years for buildings. Amortization of capital leases is included in depreciation and amortization expense.

Because most firms in the United States use the straight-line depreciation method,[11] the analyst can measure the average total life of depreciable assets by dividing average depreciable assets (gross) by depreciation expense for the year. The calculations for Coke follow (in millions):

Depreciable Assets (Gross):	
December 31, Year 6	$6,424.0
December 31, Year 7	5,377.0
Average Depreciable Assets (Gross) for Year 7	$5,900.5
Depreciation and Amortization Expense, Year 7	$ 479.0
Average Total Depreciable Life	12.3 years[12]

DEPRECIATION METHOD

The third factor in the calculation of depreciation (in addition to the acquisition cost and the expected useful life of depreciable assets) is the depreciation method. Financial reporting permits firms to write off assets evenly over their useful lives (straight-line method) or to write off larger amounts during the early years and smaller amounts in later years (accelerated depreciation methods). Note that total depreciation over an asset's life cannot exceed acquisition costs unless firms revalue such assets to current market values. Thus, straight-line and accelerated depreciation methods differ only in the timing of depreciation expense, not in the total amount of depreciation over time.

Virtually all firms in the United States use the straight-line method for financial reporting. They use accelerated depreciation methods for tax reporting, using depreciable lives specified in the income tax law. These lives are usually shorter than the depreciable lives firms use for financial reporting purposes.

Financial reporting in most countries other than the United States also permits both accelerated and straight-line depreciation methods. In countries where tax laws heavily influence financial reporting (Germany, France, and Japan are examples), most firms use accelerated depreciation methods for both financial and tax reporting. Thus, comparisons of U.S. firms with those of some other countries require the analyst to assess the effect of different depreciation methods. The analyst must either restate reported U.S. amounts to an accelerated basis or convert reported amounts for other countries to a straight-line basis.

The analyst can place U.S. firms on an accelerated depreciation basis using information in the income tax note. *Statement No. 109* requires firms to report in

---

[11]Note that all three of the airlines in Example 13 use the straight-line method for calculating depreciation expense.

[12]The average total depreciable life for Coke is slightly higher than 12.3 years because the $479 million includes both depreciation expense and amortization of intangible assets.

notes to the financial statements the deferred tax liability related to depreciation timing differences at the beginning and the end of the year.[13]

Coke, for example, reports in Note 13 (see Appendix A) that its deferred tax liability related to property, plant, and equipment was $414.0 million on December 31, Year 6, and $200.0 million on December 31, Year 7. These deferred taxes relate to differences in both depreciable lives and depreciation methods. Converting Coke's financial statements to amounts reported for tax purposes requires these *adjustments* (assuming a 35 percent income tax rate, a rate Coke discloses in the same note):

	December 31	
	Year 6	**Year 7**
Balance Sheet		
Property, Plant, and Equipment (Net):		
$414.0 ÷ 0.35; $200.0 ÷ 0.35	$−1,182.8	$−571.4
Deferred Tax Liability	−414.0	−200.0
Retained Earnings	$ −768.8	$−371.4

	For Year 7
Income Statement	
Depreciation Expense:	
($200.0 − $414.0) ÷ 0.35	$−611.4
Income Tax Expense: 0.35 × $611.4	+214.0
Net Income: 0.65 × $611.4	$+397.4

	For Year 7
Statement of Cash Flows	
Net Income	$+397.4
Depreciation Expense	−611.4
Change in the Decrease in Deferred Tax Liability for Depreciation Timing Difference ($200.0 − $414.0)	+214.0
Cash Flow from Operations	$ 0

Note that Coke's deferred tax liability related to property, plant, and equipment decreased during the year by over 50 percent ($414.0 at the beginning of the year, versus $200.0 at the end of the year). This drop accounts for the significant reduction in Year 7's depreciation expense reported for tax purposes.

IMPAIRMENT OF LONG-LIVED ASSETS

Chapter 4 addresses how the impairment of long-lived assets, including fixed assets, affects estimating future sustainable earnings. Financial reporting requires firms to assess whether the carrying amounts of long-lived assets are recoverable

---

[13]Financial Accounting Standards Board, *Statement No. 109*, "Accounting for Income Taxes," 1992. Chapter 6 provides a detailed discussion of this statement.

and, if they are not, to write down the assets to their market values and recognize an impairment loss in income from continuing operations.[14] Financial reporting does not require separate disclosure of the impaired assets, however. Chapter 4 provides an in-depth discussion of impairment accounting for fixed assets and how the analyst should interpret impairment losses.

EARNINGS SUSTAINABILITY AND FIXED ASSET REPORTING

For most firms, but particularly for firms operating in capital-intensive industries, expenditures for fixed assets are a large and recurring outflow of cash. The soft drink industry in which Coke operates is moderately capital-intensive. Coke reports capital expenditures by geographic location in Note 16 of Appendix A; they total $990 million in Year 7 ($937 million in Year 6). As Coke also reports in the Appendix, purchases of fixed assets for Year 5 through Year 7, on average, represent almost 30 percent of cash generated by operations (Consolidated Statement of Cash Flows).

Monitoring valuation and depreciation of fixed assets for the effects on the quality of financial reporting is an important task of the analyst. The analyst needs to consider:

1. The disparity between amounts reported for fixed assets and current economic values.
2. The depreciable lives established by management.
3. The depreciation method employed to match fixed asset costs to reported revenues.

Fixed Assets and Current Economic Values.   The valuation most consistent with economic value-added and high quality of financial position is the current cost of replacing fixed assets. Difficulties arise in measuring current replacement cost objectively, however. Because there are few active secondhand markets for many used fixed assets, the analyst must estimate replacement cost by looking at the cost of a similar new asset and then adjusting that replacement cost for the used asset owned (and perhaps its lower productivity).

Adjusting to replacement costs is all the more difficult because firms do not provide sufficient detailed information about the nature, location, condition, and age of their fixed assets. The most disaggregated information usually provided in dollar form is the book value of land, buildings, machinery, and equipment. (Note that Coke reports in Appendix A an additional category on the balance sheet that is unique to the soft drink industry, labeled "Containers.")

As demonstrated earlier for Coke, analysts can estimate the average age of depreciable assets by dividing the balance in the accumulated depreciation account

---

[14]Financial Accounting Standards Board, *Statement of Financial Accounting Standards No. 121,* "Accounting for the Impairment of Long-Lived Assets and for Long-Lived Assets to be Disposed of," 1995.

at the end of the most recent year by the amount of depreciation expense for the current year. The analyst can use the average age together with data on subsequent price increases to estimate current value, but the amount of subjectivity introduced is likely to be intolerable. Unless firms operate in an industry where fixed assets are at the core of their activities (real estate firms, for example), the analyst should probably work with the unadjusted numbers, and take this into consideration when interpreting the financial analysis.[15]

Choice of Depreciable Lives.   Choosing the number of years during which a firm receives benefits from fixed assets can be difficult. Moreover, firms report any change in depreciable lives as a "change in estimates" (discussed in Chapter 4) and account for its effect prospectively.

These two facts make the choice of depreciable lives a fruitful avenue for practicing earnings management. The analyst should compare the depreciable lives (or the average of the depreciable lives, a calculation illustrated earlier for Coke) across firms in the same industry to assess whether the firm under scrutiny is significantly different from the norm.

Choice of Depreciation Method.   Over 90 percent of the publicly traded firms in the United States use the straight-line method of depreciation. Although the straight-line method may not accurately reflect the actual deterioration in the usefulness of fixed assets for generating revenues, it does not appear that firms use their choice of depreciation method to manage reported earnings

There remains all the same a quality of earnings issue, because many analysts consider earnings based on accelerated depreciation methods to be of higher quality than those based on straight-line depreciation. This is because both (1) the biases caused by using acquisition costs instead of replacement cost to calculate depreciation, and (2) the opportunities to manage earnings through the choice of depreciable lives are tempered by the fact that more conservative measures of earnings result from the use of accelerated depreciation methods. In many cases, accelerated depreciation of acquisition costs also produces depreciation amounts closer to replacement cost than straight-line depreciation during the early years of assets' lives, thereby providing an enhanced measure of value-added. (Just the opposite effect occurs during the later years of assets' lives, however.)

Analysts' preference for accelerated depreciation methods is not universal. Some analysts judge earnings quality by its comparability to competitor firms. Analysts favoring the straight-line method from an earnings quality perspective observe that at least firms are using the method favored by the vast majority of publicly traded firms.

---

[15]The underlying assumption in this discussion is that fixed assets are *undervalued* on the balance sheet when compared to current economic values. If firms experience fixed asset value impairments, the analyst benefits from the reporting rules of *Statement No. 121*, which require firms to write down fixed assets to their current economic values.

ACCOUNTING FOR INTANGIBLE ASSETS

Intangible assets include trade and brand names, trademarks, patents, copyrights, franchise rights, customer lists, goodwill, and similar items. Two characteristics distinguish intangible assets: their intangibility (that is, their lack of physical attributes) and their multiple-period useful life.

Financial reporting in the United States accounts for intangible assets as follows:

1. Firms expense the cost of developing intangibles in the period in which the cost is incurred.[16] The rationale for immediate expensing of such costs is that it is difficult to ascertain whether a particular expenditure results in a future benefit (that is, an asset) or not (an expense). Accountants provide more conservative measures of earnings by expensing such costs immediately. Thus, although Coke spends millions of dollars each year promoting its products, and the name *Coke* represents one of the most valuable "assets" of the firm, financial reporting does not permit the firm to recognize an asset for the expenditures made to develop and maintain its trade name. Coke's balance sheet reported in Appendix A does not include an asset labeled "Trade Name—Coke," or "Brand Name—Coke," although this asset is undoubtedly worth hundreds of millions of dollars to the firm.

2. Firms recognize as an asset expenditures made to acquire intangible assets from others.[17] In this case the firm makes an expenditure on a specifically identifiable intangible asset. The existence of an external market transaction provides evidence of the value of the intangible asset. The acquiring firm must consider the future benefits of the intangible to at least equal the price paid.[18]

3. Firms must amortize intangible assets over their expected useful lives. If the firm cannot estimate the useful life, then financial reporting permits a maximum amortization period of 40 years. Common practice is to use straight-line amortization.

---

[16]An exception to this policy is made for certain software development costs discussed later in this section.

[17]An exception to this policy is made for "purchased in-process research and development costs." Firms immediately expense any in-process but unproven technology purchased in a corporate acquisition, a requirement stipulated by Financial Accounting Standards Board, *Interpretation No. 4*, "Applicability of FASB Statement No. 2 to Business Combinations Accounted for by the Purchase Method," 1975. In a *Barron's* article addressing this controversial requirement ("Big Blue Haze," December 23, 1996), Abraham Briloff points out that more than half the $3.2 billion IBM paid for the Lotus Development Corporation was expensed at the date of acquisition because it represented what is often labeled "in-process technology." As this book goes to press, the Financial Accounting Standards Board is reviewing this requirement under the rubric of the business combinations project.

[18]Some financial statement preparers and users have criticized the differing treatment of internally developed versus externally purchased intangibles. They point out that internally developed intangibles also result from external market exchangers (payments to advertising agencies for promotion services, payments to employees for research and development services). Supporters of the current rules point out that the market exchange in the case of externally acquired intangibles validates the existence of a "completed asset," while the market exchange in the case of internally developed intangibles validates only that the firm has made an expenditure. It does not validate the existence and value of future benefits.

RESEARCH AND DEVELOPMENT COSTS

Application of the general principles of intangible asset accounting to research and development (R&D) costs is a contentious accounting issue. Financial reporting requires firms to expense immediately all R&D costs incurred internally.[19] For industries with high R&D expenditures, this requirement is especially troublesome, because financial reporting requires firms to assume that the economic value of all R&D expenditures is zero. Thus, a major asset never appears on the balance sheet.

Consider the three examples that follow, all from financial reports of biotechnology firms. Firms in the research-intensive biotechnology industry cannot survive without making significant R&D expenditures intended to generate future revenues, and yet these expenditures are required to be expensed as incurred.

Example 14. Biogen develops biotechnology and other drug-related products internally in its research laboratories. As required by *Statement No. 2*, Biogen states in a recent annual report that "research and development costs are expensed as incurred." Its R&D expense/sales percentage averaged 54 percent in three recent years, and the firm showed no asset on its balance sheet related to this research activity.

Example 15. Genzyme Corporation is a biotechnology and health care products firm engaged in the development of medical products and services. It follows a strategy of both internal development of technology and acquisition of other companies involved in biotechnology research. Genzyme expenses the portion of the acquisition price of companies related to *in-process technology* (see footnote 17), but it capitalizes and subsequently amortizes any portion of the price related to *completed* technologies.

Genzyme's R&D expense/sales percentage for internal R&D costs and amortization of previously capitalized costs was approximately 13.6 percent for a recent year. Because it made an acquisition of a company during the same year, however, it also expensed the portion of the purchase price related to in-process technology. The total R&D expense/sales percentage for the year was 39.2 percent. In the previous year, the total R&D expense/sales percentage was 19.1 percent because only a small portion of in-process technology was purchased (and expensed).

Example 16. Amgen's top-selling product, Epogen, accounted for approximately 50 percent of the firm's sales in Year 6. (Epogen is a weight reduction drug.) Amgen is continually striving to develop new products and enhance existing ones, however. It follows a strategy of both internal development of its own biotechnology and external development through a series of joint ventures and partnerships. Amgen contributes preliminary research findings to these joint ventures and partnerships. The other participants provide funding to continue development of this preliminary research.

---

[19]Financial Accounting Standards Board, *Statement of Financial Accounting Standards No. 2*, "Accounting for Research and Development Costs," 1974.

In some cases, Amgen contracts with the joint venture or partnership to perform the continued development in its own laboratories. In this case, Amgen receives a fee each period in an amount approximately equal to the R&D costs incurred in conducting the research. In other cases, the joint venture or partnership entity conducts the research, in which case Amgen may show no R&D expense on its books. Amgen generally maintains a right of first refusal to any products developed, in which case it must pay the owners of the joint venture a periodic royalty.

Amgen's R&D expense/sales percentage for Year 6 was 16.7 percent, the lowest of the three firms for the most recent year. It shows only minor amounts on its balance sheet for investments in joint ventures and partnerships, and these relate to cash advances. Because Amgen must expense initial development costs when they are incurred, its contribution of preliminary research findings for an interest in these joint ventures and partnerships does not result in increasing an asset.

Examples 14 through 16 illustrate three different strategies that firms follow in developing biotechnologies, which highlights the problem with current R&D reporting rules. The different strategies that firms follow, especially when combined with the required accounting for R&D costs, complicate any cross-sectional analysis of firms' financial data. To the extent that the economic substance of these arrangement differs, then different accounting treatments may be appropriate. If, on the other hand, the economic substance is similar, and the principal aim is to keep R&D costs off the income statement, then the differing accounting treatments seem unwarranted.

The economic characteristics of R&D arrangements suggest a two-fold approach to dealing with these different reporting standards:

1. Capitalize and subsequently amortize all expenditures on R&D that have future service potential, whether a firm incurs the R&D cost internally or whether it purchases in-process or completed technology externally. Expense immediately all R&D costs that have no future service potential.
2. Consolidate the firm's share of the assets, liabilities, revenues, and expenses of R&D joint ventures or partnerships with its own financial statements.

Unfortunately, current financial statement disclosures do not permit the analyst to implement this two-fold approach. Without these disclosures, the analyst must proceed with caution when analyzing R&D-intensive firms. Analysis in this case will especially benefit from the scientific and other disclosures provided by these firms that are outside the financial reporting model.

SOFTWARE DEVELOPMENT COSTS

Financial reporting treats the cost of developing computer software somewhat differently from R&D costs. Firms must expense when they are incurred all costs incurred internally in developing computer software until the point that the firm establishes the "technological feasibility" of a product. Thereafter, the firm must capitalize and subsequently amortize additional development costs.[20] The FASB defines technological feasibility as completion of a detailed program design or, in its absence, completion of a working model. A key issue in applying this reporting standard is the treatment of costs to improve an existing product.

Example 17. IBM purchased Lotus Development Corporation as part of its strategic plan to remain on the cutting edge in the highly competitive information technology industry. Lotus 1-2-3, the firm's best-known product, was first developed in the early 1980s. The IBM subsidiary continually revises this software to enhance its capabilities and to adapt to changes in hardware capabilities and design.

In a recent annual report, IBM includes an introductory note on its accounting for software development costs, including the costs incurred to maintain and enhance Lotus 1-2-3:

> **Software.** Costs related to the conceptual formulation and design of licensed programs are expensed as research and development. Costs incurred subsequent to establishment of technological feasibility to produce the finished product are capitalized. The annual amortization of the capitalized amount is the greater of the amount computed based on the estimated revenue distribution over the products' revenue-producing lives, or the straight-line method, and is applied over periods ranging up to four years. Periodic reviews are performed to ensure that unamortized program costs remain recoverable from revenue. Costs to support or service license programs are charged against income as incurred, or when related revenue is recognized, whichever occurs first.

Example 18. Microsoft Corporation introduced its first version of Microsoft Word in 1983. Microsoft too continually revises this software to enhance its capabilities. Microsoft expenses all software development costs as incurred. It reports software development expense of $1,432 million (16.5 percent of sales) for Year 11 and shows no asset on its balance sheet for capitalized software development costs.

Example 19. Adobe Systems' subsidiary, Aldus Corporation, holds a leading market position in publishing and graphics software. It develops new software internally and through aggressive external acquisitions of other software companies. Aldus expenses initial software development costs incurred internally. It

---

[20]Financial Accounting Standards Board, *Statement of Financial Accounting Standards No. 86*, "Accounting for the Costs of Computer Software to Be Sold, Leased, or Otherwise Marketed," 1985.

Statement No. 86 applies to software developed for sale, not software developed or obtained for internal use. As this book goes to press, policymakers are reviewing appropriate standards for internal use software. Georgia-Pacific describes its implementation of current reporting practice for internal use software in a recent annual report by stating:

The firm capitalizes incremental costs that are directly associated with the development of software for internal use and implementation of the related systems. Amounts are amortized over five years beginning when the assets are placed in service. Capitalized costs were $121 million at December 31, Year 6 and $65 million at December 31, Year 5. Amounts are included as property, plant and equipment in the firm's balance sheet.

capitalizes such costs once a program attains technological feasibility. It also capitalizes the cost of software acquired in corporate acquisitions to the extent that the software has achieved technological feasibility.

Examples 17 through 19 illustrate the diversity in practice currently. Software development firms interpret *Statement No. 86* so differently that it is debatable whether the standard serves a purpose any longer. Furthermore, the Software Publishers Association, a trade association for firms in the software development industry, advocates expensing all software development costs at the time they are incurred. In a position paper submitted to the FASB, the Association requests rescission of *Statement No. 86,* suggesting that expensing these costs would eliminate the concerns of extremely shortened software product cycles and uncertainty over realization of software assets.

Why would the Software Publishers Association advocate immediate expensing of all software development costs, when current reporting offers the best of all worlds to software producers: capitalize *or* immediately expense the costs, depending on the company's desires? A study addressing this paradoxical position shows that in recent years enhancing reported earnings through software capitalization schemes has diminished.[21] The researchers conclude that since software capitalization no longer provides an opportunity for earnings management, nothing is lost by restricting software producers to only one allowable reporting technique. In addition, the study addresses the more substantive issue of whether software capitalization is "value-relevant" to investors. For firms that capitalize software development costs (that is, report a cumulative software intangible asset on the balance sheet), the researchers find a significant association between these costs and future earnings, concluding that this finding supports continuation of *Statement No. 86.*

The flexibility that firms enjoy in applying *Statement No. 86* currently should cause the analyst to proceed cautiously when analyzing computer software development companies. An added concern in analysis is the small size of many such companies and the rapid pace of technological change in the industry. The information technology industry, and particularly its software subsegment, are experiencing even faster change now with the surge of interest in the Internet and Internet-related services.

GOODWILL

The most common setting in which valuation of intangibles arises is in corporate acquisitions. As Chapter 7 discusses more fully, acquiring firms must allocate the purchase price of the entity acquired to the assets acquired and the liabilities assumed.[22] Acquiring firms usually allocate the purchase price to identifiable, tangible assets (inventories, land, equipment) and liabilities first. They then allo-

---

[21]David Aboody and Baruch Lev, "Politics and Substance of Standard-Setting: The Case of Software Capitalization," New York University working paper, 1997.

[22]This statement applies to corporate acquisitions accounted for using the purchase method but not the pooling of interests method.

cate any excess purchase price to identifiable, intangible assets such as patents, customer lists, or trade names, with the remainder allocated to goodwill. Goodwill is a residual, and effectively represents all intangibles that are not specifically identifiable.

Firms seldom disclose much information about their intangible assets. For example, as illustrated in Appendix A, Coke shows "Goodwill and Other Intangible Assets" on its balance sheet. Coke's Note 1 on accounting policies states only that it values these intangibles at cost and amortizes them on a straight-line basis over estimated periods of benefit (not exceeding 40 years). Coke gives no information about the type of intangibles included on the balance sheet.

How should the analyst treat goodwill that appears on a firm's balance sheet? One approach is to follow financial reporting rules, leaving goodwill among total assets and amortization of goodwill among total expenses. The justification for this approach is that the initial valuation of goodwill arose from an exchange between an independent buyer and seller of another corporate entity and simply represents valuable resources that accountants cannot separately identify. These valuable resources enable the firm to generate profits. The analyst should include these resources in the asset base on which management should be expected to generate a reasonable return. These valuable resources will not likely last forever, so amortization of their cost over some period of years seems appropriate.

Another approach eliminates goodwill from assets and subtracts its amount from retained earnings or other common shareholders' equity accounts. The analyst adds back to net income the amortization of goodwill reflected in the accounts. The justification for this approach is two-fold.

1. The amount allocated to goodwill from a corporate acquisition may occur simply because the firm paid too much; it does not necessarily indicate the presence of resources with future service potential. Subtracting the amount allocated to goodwill from retained earnings suggests that the excess purchase price is a loss for the firm.
2. Immediate subtraction of goodwill from retained earnings treats goodwill arising from an acquisition the same as goodwill developed internally. In the latter case, firms expense advertising, training, and other costs when incurred, so no asset appears on the balance sheet.

EARNINGS SUSTAINABILITY AND INTANGIBLE ASSET REPORTING

Assessing quality of financial position (and related quality of earnings) is difficult even for tangible assets, because it is often necessary to make substantial adjustments to the asset values reported on the balance sheet. At least there is a starting point in the case of tangible assets, however, in the form of historical cost. For intangible assets such as R&D, software, and goodwill, the difficulty is more acute, because intangible assets seldom are reported on the balance sheet at all, or they are reported at some mix of historical and amortized cost. Estimating the economic value of intangibles and appropriate amortization charges often entails an intolerable level of subjectivity for financial reporting.

The arguments—from an earnings quality perspective—for immediate expensing of intangibles include the following:

1. The expense occurs in the same period as the cash outflow, the latter being the economic resource sacrificed.
2. Firms must replace intangibles consumed if they are to continue operating profitably. The best measure of the replacement cost of intangibles consumed in generating revenue in a reporting period is the cost of expenditures made in the same period on such intangibles. Depreciating fixed assets using an accelerated depreciation method is analogous to this line of reasoning for intangibles consumed.
3. Immediate expensing eliminates the opportunities for earnings management that arise when firms must decide the amortization period and pattern for capitalized intangibles.[23]
4. For a stable or moderate growth firm, the expense each year from immediate expensing is approximately the same as the expense from capitalizing expenditures and subsequently amortizing them.

Most analysts tend to prefer immediate expensing of *all* intangible assets.[24] Analysts often remove from the balance sheet any R&D costs, software development costs, and goodwill reported as assets before performing a financial analysis. They eliminate the assets by subtracting them from retained earnings.

Analysts argue that through this practice (1) quality of earnings improves, because the ability to manipulate earnings is reduced, and (2) quality of financial position improves, because the balance sheet is cleansed of "soft" assets lacking physical substance. The financial analysis must be interpreted carefully, however, because a firm's asset base is undoubtedly understated when these assets are eliminated—as is the case with Coke's asset base, because the trade name *Coke* (among other important intangibles owned by the firm) is not reported on the balance sheet.

VALUING INTANGIBLES—IS IT POSSIBLE?

Robert Swieringa served as a member of the Financial Accounting Standards Board for ten years. He observes that:

> The current financial accounting model has been shaped by the existing corporate arrangements for large, complex, and more or less permanent business en-

---

[23]Note, however, that opportunities for earnings management still exist under the immediate expensing option. Firms with a poor earnings year can eliminate or delay expenditures, thereby increasing reporting earnings. Accelerating expenditures reduces current earnings.

Chapter 4 addresses whether it is good business practice to manage earnings in this way. For example, firms that cut back on research and development costs to manage earnings may earn poor quality of earnings assessments from analysts. Similarly, firms that cut back on advertising expenditures or delay maintenance expenditures as a means of increasing earnings in a reporting period may suffer the same fate.

[24]Although they may advocate immediate expensing of these costs, few analysts suggest that they are of no value. Analysts are most concerned with how to value the economic assets represented by these costs and the potential for earnings management, given the subjectivity involved in any valuation model employed.

terprises that invest heavily in tangible assets. Such a model will be challenged by more flexible and fluid organizations, increased investments in intangible or "soft" assets, more extensive use of financial instruments to manage various risks, and changes in information technology.[25]

Swieringa's point regarding "soft" assets is increasingly being made, and policymakers such as the SEC and FASB continue to explore ways for developing more relevant disclosures and measurement metrics for intangibles. Nobody doubts that the quality of a firm's financial numbers improves if the balance sheet reports the economic value of a firm's intangible resources. If these resources cannot be measured with any degree of accuracy, however, the trade-off between relevance and reliability is simply too great. The challenge for the analyst (and policymakers) involves developing robust models for valuing intangibles because, as Examples 14 through 16 above point out, intangibles often are the essential drivers of a firm's success.[26]

Recent research with respect to one intangible—future benefits accruing from R&D expenditures—is promising because it demonstrates a possible methodology for valuing intangibles.[27] The research involves studying the relation between R&D expenditures in a particular year and the revenues of subsequent years. The study shows that benefits accrue for five to nine years, depending on the industry, and that the pattern of benefits is not uniform over time.

Using this analysis, the researchers then calculate the present value of this revenue stream, net of the current R&D expenditures, to estimate the value of R&D expenditures in a particular year. By summing similar values over the past five to nine years (again, depending on the industry), the researchers obtain a value for the R&D *expenditure*. They then study the relation between this value and market prices and find a statistically significant relationship, suggesting that investors implicitly incorporate the market values of firms' R&D efforts into the valuation of firms.

The researchers stress the industry-specific nature of their work. Because of this, extensive replication of the study is necessary across many industries before a general model can be developed.

Valuing all intangibles remains an unsolved problem. Additional research emphasizing other categories of intangibles besides R&D and across a wide range of industries is appropriate and necessary.[28]

---

[25]Robert J. Swieringa, "Should Accounting be "Green and Smooth and Inviting"?" *Journal of Financial Statement Analysis*, Winter 1997, pp. 75–87.

[26]An interesting valuation "laboratory" exits involving "purchased in-process R&D costs." Firms often hire appraisers to value this work-in-process intangible when one firm acquires another firm. Baruch Lev and Zehn Deng, in a New York University working paper titled, "Flash-Then-Flush: The Valuation of Acquired R&D In-Process" (1997), point out that a systematic analysis of the valuation process employed by appraisal firms might be a fruitful avenue of research for analyzing how practitioners attempt to value intangible assets.

[27]Baruch Lev and Theodore Sougiannis, "The Capitalization, Amortization and Value-Relevance of R&D," *Journal of Accounting and Economics*, February 1996, pp. 107–138.

[28]Baruch Lev spearheads a recently announced initiative, *The Intangibles Research Project*, that has as its goal the sharing of information, ideas, and research about the valuation and disclosure of corporate intangibles. Lev is a member of the faculty at New York University's Leonard N. Stern School of Business, and a description of this long-term project, including information on how practitioners and academicians can become involved with the project, can be obtained by contacting him directly.

SUMMARY

The unifying framework for the various financial reporting rules discussed in this chapter (income recognition, inventory cost flow assumption, depreciable asset accounting, and intangible asset accounting) relies on the link between income recognition and asset valuation. The recognition of revenue usually coincides with an increase in assets (usually cash or a receivable). The recognition of expense usually coincides with a decrease in assets (cash, inventories, depreciable, or intangible assets) or an increase in liabilities (which will require a decrease in assets in a later period). Thus, the income statement and balance sheet closely interrelate. Also interrelated are the assessments of the quality of earnings and quality of financial position that analysts make as the result of the various reporting rules employed by firms.

The next chapter discusses the financial reporting rules linking expenses to liability recognition and valuation. As with asset valuation issues, liability recognition and valuation issues demonstrate the link between expenses reported on the income statement and liabilities reported on the balance sheet—and the fact that any discussion of income and economic value-added leads inevitably to a consideration of liabilities and their economic value-added as well.

APPENDIX 5.1

ACCOUNTING FOR THE EFFECTS OF CHANGING PRICES

Changing prices affect financial reports in two principal ways. The first is through a measuring unit problem. The second is through a valuation problem.

Changes in the *general level* of prices in an economy (as measured by the prices of a broad basket of goods and services) affect the purchasing power of the monetary unit (for example, the U.S. dollar). During periods of inflation, the measuring unit loses purchasing power; during deflationary periods, the unit gains purchasing power. Because the measuring unit does not reflect a constant amount of purchasing power over time, accounting measurements of assets, liabilities, revenues, and expenses made with such a measuring unit are not comparable. Adding the acquisition cost of land acquired ten years ago for $10 million to the acquisition cost of land acquired this year for $10 million is as inappropriate as adding the cost of land acquired in the U.S. for $10 million to the cost of land acquired by a subsidiary in the U.K. for £10 million. We refer to the accounting issues created by changes in the general level of prices as a *measuring unit problem*.

Changes in the *specific prices* of individual assets and liabilities (for example, inventories, fixed assets) affect the measurement of revenues and expenses on the income statement and the valuation of assets and liabilities on the balance sheet. Land acquired last year for $10 million may now have a market value of $14 million. Should the accountant report this land on the balance sheet at its acquisition cost of $10 million or at its current market value of $14 million? Should net income include an unrealized holding gain of $4 million? We refer to the accounting issues created by changes in the prices of specific assets and liabilities as a *valuation problem.*

To summarize these issues:

1. Financial reporting can use either a *nominal* measuring unit (that is, one that gives no recognition to the changing value of the measuring unit) or a *constant* measuring unit (that is, one that restates measurements made over time to reflect a constant measuring unit).
2. Financial reporting can use either *acquisition cost* valuations or *current (replacement) cost* valuations for assets and liabilities; changes in current cost valuations over time affect the measurement of net income and shareholders' equity.

The combination of alternative measuring units and valuation methods presents four possible treatments of the effects of changing prices:

1. Acquisition Cost/Nominal Dollar Accounting
2. Acquisition Cost/Constant Dollar Accounting
3. Current Cost/Nominal Dollar Accounting
4. Current Cost/Constant Dollar Accounting

We illustrate each of these four combinations using a simple example. Exhibit 5.11 summarizes the data used in the illustration. A firm begins its first year of operations, Year 1, with $400 in cash and contributed capital. On January 1, Year 1, the Consumer Price Index (CPI) is 200. The firm immediately acquires two widgets for $100 each and a piece of equipment for $100.

During the first six months of Year 1, general price inflation is 5 percent. Thus, the CPI increases from 200 to 210. On June 30, Year 1, the firm sells one widget for $240 and replaces it at the new higher replacement cost of $115. The firm also pays other expenses totaling $100 on June 30, Year 1.

During the second six months of the year, general price inflation is 10 percent (the CPI increases from 210 to 231). On December 31, Year 1, the replacement cost of the widget is $140, and the replacement cost of the equipment in new condition is $120.

EXHIBIT 5.11

Data for Inflation Accounting Illustration

Balance Sheet as of Jan. 1, Year 1

Cash: $400   **Contributed Capital: $400**

Date:	January 1, Year 1	June 30, Year 1	December 31, Year 1
CPI	200	210 (5% increase)	231 (10% increase)
Cost of One Widget	$100	$115	$140
Cost of Equipment	$100	$110	$120
Transactions	1. Buy 2 widgets at $100 each, $200	1. Sell 1 widget for $240; replace widget at $115	Close books and prepare statements
	2. Purchase equipment (5 yr. life) for $100	2. Pay other expenses of $100	

Financial statements prepared under each of the four combinations of measuring units and valuation methods appear in Exhibit 5.12 We discuss in turn each of the approaches to accounting for changing prices.

ACQUISITION COST/NOMINAL DOLLAR ACCOUNTING

Column 1 of Exhibit 5.12 shows the results for Year 1 as they would appear in the conventional financial statements prepared in the United States. These financial statements give no explicit consideration to the effects of changing prices, either in general or for specific assets and liabilities.

Sales appear at the nominal dollars received when the firm sold the widget on June 30. Other expenses appear at the nominal dollars expended on June 30. Cost of goods sold, depreciation, and equipment reflect the nominal dollars expended on January 1. Inventories on the balance sheet reflect the nominal dollars expended on January 1 and June 30. Thus, the financial statements use a measuring unit of unequal size (unequal purchasing power).

Nor do the financial statements reflect the increase in the replacement cost of the inventory and the equipment during Year 1. Is the firm better off by its $20 of net income if it must replace the widget for a higher current cost? Is $20 of depreciation a sufficient measure of the cost of the equipment used during Year 1? Might the firm be better off by more than the $20 of net income because it held inventories and equipment while their replacement cost increased?

Nominal dollars as the measuring unit can be justified when the rate of general price inflation is relatively low (less than 5 percent per year, for example). The rapid turnover of assets for most businesses will not result in serious distortions in financial statement measurements. Likewise, the use of a last-in, first-out cost flow assumption for cost of goods sold and accelerated depreciation for fixed assets provides at least a partial solution to the problems created by changes in specific prices. These accounting principles provide measures of expenses that approximate current replacement costs but result in balance sheet valuations for assets that can deviate widely from current costs.

ACQUISITION COST/CONSTANT DOLLAR ACCOUNTING

Column 2 of Exhibit 5.12 shows financial statements restated to dollars of constant general purchasing power. Acquisition cost valuations still underlie the measurement of revenues, expenses, assets, and liabilities, but the nominal dollars underlying these measurements are restated to dollars of constant purchasing power at the end of Year 1. Other constant dollar measuring units are also possible (for example, January 1, Year 1, constant dollars, or June 30, Year 1, constant dollars).

EXHIBIT 5.12

Illustration of Financial Statements Reflecting Inflation Accounting

	(1) Acquisition Cost/ Nominal Dollars		(2) Acquisition Cost/ Constant Dollars		(3) Current Cost/ Nominal Dollars		(4) Current Cost/ Constant Dollars	
Income Statement								
Sales		$240		$264.0[a]		$240		$ 264.0
Cost of Goods Sold	$100		$115.5[b]		$115		$126.5[n]	
Depreciation	20		23.1[c]		22[i]		24.2[o]	
Other Expenses	100	220	110.0[d]	248.6	100	237	110.0[d]	260.7
Operating Income		$ 20		$ 15.4		$ 3		$ 3.3
Realized Holding Gains:								
Goods Sold		—		—		15[j]		11.0[p]
Depreciable Assets Used . .		—		—		2[k]		1.1[q]
Unrealized Holding Gains:								
Inventory		—		—		65[l]		38.0[r]
Depreciable Assets		—		—		16[m]		3.6[s]
Purchasing Power Loss		—		(18.0)[e]		—		(18.0)[e]
Net Income/Loss		$ 20		$ (2.6)		$101		$ 39.0
Balance Sheet								
Cash		$125		$125.0		$125		$ 125
Inventory		215		242.0[f]		280		280
Equipment	$100		$115.5[g]		$120		$120	
Accumulated Depreciation . .	(20)	80	(23.1)	92.4	(24)	96	(24)	96
Total Assets		$420		$459.4		$501		$ 501
Contributed Capital		$400		$462.0[h]		$400		$ 462[h]
Retained Earnings		20		(2.6)		101		39
Total Equities		$420		$459.4		$501		$ 501

[a]$240 \times (231/210) = \$264.0$
[b]$100 \times (231/200) = \$115.5$
[c]$100 \times (231/200) = \$115.5; \$115.5/5 = \$23.1$
[d]$100 \times (231/210) = \$110$
[e]$[\$100 \times (10/200) \times (231/210)] + \$125 \times (21/210) = \$5.50 + \$12.50 = \$18$
[f]$100 \times (231/200) + \$115 \times (231/210) = \$242$
[g]$100 \times (231/200) = \$115.5$
[h]$400 \times (231/200) = \$462$
[i]$110/5 = \$22$
[j]$115 - \$100 = \$15$
[k]$22 - \$20 = \$2$
[l]$280 - \$215 = \$65$
[m]$96 - \$80 = \$16$
[n]$115 \times (231/210) = \$126.5$
[o]$22 \times (231/210) = \$24.2$
[p]$126.5 - \$115.5 = \$11$
[q]$24.2 - \$23.1 = \$1.1$
[r]$280 - \$242 = \$38$
[s]$96 - \$92.4 = \$3.6$

Sales revenue was originally measured in dollars of June 30, Year 1, purchasing power. The restatement expresses the $240 of sales revenue in terms of dollars of December 31, Year 1, purchasing power. Inventories and equipment are also restated from nominal dollar, acquisition-cost valuations to dollars of constant December 31, Year 1, purchasing power. Thus, an equivalent measuring unit underlies the amounts in column 2.

Note that these restated amounts do not represent the current replacement costs of the specific assets and liabilities. The specific prices of assets and liabilities could have changed in an entirely different direction and pattern from prices in general.

One new element in column 2 of Exhibit 5.12 is the *purchasing power loss on monetary items*. A firm that holds cash or claims to a fixed amount of cash (accounts receivable or marketable debt securities, for example) during a period of inflation loses general purchasing power. The dollars held or received later have less general purchasing power after the period of inflation than they had before. A firm that borrows from others, promising to pay a fixed amount in cash at a later time (this could be in the form of accounts payable or income taxes payable or bonds payable) gains general purchasing power. The dollars paid later have less general purchasing power after the period of inflation than they had before.

The purchasing power gain or loss is a measure of the increase or decrease in general purchasing power during a period because of the firm's net lending position (purchasing power loss) or net borrowing position (purchasing power gain). The accountant calculates the purchasing power gain or loss on *monetary items*. Monetary items include cash and claims receivable or payable in a fixed amount of cash regardless of changes in the general price level.

In the illustration, the firm held $100 of cash during the first six months of the year while the general purchasing power of the dollar decreased 5 percent. It therefore lost $5 of general purchasing power. This $5 loss is measured in terms of dollars of June 30, Year 1, purchasing power. Measured in dollars of December 31, Year 1, constant dollars, the purchasing power loss for the first six months of Year 1 is $5.50.

The firm held $125 of cash during the second six months of the year. With 10 percent inflation during this six-month period, an additional loss in purchasing power of $12.50 occurs. Note *e* of Exhibit 5.12 shows the calculations.

This illustration is simplified in that the firm has no receivables or payables. In more typical settings, firms that engage in long-term borrowing will often be in a net monetary liability position (that is, monetary liabilities exceed monetary assets). During periods of inflation, these firms experience purchasing power gains.

Constant dollar accounting, in contrast to current cost accounting (discussed next), provides a higher level of objectivity. Independent accountants can examine canceled checks, invoices, and other documents to verify acquisition cost valuations. The restatements to constant dollars use general price indexes published by government bodies.

Users of constant dollar financial statements must remember, however, that the amounts reported for individual assets and liabilities do not reflect the current costs of these items. Also, the firm is not necessarily better or worse off in an amount equal to the purchasing power gain or loss on monetary items. Lenders and borrowers incorporate the *expected* rate of inflation into the interest rate charged for delayed payments. Conceptually, purchasing power gains should offset interest expense, and purchasing power losses should offset interest revenue. Whether a firm is better or worse off depends on the actual rate of inflation relative to the expected rate incorporated into the interest rate.

CURRENT COST/NOMINAL DOLLAR ACCOUNTING

Column 3 of Exhibit 5.12 reports amounts in terms of the current replacement cost of specific assets and liabilities. Matched against sales are the current costs of replacing the widget sold and the current costs of the services of the equipment used. Operating income (sales minus expenses measured at current replacement cost) reports the firm's ability to maintain its operating capacity. If sales revenue is not high enough to cover the cost of replacing the goods and services used up, the firm will have to cut back its level of operations (unless it secures outside financing).

Current cost income also includes *realized and unrealized holding gains and losses*. A holding gain or loss arises from holding an asset (or liability) while its replacement cost changes. The widget purchased on January 1, Year 1, for $100 was held during the first six months of the year while its replacement cost increased to $115. When the firm sold the widget on June 30, it realized a holding gain of $15 (= $115 − $100). Likewise, the two widgets in ending inventory give rise to unrealized holding gains of $65: $40 (= $140 − $100) on the other widget acquired on January 1 and $25 (= $140 − $115) on the widget acquired on June 30.

There is no agreement on whether holding gains constitute an increase in the value of a firm. Proponents argue that firms that purchase assets early in anticipation of increases in replacement costs are better off than firms that delay purchases and must pay the higher replacement costs. Opponents argue that firms cannot use such holding gains as the basis for dividend payments without impairing the ability to replace those assets used or sold.

Current cost/nominal dollar accounting is subject to two other criticisms. First, current replacement cost valuations are not as easy to verify or audit as acquisition cost valuations. Different appraisers will likely provide different replacement cost valuations for various assets. The variation in appraisal values will be particularly wide in the case of assets specific to a firm for which active secondhand markets do not exist.

Second, the use of nominal dollars means that the measuring unit underlying current replacement cost valuations is not constant across time. Revenues and expenses reflect the purchasing power of the monetary unit during the year, while assets and liabilities reflect year-end purchasing power.

Distortions caused by changes in the general purchasing power of the measuring unit are less severe in current cost/nominal dollar accounting than in acquisition cost/nominal dollar accounting, however, because current replacement costs reflect more recent measurements.

CURRENT COST/CONSTANT DOLLAR ACCOUNTING

Column 4 of Exhibit 5.12 shows the results of accounting for changes in both general and specific prices. Sales, cost of goods sold, and other expenses measured in terms of replacement costs on June 30, Year 1 (column 3 amounts), are restated from dollars of June 30 purchasing power to dollars of December 31 purchasing power. Balance sheet amounts for assets reflect current replacement cost valuations and constant dollars on December 31, Year 1.

Perhaps the most interesting disclosures in column 4 are the holding gains. The reported amounts indicate the extent to which changes in prices of the firm's specific assets exceed (or fall short of) the change in the general price level. Economists refer to such holding gains (or losses) as *real holding gains and losses*. Column 4 also includes the purchasing power gain on monetary items.

Current cost/constant dollar accounting deals with both accounting problems caused by changing prices—the measuring unit problem and the valuation problem. Although current cost/constant dollar accounting provides a comprehensive solution to these problems, the user of financial statements based on this approach should keep in mind three concerns noted previously: (1) current cost valuations are less objective than acquisition cost valuations; (2) the firm is not necessarily better or worse off in an amount equal to the purchasing power gain or loss on monetary items; and (3) the firm cannot distribute to shareholders an amount equal to the holding gains on nonmonetary items (such as inventories or equipment) if it is to maintain its operating capacity.

PROBLEMS AND CASES

5.1 INCOME RECOGNITION FOR VARIOUS TYPES OF BUSINESSES. Discuss when the following types of businesses are likely to recognize revenues and expenses.

a. A savings and loan association lending money for home mortgages.

b. A seller of trading stamps to food stores that food store customers can redeem for various household products.

c. A travel agency that books hotels, transportation, and similar services for customers, and that earns a commission from the providers of these services.

d. A major league baseball team that sells season tickets before the season begins and signs multiyear contracts with players. These contracts typically defer the payment of a significant portion of the compensation provided by the contract until the player retires.

e. A firm that manufactures and sells limited edition figurines. The firm agrees to repurchase the figurines at any time during the twenty years after sale if the market value of the figurine does not increase by at least 10 percent annually.

f. A producer of fine whiskey that ages twelve years before sale.

g. A timber-growing firm that contracts to sell all timber in a particular tract when it reaches twenty years of age. Each year it harvests another tract. The price per board foot of timber equals the market price when the customer signs the purchase contract plus 10 percent for each year until harvest.

h. An airline that provides transportation services to customers. Each flight entitles customers to frequent flier miles. Customers earn a free flight when they accumulate sufficient frequent flier miles.

5.2 MEASURING INCOME FROM LONG-TERM CONTRACTS. Turner Construction Company agreed on January 1, Year 1, to construct an observatory for Dartmouth College for $120 million. Dartmouth College must pay $30 million upon signing and $30 million at the end of Year 1, Year 2, and Year 3. Expected construction costs are $10 million for Year 1, $60 million for Year 2, and $30 million for Year 3. Assume that these cash flows occur at the end of each year. Also assume that an appropriate interest rate for this contract is 10 percent. Amortization schedules for the deferred cash flows appear below.

		Amortization Schedule for Cash Received			
Year	**Balance Jan. 1**	**Interest Revenue**	**Payment**	**Reduction in Principal**	**Balance Dec. 31**
1	$74,606	$7,460	$30,000	$22,540	$52,066
2	52,066	5,207	30,000	24,793	27,273
3	27,273	2,727	30,000	27,273	—
		Amortization Schedule for Cash Disbursed			
Year	**Balance Jan. 1**	**Interest Expense**	**Payment**	**Reduction in Principal**	**Balance Dec. 31**
1	$81,217	$8,122	$10,000	$ 1,878	$79,339
2	79,339	7,934	60,000	52,066	27,273
3	27,273	2,727	30,000	27,273	—

Required
a. Indicate the amount and nature of income (revenue and expense) that Turner would recognize during Year 1, Year 2, and Year 3 if it uses the completed-contract method. Ignore income taxes.
b. Repeat part a using the percentage-of-completion method.
c. Repeat part a using the installment method.
d. Indicate the balance in the construction-in-process account on December 31, Year 1, Year 2, and Year 3 (just prior to completion of the contract) under the completed-contract and the percentage-of-completion methods.

5.3 ANALYZING FINANCIAL STATEMENT DISCLOSURES REGARDING INVENTORIES AND FIXED ASSETS. USX derives revenues from the manufacture of steel and the refining and marketing of petroleum products. USX uses a LIFO cost flow assumption for inventories, straight-line depreciation for financial reporting, and accelerated depreciation for tax reporting. Exhibit 5.13 presents selected data for USX for Year 7 and Year 8. The income tax rate is 35 percent.

EXHIBIT 5.13

USX
Financial Statement Data
(amounts in millions)
(Problem 5.3)

	December 31		
	Year 6	**Year 7**	**Year 8**
Inventories (LIFO)	$ 1,626	$ 1,973	$ 2,021
Property, Plant, and Equipment (net)	11,603	11,482	10,535
Total Assets	17,374	17,517	16,743
Deferred Tax Liability Relating to			
Temporary Depreciation			
Differences	2,680	2,733	2,530
Common Shareholders' Equity	3,864	4,302	4,328

	Year Ended December 31	
	Year 7	**Year 8**
Sales	$19,330	$20,922
Cost of Goods Sold	14,186	15,103
Depreciation Expense	1,065	1,160
Interest Expense	461	501
Net Income (Loss)	501	214

Required

a. The excess of FIFO over LIFO inventories was $340 million on December 31, Year 6; $260 million on December 31, Year 7; and $320 on December 31, Year 8. Compute the cost of goods sold for USX for Year 7 and Year 8, assuming that it uses a FIFO cost flow assumption.

b. Compute the inventory turnover ratio for USX for Year 7 and Year 8 using (1) a LIFO cost flow assumption and (2) a FIFO cost flow assumption.

c. Compute the amount of depreciation expense that USX recognized for income tax purposes for Year 7 and Year 8. Note that the amount reported as the deferred tax liability relating to temporary depreciation differences represents the cumulative income taxes delayed as of each balance sheet date because USX uses accelerated depreciation for tax purposes and straight-line depreciation for financial reporting.

d. Compute the fixed asset turnover ratio for Year 7 and Year 8 assuming use of (1) straight-line depreciation and (2) accelerated (tax) depreciation.

e. Compute the rate of return on assets for Year 7 and Year 8 based on the reported amounts (that is, LIFO for inventories and straight-line depreciation). Disaggregate ROA into profit margin and asset turnover components.

f. Repeat part e using FIFO for inventories and accelerated (tax) depreciation. Assume USX uses FIFO for both financial and tax reporting. Any tax effects reduce or increase cash. Disaggregate ROA into profit margin and asset turnover components.
g. Compute the rate of return on common shareholders' equity for Year 7 and Year 8 based on the reported amounts. Disaggregate ROCE into ROA, common earnings leverage, and capital structure leverage components.
h. Repeat part g using FIFO for inventories and accelerated (tax) depreciation.
i. Interpret the changes in the profitability and risk of USX between Year 7 and Year 8 in light of the preceding analyses.

5.4 ANALYZING DISCLOSURES REGARDING FIXED ASSETS. Exhibit 5.14 presents selected financial statement data for three chemical companies: Ethyl Corporation, Monsanto, and Olin Corporation.

Required
a. Compute the average total depreciable life of assets in use for each firm during Year 8.
b. Compute the average age to date of depreciable assets in use for each firm at the end of Year 8.

EXHIBIT 5.14

Three Chemical Companies
Selected Financial Statement Data on Depreciable Assets
(amounts in millions)
(Problem 5.4)

	Ethyl Corporation	Monsanto	Olin Corporation
Depreciable Assets at Cost:			
December 31, Year 7	$684	$7,237	$2,010
December 31, Year 8	713	7,588	2,406
Accumulated Depreciation:			
December 31, Year 7	250	4,405	1,353
December 31, Year 8	285	4,575	1,565
Net Income, Year 8	74	385	280
Depreciation Expense, Year 8	49	434	124
Deferred Tax Liability Relating to Depreciable Assets			
December 31, Year 7	25	35	54
December 31, Year 8	36	39	88
Income Tax Rate........................	35%	35%	35%
Depreciation Method for Financial Reporting	Straight Line	Straight Line	Straight Line
Depreciation Method for Tax Reporting	Accelerated	Accelerated	Accelerated

EXHIBIT 5.15

Deere & Company
Income Statement
(amounts in millions)
(Problem 5.5)

	Year Ended October 31	
	Year 15	**Year 16**
Revenues		
Equipment Sales Revenue (Note 1)	$ 8,830	$ 9,640
Finance Revenue (Note 2)	660	763
Insurance Premium Revenues (Note 3)	627	658
Investment Revenue	172	167
Total Revenues	$10,289	$11,228
Expenses		
Cost of Goods Sold	$ 6,922	$ 7,460
Insurance Claims	499	502
Selling and Administrative Expenses	1,374	1,567
Interest Expense	392	402
Income Tax Expense	398	480
Total Expenses	$ 9,585	$10,411
Net Income (Loss)	$ 704	$ 817

c. Compute the amount of depreciation expense recognized for tax purposes for each firm for Year 8 using the amount of the deferred taxes liability related to depreciation timing differences.

d. Compute the amount of net income for Year 8 for each firm assuming depreciation expense for financial reporting equals the amount computed in part c for tax reporting.

e. Compute the amount each company would report for property, plant, and equipment (net) on December 31, Year 8, if it had used accelerated (tax reporting) depreciation instead of straight-line depreciation.

f. What factors might explain the difference in average total life of Olin Corporation and Monsanto relative to Ethyl Corporation?

g. What factors might explain the older average age for depreciable assets of Olin Corporation and Monsanto relative to Ethyl Corporation?

5.5 INTERPRETING FINANCIAL STATEMENT DISCLOSURES RELATING TO INCOME RECOGNITION. Deere & Company manufactures agricultural and industrial equipment, and provides financing and insurance services for its independent dealers and their retail customers. Exhibit 5.15 presents an income statement, and Exhibit 5.16 presents a balance sheet, for Deere for Year 15 and Year 16. The notes to these financial statements are listed following Exhibit 5.16.

EXHIBIT 5.16

Deere & Company
Balance Sheet
(amounts in millions)
(Problem 5.5)

	October 31	
	Year 15	Year 16
Assets		
Cash	$ 364	$ 292
Marketable Securities	830	894
Accounts and Notes Receivable (Note 2)	9,099	9,615
Inventories (Note 4)	979	1,259
Property, Plant, and Equipment (Note 5)	1,335	1,351
Other Assets	1,241	1,241
Total Assets	$13,848	$14,652
Liabilities and Shareholders' Equity		
Short-Term Borrowing	$ 3,140	$ 3,144
Accounts Payable and Accrued Expenses	2,633	2,836
Insurance Claims Payable	470	438
Long-Term Borrowing	2,176	2,425
Deferred Income Taxes	16	9
Pension Liability	2,327	2,243
Total Liabilities	$10,762	$11,095
Common Stock	$ 1,729	$ 1,770
Retained Earnings	1,357	1,787
Total Shareholders' Equity	$ 3,086	$ 3,557
Total Liabilities and Shareholders' Equity	$13,848	$14,652

Note 1: Deere recognizes income from equipment sales for financial reporting at the time of shipment to dealers. Provisions for sales incentives to dealers, returns and allowances, and uncollectible accounts are made at the time of sale. There is a lag, which varies depending on the timing and level of retail demand, between the time Deere records sales to dealers and the time dealers sell equipment to retail customers. Deere recognizes income from equipment sales using the installment method for tax reporting.

Note 2: Deere provides financing to independent dealers and retail customers for Deere products. Accounts and notes receivable appear net of unearned finance income. Deere recognizes the unearned finance income as finance revenue over the period when dealer and customer notes are outstanding.

Note 3: Deere provides property and casualty insurance to purchasers of Deere products. Deere recognizes premium revenues evenly over the term of insurance coverage and recognizes expenses for actual and expected future claims arising from losses sustained by policyholders each year.

Note 4: Deere uses a LIFO cost flow assumption for inventories and cost of goods sold. The excess of FIFO over LIFO cost of inventories was $945 million on October 31, Year 15, and $1,029 on October 31, Year 16.

Note 5: Property, plant, and equipment include the following:

	October 31	
	Year 15	**Year 16**
Land	$42	$46
Buildings	891	914
Machinery and Equipment	2,764	2,784
Dies, Patterns, Tools	516	561
Total	$4,213	$4,305
Less Accumulated Depreciation	(2,878)	(2,954)
	$1,335	$1,351

Deere depreciates fixed assets using the straight-line method for financial reporting. Depreciation expense was $283 million in Year 15 and $311 in Year 16. Deere uses accelerated depreciation for tax reporting.

Required

a. Using the criteria for revenue recognition, justify the timing of revenue recognition by Deere for its equipment sales. Consider and discuss why recognition of revenue either earlier than or later than the time of shipment to dealers would not be more appropriate.

b. Describe briefly how Deere's balance sheet accounts specified below would change if the company recognized revenues during the period of production using the percentage-of-completion method. You need not give amounts, but you should indicate the likely direction of the change and describe the computation of its amount.

    Accounts and Notes Receivable

    Inventories

    Retained Earnings

c. Respond to question b for each balance sheet account assuming that Deere & Company recognizes revenue using the installment method.

d. Compute the amount of cost of goods sold for Year 16, assuming that Deere & Company uses a FIFO instead of a LIFO cost flow assumption.

e. Did the quantities and costs of inventory items likely increase or decrease during Year 16? Explain.

f. Compute the average age of Deere's depreciable assets at the end of Year 16.

g. The statement of cash flows reports this information for Year 16 (amounts in millions):

    Proceeds from sale of property, plant,
        and equipment . . . . $ 86
    Acquisition of property, plant, and equipment . . . $ 379

Compute the gain or loss recognized on the sale of property, plant, and equipment.

5.6 **INTERPRETING DISCLOSURES REGARDING CHANGING PRICES.** Chilgener S.A. is one of the largest providers of electric transmission services in Chile. The firm also provides electricity to sections of Argentina. Exhibit 5.17 presents the balance sheet for Chilgener on December 31, Year 12 and Year 13. Exhibit 5.18 presents the income statement for Chilgener for Year 12 and Year 13. Excerpts from the notes to its financial statements follow Exhibit 5.18.

EXHIBIT 5.17

Chilgener S.A
Balance Sheet.
(amounts in millions of constant December 31, Year 13 pesos)
(Problem 5.6)

	December 31	
	Year 12	**Year 13**
Assets		
Cash	P 4,031	P 30,140
Accounts Receivable	7,121	10,923
Inventories	8,664	8,622
Other Current Assets	15,053	50,746
Total Current Assets	P 34,869	P 100,431
Fixed Assets—at Cost	P 436,595	P 438,067
Technical Revaluation of Fixed Assets	29,075	29,075
Accumulated Depreciation	(165,394)	(171,353)
Net Fixed Assets	P 300,276	P 295,789
Other Assets	P 37,606	P 93,840
Total Assets	P 372,751	P 490,060
Liabilities and Shareholders' Equity		
Short-Term Borrowing	P 11,068	P 50,800
Accounts Payable	10,127	15,860
Other Current Liabilities	5,839	6,323
Total Current Liabilities	P 27,034	P 72,893
Long-Term Debt	87,360	96,482
Other Noncurrent Liabilities	5,347	9,245
Total Liabilities	P 119,741	P 178,620
Paid-in Capital	P 190,233	P 238,818
Technical Revaluation of Fixed Assets	29,075	29,075
Retained Earnings	33,702	43,547
Total Shareholders' Equity	P 253,010	P 311,440
Total Liabilities and Shareholders' Equity	P 372,751	P 490,060

EXHIBIT 5.18

Chilgener, S.A.
Income Statement
(amounts in millions of constant December 31, Year 13 pesos)
(Problem 5.6)

	December 31	
	Year 12	Year 13
Operating Revenues	P 70,514	P 90,030
Operating Costs	(38,871)	(53,556)
Operating Margin	P 31,643	P 36,474
Selling and Administrative Expense	(10,114)	(11,809)
Operating Income	P 21,529	P 24,665
Financial Income	P 3,258	P 10,415
Share of Profits of Investees	1,123	4,278
Financing Expenses	(7,136)	(7,263)
Other Nonoperating Expenses	(1,544)	(1,584)
Price Level Restatement	3,471	(1,250)
Nonoperating Income	P (828)	P 4,596
Income Before Tax	P 20,701	P 29,261
Income Tax	(3,264)	(4,030)
Net Income	P 17,437	P 25,231

SUMMARY OF SIGNIFICANT ACCOUNTING PRINCIPLES

General. The consolidated financial statements have been prepared in conformity with generally accepted accounting principles in Chile and with the regulations issued by the Superintendency of Corporations and Insurance Companies.

Price Level Restatement. These consolidated financial statements have been restated through the application of an adjustment based on the change in the consumer price index in order to reflect the effect of fluctuations in the purchasing power of the Chilean peso. Restatement is based on the official index published by the Chilean Institute of Statistics, which estimates a 12.1 percent increase for the year ended December 31, Year 13 (in Year 12, 14 percent). Income and expenses are also restated so as to express them in terms of year-end purchasing power. The Year 12 financial statements and their relevant notes have been adjusted (without being reflected in the accounting records) by 12.1 percent for the sole purpose of allowing comparison with the financial statements in constant pesos of December, Year 13.

Inventories. Inventories consist of raw materials and spares, which are valued at their replacement cost. The values thus determined do not exceed their net realizable value in accordance with generally accepted accounting principles.

Fixed Assets.   Fixed assets are presented according to contribution values or at cost, as the case may be, plus price level restatement. The value of fixed assets was adjusted on June 30, Year 6, in accordance with the Technical Appraisal Circulars of the Superintendency of Corporations and Insurance Companies. Depreciation is calculated on a straight-line basis on the adjusted value of assets, in accordance with their remaining useful life. Depreciation amounts to P10,206 for Year 13 and to P9,941 for Year 12. It is included in operating costs and includes additional depreciation for technical reappraisal of fixed assets amounting to P1,166 in Year 13 and P1,195 in Year 12.

Bonds.   Bonds are shown at nominal year-end value plus accrued interest.

Required

    a. Does Chilgener's reporting most closely resemble (1) acquisition cost/constant peso reporting; (2) current cost/nominal peso reporting; or (3) current cost/constant peso reporting? Explain.

    b. Interpret the last sentence in the note on price level restatement.

    c. What is the likely reason that Chilgener reported a price level restatement gain on its income statement for Year 12 but a price level restatement loss for Year 13?

    d. Assume that sales and price level changes occurred evenly during Year 12 and Year 13. Compute the *nominal* peso change in sales between Year 12 and Year 13.

    e. Have the current replacement costs of Chilgener's fixed assets increased at a faster or slower rate than the general price level? Explain your reasoning. If you do not think the disclosures permit an answer to this question, explain this reasoning.

    f. Why does the amount in the account, Technical Revaluation of Fixed Assets, remain at P29,075 during Year 13 if the note on fixed assets indicates that Chilgener recognized depreciation on the revalued fixed asset amount?

ARIZONA LAND DEVELOPMENT COMPANY

Joan Locker and Bill Dasher organized the Arizona Land Development Company (ALDC) on January 2, Year 1. They contributed land with a market value of $300,000 and cash of $100,000 for all of the common stock of the corporation. The land was to serve as the initial inventory of property sold to customers.

    ALDC sells undeveloped land, primarily to people approaching retirement. Within a period of nine years from the date of sale, ALDC promises to develop the land so that it is suitable for the construction of residential housing. ALDC makes all sales on an installment basis. Customers pay 10 percent of the selling price at the time of sale and remit the remainder in equal installments over the next nine years.

    ALDC estimates that development costs will equal 50 percent of the selling price of the land, and that development work will take nine years to complete from the date of sale. Actual development costs have coincided with expectations. The firm incurs 10 percent of the development costs at the time of sale and the remainder evenly over the next nine years.

    ALDC remained a privately held firm for its first six years. Exhibits 5.19 through 5.21 present the firm's income statement, balance sheet, and statement of cash flows for Year 1 to Year 6. ALDC recognizes income from sales of undeveloped land at the time of sale. The amount shown for sales each year in Exhibit 5.19 represents the gross amount ALDC

EXHIBIT 5.19

Arizona Land Development Company
Income Statements
Income Recognition at Time of Sale—No Discounting of Cash Flows
(Case 5.1)

	Year 1	Year 2	Year 3	Year 4	Year 5	Year 6
Sales	$ 650,000	$ 900,000	$1,500,000	$ 2,500,000	$ 1,200,000	$ 400,000
Less:						
Cost of Land Inventory						
Sold	(65,000)	(90,000)	(150,000)	(250,000)	(120,000)	(40,000)
Estimated Development						
Costs	(325,000)	(450,000)	(750,000)	(1,250,000)	(600,000)	(200,000)
Gross Profit	$ 260,000	$ 360,000	$ 600,000	$1,000,000	$ 480,000	$ 160,000
Selling Expenses	(65,000)	(90,000)	(150,000)	(250,000)	(120,000)	(40,000)
Net Income Before Taxes . . .	$ 195,000	$ 270,000	$ 450,000	$ 750,000	$ 360,000	$ 120,000
Income Taxes:						
Current	—	—	(9,778)	(26,091)	(73,009)	(94,902)
Deferred	(66,300)	(91,800)	(143,222)	(228,909)	(49,391)	54,102
Net Income	$ 128,700	$ 178,200	$ 297,000	$ 495,000	$ 237,600	$ 79,200

EXHIBIT 5.20

Arizona Land Development Company
Balance Sheets
Income Recognition at Time of Sale − No Discounting of Cash Flows
(Case 5.1)

	Year 1	Year 2	Year 3	Year 4	Year 5	Year 6
Assets						
Cash	$ 100,000	$ 132,500	$ 100,222	$ 126,631	$ 131,122	$ 273,720
Notes Receivable	520,000	1,175,000	2,220,000	3,915,000	4,320,000	3,965,000
Land Inventory	235,000	145,000	95,000	45,000	125,000	185,000
Total Assets	$ 855,000	$ 1,452,500	$2,415,222	$4,086,631	$ 4,576,122	$ 4,423,720
Liabilities and Shareholders' Equity						
Estimated Development						
Cost Liability	$ 260,000	$ 587,500	$1,110,000	$1,957,500	$ 2,160,000	$ 1,982,500
Deferred Income Taxes . .	66,300	158,100	301,322	530,231	579,622	525,520
Common Stock	400,000	400,000	400,000	500,000	500,000	500,000
Retained Earnings	128,700	306,900	603,900	1,098,900	1,336,500	1,415,700
Total Liabilities and						
Shareholders' Equity .	$ 855,000	$ 1,452,500	$2,415,222	$4,086,631	$ 4,576,122	$ 4,423,720

EXHIBIT 5.21

Arizona Land Development Company
Statements of Cash Flows
Income Recognition at Time of Sale—No Discounting of Cash Flows
(Case 5.1)

	Year 1	Year 2	Year 3	Year 4	Year 5	Year 6
Operations						
Net Income	$ 128,700	$ 178,200	$ 297,000	$ 495,000	$ 237,600	$ 79,200
(Increase) Decrease in						
Notes Receivable	(520,000)	(655,000)	(1,045,000)	(1,695,000)	(405,000)	355,000
(Increase) Decrease in						
Land Inventory	65,000	90,000	50,000	50,000	(80,000)	(60,000)
Increase (Decrease) in						
Estimated Development						
Cost Liability	260,000	327,500	522,500	847,500	202,500	(177,500)
Increase (Decrease) in						
Deferred Income Taxes . .	66,300	91,800	143,222	228,909	49,391	(54,102)
Cash Flow from						
Operations	$ 0	$ 32,500	$ (32,278)	$ (73,591)	$ 4,491	$ 142,598
Financing						
Common Stock Issued	—	—	—	100,000	—	—
Change in Cash	$ 0	$ 32,500	$ (32,278)	$ 26,409	$ 4,491	$ 142,598

ultimately expects to collect from customers for land sold in that year. The amount shown for estimated development costs each year is the gross amount ALDC expects ultimately to disburse in order to develop land sold in that year. The firm treats selling expenses as a period expense. It is subject to a 34 percent income tax rate. ALDC uses the installment method of income recognition for income tax purposes.

ALDC contemplates making its initial public offering of common stock early in Year 7. The firm asks you to assess whether its income recognition method, as reflected in Exhibits 5.19 through 5.21, accurately reflects its operating performance and financial position. To assist you, the firm has prepared financial statements following three other income recognition methods.

INCOME RECOGNITION AT TIME OF SALE BUT WITH DISCOUNTING OF FUTURE CASH FLOWS TO THEIR PRESENT VALUE

Exhibits 5.22 through Exhibit 5.24 present the financial statements following this income recognition method. This method discounts future cash inflows from customers and future cash outflows for development work to their present values. The gross profit recognized at the time of sale equals the present value of cash inflows net of the present value of cash outflows. One might view this gross profit as the current cash-equivalent value of the gross profit that the firm will ultimately realize over the nine year period. This method reports the

EXHIBIT 5.22

Arizona Land Development Company
Income Statements
Income Recognition at Time of Sale—With Discounting of Cash Flows
(Case 5.1)

	Year 1	Year 2	Year 3	Year 4	Year 5	Year 6
Sales	$ 411,336[a]	$ 569,543	$ 865,737	$ 1,442,895	$ 759,390	$ 253,130
Less:						
Cost of Land Inventory						
Sold	(65,000)	(90,000)	(150,000)	(250,000)	(120,000)	(40,000)
Estimated Development						
Costs	(205,668)[b]	(284,771)	(432,869)	(721,448)	(379,695)	(126,565)
Gross Profit	$ 140,668	$ 194,772	$ 282,868	$ 471,447	$ 259,695	$ 86,565
Selling Expenses	(65,000)	(90,000)	(150,000)	(250,000)	(120,000)	(40,000)
Interest Revenue	41,560[c]	96,293	196,609	361,257	411,130	400,899
Interest Expense	(20,780)[d]	(48,147)	(98,304)	(180,628)	(205,566)	(200,449)
Net Income Before						
Taxes	$ 96,448	$ 152,918	$ 231,173	$ 402,076	$ 345,259	$ 247,015
Income Taxes:						
Current	—	—	(9,778)	(26,091)	(73,009)	(94,902)
Deferred	(32,792)	(51,992)	(68,821)	(110,615)	(44,379)	10,917
Net Income	$ 63,656	$ 100,926	$ 152,574	$ 265,370	$ 227,871	$ 163,030

[a]Represents the present value of $65,000 received on January 1, Year 1, plus the present value of a series of $65,000 cash inflows on December 31, Year 1 to Year 9, discounted at 12 percent.

[b]Represents the present value of $32,500 paid on January 1, Year 1, plus the present value of a series of $32,500 cash outflows on December 31, of Year 1 to Year 9, discounted at 12 percent.

[c].12($411,336 − $65,000) = $41,560.

[d].12($205,668 − $32,500) = $20,780.

EXHIBIT 5.23

Arizona Land Development Company
Balance Sheets
Income Recognition at Time of Sale—With Discounting of Cash Flows
(Case 5.1)

	Year 1	Year 2	Year 3	Year 4	Year 5	Year 6
Assets						
Cash	$ 100,000	$ 132,500	$ 100,222	$ 126,631	$ 131,122	$ 273,720
Notes Receivable	322,896[a]	743,732	1,351,078	2,350,230	2,725,750	2,624,779
Land Inventory	235,000	145,000	95,000	45,000	125,000	185,000
Total Assets	$ 657,896	$ 1,021,232	$ 1,546,300	$ 2,521,861	$ 2,981,872	$ 3,083,499

Exh. 5.23—Continued	Year 1	Year 2	Year 3	Year 4	Year 5	Year 6
Liabilities and Shareholders' Equity						
Estimated Development						
Cost Liability	$161,448[b]	$ 371,866	$ 675,539	$1,175,115	$1,362,876	$1,312,390
Deferred Income Taxes . . .	32,792	84,784	153,605	264,220	308,599	297,682
Common Stock	400,000	400,000	400,000	500,000	500,000	500,000
Retained Earnings	63,656	164,582	317,156	582,526	810,397	973,427
Total Liabilities and						
Shareholders' Equity . . .	$657,896	$1,021,232	$1,546,300	$2,521,861	$2,981,872	$3,083,499

[a]$411,336 − $65,000 + $41,560 − $65,000 = $322,896 (see Notes a and c to Exhibit 5.22).
[b]$205,668 − $32,500 + $20,780 − $32,500 = $161,448 (see Notes b and d to Exhibit 5.22).

EXHIBIT 5.24

Arizona Land Development Company
Statements of Cash Flows
Income Recognition at Time of Sale—With Discounting of Cash Flows
(Case 5.1)

	Year 1	Year 2	Year 3	Year 4	Year 5	Year 6
Operations						
Net Income	$ 63,656	$ 100,926	$ 152,574	$ 265,370	$ 227,871	$ 163,030
(Increase) Decrease in						
Notes Receivable	(322,896)	(420,836)	(607,346)	(999,152)	(375,520)	100,971
(Increase) Decrease in						
Land Inventory	65,000	90,000	50,000	50,000	(80,000)	(60,000)
Increase (Decrease) in						
Estimated Development						
Cost Liability	161,448	210,418	303,673	499,576	187,761	(50,486)
Increase (Decrease) in						
Deferred Income Taxes . . .	32,792	51,992	68,821	110,615	44,379	(10,917)
Cash Flow from						
Operations	$ 0	$ 32,500	$ (32,278)	$ (73,591)	$ 4,491	$ 142,598
Financing						
Common Stock Issued	—	—	—	100,000	—	—
Change in Cash	$ 0	$ 32,500	$ (32,278)	$ 26,409	$ 4,491	$ 142,598

increase in the present value of cash inflows as time passes as interest revenue each year and the increase in the present value of cash outflows as interest expense.

Thus, this income recognition method results in reporting two types of income: a gross profit from the selling of land, and interest from delayed cash flows. The computations of present values underlying the financial statements in Exhibits 5.22 to 5.24 rest on several assumptions.

1. ALDC makes all sales on January 1 of each year. It receives 10 percent of the gross selling price at the time of sale and also pays 10 percent of the gross development costs immediately.

2. The firm receives 10 percent of the gross selling price from customers and pays 10 percent of the gross development costs on December 31 of each year, beginning with the year of sale.

3. The interest rates used in discounting are as follows:

Sales In:	Interest Rate
Year 1	12%
Year 2	12%
Year 3	15%
Year 4	15%
Year 5	12%
Year 6	12%

INCOME RECOGNITION USING THE INSTALLMENT METHOD—WITH DISCOUNTING OF CASH FLOWS

Exhibits 5.25 to 5.27 present the financial statements following this income recognition method. ALDC uses this income recognition method for tax reporting.

INCOME RECOGNITION USING THE PERCENTAGE-OF-COMPLETION METHOD

Exhibits 5.28 through 5.30 present the financial statements following this income recognition method. The presumption underlying this method is that ALDC is primarily a developer of real estate, and that its income should reflect its development activity, not its sales activity. The difference between the contract price and the total estimated costs of the land and development work represents the total income from development of the land. The percentage-of-completion method uses actual costs incurred to date as a percentage of estimated total costs to determine the degree of completion each period. Multiplying this percentage by the contract price yields sales revenue each year. Multiplying this percentage by the total expected costs yields cost of goods sold.

Arizona Land Development Company
Income Statements
Income Recognition Using Installment Method—With Discounting of Cash Flows
(Case 5.1)

	Year 1	Year 2	Year 3	Year 4	Year 5	Year 6
Sales Revenue	$ 88,440[a]	$ 148,707	$ 249,802	$ 427,243	$ 377,706	$ 347,017
Cost of Goods Sold ...	(58,195)[a]	(97,852)	(164,374)	(281,133)	(248,537)	(228,343)
Gross Profit	$ 30,245[a]	$ 50,855	$ 85,428	$ 146,110	$ 129,169	$ 118,674
Selling Expenses	(65,000)	(90,000)	(150,000)	(250,000)	(120,000)	(40,000)
Interest Revenue	41,560[b]	96,293	196,609	361,257	411,130	400,899
Interest Expense	(20,780)[c]	(48,147)	(98,304)	(180,628)	(205,566)	(200,449)
Net Income Before Taxes	$ (13,975)	$ 9,001	$ 33,733	$ 76,739	$ 214,733	$ 279,124
Income Taxes:						
Current	—[d]	—[d]	(9,778)[d]	(26,091)	(73,009)	(94,902)
Deferred	—	—	—	—	—	—
Net Income	$ (13,975)	$ 9,001	$ 23,955	$ 50,648	$ 141,724	$ 184,222

[a]Exhibit 5.22 indicates that the total gross profit from land sold in Year 1 is $140,668. The present value of the amounts that ALDC will receive from customers is $411,336 (see Exhibit 5.22). Thus, for each dollar of the $411,336 collected, the firm recognizes 34.2 cents (= $140,668 ÷ $411,336) of gross profit. During Year 1, ALDC collects $130,000 from sales of land made in Year 1 ($65,000 on January 1 and $65,000 on December 31). However, only $23,440 (= $65,000 − $41,560) of the December 31 payment represents payment of a portion of the $411,336 selling price. The remainder ($41,560) represents interest. Thus, the gross profit recognized in Year 1 is $30,245 [.342($65,000 + $23,440)].

[b]See Note c to Exhibit 5.22.

[c]See Note d to Exhibit 5.22.

[d]ALDC carries forward the $13,975 loss in Year 1 to offset net income before taxes in future years ($9,001 in Year 2 and $4,974 in Year 3).

Arizona Land Development Company
Balance Sheets
Income Recognition Using Installment Method − With Discounting of Cash Flows
(Case 5.1)

	Year 1	Year 2	Year 3	Year 4	Year 5	Year 6
Assets						
Cash	$ 100,000	$ 132,500	$ 100,222	$ 126,631	$ 131,122	$ 273,720
Notes Receivable	212,473[a]	489,392	899,298	1,573,113	1,818,107	1,749,245
Land Inventory	235,000	145,000	95,000	45,000	125,000	185,000
Total Assets	$ 547,473	$ 766,892	$ 1,094,520	$ 1,744,744	$ 2,074,229	$ 2,207,965

(continued)

Exh. 5.26—Continued	Year 1	Year 2	Year 3	Year 4	Year 5	Year 6
Liabilities and Shareholders' Equity						
Estimated Development						
Cost Liability	$161,448[b]	$ 371,866	$ 675,539	$ 1,175,115	$1,362,876	$1,312,390
Deferred Income Taxes ..	—	—	—	—	—	—
Common Stock	400,000	400,000	400,000	500,000	500,000	500,000
Retained Earnings	(13,975)	(4,974)	18,981	69,629	211,353	395,575
Total Liabilities and						
Shareholders' Equity ..	$547,473	$ 766,892	$1,094,520	$ 1,744,744	$2,074,229	$2,207,965

[a]The derivation of this amount is as follows:

	Notes Receivable Gross	Deferred Gross Profit	Notes Receivable Net
January 1, Year 1	$ 411,336	$ 140,668	$ 270,668
Less Cash Received, January 1, Year 1	(65,000)	—	(65,000)
Plus Interest Revenue, Year 1	41,560	—	41,560
Less Cash Received, December 31, Year 1	(65,000)	—	(65,000)
Gross Profit Recognized, Year 1	—	(30,245)	30,245
Totals	$ 322,896	$ 110,423	$ 212,473

[b]See Note b to Exhibit 5.23.

EXHIBIT 5.27

Arizona Land Development Company
Statements of Cash Flows
Income Recognition Using Installment Method—With Discounting of Cash Flows
(Case 5.1)

	Year 1	Year 2	Year 3	Year 4	Year 5	Year 6
Operations						
Net Income (Loss)	$ (13,975)	$ 9,001	$ 23,955	$ 50,648	$ 141,724	$184,222
(Increase) Decrease in						
Notes Receivable	(212,473)	(276,919)	(409,906)	(673,815)	(244,994)	68,862
(Increase) Decrease in						
Land Inventory	65,000	90,000	50,000	50,000	(80,000)	(60,000)
Increase (Decrease) in Estimated						
Development Cost Liability ..	161,448	210,418	303,673	499,576	187,761	(50,486)
Increase (Decrease) in						
Deferred Income Taxes	—	—	—	—	—	—
Cash Flow from Operations .... $	0	$ 32,500	$ (32,278)	$ (73,591)	$ 4,491	$142,598
Financing						
Common Stock Issued	—	—	—	100,000	—	—
Change in Cash .... $	0	$ 32,500	$ (32,278)	$ 26,409	$ 4,491	$142,598

EXHIBIT 5.28

Arizona Land Development Company
Income Statements
Income Recognition Using Percentage-of-Completion Method
(Case 5.1)

	Year 1	**Year 2**	**Year 3**	**Year 4**	**Year 5**	**Year 6**
Sales	$ 216,667[a]	$ 354,167	$629,167	$1,087,500	$ 862,500	$695,833
Cost of Goods Sold	(130,000)[a]	(212,500)	(377,500)	(652,500)	(517,500)	(417,500)
Gross Profit	$ 86,667[a]	$ 141,667	$251,667	$ 435,000	$ 345,000	$278,333
Selling Expenses	(65,000)	(90,000)	(150,000)	(250,000)	(120,000)	(40,000)
Net Income Before						
Taxes	$ 21,667	$ 51,667	$101,667	$ 185,000	$ 225,000	$238,333
Income Taxes:						
Current	—	—	(9,778)	(26,091)	(73,009)	(94,902)
Deferred	(7,367)	(17,567)	(24,789)	(36,809)	(3,491)	13,869
Net Income	$ 14,300	$ 34,100	$ 67,100	$ 122,100	$ 148,500	$157,300

[a]Land sold under contract in Year 1 had a contract price of $650,000 and estimated contract cost of $390,000 (= $65,000 + $325,000) (see Exhibit 5.19). ALDC incurred development costs of $130,000 (= $65,000 for land + $32,500 on January 1, Year 1 + $32,500 on December 31, Year 1) during Year 1. Thus, the percentage of completion as of the end of Year 1 is 33.3 percent (= $130,000 ÷ $390,000). Sales are 33.3 percent of $650,000 and cost of goods sold is 33.3 percent of $390,000.

Required

a. For each of the four income recognition methods illustrated in Exhibits 5.19 through 5.30, show the supporting calculations for each of the following items for Year 2:
   1. Sales Revenue for Year 2.
   2. Cost of Goods Sold for Year 2.
   3. Gross Profit for Year 2.
   4. Notes Receivable on December 31, Year 2, under the first three income recognition methods, and the Contracts in Process account on December 31, Year 2, under the fourth income recognition method.
   5. Estimated Development Costs Liability on December 31, Year 2, under the first three income recognition methods, and the Progress Billings account on December 31, Year 2, under the fourth income recognition method.

b. Evaluate each of the four income recognition methods described in the case compared to the criteria for revenue and expense recognition. Which method do you think best portrays the operating performance and financial position of ALDC? Discuss your reasoning.

c. Which income recognition method is ALDC likely to prefer in reporting to shareholders?

d. Why did ALDC choose the installment method for tax reporting?

e. With respect to maximizing cumulative reported earnings, the four income recognition methods are ranked as follows (from highest amount to lowest):
   1. Income Recognition at Time of Sale—No Discounting of Cash Flows.
   2. Income Recognition at Time of Sale—With Discounting of Cash Flows.
   3. Income Recognition Using the Percentage-of-Completion Method.
   4. Income Recognition Using the Installment Method—With Discounting of Cash Flows.

What is the reason that the income recognition methods fall in this order?

EXHIBIT 5.29

Arizona Land Development Company
Balance Sheets
Income Recognition Using Percentage-of-Completion Method
(Case 5.1)

	Year 1	Year 2	Year 3	Year 4	Year 5	Year 6
Assets						
Cash	$ 100,000	$ 132,500	$ 100,222	$ 126,631	$ 131,122	$ 273,720
Contracts in Process	216,667[a]	570,834	1,200,001	2,287,501	3,150,001	3,845,834
Less Progress Billings	(130,000)[b]	(375,000)	(830,000)	(1,635,000)	(2,430,000)	(3,185,000)
Contracts in Process (net) . . .	$ 86,667	$ 195,834	$ 370,001	$ 652,501	$ 720,001	$ 660,834
Land Inventory	235,000	145,000	95,000	45,000	125,000	185,000
Total Assets	$ 421,667	$ 473,334	$ 565,223	$ 824,132	$ 976,123	$ 1,119,554
Liabilities and Shareholders' Equity						
Deferred Income Taxes	$ 7,367	$ 24,934	$ 49,723	$ 86,532	$ 90,023	$ 76,154
Common Stock	400,000	400,000	400,000	500,000	500,000	500,000
Retained Earnings	14,300	48,400	115,500	237,600	386,100	543,400
Total Liabilities and Shareholders' Equity	$ 421,667	$ 473,334	$ 565,223	$ 824,132	$ 976,123	$ 1,119,554

[a]Accumulated costs of $130,000 + gross profit recognized in Year 1 of $86,667 (see Note a to Exhibit 5.28).

[b]Down payment of $65,000 received on January 1, Year 1, plus $65,000 installment payment received on December 31, Year 1.

EXHIBIT 5.30

Arizona Land Development Company
Statements of Cash Flows
Income Recognition Using Percentage-of-Completion Method
(Case 5.1)

	Year 1	Year 2	Year 3	Year 4	Year 5	Year 6
Operations						
Net Income	$ 14,300	$ 34,100	$ 67,100	$ 122,100	$ 148,500	$ 157,300
(Increase) Decrease in Contracts in Process ...	(216,667)	(354,167)	(629,167)	(1,087,500)	(862,500)	(695,833)
Increase (Decrease) in Progress Billings	130,000	245,000	455,000	805,000	795,000	755,000
(Increase) Decrease in Land Inventory	65,000	90,000	50,000	50,000	(80,000)	(60,000)
Increase (Decrease) in Deferred Income Taxes .	7,367	17,567	24,789	36,809	3,491	(13,869)
Cash Flow from Operations	$ 0	$ 32,500	$ (32,278)	$ (73,591)	$ 4,491	$ 142,598
Financing						
Common Stock Issued ...	—	—	—	100,000	—	—
Change in Cash	$ 0	$ 32,500	$ (32,278)	$ 26,409	$ 4,491	$ 142,598

f. The difference in cumulative reported earnings between any two income recognition methods equals (1) the difference in Notes Receivable or Contracts in Process (net) minus (2) the difference in the Estimated Development Cost Liability minus (3) the difference in the Deferred Income Taxes Liability. What is the rationale behind this relation?

g. Why is the amount shown on the income statement for "current" income taxes the same in each year for all four income recognition methods, but the amount of total income tax expenses (current plus deferred) in each year is different across income recognition methods?

h. Given that net income each year differs across the four income recognition methods, why is the amount of cash provided by operations the same? Under what conditions would a firm report different amounts of cash flow from operations for different income recognition methods?

CASE 5.2

CHIRON CORPORATION—AN R&D PUZZLE

Chiron Corporation is in the human health care industry, applying genetic engineering and other tools of biotechnology to develop products that diagnose, prevent, and treat human diseases. Exhibit 5.31 presents an income statement for Chiron for Year 5, Year 6, and Year

7. Total revenues increased from $141 million in Year 5 to $318 million in Year 7, a 49.8 percent compound annual growth rate. Net income increased from a $445 million loss in Year 5 to a $18 million profit in Year 7.

It is hard to analyze and understand the reasons for this increased profitability because of several factors:

1. The company has grown both internally and through corporate acquisitions.
2. The company uses joint ventures and collaborative research agreements to develop and market new products.
3. Sales to related parties represent 41 percent of total revenues in Year 5, 38 percent in Year 6, and 43 percent in Year 7.

EXHIBIT 5.31

Income Statement
Chiron Corporation
(amounts in thousands)
(Case 5.2)

	Year 5	Year 6	Year 7
Revenues			
Product Sales:			
Related Parties	$ 10,576	$ 11,801	$ 23,156
Unrelated Parties	40,696	99,779	124,737
	$ 51,272	$ 111,580	$ 147,893
Research Revenues:			
Related Parties	$ 18,331	$ 24,486	$ 54,552
Unrelated Parties	12,144	16,017	14,391
	$ 30,475	$ 40,503	$ 68,943
License Fees—Unrelated Parties ...	9,906	19,939	22,960
Equity in Earnings of Joint			
Ventures	49,845	74,238	77,739
Total Revenues	$ 141,498	$ 246,260	$ 317,535
Expenses			
Research and Development	$ 80,001	$ 142,265	$ 140,030
Cost of Goods Sold	28,423	54,692	68,484
Selling and Administrative Expenses .	44,068	99,707	95,790
Write-Off of In-Process Technologies	442,484	—	—
Other Operating Expenses	2,287	7,499	(1,907)
Total Expenses	$ 597,263	$ 304,163	$ 302,397
Income (Loss) from Operations	$ (455,765)	$ (57,903)	$ 15,138
Interest Income	12,997	6,973	7,949
Income (Loss) Before Income Taxes .	$ (442,768)	$ (50,930)	$ 23,087
Income Tax Expense	(1,882)	(4,024)	(4,703)
Net Income	$ (444,650)	$ (54,954)	$ 18,384

Chiron operates in four major product markets:

1. Therapeutics—The product emphasis in this segment is oncology.
2. Ophthalmic Surgical—The two principal products in this segment are equipment for removing cataracts using ultrasound technology and intraocular lenses for cataract surgeries.
3. Diagnostics—The primary product for this market is a blood screening device for hepatitis C virus. The company is researching the application of DNA probe testing technologies to develop new diagnostic products.
4. Vaccines—This segment offers immunizations for adult and pediatric diseases.

THERAPEUTICS

The company's involvement in Therapeutics is through its wholly owned, consolidated subsidiary, Cetus Corporation. Chiron acquired Cetus on December 28, Year 5, by exchanging shares of its common stock with a market value of $887.8 million. The acquisition was accounted for using the purchase method. Chiron restated the assets and liabilities of Cetus to market values on December 28, Year 5. The difference between the $887.8 million purchase price and the market value of identifiable assets and liabilities was allocated $442 million to in-process technologies and $44.8 million to base technologies. Amortization expense on the capitalized amount was $3.9 million in Year 6 and Year 7 and is included in other operating expenses in Exhibit 5.31. The amounts allocated to in-process and base technologies are not deductible for tax purposes. Under the purchase method used in this acquisition, Chiron recognizes the earnings of Cetus subsequent to the date of acquisition.

OPHTHALMIC SURGICAL

The company's involvement in Ophthalmic Surgical is through its wholly owned, consolidated subsidiary, Intra Optics. Chiron acquired Intra Optics on January 5, Year 6, by exchanging shares of its common stock. Chiron accounted for the acquisition using the pooling of interests method. Under a pooling of interests, the book values of Intra Optic's assets and liabilities carry over after the acquisition. The earnings of Chiron are retroactively restated to include the earnings of Intra Optics for all years presented.

DIAGNOSTICS

The company's involvement in Diagnostics is through a joint venture with Ortho Diagnostic Systems, a subsidiary of Johnson & Johnson. Chiron conducts research, development, and manufacturing for the Chiron/Ortho joint venture. The joint venture reimburses Chiron at cost for these services, which were as follows:

	Research and Development	Manufacturing
Year 5	$8.0	$ 9.3
Year 6	$9.2	$10.6
Year 7	$9.8	$11.3

Chiron's 50 percent share of the earnings of this joint venture totaled $49.8 million in Year 5, $73.6 million in Year 6, and $77.1 million in Year 7.

VACCINES

The company's involvement in Vaccines is through a joint venture with CIBA-GEIGY. Chiron conducts research, development, and manufacturing services for the Chiron/CIBA-GEIGY joint venture. The joint venture reimburses Chiron at cost for these services, which were as follows:

	Research and Development	Manufacturing
Year 5	$10.3	$ 1.3
Year 6	$15.3	$ 1.2
Year 7	$44.8	$11.9

Chiron's equity in the earnings of the Chiron/CIBA-GEIGY joint venture were zero in Year 5, $.638 million in Year 6, and $.639 million in Year 7.

Required
a. Recast the income statement of Chiron Corporation for Year 5, Year 6, and Year 7 into a format that enhances understanding of the changes in its profitability during the three-year period. Give particular consideration to the presentation of these items:
   1. The appropriate measure of total revenues and the classification of its components.
   2. The measurement of research and development expense, particularly with respect to the treatment of cost-reimbursed research and development services and the cost of in-process purchased technologies.
b. Identify the principal reasons for the changes in the profitability of Chiron during the three-year period.

CASE 5.3

CORPORÃCION INDUSTRIAL SANLUIS: COPING WITH CHANGING PRICES

Corporãcion Industrial Sanluis is a leading conglomerate in Mexico. It derives revenues from the manufacture of auto parts (springs and brake drums), the mining of precious metals (gold and silver), and the provision of hotel services (in several Hyatt resort hotels). The manufacture of coils, springs, and metal drums accounts for approximately 75 percent of Sanluis's revenues. Sanluis is the first Mexican company to have its shares traded in the U.S. through American Depository Receipts.

Sanluis follows generally accepted accounting principles in Mexico to prepare its financial statements. Its Year 8 financial statements are attached as Exhibit 5.32 (balance sheet),

Exhibit 5.33 (statement of income), and Exhibit 5.34 (statement of changes in financial position). Note 1 to the financial statements follows Exhibit 5.34. This case examines financial disclosures in Mexico with respect to changing prices and assesses Sanluis' success in coping with inflation.

EXHIBIT 5.32

Corporācion Industrial Sanluis, S.A. DE C.V. and Subsidiaries
Consolidated Balance Sheet
(in thousands of constant December 31, Year 8 Mexican Pesos)
(Case 5.3)

	December 31	
	Year 7	Year 8
Assets		
Cash and Short-Term Investment	P 177,670	P 219,490
Accounts Receivable	82,017	79,866
Inventories	68,027	64,075
Prepayments	2,282	9,856
Total Current Assets	P 329,966	P 373,287
Property, Plant, and Equipment	P 854,628	P 810,026
Accumulated Depreciation	(294,622)	(240,632)
Total Property, Plant, and Equipment	P 560,006	P 569,394
Other Assets	P 27,193	P 28,395
Total Assets	P 917,195	P 971,076
Liabilities and Shareholders' Equity		
Bank Loans	P 195,090	P 308,323
Accounts Payable	37,115	56,639
Accrued Liabilities	27,275	38,960
Total Current Liabilities	P 259,480	P 403,922
Long-Term Debt	184,993	125,957
Total Liabilities	P 444,473	P 529,879
Preferred Stock—Nominal Value	P 59,796	P 59,796
Restatement Increase	7,134	7,134
	P 203,902	P 203,902
Other Equity Accounts—Nominal Value	P 27,702	P 17,301
Restatement Increase	58,729	62,725
	P 86,431	P 80,026
Retained Earnings—Nominal Value	P 278,492	P 317,505
Restatement Increase	851,497	830,050
	P 1,129,989	P 1,147,555
Deficit in the Restatement of Capital	P (1,014,530)	P (1,057,216)
Total Shareholders' Equity	P 472,722	P 441,197
Total Liabilities and Shareholders' Equity ...	P 917,195	P 971,076

EXHIBIT 5.33

Corporãcion Industrial Sanluis, S.A. DE C.V. and Subsidiaries
Consolidated Statement of Income
(in thousands of constant December 31, Year 8 Mexican Pesos)
(Case 5.3)

	Year 7	Year 8
Sales	P 411,213	P 429,471
Cost of Goods Sold	(327,489)	(334,198)
Depreciation and Depletion	(17,924)	(21,032)
Gross Profit	P 65,800	P 74,241
Distribution and Selling Expenses	(13,470)	(11,806)
General and Administrative Expenses	(36,355)	(29,100)
Exploration and Development Expenses	(2,364)	(1,320)
Operating Profit	P 13,611	P 32,015
Interest Expense—Net	(18,733)	(19,536)
Exchange Loss—Net	(16,540)	(7,514)
Gain on Net Monetary Position	29,263	19,481
Other Income—Net	8,390	3,463
Income from Continuing Operations Before Tax and Statutory Employee Profit Sharing	P 15,991	P 27,909
Taxes and Statutory Employee Profit Sharing	(8,656)	(10,343)
Income from Continuing Operations	P 7,335	P 17,566

EXHIBIT 5.34

Corporãcion Industrial Sanluis, S.A. DE C.V. and Subsidiaries
Consolidated Statement of Changes in Financial Position
(in thousands of constant December 31, Year 8 Mexican Pesos)
(Case 5.3)

	Year 7	Year 8
Operations		
Income from Continuing Operations	P 7,335	P 17,566
Depreciation and Depletion	17,925	21,032
Variation in Current Assets	3,642	17,631
Resources Provided by Operations	P 28,902	P 56,229
Financing		
Increase in Capital Stock	P 66,930	—
Bank Loans—Net	(15,643)	P 53,104
Resources Provided by Financing	P 51,287	P 53,104

Exh. 5.34—Continued	Year 7	Year 8
Investing		
(Acquisition) Sale of Subsidiaries	P 16,590	P (9,963)
Acquisition of Property, Plant, and Equipment (net)	(63,965)	(57,550)
Resources Used for Investing	P (47,375)	P(67,513)
Increase in Cash and Short-Term Investments	P 32,814	P 41,820
Cash and Short-Term Investments at Beginning of Year ..	144,856	177,670
Cash and Short-Term Investments at End of Year	P 177,670	P219,490

EXCERPTS FROM NOTES TO THE FINANCIAL STATEMENTS

Note 1: Accounting Policies

a. The consolidated financial statements have been prepared in conformity with generally accepted accounting principles in Mexico and are stated in pesos of December 31, Year 8 purchasing power.

b. Marketable Securities and other investments in shares are stated at market value.

c. Inventories are stated at estimated replacement cost. Cost of goods sold is determined by the last-in, first-out (LIFO) method.

d. Property, plant and equipment are recorded at net replacement cost determined on the basis of appraisals made by independent experts registered at the National Securities Commission. Depreciation, amortization and depletion are calculated by the straight-line method based on the estimated useful lives of the assets determined by the appraisers.

e. The restatement of capital stock represents the amount necessary to maintain the shareholders' investment in terms of purchasing power at the balance sheet date, and is determined by applying to the historical amounts factors derived from the National Consumer Price Index (NCPI).

f. Retained Earnings is expressed in pesos of purchasing power as of the latest balance sheet date and is determined by applying to the historical amounts factors derived from the NCPI.

g. The gain on net monetary position represents the effect of inflation, as measured by NCPI, on the company's monthly net monetary assets and liabilities during the year, restated in pesos of purchasing power as of the end of the most recent period.

h. The gain or loss from holding nonmonetary assets represents the amount by which the increases in the values of nonmonetary assets exceeds or falls short of the inflation rate measured in terms of the NCPI, and is included in the deficit in the restatement of capital.

Required

a. Which of the methods of accounting for changing prices discussed in Appendix 5.1 does Sanluis apparently use? Indicate the evidence supporting your conclusion.

b. Prepare a balance sheet for Sanluis as of December 31, Year 8, under each of the three methodologies indicated in the columns that follow. Aggregate individual assets in preparing this analysis. You should begin with liabilities and shareholders' equity and work backward toward total assets.

	Historical Cost/ Nominal Pesos	Historical Cost/ Constant Pesos	Current Cost/ Constant Pesos
Assets	═══════	═══════	═══════
Liabilities			
Preferred Stock			
Common Stock			
Other Equity Accounts			
Retained Earnings			
Deficit in Restatement of Capital	───────	───────	───────
Total Equities	═══════	═══════	═══════

    c. What is the likely explanation for Sanluis's recognition of a purchasing power gain on its monetary items during Year 8?

    d. Did Sanluis experience a holding gain or a holding loss on its nonmonetary items (that is, inventories, fixed assets) during Year 8? What is the interpretation of this gain or loss?

    e. How well has Sanluis coped with changing prices during Year 7 and Year 8? Note: Mexico's consumer price index increased 18.8 percent in Year 7 and 11.9 percent in Year 8.

CASE 5.4

AMERICA ONLINE: ONLINE OR OFF-TRACK

America Online, Inc. (AOL) is the world's first billion-dollar new media company. AOL offers its subscribers a wide variety of interactive services including electronic mail, instant message features, entertainment, reference, financial information, computing support, and interactive magazines and newspapers, as well as easy access to all the services of the Internet. The company is headquartered in Dulles, Virginia, with current operations in the United States, Canada, the United Kingdom, France, Germany, and Japan. AOL is a leader in the Internet service provider (ISP) industry. As of January 16, Year 7, AOL subscribers reached 8 million, making the company much larger than any of its direct competitors. AOL's main source of revenue is on-line Internet service generated through customer subscriptions. The revenues are generated primarily from monthly membership fees from subscribers and, previous to December, Year 6, hourly charges based on usage in excess of the number of hours of usage provided as part of the monthly fee. Beginning in December, Year 6, AOL offered several pricing alternatives aimed at providing price points for a wide range of customers.[1]

As a result of (1) AOL's pricing policy change, (2) AOL's explosive growth over the last three years, and (3) information technology (IT) industry factors in general, analyzing the firm's earnings is extremely complicated.

---

[1]AOL announced on September 2, Year 7, that it had more than 9 million members, less than 1 million shy of its year-end goal of 10 million members worldwide.

OVERVIEW OF **ISP INDUSTRY**

Internet service providers are a subsector of the IT industry, which includes computer hardware, software, and services.

The ISP industry has evolved into four subgroups: national and international ISPs (such as UUNET Technologies Inc. and Netcom Online Communications Services Inc.); large interexchange carriers (such as AT&T Corp. and MCI Communications Corp.); regional ISPs, which are in the thousands and growing daily, and sometimes include resellers; and on-line service providers (such as America Online, Inc. and Microsoft Network).

There are 3,068 Internet service providers listed in North America, according to Boardwatch Magazine's Fall, Year 6, Directory of Internet Service Providers. The average ISP has annual revenues of $637,572 and 13 paid employees, and it provides 199 dial-up telephone ports to 1,844 Internet customers.

ISPs earned $520 million in Year 5, excluding the earnings of AOL, Compuserve, Prodigy, and Microsoft Network, according to Lorraine Sileo, senior analyst for Simba Information Inc., a Stanford, CT. based consulting firm specializing in the Internet. Despite this half-billion dollar sales figure, fierce competition and high operational costs keep most ISPs from turning a profit. To remain competitive, an ISP might adopt a flat rate for unlimited access, only to find that connection times increase substantially, raising the cost of serving customers.

Many ISPs, in fact, show large losses. PSINet, Inc., a major Internet operator, posted a $26 million loss for the first half of Year 6. Another major ISP, BBN Corp., posted a $34.7 million loss for fiscal Year 5, which ended June 30.[2]

ISPs that once trumpeted rock-bottom prices are finding out that on-line service fees are inadequate to cover costs. Advertising and electronic commerce revenues are and will be one of ISPs' important sources of income. AOL, for example, signed a major on-line shopping deal with CUC International, a major on-line marketing firm, which was announced in June of Year 7. CUC is paying AOL $50 million for the privilege of selling and marketing its services to AOL customers.

According to a Nielson Media Research report, 2.5 million persons already have bought products or services on the Web. And Forrester Research, a market research firm in Cambridge, Mass., predicts that Internet-based sales in the United States will increase from $518 million in Year 7 to $6.6 billion by Year 10. Jupiter Communication, a New York firm specializing in emerging consumer communications technologies, predicts that Internet advertising will expand from $312 million to $5 billion between Year 7 and Year 10.

As ISPs grow and change to achieve long-term profitability and differentiate themselves from competitors, they will seek to deliver value-added services to customers such as allowing users to buy or sell stock or receive real-time stock quotes or news, or providing premium channels like entertainment, games, sports, news, and children-only channels.

The number of on-line households in the U.S. passed the 10 million mark in Year 6. Future growth will be strong, given the continued development of appealing content, increased bandwidth, and expanding range of household access devices. Jupiter Communication projects that by Year 12, 57 million U.S. households will be on-line, nearly a fourfold increase over Year 6 levels of 15.2 million.

---

[2]BBN Corp. was subsequently purchased by GTE, one of the largest publicly held telecommunication companies in the world, on August 15, Year 7.

LIMITATIONS OF TRADITIONAL FINANCIAL ANALYSIS FOR IT INDUSTRY

Traditional financial analysis of firms emphasizes the use of financial statement data as key inputs for conducting both time series and cross-sectional analyses. Companies in the IT industry, however, driven primarily by highly complex human capital and technology, are following a reporting model that was fashioned a hundred years ago. What's the point of applying traditional financial analysis if the majority of the firms in the IT industry have never reported profits? Or what's the point of balance sheet analysis when the company's most important assets—its engineers—are nowhere to be found? These are important limitations of IT industry analysis.

AMERICA ONLINE

AOL launched its unlimited-use pricing on December 1, Year 6. During the quarter ended December 31, Year 6, both AOL membership and system usage showed record growth. Membership climbed 1.2 million to a total 7.8 million, with a record 546,000 new members added in December alone. This included 7.4 million members in North America and approximately 400,000 in Europe.

Industry analysts praised AOL's move to flat rate pricing, but the move also caused the company major problems. The network became so crowded that users were blocked from dialing in because there weren't enough open lines. State regulatory officials who complained to AOL on behalf of their customers obtained a settlement requiring AOL to give customer refunds.

As part of the settlement, AOL also said it would sharply reduce marketing and advertising efforts, temporarily scale back its efforts to attract new members, and, for the time being, stop airing its television advertising and reduce the distribution of free trial disks.

On January 16, Year 7, AOL announced that membership in its on-line Internet network, the world's largest, had surpassed 8 million. The company said it would increase investment in system expansion to address the extraordinary demand for its service. The increased investment in system expansion included increasing its previously announced investment to expand system capacity from $250 million to $350 million, increasing the current total of 200,000-plus modems by 75 percent to improve connectivity, and promoting and supporting alternative ways to get AOL through work or school connection.

But only months after the national controversy about its jammed networks, AOL started to recruit members again. Word of AOL's plans came from Chief Executive Steve Case in his April, Year 7, monthly letter to subscribers. On September 2, Year 7, AOL announced that the company had more than 9 million subscribers worldwide, including more than 400,000 net new members since the quarter ending June 30.

Has AOL improved its services? According to a study done by Inverse, a new Web measurement company, AOL had the highest call failure rate of the 14 major Internet service providers. Inverse tested during peak hours, 6 p.m. to midnight, in March of Year 7. CompuServe had the best connection rate, with IBM, Sprint, and Concentric following. While call failure rates for these companies were 6.5 percent, 6.8 percent, and 11.6 percent, respectively, AOL's call failure rate was 60.3 percent, most of these failures accounted for by busy phone lines.

Financial statements of AOL are presented in Exhibit 5.35, Exhibit 5.36, and Exhibit 5.37.

EXHIBIT 5.35

AOL, Inc.
Comparative Balance Sheets
(amounts in thousands)
(Case 5.4)

	June 30				
	Year 3	Year 4	Year 5	Year 6	Year 7
Assets					
Cash	$ 9,224	$ 43,891	$ 45,877	$118,421	$ 124,340
Short-Term Investments	5,105	24,052	18,672	10,712	268
Accounts Receivable	2,861	10,583	43,557	72,613	91,399
Other Current Assets	1,723	5,753	25,527	68,832	107,466
Total Current Assets	$18,913	$ 84,279	$1,323,633	$270,578	$ 323,473
Property, Plant, and Equipment (net) . .	2,402	20,306	70,919	101,277	233,129
Product Development Costs (net)	3,915	7,912	18,949	44,330	72,498
Deferred Subscriber Acquisition					
Costs (net)	6,890	26,392	77,229	314,181	—
Goodwill	—	—	54,356	51,691	41,783
Other Assets	282	15,695	50,327	176,697	175,805
Total Assets	$32,402	$154,584	$ 405,413	$958,754	$ 846,688
Liabilities and Shareholders' Equity					
Accounts Payable	$ 3,766	$ 15,642	$ 84,640	$105,904	$ 69,703
Short-Term Debt	—	2,287	2,329	2,435	1,454
Other Current Liabilities	4,851	18,460	46,393	181,567	483,313
Total Current Liabilties	$ 8,617	$ 36,389	$ 133,362	$289,906	$ 554,470
Long-Term Debt	—	7,015	17,369	19,306	50,000
Other Noncurrent Liabilities	—	12,883	37,870	137,040	114,184
Total Liabilities	$ 8,617	$ 56,287	$ 188,601	$446,252	$ 718,654
Common Stock	$ 59	$ 308	$ 767	$ 926	$ 1,002
Preferred Stock	—	—	—	1	1
Unrealized Gain on					
Available-for-Sale Securities	—	—	—	—	16,924
Additional Paid-in Capital	22,652	98,836	252,668	519,342	617,221
Accumulated Deficit	1,074	(847)	(36,623)	(7,767)	(507,114)
Total Shareholders' Equity	$23,785	$ 98,297	$ 216,812	$512,502	$ 128,034
Total Liabilities and					
Shareholders' Equity	$32,402	$154,584	$ 405,413	$958,754	$ 846,688

EXHIBIT 5.36

AOL, Inc.
Comparative Income Statements
(amounts in thousands)
(Case 5.4)

	Year Ended June 30				
	Year 3	**Year 4**	**Year 5**	**Year 6**	**Year 7**
Online Service Revenues	$ 37,648	$ 98,497	$ 344,309	$ 991,656	$ 1,429,445
Other Revenues	14,336	17,225	49,981	102,198	255,783
Total Revenues	$ 51,984	$115,722	$ 394,290	$1,093,854	$ 1,685,228
Cost of Revenues	(28,820)	(69,043)	(229,724)	(627,372)	(1,040,762)
Marketing Expenses	(9,745)	(23,548)	(77,064)	(212,710)	(409,260)
Write-Off Deferred Subscriber Acquisition Costs	—	—	—	—	(385,221)
Product Development Expenses . . .	(2,913)	(5,288)	(14,263)	(53,817)	(58,208)
Administrative Expenses	(8,581)	(13,667)	(42,700)	(110,653)	(193,537)
Acquired Research and Development	—	—	(50,335)	(16,981)	—
Amortization of Goodwill	—	—	(1,653)	(7,078)	(6,549)
Restructuring Charge	—	—	—	—	(48,627)
Contract Termination Charge	—	—	—	—	(24,506)
Settlement Charge	—	—	—	—	24,204
Total Costs and Expenses	$ 50,059	$111,546	$ 415,739	$1,028,611	$ 2,190,874
Income (Loss) from Operations	$ 1,925	$ 4,176	$ (21,449)	$ 65,243	$ (505,646)
Other Income (Expense), net	371	1,810	3,074	(2,056)	6,299
Merger Expenses	—	—	(2,207)	(848)	—
Income (Loss) Before Income Taxes	$ 2,296	$ 5,986	$ (20,582)	$ 62,339	$ (499,347)
Income Tax Expense	(764)	(3,832)	(15,169)	(32,523)	—
Net Income (Loss)	$ 1,532	$ 2,154	$ (35,751)	$ 29,816	$ (499,347)

EXHIBIT 5.37

AOL, Inc.
Comparative Statements of Cash Flows
(amounts in thousands)
(Case 5.4)

	Year Ended June 30				
	Year 3	Year 4	Year 5	Year 6	Year 7
Cash Flows from Operating Activities					
Net Income (Loss)	$ 1,532	$ 2,154	$ (35,751)	$ 29,816	$(499,347)
Write-Off of Deferred Subscriber Acquisition Costs	—	—	—	—	385,221
Non-Cash Restructuring Charges	—	—	—	—	22,478
Depreciation and Amortization	1,957	2,822	12,266	33,366	64,572
Amortization of Subscriber Acquisition Costs	7,038	17,922	60,924	126,072	59,189
Loss (Gain) on Sale of Property and Equipment	(39)	5	37	44	—
Charge for Acquired Research and Development	—	—	50,335	16,981	—
Changes in Assets and Liabilities:					
Accounts Receivable	(1,902)	(4,892)	(23,459)	(28,728)	(14,335)
Other Current Assets	(1,494)	(2,873)	(19,635)	(43,305)	(44,394)
Deferred Subscriber Acquisition Costs	(10,685)	(37,424)	(111,761)	(363,024)	(130,229)
Accounts Payable	2,119	10,224	60,805	21,150	(36,944)
Other Current Liabilities	3,209	12,193	14,787	135,316	356,210
Other Assets and Liabilities	470	1,290	8,712	5,585	(39,372)
Net Cash (used in) Provided by Operating Activities	$ 2,205	$ 1,421	$ 17,260	$ (66,727)	$ 123,049
Cash Flows from Investing Activities					
Short-Term Investments	$ (5,105)	$(18,947)	$ 5,380	$ 7,960	$ 10,444
Purchase of Property and Equipment ...	(2,041)	(18,010)	(59,255)	$ (50,262)	(149,768)
Product Development Costs	(1,831)	(5,131)	(13,054)	(32,631)	(56,795)
Sale of Property and Equipment	62	95	180	—	—
Purchase of Acquired Businesses	—	—	(20,523)	(4,133)	(475)
Net Cash Used in Investing Activities ..	$ (8,915)	$(41,993)	$ (87,272)	$ (79,066)	$(196,594)
Cash Flows from Financing Activities					
Proceeds from Issuance of Common Stock, net	$ 609	$ 68,120	$ 61,721	$ 189,359	$ 84,506
Proceeds from Issuance of Preferred Stock, net	—	—	—	28,315	—
Proceeds from Issuance of Preferred Stock of Subsidiary	—	—	—	—	15,000
Increases in Borrowings	7,187	14,260	13,488	3,000	50,000
Restricted Cash	—	—	—	—	(50,000)
Decrease in Borrowings	(7,036)	(7,878)	(3,413)	(2,337)	(20,042)

(continued)

Exh. 5.37—Continued

	Year Ended June 30				
	Year 3	Year 4	Year 5	Year 6	Year 7
Net Cash Provided by Financing Activities	$ 760	$ 74,502	$ 71,796	$ 218,337	$ 79,464
Net Increase in Cash and Cash Equivalents	$ (5,950)	$ 33,930	$ 1,784	$ 72,544	$ 5,919
Cash and Cash Equivalents— Beginning of Year	16,113	10,163	44,093	45,877	118,421
Cash and Cash Equivalents— End of Year	$ 10,163	$ 44,093	$ 45,877	$ 118,421	$ 124,340

As Exhibit 5.38 illustrates, total revenues grew along with AOL's membership. AOL's total revenues increased from $115.7 million in Year 4 to $394.3 million in Year 5, or 241 percent. The increase was primarily attributable to a 233 percent increase in the number of AOL subscribers, which contributed 250 percent growth of on-line service revenues. For Year 6, total revenues increased to $1.1 billion, or 177 percent over Year 5. On-line service revenues increased 188 percent to $991.7 million, which was primarily attributable to 93 percent growth in the number of AOL subscribers. For Year 7, on-line service revenues increased to 1.4 billion, or 44 percent over Year 6. This increase was primarily attributable to a 53 percent increase in the quarterly average number of AOL North American subscribers for Year 7. Total revenues in Year 7 were $1.7 billion, or 54 percent over Year 6.

EXHIBIT 5.38

AOL, Inc.
Total Revenues Year 2—Year 7
(Case 5.4)

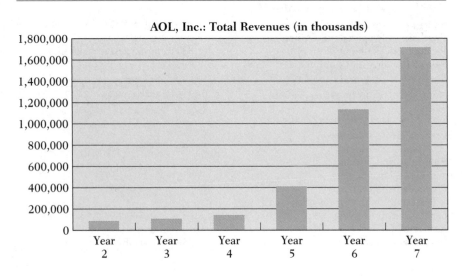

AOL, Inc.: Total Revenues (in thousands)

EXHIBIT 5.39

AOL, Inc.
Total Assets Year 2—Year 7
(Case 5.4)

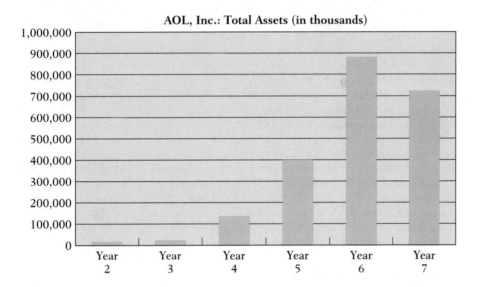

As Exhibit 5.39 illustrates, AOL's total assets increased from $155.2 million in Year 4 to $405.4 million in Year 5, or by 161 percent. In Year 6, the company's total assets increased to $958.8 million, or 136 percent over Year 5. Due to the $385.2 million write-off of deferred subscriber acquisition costs in Year 7, AOL's total assets decreased to $846.7 million, a 12 percent decrease compared to Year 6.

Two cost categories of AOL are central to analyzing the firm's earnings quality.

PRODUCT DEVELOPMENT COST

AOL capitalizes costs incurred for the production of computer software used in the sale of its services as product development costs. Costs capitalized include (1) direct labor and related overhead for software produced by the company and (2) the costs of software purchased from third parties. All costs in the software development process that are classified as research and development are expensed as incurred until technological feasibility has been established. Once technological feasibility has been established, such costs are capitalized until the software is commercially available.

Amortization is provided on a product-by-product basis, using the greater of the straight-line method or current year revenue as a percent of total revenue estimates for the related software product, not to exceed five years, commencing the month after the date of product release.

DEFERRED SUBSCRIBER ACQUISITION COSTS

AOL expenses the costs of advertising as incurred, except direct response advertising, which is classified as deferred subscriber acquisition costs. Direct response advertising consists solely of the costs of marketing programs that result in subscriber registrations without further effort required by the company. These costs, which relate directly to subscriber solicitations, principally include (1) the printing, production, and shipping of starter kits and (2) the costs of obtaining qualified prospects by various targeted direct marketing programs and from third parties.

The deferred costs are amortized, beginning the month after such costs are incurred, over a period determined by calculating the ratio of current revenues related to direct response advertising versus the total expected revenues related to this advertising, or twenty-four months, whichever is shorter. All other costs related to the acquisition of subscribers, as well as general marketing costs, are expensed as incurred.

In the first quarter of Year 7, AOL's practice of capitalizing and writing off subscriber acquisition costs over two years was abandoned. The effect of the decision was to eliminate deferred subscriber acquisition costs on the balance sheet, and charge the full amount to the income statement. Deferred subscriber acquisition costs were $314,181,000 at the end of AOL's fiscal Year 6 (see Exhibit 5.35). As a result of capitalizing and amortizing subscriber acquisition costs during the first quarter of Year 7, before the company abandoned the practice, deferred subscriber acquisition costs increased to $385,221,000. This is the writeoff amount shown on AOL's income statement for Year 7 (see Exhibit 5.36).

AOL describes the logic in its Year 7 financial statements for changing the practice:

> As a result of a change in accounting estimate, the Company recorded a charge of $385,221,000 ($4.03 per share), as of September 30, Year 6 [that is, in the first quarter of Year 7], representing the balance of deferred subscriber acquisition costs of that date. The Company previously had deferred the cost of certain marketing activities, to comply with the criteria of Statement of Position 93–7, "Reporting on Advertising Costs," and then amortized those costs over a period determined by calculating the ratio of current revenues related to direct response advertising versus the total expected revenues related to this advertising, or twenty-four months, whichever was shorter. The Company's changing business model, which includes flat-rate pricing for its online service, increasingly is expected to reduce its reliance on on-line service subscriber revenues for the generation of revenues and profits. This changing business model, coupled with a lack of historical experience with flat-rate pricing, created uncertainties regarding the level of expected future economic benefits from on-line service subscriber revenues. As a result, the Company believed it no longer had an adequate accounting basis to support recognizing deferred subscriber acquisition costs as an asset.

Required

a. Prepare an analysis that accounts for the change in the deferred subscriber acquisition costs account on the balance sheet for each of the fiscal years from Year 4 through Year 7 by using amortization of subscriber acquisition costs and deferred subscriber acquisition costs accounts from the statements of cash flows.

b. Compare the subscriber acquisition costs amortized from part a with total marketing expenses on the income statement. Calculate the percentage of this amortization to total marketing expenses for each of the fiscal year from Year 3 to Year 7.

c. Prepare an analysis of the change in the product development costs on the balance sheet account for each of the fiscal years from Year 4 through Year 7, given that the costs capitalized were $5,131,000, $13,054,000, $32,735,000, and $55,363,000, respectively, and costs amortized were $1,134,000, $2,017,000, $7,354,000, and $27,195,000, respectively.

d. Compare amortization of product development costs with total product development expenses in the income statement. Calculate the percentage that amortization bears to total product development expenses for each of the fiscal years from Year 3 through Year 7.

e. Recompute the income (loss) from operations in the income statements for AOL for each of the fiscal years Year 4 through Year 7, assuming that (1) the company expensed subscriber acquisition costs and product development costs in the year incurred instead of capitalizing, then amortizing, the costs, or (2) excludes acquired research and development costs and the writeoff of subscriber acquisition costs from the income from operations because of its materiality and nonrecurring nature.

f. Comment on America Online's quality of earnings.

CHAPTER 6

GENERALLY ACCEPTED ACCOUNTING PRINCIPLES: LIABILITY RECOGNITION AND RELATED EXPENSES

Learning Objectives

1. Review the criteria for the recognition of an accounting liability and apply these criteria to various obligations of a firm, including financing arrangements structured to keep debt off the balance sheet.
2. Understand the effect of the operating and capital lease methods on the financial statements and the adjustments required to convert operating leases to capital leases.
3. Understand the relation between the accounting records of the sponsoring employer of a pension or other retirement plan and the accounting records of the plan itself, as well as the reasons for differences between the two sets of records. Adjust the financial statements of the sponsoring employer to incorporate information from the accounting records of the retirement plan with respect to any unrecognized obligation.
4. Understand the reasons for differences between the book values of assets and liabilities for financial reporting and their tax basis, as well as the effect of such differences on the measurement of income tax expense.
5. Use information in the financial statement note on income taxes to identify reasons for changes in the income tax burden of a firm.
6. Understand the various uses of reserve accounts and their potential for management of earnings over time.

This chapter describes alternative methods of accounting for liabilities and related expenses commonly encountered in corporate annual reports. The chapter emphasizes the methods that have the greatest interpretative impact on the balance sheet and income statement. Increased business complexity in recent years precludes an exhaustive study in this chapter of all liability and related expense issues; rather, we address those reporting issues that have broad implications for analysis. We also continue our focus on how a firm's choice of accounting methods and the way it implements them affect its *quality of earnings* and *quality of financial position*, concepts introduced in Chapter 4.

The recognition and the valuation of liabilities affect the analysis of financial statements in two important ways:

1. **Profitability Analysis.** Firms use, or consume, various goods and services during a period in generating revenues, and they may not make cash payments for these goods and services until future periods. Also, firms promise to provide goods or perform services in the future for which they may receive cash and recognize revenues during the current period (under warranty plans, for example). The cost of these goods and services that the firm has already consumed or will consume in the future is an expense of the current period. Effective analysis of profitability requires that the analyst assess whether the firm has measured these expenses properly.
2. **Risk Analysis**. The amount shown on the balance sheet for liabilities indicates the present value of the cash or other assets that the firm will need to pay for obligations coming due within the next year (current liabilities) and after one year (noncurrent liabilities). A firm with inadequate resources to satisfy these obligations runs the risk of insolvency or even bankruptcy. Effective analysis of risk requires the analyst to assess whether the firm has recognized and measured its liabilities properly. Recognition issues are particularly important because many firms engage in transactions that create financial risk but do not recognize a liability for such risks on the balance sheet. In fact, financial reporting stipulates that the firm not recognize a liability in some cases.

PRINCIPLES OF LIABILITY RECOGNITION

Financial reporting recognizes an obligation as a liability if it satisfies three criteria:[1]

1. The obligation involves a probable future sacrifice of resources—a future transfer of cash, goods, or services or the forgoing of a future cash receipt—at a specified or a determinable date. The firm can measure with reasonable precision the cash-equivalent value of the resources needed to satisfy the obligation.
2. The firm has little or no discretion to avoid the transfer.
3. The transaction or event giving rise to the obligation has already occurred.

---

[1]Financial Accounting Standards Board, *Statement of Financial Accounting Concepts No. 6*, "Elements of Financial Statements," 1985.

The criteria for liability recognition may appear straightforward and subject to un-ambiguous interpretation. In fact, they really are not. Various obligations of an en-terprise fall along a continuum with respect to how well they satisfy these criteria. Exhibit 6.1 classifies obligations into six groups, which we discuss in turn.

OBLIGATIONS WITH FIXED PAYMENT DATES AND AMOUNTS

The obligations that most clearly satisfy the liability recognition criteria are those with fixed payment dates and amounts (usually set by contract). Most obligations arising from borrowing arrangements fall into this category. When a firm takes out a loan, it receives the benefit of having funds available for its use. The borrowing agreement specifies the timing and amount of interest and principal payments.

OBLIGATIONS WITH FIXED PAYMENT AMOUNTS BUT ESTIMATED PAYMENT DATES

Most current liabilities have fixed payment amounts and estimated payment dates. Either oral agreements, written agreements, or legal statutes fix the amounts payable to suppliers, employees, and governmental agencies. Firms normally settle these obligations within a few months after incurring them. The firm can estimate

---

EXHIBIT 6.1

Classification of Accounting Liabilities by Degree of Certainty

Obligations with Fixed Payment Dates and Amounts	Obligations with Fixed Payment Amounts but Estimated Payment Dates	Obligations with Estimated Payment Dates and Amounts	Obligations Arising from Advances from Cus-tomers on Unexecuted Contracts and Agreements	Obligations Under Mutually Unexecuted Contracts	Contingent Obligations
Notes Payable	Accounts Payable	Warranties Payable	Rental Fees Received in Advance	Purchase Commit-ments	Unsettled Lawsuits[a]
Interest Payable	Salaries Payable		Subscription Fees Re-ceived in Advance	Employment Commit-ments	Financial Instruments with Off-Balance Sheet Risk[a]
Bonds Payable	Taxes Payable				

Most Certain ◄───► Least Certain

◄──── Recognized as Accounting Liabilities ────►   ◄──── Not Generally Recognized as ────► Accounting Liabilities

[a]If an obligation meets certain criteria for a loss contingency, firms must recognize these obligations as liabilities. See the discussion later in this chapter.

the settlement date, although not precisely, with sufficient accuracy to warrant recognizing a liability.

OBLIGATIONS WITH ESTIMATED PAYMENT DATES AND AMOUNTS

A firm may have obligations for which both payment dates and amounts are estimated because the firm cannot identify the specific future recipients of cash, goods, or services at the time the obligation becomes a liability. The firm may also not be able to compute precisely the amount of resources it will transfer in the future.

When a firm sells products under a warranty agreement, for example, it promises to replace defective parts or perform certain repair services for a specified period of time. At the time of sale, the firm can neither identify the specific customers who will receive warranty benefits nor ascertain the amounts of their claims. Past experience, however, often provides the necessary information for estimating the likely proportion of customers who will make claims and the probable average amount of their claims. As long as the firm can estimate the probable amount of the obligation, it satisfies the first criterion for a liability. The selling price of goods sold under warranty includes an explicit or implicit charge for the warranty services. Thus, the receipt of cash or the right to receive cash in the sales transaction benefits the firm and creates the warranty liability.

OBLIGATIONS ARISING FROM ADVANCES FROM CUSTOMERS ON UNEXECUTED CONTRACTS AND AGREEMENTS

A firm sometimes receives cash from customers in advance for goods or services it will provide in a future period. For example, a rental firm may receive cash on rental property in advance of the rental period. A magazine publisher may receive subscription fees in advance of the subscription period. Organizations and associations may receive membership dues prior to the membership period.

These firms could recognize revenue upon the receipt of cash, as with the sale of products under warranty plans. In the case of advances from customers, however, all of the required transfer of resources (goods or services) will occur in the future. Revenue recognition generally requires that the firm deliver the goods or provide the services. Thus, the receipt of cash in advance creates a liability equal to the cash received. The firm might conceivably recognize a liability equal to the expected cost of delivering the promised goods or services, but doing so would result in recognizing the profit from the transaction before substantial performance had occurred.

OBLIGATIONS UNDER MUTUALLY UNEXECUTED CONTRACTS

Mutually unexecuted contracts arise when two entities agree to make a transfer of resources, but *neither* entity has yet made a transfer. For example, a firm may agree to supply its customers with specified amounts of merchandise over the next two years. A baseball organization may agree to pay its "franchise" player a certain sum as compensation over the next five years. A bank may agree to provide lines of credit to its business customers in the event that these firms need funds in the future.

In these cases, because neither party has transferred resources, no accounting liability arises. This category of obligation, called executory contracts, differs from the preceding two, where the contracts or agreements are partially executed. In the case of warranty agreements, a firm receives cash but has not fulfilled its warranty obligation. In the case of rental, subscription, and membership fees, a firm receives cash but has not provided the required goods or services.

Firms generally do not recognize obligations under mutually unexecuted contracts as accounting liabilities. If the amounts involved are material, the firm must disclose the nature of the obligation and its amount in notes to the financial statements.

CONTINGENT OBLIGATIONS

An event whose outcome is unknown today may create an obligation for the future transfer of resources. A firm may be a defendant in a lawsuit, for example, and the outcome of the suit depends on the results of the legal proceedings. The obligation in this case is *contingent* on future events.

Contingent obligations may or may not give rise to accounting liabilities. Financial reporting requires firms to recognize an estimated loss from a contingency (called a *loss contingency*) and a related liability only if both of two conditions are met:

1. Information available prior to the issuance of the financial statements indicates that it is probable that an asset has been impaired or that a liability has been incurred.
2. The firm can estimate the amount of the loss with reasonable precision.[2]

The first criterion for recognition of a loss contingency rests on the probability, or the likelihood, that an asset has been impaired or a liability has been incurred. Financial reporting does not provide clear guidance as to what probability cutoff defines *likely* or *probable*. The FASB has stated that "*probable* is used with its usual general meaning, rather than in a specific accounting or technical sense, and refers to that which can be expected or believed on the basis of available evidence or logic but is neither certain nor proved."[3]

The second criterion requires reasonable estimation of the amount of the loss. Again, financial reporting does not define *reasonably estimated* in precise terms. Instead, if the firm can narrow the amount of the loss to a reasonable range, however large, financial reporting presumes that the firm has achieved sufficient precision to justify recognition of a liability. The amount of the loss is the most likely esti-

---

[2]Financial Accounting Standards Board, *Statement of Financial Accounting Standards No. 5,* "Accounting for Contingencies," 1975.

[3]Financial Accounting Standards Board, Statement of Financial Accounting Concepts No. 6, "Elements of Financial Statements," 1985. Although the FASB has not defined probable, practice demands that firms and auditors define it. Currently, most firms and auditors appear to use probable to mean 80 percent to 85 percent or higher.

mate within the range. If no amount within the range is more likely than any other, the firm should use the amount at the lower end of the range.

Financial reporting refers to obligations meeting both of these two criteria as *loss contingencies*. One example suggested by the FASB relates to a toy manufacturer that sells toys that are later found to present a safety hazard. The toy manufacturer concludes that the likelihood of having to pay damages is high. The firm meets the second criterion if experience or other information enables it to make a reasonable estimate of the loss. The toy manufacturer recognizes a loss and a liability in this case.

As another example, firms in the tobacco industry or environmentally sensitive industries grapple with measuring loss contingencies related to litigation, and draw on lawyers and others to facilitate quantifying the loss.

CONTROVERSIAL ISSUES IN LIABILITY RECOGNITION

Most of the obligations we have given as examples clearly either are liabilities or are not liabilities. Recently, firms have structured innovative financing arrangements in ways that may not satisfy the criteria for the recognition of a liability. A principal aim of such arrangements is to reduce the amount shown as liabilities on the balance sheet. Investors often use the proportion of debt in a firm's capital structure as a measure of risk and therefore as a factor in establishing the cost of funds. (Chapter 3 discusses various ratios used by investors for measuring risk.)

Other things being equal, firms prefer to obtain funds without showing a liability on the balance sheet in the hope that future lenders will ignore such financing in setting interest rates. Although there is little empirical evidence to support the notion that lenders ignore such financing in assessing a firm's risk, some firms *act* as if lenders do overlook such borrowing.

ISSUANCE OF HYBRID SECURITIES

One means a firm can use to reduce the amount shown as liabilities is to issue securities that have both debt and equity characteristics (referred to as *hybrid securities*), but to classify them as equity on the balance sheet. Some firms do this by issuing preferred stock that is subject to mandatory redemption by the firm after some period of time. Until recently, for example, Sears, Roebuck and Co. borrowed funds though the issuance of "Series A Mandatory Exchangeable Preferred Shares." The preferred stock paid an annual, cumulative dividend of $3.75 per share before it was retired. Stock of this nature in fact often has more debt than equity characteristics.

Firms have also issued preferred stock that is subject to a call option by the issuing firm. The firm sets out provisions in the preferred stock agreement that make exercise of the call option highly probable. This preferred stock also has more debt than equity characteristics.

On the other hand, some firms issue debt securities that have more equity than debt characteristics. For example, firms might issue bonds that are convertible into common stock. The firm sets out provisions in the debt instrument that make conversion into common stock highly probable. Or, the firm might issue debt with interest payments tied to the firm's operating performance or dividend yield. (Firms treat these equity-like securities as debt in an effort to obtain a tax deduction for "interest expense.")

Although financial reporting attempts to classify all financial instruments as either a liability or shareholder equity, the securities of most firms fall along a continuum from pure debt to pure equity. The dividing line is not always clear-cut. The analyst should study the notes to the financial statements to assess whether the firm's classification of hybrid securities as debt versus equity seems reasonable.

OFF-BALANCE-SHEET FINANCING ARRANGEMENTS

Another means of reducing the amount shown as liabilities on the balance sheet is to structure a borrowing arrangement so that the firm does not recognize an obligation. This is referred to as *off-balance sheet financing*. We describe several off-balance sheet financing arrangements below.

In several cases, the FASB has issued a reporting standard setting out how firms should treat such transactions for financial reporting purposes. In other cases, it has not issued a specific financial reporting standard, and the analyst must apply the general criteria for liability recognition when deciding whether or not to recognize a liability.

A general theme runs throughout the various off-balance sheet financing arrangements. When firms leave liabilities off the balance sheet, they maintain the balance sheet equation either by reducing an existing asset or by not recognizing a newly acquired asset.

Sale of Receivables with Recourse.   Firms sometimes sell their accounts receivable with recourse as a means of obtaining short-term financing. If collections from customers are not sufficient to repay the amount borrowed plus interest, then the firm must pay the difference (that is, the lender has recourse against the borrowing firm).

Example 1.   In a recent annual report, Sears, Roebuck and Co. states that the firm "securitizes domestic credit card receivables to access intermediate-term funding in a cost-effective manner." The firm reports that $6.33 billion of credit card receivables were sold with limited recourse in Year 4, and $4.55 billion were sold in Year 3. Credit card receivables remaining on Sears' balance sheet were $21.563 billion at December 28, Year 4, and $20.106 billion at December 30, Year 3.

The question arises as to whether the recourse provision creates an accounting liability. Some argue that the arrangement is similar to a collateralized loan; the firm should leave the receivables on the books, and recognize a liability in the amount of the cash received. Others argue that the firm has sold an asset; it should recognize a liability only if it is *probable* that collections from customers will be insufficient, and the firm will be required to repay some portion of the amount received.

The FASB has ruled that firms should recognize transfers of receivables with recourse as sales if (1) the assets transferred (that is, receivables) have been completely isolated from the selling ("transferor") firm (that is, a creditor of the selling firm could not access the cash collected from the receivables in the event of the seller's bankruptcy); (2) the buying ("transferee") firm obtains the right, free of any conditions, to pledge or exchange the transferred assets; and (3) the selling firm does not maintain effective control over the assets transferred through an agreement that both entitles and obligates it to repurchase the assets.[4]

The principal refinement to the concept of an accounting liability brought out by *Statement No. 125* relates to identifying the party involved in the transaction that controls the determination of which party enjoys the economic benefits and sustains the economic risk of the *assets* (receivables in this case). If the selling (borrowing) firm controls the economic benefits/risks, then the transaction is a collateralized loan. If the arrangement transfers these benefits/risks to the buying (lending) firm, then the transaction is a sale.

Product Financing Arrangements.   Product financing arrangements occur when a firm (sponsor):

1. Sells inventory to another entity and, in a related transaction, agrees to repurchase the inventory at specified prices over specified times.
2. Arranges for another entity to purchase inventory items on the firm's behalf and, in a related transaction, agrees to purchase the inventory items from the other entity.

The first arrangement is similar to the sale of receivables with recourse, except that there is more certainty that the inventory transaction will require a future cash outflow. The second arrangement is structured so that it will appear as a purchase commitment (recall that financial reporting views purchase commitments as mutually unexecuted contracts, with a liability not normally recognized). In this case, however, the sponsoring firm usually creates the entity purchasing the inventory for the sole purpose of acquiring the inventory. The sponsoring firm usually guarantees the debt incurred by the other entity in acquiring the inventory. The other entity is often set up as a trust.

Financial reporting requires that firms recognize product financing arrangements as liabilities if they meet two conditions:

1. The arrangement requires the sponsoring firm to purchase the inventory, substantially identical inventory, or processed goods of which the inventory is a component, at specified prices.
2. The payments made to the other entity cover all acquisition, holding, and financing costs.[5]

---

[4]Financial Accounting Standards Board, *Statement of Financial Accounting Standards No. 125*, "Accounting for Transfers and Servicing of Financial Assets and Extinguishments of Liabilities," 1996.

[5]Financial Accounting Standards Board, Statement of Financial Accounting Standards No. 49, "Accounting for Product Financing Arrangements," 1981.

The second criterion suggests that the sponsoring firm recognize a liability whenever it incurs the economic risks (changing costs, interest rates) of purchasing and holding inventory, even though it may not physically control the inventory or have a legal obligation to the supplier of the inventory. Thus, as with sales of receivables with recourse, a firm recognizes a liability when it controls the determination of which party enjoys the economic benefits and incurs the economic risks of the asset involved. It also recognizes an asset of equal amount, usually inventory.

Research and Development Financing Arrangements. When a firm borrows funds to carry out research and development work, it recognizes a liability at the time of borrowing, and recognizes expenses as it incurs research and development costs.

Firms have engaged in innovative means of financing aimed at both keeping liabilities off the balance sheet and effectively excluding research and development expenses from the income statement. Example 16 in Chapter 5 details an arrangement Amgen developed that involves several joint ventures and partnerships. Amgen is always striving to develop new products and enhance existing ones, and the arrangement it developed facilitates meeting these objectives while, at the same time, minimizing the reporting of liabilities on its balance sheet for financing research and development expenditures.

Arrangements like this vary somewhat across firms, but generally operate as follows:

1. The sponsoring firm contributes either preliminary development work or rights to future products to a partnership for a general interest in the partnership. It obtains limited partners (often corporate directors or officers) who contribute cash for their partnership interests.
2. The sponsoring firm conducts research and development work for the partnership for a fee. The sponsoring firm usually performs the research and development work on a best-efforts basis, with no guarantee of success. The sponsoring firm recognizes amounts received from the partnership for research and development services as revenues. The amount of revenue generally equals or exceeds the research and development costs the firm incurs.
3. The rights to any resulting products usually reside in the partnership. At the same time, the partnership agreement usually constrains the returns and risks of the limited partners. The sponsoring firm can often acquire the limited partners' interests in the partnership if valuable products emerge. Or, the sponsoring firm may have to guarantee certain minimum royalty payments to the partnership or agree to purchase the partnership's rights to the product.

In arrangements like these, a primary objective of the sponsoring firm involves obtaining financing for its research and development work without having to recognize a liability.

There are established criteria governing when firms must recognize such financing arrangements as liabilities.[6] The sponsoring firm recognizes a liability:

1. If the contractual agreement requires the sponsoring firm to repay any of the funds provided by the other parties regardless of the outcome of the research and development work; or
2. If the circumstances indicate that the sponsoring firm bears the risk of failure of the research and development work, even though the contractual agreement does not obligate it to repay the other parties. For example, if a sponsoring firm guarantees the debt of the partnership, must make minimum royalty payments to the partnership, or must acquire the partnership's interest in any product, then the sponsoring firm bears the risk of the research and development work.

As with the two off-balance sheet financing arrangements discussed above, firms recognize liabilities when they bear the risk associated with the asset or product involved in the financing.[7]

Take-or-Pay or Throughput Contracts.   A take-or-pay contract is an agreement in which a purchaser agrees to pay specified amounts periodically to a seller for products or services. A throughput contract is similar to a take-or-pay contract except that the "product" purchased is transportation or processing services.

To understand the rationale for such arrangements, consider this example. Suppose that two petroleum companies are in need of additional refining capacity. If either company builds a refinery, it will record an asset and any related financing on its balance sheet. Suppose instead that the two companies form a joint venture to construct a refinery. The joint venture, an entity separate from the two petroleum companies, obtains financing and constructs the refinery. In order to secure financing for the joint venture, the two petroleum companies sign take-or-pay contracts agreeing to make certain payments to the joint venture each period for refining services. The payments are sufficient to cover all operating and financing costs of the refinery. The joint owners must make the payments even if they acquire no refinery services.

The economic substance of this arrangement is that each petroleum company owns half of the refinery and is obligated to the extent of half of the financing. The legal status of the arrangement is that the two firms have simply signed noncancelable purchase commitments (that is, executory contracts). Accounting likewise treats these arrangements as executory contracts. At the time of signing the contract, the firms are not viewed as having yet received any benefits that obligate

---

[6]Financial Accounting Standards Board, *Statement of Financial Accounting Standards No. 68,* "Research and Development Arrangements," 1982.

[7]A study of firms that conduct their research and development through limited partnerships finds that the stock market appears to consider the call option that firms have on research findings in the valuation of the firm. The author calls for improved disclosure of these arrangements instead of recognition of a liability in the balance sheet. See Terry Shevlin, "The Valuation of R&D Firms with R&D Limited Partnerships," *The Accounting Review, January* 1991, pp. 1–21.

them to pay. As they receive benefits over time, a liability arises. If one or the other entity guarantees the debt of the partnership, the guarantee is a contingent obligation, which is not recognized as a liability until future events indicate a high probability of payment.

Financial reporting requires firms to disclose take-or-pay and throughput commitments in the notes.[8] The analyst should examine disclosures of these commitments in notes to the financial statements to assess whether the firm incurs the risks and rewards of the arrangement and should therefore recognize a liability.

Summary of Off-Balance Sheet Financing.

The conventional accounting model based on historical cost is exchange- or transaction-oriented. Accounting recognizes events when an exchange takes place. The criteria for liability recognition discussed earlier in this chapter illustrate this exchange orientation. Accounting recognizes liabilities when a firm incurs an obligation to sacrifice resources in the future for benefits already received.

Financial reporting has typically not recognized mutually unexecuted contracts as liabilities because the parties have merely exchanged promises to perform in the future. Financial reporting also does not generally require the recognition of contingent obligations as liabilities because some future event must occur to establish the existence of a liability.

The evolving concept of an accounting liability recognizes that exchanges of promises can have economic substance, even though a legal obligation to pay does not immediately arise. When a firm controls the determination of which party enjoys the economic benefits and/or incurs the economic risks from an asset, then the firm should recognize the asset and its related financing.

The FASB closely monitors reporting issues related to off-balance sheet commitments of firms, but it continues to be challenged because of the ever-changing nature of business financing arrangements, flexible and fluid organizational arrangements, and the desire of many firms to manage risk through the use of derivatives. Firms' use of derivatives to manage risk has particularly dominated FASB regulatory efforts in recent years. The crux of the issue, as discussed next, is whether these commitments should be reported as on-balance sheet or off-balance sheet commitments.

DERIVATIVE INSTRUMENTS

Firms use derivative instruments primarily to reduce exposure to unfavorable fluctuations in interest rates, foreign exchange rates, and other market risks specific to particular firms. The practice of managing these risks is often referred to as *hedging*, or entering into *hedging activities*. Note 8 in Appendix A describes Coke's policy on the use of derivatives and hedging activities.

---

[8]Financial Accounting Standards Board, *Statement of Financial Accounting Standards No. 47*, "Disclosure of Long-Term Obligation," 1981.

Example 2. Chrysler Corporation describes its use of derivatives and hedging activities in Note 1 of a recent annual report.

> Chrysler manages risk arising from fluctuations in interest rates and currency exchange rates by using derivative financial instruments. Chrysler manages exposure to counterparty credit risk by entering into derivative financial instruments with highly rated institutions that can be expected to fully perform under the terms of such agreements. *Chrysler does not use derivative financial instruments for trading purposes.*

In the same note, Chrysler describes how its use of derivatives and hedging instruments relates specifically to the firm's international operations.

> When Chrysler sells vehicles outside the United States or purchases components from suppliers outside the United States, transactions are frequently denominated in currencies other than U.S. dollars. Periodically, Chrysler initiates hedging activities by entering into currency exchange agreements, consisting principally of currency forward contracts and purchased options, to minimize revenue and cost variation which could result from fluctuations in currency exchange rates. These instruments, consistent with the underlying purchase or sale commitments, typically mature within three years of origination. Fees paid for purchased currency options are deferred and included in other assets. The currency exchange agreements are treated as off-balance-sheet financial instruments, with the deferred fees and related gains and losses recognized in earnings upon the settlement of the underlying transactions.

The FASB first addressed reporting for derivative instruments and related off-balance sheet financing in 1986. Both the complexity of the topic and political issues have forced the FASB to move very slowly since then.[9] Beginning with quarterly reports released in 2000, however, the FASB requires firms to follow a comprehensive *measurement* and *disclosure* policy for derivative instruments and hedging activities. Prior to then, firms report following a set of *disclosure* policies established by the FASB beginning in 1990. As a result, reporting by firms in this area is in transition currently. Exhibit 6.2 lists the rulings applicable to reporting derivative instruments and hedging activities.

Analyzing financial reporting for derivative instruments and hedging activities prior to 2000 and the reporting mandated thereafter requires understanding two key concepts—*financial instruments* and *derivative instruments*—along with the concept of *hedging* defined earlier.

A financial instrument is a contractual right to receive or a contractual obligation to pay cash or some other asset in the future. Firms already recognize some "plain vanilla" financial instruments as liabilities, such as bonds payable. Other financial instruments, such as financial guarantees, standby letters of credit, and

---

[9]The deliberative process followed by the FASB has forced slow resolution of other issues addressed by the FASB in the past. Three of these are addressed subsequently in this text—accounting for pension costs, income tax reporting, and foreign currency translation.

EXHIBIT 6.2

FASB Rulings on Derivative Instruments

Statement of Financial Accounting Standards No. 105, "Disclosure of Information about Financial Instruments with Off-Balance-Sheet Risk and Financial Instruments with Concentrations of Credit Risk," 1990.

Statement of Financial Accounting Standards No. 107, "Disclosures about Fair Values of Financial Instruments," 1991.

Statement of Financial Accounting Standards No. 119, "Disclosures about Derivative Financial Instruments and Fair Value of Financial Instruments," 1994.

Statement of Financial Accounting Standards No. 133, "Accounting for Derivative and Similar Instruments and for Hedging Activities," 1998.

---

commitments under interest or exchange rate swaps, do not appear as liabilities unless payment is highly likely. The FASB defines a derivative instrument as any financial instrument or other contract that provides the holder (or writer) of the instrument the right (or the obligation) to participate in any price change of an "underlying" asset pegged to the derivative instrument.

FASB examples of "underlying" assets include financial instruments, commodities, or other assets to which a rate, an index of prices, or another market indicator is applied to determine its value and change in value over time.

Statement No. 105 Disclosures.   Changes in the market values of derivatives and financial instruments (arising, for example, from changes in interest rates or foreign exchange rates) may result in a substantial shift in value from one party to the other party and affect the willingness of the negatively affected party to perform as required. The FASB refers to these risks as *off-balance sheet risks* because they arise from events external to the firm and not under its control.

As Exhibit 6.2 reports, the FASB's first foray into this area related to disclosure of material off-balance sheet risks (*Statement No. 105*). Firms holding derivative and financial instruments with material off-balance sheet risk must disclose information as follows about the financial instruments.

1. The face, contract, or notional principal amount.
2. The terms of the instruments and a discussion of their credit and market risks, cash requirements, and related accounting policies.
3. The *accounting loss* that the entity would incur if any party to the financial instrument failed completely to perform according to the terms of the contract, and the collateral or other security, if any, for the amount due proved to be of no value to the entity.
4. The entity's policy for requiring collateral or other security on financial instruments it accepts and a description of collateral on instruments now held.

Illustrations of these disclosures appear in Coke's Notes 6 through 8 in Appendix A.

***Statement No. 119* Disclosures.**   Feeling pressure from Congress and others, the FASB addressed the topic again with *Statement No. 119*.[10] The statement is an effort to add still more disclosures regarding derivative instruments.

Firms that hold or issue derivative financial instruments for trading purposes (typically commercial and investment banks) must disclose (1) the average and end-of-the-period market value of derivative financial instruments, distinguishing between assets and liabilities, and (2) the net gains and losses arising from trading activities during the reporting period, disaggregated by class, business activity, risk or other category that is consistent with the management of those activities, and where those net trading gains and losses appear in the income statement. Entities that hold or issue derivative instruments for purposes other than trading (for example, a manufacturing firm, such as Coke, with foreign operations that hedges its foreign exchange risk using a forward contract) must disclose (1) the business or other purpose for using a derivative financial instrument, and (2) the accounting policies for reporting the derivative instrument in the financial statements. Again, illustrations of these disclosures applicable to Coke appear in Notes 6 through 8 of Appendix A.

***Statement No. 133* Accounting and Disclosures.**   *Statement No. 133* represents a paradigm shift by the FASB in accounting for derivative instruments and hedging activities. Four fundamental decisions by the FASB drive the reporting requirements of *Statement No. 133*:

1. Derivatives are assets or liabilities and should be reported in the financial statements. Derivatives are assets or liabilities because they are rights or obligations that may be settled for cash or some other asset.
2. Fair value is the most relevant measure for financial instruments and the only relevant measure for derivatives. Derivatives are measured at fair value, and adjustments to the carrying amount of hedged items reflect offsetting changes in their fair value (that is, gains and losses) arising while the hedge is in effect. The gain or loss on a hedged item is determined by focusing on the risk being hedged; as a result, the gain or loss reported may or may not be the entire change in the hedged item's fair value.
3. Only items that are assets or liabilities should be reported as such in the financial statements. Derivatives are assets or liabilities. However, changes in the gains or losses that result from changes in the fair values of the derivatives are not separate assets or liabilities.
4. Special accounting for items designed as being hedged should be provided only for qualifying transactions, and one aspect of qualification should be an assessment of offsetting changes in fair values or cash flows. As a result, hedge accounting is elective and should be limited to transactions that meet reasonable criteria.

---

[10]As Exhibit 6.2 indicates, the FASB issued *Statement No. 107* between *Statement No. 105* and *119*. However, *Statement No. 107* addresses disclosure of market values for *all* financial instruments, both on and off the balance sheet. We discuss *Statement No. 107* in the next section.

According to these fundamental decisions, beginning with quarterly reports released in 2000, firms will report all derivatives as either assets or liabilities and measure them at fair value. The change in the fair value of a derivative is recognized in net income in the period of change unless the particular instrument is designated as a hedging instrument and qualifies for hedge accounting. For derivatives qualifying for hedge accounting, the change in the fair value of the derivatives is reported either as part of net income or comprehensive income depending on what risk is being hedged and several other factors.[11] *Statement No. 133* applies to all entities and all derivative instruments, and addresses both measurement and disclosure issues for derivatives and hedging activities. This statement therefore represents a more comprehensive approach than that found in previous FASB standards addressing the topic.

Statement No. 133 defines two types of hedges: (1) fair value hedges, and (2) cash flow hedges. A fair value hedge arises when a firm obtains a derivative instrument to hedge changes in the market value of a financial instrument reported on the balance sheet. For example, a firm might issue bonds payable with a fixed interest rate. As interest rates change, the market value of the bonds will change. The firm might want to repurchase these bonds on the open market sometime before maturity but not want to subject itself to the risk that interest rates will drop and that it will have to pay more than the book value. The firm could enter into an interest rate swap with a financial instituition in which it converts the fixed-rate debt into variable-rate debt. This interest rate swap is a derivative whose value should change in the opposite direction of the bond price.

A cash flow hedge arises when a firm obtains a derivative instrument to hedge changes in periodic cash flows or commitments. Suppose a firm issues bonds payable with a variable interest rate. As interest rates change, the periodic interest payments will change (note that the market value of the bond will remain unchanged as long as the credit risk of the firm does not change). The firm might enter into an interest rate swap with a financial institution in which it converts the variable-rate debt into fixed-rate debt. The interest rate swap is a derivative whose value should change as interest rates change over time.

Example 3.   Lahey Corporation issued 8 percent, fixed-rate bonds on January 1 at par for $100 million. It simultaneously entered into an interest rate swap with National Bank under which Lahey will pay the bank each six months if interest rates rise above 8 percent, and the bank will pay Lahey if interest rates drop below 8 percent. Lahey's interest expense will therefore vary with the changes in the interest rate. The interest rate swap represents a fair value hedge. The interest rate swap has a zero market value on January 1 since the interest rate is 8 percent on this date.

Lahey would record the issuance of the bonds as follows (amounts in millions):

January 1:		
Cash	100	
Bonds Payable...		100

---

[11]Chapter 1 provides a discussion of comprehensive income, a relatively new FASB disclosure requirement.

Interest rates decrease to 6 percent during the first six months. Lahey makes these entries on June 30 for interest:

June 30
Interest Expense (0.08 × 0.5 × $100.................................... 4
    Cash 4
Cash (0.02 × 0.5 × $100)... 1
    Interest Expense 1

Lahey will report interest expense of $3, which equals the six-month portion of the annual variable interest rate of 6 percent. Lahey will also have to revalue the bonds on its books. The drop in the interest rate will increase the market value of its bonds. Assume that the market value of the bonds increases by $8. Lahey will make this entry in its accounts:

June 30
Loss on Revaluation of Bonds... 8
    Bonds Payable... 8

Accountants historically have not revalued bonds for changes in market value. *Statement No. 133* requires firms to revalue bonds when they are subject to a fair value hedge. Lahey will also have to report the derivative financial instrument (that is, the swap) at its market value on June 30.

Assume that the change in the value of the derivative exactly mirrors the change in the market value of the bond. Lahey will make this entry:

June 30
Derivative Financial Asset.. 8
    Gain on Derivative Asset.. 8

Both the loss on the revaluation of the bond and the gain on the revaluation of the derivative asset appear in net income for the period. If the derivative serves as a perfect hedge, the loss and the gain are offsetting.

Example 4. Assume now that Lahey Corporation issues $100 million of variable-rate bonds at par on January 1 at a time when the interest rate is 8 percent. The firm also enters into an interest rate swap with National Bank in which it agrees to pay the bank the difference between 8 percent interest and any variable interest rate below 8 percent, and the bank agrees to pay Lahey for the difference between 8 percent interest and any variable rate above 8 percent. In this way, Lahey converts its variable-rate debt into 8 percent fixed-rate debt.

Lahey makes the same entry on January 1 for the issuance of the bonds as the entry on the previous page. The entries on June 30, assuming that the variable rate decreases to 6 percent, are as follows:

June 30

Interest Expense (0.06 × 0.5 × $100)..................................	3	
Cash		3
Interest Expense (0.02 × 0.5 × $100)................................	1	
Cash		1

Lahey will also have to recognize a derivative liability for the decline in market value of the derivative because of the decrease in interest rates. The entry, assuming that the derivative declines in value by $8, is as follows:

Other Equity Adjustment (Comprehensive Income)	8	
Derivative Liability...		8

The loss in the value of the derivative does not affect net income immediately but it does reduce comprehensive income for the period. It also appears on a separate line in the shareholders' equity section of the balance sheet labeled "accumulated comprehensive income" or "other nonowner equity adjustments."

Over the life of the derivative contract, the market value of the interest rate swap agreement will change as interest rates change. At the end of the contract term, the market value of the contract will be zero, and the cumulative amount in comprehensive income will net to zero.

Summary. These two examples provide a simple overview of the accounting for derivatives. The types of risks needing to be hedged by firms and the wide variety of hedging vehicles available complicate the accounting far beyond the two illustrations above.

Note 8 in Appendix A reports on Coke's derivative instruments and hedging activities. Coke follows *Statement Nos. 105* and *119* reporting because *Statement No. 133* is not applicable for the years covered in the annual report. It is difficult to speculate on what Coke's reporting would look like under *Statement No. 133*; but much of the disclosure in Note 8 is required under *Statement No. 133* as well. The note confirms that Coke uses derivative instruments extensively to manage various risks incurred by the firm. The analyst must assess both the level of risk that is introduced or minimized by Coke's extensive use of derivatives and whether Coke's quality of earnings and financial position is enhanced or diminished by its method of accounting for derivatives.

PRINCIPLES OF LIABILITY VALUATION

The general principles underlying the valuation of liabilities are as follows:

1. Liabilities requiring future cash payments (bonds payable, for example) appear at the present value of the required future cash flows discounted at an interest rate that reflects the uncertainty that the firm will be able to make these cash payments. The firm establishes this discount rate at the time it initially records a liability in the accounts (it is often referred to as the *historical interest rate*), and uses this interest rate in accounting for the liability in all future periods. For some liabilities due within the next year (such as accounts payable, income taxes payable, salaries payable), the difference between the amount of the future cash flows and their present value is sufficiently small that accounting ignores the discounting process and reports the liabilities at the amounts ultimately payable.

2. Liabilities requiring the future delivery of goods or services (such as warranties payable) appear at the estimated cost of those goods and services.

3. Liabilities representing advances from customers (such as rental fees received in advance, subscription fees received in advance) appear at the amount of the cash advance.

The current market value of a liability may differ from the amount appearing on the balance sheet, particularly for long-term debt. The current market value will reflect current interest rates and assessments of the firm's ability to make the required payments. As stated earlier, the FASB requires firms to disclose the fair value of financial instruments, whether or not these financial instruments appear as liabilities (or assets) on the balance sheet. *Statement No. 107* addresses fair value disclosures for on-balance sheet financial instruments, while *Statement No. 119* addresses fair value disclosures primarily for off-balance sheet derivative instruments. *Statement No. 133* requires firms to revalue to market value each period any liabilities subject to a fair value hedge.

Example 5. Coke discloses the fair value of its financial instruments and derivative instruments in Notes 7 and 8 of Appendix A. Note 7 reports the fair values of Coke's on-balance sheet financial instruments. Note 8 reports the fair value of Coke's off-balance sheet financial instruments, which consist primarily of instruments designed to hedge certain risks of the firm. Exhibit 6.3 summarizes Coke's fair value disclosures for both its financial and derivative instruments.

As Exhibit 6.3 reveals, carrying values of Coke's on-balance sheet-financial instruments approximate fair values at the end of Year 7. Coke's derivative instruments entail an unrealized loss of $79 million because carrying values exceed fair values [$79 = $69 − ($10)].

The next three sections of the chapter discuss more fully three particularly controversial liability recognition and valuation topics: leases, retirement benefits, and deferred income taxes. A final section considers the accounting for reserves. These four topics have implications for assessing both a firm's quality of earnings and quality of financial position.

EXHIBIT 6.3		
Disclosures by Coke of the Fair Value of Financial Instruments (amounts in millions)		
December 31, Year 7	**Carrying Value**	**Fair Value**
On-balance-sheet financial instruments:	*	*
*Coke states in note 7: the carrying amounts reflected in our consolidated balance sheets for cash, cash equivalents, marketable equity securities, investments, receivables, loans and notes payable and long-term debt approximate their respective fair values. Fair values are based primarily on quoted prices for those or similar instruments.		
Off-balance-sheet financial instruments, primarily derivative instruments:		
Interest rate management		
Swap agreements-assets	$ 5	$ 13
Swap agreements-liabilities.	—	1
Interest rate caps-assets	1	—
Foreign currency management		
Forward contracts-assets	1	(2)
Forward contracts-liabilities	(53)	(42)
Swap agreements-assets	18	12
Swap agreements-liabilities.	(12)	(114)
Purchased options-assets	42	89
Other	67	33
Total.	$ 69	$ (10)

LEASES

Many firms acquire rights to use assets through long-term leases. A company might, for example, agree to lease an office suite for five years or an entire building for forty years, promising to pay a fixed periodic fee for the duration of the lease. Leasing provides benefits to lessees such as the following:

1. Ability to shift the tax benefits of depreciation and other deductions from a lessee that has little or no taxable income (such as an airline) to a lessor that has substantial taxable income. The lessee expects the lessor to share some of the benefits of these tax deductions by allowing lower lease payments.
2. Flexibility to change capacity as needed without having to purchase or sell assets.
3. Ability to reduce the risk of technological obsolescence, compared to outright ownership, by maintaining the flexibility to shift to technologically more advanced assets.
4. Ability to finance the "acquisition" of an asset using lessor financing when alternative sources of financing are unavailable.

These potential benefits of leasing to lessees do not come without a cost. When the lessor assumes the risks of ownership, it will require the lessee to make larger lease payments than if the lessee were to incur these risks. Which party bears the risks is a matter of negotiation between lessor and lessee. Promising to make an irrevocable series of lease payments commits the firm just as surely as a bond indenture or mortgage, and the accounting is similar in many cases.

We examine two methods of accounting for long-term leases: the operating lease method, and the capital lease method. The illustrations show the accounting by the lessee, the user of the leased asset. A later section discusses the accounting for the lessor, the owner of the asset.

To illustrate these two methods, suppose that Myers Company wants to acquire a computer that has a three-year life and costs $45,000. Assume that Myers Company must pay 10 percent per year to borrow money for three years. The computer manufacturer is willing to sell the equipment for $45,000 or to lease it for three years. Myers Company is responsible for property taxes, maintenance, and repairs of the computer, whether it leases or purchases it.

Assume that Myers Company signs the lease on January 1, Year 1, and must make payments on the lease on December 31, Year 1, Year 2, and Year 3. (In practice, lessees usually make lease payments in advance, but the assumption of end-of-the-year payments simplifies the computations.) Compound interest computations show that each lease payment must be $18,095. (The present value of an annuity of $1 paid at the end of this year and each of the next two years is $2.48685 when the interest rate is 10 percent per year. Because the lease payments must have a present value equal to the current cash purchase price of $45,000 if the computer manufacturer is to be indifferent between selling and leasing the computer, each payment must be $45,000/2.48685 = $18,095.)

OPERATING LEASE METHOD

In an *operating lease*, the owner, or lessor, transfers only the rights to use the property to the lessee for specified periods of time. At the end of the lease period, the lessee returns the property to the lessor. Car rental companies, for example, lease cars by the day or the week on an operating basis. In leasing arrangements where the lessee neither assumes the risks nor enjoys the rewards of ownership, the lessee treats the lease as an operating lease. Accounting gives no recognition to the signing of an operating lease (that is, the lessee reports neither the leased asset nor a lease liability on its balance sheet; the lease is simply a mutually unexecuted contract as discussed earlier in the chapter). The lessee recognizes rent expense in measuring net income each year.

Myers Company makes the following journal entry on December 31, Year 1, Year 2, and Year 3:

Rent Expense	18,095	
Cash		18,095
To recognize annual expense of leasing computer.		

CAPITAL LEASE METHOD

In leasing arrangements where the lessee assumes the risks and enjoys the rewards of ownership, the arrangement is a form of borrowing, and financial reporting treats such leases as *capital leases*. This treatment recognizes the signing of the lease as the simultaneous acquisition of a long-term asset and the incurring of a long-term liability for lease payments.

At the time Myers Company signs the lease, it makes the following entry in its records:

Leased Asset.. 45,000		
Lease Liability	45,000	
To recognize acquisition of leased asset and the		
related liability.		

Lessees recognize two expense items each year on capital leases. First, the lessee must amortize the leased asset over its useful life (that is, the term of the lease). Assuming that Myers Company uses straight-line depreciation, it recognizes depreciation expense of $15,000 (= $45,000 ÷ 3) each year as follows:

Depreciation Expense.. 15,000		
Accumulated Depreciation	15,000	
To record depreciation of leased asset.		

Second, the lease payment made each year is part interest expense on the lease liability and part reduction in the liability itself. Exhibit 6.4 shows the amortization schedule for this liability. Column (3) shows the amount of interest expense. The entries made at the end of Year 1, Year 2, and Year 3 are as follows:

EXHIBIT 6.4

Amortization Schedule for $45,000 Lease Liability, Repaid in Three Annual Installments of $18,095 Each, Interest Rate 10 Percent, Compounded Annually

Year (1)	Lease Liability, Start of Year (2)	Interest Expense for Year (3)	Payment (4)	Portion of Payment Reducing Lease Liability (5)	Lease Liability, End of Year (6)
1	$45,000	$4,500	$18,095	$13,595	$31,405
2	31,405	3,141	18,095	14,954	16,451
3	16,451	1,644[a]	18,095	16,451	0

Column (2) = column (6), previous period.   Column (5) = column (4) − column (3).
Column (3) = .10 × column (2).   Column (6) = column (2) − column (5).
Column (4) is given.   [a]Does not equal .10 × $16,451 due to rounding.

December 31, Year 1:

Interest Expense	4,500	
Lease Liability	13,595	
Cash		18,095

    To recognize lease payment, interest on liability for year
    (0.10 × $45,000 = $4,500), and the plug for reduction
    in the liability. The present value of the liability after
    this entry is $31,405 = $45,000 − $13,595.

December 31, Year 2:

Interest Expense	3,141	
Lease Liability	14,954	
Cash		18,095

    To recognize lease payment, interest on liability for year
    (0.10 × $31,405 = $3,141), and the plug for reduction
    in the liability. The present value of the liability after
    this entry is $16,451 = $31,405 − $14,954.

December 31, Year 3:

Interest Expense	1,644	
Lease Liability	16,451	
Cash		18,095

    To recognize lease payment, interest on liability for
    year (0.10 × $16,451 = $1,644), and the plug for
    reduction in the liability. The present value of the
    liability after this entry is zero (= $16,451 − $16,451).

Notice from Exhibit 6.5 that, in the capital lease method, the total expense over the three years is $54,285, which comprises $45,000 for depreciation expense (= $15,000 + $15,000 + $15,000) and $9,285 for interest expense (= $4,500 + $3,141 + $1,644). This total expense is exactly the same as that recognized under the operating lease method described previously ($18,095 × 3 = $54,285).

EXHIBIT 6.5

Comparison of Expense Recognized under Operating and Capital Lease Methods

Year	Expense Recognized Each Year Under:	
	Operating Lease Method	Capital Lease Method
1	$18,095	$19,500 (= $15,000 + $4,500)
2	18,095	18,141 (= 15,000 + 3,141)
3	18,095	16,644 (= 15,000 + 1,644)
Total	$54,285[a]	$54,285 (= $45,000[b] + $9,285[c])

[a]Rent expense.

[b]Depreciation expense.

[c]Interest expense.

One difference between the operating lease method and the capital lease method is the *timing* of the expense recognition. The capital lease method recognizes expenses sooner than does the operating lease method. But, over sufficiently long time periods, total expense equals the cash expenditure. The other difference is that the capital lease method recognizes both the asset and the liability on the balance sheet.

CHOOSING THE ACCOUNTING METHOD

When a lessee treats a lease as a capital lease, it increases both an asset account and a liability account, thereby increasing total liabilities and making the company appear more risky. Given a choice, most firms prefer not to show the asset and a related liability on the balance sheet. Their managements prefer an operating lease to either an installment purchase or a capital lease, where both the asset and liability appear on the balance sheet. Many managements also prefer to recognize expenses later rather than sooner for financial reporting. These preferences have led managements to structure asset acquisitions so that the financing takes the form of an operating lease, thereby achieving off-balance sheet financing.

Conditions Requiring Capital Lease Accounting.   Financial reporting provides detailed rules of accounting for long-term leases. The lessor and lessee must account for a lease as a capital lease if it meets any one of four conditions (we note three of them first).[12]

A lease is a capital lease (1) if it extends for at least 75 percent of the asset's life, or (2) if it transfers ownership to the lessee at the end of the lease term, or (3) if it seems likely that the lessor will transfer ownership to the lessee because of a "bargain purchase" option. A bargain purchase option gives the lessee the right to purchase the asset for a price less than the expected fair market value of the asset when the lessee exercises its option. These first three conditions are relatively easy to avoid in lease contracts if lessors and lessees prefer to treat a lease as an operating lease rather than a capital lease.

The most difficult condition to avoid is the fourth. It compares the contractual minimum lease payments discounted at an "appropriate" market interest rate with 90 percent of the fair market value of the asset at the time the lessee signs the lease. (The interest rate used must reflect the creditworthiness of the lessee.) Condition (4) is that the lease must be accounted for as a capital lease if the present value of the contractual minimum lease payments equals or exceeds 90 percent of the fair market value of the asset at the time of signing. In such cases, the lessor has less than or equal to 10 percent of the asset's value at risk until the end of the lease term. The lease therefore transfers the major risks and rewards of ownership from the lessor (landlord) to the lessee. In economic substance, the lessee has acquired an asset, and has agreed to pay for it under a long-term contract, which the

---

[12]Financial Accounting Standards Board, *Statement of Financial Accounting Standards No. 13*, "Accounting for Leases," 1976.

lessee recognizes as a liability. When the present value of the minimum lease payments is less than 90 percent of the fair market value of the asset at the time of signing, the lessor bears the major risks and rewards of ownership, and the lease is classified as an operating lease.

Firms often report both operating and capital leases because certain lease agreements meet one or more of these conditions, while others meet none of the conditions.

Example 6. Sears, Roebuck and Co. leases some of its full-line department stores, office facilities, warehouses, computers, and transportation equipment. In its notes to the financial statements, Sears reports operating lease rentals of $341, $357, and $365 million for Years 2 through 4, respectively. Sears provides a schedule of capital and operating lease commitments for Year 5 and beyond, as reported in Exhibit 6.6. The firm also reports the present value of its capital lease commitments ($340 million for Year 4, as reported in Exhibit 6.6) in another note that details all its long-term debt obligations at the end of Year 4. Capital leases represent approximately 3 percent of Sears' total long-term obligations at the end of Year 4.

Most countries outside the United States also set out criteria for distinguishing operating and capital leases. The particular criteria differ somewhat from those described above, but the common objective is to identify the party enjoying the rewards and bearing the risks of ownership.

EXHIBIT 6.6

Sears, Roebuck & Co.
Note 7—Lease and Service Agreements

Minimum lease obligations, excluding taxes, insurance and other expenses payable directly by the Company, for leases in effect as of December 28, Year 4, were:

Amounts in Millions	Capital leases	Operating leases
Year 5	$ 56	$ 279
Year 6	52	259
Year 7	49	231
Year 8	47	207
Year 9	44	189
After Year 9	611	1,006
Minimum payments	$859	$2,171
Executory costs (principally taxes)	(26)	
Imputed interest	(493)	
Present value of minimum leases payments, principally long-term	$340	

EFFECTS ON LESSOR

The lessor (landlord) generally uses the same criteria for classifying a lease as an operating lease or a capital lease as does the lessee (tenant). Under the operating lease method, the lessor recognizes rent revenue in the same amounts as the lessee recognizes rent expense. At the time of the signing of a capital lease, the lessor recognizes an asset, lease receivable, and revenue in an amount equal to the present value of all future cash flows ($45,000 in the Myers Company lease), and recognizes expense (analogous to cost of goods sold) in an amount equal to the book value of the leased asset. The difference between the revenue and expense is the lessor's gross margin from the "sale" of the asset.

The lessor records the lease receivable like any other long-term receivable at the present value of the future cash flows. It recognizes interest revenue over the term of the lease in amounts that closely mirror interest expense by the lessee. Lessors tend to prefer capital lease accounting for financial reporting because it enables them to recognize income at the time of signing. The lessor's entries, assuming that it manufactured the computer for $39,000, are as follows:

Operating Lease Method
December 31 of each year:

Cash	18,095	
Rent Revenue		18,095
To recognize annual revenue from renting computer.		
Depreciation Expense	13,000	
Accumulated Depreciation		13,000
To recognize depreciation on rented computer ($13,000 = $39,000/3).		

Capital Lease Method
January 1, Year 1:

Lease Receivable	45,000	
Sales Revenue		45,000
To recognize the "sale" of a computer for a series of future cash flows with a present value of $45,000.		
Cost of Goods Sold	39,000	
Inventory		39,000
To record the cost of the computer "sold" as an expense.		

December 31, Year 1:

Cash	18,095	
Interest Revenue		4,500
Lease Receivable		13,595
To recognize lease receipt, interest on receivable, and reduction in receivable for Year 1. See supporting calculations in the lessee's journal entries.		

December 31, Year 2:

Cash	18,095	
Interest Revenue		3,141
Lease Receivable		14,954
To recognize lease amounts for Year 2.		

December 31, Year 3:

Cash... 18,095

      Interest Revenue 1,644

      Lease Receivable 16,451

To recognize lease amounts for Year 3.

LEASE ACCOUNTING FOR TAX PURPOSES

We said earlier that one of the benefits of leasing is that it permits the user of the property (the lessee) to shift the tax benefits of depreciation, interest, and other deductions to the lessor in the expectation of lowering the required lease payments. To achieve this benefit, the lease must satisfy five criteria for an operating lease for tax purposes. These criteria differ somewhat from those GAAP uses to classify leases for financial reporting. The five criteria for operating leases for tax reporting are:

1. Use of the property at the end of the lease term by someone other than the lessee is commercially feasible.
2. The lease does not have a bargain purchase option.
3. The lessor has a minimum 20 percent of its capital at risk.
4. The lessor has a positive cash flow and profit from the lease independent of tax benefits.
5. The lessee does not have an investment in the lease and has not lent any of the purchase price to the lessor.

These criteria attempt to identify the party to the lease that enjoys the rewards and bears the risks of ownership. Because the financial and tax reporting criteria for leases differ, lessors and lessees may treat particular leases one way for financial reporting and another way for tax reporting.

CONVERTING OPERATING LEASES TO CAPITAL LEASES

The analyst must address quality of reporting issues for lessee firms that enter into substantial lease agreements, given the preference of lessees to structure leases as operating leases and the thin line that distinguishes operating and capital leases. Lease commitments accounted for off-balance sheet can negatively affect the quality of financial position reported by a firm. Off-balance sheet lease commitments also affect assessments of a firm's risk using the long-term solvency ratios discussed in Chapter 3. For these reasons, the analyst may wish to restate the financial statements of lessees to convert all operating leases into capital leases. Such a restatement provides a more conservative measure of total liabilities.

    To see the procedure followed, look at PepsiCo.'s operating lease disclosures from a recent annual report as summarized in Exhibit 6.7. Column (2) shows Pepsi's commitments on noncancelable operating leases net of sublease revenues at the end of Year 8.

EXHIBIT 6.7

PepsiCo., Inc.
Operating Lease Disclosures
(amounts in millions)

	Operating Leases Commitments at the End of Year 8		
Year (1)	Reported Lease Commitments (2)	Present Value Factor at 10%	Present Value
9	$ 356	.90909	$ 323.6
10	$ 317	.82645	262.0
11	$ 276	.75131	207.4
12	$ 243	.68301	166.0
13	$ 220	.62092	136.6
after 13	$ 1,139	.48464	552.0
			$1,647.6

Rental Expense for Year 8

Rental expense consists of minimal payments of $464 million, and contingent payments of $28 million, for Year 8. Contingent rentals are based on sales by restaurants in excess of levels stipulated in the lease agreements.

The analyst must express the lease commitments in present value terms. The discount rate that the analyst uses is the lessee's incremental borrowing rate for secured debt with similar risk as the leasing arrangement. We assume a 10 percent rate in this case. To select a present value factor for payments after Year 13, we need to know the years and amounts in which Pepsi will pay the $1,139 million. If we presume that payments after Year 13 will continue at the same amount as the $220 million payment in Year 13, then Pepsi will pay the $1,139 million over 5.2 years (= $1,139 ÷ $220), or an average 2.6 years (5.2 ÷ 2) after Year 13.

Our calculation uses the present value factor for 7.6 years. That is, Pepsi will pay the $1,139 at the rate of $220 million at the end of Year 14, $220 million at the end of Year 15, $220 million at the end of Year 16, $220 million at the end of Year 17, $220 million at the end of Year 18, and $39 million at the end of Year 19. The elapsed time for Pepsi to pay the *average* dollar in this $1,139 million aggregate amount is at Year 15.6, which is 7.6 years from the beginning of Year 9.

The analyst adds the $1,647.6 million lease amount to property, plant, and equipment and to long-term debt on the December 31, Year 8, balance sheet. For time series analysis of PepsiCo., Inc., similar calculations would be necessary for at least two previous years.

The analyst could also convert the income statement for Year 8 from the operating to the capital lease method. Assume that the January 1, Year 8, capitalized value of operating leases is $1,483, that these leased assets have a remaining lease term of 8.5 years on that date, and that all new leases signed during Year 8 are signed on December 31, Year 8. Expenses under the operating and capital lease methods are then as follows:

Operating Lease Method (as reported)

Lease Expense (see Exhibit 6.7):	
Noncontingent Rental Expense...........................	$464.0
Contingent Rental Expense.............................	28.0
Total	$492.0

Capital Lease Method (as restated)

Depreciation Expense ($1,483 ÷ 8.5).....................	174.5
Interest Expense (0.10 × $1,483)........................	148.3
Contingent Rents (see Exhibit 6.7)	28.0
Total	350.8
Decrease in Reported Expenses	$141.2

If the average lease is in the first half of its life, total expenses under the capital lease method tend to exceed total expense under the operating lease method. If the average lease is in the last half of its life, total expenses under the capital lease method tend to be less than under the operating lease method. The two expense amounts are approximately equal at the midlife point (see Exhibit 6.5). In general, balance sheet restatements are more significant than income statement restatements. Consequently, the analyst can usually ignore restatements of the income statement.[13]

The analyst could restate the statement of cash flows for the capitalization of operating leases. Under the operating lease method, the lease payment for the year is an operating use of cash. Its inclusion as a subtraction in computing net income results in reporting its negative effect on the operating section of the statement of cash flows. Under the capital lease method, a portion of the cash payment represents a repayment of the lease liability, a financing instead of an operating use of cash. The analyst should reclassify this portion of the cash payment from the operating section to the financing section of the statement of cash flows. The analyst could also reduce net income for depreciation expense on the capitalized lease assets, but this same amount appears as an addback to net income for a noncash expense. Thus, the net effect of depreciation expense on cash flows is zero.

---

[13]For an alternative procedure for converting operating into capital leases, see Eugene A. Imhoff, Jr., Robert C. Lipe, and David W. Wright, "Operating Leases: Impact of Constructive Capitalization," *Accounting Horizons*, March 1991, pp. 51–63. In this study the authors find that capitalizing operating leases decreased the rate of return on assets by 34 percent for high-lease firms and 10 percent for low-lease firms, and increased the debt-to-equity ratio 191 percent for high-lease firms and 47 percent for low-lease firms.

RETIREMENT BENEFITS[14]

Employers typically provide two types of benefits to retired employees: (1) pension benefits, and (2) health care and life insurance coverage.[15] Financial reporting, both in the United States and most other countries, requires that the employer recognize the cost of these benefits as an expense while the employees work and generate revenues rather than when the employees receive the benefits during retirement. Estimating the expected cost of the benefits requires assumptions about employee turnover, future compensation and health care costs, interest rates, and other factors. Because the employer will not know the actual costs of these benefits until many years elapse, estimating their costs while the employees work involves imprecision.

A further issue relates to the pattern for recognizing the costs as an expense. Should the employer recognize an equal amount each year over the employee's working years? Or, should the amount increase over time as compensation levels increase?

FASB pronouncements on pension and health care benefits further complicate the question of the timing of expense recognition. These pronouncements do not require immediate recognition of an expense and a liability for benefits already earned by employees at the time a firm adopts these reporting standards. Instead, the costs of benefits already earned can become expenses in future periods. One consequence of this reporting procedure is that the amount that firms show as pension or health care liabilities on the balance sheet may understate the firm's economic liability.

We discuss the accounting issues related to pensions and to health care and life insurance benefits separately.[16]

PENSIONS

Pension plans work as follows:

1. Employers agree to provide certain pension benefits to employees. The arrangement may take the form of either a defined contribution plan or a defined bene-

---

[14]Required employers' *disclosures* for pension and other postretirement benefit plans are in transition currently. *Statement of Financial Accounting Standards No. 132,* "Employers' Disclosures about Pensions and Other Postretirement Benefits," 1998, requires new disclosures for annual reports released in 1999, but does not change any of the recognition and measurement provisions discussed in this section.

[15]Some retired employees receive a third benefit from employers in the form of severance and similar benefits following active service but prior to retirement. The FASB addresses the reporting for these benefits in *Statement of Financial Accounting Standards No. 112,* "Employer's Accounting for Postemployment Benefits," 1992. The standard requires employers to accrue the cost of these benefits if they can be reasonably estimated and the employees have the unconditional right to the benefits. The statement relates only peripherally to the retiree benefits discussed in this section, however, because applying Statement No. 112 is not conditional on retirement of the employee.

In Year 8, Macy's, a subsidiary of Federated Department Stores, recognized an obligation for postemployment benefits of $11 million. Macy's indicated that the charge represents promises made to former and inactive employees after employment but before their retirement.

[16]For an expanded discussion of the many of the points discussed in this section, see Clyde P. Stickney, "Analyzing Postretirement Benefit Disclosures," *Journal of Financial Statement Analysis,* Fall 1995, pp. 15–25.

fit plan. Under a defined contribution plan, the employer agrees to contribute a certain amount to a pension fund each period (usually based on a percentage of employees' compensation), without specifying the benefits employees will receive during retirement. The amounts employees eventually receive depend on the performance of the pension fund. Under a defined benefit plan, the employer agrees to make pension payments to employees during retirement using a benefits formula based on wages earned and number of years of employment. A typical plan might provide an annual pension benefit during retirement equal to 2 percent times the number of years worked times an average of the highest five years of compensation during working years. An employee who worked 30 years at an average highest five years of compensation of $50,000 would receive an annual pension of $30,000 (= 0.02 × 30 × $50,000). The plan does not specify the amounts the employer will contribute to the pension fund. The employer must make contributions to the fund so that those amounts plus earnings from pension investments are sufficient to make the promised payments.

2. Employers periodically contribute cash to a pension fund. The trustee, or administrator, of the fund invests the cash received from the employer in stocks, bonds, and other investments. The assets in the pension fund accumulate each period both from employer contributions and income from investments. These assets appear on the balance sheet of the pension plan and not on the employer's balance sheet.

3. The employer satisfies its obligation under a defined contribution plan once it makes periodic contributions to the pension fund. The employer's obligation under a defined benefit plan increases each period because of two factors. First, employees earn increased benefits as they work each additional period at a higher compensation level. Second, the employer's obligation increases each period because time passes, and the remaining time until employees begin receiving their pensions shortens. Thus, the present value of the pension obligation increases. This obligation appears as a liability on the balance sheet of the pension plan and not on the employer's balance sheet.

4. The pension fund makes pension payments to retired employees. The employer's obligation under a defined benefit plan decreases by the amount paid.

Accounting Records of the Pension Plan. The balance sheet of a defined benefit pension plan changes each period, as summarized in Exhibit 6.8. Assets increase because of earnings on investments and contributions received from the employer and decrease from losses on investments and payments to retirees. Liabilities increase because (1) the remaining time until working employees will receive their pension shortens, and (2) employees work an additional year and earn rights to a larger pension. Liabilities decrease when the pension plan makes payments to retirees. Liabilities also increase or decrease if firms change the actuarial assumptions (discount rate, employee turnover rate, mortality rate) or the pension benefit formula underlying the pension plan.

Pension disclosures permit the analyst to assess the degree to which a firm has over- or underfunded its pension plan. These disclosures also permit an assessment of the performance of the pension fund during an accounting period.

EXHIBIT 6.8

Activity Affecting a Defined Benefit Pension Plan

Pension Fund Assets	Pension Fund Liabilities
Assets at Beginning of Period	Liabilities at Beginning of Period
± Actual Earnings on Investments	+ Increase in Liabilities Due to Passage of Time
+ Contributions Received from the Employer	+ Increase in Liabilities from Employee Services
	± Actuarial Gains and Losses Due to Changes in Assumptions
− Payments to Retirees	− Payments to Retirees
= Assets at End of Period	= Liabilities at End of Period

Obligations Under Defined Benefit Plans. Financial reporting requires firms to disclose certain information about defined benefit pension plans in notes to the financial statements. Coke's Note 12, "Pension and Other Postretirement Benefits," in Appendix A presents its disclosures, which Exhibit 6.9 summarizes.[17]

The top portion of Exhibit 6.9 shows assets and liabilities of the pension plan. The final section shows the amounts that Coke records on its books related to the pension plan. The unrecognized items (the middle three lines of the exhibit) represent amounts reflected in assets and liabilities of the pension plan but not yet recognized on the employer's books. We discuss the accounting entries on the employer's books later in the section.

Interpreting these disclosures requires several definitions:

Accumulated Benefit Obligation. The present value of amounts the employer expects to pay to retired employees (taking into consideration actuarial assumptions concerning employee turnover and mortality) based on employees' service to date and current-year compensation levels. The accumulated benefit obligation indicates the present value of the benefits earned to date, excluding any future salary increases that will serve as the base for computing the pension payment, and excluding future years of service prior to retirement. Vested benefits usually constitute the largest portion of the accumulated benefit obligation, meaning that employees will not lose the right to their pension benefit if they leave the employer prior to retirement. Employees lose nonvested benefits if they terminate

---

[17]Exhibit 6.9 summarizes pension disclosures of Coke as required by Financial Accounting Standards Board, *Statement of Financial Accounting Standards No. 87,* "Employee's Accounting for Pensions," 1985. Coke's disclosures are slightly different than those required by *Statement No. 132* because the statement is not applicable for the years covered in the annual report. The new disclosures provide additional details on the changes in the benefit obligation and fair value of plan assets during a period, and on the components of net pension expense.

EXHIBIT 6.9

Pension Disclosures by Coke
(amounts in millions)

	December 31, Year 6	December 31, Year 7
Accounting Records of Pension Plan		
Actuarial present value of benefit obligations:		
Vested	$ (1,017)	$(1,047)
Accumulated benefit obligation	$ (1,106)	$(1,152)
Projected benefit obligation	$ (1,313)	$(1,375)
Plan assets at market value	1,156	1,282
Projected benefit obligation (in excess of) or less than plan assets	$ (157)	$ (93)
Items that Reconcile the Two Sets of Records		
Unrecognized net (gain) loss	(30)	(87)
Unrecognized prior service cost	63	49
Unrecognized net assets at transition	(3)	(3)
Accounting Records of Employer		
Adjustment to recognize minimum liability	(60)	(66)
Accrued pension liability on balance sheet	$ (187)	$ (200)

employment prior to vesting. Most nonvested benefits vest after an employee works for five to ten years.

Projected Benefit Obligation. The actuarial present value of amounts the employer expects to pay to retired employees based on employees' service to date but using the expected future salaries that will serve as the base for computing the pension payment. The difference between the accumulated and projected benefit obligation is the effect of future salary increases. Consequently, the projected benefit obligation exceeds the accumulated benefit obligation. The projected benefit obligation is also closer in amount to what one might view as an economic measure of the pension obligation: the present value of amounts the employer expects to pay to employees during retirement based on total expected years of service (past and future) and expected future salaries. *Statement No. 132* does not require disclosure of this economic obligation.

The required disclosures show the relationship between the market value of pension fund assets and the projected benefit obligation at each valuation date. The amounts on the books of the pension plan reflect current market values of both assets and liabilities at each valuation date.

A pension plan can be overfunded or underfunded at any particular time. (Coke's is underfunded.) An *overfunded* pension plan has several implications for a firm:

1. The sponsoring firm can reclaim the excess assets for corporate uses. The amount reclaimed becomes immediately subject to income taxes. Corporate raiders have sometimes used excess pension assets to help finance a leveraged buyout of a firm.
2. The sponsoring firm can discontinue contributions to the pension fund until such time as the assets in the pension fund equal the projected benefit obligation.
3. The sponsoring firm can continue its historical pattern of funding on the presumption that the current overfunding is due to temporary market appreciation of investments, which could easily reverse in the future.

Although one might argue that an excess of pension fund assets over the projected benefit obligation represents an asset of the employer, *Statement No. 87* does not permit firms to recognize this resource on the balance sheet.

In Coke's case, the pension plan is *underfunded* as of the end of Year 6 by $157 million and as of the end of Year 7 by $93 million (see Exhibit 6.9). Using arguments similar to that applied to overfunded situations, one might view an excess of the projected benefit obligation over pension fund assets as a liability that firms should report on the balance sheet. The FASB, responding to criticisms that the measurement of the projected benefit obligation requires subjective projections of future salary increases, stipulates instead that firms show an excess of the *accumulated* benefit obligation over pension fund assets on the balance sheet as a liability (included in what *Statement No. 87* labels the *minimum liability*). Because the accumulated benefit obligation is usually smaller than the projected benefit obligation, relatively few firms report a liability for underfunded benefits by this measure. We discuss this minimum liability more fully below.

Accounting Records of the Employer. The employer generally makes three entries each period with respect to its pension plan:

1. Recognition of pension expense.
2. Recognition of pension contribution.
3. Adjustment to recognize the minimum liability.

We discuss each of these three entries in turn.

Recognition of Pension Expense. Firms must calculate net pension expense each year according to the projected benefit cost method, which means that actuarial calculations use accumulated service to date and projected future salaries. The firm makes an entry as follows for net pension expense:

Exhibit 6.10 summarizes the seven elements that constitute net pension expense.

EXHIBIT 6.10

Components of Pension Expense

	Effect on Pension Expense	
	Debit (Increase)	Credit (Decrease)
1. Service Cost—the increase in the projected benefit obligation because employees worked an additional year	X	
2. Interest Cost—the increase in the projected benefit obligation because of the passage of time	X	
3. Actual Return on Plan Assets—the change in the market value of plan assets due to interest, dividends, and changes in the market value of investments		X
4. Difference Between Actual Return and Expected Return on Plan Assets:		
Actual Return > Expected Return	X	
Actual Return < Expected Return		X
5. Amortization of net pension asset (pension fund assets exceed projected benefit obligation) or net pension liability (pension fund assets are less than projected benefit obligation) as of the date of initial adoption of *Statement No. 87*. The firm amortizes the net asset or net obligation straight line over the average remaining service life of employees.		
Net Pension Liability	X	
Net Pension Asset		X
6. Amortization of increases in the projected benefit obligation that arise because the firm sweetens the pension benefit formula and gives employees credit for their prior service under the sweetened benefit arrangement. The amortization period is generally the average remaining service life of employees, although a shorter period may be required if an employer regularly sweetens its pension plan.	X	
7. Amortization of gains and losses because actual experience differs from actuarial assumptions (e.g., salary, interest rate, turnover, mortality, asset returns).		
Actuarial Loss	X	
Actuarial Gain		X

Service Cost.   The present value of the projected benefit obligation on the books of the pension plan increases each year because employees work an additional year (see Exhibit 6.8). GAAP refers to this increase as the *service cost*. The employer includes this amount in pension expense on its books each year.

Interest Cost.   The present value of the projected benefit obligation on the books of the pension plan also increases each year because pension payments are one year nearer to being made. GAAP refers to this increase as the *interest cost*. The employer includes this amount in pension expense on its books each year.

Actual Return on Plan Investments.   The assets in the pension fund increase (decrease) each year because of earnings (losses) on pension investments.

The employer includes these earnings (losses) as a subtraction from (addition to) pension expense each year. The service cost and interest cost measure the increase in the obligation for pension benefits. To the extent that pension funds generate earnings, the employer will need to contribute less cash to the pension fund to pay these benefits. Earnings therefore reduce the pension expense of the employer.

Recognizing the Effects of Unexpected Changes in Pension Plan Assets and Liabilities. If the assets in a pension fund equal the liabilities of the pension plan at the beginning of the year, and the rate of return earned on pension assets exactly equals the discount rate used to compute the pension liability, then pension expense each year will equal the service cost. This precise matching seldom occurs for reasons as follows:

1. Pension funds generate actual earnings on investments at a rate that differs from the long-term rate of return that actuaries assume in deciding on the appropriate level of employer contributions to the pension fund. The firm may not immediately increase pension expense and contribute cash to the pension fund for any investment returns shortfall or reduce pension expense and its current year's contribution for any excess investment returns.
2. Firms change the pension benefit formula and give employees credit under the new formula for the years of service prior to the change (referred to as a *prior service cost*). The change immediately increases the projected benefit obligation of the pension fund. The employer, however, may not immediately increase pension expense and contribute cash to the pension fund equal to the increase in the pension obligation.
3. Actuarial experience with respect to employee turnover, mortality, compensation levels, and the discount rate may differ from the rates assumed or used at the beginning of the year. The employer may change its actuarial assumptions with respect to any of these factors, which immediately changes the amount of the projected benefit obligation of the pension fund (referred to as an *actuarial gain or loss*). The employer may again not immediately adjust pension expense for the actuarial gain or loss or contribute cash to the pension fund equal to the change in the liability.

Although these three items change either the assets or liabilities of the pension plan, GAAP does not require that firms recognize, or flow through, their full effect into the measurement of pension expense and earnings immediately at the time they occur. Instead, GAAP requires firms to defer their effects and amortize them over the remaining expected period of benefit, usually the remaining average working life of employees. The amortization smooths the effect on pension expense and earnings. Items 4 through 7 in Exhibit 6.10 include the items subject to deferral and amortization.

Difference Between Actual Return and Expected Return on Plan Assets. We have noted above that firms report the actual return on pension investments as a reduction from pension expense each year. Disclosure of the actual return lets the analyst assess the investment performance of the pension fund manager.

If the actual return exceeds the expected return, the employer must defer the excess return and amortize it as a reduction in pension expense in future years. The employer discloses the actual return as a reduction in pension expense and the excess return as an addition to pension expense. The net effect of the two amounts is a reduction in pension expense for the *expected* return on investment. If the actual return is less than the expected return, the firm again reports the actual return as a reduction of pension expense. It also reports the deficient return as a reduction of pension expense. The sum of these two amounts is a reduction in pension expense for the expected return on pension investments.

Amortization of Net Pension Asset or Liability Upon Adoption of FASB Statement No. 87.

Most firms adopted FASB *Statement No. 87* between 1986 and 1988. At the time of adoption, firms typically had either more assets in the pension fund than liabilities or more liabilities than assets. Instead of immediately reporting the difference as a gain or loss in measuring pension expense, GAAP requires employers to amortize the difference over the remaining working years of employees. This amortization is the fifth component of pension expense listed in Exhibit 6.10.

Amortization of Increases in the Projected Benefit Obligation.

Firms likewise defer and then amortize increases in the pension benefit obligation that arise from sweetening of the benefit formula. This amortization is the sixth component of pension expense in Exhibit 6.10.

Amortization of Actuarial Gains and Losses.

Actuarial gains and losses arise when actual returns on investments differ from expectations (item 4 in Exhibit 6.10) and when the actuarial assumptions underlying the pension plan change. GAAP likewise requires firms to defer and then amortize the gain or loss.

Recap.   We noted earlier that if (1) pension assets equal pension liabilities, (2) the rate of return on pension assets equals the interest rate used to compute the present value of the pension liability, and (3) actuarial assumptions turn out as expected, then the employer's pension expense will equal the current employee service cost (item 1 in Exhibit 6.10). Items 2 and 3 will net to zero, and items 4, 5, 6, and 7 will be zero.

The fact that pension assets and liabilities are unequal and the realization of a different rate of return on assets from the interest rate used to compute the pension liability result in unequal offsetting of items 2 and 3. This inequality plus changes in the pension benefit formula and an inability to realize actuarial assumptions create a need for higher or lower employer contributions to the pension fund in the future. Because the employers' total expenses must ultimately equal the cash contributed to the pension fund, pension expense must increase or decrease as well. *Statement No. 87* requires firms to smooth the effect of these excess or deficient amounts (items 4 through 7), rather than including them in the calculation of pension expense immediately.

Pension expense each period is the net of these seven elements. The seven elements may net to a pension expense or a pension credit. Coke discloses these seven components of pension expense on four lines (it combines items 4 through 7 on the line labeled net amortization and deferral) as:

	Year 5	Year 6	Year 7
Service cost benefits earned during the period. . . .	$ 46	$ 43	$ 48
Interest cost on projected benefit obligation	78	89	91
Actual return on plan assets	(25)	(211)	(169)
Net amortization and deferral	(39)	145	103
Net pension expense	$ 60	$ 66	$ 73

Note that *Statement No. 132,* not applicable for Coke's annual report covering Years 5 through 7, requires that items 4 through 7 are separately disclosed.

Recognition of Pension Contribution.   The second entry that the employer will make on its books each year is for its contribution of cash to the pension fund. The typical entry is:

Pension Liability.. Y	
Cash	Y

The amount that a firm recognizes as pension expense each period will not necessarily equal the amount the firm contributes to its pension fund. The firm measures the amount for pension expense in accordance with the provisions of *Statement No. 87.* The amount the firm contributes to its pension fund depends on actuaries' recommendations concerning the needed level of funding, minimum required funding dictated by government regulations, and decisions by the firm regarding investments of its financial resources.

For example, a firm with a significantly overfunded pension plan might delay additional contributions for a few years, and use the cash for other corporate purposes. In this case, the firm recognizes pension expense each year, but does not contribute cash to the pension fund. Alternatively, a firm might contribute more than the amount of pension expense.

Earnings on pension investments are not subject to income taxation, while earnings on cash left within the firm are subject to taxation. Within prescribed limits, firms can make excess pension contributions and delay or avoid taxes on investment earnings.

When a firm recognizes more pension expense than it contributes to the pension fund, a pension liability appears on the balance sheet. When pension expense is less than pension funding, a pension asset appears on the balance sheet. Coke, for example, reports a pension asset of $35 million at the end of Year 6 and $39 million at the end of Year 7 relating to certain overfunded pension plans (see Appendix A), suggesting that it has funded some pension plans faster than it has recognized pension expense. Note that this pension asset (or pension liability) on the balance sheet bears no necessary relation to the more important measure of the status of a pension plan: the difference between the total assets in the pension fund and the projected benefit obligation. The latter is sometimes a much larger amount.

Look again at Exhibit 6.9, Coke's pension disclosures. The combined assets in Coke's pension plans at the end of Year 7 of $1,282 million are less than the projected benefit obligation of $1,375 million by $93 million. Similar amounts for Year 6 result in an underfunded pension obligation of $157 million.

Adjustment to Recognize the Minimum Liability. Most firms maintain separate pension plans for each of their various groups of employees. If a firm has any pension plan for which the accumulated benefit obligation exceeds the assets in that pension plan, the firm must report as a minimum a liability equal to this underfunded accumulated benefit obligation on its balance sheet. The entry to recognize the minimum liability adjusts any pension liability already on the employer's books resulting from a difference between pension expenses and pension contributions from the last two journal entries. The entry to recognize the minimum liability is as follows:

Accumulated Comprehensive Income....................................	Z	
Pension Liability		Z

Coke reports an adjustment for the minimum liability of $60 million at the end of Year 6 and $66 million at the end of Year 7. Note 12 to Coke's financial statements in Appendix A indicates that Coke has some pension plans for which the accumulated benefit obligation exceeds the assets in the pension fund. Coke adjusts its pension liability account for this minimum liability.

Analysts' Treatment of Pensions. Exhibit 6.11 presents an analysis of Coke's pension plan disclosures for Year 7. The projected benefit obligation exceeds the assets in the pension fund at the beginning and the end of Year 7. Thus, Coke has an underfunded pension plan.

Pension plan investments generated earnings of $169 million during Year 7 (Coke discloses this amount in the components of its pension expense for the year). The earnings include interest, dividends, realized gains and losses from sales of investments, and unrealized gains and losses from changes in the market value of investments. The portion of the $169 million of earnings that is realized during Year 7 and that is unrealized at the end of Year 7 is not a required disclosure.

EXHIBIT 6.11

Analysis of Pension Plan Disclosures of Coke for Year 7
(amounts in millions)

Accounting Records of Pension Plan

Assets at Beginning of Year	$1,156.0
Plus Earnings from Investments	169.0
Plus Contribution from Coke	66.0[a]
Less Payments to Retirees (Plug)	(109.0)
Assets at End of Year	$1,282.0
Liability at Beginning of Year	$1,313.0
Plus Service Cost	48.0
Plus Interest Cost	91.0
Less Payments to Retirees	(109.0)
Plus (Minus) Actuarial Loss (Gain)	32.0[b]
Liability at End of Year	$1,375.0

[a]Pension Expense	$ 73.0
Increase in Pension Liability ($200.0 − 187.0)	(13.0)
Increase in Adjustment to Shareholders' Equity	
for Minimum Liability	6.0
Pension Contribution	$ 66.0
[b]Unrecognized Net (Gain) Loss, Prior Service Cost, and	
Net Transition (Asset) Liability, Beginning of Year:	
(30.0) + 63.0 + (3.0)	$ 30.0
Plus Actuarial Loss for Year 8 (Plug)	32.0
Less Amortization and Deferral (excess of actual over expected	
earnings) for Year 7	(103.0)
Unrecognized Net (Gain) Loss, Prior Service Cost, and	
Net Transition (Asset) Liability, End of Year:	
(87.0) + 49.0 + (3.0)	$ (41.0)

The entries Coke makes in its records during Year 7 relating to its pension plan are as follows:

Pension Expense	73	
Pension Liability		73
Pension Liability	66	
Cash		66
Shareholders' Equity Account (minimum		
pension liability)[18]	6	
Pension Liability		6

---

[18]The FASB requires Coke to report its minimum pension liability adjustment for Year 7 as part of comprehensive income (*Statement No. 130*, discussed in Chapter 1). The adjustment is sufficiently small for Year 7 that a separate disclosure for this component of comprehensive income is not provided by Coke in its Statement of Shareowners' Equity.

The change in the pension liability account from the three entries above is a credit change of $13 million (= $73 − $66 + $6), which equals the increase in the accrued pension liability on the balance sheet from $187 million at the end of Year 6 to $200 at the end of Year 7.

As Exhibit 6.11 reports, the projected benefit obligation increased primarily because of service cost and interest cost during Year 7. Coke discloses the amounts for these items in the components of pension expense (detailed earlier). The firm also incurred an actuarial loss for Year 7, which has the effect of increasing the projected benefit obligation. It is not clear what factors led to this loss. Note also that the $109 million payment to Coke retirees reduces the projected benefit obligation for the year.

To assess quality of financial position and a firm's profitability and risk, analysts treat a difference between pension assets and pension liabilities in various ways:

1. Make no adjustment to the employer's balance sheet for an under- or over-funded pension plan. The rationale for this approach is that the under- or over-funding is a temporary condition that will work itself out over a longer time period.
2. Recognize an underfunded projected benefit obligation as a liability. The employer may have to contribute an amount to the pension fund in the future equal to the underfunding. Including the obligation among liabilities provides better measures for assessing financial structure risk. Coke's underfunded projected benefit obligation is $93 million at the end of Year 7. Since Coke already reports a liability related to these underfunded pension plans of $239 million at the end of Year 7 (see Note 12 in Appendix A), however, no adjustment is necessary.
3. Recognize an overfunded projected benefit obligation as an asset and an underfunded projected benefit obligation as a liability. This approach shows the potential benefit of accessing excess pension assets as well as the potential cost of an underfunded obligation. Coke's pension plans that have assets in excess of the projected benefit obligation total $236 million ($1,126 million − $890 million as reported in Note 12 in Appendix A) at the end of Year 7. The balance sheet currently shows a pension asset of $39 million for these plans. The entry to reflect the net $198 million asset of these plans is (assuming a 35 percent income tax rate):

Prepaid Pension Asset ($237 − $39)...............................	198.0	
Deferred Tax Liability (0.35 × 198)..........................		69.3
Retained Earnings		128.7

4. Include both the assets and the liabilities of the pension fund on the employer's balance sheet. Include the return on pension assets as interest and dividend revenue and the interest cost component of pension expense as interest expense on the employer's income statement. This approach consolidates the financial statements of the pension fund with those of the employer, much like those for a parent company and majority-owned subsidiaries. The case for

consolidation rests on the employer's right to access pension assets and its obligation to provide for pension liabilities. The counterargument for consolidation is that federal pension law significantly constrains the operational relationship between the employer and its pension fund as compared to most parent/subsidiary relationships.

POSTRETIREMENT BENEFITS OTHER THAN PENSIONS

In addition to pensions, most employers provide health care and life insurance benefits to retired employees. This benefit may take the form of a fixed dollar amount to cover part or all of the cost of health and life insurance (analogous to the defined contribution type of pension plan), or the benefit may specify the level of health care or life insurance provided (analogous to the defined benefit type of pension plan).

The accounting issues related to these postretirement obligations are similar to the accounting issues we have discussed for pensions. The employer must recognize the cost of the postretirement benefits during the employees' years of service. The employer may or may not set aside funds to cover the cost of these benefits.

Health and life insurance expense each period includes an amount for current service plus interest on the health care or life insurance benefits obligation for the period. Expected earnings on investments in a postretirement benefits fund, if any, reduce these expenses. The employer defers and then amortizes actuarial gains and losses due to changes in employee turnover, health care costs, interest rates, and similar factors.

The major difference between the accounting for pensions and the accounting for other postretirement benefits is that firms need not report an excess of the accumulated benefits obligation over assets in a postretirement benefits fund as a liability on the balance sheet.[19] Firms must report this amount in the notes to the financial statements.

During the deliberation process on the reporting standard for postretirement benefits, many firms exerted pressure on the FASB not to require recognition of the underfunded accumulated benefits obligation, particularly for health care benefits. These firms argued that the amount of this obligation was both large (compared to other liabilities and shareholders' equity) and uncertain, because of many unknowns regarding future health care inflation rates. Some firms indicated that they would eliminate health care retirement benefits if the FASB were to require recognition of the liability. As a compromise, the FASB allows firms to recognize the obligation either in full upon adoption of *Statement No. 106* or piecemeal over employees' working years.[20]

---

[19]The accumulated benefits obligation for health care incorporates health care costs expected when employees receive benefits and is therefore more similar to the projected benefit pension obligation than the accumulated benefit pension obligation. See Financial Accounting Standards Board, *Statement of Financial Accounting Standards No. 106*, "Employer's Accounting for Postretirement Benefits Other than Pensions," 1990.

[20]The implications of the differences between the two methods allowed for adopting *Statement No. 106* are discussed in Eli Amir and Joshua Livnat, "Adoption Choices of SFAS No. 106: Implications for Financial Analysis," *Journal of Financial Statement Analysis*, Winter 1997, pp. 51–60.

Look at Note 12 to Coke's financial statements in Appendix A. When Coke adopted *Statement No. 106* in Year 3, it elected to recognize the full obligation for health care and life insurance benefits. By the end of Year 6, its balance sheet includes a liability of $273 million. This liability grew to $290 million by the end of Year 7. At the end of Year 6, the total benefit obligation exceeds plan assets by $261 million; at the end of Year 7, the total benefit obligation exceeds plan assets by $238 million. Since in both Year 6 and Year 7 the recorded liability is greater than the underfunded benefit obligation, most analysts conclude that the postretirement benefit obligation already recognized by Coke satisfactorily reflects its obligation.

Analysts' concerns with postretirement benefits other than pensions are similar to those for pensions. Should the analyst add the underfunded postretirement benefit obligation to liabilities in assessing risk? How reasonable are the firm's assumptions regarding health care cost increases, discount rates, and amortization periods? Is the postretirement benefit fund, if any, generating returns consistent with the expected rate of return?

INCOME TAXES

Income taxes affect the analysis of a firm's profitability (income tax expense is a subtraction when computing net income) and its cash flows (income taxes currently payable require cash). Deferred tax assets and deferred tax liabilities on the balance sheet affect future cash flows. The financial statements note on income taxes provides useful information for assessing a firm's income tax position. We illustrate the required income tax disclosures and discuss how the analyst might use this information when analyzing a firm's financial statements.

OVERVIEW OF INCOME TAX ACCOUNTING

Standard-setting bodies in the United States have taken the position for many years that income tax expense for a particular year is not simply the amount of income taxes currently payable on the taxable income of that year. Firms must also recognize the benefits of future tax deductions and the obligations related to future taxable incomes to the extent that revenues and expenses affect not only income for financial reporting during the current period but also affect taxable income in future periods. The underlying concept is *matching*: matching income tax expense with the income reported for financial reporting, even though the associated cash flows for income taxes will not occur until future periods.

Understanding current practice requires an appreciation of practices previously required for reporting income tax expense. Prior to the issuance of *Statement No. 109* in February 1992, the accounting for income taxes followed an *income statement approach*.[21] A diagram summarizes this approach:

---

[21]Financial Accounting Standards Board, *Statement of Financial Accounting Standards No. 109*, "Accounting for Income Taxes," 1992.

(1) Income Before Income Taxes for Financial Reporting

± (2) Additions or Subtractions to Eliminate Permanent Differences Between Income for Financial and Tax Reporting

= (3) Base for Income Tax Expense

± (4) Additions or Subtractions for Temporary Differences Between Income for Financial and Tax Reporting

= (5) Taxable Income

The journal entry to record income tax expense was:

Income Tax Expense (Tax Rate × Line 3)............................. x
Deferred Tax Asset or Deferred Tax Liability (Tax Rate
× Line 4).. x   x
    Income Tax Payable (Tax Rate × Line 5)   x

Statement No. 109 now requires firms to follow a *balance sheet approach* when computing income tax expense. The approach may be described as follows:

1. Identify at each balance sheet date all differences between the *book basis* of assets, liabilities, and tax loss carryforwards (that is, the book value for financial reporting) and the *tax basis* of assets, liabilities, and tax loss carryforwards.
2. Eliminate differences from step 1 that will not have a future tax consequence. Terminology prior to *Statement No. 109* referred to these differences as permanent differences. An example is goodwill. Firms must amortize goodwill for financial reporting, but often cannot deduct this amortization for tax purposes. Thus, the book basis and the tax basis of goodwill will differ. Note that the eliminations in this step reflect the cumulative effect of permanent differences as of the date of the balance sheet, not just the current year's permanent difference included in line (2) above following an income statement approach.
3. Separate the remaining differences after the first two steps into those that give rise to future tax deductions and those that give rise to future taxable income. Financial reporting refers to these differences as *temporary differences*. Exhibit 6.12 summarizes the possibilities. Multiply differences between the book and tax basis of assets and liabilities that give rise to future tax deductions by the *enacted* marginal tax rate expected to apply in those future periods. The result is a *deferred tax asset*. Multiply differences between the book and tax basis of assets and liabilities that give rise to future taxable income by the *enacted* marginal tax rate expected to apply in those future periods. The result is a *deferred tax liability*.

Firms may have unused net operating loss and tax credit carryforwards as of a balance sheet date. These items have the potential to reduce future taxable income (operating loss carryforwards) or future taxes payable (tax credit carryforwards). The firm includes the tax effect of these carryforwards in deferred tax assets at each balance sheet date.

EXHIBIT 6.12
Examples of Temporary Differences

	Assets	Liabilities
Future Tax Deduction	Tax Basis of Assets Exceeds Book (Financial Reporting) Basis[a]	Tax Basis of Liabilities is Less than Book (Financial Reporting) Basis[b]
Future Taxable Income	Tax Basis of Assets is Less than Book (Financial Reporting) Basis[c]	Tax Basis of Liabilities Exceeds Book (Financial Reporting) Basis[d]

Examples

[a]Accounts receivable using the direct charge-off method for uncollectible accounts for tax purposes exceeds accounts receivable (net) using the allowance method for financial reporting.

[b]Tax reporting does not recognize an estimated liability for warranty claims (firms can deduct only actual expenditures on warranty claims), whereas firms must recognize such a liability for financial reporting to match warranty expense with sales revenue in the period of sale.

[c]Depreciable assets using accelerated depreciation for tax purposes less than depreciable assets using straight-line depreciation for financial reporting.

[d]Leases recognized by a lessee as capital leases for tax reporting and operating leases for financial reporting.

4. Assess the likelihood that the firm will realize the benefits of deferred tax assets in the future. This assessment should consider the nature (whether cyclical or noncyclical, for example) and characteristics (growing, mature, or declining, for example) of the firm's business and its tax planning strategies for the future. If realization of the benefits of deferred tax assets is "more likely than not" (that is, exceeds 50 percent), then deferred tax assets equal the amounts computed in step 3 above. If it is more likely than not that a firm will *not* realize some or all of the deferred tax assets, then the firm must reduce the deferred tax assets for a *valuation allowance* (similar in concept to the allowance for uncollectible accounts). The valuation allowance reduces the deferred tax assets to the amounts the firm expects to realize by way of reduced taxes in the future.

The result of following this four-step procedure is a deferred tax asset and a deferred tax liability at each balance sheet date. Income tax expense each period equals:

1. Income taxes currently payable on taxable income.
2. Plus a net credit change in the deferred tax asset or liability and minus a net debit change in the deferred tax asset or liability between the beginning and the end of the period.

EXHIBIT 6.13

Comparison of Income Statement and Balance Approach for Measuring Income Tax Expense

Income Statement Approach (Pre-*Statement No. 109*)	**Balance Sheet Approach** (*Statement No. 109*)
(1) Taxes Current Payable on Taxable Income	(4) Taxes Current Payable on Taxable Income
(2) Taxes Potentially Saved or Payable in the Future from Timing Differences between Current Period's Income for Financial and Tax Reporting	(5) Change in Deferred Tax Assets and Deferred Tax Liabilities during the Current Period
(3) Income Tax Expense = (1) + (2)	(6) Income Tax Expense = (4) + (5)

Exhibit 6.13 provides a comparison of the components of income tax expense using the income statement approach prior to *Statement No. 109* and the balance sheet approach. The principal difference between the two approaches relates to item (2) versus item (5). Item (2) includes only temporary differences for the current year between financial and tax reporting incomes, while item (5) includes temporary differences, enacted changes during a period in future income tax rates, and changes in the valuation allowance as a result of new information regarding the realizability of deferred tax assets. When tax rates do not change, and a firm recognizes no valuation allowance, the income statement and balance sheet approaches yield identical amounts for income tax expense.

REQUIRED INCOME TAX DISCLOSURES

The amount reported as income tax expense in the income statement is the net result of applying (1) a lengthy list of rules for measuring taxable income and tax liabilities according to the Internal Revenue Code (represented by the "current" portion of income tax expense), and (2) the complex procedure discussed above to measure the deferred portion. The notes to the financial statements provide additional information to help the analyst better understand the makeup of income tax expense. Four specific disclosures are particularly useful for assessing a firm's tax position. The sections on the following pages discuss and illustrate these disclosures.

Components of Income Tax Expense. Firms must disclose the amount of income taxes currently payable and the amount deferred, broken down by government entity (federal, foreign, state, and local).

	Components of Income Tax Expense		
	Year 1	**Year 2**	**Year 3**
Current—Federal	$123	$105	$191
—Foreign	61	75	128
—State and Local	13	12	18
Total Current	$197	$192	$337
Deferred—Federal	$ 70	$ 40	$ 35
—Foreign	19	30	38
Total Deferred	$ 89	$ 70	$ 73
Total Income Tax Expense	$286	$262	$410

The journal entries made to record income taxes each year are as follows:

	Year 1	**Year 2**	**Year 3**
Income Tax Expense 286		262	410
Income Tax Payable	197	192	337
Deferred Tax Asset or			
Deferred Tax Liability.	89	70	73

Components of Income before Taxes.   Assessing a firm's tax position over time or relative to other firms requires some base for scaling the amount of income tax expense. Income before taxes serves this purpose.

	Components of Income before Taxes		
	Year 1	**Year 2**	**Year 3**
United States	$600	$450	$700
Foreign	200	250	350
Total	$800	$700	$1,050

The average, or effective, tax rates for the three years on total income before taxes are:

Year 1: $286/$800   = 35.7%

Year 2: $262/$700   = 37.4%

Year 3: $410/$1,050 = 39.0%

Thus, the effective tax rate increased over the three-year period.

Reconciliation of Income Taxes at Statutory Rate with Income Tax Expense.   The third required disclosure explains why the effective tax rates shown above differ from the statutory federal tax rate on income before taxes. Firms can express reconciling items in either dollar amounts or percentage terms.

Reconciliation of Income Taxes at Statutory Rate with Income Tax Expense

	Year 1	Year 2	Year 3
(1) Income Taxes on Income before Taxes at Statutory Rate	35.0%	35.0%	35.0%
(2) Foreign Tax Rates Greater (Less) than Statutory Federal Rate	1.3	2.5	4.1
(3) State and Local Taxes	1.1	1.1	1.1
(4) Dividend Deduction	(0.5)	(0.5)	(0.6)
(5) Tax-Exempt Income	(0.5)	(0.4)	(0.4)
(6) Goodwill Amortization	.2	.4	0.6
(7) Percentage Depletion in Excess of Cost	(0.7)	(0.7)	(0.8)
Income Tax Expense	35.7%	37.4%	39.0%

The statutory federal tax rate is 35 percent in each year, but the effective tax rates are higher than the statutory rates. The reconciliation includes two types of reconciling items: (1) tax rate differences, and (2) permanent differences. We discuss below the reconciling items most commonly encountered in corporate annual reports.

Foreign Tax Rates Greater (Less) than Statutory Federal Rate. The denominator of the effective tax rate computation combines both U.S. source and foreign source income for financial reporting. The initial assumption on line (1) is that all of this income is subject to taxes at a rate equal to the U.S. federal statutory rate. Foreign tax rates are usually different from the U.S. federal rate, however. Line (2) indicates how much the overall effective tax rate increased or decreased because of these foreign rate differences.

Look at the first two items in the components of income tax expense on the previous page. Foreign tax expense for Year 3 totals $166 (= $128 + $38). Under components of income before taxes, pretax book income from foreign sources is $350. If this income were subject to tax at the federal rate of 35 percent, foreign income tax expense would be $123 (= 0.35 × $350). Foreign tax expense of $166 exceeds the amount at the federal statutory rate by $43 (= $166 − $123). Excess taxes as a percentage of *total* pretax book income, the denominator of the effective tax rate, are 4.1 percent (= $43/$1,050). Foreign source income is thus taxed at a rate of 47.4 percent (= $166/$350).

It would be desirable to have a breakdown of total foreign income and foreign taxes by individual countries, but firms rarely disclose such information.

State and Local Taxes. The statutory tax rate on line (1) reflects federal taxes only. The reconciliation adds state and local taxes on income for financial reporting since such taxes are part of income tax expense. The amount of the reconciling item is state and local taxes net of their federal tax benefit. State and local taxes are deductible in determining taxable income for federal purposes, so the incremental effect of state and local taxes beyond the federal statutory rate appears on line (3).

Look at the disclosure of the components of income tax expense again. State and local taxes for Year 3 are $18. Net of the federal tax benefit of 35 percent, state and local taxes are $12 [(1 − 0.35)($18)]. This $12 amount increases the effective tax rate by 1.1 percent (= $12/$1,050) for Year 3.

As with foreign taxes, the income tax note to the financial statements does not give any further detail on the income and taxes by jurisdictional unit within the U.S.

Dividend Deduction. Depending on the investor's ownership percentage, only 20 percent or 30 percent of dividends received from *unconsolidated domestic* subsidiaries and affiliates is subject to federal taxation. The dividend deduction is intended to reduce the effect of triple taxation under the corporate organization form. The full dividend received is included in income for financial reporting. The calculation on line (1) presumes that the dividend is subject to tax at the statutory rate. The reduction on line (4) indicates the tax savings due to the 70 percent or 80 percent dividends received deduction.

Tax-Exempt Income. Income for financial reporting includes interest revenue on state and municipal obligations. Such interest revenue, however, is never included in taxable income. The income tax savings from this permanent difference appears on line (5).

Goodwill Amortization. A firm that acquires another firm and pays a higher price than the market value of its identifiable assets must allocate the excess to goodwill. (Chapter 7 addresses accounting for business acquisitions.) The firm must amortize goodwill over a period not exceeding 40 years for financial reporting purposes, but it often cannot amortize goodwill for tax purposes. By subtracting goodwill amortization in computing book income before taxes, line (1) presumes a tax benefit equal to the amortization times the statutory tax rate. The addition on line (6) reflects the fact that no tax benefit accrues to this permanent difference.

Percentage Depletion in Excess of Cost. The Internal Revenue Code permits firms involved in mineral extraction to claim a depletion deduction equal to a specified percentage times the gross income from the property each year. Over the life of a mineral property, total percentage depletion will likely exceed the acquisition cost of the property. For financial reporting purposes, total depletion cannot exceed acquisition cost under generally accepted accounting principles. The excess of percentage depletion over book depletion represents a permanent difference that reduces the effective tax rate.

Components of Deferred Tax Assets and Liabilities. The fourth disclosure item in the income tax note is a listing of the components of the deferred tax asset and the deferred tax liability at the beginning and the end of each year. Exhibit 6.14 presents the required disclosure. The change in deferred tax asset and deferred tax liability each year represents deferred income tax expense for that year.

Note in Exhibit 6.14 that deferred tax assets experience a net credit change of $34 (= $240 − $274) between Year 2 and Year 3, and deferred tax liabilities experience a net credit change of $39 (= $819 − $780). The total credit change in these accounts of $73 (= $34 + $39) equals the deferred component of income tax expense for Year 3 (see the first income tax disclosure item).

We discuss the components of deferred taxes in turn.

Uncollectible Accounts Receivable. Firms provide for estimated uncollectible accounts in the year of sale for financial reporting, but they cannot recognize bad debt expense for tax purposes until an actual customer's account becomes uncollectible. Thus, the book value of accounts receivable will be less than its tax basis. The difference represents the future tax deductions for bad debt expense.

These future tax benefits times the tax rate give rise to a deferred tax asset. The deferred tax asset relating to uncollectible accounts in Exhibit 6.14 increases between Year 0 and Year 2, suggesting that bad debt expense for financial reporting

---

EXHIBIT 6.14

Disclosures Related to Deferred Taxes— Components of Deferred Tax Assets and Liabilities

	December 31			
	Year 0	**Year 1**	**Year 2**	**Year 3**
Deferred Tax Asset				
(8) Uncollectible Accounts Receivable..	$ 15	$ 17	$ 19	$ 16
(9) Warranties	76	89	105	91
(10) Pensions.	53	67	83	71
(11) Leases.	32	42	54	62
(12) Net Operating Losses	—	—	13	—
Total Deferred Tax Asset	$176	$215	$274	$240
Deferred Tax Liability				
(13) Depreciable Assets	$275	$355	$421	$476
(14) Inventories	41	49	58	59
(15) Installment Receivables	149	171	205	193
(16) Intangible Drilling and Development Costs.	58	76	96	91
Total Deferred Tax Liability	$523	$651	$780	$819

continued to exceed bad debt expense for tax reporting. Such a relation characterizes a firm with increasing sales. The decrease in the deferred tax asset during Year 3 suggests that sales declined, causing bad debt expense for tax reporting to exceed the amount for financial reporting.

Warranties. Firms provide for estimated warranty costs in the year of sale for financial reporting, but they cannot recognize warranty expense for tax reporting until the firm makes actual expenditures to provide warranty services. Thus, the book value of the warranty liability (a positive amount) will exceed the tax basis of the warranty liability (zero, because the income tax law does not permit recognition of a warranty liability). The difference represents the future tax deductions for warranty expense.

The increase in the deferred tax asset relating to warranties between Year 0 and Year 2 in Exhibit 6.14 is consistent with a growing firm, while the decrease in Year 3 indicates a firm whose sales of product under warranty plans probably declined.

Pensions. Firms recognize pension expense each year as employees render services for financial reporting and when the firm contributes cash to the pension fund for tax reporting. As we discussed in the pension section, the income tax law limits a firm's ability to claim tax deductions when a pension fund is overfunded. Thus, firms may curtail making pension fund contributions even though they must recognize pension expense each year. The book basis of the pension liability (a positive amount) will exceed the tax basis (not recognized). The future tax deductions for pension expense result in a deferred tax asset.

For the firm in Exhibit 6.14, pension expense for financial reporting exceeds the amount for tax reporting during Year 1 and Year 2, and the deferred tax asset relating to pensions increased. The deferred tax asset decreased in Year 3, indicating a larger expense for tax reporting than for financial reporting (that is, the book basis of the pension liability decreased during the year).

Several explanations might account for such a decrease. First, the firm may have resumed funding the pension obligation and made a multiyear contribution. Second, the firm could have curtailed employment during Year 3 in light of the decrease in sales, reducing pension expense, but then made a pension contribution sufficient to reduce the pension liability. Third, the firm may have experienced a negative pension expense during Year 3 because of an overfunded pension plan. The negative pension expense reduces the pension liability and thereby the amount of future tax deductions previously considered available.

Leases. The firm in Exhibit 6.14 leases equipment from other entities (lessors). We know that firms may treat leases either as operating leases or as capital leases for financial and tax reporting. If a lease qualifies as an operating lease, the lessor recognizes rent revenue and depreciation expense, and the lessee recognizes rent expense. If a lease qualifies as a capital lease, the lessor recognizes a gain on the "sale" of the leased property at the inception of the lease and recognizes interest revenue each year from financing the lessee's "purchase" of the property. The lessee depreciates the assets each period and recognizes interest expense on its borrowing from the lessor.

Leasing arose as an industry in part to shift tax deductions on property from firms that need the use of property but do not have sufficient taxable income to take advantage of the tax deductions to other entities with higher tax rates that could take advantage of the deductions. If a lease qualifies as an operating lease for tax purposes, the lessor gets the tax deductions for depreciation and can possibly pass through some of these benefits to the lessee in the form of lower lease payments.

An earlier section of this chapter indicates that the operating and capital lease criteria for financial reporting are not the same as those for tax reporting. It is possible to structure a lease as an operating lease for tax reporting, even though the transaction may qualify as a capital lease for financial reporting.

The firm in Exhibit 6.14 shows a deferred tax asset relating to leases. The likely scenario is that this firm treats leases as capital leases for financial reporting and as operating leases for tax reporting. Thus, the book basis of the leased asset and lease liability (a positive amount) exceeds the tax basis of the asset and liability (not recognized). Depreciation and interest expense recognized for financial reporting exceed rent expense recognized for tax reporting. In later years, rent expense for tax reporting will exceed depreciation and interest expense. These future tax deductions give rise to a deferred tax asset.

The deferred tax asset increases each year in Exhibit 6.14, suggesting that this firm increased its involvement in leasing during the three-year period (that is, the firm has more leased assets in the early years of the lease period when the book expenses exceed the tax deduction than in the later years when the tax deduction exceeds the book expenses).

Net Operating Losses.   A firm may operate for both financial and tax reporting at a net loss for the year. The firm can carry back this net loss to offset taxable income of the two preceding years and receive a refund for income taxes paid in those years. The firm recognizes the refund as an income tax credit in the year of the net loss.

If the firm either has no positive taxable income in the two preceding years against which to carry back the net loss, or if the net loss exceeds the taxable income of those two preceding years, the firm must carry forward the net loss. This carryforward provides future tax benefits in that it can offset positive taxable incomes and thereby reduce income taxes otherwise payable. The benefits of the net operating loss carryforward give rise to a deferred tax asset.

The firm in Exhibit 6.14 recognizes a deferred tax asset during Year 2 and realizes the benefits of the net operating loss carryforward during Year 3. Looking back at the disclosure of the components of income tax expense, we see that this firm paid taxes to all three types of government units during Year 2. Thus, the firm must have been unable to offset the net operating loss incurred by some subunit during the year against the taxable income of the overall entity.

One possibility is that the firm owns a majority interest in a subsidiary and therefore consolidates it for financial reporting. Its ownership percentage, however, is less than the 80 percent required to include the subsidiary in a consolidated tax return. Thus, the net loss of the subsidiary can only offset net income of that subsidiary in a later year. The firm recognizes this future benefit as a deferred tax asset. This firm shows no valuation allowance related to the deferred tax asset, indicating a greater than 50 percent probability of realizing the tax benefits in the future.

Depreciable Assets. Firms claim depreciation on their tax returns using accelerated methods over periods shorter than the expected useful lives of depreciable assets. Most firms depreciate assets for financial reporting over the expected useful lives of such assets using the straight-line method. Thus, the book value of depreciable assets will likely exceed their tax basis. Depreciation expense for tax reporting in future years will be less than the amounts for financial reporting, giving rise to a liability for future tax payments.

For the firm in Exhibit 6.14, the deferred tax liability relating to depreciable assets increases each year, suggesting that the firm has more assets in their early years when tax depreciation exceeds book depreciation. The deferred tax liability increases, however, at a decreasing rate, suggesting a slowdown in the growth rate in capital expenditures.

Inventories. The book value of inventories for the firm in Exhibit 6.14 exceeds their tax basis, giving rise to future tax liabilities. Perhaps this firm includes certain elements of cost as part of manufacturing overhead for financial reporting, but deducts these elements when incurred for tax reporting.

Installment Receivables. Firms that sell assets on account and permit customers to pay over two or more future years often recognize revenue at the time of sale for financial reporting and when they collect cash using the installment method for tax reporting. The book basis of these receivables exceeds their tax basis and gives rise to deferred tax liabilities.

The deferred tax liability relating to installment sales for the firm in Exhibit 6.14 increases between Year 0 and Year 2, characteristic of a growing firm (that is, revenues from sales during the current period exceed collections this period from sales made in prior periods). The deferred tax liability on installment sales decreases during Year 3, consistent with the decline in sales noted above in the discussion of deferred taxes related to uncollectible accounts and warranties.

Intangible Drilling and Development Costs. Firms can deduct for tax purposes in the year of the cash expenditure certain costs of acquiring rights to drill and of actual drilling to ascertain the presence of mineral resources. These firms must capitalize and amortize such costs for financial reporting. The book basis of the property will exceed the tax basis and give rise to a deferred tax liability.

The deferred tax liability for this item in Exhibit 6.14 increases between Year 0 and Year 2, indicating a growth in drilling and development activity. The decrease in the liability during Year 3 suggests a cutback in such expenditures.

ASSESSING A FIRM'S TAX POSITION

The note to the financial statements on income taxes defines the effective tax rate as:

$$\text{Effective Tax Rate} = \frac{\text{Income Tax Expense}}{\text{Book Income before Income Taxes}}$$

Exhibit 6.15 presents an analysis of effective tax rates. This analysis separates the amounts for each year into domestic and foreign components.

The combined effective tax rate in Exhibit 6.15 based on income tax expense increases each year. The effective tax rate on the domestic portion remains relatively steady at a rate close to the 35 percent federal statutory tax rate. Differences in the domestic tax position due to rate differences and permanent differences offset each other. The effective tax rate on the foreign portion, on the other hand, exceeds 35 percent, and that rate increases each year.

The analyst should explore the reasons for this increase in the foreign effective tax rate with management. Perhaps foreign markets are growing more rapidly than domestic markets, and the firm's overall profit margin is increasing as a result of a strategic shift toward these foreign markets. Alternatively, the firm may need to search for more tax-effective ways of operating abroad. For example, the firm might:

1. Shift some operations (manufacturing, marketing) to the U.S. where the effective tax rate is lower.
2. Assess whether transfer prices or cost allocations can be adjusted to shift income from high to low tax rate jurisdictions.

EXHIBIT 6.15

Analysis of Effective Tax Rates

	Year 1		Year 2		Year 3	
	Domestic	Foreign	Domestic	Foreign	Domestic	Foreign
(1) Net Income Before Income Taxes	$600	$200	$450	$250	$700	$350
Income Taxes at 35% Statutory Fed. Rate	$210	$ 70	$157	$ 87	$245	$123
Foreign Tax Rates Greater than 35%	—	10	—	18	—	43
State and Local Taxes	9	—	8	—	11	—
Dividends Deduction	(4)	—	(3)	—	(6)	—
Tax Exempt Income	(4)	—	(3)	—	(4)	—
Goodwill Amortization	1	—	3	—	6	—
Percentage Depletion	(6)	—	(5)	—	(8)	—
(2) Income Tax Expense	$206	$ 80	$157	$105	$244	$166
Effective Tax Rates: (2) ÷ (1)	34.3%	40.0%	34.9%	42.0%	34.9%	47.4%
Combined Effective Tax Rates . . .	35.7%		37.4%		39.0%	

3. Shift from domestic to foreign borrowing to increase deductions for interest against foreign source income.
4. Shift from equity to debt financing of foreign operations to increase interest deductions against foreign source income.

The increasing tax rates abroad and an increasing proportion of income derived from abroad suggest a continuing increase in the combined effective tax rate that could hurt future profitability unless the firm takes action against that possibility.

INCOME TAX DISCLOSURES

Look at the income tax disclosures for Coke in Note 13 of Appendix A. The entry to record income tax expense for Year 7 is (amounts in millions):

Income Tax Expense ($1,249 − $145)	1,104	
Deferred Tax Assets ($753 − $778)	25	
Deferred Tax Liabilities ($878 − $676)	202	
Income Tax Payable		1,249
Income Tax Expense (Other Accounts)		82

Coke's income tax expense includes taxes currently payable of $1,249 million minus a net $227 million (= $25 + $202) debit change in deferred tax assets and liabilities. Thus, total income tax expense is $1,022 million (= $1,249 − $227). Coke reports $1,104 million as related to continuing operations, and $82 million related to other income accounts. The $82 million probably relates to equity in earnings of unconsolidated bottling operations. Coke reports in Note 3 that its ownership percentage of Coca-Cola Erfrishungsgertränke changed during Year 7, and the investment is currently accounted for using the equity method. Previously this firm was wholly owned by Coke.

The relation between income tax expense and income tax payable in the journal entry above suggests that Coke's taxable income for Year 7 exceeded book income before taxes. This does not appear to be the case for Year 5 and Year 6, however, as in those years the amount currently payable is less than income tax expense.

The largest component of deferred tax assets is for benefit plans. A deferred tax asset suggests that Coke recognized expenses for financial reporting that it has not yet recognized for tax reporting. Note 12 in Appendix A indicates that Coke has at the end of Year 7 (1) an accrued pension liability of $200 million (= $239 − $39), and (2) an accrued postretirement benefits liability of $290 million. A liability for these employee benefits is consistent with the recognition of expenses earlier than funding.

Coke reports a deferred tax asset for benefits of net operating loss carryforwards of certain international subsidiaries but also includes a valuation allowance to reflect the probability of realizing these and other deferred tax assets.

Coke shows deferred tax liabilities related to the use of accelerated depreciation for tax purposes and straight-line depreciation for financial reporting. It also reports deferred taxes for the recognition of equity method income for financial reporting earlier than the recognition of dividend revenue for tax purposes from these investments.

Coke's effective tax rate changes significantly from 31 percent in Year 6 to 24 percent in Year 7. In Note 13 in Appendix A, Coke states that a tax settlement for past years was reached with the Internal Revenue Service related to Coke's operations in Puerto Rico. The agreement resulted in a one-time reduction of $320 million in Year 7's income tax expense. Coke also acknowledges in Note 13 that the effective tax rate for Year 7 would have been 31 percent, excluding the favorable impact of the agreement reached with the Internal Revenue Service. Chapter 3 provides a time series analysis of income tax expense for Coke, taking into consideration this one-time reduction.

IS THE DEFERRED TAX LIABILITY REALLY A LIABILITY?

There is considerable disagreement about the accounting for deferred income taxes, particularly with respect to whether the account *Deferred Income Tax Liability* is really a liability. Proponents of the required accounting point out that temporary differences eventually reverse. When they do, taxable income will likely exceed income before taxes for financial reporting, and the firm's cash payment for taxes will exceed income tax expense. Thus, a future cash outflow in the amount of the deferred tax liability will occur.

Opponents point out that, for a growing firm, temporary differences originating in a period will exceed temporary differences reversing in the period, so that the deferred tax liability account continually increases. Opponents therefore argue that net timing differences never require future cash flows. They further point out that the deferred tax liability account does not represent a legal obligation of a firm. If the firm files for bankruptcy, it will not owe the amount in the deferred tax liability account to government entities. The firm pays the required taxes to government entities each year depending on its taxable income. The amount in the deferred tax liability account arises only because accountants attempt to smooth income tax expense so that it matches income before taxes for financial reporting.

The analyst obtains a more conservative measure of liabilities by leaving the deferred income tax liability account on the balance sheet as a liability. An alternative approach involves studying the behavior of deferred income taxes during recent years. If the deferred tax liability account has increased constantly, the analyst might eliminate it from liabilities and add it to retained earnings. This treatment presumes that the firm should not have provided deferred taxes to begin with. If the deferred tax liability account increases in some years, and decreases in other years, then the analyst can leave the account among liabilities.

The treatment of deferred taxes assumes even greater importance when analysts are comparing U.S. firms with non-U.S. firms. Firms in France, Germany, and Japan use similar accounting methods for financial and tax reporting, so in this case the issue of deferred tax accounting does not arise. Firms in Great Britain provide deferred taxes for timing differences only when a high probability exists that a liability will become due. Deferred tax accounting in Canada closely mirrors U.S. reporting practices.

UNDERSTANDING RESERVES IN THE FINANCIAL STATEMENTS

This chapter and the previous one emphasize two important concepts underlying the financial statements:

1. Income over sufficiently long time periods equals cash inflows minus cash outflows from operating, investing, and financing activities (except dividends and capital transactions).
2. Because accountants prepare financial statements for discrete periods of time shorter than the life of a firm, the recognition of revenues does not necessarily coincide with the receipt of cash, and the recognition of expenses does not necessarily coincide with the disbursement of cash.

Assets such as inventories, investments, property, plant, equipment, and intangibles result from past cash outflows. The costs of these assets become expenses in future periods when the firm uses the services of these assets in operations or through sale. Liabilities, such as salaries payable, interest payable, taxes payable, and pensions payable, reflect the cost of services already received by a firm. They generally require a future cash outflow. Thus, most asset and liability accounts result from efforts to match revenues with expenses for discrete periods of time.

Because revenues must ultimately equal the total cash inflows and expenses must ultimately equal the total cash outflows (except for dividends and capital transactions), firms in the long run cannot alter the total *amount* of revenues and expenses. In the short run, however, they can only estimate ultimate cash flows.

In addition, the allocation of benefits received in the form of revenues and services consumed in the form of expenses to discrete accounting periods is subject to some imprecision. As Chapter 4 discusses, management may have incentives to shift revenues or expenses between accounting periods to accomplish certain reporting objectives. Audits by the firm's independent accountants, taxing authorities, and government regulators serve as control mechanisms on management's behavior in this regard.

The analyst will develop a sensitivity to financial reporting areas where firms enjoy flexibility in measuring revenues, expenses, assets, and liabilities. This chapter and the previous one discuss reporting areas that allow management to select from acceptable alternatives to influence reported earnings (FIFO versus LIFO cost flow assumptions, or depreciation methods, for example). These chapters also discuss reporting areas that require firms to make estimates in applying accounting principles (such as in the case of useful lives for depreciable assets or future salary increases for pensions). Management's latitude for influencing reported earnings correlates directly with the role or significance of estimates in applying accounting principles.

In the United States, all major revenues, gains, expenses, and losses flow through the income statement. The analyst can study the time series pattern of earnings to assess the extent to which firms attempt to shift income through time.

In some countries outside the United States, certain income items do not flow through the income statement, but instead increase or decrease a shareholders' equity account directly. In addition, common practice in certain countries permits liberal shifting of income between accounting periods either to minimize income taxes or to smooth earnings. The accounting mechanism used to accomplish these reporting results is called a *reserve account*.

NATURE OF A RESERVE ACCOUNT

Reserve accounts may appear on the balance sheet as a deduction from an asset, as a liability, or as a component of shareholders' equity. (Thus, reserve accounts always carry a credit balance.) They may appear for a limited period of time or represent a permanent account. Firms may use reserve accounts to shift earnings between periods, or they may not affect earnings in any period. These multiple uses of reserve accounts and the implication that firms have set aside assets equal to the reserve result in considerable confusion among financial statement users and even among some professional analysts.

Using the term *reserve* in the title of an account in the United States is generally unacceptable. When firms use an account that functions similarly to a reserve, U.S. firms must use more descriptive terminology. Reserve accounts commonly appear in the financial statements of non-U.S. firms. Reserve accounts customarily raise a number of issues for analysts.

USE OF RESERVE ACCOUNTS

Matching Expenses with Associated Revenues.   The recognition of an expense during the current period could result in an increase in a reserve account. The reserve account might appear on the balance sheet as a reduction in an asset. For example, firms provide for bad debt expense and increase the account, reserve for bad debts (U.S. firms use the account, allowance for uncollectible accounts). This reserve account appears as a subtraction from accounts receivable on the balance sheet.

Likewise, firms recognize depreciation expense and increase the account, reserve for depreciation (U.S. firms use the account, accumulated depreciation). The reserve account appears as a reduction from fixed assets on the balance sheet.

Alternatively, the reserve account might appear as a liability on the balance sheet. For example, a firm might provide for warranty expense or pension expense and increase the accounts, reserve for warranties (estimated warranty liability in the United States) or reserve for retirement benefits (accrued retirement liability in the United States).

When used properly, reserve accounts serve the same functions as the corresponding accounts that U.S. firms use: to permit an appropriate matching of revenues and expenses and an appropriate valuation of assets and liabilities. Of course, firms in both the United States and abroad can misuse these accounts (that is, under or overstate the provisions each year) to manage earnings as discussed in Chapter 4. Besides searching for situations where such management occurs, the analyst's main concern with reserves is to understand the nature of the reserve account in each case. There is usually an analogous account used in the United States that helps the analyst in this interpretation.

Keeping Expenses Out of the Income Statement. A practice in some countries is to create a reserve account by reducing the retained earnings account. For example, a firm might decrease retained earnings and increase the reserve for price increases or reserve for contingencies. These accounts appear among the shareholders' equity accounts and may carry a title such as retained earnings appropriated for price increases or retained earnings appropriated for contingencies. When firms later experience the price increase or contingency, they charge the cost against the reserve account rather than include it in expenses. These costs therefore bypass the income statement and usually result in an overstatement of earnings.

Note that this use of reserves does not misstate total shareholders' equity because all of the affected accounts (retained earnings, reserve accounts, expense accounts) are components of shareholders' equity. Thus, the analyst's primary concern with these reserves is assessing whether the resulting net income is an appropriate base for estimating future sustainable earnings. The analyst can study the shareholders' equity portion of the balance sheet to ascertain whether firms have used reserve accounts to avoid sending legitimate expenses through the income statement.

Revaluing Assets But Delaying Income Recognition Effect. Firms might use reserves when they revalue assets but do not want the income effect of the revaluation to affect income of the current period. In the next chapter we point out that firms in the United States account for investments in marketable equity securities using the market value method. When market value differs from acquisition cost, U.S. firms write up or write down the investment account.

Financial reporting in the United States does not generally permit the immediate recognition of this increase or decrease in market value in measuring income (except for securities held for trading purposes, as we discuss in Chapter 7). Instead, these firms increase or decrease an account titled unrealized gain or loss in market value of investments and include it as an element among shareholders' equity accounts (see Coke's balance sheet in Appendix A, and the account titled unrealized gain on securities available for sale). When the firm sells the securities, it eliminates the unrealized gain or loss account, and recognizes a realized gain or loss in measuring net income.

Another example of this use of the reserve account relates to foreign currency translation (also discussed in the next chapter). U.S. firms with foreign operations usually translate the financial statements of their foreign entities into U.S. dollars each period using the exchange rate at the end of the period. Changes in the exchange rate cause an unrealized foreign currency gain or loss.

Firms do not recognize this gain or loss in measuring income each period but instead use a shareholders' equity account titled unrealized foreign currency adjustment (see Coke's balance sheets in Appendix A, and the account titled foreign currency translation adjustment). When the firm disposes of the foreign unit, it eliminates the unrealized foreign currency adjustment account, and recognizes a gain or loss on disposal. U.S. firms could use titles such as reserve for price declines in investments or reserves for foreign currency gains and losses, as is common practice in some countries, but U.S. financial reporting requires a more descriptive title.

Financial reporting in the United Kingdom permits periodic revaluations of fixed assets and intangible assets to their current market value. The increased valuation of assets that usually occurs leads to an increase in a revaluation reserve account included in the shareholders' equity section of the balance sheet. Depreciation or amortization of the revalued assets may appear fully on the income statement each period as an expense, or may be split between the income statement (depreciation or amortization based on acquisition cost) and a reduction in the revaluation reserve (depreciation or amortization based on the excess of current market value over acquisition cost).

The analyst's concern with this type of reserve is the appropriateness of revaluing the asset and delaying recognition of its income effect. Note that total shareholders' equity is the same, whether or not the unrealized gain or loss immediately affects net income or whether it affects another shareholders' equity account and later affects net income. This use of reserves does affect net income of the current period. The analyst may wish to restate reported net income of the current period to incorporate changes in these reserves.

Permanently Reclassifying Retained Earnings.   Local laws or practices may dictate that firms transfer an amount from retained earnings, which are available for dividends, to a more permanent account that is not available for dividends. U.S. firms typically "capitalize" a portion of retained earnings when they issue a stock dividend. Several other countries require firms to report a certain amount of legal capital on the balance sheet. Such firms reduce retained earnings and increase an account titled legal capital or legal reserve. The implication of such disclosures is that assets equal to the amount of this legal capital are not available for dividends. This use of reserves has no effect on net income of the current or future periods.

SUMMARY OF RESERVES

The quality of disclosures regarding reserves varies considerably across countries. Analysts will often encounter difficulties attempting to understand, much less adjust for, the effect of changes in reserves. An awareness of the ways that firms can use reserve accounts should help the analyst know the kinds of questions to raise in the study of financial statements. Until greater standardization in the use of reserves occurs across countries, the analyst must recognize the lack of comparability of net income and balance sheet amounts and perhaps the increased importance of a statement of cash flows.

SUMMARY

This chapter has explored various reporting areas where expense measurement and liability recognition interact. These reporting areas therefore affect both profitability analysis and risk analysis. A firm's desire to keep debt off the balance sheet, with the aim of lowering the cost of financing, should put the analyst on guard for the presence of unreported liabilities and the potential for poorer-quality financial reporting. Because liabilities (unlike most assets) may not physically exist, it is harder for both the independent auditor and the analyst to identify the presence of unreported liabilities. This chapter highlights some of the areas that the analyst should consider when engaging in this search.

PROBLEMS AND CASES

6.1 ACHIEVING OFF-BALANCE SHEET FINANCING (ADAPTED FROM MATERIALS BY R. DIETER, D. LANDSITTEL, J. STEWART, AND A. WYATT). Brion Company wants to raise $50 million cash but, for various reasons, not in a way that results in a newly recorded liability. It is sufficiently solvent and profitable that its bank is willing to lend up to $50 million at the prime interest rate. Brion Company's financial executives have devised six different plans, described as follows.

TRANSFER OF RECEIVABLES WITH RECOURSE

Brion Company will transfer to Credit Company its long-term accounts receivable, which call for payments over the next two years. Credit Company will pay an amount equal to the present value of the receivables, less an allowance for uncollectibles, as well as a discount because it is paying now but will collect cash later. Brion Company must repurchase from Credit Company at face value any receivables that become uncollectible in excess of the allowance. In addition, Brion Company may repurchase any of the receivables not yet due at face value less a discount specified by formula and based on the prime rate at the time of the initial transfer. (This option permits Brion Company to benefit if an unexpected drop in interest rates occurs after the transfer.)

The accounting issue is whether the transfer is a sale (where Brion Company increases cash, reduces accounts receivable, and recognizes expense or loss on transfer), or whether it is merely a loan collateralized by the receivables (where Brion Company increases cash and increases notes payable at the time of transfer).

PRODUCT FINANCING ARRANGEMENT

Brion Company will transfer inventory to Credit Company, which will store the inventory in a public warehouse. Credit Company may use the inventory as collateral for its own borrowings, whose proceeds will be used to pay Brion Company. Brion Company will pay storage costs, and will repurchase all the inventory within the next four years at contractually fixed prices plus interest accrued for the time elapsed between the transfer and later repurchase. The accounting issue is whether the inventory is sold to Credit Company, with later repurchases treated as new acquisitions for Brion's inventory, or whether the transaction is merely a loan, with the inventory remaining on Brion's balance sheet.

THROUGHPUT CONTRACT

Brion Company wants a branch line of a railroad built from the main rail line to carry raw material directly to its own plant. It could, of course, borrow the funds and build the branch line itself. Instead, it will sign an agreement with the railroad to ship specified amounts of material each month for ten years. Even if it does not ship the specified amounts of material, it will pay the agreed shipping costs. The railroad will take the contract to its bank and, using it as collateral, borrow the funds to build the branch line.

The accounting issue is whether Brion Company would increase an asset for future rail services and increase a liability for payments to the railroad. The alternative is to make no accounting entry except when Brion makes payments to the railroad.

CONSTRUCTION PARTNERSHIP

Brion Company and Mission Company will jointly build a plant to manufacture chemicals that both need in their own production processes. Each will contribute $5 million to the project, called Chemical. Chemical will borrow another $40 million from a bank, with Brion the only guarantor for the debt. Brion and Mission are each to contribute equally to future operating expenses and debt service payments of Chemical, but, in return for its guaranteeing the debt, Brion will have an option to purchase Mission's interest for $20 million four years hence.

The accounting issue is whether Brion Company should recognize a liability for the funds borrowed by Chemical. Because of the debt guarantee, debt service payments will ultimately be Brion Company's responsibility. Alternatively, the debt guarantee is a commitment merely to be disclosed in notes to Brion Company's financial statements.

RESEARCH AND DEVELOPMENT PARTNERSHIP

Brion Company will contribute a laboratory and a preliminary finding about a potentially profitable gene-splicing discovery to a partnership, called Venture. Venture will raise funds by selling the remaining interest in the partnership to outside investors for $2 million and borrowing $48 million from a bank, with Brion Company guaranteeing the debt. Although Venture will operate under the management of Brion Company, it will be free to sell the results of its further discoveries and development efforts to anyone, including Brion Company. Brion Company is not obligated to purchase any of Venture's output.

The accounting issue is whether Brion Company would recognize the liability. (Would it make any difference if Brion Company has either the *option* to purchase or an *obligation* to purchase the results of Venture's work?)

HOTEL FINANCING

Brion Company owns and operates a profitable hotel. It could use the hotel as collateral for a conventional mortgage loan. Instead, it considers selling the hotel to a partnership for $50 million cash. The partnership will sell ownership interests to outside investors for $5 million and borrow $45 million from a bank on a conventional mortgage loan, using the hotel as collateral. Brion Company guarantees the debt.

The accounting issue is whether Brion Company would record the liability for the guaranteed debt of the partnership.

Required
Discuss the appropriate treatment of each of these proposed arrangements from the viewpoint of the auditor (who must decide whether the transaction will result in a liability to be

recorded, or whether footnote disclosure will suffice) and from the viewpoint of an investment banker (who must assess the financing structure of Brion Company in order to make a competitive bid on a proposed new underwriting of Brion company's common shares).

6.2 ACCOUNTING FOR ATTEMPTED OFF-BALANCE-SHEET FINANCING ARRANGEMENTS.
Part A. International Paper Company (IP) is in need of $100 million of additional financing, but because of restrictions in existing debt covenants cannot place any more debt on its balance sheet. To obtain the needed funds, it plans to transfer cutting rights to a mature timber tract to a newly created trust as of January 1, Year 8. The trust will use the cutting rights to obtain a $100 million, five-year, 10 percent interest rate bank loan due in five equal installments with interest on December 31 of each year.

The timber will be harvested each year, and sold to obtain funds to service the loan and pay operating costs. According to current prices, there is 10 percent more standing wood available for cutting than should be needed to service the loan and pay ongoing operating costs of the tract (including wind, fire, and erosion insurance). If the selling price of timber decreases in the future, the volume of the timber harvested will be increased sufficiently to service the debt. If the selling price of timber increases in the future, the volume harvested will remain as originally anticipated, but any cash left over after debt service and coverage of operating costs will be invested by the trust to provide a cushion for possible future price decreases. The value of any cash or uncut timber at the end of five years will revert to IP.

IP will not guarantee the debt. The bank, however, has the right to inspect the tract at any time and to replace IP's forest management personnel with managers of its own choosing if it feels the tract is being mismanaged.

Required (Part A)
Discuss the appropriate accounting for this transaction by IP in light of FASB pronouncements on off-balance-sheet financing.

Part B. On June 24, Year 4, Delta Airlines entered into a revolving accounts receivable facility (Facility) providing for the sale of $489 million of a defined pool of accounts receivable (Receivables) through a wholly owned subsidiary to a trust in exchange for a senior certificate in the principal amount of $300 million (Senior Certificate) and a subordinate certificate in the principal amount of $189 million (Subordinate Certificate). The subsidiary retains the Subordinate Certificate and the Company receives $300 million in cash from the sale of the Senior Certificate to a third party. The principal amount of the Subordinate Certificate fluctuates daily depending upon the volume of Receivables sold, and is payable to the subsidiary only to the extent that the collections received on the Receivables exceed amounts due on the Senior Certificate. The full amount of the allowance for doubtful accounts related to the Receivables sold has been retained, as the Company has substantially the same credit risk as if the Receivables had not been sold. Under the terms of the Facility, the company is obligated to pay fees that approximate the purchaser's cost of issuing a like amount of commercial paper plus certain administrative costs.

Required (Part B)
Delta requests your advice on the appropriate accounting for this transaction. How would you respond?

Part C. In Year 2, a wholly owned subsidiary of the Sun Company became a one-third partner in Belvieu Environmental Fuels (BEF), a joint venture formed for the purpose of constructing, owning, and operating a $220 million methyl tertiary butyl ether (MTBE) production facility in Mont Belvieu, Texas. As of December 31, Year 3, BEF had borrowed $128 million against a construction loan facility of which the Company guarantees one-third or $43 million. The plant, which has a designed capacity of 12,600 barrels daily of MTBE, is expected to begin production in mid-Year 4. When production commences, the construction loan will be converted into a five-year, nonrecourse term loan with a first-priority lien on all project assets.

In order to obtain a secure supply of oxygenates for the manufacture of reformulated fuels, Sun has entered into a ten-year take-or-pay agreement with BEF, which commences when the plant becomes operational. Pursuant to this agreement, Sun will purchase all of the MTBE production from the plant. The minimum per unit price to be paid for the MTBE production while the nonrecourse term loan is outstanding will be equal to BEF's annual raw material and operating costs and debt service payments divided by the plant's annual designed capacity. Notwithstanding this minimum price, Sun has agreed to pay BEF a price during the first three years of the offtake agreement that approximates prices in current MTBE long-term sales agreements in the marketplace. This price is expected to exceed the minimum price required by the loan agreement. Sun will negotiate a new pricing arrangement with BEF for the remaining years the take-or-pay agreement is in effect, which will be based upon the expected market conditions existing at the time.

Required (Part C)

How should Sun account for this transaction?

6.3 ACCOUNTING FOR A LEASE BY THE LESSOR AND THE LESSEE. Delta Airlines needs to acquire computer equipment from Hewlett-Packard (HP) as of January 1, Year 4. Delta can borrow the necessary funds to purchase the computer for $2 million. Delta, however, wants to keep debt off its balance sheet and instead structures an operating lease with HP. The computer has an estimated life to HP of eight years. Delta will lease the computer for five years, at which time the computer reverts to HP. The cost to HP to manufacture the computer is $1.6 million. Delta's borrowing rate for five-year, secured financing is 10 percent.

Required

    a. Assume that Delta must make rental payments on December 31 of Year 4 through December 31 of Year 8. What is the maximum annual rental (to the nearest dollar) that Delta can make and still permit this lease to qualify as an operating lease?

    b. Assume that Delta must make rental payments on January 1, Year 4, through January 1, Year 8. What is the maximum annual rental (to the nearest dollar) that Delta can make and still permit this lease to qualify as an operating lease?

    c. Assume for the remaining parts of this problem that Delta will make annual payments of $527,595 on December 31, Year 4, through December 31, Year 8. Indicate the nature and amount of revenues and expenses (excluding income taxes) each company would report for each of the Years 4 through 8, assuming that each company accounts for the lease as an operating lease.

    d. Repeat part c assuming each company accounts for the lease as a capital lease.

    e. Assume that these firms treat the lease as a capital lease for financial reporting and an operating lease for tax reporting. Compute the amount of deferred tax asset or deferred tax liability each firm would report related to the lease on December 31, Year 4, through December 31, Year 8. The income tax rate is 35 percent.

6.4 ACCOUNTING FOR CAPITAL LEASES. Wal-Mart leases most of its office, warehouse, and retail space under a combination of capital and operating leases. The disclosures related to *capital leases* for its fiscal year ending January 31, Year 11, appear below (amounts in millions):

	January 31	
	Year 10	**Year 11**
Property, Plant, and Equipment under Capital Leases	$2,476	$2,782
Less Accumulated Depreciation	(680)	(791)
Net Property, Plant, and Equipment under Capital Leases	$1,796	$1,991
Capitalized Lease Obligation	$2,092	$2,307

Fully depreciated leased assets originally capitalized for $38 million were written off during fiscal Year 11. The weighted average discount rate used to compute the present value of the capitalized lease obligation is 11 percent. Assume that new leases capitalized and lease payments occur evenly throughout the year.

Required

    a. Prepare an analysis that explains the change in the accounts below during the Year 11 fiscal year.

        (1) Property, Plant, and Equipment under Capital Leases

        (2) Accumulated Depreciation

        (3) Capitalized Lease Obligation

    b. Assume that Wal-Mart treats these capitalized leases as operating leases for income tax purposes. The income tax rate is 35 percent. Compute the total amount of pretax expenses related to these leased assets for financial and tax reporting for the Year 11 fiscal year.

    c. Compute the amount of deferred tax asset and/or deferred tax liability that Wal-Mart would report on its January 31, Year 11, balance sheet related to these leases.

6.5 **EFFECT OF CAPITALIZING OPERATING LEASES ON BALANCE SHEET RATIOS.** Some retailing companies own their own stores or acquire their premises under capital leases. Other retailers acquire the use of store facilities under operating leases, contracting to make future payments. An analyst comparing the capital structure risks of retailing companies may wish to make adjustments to reported financial statement data to put all firms on a comparable basis.

    Certain data from the financial statements of The Gap and The Limited appear below (amounts in millions):

	The Gap	**Limited**
Balance Sheet as of End of Year 3		
Current Liabilities	$ 462	$ 707
Long-Term Debt	75	650
Other Noncurrent Liabilities	99	336
Shareholders' Equity	1,127	2,442
Total	$1,763	$4,135

(continued)

	The Gap	Limited
Minimum Payments Under Operating Leases		
Year 4	$ 233	$ 568
Year 5	235	559
Year 6	234	542
Year 7	227	523
Year 8	218	504
After Year 8	2,231	2,695
Total	$3,378	$5,391

Required

a. Compute the present value of operating lease obligations using a 10 percent discount rate for The Gap and The Limited at the end of Year 3. Assume that all cash flows occur at the end of each year.

b. Compute each of the following ratios for The Gap and The Limited as of the end of Year 3 using the amounts as originally reported in their balance sheets for the year.

$$\text{Liabilities to Assets Ratio} = \text{Total Liabilities/Total Assets}$$

$$\text{Long-Term Debt Ratio} = \text{Long-Term Debt} /$$
$$(\text{Long-Term Debt} + \text{Shareholders' Equity})$$

c. Repeat part b but assume that these firms capitalize operating leases.

d. Comment on the results from parts b. and c.

6.6 FINANCIAL STATEMENT EFFECTS OF CAPITAL AND OPERATING LEASES. Delta Airlines leases aircraft used in its operations. Information taken from its financial statements and notes for Year 8 and Year 9 appears below (amounts in millions).

Balance Sheet	June 30, Year 8	June 30, Year 9
Property Rights under Capital Leases (net of accumulated depreciation) ...	$388	$347
Capitalized Lease Obligation	$322	$240

NOTES TO THE FINANCIAL STATEMENTS

Leases: Minimum lease payments under *capital leases* as of June 30, Year 8 and Year 9, are (assume all cash flows occur at the end of each year):

	June 30, Year 8	**June 30, Year 9**
Lease Payments on June 30 of		
Year 9	$ 105	—
Year 10	101	$ 101
Year 11	100	100
Year 12	68	68
Year 13	57	57
After Year 13	152	152
Total	$ 583	$478
Less Discount	(159)	(94)
Present Value	$ 424	$ 384

Minimum lease payments under *operating leases* as of June 30, Year 3 and Year 4, appear below:

	June 30, Year 8	**June 30, Year 9**
Lease Payment on June 30 of		
Year 9	$ 817	—
Year 10	816	$ 860
Year 11	830	860
Year 12	831	840
Year 13	819	830
After Year 13	10,086	10,643
Total	$14,199	$14,033

a. Complete the analyses below relating to capital leases for Year 9:

Property Rights under Capital Leases, June 30, Year 8 ....
New Capital Leases Entered into During Year 9 ....
Amortization of Property Rights for Year 9 ....   ———
Property Rights under Capital Leases, June 30, Year 9 ....   ═══

Capitalized Lease Obligation, June 30, Year 8 ....
Increase in Capitalized Lease Obligation for Interest During Year 9 ....
New Capitalized Lease Obligations Entered into During Year 9 ....
Cash Payments under Capital Leases During Year 9 ....
Capitalized Lease Obligation, June 30, Year 9 ....

   b. Compute the average interest rate for leases capitalized as of June 30, Year 9.
   c. Determine the amount that Delta would have reported as rent expense for Year 9 if it had treated all capital leases as operating leases.
   d. Determine the amount reported as rent expense for Year 9 for all operating leases.
   e. Compute the present value of commitments under operating leases on June 30, Year 8 and Year 9, assuming that 10 percent is an appropriate discount rate.
   f. Assume that Delta had capitalized all operating leases using the amounts computed in part e. Complete the analyses below for Year 9:

Capitalized Value of Operating Leases, June 30, Year 8	
Increase in Capitalized Value for Interest During Year 9	
New Operating Leases Capitalized During Year 9	
Cash Payments under Capitalized Operating Leases During Year 9.	_____
Capitalized Value of Operating Leases, June 30, Year 9	=========

   g. Delta Airlines treats *all* its leases as operating leases for tax purposes. The income tax rate is 35 percent, and Delta expects this rate to continue into the foreseeable future. Compute the amount of deferred tax asset or liability that Delta Airlines will recognize at the end of Year 8 and the end of Year 9. Indicate whether the change in the deferred tax asset or liability during Year 9 increases or decreases income tax expense for the year.

6.7   ANALYZING PENSION BENEFIT DISCLOSURES. Deere & Company discloses the information below with respect to its health care obligation (amounts in millions):

Components of Health Care Cost	Year 7	Year 8
Service Cost	$ 55	$ 61
Interest Cost	122	135
Return on Assets:		
Actual	(30)	(37)
Deferred	15	17
Net Amortization	(40)	(23)
Net Health Care Cost	$ 122	$ 153

	October 31	
	Year 7	**Year 8**
Accumulated Health Care Benefits Obligation	$(1,761)	$(1,870)
Plan Assets at Fair Value	192	271
Accumulated Health Care Benefits Obligation in Excess of Plan Assets	$(1,569)	$(1,599)
Unrecognized Net Loss	143	108
Unrecognized Prior Service Credit	(91)	(30)
Health Care Benefits Liability Recognized in Consolidated Balance Sheet	$(1,517)	$(1,521)

	October 31	
	Year 7	**Year 8**
Expected Long-Term Rate of Return on Assets	9.7%	9.7%
Discount Rate for Obligation	7.75%	7.75%
Health Care Cost Inflation Rate:		
Initial Year	9.1%	9.2%
Steady State	4.5%	4.5%

An increase of one percentage point in the assumed health care inflation rate would increase the accumulated health care benefits obligation by $213 million and the net health care cost for the year by $26 million.

Required

  a. Complete the analysis below (description and amounts) to explain the reasons for the changes in the assets and the obligations of the health care benefits fund for fiscal Year 8.

Assets, October 31, Year 7	$ 192
Assets, October 31, Year 8	$ 271
Obligation, October 31, Year 7	$1,761
Obligation, October 31, Year 8	$1,870

  b. What is the likely reason for the actuarial gain or loss related to the accumulated health care benefits obligation during fiscal Year 8? Explain your answer.

  c. What is the likely reason that Deere reports a prior service credit instead of a prior service cost?

  d. Complete the analysis below (description and amounts) to explain the reasons for the changes in the unrecognized net loss and the unrecognized prior service credit during fiscal Year 8 to the maximum extent permitted by the given disclosures.

Unrecognized Net Loss, October 31, Year 7	$143
Unrecognized Net Loss, October 31, Year 8	$108
Unrecognized Prior Service Credit, October 31, Year 7	$ (91)
Unrecognized Prior Service Credit, October 31, Year 8	$ (30)

  e. Give the appropriate entry that the financial analysts would make to recognize any underfunded health care benefits obligation on October 31, Year 8. The income tax rate is 35 percent.

6.8　ANALYZING PENSION DISCLOSURES. Westinghouse Corporation changed its name to CBS in Year 5 after it sold several major defense and electronic businesses the previous year in order to concentrate on the communications industry. The note on pensions for CBS for Year 4 appears in Exhibit 6.16. CBS uses a 7.75 percent discount rate and a 6 percent rate of increase in future compensation levels to compute the projected benefits obligation, and an 11 percent expected long-term rate of return on assets for Year 4. In Year 3, CBS uses a 6.75 percent discount rate. CBS contributed $160 million to its pension fund during Year 4. The income tax rate was 35 percent.

EXHIBIT 6.16

CBS
Pension Disclosures
(amounts in millions)
(Problem 6.8)

	Year 2	Year 3	Year 4
Net Periodic Cost			
Service Cost	$ 79	$ 53	$ 70
Interest Cost	404	391	371
Amortization of:			
Unrecognized Net Obligation	36	35	25
Unrecognized Prior Service Cost	6	(11)	(7)
Unrecognized Net Loss	112	68	108
	$ 637	$ 536	$ 567
Return on Plan Assets:			
Actual Return	$ (18)	$(584)	$ (437)
Unrecognized Return on Plan Assets . .	(385)	245	90
Deferred Gain (Loss)	$(403)	$(339)	$ (347)
Net Periodic Pension Cost	$ 234	$ 197	$ 220

	Year 3	Year 4
Funded Status of Pension Plan		
Accumulated Benefit Obligation	$ 5,864	$ 4,880
Effect of Projected Compensation Levels	383	314
Projected Benefit Obligation	$ 6,247	$ 5,194
Plan Assets at Fair Value	(4,137)	(3,930)
Projected Benefits Obligation in		
Excess of Plan Assets	$ 2,110	$ 1,264
Unrecognized Transition Obligation	(161)	(117)
Unrecognized Prior Service Cost	(95)	(77)
Unrecognized Net Loss	(2,110)	(1,402)
Adjustment to Recognize Minimum Liability	2,080	1,421
Accrued Pension (Asset) Liability on Balance Sheet . . .	$ 1,824	$ 1,089

a. Complete the analysis below of changes in pension fund assets during Year 4.

Pension Fund Assets, Beginning of Year 4 ....

Plus Earnings on Pension Fund Investments during Year 4 ....

Plus Contributions Received from CBS during Year 4 ....

Less Pension Payments to Retirees during Year 4 ....   _____

Pension Fund Assets, End of Year 4 ....   ========

---

b. Complete the analysis below of changes in the projected benefits obligation of the pension plan during Year 4.

Projected Benefits Obligation, Beginning of Year 4 ....

Plus Service Cost for Year 4 ....

Plus Interest Cost for Year 4 ....

Less Pension Payments to Retirees during Year 4 ....

Plus (Minus) Actuarial Losses (Gains) during Year 4 ....   _____

Projected Benefits Obligation, End of Year 4 ....   ========

---

c. Complete the analysis below of changes in the unrecognized net loss during Year 4.

Unrecognized Net Loss, Beginning of Year 4 ....

Plus (Minus) Actuarial (Gain) Loss during Year 4 ....

Plus (Minus) Unrecognized Deficient (Excess) Returns on
  Plan Assets during Year 4 ....

Less Amortization of Unrecognized Net Loss during Year 4 ....   _____

Unrecognized Net Loss, End of Year 4 ....   ========

---

d. Did CBS sweeten its pension plan during Year 4 and make the benefits retroactive? Explain.

e. What are possible explanations for the decrease in the unrecognized net loss from $2,110 million at the end of Year 3 to $1,402 million at the end of Year 4?

f. Suggest reasons for the decrease in the accumulated benefits obligations during Year 4.

g. Give the journal entry that you would make as an analyst to recognize the underfunded projected benefits obligation at the end of Year 3. The income tax rate is 35 percent.

h. Repeat part g for Year 4.

6.9 **INTERPRETING PENSION DISCLOSURES.** Exhibit 6.17 reveals information with respect to the pension plan of Chrysler Corporation. Chrysler contributed $1,153 million to its pension fund during Year 11, $838 million in Year 10, and $2,600 million in Year 9.

 a. Complete the analyses below of changes in pension fund assets during Year 11.

Pension Fund Assets, Beginning of Year 11 . . . .

Plus Earnings on Pension Fund Investments . . . .

Plus Contributions Received from Chrysler . . . .

Less Pension Payments to Retirees . . . . _____

Pension Fund Assets, End of Year 11 . . . . _____

EXHIBIT 6.17

Chrysler Corporation
Pension Disclosures
(amounts in millions)
(Problem 6.9)

	Year 10	Year 11
Components of Pension Expense		
Service Cost.	$ 253	$ 334
Interest Cost	993	1,014
Return on Plan Assets:		
Actual Return.	(2,740)	(2,202)
Deferred Gain.	1532	826
Expected Return on Plan Assets.	(1,208)	(1,376)
Net Amortization	367	585
Total	$ 405	$ 557
Actuarial Assumptions		
Discount Rate	7.00%	7.25%
Rate of Increase in Compensation	6.00%	6.00%
Long-Term Rate of Return on Plan Assets	10.00%	10.00%
Funded Status of Pension Plan		
Accumulated Benefit Obligation	$13,886	$15,143
Effect of Salary Increases.	275	344
Projected Benefit Obligation	$14,161	$15,487
Plan Assets at Market Value.	14,657	16,867
PBO Less than Plan Assets	$ 496	$ 1,380
Unrecognized Net Loss	1,855	1,022
Unrecognized Prior Service Cost	1,484	2,173
Unamortized Net Obligation at Date of Adoption.	864	720
Adjustment to Recognize Minimum Liability	(115)	(200)
Net Prepaid Pension Asset on Balance Sheet.	$ 4,584	$ 5,095

b. Complete the analyses below of changes in the projected benefits obligation during Year 11.

Projected Benefits Obligation, Beginning of Year 11 . . . .
Plus Service Cost for Year 11 . . . .
Plus Interest Cost for Year 11 . . . .
Minus Pension Payments to Retirees for Year 11 . . . .
Plus (Minus) Actuarial Loss (Gain) for Year 11 . . . .   _____
Projected Benefits Obligation, End of Year 11 . . . .   ========

c. Complete the analyses below of changes in the unrecognized net loss, unrecognized prior service cost, and unamortized net obligation at date of adoption.

Unrecognized Net Loss, Prior Service Cost, and Net
   Obligation at Beginning of Year 11 . . . .
Plus (Minus) Actuarial Loss (Gain) for Year 11 . . . .
Plus (Minus) Deferred Loss (Gain) from Pension Fund
   Investments for Year 11 . . . .
Minus Net Amortization for Year 11 Included in Pension Expense . . . . .   _____
Unrecognized Net Loss, Prior Service Cost, and Net Obligation
   at End of Year 11 . . . .   ========

d. Prepare an analysis that explains the change in the net prepaid pension asset on the balance sheet of Chrysler between the beginning and end of Year 11.
e. What is the likely reason for the increase in pension expense between Year 10 and Year 11?
f. What is the likely reason for the change in the unrecognized net loss between Year 10 and Year 11?
g. What is the likely reason for the change in the unrecognized prior service cost between Year 10 and Year 11?

6.10 INTERPRETING POSTRETIREMENT BENEFITS DISCLOSURES. The notes to the financial statements of Chrysler Corporation reveal the information below with respect to its postretirement benefits plan (amounts in millions):

	Year 11
Components of Postretirement Benefits Expense	
Benefits Attributed to Employees' Service	$191
Interest on Accumulated Postretirement Benefits Obligation	666
Total	$857

	Year 10	Year 11
Discount Rate	7.0%	7.3%
Average Health Care Inflation Rate	7.0%	7.5%
Accumulated Postretirement Benefits Obligation	$ 9,832	$9,921
Assets in Postretirement Benefits Fund	—	—
Net Obligation	$ 9,832	$9,921
Unrecognized Net Loss	(1,107)	(796)
Postretirement Benefits Obligation Recognized in Balance Sheet	$ 8,725	$9,125

a. Give the journal entry that Chrysler made to recognize postretirement benefits expense and funding during Year 11. Be sure to consider any deferred tax effect.
b. What is the likely reason for the decrease in the unrecognized net loss during year 11?
c. Why does Chrysler not include in postretirement benefits expense for Year 11 a reduction for the expected return on assets?
d. Give the journal entry that the analyst would make at the end of Year 11 to recognize any unrecognized postretirement benefits obligations.

6.11 INTERPRETING INCOME TAX DISCLOSURES. Exhibit 6.18 presents information from the income tax note of Borden, Inc. for Year 5.
a. Was taxable income greater or less than book income before taxes for Year 4? Explain.
b. Was taxable income greater or less than book income before taxes for Year 5? Explain.
c. Compute the amount of state and local income tax expense (credit) for Year 5.
d. What is the likely reason that amounts for restructuring programs appear in both the income tax reconciliation and in deferred tax assets?
e. Was postemployment benefits expense (other than pensions) greater or less than the contribution to this benefits fund during Year 5? Explain.
f. Depreciation expense for financial reporting was $224 million during Year 5. Compute the amount of depreciation expense for tax reporting.
g. Has Borden funded its pension plan faster or slower than it has recognized pension expense? Explain.

6.12 ANALYZING INCOME TAX DISCLOSURES. Exhibit 6.19 presents information from the income tax notes of TRW, Inc. for Year 6.
a. Give the journal entry to record income tax expense for Year 5.
b. Was taxable income greater or less than book income before income taxes for Year 5? Explain.
c. Why is there a positive amount for income tax expense for Year 5 if earnings before income taxes are negative for the year?
d. Give the journal entry to record income tax expense for Year 6.
e. Was taxable income greater or less than book income before income taxes for Year 6? Explain.
f. Why do restructuring charges appear in both the income tax reconciliation and in deferred tax assets?
g. What is the likely reason for the change in the deferred tax asset for postretirement benefits other than pensions?
h. What is the likely reason for the change in deferred taxes related to pensions from a deferred tax asset at the end of Year 4 to a deferred tax liability at the end of Year 5?

EXHIBIT 6.18

Income Tax Disclosures for Borden, Inc.
(amounts in million)
(Problem 6.11)

	Year 4	Year 5
Income Tax Expense		
Current	$ 58.8	$ (1.9)
Deferred	(89.7)	(208.9)
Income Tax Expense (credit)	$(30.9)	$(210.8)
Income Tax Reconciliation		
Income Taxes at Statutory Rate of 35%	$(52.8)	$(280.0)
State and Local Taxes (net of Federal tax benefit)	(2.2)	(22.6)
Foreign Tax Differentials	1.7	.1
Capital Loss Benefit	(17.9)	—
Restructuring Programs	40.0	4.3
Loss on Disposal of Discontinued Operation	—	81.3
Other—net	.3	6.1
Income Tax Expense (credit)	$(30.9)	$(210.8)
Component of Deferred Tax Assets		
Post-Employment Benefits Other than Pensions	118.4	131.7
Restructuring Programs	113.8	140.1
Loss Carryforwards	42.9	108.6
Divestiture Reserve	—	147.4
Other	95.7	130.7
	370.8	658.5
Valuation Reserve	(42.9)	(58.7)
Deferred Tax Asset	$327.9	$ 599.8
Components of Deferred Tax Liabilities		
Property Plant and Equipment	$212.5	$ 236.5
Pension Contributions	22.9	26.5
Deferred Charges	50.8	52.4
Other	67.2	62.1
Deferred Tax Liability	$353.4	$ 377.5

i. What is the likely reason for the valuation allowance related to deferred tax assets?

j. What is the likely explanation for the behavior of the deferred tax liability related to depreciation?

6.13 ANALYZING INCOME TAX DISCLOSURES. Exhibit 6.20 presents income tax disclosures for Sun Company for Year 16 and Year 17.

a. Give the journal entry to record the provision for income taxes for Year 16. Use a single deferred tax asset or deferred tax liability account.

EXHIBIT 6.19

Income Tax Disclosures for TRW, Inc.
(amounts in millions)
(Problem 6.12)

	Year 4	Year 5	Year 6
Earnings Before Income Taxes			
U.S.	$ 178	$(156)	$ 213
Non-U.S.	165	27	135
	$ 343	$(129)	$ 348
Provision for Income Taxes			
Current: U.S.	$ 97	$ 25	$ 81
Non-U.S.	75	39	59
Deferred: U.S.	(44)	(39)	11
Non-U.S.	7	(14)	3
	$ 135	$ 11	$ 154
Effective Tax Rate Reconciliation			
U.S. Statutory Tax Rate	35.0%	(35.0%)	35.0%
U.S. State and Local Taxes	4.2	.3	3.6
Non-U.S. Tax Rate Variances	3.0	14.9	4.2
Losses on Restructuring Without Income Tax Benefit	—	23.1	3.6
Other	(2.8)	4.9	(2.1)
Effective Income Tax Rate	39.4%	8.2%	44.3%
Components of Deferred Taxes			
Deferred Tax Assets:			
Post Retirement Benefits Other than Pensions	—	$ 232	$ 244
Restructuring Charges	$ 50	121	124
Pensions	115	—	—
Non-U.S. Net Operating Loss Carryforwards	—	30	36
Valuation Allowance	—	(30)	(36)
Total	$ 165	$ 353	$ 368
Deferred Tax Liabilities:			
Depreciation	$ 351	$ 431	$ 470
Pensions	—	55	45
Total	$ 351	$ 486	$ 515

EXHIBIT 6.20

Income Tax Disclosures for Sun Company
(amounts in millions)
(Problem 6.13)

	Year 16	Year 17
Components of Income Before Taxes		
U.S.	$ (79)	$ 184
Foreign	199	135
Total	$ 120	$ 319

	Year 16	Year 13
Income Tax Expense (Credit)		
Current:		
U.S.	$ 17	$ (3)
Foreign	66	34
Total Current	$ 83	$ 31
Deferred:		
U.S.	$ (86)	$ 53
Foreign	26	8
Total Deferred	$ (60)	$ 61
Total Income Tax Expense	$ 23	$ 92

	December 31	
	Year 16	Year 17
Components of Deferred Taxes		
Deferred Tax Assets:		
Retirement Benefit Obligations	$ 166	$ 165
Estimated Expenses Not Yet Deductible	272	306
Tax Loss Carryforwards	90	29
Restructuring Charges	113	37
Other	96	93
Valuation Allowance	(106)	(101)
Total Deferred Tax Assets	$ 631	$ 529
Deferred Tax Liabilities:		
Depreciation and Depletion	$(711)	$(694)
Investment in Foreign Subsidiaries	(27)	(12)
Other	(71)	(62)
Total Deferred Tax Liabilities	$(809)	$(768)
Net Deferred Tax Asset (Liability)	$(178)	$(239)

(continued)

| | December 31 | |
Exh. 6.20—Continued	Year 16	Year 17
Tax Rate Reconciliation		
Income Taxes at U.S. Statutory Rate	$ 42	$ 112
Foreign Tax Rates in Excess of (less than) U.S. Tax Rate ..	13	4
Benefits of Nonconventional Fuels Credit	(18)	(8)
Other	(14)	(16)
Income Tax Provision	$ 23	$ 92

b. What is the relation between the amount of income before taxes for financial report-ing and taxable income for Year 16? Explain.

c. Give the journal entry to record the provision for income taxes for Year 17. Use separate deferred tax asset and deferred tax liability accounts.

d. What is the relation between the amount of income before taxes for financial report-ing and taxable income for Year 17? Explain.

e. What is the likely event that gave rise to the deferred tax asset for retirement benefits obligations?

f. Why do restructuring charges give rise to a deferred tax asset?

g. What does the decrease in the deferred tax liability for depreciation and depletion suggest about Sun's capital expenditures?

CASE 6.1

AMERICAN AIRLINES AND UNITED AIRLINES: A PENSION FOR DEBT

American Airlines and United Airlines maintain dominant market positions in the airline market in the United States. Airlines carry heavy investments in fixed assets. Their high pro-portions of fixed operating costs provide potential benefits and risks of economies and disec-onomies of scale.

Airlines rely heavily on debt financing for their fixed asset investments. The financing may take the form of borrowing to purchase fixed assets or leasing under a capital lease arrangement. Airlines have turned increasingly in recent years to operating leases as a means to keep debt off their balance sheets. The fixed costs of servicing on-balance sheet debt and off-balance sheet leasing commitments add to the potential scale economies and diseconomies.

Most airlines are unionized and provide pension, health care, and other postretirement benefits to employees. The obligations under various benefits plans are not fully reflected in liabilities on the balance sheet.

An effective analysis of the risk of airlines requires consideration of the effects of both commitments under operating leases and underfunded retirement benefits obligations. This case analyzes the disclosures of American and United with respect to leases, pensions, and health care benefits.

Data for American and United appear in the exhibits:
Exhibit 6.21: Balance sheet data.
Exhibit 6.22: Income and cash flow data.
Exhibit 6.23: Capital and operating lease data.
Exhibit 6.24: Pension data.
Exhibit 6.25: Postretirement benefits data.

EXHIBIT 6.21

Balance Sheet Data for American Airlines and United Airlines
(amounts in millions)
(Case 6.1)

	American		United	
	December 31		December 31	
	Year 5	Year 6	Year 5	Year 6
Assets				
Current Assets	$ 3,137	$ 4,470	$ 3,043	$ 2,682
Property, Plant and Equipment:				
Cost	$17,600	$17,205	$11,213	$12,325
Accumulated Depreciation	(5,784)	(6,072)	(5,153)	(5,380)
Net	$11,816	$11,133	$ 6,060	$ 6,945
Property, Plant, and Equipment under Capital Leases:				
Cost	$ 2,624	$ 3,143	$ 1,464	$ 1,881
Accumulated Depreciation	(875)	(971)	(503)	(583)
Net	$ 1,749	$ 2,172	$ 961	$ 1,298
Other Assets	$ 2,854	$ 2,722	$ 1,577	$ 1,752
Total Assets	$19,556	$20,497	$11,641	$12,677
Liabilities and Shareholders' Equity				
Current Operating Liabilities	$ 4,282	$ 4,665	$ 4,244	$ 4,706
Current Maturities of Long-Term Debt	228	424	90	165
Current Maturities of Capital Leases	122	130	99	132
Total Current Liabilities	$ 4,632	$ 5,219	$ 4,433	$ 5,003
Long-Term Debt	4,983	2,752	2,919	1,661
Capital Leases	2,069	2,507	994	1,325
Other Noncurrent Liabilities	4,152	4,351	3,415	3,497
Total Liabilities	$15,836	$14,829	$11,761	$11,486
Preferred Stock	$ 78	—	$ 60	$ 165
Common Stock	2,224	$ 3,234	1,412	2,192
Retained Earnings	1,418	2,434	(1,039)	(566)
Other Equity Adjustments	—	—	(271)	(215)
Treasury Stock	—	—	(282)	(385)
Total Shareholders' Equity	$ 3,720	$ 5,668	$ (120)	$ 1,191
Total Liabilities and Shareholders' Equity	$19,556	$20,497	$11,641	$12,677

EXHIBIT 6.22

Income and Cash Flow Data for American Airlines and United Airlines
(amounts in millions)
(Case 6.1)

	American		United	
	Year 5	Year 6	Year 5	Year 6
Operating Revenues	$ 16,910	$ 17,753	$14,943	$ 16,362
Operating Expenses	(15,895)	(15,914)	(14,114)	(15,239)
Operating Income	$ 1,015	$ 1,839	$ 829	$ 1,123
Interest Expense	(670)	(499)	(399)	(295)
Other Income (Expense)	8	293	191	142
Income Before Taxes	$ 353	$ 1,633	$ 621	$ 970
Income Taxes	(162)	(528)	(243)	(370)
Net Income	$ 191	$ 1,105	$ 378	$ 600
Cash Flow from:				
Operations	$ 2,180	$ 2,716	$ 1,624	$ 2,453
Investing	(925)	(1,214)	(478)	(983)
Financing	(1,196)	(1,516)	(1,452)	(1,435)
Change in Cash	$ 59	$ (14)	$ (306)	$ 35
Capital Lease Obligations				
Incurred		$ 519		$ 417
Rent Expense	$ 1,300	$ 1,200	$ 1,439	$ 1,424

EXHIBIT 6.23

Capital and Operating Lease Data for American Airlines and United Airlines
(amounts in millions)
(Case 6.1)

| | American | | United | |
	Year 5	Year 6	Year 5	Year 6
Commitments Under Capital Leases				
Payable In:				
Year 6	$ 248	—	$ 182	—
Year 7	273	$ 357	180	$ 233
Year 8	268	350	183	236
Year 9	263	343	158	210
Year 10	328	433	136	186
Year 11	*	408	*	261
Subsequent	1,954	2,032	835	1,036
Total	$ 3,334	$ 3,923	$ 1,674	$ 2,162
Less Imputed Interest	(1,143)	(1,286)	(581)	(705)
	$ 2,191	$ 2,637	$ 1,093	$ 1,457
Current Portion	(122)	(130)	(99)	(132)
Long-Term Portion	$ 2,069	$ 2,507	$ 994	$ 1,325
Commitments Under Operating Leases				
Payable In:				
Year 6	$ 879	—	$ 1,291	—
Year 7	919	$ 992	1,274	1,416
Year 8	926	987	1,272	1,405
Year 9	918	974	1,269	1,386
Year 10	874	924	1,275	1,392
Year 11	*	919	*	1,398
Subsequent	14,402	14,122	20,342	21,274
Total	$18,918	$18,918	$26,723	$28,271

*Amount included on next line.

EXHIBIT 6.24

Pension Data for American Airlines and United Airlines
(amounts in millions)
(Case 6.1)

	American		United	
	Year 5	**Year 6**	**Year 5**	**Year 6**
Net Periodic Pension Cost				
Service Cost	$ 165	$ 204	$ 173	$ 237
Interest Cost	323	375	396	440
Actual (Return) Loss on Plan Assets .	(1,288)	(91)	(934)	(703)
Net Amortization and Deferral	1,008	(322)	545	268
Total	$ 208	$ 166	$ 180	$ 242
	December 31		**December 31**	
	Year 5	**Year 6**	**Year 5**	**Year 6**
Status of Pension Plan				
Accumulated Benefit Obligation	$4,325	$4,392	$5,309	$5,579
Effect of Salary Increases	748	852	465	568
Projected Benefit Obligation	$5,073	$5,244	$5,774	$6,147
Plan Assets at Fair Value	(4,551)	(4,617)	(4,947)	(5,910)
Underfunded Projected Benefit Obligation	$ 522	$ 627	$ 827	$ 237
Unrecognized Net Loss	(722)	(966)	(356)	(68)
Unrecognized Prior Service Cost	(23)	(66)	(482)	(446)
Unrecognized Transition Asset (Loss)	46	32	(15)	(21)
Adjustment for Minimum Liability ..	12	69	400	86
Prepaid Pension Cost	$ (165)	$ (304)	—	$ (212)
Accrued Pension Liability	—	—	$ 374	
Actuarial Assumptions				
Expected Return on Assets	9.50%	9.50%	9.75%	9.75%
Discount Rate	7.25%	7.75%	7.25%	7.75%
Salary Inflation	4.20%	4.20%	3.15%	3.15%

EXHIBIT 6.25

Postretirement Benefits Data for American Airlines and United Airlines
(amounts in millions)
(Case 6.1)

	American		United	
	Year 5	**Year 6**	**Year 5**	**Year 6**
Net Postretirement Benefits Cost				
Service Cost	$ 48	$ 58	$ 37	$ 44
Interest Cost	101	102	100	98
(Return) Loss on Assets	(2)	(3)	(7)	(7)
Net Amortization and Deferral	(6)	(5)	(5)	(5)
Total	$ 141	$ 152	$ 125	$ 130
	December 31		**December 31**	
	Year 5	**Year 6**	**Year 5**	**Year 6**
Status of Postretirement Benefit Plan				
Accumulated Postretirement Benefits Obligation	$1,435	$1,213	$1,422	$1,339
Plan Assets at Fair Value	(28)	(39)	(99)	(103)
Underfunded Postretirements Benefits Obligation	$1,407	$1,174	$1,323	$1,236
Unrecognized Prior Service Benefit . . .	61	56	—	—
Unrecognized Net Gain (Loss)	(29)	300	(54)	109
Accrued Postretirement Benefits Obligation	$1,439	$1,530	$1,269	$1,345
Actuarial Assumptions				
Discount Rate	7.25%	7.75%	7.25%	7.75%
Health Care Inflation Rate:				
Initial Year	8.00%	6.00%	8.50%	7.40%
Steady State	4.00%	4.00%	4.00%	4.00%

PART A: CAPITAL LEASES

a. Complete the analyses below of changes in the capitalized lease assets and capitalized lease obligation of American for Year 6.

Capitalized Lease Assets (net), December 31, Year 5. . . . .
Plus New Leases Capitalized during Year 6 . . . .
Less Depreciation Recognized for Year 6 . . . .   _____
Capitalized Lease Assets (Net), December 31, Year 6 . . . .   _____

Capitalized Lease Liability, December 31, Year 5* . . . .
Plus Interest on Lease Liability for Year 6 . . . .
Plus New Leases Capitalized During Year 6. . . . .
Less Cash Payments Made on Capital Leases during Year 6 . . . .   _____
Capitalized Lease Liability, December 31, Year 6 . . . .   _____

---

*Be sure to include current and noncurrent portions.

b. Repeat part a, for United for Year 6.

PART B: OPERATING LEASES

a. Assume for this part that 8 percent is the appropriate interest rate to capitalize the operating lease commitments of American and United. Also assume that all lease payments occur at the end of each year. Compute the present value of the operating lease commitments of each airline as of December 31, Year 5 and Year 6.

b. Compare the total expenses for operating leases for Year 6 assuming that American and United account for these leases as operating leases (that is, as reported) and not as capital leases.

c. Compute the long-term debt ratio [Long-Term Debt/(Long-Term Debt + Shareholders' Equity)] as of December 31, Year 6, with and without capitalization of operating leases. Assume no change in retained earnings as a result of capitalizing operating leases.

PART C: PENSION OBLIGATIONS

a. Prepare an analysis that accounts for the change in pension fund assets and the projected benefits obligation during Year 6 for each airline's pension fund using the format as follows:

Pension Fund Assets
Balance, December 31, Year 5 . . . .
Plus Return on Pension Investments during Year 6 . . . .
Plus Contributions Received from the Employer during Year 6 . . . .
Less Payments to Retirees during Year 6 . . . .   _____
Balance, December 31, Year 6 . . . .   _____

Projected Benefit Obligation
Balance, December 31, Year 5. . . . .
Plus Service Cost for Year 6. . . . .
Plus Interest Cost for Year 6 . . . .
Less Payments to Retirees during Year 6 . . . .
Plus or Minus Actuarial Gains or Losses for Year 6 . . . .   ———
Balance, December 31, Year 6. . . . ., ...   ═══

b. Evaluate the investment performance of each airline's pension fund during Year 6.
c. Present the journal entry that the analyst would make to recognize the net underfunded projected benefit obligation of each airline as of December 31, Year 6. The income tax rate is 35 percent.

PART D: POSTRETIREMENT BENEFITS OTHER THAN PENSIONS

a. Repeat part a above relating to pensions for the postretirement benefits obligation (other than pensions) for American and United.
b. Give the journal entry that the analyst would make to recognize the underfunded, unrecognized liability for postretirement benefits other than pensions as of December 31, Year 6.

PART E: SYNTHESIS

a. Compute the long-term debt ratio [Long-Term Debt/(Long-Term Debt + Shareholders' Equity)] for American and United on December 31, Year 6, based on (1) reported data that include long-term debt, capital leases, and recorded postretirement benefit obligations, and (2) restated data that include operating leases, underfunded pension obligations, and underfunded postretirement benefits obligations.

CASE 6.2

SUN MICROSYSTEMS: A NOT-TOO-TAXING EXPERIENCE

Sun Microsystems designs, manufactures, and sells computer hardware aimed primarily at engineers, architects, and others with sophisticated graphics needs. It also sells software designed to enhance interaction among multiple users on interactive networks. Exhibit 6.26 presents geographical segment data for Sun Microsystems for Year 5, Year 6, and Year 7. Exhibit 6.27 presents information taken from the financial statement note on income taxes.

EXHIBIT 6.26

Sales and Income Mix Data for Sun Microsystems
(amounts in millions)
(Case 6.2)

	Year 5	Year 6	Year 7
Sales:			
Domestic	$3,452	$4,082	$4,736
Foreign	1,238	1,820	2,359
Total	$4,690	$5,902	$7,095
Income Before Income Taxes:			
Domestic	$ 48	$ 249	$ 291
Foreign	235	274	418
Total	$ 283	$ 523	$ 709

Required

a. Give the journal entries to record income tax expense for Year 6 and Year 7.

b. Did income before taxes for financial reporting exceed or fall short of taxable income for Year 6? For Year 7? Explain.

c. Discuss briefly the major factors that cause the relation between income before taxes for financial reporting and taxable income (see part b) to change between Year 6 and Year 7.

d. Prepare a tax reconciliation similar to Exhibit 6.15 in the text. Include a total column (that is, domestic plus foreign) for each year.

e. Analyze the level and changes in the effective tax rate on domestic income between Year 5 and Year 7.

f. Repeat part e for foreign-source income.

g. Compute the pretax and after-tax profit margin for the domestic, foreign, and overall operations of Sun Microsystems for Year 5, Year 6, and Year 7. How does the change in Sun's effective tax rate affect the interpretation of its changing profit margin?

EXHIBIT 6.27

Income Tax Disclosures for Sun Microsystems
(amounts in millions)
(Case 6.2)

	Year 5	Year 6	Year 7
Provision for Income Taxes			
Current			
U.S. Federal	$ 28	$123	$153
State	4	10	16
Foreign	60	57	62
Total Current	$ 92	$190	$231
Deferred			
U.S. Federal	$ (5)	$ (17)	$ (3)
State	5	5	1
Foreign	(4)	(11)	4
Total Deferred	$ (4)	$ (23)	$ (2)
Provision for Income Taxes	$ 88	$167	$233
Components of Deferred Taxes			
Deferred Tax Assets			
Inventory Valuation	$ 41	$ 49	$ 43
Warranty Reserves	48	57	56
Fixed Asset Basis Differences	31	46	50
Compensation Not Currently Deductible	24	35	29
Other	30	14	15
Total Deferred Tax Assets	$174	$196	$193
Deferred Tax Liabilities			
Undistributed Profits of Subsidiaries	$ (22)	$ (24)	$ (20)
Other	(5)	(2)	(5)
Total Deferred Tax Liabilities	$ (27)	$ (26)	$ (25)
Net Deferred Tax Assets	$147	$170	$168
Income Tax Reconciliation			
Expected Tax at 35 percent	$ 99	$183	$248
State Tax, Net of Federal Tax Benefit	6	10	11
Interest on State and Municipal Securities	(6)	(7)	(5)
Utilization of Foreign Losses	(5)	(1)	—
Foreign Earnings Permanently Reinvested	(3)	(21)	(36)
Other	(3)	3	15
Provision for Income Taxes	$ 88	$167	$233

CASE 6.3

CIFRA: REMODELING THE FINANCIAL STATEMENTS

CIFRA, S.A. de C.V. and Subsidiaries (CIFRA) is a leading retailer in Mexico. At the end of Year 8, Year 9, and Year 10, it operated retailing establishments as follows:

	Year 8		Year 9		Year 10	
	No. of Stores	Square Feet	No. of Stores	Square Feet	No. of Stores	Square Feet
Self-Service Stores	38	2,775,508	33	2,253,788	33	2,285,800
Discount Warehouse Stores	29	1,308,127	39	1,821,193	45	2,216,577
Supermarkets ..	34	479,030	35	505,176	37	568,371
Department Stores	29	1,545,771	28	1,501,578	31	1,698,075
Restaurants	78	16,616*	89	18,274*	106	21,818*
Hypermarkets ..	—	—	2	361,832	5	871,819
Membership Clubs	—	—	3	291,704	7	688,788

*Seating capacity.

CIFRA follows an "everyday-low-price" strategy in its stores. The company commenced a major remodeling effort in all its retailing establishments in Year 8. It expects to complete these renovations by the end of Year 11. CIFRA created an account, Fund for Remodeling, which it uses to cover the cost of remodeling. Financial statements for CIFRA for Year 8, Year 9, and Year 10 appear in Exhibit 6.28 (balance sheet), Exhibit 6.29 (statement of earnings), and Exhibit 6.30 (statement of changes in financial position). Selected notes follow these financial statements.

Required

    a. Prepare an analysis of the changes in the Funds for Remodeling account during Year 8, Year 9, and Year 10.
    b. Which of the amounts from part a did CIFRA charge against earnings for each year?
    c. Which amounts (if any) related to remodeling do you think CIFRA should have charged against earnings each year? Explain your reasoning.
    d. What adjustments must be made to the financial statements for Year 8, Year 9, and Year 10 to conform to the accounting suggested in your response to part c?
    e. Suggest reasons why CIFRA chose to account for remodeling costs the way it did.
    f. Using your restated financial statements from part d, assess the profitability and risk of CIFRA for Year 8 through Year 10.

EXHIBIT 6.28

CIFRA, S.A. de C.V. and Subsidiaries
Consolidated Balance Sheet
(in millions of constant December 31, Year 10 Mexican Pesos)
(Case 6.3)

	December 31			
	Year 7	Year 8	Year 9	Year 10
Assets				
Current Assets				
Cash and Short-Term Investments	P 942	P 1,382	P 2,180	P 1,940
Accounts Receivable	144	231	152	234
Inventories	814	804	1,080	1,319
Prepayments	8	15	47	38
Total Current Assets	P 1,908	P 2,432	P 3,459	P 3,531
Property, Plant, and Equipment	P 3,668	P 4,188	P 5,389	P 7,378
Accumulated Depreciation	(930)	(1,013)	(1,079)	(1,298)
Net Property, Plant, and Equipment	P 2,738	P 3,175	P 4,310	P 6,080
Investments in Securities	—	P 69	—	—
Surplus Pension Funds	—	—	—	P 593
Total Assets	P 4,646	P 5,676	P 7,769	P 10,204
Current Liabilities				
Accounts Payable-Trade	P 1,336	P 1,494	P 1,882	P 2,279
Other Accounts Payable	496	570	627	571
Fund for Remodeling (Note 1)	—	111	261	51
Total Current Liabilities	P 1,832	P 2,175	P 2,770	P 2,901
Reserve for Seniority Premiums (Note 2)	—	—	P 21	P 22
Shareholders' Equity				
Capital Stock	P 900	P 900	P 900	P 900
Legal Reserve	201	229	264	264
Retained Earnings	1,469	1,995	2,678	3,726
Surplus on Restatement of Fixed Assets and Capital Stock	410	501	782	1,447
Treasury Stock	(166)	(124)	(38)	(124)
Majority Shareholders' Equity	P 2,814	P 3,501	P 4,586	P 6,213
Minority Shareholders' Equity	—	—	392	1,068
Total Shareholders' Equity	P 2,814	P 3,501	P 4,978	P 7,281
Total Liabilities and Shareholders' Equity	P 4,646	P 5,676	P 7,769	P 10,204

EXHIBIT 6.29

CIFRA, S.A. de C.V. and Subsidiaries
Consolidated Statement of Earnings
(in millions of constant December 31, Year 10 Mexican Pesos)
(Case 6.3)

	Year 8	Year 9	Year 10
Net Sales	P10,287	P 12,417	P 14,231
Cost of Goods Sold	(7,870)	(9,525)	(11,135)
Operating Expenses	(1,859)	(2,154)	(2,306)
Operating Income	P 558	P 738	P 790
Comprehensive Financing Income:			
Financial Income	P 239	P 338	P 324
Gain on Monetary Position	91	42	9
Other Income (Expenses)—Net	16	(39)	(17)
Earnings Before Taxes	P 904	P 1,079	P 1,106
Income Taxes and Employees'			
Statutory Profit Sharing	(250)	(309)	(308)
Earnings Before Special Items	P 654	P 770	P 798
Special Items Net of Applicable Income Taxes			
Net Effect of Bulletin D-3 on			
Labor Obligations (Note 2)	—	—	233
Reversion of Surplus in			
Pension Funds (Note 2)	309	549	—
Fund for Remodeling (Note 1)	(179)	(270)	—
Reserve for Seniority Premiums (Note 2)	—	(21)	—
Net Earnings	P 784	P 1,028	P 1,031
Minority Interest in Earnings	—	(15)	3
Majority Share	P 784	P 1,013	P 1,034

EXHIBIT 6.30

CIFRA, S.A. de C.V. and Subsidiaries
Consolidated Statement of Changes in Financial Position
(in millions of constant December 31, Year 10 Mexican Pesos)
(Case 6.3)

	Year 8	Year 9	Year 10
Net Earnings Before Special Items	P 654	P 770	P 798
Depreciation and Amortization	174	199	237
Other Addbacks	—	—	3
Change in:			
Accounts Receivable	(87)	77	(83)
Inventories	19	(285)	(245)
Prepayments	(8)	(32)	11
Accounts Payable—Trade	158	388	397
Other Accounts Payable	(17)	15	(41)
Resources Provided by Operations	P 893	P 1,132	P 1,077
Reimbursement of Pension Surplus (Note 2)	P 309	P 549	P —
Investment of Minority Shareholders	—	P 446	P 676
Other Investments	P (69)	—	—
Payment of Dividends	(210)	(289)	(323)
Premium on Sale of Shares	5	71	279
Resources Provided by Financing	P (274)	P 228	P 632
Acquisition of Property and Equipment	P (420)	P (991)	P(1,739)
Application of Fund for Remodeling (Note 1)	(68)	(120)	(210)
Resources Used for Investing	P (488)	P(1,111)	P(1,949)
(Decrease) Increase in Cash and			
Short-term Investments	P 440	P 798	P (240)
Cash and Short-Term Investments—			
Beginning of Year	942	1,382	2,180
Cash and Short-Term Investments—			
End of Year	P1,382	P 2,180	P 1,940

NOTES TO EXHIBITS 6.28–6.30

Note 1: CIFRA commenced a major remodeling effort of its retailing establishments in Year 8. It created a Fund for Remodeling account on its balance sheet, which CIFRA increased by provisions of P179 million (net of taxes) in Year 8 and P270 million (net of taxes) in Year 9. CIFRA charges a portion of remodeling expenditures (net of taxes) each year against the Fund for Remodeling account and capitalizes a portion in fixed assets.

Note 2: The Mexican government instituted a mandatory pension program on May 1 of Year 9. All CIFRA employees participate in this program from that date forward. Retirement benefits earned in CIFRA's retirement plans prior to the effective date remain the responsibility of CIFRA. CIFRA's pension plan for nonsenior employees had pension assets in excess of pension liabilities. CIFRA reverted part of the excess to the Company during Year 8 and Year 9. Its pension plan for senior employees had pension liabilities in excess of pension assets on May 1, Year 9. CIFRA recognized a liability for the excess. On December 31, Year 10, the pension plan for nonsenior employees had pension assets in excess of pension liabilities of P593 million. CIFRA recognized this excess as an asset on this date. It credited retained earnings for P360 million (related to returns on pension fund investments for years prior to Year 10) and earnings for Year 10 for P233 million (related to returns on pension fund investments during Year 10).

Note 3: CIFRA recognizes deferred taxes for *nonrecurring* timing differences between income before taxes for financial reporting and taxable income. There were no *recurring* timing differences qualifying for the recognition of deferred taxes under Mexican accounting principles in Year 8, Year 9, or Year 10.

CHAPTER 7

GENERALLY ACCEPTED ACCOUNTING PRINCIPLES: INTERCORPORATE ENTITIES

Learning Objectives

1. Apply the criteria for the purchase and pooling of interests methods of accounting for a corporate acquisition, and understand the effects of each method on the financial statements at the time of the acquisition and in subsequent years.
2. Understand the financial statement effects of the market value, equity, proportionate consolidation, and full consolidation methods.
3. Prepare a set of translated financial statements using the all-current method and the monetary/nonmonetary method, and understand in what circumstances each method best portrays the operating relationship between a U.S. parent firm and its foreign subsidiary.
4. Understand the reporting issues in preparing financial statement data for segments of a firm and the appropriate use of segment data when analyzing a firm's profitability.

This chapter continues the discussion of generally accepted accounting principles for selected intercorporate transactions and related activities commonly encountered in corporate annual reports. The chapter emphasizes the transactions and activities that have the greatest impact on the interpretation of financial statements issued by firms. We continue our focus on how a firm's choice of reporting for intercorporate transactions and activities affects its *quality of earnings* and *quality of financial position*, concepts introduced in Chapter 4. We also note significant intercorporate reporting differences worldwide, although the primary focus is reporting in the United States.

This chapter addresses four reporting topics:

1. Corporate acquisitions.
2. Investments in securities.
3. Foreign currency translation.
4. Segment reporting.

Investing in other corporations became a popular form of growth and expansion for firms many years ago. For various strategic reasons, its popularity as a corporate investment remains today. Analysts thus need to understand the reporting for corporate acquisitions and investments in securities. Coke, for example, reports in Appendix B that it owns securities of companies that in total account for 45 percent of the worldwide volume sales of its soft drinks.

Corporate activity of U.S. firms overseas also constitutes an important area for growth and expansion. In Note 16 of Appendix A, Coke reports that over two-thirds of its revenues are generated outside North America. Foreign currency translation, therefore, takes on special importance for Coke and many other firms with significant foreign operations.

Finally, the required reporting for a firm's segments presented in this chapter confirms the importance of disaggregating the information that a firm aggregates in its consolidated financial statements. To understand firms with diverse operating activities, analysts need to work with segment data, rather than combined data.

CORPORATE ACQUISITIONS

Corporate acquisitions occur when one corporation acquires all, or substantially all, of another corporation's common stock in a single transaction. *Opinion No. 16*, a controversial ruling when it was issued in 1970, permits two methods of accounting for corporate acquisitions, depending on the structure of the transaction: the purchase method and the pooling of interests method.[1]

Exhibit 7.1 shows financial statement information for Company P and Company S, which we use to illustrate these two accounting methods. Company P acquires 100 percent of the outstanding common stock of Company S. Management estimates that the combination will save $50,000 a year in operating expenses before income taxes. Columns (1) and (2) of Exhibit 7.1 show abbreviated single-company financial statements of each company prior to the combination.

---

[1]Accounting Principles Board, *Accounting Principles Board Opinion No. 16*, "Business Combinations," 1970. *Opinion No. 16*, together with Accounting Principles Board, *Accounting Principles Board Opinion No. 17*, "Intangible Assets," are under reconsideration by the FASB as this book goes to press. Linda Vincent describes the controversy that surrounds these two opinions in "Equity Valuation Implications of Purchase versus Pooling Accounting," *Journal of Financial Statement Analysis*, Summer 1997, pp. 5–19.

EXHIBIT 7.1

Consolidated Statements Comparing Purchase and Pooling of Interests Methods

	Historical Cost		S Shown at Current Market Values	Consolidated at Date of Acquisition	
	P	S		Purchase	Pooling of Interests
	(1)	(2)	(3)	(4)	(5)
Balance Sheets					
Assets:					
Current Assets	$ 1,500,000	$ 450,000	$ 450,000	$1,950,000	$1,950,000
Depreciable Assets less					
Accum. Depr.	1,700,000	450,000	850,000	2,550,000	2,150,000
Goodwill	—	—	1,138,000	1,138,000	—
Total Assets	$ 3,200,000	$ 900,000	$2,438,000	$5,638,000	$4,100,000
Equities:					
Liabilities	$ 1,300,000	$ 450,000	$ 450,000	$1,750,000	$1,750,000
Deferred Income					
Tax Liability	—	—	140,000	140,000	—
Shareholders' Equity	1,900,000	450,000	1,848,000	3,748,000	2,350,000
Total Equities	$ 3,200,000	$ 900,000	$2,438,000	$5,638,000	$4,100,000
Income Statements					
Precombination Income					
Before Income					
Taxes	$ 300,000	$ 160,000		$ 460,000	$ 460,000
From Combination:					
Cost Savings	—	—	.	50,000	50,000
Extra Depreciation					
Expense	—	—		(80,000)	—
Base for Income Tax Expense . .	$ 300,000	$ 160,000		$ 430,000	$ 510,000
Income Tax Expense	(105,000)	(56,000)		(150,500)	(178,500)
Goodwill Amort	—	—		(28,450)	—
Net Income	$ 195,000	$ 104,000		$ 251,050	$ 331,500
Number of Common					
Shares Outstanding	100,000	22,000		144,000	144,000
Earnings per Share	$ 1.95	$ 4.73		$ 1.74	$ 2.30

Column (3) shows the market values of the assets, liabilities, and shareholders' equity of Company S. Company S has 22,000 shares of common stock outstanding, which sell for $84 per share in the market. The market value of Company S's shareholders' equity is therefore $1,848,000 (= 22,000 × $84). The market value ($1,848,000) exceeds the book value ($450,000) of shareholders' equity by $1,398,000.

There are three reasons for this difference:

1. Long-term depreciable assets have a market value of $850,000 but a book value of only $450,000. The lower book value of depreciable assets results from the fact that in accounting historical cost valuations are used for assets. Company S initially recorded its depreciable assets at acquisition cost. Over time, Company S recognized a portion of this acquisition cost as depreciation expense. Financial reporting does not permit the firm to recognize increases in the market values of these assets. The market value of Company S, as measured by the market value of its common stock, reflects the economic values, not book values, of assets.

2. Deferred income taxes of $140,000 arise because the acquiring firm cannot deduct the $400,000 excess of the market value over the book value of depreciable assets as depreciation expense for income tax purposes in future years ($400,000 $\times$ 0.35 = $140,000). This $140,000 amount represents the extra income taxes that the firm will pay in future years because taxable income will exceed book income before income taxes. To put it another way, the $140,000 represents the loss in future tax benefits because the company cannot base depreciation on the $850,000 market value of depreciable assets. We might show the $140,000 as a reduction in the market value of depreciable assets ($850,000 − $140,000 = $710,000) on the premise that the market value of these assets *to Company P* is only $710,000, not $850,000. As discussed later, financial reporting includes the $140,000 in the deferred income tax liability account. (Accounting for deferred income taxes is discussed in Chapter 6.)

3. Goodwill of $1,138,000 exists. The $1,138,000 amount for goodwill equals the difference between the acquisition cost ($1,848,000) and the market value of identifiable assets and liabilities ($450,000 + $850,000 − $450,000 − $140,000 = $710,000). Goodwill includes intangible attributes that a firm cannot separately identify (such as a well-trained labor force, reputation for high-quality products, superior managerial skills), as well as any merger premium that the acquirer had to pay to consummate the corporate acquisition. Goodwill generates no deferred income tax liability account in this case because the merger is structured so that amortization of goodwill (discussed below) is not a deductible expense for income tax purposes. Chapter 6 uses the term *permanent difference* for items that have no future tax consequences, such as amortization of goodwill in this example.

Company P, the acquiring company, has 100,000 shares of common stock outstanding, which sell for $42 each in the market.

PURCHASE METHOD

With the *purchase method*, the acquirer (Company P) records the assets and liabilities of the acquired company (Company S) at the amount of cash or market value of other consideration given in the exchange. The purchase method therefore follows the principles of acquisition cost accounting; that is, the acquiring company records assets and liabilities at the price it pays for them.

To see this, assume that P issues (sells) 44,000 additional shares of its common stock on the market for $42 each, or $1,848,000 in total, and uses the proceeds to purchase 100 percent of the outstanding common shares of S. When cash is the only consideration used in a corporate acquisition, financial reporting requires the purchase method.

Column (4) of Exhibit 7.1 shows the combined, or consolidated, balance sheet of P and S on the date of the combination under the purchase method. The consolidation combines book values of P's assets, liabilities, and shareholders' equity with the market values of S's assets, liabilities, and shareholders' equity in applying the purchase method.

The lower panel of Exhibit 7.1 shows the effect of using the purchase method for the acquisition on income statements of subsequent years.[2] The consolidated income statement begins with the combined pretax incomes of P and S, assuming no acquisition had occurred. We add the $50,000 of cost savings resulting from more efficient operations after the combination. (Actually, you will learn that this savings occurs whether the combination is structured as a purchase or a pooling of interests transaction.) We subtract the additional depreciation arising from the asset revaluation. The additional depreciation expense of $80,000 reflects a five-year life and use of the straight-line depreciation method [$80,000 = 0.20($850,000 − $450,000)].

The $430,000 of book income before taxes and before amortization of goodwill is the basis for income tax *expense* of $150,500 for the purchase method. Taxable income of $510,000 (= $460,000 + $50,000) is the basis for income taxes payable of $178,500.

The combined companies report the difference between income tax expense of $150,500 and income tax payable of $178,500, or $28,000, as a reduction in deferred income tax liability established at the date of acquisition. This $28,000 equals the income tax rate of 35 percent times the extra depreciation expense of $80,000. Goodwill amortization of $28,450 assumes straight-line amortization over 40 years ($28,450 = $1,138,000 ÷ 40).[3]

POOLING OF INTERESTS METHOD

The pooling of interests method accounts for a corporate acquisition as the uniting of the ownership interests of two companies by an exchange of common stock. The pooling of interests method views the exchange of shares as a change in *form*, not in *substance*. That is, the shareholders of the predecessor companies become shareholders in the new combined enterprise. Each of the predecessor companies continues its operations as before.

---

[2]The actual income statement of the combined firm would not appear as detailed in the lower panel of Exhibit 7.1. Rather, the line items reported in the exhibit showing the *effects* of the purchase method would be reported on the applicable line items of the firms' combined income statement (cost of goods sold, depreciation expense, income tax expense and so on).

[3]*Opinion No. 17* stipulates that the amortization period for goodwill should be the expected useful life of the goodwill, but the period cannot exceed 40 years. Virtually all firms use the 40-year period allowed.

Because no change occurs in either the ownership interests or the nature of the activities of the enterprises involved, no new basis of accountability arises. The accountant merely adds the book values of the assets and the liabilities of each company when accounting for a "corporate acquisition" as a pooling of interests. Unlike the purchase method, the consolidated balance sheet does not reflect the market values of the acquired company's assets and liabilities on the date of acquisition.[4]

To see the pooling of interests method, assume that P issues the 44,000 additional shares of its common stock directly to the shareholders of S in return for their shares. Note that under the purchase method discussed in the preceding section, these 44,000 shares were sold on the market, and the *cash* received is used to buy all the stock of S.

Under the pooling of interests method, previous shareholders of P and S now own the outstanding shares of P and S combined. The consolidated balance sheet in column (5) of Exhibit 7.1 is the sum of the separate company amounts in columns (1) and (2). The pooling of interests method requires no revaluation of assets; nor does it result in the recognition of goodwill.

The consolidated income statement is likewise the sum of the amounts for the separate companies (except for recognizing the projected cost savings). Because the balance sheet does not reflect asset revaluations and goodwill under the pooling of interests method, the accountant records no additional depreciation or amortization. For this reason, income under the pooling of interests method is usually higher than under the purchase method. Furthermore, assets and shareholders' equities are usually less under the pooling of interests method than under the purchase method. Rates of return on assets and on shareholders' equity will likely exceed those under the purchase method.

CRITERIA FOR POOLING OF INTERESTS

The concept of a pooling of interests envisions two independent companies agreeing to combine their shareholder groups and their operations and continuing to operate in a new combined form. It does not view the transaction as one company buying out the other.

To qualify for the pooling of interests method, the transaction must meet the twelve criteria set out in Exhibit 7.2. Unless the transaction satisfies all twelve criteria, the combining firms cannot use the pooling method. If the transaction satisfies all criteria, however, the combining firms must use the pooling method.

The first two criteria attempt to operationalize the notion that the combining companies acted independently in their decision to combine. The next seven criteria attempt to ensure that the shareholders of the predecessor companies become common equityholders in the new combined enterprise. Financial reporting includes several of these criteria to circumvent abuses of the pooling method. The aim of the last three criteria is to ensure continuity of the shareholder groups and of operations after the combination.

---

[4]Many U.S. money center bank combinations in recent years were accounted for using the pooling of interests method. Accountants reported the merger of Chemical Bank and Chase Manhattan Bank, for example, using the pooling of interests method. Regional banks use the technique as well, however, as illustrated in Example 3.

EXHIBIT 7.2
Criteria for Pooling of Interests Method

Prior to the Combination

1. Each of the combining companies is autonomous and has not been a subsidiary or division of another corporation within two years before initiation of the plan to combine.
2. Each of the combining companies is independent of the other combining companies.

At the Time of the Combination

3. The combination occurs in a single transaction or in accordance with a specific plan that the combining entities complete within one year.
4. A corporation issues only common stock with rights identical to the majority of its outstanding voting stock in exchange for substantially all (at least 90 percent) of the voting stock of another company.
5. None of the combining companies changes the equity interest of the voting common stock in contemplation of the combination either within two years before initiating the plan of combination or between the initiation and consummation dates; changes in contemplation of the combination may include distributions to shareholders and additional issuances, exchanges, and retirements of securities.
6. Each of the combining companies only acquires shares of voting common stock for purposes other than business combinations, and no company reacquires more than a normal number of shares between the initiation and consummation dates.
7. The ratio of the interest of an individual common shareholder to those of other common shareholders in a combining company remains the same as a result of the exchange of stock in the combination.
8. Shareholders can exercise the voting rights to which the common stock in the combined corporation entitle them; the combined company can neither deprive nor restrict the shareholders from exercising those rights.
9. The combining entities resolve all issues at the consummation date of the plan; no provisions of the plan relating to the issue of securities or other consideration are pending.

Subsequent to the Combination

10. The combined corporation does not agree directly or indirectly to retire or reacquire all or part of the common stock issued in the combination.
11. The combined corporation does not make special financial arrangements for the benefit of the former shareholders of a combining company, such as guaranteeing loans secured by stock issued in the combination, which in effect negate the exchange of equity securities.
12. The combined corporation does not intend or plan to dispose of a significant part of the assets of the combining companies within two years after the combination other than disposals in the ordinary course of business of the formerly separate companies and to eliminate duplicate facilities or excess capacity.

SOURCE: Accounting Principles Board, *Accounting Principles Board Opinion No. 16*, "Business Combinations " 1970.

PURCHASE VERSUS POOLING OF INTERESTS REPORTING: WHICH IS PREFERABLE TO ANALYSTS?

Critics of the pooling of interests method argue that not only does it keep reported expenses from increasing after the merger, but it may also allow the management of the pooled companies to manage reported earnings in an arbitrary way. As Chapter 4 discusses, estimating future sustainable earnings requires assessing to what degree management manipulates current earnings.

Suppose, as has happened, that Company P merges with an old, established firm, Company F, which has produced commercial movies. Company F has amortized these movies, made in the 1940s and 1950s, so that by the 1990s their book value is close to zero. But in fact the market value of the films is much higher than zero, because television stations and cable networks find that old movies attract audiences.

If Company P acquires Company F and uses the purchase method, the old films appear on the consolidated balance sheet at the films' current market values. If Company P merges with Company F, and uses the pooling of interests method, the films appear on the consolidated balance sheet at their near-zero book values. Then, when Company P wants to boost reported earnings for the year, it can sell some old movies to a television or cable network and report a large gain. Actually, of course, the owners of Company F enjoyed this gain when they "sold" to Company P for current asset values, not the obsolete book values.

Those who defend pooling of interests accounting argue that the managers of the pooled enterprise have no more opportunity to manage earnings than did the managers of Company F before the pooling. Managers of Company F can sell old movies any time they choose and report handsome gains. It is the use of the historical cost basis of accounting that creates the opportunity for managing earnings.

Defenders of pooling of interests accounting argue that there is no reason to penalize the management of a merged company more than the management of an established company that has many undervalued assets on its books. Opponents of the pooling of interests method reply that it is the managers of Company F who earned the holding gains, but it is the managers of Company P who can report them as realized gains when using this method.

Proponents of the pooling of interests method point out that the purchase method also provides at least two opportunities for managing *future* earnings.

1. Under the purchase method, the combining companies allocate the aggregate purchase price to identifiable assets and liabilities on the basis of their market values. The market values of many assets, particularly depreciable assets, patents, copyrights, and similar items, are difficult to measure objectively because of the absence of well-organized, used asset markets. Thus, the combining companies can allocate relatively low amounts to assets that the firm will write off quickly as expenses (such as machinery) and relatively high amounts to assets that it will write off over longer periods (such as buildings) or not at all (such as land). The combining companies must use appraisals or other independent evidence of market values to validate the purchase price allocation, but there is considerable latitude in selecting appraisers.

2. The purchase method commonly entails establishing "acquisition reserves" at the time one company acquires another company, because the acquiring company may not know fully the potential losses inherent in the acquired assets or the potential liabilities of the acquired company. Chapter 6 provides a discussion of the various types of reserves employed in U.S. and non-U.S. reporting systems, and how they are used and abused.

    The acquiring company will allocate a portion of the purchase price to various types of acquisition reserves (for example, estimated losses on long-term contracts, estimated liabilities for unsettled lawsuits). An acquiring company has up to one year after the date of acquisition to revalue these acquisition reserves as new information becomes available. After that, the acquisition reserve amounts remain in the accounts and absorb losses as they occur. That is, the acquiring firm charges actual losses against the acquisition reserves instead of against income for the period of the loss.

To see this, assume that at the date of acquisition there is unsettled litigation involving an acquired company. The acquiring company, based on the information it has available, estimates that a pretax loss of $3 million will ultimately result. It allocates $3 million to an acquisition reserve (liability account) and debits deferred tax assets for the $1.05 million tax effect (= 0.35 × $3 million). The acquiring firm would presumably pay less for this company because of this potential liability.

Assume that settlement of the lawsuit occurs three years after the date of the acquisition for $2 million (pretax). The accountant charges the $2 million loss against the $3 million reserve instead of against net income for the year and reduces deferred tax assets by $.7 million (= 0.35 × $2 million). Furthermore, the accountant eliminates the $1 million remaining in the acquisition reserve and the $0.35 million remaining in deferred tax assets, increasing net income by $0.65 million (0 = $1 million − 0.35 million) in the year of the settlement.

The benefit of this scenario to the acquiring firm is twofold: (1) no *charges* for the settlement reduce net income; but (2) the "cleaning up" *credit* increases net income in the year of the settlement.

When used properly, acquisition reserves are an accounting mechanism that helps ensure that the assets and liabilities of an acquired company reflect market values. Given the estimates required in establishing such reserves, however, management has some latitude in managing earnings under the purchase method.

Analysts generally prefer the purchase method over the pooling of interests method because of the perceived greater opportunities to manage earnings under the latter method. Most analysts also emphasize that asset and subsequent expense amounts under the purchase method more closely approximate replacement costs than do the corresponding amounts under the pooling of interests method. These amounts, analysts conclude, serve as better measures of the economic value of assets consumed each period.

Researchers have examined the postacquisition performance of equity securities of firms that accounted for an acquisition using the purchase method versus the pooling of interests method.[5] Excess, or unexpected, returns for firms using the purchase method generally exceed those for firms using the pooling of interests method. One interpretation of this result is that firms using the purchase method expected higher future earnings that could absorb the goodwill amortization. The market interprets the decision to use the purchase method as a positive signal

---

[5] For a summary of this research, see Michael L. Davis, "The Purchase vs. Pooling Controversy: How the Stock Market Responds to Goodwill," *Journal of Applied Corporate Finance,* Spring 1996, pp. 50–59.

about future earnings. The excess returns after acquisitions accounted for as pooling of interests were not significantly different from zero. One interpretation of this result is that the market saw no value added from the merger.

Studies also show that the merger premium (excess of market value over book value) is larger for acquisitions accounted for as pooling of interests than as purchases. One possible interpretation is that firms overpay in order to use the pooling of interests method and avoid the negative impact of goodwill amortization that arises under the purchase method. Another interpretation is that the earnings benefits under the pooling of interests method increase as the merger premium increases.

CORPORATE ACQUISITIONS AND INCOME TAXES

Most corporate acquisitions involve a transaction between the acquiring corporation and the *shareholders* of the acquired corporation. Although the board of directors and management of the acquired company may closely monitor the discussions and negotiations, the acquisition usually takes place through the acquiring corporation's provision of some type of consideration to the shareholders of the acquired corporation in exchange for their stock. From a legal viewpoint, the acquired corporation remains a legally separate entity that has simply had a change in the makeup of its shareholder group.

The income tax treatment of corporate acquisitions follows these legal entity notions. In most acquisitions, the acquired company does not restate its assets and liabilities for tax purposes to reflect the amount that the acquired corporation paid for the shares of common stock. Instead, the tax basis of assets and liabilities of the acquired company before the acquisition carries over after the acquisition.[6] In this sense, the tax treatment of a corporate acquisition is analogous to a pooling of interests. Thus, even if the combining entities use the purchase method for financial reporting, they treat the transaction like a pooling of interests for tax purposes (termed a *nontaxable reorganization* by the Internal Revenue Service).

Example 1. Kimberly-Clark operates in three major businesses: personal care products, consumer tissue projects, and away-from-home products. The company merged with Scott Paper in an effort to become what the chairman described in the firm's annual report as "a global consumer products powerhouse." Note 2 of the annual report, labeled "Business Combinations," states:

> The corporation issued 119.7 million shares of its common stock for all of the outstanding stock of Scott, a worldwide producer of sanitary tissue products. Scott shareholders received .78 of a share of the corporation's common stock for

---

[6]An acquiring company can elect Section 338 of the Internal Revenue Code and thereby record assets and liabilities at their market values for tax purposes, but the acquired company must pay taxes immediately on differences between these market values and the tax basis of assets and liabilities.

Any goodwill resulting from the restatement of assets and liabilities that qualifies as a Section 197 intangible is amortized over a 15-year period as specified in the Revenue Recognition Act of 1993. To qualify for the amortization deduction, the goodwill had to be acquired after August 10, 1993. Goodwill amortization usually is not deducted for tax purposes, however, because few acquired firms pay taxes immediately on the excess of market values over tax basis.

each share of Scott's common stock, for a total value of $9.4 billion. The merger qualified as a tax-free reorganization.

CORPORATE DISCLOSURES ON ACQUISITIONS

As should be clear, acquisitions are accounted for differently, depending on the structure of the transaction. We illustrate this in three examples that follow—two transactions accounted for using the pooling of interest methods, and one accounted for using the purchase method.

Example 2. Kimberly-Clark accounted for its merger with Scott Paper as a pooling of interests for financial reporting purposes. Note that the transaction involved an exchange of Scott Paper common stock for Kimberly-Clark common stock, one of the criteria (Item 4 in Exhibit 7.2) for the pooling of interests method. The firm states in Note 2:

> The merger was accounted for as a pooling of interests. Accordingly, the corporation's consolidated financial statements were restated for all periods prior to the business combination to include the results of operations, financial positions, and cash flows of Scott. In conjunction with the restatement, accounting practices of Scott were conformed to those of Kimberly-Clark.

Before the merger actually took place but after it was announced, the chairman of Kimberly-Clark estimated that the Scott Paper merger would save the firm approximately $250 million. (Recall that Exhibit 7.1 assumes a cost savings in the combination of company P and S of $50,000.) In the chairman's letter in the annual report quoted above, the firm reports an actual savings of $280 million, and anticipates an annual savings of $500 million in future years. Not surprisingly, the chairman highlights these points in the annual report and analysts' meetings.

Example 3. Regions Financial Corporation's banking operations are principally in Alabama, Georgia, Louisiana, Florida, and Tennessee. Regions grows substantially through acquisition, with 28 firms acquired in Year 8 alone. Regions describes the largest of these mergers in Note Q, "Business Combinations," of Year 8's annual report:

> On March 1, Year 8, First National Bankcorp of Gainesville, Georgia, with approximately $3.2 billion in assets merged with and into Regions. Under the terms of the transaction, Regions issued 15,920,108 shares of its common stock for all of First National's outstanding common stock (based on an exchange ratio of 0.76 of a share of Regions common stock for each share of First National's common stock). The transaction was accounted for as a pooling of interests and accordingly, all prior period financial statements have been restated to include the effect of the First National transaction.

For comparative purposes, the note also presents net interest income, net income and net income per share as reported by Regions, First National and on a combined basis.

Example 4.   Ten days into Year 6, Sherwin-Williams acquired Pratt & Lambert for approximately $400 million. The firm accounted for the acquisition using the purchase method, and included essentially the full year's results of Pratt & Lambert's operations in the firm's financial statements for Year 6. Sherwin-Williams acquired various other paint and coating businesses during the same year, resulting in a total of $671 million spent on acquisitions. As a result of these acquisitions, goodwill increased $510 million during the year. Goodwill at the end of Year 6 represented almost 20 percent of Sherwin-Williams' total assets, compared to only 2 percent of total assets at the end of the previous year.

The firm indicates that goodwill is amortized over 40 years using the straight-line method. As a result of the Pratt & Lambert and other acquisitions during the year, Sherwin-Williams' goodwill amortization expense almost doubled for Year 6, to $27 million. The firm does *not* restate prior period financial statements (as is the case with the preceding two examples), but does provide the pro forma information for Year 5 as follows:

Condensed Statement of Consolidated Income (Unaudited)
For the year ending December 31, Year 5
(in thousands)

	As reported	Pratt & Lambert and Sherwin-Williams
Net sales	$ 3,273,819	$ 3,670,181
Net income	$ 200,654	$ 183,806
Net income per share	$ 1.17	$ 1.07

Sherwin-Williams indicates that the pro forma income statement information reflects adjustments for interest expense, net investment income, depreciation expense, and amortization of goodwill.

For firms that use the purchase method of accounting, analysts assess (1) the portion of total assets represented by goodwill, and (2) the period over which the firms amortize the goodwill. Large percentages of total assets represented by goodwill negatively affect quality of financial position assessments. Since most firms amortize goodwill over 40 years, the quality of earnings generally is not affected; firms are following the same policy. For firms operating in certain industries, however, 40 years might be inappropriate. For example, 40 years appears too long for firms operating in technology-based industries and mature, highly competitive industries.

For mergers accounted for as a pooling of interests, the analyst should carefully examine the resulting consolidated financial statements. The market values for assets and liabilities often far exceed their recorded values, as discussed earlier. For example, May Department Stores merged with Associated Dry Goods in a transaction treated as a pooling of interests. The book values for Associated at the time of the merger were as follows (in millions):

Assets	$ 2,489
Liabilities	$ 1,589
Shareholders' Equity	900
	$ 2,489

May used these amounts to record the merger. The financial statements indicate that May exchanged 69.7 million shares of its common stock for all of the outstanding common stock of Associated. Based on a market price per share for May of approximately $38 on the date of the merger, the market value of Associated's shareholders' equity was $2,648.6 million (= 69.7 million × $38). The book value of shareholders' equity was $900 million. The excess of market value over book value of shareholders' equity of $1,748.6 million (= $2,648.6 − $900.0) represents undervalued or nonrecorded assets and liabilities.

If the analyst assumes that all of the difference is goodwill and amortizes it over 40 years, then goodwill amortization of the merged enterprise increases $43.7 million ($1,748.6 ÷ 40) using the purchase method instead of the pooling of interests method. Reported earnings of the combined enterprise for the year of the merger were $381 million. If the entities had used the purchase method, net income would be no greater than $337.3 million (= $381.0 − $43.7), an 11.5 percent decrease. If a portion of the excess purchase price were allocated to assets with lives shorter than the 40-year amortization period for goodwill, net income would be even less than $337.3 million.

The analyst should also be cautious when comparing U.S. and non-U.S. firms engaged in corporate acquisitions. The pooling of interests method is either disallowed or allowed only under unusual circumstances in most other countries (such as an inability to identify which company is the purchaser when the merging firms are of similar size).[7]

There is considerable diversity across countries in accounting for goodwill. Firms in the United Kingdom can charge off goodwill directly against shareholders' equity accounts, bypassing the income statement. Firms in Japan amortize goodwill over 5 years, while firms in Germany use a period between 5 and 15 years. These differences in accounting methods for corporate acquisitions will likely gain further importance as international acquisition activity accelerates in the years ahead.

INVESTMENTS IN SECURITIES

Firms invest in the securities (debt, preferred stock, common stock) of other entities (corporations, government units) for a variety of reasons:

---

[7]*International Accounting Standard No. 22*, "Business Combination," issued in 1983 and revised in 1993, prohibits the use of the pooling of interests method except in those circumstances when the accountant cannot identify which firm is the acquirer and which firm is the acquiree.

1. Short-term investments of temporarily excess cash.
2. Long-term investments to:
   a. Lock in high yields on debt securities.
   b. Exert significant influence on an important raw materials supplier, customer, technological innovator, or other valued entity.
   c. Gain voting control of another entity whose operations mesh well strategically with the investing firm.

Firms report investments of the first type in the current assets section of the balance sheet under the title, Marketable Securities. These investments tend to be in government securities. Firms report investments of the second type in the noncurrent asset section of the balance sheet under Investments. These longer-term investments tend to be in equity, rather than debt, securities.

TYPES OF INVESTMENTS

The accounting for investments depends on the purpose of the investment and on the percentage of voting stock that one firm owns of another.[8] Exhibit 7.3 identifies three types of investments:

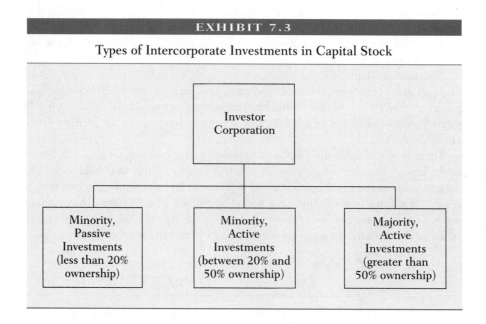

EXHIBIT 7.3

Types of Intercorporate Investments in Capital Stock

Investor Corporation

| Minority, Passive Investments (less than 20% ownership) | Minority, Active Investments (between 20% and 50% ownership) | Majority, Active Investments (greater than 50% ownership) |

---

[8]As this book goes to press, the FASB is reconsidering the use of percentage of voting stock that one firm owns of another as a criterion for determining how to account for investments. The FASB proposes using the concept of *effective control* for determining the appropriate reporting, and not simply the percentage of ownership. The proposed standard would affect only the accounting for investments defined by categories two and three in this section.

1. *Minority, passive investments.* Firms view debt securities or shares of capital stock of another corporation as a good investment, and acquire them for their anticipated interest or dividends and capital gains (increases in the market prices of the securities). The percentage owned of another corporation's voting shares is not so large that the acquiring company can control or exert significant influence over the other company. Financial reporting views investments in debt securities, preferred stock, or common stock in which the firm holds less than 20 percent of the voting stock as a minority, passive investment.

2. *Minority, active investments.* Firms acquire shares of another corporation so that the acquiring corporation can exert significant influence over the other company's activities. This significant influence is usually at a broad policymaking level through representation on the other corporation's board of directors. Because of the wide dispersion of ownership of most publicly held corporations, many of whose shareholders do not vote their shares, firms can exert significant influence over another corporation even with ownership of less than a majority of the voting stock. Financial reporting views investments of between 20 percent and 50 percent of the voting stock of another company as a minority, active investment unless evidence indicates that the acquiring firm cannot exert significant influence.

3. *Majority, active investments.* Firms acquire shares of another corporation so that the acquiring corporation can control the other company. This control is typically at both the broad policymaking level and the day-to-day operational level. Ownership of more than 50 percent of the voting stock of another company implies an ability to control, unless there is evidence to the contrary.

The accounting for these three types of investments attempts to reflect the different purpose of each. Exhibit 7.4 summarizes the reporting for each type of investment in the financial statements.

MINORITY, PASSIVE INVESTMENTS

If a firm does not own a sufficient percentage of the voting stock of another corporation to control or influence it significantly, the management of the investment involves two activities: awaiting the receipt of interest or dividends, and deciding when to sell the investment for a capital gain or loss. Financial reporting requires firms to account for minority, passive investments using either amortized acquisition cost or the market value method.[9] A summary of the accounting follows.

1. Firms initially record investments at acquisition cost.
2. Revenues each period equal interest and dividends received or receivable.
3. The accounting at the end of each period depends on the type of security and the firm's reason for holding it. *Statement No. 115* classifies securities into three categories:

[9]Financial Accounting Standards Board, *Statement of Financial Accounting Standards No. 115*, "Accounting for Certain Investments in Debt and Equity Securities," 1993.

EXHIBIT 7.4

Reporting Investments in Securities in the Financial Statements

Financial Statement	Minority Passive Investments	Minority Active Investments	Majority Active Investments
Income Statement	Interest and dividend revenue Unrealized increases and decreases in the market value of securities classified as trading securities Realized gains and losses on sales of securities	Investor's share of investee's net income minus amortization of any excess of the purchase price over the book value of the investee's shareholders' equity at the time of acquisition	Individual revenues and expenses of investee minus the minority interest's share of investee's net income included in consolidated net income
Balance Sheet	Marketable securities and investments in securities reported at market value (except that debt securities held to maturity appear at amortized acquisition cost) Unrealized increases and decreases in the market value of securities classified as available for sale included in shareholders' equity section of the balance sheet	Investments reported at acquisition cost plus investor's cumulative share of investee's net income minus cumulative amortization of excess purchase price over book value acquired minus dividends received from investee since acquisition	Investment in securities account eliminated and replaced by investee's individual assets and liabilities in preparing consolidated balance sheet Minority interest's claim on investee's net assets shown in the shareholders' equity section of consolidated balance sheet.
Statement of Cash Flows	Cash received from interest and dividends included in cash flow from operations; cash flows associated with purchases and sales included in cash flows from investing	Cash received from interest and dividends included in cash flow from operations. Cash flows associated with purchases and sales included in cash flows from investing	Individual cash flows from operating, investing, and financing activities of investee included in consolidated statement of cash flows

a. Debt securities that a firm has a positive intent and ability to hold to maturity.

b. Debt and equity securities held as *trading securities*.

c. Debt and equity securities held as *available for sale*.

Firms must account for debt securities expected to be held until maturity at amortized acquisition cost. That is, the firm must amortize any difference between the acquisition cost and the maturity value of these debt securities as an adjustment to interest revenue over the life of the debt. Firms report all other debt and equity securities at market value at the end of each period.

The reporting of any unrealized holding gain or loss depends on the purpose of holding the securities. If firms actively buy and sell securities to take advantage of short-term differences or changes in market values, then these firms classify the securities as *trading securities*, a current asset on the balance sheet. Commercial banks, for example, often trade securities in different capital markets worldwide to take advantage of temporary differences in market prices. Manufacturers, retailers, and other nonfinancial firms occasionally invest funds for trading purposes, but such situations are unusual. Firms include unrealized holding gains and losses on trading securities in the calculation of net income each period.

Firms classify debt and equity securities that do not fit either of these first two categories as securities *available for sale*, including them as either current assets or noncurrent assets depending on the expected holding period. Unrealized holding "gains" or "losses" on securities available for sale are not included in net income each period, but appear instead as a component of comprehensive income, labeled Unrealized Holding Gain or Loss on Securities Available for Sale. The cumulative unrealized holding gain or loss on securities available for sale appears in the shareholders' equity section of the balance sheet as part of Accumulated Other Comprehensive Income.

4. When a firm sells a trading security, it recognizes the difference between the selling price and the book value (that is, the market value at the end of the most recent accounting period prior to sale) as a gain or a loss in measuring net income. When a firm sells a security classified as available for sale, it recognizes the difference between the selling price and the *acquisition cost* of the security as a realized gain or loss. The firm must eliminate at the time of sale any amount in the shareholders' equity account, Accumulated Other Comprehensive Income, for the unrealized holding gain or loss related to that security.

Example 5. Note 7 of Appendix A reports Coke's investments in debt and marketable equity securities. Coke states:

On December 31, Year 6 and Year 7, we had no trading securities. Securities categorized as available for sale are stated at fair value, with unrealized gains and losses, net of deferred income taxes, reported in share-owners' equity. Debt securities categorized as held to maturity are stated at amortized cost.

Coke reports (in millions):

Balance Sheet—Assets at December 31, Year 7
Securities Available for Sale (historical cost of $546) $797
Securities Held to Maturity (estimate fair value of $1599) $1608

Balance Sheet—Share-Owners' Equity at December 31, Year 7
Unrealized gain on securities available for sale, net of deferred taxes $156

Component of Comprehensive Income for Year 7
Net change in unrealized gain on securities, net of deferred taxes $74

Financial reporting requires Coke to disclose the $74 million unrealized gain on securities as a separate component of comprehensive income. Exhibit 1.9 in Chapter 1 illustrates a possible disclosure format for Coke.

Interpreting Changes.   In assessing earnings quality, analysts must decide whether or not to include any change in the holding gain or loss on securities classified as available for sale in earnings for the period. The principal argument for excluding it is that the unrealized "gain" or "loss" may well reverse, and perhaps will not be realized for many years, if ever. The principal argument for including it relates to the fact that firms have some latitude in deciding how to classify securities; firms can therefore manage earnings by classifying securities as available for sale versus trading. If pro forma income statements include *all* changes in holding gain or losses on securities, then any earnings management practiced by firms is eliminated. For Coke, the amounts are small enough that no adjustment is warranted.

Because firms invest in marketable securities with temporarily excess cash, the analyst can generally presume that firms could sell these securities for an amount at least equal to the amount shown on the balance sheet. This is a reasonable presumption for firms located in countries that require the market method, such as France and Great Britain. Certain countries, such as Canada, Japan, and Germany, require the valuation of marketable securities at acquisition cost unless firms consider a price decline to be permanent. Firms in these latter countries seldom disclose the market value of their marketable securities. If interest rates have increased or stock prices have declined materially in one of these countries during the last several months of the accounting period, the analyst should interpret the reported amounts for these securities cautiously.

MINORITY, ACTIVE INVESTMENTS

When a firm owns less than a majority of the voting stock of another corporation, the accountant must exercise judgment in ascertaining whether the firm can exert significant influence. For the sake of uniformity, financial reporting presumes that one company can significantly influence another company when it owns 20 percent or more of the voting stock of the other company. Ownership of less than 20 percent may permit a firm to exert significant influence, but in these cases management must demonstrate to the independent accountant that it is possible (for example, by placing individuals on the investee's board of directors).

Financial reporting requires firms to account for minority, active investments, generally those where ownership is between 20 percent and 50 percent, using the *equity method*.[10] Under the equity method, the firm owning shares in another firm recognizes as revenue (expense) each period its share of the net income (loss) of the other firm. See, for example, the income statement of Coke in Appendix A. The line, Equity Income, includes Coke's share of the earnings from 20 percent-

---

[10]Accounting Principles Board, *Accounting Principles Board Opinion No. 18*, "The Equity Method of Accounting for Investments in Common Stock," 1971. See footnote 8 for a discussion of changes proposed by the FASB, however.

to 50 percent-owned affiliates. If the investor pays more for the shares of an investee than the book value of the common shareholders' equity underlying the shares, the investor must amortize the excess purchase price over a period not exceeding 40 years. The investor treats dividends received from the investee as a return of investment and not as income. In the discussion that follows, we designate the firm owning shares as P and the firm whose shares P owns as S.

The rationale for using the equity method when significant influence is present is best understood by considering the financial statement effects of using the market value method for securities classified as available for sale in these circumstances. Under the market value method, P recognizes income or loss on the income statement only when it receives a dividend or sells all or part of the investment. Suppose, as often happens, that S follows a policy of financing its own growing operations through retention of earnings and consistently declares dividends that are significantly lower than its net income. The market price of S's shares will probably increase to reflect the retention of assets generated by earnings. Under the market value method, P's only reported income from the investment will be the modest dividends received.

P, because of its ownership percentage, can influence S's dividend policy, and thereby the amount of income recognized under the market value method. Under these conditions, the market value method may not reasonably reflect the earnings of S generated under P's influence. The equity method provides a better measure of a firm's earnings and of its investment when, because of its ownership interest, one firm can significantly influence the operations and dividend policy of another firm.

Under the equity method, firms report investments on the balance sheet at acquisition cost plus (minus) the investor's share of the investee's net income (loss) each period, minus amortization of any excess purchase price, minus the dividends received from the investee each period.

The statement of cash flows reports cash flows and not equity method earnings. Thus, in deriving cash flow from operations, the statement of cash flows subtracts the investor's share of the investee's earnings from net income, and adds the cash dividends received. Most firms (including Coke) report this adjustment as a subtraction for the investor's share of the *undistributed* earnings (equity income minus dividends) of the investee.

Example 6. Look at the financial statements for Coke in Appendix A. Its balance sheet reports "equity method investments" in Coca-Cola Enterprises, Coca-Cola Amatil Limited, and Other, principally bottling operations. (Chapter 1 presents a framework for analyzing a firm's operating strategy, and also specifically discusses Coke's rationale for substantial *equity* investments in bottlers, but not 100 percent ownership.) Coca-Cola Enterprises is a 45 percent-owned bottler. Coca-Cola Amatil Limited is a 36 percent-owned bottler. Coke does not disclose the percentage of common stock it owns of the other bottler operations, but the firm indicates that the investments are accounted for using the equity method as well.

For these investments, Coke's statement of income shows equity income of $211 million. Coke's statement of cash flows shows a subtraction from net income of $89 million for "equity income, net of dividends" in deriving cash flow from operations. Coke therefore received cash dividends of $122 million (= $211 − $89) from these investments during Year 7.

Questioning Equity Method Intercorporate Investments.   The analyst should address two questions in particular when examining the financial statements of firms with significant equity method intercorporate investments:

1. What is the relation between equity method income and cash flows received from the investees?
2. Are assets and liabilities essential to a firm's operations submerged in the intercorporate investment account?

The analyst answers the first question by comparing equity method income on the income statement with the adjustment to net income for undistributed earnings of investees in the statement of cash flows. Coke, for example, derived less than 5 percent of its pretax earnings during Year 7 from equity method investees and received only a minor amount of cash from these investments.

The analyst answers the second question by studying the notes on intercorporate investments. Firms must disclose partial balance sheet and income statement information for significant intercorporate investments. We know that Coke maintains less than a controlling interest in its major bottling operations. The assets and liabilities of these bottlers do not appear on Coke's balance sheet. A later section discusses the procedure an analyst might follow to incorporate amounts for such investments on the balance sheet (illustrated in Exhibit 7.6).

The analyst should also exert caution when examining the financial statements of firms in other countries. Firms commonly use the equity method for minority, active investments in Canada, France, and Great Britain and in certain filings with the Ministry of Finance in Japan. Countries that follow a strict legal definition of the corporate entity, such as Germany, tend to report these intercorporate investments at acquisition cost, even when significant influence is present.

MAJORITY, ACTIVE INVESTMENTS

When one firm, P, owns more than 50 percent of the voting stock of another company, S, P can control the activities of S. This control may occur at both a broad policymaking level and a day-to-day operational level. The majority investor in this case is the *parent* and the majority-owned company is the *subsidiary*. Financial reporting requires the combining or *consolidating* of the financial statements of majority-owned companies with those of the parent (unless the parent cannot for legal or other reasons exercise control).[11]

---

[11]Financial Accounting Standards Board, *Statement of Financial Accounting Standards No. 94*, "Consolidation of Majority-Owned Subsidiaries," 1987.

Reasons for Legally Separate Corporations. There are many reasons why a business firm prefers to operate as a group of legally separate corporations rather than as a single legal entity. From the viewpoint of the parent company, the more important reasons for maintaining legally separate subsidiary companies include the following:

1. **To reduce financial risk.** Separate corporations may mine raw materials, transport them to a manufacturing plant, produce the product, and sell the finished product to the public. If any one part of the total process proves to be unprofitable or inefficient, losses from insolvency fall only on the owners and creditors of the one subsidiary corporation. Furthermore, creditors have a claim on the assets of the subsidiary corporation only, not on the assets of the parent company.
2. **To meet the requirements of state corporation laws and tax legislation more effectively.** If a firm does business in many states, it must often contend with overlapping and inconsistent taxation, regulations, and requirements. Organizing separate corporations to conduct the operations in the various states may reduce administrative costs.
3. **To expand or diversify with a minimum of capital investment.** One way to absorb a company is by acquiring a controlling interest in its voting stock. The acquirer may accomplish this result with a substantially smaller capital investment, as well as with less difficulty, inconvenience, and risk, than if it were to construct a new plant or gear up for a new line of business.

Purpose of Consolidated Statements. For a variety of reasons, then, a parent and several legally separate subsidiaries may exist as a single economic entity. A consolidation of the financial statements of the parent and each of its subsidiaries presents the results of operations, financial position, and changes in cash flows of an affiliated group of companies under the control of a parent, essentially as if the group of companies were a single entity. The parent and each subsidiary are legally separate entities, but they operate as one centrally controlled *economic entity*. Consolidated financial statements generally provide more useful information to the shareholders of the parent corporation than would separate financial statements of the parent and each subsidiary.

Consolidated financial statements also generally provide more useful information than does the equity method. The parent, because of its voting interest, can effectively control the use of the subsidiary's individual assets. Consolidation of the individual assets, liabilities, revenues, and expenses of both the parent and the subsidiary provides a more realistic picture of the operations and financial position of the single economic entity.

In a legal sense, consolidated statements merely supplement, and do not replace, the separate statements of the individual corporations, although it is common practice in the United States to present only the consolidated statements in published annual reports.

Consolidation Policy.   Financial reporting requires that firms prepare consolidated financial statements when they meet two criteria:

1. The parent owns more than 50 percent of the voting stock of the subsidiary.
2. There are no important restrictions on the ability of the parent to exercise control of the subsidiary.

Ownership of more than 50 percent of the subsidiary's voting stock implies an ability to exert control over the activities of the subsidiary. The parent, for example, can control the subsidiary's corporate policies and dividend declarations. Sometimes, however, the parent cannot control the subsidiary's activities, despite the ownership of a majority of the voting stock. This could happen if the subsidiary is in a foreign country that severely restricts the withdrawal of funds from the country. Or, the subsidiary may be in bankruptcy and under the control of court-appointed trustees. In these cases, the parent will probably not consolidate its financial statements with those of the subsidiary. When the parent owns more than 50 percent of the shares but cannot exercise control, it uses the market value method.

Disclosure of Consolidation Policy.   The note to the financial statements that describes significant accounting policies includes a statement about the consolidation policy of the parent. If a parent does not consolidate a significant majority-owned subsidiary, the notes will disclose that fact. Note 1 in Appendix A states that Coke consolidates "all subsidiaries except where control is temporary or does not rest with the firm."[12]

Understanding Consolidated Statements.   There are three concepts essential for understanding consolidated financial statements:

1. The need for intercompany eliminations.
2. The meaning of consolidated net income.
3. The nature of the external minority interest.

The Need for Intercompany Eliminations.   State corporation laws typically require each legally separate corporation to maintain its own set of books. Thus, during the accounting period, the accounting system of each corporation records transactions of that entity with all other entities (both affiliated and nonaffiliated). At the end of the period, each corporation prepares its own set of financial statements.

The consolidation of these financial statements involves summing the amounts for various financial statement items across the separate company

---

[12]For example, several years ago Coke owned more than 50 percent of Coca-Cola Amatil Limited (it currently owns 45 percent as discussed in the previous section) but did not consolidate the subsidiary. Coke stated that its controlling interest was temporary and that it intended to reduce its interest below 50 percent (which it subsequently did). Coke used the equity method of accounting for the subsidiary then, as it does now.

statements. The amounts resulting from the summation require adjustments, however, to eliminate double counting resulting from *intercompany transactions*. Consolidated financial statements reflect the results of an affiliated group of companies operating as a single company. Thus, consolidated financial statements include only the transactions between the consolidated entity and others outside the group.

The eliminations to remove intercompany transactions typically appear on a *consolidation worksheet* and not on the books of any of the legal entities constituting the consolidated group. The accountant prepares the consolidated financial statements directly from the worksheet. The consolidated entity generally maintains no separate set of books.

To see the need for, and the nature of, *elimination entries*, look at the data for Company P and Company S in Exhibit 7.5. Column (1) shows the balance sheet and income statement data for Company P taken from its separate company books. Column (2) shows similar data for Company S. Column (3) sums the amounts from columns (1) and (2). The amounts in column (3) include the effects of several intercompany items and therefore do not represent the correct amounts for *consolidated* assets, equities, revenues, or expenses.

Eliminating Double Counting of Intercompany Payables.   Separate company records indicate that $12,000 of Company S's accounts receivable represent amounts payable by Company P. The amounts in column (3) count the current assets underlying this transaction twice: once as part of accounts receivable on Company S's books and a second time as cash (or other assets) on Company P's books. Also, accounts payable in column (3) includes the liability shown on Company P's books, even though the amount is not payable to an entity external to the consolidated group. To eliminate double counting on the asset side and to report accounts payable at the amount payable to external entities, the elimination entry reduces the amounts for accounts receivable and accounts payable in column (3) by $12,000.

Eliminating Double Counting of Investment.   Company P's balance sheet shows an asset, Investment in Stock of Company S. The subsidiary's balance sheet shows its individual assets and liabilities. The combined balance sheets in column (3) include both Company P's investment in Company S's net assets and the assets and liabilities themselves. We must eliminate Company P's account, Investment in Stock of Company S, from the sum of the balance sheets.

Because the consolidated balance sheet must maintain the accounting equation, we must make corresponding eliminations on the right-hand, or equities, side as well. To understand the eliminations from the right-hand side of the balance sheet, recall that the right-hand side shows the sources of the firm's financing. Creditors (liabilities) and owners (shareholders' equity) finance Company S. Company P owns 100 percent of Company S's voting shares. Thus, the creditors of both companies and Company P's shareholders finance the assets on the consolidated balance sheet of the single economic entity. In other words, the equities of

---

EXHIBIT 7.5

Illustrative Data for Preparation of Consolidated Financial Statements

	Single-Company Statements		
	Company P (1)	Company S (2)	Combined (3) = (1) + (2)
Condensed Balance Sheets on December 31			
Assets:			
Accounts Receivable	$ 200,000	$ 25,000	$ 225,000
Investment in Stock of Company S (at equity)	705,000	—	705,000
Other Assets	2,150,000	975,000	3,125,000
Total Assets	$3,055,000	$1,000,000	$4,055,000
Equities:			
Accounts Payable	$ 75,000	$ 15,000	$ 90,000
Other Liabilities	70,000	280,000	350,000
Common Stock	2,500,000	500,000	3,000,000
Retained Earnings	410,000	205,000	615,000
Total Equities	$3,055,000	$1,000,000	$4,055,000
Condensed Income Statement for Current Year			
Revenues:			
Sales	$ 900,000	$ 250,000	$1,150,000
Equity in Earnings of Company S	48,000	—	48,000
Total Revenues	$ 948,000	$ 250,000	$1,198,000
Expenses:			
Cost of Goods Sold (excluding depreciation)	$ 440,000	$ 80,000	$ 520,000
Depreciation Expense	120,000	50,000	170,000
Administrative Expenses	80,000	40,000	120,000
Income Tax Expense	104,000	32,000	136,000
Total Expenses	$ 744,000	$ 202,000	$ 946,000
Net Income	$ 204,000	$ 48,000	$ 252,000
Dividend Declarations	50,000	13,000	63,000
Increase in Retained Earnings for the Year	$ 154,000	$ 35,000	$ 189,000

the consolidated entity are the liabilities of both companies but the shareholders' equity of Company P alone.

If we add the shareholders' equity accounts of Company S to those of Company P, we would double count the financing from Company P's shareholders (once on the parent's books and once on the subsidiary's books). Hence, when we eliminate Company P's investment account from the sum of the two companies' assets, we maintain the accounting equation by eliminating the shareholders' equity accounts of Company S.

Eliminating Double Counting of Income. Similarly, we must eliminate certain intercompany items from the sum of income statement accounts for a meaningful presentation of the operating performance of the consolidated entity. Company P's accounts show Equity in Earnings of Company S of $48,000. Company S's records show individual revenues and expenses that net to $48,000. If we merely sum the revenues and expenses of the two companies, as column (3) of Exhibit 7.5 illustrates, we would double count the earnings of Company S. We must eliminate the account, Equity in Earnings of Company S, in preparing consolidated statements.

Eliminating Intercompany Sales. Another example of an intercompany item involves intercompany sales of inventory. Separate company records indicate that Company S sold merchandise to Company P for $40,000 during the year. None of this inventory remains in Company P's inventory on December 31. The sale of the merchandise inventory increases sales revenue on both Company S's books (sale to Company P for $40,000) and on Company P's books (sale to an external entity for probably a higher price). Thus, the combined amounts for sales revenue overstate sales from the standpoint of the consolidated entity by $40,000. Likewise, cost of goods sold of both companies includes the separate-company costs of the goods sold. To eliminate double counting, we must eliminate $40,000 from consolidated cost of goods sold.

The Meaning of Consolidated Income. The amount of consolidated net income for a period exactly equals the amount that the parent shows on its separate company books from applying the equity method. That is, consolidated net income equals

Parent Company's Net Income from Its Own Activities	+	Parent Company's Share of Subsidiary's Net Income	−	Profit (or + Loss) on Intercompany Transactions	−	Amortization of Goodwill from the Acquisition

A consolidated income statement differs from an equity method income statement in the *components* presented. When a firm uses the equity method for reporting an unconsolidated subsidiary, the parent's share of the subsidiary's net income minus gain (or plus loss) on intercompany transactions and minus amortization of goodwill appears on a single line entitled, Equity in Earnings of Unconsolidated Subsidiary. In a consolidated income statement, we combine the individual revenues and expenses of the subsidiary (less intercompany adjustments) with those of the parent, and eliminate the account, Equity in Earnings of Unconsolidated Subsidiary, shown on the parent's books.

Some accountants refer to the equity method as a *one-line consolidation* because it nets the individual revenues and expenses of the subsidiary into the one account, Equity in Earnings of Unconsolidated Subsidiary.

The Nature of External Minority Interest in Consolidated Subsidiary.   The parent does not always own 100 percent of the voting stock of a consolidated subsidiary. Accountants refer to the owners of the remaining shares of voting stock as the minority interest. These shareholders have a proportionate interest in the net assets (= total assets − total liabilities) of the subsidiary as shown on the subsidiary's separate corporate records. They also have a proportionate interest in the earnings of the subsidiary.

One issue that the accountant must confront in preparing consolidated statements is whether the statements should show only the parent's share of the assets and liabilities of the subsidiary or whether they should show all of the subsidiary's assets and liabilities along with the minority interests' claim on them. Financial reporting shows all of the assets and liabilities of the subsidiary, because the parent, with its controlling voting interest, effectively directs the use of all the assets and liabilities, not merely an amount equal to the parent's percentage of ownership. The consolidated balance sheet and income statement in these instances, however, must disclose the interest of the minority shareholders in the consolidated subsidiary.

The amount of the minority interest appearing on the balance sheet results from multiplying the common shareholders' equity of the subsidiary by the minority's percentage of ownership. For example, if the common shareholders' equity (or assets minus liabilities) of a consolidated subsidiary totals $500,000, and the minority owns 20 percent of the common stock, the minority interest appears on the consolidated balance sheet at $100,000 (= .20 × $500,000). The consolidated balance sheet shows the minority interest as part of shareholders' equity. The financial statements of Coke give no indication that a minority interest exists in any of its consolidated subsidiaries.

The amount of the minority interest in the subsidiary's income is calculated by multiplying the subsidiary's net income by the minority's percentage of ownership. The consolidated income statement shows the proportion of consolidated income applicable to the parent company and the proportion of the subsidiary's income applicable to the minority interest. Typically, the minority interest in the subsidiary's income appears as a subtraction in calculating consolidated net income.

Limitations of Consolidated Statements.   Consolidated statements do not replace statements of individual corporations; rather, they supplement those statements and aid in their interpretation. Creditors must rely on the resources of one corporation, and they may be misled if forced to rely entirely on consolidated statements that combine the data of a company in good financial condition with that of one verging on insolvency. Firms can legally declare dividends only from their own retained earnings. When the parent company does not own all of the shares of the subsidiary, the outside or minority shareholders can judge the dividend constraints, both legal and financial, only by inspecting the subsidiary's statements.

Consolidation of Unconsolidated Subsidiaries and Affiliates.
The analyst may wish to assess the financial position of a firm with all important majority-owned subsidiaries and minority-owned affiliates consolidated. As dis-

cussed in this chapter and in Chapter 1, Coca-Cola has significant investments in bottlers that are integral to its operations. Consolidation of the financial statements of these affiliates with those of Coke presents a more realistic picture of the assets and liabilities of Coke as an operating enterprise. Consolidation also places Coke on a more comparable basis with its most direct competitor, Pepsi, which owns most of its bottling operations.

Exhibit 7.6 presents a consolidation worksheet for Coke and its bottlers. Coke's balance sheet (from Appendix A) provides the amounts in column (1). Note 2 to Coke's financial statements provides the amounts for columns (2), (3), and (4).

The amounts in column (5) eliminate amounts in the intercorporate investment accounts on Coke's books against the shareholders' equity accounts of the affiliates. The column also shows the reclassification of a portion of the shareholders' equity accounts of the affiliates to recognize the minority or external interests' claims. The amount that Exhibit 7.6 shows for the external interest equals the total shareholders' equity of the affiliates times the external interests' ownership percentage. This percentage is 55 percent for Coca-Cola Enterprises, and 64 percent for Coca-Cola Amatil Limited.

Coke does not disclose its ownership percentage in Other Equity Investments. We can approximate this percentage by comparing Coke's equity income from these investments ($131 million in Note 2) to the total net income of the investees ($366 million in Note 2). Coke appears to own 35.8 percent (= $131 ÷ $366), and the external interests own 64.2 percent.

This procedure probably includes some measurement error. The amounts that Coke shows for its intercorporate investments ($547, $881, and $2,004) do not equal Coke's share (45 percent, 36 percent, and 35.8 percent) of the shareholders' equity of the investees. The difference represents negative goodwill of $151 million and positive goodwill of $720 million ($137 + 583). Exhibit 7.6 includes this goodwill in noncurrent assets.

The consolidated amounts in column (6) provide a better sense of the assets and obligations under Coke's influence and integral to its operations. Net income for Coke remains the same, whether Coke accounts for these investments using the equity method or consolidates them. The components of net income do change (sales, cost of goods sold), but net income does not.

Consider now the effect of consolidating Coke's bottlers on its rate of return on assets. For Year 7, Chapter 3 calculates an ROA based on Coke's reported amounts of 23.6 percent as follows:

$$\text{ROA} = \frac{[\$3,492 + 1 - 0.35\,(\$286) + \$0]}{[0.5(\$15,041 + \$16,161)]}.$$

Operating income in the numerator of ROA does not change as a result of consolidation.

To exclude the effect of financing from the numerator of ROA, we must add back the interest expense (net of taxes) recognized by Coke's bottlers. Coke's Note 2 does not provide the amount of interest expense for those entities. We might approximate this amount by assuming that the noncurrent liabilities

EXHIBIT 7.6

Coke and Equity Method Affiliates
Consolidation Worksheet
December 31, Year 7
(in millions)

	Coke (1)	Coca-Cola Enterprises (2)	Coca-Cola Amatil (3)	Other Equity Investments (4)	Eliminations (5)		Consolidated (6)
Current Assets	$ 5,910	$ 1,319	$ 1,847	$ 2,792	(A)	−547[a]	$11,868
Investments in Securities	5,948	—	—		(B)	−881[a]	
					(C)	−2,004[a]	2,516
Noncurrent Assets	4,303	9,915	2,913	8,783	(A)	−151[c]	26,484
					(B)	+137[e]	
					(C)	+583[g]	
Total Assets	$16,161	$11,234	$ 4,760	$11,575			$40,868
Current Liabilities	$ 7,406	$ 1,390	$ 1,247	$ 2,758			$12,801
Noncurrent Liabilities	2,599	8,294	1,445	4,849			17,187
External Interests	—	—	—	—	(A)	+853[b]	4,724
					(B)	+1,324[d]	
					(C)	+2,547[f]	
Shareholders' Equity	$ 6,156	$ 1,550	$ 2,068	$ 3,968	(A)	−1,550[a]	6,156
					(B)	−2,068[a]	
					(C)	−3,968[a]	
	$16,161	$11,234	$ 4,760	$11,575			$40,868

[a]Given in Coke's Note 3.

[b]$853 = .55 × $1,550.

[c]−$151 = [$547 − (.45 × $1,550)].

[d]$1,324 = .64 × $2,068.

[e]$137 = [($881 − (.36 × $2,068).

[f]$2,547 = (1 − .0358) × ($3,968).

[g]$583 = [$2,004 − (.358 × $3,968)].

represent interest-bearing debt. According to the disclosures in Coke's Note 6, the weighted average interest rate on its long-term debt was 6.5 percent at the end of Year 6 and 5.9 percent at the end of Year 7. Using an assumed interest rate of 6.2 percent (= [0.5(6.2 percent + 5.9 percent)]) on the debt of Coke's investees, amounts for noncurrent liabilities from Note 2 for Year 7, and corresponding disclosures from its Year 6 annual report yields interest expense of $769 million [0.062 × 0.5($6,770 + $8,294 + $881 + $1,445 + $2,555 + $4,849)] for Year 7. We inject some error into the calculation of ROA to the extent that some of the current liabilities of these entities bear interest, that some of the noncurrent liabilities do not bear interest, and that 6.2 percent is not a reasonable interest rate.

The final adjustment to the numerator of ROA to consolidate these bottlers is to add the external interest in earnings. This adjustment permits the numerator to include 100 percent of the operating income of Coke and its bottlers and the denominator to include 100 percent of the assets of these entities.

Coke's Note 2 shows the total income of these bottlers for Year 7 ($114 + $80 + $366 = $560), as well as Coke's equity share ($53 + $27 + $131 = $211). The share of the external interest is therefore $349 million (= $560 − $211). Consolidating Coke's bottlers results in a recomputed ROA for Year 7 as follows:

$$\text{ROA} = \frac{\$3{,}492 + (1 - .35)(\$286 + \$769) + \$349}{.5(\$32{,}398 + \$40{,}868)} = \frac{\$4{,}527}{\$36{,}663} = 12.4\%$$

Thus, Coke's ROA for Year 7 drops from 23.6 percent to 12.4 percent, almost a 50 percent decline. The capital-intensive nature of bottling reveals itself in this pro forma ratio analysis in that Coke's asset base increases dramatically when the bottling companies are consolidated. The analysis clearly points out the benefit to Coke of not bottling its own product.

The consolidation of majority-owned subsidiaries is a relatively recent phenomenon in some countries (Germany and Japan for example). These countries had tended to follow strict legal definitions of the reporting entity. Financial reporting in these countries now generally requires the preparation of consolidated financial statements, although the requirement in Japan applies only to filings with the Ministry of Finance.

JOINT VENTURE INVESTMENTS

Firms frequently come together in joint ventures to carry out their business activities. Example 16 in Chapter 5 describes how Amgen, a leading biotechnology company, contributes preliminary research findings to joint ventures that it has formed with other biotechnology firms. As another example, two chemical firms may join together to construct a chemical processing plant. In this case, typically each firm agrees to purchase 50 percent of the output of the plant and to pay 50 percent of the operating and debt service costs. When they sell the plant, each firm receives one-half of the net cash proceeds. By joining together, they can perhaps construct a larger, more efficient plant than if each firm were to build its own smaller plant.

Joint ventures are unique in that joint control is present. Neither firm has a majority, voting position. Both firms must generally agree to make significant policy changes. These investments therefore fall between minority, active investments and majority, active investments.

Firms account for joint ventures using the equity method. They include the investment in the joint venture in the noncurrent asset section entitled investments on the balance sheet. The assets and liabilities of the joint venture do not appear on the balance sheet of either owner.

Long-term debt typically finances most joint ventures. By accounting for the joint venture using the equity method, firms keep this debt off the balance sheet. As Chapter 6 discusses, firms commonly attempt to keep debt off the balance sheet in an effort to present a less risky profile to potential lenders. Joint ventures have increased in popularity in recent years.

The FASB is currently studying the accounting for joint ventures under the rubric of its consolidation project (see footnote 8). At issue is whether firms should use the equity method, or whether proportionate consolidation is more appropriate. Under proportionate consolidation, the investor's share of the assets and liabilities of the joint venture appear in separate sections on the asset and liabilities sides of the balance sheet, with the investment account eliminated. Some accountants argue that proportionate consolidation better captures the economics of transactions where joint control is present.

INCOME TAX CONSEQUENCES OF INVESTMENTS IN SECURITIES

For income tax purposes, investments fall into two categories:

1. Investments in debt securities, in preferred stock, and in less than 80 percent of the common stock of another entity. Firms recognize interest or dividends received or receivable each period as taxable income (subject to a partial dividend exclusion), as well as gains or losses when they sell the securities.
2. Investments in 80 percent or more of the common stock of another entity. Firms can prepare consolidated tax returns for these investments.

As is evident, the methods of accounting for investments for financial and tax reporting do not overlap precisely. Thus, temporary differences will likely arise for which firms must recognize deferred taxes. Coke, for example, cannot file consolidated tax returns with Coca-Cola Enterprises or other equity investments because its ownership percentage is less than 80 percent. Coke reports in Note 13 of Appendix A deferred tax liabilities relating to these equity investments ($369 million at December 31, Year 7), because it includes its share of the investees' earnings each year for financial reporting but recognizes dividends received as income on its tax return.

FOREIGN CURRENCY TRANSLATION

U.S. parent companies must translate the financial statements of foreign branches and subsidiaries into U.S. dollars before preparing consolidated financial statements for shareholders and creditors. We describe and illustrate the translation methodology, and discuss the implications of the methodology both for managing international operations and for interpreting financial statement disclosures regarding such operations.

Two general issues arise in translating the financial statements of a foreign branch or subsidiary.

1. Should the firm translate individual financial statement items at the exchange rate at the time of the transaction (referred to as the historical exchange rate), or at the exchange rate during or at the end of the current period (referred to as the current exchange rate)?

   Financial statement items that firms translate using the historical exchange rates appear in the financial statements at the same U.S. dollar-equivalent amount each period, regardless of changes in the exchange rate. For example, land acquired in France for 10,000 French francs when the exchange rate was $0.40 per French francs appears on the balance sheet at $4,000 each period.

   Financial statement items that firms translate using the current exchange rate appear in the financial statements at a different U.S. dollar amount each period when exchange rates change. Thus, a change in the exchange rate to $0.60 per French franc results in reporting the land at $6,000 on the balance sheet. Financial statement items for which firms use the current exchange rate give rise to a *foreign exchange adjustment* each period.

2. Should the firm recognize the foreign exchange adjustment as a gain or loss in measuring net income each period as it arises, or should the firm defer its recognition until a future period? The foreign exchange adjustment represents an unrealized gain or loss, much the same as changes in the market value of marketable securities, inventories, or other assets. Should financial reporting require realization of the gain or loss through sale of the foreign operation before recognizing it, or should the unrealized gain or loss flow directly to the income statement as the exchange rate changes?

The foreign currency translation methods differ across countries primarily with regard to the answers to these two questions. First we describe financial reporting in the United States, and then reporting in other countries.

FUNCTIONAL CURRENCY CONCEPT

Central to the translation of foreign currency items is the *functional currency concept*.[13]

---

[13]Financial Accounting Standards Board, *Statement of Financial Accounting Standards No. 52* (as amended by *Statement No. 130*), "Foreign Currency Translation," 1981.

Foreign entities (whether branches or subsidiaries) are of two general types:

1. A foreign entity operates as a relatively self-contained and integrated unit within a particular foreign country. The functional currency for these operations is the currency of that foreign country.
2. The operations of a foreign entity are a direct and integral component or extension of the parent company's operations. The functional currency for these operations is the U.S. dollar.

Statement No. 52 sets out characteristics for determining whether the currency of the foreign unit or the U.S. dollar is the functional currency. Exhibit 7.7 summarizes these characteristics.

The operating characteristics of a particular foreign operation may provide mixed signals regarding which currency is the functional currency. Managers must exercise judgment in determining which functional currency best captures the economic effects of a foreign entity's operations and financial position. As we discuss later, managers may wish to structure certain financing or other transactions to swing the balance to favor selecting either the foreign currency or the U.S. dollar as the functional currency. Once a firm determines the functional currency of a foreign entity, it must use that currency consistently over time unless changes in economic circumstances clearly indicate a change in the functional currency.

EXHIBIT 7.7

Factors for Determining Functional Currency of Foreign Unit

	Foreign Currency Is Functional Currency	U.S. Dollar Is Functional Currency
Cash Flows of Foreign Entity	Receivables and payables denominated in foreign currency and not usually remitted to parent currently	Receivables and payables denominated in U.S. dollars and readily available for remittance to parent
Sales Prices	Influenced primarily by local competitive conditions and not responsive on a short-term basis to exchange rate changes	Influenced by worldwide competitive conditions and responsive on a short-term basis to exchange rate changes
Cost Factors	Foreign unit obtains labor, materials, and other inputs primarily from its own country	Foreign unit obtains labor, materials, and other inputs primarily from the United States
Financing	Financing denominated in currency of foreign unit or generated internally by the foreign unit	Financing denominated in U.S. dollars or ongoing fund transfers by the parent
Relations between Parent and Foreign Unit	Low volume of intercompany transactions and little operational interrelations between parent and foreign unit	High volume of intercompany transactions and extensive operational interrelations between parent and foreign unit

Statement No. 52 provides for one exception to the guidelines in Exhibit 7.7 for determining the functional currency. If the foreign entity operates in a highly inflationary country, financial reporting considers its currency to be too unstable to serve as the functional currency, and the firm must use the U.S. dollar instead. A highly inflationary country is one that has experienced cumulative inflation of at least 100 percent over a three-year period. Some developing nations fall within this exception and pose particular problems for the U.S. parent company, as we note later.

TRANSLATION METHODOLOGY—FOREIGN CURRENCY IS FUNCTIONAL CURRENCY

When the functional currency is the currency of the foreign unit, financial reporting requires firms to use the *all-current translation method*. The left-hand column of Exhibit 7.8 summarizes the translation procedure under the all-current method.

Firms translate revenues and expenses at the average exchange rate during the period and translate balance sheet items at the end-of-the-period exchange rate. Net income includes only *transaction* exchange gains and losses of the foreign unit. That is, a foreign unit that has receivables and payables denominated in a currency other than its own must make a currency conversion on settlement of the account. The gain or loss from changes in the exchange rate between the time the account originated and the time of settlement is a transaction gain or loss. Firms recognize this gain or loss during the period the account is outstanding, even though it is not yet realized or settled.

When a foreign unit operates more or less independently of the U.S. parent, financial reporting assumes that only the parent's equity investment in the foreign unit is subject to exchange rate risk. The firm measures the effect of exchange rate changes on this investment each period, but includes the resulting "translation adjustment" as a component of comprehensive income, rather than net income. The GAAP rationale for this treatment is that the firm's investment in the foreign unit is for the long term; short-term changes in exchange rates, therefore, should not affect periodic net income. Firms recognize the cumulative amount in the translation adjustment account when they measure any gain or loss from disposing of the foreign unit.

Illustration—Foreign Currency is Functional Currency. Exhibit 7.9 illustrates the all-current method for a foreign unit during its first year of operations. The exchange rate was $1:1FC (foreign currency) on January 1, $2:1FC on December 31, and $1.5:1FC on average during the year. Thus, the foreign currency increased in value compared to the U.S. dollar during the year.

The firm translates all assets and liabilities on the balance sheet at the exchange rate on December 31. It translates common stock at the exchange rate on the date of issuance; the translation adjustment account includes the effects of changes in exchange rates on this investment. The translated amount of retained earnings results from translating the income statement and dividends. Note that the firm translates all revenues and expenses of the foreign unit at the average exchange rate.

EXHIBIT 7.8

Summary of Translation Methodology

	Foreign Currency Is the Functional Currency (all-current method)	U.S. Dollar Is the Functional Currency (monetary/non-monetary method)
Income Statement	Firms translate revenues and expenses as measured in foreign currency into U.S. dollars using the average exchange rate during the period. Income includes (1) realized and unrealized transaction gains and losses and (2) realized translation gains and losses when the firm sells the foreign unit.	Firms translate revenues and expenses using the exchange rate in effect when the firm made the original measurements underlying the valuations. Firms translate revenues and most operating expenses using the average exchange rate during the period. However, they translate cost of goods sold and depreciation using the historical exchange rate appropriate to the related asset (inventory, fixed assets). Net income includes (1) realized and unrealized transaction gains and losses and (2) unrealized translation gains and losses on the net monetary position of the foreign unit each period.
Balance Sheet	Firms translate assets and liabilities as measured in foreign currency into U.S. dollars using the end-of-the-period exchange rate. Use of the end-of-the-period exchange rate gives rise to unrealized transaction gains and losses on receivables and payables requiring currency conversions in the future. Firms include an unrealized translation adjustment on the net asset position of the foreign unit in a separate shareholders' equity account, not in net income, until the firm sells the foreign unit.	Firms translate monetary assets and liabilities using the end-of-the-period exchange rate. They translate nonmonetary assets and equities using the historical exchange rate.

The foreign unit realizes a transaction gain during the year and records this on its books. In addition, the translated amounts for the foreign unit include an unrealized transaction gain arising from exposed accounts that are not yet settled. Note a to Exhibit 7.9 shows the computation of translated retained earnings. The foreign unit pays the dividend on December 31.

Note b shows the calculation of the translation adjustment. By investing $30 in the foreign unit on January 1 and allowing the $22.5 of earnings to remain in the foreign unit throughout the year while the foreign currency was increasing in value relative to the U.S. dollar, the parent has a potential exchange "gain" of $37.5. It reports this amount as a component of comprehensive income.

(continued)

EXHIBIT 7.9

Illustration of Translation Methodology when the Foreign Currency
Is the Functional Currency

	Foreign Currency		U.S. Dollars
Balance Sheet			
Assets			
Cash	FC 10	$2.0:1FC	$ 20.0
Receivables	20	$2.0:1FC	40.0
Inventories	30	$2.0:1FC	60.0
Fixed Assets (net)	40	$2.0:1FC	80.0
Total	FC 100		$200.0
Liabilities and Shareholders' Equity			
Accounts Payable	FC 40	$2.0:1FC	$ 80.0
Bonds Payable	20	$2.0:1FC	40.0
Total	FC 60		$120.0
Common Stock	FC 30	$1.0:1FC	$ 30.0
Retained Earnings	10		12.5[a]
Unrealized Translation Adjustment	—		37.5[b]
Total	FC 40		$ 80.0
Total	FC 100		$200.0
Income Statement			
Sales Revenue	FC 200	$1.5:1FC	$300.0
Realized Transaction Gain	2[c]	$1.5:1FC	3.0[c]
Unrealized Transaction Gain	1[d]	$1.5:1FC	1.5[d]
Cost of Goods Sold	(120)	$1.5:1FC	(180.0)
Selling & Administrative Expense	(40)	$1.5:1FC	(60.0)
Depreciation Expense	(10)	$1.5:1FC	(15.0)
Interest Expense	(2)	$1.5:1FC	(3.0)
Income Tax Expense	(16)	$1.5:1FC	(24.0)
Net Income	FC 15		$ 22.5

	Foreign Currency		U.S. Dollars
[a]Retained Earnings, Jan. 1	FC 0.0		$ 0.0
Plus Net Income	15.0		22.5
Less Dividends	(5.0)	$2.0:1FC	$(10.0)
Retained Earnings, Dec. 31	FC 10.0		$ 12.5

(continued)

Exh. 7.9—Continued	Foreign Currency		U.S. Dollars
[b]Net Asset Position, Jan. 1	FC 30.0	$1.0:1FC	$ 30.0
Plus Net Income	15.0		22.5
Less Dividends	(5.0)	$2.0:1FC	$(10.0)
Net Asset Position, Dec. 31	FC 40.0		$42.5
Net Asset Position, Dec. 31	$2.0:1FC	80.0
Unrealized Translation "Gain"			$ 37.5

[c]The foreign unit had receivables and payables denominated in a currency other than its own. When it settled these accounts during the period, the foreign unit made a currency conversion and realized a transaction gain of FC2.

[d]The foreign unit has receivables and payables outstanding that will require a currency conversion in a future period when the foreign unit settles the accounts. Because the exchange rate changed while the receivables/payables were outstanding, the foreign unit reports an unrealized transaction gain for financial reporting.

TRANSLATION METHODOLOGY—U.S. DOLLAR IS FUNCTIONAL CURRENCY

When the functional currency is the U.S. dollar, financial reporting requires firms to use the *monetary/nonmonetary translation method*. The right-hand column of Exhibit 7.8 summarizes the translation procedure under the monetary/nonmonetary method.

The underlying premise of the monetary/nonmonetary method is that the translated amounts reflect amounts that the firm would have reported if it had originally made all measurements in U.S. dollars. To implement this underlying premise, financial reporting makes a distinction between monetary items and nonmonetary items.

A monetary item is an account whose maturity amount does not change as the exchange rate changes. From a U.S. dollar perspective, these accounts give rise to exchange gains and losses, because the number of U.S. dollars required to settle the fixed foreign currency amounts fluctuates over time with exchange rate changes.

Monetary items include cash, receivables, accounts payable and other accrued liabilities, and long-term debt. Firms translate these items using the end-of-the-period exchange rate and recognize translation gains and losses. These translation gains and losses increase or decrease net income each period, whether or not the foreign unit must make an actual currency conversion to settle the monetary item.

A nonmonetary item is any account that is not monetary, and includes inventories, fixed assets, common stock, revenues, and expenses. Firms translate these accounts using the historical exchange rate in effect when the foreign unit initially made the measurements underlying these accounts.

EXHIBIT 7.10

Illustration of Translation Methodology when the U.S. Dollar Is the Functional Currency

	Foreign Currency		U.S. Dollars
Balance Sheet			
Assets			
Cash	FC 10	$2.0:1FC	$ 20.0
Receivables	20	$2.0:1FC	40.0
Inventories	30	$1.5:1FC	45.0
Fixed Assets (net)	40	$1.0:1FC	40.0
Total	FC 100		$145.0
Liabilities and Shareholders' Equity			
Accounts Payable	FC 40	$2.0:1FC	$ 80.0
Bonds Payable	20	$2.0:1FC	40.0
Total	FC 60		$ 120.0
Common Stock	FC 30	$1.0:1FC	$ 30.0
Retained Earnings	10		(5.0)[a]
Total	FC 40		$ 25.0
Total	FC 100		$ 145.0
Income Statement			
Sales Revenue	FC 200	$1.5:1FC	$ 300.0
Realized Transaction Gain	2	$1.5:1FC	3.0
Unrealized Transaction Gain	1	$1.5:1FC	1.5
Unrealized Translation Loss	—		(22.5)[b]
Cost of Goods Sold	(120)	$1.5:1FC	(180.0)
Selling & Administrative Expense	(40)	$1.5:1FC	(60.0)
Depreciation Expense	(10)	$1.0:1FC	(10.0)
Interest Expense	(2)	$1.5:1FC	(3.0)
Income Tax Expense	(16)	$1.5:1FC	(24.0)
Net Income	FC 15		$ 5.0

[a]Retained Earnings, Jan. 1	FC 0	—	$ 0.0
Plus Net Income	15		5.0
Less Dividends	(5)	$2.0:1FC	(10.0)
Retained Earnings, Dec. 31	FC 10		$ (5.0)

[b]Income for financial reporting includes any unrealized translation gain or loss for the period. The net monetary position of a foreign unit during the period serves as the basis for computing the translation gain or loss. The foreign unit was in a net monetary liability position during a period when the U.S. dollar decreased in value relative to the foreign currency. The translation loss arises because the U.S. dollars required to settle the net monetary liability position at the end of the year exceed the U.S. dollars required to settle the obligation at the time the firm initially recorded the transactions giving rise to change in net monetary liabilities during the period. The calculations appear below:

(continued)

Exh. 7.10—Continued	Foreign Currency		U.S. Dollars
Net Monetary Position, Jan. 1	FC 0.0	—	$ 0.0
Plus:			
Issue of Common Stock	30.0	$1.0:1FC	$ 30.0
Sales for Cash and on Account	200.0	$1.5:1FC	300.0
Settlement of Exposed Receivable/Payable at a Gain	2.0	$1.5:1FC	3.0
Unrealized Gain on Exposed Receivable/Payable	1.0	$1.5:1FC	1.5
Less:			
Acquisition of Fixed Assets	(50.0)	$1.0:1FC	(50.0)
Acquisition of Inventory	(150.0)	$1.5:1FC	(225.0)
Selling & Admin. Costs Incurred	(40.0)	$1.5:1FC	(60.0)
Interest Cost Incurred	(2.0)	$1.5:1FC	(3.0)
Income Taxes Paid	(16.0)	$1.5:1FC	(24.0)
Dividend Paid	(5.0)	$2.0:1FC	(10.0)
Net Monetary Liability Position, Dec. 31	(30.0)		$ (37.5)
	→ $2.0:1FC		(60.0)
Unrealized Translation Loss			$ 22.5

Inventories and cost of goods sold translate at the exchange rate at the time the foreign unit acquired the inventory items. Fixed assets and depreciation expense translate at the exchange rate at the time the foreign unit acquired the fixed assets. Most revenues and operating expenses other than cost of goods sold and depreciation translate at the average exchange rate during the period.

The objective is to state these accounts at their U.S. dollar-equivalent historical cost amounts. In this way the translated amounts will reflect the U.S. dollar perspective that is appropriate when the U.S. dollar is the functional currency.

Illustration—U.S. Dollar is Functional Currency.   Exhibit 7.10 shows the application of the monetary/nonmonetary method to the same data considered in Exhibit 7.9. Net income again includes both realized and unrealized transaction gains and losses. Net income under the monetary/nonmonetary translation method also includes a $22.5 translation loss.

As Exhibit 7.10 (note b) shows, the firm was in a net monetary liability position during a period in which the U.S. dollar decreased in value relative to the foreign currency. The translation loss arises because the U.S. dollars required to settle the firm's foreign-denominated net liabilities at the end of the year exceed the U.S. dollar amount required to settle the net liability position before the exchange rate changed.

IMPLICATIONS OF FUNCTIONAL CURRENCY DETERMINATION

As Exhibit 7.9 and Exhibit 7.10 demonstrate, the functional currency and the related translation method can significantly affect translated financial statement amounts for a foreign unit. Here are some summary comparisons:

	Functional Currency Is:	
	Foreign Currency	**U.S. Dollar**
Net Income	$ 22.5	$ 5.0
Total Assets	200.0	145.0
Shareholders' Equity	80.0	25.0
Return on Assets	11.3%	3.4%
Return on Equity	28.1%	20.0%

These differences arise for two principal reasons:

1. The all-current translation method (foreign currency is the functional currency) uses current exchange rates, while the monetary/nonmonetary translation method (U.S. dollar is the functional currency) uses a mixture of current and historical rates. Not only are net income and total asset amounts different, but the relative proportions of receivables, inventories, and fixed assets to total assets, debt/equity ratios, and gross and net profit margins also differ. When firms use the all-current translation method, the translated amounts reflect the same financial statement relationships (for example, debt/equity ratios) as when measured in the foreign currency. When the U.S. dollar is the functional currency, financial statement relationships get measured in U.S. dollar-equivalent amounts and financial ratios differ from their foreign currency amounts.

2. The other major reason for differences between the two translation methods is the inclusion of unrealized translation gains and losses in net income under the monetary/nonmonetary method. Much of the debate with respect to the predecessor to *Statement No. 52*, which was *Statement No. 8*, involved the inclusion of this unrealized translation gain or loss in net income. Many companies argued that the gain or loss was a bookkeeping adjustment only, and that it lacked economic significance, particularly when the transaction required no currency conversion to settle a monetary item. Also, its inclusion in net income often caused wide, unexpected swings in earnings, particularly in quarterly reports.

As discussed earlier, the organizational structure and operating policies of a particular foreign unit determine its functional currency. The two acceptable choices and the corresponding translation methods are designed to capture the different economic and operational relationships between a parent and its foreign affiliates. Firms still have some discretion in deciding the function currency, however, and therefore the translation method, for each foreign unit.

In many cases the signals about the appropriate functional currency will be mixed, and firms will have latitude to select between them. Some actions that management might consider to swing the balance of factors toward use of the foreign currency as the functional currency include:

1. *Decentralize decision making into the foreign unit.* The greater the degree of autonomy of the foreign unit, the more likely its currency will be the functional currency. The U.S. parent company can design effective control systems to monitor the activities of the foreign unit while at the same time permitting the foreign unit to operate with considerable freedom.
2. *Minimize remittances/dividends.* The greater the degree of earnings retention by the foreign unit, the more likely its currency will be the functional currency. The parent may obtain cash from a foreign unit indirectly rather than directly through remittances or dividends. For example, a foreign unit with mixed signals about its functional currency might, through loans or transfer prices for goods or services, send cash to another foreign unit whose functional currency is clearly its own currency. This second foreign unit can then remit it to the parent. Other possibilities for interunit transactions are possible to ensure that *some* foreign currency rather than the U.S. dollar is the functional currency.

Research suggests that approximately 80 percent of U.S. firms with foreign operations use the foreign currency as the functional currency; the remainder use the U.S. dollar.[14] Few firms select the foreign currency for some operations and the U.S. dollar for other operations (except for operations in highly inflationary countries, when firms must use the U.S. dollar as the functional currency). Thus, it appears that firms have a preference for the all-current translation method, in large part because they can exclude unrealized foreign currency "gains and losses" from earnings each period, and experience fewer earnings surprises. Inclusion of the change in the foreign currency translation adjustment account each period in earnings can cause large, unexpected variations in reporting earnings, a result that most managers prefer to avoid.

The question for the analyst assessing earnings quality is whether to include the change in the foreign currency translation account in earnings, or to leave it as a component of comprehensive income. The principal argument for excluding it is that the unrealized "gains or losses" may well reverse in the long term, and, in any case, will not be realized perhaps for many years. The principal arguments for including it in earnings are (1) management has purposely chosen the foreign currency as the functional currency in order to avoid including such "gains or losses" in earnings, not because the firm allows its foreign units to operate as independent units, and (2) the change in the foreign currency translation adjustment represents the current period's portion of the eventual net gain or loss that *will* be realized.

A study examining the valuation relevance of the translation adjustment regresses excess, or unexpected, returns on (1) earnings excluding exchange gains and losses, (2) transaction exchange gains and losses included in earnings, and (3) changes in the translation adjustment reported as a component of comprehensive income.[15] The study finds that the coefficient on the translation adjustment is sta-

---

[14]Eli Bartov and Gordon M. Bodnar, "Alternative Accounting Methods, Information Asymmetry and Liquidity: Theory and Evidence," *The Accounting Review*, July 1996, pp. 397–418.

[15]Billy S. Soo and Lisa Gilbert Soo, "Accounting for the Multinational Firm: Is the Translation Process Valued by the Stock Market?" *The Accounting Review*, October 1995, pp. 617–637.

tistically significant, but smaller than that on earnings excluding all exchange gains and losses. This suggests that the market considers the translation adjustment relevant for security valuation but less persistent (more transitory, as defined in Chapter 4) than earnings excluding gains and losses. Given this finding, the FASB's relatively recent decision to require firms to report the translation adjustment change as a *separate and distinct* component of comprehensive income appears on target in that it mandates highlighting of the change.

INTERPRETING FINANCIAL STATEMENT DISCLOSURES

Look at the financial statements for Coke in Appendix A. Coke's Note 1 on accounting policies does not indicate the foreign currency translation method it uses for foreign operations. Note 16 discloses that Coke has substantial foreign involvements (67 percent of sales and 51 percent of assets in Year 7).[16] Coke conducts a portion of these operations in Latin American and Africa, where high inflation rates often dictate use of the monetary/nonmonetary translation method.

Coke's balance sheet shows an account, "foreign currency translation adjustment," in the shareholders' equity section, suggesting that Coke uses the all-current translation method for a portion of its foreign operations. These operations result in a negative translation adjustment of $424 million at the end of Year 6 and a negative adjustment of $662 million at the end of Year 7, an increase of $238 million during Year 7. The $238 million increase is reported as a component of comprehensive income, as Chapter 1 illustrates in Exhibit 1.9.

The all-current translation method assumes that Coke's net asset position (that is, assets minus liabilities, or shareholders' equity) is at risk to exchange rate changes. The reporting of a larger negative amount in the translation adjustment at the end of Year 7 than at the beginning suggests that on average foreign currencies decreased in value relative to the U.S. dollar during Year 7.

As noted before, Coke has significant foreign operations. Changes in exchange rates can significantly affect interpretations of its profitability, independent of the translation method used. Consider the example in Exhibit 7.11.

Under the first scenario, the average exchange rate was $10:1FC during the period. Foreign sales represent 40 percent of consolidated sales (= $1,000 ÷ $2,500), and the consolidated profit margin is 28 percent.

Under the second scenario, foreign operations as measured in the local currency are identical to those above. In this case, however, the average exchange rate was $15:1FC. After translation, foreign sales represent 50 percent of consolidated sales ($1,500 ÷ $3,000), and the profit margin is now 26.7 percent. Although the operations of this foreign unit are largely self-contained within the foreign country and, on an operational level at least, not affected by exchange rate changes, the extent to which the exchange rate changes does have an effect on consolidated financial statements in U.S. dollars.

---

[16]These percentages are approximations because Coke combines the United States and Canada in its segment disclosures.

EXHIBIT 7.11

Effect of Foreign Sales on Consolidated Profit Margin

	Foreign Subsidiary		U.S. Parent	
	Foreign Currency	U.S. Dollars	U.S. Dollars	Consolidated
Scenario 1:				
Sales	FC 100	$10:1FC $1,000	$1,500	$2,500
Expenses	80	$10:1FC 800	1,000	1,800
Net Income	FC 20	$10:1FC $ 200	$ 500	$ 700
Profit Margin		20%	33%	28%
Scenario 2:				
Sales	FC 100	$15:1FC $1,500	$1,500	$3,000
Expenses	80	$15:1FC 1,200	1,000	2,200
Net Income	FC 20	$15:1FC $ 300	$ 500	$ 800
Profit Margin		20%	33%	26.7%

Coke's disclosures regarding foreign operations, though scanty, are not unusual. Most firms aggregate information for all foreign operations, so the analyst will find it hard to interpret the impact of international activities on profitability and risk.

The interpretive difficulties increase when comparing U.S. companies with non-U.S. companies. Reporting practices vary widely. In addition to the all-current and monetary/nonmonetary translation methods, some countries permit the current/noncurrent method in which current assets and liabilities translate at the current exchange rate; noncurrent assets and liabilities translate at the historical exchange rate. Besides recognizing translation adjustments in income immediately or in a separate shareholders' equity account, some countries require firms to amortize this adjustment into income over a period of future years.

As capital markets become more integrated internationally, one would hope that greater uniformity in translation methods will evolve.

FOREIGN CURRENCY TRANSLATION AND INCOME TAXES

Income tax laws make a distinction between a foreign branch of a U.S. parent and a subsidiary of a U.S. parent. A subsidiary is a legally separate entity from the parent, while a branch is not. The translation procedure for foreign branches is essentially the same as for financial reporting (except that taxable income does not include translation gains and losses until realized). That is, a firm selects a functional currency for each foreign branch and uses the all-current or monetary/nonmonetary translation method as appropriate.

For foreign subsidiaries, taxable income includes only dividends received each period (translated at the exchange rate on the date of remittance). Because parent companies typically consolidate foreign subsidiaries for financial reporting but cannot consolidate them for tax reporting, temporary differences that require the provision of deferred taxes are likely to arise.

SEGMENT REPORTING

The three topics discussed thus far in this chapter—corporate acquisitions, investments in securities, and foreign currency translation—involve the aggregation of information about various entities or units into a single set of financial statements. When these entities or units operate in an integrated or coordinated manner, it is useful to examine the results of operations and financial position for the combined entities as a whole.

The process of combining or aggregating information for various entities, however, can hinder analysis of the returns and risks of the subunits. For example, General Electric Company (GE) manufactures and distributes a wide line of industrial and consumer products. Its wholly owned, consolidated subsidiary, General Electric Capital Services (GECS), operates in leasing and other financial services. GE's consolidated financial statements merge these different activities. Yet GE's assets are primarily inventories and fixed assets, while those of GECS are largely receivables. The capital structure of GECS includes considerably more debt than that of GE.

To provide useful information about its subunits, financial reporting requires firms to provide certain segment information.[17]

DEFINITION OF SEGMENTS

Financial reporting requires firms to disclose segment data in three ways, according to (1) reportable operating segments, (2) geographic location (foreign versus domestic), and (3) major customers (U.S. government for example). Firms provide segment data, however, only for those segments that make up 10 percent or more of total sales, income, or assets.

Statement No. 131 does not prescribe a list of acceptable segment classes. Instead, firms chose appropriate segment classes following what the FASB refers to as the *management approach*. The management approach is meant to reflect the way that a firm organizes its segments for making operating decisions and assessing performance. By stressing management's choice of how a firm is structured as a basis for defining segment classes, *Statement No. 131* places more emphasis on the consistent reporting of segment data for a *particular firm over time* than on comparable segment data across firms. Financial reporting defines a *reportable operating segment* as a subunit of the firm:

---

[17]Financial Accounting Standards Board, *Statement of Financial Accounting Standards No. 131*, "Disclosures about Segments of an Enterprise and Related Information," 1997.

1. That engages in business activities from which it may earn revenues and incur expenses (including revenues and expenses relating to transactions with other subunits of the firm).
2. Whose operating results are regularly reviewed by the firm's chief operating officer to make decisions about resources to be allocated to the segment and assess its performance.
3. For which discrete financial information is available.

Financial reporting labels these three criteria collectively the management approach, because the aim is that the segment results reported externally are the same segment results that are used internally for evaluating performance and determining resource allocation.

TRANSFER PRICING AND TREATMENT OF CENTRAL CORPORATE EXPENSES

Most firms operate with some degree of integration. As a consequence, most segments sell a portion of their output to other segments within the firm. Two questions arise with respect to intersegment sales:

1. Should segment sales include intersegment sales, or should firms eliminate intersegment sales from the segment data?
2. At what transfer price should segments report intersegment sales (cost or market price)?

Statement No. 131 requires firms to disclose material intercompany sales in their segment reports, and also to disclose the transfer price used. Coke indicates in Note 16 of Appendix A that intersegment transfers are not material.

A second reporting issue is the treatment of central corporate costs (senior management compensation, corporate office expenses). Should firms allocate these costs to segments in measuring segment operating income, or should they remain unallocated? *Statement No. 131* does not prescribe one treatment or the other, but requires firms to disclose the nature and the amount of corporate expenses, and to indicate clearly how they treat such costs in the segment report.

Coke includes in Note 16 a "corporate" column in its segment disclosures. This column includes amounts that Coke chooses not to allocate to the segments. It does not disclose the items included in the $602 million on the operating income line for Year 7. An examination of Coke's income statement suggests that it includes primarily interest expense. Note that the consolidated operating income reported in the segment disclosures is pretax income.

SEGMENT ITEMS DISCLOSED

Statement No. 131 requires firms to identify the factors used for determining the reportable operating segments, as well as the types of products and services from which each segment derives its revenues. For each reportable operating segment, firms must disclose:

1. **Sales.** Financial reporting requires disclosure of sales from external customers and those with other operating segments.
2. **Profit or loss.** *Statement No. 131* does not define segment profit or loss, but allows any measure of performance to be displayed, as long as that measure is reviewed by the chief operating officer. Key components of profit or loss must be disclosed if they are included in the *measure* of segment profit of loss, including interest revenue and expense, depreciation, equity income, and income tax expense.
3. **Assets.** Similar to its treatment of segment profit or loss, *Statement No. 131* does not define segment assets. Key components of segment assets must be disclosed if they are included in the determination of segment assets, including capital expenditures and investments in equity method investees.

For geographic segments, firms must report only segment sales and fixed assets. For segment disclosures by major customers, firms need report sales only if a single external customer represents 10 percent or more of a firm's revenues. Firms need not disclose the customer, but often they do.

The required segment disclosures in Canada closely parallel those in the United States. In fact, policy bodies in the United States (FASB) and Canada (Accounting Standards Board) jointly drafted *Statement No. 131*. European countries and Japan tend to require the reporting of sales by major industry grouping and by geographic location. Firms in these countries seldom disclose information about segment operating income or assets.

SUMMARY

Unlike reporting topics such as inventories, leases, and deferred taxes (covered in Chapters 5 and 6), which affect one line or only a few lines in the financial statements, the topics discussed in this chapter tend to affect many line items. The accounting for corporate acquisitions, intercorporate investments, foreign currency translation, and segment reporting therefore has a more pervasive effect on financial statements. This pervasiveness both increases the potential significance of the reporting in these areas to the financial analyst and provides a source for concern. Full disclosure of the effects of using the purchase method instead of the pooling of interests method, or translating the financial statements of a foreign unit using the all-current method instead of the monetary/nonmonetary method, is cumbersome and possibly confusing. The analyst must often contend with less than sufficient disclosures when interpreting financial statements affected by the topics considered in this chapter.

PROBLEMS AND CASES

7.1 **EFFECT OF THE PURCHASE METHOD AND THE POOLING OF INTERESTS METHOD ON THE BALANCE SHEET.** Sun Company acquired all the outstanding common stock of Snow Company on January 1, Year 5. Sun gave shares of its common stock with a market value of

$504 million in exchange for the Snow common stock. Snow will remain a legally separate entity after the exchange, but Sun will prepare consolidated financial statements each period with Snow. The transaction qualifies as a nontaxable exchange for income tax purposes.

Exhibit 7.12 presents the balance sheets of Sun and Snow on January 1, Year 5 just prior to the acquisition. The income tax rate is 40 percent. The information below applies to Snow:

1. The market value of Snow's fixed assets exceeds book value of the assets by $80 million.
2. Snow owns a copyright with a market value of $50 million.
3. Snow is a defendant in a lawsuit that it expects to settle during Year 5 at a pretax cost of $30 million. The firm carries no insurance against such lawsuits. Sun wants to establish an acquisition reserve for this lawsuit.
4. Snow has an unrecognized and unfunded pension benefits obligation totaling $40 million on January 1, Year 5.

Required

a. Prepare an analysis that determines the excess purchase price, and show the allocation of the excess to individual assets and liabilities under the purchase method and the pooling of interests method.
b. Prepare a consolidated balance sheet for Sun and Snow on January 1, Year 5, under (1) the purchase method, and (2) the pooling of interests method. Show your sup-

---

EXHIBIT 7.12

Sun Company and Snow Company
Balance Sheets
January 1, Year, 5
(amounts in millions)
(Problem 7.1)

	Sun Company	Snow Company
Cash	$ 100	$ 30
Accounts Receivable	240	90
Fixed Assets (net)	1,000	360
Copyright	—	—
Deferred Tax Asset	40	—
Goodwill	—	—
Total Assets	$1,380	$480
Accounts Payable and Accruals	$ 240	$ 80
Long-term Debt	480	100
Deferred Tax Liability	160	—
Other Noncurrent Liabilities	120	—
Common Stock	320	100
Retained Earnings	60	200
Total Equities	$1,380	$480

porting calculations for any amount that is not simply the sum of the amounts for Sun and Snow from their separate financial records.

7.2 EFFECT OF THE PURCHASE METHOD AND THE POOLING OF INTERESTS METHOD ON THE BALANCE SHEET AND THE INCOME STATEMENT. Condensed balance sheet data for Moran Corporation and Walther Corporation as of January 1, Year 8, appear below.

	Book Values		Market Values
	Moran (1)	**Walther** (2)	**Walther** (3)
Current Assets	$ 1,200	$ 800	$ 900
Fixed Assets	1,800	1,200	1,500
Goodwill	—	—	
	$ 3,000	$2,000	$
Current Liabilities	$ 1,000	$ 600	$ 600
Noncurrent Liabilities	1,400	1,000	1,000
Shareholders' Equity	600	400	
	$ 3,000	$2,000	$

The shares of Moran Corporation currently sell on the market for $40 per share. Moran Corporation wants to acquire all the common stock of Walther Corporation as of January 1, Year 8, and is considering two ways of structuring the acquisition.

ALTERNATIVE A

Moran Corporation will issue at par 10 percent, 20-year bonds for $1,200. It will use the proceeds to acquire all the common stock of Walther Corporation. The firms will account for the transaction using the purchase method for financial reporting. This transaction is a taxable exchange for the shareholders of Walther Corporation but a nontaxable exchange for the corporation itself.

ALTERNATIVE B

Moran Corporation will issue 25 shares of its common stock for all the common stock of Walther Corporation. The firms will account for the transaction using the pooling of interests method for financial reporting. This transaction is a nontaxable exchange for both Walther Corporation and its shareholders.

Required
    a. Prepare proforma balance sheets under Alternative A and Alternative B as of January 1, Year 8. The income tax rate is 40 percent.
    b. Before considering the effects of the acquisition, Moran Corporation projects net income of $300, and Walther Corporation projects net income of $200 for Year 8.

Compute the amount of proforma net income for Year 8 for the merged firm under each alternative. Both firms use a LIFO cost flow assumption for inventories and neither expects to liquidate a LIFO layer during Year 8. Depreciable assets have a 10-year remaining life as of January 1, Year 8. Both firms use the straight-line depreciation method. Amortize any goodwill over 20 years.

7.3   EFFECT OF THE PURCHASE METHOD AND THE POOLING OF INTERESTS METHOD ON CONSOLIDATED BALANCE SHEET AND INCOME STATEMENT. AT&T launched a hostile takeover bid for NCR early in Year 6. AT&T was successful in acquiring all the common stock of NCR for $7,800 million of AT&T common stock. Financial statement data for these companies for Year 5, taken from their most recent annual reports prior to the transaction, reveal the following (amounts in millions):

	AT&T	NCR
December 31, Year 5 (Before Takeover)		
Total Assets	$43,775	$4,547
Total Liabilities	29,682	2,757
Total Shareholders' Equity .	14,093	1,790
	$43,775	$4,547

Required

a. Assume for this part that AT&T uses the purchase method to account for its acquisition of NCR. Also assume that $2 billion of any excess purchase price relates to depreciable assets with a market value in excess of their book value. These depreciable assets have an average remaining life of 10 years at the date of acquisition. AT&T uses the straight-line depreciation method. AT&T amortizes goodwill over 40 years. The income tax rate is 34 percent. Prepare a consolidated balance sheet as of January 2, Year 6.

b. Repeat part a, but assume that all of any excess purchase price relates to goodwill.

c. Assume now that AT&T accounts for the transaction using the pooling of interests method. Prepare a consolidated balance sheet as of January 2, Year 6.

d. AT&T actually accounted for this transaction using the pooling of interests method. It reported consolidated net income for Year 6 of $2,880 million (excluding a restructuring charge). Compute the amount of consolidated net income for Year 6 if AT&T had accounted for the acquisition following the assumptions in part a.

e. Repeat the computations in part d following the assumptions in part b.

7.4   EFFECT OF THE PURCHASE METHOD AND THE POOLING OF INTERESTS METHOD ON BALANCE SHEET AND INCOME STATEMENT. Bristol-Myers Company and Squibb Company, both pharmaceutical firms, agreed to merge as of October 1, Year 9. Bristol-Myers exchanged 234 million shares of its common stock for Squibb's outstanding shares. Bristol-Myers shares sold for $55 per share on the merger date, resulting in a transaction with a market value of $12.87 billion. The firms accounted for the merger as a pooling of interests.

Required

a. The most recent balance sheets of Bristol-Myers and Squibb prior to the merger reveal the following (amounts in millions):

	Bristol-Myers	Squibb
Assets	$5,190	$3,083
Liabilities	$1,643	$1,682
Shareholders' Equity	3,547	1,401
	$5,190	$3,083

Prepare a summary consolidated balance sheet such as those above for Bristol-Myers and Squibb, assuming that the firms account for the merger using the (1) pooling of interests method, and (2) the purchase method. Assume that any excess of market value over book value relates to goodwill.

b. Net income of Bristol-Myers and Squibb prior to and subsequent to the merger appears below (amounts in millions). The amounts for Year 9 exclude a special charge for merger-related expenses.

	Pre-Merger			Post-Merger	
			First Nine Months of	Last Three Months of	
	Year 7	Year 8	Year 9	Year 9	Year 10
Bristol-Myers	$710	$829	$716	—	—
Squibb	$358	$425	$384	—	—
Combined	—	—	—	$340	$1,748

Compute the amount of net income that Bristol-Myers Squibb would report for Year 9 using the pooling of interests method.

c. Compute the amount of net income that Bristol-Myers Squibb would report for Year 9 using the purchase method. Assume that the firm amortizes goodwill over 40 years. Note that net income under the purchase method excludes earnings of Squibb prior to the merger.

d. Compute the amount of net income that Bristol-Myers Squibb would report for Year 10 using the purchase method.

e. Complete the schedule of net income below:

	Bristol-Myers Company		Bristol-Myers Squibb Company	
	Year 7	Year 8	Year 9	Year 10
Pooling of Interests Method				
Purchase Method				

f. Look at the analysis in question e. Compare the levels and growth rates in net income for the purchase and pooling of interests methods.

7.5 EFFECT OF THE PURCHASE METHOD AND THE POOLING OF INTERESTS METHOD ON BALANCE SHEET AND INCOME STATEMENT. Ormond Co. acquired all the outstanding common stock of Daytona Co. on January 1, Year 5. Ormond Co. gave shares of its common stock with a market value of $312 million in exchange for the Daytona Co. common stock. Daytona Co. will remain a legally separate entity after the exchange, but Ormond Co. will prepare consolidated financial statements each period with Daytona Co. The transaction qualifies as a nontaxable exchange for income tax purposes.

Exhibit 7.13 presents the balance sheets of Ormond Co. and Daytona Co. on January 1, Year 5, just prior to the acquisition. The income tax rate is 40 percent. The information below applies to Daytona Co.

1. The market value of Daytona Co.'s fixed assets exceeds their book value by $50 million.
2. Daytona Co. owns a patent with a market value of $40 million.

EXHIBIT 7.13

Ormond Co. and Daytona Co.
Balance Sheets on January 1, Year 5
(amounts in millions)
(Problem 7.5)

	Ormond Co.	Daytona Co.
Cash	$ 25	$ 15
Accounts Receivable	60	40
Fixed Assets (net)	250	170
Patent	—	—
Deferred Tax Asset	10	—
Goodwill	—	—
Total Assets	$345	$225
Accounts Payable & Accruals	$ 60	$ 40
Long-Term Debt	120	60
Deferred Tax Liability	40	—
Other Noncurrent Liabilities	30	—
Common Stock	80	50
Retained Earnings	15	75
Total Equities	$345	$225

3. Daytona Co. is a defendant in a lawsuit that it expects to settle during Year 5 at a pretax cost of $25 million. The firm carries no insurance against such lawsuits. If permitted, Ormond Co. desires to establish an "acquisition reserve" for this lawsuit.
4. Daytona Co. has an unrecognized and unfunded retirement health care benefits obligation totaling $20 million on January 1, Year 5.

Required

a. Prepare a consolidated balance sheet for Ormond Co. and Daytona Co. on January 1, Year 5, assuming that Ormond Co. accounts for the acquisition using the purchase method.
b. Repeat part a, assuming that Ormond Co. accounts for the acquisition using the pooling of interests method.
c. Exhibit 7.14 presents income statements and balance sheets taken from the separate company books at the end of Year 5, assuming that Ormond Co. accounts for its

---

EXHIBIT 7.14

Ormond Co. and Daytona Co.
Consolidation Worksheet for Year 5
(amounts in millions)
(Problem 7.5)

	Ormond Co.	Daytona Co.
Income Statement for Year 5		
Sales	$ 600	$ 450
Equity in Earnings of Daytona Co.	18	—
Operating Expenses	(550)	(395)
Interest Expense	(10)	(5)
Loss on Lawsuit	—	(20)
Income Tax Expense	(23)	(12)
Net Income	$ 35	$ 18
Balance Sheet on December 31, Year 5		
Cash	$ 45	$ 25
Accounts Receivable	80	50
Investment in Daytona Co.	327[a]	—
Fixed Assets	280	195
Patent	—	—
Deferred Tax Asset	15	—
Goodwill	—	—
Total Assets	$ 747	$ 270
Accounts Payable & Accruals	$ 85	$ 55
Long-Term Debt	140	75
Deferred Tax Liability	50	—
Other Noncurrent Liabilities	40	—
Common Stock	392	50
Retained Earnings	40	90
Total Equities	$ 747	$ 270

[a]$312 initial investment + $18 equity in earnings − $3 dividend received = $327.

acquisition of Daytona Co. using the *purchase* method. The information below applies to these companies.

1. The fixed assets of Daytona Co. have an average remaining life of 5 years on January 1, Year 5. The firms use the straight-line depreciation method.
2. The patent of Daytona Co. has a remaining life of 10 years on January 1, Year 5.
3. Daytona Co. settled its lawsuit during Year 5 and expects no further liability.
4. Daytona Co. will amortize and fund its retirement health care benefits obligation over 20 years. It included $1 million in operating expenses during Year 5 related to amounts unrecognized and unfunded as of January 1, Year 5.
5. Goodwill is amortized on a straight-line basis over 40 years.

Prepare a consolidated income statement for Year 5 and a consolidated balance sheet on December 31, Year 5, using the purchase method of accounting.

7.6 APPLICATION OF STATEMENT NO. 115 FOR INVESTMENTS ON MARKETABLE EQUITY SECURITIES. Suntrust Bank owns a large block of Coca-Cola Company common stock that it has held for many years. Suntrust indicates in a note to its financial statements that all equity securities held by the bank, including its investment in Coke stock, are classified as *available for sale*. A recent annual report of Suntrust reports this information for its Coke investment (in thousands):

Coke common stock investment, market value at December 31, Year 8	$1,791,894
Coke common stock investment, market value at December 31, Year 9	$1,242,862
Net income for Year 9	$ 565,476

Required

a. Calculate the effect of the change in the market value of Suntrust's investment in Coke common stock on Year 9's (1) net income, and (2) shareholders' equity for the bank. The income tax rate is 35 percent.
b. How does your answer to part a differ if Suntrust classified its investment in Coke's common stock as a *trading* security?
c. Does the value reported on Suntrust's balance sheet for the investment in Coke's stock differ depending on the firm's reason for holding the stock (that is, whether it is classified as available for sale versus trading by management)? Explain your answer.

7.7 EFFECT OF MARKET VALUE AND EQUITY METHODS ON BALANCE SHEET AND INCOME STATEMENT. Seagram acquired 11.7 percent of Time Warner on January 2, Year 3. Financial statement data for these firms at the end of Year 3 reveal the following (amounts in millions):

Seagram
Assets — December 31, Year 3

Investment in Time Warner at Market Value (11.7% ownership)	$ 1,769
All Other Assets	9,949
Total Assets	$11,718

Liabilities	$ 6,717

Shareholders' Equity

Unrealized Appreciation in Market Value of Time Warner (pre-tax) ...	13
All Other Shareholders' Equity	4,988
Total Liabilities and Shareholders' Equity	$11,718

Income Statement for Year 3

Dividend Revenue from Time Warner (net of taxes)	$ 8
All Other Revenue and Expenses (net of taxes)	371
Net Income	$ 379

Time Warner — December 31, Year 3

Assets	$16,892
Liabilities	$15,522
Shareholders' Equity	1,370
	$16,892
Net Loss for Year 3	$ (339)

Required

a. The total common shareholders' equity of Time Warner on January 1, Year 3, is $1,810. Assume that any excess purchase price relates to goodwill. Compute the amount of goodwill related to Seagram's investment in Time Warner on the date of acquisition.

b. Assume for this part that Seagram had used the equity method instead of the market value method to account for its investment in Time Warner during Year 3. Compute the maximum amount of net income that Seagram would report for Year 3. The income tax rate is 35 percent.

c. Compute the total assets for Seagram on December 31, Year 3, if it had used the equity method instead of the market value method throughout Year 3.

7.8 APPLYING THE EQUITY, PROPORTIONATE CONSOLIDATION, AND FULL CONSOLIDATION METHODS. Mylan Laboratories (Mylan) is a leading firm in the generic pharmaceutical industry. Generic drugs have chemical compositions similar to ethical drugs, but sell for a significantly lower price. Once the patent period ends on an ethical drug, generic drug company chemists break the drug into its basic chemical elements. The company then submits an application to the Food and Drug Administration to sell a generic equivalent of the ethical drug. Generic drugs may be sold at a lower price because of reduced research and development, marketing, and other costs.

Mylan owns 50 percent of the common stock of Somerset Pharmaceuticals, which sells an ethical drug for Parkinson's Disease. Mylan accounts for its investment in Somerset using the equity method. Equity in earnings of Somerset includes Mylan's 50 percent share of Somerset's earnings minus amortization of intangible assets resulting from the acquisition of Somerset. Such intangible assets are amortized over 15 years. Amortization expense totals $924,000 in each of the Years 6 through 8. Additionally, Mylan charges Somerset a management services fee each year, and includes it in the Equity in Earnings of Somerset account. Somerset records this fee as an expense in measuring earnings.

Exhibit 7.15 presents financial statement data for Mylan. Exhibit 7.16 presents financial statement data for Somerset.

EXHIBIT 7.15

Mylan Laboratories
Financial Statement Data
(amounts in thousands)
(Problem 7.8)

	Year 5	Year 6	Year 7	Year 8
Balance Sheet				
Current Assets	$ 94,502	$120,014	$180,482	$209,572
Investment in and Advances				
to Somerset	18,045	13,674	14,844	17,964
Noncurrent Assets	74,408	93,032	155,779	175,789
Total Assets	$186,955	$226,720	$351,105	$403,325
Current Liabilities	$ 12,931	$ 17,909	$ 26,482	$ 17,926
Noncurrent Liabilities	6,493	5,359	7,348	5,430
Shareholders' Equity	167,531	203,452	317,275	379,969
Total Liabilities and				
Shareholders' Equity	$186,955	$726,720	$351,105	$403,325

	Year 6	Year 7	Year 8
Income Statement			
Sales	$131,936	$ 211,964	$ 251,773
Costs and Expenses	(100,458)	(135,759)	(188,304)
Operating Income	$ 31,478	$ 76,205	$ 63,469
Equity in Earnings of Somerset	18,664	21,136	23,596
Income Before Taxes	$ 50,142	$ 97,341	$ 87,065
Income Tax Expense	(10,028)	(26,720)	(13,998)
Net Income	$ 40,114	$ 70,621	$ 73,067

	Year 6	Year 7	Year 8
Cash Flow Statement			
Net Income	$ 40,114	$ 70,621	$ 73,067
Equity in Earnings of Somerset	(18,664)	(21,136)	(23,596)
Cash Received from Somerset	23,035	19,966	20,676
Other Addbacks and Subtractions	5,962	7,959	14,690
Changes in Working Capital Accounts ...	(4,519)	(9,073)	(49,204)
Cash Flow from Operations	$ 45,928	$ 68,337	$ 35,633

EXHIBIT 7.16

Somerset Pharmaceuticals
Financial Statement Data
(amounts in thousands)
(Problem 7.8)

	Year 5	Year 6	Year 7	Year 8
Balance Sheet				
Current Assets	$22,801	$24,597	$30,409	$27,931
Noncurrent Assets	2,802	2,791	2,670	6,043
Total Assets	$25,603	$27,388	$33,079	$33,974
Current Liabilities	$ 7,952	$15,413	$20,675	$14,918
Payable to Owners	7,274	1,490	1,796	1,002
Other Noncurrent Liabilities	3,302	975	808	642
Shareholders' Equity	7,075	9,510	9,800	17,412
Total Liabilities and Share-holders' Equity	$25,603	$27,388	$33,079	$33,974

	Year 6	Year 7	Year 8
Income Statement			
Sales	$93,513	$108,518	$111,970
Costs and Expenses	(42,041)	(49,872)	(50,465)
Income Before Taxes	$51,472	$ 58,646	$ 61,505
Income Tax Expense	(18,806)	(21,789)	(19,547)
Net Income	$32,666	$ 36,857	$ 41,958

Required

a. Prepare an analysis of the changes in the shareholders' equity of Somerset for each of the Years 6 through 8.

b. Prepare an analysis of the changes in the investment in and advances to Somerset account on Mylan's books for each of the Years 6 through 8. Be sure to indicate the amounts for equity in earnings of Somerset, management fee, goodwill amortization, dividend received, and other cash payments received.

c. Does the equity method, proportionate consolidation method, or full consolidation method best reflect the operating relationships between Mylan and Somerset? Explain.

d. Prepare an income statement for Mylan and Somerset for Year 6, Year 7, and Year 8 using the proportionate consolidation method.

e. Repeat part d using the full consolidation method.

f. Compute the ratio of operating income before income taxes to sales for Year 6, Year 7, and Year 8, using the equity method, proportionate consolidation method, and full consolidation method.

g. Why do the ratios computed in part f differ across the three methods of accounting for the investment in Somerset?

h. Compute the effective tax rate (that is, income tax expense divided by income before income taxes) for Year 6, Year 7, and Year 8 using the equity method, the proportionate consolidation method, and full consolidation method.

i. Why do the measures of the effective tax rate computed in part h differ across the three methods of accounting for the investment in Somerset?

7.9 CALCULATING THE TRANSLATION ADJUSTMENT UNDER THE ALL-CURRENT METHOD AND THE MONETARY/NONMONETARY METHOD. Foreign Sub is a wholly owned subsidiary of U.S. Domestic Corporation. U.S. Domestic Corporation acquired the subsidiary several years ago. The financial statements for Foreign Sub for Year 4 in its own currency appear in Exhibit 7.17.

The exchange rates between the U.S. dollar and the foreign currency of the subsidiary follow:

December 31, Year 3:	$10:1 FC
Average—Year 4:	$8:1 FC
December 31, Year 4:	$6:1 FC

On January 1, Year 4, Foreign Sub issued FC100 of long-term debt and FC100 of common stock in the acquisition of land costing FC200. Operating activities occurred evenly over the year.

EXHIBIT 7.17

Foreign Sub
Financial Statement Data
(Problem 7.9)

	December 31	
	Year 3	**Year 4**
Cash	FC 100	FC 150
Accounts Receivable	300	350
Inventories	350	400
Land	500	700
	FC 1,250	FC 1,600
Accounts Payable	FC 150	FC 250
Long-Term Debt	200	300
Common Stock	500	600
Retained Earnings	400	450
	FC 1,250	FC 1,600

	For Year 4
Sales	FC 4,000
Cost of Goods Sold	(3,200)
Selling and Administrative	(400)
Income Taxes	(160)
Net Income	FC 240
Dividend Declared and Paid on December 31	(190)
Increase in Retained Earnings	FC 50

Required

    a. Assume that the currency of Foreign Sub is the functional currency. Compute the change in the cumulative translation adjustment for Year 4. Indicate whether the change increases or decreases shareholders' equity.

    b. Assume that the U.S. dollar is the functional currency. Compute the amount of the translation gain or loss for Year 4. Indicate whether the amount is a gain or loss.

7.10 TRANSLATING THE FINANCIAL STATEMENTS OF A FOREIGN SUBSIDIARY—COMPARISON OF TRANSLATION METHODS. Stebbins Corporation established a wholly owned Canadian subsidiary on January 1, Year 6, by contributing US$500,000 for all the subsidiary's common stock. The exchange rate on that date was C$1:US$0.90 (that is, one Canadian dollar equals 90 U.S. cents). The Canadian subsidiary invested C$500,000 in a building with an expected life of 20 years, and rented it to various tenants for the year. The average exchange rate during Year 6 was C$1:US$0.85, and the exchange rate on December 31, Year 6, was C$1:US$0.80. Exhibit 7.18 shows the amounts taken from the books of the Canadian subsidiary at the end of Year 6, measured in Canadian dollars.

EXHIBIT 7.18

Canadian Subsidiary
Financial Statements
Year 6
(Problem 7.10)

Balance Sheet: December 31, Year 6
Assets

Cash	C$ 77,555
Rent Receivable	25,000
Building (net)	475,000
	C$577,555

Liabilities and Equity

Accounts Payable	6,000
Salaries Payable	4,000
Common Stock	555,555
Retained Earnings	12,000
	C$577,555

Income Statement For Year 6

Rent Revenue	C$125,000
Operating Expenses	(28,000)
Depreciation Expense	(25,000)
Translation Exchange Loss	—
Net Income	C$ 72,000

Retained Earnings Statement for Year 6

Balance, January 1, Year 6	C$ —
Net Income	72,000
Dividends	(60,000)
Balance, December 31, Year 6	C$ 12,000

Required

a. Prepare a balance sheet, income statement, and retained earnings statement for the Canadian subsidiary for Year 6 in U.S. dollars, assuming that the Canadian dollar is the functional currency. Include a separate schedule showing the computation of the translation adjustment account.

b. Repeat the computations in a, but assume that the U.S. dollar is the functional currency. Include a separate schedule showing the computation of the translation gain or loss.

c. Why are the signs of the translation adjustment for Year 6 under the all-current translation method and the translation gain or loss for Year 6 under the monetary/nonmonetary translation method the same? Why do the amounts differ?

d. Assuming that the firm could justify either translation method, which method would the management of Stebbins Corporation likely prefer for Year 6?

EXHIBIT 7.19

Canadian Subsidiary
Financial Statements
Year 7
(Problem 7.11)

Balance Sheet:
Assets

Cash	C$116,555
Rent Receivable	30,000
Building (net)	450,000
	C$596,555

Liabilities and Equity

Accounts Payable	7,500
Salaries Payable	5,500
Common Stock	555,555
Retained Earnings	28,000
	C$596,555

Income Statement

Rent Revenue	C$150,000
Operating Expenses	(34,000)
Depreciation Expense	(25,000)
Translation Exchange Gain	—
Net Income	C$ 91,000

Retained Earnings Statement

Balance, January 1, Year 7	C$ 12,000
Net Income	91,000
Dividends	(75,000)
Balance, December 31, Year 7	C$ 28,000

**7.11 TRANSLATING THE FINANCIAL STATEMENTS OF A FOREIGN SUBSIDIARY—SEC-
OND YEAR OF OPERATIONS.** Look at Problem 7.10 for Stebbins Corporation for Year 6, its
first year of operations. Exhibit 7.19 shows the amounts for the Canadian subsidiary for
Year 7. The average exchange rate during Year 7 was C$1:US$0.82, and the exchange rate
on December 31, Year 7, was C$1:US$0.84. The Canadian subsidiary declared and paid
dividends on December 31, Year 7.

Required

    a. Prepare a balance sheet, income statement, and retained earnings statement for the
        Canadian subsidiary for Year 7 in U.S. dollars, assuming that the Canadian dollar is
        the functional currency. Include a separate schedule showing the computation of
        the translation adjustment for Year 7 and the change in the translation adjustment
        account.

    b. Repeat the computations in question a, but assume that the U.S. dollar is the func-
        tional currency. Include a separate schedule showing the computation of the transla-
        tion gain or loss.

    c. Why are the signs of the translation adjustment for Year 7 under the all current trans-
        lation method and the translation gain or loss under the monetary/nonmonetary trans-
        lation method the same? Why do the amounts differ?

    d. Assuming that the firm could justify either translation method, which method would
        the management of Stebbins Corporation likely prefer for Year 7?

7.12 INTERPRETING FOREIGN CURRENCY TRANSLATION DISCLOSURES. Hewlett-
Packard and Sun Microsystems derive similar proportions of their sales from the United
States., Europe, Japan, and other countries. Recent annual reports of the two companies indicate that HP uses the U.S. dollar as its functional currency, while Sun uses the currency
of each foreign operation as its functional currency.

    The shareholders' equity section of Sun's balance sheet reveals the following (amounts
in thousands):

	June 30	
	Year 8	**Year 9**
Common Stock	$1,089,550	$1,164,421
Retained Earnings	1,205,483	1,662,355
Cumulative Translation Adjustment	33,629	21,620
Treasury Stock	(206,067)	(596,910)
Total	$2,122,595	$2,251,486

Required

    a. Did the U.S. dollar likely increase or decrease in value on average during the year
        ended June 30, Year 9, against the foreign currencies of the countries in which Sun
        conducts its operations? Explain.

    b. Sun uses a FIFO cost flow assumption for inventories and cost of goods sold. Would
        Sun's gross margin in U.S. dollars (that is, sales minus cost of goods sold) likely have
        increased or decreased for the year ended June 30, Year 9, if it had used the U.S.
        dollar as its functional currency instead of the currency of its foreign operations?
        Explain.

c. HP also uses a FIFO cost flow assumption for inventories and cost of goods sold. Both companies maintain net monetary asset positions in their foreign operations. HP generated a pretax return from foreign operations of 12.3 percent for the year ended June 30, Year 9, while Sun generated a pretax return of 5.1 percent. Would the profit margin of HP likely increase or decrease if it had used the currency of its foreign units as the functional currency? Explain.

7.13 IDENTIFYING THE FUNCTIONAL CURRENCY. Electronic Computer Systems (ECS) designs, manufactures, sells, and services networked computer systems, associated peripheral equipment, and related network, communications, and software products.

ECS conducts sales and marketing operations outside the United States principally through sales subsidiaries in Canada, Europe, Central and South America, and the Far East, by direct sales from the parent corporation, and through various representative and distributorship arrangements. The company's international manufacturing operations include plants in Canada, the Far East, and Europe. These manufacturing plants sell their output to the company's sales subsidiaries, the parent corporation, or other manufacturing plants for further processing. ECS accounts for intercompany transfers between geographic areas at prices representative of unaffiliated party transactions.

Exhibit 7.20 presents segment geographic data.

Sales to unaffiliated customers outside the United States, including U.S. export sales, were $5,729,879,000 for Year 5, $4,412,527,000 for Year 4, and $3,179,143,000 for Year 3; which represented 50 percent, 47 percent and 42 percent, respectively, of total operating revenues. The international subsidiaries have reinvested substantially all their earnings to support operations. These accumulated retained earnings, before elimination of intercompany transactions, aggregated $2,793,239,000 at the end of Year 5, $2,070,337,000 at the end of Year 4, and $1,473,081,000 at the end of Year 3.

ECS enters into forward exchange contracts to reduce the impact of foreign currency fluctuations on operations and on the asset and liability positions of foreign subsidiaries. The gains and losses on these contracts increase or decrease net income in the same period as the related revenues and expenses, and for assets and liabilities, in the period in which the exchange rate changes.

Required

Discuss whether ECS should use the U.S. dollar or the currencies of its foreign subsidiaries as its functional currency.

7.14 SEGMENT DEFINITION AND DISCLOSURES. Lara Corporation reports on four segments in its annual report: plastic truck moldings, computer-aided design services, electronic truck components, and finance. The first three segments produce products sold primarily to custom truck manufacturers. The finance segment is responsible for portions of the firm's financial operations, including financing customer purchases of products from other segments.

Each of the firms' reportable segments is a strategic business unit that offers different products and services. The segments are managed separately because each business requires different technology and marketing strategies.

With the exception of the finance segment, each business was acquired as a unit, and, for the most part, the management at the time of the acquisition was retained. Each of four segments generates revenues and reports profits—with the exception of the electronic truck components segment, which reported losses in the last two years.

Required

a. *Statement No. 131* requires firm to choose segment classes following what the FASB refers to as the *management approach*. What characteristics of these four lines of business are indicative of the management approach as defined by the FASB?

b. Describe the disclosures that Lara Corporation should provide in its annual report for each of these segments.

EXHIBIT 7.20

**Electronic Computer Systems
Geographic Segment Data
(amounts in thousands)
(Problem 7.13)**

	Year 3	Year 4	Year 5
Revenues			
United States customers	$ 4,472,195	$5,016,606	$ 5,810,598
Intercompany	1,354,339	1,921,043	2,017,928
Total	$ 5,826,534	$6,937,649	$ 7,828,526
Europe customers	2,259,743	3,252,482	4,221,631
Intercompany	82,649	114,582	137,669
Total	$ 2,342,392	$3,367,064	$ 4,359,300
Canada, Far East,			
Americas customers	858,419	1,120,356	1,443,217
Intercompany	577,934	659,204	912,786
Total	$ 1,436,353	$1,779,560	$ 2,356,003
Eliminations	(2,014,922)	(2,694,829)	(3,068,383)
Net revenue	$ 7,590,357	$9,389,444	$11,475,446
Income			
United States	$ 342,657	$ 758,795	$ 512,754
Europe	405,636	634,543	770,135
Canada, Far East, Americas	207,187	278,359	390,787
Eliminations	(126,771)	(59,690)	(38,676)
Operating income	828,709	1,612,007	1,635,000
Interest income	116,899	122,149	143,665
Interest expense	(88,079)	(45,203)	(37,820)
Income before income taxes	$ 857,529	$1,688,953	$ 1,740,845
Assets			
United States	$ 3,911,491	$4,627,838	$ 5,245,439
Europe	1,817,584	2,246,333	3,093,818
Canada, Far East, Americas	815,067	843,067	1,293,906
Corporate assets (temporary cash			
investments)	2,035,557	1,979,470	2,057,528
Eliminations	(1,406,373)	(1,289,322)	(1,579,135)
Total assets	$ 7,173,326	$8,407,386	$10,111,556

CASE 7.1

FISHER CORPORATION*

Effective January 1, 1999, Weston Corporation (Weston) and Fisher Corporation (Fisher) are merging their companies. Under the terms of the merger agreement, Weston will acquire all the outstanding common shares of Fisher. Fisher will remain a legally separate entity, but Weston will consolidate its financial statements with Fisher's at the end of each accounting period. According to the merger agreement, Weston can structure the transaction under any one of three alternatives:

ALTERNATIVE A

Weston would acquire all the outstanding common shares of Fisher for $58.5 million in cash. To obtain the necessary cash, Weston would issue $59 million of 10 percent 20-year bonds on the open market. For financial reporting purposes, Weston would account for the merger using the purchase method. For tax purposes, the merger transaction is a taxable event to Fisher's shareholders. The tax basis of Fisher's net assets remains the same after the acquisition as before the acquisition; the tax law does not allow a revaluation of these net assets to market value.

ALTERNATIVE B

Weston would acquire all the outstanding common shares of Fisher for the issuance of 1,800,000 shares of new Weston preferred stock. The preferred stock would carry an annual dividend of $2 per share, and would be convertible into 0.75 shares of Weston stock at any time. The exchange ratio would be one share of the new preferred stock for each outstanding common share of Fisher. An independent investment banking firm has valued the preferred shares at $50 million. For financial reporting purposes, Weston would account for the merger using the purchase method. For tax purposes, the merger transaction is a nontaxable event to Fisher's shareholders. The tax bases of Fisher's net assets carry over after the acquisition.

ALTERNATIVE C

Weston would acquire all the outstanding common shares of Fisher in exchange for 1,517,787 shares of Weston's $.30 par value common stock. Based on the market price at the merger date, these shares would have a market value of $48 million. For financial reporting purposes, Weston would account for the merger using the pooling of interests method. For tax purposes, the merger transaction is a nontaxable event to Fisher's shareholders. The tax basis of Fisher's net assets carries over after the acquisition.

---

*The authors gratefully acknowledge the assistance of Gary M. Cypres in the preparation of this case.

ALTERNATIVES

Summarizing the alternatives:

	Alternative A	Alternative B	Alternative C
Type of Consideration Given	Cash	Convertible Preferred Stock	Common Stock
Value of Consideration Given	$58,500,000	$50,000,000	$48,000,000
Financial Reporting Method	Purchase	Purchase	Pooling of Interests
Tax Reporting Method— Shareholders	Taxable	Nontaxable	Nontaxable
Tax Reporting Method—Fisher	Nontaxable	Nontaxable	Nontaxable

WESTON COMPANY BACKGROUND (AS OF JANUARY 1, 1999)

Weston was formed on November 4, 1966, in a merger of four companies, and has grown continually since that date. Weston is a worldwide Fortune 500 company with 1998 revenues of $482 million. The company designs and manufactures environmental, energy, and engineered products, and makes chemicals and specialty products.

The company's long involvement with environmental protection systems began in 1937, with the development of the Weston machine for cleaning rust and scale from structural steel and other materials. Each Weston machine included air pollution controls to prevent the debris of the cleaning process from spreading. The Weston requires less time and less than one-tenth the energy of sandblasting. Further savings resulted from recycling the abrasive shot used in the cleaning process.

As the Weston business grew, the company expanded its manufacturing capability. In addition to making Westons, spare parts, and associated pollution control equipment, the company began to produce consumables, such as the abrasives used by the Westons and the replacement filter bags that collect the fine particulate matter resulting from the cleaning process.

Soon after the development of the Weston, growing customer interest in separately purchasing the pollution control devices incorporated in the Weston machines resulted in the company's entry into the air pollution control business. By the early 1950s, it was offering a full range of fabric filter systems for a variety of industrial and utility uses. In the mid-1960s, the company became the North American licensee for certain European air pollution technologies, including "Lurgi" electrostatic precipitators.

To enable the company to offer more comprehensive systems to solve environmental problems and to broaden its activities into related energy areas, Weston sought an engineering and technological capability to complement its established manufacturing capacity. In 1988 it acquired Metallurgical Engineering Company. Weston also increased its manufacturing capacity in two ways. It constructed new facilities for its existing product lines, and it acquired additional facilities for the production of industrial fans and blowers and the means to design, erect, and service industrial chimneys. It further augmented its manufacturing capabilities by purchasing, in 1992, BPM Corporation, a manufacturer of precision and industrial ball and roller bearings, motion transmission devices, and related products.

Weston is the exclusive licensee in the United States of certain European technology for the production of steam through the combustion of refuse. The same process permits the recovery of metal and other commercially valuable resources. The steam is used for a variety of purposes, including heating and electricity generation.

In 1991, the company completed the construction of its first refuse-to-energy plant using this technology, at Saugus, Massachusetts. Weston is active in designing facilities and seeking to develop processes that allow the efficient and economical use of high-sulfur coal in an environmentally acceptable way on a commercial scale. The company also participates in developing other clean energy technologies such as the burning of biomass (primarily wood refuse).

Weston's other broad product category is its chemicals and specialty products. It manufactures chemicals, including urethane-based products, pigments, resins, varnishes, dispersions, and color flushes. The company offers various specialty products used in numerous printing processes including letterpress, offset, silk screen, flexographic, and rotogravure processes. The company also produces one-time carbon paper and carbonless reproduction paper for business forms and for data processing.

For the five years ended 1998, Weston's revenues, net income, and earnings per share each grew at an average compounded annual rate of 23 percent (see Exhibit 7.21). Growth in 1998 exceeded the average in all categories. These five-year growth rates include the

EXHIBIT 7.21

Weston Corporation
Income Statements
For the Years Ended December 31,
(Amounts in thousands)
(Case 7.1)

	1994	1995	1996	1997	1998	Estimated 1999*
Sales	$233,000	$321,300	$306,500	$361,500	$482,100	$560,000
Cost & Expenses						
Cost of Sales	(180,700)	(251,100)	(232,800)	(273,900)	(360,600)	(415,700)
Selling & Admin.	(36,500)	(51,600)	(51,900)	(58,300)	(86,921)	(105,632)
Operating Income	$ 15,800	$ 18,600	$ 21,800	$ 29,300	$ 34,579	$ 38,668
Equity in net income of nonconsolidated entities	2,300	3,800	3,600	2,600	3,200	4,000
Other income (expense)	(1,300)	(2,100)	(900)	(400)	(1,600)	(1,000)
Income before taxes	$ 16,800	$ 20,300	$ 24,500	$ 31,500	$ 36,179	$ 41,668
Provision for income taxes	(6,800)	(7,500)	(9,900)	(14,000)	(14,179)	(14,584)
Net income	$ 10,000	$ 12,800	$ 14,600	$ 17,500	$ 22,000	$ 27,084
Earnings per share	$1.25	$1.60	$1.83	$2.22	$2.82	$3.47
Dividends per share of common stock	$ .40	$ .40	$ .45	$ .63	$ .88	$1.20
Ave. number of shares of common stock outstanding	8,000	8,000	8,000	7,900	7,800	7,800

*Before consideration of the merger with Fisher.

EXHIBIT 7.22

Weston Corporation
Consolidated Balance Sheets
December 31,
(Amounts in Thousands)
(Case 7.1)

	1997	1998	Estimated 1999*
Assets			
Cash	$ 28,000	$ 28,000	$ 32,000
Accounts Receivable	84,000	90,000	100,000
Inventory	58,000	71,000	82,000
Other	4,000	13,000	13,000
Total Current Assets	$ 174,000	$202,000	$227,000
Property, Plant, and Equipment	$ 96,000	$116,000	$131,000
Less Accumulated Depreciation	(29,000)	(38,000)	(48,000)
Net	$ 67,000	$ 78,000	$ 83,000
Investment in Nonconsolidated Entities	42,000	45,000	47,000
Goodwill	8,400	8,000	7,800
Other Assets	6,000	7,000	7,200
Total Assets	$ 297,400	$340,000	$372,000
Liabilities			
Current Portion Long-Term Debt	$ 400	$ 2,000	$ —
Accounts Payable	23,000	30,000	40,000
Accrued Liabilities and Advances	67,000	78,000	91,000
Income Taxes	12,000	21,000	14,000
Total Current Liabilities	$ 102,400	$131,000	$145,000
Long-Term Debt	48,000	48,000	48,000
Deferred Taxes	9,000	10,000	10,000
Total Liabilities	$ 159,400	$189,000	$203,000
Shareholders' Equity			
Common Stock	$ 11,000	$ 11,000	$ 11,000
Capital Surplus	55,000	55,000	55,000
Retained Earnings	72,000	85,000	103,000
Total Shareholders' Equity	$ 138,000	$151,000	$169,000
Total Liabilities and Shareholders' Equity	$ 297,400	$340,000	$372,000

*Before consideration of the merger with Fisher.

EXHIBIT 7.23

Weston Corporation
Key Financial Highlights
1995–1999 Estimated
(Case 7.1)

	1995	1996	1997	1998	Estimated 1999*
Earnings per Share	$ 1.60	$ 1.83	$ 2.22	$ 2.82	$ 3.53
Dividends per Share	$ .40	$ .45	$ .63	$ .88	$ 1.20
Current Ratio	1.8	2.0	1.7	1.5	1.6
Long-Term Debt as a Percentage of Long-Term Capital	28.9%	26.5%	25.8%	24.1%	22.1%
Return on Average Common Shareholders' Equity	12.4%	12.9%	13.6%	15.2%	16.9%
Book Value per Share	$ 13.50	$ 14.88	$ 17.69	$ 19.36	$ 21.68
Tangible Net Worth ($000)	$99,300	$ 111,600	$129,600	$143,000	$161,200
Times Interest Earned	5.7	7.8	9.8	10.9	10.0

*Before consideration of the merger with Fisher.

recession year of 1996 when the company's net income increased by 14 percent despite a sales decline of 5 percent. Weston accomplished this growth rate both through operations and through aggressive corporate acquisitions. The company intends to continue making acquisitions in the future.

Although Weston has exhibited strong financial growth, it has consistently maintained a conservative balance sheet (see Exhibit 7.22). The company's debt has steadily declined from 29 percent of long-term capital in 1995 to 24 percent in 1998 (see Exhibit 7.23). Dividends per share have ranged between 27 percent and 32 percent of earnings per share in each of the last five years.

Weston currently projects 25 percent growth in net income and earnings per share in 1999, with revenues increasing by 16 percent.

COMPANY BACKGROUND—FISHER (AS OF JANUARY 1, 1999)

Fisher Corporation is a leading designer and manufacturer of material handling and process equipment for heavy industry in the United States and abroad. Its sales have more than doubled, and its earnings increased more than sixfold, in the past five years. In material handling, Fisher is a major producer of electric overhead and gantry cranes, ranging in capacity from 5 tons to 600-ton giants, the latter used primarily in nuclear and conventional power generating plants. It also builds underhung cranes and monorail systems for general industrial use of loads up to 40 tons, railcar movers, railroad and mass transit shop maintenance equipment, and a broad line of advanced package conveyors. Fisher is a world leader in evaporation and crystallization systems, and also furnishes dryers, heat exchangers, and filters to complete its line of chemical processing equipment sold internationally to the chemical, fertilizer, food, drug, and paper industries. For the metallurgical industry, it designs and manufactures electric arc and induction furnaces, cupolas, ladles, and hot metal distribution equipment.

Exhibit 7.24 presents comparative income statements, and Exhibit 7.25 presents comparative balance sheets for Fisher.

EXHIBIT 7.24

Fisher Corporation
Income Statement
(amounts in thousands)
(Case 7.1)

	1994	1995	1996	1997	1998	Estimated 1999
Sales	$41,428	$53,541	$76,328	$109,373	$102,699	$100,000
Other Revenue & Gains	0	41	0	0	211	200
Cost of Goods Sold	(33,269)	(43,142)	(60,000)	(85,364)	(80,260)	(85,600)
Sell. & Admin. Expense	(6,175)	(7,215)	(9,325)	(13,416)	(12,090)	(10,820)
Other Expenses & Losses	(2)	0	(11)	(31)	(1)	—
Earnings before Interest and Taxes	$ 1,982	$ 3,225	$ 6,992	$ 10,562	$ 10,559	$ 3,780
Interest Expense	(43)	(21)	(284)	(276)	(13)	—
Income Tax Expense	(894)	(1,471)	(2,992)	(3,703)	(3,944)	(1,323)
Income from Contin. Ops	$ 1,045	$ 1,733	$ 3,716	$ 6,583	$ 6,602	$ 2,457

Fisher's management estimates that revenues will remain approximately flat between 1998 and 1999, but that its net income for 1999 will decline to $2,500,000, compared with $6,602,000 in 1998. This decrease in net income results from a $1 million increase in labor costs in 1999, a $3 million loss in the construction of a crystallization system, a $1 million expenditure to meet expected OSHA requirements, and a $1 million expenditure to relocate one of its product lines to a new plant facility. Fisher has 1,800,000 shares outstanding on January 1, 1999. It currently pays a dividend of $1.22 per share.

ALLOCATION OF PURCHASE PRICE

Exhibit 7.26 shows the calculation of the purchase price and the allocation of any excess cost under each of the three alternatives for structuring the acquisition of Fisher. Notes to the calculations are as follows:

Note 1: Acquisition costs consist of printing, legal, auditing, and finders' fees, and increase the cost of the shares of Fisher acquired under Alternatives A and B.

Note 2: The book value of certain long-term contracts of Fisher (relating to a crystallization system) exceeds their market value by $3 million. Fisher expects to complete these contracts during 1999. Weston establishes a "reserve" for this loss as of the date of acquisition and includes it among current liabilities. When Fisher completes the contracts in 1999, the consolidated entity will charge the actual loss against the reserve for financial reporting. It will then claim a deduction for the loss in calculating taxable income.

Note 3: The market value of Fisher's property, plant, and equipment on January 1, 1999, is $23,000. The book value and tax basis is $6,000. Thus, Weston allocates $17,000 (= 23,000 − $6,000) of the excess cost to property, plant, and equipment. The consolidated entity will depreciate the excess using the straight-line method over ten years for financial reporting. It cannot depreciate the excess for tax purposes.

EXHIBIT 7.25

Fisher Corporation
Balance Sheet
(amounts in thousands)
(Case 7.1)

	1993	1994	1995	1996	1997	1998
Cash	$ 955	$ 961	$ 865	$ 1,247	$ 1,540	$ 3,100
Marketable Securities	0	0	0	0	0	2,900
Accts./Notes Receivable	6,545	7,295	9,718	13,307	18,759	15,000
Inventories	7,298	8,686	12,797	20,426	18,559	18,000
Current Assets	$14,798	$16,942	$23,380	$34,980	$38,858	$39,000
Property, Plant, and Equipment .	12,216	12,445	13,126	13,792	14,903	15,000
Less: Accum. Depreciation	(7,846)	(8,236)	(8,558)	(8,988)	(9,258)	(9,000)
Other Assets	470	420	400	299	343	1,000
Total Assets	$19,638	$21,571	$28,348	$40,083	$44,846	$46,000
Accts. Payable—Trade	$ 2,894	$ 4,122	$ 6,496	$ 7,889	$ 6,779	$ 7,000
Notes Payable—Non-trade	0	0	700	3,500	0	0
Current Part LT Debt	170	170	170	170	170	0
Other Current Liab	550	1,022	3,888	8,624	12,879	8,000
Current Liabilities	$ 3,614	$ 5,314	$11,254	$20,183	$19,828	$15,000
Long-Term Debt	680	510	340	170	0	0
Deferred Taxes	0	0	5	228	357	1,000
Total Liabilities	$ 4,294	$ 5,824	$11,599	$20,581	$20,185	$16,000
Preferred Stock	$ 0	$ 0	$ 0	$ 0	$ 0	$ 0
Common Stock	2,927	2,927	2,927	5,855	7,303	9,000
Additional Paid-in Capital	5,075	5,075	5,075	5,075	5,061	5,000
Retained Earnings	7,342	7,772	8,774	8,599	12,297	16,000
Treasury Stock	0	-27	-27	-27	0	0
Shareholders' Equity	$15,344	$15,747	$16,749	$19,502	$24,661	$30,000
Total Equities	$19,638	$21,571	$28,348	$40,083	$44,846	$46,000

Note 4: Fisher has an unfunded pension obligation of $5,000 on January 1, 1999. Fisher had planned to amortize this obligation straight-line over 20 years from January 1, 1999. Weston allocates a portion of the purchase price to this obligation on the date of the acquisition.

Note 5: Fisher expects to incur $1,000 of costs during 1999 on its facilities to comply with various health and safety provisions of OSHA. Weston allocates a portion of the purchase price to recognize this expected cost.

Note 6: Weston intends to relocate the manufacture of certain product lines of Fisher to a new plant facility during 1999. The estimated costs of relocation are $1,000. Weston allocates a portion of the purchase price to recognize this expected cost.

Note 7: FASB *Statement No. 109* requires firms to provide deferred taxes for differences between the book basis and tax basis of assets and liabilities. Weston allocates the $7,000 amount of excess cost shown in Exhibit 7.26 to individual assets and liabilities for financial reporting. For tax reporting, the bases of these assets and liabilities remain the same

EXHIBIT 7.26

Calculation of Purchase Price and Allocation of Excess Cost
(amounts in thousands)
(Case 7.1)

	Alternative A	Alternative B	Alternative C*
Purchase Price:			
Base Price	$ 58,500	$50,000	$ 14,000
Acquisition Costs (Note 1)	500	500	500
Total	$ 59,000	$50,500	$ 14,500
Book Value of Contributed			
Capital of Fisher	(30,000)	(30,000)	(14,000)
Excess of Cost over Book Value to be Allocated to Assets and Liabilities	$ 29,000	$20,500	$ 500
Allocation of Excess Cost:			
Recognition of "Reserve" for Losses on Long-Term Contracts (Note 2)	3,000 Cr.	3,000 Cr.	—
Write-up of Building and Equipment (Note 3)	17,000 Dr.	17,000 Dr.	—
Recognition of Unfunded Pension Liability (Note 4)	5,000 Cr.	5,000 Cr.	—
Recognition of Estimated Liability to meet OSHA Requirements (Note 5)	1,000 Cr.	1,000 Cr.	—
Recognition of Estimated Costs to Relocate Facilities in Connection with Product Move (Note 6) ..	1,000 Cr.	1,000 Cr.	—
Total Allocated to Identifiable Assets and Liabilities	7,000 Dr.	7,000 Dr.	—
Deferred Tax Effect (Note 7)	2,450 Cr.	2,450 Cr.	—
Residual to Goodwill (Note 8) ...	24,450 Dr.	15,950 Dr.	—
Total Allocated	$ 29,000 Dr.	$ 20,500 Dr.	—

*The pooling of interests method ignores the market value of Weston's common shares of $48,000,000. The shares exchanged receive a value equal to the book value of Fisher's contributed capital, $14,000,000. Weston must expense the acquisition costs in the year incurred.

as the amounts shown on Fisher's books before the acquisition. Thus, Weston provides deferred taxes of $2,450 (0.35 × $7,000), of which $1,750 [= 0.35 × ($3,000 Cr. + $1,000 Cr. + $1,000 Cr.)] is a current asset, $1,750 (= 0.35 × $5,000) is a noncurrent asset, and $5,950 (= 0.35 × $17,000) is a noncurrent liability. The consolidated entity eliminates these deferred taxes as it amortizes the related asset or liability.

Note 8: Weston allocates the remaining excess cost to goodwill. The consolidated entity amortizes goodwill over 40 years.

Exhibits 7.27 through 7.33 present pro forma consolidated financial statements for Weston and Fisher under each of the three alternatives.

EXHIBIT 7.27

Weston Corporation and Fisher Corporation
Pro Forma Consolidated Balance Sheet As Of January 1, 1999
Assuming Cash Exchange
(amounts in thousands)
(Case 7.1)

	Weston (Before Acquisition)	To Record Acquisition of Fisher's Shares		Weston (After Acquisition)	Fisher (After Acquisition)	Worksheet Consolidation Entries		Pro Forma Consolidated
	(1)	(2)	(3)	(4)	(5)	(6)	(7)	(8)
Assets								
Cash	$ 28,000	(A)59,000	(B)59,000	$ 28,000	$ 6,000			$ 34,000
Accounts Receivable	90,000			90,000	15,000			105,000
Inventory	71,000			71,000	18,000			89,000
Other	13,000			13,000	—	(C) 1,750		14,750
Total Current Assets	$202,000			$202,000	$39,000			$242,750
Property, Plant, and Equipment	$116,000			$116,000	$15,000	(C) 8,000		$139,000
Less: Accumulated Depr.	(38,000)			(38,000)	(9,000)	(C) 9,000		(38,000)
Net Property, Plant, and Equipment	$ 78,000			$ 78,000	$ 6,000			$101,000
Investment in Nonconsolidated Entities	45,000			$ 45,000	—			$ 45,000
Investment in Fisher	—	(B)59,000		59,000	—		(C)59,000	
Goodwill	8,000			8,000	—	(C)24,450		32,450
Other Assets	7,000			7,000	1,000	(C) 1,750		9,750
Total Assets	$340,000			$399,000	$46,000			$430,950

Liabilities

Current Portion Long-Term Debt	$ 2,000		$ —	$ 2,000
Accounts Payable	30,000		7,000	(C) 3,000	37,000
Accrued Liabilities and Advances	78,000		7,000	(C) 1,000	90,000
Income Taxes	21,000		1,000	(C) 1,000	22,000
Total Current Liabilities	$131,000		$15,000		$151,000
Long-Term Debt	48,000	(A)59,000	—		107,000
Other Liabilities	—		1,000	(C) 5,000	6,000
Deferred Taxes	10,000		—	(C) 5,950	15,950
Total Liabilities	$189,000		$16,000		$279,950

Shareholders' Equity

Preferred Stock	$ —		$ —		$ —
Common Stock	11,000		9,000	(C) 9,000	11,000
Additional Paid-In Capital	55,000		5,000	(C) 5,000	55,000
Retained Earnings	85,000		16,000	(C)16,000	85,000
Total Shareholders' Equity	$151,000		$30,000		$151,000
Total Liabilities and Shareholders' Equity	$340,000		$46,000		$430,950

(A) Issue of bonds for cash and payment of acquisition costs.
(B) Purchase of Fisher's outstanding common stock.
(C) Elimination of investment in Fisher and Fisher's shareholders' equity accounts and allocation of excess purchase price (see Exhibit 7.26 for amounts).

EXHIBIT 7.28

Weston Corporation and Fisher Corporation
Proforma Consolidated Income Statement
For The Year Ending December 31, 1999
Assuming Cash Exchange
(amounts in thousands)
(Case 7.1)

	Weston	Fisher	Consolidated Worksheet Entries Dr.	Consolidated Worksheet Entries Cr.	Pro Forma
Sales	$560,000	$ 100,000			$ 660,000
Cost of Sales					
Cost of Sales	(415,700)	(85,600)	(B) 1,700	(E) 5,000	(498,000)
Selling and Administrative	(105,632)	(10,820)	(C) 611	(D) 250	(116,813)
Operating Income	38,668	3,580			$ 45,187
Equity in Net Income of					
Non-Consolidated Entities	4,000	—			4,000
Other Income (expense)	(1,000)	200	(A) 5,900		(6,700)
Income before Taxes	41,668	3,780			$ 42,487
Provision for Income Taxes	(14,584)	(1,323)	(D) 88	(A) 2,065	(15,085)
			(E) 1,750	(B) 595	
Net Income	$ 27,500	$ 2,500			$ 27,402
Basic Earnings per Share	$ 3.47	$ 1.37			$ 3.51
Average Number Shares of					
Common Stock Outstanding ...	7,800	1,800			7,800

(A) Interest on debt: .10 × $59,000 = $5,900, Tax effect = $2,065
(B) Depreciation expense: $17,000 ÷ 10 = $1,700; Deferred tax effect = .35 × $1,700 = $595
(C) Goodwill amortization: $24,450 ÷ 40 = $611; Tax effect = 0
(D) Elimination of pension expense: $5,000 ÷ 20 = $250, Deferred tax effect = .35 × $250 = $88
(E) Elimination of contract loss, OSHA cost, and relocation costs = $5,000; Deferred tax effect: .35 × $5,000 = $1,750

EXHIBIT 7.29

Weston Corporation and Fisher Corporation
Pro Forma Consolidated Balance Sheet As Of January 1, 1999
Assuming Preferred Stock Exchange
(amounts in thousands)
(Case 7.1)

	Weston (Before Acquisition)	To Record Acquisition of Fisher's Shares		Weston (After Acquisition)	Fisher (After Acquisition)	Consolidation Worksheet Entries		Pro Forma Consolidated
	(1)	(2)	(3)	(4)	(5)	(6)	(7)	(8)
Assets								
Cash	$ 28,000		(A) 500	$ 27,500	$ 6,000			$ 33,500
Accounts Receivable	90,000			90,000	15,000			105,000
Inventory	71,000			71,000	18,000			89,000
Other	13,000			13,000	–	(B) 1,750		14,750
Total Current Assets	$ 202,000			$201,500	$ 39,000			$ 242,250
Property, Plant, and Equipment	$ 116,000			$116,000	$ 15,000	(B) 8,000		$ 139,000
Less: Accumulated Depr.	(38,000)			(38,000)	(9,000)	(B) 9,000		(38,000)
Net Property, Plant, and Equipment	$ 78,000			$ 78,000	$ 6,000			$ 101,000
Investment in Nonconsolidated Entities	45,000			$ 45,000	–			$ 45,000
Investment in Fisher	–	(A) 50,500		50,500	–		50,500 (B)	–
Goodwill	8,000			8,000	–	(B) 15,950		23,950
Other Assets	7,000			7,000	1,000	(B) 1,750		9,750
Total Assets	$ 340,000			$390,000	$ 46,000			$ 421,950

(continued)

533

Exh. 7.29—Continued

	Weston (Before Acquisition)	To Record Acquisition of Fisher's Shares		Weston (After Acquisition)	Fisher (After Acquisition)	Worksheet Consolidation Entries		Pro Forma Consolidated
	(1)	(2)	(3)	(4)	(5)	(6)	(7)	(8)
Liabilities								
Current Portion Long-Term Debt	$ 2,000			$ 2,000	$ —			$ 2,000
Accounts Payable	30,000			30,000	7,000		3,000 (B)	37,000
Accrued Liabilities and Advances	78,000			78,000	7,000		1,000 (B)	90,000
Income Taxes	21,000			21,000	1,000		1,000 (B)	22,000
Total Current Liabilities	$131,000			$131,000	$15,000			$151,000
Long-Term Debt	48,000			48,000	—			48,000
Other Liabilities	—			—	1,000		5,000 (B)	6,000
Deferred Taxes	10,000			10,000	—		5,950 (B)	15,950
Total Liabilities	$189,000			$189,000	$16,000			$220,950
Shareholders' Equity								
Preferred Stock	$ —		(A) 50,000	$ 50,000	$ —			$ 50,000
Common Stock	11,000			11,000	9,000	(B) 9,000		11,000
Additional Paid-In Capital	55,000			55,000	5,000	(B) 5,000		55,000
Retained Earnings	85,000			85,000	16,000	(B) 16,000		85,000
Total Shareholders' Equity	$151,000			$201,000	$30,000			$201,000
Total Liabilities and Shareholders' Equity	$ 340,000			$390,000	$ 46,000			$ 421,950

(A) Issue of preferred stock for the outstanding common shares of Fisher and payment of acquisition costs.
(B) Elimination of investment in Fisher and Fisher's shareholders' equity accounts and allocation of excess purchase price (see Exhibit 7.26 for amounts).

EXHIBIT 7.30

Weston Corporation and Fisher Corporation
Pro Forma Consolidated Income Statement
For The Year Ending December 31, 1999
Assuming Preferred Stock Exchange
(amounts in thousands)
(Case 7.1)

	Weston	Fisher	Consolidation Worksheet Entries Dr.	Cr.	Consolidated Pro Forma
Sales	$ 560,000	$100,000			$ 660,000
Cost of Sales					
Cost of Sales	(415,700)	(85,600)	(A)1,700	(D) 5,000	(498,000)
Selling and Administrative	(105,632)	(10,820)	(B) 399	(E) 250	(116,601)
Operating Income	38,668	3,580			$ 45,399
Equity in Net Income of					
Non-Consolidated Entities	4,000	—			4,000
Other Income (expense)	(1,000)	200			(800)
Income before Taxes	$ 41,668	$ 3,780			$ 48,599
Provision for Income Taxes	(14,584)	(1,323)	(C) 88	(A) 595	(17,150)
			(D)1,750		
Net Income	$ 27,084	$ 2,457			$ 31,449
Basic Earnings per Share	$ 3.47	$ 1.37			*
Average Number Shares of					
Common Stock Outstanding	7,800	1,800			7,800

(A) Depreciation expense = $17,000 ÷ 10 = $1,700; Deferred tax effect = .35 × $1,700 = $595.

(B) Goodwill amortization = $15,950 ÷ 40 = $399; Tax effect = 0.

(C) Pension expense: $5,000 ÷ 20 = $250; Deferred tax effect = .35 × $250 = $88.

(D) Loss on contract, OSHA and relocation costs = $5,000; Deferred tax effect = .35 × $5,000 = $1,750.

*Basic EPS: $\dfrac{\$(31,499 - \$3,600)}{7,800} = \$3.58$

Diluted EPS: $\dfrac{\$31,499}{7,800 + 1,350} = \$3.44$

EXHIBIT 7.31

Weston Corporation and Fisher Corporation
Pro Forma Consolidated Balance Sheet As Of January 1, 1999
Assuming Common Stock Exchange
(amounts in thousands)
(Case 7.1)

	Weston (Before Acquisition)	To Record Acquisition of Fisher's Shares		Weston (After Acquisition)	Fisher (After Acquisition)	Worksheet Elimination Entries		Pro Forma Consolidated
	(1)	(2)	(3)	(4)	(5)	(6)	(7)	(8)
Assets								
Cash	$ 28,000		(B) 500	$ 27,500	$ 6,000			$ 33,500
Accounts Receivable	90,000			90,000	15,000			105,000
Inventory	71,000			71,000	18,000			89,000
Other	13,000			13,000	—			13,000
Total Current Assets	$202,000			$ 201,500	$ 39,000			$ 240,500
Property, Plant, and Equipment	$116,000			$ 116,000	$ 15,000			$ 131,000
Less: Accumulated Depr.	(38,000)			(38,000)	(9,000)			(47,000)
Net Property, Plant, and Equipment	$ 78,000			$ 78,000	$ 6,000			$ 84,000
Investment in Nonconsolidated Entities	45,000			45,000	—			45,000
Investment in Fisher	—	(A) 14,000		14,000	—		14,000 (C)	—
Goodwill	8,000			8,000	—			8,000
Other Assets	7,000			7,000	1,000			8,000
Total Assets	$340,000			$ 353,500	$ 46,000			$ 385,500

Liabilities

Current Portion Long-Term Debt	$ 2,000			$ —				$ 2,000
Accounts Payable	30,000			7,000				37,000
Accrued Liabilities and Advances	78,000			7,000				85,000
Income Taxes	21,000			1,000				22,000
Total Current Liabilities	$131,000			$15,000				$146,000
Long-Term Debt	48,000			—				48,000
Other Liabilities	—			1,000				1,000
Deferred Taxes	10,000			—				10,000
Total Liabilities	$189,000			$16,000				$205,000

Shareholders' Equity

Preferred Stock	$ —			$ —				$ 0
Common Stock	11,000	(A)	455	9,000	(C)	9,000		11,455
Additional Paid-In Capital	55,000	(A)	13,545	5,000	(C)	5,000		68,545
Retained Earnings	85,000	(B)	500	16,000				84,500
Total Shareholders' Equity	$151,000			$30,000				$180,500
Total Liabilities and Shareholders' Equity	$340,000			$46,000				$385,500

(A) Issue of common stock for the outstanding common shares of Fisher.

(B) Immediate expensing of the acquisition costs of $500. See Exhibit 7.26 for the explanation. The same amount affects net income for 1999; see Exhibit 7.32.

(C) Elimination of investment in Fisher and Fisher's shareholders' equity accounts.

537

EXHIBIT 7.32

Weston Corporation and Fisher Corporation
Pro Forma Consolidated Income Statement
For The Year Ending December 31, 1999
Assuming Common Stock Exchange
(amounts in thousands)
(Case 7.1)

	Weston	Fisher	Consolidation Worksheet Entries Dr.	Cr.	Consolidated Pro Forma
Sales	$560,000	$100,000			$ 660,000
Cost of Sales					
Cost of Sales	(415,700)	(85,600)			(501,300)
Selling and Administrative	(105,632)	(10,820)			(116,452)
Operating Income	38,668	3,580			$ 42,248
Equity in Net Income of					
Non-Consolidated Entities	4,000	—			4,000
Other Income (expense)	(1,000)	200	(A) 500		(1,300)
Income before Taxes	$ 41,668	$ 3,780			$ 44,948
Provision for Income Taxes	(14,584)	(1,323)		(A) 175	(15,732)
Net Income	$ 27,084	$ 2,457			$ 29,216
Basic Earnings per Share	$ 3.47	$ 1.37			$ 3.14
Average number shares of common stock outstanding	7,800	1,800			9,318

(A) Expensing the cost of acquisition = $500. Income tax effect = .35 × $500 = $170.

EXHIBIT 7.33

Weston Corporation and Fisher Corporation
Key Financial Highlights
(Case 7.1)

	Actual for Weston Corporation				Weston Corporation and Fisher Corporation —Proforma for 1999		
	1995	1996	1997	1998	Alter. A	Alter. B	Alter. C
Earnings per Common Share							
(basic)	$ 1.60	$ 1.83	$ 2.22	$ 2.82	$ 3.51	$ 3.58	$ 3.14
(diluted)					—	3.44	
Dividends per Common Share	$ .40	$ .45	$ .63	$ .88	$ 1.20	$ 1.20	$ 1.20
Current Ratio*	1.8	2.0	1.7	1.5	1.6	1.6	1.6
Long-Term Debt as Percentage of Long-Term Capital*	28.9%	26.5%	25.8%	24.1%	41.5%	19.3%	21.0%
Return on Average Common Shareholders' Equity	12.4%	12.9%	13.6%	15.2%	17.1%	17.4%	15.4%
Book Value per Common Share	$ 13.50	$ 14.88	$ 17.69	$ 19.36	$ 19.36	$ 19.36	$ 19.37
Tangible Net Worth ($000)*	$99,300	$111,600	$129,600	$143,000	$118,550	$127,050	$172,500
Times Interest Earned	5.7	7.8	9.8	10.9	5.0	11.3	10.5
(with preferred dividend)					—	6.4	—

*Proforma amounts for these ratios are at date of acquisition of Fisher.

Calculation of Key Financial Ratios—Alternative A

Basic Earnings per Share: $27,402 ÷ 7,800 = $3.51

Current Ratio: $242,750 ÷ $151,000 = 1.6

Long-Term Debt to Long-Term Capital: $107,000 ÷ ($107,000 + $151,000) = 41.5%

Return on Common Equity: $27,402 ÷ 0.5[$151,000 + ($151,000 + $27,402 − $9,360)] = 17.1%

Common Dividend = 7,800 × $1.20 = $9,360

Book Value per Share: $151,000 ÷ 7,800 = $19.36

Tangible Net Worth: $430,950 − $32,450 − $279,950 = $118,550.

Times Interest Earned: ($27,402 + $15,085 + $4,741 + $5,900) ÷ ($4,741 + $5,900) = 5.0

Interest Expense with No Merger: ($27,084 + $15,584 + X) ÷ X = 10.0; X = $4,741

Calculation of Key Financial Ratios—Alternative B

Basic Earnings Per Share: ($31,449 − $3,600) ÷ 7,800 = $3.58

Preferred Dividend = 1,800 × $2.00 = $3,600

Diluted Earnings Per Share: $31,449 ÷ (7,800 + 1,350) = 3.44

Common Shares Issued Upon Conversion of Preferred: 1,800 × 0.75 = 1,350.

Current Ratio: $242,250 ÷ $151,000 = 1.6

Long-Term Debt to Long-Term Capital: $48,000 ÷ ($48,000 + $201,000) = 19.3%

Return on Common Equity: ($31,449 − $3,600) ÷ 0.5[$151,000 + ($151,000 + $31,449 − $3,600 − $9,360)] = 17.4%

Book Value per Common Share: $151,000 ÷ 7,800 = $19.36

Tangible Net Worth: $421,950 − $23,950 − $220,950 − $50,000 = $127,050.

Times Interest Earned: ($31,449 + $17,150 + $4,741) ÷ $4,741 = 11.3

With Preferred Dividend: ($31,449 + $17,150 + $4,741) ÷ ($4,741 + $3,600) = 6.4

Calculation of Key Financial Ratios—Alternative C

Basic Earnings Per Share: $29,216 ÷ (7,800 + 1,518) = $3.14

Current Ratio: $240,500 ÷ $146,000 = 1.6

Long-Term Debt to Long-Term Capital: $48,000 ÷ ($48,000 + $180,500) = 21.0%

Return on Common Equity: $29,216 ÷ 0.5[$180,500 + ($180,500 + $29,216 − $11,182)] = 15.4%

Common Dividend: (7,800 + 1,518) × $1.20 = $11,182.

Book Value per Common Share: $180,500 ÷ (7,800 + 1,518) = $19.37

Tangible Net Worth: $385,500 − $8,000 − $205,000 = $172,500

Times Interest Earned: ($29,216 + $15,732 + $4,741) ÷ 4,741 = 10.5

Required

a. As a shareholder of Fisher, which alternative would you choose and why? The income tax rate on capital gains is 28 percent. Would the answers of an individual investor and a pension fund differ?

b. As the chief financial officer of Weston, which alternative would you choose, and why?

CLARK EQUIPMENT COMPANY: ANALYZING A JOINT PROBLEM

Clark Equipment Company, through its wholly owned subsidiaries, operates in three principal product markets:

1. Small "lift and carry" products, including excavators for digging and loaders for hauling various materials. Its Bobcat® skid steer loader has a 50 percent worldwide market share.
2. Axles and transmissions for use by manufacturers of cranes and large materials handling machinery used in construction, mining, logging, and industrial applications.
3. Axles and transmissions for use by manufacturers of automobiles, trucks, and tractors in the Brazilian market.

Sales for these product groups for Year 10 through Year 12 appear below:

	Year 10		Year 11		Year 12	
Off-highway:						
Lift-and-carry products ...	$385	44%	$347	48%	$410	51%
Axles and Transmissions ..	274	32	240	33	241	30
On-highway:						
Axles and Transmissions ..	205	24	140	19	152	19
	$864	100%	$727	100%	$803	100%

The geographic sources of Clark's product sales (that is, the location of its manufacturing facilities) for Year 10 through Year 12 are as follows:

	Year 10		Year 11		Year 12	
North America	$504	58%	$439	60%	$501	62%
Europe	165	19	153	21	157	20
South America	195	23	135	19	145	18
	$864	100%	$727	100%	$803	100%

Since Year 5, Clark Equipment Company has engaged in a 50 percent-owned joint venture with Volvo of Sweden. The joint venture, called VME Group, manufactures heavy earthmoving construction and mining equipment worldwide. Its principal competitors are Caterpillar, Komatsu, and to a lesser extent Deere & Company. Clark Equipment Company accounts for its investment in this joint venture using the equity method.

Key economic characteristics of the equipment manufacturing industry, which includes industrial, construction, and agricultural equipment, are as follows:

1. **Product Lines**. Products include tractors, excavators, loaders, haulers, cranes, compactors, and similar products. Manufacturers range from worldwide full-line producers to regional niche players. There are currently over 700 producers in the U.S., yet six companies command over 70 percent of the domestic market. Manufacturers compete on the basis of machine performance, price, after-market support and parts availability. Approximately 20 percent to 30 percent of a manufacturer's sales typically come from the after-market. A large tractor, for example, will usually consume parts and service equal to the cost of the equipment within approximately two years of initial purchase.

2. **Production**. Equipment manufacturing is capital-intensive. Manufacturers tend to centralize production around key machine components, such as engines, axles, transmissions, and hydraulics. Customizing products to particular customers' needs typically occurs at the assembly stage.

3. **Technology**. Electronic and computer-based technologies have played an increasingly important role in recent years, both in the design of the final product and its manufacturing. Robotics in particular has been applied successfully in the manufacturing process.

4. **Demand**. The relatively high cost of equipment and the cyclicality of many of the industries to which manufacturers sell their products (such as the construction, mining, and automotive industries) result in highly cyclical sales patterns for equipment manufacturers. The level of interest rates, general conditions in the economy, and income tax considerations (such as depreciation rates) significantly impact sales.

5. **Marketing**. Manufacturers use a distributor network to sell their products (original equipment and parts). Distributors usually sell a single manufacturer's products, but complement their product offerings by selling other products unique to the market that the manufacturer does not offer.

6. **Financing**. The capital-intensive nature of the manufacturing process leads equipment manufacturers to rely on extensive long-term debt financing. Responsibility for arranging customer financing for equipment purchases may fall on the manufacturer, the distributor, or both.

Exhibit 7.34 presents condensed balance sheets for Clark Equipment Company as of December 31, Year 9, through December 31, Year 12, and condensed income statements for Year 10 through Year 12. These financial statements report Clark Equipment Company's investment in VME Group using the equity method. Exhibit 7.35 presents similar condensed financial statement data for VME Group.

Required

a. Prepare an analysis of the changes in the Investment in VME Group account on Clark's books for Year 9 through Year 11.

b. Exhibit 7.36 presents partial condensed balance sheets and income statements for Clark Equipment Company assuming that it accounted for its investment in VME Group using the proportionate consolidation method (that is, Clark Equipment Company recognizes its 50 percent share of the assets, liabilities, revenues, and expenses of VME Group). Complete Exhibit 7.36 by preparing a balance sheet as of December 31, Year 12, and an income statement for Year 12 following the proportionate consolidation method.

EXHIBIT 7.34

Condensed Financial Statement Data for Clark Equipment Company with VME Group Accounted for Using the Equity Method
(amounts in millions)
(Case 7.2)

		December 31:		
	Year 9	**Year 10**	**Year 11**	**Year 12**
Balance Sheet				
Current Assets	$ 551	$ 468	$ 520	$396
Investment in VME Group	142	166	135	119
Noncurrent Assets	319	466	465	444
Total Assets	$1,012	$1,100	$1,120	$959
Current Liabilities	$ 265	$ 282	$ 328	$187
Noncurrent Liabilities	255	238	554	519
Shareholders' Equity	492	580	238	253
Total Equities	$1,012	$1,100	$1,120	$959

	For the Year:		
	Year 10	**Year 11**	**Year 12**
Income Statement			
Sales	$ 864	$727	$803
Equity in Earnings of VME	26	(29)	(47)
Cost of Goods Sold	(717)	(638)[a]	(664)
Interest Expense	(22)	(26)	(26)
Other Expenses, including Taxes ..	(111)	(87)	(94)
Net Income (Loss)	$ 40	$ (53)	$ (28)

[a]Includes $20 million of charges for restructuring operations and environmental cleanup.

EXHIBIT 7.35

Condensed Financial Statement Data for VME Group
(amounts in millions)
(Case 7.2)

		December 31:		
	Year 9	**Year 10**	**Year 11**	**Year 12**
Balance Sheet				
Current Assets	$594	$665	$ 801	$649
Noncurrent Assets	177	231	392	321
Total Assets	$771	$896	$1,193	$970

(continued)

Exh. 7.35—Continued	December 31:			
	Year 9	Year 10	Year 11	Year 12
Balance Sheet				
Current Liabilities	$326	$354	$ 642	$516
Noncurrent Liabilities	187	232	299	230
Shareholders' Equity	258	310	252	224
Total Equities	$771	$896	$1,193	$970

	For the Year:		
	Year 10	Year 11	Year 12
Income Statement			
Sales	$ 1,325	$ 1,368	$ 1,357
Cost of Goods Sold	(1,037)	(1,110)	(1,159)
Interest Expense	(20)	(33)	(29)
Other Expenses, including Taxes	(216)	(283)	(263)
Net Income (Loss)	$ 52	$ (58)	$ (94)

EXHIBIT 7.36

Condensed Financial Statement Data for Clark Equipment Company with
VME Group Accounted for Using the Proportionate Consolidation Method
(amounts in millions)
(Case 7.2)

	December 31:			
	Year 9	Year 10	Year 11	Year 12
Balance Sheet				
Current Assets	$ 848.0	$ 800.5	$ 920.5	
Noncurrent Assets	407.5	581.5	661.0	
Goodwill	13.0	11.0	9.0	
Total Assets	$1,268.5	$1,393.0	$1,590.5	
Current Liabilities	$ 428.0	$ 459.0	$ 649.0	
Noncurrent Liabilities	348.5	354.0	703.5	
Shareholders' Equity	492.0	580.0	238.0	
Total Equities	$1,268.5	$1,393.0	$1,590.5	

	For the Year:		
	Year 10	Year 11	Year 12
Income Statement			
Sales	$ 1,526.5	$ 1,411.0	
Cost of Goods Sold	(1,235.5)	(1,193.0)	
Interest Expense	(32.0)	(42.5)	
Other Expenses, including Taxes ...	(219.0)	(228.5)	
Net Income (Loss)	$ 40.0	$ (53.0)	

EXHIBIT 7.37

Condensed Financial Statement Data for Clark Equipment Company with VME Group Accounted for Using the Full Consolidation Method (amounts in millions) (Case 7.2)

	December 31:			
	Year 9	**Year 10**	**Year 11**	**Year 12**
Balance Sheet				
Current Assets	$1,145	$1,133	$1,321	
Noncurrent Assets	496	697	857	
Goodwill	13	11	9	
Total Assets	$1,654	$1,841	$2,187	
Current Liabilities	$ 591	$ 636	$ 970	
Noncurrent Liabilities	442	470	853	
Joint-Owner's Interest	129	155	126	
Shareholders' Equity	492	580	238	
Total Equities	$1,654	$1,841	$2,187	

	For the Year:		
	Year 10	**Year 11**	**Year 12**
Income Statement			
Sales	$ 2,189	$ 2,095	
Cost of Goods Sold	(1,754)	(1,748)	
Interest Expense	(42)	(59)	
Other Expenses, including Taxes	(327)	(370)	
Joint-Owners Interest	(26)	29	
Net Income (Loss)	$ 40	$ (53)	

c. Exhibit 7.37 presents partial condensed balance sheets and income statements for Clark Equipment Company assuming that it accounted for its investment in VME Group using the full consolidation method (that is, Clark Equipment Company consolidates 100 percent of the assets, liabilities, revenues, and expenses of VME Group, and reports Volvo's share of these items as a joint owner's interest. Complete Exhibit 7.37 by preparing a balance sheet as of December 31, Year 12, and an income statement for Year 12 following the full consolidation method.

d. Which of three methods of accounting for Clark's investment in VME Group—equity, proportionate consolidation, full consolidation—better portrays the economics of the relationship between the entities? Explain.

e. Exhibit 7.38 presents selected financial statement ratios for Clark Equipment Company and VME Group under each of the three methods of accounting. Calculate these ratios for Year 12. The income tax rate is 34 percent.

f. Identify the likely reasons for changes in the profitability and risk of Clark Equipment Company during the period covering Year 10 through Year 12.

EXHIBIT 7.38

Clark Equipment Company
Profitability and Risk Ratios
(Case 7.2)

	Equity Method			Proportionate Consolidation			Full Consolidation		
	Year 10	Year 11	Year 12	Year 10	Year 11	Year 12	Year 10	Year 11	Year 12
Profit Margin for ROA	6.31%	(4.93%)		4.00%	(1.77%)		4.28%	(2.06%)	
Assets Turnover	.82	.65		1.15	.95		1.25	1.04	
Return on Assets	5.16%	(3.23%)		4.59%	(1.67%)		5.36%	(2.14%)	
Common Earnings Leverage	.73	1.48		.65	2.12		.43	1.23	
Capital Structure Leverage	1.97	2.71		2.48	3.65		3.26	4.92	
Return on Common Equity	7.46%	(12.96%)		7.46%	(12.96%)		7.46%	(12.96%)	
Current Ratios (December 31)	1.66	1.59		1.74	1.42		1.78	1.36	
Fixed Asset Turnover[a]	2.20	1.56		3.09	2.27		3.67	2.70	
Long-Term Debt Ratio (Dec. 31)[b]	29.10%	69.95%		37.90%	74.72%		39.00%	70.09%	
Cost of Goods Sold/Sales	82.99%	87.76%		80.94%	84.55%		80.13%	83.44%	

	Clark-Separate Co.			VME-Separate Co.		
	Year 10	Year 11	Year 12	Year 10	Year 11	Year 12
Profit Margin for ROA	3.30%	.88%		4.92%	(2.65%)	
Assets Turnover	.96	.76		1.59	1.31	
Return on Assets	3.16%	.66%		7.82%	(3.47%)	
Common Earnings Leverage	.49	(1.70)		.80	1.60	
Capital Structure Leverage	1.68	2.35		2.94	3.72	
Return on Common Equity	2.61%	(2.64%)		18.3%	(20.64%)	
Current Ratios (December 31)	1.66	1.59		1.88	1.25	
Fixed Asset Turnover[a]	2.20	1.56		6.50	4.39	
Long-Term Debt Ratio (Dec. 31)[b]	29.10%	69.95%		42.80%	54.27%	
Cost of Goods Sold/Sales	82.99%	87.76%		78.26%	81.14%	

[a]Assuming that noncurrent assets represent property, plant and equipment.
[b]Assuming that noncurrent liabilities represent long-term debt.

LOUCKS CORPORATION: OBTAINING SECURITY IN TRANSLATION

Loucks Corporation, a U.S. company, manufactures and markets security alarm systems. Because of predictions of rapid economic growth in South America during the next decade, Loucks plans to establish a wholly owned subsidiary in Colombia as of January 1, Year 8, to manufacture and market security alarm systems in that country. The Colombian subsidiary will use technology developed by Loucks for the alarm systems. It will import from Loucks a portion of the electronic software needed for the systems. Assembly will take place in Colombia.

Loucks plans to contribute $100,000 to establish the subsidiary on January 1, Year 8. The exchange rate between the U.S. dollar and the Colombian peso is expected to be $0.02:P1 on this date. Exhibit 7.39 presents proforma financial statements for Year 8 for the Colombian subsidiary during its first year of operations. Exhibit 7.40 presents a partial proforma consolidation worksheet for Loucks and its Colombian subsidiary for Year 8.

Additional information pertaining to these companies during Year 8 includes:

1. Loucks expects to sell electronic software to its Colombian subsidiary during Year 8 at a transfer (selling) price of P3 million. The Colombian subsidiary expects to sell all alarm systems in which this software is a component by the end of Year 8. Transfers will be denominated in Colombian pesos. Loucks plans to hedge its exchange exposure, including any transaction gain or loss and related gain or loss on the hedging instrument in other expenses.
2. The subsidiary expects to declare and pay a dividend to Loucks on December 31, Year 8.

Required

a. Discuss whether Loucks should use the U.S. dollar or the Colombian peso as the functional currency for its Colombian subsidiary.
b. Loucks expects the exchange rate between the U.S. dollar and the Colombian peso to change as follows during Year 8:

January 1, Year 8	$0.020:P1
Average, Year 8	$0.018:P1
December 31, Year 8	$0.015:P1

Complete Exhibit 7.39 showing the translation of the subsidiary's accounts into U.S. dollars, assuming that the Colombian peso is the functional currency. Include a separate calculation of the translation adjustment. Using the translated amounts from part b, complete the consolidation worksheet in Exhibit 7.40.
c. Repeat part b, assuming that the U.S. dollar is the functional currency. Include a separate calculation of the translation gain or loss. The Colombian subsidiary expects to issue bonds denominated in Colombian pesos and acquire fixed assets on January 1, Year 8.

EXHIBIT 7.39

Columbia Subsidiary
Translation of Financial Statements – Year 8
(Case 7.3)

	Colombian Pesos	Exchange Rate	U.S. Dollars
Balance Sheet:			
Assets			
Cash	P 700,000		
Accounts Receivable	2,000,000		
Inventories	3,500,000		
Fixed Assets (net)	5,700,000		
	P 11,900,000		
Liabilities and Equity			
Accounts Payable	P 2,400,000		
Bonds Payable	4,000,000		
Common Stock	5,000,000		
Translation Adjustment	—		
Retained Earnings	500,000		
	P 11,900,000		
Income Statement:			
Revenues	P 15,000,000		
Cost of Goods Sold	(10,000,000)		
Depreciation Expense	(300,000)		
Other Expenses	(2,500,000)		
Net Income	P 2,200,000		
Retained Earnings Statement:			
Balance, January 1, Year 1	P —		
Plus Net Income	2,200,000		
Less Dividends	(1,700,000)		
Balance, December 31, Year 1	P 500,000		

---

d. Why does the sign of the translation adjustment in part b differ from the sign of the translation gain or loss in part c?

e. Assume that actual financial statement amounts for Year 8 turn out to be exactly as projected in Exhibits 7.39 and 7.40, but that the exchange rate changes as follows:

January 1, Year 8	$0.020:P1
Average, Year 8	$0.022:P1
December 31, Year 8	$0.025:P1

EXHIBIT 7.40

Loucks Corporation and Colombian Subsidiary
Consolidation Worksheet for
(Case 7.3)

	Loucks Corp.	Colombian Subsidiary	Adjustments and Eliminations	Consolidated
Balance Sheet				
Cash	$ 48,000			
Accounts Receivable	125,000			
Inventories	260,000			
Investment in Colombian Subsidiary	?			
Fixed Assets (net)	120,000			
Total Assets	$?			
Accounts Payable	$ 280,000			
Bonds Payable	50,000			
Common Stock	100,000			
Translation Adjustment	—			
Retained Earnings	?			
Total Equities	$?			
Income Statement				
Sales Revenue	$ 500,000			
Equity in Earnings of Colombian Subs. ...	?			
Cost of Goods Sold	(400,000)			
Depreciation Expense	(20,000)			
Other Expenses	(30,000)			
Net Income	$ 89,600			
Dividends	(20,000)			
Increase in Retained Earnings	$?			
Retained Earnings, Jan. 1	167,500			
Retained Earnings, Dec. 31	$?			

Calculate the amount of the translation adjustment under the all-current method and the amount under the monetary/nonmonetary method for Year 8. Why do the signs of the translation adjustments in part e differ from those in parts b and c?

f. Compute the net income to revenues ratio based on (1) amounts originally measured in Colombian pesos, (2) amounts measured in U.S. dollars from part b and (3) amounts measured in U.S. dollars from part c. Why is the net income to revenues percentage the same under (1) and (2) but different under (3)?

PART III

EXPLORING PROFITABILITY AND RISK ANALYSIS IN MORE DEPTH

INTERRELATED SEQUENTIAL STEPS IN FINANCIAL STATEMENT ANALYSIS

1. Identify Economic Characteristics

2. Identify Company Strategies

3. Understand and Cleanse the Financial Statements

4. Analyze Profitability and Risk

5. Value the Firm

Part III provides an extended look at the profitability and risk analysis introduced in Chapter 3. This part emphasizes step four of the five interrelated sequential steps in financial statement analysis by providing a more in-depth discussion of how to effectively analyze the profitability and risk of a firm.

Meaningful interpretations of a firm's profitability are enhanced by analyzing ROA and ROCE in relation to various economic attributes and strategic choices of a firm. Likewise, meaningful interpretations of the levels of risk taken on by a firm are enhanced by examining the relation between economic and market measures of risk and accounting measures of risk. As emphasized in Parts I and II, the profitability and risk analysis discussed in this part stresses the importance of an industry context to be most effective.

Part III, Chapters 8 and 9, explore profitability and risk analysis in greater depth. ROA and ROCE are used as a framework for extending the profitability discussion introduced in Chapter 3. Key short-term liquidity and long-term solvency ratios introduced in Chapter 3 are used to study credit and bankruptcy risk of a firm.

CHAPTER 8   PROFITABILITY ANALYSIS: AN EXTENDED LOOK
Operating Risk Characteristics and ROA Differences; Profit Margins, Assets Turnover, and Economic Attributes of a Firm; Financial Leverage; and ROCE Differences.

CHAPTER 9   RISK ANALYSIS: AN EXTENDED LOOK
Assessing Credit Risk; Univariate and Multivariate Models for Predicting Bankruptcy; Application of Bankruptcy Models in Practice; Relation Between Financial Statement Measures of Risk; and Market Equity Beta.

CHAPTER 8

PROFITABILITY ANALYSIS: AN EXTENDED LOOK

Learning Objectives

1. Use differences in the operating risk characteristics of firms (such as operating leverage, sales cyclicality, stage and length of product life cycle) to explain differences in firms' returns on assets (ROA).
2. Use differences in the extent of barriers to entry, degrees of competition, and nature of products to explain differences in the mix of profit margin and assets turnover.
3. Identify industries for which some base other than total assets serves as a more effective basis for assessing operating performance.
4. Understand the role of ROA and financial leverage in explaining differences in firms' returns on common shareholders' equity (ROCE).

Chapter 3 introduced two financial statement ratios that are commonly used for analyzing the overall profitability of a firm: the rate of return on assets (ROA) and the rate of return on common shareholders' equity (ROCE). This chapter explores these financial ratios more fully.

RATE OF RETURN ON ASSETS

ROA measures the return from using assets to generate earnings, independent of the financing of those assets. The analyst uses ROA to assess a firm's operating performance relative to investments made in assets without regard to whether the firm uses debt or equity capital to finance the investments. ROA is computed as follows (level 1 analysis):

$$\text{ROA} = \frac{\text{Net Income} + (1 - \text{Tax Rate})(\text{Interest Expense}) + \text{Minority Interest in Earnings}}{\text{Average Total Assets}}$$

The analyst obtains enhanced understanding of the behavior of ROA by disaggregating it into profit margin and total assets turnover components as follows (level 2 analysis):[1]

ROA	=	**Profit Margin**	×	**Total Assets Turnover**
$\dfrac{\text{Net Income} + (1 - \text{Tax Rate})(\text{Interest Expense}) + \text{Minority Interest in Earnings}}{\text{Average Total Assets}}$	=	$\dfrac{\text{Net Income} + (1 - \text{Tax Rate})(\text{Interest Expense}) + \text{Minority Interest in Earnings}}{\text{Sales}}$	×	$\dfrac{\text{Sales}}{\text{Average Total Assets}}$

In the first section of this chapter we examine more fully the economic and strategic significance of ROA, profit margin, and total assets turnover.

INTERPRETING THE RATE OF RETURN ON ASSETS[2]

Exhibit 8.1 graphs the ten-year average of the median annual ROAs, profit margins, and assets turnovers of 22 industries for each of the years 1987 through 1996. The two isoquants reflect ROAs of 3 percent and 6 percent. The isoquants show the various combinations of profit margin and assets turnover that yield an ROA of 3 percent and 6 percent. For instance, an ROA of 6 percent results from any of these profit margin/assets turnover combinations: 6%/1.0, 3%/2.0, 2%/3.0, and 1%/6.0.

The data underlying the plots for ROA, profit margin, and assets turnover in Exhibit 8.1 reflect aggregated amounts across firms and across years. The focus of financial statement analysis is of course on the ROAs of specific firms, or even segments of specific firms, for particular years (or even quarters). The analyst can nevertheless obtain useful insights about the behavior of ROA at the segment or firm level by examining average industry-level data. In particular:

1. What factors explain the consistently high or consistently low ROAs of some industries compared to the average of all industries? That is, what are the rea-

---

[1]Chapter 3 demonstrates that various expense-to-sales percentages enhance analysis of differences in profit margins, and various asset turnovers (for example, accounts receivable turnover, inventory turnover) enhance understanding of differences in total assets turnovers (level 3 analysis). The analyst gains additional insight by studying ROA, profit margins, and total assets turnovers for the product and geographical segments of a firm (level 4 analysis).

[2]The material in this section draws heavily from Thomas I. Selling and Clyde P. Stickney, "The Effects of Business Environments and Strategy on a Firm's Rate of Return on Assets," *Financial Analysts Journal* (January/February 1989), pp. 43–52.

sons for differences in the distribution of industries in the bottom left versus the top right in Exhibit 8.1?

2. What factors explain the fact that certain industries have high profit margins and low assets turnovers, while other industries experience low profit margins and high assets turnovers? That is, what are the reasons for differences in the distribution of industries in the upper left versus the lower right in Exhibit 8.1?

The microeconomics and business strategy literatures provide useful background for interpreting the behavior of ROA, profit margin, and assets turnover.

Differences or Changes in ROA. Economic theory suggests that higher levels of perceived risk in any activity should lead to higher levels of

---

EXHIBIT 8.1

Average Median ROAs, Profit Margins, and Assets Turnovers For 22 Industries 1987–1996

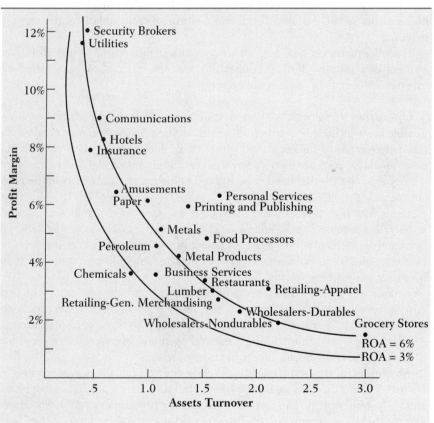

expected return if that activity is to attract capital. The extra return compensates for the extra risk assumed. This is not a direct or simple relationship, however. There are a variety of reasons why realized rates of return on assets derived from financial statement data for any particular period will not necessarily correlate as predicted with the level of risk involved in an activity as economic theory suggests. It could be that:

1. Faulty assumptions were used in deriving expected ROAs. These assumptions might relate to, for example, growth rate in sales, mix of variable and fixed costs, or income tax rate.
2. Changes in the environment after forming expectations cause realized ROAs to deviate from expectations.
3. ROA may provide a biased measure of economic rates of return (that is, rates of return that include all changes in economic value) because generally accepted accounting principles often place greater weight on conservatism than on reflection of economic reality.

Despite these weaknesses, ROAs based on reported financial statement data do provide useful information for tracking the periodic performance of a firm and its segments in the past and for developing expectations about future earnings potential.

Three elements of risk help in understanding differences across firms and changes over time in ROAs: (1) operating leverage, (2) cyclicality of sales, and (3) stage and length of product life cycles.

Operating Leverage.   Firms operate with different mixtures of fixed and variable costs in their cost structures. Firms in the utilities, communications, hotels, petroleum, and chemicals industries are capital-intensive. Depreciation and many operating costs are more or less fixed for any given period. Most retailers and wholesalers, on the other hand, have high proportions of variable costs in their cost structures.

Firms with high proportions of fixed costs will experience significant increases in operating income as sales increase. The increased income occurs because the firms spread fixed costs over a larger number of units sold, resulting in a decrease in average unit cost. Similarly, when sales decrease, such firms experience sharp decreases in operating income.

Economists refer to this process of operating with high proportions of fixed costs as *operating leverage*. Firms with high levels of operating leverage experience greater variability in their ROAs than firms with low levels of operating leverage. All else being equal, firms with high levels of operating leverage incur more risk in their operations and should earn higher rates of return.

Measuring the degree of operating leverage of a firm or its segments requires information about the fixed and variable cost structure. The top panel of Exhibit 8.2 shows the total revenue and total cost functions of two firms, A and B. The graphs assume that the two firms are the same size and have the same total revenue function and break-even points. These assumptions simplify the discussion of operating leverage, but are not necessary when comparing actual companies.

Firm B has a higher level of fixed costs than Firm A, as measured by the intersection of the vertical axis at zero sales in the top panel of Exhibit 8.2. Firm A has a higher level of variable costs than Firm B, as measured by the slope of its total cost functions as revenues increase above zero.

The lower panel nets the total revenue and total cost functions to derive the operating income function. Operating income is negative in an amount equal to fixed costs when revenues are zero and operating income is zero at break-even revenues.

We use the slope of the operating income line as a measure of the extent of operating leverage. Firm B, with its higher fixed-cost and lower variable-cost mix, has more operating leverage. As revenues increase, its operating income increases more than Firm A's operating income does. On the down side, however, income decreases more sharply as revenues decrease.

Unfortunately, firms do not publicly disclose information about their fixed and variable cost structures. To examine the influence of operating leverage on the behavior of ROA for a particular firm or its segments, the analyst must make estimates about the fixed/variable cost structure. One approach to such estimation is to study the various cost items of a firm and attempt to identify the items that are likely to behave as fixed costs.

Firms incur some costs in particular amounts, referred to as *committed fixed costs*, regardless of their actual level of activity during a period. Examples of such

EXHIBIT 8.2

Cost Structure and Operating Leverage

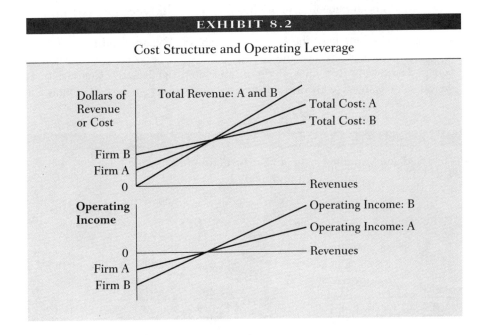

costs are depreciation, amortization, and rent. Firms can alter the amount of some other costs, referred to as *discretionary fixed costs*, in the short run in response to operating conditions, but, in general, these costs do not vary directly with the level of activity. Examples of discretionary fixed costs would be research and development, maintenance, advertising, and central corporate staff expenses. Whether the analyst should classify these latter costs as fixed costs or as variable costs in measuring operating leverage depends on their behavior in a particular firm.

Exhibit 8.3 presents cost data for firms in four industries, showing the amount of depreciation and amortization and the amount of all other operating (variable) costs for a recent year, assuming that depreciation and amortization are the only fixed costs. The proportion of total costs that fixed costs represent is a rough gauge of the extent of operating leverage. This is an admittedly imprecise approach to measuring operating leverage, because the fixed cost proportion by definition should vary as the level of operations varies.

These calculations show that Kelly Services has the least operating leverage. It incurs fixed costs for its office facilities, but its employees receive compensation based on the number of hours worked (thereby making their compensation a variable cost). Coke has more operating leverage than Kelly Services, because of the fixed costs of its bottling plants. It has less operating leverage than USX, which manufactures steel and petroleum products in capital-intensive plants. Consolidated Edison has even more operating leverage, because its plants operate with fewer employees than USX plants.

Cyclicality of Sales.   The sales of certain goods and services are sensitive to conditions in the economy. Examples are construction services, industrial equipment, computers, automobiles, and other durable goods. When the economy is in an upswing—there is healthy GNP growth, low unemployment, low interest rates—customers purchase these relatively high-priced items, and sales of these firms grow accordingly. When the economy enters a recession, customers curtail their purchases, and the sales of these firms drop significantly. Contrast these cyclical sales patterns with those of grocery stores, food processors, nonfashion

---

EXHIBIT 8.3

Proportions of Fixed and Variable Costs in Cost Structure of Selected Firms
(amounts in millions)

	Kelly Services		Coke		USX		Consolidated Edison	
Depreciation and Amortization	$ 26	.8%	$ 479	3.2%	$ 1,012	4.6%	$ 951	18.3%
Other Operating Expenses	3,181	99.2	14,631	96.8	21,207	95.4	4,250	81.7
Total	$3,207	100.0%	$15,110	100.0%	$22,219	100.0%	$5,201	100.0%

clothing producers, and electric utilities. These latter industries sell products that most consumers consider necessities. Products in these industries also tend to carry lower per unit costs, reducing the benefits to the buyer of delaying purchases in order to realize cost savings. Firms with cyclical sales patterns incur more risk than firms with noncyclical sales.

One way a firm can reduce the risk inherent in cyclical sales is to strive for a high proportion of variable cost in its cost structure. It could pay employees an hourly wage instead of a fixed salary, and rent buildings and equipment under short-term cancelable leases instead of purchasing these facilities. Cost levels should thus change proportionally with sales, thereby maintaining profit margin percentages and reducing risk.

For some firms, the nature of their activities is such that they must carry high levels of fixed costs (that is, operating leverage). Examples are capital-intensive service firms such as airlines and railroads. Firms in these industries may attempt to transform the cost of their physical capacity from a fixed cost to a variable cost by entering into short-term leases. Of course, lessors will then bear the risk of cyclical sales and demand higher returns (in the form of higher rental fees). Thus, some firms bear a combination of operating leverage and cyclical sales risks.

A noncyclical sales pattern can compensate for high operating leverage and effectively neutralize this latter element of risk. Electric utilities and telecommunications firms, for example, carry high levels of fixed costs. Their dominant positions in most service areas, however, mitigate their operating risks and permit them to achieve stable profitability.

Product Life Cycle. A third element of risk that affects ROA relates to the stage and length of a firm's product life cycle. Products move through four identifiable phases: introduction, growth, maturity, and decline. During the introduction and growth phases, a firm focuses on product development (product R&D spending) and capacity enlargement (capital spending). The objective is to gain market acceptance and market share. There may be considerable uncertainty during these phases regarding the market viability of a firm's products.

Products that survive into the maturity phase have gained market acceptance. At this time, firms may have been able to reduce capital expenditures on new operating capacity. During the maturity phase, however, competition becomes more intense, and the emphasis shifts to reducing costs through improved capacity utilization (economies of scale) and more efficient production (process R&D spending aimed at reducing manufacturing costs through better use of labor and materials).

During the decline phase, firms exit the industry as sales decline and profit opportunities diminish.

Exhibit 8.4 depicts the typical behavior of revenues, operating income, investment, and ROA in these four product life cycles. During the introduction and early growth phases, expenditures on product development and marketing, coupled with relatively low sales levels, lead to operating losses and negative ROAs.

As sales accelerate during the high growth phase, operating income and ROAs turn positive. Extensive product development, marketing, and depreciation

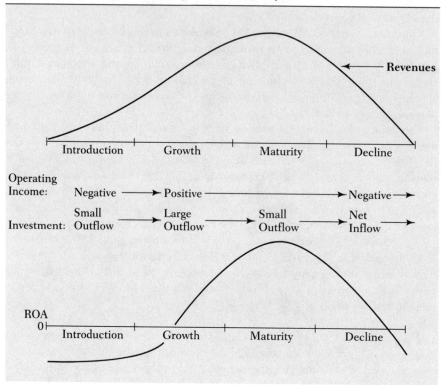

EXHIBIT 8.4

Relationships Among Sales, Operating Income, Investment, and ROA
During Product Life Cycle

expenses during this phase moderate operating income, while heavy capital expenditures to build capacity for expected higher future sales increase the denominator of ROA. Thus, ROA does not grow as rapidly as sales.

ROA increases significantly during the maturity phase because of the benefits of economies of scale and learning curve phenomena and curtailments of capital expenditures. ROA deteriorates during the decline phase as operating income decreases, but may remain positive or even increase for some time into this phase.

Thus, as products move through their life cycles, their ROAs should move to the upper right area in Exhibit 8.1, peak during the maturity stage, and then move to the lower left area as the decline phase sets in.

This movement in ROA appears negatively correlated with the level of risk. That is, risks are probably highest in the introduction and growth stages, when ROA is low or negative, and lowest in the maturity phase, when ROA is high. Taking a weighted average of ROAs over several years will more accurately reflect the economic returns generated by high growth firms.

Note that the product life cycle theory focuses on individual products. We can extend the theory to an industry level by examining the average stage in the product life cycle of all products within that industry. For instance, products offered in the computer industry are in all phases from introduction to decline, but the industry overall is probably in the latter part of the high growth phase. The soft drink and food processing industries, Coke's primary involvement, are mature, although Coke and its competitors constantly introduce new products. We might view the steel industry, at least in the United States, as in the early decline phase, although some companies have modernized production sufficiently to stave off the decline.[3]

Besides product life cycle stage, the length of the life cycle also figures into risk that affects ROA. Products with short product life cycles require a firm to make more frequent expenditures to develop replacement or new products, which thereby increases risks. The product life cycles of most computer products run one to two years. Most pharmaceutical products experience product life cycles of approximately seven years. The life cycles of Coke's soft drinks, branded food products, and some toys are much longer. Consider the Barbie doll, for example.

Look again at the average industry ROAs in Exhibit 8.1. The positioning of several industries is consistent with the fact that they incur one or more of these elements of risk. The relatively high ROAs of the amusements industry reflect its high operating leverage, growth, and dominant market positions in particular geographic locations. Apparel retailers face the risk of fashion obsolescence of their products. Insurance companies bear little risk from operating leverage, sales cyclicality, or life cycle phenomena and have relatively low ROAs.

Some of the industry positionings in Exhibit 8.1 appear inconsistent with these elements of risk. The petroleum, chemicals, and hotel industries are capital-intensive and experience sales cyclicality. Their ROAs are lower than risk theory would suggest. Excess capacity and obsolete plant assets characterize all three industries, however. Thus, the low ROAs may reflect the need for restructuring in these industries (that is, the lower ROAs represent disequilibrium positions).

The ROA positioning of several industries appears to be affected by generally accepted accounting principles (GAAP). A major asset for food processors, for example, is the value of their brand names. Yet, GAAP requires these firms to immediately expense advertising and other costs incurred to develop these brand names. Thus, their asset bases are understated and their ROAs are overstated.[4] Similarly, the publishing industry does not recognize the value of copyrights or authors' contracts as assets, which results in an overstatement of ROAs. A similar overstatement problem occurs for service firms, where the value of employees does not appear as an asset.

One approach to dealing with these "off-balance sheet assets" is to reverse the immediate expensing of a portion of advertising, research and development

---

[3]Empirical support for a link between life cycle stage, sales growth, capital expenditure growth and stock market reaction appears in Joseph H. Anthony and K. Ramesh, "Association Between Accounting Performance Measures and Stock Prices: A Test and the Life Cycle Hypothesis," *Journal of Accounting and Economics*, 15 (1992), pp. 203–227.

[4]The immediate expensing of advertising costs understates net income as well, but the difference between the amount expensed and amortization of amounts from the current and prior periods that perhaps should have been capitalized will result in less distortion of net income than of total assets.

(R&D), and similar costs for some period of prior years, and recognize that amount as an asset. For example, suppose the experience of a branded food processing firm is that brands have a 20-year life; and 20 percent of expenditures on advertising maintain brand recognition; the remaining 80 percent serve to stimulate current demand. The analyst might recognize an asset equal to one-half of 20 percent of total advertising expenditures (assuming straight-line amortization) during the last 20 years. The analyst should add back to net income for the current year 20 percent of advertising expense, and subtract amortization of the capitalized advertising amount (along with related tax effects).

Differences in the Profit Margin/Assets Turnover Mix.   In addition to differences in ROA depicted in Exhibit 8.1, we must also examine reasons for differences in the relative mix of profit margin and assets turnover. Explanations come from both the microeconomics and business strategy literatures.

Microeconomic Theory.   Exhibit 8.5 sets out some important economic factors that constrain certain firms and industries to operate with particular combinations of profit margins and asset turnovers. Firms and industries characterized by heavy fixed capacity costs and lengthy periods required to add new capacity operate under a capacity constraint. There is an upper limit on the size of assets turnover achievable. In order to attract sufficient capital, these firms must generate a relatively high profit margin. Such firms will therefore operate in the area of Exhibit 8.5 marked Ⓐ.

These firms usually achieve their high profit margin through some form of entry barrier. The entry barrier may take the form of large required capital outlays, high risks, or regulation. Such factors help explain the profit margin/assets turnover mix of communications, utilities, hotels, and amusements industries in Exhibit 8.1. The absence of such barriers, coupled with excess capacity and high fixed costs, helps explain the low ROAs in recent years of firms in the chemical and petroleum industries.

Firms whose products are commodity-like in nature, where there are few entry barriers and where competition is intense, operate under a competitive constraint. There is an upper limit on their achievable levels of profit margin. To attract sufficient capital, these firms must strive for high asset turnovers. Such firms will therefore operate in the area of Exhibit 8.5 marked Ⓒ.

These firms achieve their high asset turnovers by keeping costs as low as possible; they may, for example, minimize fixed overhead costs, purchase in sufficient quantities to realize discounts, and integrate vertically or horizontally to obtain cost savings. They match such actions to control costs with aggressively low prices to gain market share and drive out marginal firms. Most retailers and wholesalers operate in the Ⓒ area of Exhibit 8.5.

Firms that operate in the area of Exhibit 8.5 marked Ⓑ are not as subject to either capacity or competitive constraints as those that operate in the tails of the ROA curves. They therefore have more flexibility to take actions that will increase profit margin, assets turnover, or both, to achieve a higher ROA.

EXHIBIT 8.5

Economic Factors Affecting the Profit Margin/Assets Turnover Mix

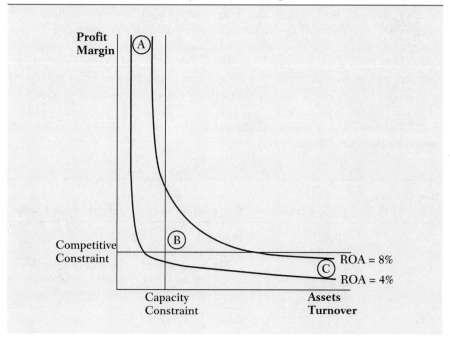

The notion of flexibility in trading off profit margin for assets turnover (or vice versa) is important when a firm considers strategic alternatives. The underlying economic concept is the marginal rate of substitution.

Consider first a firm with a profit margin/assets turnover combination that puts it in the Ⓐ area of Exhibit 8.5. Such a firm will have to give up a significant amount of profit margin to obtain a meaningful increase in assets turnover. To increase ROA, this firm should therefore emphasize actions that increase profit margin; it might, for example, increase selling prices or reduce variable costs. Likewise, a firm in area Ⓒ of Exhibit 8.5 will have to give up considerable assets turnover to achieve a higher profit margin. To increase ROA, such a firm should emphasize actions that increase assets turnover. For firms operating in the tails of the ROA curves, the poor marginal rates of substitution do not favor trading off one variable for the other. Such firms must generally emphasize only one of these factors.

For firms operating in the area marked Ⓑ in Exhibit 8.5, the marginal rates of substitution of profit margin for assets turnover are more equal. Such firms therefore have more flexibility to design strategies that promote profit margin, assets turnover, or some combination, when striving to increase ROA. Unless the economic characteristics of a business constrain it to operate in area Ⓐ or Ⓒ, firms should strive to position themselves in area Ⓑ. Such positioning provides greater potential to adapt to changing economic and business conditions.

Firms operating in areas Ⓐ might attempt to reposition the capacity constraint to the right by outsourcing some of their production. Such an action reduces the amount of fixed assets needed per dollar of sales (that is, increases the fixed asset turnover), but will likely reduce the profit margin (because of the need to share some of the margin with the outsourcing company). Firms operating in area Ⓒ might add products with a higher profit margin. Grocery stores, for example, have added fresh flowers, salad bars, bakery products, and pharmaceutical prescription services to their product offerings in recent years in an effort to increase their profit margins and advance beyond the competitive constraint common for the grocery products industry.

In summary, the economic concepts underlying the profit margin/assets turnover mix are the following:

Area of Firm In Exhibit 8.5	Capital Intensity	Competition	Likely Strategic Focus
Ⓐ	High	Monopoly	Profit Margin
Ⓑ	Medium	Oligopolistic or Monopolistic Competition	Profit Margin, Assets Turnover, or Some Combination
Ⓒ	Low	Pure Competition	Assets Turnover

Business Strategy.   Both Hall and Porter suggest that firms have two generic, alternative strategies for any particular product: product differentiation and low-cost leadership.[5] The thrust of a product differentiation strategy is to differentiate an offering in such a way as to obtain market power over revenues and therefore profit margins. Differentiation could relate to product capabilities, product quality, service, channels of distribution, or some other factor. The thrust of a low-cost leadership strategy is to become the lowest-cost producer, thereby enabling the firm to charge the lowest prices and to achieve higher volumes. Firms can achieve a low-cost position through economies of scale, production efficiencies, outsourcing, or similar factors, or by asset parsimony (maintaining strict controls on investments in receivables, inventories, and capital expenditures).[6]

To see this in terms of Exhibit 8.5, movements in the direction of area Ⓐ from any point along the ROA curves emphasize product differentiation. Likewise,

---

[5]W.K. Hall, "Survival Strategies in a Hostile Environment," *Harvard Business Review* (September–October 1980), pp. 78–85. M.E. Porter, *Competitive Strategy* (New York: Free Press, 1980). Porter suggests that firms might also pursue a niche strategy. Because a niche strategy essentially represents differentiation within a market segment, we include it here under product differentiation strategy.

[6]Recent research in business strategy suggests that firms can pursue product differentiation and low-cost leadership simultaneously, since product differentiation is revenue (output) oriented, and low-cost leadership is more expense (input) oriented.

movements in the direction of area © from any point along the ROA curves emphasize low-cost leadership. To illustrate, let us look at the average profit margins and assets turnovers for three types of retailers during the period 1987 through 1996:

	Profit Margin	Assets Turnover
Specialty Retailers	3.10%	2.26
General Merchandise Stores	2.90%	2.15
Grocery Stores	1.90%	3.27

Within the retailing industry, specialty retailers have differentiated themselves by following a niche strategy, achieving a higher profit margin than the other two segments. Competition severely constrains the profit margin of grocery stores, and they must pursue more low-cost leadership strategies. Thus, a firm does not have to be in the tails of the ROA curves to be described as a product differentiator or low-cost leader. The appropriate basis of comparison is not other industries but other firms in the same industry. Remember, however, that the relative location along the ROA curve affects a firm's flexibility to trade off profit margin (product differentiation) for assets turnover (low-cost leadership).

Exhibit 8.6 shows the ROA, profit margin, and assets turnover of Coke for Year 3 through Year 7. It also shows the average ROA, profit margin, and assets turnover for the consumer foods industry during this five-year period. Note that:

1. Coke's ROA is significantly higher than the consumer foods industry average.
2. Coke experiences higher profit margins than the consumer foods industry average. This performance reflects brand recognition and brand loyalty as well as a lack of major competitors.
3. Coke has slower asset turnovers than the consumer foods industry average. Possible explanations include greater capital intensity of bottling operations and more extensive foreign involvements.
4. Coke's ROA has trended upward during the five-year period, primarily as a result of a higher profit margin.

Generalizations like this provide a useful first pass, but more in-depth analysis would be required before an analyst draws meaningful conclusions.

Summarizing, differences in the profit margin/assets turnover mix relate to factors external to a firm, such as degree of competition, extent of regulation, entry barriers, and similar factors, and to internal strategic choices, such as product differentiation and low-cost leadership. The external and internal factors are, of course, interdependent and in a continual state of change.

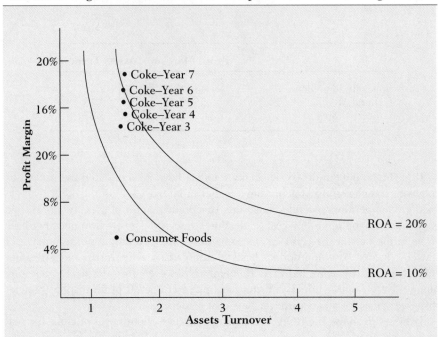

EXHIBIT 8.6

ROA, Profit Margin, and Assets Turnover for Coke for Year 3 through Year 7 and the Average for Consumer Foods Companies for Year 4 through Year 8

RELATING ROAs AND VALUE CHAIN ANALYSIS

Chapter 1 introduced the concept of the value chain and its usefulness in studying the economic characteristics of a firm and its industry. We illustrate an application of value chain analysis using industry-level profit margins, asset turnovers, and ROAs. The data used are the data underlying Exhibit 8.1, which represent the average over the period 1987–1996 of the annual median profit margin, assets turnover, and ROA for firms in various industries. The average median values for ROA will not precisely equal the product of the average median values for profit margin and assets turnover at the aggregate industry level, even though this relation holds for each firm.

Forest Products Industry.   The profit margins, asset turnovers, and ROAs of three segments of the forest products industry appear in the first section of Exhibit 8.7. The lumber segment grows and harvests trees. The cut timber is either converted into lumber for construction or ground up as pulp for subsequent conversion into various grades of paper. The paper processing segment converts pulp into commodity paper products, such as newsprint and linerboard for boxes,

EXHIBIT 8.7

Average Annual Median Profit Margins,
Assets Turnovers, and ROAs for Selected Industries, 1987 to 1996

	Profit Margin	Assets Turnover	ROA
Forest Products Industry			
Lumber	3.1%	1.56	5.9%
Paper Processing	6.1%	1.12	6.9%
Printing and Publishing . . .	6.1%	1.21	7.5%
Apparel Industry			
Textile Manufacturing	4.3%	1.45	6.1%
Apparel Manufacturing	3.9%	1.74	6.4%
Apparel Retailing	3.1%	2.26	6.9%
Food Industry			
Food Processors	4.7%	1.48	7.2%
Grocery Stores	1.9%	3.27	6.3%
Restaurants	3.3%	1.53	5.4%

or specialty paper products, such as photographic film and glossy papers used in corporate annual reports. The printing and publishing segment publishes newspapers, magazines, and books.

In this industry, the products of the lumber segment are the most difficult products to differentiate from each other. This commodity characteristic tends to limit the profit margin achievable. Some paper products also display commodity characteristics, while others are targeted to specific market niches. Thus, the profit margins of paper processing companies on average exceed those of lumber firms. The printing and publishing segment also produces a mixture of products that are non-differentiated (like printed stationery or business forms) and differentiated (books by well-known authors, newspapers with dominant market shares in their locales), and thus this segment achieves profit margins similar to those of paper companies.

The assets turnover of the lumber segment is the largest of the three segments. A principal asset of these firms is their forests, which appear on the balance sheet at acquisition cost, which is likely to be much less than replacement cost. This undervaluation of fixed assets overstates the lumber segment's assets turnover. Lumber companies also do not need to invest in capital-intensive paper processing facilities or capital-intensive printing facilities, another factor that gives the segment a higher assets turnover than the paper and printing and publishing segments. Printing facilities are less capital-intensive than paper processing plants. Also, publishing companies have increasingly outsourced their printing activity in recent years, resulting in a higher assets turnover for printing and publishing than for paper processing.

The ROAs in this industry increase as one moves down the value chain. The upstream activities (lumber, pulp) are less differentiable than those downstream.

Some printing and publishing firms dominate in some markets (local newspapers, books by popular authors), resulting in higher ROAs. The downstream activities bear risk of diseconomies of scale from their capital-intensive facilities. Lumber companies can simply delay harvesting trees if demand is weak, but fixed capacity not used in a particular year in a paper processing or printing plant is lost. Thus, a combination of differentiated products and higher risk appears to explain the higher ROAs as one moves downstream.

Apparel Industry.   The second section of Exhibit 8.7 shows the profit margins, asset turnovers, and ROAs of segments of the apparel industry. The textile manufacturing segment processes various natural and synthetic materials into fabric. The apparel manufacturing segment transforms the fabric into men's, women's, and children's apparel. The apparel retailing segment operates retail stores to sell the clothing to the final consumer.

The textile manufacturing segment produces various fabrics that are difficult to differentiate from each other. Thus, one would expect it to have the smallest profit margin. Textile manufacturing, however, is capital-intensive, as the total assets turnover suggests. To attract capital to this segment, firms must obtain a sufficient profit margin to offset the lower assets turnover.

The higher profit margin for the apparel manufacturing segment over the retailing segment reflects the outsourcing of manufacturing to lower wage rate countries and to the brand names of many apparel products. The low profit margin in apparel retailing reflects both the small value-added by the retailing function and the mixture of branded apparel and discount apparel firms in this segment.

The pattern of ROAs in the apparel industry mirror those in the forest products industry: downstream operations generate a higher ROA than upstream operations. The textile manufacturing firms face the risk of diseconomies of scale in their capital-intensive manufacturing facilities. The apparel manufacturers face the risk of exchange rate changes, political risk in developing countries, and fashion changes. The apparel retailing firms face the risk of fashion changes and swings in consumer spending. The rank ordering on ROAs suggests that the ability to differentiate by product and store concept as one moves downstream dominates the risk inherent in capital-intensive manufacturing operations upstream.

Food Industry.   The last section of Exhibit 8.7 shows the profit margins, asset turnovers, and ROAs of food processors, grocery stores, and restaurants. Food processors, with their brand-name food products, command the highest profit margins. Restaurants also enjoy brand recognition, but intense competition among similar eating establishments dampens profit margins. Various grocery stores carry similar products, so differentiation is difficult. Competition among grocery stores on the basis of price is intense, driving down profit margins.

The lower asset turnovers of food processors reflect the mechanized nature of food manufacturing. The lower asset turnovers of restaurants result from their land and restaurant buildings. The faster asset turnovers of grocery stores reflect the rapid turnover of perishable foods and the less complicated nature of their building structures.

The ROAs in the food industry indicate that the upstream operations generate the highest ROAs. Brand recognition and the omission of brand names from the balance sheet tend to elevate the ROAs of food processors. Competition tends to dampen the ROAs of the downstream operations. The ROAs of restaurants in particular trended downward during the last five years studied.

SUPPLEMENTING ROAs IN PROFITABILITY ANALYSIS

ROA uses total assets as a base for assessing a firm's effectiveness in using resources to generate earnings from operations. For some firms and industries, total assets may not serve an informative role for this purpose because GAAP (1) excludes certain valuable resources from assets (brand names, technological knowledge), and (2) reports assets at their acquisition costs instead of current market values (forests for forest products companies, land and buildings for retail stores). Analysts often supplement ROA by relating sales, expenses, and earnings to other bases when evaluating profitability.

We discuss several techniques for assessing profitability unique to certain industries. Our discussion is not intended to be exhaustive or to cover all industries but rather to provide a sense of the types of supplemental measures analysts use.

Analyzing Retailers.   A key resource retailers have is their retail space. Some retailers own their stores, while others lease space. The analyst can capitalize the present value of operating lease commitments to insure that total assets include store buildings under operating leases.

A common practice in analyzing retailers is to express sales, operating expenses, and operating income on a per square foot basis. This approach to evaluating profitability avoids the need to address whether firms own or lease their space. It also eliminates the effects of different depreciation methods and depreciable lives and the problem of comparing fixed assets with different ages.

Exhibit 8.8 presents per square foot data for The GAP and The Limited for a recent year, as well as profit margin, assets turnover, and ROA. The GAP's superior

EXHIBIT 8.8		
Profitability Ratios for The GAP and The Limited		
	The GAP	**The Limited**
Per Square Foot		
Sales	$ 418	$304
Cost of Goods Sold	(243)	(202)
Selling and Administrative	(100)	(65)
Operating Income	$ 75	$ 37
Profit Margin for ROA	11.2%	8.0%
Assets Turnover	1.13	.99
ROA	12.6%	7.9%

ROA results from its much higher sales per square foot. Although its expenses per square foot are higher than those of The Limited, its ability to obtain higher sales from its space largely accounts for its superior profitability.

Analyzing Airlines. Their aircraft fleets provide airlines with a fixed amount of capacity during any particular period. The total number of seats available to carry passengers times the number of miles flown equals the available seat-mile capacity. The number of seats occupied times the number of miles flown equals the amount of capacity used (referred to as revenue passenger miles). Common practice in the airline industry is to compute revenues and expenses per available seat mile and per seat miles flown to judge both cost structure and profitability.

Exhibit 8.9 presents selected profitability data for American Airlines, Southwest Airlines, and United Airlines for a recent year. The first three columns present revenues, expenses, and operating income before income taxes per available seat mile, and the last three columns present the same income items per seat miles flown.

American and United operate both domestic and international routes, while Southwest provides primarily domestic services. American and United employees are unionized; Southwest's are not. All three airlines are publicly owned, although employees own a majority of United's common stock.

The costs of an airline, such as depreciation, fuel, and compensation, are largely fixed for any particular year. Thus, the operating expenses per available seat mile indicate the costs of operating each airline. Southwest's operating costs are lower than those of American and United. Southwest's advantage relates to lower compensation costs and lower other operating expenses.

The income data per seat mile flown indicate the usage of the available capacity. American generates the highest revenues per seat mile flown, but also has the highest costs. Its compensation costs and other operating expenses are the highest

---

EXHIBIT 8.9

Profitability Ratios for American Airlines, Southwest Airlines, and United Airlines

	Per Available Seat Mile			Per Seat Mile Flown		
	American	Southwest	United	American	Southwest	United
Operating Revenues	10.60¢	8.36¢	10.05¢	15.48¢	12.58¢	14.02¢
Compensation	(3.56)	(2.45)	(3.31)	(5.20)	(3.69)	(4.63)
Fuel	(1.16)	(1.19)	(1.28)	(1.69)	(1.79)	(1.78)
Other Operating Expenses ...	(4.94)	(3.86)	(4.77)	(7.21)	(5.80)	(6.65)
Operating Income	.94¢	.86¢	.69¢	1.38¢	1.30¢	.96¢
Profit Margin for ROA				6.2%	6.8%	4.5%
Assets Turnover				.61	.65	.65
ROA				3.8%	4.4%	2.9%

of the three airlines. Southwest realizes lower revenues per seat mile flown than American, but its lower cost structure permits it to generate almost the same operating income before income taxes. United falls between American and Southwest on both revenues and operating expenses per seat mile flown, but has the lowest operating income before income taxes. The ROA data are consistent with the seat mile data, except that the profit margin of Southwest reflects higher interest revenues from investments of excess cash relative to American and United.

The analyst can apply similar metrics to other firms with fixed capacity. The analysis of hospitals, for example, focuses on income data per available bed or per patient day. The analysis of hotels uses income data per room. The analysis of cable or telecommunications companies examines income data per subscriber or customer.

Analyzing Advertising Firms.   Analysis of the profitability of firms that provide services using ROA can result in misleading conclusions, because the most important resource of a service firm, its employees, does not appear on the balance sheet as an asset under GAAP. One approach to deal with this omission is to express income data on a per employee basis. The analyst must use this data cautiously because of differences among firms in their use of full- versus part-time employees and their mix of direct service providers versus support personnel.

Exhibit 8.10 presents profitability data for three advertising agencies: Interpublic Group, Omnicom Group, and Grey Advertising. Grey Advertising has the highest revenue per employee but also the highest compensation per employee. Its administrative expenses are similar to those of Interpublic, but its higher compensation leads to the lowest operating income before income taxes per employee and the lowest profit margin and ROA. Interpublic and Omnicom have similar operating revenues per employee but Omnicom's higher compensation offset by its lower

---

EXHIBIT 8.10

Profitability Data for Interpublic Group, Omnicom Group and Grey Advertising

	Interpublic Group	Omnicom Group	Grey Advertising
Per Employee			
Operating Revenues	$116,936	$116,373	$121,508
Compensation	(61,946)	(68,527)	(75,347)
Administration Expenses	(36,653)	(33,460)	(36,870)
Operating Income Before Income Taxes	$ 18,337	$ 14,386	$ 9,291
Profit Margin for ROA	9.7%	9.2%	4.6%
Assets Turnover	.56	.70	.75
ROA	5.4%	6.4%	3.9%

administrative expenses yields it less operating income per employee and a lower profit margin. Omnicom has a faster assets turnover than Interpublic, so it has the highest ROA.

Other service industries for which per employee data might usefully supplement traditional financial ratios include management consulting, temporary help services, and engineering services. The use of per employee data might also supplement the analysis of firms that use fixed assets in the provision of services, such as airlines, healthcare providers, and hotels.

Analyzing Technology-Based Firms.   ROA can be an even more misleading ratio for analyzing technology-based firms than for services firms because the two most important resources of technology firms do not appear in their assets: (1) their people, and (2) their technologies. Employees contribute to the creation of technologies, but the most important resource not recognized is the value of the technologies themselves. GAAP requires firms to expense research and development (R&D) cost in the year incurred. Thus, both assets and net income are understated.

Chapter 5 discusses work by Lev and Sougiannis to document the value of technologies that might provide a basis for recognizing a technology asset on the balance sheet and recomputing net income each year.[7] The methodology involves studying the relationship between R&D expenditures in a particular year and revenues of subsequent years. The technology "asset" equals the present value of the future revenue stream net of the R&D expenditure during the year. The analyst would then amortize this "asset" over the future periods of benefit based on the projected stream of revenues.

Such research is in an early development stage and not yet widely used by analysts of technology companies. Traditional financial ratio analysis works reasonably well for established technology firms that have products in all stages of their life cycles. The traditional approach does not work as well for start-up firms and firms with most of their products in the early, high-growth stages of their life cycles.

RATE OF RETURN ON COMMON SHAREHOLDERS' EQUITY

The rate of return on common shareholders' equity (ROCE) measures the accounting return to common shareholders after subtracting all payments to providers of capital senior to the common shareholders; these providers are creditors and preferred shareholders. The analyst calculates ROCE as follows:

$$\text{ROCE} = \frac{\text{Net Income} - \text{Preferred Dividends}}{\text{Average Common Shareholders' Equity}}$$

---

[7]Baruch Lev and Theodore Sougiannis, "The Capitalization, Amortization and Value-Relevance of R&D," *Journal of Accounting and Economics*, 1996, pp. 107–138.

We can obtain enhanced understanding of the behavior of ROCE by disaggregating it into three components as follows:

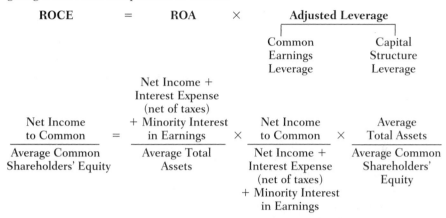

ROA indicates the return from operations independent of financing. Adjusted leverage indicates the multiplier effect of using debt and preferred stock financing to increase the return to common shareholders.

Adjusted leverage is the product of two components: common earnings leverage and capital structure leverage. The common earnings leverage (CEL) ratio indicates the proportion of operating income (that is, net income before financing costs and related tax effects) allocable to the common shareholders. The capital structure leverage (CSL) ratio measures the degree to which firms use common shareholders to finance assets.

We discuss the behavior of ROCE and the role of the three disaggregated components in explaining changes in ROCE. Our emphasis in this chapter is on using ROCE to measure the profitability of a firm. Chapter 12 discusses its use in the valuation of firms.

BEHAVIOR OF ROCE

Relation to Market Rates of Return.   To the extent that accounting earnings serve as surrogates for economic earnings, one might expect a correlation between ROCE and market rates of return (that is dividends plus changes in the market prices of common stock divided by market price of the stock at the beginning of the period). Penman regresses market rates of return on ROCE for each of the years 1969 through 1985 for all firms in the Compustat data file (which includes all firms listed on the New York and American Stock Exchanges).[8] The regression takes the form:

$$\text{Market Rate of Return}_t = a + b(\text{ROCE}_t)$$

Values of 0 for the alpha coefficient and 1 for the beta coefficient are consistent with the idea that market rates of return and ROCE are the same, on average. Penman

[8]Stephen H. Penman, "An Evaluation of Accounting Rates-of-Return," *Journal of Accounting, Auditing and Finance* (Spring 1991), pp. 233–255.

finds a mean of the alpha coefficients across the 18 annual regressions of 0.049. The t-statistic of 0.95 suggests that the alpha coefficient is not significantly different from zero. The mean of the beta coefficients across years is 0.879. The t-statistic when assessed against zero is 10.98 and when assessed against unity is -1.92.

These results suggest a relation between ROCE and market rates of return. The mean R^2 for the 18 years is only 0.09, however, indicating that ROCE explains only a small portion of the cross-sectional variation in market returns. We explore these relations more fully in Chapter 12.

Time Series Behavior of ROCE. Two hypotheses regarding the time series behavior of ROCE have been advanced in the literature. One hypothesis draws on the economic theory that different rates of return reflect different levels of risk. Firms engaged in more risky activities must generate higher returns to compensate investors for the higher risk incurred. As long as firms maintain their risk levels over time, their ROCEs should fluctuate randomly around the level of return commensurate with their level of risk. (This view of the behavior of ROCE has been labeled the random walk hypothesis, similar in concept to the random walk hypothesis of stock prices.) Thus, firms generating ROCEs higher than the average of all firms in the economy should, because of their risk level, continue to earn higher ROCEs in the future; those generating lower ROCEs should earn lower ROCEs in the future.

An alternative hypothesis is that the ROCEs of individual firms revert over time to the average ROCE of all firms in the economy. The underlying rationale is that generation of high or low ROCEs, relative to the economywide average, represents a disequilibrium position. Competition will enter markets with firms generating returns higher than the economywide average and force ROCEs down. Firms will exit industries generating lower than the economywide average ROCEs until the surviving firms generate returns consistent with the economywide average. Firms earning the economywide average ROCE will continue to earn at this rate. Thus, firms with ROCEs higher (lower) than the average of all firms should experience lower (higher) ROCEs in the future. Firms with ROCEs close to the economywide average should experience little change in their ROCEs over time.

Penman also studies the time series behavior of ROCE for his sample firms and time period. *For each year,* he groups companies into 20 equal-sized portfolios according to the level of their ROCE for the year. ROCE was based on income from continuing operations. He computes the median ROCE for these 20 portfolios of firms during each of the 15 years following the base year, and repeats this process for each year between 1969 and 1985.[9] He then computes the mean of these portfolio medians for the base year and each subsequent year. Exhibit 8.11 presents the results.

The column labeled Year 0 shows the mean of portfolio median ROCEs in the base year. Note that portfolio 1 represents firms with the highest ROCE, and portfolio 20 represents firms with the lowest ROCE. The mean of the portfolio median ROCEs one year after the base year appears in the second column; the mean two

---

[9]Portfolios formed after 1971 do not have a full 15 years of subsequent ROCEs.

EXHIBIT 8.11

Median Accounting Rates-of-Return (ROE) for Portfolios Formed on ROE, for Portfolio Formation Year and Subsequent Years; 1969–85

| ROE Portfolio | Year Ahead of Formation Year (Year 0) | | | | | | | | | | |
	0	1	2	3	4	5	6	9	12	15	N_0
1	0.433	0.313	0.239	0.205	0.183	0.171	0.171	0.153	0.136	0.130	2330
2	0.287	0.247	0.208	0.190	0.180	0.177	0.168	0.164	0.152	0.146	2330
3	0.238	0.217	0.193	0.182	0.173	0.162	0.165	0.157	0.156	0.148	2330
4	0.210	0.200	0.182	0.170	0.166	0.168	0.167	0.159	0.157	0.151	2330
5	0.191	0.183	0.169	0.162	0.157	0.155	0.155	0.150	0.144	0.140	2330
6	0.177	0.172	0.163	0.156	0.153	0.152	0.144	0.146	0.141	0.133	2330
7	0.165	0.161	0.153	0.151	0.145	0.144	0.143	0.142	0.142	0.142	2330
8	0.154	0.151	0.147	0.143	0.143	0.142	0.139	0.138	0.135	0.143	2330
9	0.144	0.144	0.141	0.138	0.138	0.136	0.138	0.136	0.137	0.131	2330
10	0.135	0.135	0.131	0.132	0.130	0.132	0.133	0.136	0.137	0.135	2330
11	0.126	0.127	0.129	0.129	0.131	0.132	0.130	0.133	0.128	0.134	2335
12	0.117	0.120	0.122	0.124	0.128	0.128	0.129	0.135	0.137	0.125	2330
13	0.106	0.112	0.117	0.122	0.124	0.126	0.127	0.133	0.128	0.127	2330
14	0.095	0.100	0.108	0.115	0.120	0.117	0.121	0.129	0.111	0.100	2330
15	0.083	0.088	0.097	0.105	0.111	0.115	0.112	0.113	0.099	0.096	2330
16	0.068	0.073	0.085	0.093	0.101	0.106	0.109	0.116	0.099	0.097	2330
17	0.049	0.061	0.074	0.087	0.094	0.099	0.104	0.116	0.097	0.087	2330
18	0.022	0.041	0.059	0.072	0.082	0.087	0.092	0.106	0.093	0.076	2330
19	−0.032	0.011	0.045	0.061	0.080	0.082	0.085	0.102	0.094	0.075	2330
20	−0.225	−0.060	0.030	0.064	0.088	0.096	0.100	0.115	0.105	0.056	2330
1–20	0.657	0.373	0.210	0.141	0.095	0.075	0.071	0.039	0.030	0.074	
2–19	0.319	0.235	0.164	0.129	0.101	0.095	0.082	0.062	0.058	0.071	
Mean Rank Correlation	1.000	0.999	0.989	0.968	0.907	0.871	0.857	0.698	0.821	0.764	

NOTES: Accounting Rate-of-Return is annual earnings before extraordinary times divided by beginning-of-year book values. Each calendar year, 1969–1985, is a base year (year 0). Reported ROE values are means of portfolio medians over years for the base year and subsequent years indicated at the head of the columns.

N_0 is the number of firms in the portfolio for all base years.

SOURCE: Stephen H. Penman, "An Evaluation of Accounting Rates-of-Return," *Journal of Accounting, Auditing, and Finance*, Spring 1991, vol. 6, no. 2, pp. 233–255. (Greenwood Subscription Publications, Westport, CT). Reprinted with permission. All rights reserved.

years after the base year in the third column, and so forth. The mean ROCE in the base year for all firms is approximately 13 percent.

Penman's results are supportive of the second hypothesis, reversion to economy-wide ROCEs, but the mean reversion process is slow. Firms with high ROCEs in the base year experience declines in their ROCEs over time to levels in the middle teens. Firms with low ROCEs in the base year experience increases in their ROCEs over time, but the levels remain around 10 percent. Firms in the middle portfolios (portfolios 10 and 11) continue to generate ROCEs near the average for all firms throughout the years studied.

The mean rank correlations at the bottom of Exhibit 8.11 represent the means of the rank order correlations for each year subsequent to the base year with the rank orders in the base year. The rank order correlations remain relatively high until some time after the sixth year, evidence that supports the first hypothesis of the behavior of ROCE over time. That is, differences in ROCE tend to persist for at least six years on average, reverting to the economywide average only over an extended period of years.

The implication of these results for the analyst is that ROCE of the current period should *on average* serve as a useful predictor of ROCE for the next several periods. Any long-term reversion toward the economywide average ROCE should take many years, and is not likely to have a major influence on the market valuation of the firm. These results, of course, reflect amounts for the particular large group of firms studied. An analyst could identify a particular firm whose future ROCE will remain significantly higher or lower than the economywide average or that will revert to the mean more quickly than the average results in Exhibit 8.11 indicate.

Disaggregated Components of ROCE.   The disaggregated components of ROCE suggest that ROCE relates to (1) an ability to generate a return from using assets in operations (that is, ROA), and (2) an ability to leverage this return successfully for the benefit of shareholders. What then is the association of ROA and financial leverage with ROCE?

Exhibit 8.12 classifies the 22 industries mentioned earlier in the chapter into a three-by-three matrix according to the level of the average of their median annual ROAs and capital structure leverage ratios for each of the years 1987 through 1996. The cells represent the lower, middle, and upper thirds in the rank orderings on each of these ratios. The averages of the median ROCEs for each industry over the same time period appear in parentheses.

Note the high degree of association between the level of ROA and the level of ROCE. The Spearman rank order correlation coefficient is 0.52. If we remove security brokerage and insurance companies, which have very low ROAs and very high capital structure leverage ratios, the Spearman rank order correlation is 0.89.

Although we would expect firms with high ROAs to have high ROCEs, and vice versa, the important insight from Exhibit 8.12 is that the extent of financial leverage does not seem to make much difference in the rank ordering of ROA and ROCE (that is, the industries do not line up on an upward-sloping diagonal suggestive of a positive relation between ROA and capital structure leverage). The Spearman rank order correlation coefficient between the capital structure leverage ratio and ROCE is only 0.31. The lack of association between ROCE and the capital structure leverage ratio suggests that enhancing ROCE does not appear to drive firms' capital structure decisions.

EXHIBIT 8.12

Relation of ROCE to ROA and Capital Structure Leverage Ratio
1987 to 1996
(ROCE in Parentheses)

				Mean ROCE =
Upper Third	Printing and Publishing (12.0%) Retailing-Apparel (10.9%) Personal Services (12.2%)	Paper (11.4%) Food Processors (11.5%) Metal Products (9.4%)	Grocery Stores (12.1%)	11.4%
Middle Third ROA	Metals (9.2%) Restaurants (6.2%)	Lumber (9.5%) Retailing-General Merchandise (10.0%) Communications (6.9%)	Petroleum (9.7%) Utilities (11.5%)	9.0%
Lower Third	Chemicals (4.5%) Business Services (7.8%)	Wholesalers-Durables (7.4%) Amusements (2.9%)	Wholesalers-Nondur. (8.7%) Security Brokers (13.9%) Insurance (12.8%) Hotels (3.7%)	7.7%
	Lower Third	Middle Third	Upper Third	

Capital Structure Leverage Ratio

Mean ROCE =	9.0%	8.2%	10.3%

A research study of firms in 22 industries for the years 1977 to 1986 finds that the major portion of the annual changes in ROCE resulted from changes in ROA and not from financial leveraging activities.[10] Firms did not appear to make significant changes in their capital structure, at least during the annual reporting periods studied, to compensate for changes in ROA.

This result makes intuitive sense, because major changes in capital structure take time and are costly to execute. The results are also consistent with the idea that a firm identifies and maintains an optimal or desired capital structure over time, independent of short-term changes in operating profitability. Chapter 9 explores more fully the factors that explain differences in debt levels.

SUMMARY

The objective of this chapter has been to enhance understanding of the behavior of ROA and ROCE so that the analyst can make more meaningful interpretations of a firm's profitability. The chapter's principal insights may be summarized as follows:

[10]Thomas I. Selling and Clyde P. Stickney, "Disaggregating the Rate of Return on Common Shareholders' Equity: A New Approach," *Accounting Horizons* (December 1990), pp. 9–17.

1. Differences in ROA appear related to differences in risk, including degree of operating leverage, sales cyclicality, and stage and length of product life cycles.
2. Differences in the mix of profit margin and assets turnover relate to the extent of capital intensity and the presence or absence of entry barriers (in the form of brand name recognition, patents, regulated monopoly positions, and differentiated versus commodity products).
3. Differences in ROCE correlate highly with differences in ROA. Differences in the use of financial leverage do not seem to explain much about differences in ROCE.

PROBLEMS AND CASES

8.1 EFFECT OF INDUSTRY CHARACTERISTICS ON FINANCIAL STATEMENT RELATIONS. Prepare problem 1.1 in Chapter 1.

8.2 EFFECT OF INDUSTRY CHARACTERISTICS ON FINANCIAL STATEMENT RELATIONS. Prepare problem 1.2 in Chapter 1.

8.3 VALUE CHAIN ANALYSIS AND FINANCIAL STATEMENT RELATIONSHIPS. Prepare problem 1.3 in Chapter 1.

EXHIBIT 8.13

Relations Between Profitability and Risk Ratios
(Problem 8.4)

Financial Statement Ratio	Numerator	Denominator
Profit Margin	Net Income Excluding Financing Costs	Sales
×		
Assets Turnover	Sales	Average Total Assets
=		
Return on Assets	Net Income Excluding Financing Costs	Average Total Assets
×		
Common Earnings Leverage	Net Income	Net Income Excluding Financing Costs
×		
Capital Structure Leverage	Average Total Assets	Average Common Shareholders' Equity
=		
Return on Common Shareholders' Equity	Net Income	Average Common Shareholders' Equity

8.4   **INTERPRETING INDUSTRY-LEVEL ROAs AND ROCEs.** The rate of return on assets (ROA) measures the earnings generated by a firm from the use of assets in its principal operating activities. ROA disregards the manner in which the firm finances its assets (that is, debt versus equity).

The rate of return on common shareholders' equity (ROCE) measures the earnings generated by a firm on resources provided by common shareholders. ROCE considers both the firm's ability to generate earnings from operations and to use financial leverage (debt financing) successfully.

This problem uses the framework in Exhibit 8.13 to gain insight into the operating and financing characteristics of various related industry segments. Exhibit 8.14 presents financial statement ratios for various industry segments based on data provided by Compustat for each of the years 1987 through 1996. Six ratios are computed for each firm and each year. The median value for each year for each ratio for each two-digit SIC industry code is then determined. Using the median value instead of the mean value reduces the impact of outliers.

The means of the ten annual median values for each ratio for each two-digit SIC industry code are then computed. The mean of the medians serves as a long-term (ten-year) measure for each financial ratio by industry.

At the level of the individual firm, the six financial ratios are mathematically related as indicated in Exhibit 8.13. Because the firm that represents the median value differs across the six ratios in any single year and across years, the means of the medians of the six ratios will not precisely net mathematically at the aggregate industry level as

EXHIBIT 8.14

Average Median Financial Statement Ratios
for Selected Industries—1987 to 1996
(Problem 8.4)

Industry	Profit Margin for ROA	Assets Turnover	ROA	Common Earnings Leverage	Capital Structure Leverage	ROCE
Group 1 (Wholesalers)						
Wholesalers—Durables	2.30%	1.96	4.80%	.82	2.40	7.40%
Wholesalers—Nondurables	1.90%	2.20	5.00%	.77	2.66	8.70%
Group 2 (Services)						
Personal Services	6.30%	1.26	7.20%	.90	1.94	12.20%
Business Services	3.50%	1.15	5.00%	.99	1.84	7.80%
Group 3 (Financial Institutions)						
Depository Financial Institutions . . .	10.40%	.09	.90%	1.00	14.40	12.40%
Security Brokerage Firms	11.90%	.50	5.00%	.79	3.22	13.90%
Insurance Companies	8.00%	.36	3.20%	.92	4.24	12.80%
Group 4 (Transportation)						
Air Transportation	3.60%	1.20	4.40%	.79	3.36	7.40%
Motor Freight Transportation	3.90%	1.50	5.90%	.82	2.43	9.30%
Railroad Transportation	10.20%	.48	5.10%	.67	2.94	8.70%
Water Transportation	10.00%	.53	5.20%	.74	2.25	7.30%

summarized in Exhibit 8.13. The average median ratios for various related industries nevertheless provide useful information about the operating profitability and financial risk of these industries.

Additional information regarding these industries follows.

Wholesalers. Durable goods include furniture, appliances, and automobiles. Nondurable goods include groceries, apparel, and paper products.

Services. Personal services include dry cleaning, beauty, barber, shoe repair, and funeral services. Business services include advertising, computer and data processing, equipment rental, and secretarial services.

Financial Institutions. Depository financial institutions include commercial banks and savings and loans associations. These firms obtain deposits from customers and lend to businesses and consumers. Security brokerage firms conduct securities trades for customers and also provide financial consulting services (such as arranging mergers and acquisitions). Insurance companies receive premium revenues from insured customers, invest the cash received, and subsequently pay claims by customers.

Transportation. Air transportation includes commercial airlines. The airline industry experienced considerable competition during the decade under consideration as bankruptcies eliminated excess capacity in the industry. Motor freight transportation includes trucks that transport goods over land. Railroad transportation includes the movement of freight by rail. Water transportation includes the movement of freight by large ships, as well as passenger transportation.

Required
For each group:
- a. Suggest reasons for the differences in profit margins and asset turnovers.
- b. Suggest reasons for the differences in ROAs.
- c. Suggest reasons for the differences in the use of financial leverage and its effectiveness in enhancing ROCEs.

8.5 INTERPRETING PROFITABILITY RATIOS FOR THE ELECTRONIC EQUIPMENT INDUSTRY. Exhibit 8.15 presents selected median financial ratios for the electronic equipment industry, which includes computers and communication equipment, for each of the years 1992 through 1996. At the level of the individual firms in this industry, the six ratios are mathematically related in the manner discussed in this chapter. Because the firm that represents the median value differs for each ratio, the medians for a particular year will not net precisely at the aggregate industry level as the mathematical relations suggest.

The electronic equipment industry has experienced rapid growth in recent years with the introduction of new technologies and the emergence of the Internet.

EXHIBIT 8.15

Average Median Financial Ratios for the Electronic Equipment Industry
(Problem 8.5)

	1992	1993	1994	1995	1996
Profit Margin for ROA	3.4%	3.5%	4.6%	4.7%	5.2%
Assets Turnover	1.29	1.28	1.33	1.28	1.25
Return on Assets	4.3%	4.2%	6.0%	6.2%	7.2%
Common Earnings Leverage	96.1%	96.2%	96.6%	97.1%	97.6%
Capital Structure Leverage	1.84	1.85	1.80	1.76	1.71
Rate of Return on Common Shareholders' Equity	5.8%	5.9%	9.9%	10.4%	11.5%

Required
   a. Suggest possible reasons for changes in yearly profit margins and asset turnovers during this five-year period.
   b. Suggest possible reasons for the increasing common earnings leverage ratio.
   c. Suggest possible reasons for the decreasing capital structure leverage ratio.
   d. Does the increased rate of return on common shareholders' equity appear related primarily to improved operating performance or to increased financial leverage? Explain.

8.6 **INTERPRETING PROFITABILITY RATIOS FOR THE FOOD PROCESSING INDUSTRY.**
The food processing industry includes firms that transform food ingredients into brand-name food products. This industry has experienced growth in sales approximately equal to the growth rate in the population in recent years (approximately 2 percent per year). This relatively slow growth rate reflects heightened competition for the consumers' food dollar both among food processors and from restaurants.

Exhibit 8.16 presents selected median profitability ratios for the food processing industry for each of the years 1992 through 1996. At the level of the individual firms in

---

EXHIBIT 8.16

Profitability Ratios for the Food Processing Industry
(Problem 8.6)

	1992	1993	1994	1995	1996
Profit Margin for ROA	4.9%	4.8%	4.7%	4.6%	3.7%
Assets Turnover	1.51	1.44	1.41	1.38	1.33
Rate of Return on Assets (ROA) ..	7.4%	6.8%	6.5%	6.7%	5.2%
Common Earnings Leverage	84.6%	85.6%	86.2%	85.8%	84.8%
Capital Structure Leverage	2.23	2.26	2.12	2.09	1.95
Rate of Return on Common Shareholders' Equity	12.0%	11.8%	10.5%	10.2%	7.5%

this industry, the six ratios are related in the manner discussed in this chaper. Because the firm that represents the median value differs for each ratio, the medians for a particular year will not net precisely at the aggregate industry level as the mathematical relations suggest.

Required

   a. Suggest possible reasons for changes in the profit margin and asset turnover ratios during the five-year period.
   b. Suggest possible reasons for changes in the capital structure leverage ratios during the five-year period.
   c. Does the decreased ROCE appear related primarily to decreased operating performance or to decreased financial leverage? Explain.

8.7   ANALYZING THE PROFITABILITY OF A SERVICE FIRM. Kelly Services places employees at clients' businesses on a temporary basis. Kelly charges the client a fee intended to cover the payroll cost of the temporary employee plus administrative costs of operating its personnel supply offices. The latter includes payroll costs for permanent employees who run the offices, data processing costs relating primarily to payroll for all employees, and rent, taxes, and insurance on office space. Amounts receivable from clients appear in accounts receivable, and amounts payable to permanent and temporary employees appear in current liabilities.

The temporary employee business offers clients flexibility to adjust the number of workers to meet changing capacity needs. Clients can observe the quality of work of temporary employees before hiring them permanently. Temporary employees are typically less costly than permanent workers because they have fewer fringe benefits. Temporary workers, however, generally are less well trained than permanent workers and have less loyalty to clients.

Barriers to entry in the personnel supply business are low. This business does not require capital for physical facilities (most space is rented), does not need specialized assets (most temporary employees do not have unique skills, and the requisite data processing technology is readily available), and operates with little government regulation. Thus, competition is intense, and margins tend to be thin.

The growth in the U.S. economy in recent years has had two effects on the temporary personnel business. Business firms have needed additional personnel to support their growth and have relied on temporary employees for a portion of their employment needs. The shortage of available full-time employees and the attractiveness of fringe benefits, however, have led many temporary employees to move to permanent status.

Exhibit 8.17 presents selected profitability ratios and other data for Kelly, the largest temporary personnel supply firm in the United States. These amounts reflect the capitalization of operating lease commitments in property, plant, and equipment and long-term debt.

Required

Analyze the changes in the profitability of Kelly Services during the three-year period in as much detail as permitted by the data provided.

8.8   ANALYZING THE PROFITABILITY OF TWO HOTELS. La Quinta Inns operates a chain of mid-price hotels aimed at the cost-conscious business traveler. Its targeted guests are those who want quality rooms in convenient locations at attractive prices but do not require banquet and convention facilities, in-house restaurants, cocktail lounges or room service. Exhibit 8.18 presents selected profitability ratios and other data for La Quinta.

EXHIBIT 8.17

Profitability Ratios and Other Data for Kelly Services
(Problem 8.7)

	Year 5	Year 6	Year 7
Profit Margin for ROA	2.6%	2.6%	2.3%
Assets Turnover	3.63	3.59	3.84
Rate of Return on Assets	9.5%	9.2%	8.6%
Common Earnings			
Leverage Ratio	100.0%	100.0%	98.3%
Capital Structure Leverage Ratio	1.6	1.7	1.7
Rate of Return on Common			
Shareholders' Equity	15.2%	15.2%	14.7%
Cash Flow from Operations/			
Average Current Liabilities ...	34.4%	9.7%	(5.0%)
Revenues	100.0%	100.0%	100.0%
Other Income/Revenues	.3%	.3%	.1
Compensation of Temporary			
Employees/Revenues	80.4%	79.9%	81.4%
Selling and Administrative			
Expense/Revenues	15.7%	16.2%	14.9%
Income Tax Expense/Revenues ..	1.6%	1.6%	1.5%
Accounts Receivable Turnover ..	8.5	7.6	6.9
Fixed Asset Turnover	18.5	18.3	19.1
Number of Offices	1,000	1,300	1,500
Number of Permanent			
Employees	4,800	5,600	6,100
Number of Temporary			
Employees	665,000	655,000	686,000
Growth Rate in Revenues	20.9%	13.8%	22.8%
Per Office Data:			
Revenues	$2,363,000	$2,069,231	$2,201,337
Net Income	61,000	53,077	48,667
Permanent Employees	4.8	4.3	4.1
Temporary Employees	665	504	457
Per Permanent Employee Data:			
Revenues	$ 492,292	$ 480,357	$ 541,311
Net Income	$ 12,708	$ 12,321	$ 11,967
Temporary Employees	138.5	117.0	112.5
Per Temporary Employee Data:			
Revenues	$ 3,553	$ 4,107	$ 4,813
Net Income	92	105	106

EXHIBIT 8.18

Profitability Ratios and Other Data for La Quinta Inns
(Problem 8.8)

	Year 7	Year 8	Year 9
Profit Margin for ROA	17.4%	18.8%	19.9%
Assets Turnover	.45	.46	.43
Rate of Return on Assets	7.9%	8.6%	8.6%
Common Earnings Leverage			
Ratio	60.0%	66.2%	68.7%
Capital Structure Leverage			
Ratio	4.7	3.5	3.0
Rate of Return on Common			
Shareholders' Equity	22.4%	19.7%	17.4%
Number of Hotels	228	237	248
Number of Rooms	29,712	31,363	32,728
Rooms/Hotel	130	132	132
Occupancy Rate	70.1%	70.8%	68.9%
Revenue/Available Room Night . .	$33.40	$36.16	$37.09
Operating Income/			
Available Room Night	$5.82	$6.78	$7.39
Revenue/Occupied Room Night . .	$47.65	$51.07	$53.83
Operating Income/			
Occupied Room Night	$8.30	$9.58	$10.73
Revenue/Hotel	$1,588,781	$1,746,494	$1,786,528
Operating Income/Hotel	$276,640	$327,629	$356,141

Prime Hospitality Corporation operates several hotel chains with different targeted customers. Its AmeriSuites and Wellesley Inns offer hotel suites in primarily suburban commercial centers and corporate office parks. These hotels are located with easy access to shopping, food, and entertainment amenities. Prime also operates full-service hotels under national brand names (Marriott, Sheraton, Crown Plaza), which offer banquet and convention facilities. Exhibit 8.19 presents selected profitability and other data for Prime.

Required

Analyze the changes and the differences in the profitability of these two hotel chains in as much detail as permitted by the data provided.

8.9 ANALYZING THE PROFITABILITY OF TWO RESTAURANTS. Analyzing the profitability of restaurants requires consideration of their strategies with respect to ownership of restaurants versus franchising. Firms that own and operate their restaurants will report the assets and financing of the restaurants on their balance sheet and the revenues and operating expenses of the restaurants on their income statement. Firms that franchise their restaurants to others (that is, to franchisees) will often own the land and buildings of franchised restaurants and lease them to the franchisees. Their income statement includes fees received from franchisees in the form of license fees for using the franchiser's name, rent for facilities and equipment, and various fees for advertising, menu planning, and food and paper

EXHIBIT 8.19

Profitability Ratios and Other Data for Prime Hospitality Corporation
(Problem 8.8)

	Year 7	Year 8	Year 9
Profit Margin for ROA	20.4%	15.3%	13.8%
Assets Turnover	.32	.41	.38
Rate of Return on Assets	6.5%	6.3%	5.2%
Common Earnings Leverage Ratio . .	66.7%	55.4%	62.6%
Capital Structure Leverage Ratio . . .	2.3	2.3	2.1
Rate of Return on Common			
Shareholders' Equity	9.7%	8.0%	6.8%
Number of Hotels	86	95	108
Number of Rooms	8,965	11,110	16,232
Rooms/Hotel	104	117	150
Occupancy Rate	68.0%	69.2%	69.0%
Revenue/Available Room Night	$41.04	$50.71	$43.09
Operating Income/			
Available Room Night	$8.36	$7.77	$5.96
Revenue/Occupied Room Night	$60.36	$73.28	$62.45
Operating Income/			
Occupied Room Night	$12.30	$11.23	$8.64
Revenue/Hotel	$1,561,663	$2,164,505	$2,363,944
Operating Income/Hotel	$318,058	$331,653	$208,620

products used by the franchisee. The revenues and operating expenses of the franchised restaurants appear on the financial statements of the franchisee.

Exhibit 8.20 presents profitability ratios and other data for Brinker International, and Exhibit 8.21 presents similar data for Wendy's International.

Brinker operates chains of specialty sit-down restaurants under the names of Chili's, Macaroni Grill, and On The Border. Its restaurants average approximately 7,000 square feet. Brinker owns and operates approximately 78 percent of its restaurants.

Wendy's operates chains of fast food restaurants under the names of Wendy's and Tom Hortons. Its restaurants average 2,800 square feet. Wendy's owns and operates approximately 23 percent of its restaurants. It also owns approximately 28 percent of the restaurant land and buildings of franchisees.

The financial ratios and other data in Exhibits 8.20 and 8.21 reflect the capitalization of operating leases in property, plant, and equipment and long-term debt.

Required

  a. Suggest reasons for the changes in Brinker's profitability during the three-year period.
  b. Suggest reasons for the changes in Wendy's profitability during the three-year period.
  c. Suggest reasons for differences in the profitability of the two chains during the three-year period.

8.10 ANALYZING TWO COMMERCIAL BANKS. Commercial banks generate their revenues from two principal sources: (1) lending and investing, and (2) fee-based services.

EXHIBIT 8.20

Profitability Ratios and Other Data for Brinker International
(Problem 8.9)

	Year 4	Year 5	Year 6
Profit Margin for Rate of Return on Assets	7.0%	5.5%	5.0%
Assets Turnover	1.22	1.13	1.14
Rate of Return on Assets	8.6%	6.2%	5.7%
Common Earnings Leverage	99.5%	95.3%	90.8%
Capital Structure Leverage	1.9	1.9	2.1
Rate of Return on Common Shareholders' Equity	15.9%	11.0%	10.7%
Cost of Goods Sold ÷ Revenues	84.7%	87.3%	87.9%
Selling and Administrative Expenses ÷ Revenues	4.8%	4.7%	4.8%
Income Tax Expense (excluding tax effects of interest expense) ÷ Revenues	3.7%	2.9%	2.5%
Accounts Receivable Turnover	68.1	72.5	90.8
Inventory Turnover	95.3	96.0	98.4
Fixed Asset Turnover	1.5	1.4	1.5
Revenues per Restaurants (000's)	$1,861	$1,897	$1,881
Operating Income per Restaurant (000's)	$131	$104	$94
Fixed Assets per Restaurant (000's)	$1,405	$1,350	$1,408
Percentage of Restaurants Owned	78.9%	76.5%	78.5%
Growth in Revenues	20.3%	11.6%	14.8%
Growth in Number of Restaurants	22.2%	9.5%	15.8%

Commercial banks obtain the majority of their funds from deposits by customers and short-term borrowing. They invest a portion of the funds in relatively liquid government and high-grade corporate debt securities, and lend most of the remainder to businesses and consumers. Some banks conduct trading activities in various securities both to help establish an active market and to trade on their own account for profit.

Competition among banks and other financial institutions has reduced the net interest margin that banks generate from the spread between the rate paid for funds and the return generated from lending. As a consequence, commercial banks have increasingly turned to fee-based revenues to improve their profitability. Service charges for bank services (checking accounts, trust services, and investment advisory and management services) are one form of fee-based revenues. Another avenue involves structuring new financing and providing mergers and acquisition and other advisory services for businesses.

The principal expenses of commercial banks, besides interest, are compensation of employees, occupancy costs, information systems costs, and uncollectible accounts.

The commercial banking industry has experienced major consolidation during the last decade, the result of (1) reduced restrictions on interstate banking, (2) bank desires to build a national, and even international, presence to serve customers more effectively, and (3) the perceived benefits of economies of scale in information processing and one-stop customer shopping for financial services. Mergers between commercial banks and investment banks are occurring rapidly with the relaxation of restrictions originally imposed by the Glass-Steagall Act of 1933.

EXHIBIT 8.21

Profitability Ratios and Other Data for Wendy's International
(Problem 8.9)

	Year 4	Year 5	Year 6
Profit Margin for Rate of Return on Assets	8.2%	8.9%	9.0%
Assets Turnover	1.35	1.17	.99
Rate of Return on Assets	11.0%	10.4%	8.9%
Common Earnings Leverage	89.0%	91.5%	91.2%
Capital Structure Leverage	1.8	2.0	2.0
Rate of Return on Common			
Shareholders' Equity	18.1%	19.0%	16.6%
Cost of Goods Sold ÷ Revenues	80.3%	79.2%	79.1%
Selling and Administrative			
Expenses ÷ Revenues	7.7%	8.0%	7.2%
Income Tax Expense (excluding tax			
effects of interest expense) ÷ Revenues	4.4%	4.6%	5.6%
Accounts Receivable Turnover	46.7	35.9	30.1
Inventory Turnover	99.0	96.0	93.7
Fixed Asset Turnover	1.8	1.6	1.4
Revenues per Restaurants (000's)	$291	$298	$302
Operating Income per Restaurant (000's)	$24	$27	$27
Fixed Assets per Restaurant (000's)	$165	$216	$237
Percentage of Restaurants Owned	23.7%	23.0%	22.0%
Growth in Revenues	4.9%	9.7%	8.6%
Growth in Number of Restaurants	5.8%	7.1%	7.0%

Analyzing the profitability of a commercial bank uses rate of return on assets and on common shareholders' equity and their disaggregated components, profit margin, assets turnover, and capital structure leverage ratios. One difference in the calculation of these ratios in the banking industry is that the analyst makes no adjustment to ROA and profit margin for interest expense, since interest expense for a commercial bank is similar to cost of goods sold for a manufacturing or retailing firm. Commercial banks provide sufficient information to compute the return from loans, bank deposits, investments in securities, and trading securities, and the cost of deposits and other borrowing. Because most balance sheet accounts experience significant increases and decreases each day, commercial banks provide average daily balances in various accounts to serve as the basis for computing various rates of return.

The sources of risks for commercial banks include (1) credit risk from lending, (2) interest rate risk from borrowing and lending activities, and (3) liquidity risk. Analysis of credit risk uses the ratios as follows:

1. Loan Loss Reserve Ratio = Loan Loss Reserve/Loans Receivable.
2. Net Charge-Off Ratio = Net Charge-Offs/Average Loans Receivable during the Year. Net charge-offs equal loans charged off minus recoveries of loans charged off in a previous year.
3. Nonperforming Loan Percentage = Nonperforming Loans/Total Loans Receivable. Nonperforming loans are loans that the bank does not expect to collect in full in

accordance with the original lending agreement. Some of these loans no longer accrue interest and some have been restructured.

Commercial banks have become quite sophisticated in managing their interest rate risk. They use a variety of computer software to ensure that the level and the term structure of their interest-sensitive assets match their interest-sensitive liabilities on a daily basis. Commercial banks disclose their interest-sensitive position by maturity date.

The analyst assesses liquidity risk by examining the proportion of long-term debt and shareholders' equity in the capital structure. The higher this proportion, the more cushion the banks have to cover deposits by customers and to repay short-term borrowing.

The Federal Reserve Board establishes minimum capital requirements that are a stated percentage of risk-adjusted assets. Tier 1 capital includes primarily common and preferred stock. Tier 2 capital includes certain long-term debt. Risk-adjusted assets include most assets reported on the balance sheet plus various off-balance sheet commitments. Commercial

---

EXHIBIT 8.22

Profitability and Risk Ratios for Wells Fargo
(Problem 8.10)

	Year 6	Year 7	Year 8
Company-Level Profitability Analysis			
Profit Margin for Rate of Return on Assets	16.94%	21.92%	12.28%
Assets Turnover	.10	.11	.09
Rate of Return on Assets	1.62%	2.44%	1.15%
Capital Structure Leverage Ratio	14.57	14.93	8.21
Rate of Return on Shareholders' Equity	22.68%	35.21%	8.78%
Operating Performance Analysis			
Gross Yield on Earning Assets	8.01%	9.14%	8.80%
Rate Paid on Funds	2.46%	3.20%	2.70%
Net Interest Margin	5.55%	5.94%	6.10%
Non-Interest Revenue Percentage	24.17%	26.36%	25.22%
Non-Interest Expense Percentage	65.12%	60.60%	69.84%
Loan Loss Provision Percentage	5.31%	0.00%	1.61%
Segment Profitability Analysis			
Return on Bank Deposits	2.88%	3.05%	3.04%
Return on Domestic Loans	8.86%	9.86%	9.40%
Return on Foreign Loans	6.45%	8.70%	6.90%
Return on Investment Securities	5.85%	6.75%	6.40%
Cost of Domestic Deposits	2.62%	3.19%	3.23%
Cost of Foreign Deposits	4.76%	5.93%	5.06%
Cost of Other Borrowing	5.11%	6.18%	6.09%
Risk Analysis			
Loan Loss Reserve Ratio	5.73%	5.04%	2.99%
Net Charge-Off Ratio	.71%	.83%	1.06%
Non-Performing Loan Percentage	1.56%	1.51%	1.06%
Risk-Adjusted Capital Ratio—Tier 1	9.09%	8.81%	7.68%
Tier 1 and 2	13.16%	12.46%	11.70%

banks apply various risk adjustment factors to these assets to form the denominator of the capital ratios. Tier 1 capital as a percentage of risk-adjusted assets must reach a minimum of 4 percent. Tier 1 plus Tier 2 capital must reach a minimum of 8 percent of risk-adjusted assets.

Exhibit 8.22 presents various profitability and risk ratios, and Exhibit 8.23 presents a common size balance sheet, for Wells Fargo for Year 6 through Year 8. Exhibits 8.24 and 8.25 present similar information for J.P. Morgan.

Wells Fargo maintains its principal presence in the West and Southwest United States. It maintains a network of branch banks to obtain deposits from customers and to lend to businesses and consumers. It emphasizes the traditional borrowing and lending activities of commercial banks. Wells Fargo acquired First Interstate Bancorp during the second quarter of Year 8 by an exchange of common stock in a transaction accounted for using the purchase method. J.P. Morgan maintains a minor presence in traditional borrowing and lending. Instead it emphasizes investing and trading activities and the offering of fee-based financial advisory services.

Required

a. Analyze the changes in the profitability and risk of Well Fargo during the three-year period.
b. Analyze the changes in the profitability and risk of J.P. Morgan during the three-year period.
c. Analyze the differences in the profitability and risk of Wells Fargo and J.P. Morgan, indicating how differences in their strategies affect their operating performance and risk.

EXHIBIT 8.23

Common Size Balance Sheets for Wells Fargo
(Problem 8.10)

	Year 6	Year 7	Year 8
Interest Bearing Deposits	.5%	.3%	1.1%
Investment Securities	24.5	20.2	13.5
Domestic Loans	65.6	69.3	64.7
Foreign Loans	.1	.1	.2
Total Earning Assets	90.7%	89.9%	79.5%
Other Assets	9.3	10.1	20.5
Total Assets	100.0%	100.0%	100.0%
Domestic Interest Bearing Deposits	59.6%	55.0%	52.0%
Foreign Interest Bearing Deposits	1.8	3.5	.4
Non-Interest Bearing Deposits	17.4	17.9	24.3
Short-Term Borrowing	4.7	7.8	2.3
Long-Term Borrowing	6.6	6.1	5.0
Other Non-Interest Bearing Liabilities	2.0	2.2	3.0
Total Liabilities	92.1%	92.5%	87.0%
Preferred Stock Equity	1.0%	1.0%	.8%
Common Stock Equity	6.9	6.5	12.2
Total Shareholders' Equity	7.9%	7.5%	13.0%
Total Liabilities and Shareholders' Equity	100.0%	100.0%	100.0%

EXHIBIT 8.24

Profitability and Risk Ratios for J. P. Morgan
(Problem 8.10)

	Year 6	Year 7	Year 8
Company-Level Profitability Analysis			
Profit Margin for Rate of Return on Assets	10.20%	9.37%	9.92%
Assets Turnover	.07	.08	.07
Rate of Return on Assets	.70%	.73%	.73%
Capital Structure Leverage Ratio	18.63	19.06	20.68
Rate of Return on Shareholders' Equity	12.90%	13.58%	15.14%
Operating Performance Analysis			
Gross Yield on Earning Assets	6.24%	7.30%	6.24%
Rate Paid on Funds	4.76%	5.83%	5.25%
Net Interest Margin	1.47%	1.47%	.99%
Non-Interest Revenue Percentage	29.68%	28.19%	32.48%
Non-Interest Expense Percentage	36.59%	33.51%	33.42%
Loan Loss Provision Percentage	0.00%	0.00%	0.00%
Segment Profitability Analysis			
Return on Bank Deposits	5.17%	3.64%	2.76%
Return on Resale Agreements	4.63%	6.00%	5.17%
Return on Domestic Loans	5.58%	7.21%	6.66%
Return on Foreign Loans	6.02%	6.97%	6.24%
Return on Trading Account Securities	9.84%	11.50%	12.44%
Return on Investment Securities	13.90%	16.33%	17.95%
Cost of Domestic Deposits	4.64%	4.79%	5.15%
Cost of Foreign Deposits	4.89%	5.80%	5.18%
Cost of Other Borrowing	5.06%	6.27%	5.67%
Risk Analysis			
Loan Loss Reserve Ratio	6.06%	5.06%	4.06%
Net Charge-Off Ratio	.11%	.00%	.05%
Non-Performing Loan Percentage	1.01%	.52%	.44%
Risk-Adjusted Capital Ratio—Tier 1	9.6%	8.8%	8.8%
Tier 1 and 2	14.2%	13.0%	12.2%

8.11 ANALYZING GLOBAL TELECOMMUNICATIONS COMPANIES. The telecommunications industry is experiencing rapid change along several dimensions:

1. Removal of entry barriers in both local and long-distance services, as governments privatize or deregulate their telephone systems and encourage increased competition.
2. Advancements in technology that permit a wider geographic mix of customers and the offering of new services (cellular phones, Internet access, data and image transmission).

Exhibit 8.26 presents selected financial statement ratios for three major telecommunications companies: American Telephone & Telegraph (AT&T), British Telecommunications (BT), and Nippon Telegraph & Telegraph (NTT). The ratios present the average for each company for three recent years.

EXHIBIT 8.25

Common Size Balance Sheets for J. P. Morgan
(Problem 8.10)

	Year 6	Year 7	Year 8
Interest Bearing Deposits	2.2%	2.6%	1.9%
Resale Agreements	27.7	26.3	31.8
Investment Securities	11.6	12.3	11.6
Trading Account Securities	22.4	21.5	21.5
Domestic Loans	4.5	3.7	2.9
Foreign Loans	9.4	9.8	10.1
Total Earning Assets	77.8%	76.2%	79.8%
Other Assets	22.2	23.8	20.2
Total Assets	100.0%	100.0%	100.0%
Domestic Interest Bearing Deposits	1.3%	1.2%	1.8%
Foreign Interest Bearing Deposits	21.9	23.4	21.0
Non-Interest Bearing Deposits	3.0	2.6	1.4
Short-Term Borrowing	47.6	43.5	48.1
Long-Term Borrowing	3.4	4.9	5.0
Other Non-Interest Bearing Liabilities	17.1	18.9	17.6
Total Liabilities	94.3%	94.5%	94.9%
Preferred Stock Equity	.3%	.3%	.3%
Common Stock Equity	5.4	5.2	4.8
Total Shareholders' Equity	5.7%	5.5%	5.1%
Total Liabilities and Shareholders' Equity	100.0%	100.0%	100.0%

EXHIBIT 8.26

Selected Three-Year Average Financial Statement Ratios
for AT&T, BT, and NTT
(Problem 8.11)

	AT&T	BT	NTT
Profit Margin for ROA	8.0%	15.4%	3.7%
Assets Turnover	.7	.6	.5
Rate of Return on Assets	6.0%	8.7%	1.7%
Common Earnings Leverage	92.0%	86.6%	47.0%
Capital Structure Leverage	3.9	1.8	3.4
Rate of Return on Common Equity	21.4%	13.8%	2.9%
Accounts Receivable Turnover	2.3	9.6	10.1
Fixed Asset Turnover	2.6	.9	.7
Current Ratio	1.1	1.0	.7
Operating Cash Flow/Average Current Liabilities	29.7%	79.2%	92.3%
Long-Term Debt/Shareholders' Equity	50.6%	23.8%	85.2%
Interest Coverage Ratio	18.4	8.2	2.0

AT&T.   AT&T has a 65 percent market share of long distance within the United States, competing aggressively with Sprint and MCI. AT&T has the largest market share within the United States of international long-distance. This firm currently does not have a presence in local telephone services. It pays local telephone companies a fee to access their telephone lines. AT&T offers its own credit card for the making of long-distance telephone calls and purchasing consumer goods and services. Its current strategic emphasis is on one-stop communications services, including wireless, on-line, electronic commerce, and similar services. AT&T is a publicly traded company.

BT.   BT has a greater than 80 percent market share in the U.K. for local, long-distance, and wireless services. BT competes against Deutsche Telecom, AT&T, and France Telecom in long- distance service. BT is a publicly traded company. The U.K. government has oversight of BT in the offering of its domestic services, although it stops short of setting telephone rates.

NTT.   NTT maintains a greater than 90 percent market share in Japan for local and long-distance services. NTT was originally owned by the Japanese government, but has been privatized (that is, it is now publicly owned), although the Japanese government still owns 66 percent of the outstanding common stock and maintains close oversight of the firm's operating activities.

Required

    a. What are the likely reasons for the relative rankings of the three firms on their profit margins for ROA?

    b. What are the likely reasons for the relative rankings of these firms on their capital structure leverage ratios?

    c. Suggest possible reasons for the slower accounts receivable turnover ratio for AT&T relative to BT and NTT.

    d. Suggest possible reasons for the higher fixed assets turnover for AT&T than for BT and NTT.

    e. Suggest possible reasons for the lower operating cash flow to average current liabilities ratio for AT&T than for BT and NTT.

    f. AT&T has a higher capital structure leverage ratio than NTT, but a much lower interest coverage ratio. Explain this apparent paradox.

CASE 8.1

COMPUTER WORKSTATION INDUSTRY ANALYSIS: HEWLETT-PACKARD AND SUN MICROSYSTEMS

Experiencing rapid growth of over 25 percent per year during the 1970s and 1980s, only to encounter economic recession accompanied by restructurings and layoffs during the early 1990s, the computer hardware industry has now found new life. Economic expansion along with advances in technology, lower selling prices, and increased avenues for applying computer technology (such as Internet, corporate intranets) have breathed new life into the industry. The industry landscape has changed dramatically since its earlier growth phase, and increased competition, more commodity-like products, and short product life cycles are now the name of the game.

The workstation segment of the computer industry has been a bright spot throughout the 1980s and 1990s. Workstations, originally developed in the early 1980s to serve the design, graphic, and networking needs of engineers and scientists, then enjoyed growth rates of 40 percent per year. Although industry analysts now project growth rates in the mid-teens during the remainder of the 1990s, the industry is poised to target business users who want to establish networked systems.

This case analyzes the two leading firms in the workstation segment of the computer industry: Hewlett-Packard Corporation (HP) and Sun Microsystems (Sun). The two firms commanded a 61 percent market share in 1996.

OVERVIEW OF COMPUTER INDUSTRY

Information technologies include computer hardware, software, and services. Computer hardware, the largest segment, represented 40 percent of spending on computer technologies worldwide during 1996. Computer hardware includes (1) personal computers (PCs); (2) large, multiuser systems based on supercomputers, mainframes, minicomputers; and servers; and (3) workstations. Their relative shares of computer hardware spending during 1996 were 60 percent, 35 percent, and 5 percent, respectively.

The PC segment experienced a 20 percent growth rate in 1996, with a 19 percent growth rate projected for 1997. Growth of 10 to 15 percent is likely in this segment during the next several years. The principal growth opportunities are international sales, the home computer market (particularly centered on Internet access), and upgrades by business firms. The market share leaders in the PC segment are Compaq Computer, IBM, Packard Bell NEC, Dell, and Toshiba.

Industry analysts project sales of supercomputers, mainframes, and minicomputers to remain relatively flat during the rest of the 1990s. Governmental entities remain a primary customer. The traditional midrange systems are under attack from networked PCs within business firms. The market share leaders in this segment are IBM, Hitachi, and Amdahl.

Local area network servers, the fastest-growing segment of the computer hardware industry, tie mainframes, PCs, and other computers together, permitting them to share data, access system software, and share excess processing and storage capacity within a system. Market share leaders for servers are Compaq Computer, IBM, HP, Digital Equipment, and Sun. Profit margins on servers are higher than on PCs because of the heavy demand currently to develop networked systems and the smaller number of suppliers.

Workstation units shipped grew 18 percent in 1996 and are projected to maintain growth in the low to mid-teens throughout the remainder of the 1990s. The principal growth avenue is in developing networked systems for business firms. Market share leaders include Sun, HP, Silicon Graphics, Digital Equipment, and IBM.

ECONOMICS OF THE COMPUTER INDUSTRY

DEMAND

Industry analysts project overall revenue growth in the mid-teens during the remainder of the 1990s, although growth rates will vary considerably by segment, as discussed above. International sales are currently growing more rapidly than domestic sales.

Demand tends to follow cyclical trends in the economy. With 24 percent of capital expenditures by business firms going into computers, discretionary changes that firms make in their capital budgets in response to economic conditions impact the revenues of computer firms. Demand also tends to be seasonal; there is significant year-end shopping by consumers during the holidays and by business firms to spend annual capital budget allowances. Computer firms also tend to offer sales incentives during the last quarter of the year in an effort to meet annual sales goals.

Customers are now demanding greater standardization across hardware and software to minimize difficulties in systems integration. Customers are also showing a tendency for one-stop shopping to enhance the likelihood of internal systems compatibility.

SUPPLY

In most segments of the computer industry, there are multiple suppliers who offer products that differ very little from each other in term of technical capabilities. Thus, competition is fierce. New technologies are copied quickly, and product life cycles run for only six to twelve months.

Industry analysts estimate that 50 percent of the profits of a new computer accrue during the first six months. Thus, firms must carefully debug new computers prior to launching. Waiting too late to introduce new products, however, will almost certainly allow competitors time to introduce similar technologies. Lowering prices to gain market share has sometimes worked in the past, but most firms quickly follow price reductions by their competitors.

Japanese companies (NEC, Sony, Toshiba, and Fujitsu) are aggressively entering the PC segment, some with considerable brand-name recognition among consumers. Suppliers attempt to differentiate themselves on networking capabilities, installed base, software, product quality, and service.

TECHNOLOGY

The creation of new technologies and its effective incorporation into new products are essential for survival in the rapidly changing computer industry. The list of casualties or ailing firms, such as Wang, Data General, Sperry, Honeywell, and Digital Equipment, attests to the importance of constant technology investment. The ratio of price to performance continues to decline exponentially. Company size appears to be a rapidly evolving competitive weapon in the creation of technology, leading some firms to form strategic alliances for specific technology initiatives.

Two recent technological developments are expected to have a major effect on the industry in the next several years: the Pentium Pro processing chip by Intel and the Windows NT operating system by Microsoft. The networking ability provided by these two technologies, termed Wintel, will likely provide a competitive advantage to computer hardware firms that incorporate them into their products.

MANUFACTURING

Most computer hardware firms outsource the manufacture of computer components, and then assemble and test final products at plants worldwide. This sort of assembly strategy reduces the need for capital-intensive plants with their attendant high fixed costs, and provides flexibility to adapt to changing demand. Some firms have even begun outsourcing the assembly function. Short product life cycles also increase the need for outsourcing because of the difficulty of matching component purchases, assembled products, and customer demand. Some firms, particularly those marketing through mail order, manufacture on a build-to-order basis.

MARKETING

Distribution of computer products varies by type of computer and customer. Retail outlets, including mass merchandisers, consumer electronics stores, office products stores, and warehouse clubs, are the primary avenue for PCs sold to consumers. With consumers becoming more computer-literate, mail order is an increasingly important distribution mechanism for PCs, posting sales increases in the mid-40 percent range in 1997.

Most computer firms maintain a direct sales force for selling to business firms, although the role of indirect sellers is increasing. The latter includes value-added resellers and systems integrators. The use of indirect sellers reduces the cost of a firm's in-house sales staff and increases its market reach to customers. In this case, however, computer firms must share some of their profit margin with the indirect sellers, as well as incur costs to monitor the indirect distribution channels.

FINANCE

Profitable computer firms tend to generate sufficient cash flow from operations to finance their relatively modest investments in property, plant, and equipment. Their relatively low level of fixed assets on the balance sheet coupled with short product life cycles allow firms to minimize their use of long-term debt. Start-up technology firms are generally able to attract venture capitalists willing to take equity stakes, thus obviating the need for debt financing.

Because computer firms source components and sell assembled products worldwide, foreign currency risk is significant. Firms engage in various risk reducing mechanisms, including local currency borrowing, futures contracts, and currency swaps. Changes in exchange rates also affect reported earnings of computer firms, the effect depending on the direction of exchange rate changes and the foreign currency translation method used.

COMPUTER WORKSTATION MARKET

The workstation market initially developed to meet the computation, design, and graphics needs of technical users such as scientists, architects, and engineers. High-quality graphics, design flexibility, and the need to integrate the work of several individuals on a design team were the primary product objectives. The workstation segment has experienced continual growth during the last two decades as the price-performance ratio has steadily declined.

Although firms offered proprietary systems during the 1980s in an attempt to lock in customers, these customers have increasingly demanded greater standardization during the 1990s so that workstations purchased from various vendors can be integrated effectively. The UNIX operating system is now the accepted industry standard.

Most workstations rely on reduced instruction set computing, or RISC, chips. The recent introduction of Microsoft's Windows NT operating system and Intel's Pentium Pro processing chip, based on complex instruction set computing, or CISC, is expected to challenge the use of UNIX and RISC chips. The willingness of workstation manufacturers to embrace these two new technologies may be a major factor in their profitability going forward.

The traditional workstation market geared to technical users is currently subject to two major challenges. First, technological developments now provide high-end PCs with the data analysis and graphic capabilities of workstations. Thus, increased competition from PC manufacturers seems likely.

Second, business firms are rapidly expanding their networked systems in order to link PCs, mainframes, and other computers. The technology needed for such integration, including RISC-based servers, has been integral to workstation design for years. Thus, workstation firms have the expertise and experience in systems integration needed to move into the office market. Also, high-end workstations have the storage and data processing capacities of low-end mainframe computers, providing workstation firms another opening into the office market.

Several impediments will limit the speed at which traditional PC, mainframe, and workstation firms enter each other's markets. First, software designed to run on Microsoft's DOS, Windows 95, and Windows NT operating systems dominates the PC market, while UNIX dominates the workstation market. Which systems will become the industry standard remains an open question.

Second, firms start with different positionings in this rapidly changing environment. Sun's primary emphasis is workstations, with little involvement with PCs and mainframes. Its traditional emphasis has been on low-end workstations, but it has recently moved to the high-end of the line. HP has focused on high-end workstations and midsize minicomputers, with a recent movement into PCs. IBM is a dominant player in mainframes and PCs, and has only a minor presence in workstations. Silicon Graphics has its primary presence in the workstation market. Compaq Computer and Apple have their primary presence in PCs (although Compaq Computer is now branching into workstations and servers). The extent to which industry-level standardization will permit firms to remain in a product niche or force firms to expand their product offerings remains an open question.

Third, business firms have increasingly used network systems specialists instead of hardware manufacturers to design, implement, and manage their network systems. The use of network specialists reflects in part the presence of in-place hardware from several manufacturers but also a desire on the part of business firms to disentangle the design of network systems from the particular hardware offered by any one manufacturer.

COMPANIES STUDIED

HP has traditionally maintained its primary presence in the market for midsized computers for business. HP acquired Apollo Computer in 1989, providing it with a major presence in the high end of the workstation market. Sales of its LaserJet and DeskJet printers have become an increasing proportion of its sales mix in recent years.

HP entered the PC market in mid-1995. In addition to offering workstations with its own RISC-based processor, HP is now also offering products that incorporate Intel's Pentium Pro processing chip. HP is more vertically integrated in its manufacturing than Sun, although it outsources significant components. HP has shifted increasing responsibility for the distribution function to retailers and indirect sellers.

Exhibits 8.27 through 8.29 present financial statements for HP for 1995 through 1997, and Exhibit 8.30 presents geographic segment data. The present values of operating lease commitments for HP at a 10 percent discount rate are as follows (in millions): 1994, $496; 1995, $557; 1996, $631; 1997, $788.

EXHIBIT 8.27

Hewlett-Packard
Balance Sheets
(amounts in millions)
(Case 8.1)

	October 31			
	1994	1995	1996	1997
Assets				
Cash	$ 1,357	$ 1,973	$ 2,885	$ 3,072
Marketable Securities	1,121	643	442	1,497
Accounts Receivable	5,028	6,735	7,126	8,173
Inventories.....................	4,273	6,013	6,401	6,763
Prepayments	730	875	1,137	1,442
Total Current Assets	$12,509	$16,239	$17,991	$20,947
Property, Plant, and Equipment (cost) .	$ 7,938	$ 8,747	$10,198	$11,776
Accumulated Depreciation	(3,610)	(4,036)	(4,662)	(5,464)
Property, Plant, and Equipment (net) .	$ 4,328	$ 4,711	$ 5,536	$ 6,312
Other Assets	$ 2,730	$ 3,477	$ 4,172	$ 4,490
Total Assets	$19,567	$24,427	$27,699	$31,749
Liabilities and Shareholders' Equity				
Accounts Payable	$ 1,466	$ 2,422	$ 2,375	$ 3,185
Notes Payable	2,469	3,214	2,125	1,226
Other Current Liabilities	4,295	5,308	6,123	6,808
Total Current Liabilities	$ 8,230	$10,944	$10,623	$11,219
Long-Term Debt	547	663	2,579	3,158
Deferred Income Taxes	—	—	—	—
Other Noncurrent Liabilities	864	981	1,059	1,217
Total Liabilities	$ 9,641	$12,588	$14,261	$15,594
Common Stock	$ 1,033	$ 1,381	$ 1,014	$ 1,187
Retained Earnings	8,893	10,458	12,424	14,968
Total Shareholders' Equity	$ 9,926	$11,839	$13,438	$16,155
Total Liabilities and Shareholders' Equity	$19,567	$24,427	$27,699	$31,749

EXHIBIT 8.28

Hewlett-Packard
Income Statements
(amounts in millions)
(Case 8.1)

	Fiscal Year Ended October 31		
	1995	**1996**	**1997**
Sales	$31,519	$38,420	$42,895
Other Revenues	270	295	331
Cost of Goods Sold	(20,014)	(25,499)	(28,319)
Selling and Administrative	(5,635)	(6,477)	(7,159)
Research and Development	(2,302)	(2,718)	(3,078)
Interest	(206)	(327)	(215)
Income Taxes	(1,199)	(1,108)	(1,336)
Net Income	$ 2,433	$ 2,586	$ 3,119

EXHIBIT 8.29

Hewlett-Packard
Statements of Cash Flows
(amounts in millions)
(Case 8.1)

	Fiscal Year Ended October 31		
	1995	**1996**	**1997**
Operations			
Net Income	$ 2,433	$ 2,586	$ 3,119
Depreciation and Amortization	1,139	1,297	1,556
Other Addbacks	—	—	—
Other Subtractions	(322)	(378)	(481)
(Increase) Decrease in Accounts Receivable	(1,696)	(293)	(752)
(Increase) Decrease in Inventories	(1,740)	(356)	(279)
(Increase) Decrease in Prepayments	(145)	(262)	(305)
Increase (Decrease) in Accounts Payable	956	(55)	775
Increase (Decrease) in Other Current Liabilities	988	917	688
Cash Flow from Operations	$ 1,613	$ 3,456	$ 4,321
Investing			
Sale of Marketable Securities	$ 3,669	$ 7,074	$ 4,158
Acquisition of Marketable Securities	(3,499)	(7,386)	(5,213)
Sale of Property, Plant, and Equipment	294	316	333
Acquisition of Property, Plant, and Equipment	(1,601)	(2,201)	(2,338)
Other Investing Transactions	(38)	22	48
Cash Flow from Investing	$(1,175)	$(2,175)	$(3,012)

	Fiscal Year Ended October 31		
Exh. 8.29—Continued	**1995**	**1996**	**1997**

Financing

Increase (Decrease) in Short-Term Borrowing	$ 755	$(1,137)	$(1,194)
Increase in Long-Term Borrowing	434	1,989	1,182
Issue of Common Stock	361	363	419
Decrease in Long-Term Borrowing	(332)	(41)	(273)
Acquisition of Common Stock	(686)	(1,089)	(724)
Dividends	(358)	(450)	(532)
Other Financing Transactions	4	(4)	0
Cash Flow from Financing	$ 178	$ (369)	$(1,122)
Change in Cash	$ 616	$ 912	$ 187
Cash—Beginning of Year	1,357	1,973	2,885
Cash—End of Year	$ 1,973	$ 2,885	$ 3,072

EXHIBIT 8.30

Hewlett-Packard
Selected Geographic Segment Data
(Case 8.1)

	Sales Mix			Asset Mix		
	1995	**1996**	**1997**	**1995**	**1996**	**1997**
United States	44.3%	44.4%	44.5%	48.7%	48.5%	46.2%
Europe	35.4	34.5	33.4	28.2	27.1	28.6
Other	20.3	21.1	22.1	23.1	24.4	25.2
	100.0%	100.0%	100.0%	100.0%	100.0%	100.0%

	ROA			Profit Margin			Assets Turnover		
	1995	**1996**	**1997**	**1995**	**1996**	**1997**	**1995**	**1996**	**1997**
United States	18.3%	17.2%	16.3%	16.2%	14.5%	13.4%	1.13	1.19	1.22
Europe	13.0%	9.6%	13.3%	8.3%	5.8%	9.0%	1.55	1.66	1.47
Other	21.2%	16.3%	14.9%	19.3%	14.4%	13.5%	1.10	1.13	1.11

Sun has traditionally operated primarily in the workstation market, with an emphasis on the low end of this market. It introduced new high-end workstations in November 1995. Sun has emphasized networking capabilities and open system architecture as its principal strategic focus for many years. Sun is currently attempting to differentiate itself by emphasizing its experience and long-term commitment to these two needed qualities of integrated systems. Sun now characterizes itself as a "supplier of enterprise network computing prod-

EXHIBIT 8.31

Sun Microsystems
Balance Sheets
(amounts in millions)
(Case 8.1)

	June 30			
	1994	**1995**	**1996**	**1997**
Assets				
Cash	$ 434	$ 414	$ 529	$ 660
Marketable Securities	449	814	461	453
Accounts Receivable	853	1,042	1,207	1,667
Inventories	295	320	461	438
Prepayments	274	345	376	510
Total Current Assets	$2,305	$2,935	$3,034	$3,728
Property, Plant, and Equipment (cost) . . .	$ 877	$1,046	$1,282	$1,658
Accumulated Depreciation	(517)	(617)	(748)	(859)
Property, Plant, and Equipment (net)	$ 360	$ 429	$ 534	$ 799
Other Assets	$ 233	$ 181	$ 233	$ 170
Total Assets	$2,898	$3,545	$3,801	$4,697
Liabilities and Shareholders' Equity				
Accounts Payable	$ 364	$ 304	$ 325	$ 469
Notes Payable	79	51	49	101
Current Portion of Long-Term Debt	38	38	38	0
Other Current Liabilities	667	938	1,077	1,279
Total Current Liabilities	$1,148	$1,331	$1,489	$1,849
Long-Term Debt	122	91	60	106
Total Liabilities	$1,270	$1,422	$1,549	$1,955
Common Stock	$1,066	$1,090	$1,164	$1,230
Retained Earnings	879	1,205	1,663	2,410
Cumulative Translation Adjustment	12	34	22	17
Treasury Stock	(329)	(206)	(597)	(915)
Total Shareholders' Equity	$1,628	$2,123	$2,252	$2,742
Total Liabilities and Shareholders' Equity	$2,898	$3,545	$3,801	$4,697

ucts, including workstations, servers, software, microprocessors, and a full range of services and support."

Sun outsources virtually all the components of its computers, employing an assembly manufacturing strategy for the final product. It currently relies on indirect sellers for over 50 percent of its revenues, and its own sales force accounts for the remainder. In addition to emphasizing its experience in network systems, two other strategic decisions affect Sun going forward. First, Sun has decided to remain with its proprietary RISC-based processing chip, disregarding Intel's Pentium Pro chip. Second, Sun has developed the Java computer language to be used in writing software for complex networks such as the Internet and corporate intranets. It has obtained agreements whereby IBM, Microsoft, Oracle Systems, and Netscape Communications will use Java in their network software.

Exhibits 8.31 through 8.33 present financial statements for Sun for 1995 through 1997, and Exhibit 8.34 presents geographic segment data. The present values of operating lease commitments for Sun at a 10 percent discount rate are as follows (amounts in millions): 1994, $265; 1995, $257; 1996, $252; 1997, $363.

Sun acquired two firms during its 1996 and 1997 fiscal years. It allocated $58 million to in-process technologies in fiscal 1996 and $23 million in fiscal 1997, which is included in research and development expense in Exhibit 8.32. The amounts expensed do not give rise to an income tax deduction. Other income for fiscal 1997 includes a $62 million gain on sale of an equity investment.

Required

    a. Make any adjustments to the reported financial statements for HP and Sun that you think appropriate in order to assess their profitability and risk. Briefly describe your reasoning for the adjustments.

    b. Assess the relative profitability and risk of HP and Sun, identifying the likely reasons for (1) changes across time for each company (time series analysis), and (2) differences between the firms (cross-sectional analysis).

EXHIBIT 8.32

Sun Microsystems
Income Statements
(amounts in millions)
(Case 8.1)

	Fiscal Year Ended June 30		
	1995	**1996**	**1997**
Sales	$ 5,902	$ 7,095	$ 8,598
Other Revenues	41	43	102
Cost of Goods Sold	(3,399)	(3,972)	(4,320)
Selling and Administrative	(1,440)	(1,791)	(2,402)
Research and Development	(563)	(657)	(849)
Interest	(18)	(9)	(8)
Income Taxes	(167)	(233)	(359)
Net Income	$ 356	$ 476	$ 762

EXHIBIT 8.33

Sun Microsystems
Statements of Cash Flows
(amounts in millions)
(Case 8.1)

	Fiscal Year Ended June 30		
	1995	1996	1997
Operations			
Net Income	$ 356	$ 476	$ 762
Depreciation and Amortization	241	284	342
Other Addbacks	23	121	101
(Increase) Decrease in Accounts Receivable	(189)	(160)	(335)
(Increase) Decrease in Inventories	(25)	(136)	23
(Increase) Decrease in Prepayments	(2)	(31)	(134)
Increase (Decrease) in Accounts Payable	(60)	17	144
Increase (Decrease) in Other Current Liabilities	293	117	202
Cash Flow from Operations	$ 637	$ 688	$1,105
Investing			
Sale of Marketable Securities	$3,106	$1,653	$1,045
Acquisition of Marketable Securities	(3,471)	(1,398)	(997)
Acquisition of Property, Plant, and Equipment	(242)	(296)	(554)
Other Investing Transactions	(68)	(84)	(38)
Cash Flow from Investing	$ (675)	$ (125)	$ (544)
Financing			
Increase (Decrease) in Short-Term Borrowing	$ (28)	$ (1)	$ 52
Issue of Common Stock	122	114	134
Decrease in Long-Term Borrowing	(40)	(39)	(160)
Acquisition of Common Stock	(36)	(522)	(456)
Cash Flow from Financing	$ 18	$ (448)	$ (430)
Change in Cash	$ (20)	$ 115	$ 131
Cash—Beginning of Year	434	414	529
Cash—End of Year	$ 414	$ 529	$ 660

EXHIBIT 8.34

Sun Microsystems
Selected Geographic Data
(Case 8.1)

	Sales Mix			Asset Mix		
	1995	1996	1997	1995	1996	1997
United States	53.1%	56.0%	48.7%	65.3%	63.0%	56.5%
Europe	25.3	25.1	35.9	23.8	26.1	33.4
Other	21.6	18.9	15.4	10.9	10.9	10.1
	100.0%	100.0%	100.0%	100.0%	100.0%	100.0%

	ROA			Profit Margin			Assets Turnover		
	1995	1996	1997	1995	1996	1997	1995	1996	1997
United States	6.8%	7.5%	11.7%	7.7%	7.4%	8.4%	0.88	1.02	1.39
Europe	19.3%	24.0%	21.7%	16.9%	20.8%	12.5%	1.15	1.15	1.74
Other	4.5%	4.7%	3.0%	2.1%	2.0%	1.2%	2.15	2.37	2.40

CASE 8.2

WIRELESS TELECOMMUNICATIONS INDUSTRY ANALYSIS: MOTOROLA, NOKIA, AND ERICSSON

The wireless telecommunications equipment market, which includes cellular telephones and the infrastructure to support cellular communications, grew significantly during the last decade. This growth is expected not only to continue during the next decade but also to increase substantially. This case analyzes the three leading companies in this industry: Motorola (a U.S. company), Ericsson (a Swedish company), and Nokia (a Finnish company). Together, these firms command over 65 percent of worldwide wireless telecommunication revenues.

INDUSTRY OVERVIEW

A simplified value chain for the wireless telecommunications industry appears below:

Semiconductors	Infrastructure Systems	Cellular Phones

Semiconductors, or microprocessors, represent the brains of telecommunications products. Firms operating in this segment must make substantial ongoing research and development expenditures to remain competitive. The manufacturing process is highly automated, with heavy fixed costs.

Market prices respond quickly to cyclical swings in demand for products that use semi-conductors and to the amount of unused manufacturing capacity. Firms will lower prices to use their fixed capacity when demand is weak, and raise prices when demand exceeds existing capacity. Motorola is the only one of the three firms studied that has a major presence in semiconductors, although Ericsson maintains a minor presence.

Infrastructure systems comprise the base stations and switches needed to conduct communication between users of cellular telephones. Equipment providers compete on the basis of price, service, warranties, product features (including technology and quality), and financing. Most wireless systems currently in place, particularly in the United States, use analogue technology, but digital technology is expected to become the worldwide standard within a year or two. Over 80 percent of new systems under construction rely on digital technology.

Digital technology has higher throughput capacity and permits expanded applications in data and video transmission. It is uncertain today which digital technology will become the industry standard; GSM is the accepted standard in Europe, and CDMA the more common standard in the United States.

Purchasers of infrastructure systems increasingly rely on the equipment manufacturers to provide financing. Research and development expenditures represent a significant barrier to entry in this segment. The manufacturing process is capital-intensive but less so than for semiconductor manufacturing. Firms use their own sales staffs and independent distributors to market their products. Motorola, Ericsson, and Nokia maintain a presence in the infrastructure systems segment, combining for approximately a 65 percent market share in 1997. Ericsson is the worldwide market share leader in this segment.

The cellular telephone segment includes the handsets that customers use to conduct wireless communications. Two key factors drive demand in this segment: subscriber growth and new products. Subscriber growth is expected to increase dramatically in coming years, as current users switch from analogue to digital phones, new opportunities for data and video transmission emerge, markets become deregulated, governments allocate additional spectrum to increase competition, and new wireless systems are built in more remote areas.

Barriers to entry are lower in cellular telephones than in semiconductors and infrastructure systems. Increased competition and new product offerings in this segment will likely lead customers to purchase new cellular telephones. Market prices for cellular phones are expected to decrease 10 percent to 20 percent per year during the next several years, increasing the volume of telephones sold but dampening the growth in total revenues.

The manufacturing process for cellular telephones is primarily an assembly operation, and firms frequently outsource some of the components. Retail outlets remain the principal distribution channel. Advertising plays an important role in building brand awareness in this segment. Motorola, Ericsson, and Nokia maintained an 80 percent market share in cellular telephones in 1997, down from 90 percent as new competitors entered the market. Nokia was the market share leader in digital telephones in 1997. Motorola tends to target the low end of the cellular telephone market, while Ericsson and Nokia target the high end.

Thus, Motorola maintains a presence in all three industry segments; Ericsson operates in infrastructure systems and cellular telephones, with an emphasis on infrastructure systems; and Nokia operates in infrastructure systems and cellular telephones but with an emphasis on cellular telephones.

There are obvious integration advantages between the infrastructure systems and cellular telephone segments. Given the alternative uses of semiconductors in a wide range of industries, the need to invest heavily in research and development to remain competitive, and the need to use capital-intensive plants efficiently, it is not clear that vertical integration backward into semiconductor manufacturing represents a sustainable, competitive advantage in this industry.

COMPANIES ANALYZED

MOTOROLA

Motorola segments its operations into five groups. Exhibit 8.35 presents segment data for 1995, 1996, and 1997. The five groups include:

Cellular Products The cellular products segment designs, manufactures, sells, and services cellular infrastructure and cellular telephone equipment and computer systems products. Motorola has historically emphasized products using analogue technology but now offers products using all the leading digital technologies (GSM, CDMA, TDMA).

Semiconductor Products The semiconductor products segment designs and manufactures semiconductor chips for use in Motorola's products as well products of companies in the aerospace, automotive, home appliance, computer, and other industries.

Land Mobile Products The land mobile products segment manufactures products used in two-way communications by police and fire departments, and construction, mining, and other industries.

EXHIBIT 8.35

Segment Data for Motorola
(Case 8.2)

	Sales Mix			Income Mix			Asset Mix		
	1995	1996	1997	1995	1996	1997	1995	1996	1997
Cellular Products	34%	35%	36%	39%	55%	59%	29%	30%	34%
Semiconductor Products . .	29	26	24	37	16	14	39	37	33
Land Mobile Products	12	13	15	10	21	25	10	10	11
Messaging, Information, and Media Products	12	13	12	10	4	4	12	12	10
Other Products	13	13	13	4	4	(2)	10	11	12
	100%	100%	100%	100%	100%	100%	100%	100%	100%
United States	53%	55%	55%	47%	47%	42	60%	60%	58%
Other Nations	47	45	45	53	53	58	40	40	42
	100%	100%	100%	100%	100%	100%	100%	100%	100%

	Profit Margin			Assets Turnover			Return on Assets		
	1995	1996	1997	1995	1996	1997	1995	1996	1997
Cellular Products	12.5%	11.9%	11.7%	1.7	1.7	1.5	21.9%	20.4%	17.4%
Semiconductor Products . .	14.3%	4.9%	4.1%	1.1	1.0	1.0	15.3%	4.8%	4.2%
Land Mobile Products	8.7%	12.4%	11.9%	1.7	1.9	1.9	14.9%	23.4%	23.2%
Messaging, Information, and Media Products	8.4%	2.3%	2.1%	1.5	1.6	1.6	12.3%	3.6%	3.3%
Other Products	3.4%	2.0%	(.9%)	1.8	1.8	1.5	6.0%	3.5%	(1.4%)
United States	8.8%	6.1%	4.9%	1.5	1.6	1.6	13.4%	9.8%	7.7%
Other Nations	11.2%	8.5%	8.3%	2.1	2.0	1.8	23.2%	16.6%	14.8%

Messaging, Information, and Media Products The products of the messaging, information, and media products segment include paging systems and modems for data transmission.

Other Products "Other products" includes a variety of electronic-based products used in automotive, energy, space, and satellite products of other companies.

ERICSSON

Ericsson operates in four segments as follows:

Mobile Systems This segment provides infrastructure systems and equipment for mobile networks. Although Ericsson offers products employing analogue technology, most of its products use digital technology.

Infocom Systems This segment provides network telecommunication products and services for public and business customers.

Mobile Telephones and Terminals This segment represents Ericsson's cellular telephone products sold to consumers.

Other Operations This segment includes components and microwave systems products.

Exhibit 8.36 presents sales mix data by product and geographical segment for Ericsson.

EXHIBIT 8.36

Segment Data for Ericsson
(Case 8.2)

	1995	1996	1997
Sales Mix			
Mobile Systems	37%	43%	41%
Inforcom Systems	35	30	28
Mobile Phones and Terminals	15	17	21
Other Operations	13	10	10
	100%	100%	100%
Sweden	9%	6%	6%
Europe (excluding Sweden)	41	39	40
United States and Canada	11	13	11
Latin America	7	10	12
Africa	2	2	2
Middle East	4	3	3
Asia (excluding Middle East)	20	23	22
Australia, New Zealand, and Oceania	6	4	4
	100%	100%	100%

NOKIA

Nokia is Europe's largest manufacturer of cellular infrastructure and cellular telephones, the world's largest manufacturer of digital cellular telephones, and one of the world's leaders in digital and analogue cellular infrastructure systems. Exhibit 8.37 presents segment data for Nokia for 1995, 1996, and 1997. Nokia organizes its business into three segments:

Telecommunications   The telecommunications segment provides infrastructure systems and equipment for use in fixed and cellular telephone networks. Nokia products rely on GSM digital technology.

Mobile Telephones   The mobile telephones segment manufactures cellular telephones for distribution worldwide.

Other Operations   The other operations segment now includes digital satellite and cable network systems, focusing on Internet protocols, and PC and workstation monitors. Nokia has divested its investment in cable, color television, and chemical businesses in recent years.

EXHIBIT 8.37

Segment Data for Nokia
(Case 8.2)

	Sales Mix			Income Mix			Asset Mix		
	1995	1996	1997	1995	1996	1997	1995	1996	1997
Telecommunications	28%	33%	35%	54%	70%	48%	24%	29%	27%
Mobile Phones	43	54	51	35	34	45	37	26	23
Other	29	13	14	11	(4)	7	39	45	50
	100%	100%	100%	100%	100%	100%	100%	100%	100%
Nordic Countries	47%	42%	45%	78%	82%	49%	47%	56%	54%
Other European Countries .	31	30	26	22	19	32	33	32	30
Other Countries	22	28	29	—	(1)	19	20	12	16
	100%	100%	100%	100%	100%	100%	100%	100%	100%

	Profit Margin			Assets Turnover			Return on Assets		
	1995	1996	1997	1995	1996	1997	1995	1996	1997
Telecommunications	26.3%	22.4%	21.5%	1.3	1.3	1.3	33.2%	29.2%	28.1%
Mobile Phones	10.9%	6.6%	13.9%	1.3	2.3	2.2	13.7%	15.3%	30.3%
Other	4.8%	(2.8%)	7.8%	.8	.3	.3	4.1%	(.9%)	2.1%
Nordic Countries	15.3%	13.6%	11.4%	1.5	1.0	1.2	23.3%	13.7%	14.3%
Other European Countries .	6.5%	4.5%	12.7%	1.4	1.4	1.3	9.2%	6.4%	16.5%
Other Countries	(.2%)	(.4%)	6.5%	1.7	3.0	2.8	(.3%)	(1.2%)	18.5%

DATA ISSUES

MOTOROLA

Exhibits 8.38 through 8.40 present the financial statements for Motorola for 1994 through 1997. Motorola prepares its financial statements in accordance with generally accepted accounting principles (GAAP) in the United States. The present values of operating lease commitments for Motorola on December 31 of each year at a discount rate of 8 percent are as follows (in millions): 1994, $391; 1995, $442; 1996, $534; 1997, $407. These amounts do not appear on the balance sheet as assets and liabilities under GAAP in the United States. Other income for 1995 includes a pre-tax gain of $443 ($267 after taxes) on the sale of a portion of mobile radio business.

ERICSSON

Exhibits 8.41 through 8.43 present the financial statements for Ericsson for 1994 through 1997. The present values of operating lease commitments for Ericsson on December 31 of each year at a discount rate of 8 percent are as follows (in millions): 1994, SEK4,493; 1995, SEK4,076; 1996, SEK5,051; 1997, SEK5,094.

EXHIBIT 8.38

Motorola
Balance Sheets
(amounts in millions)
(Case 8.2)

	December 31			
	1994	**1995**	**1996**	**1997**
Assets				
Cash	$ 741	$ 725	$ 1,513	$ 1,445
Marketable Securities	318	350	298	335
Accounts Receivable	3,421	4,081	4,035	4,847
Inventories	2,670	3,528	3,220	4,096
Other Current Assets	1,775	1,826	2,253	2,513
Total Current Assets	$ 8,925	$10,510	$11,319	$13,236
Investments	$ 0	$ 0	$ 0	$ 0
Property, Plant, and Equipment (cost)	$13,730	$17,466	$19,598	$21,380
Accumulated Depreciation	(6,657)	(8,110)	(9,830)	(11,524)
Property, Plant, and Equipment (net)	$ 7,073	$ 9,356	$ 9,768	$ 9,856
Other Assets	$ 1,538	$ 2,872	$ 2,989	$ 4,186
Total Assets	$17,536	$22,738	$24,076	$27,278

| | December 31 | | | |
Exh. 8.38—Continued	1994	1995	1996	1997
Liabilities and Shareholders' Equity				
Accounts Payable	$ 1,678	$ 2,018	$ 2,050	$ 2,297
Notes Payable	916	1,605	1,382	1,282
Other Current Liabilities	3,323	4,170	4,563	5,476
Total Current Liabilities	$ 5,917	$ 7,793	$ 7,995	$ 9,055
Long-Term Debt	1,127	1,949	1,931	2,144
Deferred Income Taxes	509	968	1,108	1,522
Other Noncurrent Liabilities	887	1,043	1,247	1,285
Total Liabilities	$ 8,440	$11,753	$12,281	$14,006
Common Stock	$ 1,764	$ 1,774	$ 1,780	$ 1,792
Additional Paid-in Capital	1,415	1,483	1,405	1,976
Retained Earnings	5,917	7,728	8,610	9,504
Total Shareholders' Equity	$ 9,096	$10,985	$11,795	$13,272
Total Liabilities and Shareholders' Equity	$17,536	$22,738	$24,076	$27,278

EXHIBIT 8.39

Motorola
Income Statements
(amounts in millions)
(Case 8.2)

| | Year Ended December 31 | | |
	1995	1996	1997
Sales	$ 27,037	$ 27,973	$ 29,794
Other Revenues	507	7	85
Cost of Goods Sold	(19,464)	(21,298)	(22,332)
Selling and Administrative Expense	(2,445)	(2,321)	(2,767)
Research and Development Expense	(2,197)	(2,394)	(2,748)
Interest Expense	(213)	(192)	(216)
Income Tax Expense	(1,177)	(621)	(636)
Net Income	$ 2,048	$ 1,154	$ 1,180

EXHIBIT 8.40

Motorola
Statements of Cash Flows
(amounts in millions)
(Case 8.2)

	Year Ended December 31		
	1995	1996	1997
Operations			
Net Income	$ 2,048	$ 1,154	$ 1,180
Depreciation and Amortization	1,919	2,308	2,329
Other Addbacks	12	8	10
Other Subtractions	(433)	(238)	(214)
(Increase) Decrease in Accounts Receivable	(653)	101	(812)
(Increase) Decrease in Inventories	(856)	308	(880)
(Increase) Decrease in Prepayments	(100)	(69)	(114)
Increase (Decrease) in Accounts Payable	340	32	247
Increase (Decrease) in Other Current Liabilities	988	586	850
Cash Flow from Operations	$ 3,265	$ 4,190	$ 2,596
Investing			
Sale of Marketable Securities	$ 252	$ 119	$ 248
Acquisition of Marketable Securities	(563)	(346)	(286)
Sale of Property, Plant, and Equipment	0	0	0
Acquisition of Property, Plant, and Equipment	(4,225)	(2,973)	(2,874)
Other Investing Transactions	(43)	294	287
Cash Flow from Investing	$(4,579)	$(2,906)	$(2,625)
Financing			
Increase (Decrease) in Short-Term Borrowing	686	0	0
Increase in Long-Term Borrowing	851	55	312
Issue of Common Stock	71	7	137
Decrease in Short-Term Borrowing	0	(260)	(100)
Decrease in Long-Term Borrowing	(74)	(37)	(102)
Acquisition of Common Stock	0	0	0
Dividends	(236)	(261)	(286)
Other Financing Transactions	0	0	0
Cash Flow from Financing	$ 1,298	$ (496)	(39)
Change in Cash	$ (16)	$ 788	(68)
Cash—Beginning of Year	741	725	1,513
Cash—End of Year	$ 725	$ 1,513	1,445

EXHIBIT 8.41

Ericsson
Balance Sheets
(amounts in millions)
(Case 8.2)

	December 31			
	1994	1995	1996	1997
Assets				
Cash	SEK 11,892	SEK 15,385	SEK 19,060	SEK 29,127
Marketable Securities	0	0	0	0
Accounts Receivable	20,666	25,379	35,384	46,151
Inventories	12,805	19,351	19,619	23,614
Other Current Assets	5,851	7,719	10,514	19,133
Total Current Assets	SEK 51,214	SEK 67,834	SEK 84,577	SEK 118,025
Investments	SEK 3,019	SEK 3,564	SEK 3,773	SEK 4,077
Property, Plant, and Equipment (cost)	SEK 28,993	SEK 31,973	SEK 36,807	SEK 41,159
Accumulated Depreciation	(15,315)	(16,452)	(19,053)	(21,934)
Property, Plant, and Equipment (net)	SEK 13,678	SEK 15,521	SEK 17,754	SEK 19,225
Other Assets	SEK 5,088	SEK 3,913	SEK 6,048	SEK 6,113
Total Assets	SEK 72,999	SEK 90,832	SEK 112,152	SEK 147,440
Liabilities and Shareholders' Equity				
Accounts Payable	SEK 7,870	SEK 10,018	SEK 11,371	SEK 14,803
Notes Payable	2,598	2,198	4,340	4,242
Current Portion of Long-Term Debt	271	1,715	2,185	742
Other Current Liabilities	22,445	28,422	37,026	49,860
Total Current Liabilities	SEK 33,184	SEK 42,353	SEK 54,922	SEK 69,647
Long-Term Debt	4,891	3,523	2,272	8,510
Deferred Income Taxes	1,073	826	800	2,344
Other Noncurrent Liabilities	8,762	8,118	10,292	9,920
Minority Interest in Subsidiary	1,787	1,749	3,410	4,395
Total Liabilities	SEK 49,697	SEK 56,569	SEK 71,696	SEK 94,816
Common Stock	SEK 2,172	SEK 2,394	SEK 2,403	SEK 2,436
Additional Paid-in Capital	13,660	22,061	24,185	29,172
Retained Earnings	7,470	9,808	13,868	21,016
Total Shareholders' Equity	SEK 23,302	SEK 34,263	SEK 40,456	SEK 52,624
Total Liabilities and Shareholders' Equity .	SEK 72,999	SEK 90,832	SEK 112,152	SEK 147,440

EXHIBIT 8.42

Ericsson
Income Statements
(amounts in millions)
(Case 8.2)

	Year Ended December 31		
	1995	1996	1997
Sales	SEK 98,780	SEK 124,266	SEK 167,740
Other Revenues	2,398	3,525	3,759
Cost of Goods Sold	(57,755)	(74,179)	(97,868)
Selling and Administrative Expense	(16,871)	(21,109)	(28,219)
Research and Development Expense	(16,891)	(19,837)	(24,242)
Interest Expense	(1,439)	(1,496)	(2,365)
Income Tax Expense	(2,341)	(3,399)	(5,755)
Minority Interest in Earnings	(442)	(661)	(1,109)
Net Income	SEK 5,439	SEK 7,110	SEK 11,941

Ericsson prepares its financial statements in accordance with generally accepted accounting principles in Sweden. Exhibit 8.44 presents the necessary adjustments to balance sheet and income statement accounts to convert Ericsson's financial statements to U.S. GAAP. The principal differences relate to the items as follows:

1. Revaluation of certain property, plant, and equipment to an amount exceeding acquisition cost, a procedure not allowed under GAAP in the United States.
2. Treatment of all interest cost incurred as an expense each period; United States companies must capitalize interest incurred in connection with the construction of property, plant, and equipment.
3. Expensing of all software development costs in the year incurred; U.S. GAAP requires firms to capitalize and then amortize these costs once the software reaches the stage of commercial feasibility.
4. Recognition of deferred income taxes for temporary differences between book and taxable income. Although Swedish GAAP does not require the recognition of deferred taxes, Ericsson does recognize deferred taxes for some temporary differences, but the accounting is not the same as U.S. GAAP requires.
5. Recognition of expenses and liabilities for pensions and retiree health benefits. Ericsson follows local laws and accounting principles with respect to these items, which differ from those under U.S. GAAP with respect to actuarial assumptions.

EXHIBIT 8.43

Ericsson
Statements of Cash Flows
(amounts in millions)
(Case 8.2)

	Year Ended December 31		
	1995	1996	1997
Operations			
Net Income	SEK 5,439	SEK 7,110	SEK 11,941
Depreciation and Amortization	4,156	4,659	5,756
Other Addbacks	510	661	1,261
Other Subtractions	0	(345)	0
(Increase) Decrease in Accounts Receivable	(4,713)	(10,005)	(10,767)
(Increase) Decrease in Inventories	(7,237)	1,118	(3,965)
(Increase) Decrease in Prepayments	(3,704)	491	(8,619)
Increase (Decrease) in Accounts Payable	2,148	1,353	3,432
Increase (Decrease) in Other Current Liabilities	6,547	4,256	15,863
Cash Flow from Operations	SEK 3,146	SEK 9,298	SEK 14,902
Investing			
Sale of Property, Plant, and Equipment	SEK 397	SEK 767	SEK 642
Acquisition of Property, Plant, and Equipment	(6,423)	(6,290)	(7,237)
Other Investing Transactions	368	1,673	(561)
Cash Flow from Investing	SEK (5,658)	SEK (3,850)	SEK (7,156)
Financing			
Increase (Decrease) in Short-Term Borrowing	SEK 0	SEK 1,453	SEK 96
Increase in Long-Term Borrowing	247	682	7,446
Issue of Common Stock	7,831	0	0
Decrease in Short-Term Borrowing	(217)	0	0
Decrease in Long-Term Borrowing	(615)	(2,029)	(2,672)
Acquisition of Common Stock	0	0	0
Dividends	(1,510)	(1,917)	(2,805)
Other Financing Transactions	269	38	256
Cash Flow from Financing	SEK 6,005	SEK (1,773)	SEK 2,321
Change in Cash	SEK 3,493	SEK 3,675	SEK 10,067
Cash—Beginning of Year	11,892	15,385	19,060
Cash—End of Year	SEK15,385	SEK 19,060	SEK 29,127

EXHIBIT 8.44

Adjustments to Convert Ericsson to U.S. GAAP
(in millions of Swedish kroner)
(Case 8.2)

	December 31			
	1994	1995	1996	1997
Balance Sheet				
Other Current Assets	−	−	+ 898	+1,043
Property, Plant, and Equipment	+ 3,702	+4,991	+5,954	+7,221
Other Noncurrent Assets	+ 62	+ 59	− 100	+ 49
Deferred Tax Liabilities	+ 1,549	+1,946	+2,230	+2,138
Other Noncurrent Liabilities	− 178	− 511	+ 57	+1,176
Retained Earnings	+ 2,393	+3,615	+4,465	+4,740
Minority Interest	−	−	−	+ 32
Other Current Liabilities	−	−	−	+ 227

	Year Ended December 31		
	1995	1996	1997
Cost of Goods Sold	− 23	− 24	− 22
Selling Expenses	− 361	− 156	+ 266
Research and Development Expenditures	−1,242	− 942	− 1,298
Interest Expense	− 15	− 24	+ 10
Income Tax Expense	+ 433	+ 280	+ 137
Net Income	+1,208	+ 866	+ 907

NOKIA

Exhibits 8.45 through 8.47 present the financial statements for Nokia for 1994 through 1997. The present values of operating lease commitments are as follows (in millions): 1994, FIM845; 1995, FIM1,139; 1996, FIM913; 1997, FIM1,046.

Nokia prepares its financial statements in accordance with both Finnish accounting standards and standards of the International Accounting Standards Committee (IASC). The financial statements included with this case use IASC accounting standards. These standards differ from those in the United States. Exhibit 8.48 shows the necessary adjustments to the balance sheet and income statements to covert from IASC GAAP to U.S. GAAP. The most important differences are as follows:

1. Recognition of deferred income taxes only for temporary differences expected to reverse in the near future; U.S. GAAP requires instead the recognition of deferred taxes for all temporary differences between book income and taxable income.

EXHIBIT 8.45

Nokia
Balance Sheets
(amounts in millions)
(Case 8.2)

	December 31			
	1994	1995	1996	1997
Assets				
Cash	FIM 5,268	FIM 4,214	FIM 7,545	FIM 12,247
Marketable Securities	0	0	0	0
Accounts Receivable	7,835	9,518	10,898	12,732
Inventories	6,803	9,982	6,423	7,314
Other Current Assets	0	0	0	0
Total Current Assets	FIM 19,906	FIM 23,714	FIM 24,866	FIM 32,293
Investments	FIM 1,810	FIM 837	FIM 901	FIM 789
Property, Plant, and Equipment (cost)	FIM 10,683	FIM 11,338	FIM 10,281	FIM 12,122
Accumulated Depreciation	(5,586)	(5,229)	(4,619)	(5,882)
Property, Plant, and Equipment (net)	FIM 5,097	FIM 6,109	FIM 5,662	FIM 6,240
Other Assets	FIM 1,521	FIM 2,101	FIM 1,846	FIM 2,416
Total Assets	FIM 28,334	FIM 32,761	FIM 33,275	FIM 41,738
Liabilities and Shareholders' Equity				
Accounts Payable	FIM 3,353	FIM 4,077	FIM 3,559	FIM 4,865
Notes Payable	2,453	4,332	3,404	3,008
Current Portion of Long-Term Debt	278	187	555	285
Other Current Liabilities	5,235	7,359	7,389	10,218
Total Current Liabilities	FIM 11,319	FIM 15,955	FIM 14,907	FIM 18,376
Long-Term Debt	3,071	2,121	2,117	1,348
Deferred Income Taxes	0	0	0	0
Other Noncurrent Liabilities	486	457	297	295
Minority Interest in Subsidiary	555	422	29	195
Total Liabilities	FIM 15,431	FIM 18,955	FIM 17,350	FIM 20,214
Common Stock	FIM 1,498	FIM 1,498	FIM 1,498	FIM 1,499
Additional Paid-in Capital	5,494	5,455	5,298	5,542
Retained Earnings	6,348	7,323	9,786	15,137
Treasury Stock	(437)	(470)	(657)	(654)
Total Shareholders' Equity	FIM 12,903	FIM 13,806	FIM 15,925	FIM 21,524
Total Liabilities and Shareholders' Equity	FIM 28,334	FIM 32,761	FIM 33,275	FIM 41,738

EXHIBIT 8.46

Nokia
Income Statements
(amounts in millions)
(Case 8.2)

	Year Ended December 31		
	1995	**1996**	**1997**
Sales	FIM 36,810	FIM 39,321	FIM 52,612
Other Revenues	666	598	923
Cost of Goods Sold	(25,518)	(28,029)	(33,999)
Selling and Administrative Expense	(3,749)	(3,512)	(5,599)
Research and Development Expense	(2,531)	(3,514)	(4,560)
Interest Expense	(745)	(966)	(1,006)
Income Tax Expense	(769)	(856)	(2,274)
Minority Interest in Earnings	(77)	2	(99)
Income from Continuing Operations	FIM 4,087	FIM 3,044	FIM 5,998
Income from Discontinued Operations	(2,340)	219	261
Net Income	FIM 1,747	FIM 3,263	FIM 6,259

2. Recognition of expenses and liabilities for pensions following IASC rules that differ from those in the United States with respect to actuarial assumptions.
3. Capitalization of certain nonsoftware development costs after a product reaches commercial feasibility under IASC rules that U.S. GAAP requires companies to expense in the year incurred.
4. Recognition of gains on certain sale and leaseback transactions. U.S. GAAP treats these as financing transactions and defers and then amortizes the gain over the term of the financing.
5. Classification of the sale of some divisions as Discontinued Operations under IASC GAAP that would appear as part of Continuing Operations under U.S. GAAP.

Required
   a. Adjust the financial statements of these three companies to achieve data comparability to the extent you think it appropriate.
   b. Analyze the time series and cross-sectional profitability and risk of these companies, identifying strategic and other factors that might explain differences across time and across firms.

EXHIBIT 8.47

Nokia
Statements of Cash Flows
(amounts in millions)
(Case 8.2)

	Year Ended December 31		
	1995	1996	1997
Operations			
Net Income	FIM 4,087	FIM 3,044	FIM 5,998
Depreciation and Amortization	1,825	2,236	2,762
Other Addbacks	0	73	800
Other Subtractions	(632)	(27)	(210)
(Increase) Decrease in Accounts Receivable	(3,430)	(917)	(1,616)
(Increase) Decrease in Inventories	(3,478)	3,113	(718)
(Increase) Decrease in Prepayments	0	0	0
Increase (Decrease) in Accounts Payable	724	(518)	1,306
Increase (Decrease) in Other Current Liabilities	833	1,342	1,905
Cash Flow from Continuing Operations	FIM (71)	FIM 8,346	FIM 10,227
Cash from Discontinued Operations	(496)	(378)	86
Cash Flow from Operations	FIM (567)	FIM 7,968	FIM 10,313
Investing			
Sale of Marketable Securities	FIM 0	FIM 0	FIM 0
Acquisition of Marketable Securities	(0)	(0)	0
Sale of Property, Plant, and Equipment	396	293	506
Acquisition of Property, Plant, and Equipment	(3,299)	(2,028)	(2,402)
Other Investing Transactions	2,033	(1,208)	(1,269)
Cash Flow from Investing	FIM (870)	FIM (3,118)	FIM (3,165)
Financing			
Increase (Decrease) in Short-Term Borrowing	FIM 1,976	FIM 0	FIM 0
Increase in Long-Term Borrowing	37	242	0
Issue of Common Stock	0	0	153
Decrease in Short-Term Borrowing	0	(675)	(980)
Decrease in Long-Term Borrowing	(754)	0	(1,027)
Acquisition of Common Stock	0	(210)	0
Dividends	(789)	(901)	(1,061)
Other Financing Transactions	(87)	25	469
Cash Flow from Financing	FIM 383	FIM (1,519)	FIM (2,446)
Change in Cash	FIM (1,054)	FIM 3,331	FIM 4,702
Cash—Beginning of Year	5,268	4,214	7,545
Cash—End of Year	FIM 4,214	FIM 7,545	FIM 12,247

EXHIBIT 8.48

Adjustments to Convert Nokia to U.S. GAAP
(in millions of Finnish markka)
(Case 8.2)

	December 31			
	1994	**1995**	**1996**	**1997**
Balance Sheet				
Property, Plant, and Equipment	+277	−567	−535	−715
Other Noncurrent Assets	− 20	+578	+365	+534
Other Noncurrent Liabilities	+448	+244	− 85	−259
Retained Earnings	−191	−233	− 85	+ 78

	Year Ended December 31		
	1995	**1996**	**1997**
Other Income	−134	−129	—
Selling and Administrative Expenses	−173	−220	−148
Research and Development Expenditures ..	+844	−32	+180
Income Tax Expense	−602	+213	−169
Income from Continuing Operations	−203	−90	+137
Income from Discontinued Operations	+619	+129	—

CHAPTER 9

RISK ANALYSIS:
AN EXTENDED LOOK

Learning Objectives

1. Apply financial statement ratios and other analytical tools to assess the credit risk of a firm.
2. Explore the strengths and weaknesses of various univariate and multivariate statistical models for predicting bankruptcy.
3. Apply multivariate statistical models for predicting bankruptcy to the financial statements of actual companies.
4. Explore the relation between financial statement measures of risk and market equity beta.

Chapter 8 extended the discussion in Chapter 3 of profitability analysis by examining the relation between various economic attributes and strategic choices of a firm and accounting measures of its profitability (ROA, ROCE). This chapter extends Chapter 3's discussion of risk analysis by examining the relation between economic and market measures of risk (financial distress, market beta) and accounting measures of risk (short-term liquidity ratios, long-term solvency ratios).

Research on the risk of a firm has not evolved to the point where a well-structured and well-accepted theory of risk exists. Multiple research streams have studied various dimensions of risk using a variety of research methodologies. This chapter incorporates the findings of these multiple research streams into a framework for analyzing risk using financial statement data.

DEFINITION OF RISK

The field of finance identifies two types of firm-specific risk: *credit risk* and *bankruptcy risk*. Credit risk relates to a firm's ability to make interest and principal payments on borrowings. Bankruptcy risk relates to the likelihood that a firm will file for bankruptcy and perhaps subsequently liquidate. We might view these two types of risk as states of *financial distress* that fall along a continuum of increasing gravity from (1) failing to make a required interest payment on time, to (2) defaulting on a principal payment on debt, to (3) filing for bankruptcy, to (4) liquidating a firm. Analysts concerned with the economic loss of a portion or all of the amount lent to or invested in a firm can examine a firm's position on this financial distress continuum. We describe and illustrate tools for analyzing credit risk and bankruptcy risk in this chapter.

Not even 5 percent of publicly traded firms experience financial distress as defined by one of the four states above. In the normal course of events, we therefore need a broader definition that encompasses elements of risk common to all firms. One broader definition of risk is based on attempts to explain differences in market rates of return of common stocks. Economic theory holds that differences in market returns must relate to differences in perceived risk.

Studies of this returns/risk relationship use market equity beta as the measure of risk. Market equity beta measures the covariability of a firm's returns with the returns of all securities in the market.

Because only a small percentage of publicly traded firms experience significant risk from financial distress, additional factors besides credit risk and bankruptcy risk must explain market beta. We discuss the research relating financial statement data and market equity beta later in the chapter.

ANALYZING CREDIT RISK

This section describes the sources of debt financing and the tools for analyzing credit risk.

SOURCES OF DEBT FINANCING

Firms obtain debt, or creditor, financing from various sources, depending on the use of the funds, the elapsed time to repayment, and the degree of security required by the lender. The most common sources of debt financing include:

1. **Commercial Banks** Commercial banks lend funds to firms to finance working capital needs, such as to carry accounts receivable until customers pay or to hold inventory until sold. These loans typically extend for periods of less than one year and therefore appear in current liabilities on the balance sheet under notes payable. Often, accounts receivable and inventory serve as collateral in the event the firm is unable to repay the loan at maturity. Commercial banks

also provide funds to purchase equipment, buildings, and other long-term assets. These loans extend for periods of 20 or more years and are collateralized by the specific asset financed. These loans appear in the long-term debt payable category among other noncurrent liabilities on the balance sheet. The notes to the financial statements disclose whether certain assets serve as collateral for borrowings.

2. **Other Financial Institutions** Firms may also obtain funds from insurance companies, finance companies, and other financial institutions. Such loans typically finance long-term assets, with the assets serving as collateral for the borrowing.

3. **Commercial Paper Market** Firms with very short-term needs for cash, such as to meet semimonthly payroll before collecting cash from accounts receivable monthly, may issue commercial paper. Commercial paper is typically unsecured (that is, not collateralized by specific assets). As a consequence, large, established firms with solid credit status most easily access the commercial paper market for funds. Firms generally include commercial paper in notes payable among current liabilities on the balance sheet. Lenders, or investors in the commercial paper, include financial institutions, other business enterprises with temporarily excess cash, and money market mutual funds.

4. **Unsecured Debt Market** Firms needing long-term sources of funds can issue bonds on the open market. These bonds are typically unsecured (that is, not collateralized by specific assets), and are priced according to the overall credit quality of the issuer, the term to maturity of the bonds, and the general level of interest rates in the market. In the event of bankruptcy, investors in these bonds have a secondary claim on a firm's assets after secured (collateralized) lenders receive payment. Unsecured creditors, however, have senior claims to preferred or common shareholders in the event of bankruptcy. These bonds appear in long-term debt payable on the balance sheet. Investors in these bonds include financial institutions, mutual funds, pension funds, and individuals.

5. **Suppliers** Suppliers of various goods and services that do not require firms to pay immediately implicitly provide funds to the firm. Such financing may either carry no explicit interest charge for the right to delay payment (suppliers may include an implicit interest charge in the price of the good or service) or specify explicit interest that the firm is to pay. Suppliers of raw materials or merchandise inventories may require that the inventories serve as collateral for the delayed payment.

THE C'S OF CREDIT RISK ANALYSIS

Common practice is to characterize the factors that an analyst should examine when assessing credit risk in terms of a series of terms that begin with the letter "C." Although the list below is not an exhaustive catalogue of the "C" terms that we have seen from various financial institutions, it includes the factors of primary importance in credit analysis.

Circumstances Leading to Need for the Loan.   The reason that a firm needs to borrow affects the riskiness of the loan and the likelihood of repayment. Consider some examples.

Example 1.   W.T. Grant Company, a discount retail chain, filed for bankruptcy in 1975. Its bankruptcy has become a classic example of how poorly designed and implemented controls can lead a firm into financial distress (see Case 2.1). Between 1968 and 1975, Grant experienced increasing difficulty collecting its accounts receivable from credit card customers. The number of days that accounts receivable were outstanding continually increased. To finance the buildup of its accounts receivable, Grant borrowed short-term funds from commercial banks. The company failed, however, to fix the credit extension and cash collection problems with its receivables. The bank loans simply kept Grant in business in an ever-worsening credit situation. Lending to satisfy cash flow needs related to an unsolved problem or difficulty can be highly risky.

Example 2.   Toys "R" Us purchases toys, games, and other entertainment products in September and October in anticipation of heavy demand during the end-of-the year holiday season. It typically pays its suppliers within 30 days for these purchases, but doesn't collect cash from customers until December, January, or later. To finance its inventory, Toys "R" Us borrows short term from its banks. It repays these loans with cash collected from customers. Lending to satisfy cash flow needs related to ongoing seasonal business operations is generally relatively low risk. Toys "R" Us has an established brand name and predictable demand. Although some risk exists that the products offered will not meet customer preferences in a particular year, Toys "R" Us offers a sufficiently diverse product line that failure to collect sufficient cash to repay the bank loan is low.

Example 3.   Wal-Mart Stores has grown the number of its stores at a rate of approximately 12 percent per year during the last five years. The fastest growth is in its superstores, which represent a combination of its traditional discount store and a grocery store. Wal-Mart borrows a large portion of the funds needed to construct new stores using 20- to 25-year loans (Wal-Mart also enters into leases for a significant portion of the space needed for its new stores). Such loans are relatively low risk, given Wal-Mart's operating success in the past and the existence of land and buildings that serve as collateral for the loans.

Example 4.   Data General Corporation has maintained a presence in the midsize computer market for several decades. Technological advances and aggressive marketing by competitors have eroded its share of the computer market more recently. If Data General wanted to develop new technologies for Internet products and needed to borrow funds to finance its research and development effort, such a loan would likely be relatively high-risk. Data General would be embarking on a new line of business for which it does not necessarily have a competitive advantage. Technological change occurs rapidly in Internet products, which could make any products developed by Data General obsolete. In addition, expenditures on research and development will not likely result in assets that can serve as collateral for the loan.

Thus, lending to established firms for ongoing operating needs presents the lowest credit risk. Lending to firms experiencing operating problems, lending to emerging businesses, and lending to support investments in intangible assets typically carry higher risks. Lenders should be wary of borrowers that have only a vague idea of how they intend to use the proceeds of a loan.

Cash Flows.   A second "C" term is cash flow. Lenders want firms to generate sufficient cash flow to pay interest and repay principal on a loan so they don't have to rely on selling the collateral. Tools for studying the cash-generating ability of a firm include examination of the statement of cash flows for recent years, computation of various cash flow-based financial ratios, and the study of projected financial statements.

Statement of Cash Flows.   Chapter 2 discussed in detail the relation between net income and cash flow from operations for various types of businesses and the relation between cash flows from operating, investing, and financing activities for firms at various stages of their life cycles. An examination of a firm's statement of cash flows for the most recent three or four years will indicate whether the relations expected for a particular business occurred.

Some of the indicators of potential cash flow problems, if observed for several years in a row, include:

1. Growth in accounts receivable or inventories that exceeds the growth rate in sales.
2. Increases in accounts payable that exceed the increase in inventories.
3. Other current liabilities that grow at a faster rate than sales.
4. Persistent negative cash flow from operations, either because of net losses or substantial increases in net working capital.
5. Capital expenditures that substantially exceed cash flow from operations. Although the analyst should expect this shortfall pattern for a rapidly growing, capital-intensive firm, a negative free cash flow (cash flow from operations minus capital expenditures) indicates a firm's continuing need for external financing to sustain that growth.
6. Reductions in capital expenditures over time. Although such reductions conserve cash in the near term, they might signal that the firm expects declines in future sales, earnings, and operating cash flows.
7. Sales of marketable securities in excess of purchases of marketable securities. Such sales provide cash immediately, but might signal the inability of a firm's operations to provide adequate cash flow to finance working capital and long-term investments. Firms may sell marketable securities to obtain the cash needed for these purposes. Marketable securities sales, however, may not be an indicator of cash flow problems if the firm were to invest the temporarily excess cash in order to subsequently make a corporate acquisition or acquire fixed assets.
8. A substantial shift from long-term borrowing to short-term borrowing. An increase in short-term borrowing may signal a firm's inability to obtain long-term loans because lenders are uncertain about a firm's future.
9. A reduction or elimination of dividend payments. Although such actions conserve cash in the near term, the stock market generally interprets such dividend changes as a negative signal about a firm's future prospects.

Although one of these indicators by itself would not represent conclusive evidence of cash flow problems, the presence of any of these circumstances signals the need to obtain explanations from management to see if an emerging cash flow problem may exist.

Cash Flow Financial Ratios.   In Chapter 3 we considered several financial statement ratios that might signal a cash flow problem:

1. **Cash Flow from Operations to Average Current Liabilities** This ratio indicates the ability of a firm to generate sufficient cash flows from operations to repay liabilities coming due within the next year. As Chapter 3 indicated, a ratio in excess of 40 percent is common for a financially healthy firm.
2. **Cash Flow from Operations to Average Total Liabilities** This ratio indicates the ability of a firm to generate sufficient cash flow to repay all liabilities. Chapter 3 indicated that a ratio in excess of 20 percent is common for a financially healthy firm.
3. **Cash Flow from Operations to Capital Expenditures** This ratio indicates the ability of a firm to finance capital expenditures with operating cash flows. A ratio lower than 1.0 indicates a need to access other sources of capital to finance capital expenditures. Although the analyst might expect a ratio lower than 1.0 for a rapidly growing, capital-intensive firm, such a ratio does indicate that the firm will need to continue to find various sources of external capital if its growth is to continue.

Projected Financial Statements.   Projected financial statements, sometimes referred to as *pro forma* financial statements, represent forecasted income statements, balance sheets, and statements of cash flows for some number of years into the future. (The next chapter describes the procedures for preparing projected financial statements.) Lenders may require potential borrowers to prepare such statements to demonstrate the borrower's ability to repay the loan with interest as it comes due. The credit analyst should question each of the important assumptions underlying these projected financial statements (such as sales growth, cost structure, capital expenditure plans).

The analyst should also assess the sensitivity of the projected cash flows to changes in key assumptions. Suppose, for example, that sales grow by 4 percent instead of the 6 percent projected. Suppose that raw materials costs increase 5 percent instead of the 3 percent projected. Suppose that additional plant expenditures are necessary because a firm reaches capacity limits with a higher-than-expected sales increase? What impact will each of these changed assumptions have on cash flow from operations?

Collateral.   A third consideration when assessing credit risk is the availability and value of collateral for a loan. If cash flows are insufficient to pay interest and repay the principal on a loan, the lender has the right to obtain any collateral pledged in support of the loan. Depending on the nature of the collateral pledged, the analyst might examine the following:

1. **Marketable Securities** Marketable equity securities representing less than a 20 percent ownership appear on the balance sheet at market value. The analyst can assess whether the market value of securities pledged as collateral exceeds the unpaid balance of a loan. Marketable securities representing 20 percent or more of another entity appear on the balance sheet using the equity method (discussed in Chapter 7). Determining whether the market value of such securities adequately covers the unpaid balance of a loan is more difficult. The analyst might examine the amount reported as equity in earnings of affiliates in recent years to assess the level and changes in profitability of the investee.

2. **Accounts Receivable** A lender should assess whether the current value of accounts receivable is sufficient to cover the unpaid portion of a loan collateralized by accounts receivable. Determining whether the book value of accounts receivable accurately reflects their market value involves an examination of changes in the provision for uncollectible accounts relative to sales, the balance in allowance for uncollectible accounts relative to gross accounts receivable, the amount of accounts written off as uncollectible relative to gross accounts receivable, and the number of days receivables are outstanding.

3. **Inventories** The analyst should examine changes in the inventory turnover rate, in the cost of goods sold to sales percentage, and in the mix of raw materials, work in process inventories, and finished goods inventories to identify possible inventory obsolescence problems. The analyst should remember that the market value of LIFO inventories will likely exceed their book value, while FIFO inventories will appear at an amount closer to market value. Firms using LIFO must report the excess of market or FIFO value over LIFO cost, permitting the analyst to assess the adequacy of LIFO inventories to cover the unpaid balance on a loan collateralized by inventories.

4. **Property, Plant, and Equipment** Firms often pledge fixed assets as collateral for long-term borrowing. Determining the market values of such assets is difficult using reported financial statement information because of the use of historical cost valuations. Market values of unique, firm-specific assets are particularly difficult to ascertain. Clues indicating market value declines include restructuring charges or asset impairment charges related to such assets or recent sales at a loss.

Earlier we indicated that some lending occurs on a nonsecured basis (that is, the borrower pledges no specific collateral in support of the loan). In these cases, the analyst should study the notes to the financial statements to ascertain how much, if any, of the borrower's assets are not already pledged or otherwise restricted. The liquidation value of such assets represents the available resources of a firm to repay unsecured creditors. For smaller, family-owned businesses, an additional source of collateral may be the personal assets of management or major shareholders. Have managers or shareholders pledged their personal residences, debt or equity securities owned, or other assets to serve as additional collateral for a business loan?

Capacity for Debt.   Closely related to a firm's cash-generating ability and available collateral is a firm's capacity to assume additional debt. A firm's cash flows and collateral represent the means to repay the debt. Most firms do not borrow up to the limit of their debt capacity. Lenders want to be sure that a margin of safety exists. Although no precise methodology exists to measure debt capacity, the analyst can study various financial statement ratios when assessing debt capacity.

1. **Debt Ratios** Chapter 3 describes several ratios that relate the amount of long-term debt or total liabilities to shareholders' equity or total assets as measures of the proportion of liabilities in the capital structure. In general, the higher the debt ratios, the higher the credit risk and the lower the unused debt capacity of the firm. When measuring debt ratios, the analyst must be careful to consider possible off-balance sheet obligations (such as operating lease commitments, or underfunded pension or health care benefit obligations). The analyst can compare a particular firm's debt ratios with those of similar firms in the same industry.
2. **Interest Coverage Ratio** The number of times that interest payments are covered by operating income before interest and income taxes serves as a gauge of the margin of safety provided by operations to service debt. When firms make heavy use of operating leases for their fixed assets, as is common for airlines and retail stores, the analyst might convert the operating leases to capital leases for the purpose of computing the interest coverage ratio. The analyst adds back the lease payments (that is, rent expense) to net income when computing cash flows from operations in the numerator of this ratio and includes the lease payments in the denominator. When the interest coverage ratio falls below approximately 2.0, the credit risk is generally considered high. Interest coverage ratios that exceed 4.0 or 5.0 usually suggest a capacity to carry additional debt.

Contingencies.   The credit standing of a firm could change abruptly in the future if current uncertainties turn out negatively for the firm. Questions that the analyst might ask include the following:

1. Is the firm a defendant in a major lawsuit involving its principal products, its technological advantages, its income tax returns, or other core endeavors whose outcome could change its profitability and cash flows in the future? Consider, for example, the uncertainty facing the tobacco industry at the present time as lawsuits in the United States remain unsettled. Many large firms are engaged in lawsuits all the time as a normal part of their business. Most of their losses are insured. Negative legal judgments will likely have a more pronounced effect on smaller firms, however, because they have less of a resource base to defend themselves and sustain such losses, and may not carry adequate insurance.
2. Has the firm served as guarantor on a loan by a subsidiary, joint venture, or corporate officer that, if payment is required, will consume cash flows otherwise available to service other debt obligations?
3. Has the firm committed itself to make payments related to derivative financial instruments that could adversely affect future cash flows if interest rates, exchange rates, or other prices change significantly in an unexpected direction?

4. Is the firm dependent on one or a few key employees, contracts or license agreements, or technologies, whose loss could substantially affect the viability of the business?

Obtaining answers to such questions will require the analyst to read the notes to the financial statement carefully, and to ask astute questions of management, attorneys, and others.

Character of Management. An intangible that can offset to some extent otherwise weak signals about the creditworthiness of a firm is the character of its management. Has the management team successfully weathered previous operating problems and challenges that could have bankrupted most firms? Has the management team delivered in the past on projections made with regard to sales levels, cost reductions, new product development, and similar operating targets? Does a firm have a reputation for honest and fair dealings with suppliers, customers, bankers, and others? Lenders are also more comfortable lending to firms whose managers have a substantial portion of their personal wealth invested in the firm's common equity. Managers in these situations have incentives to operate the firm profitably and avoid defaulting on debt to increase the value of their equity holding.

Conditions. Lenders often place restrictions, or constraints, on a firm to protect their interests. Such restrictions might include minimum or maximum levels of certain financial ratios; an example might be that the current ratio cannot decline below 1.2, or the debt/equity ratio cannot exceed 75 percent. Firms may also be precluded from paying dividends or taking on new financing that gives the creditors rights senior to existing lenders in the event of bankruptcy. Violation of these debt constraints, or covenants, could result in the need to repay borrowing immediately.

Although debt covenants can protect the interest of senior, collateralized lenders, they can place less senior lenders in jeopardy if the firm must quickly liquidate assets to repay debt. Thus, debt covenants are a two-edged sword from the viewpoint of credit risk. They provide protection against undue deterioration in the financial condition of a firm but at the same time increase the likelihood of default or bankruptcy if the constraints are too tight.

SUMMARY OF CREDIT RISK ANALYSIS

Existing lenders should monitor a firm's credit risk on an ongoing basis. New lenders should assess how their loan will incrementally affect the firm's credit risk.

The analysis of credit risk is a multifaceted endeavor. The financial statements and notes provide evidence on a firm's cash-generating ability, extent of collateralized assets, amount of unused debt capacity, and constraints imposed by existing borrowing agreements. Although the financial statements might provide some clues, the credit analyst must search beyond the financial statements for information on the market value of collateral, contingencies confronting the firm, and the character of management.

ANALYZING BANKRUPTCY RISK

This section discusses the analysis of bankruptcy risk using information in the financial statements.

THE BANKRUPTCY PROCESS

Firms may file a petition for bankruptcy with the relevant bankruptcy federal court. The majority of firms file under Chapter XI of the National Bankruptcy Code. Under Chapter XI, firms have four months in which to present a plan of reorganization to the court. After that period elapses, creditors, employees, and others can file their plans of reorganization. One such plan might include immediately selling the assets of the business and paying creditors the amounts due.

The court decides which plan provides the fairest treatment for all parties concerned. While in bankruptcy, creditors cannot demand payment of their claims. The court oversees the execution of the reorganization. When the court determines that the firm has executed the plan of reorganization successfully and appears to be a viable entity, the firm is released from bankruptcy.

A Chapter VII filing for bankruptcy entails an immediate sale, or liquidation, of the firm's assets and a distribution of the proceeds to the various claimants in the order of their priority.

Firms typically file for bankruptcy when they have insufficient cash to pay creditors' claims coming due. If a firm did not file for bankruptcy, creditors could exercise their right to any collateral pledged to secure their lending and effectively begin liquidation of the firm. In an effort to keep assets intact and allow time for the firm to reorganize itself, the firm instead files for bankruptcy.

In recent years, some firms have filed for bankruptcy for reasons other than insufficient liquid resources to pay creditors. Some firms have filed to avoid labor contracts that they consider too costly. Other firms facing potentially costly litigation have filed for bankruptcy as a means of forcing the contending party to negotiate a settlement.

MODELS OF BANKRUPTCY PREDICTION

Empirical studies of bankruptcy attempt to distinguish the financial characteristics of firms that file for bankruptcy from those that do not, a *dichotomous outcome* state. The objective is to develop a model that predicts which firms will likely file for bankruptcy one or more years before the filing takes place.

Univariate Bankruptcy Prediction Models.   Research in the mid-1960s used univariate analysis in developing bankruptcy prediction models. Univariate models examine the relation between a particular financial statement ratio and bankruptcy. Multivariate models, discussed later, combine several financial statement ratios to determine if the set of ratios together can improve bankruptcy prediction.

Beaver studied 29 financial statement ratios for the five years preceding bankruptcy for a sample of bankrupt and nonbankrupt firms.[1] The objective was to identify the ratios that distinguish best between these two groups of firms and to determine how many years prior to bankruptcy the differences in the ratios emerged. The six ratios with the best discriminating power (and the nature of the risk each ratio measures) are:

1. Net Income before Depreciation, Depletion, and Amortization/Total Liabilities (long-term solvency risk).[2]
2. Net Income/Total Assets (profitability).
3. Total Debt/Total Assets (long-term solvency risk).
4. Net Working Capital/Total Assets (short-term liquidity risk).
5. Current Assets/Current Liabilities (short-term liquidity risk).
6. Cash, Marketable Securities, Accounts Receivable/Operating Expenses excluding Depreciation, Depletion, and Amortization (short-term liquidity risk).[3]

Note that this list includes profitability, short-term liquidity risk, and long-term solvency risk ratios. Beaver's best predictor was net income before depreciation, depletion, and amortization divided by total liabilities.

Exhibit 9.1 summarizes the success of this ratio in correctly classifying sample firms as bankrupt or not for each of the five years preceding bankruptcy. The classification accuracy increases as bankruptcy approached, but is close to 80 percent for as early as five years preceding bankruptcy.

The error rates deserve particular attention, however. A Type I error is classifying a firm as nonbankrupt when it ultimately goes bankrupt. A Type II error is classifying a firm as bankrupt that ultimately survives. A Type I error is more costly to an investor because it subjects the investor to the likelihood of losing the full amount invested. A Type II error costs the investor the opportunity cost of funds invested.

Note that the Type I error rates are much higher than the Type II error rates in Beaver's study. Four years prior to bankruptcy, the net income before depreciation, depletion, and amortization to total liabilities ratio does only slightly better in predicting which firms will enter bankruptcy than flipping a coin.

Univariate analysis helps to identify factors related to bankruptcy and is therefore a necessary step in the initial development of a theory of risk. What univariate analysis does not provide is a means of measuring the relative importance of individual financial statement ratios or of combining them when assessing risk. For example,

---

[1] William Beaver, "Financial Ratios as Predictors of Failure," *Empirical Research in Accounting: Selected Studies, 1966,* supplement to *Journal of Accounting Research* (1966), pp. 71–102.

[2] This ratio is similar to the cash flow from operations to total liabilities ratio discussed earlier (and in Chapter 3) except that the numerator of Beaver's ratio does not include changes in working capital accounts. Published "funds flow" statements at the time of Beaver's study defined funds as working capital (instead of cash).

[3] This ratio, referred to as the defensive interval, indicates the proportion of a year that a firm could continue to operate by paying cash operating expenses with cash and near-cash assets.

EXHIBIT 9.1

Classification Accuracy and Error Rates for Net Income before Depreciation, Depletion and Amortization/Total Liabilities

Years Prior To Bankruptcy	Proportion Correctly Classified	Error Rate	
		Type I	Type II
5	78%	42%	4%
4	76%	47%	3%
3	77%	37%	8%
2	79%	34%	8%
1	87%	22%	5%

SOURCE: William Beaver, "Financial Ratios as Predictors of Failure," *Empirical Research in Accounting: Selected Studies*, 1966, supplement to *Journal of Accounting Research* (1966), p. 90.

does a firm with a high current ratio and a high debt to assets ratio have more bankruptcy risk than a firm with a low current ratio and low debt to assets ratio?

Multivariate Bankruptcy Prediction Models Using Multiple Discriminant Analysis.   The deficiencies of univariate analysis led researchers during the late 1960s and throughout the 1970s to use multiple discriminant analysis (MDA), a multivariate statistical technique, to develop bankruptcy prediction models. Researchers typically select a sample of bankrupt firms and match these firms with healthy firms of approximately the same size and in the same industry. The matching procedure attempts to control for size and industry factors so that the researcher can examine the impact of other factors that might explain bankruptcy.

The researcher then calculates a large number of financial statement ratios expected *a priori* to explain bankruptcy. Using these financial ratios as inputs, the MDA model selects the subset of ratios that best discriminates between bankrupt and nonbankrupt firms (usually four to six ratios). The resulting MDA model includes a set of coefficients that, when multiplied by the particular financial statement ratios and then summed, yield a multivariate score. Scores below a critical cutoff point suggest a high probability of bankruptcy, and scores above that point suggest a low probability. Researchers usually develop the MDA model on an estimation sample and then apply the resulting model to a separate holdout, or prediction, sample to check on the generalizability and predictability of the model.

Perhaps the best-known MDA bankruptcy prediction model is Altman's Z-score.[4] Altman used data for manufacturing firms to develop the model. The calculation of the Z-score appears on the following page:

---

[4]Edward Altman, "Financial Ratios, Discriminant Analysis, and the Prediction of Corporate Bankruptcy," *Journal of Finance* (September 1968), pp. 589–609.

$$\text{Z-score} = 1.2 \left[\frac{\text{Net Working Capital}}{\text{Total Assets}}\right] + 1.4 \left[\frac{\text{Retained Earnings}}{\text{Total Assets}}\right]$$

$$+ 3.3 \left[\frac{\text{Earnings Before Interest and Taxes}}{\text{Total Assets}}\right]$$

$$+ 0.6 \left[\frac{\text{Market Value of Equity}}{\text{Book Value of Liabilities}}\right] + 1.0 \left[\frac{\text{Sales}}{\text{Total Assets}}\right]$$

Each of the ratios captures a different dimension of profitability or risk:

1. **Net Working Capital/Total Assets** This ratio measure the proportion of total assets representing relatively liquid net current assets (current assets minus current liabilities). It serves as a measure of short-term liquidity risk.
2. **Retained Earnings/Total Assets** This ratio captures accumulated profitability and relative age of a firm.
3. **Earnings before Interest and Taxes/Total Assets** This ratio is a version of ROA. It measures current profitability.
4. **Market Value of Equity/Book Value of Liabilities** This is a form of the debt/equity ratio, but it incorporates the market's assessment of the value of the firm's shareholders' equity. This ratio therefore measures long-term solvency risk and the market's overall assessment of the profitability and risk of the firm.
5. **Sales/Total Assets** This ratio is similar to the total assets turnover ratio and indicates the ability of a firm to use assets to generate sales.

In applying this model, Altman found that Z-scores of less than 1.81 indicate a high probability of bankruptcy, while Z-scores higher than 3.00 indicate a low probability of bankruptcy. Scores between 1.81 and 3.00 are in the gray area.

Altman obtained a 95 percent correct classification accuracy rate one year prior to bankruptcy, with a Type I error rate of 6 percent and a Type II error rate of 3 percent. The correct classification rate two years before bankruptcy was 83 percent, with a Type I error rate of 28 percent and a Type II error rate of 6 percent. As with Beaver's study, the more costly Type I error rate is larger than the Type II error rate.

The first column of Exhibit 9.2 shows the calculation of Altman's Z-score for Coke for Year 7, the most recent year reported in Appendix A. Coke's Z-score clearly indicates a low probability of bankruptcy. Its policy of not consolidating its bottlers, however, significantly affects its Z-score.

Exhibit 7.6 (see Chapter 7) presents the worksheet to consolidate Coke with its bottlers. The second column of Exhibit 9.2 shows the revised Z-score for Coke based on these consolidated amounts. Revised retained earnings include the full equity of the external interest in the bottlers, although a portion of this equity interest represents contributed capital instead of retained earnings. Earnings before interest, taxes, and the external interest in earnings assumes that interest expense for the bottlers is $769 million (see the discussion in Chapter 7), and that the external interest in earnings is the total earnings of the affiliates minus Coke's share.

EXHIBIT 9.2

Altman's Z-Score for Coke with Its Bottlers Unconsolidated and Consolidated

	Unconsolidated	Consolidated
Net Working Capital/Total Assets		
1.2[($5,910 − $7,406)/$16,161]	−.1111	
1.2[($11,686 − $12,801)/$40,868]		−.0327
Retained Earnings/Total Assets		
1.4[$15,127/$16,161]	1.3104	
1.4[($15,127 + $4,724)/$40,868]		.6800
Earnings before Interest and Taxes/Total Assets		
3.3[($4,596 + $286)/$16,161]	.9969	
3.3[($4,596 + $286 + $769 + $341)/$40,868]		.4838
Market Value of Equity/Book Value of Liabilities		
.6[($52.63 × 2,481)/$10,005]	7.8306	
.6[[($52.63 × 2,481) + $4,724]/$34,712]		2.3387
Sales/Total Assets		
1.0[$18,546/$16,161]	1.1476	
1.0[($18,546 + $7,921 + $2,905 + $11,640)/$40,868]		1.0035
Z-score	11.1744	4.4733

The market value of common stock includes the market value of Coke plus the book value of the external interest in the bottlers. The revised Z-score for Coke of 4.47333, however, still clearly indicates a low probability of bankruptcy.

The principal strengths of MDA are:

1. It incorporates multiple financial ratios simultaneously.
2. It provides the appropriate coefficients for combining the independent variables.
3. It is easy to apply once the initial model has been developed.

The principal criticisms of MDA are:

1. As in univariate applications, the researcher cannot be sure that the MDA model includes all relevant discriminating financial ratios. Most early studies, for example, used accrual basis income statement and balance sheet data instead of cash flow data. MDA selects the best ratios from the ratios provided to it, but that set does not necessarily provide the best explanatory power.
2. The researcher must judge subjectively the value of the cutoff score that best distinguishes bankrupt from nonbankrupt firms.
3. The development and application of the MDA model requires firms to disclose the necessary information to compute each financial ratio. Exclusion of firms because they do not provide the necessary data may bias the MDA model.

4. MDA assumes that each of the financial ratios for bankrupt and nonbankrupt firms is normally distributed. Firms experiencing financial distress often display unusually large or small ratios that can skew the distribution away from normality. In addition, the researcher cannot include dummy variables (for example: 0 if financial statements are audited, 1 if they are not audited). Dummy variables are not normally distributed.
5. MDA requires that the variance-covariance matrix of the explanatory variables be the same for bankrupt and nonbankrupt firms.[5]

Multivariate Bankruptcy Prediction Models Using Logit Analysis. A third stage in the methodological development of bankruptcy prediction research was the move during the 1980s and early 1990s to the use of logit analysis instead of MDA. Logit does not require that the data display the underlying statistical properties described above for MDA. In addition, logit provides a probability of bankruptcy, which is more easily interpretable than the numerical score obtained from MDA. Interpreting the MDA score requires the researcher to choose subjectively the range of scores that indicate high, low, and uncertain likelihoods of bankruptcy.

The development of the logit model proceeds much like that for MDA: (1) initial calculation of a large set of financial ratios, (2) reduction of the set of financial ratios to a subset that best discriminates bankrupt and nonbankrupt firms, and (3) specification of coefficients for each included variable.

The logit model defines the probability of bankruptcy as follows:

$$\text{Probability of Bankruptcy for a Firm} = \frac{1}{1 + e^{-y}}$$

where e equals approximately 2.718282. The exponent y is a multivariate function that includes a constant and coefficients for a set of explanatory variables (that is, financial statement ratios).

Ohlson uses logit to discriminate bankrupt from nonbankrupt firms.[6] Ohlson's model for one year prior to bankruptcy defines y as follows:

$$y = -1.32 - 0.407(\text{SIZE}) + 6.03(\text{TLTA}) - 1.43(\text{WCTA}) + 0.0757(\text{CLCA})$$

$$- 2.37(\text{NITA}) - 1.83(\text{FUTL}) + 0.285(\text{INTWO}) - 1.72(\text{OENEG})$$

$$- 0.521(\text{CHIN})$$

---

[5]For an elaboration of these criticisms, see James A. Ohlson, "Financial Ratios and the Probabilistic Prediction of Bankruptcy," *Journal of Accounting Research* (Spring 1980), pp. 109–131, and Mark E. Zmijewski, "Methodological Issues Related to the Estimation of Financial Distress Prediction Models," *Journal of Accounting Research—Supplement 1984*, pp. 59–82.

[6]Ohlson, op. cit.

The explanatory variables are defined as follows:

SIZE = Natural log of (Total Assets/GNP Implicit Price Deflator Index). The price index is as of the end of the year prior to the year-end of the balance sheet to allow for real-time implementation of the model. Ohlson's model was developed using a GNP index of 100 in 1978.[7] Total assets equal the full dollar value of assets, not the amount reported on the balance sheet with zeros omitted (for example, when the balance sheet reports amounts in thousands or millions).[8]

TLTA = Total Liabilities/Total Assets.

WCTA = (Current Assets − Current Liabilities)/Total Assets.

CLCA = Current Liabilities/Current Assets.

NITA = Net Income/Total Assets.

FUTL = Funds (Working Capital) from Operations/Total Liabilities.

Ohlson developed his model when firms presented a statement of sources and uses of funds, with funds defined as working capital, instead of a statement of cash flows. As Chapter 2 discusses, working capital from operations equals net income plus addbacks for expenses (such as depreciation) and subtractions for revenues (such as equity in earnings of affiliates in excess of dividends received) that do not provide cash. Thus, working capital from operations is an intermediate subtotal between net income and cash flow from operations before adjusting for changes in working capital accounts.

INTWO = One if net income was negative for the last two years and zero otherwise.

OENEG = One if total liabilities exceed total assets and zero otherwise.

CHIN = (Net Income$_t$ − Net Income$_{t-1}$)/(|Net Income$_t$|+|Net Income$_{t-1}$|).

Explanatory variables with a positive coefficient increase the probability of bankruptcy because they decrease e^{-y} toward zero, with the result that the bankruptcy probability function approaches 1/1 or 100 percent. Likewise, independent variables with a negative coefficient decrease the probability of bankruptcy. The analyst must interpret the sign of the coefficient for a particular financial statement ratio cautiously because the coefficients of the various ratios in a multivariate model are not independent of each other. With this caveat in mind, consider each of the nine independent variables in Ohlson's logit model.

1. **SIZE** Larger firms have greater flexibility to curtail capacity, sell assets, and attract debt or equity capital than smaller firms. Thus, the coefficient on SIZE carries a negative coefficient.

---

[7]The GNP index for the fourth quarter of 1996 was 111.05 when 1992 = 100. With 1978 = 100, the equivalent index for the fourth quarter of 1996 is 212.1 (111.05/52.35). The *Survey of Current Business* regularly publishes values for the GNP implicit price deflator index.

[8]Most calculators have a button labeled "In" for calculating natural logs.

2. **TLTA** Higher debt ratios increase the probability of bankruptcy. TLTA is a measure of long-term solvency risk. Thus, the coefficient on TLTA is appropriately positive.

3. **WCTA** The higher the proportion of net working capital to total assets, the more liquid are the assets and the lower the probability (negative coefficient) of bankruptcy. WCTA is a measure of short-term liquidity risk.

4. **CLCA** An excess of current liabilities over current assets is also an indicator of short-term liquidity risk, consistent with the positive sign for this coefficient.

5. **NITA** The higher the rate of profitability, the less likely a firm will experience difficulty servicing debt, and therefore the lower the probability (negative coefficient) of bankruptcy.

6. **FUTL** The greater the ability of working capital from operations to cover total liabilities, the lower the probability (negative coefficient) of bankruptcy. This reasoning is similar to that for the cash flow from operations to total liabilities ratio discussed in Chapter 3 (and earlier in this chapter) in connection with assessing credit risk. Thus, FUTL is a measure of short- and long-term solvency risk.

7. **INTWO** A recent history of net losses increases the probability of bankruptcy and results in the positive coefficient for this explanatory variable.

8. **OENEG** This variable would appear to be redundant with TLTA. One would also expect that this variable would carry a positive, instead of a negative, coefficient. The appearance and sign of this variable in the logit model illustrates the difficulty of interpreting individual coefficients in a multivariate statistical model.

9. **CHIN** The change in net income indicates the direction and magnitude of earnings growth or decline. Increased earnings coupled with the negative coefficient suggest a lower probability of bankruptcy. Decreased earnings coupled with the negative coefficient (net positive effect on y) suggest a higher probability of bankruptcy.

Ohlson developed this logit model on 105 bankrupt and 2,058 nonbankrupt firms. He found that using a probability cutoff of 3.8 percent for classifying firms as bankrupt (that is, firms are likely to go bankrupt if the probability derived from applying the logit model exceeds 3.8 percent) minimizes Type I and Type II errors. At this probability cutoff point, the model correctly classified 87.6 percent of his bankrupt firm sample and 82.6 percent of the nonbankrupt firms.

Exhibit 9.3 shows calculation of the value of y in Ohlson's logit model for Coke for Year 7. The calculation of the probability of bankruptcy is as follows:[9]

$$1/(1 + e^{-(-5.935)}) = 1/(1 + 378.0) = 0.26\%$$

As one would expect, the probability of bankruptcy for Coke is very small. The value of the SIZE variable for Coke dominates the value of y. Coke's recent acquisitions of its own stock reduce shareholders' equity and tend to increase the value of the TLTA

---

[9]Most calculators have a function for computing e.

EXHIBIT 9.3	
Ohlson's Probability for Coke	
Constant	−1.320
SIZE: −.407(18.171)[a]	−7.396
TLTA: 6.03($10,005/$16,161)	3.733
WCTA: −1.43[($5,910 − $7,406)/$16,161]	.133
CLCA: .0757($7,406/$5,910)	.095
NITA: −2.37($3,492/$16,161)	−.512
FUTL: −1.83[($3,463 − $36)/$10,005]	−.627
INTWO: .285(0)	.000
OENEG: −1.72(0)	.000
CHIN: −.521[($3,492 − $2,986)/($3,492 + $2,986)]	−.041
Value of y	−5.935
[a]Natural log of ($16,161,000,000/207.5) = 18.171.	

variable in the calculation of y. Its excess of current liabilities over current assets has only a minor effect. Its healthy profitability increases the values for NITA, FUTL, and CHIN and lowers the value of y (that is, makes it more negative).

APPLICATION OF BANKRUPTCY PREDICTION MODELS TO W.T. GRANT COMPANY

W. T. Grant Company, one of the largest retailers in the United States, filed for bankruptcy in October 1975. Case 2.1 in Chapter 2 includes financial statement data for Grant for its fiscal years ended January 31, 1968, through 1975. Exhibit 9.4 shows the calculation of Altman's Z-score and Ohlson's probability of bankruptcy for each of these fiscal years using amounts from Exhibits 2.27 and 2.28 of Case 2.1.

Altman's model shows a low probability of bankruptcy prior to 1973, a move into the gray area in 1973 and 1974, and a high probability of bankruptcy in 1975. The absolute levels of these Z-scores are inflated because Grant is a retailer, and Altman's model was developed using manufacturing firms. Retailing firms typically have a faster assets turnover than manufacturing firms. In this case, the trend of the Z-score is more meaningful than its absolute level. Note that the Z-score declined steadily beginning in 1970. With a few exceptions in individual years, each of the five components also declined steadily.[10]

The lower panel of Exhibit 9.4 shows the probability of bankruptcy using Ohlson's model. The model indicates a steady increase in the probability of

---

[10]The teaching note to the Grant case indicates that prior to its 1975 fiscal year Grant failed to provide adequately for uncollectible accounts. The effect of this action was to overstate the net working capital/assets, retained earnings/assets, and EBIT/assets components of the Z-score, understate the sales/assets component, and probably overstate the overall Z-score.

EXHIBIT 9.4

Application of Altman's and Ohlson's Bankruptcy Prediction Models to W.T. Grant

Fiscal Year	1968	1969	1970	1971	1972	1973	1974	1975
Altman's Z-Score Model								
Net Working Capital/Assets	.54353	.51341	.44430	.37791	.44814	.36508	.38524	.19390
Retained Earnings/Assets	.43738	.42669	.41929	.38511	.34513	.31023	.25712	.04873
EBIT/Assets	.41358	.44611	.44228	.38848	.27820	.26029	.25470	−.63644
Market Value Equity/ Bank Value Liabilities	.86643	1.01740	.95543	.89539	.69788	.50578	.10211	.01730
Sales/Assets	1.77564	1.76199	1.71325	1.67974	1.57005	1.58678	1.54797	1.62802
Score	4.03656	4.16560	3.97455	3.72663	3.33940	3.02816	2.54714	1.25151
Probability of Bankruptcy Range	Low	Low	Low	Low	Low	Gray	Gray	High
Ohlson's Logit Model								
Constant	−1.320	−1.320	−1.320	−1.320	−1.320	−1.320	−1.320	−1.320
SIZE	−6.504	−6.536	−6.652	−6.686	−6.730	−6.779	−6.801	−6.700
TLTA	3.399	3.315	3.550	3.793	3.984	4.268	4.543	5.396
WCTA	−.648	−.612	−.529	−.450	−.534	−.435	−.459	−.231
CLCA	.037	.039	.044	.049	.043	.049	.048	.061
NITA	−.142	−.148	−.139	−.116	−.086	−.080	−.022	.398
FVTL	−.237	−.243	−.216	−.170	−.128	−.113	−.047	.340
INTWO	.000	.000	.000	.000	.000	.000	.000	.000
OENEG	.000	.000	.000	.000	.000	.000	.000	.000
CHIN	−.011	−.042	−.018	.034	.037	−.026	.273	.521
Total	−5.426	−5.547	−5.280	−4.866	−4.734	−4.436	−3.785	−1.535
Probability of Bankruptcy	.4%	.4%	.5%	.8%	.9%	1.2%	2.2%	17.7%

bankruptcy beginning with the 1970 fiscal year, primarily as a result of increased borrowing. It is not until 1975, however, that the probability of bankruptcy would show cause for alarm (the Ohlson model, using a 3.8 percent cutoff, would not classify Grant as a likely bankruptcy candidate prior to this time).

The seemingly late classification of Grant as a bankruptcy candidate relates again to the influence of the SIZE variable in Ohlson's model. An alternative logit model by Zavgren that does not use size as an explanatory variable shows an increase in the probability of bankruptcy for Grant from 35.0 percent in 1967 to 93.5 percent in 1975.[11]

OTHER METHODOLOGICAL ISSUES IN BANKRUPTCY PREDICTION RESEARCH

Bankruptcy prediction research has addressed several other methodological issues.

Equal Sample Sizes of Bankrupt and Nonbankrupt Firms.
The proportion of bankrupt firms in the economy is substantially smaller than the proportion of nonbankrupt firms. The matched pairs research design common in most studies results in overfitting the MDA and logit models toward the characteristics of bankrupt firms. This overfitting is not necessarily a problem if the objective is to identify characteristics of bankrupt firms. It will, however, likely result in classifying too many nonbankrupt firms as bankrupt (a Type II error) when the model is applied to the broader population of firms. Researchers such as Ohlson have addressed this criticism by using a larger proportion of nonbankrupt firms.

Matching Bankrupt and Nonbankrupt Firms on Size and Industry Characteristics.
The matching process precludes consideration of either size or industry factors as possible explanatory variables for bankruptcy. Yet, small firms may experience greater difficulty obtaining funds when needed than larger firms (consistent with the results for Ohlson's SIZE variable). Industry membership, particularly for cyclical industries, may be an important factor explaining bankruptcy. Some researchers select a random sample of nonbankrupt firms. Another approach is to develop the MDA or logit models for each industry. Platt, for example, develops models for sixteen two-digit SIC industries in which explanatory variables and their coefficients vary across industries.[12] Platt and Platt normalize the financial ratios of each firm by relating them to the corresponding average industry ratio of the firm's industry. They find that normalized financial ratios increase the classification accuracy of their sample to 90 percent, versus 78 percent based on a model of nonnormalized ratios.[13]

---

[11]Christine V. Zavgren, "Assessing the Vulnerability to Failure of American Industrial Firms: A Logistic Analysis," *Journal of Business Finance and Accounting* (Spring 1985), pp. 19–45.

[12]Harlan D. Platt, "The Determinants of Interindustry Failure," *Journal of Economics and Business* (1989), pp. 107–126.

[13]Harlan D. Platt and Marjorie B. Platt, "Development of a Class of Stable Predictive Variables: The Case of Bankruptcy Prediction," *Journal of Business, Finance, and Accounting* (Spring 1990), pp. 31–51.

Use of Accrual versus Cash Flow Variables.   Until the mid-1980s, most bankruptcy research used accrual basis balance sheet and income statement ratios or ratios from the "funds flow" statement, which defined funds as working capital. The transition to a cash definition of funds in the statement of cash flows led researchers to add cash flow variables to bankruptcy prediction models. Casey and Bartczak, among others, find that adding cash flow from operations/current liabilities and cash flow from operations/total liabilities does not add significant explanatory power to models based on accrual basis amounts.[14] Other researchers find contrary results.[15]

Stability in Bankruptcy Prediction Models over Time.   A final methodological issue in bankruptcy prediction research concerns the stability of the bankruptcy prediction models over time, both with regard to the explanatory variables included and their coefficients. Bankruptcy laws and their judicial interpretation change from time to time. The frequency of bankruptcy filings changes as economic conditions change. New financing vehicles emerge that previous MDA or logit models did not consider in their formulation. Examples might be redeemable preferred stock or debt and equity securities with various option rights. To apply bankruptcy models in practical settings, the analyst should periodically update them for these circumstances.

When Begley, Ming, and Watts applied Altman's MDA model and Ohlson's logit model to a sample of bankrupt and nonbankrupt firms in the 1980s—after the periods that the Altman and Ohlson models are based on—they found substantially higher Type I and Type II error rates than those in the original studies.[16] They then reestimated the coefficients for each model using data for a portion of their 1980s sample. The coefficients on the liquidity ratios increased, and the coefficients on the debt ratio decreased, relative to those in the original studies. When they applied the original and reestimated coefficients to the 1980s sample, they observed a reduction in Type II errors but no improvement in Type I errors for the Altman model. For the Ohlson model, they found that a reduction in Type II errors was offset by an increase in Type I error of equal amount. Thus, the revised coefficients result in fewer errors in classifying nonbankrupt firms as bankrupt but similar or worse errors in classifying bankrupt firms as nonbankrupt.

Promising areas for research in bankruptcy prediction include the use of neural networks to carry out the updating process and recent developments in chaos theory.[17]

---

[14]Cornelius J. Casey and Norman J. Bartczak, "Cash Flow—It's Not the Bottom Line," *Harvard Business Review* (June 1984), pp. 61–67.

[15]For a summary of this research, see M. F. Gombola, M. E. Haskins, J. E. Ketz, and D. D. Williams, "Cash Flow in Bankruptcy Prediction," *Financial Management* (Winter 1987), pp. 55–65.

[16]Joy Begley, Jin Ming, and Susan Watts, "Bankruptcy Classification Errors in the 1980s: An Empirical Analysis of Altman's and Ohlson's Models," *Review of Accounting Studies*, vol. 1 (4), (1996), pp. 267–284.

[17]See Delvin D. Hawlay, John D. Johnson, and Dijjotam Raina, "Artificial Neural Systems: A New Tool for Financial Decision Making," *Financial Analysts Journal* (November–December 1990), pp. 63–72; Rick L. Wilson and Ramesh Sharda, "Bankruptcy Prediction Using Neural Networks," *Decision Support Systems* 11 (1994), pp. 545–557; Kun Chang Lee, Ingoo Han, and Youngsig Kwon, "Hybrid Neural Network Models for Bankruptcy Predictions," *Decision Support Systems* 18 (1996), pp. 63–72. See also David H. Lindsay and Annhenrie Campbell, "A Chaos Approach to Bankruptcy Prediction," *Journal of Applied Business Research* (Fall 1996), pp. 1–9.

SYNTHESIS OF BANKRUPTCY PREDICTION RESEARCH

Research similar to the bankruptcy prediction models we have discussed relates to commercial bank lending, bond ratings, corporate restructurings, and corporate liquidations.[18] Although the statistical models used and the relevant financial statement ratios vary across the numerous studies, certain commonalities occur as well. We summarize the factors that seem to explain bankruptcy most consistently across various studies.

Investment Factors.   Two factors relate to the asset side of the balance sheet.

Relative Liquidity of a Firm's Assets.

The probability of financial distress decreases as the relative liquidity of a firm's assets increases. Firms with relatively large proportions of current assets tend to experience less financial distress than firms whose dominant assets are fixed assets or intangible assets. Greater asset liquidity means that a firm will either have or will generate soon the necessary cash to meet creditors' claims.

In this respect, it should be noted that the expected return on the more liquid assets such as cash, marketable securities, and accounts receivable is usually less than the expected return from fixed and intangible assets; this reflects its lower risk. Thus, firms must balance their mix of assets to obtain the desired return/risk profile. The ratios analysts typically use to measure relative liquidity include: cash/total assets, current assets/total assets, and net working capital/total assets. To measure relative illiquidity they use the fixed assets/total assets ratio.

Rate of Asset Turnover.

The investment of funds in any asset eventually ends up in a firm's cash. Firms acquire fixed assets or develop intangibles to produce a salable product (inventory) or deliver a desired service. Goods or services are often sold on account (accounts receivable) and later collected in cash. The more quickly assets turn over, the more quickly funds work their way toward cash on the balance sheet. Thus, a retailer may have the same proportion of fixed assets to total assets as a manufacturing firm, but its other assets, such as accounts receivable or inventories, likely turn over more quickly and are thus more liquid.

Commonly used financial ratios for how quickly assets are turned into cash are total assets turnover, accounts receivable turnover, and inventory turnover. The working capital turnover ratio [= sales/(current assets minus current liabilities)] and fixed asset turnover ratios have not generally showed statistical significance in studies of financial distress.

---

[18]Commercial banking: Edward Altman, *Corporate Financial Distress and Bankruptcy*, 2nd edition, New York: John Wiley & Sons (1993), pp. 245–266; bond ratings: G. E. Pinches and K. A. Mingo, "A Multivariate Analysis of Industrial Bond Ratings," *Journal of Finance* (March 1973), pp. 1–18; corporate restructurings: James E. Seward, "Corporate Restructuring and Reorganization," in *Handbook of Modern Finance*, edited by Dennis Logue, New York: Warren, Gorham & Lamont (1993), pp. E8-1–E8-36; and corporate liquidations: Cornelius J. Casey, Victor McGee, and Clyde P. Stickney, "Discriminating Between Reorganized and Liquidated Firms in Bankruptcy," *Accounting Review* (April 1986), pp. 249–262.

Financing Factors.　Two factors relate to the liability side of the balance sheet.

Relative Proportion of Debt in the Capital Structure.　Firms experience bankruptcy because they are unable to pay liabilities as they come due. The higher the proportion of liabilities in the capital structure, the higher the probability that firms will experience bankruptcy. Firms with lower levels of debt tend to have unused borrowing capacity that they can depend on in times of difficulty. Some measure of the proportion of debt in the capital structure appears in virtually all bankruptcy prediction models. Commonly used debt level ratios include total liabilities/total assets and total liabilities/shareholders' equity.

Relative Proportion of Short-Term Debt in the Capital Structure. A short-term debt factor is relevant because more imminent due dates of debt exacerbate the risk of bankruptcy. Thus, considering only the financing side of the balance sheet, a retailer using extensive short-term bank and creditor financing is likely at greater risk of bankruptcy than a manufacturer using a similar proportion of total liabilities but primarily in the form of long-term debt. A commonly used ratio for the short-term debt factor is current liabilities/total assets.

Operating Factors.　Two factors relate to the operating activities of a firm.

Relative Level of Profitability.　Profitable firms ultimately turn their earnings into cash. Firms with low or negative profitability must often rely on available cash or additional borrowing to meet financial commitments as they come due. Profitable firms are usually able to borrow funds more easily than unprofitable firms. Research indicates that most bankruptcies are preceded by one or more years of poor operating performance. Firms with unused debt capacity can often borrow for a year or two until the operating difficulties reverse. A combination of weak profitability and high debt ratios usually spells financial distress.

Commonly used financial ratios for profitability are: (1) net income/assets, (2) income before interest and taxes/assets, (3) net income/sales, and (4) cash flow from operations/assets. The second profitability measure identifies profitability problems in the core input/output markets of a firm before considering debt service costs and income taxes. The third measure appears in bankruptcy distress prediction models because profit margin, rather than assets turnover, is usually the driving force behind return on assets. The fourth measure substitutes cash flow from operations for net income in measuring profitability, on the premise that cash pays the bills, not earnings.

Variability of Operations.　Firms that experience variability in their operations, perhaps because of cyclical sales patterns, are more in danger of bankruptcy than firms with less variability. During down times in their cycle, such firms must obtain financing to meet financial commitments and maintain operating levels. The risk of bankruptcy in this case relates to the unknown duration of the down portion of the cycle. How many years can a firm hold on until a down cycle reverses? Researchers typically use the change in sales or the change in net income from the previous year to measure variability, although a longer period would seem more reasonable.

Other Possible Explanatory Variables.   Three other factors examined in bankruptcy research warrant discussion.

Size.   Studies of bankruptcy since the early 1980s increasingly identify size as an important explanatory variable. Larger firms generally have access to a wider range of financing sources as well as more flexibility to redeploy assets than smaller firms. Larger firms therefore are less subject to bankruptcy than smaller firms. Most studies use total assets as the measure of size.

Growth.   Studies of bankruptcy often include some measure of growth as a possible explanatory variable; examples are growth in sales, in assets, or in net income. The statistical significance of growth as an independent variable has varied

---

EXHIBIT 9.5

Relation Between Profitability and Risk Ratios and Financial Distress Factors

	Financial Statement Ratio	**Financial Distress Factor**
Profitability Ratios	Profit Margin for ROA	Operating Profitability
	Total Assets Turnover	Liquidity of Assets
	Rate of Return on Assets	Operating Profitability
	Common Earnings Leverage	Operating Profitability; Proportion of Debt in Capital Structure
	Capital Structure Leverage	Proportion of Debt in Capital Structure
	Rate of Return on Common Shareholders' Equity	Operating Profitability
Short-Term Liquidity Ratios	Current Ratio	Liquidity of Assets; Proportion of Short-Term Debt in Capital Structure
	Quick Ratio	Liquidity of Assets; Proportion of Short-Term Debt in Capital Structure
	Cash Flow from Operations to Current Liabilities	Liquidity of Operations; Proportion of Short-Term Debt in Capital Structure
	Days Accounts Receivable	Liquidity of Assets; Assets Turnover
	Days Inventory	Liquidity of Assets; Assets Turnover
	Days Payable	Proportion of Short-Term Debt in Capital Structure
Long-Term Solvency Ratios	Total Liabilities/Total Assets	Proportion of Debt in Capital Structure
	Long-Term Debt Ratio	Proportion of Debt in Capital Structure
	Debt/Equity Ratio Equity	Proportion of Debt in Capital Structure
	Cash Flow from Operations to Total Liabilities	Liquidity of Operations; Proportion of Debt in Capital Structure
	Interest Coverage	Operating Profitability; Proportion of Debt in Capital Structure
	Cash Flow from Operations to Capital Expenditures	Liquidity of Operations; Liquidity of Assets

considerably across studies. It is therefore difficult to conclude much about its relative importance. The mixed results may relate in part to ambiguity as to the way growth relates to bankruptcy. Rapidly growing firms often need external financing to cover cash shortfalls from operations and permit acquisitions of fixed assets. These firms often display financial ratios typical of a firm in financial difficulty (that is, high debt ratios, weak profitability). Yet their growth potential provides access to capital that permits them to survive. Conversely, firms in the late maturity or early decline phases of their life cycles may display healthy financial ratios yet have sufficiently poor prospects that the probability of future financial difficulty is high.

Qualified Audit Opinion. Some studies have examined the information value of a qualified audit opinion in predicting bankruptcy. Hopwood, McKeown, and Mutchler compare the predictive accuracy of qualified audit opinions and models that include only financial ratios in predicting bankruptcy.[19] They find that the qualified audit opinion has much the same predictive accuracy as the models based on financial ratios. This result is not surprising, assuming auditors use bankruptcy prediction models in deciding whether to issue a qualified opinion. Chen and Church find that the negative stock price reaction at the time of a bankruptcy filing is lower for firms that have had previous qualified audit opinions than for firms that have had only clean audit opinions, suggesting that the audit opinion has information content.[20]

Exhibit 9.5 relates financial distress factors to the profitability and risk ratios discussed in Chapter 3.

MARKET RISK

Firms face other risks besides credit and bankruptcy risk. Firms that operate internationally experience in some countries political risks related to changes in governments and the possibility of expropriation of assets. Firms that are unionized face the risk of labor strikes. Firms that are in high technology industries encounter product obsolescence risks.

These and similar sources of risk lead firms only infrequently into financial distress. Yet the investor in a firm's common stock must consider these dimensions of risk when making investment decisions. Economic theory teaches that differences in expected rates of return for different investment alternatives should relate to differences in risk. One way to obtain a comprehensive measure of risk therefore is to look at the equity markets . We can then relate this market measure of risk to financial statement information.

---

[19]William Hopwood, James C. McKeown, and Jane F. Mutchler, "A Reexamination of Auditor versus Model Accuracy within the Context of the Going-Concern Opinion Decision," *Contemporary Accounting Research* (Spring 1994), pp. 409–431.

[20]Kevin C. W. Chen and Bryan K. Church, "Going Concern Opinions and the Market's Reaction to Bankruptcy Filings," *Accounting Review* (January 1996), pp. 117–128.

Studies of market rates of return traditionally use the capital asset pricing model (CAPM). The research typically regresses the returns on a particular firm's common shares [dividends plus (minus) capital gains (losses)] over some period of time on the excess of the returns of all common stocks over the risk-free rate. The regression takes the form:

$$
\begin{array}{c}\text{Returns on}\\\text{Common Stock}\\\text{of a Particular}\\\text{Firm}\end{array} = \begin{array}{c}\text{Risk-Free}\\\text{Interest Rate}\end{array} + \begin{array}{c}\text{Market}\\\text{Beta}\end{array} \left[\begin{array}{c}\text{Market}\\\text{Return}\end{array} - \begin{array}{c}\text{Risk-Free}\\\text{Interest Rate}\end{array}\right]
$$

The beta coefficient measures the covariability of a firm's returns with those of all shares traded on the market (in excess of the risk-free interest rate). Beta captures the *systematic risk* of the firm. The market, through the pricing of a firm's shares, rewards shareholders for the systematic risk that they assume. Elements of risk that do not contribute to systematic risk are referred to as *nonsystematic risk*. By constructing a diversified portfolio of securities, the investor can eliminate nonsystematic risk. Thus, market pricing should provide no returns for the assumption of nonsystematic risk.

Studies of the determinants of market beta have identified three principal explanatory variables:[21]

1. Degree of operating leverage.
2. Degree of financial leverage.
3. Variability of sales.

All these factors cause the earnings of a particular firm to vary over time.

Operating leverage refers to the extent of fixed operating costs in the cost structure. Fixed costs such as depreciation and amortization do not vary with the level of sales. Other costs such as research and development and advertising may vary somewhat with the level of sales, yet even these costs remain relatively fixed for any particular period. The presence of fixed operating costs leads to variations in operating earnings as sales increase and decrease. Likewise, the presence of debt in the capital structure adds a fixed cost for interest and creates the potential that earnings may increase or decrease as the level of sales varies.

The presence of these fixed costs does not necessarily lead to earnings fluctuations over time, however. A firm with stable or growing sales may be able to resort to leasing to adjust the level of fixed assets and related financing to its level of sales, in effect converting fixed costs into variable costs. Firms such as electric utilities, which have high fixed costs because of operating and financial leverage,

---

[21]Robert S. Hamada, "The Effect of a Firm's Capital Structure on the Systematic Risk of Common Stocks," *Journal of Finance* (May 1972), pp. 435–452; Barr Rosenberg and Walk McKibben, "The Prediction of Systematic and Specific Risk in Common Stocks," *Journal of Financial and Quantitative Analysis* (March 1973), pp. 317–333; James M. Gahlon and James A. Gentry, "On the Relationship Between Systematic Risk and Degrees of Operating and Financial Leverage," *Financial Management* (Summer 1982), pp. 15–23.

have historically had monopoly power to price their services to cover costs regardless of demand. They thus do not experience wide variations in earnings.

Operating and financial leverage create variations in earnings when sales vary and firms cannot alter their level of fixed costs. It is typical that capital-intensive firms in cyclical industries experience wide variations in earnings over the business cycle.

Research shows a link between changes in earnings and changes in stock prices.[22] Operating leverage, financial leverage, and variability of sales should therefore result in fluctuations in the market returns for a particular firm's common shares. The average returns for all firms in the market should reflect the average level of operating leverage, financial leverage, and sales variability of these firms; thus, the market beta for a particular firm reflects its degree of variability relative to the average firm. Firms with a market beta of 1.0 experience variability equal to the average. Firms with a beta of more than 1.0 experience greater variability than the average. Firms with a beta of less than 1.0 experience less variability than the average firm. A beta of 1.20 suggests 20 percent greater variability. A beta of 0.80 suggests 20 percent less variability.

Exhibit 9.6 presents data for the 22 industries considered in Chapter 8 that we can use to assess these explanations for market beta. The amounts for market equity beta, assets turnover, capital structure leverage ratio, and ROCE represent the mean of the industry medians for each of the years 1992 through 1996. The standard deviation of ROCE measures the variability in the medians for each industry for the period. The industries are ordered in terms of the level of their average beta.

Although it is not a precise measure, total assets turnover serves as an indicator of the asset intensity of a business. This measure works well for industrial firms, but less well for financial institutions (because their revenues are dissimilar to sales of industrial firms) and retailers (because of the heavy use of operating leases).

The capital structure leverage ratio is an indicator of the amount of financial leverage. An industry's variability in sales, coupled with high fixed operating and financing costs, should show up in a variability in ROCE. The last column of Exhibit 9.6 shows the mean ROCE of each industry relative to its standard deviation.

Betas in certain industries appear to support the theoretical framework we have discussed.

Utilities.   Electric utilities have capital-intensive facilities and use extensive borrowing to finance their acquisition. Thus, utilities have one of the lowest assets turnover ratios and one of the highest capital structure leverage ratios of the industries in Exhibit 9.6. Their standard deviation of ROCE is the smallest of all the industries, consistent with their regulated status during the period analyzed. Thus, their market beta is the smallest.

---

[22]Ray Ball and Philip Brown, "An Empirical Evaluation of Accounting Income Numbers," *Journal of Accounting Research* (Accounting 1968), pp. 159–178.

EXHIBIT 9.6					
Average Industry Median Financial Ratios for 1992 to 1996					
	Market Beta	Assets Turnover	Capital Structure Leverage	ROCE	Standard Deviation of ROCE	ROCE/ Standard Deviation
Industry						
Utilities	.50	.49	3.09	10.99%	.26	42.27
Petroleum	.68	1.19	2.71	9.46%	3.46	2.73
Metal Products	.70	1.32	2.19	10.67%	2.31	4.62
Amusements	.74	.74	2.17	3.57%	.97	3.68
Grocery Stores	.74	3.10	2.73	10.86%	1.21	8.98
Wholesalers–Nondurables	.74	2.23	2.69	9.73%	2.50	3.98
Food Processors	.79	1.41	2.13	10.39%	1.79	5.80
Insurance	.84	.32	4.19	12.88%	1.04	12.38
Wholesalers–Durables	.87	2.05	2.37	7.62%	1.66	4.59
Printing & Publishing	.88	1.19	2.03	12.49%	.65	19.22
Lumber	.89	1.48	2.24	12.53%	3.63	3.45
Metals	.89	1.09	2.20	8.71%	5.27	1.65
Paper	.89	1.04	2.43	9.68%	4.10	2.36
Communication	.90	.49	2.45	4.35%	2.97	1.46
Personal Services	.90	1.20	1.93	10.87%	1.35	8.05
Restaurants	.90	1.48	1.76	6.75%	3.39	1.99
Hotels	.95	.54	2.54	7.65%	4.92	1.55
Business Services	1.01	1.13	1.73	8.45%	1.37	6.17
Retailers–Gen. Merchandise . . .	1.02	2.14	2.51	9.52%	3.29	2.89
Security Brokers	1.02	.55	2.98	17.77%	3.08	5.77
Chemicals	1.13	.75	1.54	1.79%	1.69	1.06
Retailing–Apparel	1.20	2.25	1.75	10.19%	1.65	6.18

Metals and Metal Products.   The metals industry takes iron ore and other minerals and processes them into steel and other intermediate products. This manufacturing process is capital-intensive, and the products tend to portray commodity characteristics. The metal products industry takes steel and other intermediate products and processes them into final products that have an element of differentiation. This manufacturing process is less capital-intensive. Thus, the metal products industry has a faster assets turnover than the metals industry.

The two industry segments have similar capital structure leverage ratios, but the level of ROCE is higher and the standard deviation of ROCE is lower for the metal products segment, consistent with a more differentiated product and lower capital intensity. The market beta of metal products is less than that for metals.

Grocery Stores, Food Processors, and Restaurants.   The market betas of these three segments line up in the order of the standard deviation of their ROCEs. One would expect less variability in the ROCEs of grocery stores and food processors, where demand is relatively price-inelastic, than restaurants, where demand has somewhat greater price elasticity.

Amusements and Hotels.   The amusements and the hotel industry are subject to heavy investments in fixed assets and debt. Economic conditions affect the demand for their products. The amusements industry experienced much less variability in its ROCE than hotels during the period studied, perhaps because some segments of the amusement industry (such as movie theaters and movie rentals) are less affected by economic conditions than travel-related hotel demand. The amusements industry is also somewhat less capital-intensive and debt-intensive than hotels. Thus, amusements show a smaller market beta than hotels.

The market betas for some industry groupings seem inconsistent with the theoretical framework we have described above.

Printing and Publishing, Lumber, and Paper.   The paper industry is more capital-intensive and debt-intensive than the printing and publishing industry and the lumber industry. The paper industry also has a higher standard deviation of ROCE in Exhibit 9.6 than these two segments. Furthermore, the lumber industry has considerably more variability in its ROCE than the printing and publishing segments. Thus, one would expect the market beta of the printing and publishing segment to be much lower than that for lumber, and the market beta for lumber in turn to be much lower than that for paper. Yet, their market betas are quite similar.

Petroleum.   The petroleum industry is relatively capital- and debt-intensive (the same assets turnover and a higher capital structure leverage, for example, as printing and publishing). The standard deviation of its ROCE is also relatively high (contrast with that of printing and publishing). Yet the market beta for petroleum is the second smallest of the 22 industries.

Although operating leverage, financial leverage, and variability of sales appear to explain some of the industry differences in market beta, the manner in which the market trades off one factor against another is not clear.

Bankruptcy risk and market beta risk share several similar explanatory factors. High proportions of fixed assets in the asset structure provide relatively illiquid assets (increasing bankruptcy risk) and high fixed costs (increasing market beta risk). High proportions of debt in the capital structure require regular debt servicing (increasing bankruptcy risk) and high fixed costs for interest (increasing market beta risk). Variability of sales raises the possibility that a firm may not have sufficient liquid assets to service debt (increasing bankruptcy risk) and creates fluctuations in earnings (increasing market beta risk). Bankruptcy risk relates primarily to an illiquidity problem, while market beta risk relates more to an earnings problem. Bankruptcy risk, when it becomes important for a particular firm, intensifies the underlying market beta risk.

Research has shown that the market betas for a sample of firms filing for bankruptcy increased from week 25 prior to filing up to week 9 prior to filing, at the same time that the beta of a matched pair of nonbankrupt firms decreased slightly.[23] The market beta of the bankrupt firms remained relatively stable for the nine weeks preceding the bankruptcy, suggesting that the market had fully reflected the effects of the filing by that time.

The use of market beta as a measure of risk continues to be controversial. Finance textbooks discuss the issues more fully, but the questions below identify some of the concerns.

1. Should the risk-free rate be the rate on short-term U.S. Treasury bills (three- to six-month maturities) or the rate on U.S. Treasury bonds that have maturities similar to the average holding period for common stock investments?
2. Should the measure of market return represent the return on publicly traded common stocks only or on other investments as well (such as bonds, preferred stock, real estate)?
3. What index of market returns should be used: Dow Jones 30 industrials, S&P 500 industrials, all exchange-listed stocks, all publicly traded stocks, all domestic and foreign stocks?
4. Does a single factor (excess of market return over the risk-free rate) adequately capture firm-specific returns, or should the set of independent variables be expanded or replaced with other independent variables (such as size or market value to book value ratios)?
5. Are market betas sufficiently stable over time to serve as a measure of risk?

SUMMARY

An effective analysis of risk requires the analyst to consider a wide range of factors that may include government regulatory status, technological change, management's health, and competitors' actions. This chapter examines those dimensions of risk that have financial consequences and thus impact a firm's financial statements. We have emphasized the need to consider risk as falling along a continuum from low risk to high risk. Most credit analysis falls on the low- to medium-risk side of this continuum. Most bankruptcy risk analysis falls on the medium- to high-risk side. Market equity risk analysis is relevant anywhere along this continuum, but its application is generally to healthy, publicly traded firms.

Common factors come into play in all three settings of risk analysis. Fixed costs related either to operations or to financing constrain the flexibility of a firm to adapt to changing economic, business, and firm-specific conditions. The profitability and cash-generating ability of a firm permit it either to operate within its constraints or to change the constraints in some desirable direction. If the constraints are too strict or a firm's capacity to adapt is too limited, a firm faces the risk of financial distress.

---

[23]Byung T. Ro, Christine V. Zavgren, and Su-Jane Hsieh, "The Effect of Bankruptcy on Systematic Risk of Common Stock: An Empirical Assessment," *Journal of Business, Finance and Accounting* (April 1992), pp. 309–328.

PROBLEMS AND CASES

9.1   COMPUTING AND INTERPRETING BANKRUPTCY PREDICTION RATIOS. Payless Cashways operates a chain of retail stores that offers home improvement products for professional craftspeople such as carpenters, plumbers, and painters as well as do-it-yourself homeowners. The firm filed for Chapter 11 bankruptcy protection on July 21, Year 7. Exhibit 9.7 presents selected financial data for Payless Cashways for each of the four fiscal years ending November 30, Year 3, Year 4, Year 5, and Year 6 that preceded its bankruptcy filing.

Required

a. Compute the value of each the following risk ratios for Year 4, Year 5, and Year 6:
   1. Current ratio (at year-end).
   2. Cash flow from operations to average current liabilities.
   3. Debt equity ratio (at year-end).
   4. Total liabilities to total assets ratio (at year-end).
   5. Cash flow from operations to average total liabilities.
   6. Interest coverage ratio.
   7. Cash flow from operations to capital expenditures.

EXHIBIT 9.7

Financial Data for Payless Cashways
(amounts in thousands)
(Problem 9.1)

Year Ended November	Year 3	Year 4	Year 5	Year 6
Sales	$2,601,003	$ 2,722,539	$ 2,680,186	$ 2,642,829
Net Income (Loss)				
Before Interest and Taxes	$ 151,086	$ 161,792	$ (60,562)	$ 10,458
Interest Expense	$ 125,247	$ 65,571	$ 61,067	$ 60,488
Net Income (Loss)	$ (36,159)	$ 44,889	$ (128,549)	$ (19,078)
Current Assets	$ 427,702	$ 449,870	$ 442,679	$ 450,497
Total Assets	$1,458,481	$ 1,495,882	$ 1,344,436	$1,293,118
Current Liabilities	$ 345,560	$ 310,742	$ 344,279	$ 319,593
Long-Term Debt	$ 640,127	$ 654,131	$ 608,627	$ 618,667
Total Liabilities	$1,071,170	$ 1,060,017	$ 1,036,273	$1,003,387
Retained Earnings (Deficit)	$ (136,259)	$ (91,370)	$ (219,919)	$ (238,997)
Working Capital Provided				
by Operations	$ 96,411	$ 127,335	$ 78,257	$ 95,400
Cash Flow Provided by				
Operations	$ 109,027	$ 117,330	$ 108,428	$ 32,447
Capital Expenditures	$ 49,982	$ 81,906	$ 67,281	$ 40,117
Common Shares Outstanding	39,537	39,874	39,914	39,959
Market Price per Share	$ 11.00	$ 8.25	$ 3.625	$ 1.125
Applicable GNP Implicit Price				
Deflation for Ohlson Model	192.7	197.7	202.7	207.5

b. Compute the value of Altman's Z-score for Payless Cashways for Year 3, Year 4, Year 5, and Year 6.

c. Compute the value of Ohlson's probability of bankruptcy for Payless Cashways for Year 3, Year 4, Year 6, and Year 6. The firm generated a net loss of $15,902,000 in Year 2.

d. Using the analyses in parts a, b. and c above, discuss the most important factors that signal the bankruptcy of Payless Cashways in Year 7.

9.2 APPLYING AND INTERPRETING BANKRUPTCY PREDICTION MODELS. Exhibit 9.8 presents selected financial data for Harvard Industries and Marvel Entertainment for fiscal Year 5 and Year 6. Harvard Industries manufactures automobile components that it sells to automobile manufacturers. Competitive conditions in the automobile industry in recent years have led automobile manufacturers to put pressure on suppliers like Harvard Industries to reduce costs and selling prices. Marvel Entertainment creates and sells comic books, trading cards, and other youth entertainment products, and licenses others to use fictional characters created by Marvel Entertainment in their products. Youth readership of comic books and interest in trading cards have been in steady decline in recent years. Marvel Entertainment recognized a significant asset impairment charge in fiscal Year 6.

Required

a. Compute Altman's Z-score for Harvard Industries and Marvel Entertainment for fiscal Year 5 and Year 6.

EXHIBIT 9.8

Financial Data for Harvard Industries and Marvel Entertainment
(amounts in thousands)
(Problem 9.2)

	Harvard Industries		Marvel Entertainment	
	Year 5	Year 6	Year 5	Year 6
Sales	$ 631,832	$ 824,835	$ 828,900	$ 745,400
Net Income (Loss)				
Before Interest and Taxes	$ 40,258	$ (11,012)	$ 25,100	$ (370,200)
Net Income (Loss) Current Year	$ 6,921	$ (68,712)	$ (48,400)	$ (464,400)
Net Income (Loss) Previous Year	$ 7,630	$ 6,921	$ 61,800	$ (48,400)
Current Assets	$ 195,417	$ 156,226	$ 490,600	$ 399,500
Total Assets	$ 662,262	$ 617,705	$1,226,310	$ 844,000
Current Liabilities	$ 176,000	$ 163,384	$ 318,100	$ 345,800
Total Liabilities	$ 624,817	$ 648,934	$ 948,100	$ 999,700
Retained Earnings (Deficit)	$(115,596)	$(184,308)	$ 114,100	$ (350,300)
Working Capital Provided (Used)				
by Operations	$ 55,054	$ 12,321	$ (7,200)	$(116,200)
Common Shares Outstanding	6,995	7,014	101,703	101,810
Market Price per Share	$ 100.50	$ 85.00	$ 10.625	$ 1.625
Applicable GNP Implicit Price				
Deflator Index for Ohlson Model ...	201.3	206.3	202.7	207.5

b. Compute Ohlson's probability of bankruptcy for Harvard Industries and Marvel Entertainment for fiscal Year 5 and Year 6.
c. How did the bankruptcy risk of Harvard Industries change between fiscal Year 5 and Year 6? Explain.
d. How did the bankruptcy risk of Marvel Entertainment change between Year 5 and Year 6? Explain.
e. Which firm do you think is more likely to file for bankruptcy during fiscal Year 7? Explain, using your analyses from parts a and b.

9.3 APPLYING AND INTERPRETING BANKRUPTCY PREDICTION MODELS. Exhibit 9.9 presents selected financial data for Old America Stores and Levitz Furniture for fiscal Year 6 and Year 7. Old America Stores operates a chain of retail stores that sells craft supplies, framing services, artificial flowers and flower arranging services, baskets, and knick-knacks. Levitz Furniture operates a chain of retail stores offering furniture in a warehouse-showroom format. The firm switched to a value pricing strategy beginning in fiscal Year 6.

Required

a. Compute Altman's Z-score for Old America Stores and Levitz Furniture for fiscal Year 6 and Year 7.

EXHIBIT 9.9

Financial Data for Old America Stores and Levitz Furniture
(amounts in thousands)
(Problem 9.3)

	Old America Stores		Levitz Furniture	
	Year Ended January		Year Ended March	
	Year 6	Year 7	Year 6	Year 7
Sales	$117,943	$134,605	$ 986,622	$ 965,855
Net Income (Loss)				
Before Interest and Taxes	$ 7,986	$ 7,560	$ 42,208	$ 43,859
Net Income (Loss)—Current Year	$ 4,154	$ 3,911	$ (23,753)	$ (27,586)
Net Income (Loss)—Previous Year	$ 2,937	$ 4,154	$ 2,386	$ (23,753)
Current Assets	$ 48,944	$ 56,753	$ 198,046	$ 222,859
Total Assets	$ 76,059	$ 87,991	$ 606,867	$ 934,368
Current Liabilities	$ 19,779	$ 19,002	$ 217,915	$ 271,276
Total Liabilities	$ 28,323	$ 36,150	$ 674,539	$1,028,440
Retained Earnings (Deficit)	$ 5,627	$ 9,537	$(278,365)	$ (305,951)
Working Capital Provided (Used)				
by Operations	$ 6,071	$ 6,603	$ (800)	$ (3,653)
Common Shares Outstanding	4,483	4,515	30,321	$ 30,321
Market Price per Share	$ 8.137	$ 7.50	$ 2.50	$ 2.125
Applicable GNP Implicit Price				
Deflator Index for Ohlson Model	202.7	207.5	204.3	209.0

b. Compute Ohlson's probability of bankruptcy for Old America Stores and Levitz Furniture for fiscal Year 6 and Year 7.

c. How did the bankruptcy risk of Old America Stores change between fiscal Year 6 and Year 7? Explain.

d. How did the bankruptcy risk of Levitz Furniture change between fiscal Year 6 and Year 7? Explain.

e. Which firm do you think is more likely to file for bankruptcy during fiscal Year 8? Explain, using your analyses from parts a and b.

9.4   RELATING MARKET EQUITY BETA TO FINANCIAL STATEMENT ITEMS. Exhibit 9.10 presents average median market equity betas for 1992 through 1996 for firms in five broad industry groups. It also presents ratios based on items taken from the financial statements of firms in these industries. For each of the five broad industry groups, discuss the extent to which the rank ordering of average median market equity betas of the subindustries within each group is consistent with the theory discussed in the chapter relating market equity beta to financial statement items.

EXHIBIT 9.10

Average Median Industry Market Betas and Financial Ratios
for 1992 to 1996
(Problem 9.4)

	Market Beta	Assets Turnover	Capital Structure Leverage	ROCE	Standard Deviation of ROCE	ROCE/ Standard Deviation
Industry						
Group 1 (Wholesalers)						
Wholesalers–Durables	.87	2.05	2.32	7.62%	1.66	4.59
Wholesalers–Non-durables	.74	2.23	2.69	9.93%	2.50	3.98
Group 2 (Services)						
Business Services	1.01	1.13	1.73	8.45%	1.37	6.17
Personal Services	.90	1.20	1.93	10.87%	1.35	8.05
Group 3 (Financial Institutions)						
Security Brokerage Firms	1.02	.55	2.98	17.77%	3.08	5.77
Insurance Companies	.84	.32	4.19	12.88%	1.04	12.38
Depository Financial Institutions . .	.70	.08	12.70	12.53%	1.27	9.87
Group 4 (Transportation)						
Air Transportation	1.35	1.17	3.42	7.78%	3.17	2.45
Railroad Transportation	.94	.46	2.91	9.79%	2.92	3.35
Water Transportation	.81	.51	2.45	5.66%	3.68	1.54
Motor Freight Transportation	.80	1.51	2.42	11.31%	3.16	3.58
Group 5 (Equipment Manufacturing)						
Industrial Equipment	1.00	1.29	1.79	8.68%	2.65	3.28
Electrical Equipment	.95	1.26	1.71	8.73%	2.29	3.81
Transportation Equipment	.84	1.38	2.45	12.63%	2.51	5.03

MASSACHUSETTS STOVE COMPANY— BANK LENDING DECISION

Massachusetts Stove Company manufactures wood burning stoves for the heating of homes and businesses. The company has approached you as chief lending officer for the Massachusetts Regional Bank, seeking to increase its loan from the current level of $93,091 as of January 15, Year 6, to $125,000. Jane O'Neil, Chief Executive Officer and majority stockholder of the company, indicates that the company needs the loan to finance the working capital required for an expected 25 percent annual increase in sales during the next two years, to repay suppliers, and to provide funds for expected nonrecurring legal and retooling costs.

The company's wood stoves have two distinguishing characteristics: (1) they are inlaid with ceramic tile, which increases the intensity and duration of the heat provided and enhances the stove's appearance, and (2) a catalytic combuster, which adds heating potential to the stoves and reduces air pollution.

The company manufactures wood burning stoves in a single plant located in Greenfield, Massachusetts. It purchases metal castings for the stoves from foundries in Germany and Belgium. The ceramic tile comes from a supplier in Canada. These purchases are denominated in U.S. dollars. The catalytic combuster is purchased from a supplier in the United States. The manufacturing process is essentially an assembly operation. The plant employs an average of eight workers. The two keys to quality control are structural air tightness and effective operation of the catalytic combuster.

The company rents approximately 60 percent of the 25,000 square foot building that it uses for manufacturing and administrative activities. This building also houses the company's factory showroom. The remaining 40 percent of the building is not currently rented.

The company's marketing of wood stoves follows three channels:

1. **Wholesaling of stoves to retail hardware stores** This channel represents approximately 20 percent of the company's sales in units.
2. **Retail direct marketing to individuals in all 50 states** Direct marketing occurs through (a) national advertising in construction and design magazines, and (b) brochures mailed to potential customers identified from personal inquiries. This channel represents approximately 70 percent of the company's sales in units. The company is the only firm in the industry with a strategic emphasis on retail direct marketing.
3. **Retailing from the company's showroom** This channel represents approximately 10 percent of the company's sales in units.

The company offers three payment options to retail purchasers of its stoves:

1. **Full payment** Check, money order, or charge to a third-party credit card.
2. **Lay-away plan** Monthly payments over a period not exceeding one year. The company ships the stove after receiving the final payment.
3. **Installment financing plan** The company has a financing arrangement with a local bank to finance the purchase of stoves by credit-approved customers. The company is not liable if customers fail to repay their installment bank loans.

The imposition of strict air emission standards by the Environmental Protection Agency has resulted in a major change in the wood stove industry. By Year 4, firms were required by

EPA regulations to demonstrate that their wood stoves met or surpassed specified air emission standards. These standards were not only more strict than industry practices at the time, but also required firms to engage in extensive company-sponsored and independent testing of their stoves to satisfy EPA regulators. As a consequence, the number of firms in the wood stove industry decreased from over 200 in the years prior to Year 4 to approximately 35 by Year 5.

The company received approval for its Tile Stove I in Year 4, after incurring retooling and testing costs of $63,001. It capitalized these costs in the property, plant, and equipment account. It depreciates these costs over the five-year EPA approval period. A second stove, Tile Stove II, is currently undergoing retooling and testing. The company incurred costs of $19,311 in Year 4 and $8,548 in Year 5 on this stove, which has received preliminary EPA approval. It anticipates additional design, tooling, and testing costs of approximately $55,000 in Year 6 and $33,000 in Year 7 in order to obtain final EPA approval.

The company holds an option to purchase the building in which it is located for $608,400. The option also permits the company to assume the unpaid balance on a low interest rate loan on the building from the New England Regional Industrial Development Authority. The interest rate on this loan is adjusted annually and equals 80 percent of the bank prime interest rate. The unpaid balance on the loan exceeds the option price, and will result in a cash transfer to the company from the owner of the building at the time of transfer. The company exercised its option in Year 4, but the owner of the building refused to comply with the option provisions. The company sued the owner. The case has gone through the lower court system in Massachusetts and is currently under review at the Massachusetts Supreme Court. The company incurred legal costs totaling $68,465 through Year 5 and anticipates additional costs of approximately $45,000 in Year 6. The lower courts have ruled in favor of the company's position on all the major issues in the case. The company expects the Massachusetts Supreme Court to concur with the decision of the lower court when it renders its final decision in the spring of Year 6. The company has held discussions with two prospective tenants for the 10,000 square feet of the building that it does not use in its operations.

Jane O'Neil owns 51 percent of the company's common stock. The remaining stockholders include John O'Neil (Chief Financial Officer and father of Jane O'Neil), Mark Forest (Vice President for Manufacturing), and four independent local investors.

EXHIBIT 9.11

Massachusetts Stove Company
Income Statements
(Case 9.1)

| | Actual | | | Pro Forma | |
	Year 3	Year 4	Year 5	Year 6	Year 7
Sales	$665,771	$783,754	$955,629	$1,194,537	$1,493,171
Cost of Goods Sold	(460,797)	(474,156)	(514,907)	(597,268)	(746,585)
Selling and Administrative	(165,470)	(278,658)	(378,532)	(477,815)	(597,268)
Legal (Note 1)	(28,577)	(30,092)	(9,796)	(45,000)	—
Interest	(38,109)	(36,183)	(35,945)	(38,138)	(38,138)
Income Tax (Note 2)	—	—	—	—	—
Net Income (Loss)	$ (27,182)	$ (35,335)	$ 16,449	$ 36,316	$ 111,180

EXHIBIT 9.12

Massachusetts Stove Company
Balance Sheets
(Case 9.1)

	Actual				Pro Forma	
	Year 2	**Year 3**	**Year 4**	**Year 5**	**Year 6**	**Year 7**
Assets						
Cash	$ 3,925	$ 11,707	$ 8,344	$ 37,726	$ 5,094	$ 27,477
Accounts Receivable	94,606	54,772	44,397	31,964	39,955	49,944
Inventories	239,458	208,260	209,004	225,490	281,863	352,328
Total Current Assets	$337,989	$274,739	$261,745	$295,180	$326,912	$429,749
Property, Plant, and Equipment (at Cost)	$258,870	$316,854	$362,399	$377,784	$440,284	$487,784
Accumulated Depreciation	(205,338)	(228,985)	(250,189)	(274,347)	(304,570)	(339,792)
Property, Plant, and Equipment (Net)	$ 53,532	$ 87,869	$112,210	$103,437	$135,714	$147,992
Other Assets	$ 17,888	$ 17,888	$ 17,594	$ 17,006	$ 16,418	$ 15,830
Total Assets	$409,409	$380,496	$391,549	$415,623	$479,044	$593,571
Liabilities and Shareholders' Equity						
Accounts Payable	$148,579	$139,879	$189,889	$160,905	$185,041	$212,797
Notes Payable—Banks (Note 3)	152,985	140,854	125,256	93,091	125,000	93,091
Other Current Liabilities (Note 4)	13,340	11,440	23,466	62,440	33,500	41,000
Total Current Liabilities	$314,904	$292,173	$338,611	$316,436	$343,541	$346,888
Long-Term Debt (Note 3)	248,000	269,000	268,950	298,750	298,750	298,750
Total Liabilities	$562,904	$561,173	$607,561	$615,186	$642,291	$645,638
Common Stock	$ 2,000	$ 2,000	$ 2,000	$ 2,000	$ 2,000	$ 2,000
Additional Paid-in Capital	435,630	435,630	435,630	435,630	435,630	435,630
Accumulated Deficit	(591,125)	(618,307)	(653,642)	(637,193)	(600,877)	(489,697)
Total Shareholders' Equity	$(153,495)	$(180,677)	$(216,012)	$(199,563)	$(163,247)	$ (52,067)
Total Liabilities and Shareholders' Equity	$409,409	$380,496	$391,549	$415,623	$479,044	$593,571

To assist in the loan decision, the company provides you with financial statements and notes for the three years ending December 31, Year 3, Year 4, and Year 5 (Exhibits 9.11 through 9.14). These financial statements were prepared by John O'Neil, Chief Financial Officer, and are not audited. The company also provides you with pro forma financial statements for Year 6 and Year 7 to demonstrate both its need for the loan and its ability to repay. The loan requested involves an increase in the current loan amount from $93,091 to $125,000. The company will pay interest monthly and repay the $31,909 additional amount borrowed by December 31, Year 7.

The assumptions underlying the pro forma financial statements are as follows:

Sales: Sales are projected to increase 25 percent annually during the next two years, after increasing 17.7 percent in Year 4 and 21.9 percent Year 5. The increase reflects continuing market opportunities related to the company's strategic emphasis on retail direct marketing and to the expected continuing contraction in the number of competitors in the industry.

EXHIBIT 9.13

Massachusetts Stove Company
Statement of Cash Flows
(Case 9.1)

	Actual			Pro Forma	
	Year 3	**Year 4**	**Year 5**	**Year 6**	**Year 7**
Operations					
Net Income (Loss)	$(27,182)	$(35,335)	$ 16,449	$ 36,316	$111,180
Depreciation and Amortization	23,647	21,498	24,746	30,811	35,811
(Increase) Decrease in					
Accounts Receivable	39,834	10,375	12,433	(7,991)	(9,989)
(Increase) Decrease in Inventories ...	31,198	(744)	(16,486)	(56,373)	(70,466)
Increase (Decrease) in					
Accounts Payable	(8,700)	50,010	(28,984)	24,136	27,756
Increase (Decrease) in					
Other Current Liabilities	(1,900)	12,026	38,974	(28,940)	7,500
Cash Flow from Operations	$ 56,897	$ 57,830	$ 47,132	$ (2,041)	$101,792
Investing					
Fixed Assets Acquired	$(57,984)	$(45,545)	$(15,385)	$ (62,500)	$ (47,500)
Financing					
Increase (Decrease) in					
Short-Term Borrowing	$(12,131)	$(15,598)	$(32,165)	$ 31,909	$ (31,909)
Increase (Decrease) in					
Long-Term Borrowing	21,000	(50)	29,800	—	—
Cash Flow from Financing	$ 8,869	$(15,648)	$ (2,365)	$ 31,909	$(31,909)
Change in Cash	$ 7,782	$ (3,363)	$ 29,382	$ (32,632)	$ 22,383
Cash—Beginning of Year	3,925	11,707	8,344	37,726	5,094
Cash—End of Year	$ 11,707	$ 8,344	$ 37,726	$ 5,094	$ 27,477

EXHIBIT 9.14

Financial Ratios for Massachusetts Stove Company
(Case 9.1)

	Actual			Pro Forma	
	Year 3	Year 4	Year 5	Year 6	Year 7
Profit Margin for Return on Assets	1.6%	.1%	5.5%	6.2%	10.0%
Assets Turnover	1.7	2.0	2.4	2.7	2.8
Return on Assets	2.8%	.2%	13.0%	16.6%	27.8%
Cost of Goods Sold ÷ Sales	69.2%	60.5%	53.9%	50.0%	50.0%
Selling and Administrative ÷ Sales	24.9%	35.6%	39.6%	40.0%	40.0%
Days Accounts Receivable	41	23	15	11	11
Days Inventory	177	161	154	155	155
Days Accounts Payable	123	127	120	97	89
Current Ratio	.9	.8	.9	1.0	1.2
Quick Ratio	.2	.2	.2	.1	.2
Cash Flow from Operations ÷ Average					
Current Liabilities	18.7%	18.3%	14.4%	(.6%)	29.5%
Total Liabilities ÷ Total Assets	147.5%	155.2%	148.0%	134.1%	108.8%
Long-Term Debt ÷ Total Assets	70.7%	68.7%	71.9%	62.4%	50.3%
Cash Flow from Operations ÷ Average					
Total Liabilities	10.1%	9.9%	7.7%	(.3%)	15.8%
Interest Coverage Ratio	.3	—	1.5	2.0	3.9
Cash Flow from Operations ÷					
Capital Expenditures	1.0	1.3	3.1	—	2.1

Cost of Goods Sold: Most manufacturing costs vary with sales. The company projects the cost of goods sold to equal 50 percent of sales, after declining from 69.2 percent of sales in Year 3 to 53.9 percent of sales in Year 5. These reductions resulted from a higher proportion of retail sales in the sales mix (which have a higher gross margin than wholesale sales), a more favorable pricing environment in the industry (fewer competitors), a switch to lower-cost suppliers, and more efficient production.

Selling and Administrative Expenses: The company projects selling and administrative costs to equal 40 percent of sales, having increased from 24.9 percent of sales in Year 3 to 39.6 percent of sales in Year 5. The increases resulted from a heavier emphasis on retail sales, which require more aggressive marketing than wholesale sales.

Legal Expenses: The additional $45,000 of legal costs represent the best estimate by the company's attorneys.

Interest Expense: Interest expense has averaged approximately 9 percent of short- and long-term borrowing during the last three years. The pro forma income statement assumes a continuation of the 9 percent average rate.

Income Tax Expense: The company has a tax loss carryforward of $617,285 as of December 31, Year 5. This tax loss carryforward comes almost entirely from the acquisition of a lawn products company ten years ago. The company discontinued the lawn products business in Year 3. It does not anticipate having to pay income taxes during the next two years.

Cash: The pro forma amounts for cash represent a plug to equate projected assets with projected liabilities and shareholders' equity. Projected liabilities include the requested loan during Year 6 and its repayment during Year 7.

Accounts Receivable and Inventories: Accounts receivable and inventories are projected to grow at the growth rate in sales.

Property, Plant, and Equipment: Capital expenditures for Year 6 include $55,000 cost for retooling the Tile Stove II and $7,500 for other equipment. For Year 7 they include $33,000 for retooling the Tile Stove II and $14,500 for other equipment. The pro formas exclude the cost of acquiring the building, its related debt, the cash to be received at the time of transfer, and rental revenues from leasing the unused 40 percent of the building to other businesses.

Accumulated Depreciation: The historical relation between depreciation expense and the cost of property, plant and equipment is expected to continue.

Other Assets: The historical amortization rate for intangibles is expected to continue.

Accounts Payable: Accounts payable are projected to increase each year by the 25 percent growth rate in sales but also then to decrease by 10 percent each year due to the ability to repay suppliers more quickly with proceeds of the increased bank loan for a net growth rate of 15 percent per year.

Notes Payable: Notes payable are projected to increase by the amount of the bank loan in Year 6 and to decrease by the loan repayment in Year 7.

Other Current Liabilities: The large increase in current liabilities at the end of Year 5 resulted from a major promotional offer in the fall of Year 5, which increased the amount of deposits by customers. The projected amounts for Year 5 and Year 6 represent more normal expected levels of deposits.

Long-term Debt: Long-term borrowing represents loans from shareholders to the company. The company does not plan to repay any of these loans in the near future.

Retained Earnings: The change in retained earnings each year represents net income or net loss from operations. The company does not pay dividends.

Statement of Cash Flows: Cash flow amounts are taken from the change in various accounts on the actual and pro forma balance sheets.

Required

Would you make the loan to the company in accordance with the stated terms? In responding, consider the reasonableness of the company's projections, positive and negative factors affecting the industry and the company, and the likely ability of the company to repay the loan.

NOTES TO FINANCIAL STATEMENTS

Note 1: The company has incurred legal costs to enforce its option to purchase the building used in its manufacturing and administrative activities. The case is under review at the Massachusetts Supreme Court, with a decision expected in the spring of Year 6.

Note 2: The company has a tax loss carryforward of $617,285 as of December 31, Year 5.

Note 3: The notes payable to banks are secured by machinery and equipment, shares of common stock of companies traded on the New York Stock Exchange owned by two shareholders, and by personal guarantees of three of the shareholders. The long-term debt consists of unsecured loans from three shareholders.

Note 4: Other current liabilities include the following:

	Year 2	Year 3	Year 4	Year 5
Customer Deposits	$11,278	$ 9,132	$20,236	$59,072
Employee Taxes Withheld	2,062	2,308	3,230	3,368
	$13,340	$11,440	$23,466	$62,440

FLY-BY-NIGHT INTERNATIONAL GROUP: CAN THIS COMPANY BE SAVED?*

Douglas C. Mather, Founder, Chairman, and Chief Executive of Fly-By-Night International Group (FBN), lived the fast-paced, risk-seeking life that he tried to inject into his company. Flying the company's Learjets, he logged 28 world speed records. Once he throttled a company plane to the top of Mount Everest in 3½ minutes.

These activities seemed perfectly appropriate at the time. Mather was a Navy fighter pilot in Vietnam and then flew commercial airlines. In the mid-1970s, he started FBN as a pilot training school. With the defense buildup beginning in the early 1980s, Mather branched out into government contracting. He equipped the company's Learjets with radar jammers and other sophisticated electronic devices to mimic enemy aircraft. He then contracted his "rent-an-enemy" fleet to the Navy and Air Force for use in fighter pilot training. The Pentagon liked the idea and FBN's revenues grew to $55 million in the fiscal year ending April 30, Year 14. Its common stock, issued to the public in Year 9 at $8.50 a share, reached a high of $16.50 in mid-Year 13. Mather and FBN received glowing writeups in *BusinessWeek* and *Fortune*.

In mid-Year 14, however, FBN began a rapid descent. Although still growing rapidly, its cash flow was inadequate to service its debt. According to Mather, he was "just dumbfounded. There was never an inkling of a problem with cash."

In the fall of Year 14, the Board of Directors withdrew the company's financial statements for the year ending April 30, Year 14, stating that there appeared to be material misstatements that needed investigation. In December of Year 14, Mather was asked to step aside as manager and director pending completion of an investigation of certain transactions between Mather and the company. On December 29, Year 14, Nasdaq (the over-the-counter stock market) discontinued quoting the company's common shares. In February, Year 15, the Board of Directors, following its investigation, terminated Mather's employment and membership on the Board.

Exhibits 9.15 through 9.17 present the financial statements and related notes of FBN for the five years ending April Year 10 through April Year 14. The financial statements for Year 10 through Year 12 use the amounts as originally reported for each year. The amounts

---

*The authors gratefully acknowledge the assistance of Lawrence C. Calcano in the preparation of this case.

EXHIBIT 9.15

Fly-By-Night International Group
Comparative Balance Sheets
(amounts in thousands)
(Case 9.2)

	April 30					
	Year 9	**Year 10**	**Year 11**	**Year 12**	**Year 13**	**Year 14**
Assets						
Cash	$ 192	$ 753	$ 142	$ 313	$ 583	$ 159
Notes Receivable	—	—	1,000	—	—	—
Accounts Receivable	2,036	1,083	1,490	2,675	4,874	6,545
Inventories	686	642	602	1,552	2,514	5,106
Prepayments	387	303	57	469	829	665
Net Assets of Discontinued Businesses	—	1,926	—	—	—	—
Total Current Assets	$ 3,301	$ 4,707	$ 3,291	$ 5,009	$ 8,800	$ 12,475
Property, Plant, and Equipment	$17,471	$37,250	$17,809	$24,039	$76,975	$106,529
Less Accumulated Depreciation	(2,593)	(4,462)	(4,288)	(5,713)	(8,843)	(17,231)
Net	$14,878	$32,788	$13,521	$18,326	$68,132	$ 89,298
Other Assets	$ 1,278	$ 1,566	$ 1,112	$ 641	$ 665	$ 470
Total Assets	$19,457	$39,061	$17,924	$23,976	$77,597	$102,243
Liabilities and Shareholders' Equity						
Accounts Payable	$ 1,436	$ 2,285	$ 939	$ 993	$ 6,279	$ 12,428
Notes Payable	—	4,766	1,021	140	945	—
Current Portion of Long-Term Debt	1,239	2,774	1,104	1,789	7,018	60,590
Other Current Liabilities	435	1,845	1,310	2,423	12,124	12,903
Total Current Liabilities	$ 3,110	$11,670	$ 4,374	$ 5,345	$26,366	$ 85,921
Long-Term Debt	9,060	20,041	6,738	9,804	41,021	—
Deferred Income Taxes	1,412	1,322	—	803	900	—
Other Noncurrent Liabilities	—	248	—	226	—	—
Total Liabilities	$13,582	$33,281	$11,112	$16,178	$68,287	$ 85,921
Common Stock	$ 20	$ 20	$ 20	$ 21	$ 22	$ 34
Additional Paid-in Capital	3,611	3,611	4,323	4,569	5,685	16,516
Retained Earnings	2,244	2,149	2,469	3,208	3,802	(29)
Treasury Stock	—	—	—	—	(199)	(199)
Total Shareholders' Equity	$ 5,875	$ 5,780	$ 6,812	$ 7,798	$ 9,310	$ 16,322
Total Liabilities and Shareholders' Equity	$19,457	$39,061	$17,924	$23,976	$77,597	$102,243

EXHIBIT 9.16

Fly-By-Night International Group
Comparative Income Statements
For the Year Ended April 30
(amounts in thousands)
(Case 9.2)

	Year 10	Year 11	Year 12	Year 13	Year 14
Sales	$31,992	$19,266	$20,758	$36,597	$54,988
Expenses					
Cost of Services	22,003	9,087	12,544	26,444	38,187
Selling and					
Administrative	4,236	2,989	3,467	3,020	5,880
Depreciation	3,003	2,798	1,703	3,150	9,810
Interest	2,600	2,743	1,101	3,058	5,841
Income Taxes	74	671	803	379	(900)
Total Expenses	$31,916	$18,288	$19,618	$36,051	$58,818
Income—Continuing					
Operations	$ 76	$ 978	$ 1,140	$ 546	$(3,830)
Income—Discontinued					
Operations	(171)	(659)	(400)	47	—
Net Income	$ (95)	$ 319	$ 740	$ 593	$(3,830)

---

reported on the statement of cash flows for Year 10 (such as the change in accounts receivable) do not precisely agree with the amounts on the balance sheet at the beginning and the end of the year because certain items classified as relating to continuing operations on the balance sheet at the end of Year 9 were reclassified as relating to discontinued operations on the balance sheet at the end of Year 10. The financial statements for Year 13 and Year 14 represent the restated financial statements for the years after the Board of Directors completed its investigation of suspected material misstatements that caused it to withdraw the originally issued financial statements for fiscal Year 14.

Required

You are asked to study these financial statements and notes and respond to these questions:

a. What evidence can you observe from analyzing the financial statements that might signal the cash flow problems experienced in mid-Year 14?

b. Can FBN avoid bankruptcy during Year 15? What changes in either the design or implementation of FBN's strategy would you recommend? To compute Altman's Z-score, use the low bid market price for the year to determine the market value of common shareholders' equity. To compute Ohlson's probability of bankruptcy, use these values for the GNP implicit price deflator: Year 11: 148.29; Year 12: 152.45; Year 13, 156.81; Year 14, 161.74. Note that the case does not provide sufficient information to compute the probability of bankruptcy for Year 10.

EXHIBIT 9.17

Fly-By-Night International Group
Comparative Statements of Cash Flows For the Year Ended April 30
(amounts in thousands)
(Case 9.2)

	Year 10	Year 11	Year 12	Year 13	Year 14
Operations					
Income—Continuing Operations	$ 76	$ 978	$ 1,140	$ 546	$ (3,830)
Depreciation	3,003	2,798	1,703	3,150	9,810
Other Adjustments	74	671	1,119	1,817	1,074
Working Capital from Operations	$ 3,153	$ 4,447	$ 3,962	$ 5,513	$ 7,054
Changes in Working Capital					
(Increase) Decrease in Receivables	403	(407)	(1,185)	(2,199)	(1,671)
(Increase) Decrease in Inventories	19	40	(950)	(962)	(2,592)
(Increase) Decrease in Prepayments	36	246	(412)	(360)	164
Increase (Decrease) in Accounts Payable	359	(1,346)	54	5,286	6,149
Increase (Decrease) in Other					
Current Liabilities	596	(535)	1,113	9,701	779
Cash Flow from Continuing Operations	$ 4,566	$ 2,445	$ 2,582	$ 16,979	$ 9,883
Cash Flow from Discontinued Operations	(335)	(752)	(472)	(77)	—
Net Cash Flow from Operations	$ 4,231	$ 1,693	$ 2,110	$ 16,902	$ 9,883
Investing					
Sale of Property, Plant, and Equipment	$ 12	$ 18,387	$ 119	$ 3	$ 259
Acquisition of Property, Plant,					
and Equipment	(20,953)	(2,424)	(6,573)	(52,960)	(33,035)
Other	30	(679)	1,017	78	(1,484)
Net Cash Flow from Investing	$(20,911)	$ 15,284	$(5,437)	$(52,879)	$(34,260)
Financing					
Increase in Short-Term Borrowing	$ 4,766	$ —	$ —	$ 805	$ —
Increase in Long-Term Borrowing	14,739	5,869	5,397	42,152	43,279
Issue of Common Stock	—	—	428	191	12,266
Decrease in Short-Term Borrowing	—	(3,745)	(881)	—	(945)
Decrease in Long-Term Borrowing	(2,264)	(19,712)	(1,647)	(7,024)	(30,522)
Acquisition of Common Stock	—	—	—	(198)	—
Other	—	—	201	321	(125)
Net Cash Flow from Financing	$ 17,241	$(17,588)	$ 3,498	$ 36,247	$ 23,953
Change in Cash	$ 561	$ (611)	$ 171	$ 270	$ (424)

NOTES TO FINANCIAL STATEMENTS

1. *Summary of Significant Accounting Policies*

Consolidation. The consolidated financial statements include the accounts of the company and its wholly owned subsidiaries. The company uses the equity method for subsidiaries not majority owned (50 percent or less) and eliminates significant intercompany transactions and balances.

Inventories. Inventories, which consist of aircraft fuel, spare parts, and supplies, appear at lower of FIFO cost or market.

Property and Equipment. Property and equipment appear at acquisition cost. The company capitalizes major inspections, renewals, and improvements, while it expenses replacements, maintenance, and repairs that do not improve or extend the life of the respective assets. The company computes depreciation of property and equipment using the straight-line method.

Contract Income Recognition. Contractual specifications (that is, revenue rates, reimbursement terms, functional considerations) vary among contracts. Accordingly, the company recognizes guaranteed contract income (guaranteed revenue less related direct costs) either as it logs flight hours or on a straight-line monthly basis over the contract year, whichever method better reflects the economics of the contract. The company recognizes income from discretionary hours flown in excess of the minimum guaranteed amount each month as it logs such discretionary hours.

Income Taxes. The company recognizes deferred income taxes for temporary differences between financial and tax reporting amounts.

2. *Transactions with Major Customers.* The company provides contract flight services to three major customers: the U.S. Air Force, the U.S. Navy, and the Federal Reserve Bank System. These contracts have termination dates in Year 16 or Year 17. Revenues from all government contracts as a percentage of total revenues were as follows: Year 10, 31 percent; Year 11, 68 percent; Year 12, 73 percent; Year 13, 72 percent; Year 14, 62 percent.

3. *Segment Data.* During Year 10, the company operated in five business segments as follows:

Flight Operations—Business. Provides combat readiness training to the military and nightly transfer of negotiable instruments for the Federal Reserve Bank System, both under multiyear contracts.

Flight Operations—Transport. Provides charter transport services to a variety of customers.

Fixed Base Operations. Provides ground support operations (fuel, maintenance) to commercial airlines at several major airports.

Education and Training. Provides training for nonmilitary pilots.

Aircraft Sales and Leasing. Acquires aircraft that the company then either resells or leases to various firms.

The Company discontinued the Flight Operations—Transport and the Education and Training segments in Year 11. It sold most of the assets of the Aircraft Sales and Leasing segment in Year 11.

Segment revenue, operating profit, and asset data for the various segments are as follows (amounts in thousands).

| | April 30 | | | | |
	Year 10	Year 11	Year 12	Year 13	Year 14
Revenues					
Flight Operations— Business	$10,803	$11,236	$16,026	$31,297	$ 44,062
Flight Operations— Transport	13,805	—	—	—	—
Fixed Base Operations	3,647	3,911	4,651	4,832	9,597
Education and Training . . .	542	—	—	—	—
Aircraft Sales and Leasing	3,195	4,119	81	468	1,329
Total	$31,992	$19,266	$20,758	$36,597	$ 54,988
Operating Profit					
Flight Operations— Business	$ 849	$ 2,463	$ 3,455	$ 4,863	$ 5,707
Flight Operations— Transport	(994)	—	—	—	—
Fixed Base Operations	332	174	1,038	1,362	(2,041)
Education and Training . . .	12	—	—	—	—
Aircraft Sales and Leasing	2,726[a]	1,217[b]	(15)	378	1,175
Total	$ 2,925	$ 3,854	$ 4,478	$ 6,603	$ 4,841
Assets					
Flight Operations— Business	$13,684	$11,130	$17,738	$64,162	$ 85,263
Flight Operations— Transport	1,771	—	—	—	—
Fixed Base Operations	4,784	5,011	5,754	13,209	16,544
Education and Training . . .	1,789	—	—	—	—
Aircraft Sales and Leasing	18,524	1,262	438	226	436
Total	$40,552	$17,403	$23,930	$77,597	$102,243

[a]Includes a gain of $2.6 million on the sale of aircraft.

[b]Includes a gain of $1.2 million on the sale of aircraft.

4. *Discontinued Operations.* Income from discontinued operations consists of the following (amounts in thousands):

Year 10

Loss from Operations of Charter Tour Business, net of income tax
benefits of $164 . . . . $ (171)

Year 11

Loss from Operations of Flight Operations—Transport
($1,261) and Education and Training ($172) Segments,
net of income tax benefits of $685 .... $ (748)

Gain on Disposal of Education and Training Business, net of income taxes
of $85 89

Total .... $ (659)

Year 12

Loss from write-off of Airline Operations Certificates in Flight
Operations—Transport Business .... $ (400)

Year 13

Income from Operations of Flight Operations—Transport ($78), net of
income taxes of $31 .... $ 47

5. *Related Party Transactions.* On April 30, Year 11, the company sold most of the net assets of the Aircraft Sales and Leasing segment to Interlease, Inc., a Georgia corporation wholly owned by the company's majority stockholder, whose personal holdings represented at that time approximately 75 percent of the company.

Under the terms of the sale, the sales price was $1,368,000, of which the buyer paid $368,000 in cash and gave a promissory note for the remaining $1,000,000. The company treated the proceeds received in excess of the book value of the net assets sold of $712,367 as a capital contribution due to the related party nature of the transaction. FBN originally acquired the assets of the Aircraft Sales and Leasing segment during Year 10.

On September 29, Year 14, the company's Board of Directors established a Transaction Committee to examine certain transactions between the company and Douglas Mather, its Chairman, President, and majority stockholder. These transactions were as follows:

Certain Loans to Mr. Mather. In early September, Year 13, the Board of Directors authorized a $1 million loan to Mr. Mather at the company's cost of borrowing plus ⅛ percent. On September 19, Year 13, Mr. Mather tendered a $1 million check to the company in repayment of the loan. On September 22, Year 13, at Mr. Mather's direction, the company made an additional $1 million loan to him, the proceeds of which Mather apparently used to cover his check in repayment of the first $1 million loan. The Transaction Committee concluded that the Board of Directors did not authorize the September 22, Year 13, loan to Mr. Mather nor that any director was aware of the loan at the time other than Mr. Mather. The company's Year 13 Proxy Statement, dated September 27, Year 13, incorrectly stated that "as of September 19, Year 13, Mr. Mather had repaid the principal amount of his indebtedness to the Company." Mr. Mather's $1 million loan remained outstanding until it was cancelled in connection with the ESOP transaction discussed below.

ESOP Transaction. On February 28, Year 14, the company's Employee Stock Ownership Plan (ESOP) acquired 100,000 shares of the company's common stock from Mr. Mather at $14.25 per share. FBN financed the purchase. The ESOP gave the company a $1,425,000 unsecured demand note. To complete the transaction, the company cancelled a $1 million promissory note from Mr. Mather and paid the remaining $425,000 in cash. The Transaction Committee determined that the Board of Directors authorized neither the $1,425,000 loan to the ESOP, the cancellation of Mather's $1,000,000 note, or the payment of $425,000 in cash.

Eastwind Transaction. On April 27, Year 14, the company acquired four Eastwind aircraft from a German company. FBN subsequently sold these aircraft to Transreco, a corporation owned by Douglas Mather, for a profit of $1,600,000. In late September and early October, Transreco sold these four aircraft at a profit of $780,000 to unaffiliated third parties. The Transactions Committee determined that none of the officers or directors of the Company were aware of the Eastwind transaction until late September, Year 14.

On December 12, Year 14, the company announced that Mr. Mather had agreed to step aside as Chairman and a Director and take no part in the management of the company pending resolution of the matters presented to the Board by the Transactions Committee. On February 13, Year 15, the company announced that it had entered into a settlement agreement with Mr. Mather and Transreco resolving certain of the issues addressed by the Transactions Committee. Pursuant to the agreement, the company will receive $211,000, the bonus paid to Mr. Mather for fiscal Year 14, and $780,000, the gain recognized by Transreco on the sale of the Eastwind aircraft. Also pursuant to the settlement, Mr. Mather will resign all positions with the company and waive rights under his employment agreement to any future compensation or benefits on which he might otherwise have a claim.

6. *Long-Term Debt.* Long-term debt consists of the following (amounts in thousands):

	April 30				
	Year 10	**Year 11**	**Year 12**	**Year 13**	**Year 14**
Notes Payable to Banks:					
Variable Rate	$ 3,497	$2,504	$ 2,086	$30,495	$44,702
Fixed Rate	1,228	3,562	6,292	14,679	13,555
Notes Payable to Finance Companies:					
Variable Rate	10,808	1,667	1,320	—	—
Fixed Rate	325	—	—	—	—
Capitalized Lease Obligations	5,297	70	1,295	2,865	2,333
Other	1,660	39	600	—	—
Total	$22,815	$7,842	$11,593	$48,039	$60,590
Less Current Portion	(2,774)	(1,104)	(1,789)	(7,018)	(60,590)
Net	$20,041	$6,738	$ 9,804	$41,021	$ —

Substantially all of the company's property, plant, and equipment serves as collateral for this debt. The borrowings from bank and finance companies include restrictive covenants, the most restrictive of which appear on the following page:

	Year 10	Year 11	Year 12	Year 13	Year 14
Liabilities/Tangible Net Worth	≤6.7	≤5.5	≤4.2	≤3.0	≤2.5
Tangible Net Worth ..	≥$5,100	≥$5,300	≥$5,400	≥$5,800	≥$20,000
Working Capital	—	—	—	—	≥$5,000
Interest Coverage Ratio	—	—	—	—	≥1.15

As of April 30, Year 14, the company is in default on its debt covenants. It is also in default with respect to covenants underlying its capitalized lease obligations. As a result, lenders have the right to accelerate repayment of their loans. Accordingly, the company has classified all its long-term debt as a current liability.

The company has entered into operating leases for aircraft and other equipment. The estimated present value of the minimum lease payments under these operating leases as of April 30 of each year is

Year 10:	$4,083
Year 11:	3,971
Year 12:	3,594
Year 13:	3,142
Year 14:	2,706

7. *Income Taxes.* Income tax expense consists of the following:

	Year Ended April 30				
	Year 10	Year 11	Year 12	Year 13	Year 14
Current					
Federal	$ —	$—	$ —	$ —	$ —
State	—	—	—	—	—
Deferred					
Federal	$(85)	$67	$685	$380	$(845)
State	(5)	4	118	30	(55)
Total	$(90)	$71	$803	$410	$(900)

The cumulative tax loss and tax credit carryovers as of April 30 of each year are as follows:

April 30	Tax Loss	Tax Credit
Year 10	$ 4,500	$750
Year 11	2,100	450
Year 12	1,400	300
Year 13	5,200	280
Year 14	10,300	250

The deferred tax provision results from temporary differences in the recognition of revenues and expenses for income tax and financial reporting. The sources and amounts of these differences for each year are as follows:

	Year 10	Year 11	Year 12	Year 13	Year 14
Depreciation	$ 778	$ (770)	$ 336	$ 503	$ —
Aircraft Modification Costs ..	703	982	382	1,218	—
Net Operating Losses	(1,729)	—	290	(1,384)	(900)
Other	158	(141)	(205)	73	—
	$ (90)	$ 71	$ 803	$ 410	$ (900)

A reconciliation of the effective tax rate with the statutory tax rate is as follows:

	Year 10	Year 11	Year 12	Year 13	Year 14
Federal Taxes at Statutory Rate	(34.0)%	34.0%	34.0%	35.0%	(35.0)%
State Income Taxes	(3.0)	3.0	3.0	3.0	(2.5)
Effect of Net Operating Loss and Investment Credits ...	—	(29.9)	(7.2)	—	16.5
Other	(12.0)	11.1	22.2	2.9	2.0
	(49.0)%	18.2%	52.0%	40.9%	(19.0)%

8. *Market Price Information.* The company's common stock trades on the Nasdaq National Market System under the symbol FBN. Trading in the company's common stock commenced on January 10, Year 10. High and low bid prices during each fiscal year are as follows:

	High Bid	**Low Bid**
Fiscal Year		
Year 10	$ 5.25	$3.25
Year 11	$ 4.63	$3.00
Year 12	$11.25	$3.25
Year 13	$14.63	$6.25
Year 14	$16.50	$9.50

On December 29, Year 14, the company announced that Nasdaq had decided to discontinue quoting the company's common stock because of the company's failure to comply with Nasdaq's filing requirements.

Ownership of the company's stock at various dates appears below:

	April 30				
	Year 10	**Year 11**	**Year 12**	**Year 13**	**Year 14**
Douglas Mather	75%	75%	72%	68%	42%
Public	25	25	24	23	48
Company ESOP	—	—	4	9	10
	100%	100%	100%	100%	100%
Common Shares Outstanding (000s)	2,000.0	2,000.0	2,095.0	2,222.8	3,357.5

MILLENNIAL TECHNOLOGIES: APOCALYPSE NOW?

Millennial Technologies, a designer, manufacturer, and marketer of PC cards for portable computers, printers, telecommunications equipment, and equipment diagnostic systems, was the darling of Wall Street during Year 6. Its common stock was the leading gainer for the year on the New York Stock Exchange. The bubble burst, however, during the third quarter of Year 7 when revelations about seriously misstated financial statements for prior years became known. This case seeks to identify signals of the financial shenanigans and to assess the likelihood of the firm's future survival.

INDUSTRY AND PRODUCTS

Digital computing and processing have expanded beyond desktop computing systems in recent years to include a broad array of more mobile applications, including portable computers, cellular telephones, digital cameras, and medical and automobile diagnostic equipment. A PC card is a rugged but lightweight credit-card sized device inserted into a dedicated slot in these products to provide programming, processing, and storage capabilities normally provided on hard drives and floppy disks in conventional desktop computers. The PC card has high shock and vibration tolerance, low power consumption, small size, and high access speed. The market for PC cards is one of the fastest growing segments of the electronics industry.

Millennial Technologies designs PC cards for four principal industries: (1) communications (routers, cellular telephones, and local area networks), (2) transportation (vehicle diagnostics, navigation), (3) mobile computing (hand-held data collection terminals, notebook computers), and (4) medical (blood gas analysis systems, defibrillators). The firm targets its engineering and product development, all of it conducted in-house, to these four industry groups. It works closely with original equipment manufacturers (OEMs) to design PC cards that meet specific needs of products for these four industries. Millennial's customers include Lucent Technologies, Philips Electronics, 3Com Corporation, and Bay Networks. The company also keeps its manufacturing in-house, which allows it to respond quickly to changing requirements and schedules of these OEMs. The firm markets its products using its own sales force.

Millennial Technologies was incorporated in Year 4 in Delaware as the successor of M. Millennial, a Massachusetts corporation. The firm made its initial public offering of common stock (1 million shares) on April 19, Year 4, at a price of $5.625 per share. Each common share issued at that time included a redeemable stock purchase warrant that permitted the holder to purchase one share of the firm's common stock for $7.20. Prior to its initial public offering, Millennial Technologies obtained a $550,000 bridge loan during Year 4, which it repaid with proceeds from the initial public offering. Holders of the stock warrants exercised their options during Year 5 and Year 6.

The firm obtained additional equity capital during Year 5 as a result of a private placement of its common stock at $5.83 a share. It issued additional shares to the public during Year 6 at $18 a share. Its stock price was $5.25 on June 30, Year 4; $22.625 on June 30, Year 5; $29.875 on June 30, Year 6; and $52.00 on December 31, Year 6.

Throughout Year 4 through Year 6, Millennial Technologies maintained a line of credit with a major Boston bank to finance its accounts receivable and inventories. The borrowing is at the bank's prime lending rate. Substantially all the assets of the firm are pledged as collateral for this borrowing.

The firm's chief executive officer, Manuel Pinoza, is also its major shareholder. The firm maintains an employment agreement with Mr. Pinoza under which it pays his compensation to a Swiss executive search firm, which then pays Mr. Pinoza.

Beginning in Year 6, Millennial Technologies made minority investments in five corporations engaged in technology development. The firm accounts for four of these investments using the cost method and one using the equity method. Products developed by these companies could conceivably use PC cards. Millennial Technologies also advanced amounts to some of these companies using interest-bearing notes.

Exhibits 9.18 to 9.20 present the financial statements for the fiscal years ended June 30, Year 4, Year 5, and Year 6 for Millennial Technologies, based on the amounts originally reported for each year. Exhibit 9.21 presents selected financial statement ratios based on these reported amounts.

EXHIBIT 9.18

Millennial Technologies
Balance Sheets as Originally Reported
(amounts in thousands)
(Case 9.3)

	June 30			
	Year 3	**Year 4**	**Year 5**	**Year 6**
Assets				
Cash	—	$ 981	$ 970	$ 6,182
Marketable Securities	—	—	—	4,932
Accounts Receivable	$ 730	1,662	3,932	12,592
Inventories........................	2,257	3,371	8,609	18,229
Other Current Assets	234	306	1,932	6,256
Total Current Assets	$3,221	$6,320	$15,443	$48,191
Investments in Securities	—	—	—	2,472
Property, Plant, and Equipment (net) ...	208	669	1,323	4,698
Other Assets	666	601	1,433	421
Total Assets	$4,095	$7,590	$18,199	$55,782
Liabilities and Shareholders' Equity				
Accounts Payable	$1,590	$ 616	$ 3,571	$ 3,494
Notes Payable	980	—	1,153	4,684
Current Portion of Long-Term Debt	—	—	103	336
Other Current Liabilities	457	516	765	614
Total Current Liabilities	$3,027	$1,132	$ 5,592	$ 9,128
Long-Term Debt	—	—	162	367
Deferred Tax Liability	24	39	—	242
Total Liabilities	$3,051	$1,171	$ 5,754	$ 9,737
Common Stock	$ 60	$ 90	$ 110	$ 165
Additional Paid-in Capital	146	5,027	10,159	38,802
Retained Earnings	838	1,302	2,176	7,078
Total Shareholders' Equity	$1,044	$6,419	$12,445	$46,045
Total Liabilities and Shareholders' Equity	$4,095	$7,590	$18,199	$55,782

EXHIBIT 9.19

Millennial Technologies
Income Statements as Originally Reported
(amounts in thousands)
(Case 9.3)

	For the Year Ended June 30		
	Year 4	Year 5	Year 6
Sales	$ 8,213	$12,445	$ 37,848
Other Revenues	9	10	353
Cost of Goods Sold	(4,523)	(6,833)	(23,636)
Selling and Administrative	(1,889)	(3,366)	(4,591)
Research and Development	(567)	(752)	(1,434)
Interest	(495)[a]	(74)	(370)
Income Taxes	(284)	(556)	(3,268)
Net Income	$ 464	$ 874	$ 4,902

[a]Includes the cost of selling receivables to a factor and interest on bridge financing obtained and repaid during the year.

EXHIBIT 9.20

Millennial Technologies
Statements of Cash Flows as Originally Reported
(amounts in thousands)
(Case 9.3)

	For the Year Ended June 30		
	Year 4	Year 5	Year 6
Operations			
Net Income	$ 464	$ 874	$ 4,902
Depreciation and Amortization	193	337	645
Other Addbacks and Subtractions (net)	219	(5)	1,159
Working Capital Provided by Operations	$ 876	$ 1,206	$ 6,706
(Increase) Decrease in Accounts Receivables ...	(981)	(2,433)	(8,940)
(Increase) Decrease in Inventories	(1,115)	(5,238)	(9,620)
(Increase) Decrease in Other Current Assets	(71)	(2,406)	(836)
Increase (Decrease) in Accounts Payable	(974)	2,955	(76)
Increase (Decrease) in Other Current Liabilities	87	251	(152)
Cash Flow from Operations	$(2,178)	$(5,665)	$(12,918)
Investing			
Sale of Investments	—	—	$ 3,981
Acquisition of Fixed Assets	$ (525)	$ (862)	(3,899)
Acquisitions of Investments	—	—	(11,186)
Other Investing Transactions	—	—	(2,800)
Cash Flow from Investing	$ (525)	$ (862)	$(13,904)

Exh. 9.20—Continued	For the Year Ended June 30		
	Year 4	Year 5	Year 6

Financing

	Year 4	Year 5	Year 6
Increase in Short-Term Borrowing	$ 550	$ 1,153	$ 3,531
Increase in Long-Term Borrowing	—	320	691
Increase in Common Stock	4,663	5,099	28,064
Decrease in Short-Term Borrowing	(1,529)	—	—
Decrease in Long-Term Borrowing	—	(56)	(252)
Cash Flow from Financing	$ 3,684	$ 6,516	$ 32,034
Net Change in Cash	$ 981	$ (11)	$ 5,212
Cash—Beginning of Year	—	981	970
Cash—End of Year	$ 981	$ 970	$ 6,182

EXHIBIT 9.21

Millennial Technologies
Financial Ratios Based on Originally Reported Amounts
(Case 9.3)

	Year 4	Year 5	Year 6
Profit Margin for Rate of Return on Assets	9.6%	7.4%	13.6%
Assets Turnover	1.4	1.0	1.0
Rate of Return on Assets	13.5%	7.2%	13.9%
Common Earnings Leverage	58.7%	94.7%	95.3%
Capital Structure Leverage	1.6	1.4	1.3
Rate of Return on Common Shareholders' Equity	12.4%	9.3%	16.8%
Cost of Goods Sold/Sales	55.1%	54.9%	62.4%
Selling and Administrative/Sales	23.0%	27.0%	12.1%
Research and Development/Sales	6.9%	6.0%	3.8%
Income Tax Expense (excluding tax effects of interest expense)/Sales	5.5%	4.7%	9.0%
Accounts Receivable Turnover	6.9	4.4	4.6
Inventory Turnover	1.6	1.1	1.8
Fixed Asset Turnover	18.7	12.5	12.6
Current Ratio	5.6	2.8	5.3
Quick Ratio	2.3	.9	2.6
Days Accounts Payable	71	63	39
Cash flow from Operations/Current Liabilities ..	(104.7%)	(168.5%)	(175.5%)
Long-Term Debt Ratio	—	1.3%	.8%
Liabilities/Assets	15.4%	31.6%	17.5%
Cash Flow from Operations/Total Liabilities	(103.2%)	(163.6%)	(166.8%)
Interest Coverage Ratio	2.5	20.3	23.1

FINANCIAL STATEMENT IRREGULARITIES

On February 10, Year 7, after receiving information regarding various accounting and reporting irregularities, the Board of Directors fired Mr. Pinoza and relieved the Chief Financial Officer of his duties. The Board formed a special committee of outside directors to investigate the purported irregularities, obtaining the assistance of legal counsel and the firm's independent accountants. On February 21, Year 7, the New York Stock Exchange announced the suspension of trading in the firm's common stock. The stock was delisted on April 25, Year 7. On February 14, Year 7, the major Boston bank providing working capital financing notified the firm that it had defaulted on the line of credit agreement. Although the bank subsequently extended the line of credit through July 31, Year 7, it increased the interest rate significantly above prime. Millennial Technologies decided to seek a new lender.

The investigation by the Board's special committee revealed the following accounting and reporting irregularities:

1. Recording of invalid sales transactions. The firm fabricated fictitious purchase orders from regular customers using their purchase order forms from legitimate purchase transactions. The firm then shipped empty PC card housings, purportedly to these customers but at bogus addresses. Mr. Pinoza then apparently paid the accounts receivable underlying these sales with his personal funds.
2. Recording of revenues from bill and hold transactions. The firm kept its books open beyond June 30 each year and recorded as sales in that fiscal year products that were shipped in July and should have been recorded as revenues of the next fiscal year.
3. Manipulation of physical counts of inventory balances and inclusion of empty PC card housings in finished goods inventories.
4. Failure to write down inventories adequately for product obsolescence.
5. Inclusion of certain costs in property, plant, and equipment that the firm should have expensed in the period incurred.
6. Inclusion in advances to other technology companies of amounts that represent prepaid license fees. The firm should have amortized these fees over the license period.
7. Failure to provide adequately for uncollectible amounts related to advances to other technology companies.
8. Failure to write down or write off investments in other technology companies when their market value was less than the cost of the investment.

Exhibits 9.22 through 9.24 present the restated financial statements for Millennial Technologies for the fiscal years ending June 30, Year 4, Year 5, and Year 6 after correcting for the irregularities described above. These exhibits also present the financial statements for the nine months ended March 30, Year 7. The firm decided during February of Year 7 to change its fiscal year to a March year-end. Exhibit 9.25 presents selected financial ratios based on the restated financial statements.

Required

a. Using information in the financial statements as originally reported in Exhibits 9.18 through 9.20 and the financial ratios in Exhibit 9.21, indicate possible signals that Millennial Technologies might have been manipulating its financial statements.

EXHIBIT 9.22

Millennial Technologies
Balance Sheets Using Restated Data
(amounts in thousands)
(Case 9.3)

		June 30			March 31
	Year 3	Year 4	Year 5	Year 6	Year 7
Assets					
Cash	—	$ 981	$ 970	$ 6,182	$ 57
Marketable Securities	—	—	—	4,932	—
Accounts Receivable	$ 730	1,280	2,802	11,260	5,571
Inventories	2,257	1,581	2,181	8,248	7,356
Other Current Assets	669	839	2,284	6,395	14,229
Total Current Assets	$3,656	$4,681	$ 8,237	$ 37,017	$ 27,213
Investments in Securities	—	—	—	1,783	20,332
Property, Plant, and Equipment (net)	243	399	923	2,033	3,087
Other Assets	172	123	390	299	566
Total Assets	$4,071	$5,203	$ 9,550	$ 41,132	$ 51,198
Liabilities and Shareholders' Equity					
Accounts Payable	$1,590	$ 772	$ 3,303	$ 3,025	$ 4,766
Notes Payable	980	—	1,153	4,684	10,090
Current Portion of Long-Term Debt	—	—	103	336	671
Other Current Liabilities	457	116	562	811	7,117
Total Current Liabilities	$3,027	$ 888	$ 5,121	$ 8,856	$ 22,644
Long-Term Debt	—	—	162	367	—
Total Liabilities	$3,027	$ 888	$ 5,283	$ 9,223	$ 22,644
Common Stock	$ 60	$ 90	$ 110	$ 165	$ 177
Additional Paid-in Capital	146	5,059	10,843	42,712	82,240
Retained Earnings	838	(834)	(6,686)	(10,968)	(53,630)
Foreign Currency Adjustment	—	—	—	—	(233)
Total Shareholders' Equity	$1,044	$4,315	$ 4,267	$ 31,909	$ 28,554
Total Liabilities and Shareholders' Equity	$4,071	$5,203	$ 9,550	$ 41,132	$ 51,198

b. Describe the effect of each of the eight accounting irregularities listed above on the balance sheet, income statement, and statement of cash flows.

c. Using information in the restated financial statements in Exhibits 9.22 through 9.24, the financial ratios in Exhibit 9.25, and the information provided in this case, would you as a commercial banker be willing to offer Millennial Technologies a line of credit as of July 31, Year 7? State the conditions that would induce you to offer such a line of credit.

EXHIBIT 9.23

Millennial Technologies
Income Statements Using Restated Data
(amounts in thousands)
(Case 9.3)

	Year Ended June 30			Nine Months Ended March 31
	Year 4	**Year 5**	**Year 6**	**Year 7**
Sales	$ 7,801	$ 8,982	$ 33,412	$ 28,263
Other Revenues	9	10	353	67
Cost of Goods Sold	(6,508)	(11,575)	(29,778)	(24,453)
Selling and Administrative ..	(2,083)	(2,442)	(3,803)	(7,318)
Research and Development	(567)	(753)	(1,434)	(1,061)
Loss on Investments	—	—	(2,662)[a]	(14,096)[a]
Investigation Costs	—	—	—	(3,673)[b]
Provision for Settlement of Shareholder Litigation ..	—	—	—	(20,000)[c]
Interest	(495)	(74)	(370)	(391)
Income Taxes	171	—[d]	—[d]	—[d]
Net Income (Loss)	$(1,672)	$ (5,852)	$ (4,282)	$(42,662)

[a]Writeoffs of advances and writedowns or write-offs of investments in technology companies.

[b]Legal, accounting, and related costs of investigating misstatements of financial statements.

[c]Estimated cost of class action lawsuits arising from misstatements of financial statements. Millennial Technologies reached an agreement on June 18, Year 7 to pay the plaintiffs $1,475,000 in cash (included in Accounts Payable on March 31, Year 7 balance sheet) and common stock of $18,525,000 (included in Additional Paid-in Capital on March 31, Year 7 balance sheet). The common stock portion of the settlement represents 37 percent of the common stock of Millennial Technologies.

[d]Millennial Technologies incurred net losses for income tax purposes and maintains a valuation allowance equal to the balance in deferred tax assets.

d. Exhibit 9.26 presents the values of Altman's Z-score for fiscal Year 4, Year 5, and Year 6 based on both the originally reported amounts and the restated amounts. Compute the value of Altman's Z-score for the fiscal year ended March 31, Year 7. Although this procedure is not technically correct, use the income amounts for the nine-month period ending March 31, Year 7. According to the amounts in the proposed settlement of the class action lawsuits, the value of the common equity on March 31, Year 7, is $50,068,568.

e. Exhibit 9.27 presents the values of y and the probability of bankruptcy for Millennial Technologies according to Ohlson's model for fiscal Year 4, Year 5, and Year 6. Compute the value of y and the probability of bankruptcy for the fiscal year ended March 31, Year 7. The GNP implicit price index on March 31, Year 7, was 209.0. Use the income amounts for the nine-month period ending March 31, Year 7.

f. Can Millennial Technologies avoid bankruptcy as of mid-Year 7? Why don't the Altman and Ohlson models signal the financial difficulties earlier than they do?

EXHIBIT 9.24

Millennial Technologies
Statements of Cash Flows Using Restated Data
(amounts in thousands)
(Case 9.3)

	Year Ended June 30			Nine Months Ended March 31
	Year 4	Year 5	Year 6	Year 7
Operations				
Net Loss	$(1,672)	$(5,852)	$ (4,282)	$(42,662)
Depreciation and Amortization	176	281	471	831
Other Addbacks and Subtractions (net)	352	224	2,005	28,812
Working Capital Provided by Operations	$(1,144)	$(5,347)	$ (1,806)	$(13,019)
(Increase) Decrease in Accounts Receivable	(599)	(1,693)	(8,883)	5,289
Increase (Decrease) in Inventories	676	(600)	(6,067)	454
(Increase) Decrease in Other Current Assets	(176)	(1,932)	(5,213)	(8,092)
Increase (Decrease) in Accounts Payable	(818)	3,072	(9)	6,572
Increase (Decrease) in Other Current Liabilities	(340)	(96)	(20)	—
Cash Flow from Operations	$(2,401)	$(6,596)	$(21,998)	$ (8,796)
Investing				
Sale of Investments	—	—	$ 3,981	$ 32,182
Acquisition of Fixed Assets	$ (332)	$ (583)	(1,459)	(2,074)
Acquisition of Investments	—	—	(11,186)	(38,892)
Cash Flow from Investing	$ (332)	$ (583)	$ (8,664)	$ (8,784)
Financing				
Increase in Short-Term Borrowing	$ 550	$ 1,153	$ 3,531	$ 5,406
Increase in Long-Term Borrowing	—	320	691	250
Increase in Capital Stock	4,663	5,099	28,813	4,060
Decrease in Short-Term Borrowing	(1,529)	—	—	—
Decrease in Long-Term Borrowing	—	(56)	(252)	(282)
Proceeds from Related Party Transaction	30	652	3,091	2,021
Cash Flow from Financing	$ 3,714	$ 7,168	$ 35,874	$ 11,455
Change in Cash	$ 981	$ (11)	$ 5,212	$ (6,125)
Cash—Beginning of Year	—	981	970	6,182
Cash—End of Year	$ 981	$ 970	$ 6,182	$ 57

EXHIBIT 9.25

Millennial Technologies
Financial Ratios Based on Restated Data
(Case 9.3)

	Year 4	Year 5	Year 6	Year 7[a]
Profit Margin for Rate of				
Return on Assets	(17.2%)	(64.6%)	(12.1%)	(150.0%)
Assets Turnover	1.7	1.2	1.3	.6
Rate of Return on Assets	(29.0%)	(78.7%)	(15.9%)	(91.9%)
Common Earnings Leverage	124.3%	100.8%	106.0%	100.6%
Capital Structure Leverage	1.7	1.7	1.4	1.5
Rate of Return on Common				
Shareholders' Equity	(62.4%)	(136.4%)	(23.7%)	(141.1%)
Cost of Goods Sold/Sales	83.4%	128.9%	89.1%	86.5%
Selling and Administrative/Sales	26.7%	27.2%	11.4%	25.9%
Research and Development/Sales	7.3%	8.4%	4.3%	3.8%
Special Provisions/Sales	—	—	8.0%	133.6%
Accounts Receivable Turnover	7.8	4.4	4.8	3.4
Inventory Turnover	3.4	6.2	5.7	3.1
Fixed Asset Turnover	24.3	13.6	22.6	11.0
Current Ratio	5.3	1.6	4.2	1.2
Quick Ratio	2.6	.7	2.5	.3
Days Accounts Payable	74	61	32	60
Cash flow from Operations/				
Current Liabilities	(122.7%)	(219.5%)	(314.8%)	(55.8%)
Long-Term Debt Ratio	—	3.7%	1.1%	—
Liabilities/Assets	17.1%	55.3%	22.4%	44.2%
Cash Flow from Operations/				
Total Liabilities	(122.7%)	(213.8%)	(303.3%)	(55.2%)
Interest Coverage Ratio	(2.7)	(78.1)	(10.6)	(108.1)

[a]Amounts based on a nine-month fiscal year.

EXHIBIT 9.26

Altman's Z-score for Millennial Technologies
(Case 9.3)

	Originally Reported Data			Restated Data		
	Year 4	Year 5	Year 6	Year 4	Year 5	Year 6
Net Working Capital/Total Assets	.8203	.6496	.8403	.8748	.3915	.8216
Retained Earnings/Total Assets	.2402	.1674	.1776	−.2244	−.9801	−.3733
Income Before Interest and Taxes/Total Assets	.5404	.2727	.5052	−.8550	−1.9966	−.3139
Market Value of Equity/ Book Value of Liabilities	8.0700	13.1911	15.3089	10.6419	14.3672	16.1620
Sales/Total Assets	1.0821	.6838	.6785	1.4993	.9405	.8123
Z-score	10.7530	14.9646	17.5106	11.9366	12.7225	17.1088

EXHIBIT 9.27

Ohlson's Probability of Bankruptcy for Millennial Technologies
(Case 9.3)

	Originally Reported Data			Restated Data		
	Year 4	Year 5	Year 6	Year 4	Year 5	Year 6
Size	−4.3007	−4.6474	−5.0926	−4.1470	−4.3849	−4.9866
TLTA	.9303	1.9065	1.0526	1.0291	3.3357	1.3521
WCTA	−.9774	−.7740	−1.0014	−1.0425	−.4666	−.9790
CLCA	.0136	.0274	.0143	.0144	.0471	.0181
NITA	−.1449	−.1138	−.2083	.7616	1.4523	.2467
FUTL	−1.3690	−.3836	−1.2603	2.3576	1.8522	.3583
INTWO	—	—	—	—	.2850	.2850
OENEG	—	—	—	—	—	—
CHIN	−.0127	−.1596	−.3633	.5210	.2894	−.0807
CONSTANT	−1.3200	−1.3200	−1.3200	−1.3200	−1.3200	−1.3200
Value of Y	−7.1808	−5.4645	−8.1790	−1.8258	1.0902	−5.0881
Probability of Bankruptcy ...	.08%	4.2%	.03%	13.9%	74.8%	.6%

CASE 9.4

KROGER COMPANY: RISKY TIMES*

The Kroger Company operates one of the largest supermarket chains in the United States. During the fall of Year 8, Kroger became the target of unfriendly takeover bids by the Haft family and Kohlberg, Kravis, and Roberts. Prior to these bids, Kroger's common stock traded at a price of $34 per share. The bidding was started at a price of $55 per share and increased to $64 per share.

To defend itself against a takeover, Kroger issued a package of senior and subordinated debt totaling $3.6 billion and used the proceeds to partially fund a special dividend of $3.9 billion. The special dividend included cash of $40 per share (for a total of $3.2 billion) and a senior subordinated, increasing rate debenture with a face value of $12.50 and a market value of $8.69 per share (for a total of $695 million).

This case analyzes the factors that made Kroger an attractive buyout candidate in Year 8 as well as the subsequent effect of the special dividend on its profitability and risk. Exhibits 9.28, 9.29, and 9.30 present Kroger's financial statements for its fiscal years ending December, Year 6, through December, Year 10. Several unusual items affect these financial statements:

1. **Disposal of drug store operations** Kroger sold its drug store operations in Year 6 and included a loss in discontinued operations for that year.

---

*The authors gratefully acknowledge the assistance of Yannis Vasatis in the preparation of this case.

EXHIBIT 9.28

Kroger Company
Comparative Income Statements
(in millions)
(Case 9.4)

	Year 6	Year 7	Year 8	Year 9	Year 10
Sales	$17,123	$17,660	$19,053	$19,104	$20,261
Other Revenues and Gains	13	11	10	16	6
Cost of Goods Sold	(13,163)	(13,696)	(14,824)	(14,846)	(15,670)
Selling and Administrative Expense	(3,609)	(3,553)	(3,784)	(3,652)	(3,918)
Restructuring (Charges) Credits[a]	(164)	8	(195)	18	27
Interest Expense	(104)	(107)	(208)	(649)	(564)
Income Tax Expense[a]	(40)	(140)	(17)	(7)	(59)
Income from Continuing Operations	$ 56	$ 183	$ 35	$ (16)	$ 83
Income from Discontinued Operations ...	(4)[b]	0	0	0	0
Extraordinary Gains (Losses)	0	0	0	(56)[d]	(1)[d]
Changes in Accounting Principles	0	63[c]	0	0	0
Preferred Stock Dividend	(3)	(6)	(16)	(2)	0
Net Income to Common	$ 49	$ 240	$ 19	$ (74)	$ 82
Average Number of Shares Outstanding ..	86.9	80.4	79.3	81.6	86.6

[a]Includes restructuring changes and credits (and related tax effects) as follows:
 Year 6: Provision for downsizing corporate overhead staff and closing of 100 stores, $164 million charge; tax effect, $82 million.
 Year 7: Reversal of provision in Year 6 when actual charges and costs were less than expected, $8 million credit; tax effect, $4 million.
 Year 8: Provision for corporate restructuring relating to issue of debt and distribution of special dividend, $195 million charge; tax effect, $67 million.
 Year 9, Year 10: Reversal of provision for corporate restructuring when actual charges were less than anticipated, $18 million credit in Year 9 (tax effect 6 million); $27 million credit in Year 10 (tax effect, $9 million).

[b]Loss from operations of drug store operations sold during Year 6.

[c]Change to the liability method of accounting for deferred income taxes.

[d]Writeoff of deferred costs incurred in corporate structuring in Year 8 (net of tax effects).

2. **Restructuring provisions** Kroger made two major provisions for restructuring of its business. It made a pretax provision of $164 million in Year 6 to reduce corporate headquarters staff and close 100 stores and related manufacturing operations. It made a pretax provision of $195 million in Year 8 to cover a portion of the cost of its financial restructuring and special dividend.

3. **Change in accounting for income taxes** Kroger adopted the liability method of accounting for deferred income taxes in Year 7. Because income tax rates declined as a result of recent changes in the income tax law, Kroger's deferred tax liability overstated the amount of taxes it expected to pay when timing differences reversed. Kroger reduced its deferred tax liability and included a special credit in earnings of $63 million in Year 7.

4. **Writeoff of deferred restructuring costs** Kroger originally capitalized as assets certain debt issue costs incurred in connection with its corporate restructuring in Year 8. It

EXHIBIT 9.29

Kroger Company
Comparative Balance Sheets
(in millions)
(Case 9.4)

	Year 5	Year 6	Year 7	Year 8	Year 9	Year 10
Cash	$ 106	$ 212	$ 113	$ 211	$ 115	$ 55
Accounts Receivable	215	262	253	258	280	277
Inventories	1,473	1,197	1,448	1,275	1,395	1,448
Other Current Assets[a]	208	277	341	726	258	170
Current Assets	$2,002	$1,948	$2,155	$ 2,470	$ 2,048	$ 1,950
Investments	0	0	0	0	0	0
Property, Plant, and Equip. (net) ..	1,991	1,968	2,137	1,910	1,912	1,874
Other Assets	185	170	168	234	282	295
Total Assets	$4,178	$4,086	$4,460	$ 4,614	$ 4,242	$ 4,119
Accts. Payable—Trade	$ 986	$ 912	$1,005	$ 1,095	$ 1,132	$ 1,198
Notes Payable—Non-Trade	122	10	315	6	13	0
Current Part Long-Term Debt	42	50	29	341	171	96
Other Current Liab.	577	738	614	723	753	768
Current Liabilities	$1,727	$1,710	$1,963	$ 2,165	$ 2,069	$ 2,062
Long-Term Debt	925	830	987	4,724	4,724	4,558
Deferred Tax	314	292	292	302	294	273
Other Non-Current Liabilities	23	99	84	102	120	86
Total Liabilities	$2,989	$2,931	$3,326	$ 7,293	$ 7,207	$ 6,979
Preferred Stock	$ 0	$ 125	$ 125	$ 250	$ 0	$ 0
Common Stock	396	410	424	101	102	104
Retained Earnings	980	939	1,095	(2,517)	(2,609)	(2,541)
Treasury Stock	(187)	(319)	(510)	(513)	(458)	(423)
Shareholders' Equity	$1,189	$1,155	$1,134	$(2,679)	$(2,965)	$(2,860)
Total Equities	$4,178	$4,086	$4,460	$ 4,614	$ 4,242	$ 4,119

[a]Includes assets that Kroger expects to sell at a net realizable value of $88 million in Year 5, $101 million in Year 6, $115 in Year 7, $483 in Year 8, $37 million in Year 9, and $23 million in Year 10.

later refinanced some of the debt in Year 9 and wrote off deferred costs totaling $56 million in Year 9 and $1 million in Year 10.

5. **Operating lease commitments** Kroger leases a substantial portion of its stores under operating lease arrangements. The present values of these operating lease commitments when discounted at 10 percent appear below (in millions):

Year 5: $1,785	Year 7: $1,823	Year 9: $1,692
Year 6: $1,693	Year 8: $1,732	Year 10: $2,936

EXHIBIT 9.30

Kroger Company
Comparative Statement of Cash Flows
(in millions)
(Case 9.4)

	Year 6	Year 7	Year 8	Year 9	Year 10
Operations					
Income from Continuing Operations	$ 56	$ 183	$ 35	$ (16)	$ 83
Depreciation and Amortization	231	223	254	241	245
Other Addbacks	52	0	8	104	113
Other Subtractions	0	(20)	0	0	0
WC Provided by Operations	$ 339	$ 386	$ 297	$ 329	$ 441
(Increase) Decrease in Receivables	(45)	8	(6)	(1)	4
(Increase) Decrease in Inventories	83	(261)	15	(84)	(53)
(Increase) Decrease in Other CA	(50)	(39)	(24)	42	75
Increase (Decrease) Accounts Payable–Trade ...	(74)	93	90	37	66
Increase (Decrease) in Other CL	120	(7)	157	85	(35)
Cash from Continued Operations	$ 373	$ 180	$ 529	$ 408	$ 498
Cash from Discontinued Operations	(4)	0	0	0	0
Cash from Extraordinary Gain/Loss	0	0	0	0	0
Net Cash Flow from Operations	$ 369	$ 180	$ 529	$ 408	$ 498
Investing					
Fixed Assets Sold	$ 129	$ 62	$ 93	$ 13	$ 25
Investments Sold	406[a]	21	0	0	30
Fixed Assets Acquired	(475)	(416)	(324)	(131)	(219)
Investments Acquired	(26)	0	(86)	(15)	(14)
Other Investment Transact.	(22)	(76)	7	299[b]	(13)
Net Cash Flow from Investing	$ 12	$(409)	$ (310)	$ 166	$ (191)
Financing					
Increase Short-Term Borrowing	$ 0	$ 305	$ 0	$ 0	$ 0
Increase Long-Term Borrowing	164	141	4,191[c]	2,706[f]	306
Issue of Capital Stock	146	12	181	16	22
Decrease Short-Term Borrowing	(112)	0	(309)	0	0
Decrease Long-Term Borrowing	(241)	(48)	(861)[d]	(3,141)[f]	(697)
Acquisition of Capital Stock	(140)	(191)	(3)	(251)	0
Dividends	(93)	(91)	(3,347)[e]	(2)	0
Other Financing Transactions	2	2	26	2	1
Net Cash Flow from Financing.	$(274)	$ 130	$ (122)	$ (670)	$ (368)
Net Change in Cash	$ 107	$ (99)	$ 97	$ (96)	$ (61)

[a]Represents proceeds from the sale of drug store operations.

[b]Includes $224 million from the sale of assets; see Note a to Exhibit 9.29.

[c]Includes $3.6 billion of financing for payment of special dividend.

[d]Includes $360 million of existing debt obligations refinanced as part of restructuring.

[e]Includes approximately $3.2 billion in the cash portion of the special dividend.

[f]Includes $625 million of senior debentures and $625 million of subordinated debentures, the proceeds of which refinanced $1,000 million of senior, increasing rate subordinated debentures issued in Year 8 to finance the special dividend.

EXHIBIT 9.31

Comparative Data for Supermarket Competitors
(Case 9.4)

Fiscal Year	Total Assets	Return on Assets	Long-Term Debt/ Long-Term Capital	Return on Common Equity	Current Ratio	Price-Earnings Ratio
Kroger						
Year 5	$4,178	4.7%	38.1%	15.7%	1.2	12
Year 6	$4,076	3.4%[a]	34.4%[a]	11.8%[a]	1.1	11[a]
Year 7	$4,460	4.4%	40.9%	18.0%	1.1	11
A&P						
Year 5	$1,664	3.7%	33.6%	8.9%	1.3	15
Year 6	$2,080	3.7%	35.3%	9.7%	1.1	14
Year 7	$2,243	4.8%	30.4%	12.9%	1.1	14
American Stores						
Year 5	$3,463	4.4%	50.5%	18.0%	1.2	15
Year 6	$3,590	4.1%	47.0%	14.9%	1.2	15
Year 7	$3,650	4.3%	46.6%	15.2%	1.2	15
Winn Dixie Stores						
Year 5	$705	9.0%	12.8%	17.7%	1.6	14
Year 6	$830	8.9%	12.3%	17.1%	1.7	16
Year 7	$851	8.1%	12.2%	15.6%	1.6	17

[a]The amounts for Kroger for Year 6 exclude a $164 million ($82 million net of taxes) restructuring charge.

SOURCE: Standard & Poor, *Stock Reports*.

Exhibit 9.31 presents selected financial statement and market price data for Kroger and three leading competitors for fiscal Year 5, Year 6, and Year 7, the three years prior to payment of Kroger's special dividend. These data use the originally reported amounts for each company (except for the elimination of Kroger's restructuring charge for Year 6). The rate of return ratios use end-of-the-period values for assets and common shareholders' equity instead of the average values for these items.

Required

a. An analyst desires to study the changes in Kroger's profitability and risk prior to and subsequent to the special dividend to assess why Kroger needed to pay the special dividend and how well it performed with its heavier debt load after the special dividend. Discuss the adjustments that the analyst should make to the financial statement data in Exhibits 9.28 through 9.30 before performing the profitability and risk analysis.

b. Prepare a profitability and risk analysis of Kroger for Year 6 and Year 7. Using this analysis and the data in Exhibit 9.31, indicate the apparent reasons that Kroger became a takeover target in the fall of Year 8.

c. Prepare a profitability and risk analysis of Kroger for Year 8 through Year 10. The appropriate GNP implicit price deflator index values for Ohlson's bankruptcy prediction model are as follows: Year 7, 155.6; Year 8, 160.6; Year 9, 167.0; Year 10, 173.6. Evaluate the changes in Kroger's profitability and risk since payment of the special dividend.

PART IV

FINANCIAL STATEMENT ANALYSIS AND VALUATION

INTERRELATED SEQUENTIAL STEPS IN FINANCIAL STATEMENT ANALYSIS

1. Identify Economic Characteristics

2. Identify Company Strategies

3. Understand and Cleanse the Financial Statements

4. Analyze Profitability and Risk

5. Value the Firm

Part IV, chapters 10 to 12, completes the five sequential steps in financial statement analysis introduced in Chapter 1. It provides an opportunity to synthesize industry economics, firm strategies, GAAP reporting, profitability and risk analysis, and valuation into an integrated whole.

Examining the recent profitability and risk of a firm, the subject matter of the first nine chapters, aids in understanding how well the firm has adapted to economic conditions, competitors' actions, and other external factors. We now shift the time perspective to the future and project a firm's future course through the lens of its financial statements. Pro forma financial statements are the analytical tool used to summarize these projections. We then use multiple valuation methods to value firms. Projected cash flows are the principal input to valuation using the present value of cash flows. Projected earnings serve a similar function in the price-earnings valuation method. Projected ROCE is the critical ingredient in the price-book value valuation method. This part also summarizes the results of recent empirical research examining the relationship between accounting information and market prices.

CHAPTER 10

PRO FORMA FINANCIAL STATEMENTS

Learning Objectives

1. Observe the flow of preparing pro forma financial statements, which includes projecting amounts in the following order: (a) sales and other revenues, (b) operating expenses excluding the cost of debt financing and income taxes, (c) assets, (d) liabilities and shareholders' equity excluding retained earnings, (e) interest expense on debt financing, income tax expense, net income, dividends, and the change in retained earnings, and (f) the statement of cash flows.
2. Observe the critical role of sales projections in preparing pro forma financial statements.
3. Understand under what conditions common size percentages, growth rates, and turnovers provide the best projections of financial statement amounts.
4. Prepare comprehensive pro forma financial statements.
5. Design a computer spreadsheet for the preparation of pro forma financial statements.

The economic value of any resource is a function of the returns that are expected from that resource relative to the risk involved. In previous chapters we have discussed tools for analyzing the profitability of a firm (its returns) and the risks of a firm using published financial statement data. This analytical task is a backward-looking exercise. Valuing any economic resource, however, is a forward-looking exercise. It requires us to project future returns and risks.

The analytical tool used to make these projections is the *pro forma financial statements*. The analyst makes predictions about likely future general economic conditions, specific industry conditions, and firm-specific abilities and strategies. The analyst then incorporates these predictions into a set of pro forma, or projected, financial statements. A study of the past profitability and risks of a firm is often helpful in making these projections.

This chapter describes and illustrates the techniques for preparing pro forma financial statements for Coke. Chapters 11 and 12 explore the use of pro forma financial statements in valuation. Chapter 11 presumes that *projected cash flow* is the appropriate measure of returns for valuing a firm. Chapter 12 presumes that *projected earnings* is the appropriate measure of returns.

Pro forma financial statements have applications besides valuation. The managers of a firm might be interested in acquiring another firm and want to see the impact of the acquisition on consolidated financial statements of future years (see Case 7.1 for an illustration of this use of pro forma financial statements). A commercial lender might ask a borrower to prepare pro forma financial statements to demonstrate the borrower's ability to repay the loan with interest (see Case 9.2 for an illustration of this use of pro forma financial statements).

Computer-based spreadsheet programs speed the preparation of pro forma financial statements and make it easier to assess the sensitivity of certain projected amounts to changes in various assumptions. Appendix 10.1 describes and illustrates the preparation of a spreadsheet program for the pro forma financial statements of Coke discussed in this chapter.

PREPARING PRO FORMA FINANCIAL STATEMENTS

Some general principles guide the preparation of pro forma financial statements.

Establish at the outset a flow, or sequence of steps, to project the three principal financial statements. The preparation of pro forma financial statements can be an overwhelming task because of the numerous assumptions and relations that the analyst must consider. Establishing a game plan at the outset can keep the task on course. The particular sequence of steps might vary, depending on the reason for preparing the pro forma financial statements. For most applications, this sequence works well:

1. Project sales revenue and other revenues for the desired number of future periods.
2. Project operating expenses (cost of goods sold, selling and administrative), and derive projected net income before interest expense and income taxes.
3. Project the assets needed to support the level of operations projected in steps 1 and 2.
4. Project the financing (liabilities and shareholders' equity, except retained earnings) needed to support the level of assets projected in step 3.
5. Determine the cost of financing the capital structure derived in step 4. Subtract the cost of this financing from pretax operating income to obtain projected

EXHIBIT 10.1

Preparing Pro Forma Financial Statements

Statement of Income and Retained Earnings

STEP 1: Project Operating Revenues
  Sales Revenue
  Other Revenues

STEP 2: Project Operating Expenses
  Cost of Goods Sold
  Selling and Administrative Expenses
  Net Income Before Interest Expense
    and Income Taxes

STEP 5: Project Cost of Financing, Income
  Tax Expense and the Change in
  Retained Earnings
  Interest Expense
  Income Tax Expense
  Net Income
  Dividends
  Change in Retained Earnings

Operations
Net Income
Depreciation
Other Adjustments
Change in Receivables
Change in Inventories
Change in Other Current Assets
Change in Accounts Payable
Change in Other Current Liabilities
CASH FLOW FROM OPERATIONS

Balance Sheet

STEP 4: Project Liabilities and
  Contributed Capital
  Accounts Payable
  Notes Payable
  Other Current Liabilities
  Long-Term Debt
  Other Liabilities
  Contributed Capital

STEP 5: Project Retained Earnings
  Retained Earnings

STEP 3: Project Assets
  Cash
  Accounts Receivable
  Inventories
  Other Current Assets
  Investments
  Fixed Assets
  Other Assets

Statement of Cash Flows

STEP 6: Project the Statement of Cash Flows

Investing
Acquisition of Fixed Assets
Sale of Investments
Acquisition of Investments
Other Investing Transactions
CASH FLOW FROM INVESTING

Financing
Change in Notes Payable
Change in Long-Term Debt
Change in Common Stock
Dividends
Other Financing Transactions
CASH FLOW FROM FINANCING

net income before income taxes. Subtract income tax expense from net income before income taxes to obtain projected net income. Subtract dividends from projected net income to obtain the projected change in retained earnings.

6. Derive the statement of cash flows from the projected income statements and comparative balance sheets.

Exhibit 10.1 summarizes this six-step procedure.

Be sure that the amounts on the three pro forma financial statements articulate with each other. For example, projected net income and dividends should agree with the change in retained earnings on the balance sheet. The amounts for the depreciation addback and capital expenditures on the statement of cash flows should agree with the change in net property, plant, and equipment on the balance sheet. If the balance sheet does not balance or the change in cash on the balance sheet disagrees with the net change in cash on the statement of cash flows, it is likely that other important relations between financial statement items have been violated.

Be sure that the assumptions made in preparing the pro forma financial statements are consistent with the past or reflect changes that management intends to make in the future. The quality of pro forma financial statements is no better than the quality of the assumptions on which they are based. The analyst should spend time thinking through and justifying each assumption made. The analyst should also assess the sensitivity of projected amounts to the assumptions made. Some assumptions are more critical to the resulting projections than others.

In successive sections of this chapter we illustrate the six-step procedure described above by preparing pro forma financial statements for Coke for Year 8 through Year 12. Appendix A presents the financial statements and notes for Coke for Year 7. Appendix C presents printouts for Coke of FSAP, the financial statement analysis package discussed in Chapter 1. We use selected data from these printouts to make the projections for Coke. We derive the amounts using the computer spreadsheets discussed in Appendix 10.1.

All financial statement amounts throughout the chapter appear in millions. The spreadsheets take all computations to multiple decimal places. Because we express all amounts in millions, rounding differences will occasionally make it seem that some subtotals and totals disagree with the sum of the individual items that make up the subtotal or total.

STEP 1: PROJECT SALES AND OTHER REVENUES

Projecting Sales. The key starting point is to project sales. The expected level of sales serves as a basis for deriving most of the other amounts in the pro forma financial statements.

Sales has both a volume component and a price component. Although firms typically do not report these two elements of total sales separately, the analyst might use them as a framework for thinking about likely future sales.

In the case of *volume*, a firm in a mature industry with little expected change in its market share (a consumer foods company, for example) might anticipate volume increases equal to the growth rate in the general population. A firm that has increased its operating capacity consistent with the high growth rate anticipated in a particular industry (a biotechnology or computer software company, for example) might use the industry growth rate to project volume increases.

Projecting *price* increases involves consideration of the expected rate of general price inflation in the economy as well as specific industry factors that might affect demand, such as excess capacity, shortages of raw materials, prices of substitute products, and similar factors. A capital-intensive industry, such as paper manufacturing, often takes several years to add new capacity. If firms in an industry anticipate operating near capacity for the next few years, then price increases are likely to occur. If excess capacity already exists or new capacity is expected to become available soon, however, price increases are less likely. A firm operating in an industry that is expected to transition from the high-growth to the maturity phase of its life cycle (such as some segments of the computer industry) might expect lessening growth rates from the recent historical rate of volume and price increases.

If sales have grown at a reasonably steady rate in prior periods, and there is no indication that economic, industry, or firm-specific factors will change significantly, then the analyst can project this growth rate into the future. If a major acquisition or sale affected the historical growth rate, then the analyst should filter out the effect of this event when making projections (unless the firm's strategy is to make additional acquisitions). The most difficult sales projections occur for firms with cyclical sales patterns (heavy machinery, computers, for example). The historical growth rates for sales in such firms might reflect wide variations in both direction and amount from year to year. The analyst should then project a varying growth rate that maintains this cyclical sales pattern in these cases.

The historical growth rates in sales for Coke are as follows:

Year 3	13.0%
Year 4	6.8%
Year 5	15.9%
Year 6	11.4%
Year 7	2.9%
Five-year compound average	9.1%

We have noted that the consumer foods industry in the United States is in its maturity phase. Industry sales have grown recently at the growth rate for the general population, approximately 2 percent per year. The primary vehicles for growth by consumer foods companies are international sales and corporate acquisitions.

With respect to international sales, Note 16 to Coke's financial statements in Appendix A indicates that sales in the United States grew at a 6 percent compound annual rate during the preceding five years, while international sales grew at a rate in the mid-teens. Increasing competition in international markets and increases in the value of the U.S. dollar will dampen future sales increases in other countries.

With respect to acquisition activity, Coke has followed the policy of establishing bottling operations and later selling them to various investors. Coke sometimes reacquires particular bottlers for short periods if their operations seem to be in need of Coke's managerial expertise. The acquisition or divestment of a bottler in which Coke owns a controlling interest impacts the change in sales each year, a factor that is behind some changes in Coke's growth rates. The decrease in the growth rate in sales during Year 7 from its historical level results from Coke's sale of previously consolidated bottling operations in France and Belgium during the year. Coke states in Appendix B that it intends to continue selling interests in its bottling operations in the future.

We assume that Coke's sales will increase at a rate of 6 percent per year between Year 8 and Year 12. This rate of growth is slower than that during the last five years, and reflects increasing competition in international markets and continuing sales of operations that were previously consolidated. Projected sales are as follows:

	Amount	Percentage Change
Year 7 Actual Sales	$18,546	—
Year 8 Projected Sales	$19,659	6.0%
Year 9 Projected Sales	$20,838	6.0%
Year 10 Projected Sales	$22,089	6.0%
Year 11 Projected Sales	$23,414	6.0%
Year 12 Projected Sales	$24,819	6.0%

Projecting Other Revenues.   Other revenues for Coke include interest on marketable securities and investments in securities and earnings in equity-method affiliates. Other income as a percentage of sales has gradually increased from 1.1 percent during Year 3 to 5.2 percent during Year 7. The percentage during Year 7, however, includes an unusually large gain of 2.3 percent (= $431/$18,546) from the issuance of common stock by unconsolidated affiliates. For projection purposes, we assume that gains of this magnitude will not recur. Thus, we project other revenues equal to 3.0 percent of sales.

The projected amounts are as follows:

	Projected Sales	Projected Other Revenues	Percentage of Sales
Year 8 Projected	$19,659	$590	3.0%
Year 9 Projected	$20,838	$625	3.0%
Year 10 Projected	$22,089	$663	3.0%
Year 11 Projected	$23,414	$702	3.0%
Year 12 Projected	$24,819	$745	3.0%

STEP 2: PROJECT OPERATING EXPENSES

The procedure for projecting operating expenses depends on the behavior of the particular cost items. If all costs behave like variable costs, and the analyst anticipates no changes in their behavior relative to sales, then the common size income statement percentages can serve as the basis for projecting future operating expenses. The analyst would multiply projected sales by the cost of goods sold percentage, selling and administrative expense percentage, and so on to derive the amounts for operating expenses. Alternatively, each operating expense can be projected to grow at the same rate as sales (6.0 percent for Coke).

If the cost structure reflects a high proportion of fixed cost that will not change as sales increase, however, then using the common size income statement approach can result in poor projections. In this case, the analyst should attempt to estimate the variable and fixed cost structure of the firm. Alternatively, the analyst can use the historical growth rates for individual cost items.

Capital-intensive manufacturing firms are often subject to high proportions of fixed costs. One clue suggesting the presence of fixed costs is that the percentage change in cost of goods sold or selling and administrative expenses in prior years differs significantly from the percentage change in sales. Using historical growth rates for individual cost items is one way to reflect the effects of different mixes of variable and fixed costs.

Coke has a relatively low level of fixed costs. Thus, we project Coke's operating expenses using the common size income statement percentages.

Cost of Goods Sold.   Coke's cost of goods sold percentage varied between 37.0 percent and 38.7 percent of sales during Year 3 through Year 6, but declined to 36.3 percent during Year 7. Coke sold previously consolidated bottlers during Year 7 and now sells concentrate to these bottlers. Coke's gross margin on sales of concentrate is higher than on bottling operations. Thus, the cost of goods sold percentage decreased. We assume that continuing sales of bottling operations will lower the cost of goods sold percentage, but increased competition will dampen selling price increases and tend to moderate such reductions. Thus, we assume that cost of goods sold will be 36 percent of sales for Year 8 through Year 12.

Selling and Administrative Expenses.   The selling and administrative expense to sales percentage varied between 39.4 percent and 42.6 percent between Year 3 and Year 7. The 42.6 percent during year 7 includes unusually large nonrecurring charges of $384.5 million (see Coke's Note 14 in Appendix A). These charges amount to 2.1 percent ($384.5/$18,546) of sales. We assume that charges of this size will not recur during the next five years. We therefore project selling and administrative expenses to equal 40 percent of sales between Year 8 and Year 12.

Exhibit 10.2 presents the pro forma statement of income and retained earnings for Year 8 through Year 12. We consider the projection of interest and income tax

		EXHIBIT 10.2			
	Pro Forma Statement of Income and Retained Earnings for Coke				
		(amounts in millions)			

	Year 8 Projected	Year 9 Projected	Year 10 Projected	Year 11 Projected	Year 12 Projected
Sales[a]	$19,659	$20,838	$22,089	$23,414	$24,819
Other Revenues[b]	590	625	663	702	745
Cost of Goods Sold[c]	(7,077)	(7,502)	(7,952)	(8,429)	(8,935)
Selling andAdministrative[d]	(7,864)	(8,335)	(8,835)	(9,366)	(9,927)
Interest Expense[e]	(325)	(403)	(494)	(599)	(716)
Net Income before Income Taxes	$ 4,983	$ 5,223	$ 5,470	$ 5,723	$ 5,985
Income Tax Expense[f]	(1,545)	(1,619)	(1,696)	(1,774)	(1,855)
Net Income	$ 3,438	$ 3,604	$ 3,774	$ 3,949	$ 4,130
Dividends	(1,397)	(1,564)	(1,752)	(1,962)	(2,198)
Change in Retained Earnings	$ 2,042	$ 2,040	$ 2,022	$ 1,987	$ 1,932

[a]Projected using 6 percent growth rate.

[b]Projected assuming 3 percent of sales.

[c]Projected assuming 36 percent of sales.

[d]Projected assuming 40 percent of sales.

[e]Projected assuming an interest rate of 6 percent of average notes payable and 8 percent of average long-term debt and a 35 percent tax savings at the statutory marginal tax rate.

[f]Projected assuming 31 percent of operating income before taxes.

expense, net income, and the change in retained earnings after projecting the firm's financing.

STEP 3: PROJECT THE ASSETS ON THE BALANCE SHEET

We prepare the asset side of the pro forma balance sheet next. Two general approaches to projecting assets are:

1. Project total assets, and then use the common size balance sheet percentages to allocate this total among individual asset items.
2. Project individual assets, and then sum individual asset amounts to obtain total assets.

Projected Total Assets Approach. We can project total assets using the historical growth rate in assets. Coke's assets grew at a 9.7 percent compound annual growth rate during the last five years. If this growth rate continues, total assets will increase as follows:

	Amount	Percentage Change
Year 7 Actual Assets	$16,161	—
Year 8 Projected Assets	$17,729	9.7%
Year 9 Projected Assets	$19,448	9.7%
Year 10 Projected Assets	$21,335	9.7%
Year 11 Projected Assets	$23,404	9.7%
Year 12 Projected Assets	$25,674	9.7%

Using historical growth rates to project total assets can result in erroneous projections if the analyst fails to consider the link between sales growth and asset growth. We assume a sales growth rate for Coke of 6.0 percent in Exhibit 10.2. Coke would not likely increase assets by 9.7 percent each year if sales continue to grow by only 6.0 percent. The analyst should probably use a smaller growth rate for assets than the historical rate in this case.

An alternative approach to projecting total assets uses the total assets turnover ratio. This approach ties the projection of total assets to the level of projected sales. Coke's total assets turnover was 1.2 in Year 3 through Year 7. Assume that Coke's total assets turnover will remain at 1.2 over the next five years. The calculation of projected total assets using the assets turnover is as follows:

				Total Assets	
	Sales	Total Assets Turnover	Average Total Assets	Beginning of Year	End of Year
Year 8 Projected ...	$19,659	1.2	$16,382	$16,161	$16,604
Year 9 Projected ...	$20,838	1.2	$17,365	$16,604	$18,126
Year 10 Projected ..	$22,089	1.2	$18,407	$18,126	$18,689
Year 11 Projected ..	$23,414	1.2	$19,512	$18,689	$20,334
Year 12 Projected ..	$24,819	1.2	$20,682	$20,334	$21,031

One difficulty we sometimes encounter in using total assets turnover to project total assets is that it can result in unusual patterns for projected total assets. The total assets turnover uses *average* total assets in the denominator. If total assets changed by an unusually large (small) percentage in the most recent year before projections are made, then the next year's assets must change by an unusually small (large) proportion to compensate.

Look at Exhibit 10.3. Assume that a firm has historically experienced a total assets turnover of 2.0. An acquisition late in Year 3 causes its total assets to increase, but the firm expects the assets turnover to remain at 2.0 for the longer term (dotted line). Projecting Year 4 assets using an assets turnover of 2.0 means that

EXHIBIT 10.3

**Illustration of Difficulty Sometimes Encountered
When Projecting Total Assets Using Assets Turnover**

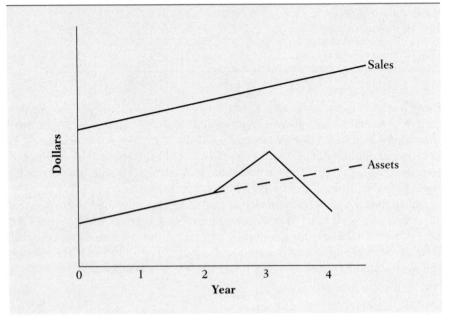

projected assets must decrease to maintain the *average* total assets commensurate with an assets turnover of 2.0. This "sawtooth" pattern makes little sense, given the growth rate in sales.

We encounter this problem projecting total assets for Coke using its total assets turnover. Note that Coke's total assets increased 7.4 percent during Year 7. Using an assets turnover of 1.2 to project total assets, we determine above that total assets would increase as shown in the first two columns below:

	Year-End Assets	Percentage Increase	Year End Assets	Percentage Increase
Year 7	$16,161	7.4%	$16,161	
Year 8	$16,604	2.7%	$17,035	5.41%
Year 9	$18,126	9.2%	$17,957	5.41%
Year 10	$18,689	3.1%	$18,928	5.41%
Year 11	$20,334	8.8%	$19,952	5.41%
Year 12	$21,031	3.4%	$21,031	5.41%

Note that the growth rate in total assets fluctuates in a systematic pattern each year. The analyst can deal with this "sawtooth problem" by smoothing the rate of increase in assets. An increase in assets from $16,161 million to $21,031 million over five years represents a compound average annual rate of 5.41 percent. The last two columns show the revised projected assets applying this rate to smooth the growth of assets. Note that total assets equal $21,031 million at the end of Year 12 in both cases. We could use these revised total asset amounts to prepare the pro forma balance sheet for Coke.

An alternative approach to dealing with the "sawtooth problem" is to base the asset turnover on the ending balance, instead of the average balance, in total assets. Coke's actual sales for Year 7 were 1.15 times the total assets on December 31, Year 7 (1.15 = $18,546/$16,161). The projection of total assets following this alternative approach yields total assets as follows:

	Sales	Total Assets Turnover	Year-End Assets	Percentage Increase
Year 7 Actual	$18,546	1.15	$16,161	
Year 8 Projected	19,659	1.15	17,095	6%
Year 9 Projected	20,838	1.15	18,120	6%
Year 10 Projected	22,089	1.15	19,208	6%
Year 11 Projected	23,414	1.15	20,360	6%
Year 12 Projected	24,819	1.15	21,582	6%

The growth rate in total assets equals the projected growth rate in sales only because we assume that the projected total assets turnover would be the same as for Year 7. We could have assumed a different total assets turnover and accomplished the smoothing as above using year-end assets.

Once the analyst projects total assets, common size balance sheet percentages provide the basis for allocating this total to individual assets. The assumption behind using these common size percentages is that the firm maintains a constant mix of assets, regardless of the level of total assets. The common size balance sheet for Coke in Appendix C indicates that the composition of total assets displayed a relatively stable pattern during the last five years (with the exception of an unusual increase in the percentage for investments and an unusual decrease in the percentage for property, plant, and equipment in Year 7). We might use an average of the common size percentages during this period to allocate projected total assets to individual asset components.

Using common size balance sheet percentages to project individual assets has two shortcomings, however. First, the common size percentages for individual assets are not independent of each other. For example, for a firm like Coke, which acquires and disposes of its bottlers on an ongoing basis, the analyst would see a changing proportion for investments in securities. Other asset categories may show decreasing percentages in some years, even though their dollar amounts are increasing. The analyst must interpret these decreasing percentages carefully.

Second, using the common size percentages does not permit the analyst to change assumptions about the future behavior of an individual asset easily. For example, assume that Coke intends to implement inventory control systems that should increase its inventory turnover in the future. Inventory will likely constitute a smaller percentage of total assets in the future than it has in the past. The analyst will have difficulty adjusting the common size balance sheet percentages to reflect such changes in inventory policies.

Projected Individual Asset Approach. The second general approach to project total assets focuses on individual assets. We can again use either historical growth rates or asset turnovers.

As in the case of using historical growth rates to project total assets, the analyst must link historical growth rates for individual assets to the assumption made regarding the growth in sales, particularly for assets integrally related to operations (such as accounts receivable, inventories, or fixed assets). For example, Coke's inventories decreased at a 0.7 percent compound annual rate during the last five years. It is unlikely that inventories will continue to decrease at such a rate if sales grow at 6.0 percent each year. Asset turnovers probably are a better basis for projecting individual assets because they incorporate the projected level of operating activity and permit changes in the expected behavior of individual assets.

Our projections of individual assets for Coke use a combination of common size percentages, growth rates, and asset turnovers. Exhibit 10.4 presents the projected balance sheet. We discuss in turn the projection of individual assets.

Cash and Marketable Securities. Cash has constituted approximately 9 percent of total assets, and marketable securities have constituted approximately 1 percent of total assets, during the last five years. Coke apparently needs a certain amount of cash on hand to maintain its operations. We assume a continuation of these common size percentages in the future. We project the dollar amount for cash and for marketable securities after projecting the amounts for all other assets.

As discussed later, projecting balance sheet amounts by projecting individual assets, liabilities, and shareholders' equity items requires the analyst to plug some item on the balance sheet to make assets equal liabilities and shareholders' equity. The plug is often cash. The change in cash on the balance sheet for the year should then agree with the change in cash on the projected statement of cash flows. If the projected level of cash is considered too high, the analyst can then assume that the firm will either invest the excess in marketable securities (if the excess is considered temporary) or pay down other borrowing. If the projected balance in cash is negative, the analyst might assume that the firm engages in short-term borrowing to bring about a desired level of cash.

EXHIBIT 10.4

Pro Forma Balance Sheet for Coke
(amounts in millions)

	Year 8 Projected	Year 9 Projected	Year 10 Projected	Year 11 Projected	Year 12 Projected
Assets					
Cash	$ 1,585	$ 1,732	$ 1,894	$ 2,071	$ 2,265
Marketable Securities	176	192	210	230	252
Accounts Receivable	1,768	1,904	2,051	2,210	2,380
Inventories	1,045	1,148	1,261	1,384	1,520
Other Current Assets	1,759	1,864	1,976	2,094	2,220
Total Current Assets	$ 6,333	$ 6,841	$ 7,392	$ 7,990	$ 8,637
Investments	6,543	7,197	7,917	8,708	9,579
Property, Plant, and Equipment (cost) ..	6,188	6,859	7,604	8,430	9,346
Accumulated Depreciation	(2,252)	(2,496)	(2,767)	(3,068)	(3,401)
Other Assets	798	846	897	951	1,008
Total Assets	$17,610	$19,247	$21,043	$23,011	$25,169
Liabilities and Shareholders' Equity					
Accounts Payable	$ 3,125	$ 3,285	$ 3,454	$ 3,632	$ 3,819
Notes Payable	4,288	5,115	7,015	8,470	10,563
Current Maturities of Long-Term Debt .	9	422	16	257	2
Other Current Liabilities	1,099	1,165	1,235	1,309	1,388
Total Current Liabilities	$ 8,521	$ 9,987	$11,720	$13,669	$15,771
Long-Term Debt	1,233	1,347	1,473	1,611	1,762
Deferred Income Taxes	319	338	358	380	403
Other Noncurrent Liabilities	1,253	1,328	1,408	1,492	1,582
Total Liabilities	$11,326	$13,001	$14,959	$17,152	$19,518
Common Stock	$ 2,203	$ 2,534	$ 2,914	$ 3,351	$ 3,854
Retained Earnings	17,169	19,209	21,231	23,218	25,149
Other Equity Adjustments	(601)	(637)	(675)	(716)	(759)
Treasury Stock	(12,487)	(14,860)	(17,386)	(19,994)	(22,593)
Total Shareholders' Equity	$ 6,284	$ 6,246	$ 6,084	$ 5,859	$ 5,651
Total Liabilities and Shareholders' Equity	$17,610	$19,247	$21,043	$23,011	$25,169

Accounts Receivable. Coke's accounts receivable turnover declined steadily from 12.7 in Year 3 to 11.1 in Year 7. The decline results from an increase in the number of unconsolidated bottlers to which Coke sells concentrate on account. We project accounts receivable assuming a turnover of 11.1 for Year 8 through Year 12. The projected amounts are as follows:

Accounts	Sales	Receivable Turnover	Average Accounts Receivable	Accounts Receivable Beginning of Year	End of Year
Year 8 Projected	$19,659	11.1	$1,771	$1,641	$1,901
Year 9 Projected	$20,838	11.1	$1,877	$1,901	$1,854
Year 10 Projected	$22,089	11.1	$1,990	$1,854	$2,126
Year 11 Projected	$23,414	11.1	$2,109	$2,126	$2,092
Year 12 Projected	$24,819	11.1	$2,236	$2,092	$2,380

The increase in accounts receivable portrays the sawtooth pattern depicted in Exhibit 10.3. We smooth this increase over time using the compound growth rate procedure illustrated earlier for total assets. An increase in accounts receivable from $1,641 million to $2,380 million over five years represents a compound annual rate of increase of 7.72 percent. Thus, projected accounts receivable are:

	Year-End Accounts Receivable	Percentage Increase
Year 7 Actual	$1,641	
Year 8 Projected	$1,768	7.72%
Year 9 Projected	$1,904	7.72%
Year 10 Projected	$2,051	7.72%
Year 11 Projected	$2,210	7.72%
Year 12 Projected	$2,380	7.72%

Inventories. Coke experienced an increasing inventory turnover during the last four years. It is likely that Coke's sale of previously consolidated bottlers increased the inventory turnover. We project inventories using an inventory turnover of 6.5, the level in Year 7. The projected amounts are as follows:

	Cost of Goods Sold	Inventory Turnover	Average Inventories	Inventories Beginning of Year	End of Year
Year 8 Projected	$7,077	6.5	$1,089	$ 952	$1,226
Year 9 Projected	$7,502	6.5	$1,154	$1,226	$1,082
Year 10 Projected	$7,952	6.5	$1,223	$1,082	$1,365
Year 11 Projected	$8,429	6.5	$1,297	$1,365	$1,229
Year 12 Projected	$8,935	6.5	$1,375	$1,229	$1,520

The increases in inventories also display a sawtooth pattern. We smooth the increases using a compound annual rate of increase of 9.81 percent as follows:

	Year-End Inventories	Percentage Increase
Year 7 Actual	$ 952	
Year 8 Projected	$1,045	9.81%
Year 9 Projected	$1,148	9.81%
Year 10 Projected	$1,261	9.81%
Year 11 Projected	$1,384	9.81%
Year 12 Projected..	$1,520	9.81%

Other Current Assets.   Other current assets usually vary in relation to the level of operating activity. We assume that other current assets will increase at the growth rate of sales as follows:

	Year-End Other Current Assets	Percentage Increase
Year 7 Actual	$1,659	
Year 8 Projected	$1,759	6.0%
Year 9 Projected	$1,864	6.0%
Year 10 Projected	$1,976	6.0%
Year 11 Projected	$2,094	6.0%
Year 12 Projected	$2,220	6.0%

Investments in Securities.   Coke's investments in securities primarily represent its interest in unconsolidated bottlers. These investments grew at a compound annual rate of 16.8 percent during the last five years. The growth reflects the effects of (1) Coke's accrual of its share of earnings of equity method investees, and (2) Coke's sale of a portion of the stock of previously consolidated subsidiaries that Coke now treats as equity method investments. Much of the growth occurred in Year 7.

Assuming that the increase in Year 7 was unusual, we project that equity method investments will increase 10.0 percent each year from Year 8 through Year 12. The projected amounts are as follows:

	Year-End Investments in Securities	Percentage Increase
Year 7 Actual	$5,948	
Year 8 Projected	$6,543	10.0%
Year 9 Projected	$7,197	10.0%
Year 10 Projected	$7,917	10.0%
Year 11 Projected	$8,708	10.0%
Year 12 Projected	$9,579	10.0%

Property, Plant, and Equipment.   Coke's fixed assets turnover increased steadily from 3.8 to 4.7 between Year 4 and Year 7. The increase likely results from the sale of interests in previously consolidated bottlers. We assume that the fixed asset turnover will remain at 4.7 for Year 8 through Year 12.

	Sales	Fixed Asset Turnover	Average Net Fixed Assets	Net Fixed Assets Beginning of Year	End of Year
Year 8 Projected	$19,659	4.7	$4,183	$3,550	$4,815
Year 9 Projected	$20,838	4.7	$4,434	$4,815	$4,052
Year 10 Projected	$22,089	4.7	$4,700	$4,052	$5,347
Year 11 Projected	$23,414	4.7	$4,982	$5,347	$4,616
Year 12 Projected	$24,819	4.7	$5,281	$4,616	$5,945

Smoothing the sawtooth rate of increase in net fixed assets yields a compound annual rate of increase of 10.86 percent. We use this rate to project both gross property, plant, and equipment and accumulated depreciation.

	Year-End Gross Fixed Assets	Year-End Accumulated Depreciation	Percentage Increases
Year 7 Actual	$5,581	$2,031	
Year 8 Projected	$6,188	$2,252	10.86%
Year 9 Projected	$6,859	$2,496	10.86%
Year 10 Projected	$7,604	$2,767	10.86%
Year 11 Projected	$8,430	$3,068	10.86%
Year 12 Projected	$9,346	$3,401	10.86%

Other Assets.   Other assets for Coke primarily include goodwill and other intangibles from acquisitions. These assets increased at a compound annual rate of 13.7 percent during the last five years. The amount of other assets for Coke represents only 4.7 percent of assets at the end of Year 7. Because of their lack of materiality (Coke is not heavily involved in making majority ownership investments), we assume that other assets will grow at the growth rate in sales.

The projected amounts for other assets are:

	Year-End Other Assets	Percentage Increase
Year 7 Actual	$ 753	
Year 8 Projected	$ 798	6.0%
Year 9 Projected	$ 846	6.0%
Year 10 Projected	$ 897	6.0%
Year 11 Projected	$ 951	6.0%
Year 12 Projected	$ 1,008	6.0%

Cash and Marketable Securities.   The analyst can now project cash and marketable securities. Projected assets for Year 8, other than cash and marketable securities, are as follows:

Accounts Receivable	$ 1,768
Inventories	1,045
Other Current Assets	1,759
Investments	6,543
Property, Plant, and Equipment (net)	3,936
Other Assets	798
Total Assets Excluding Cash and Marketable Securities	$15,849

The $15,849 total represents 90 percent of total assets. Total assets therefore equal $17,610 (= $15,849/0.90). Cash equals $1,585 (= 0.09 × $17,610), and marketable securities equal $176 (= 0.01 × $17,610).

We can use a diagram to summarize the approaches to projecting assets:

	Project Total Assets	**Project Individual Assets**
Use Historical Growth Rates for Projections		
Use Asset Turnovers for Projections		

The four possible combinations in the diagram yield similar projections for assets when a firm has experienced relatively stable historical growth rates for total assets and individual asset items and relatively stable asset turnovers. If historical growth rates have varied significantly from year to year, then using *average* historical growth rates provides more reasonable projections than asset turnovers.

One desirable feature of using asset turnovers, however, is that projected asset amounts incorporate projections of the level of sales. Also, management's actions to improve profitability often focus on improving asset turnovers. The analyst can incorporate the effects of these actions into the projections more easily by using the asset turnovers approach than by adjusting the compound annual growth rates or common size balance sheet percentages.

STEP 4: PROJECT LIABILITIES AND SHAREHOLDERS' EQUITY

Once the analyst completes the asset side of the pro forma balance sheet, projections of liabilities and shareholders' equity come next. For firms that target and maintain a particular capital structure over time, the analyst can use the common size balance sheet percentages to project amounts of individual liabilities and shareholders' equity. The common size balance sheet for Coke in Appendix C shows that the balance sheet percentages for total liabilities fluctuated between 61.9 percent and 65.4 percent, with shareholders' equity fluctuating between 34.6 percent and 38.1 percent during the last five years. Thus, using the common size percentages appears reasonable in this case. Alternatively, the analyst can project individual liabilities and shareholders' equity accounts using historical growth rates or turnover ratios.

We use a combination of common size percentages, growth rates, and turnover ratios to project the liabilities and shareholders' equity for Coke. Each account is discussed in turn.

Accounts Payable. Coke includes accounts payable and accrued expenses on a single line on its balance sheet. Thus, the average days payable do not accurately reflect the number of days accounts payable are outstanding to suppliers of inventories. We use the days payable, however, to project the combined amounts for accounts payable and accrued expenses. Coke's days payable varied between 142 and 169 days during the last five years. These days payable translate into an accounts payable turnover between 2.2 (= 365/169) and 2.6 (= 365/142). We assume an accounts payable turnover of 2.4 for Year 8 through Year 12. We begin by calculating purchases on account.

	Year 8	Year 9	Year 10	Year 11	Year 12
Cost of Goods Sold	$7,077	$7,502	$7,952	$8,429	$8,935
Plus Ending Inventory	1,045	1,148	1,261	1,384	1,520
Less Beginning Inventory . . .	(952)	(1,045)	(1,148)	(1,261)	(1,384)
Purchases	$7,170	$7,605	$8,065	$8,552	$9,071

The projection of accounts payable is as follows:

	Purchases	Accounts Payable Turnover	Average Accounts Payable	Accounts Payable Beginning of Year	Accounts Payable End of Year
Year 8 Projected	$7,170	2.4	$2,987	$2,972	$3,003
Year 9 Projected	$7,605	2.4	$3,169	$3,003	$3,334
Year 10 Projected	$8,065	2.4	$3,360	$3,334	$3,387
Year 11 Projected	$8,552	2.4	$3,563	$3,387	$3,740
Year 12 Projected	$9,071	2.4	$3,780	$3,740	$3,819

Projected accounts payable display a sawtooth pattern over time. We smooth the variations in growth rates using a 5.14 percent compound annual growth rate as follows:

	Year-End Accounts Payable	Percentage Increase
Year 7 Actual	$2,972	
Year 8 Projected	$3,125	5.14%
Year 9 Projected	$3,285	5.14%
Year 10 Projected	$3,454	5.14%
Year 11 Projected	$3,632	5.14%
Year 12 Projected	$3,819	5.14%

Notes Payable. Coke's short-term borrowing varied between $1,653 million and $3,388 million during the last five years. Given that Coke maintains approximately 10 percent of its assets in cash and marketable securities, it is unlikely that Coke borrows short-term for temporary operating needs. It is likely, however, that it borrows to help finance the repurchase of its common stock. Note from the statement of cash flows for Coke in Appendix A that the firm generates approximately $2 billion of free cash flow each year (that is, cash flow from operations net of cash flow for investing). Thus, Coke uses free cash flow primarily to pay dividends and repurchase common stock. It engages in short-term borrowing to make up temporary cash shortages for these purposes. We treat notes payable as the plug to equate projected assets with projected liabilities and shareholders' equity.

Current Maturities of Long-Term Debt. Note 6 to Coke's financial statements discloses the amounts due on long-term debt during Year 8 through Year 12. We use these amounts in the pro forma balance sheet.

Other Current Liabilities. Other current liabilities relate primarily to operating activities (such as salaries payable, utilities payable, taxes payable). We project this account to grow at the growth rate in sales of 6.0 percent.

	Year-End Other Current Liabilities	Percentage Increase
Year 7 Actual	$1,037	
Year 8 Projected	$1,099	6.0%
Year 9 Projected	$1,165	6.0%
Year 10 Projected	$1,235	6.0%
Year 11 Projected	$1,309	6.0%
Year 12 Projected	$1,388	6.0%

Long-Term Debt. Long-term debt as a percentage of total assets declined steadily from 11.9 percent in Year 4 to 6.9 percent in Year 7. Coke likely repaid debt with proceeds from the sale of previously consolidated bottlers. We assume that Coke will maintain a long-term debt to total assets ratio of 7.0 percent between Year 8 and Year 12, approximately its level at the end of Year 7. The projected amounts are as follows:

	Year-End Long-Term Debt	Common Size Balance Sheet Percentage
Year 8 Projected	$1,233	7.0%
Year 9 Projected	$1,347	7.0%
Year 10 Projected	$1,473	7.0%
Year 11 Projected	$1,611	7.0%
Year 12 Projected	$1,762	7.0%

Deferred Income Taxes. The income tax note for Coke indicates that deferred taxes relate to a variety of operating items (employee benefits plans, property, plant, and equipment, equity investments, intangible assets). Thus, we assume that deferred tax liabilities will increase at the growth rate in sales. The amounts are as follows:

	Year-End Deferred Income Taxes	Percentage Increase
Year 7 Actual	$301	
Year 8 Projected	$319	6.0%
Year 9 Projected	$338	6.0%
Year 10 Projected	$358	6.0%
Year 11 Projected	$380	6.0%
Year 12 Projected	$403	6.0%

Other Noncurrent Liabilities.　Other noncurrent liabilities relate to pension obligations, health care obligations, and other operating-related items. We therefore project other noncurrent liabilities to grow at the growth rate in sales of 6.0 percent.

	Year-End Other Noncurrent Liabilities	Percentage Increase
Year 7 Actual	$1,182	
Year 8 Projected	$1,253	6.0%
Year 9 Projected	$1,328	6.0%
Year 10 Projected	$1,408	6.0%
Year 11 Projected	$1,492	6.0%
Year 12 Projected	$1,582	6.0%

Contributed Capital.　Common stock and additional paid-in capital have increased through the issuance of stock in connection with employee stock option plans. These accounts increased at a compound annual rate of approximately 15 percent between Year 3 and Year 7. We assume this same rate of increase for Year 8 through Year 12.

	Year-End Common Stock	Percentage Increase
Year 7 Actual	$1,916	
Year 8 Projected	$2,203	15.0%
Year 9 Projected	$2,534	15.0%
Year 10 Projected	$2,914	15.0%
Year 11 Projected	$3,351	15.0%
Year 12 Projected	$3,834	15.0%

Other Equity Adjustments. Other equity adjustments primarily include the foreign currency translation adjustment (as well as amounts for unrealized gains on securities available for sale). The cumulative translation adjustment account has consistently been a negative amount during the last five years. Coke has expanded into developing countries whose currencies have decreased in value relative to the U.S. dollar. The company will likely continue to expand its international operations.

We assume that the U.S. dollar will continue to increase in value relative to the foreign currencies of Coke's foreign operations. Thus, we project a continuing negative other equity adjustment that will increase at the growth rate in sales as follows:

	Year-End Other Equity Adjustments	Percentage Increase
Year 7 Actual	$-567	
Year 8 Projected	$-601	6.0%
Year 9 Projected	$-637	6.0%
Year 10 Projected	$-675	6.0%
Year 11 Projected	$-716	6.0%
Year 12 Projected	$-759	6.0%

Treasury Stock. Coke has repurchased significant amounts of its common stock in recent years. One advantage of stock repurchases is that they reduce the amount of dividends a company must subsequently pay (that is, they reduce the number of shares outstanding). Another advantage is that the stock market often interprets such repurchases as good news, concluding that managers with their inside knowledge of the firm think that the market is underpricing the firm's stock. The stock market reacts to this positive signal by bidding up the price of the firm's shares.

The amount in Coke's treasury stock account increased at a compound annual rate of 21.2 percent during the last five years. It is unlikely that Coke will be able to continue this pace of stock reacquisitions. We assume the treasury stock accounts will increase 21 percent in Year 8, 19 percent in Year 9, 17 percent in Year 10, 15 percent in Year 11, and 13 percent in Year 12. The projected amounts for treasury stock are as follows:

	Year-End Treasury Stock	Percentage Increase
Year 7 Actual	$10,320	
Year 8 Projected	$12,487	21.0%
Year 9 Projected	$14,860	19.0%
Year 10 Projected	$17,386	17.0%
Year 11 Projected	$19,994	15.0%
Year 12 Projected	$22,593	13.0%

STEP 5: PROJECT THE COST OF FINANCING, INCOME TAX EXPENSE, AND THE CHANGE IN RETAINED EARNINGS

Interest Expense. We can now project interest expense. Note 5 to Coke's financial statements indicates that the interest rate on short-term borrowing was 5.6 percent at the end of Year 7. Note 6 indicates that the interest rate on long-term debt varied between 5.75 percent and 7.875 percent at the end of Year 7. We assume that interest expense will equal 6 percent of average notes payable and 8 percent of average long-term debt between Year 8 and Year 12. Projected interest expense is as follows:

	Year 8	Year 9	Year 10	Year 11	Year 12
Average Notes Payable	$3,838	$4,702	$6,065	$7,743	$ 9,517
Interest Rate	0.06	0.06	0.06	0.06	0.06
Interest Expense on Notes Payable	$ 230	$ 282	$ 364	$ 465	$ 571
Average Long-Term Debt	$1,183	$1,506	$1,629	$1,679	$ 1,816
Interest Rate	0.08	0.08	0.08	0.08	0.08
Interest Expense on Long-Term Debt	$ 95	$ 121	$ 130	$ 134	$ 145
Total Interest Expense	$ 325	$ 403	$ 494	$ 599	$ 716

We can now enter these interest expense amounts in the projected income statement in Exhibit 10.2.

Income Taxes. Coke's income tax note (Note 13) shows the reconciliation between the statutory tax rate and the average, or effective, tax rate. The statutory tax rate was 35 percent during Year 5 through Year 7. Coke experienced increases in its effective tax rate of 1.0 percentage point from state income taxes and decreases in its effective tax rate of approximately 5.0 percentage points from lower tax rates in other tax jurisdictions and equity method income, yielding an effective tax rate of approximately 31 percent. Coke realized a one-time benefit from a tax settlement during Year 7 that reduced its effective tax rate in that year to 24 percent. We assume that the effective tax rate for Year 8 to Year 12 will be 31 percent.

Retained Earnings. Retained earnings increase by the amount of projected net income and decrease for dividends. Dividends grew at a compound annual rate of 17.55 percent during the last five years. We project dividends to grow at 12 percent a year between Year 8 and Year 12. The slower growth rate reflects the slower assumed growth rate in sales. Projected dividends are as follows:

	Dividends For Year	Percentage Increase
Year 7 Actual	$1,247	
Year 8 Projected	$1,397	12.0%
Year 9 Projected	$1,564	12.0%
Year 10 Projected	$1,752	12.0%
Year 11 Projected	$1,962	12.0%
Year 12 Projected	$2,198	12.0%

Thus, the change in retained earnings is as follows:

	Year 8	Year 9	Year 10	Year 11	Year 12
Beginning of Year	$15,127	$17,169	$19,209	$21,231	$23,218
Plus Net Income	3,438	3,604	3,774	3,949	4,130
Less Dividends	(1,397)	(1,564)	(1,752)	(1,962)	(2,198)
End of Year	$17,169	$19,209	$21,231	$23,218	$25,149

Notes Payable.   We can now plug for the amount of notes payable for each year. Projected total assets equal $17,610 for Year 8. To obtain total liabilities plus shareholders' equity of $17,610 requires a plug to notes payable of $4,288.

STEP 6: PROJECT THE STATEMENT OF CASH FLOWS

The final step involves preparing a projected statement of cash flows. We prepare the statement of cash flows directly from the projected income statement and projected balance sheet. We follow the usual procedure for preparing this statement described in Chapter 2.

Exhibit 10.5 presents the pro forma statement of cash flows for Coke. The derivation of each of the line items is as follows:

1. Net income: We use the amounts in the pro forma income statement (Exhibit 10.2).
2. Depreciation: We assume that the addback for depreciation equals the change in accumulated depreciation on the pro forma balance sheet. There is some error here because we have excluded the addback for amortization of goodwill. The other assets item on the pro forma balance sheet, which includes goodwill, is a relatively small amount. Thus, the error here is not material. The error primarily affects the amount for cash flow from operations (the goodwill amortization addback) and cash flow from investing (where the change in other assets appears). There is also some error here in that we assume that Coke did not sell or retire depreciable assets each year.

EXHIBIT 10.5

Pro Forma Statement of Cash Flows for Coke
(amounts in millions)

	Year 8 Projected	Year 9 Projected	Year 10 Projected	Year 11 Projected	Year 12 Projected
Operations					
(1) Net Income	$ 3,438	$ 3,604	$ 3,774	$ 3,949	$ 4,130
(2) Depreciation	221	244	271	300	334
(3) Other Addbacks (net)	55	58	62	65	69
(4) (Increase) Decrease in Accounts Receivable	(127)	(136)	(147)	(159)	(170)
(5) (Increase) Decrease in Inventories ...	(93)	(103)	(113)	(123)	(136)
(6) (Increase) Decrease in Prepayments ..	(100)	(106)	(112)	(119)	(126)
(7) Increase (Decrease) in Accounts Payable	153	160	169	178	187
(8) Increase (Decrease) in Other Current Liabilities	62	66	70	74	79
Cash Flow from Operations	$ 3,610	$ 3,788	$ 3,974	$ 4,166	$ 4,366
Investing					
(9) Acquisition of Marketable Securities and Investments (net) ...	$ (546)	$ (671)	$ (738)	$ (811)	$ (892)
(10) Acquisition of Property, Plant, and Equipment (net)	(607)	(671)	(745)	(825)	(917)
(11) Other Investing Transactions	(45)	(48)	(51)	(54)	(57)
Cash Flow from Investing	$(1,198)	$(1,390)	$(1,534)	$(1,691)	$(1,866)
Financing					
(12) Increase (Decrease) in Short-Term Borrowing	$ 900	$ 827	$ 1,899	$ 1,456	$ 2,092
(13) Increase in Long-Term Debt	117	528	(280)	379	(104)
(14) Increase in Common Stock	287	331	380	437	503
(15) Dividends	(1,397)	(1,564)	(1,752)	(1,962)	(2,198)
(16) Acquisition of Common Stock	(2,167)	(2,373)	(2,526)	(2,608)	(2,599)
Cash Flow from Financing	$(2,260)	$(2,251)	$(2,279)	$(2,299)	$(2,306)
(17) Change in Cash	$ 152	$ 147	$ 162	$ 177	$ 194
Cash—Beginning of Year	1,433	1,585	1,732	1,894	2,071
Cash—End of Year	$ 1,585	$ 1,732	$ 1,894	$ 2,071	$ 2,265

---

3. Other addbacks (net): This item includes the increase in deferred income taxes and other noncurrent liabilities on the projected balance sheet. There is likely to be some error here as well. A subtraction should appear for the excess of equity earnings over dividends received from affiliates. Rather than making assumptions about this relatively immaterial item, we choose simply to treat the change in investments fully as an investing transaction. Excluding this item from other addbacks (net) affects the classification of cash flows as relating to operating and investing activities, but does not affect the net change in cash each year.

4.–8. Changes in operating current asset and current liability accounts other than cash appearing on the pro forma balance sheet.

9. Acquisition of marketable securities and investments (net): The statement of cash flows classifies purchases and sales of marketable securities (current asset) and investments in securities (noncurrent asset) as investing transactions. We use the changes in these accounts on the pro forma balance sheet to derive the amounts for these items on the statement of cash flows.

10. Acquisition of property, plant, and equipment (net): The amount on this line equals the change in property, plant, and equipment (at cost) on the pro forma balance sheet in Exhibit 10.4. We assume that Coke did not sell or retire depreciable assets each year.

11. Other investing transactions: We enter the acquisition of other assets (intangibles and goodwill) on this line. The change in other assets on the pro forma balance sheet is the net of acquisitions and amortization. As discussed above, we assume that the amount of amortization is sufficiently immaterial that we treat the change in other assets fully as an investing transaction.

12.–13. Increases in borrowings (notes payable and long-term debt) are financing activities.

14., 16. Changes in common stock: The amounts entered on lines (14) and (16) represent the changes in the common stock, additional paid-in capital, and treasury stock accounts on the pro forma balance sheet.

15. Dividends: The amount for dividends equals the projected amount each year (discussed earlier under "retained earnings").

17. Change in cash: The amounts on lines (1) through (16) net to the change in cash on the comparative balance sheet.

ANALYZING PRO FORMA FINANCIAL STATEMENTS

We can analyze pro forma financial statements using the same ratios and other analytical tools discussed in previous chapters. Exhibit 10.6 presents a ratio analysis for Coke based on the pro forma results for Year 8 through Year 12.

The projected profit margin for the rate of return on assets remains the same. This occurs because we have assumed that the cost of goods sold and selling and administrative expenses vary directly with changes in sales.

The total assets turnover and the accounts receivable, inventory, and fixed assets turnovers show a gradual decline. These declines occur because of the smoothing applied in deriving the balance sheet amounts for these accounts. Recall that we assumed that the asset turnovers for these accounts for Year 8 through Year 12 would be approximately equal to the actual amounts for Year 7. Thus, the asset turnovers for *nonsmoothed* balance sheet amounts would portray steady levels. By smoothing, the asset turnovers for Year 8 and Year 9 exceed the assumed turnover levels; those for Year 10 approximately equal the assumed amounts; and

EXHIBIT 10.6

Ratio Analysis for Coke
Based on Pro Forma Financial Statements

	Year 8 Projected	Year 9 Projected	Year 10 Projected	Year 11 Projected	Year 12 Projected
Profitability					
Profit Margin for ROA	18.6	18.6%	18.6%	18.6%	18.6%
Asset Turnover	1.16	1.13	1.10	1.06	1.03
Rate of Return on Assets	21.6%	21.0%	20.3%	19.7%	19.1%
Common Earnings Leverage	94.2%	93.2%	92.2%	91.0%	89.9%
Capital Structure Leverage	2.71	2.94	3.27	3.69	4.19
Rate of Return on Common Shareholders' Equity	55.3%	57.5%	61.2%	66.1%	71.8%
Cost of Goods Sold/Sales	36.0%	36.0%	36.0%	36.0%	36.0%
Selling and Administrative Expense/Sales	40.0%	40.0%	40.0%	40.0%	40.0%
Interest Expense/Sales	1.7%	1.9%	2.2%	2.6%	2.9%
Income Tax Expense/Sales	7.9%	7.8%	7.7%	7.7%	7.5%
Accounts Receivable Turnover	11.5	11.3	11.2	11.0	10.8
Inventory Turnover	7.1	6.8	6.6	6.4	6.2
Fixed Asset Turnover	5.3	5.0	4.8	4.6	4.4
Short-Term Liquidity					
Current Ratio	.74	.68	.63	.58	.55
Quick Ratio	.41	.38	.35	.33	.31
Operating Cash Flow to Current Liabilities	44.9%	40.5%	36.2%	32.5%	29.3%
Long-Term Solvency					
Total Liabilities to Total Assets	64.3%	67.5%	71.1%	74.5%	77.5%
Long-Term Debt Ratio	16.4%	17.7%	19.5%	21.6%	23.8%
Debt Equity Ratio	19.6%	21.6%	24.2%	27.5%	31.2%
Times Interest Earned	16.3	14.0	12.1	10.6	9.4
Operating Cash Flow to Total Liabilities	33.5%	30.8%	28.1%	25.7%	23.6%
Operating Cash Flow to Capital Expenditures	5.9	5.5	5.3	5.0	4.7

those for Year 11 and Year 12 are lower than the assumed amounts. Thus, the decline in the asset turnover and the resulting effects on the rate of return on assets are not cause for concern.

We assumed that Coke would continue to make significant repurchases of its common stock. Coke would finance these repurchases with cash flow from operations and with short-term borrowing. The effect of this shift from shareholders' equity to debt is an increase in the capital structure leverage ratio. The net effect of a decreasing ROA and an increasing capital structure leverage ratio is an increase in the rate of return on common shareholders' equity.

The short-term liquidity ratios decline over time, primarily because of the increase in notes payable. The long-term solvency ratios also decline, the result of both the buildup of notes payable and the decrease in shareholders' equity.

These pro forma financial statements can serve as a base case that an analyst can use to assess the impact of various changes for Coke. For example, suppose Coke were to discontinue purchases of its treasury stock. Coke's revised profitability ratios for Year 8 would then be:

	Year 8 Originally Projected	Year 8 Revised Projected
Profit Margin	18.6%	18.6%
Assets Turnover	1.16	1.16
Rate of Return on Assets	21.6%	21.6%
Common Earnings Leverage	94.2%	95.4%
Capital Structure Leverage	2.71	2.3
Rate of Return on Common Shareholders' Equity	55.3%	47.6%
Current Ratio	0.74	1.00
Cash Flow from Operations to Average Current Liabilities	44.9%	52.8%
Cash Flow from Operations to Average Total Liabilities	33.5%	37.9%
Interest Coverage Ratio	16.3	20.5

The assumption about the growth in treasury stock has a significant effect on pro forma amounts for Coke. Various other changes in assumptions will have a variety of possible effects. By designing a flexible computer spreadsheet, the analyst can change any one assumption or a combination of assumptions and observe the effect on the financial statement ratios. Appendix 10.1 describes a procedure for designing a flexible spreadsheet.

SUMMARY

The preparation of pro forma financial statements requires numerous assumptions (growth rate in sales, cost behavior of various expenses, levels of investment in working capital and fixed assets, or mix of financing). The analyst should study the sensitivity of the pro forma financial statements to the assumptions made and to the impact of different assumptions. Spreadsheet computer programs are useful in this sensitivity analysis. The analyst can study alternative assumptions quickly and trace their effects on the financial statements.

Pro forma financial statement preparation and use are subject to two dangers, however:

1. The preparation of pro forma financial statements can easily become merely a mechanical exercise. Spreadsheet computer programs let the analyst put in a handful of assumptions, and the program outputs financial statements for

many years into the future. The familiar adage, "garbage-in, garbage-out," is particularly apt to describe the preparation of pro forma financial statements. The analyst should (a) carefully study past financial statement relationships to gain an understanding of the economic characteristics of the business, and (b) consider changes in economic conditions, business strategy, and other factors that affect the projections. Pro forma financial statements that attempt to project more than four or five years into the future are not likely to be reliable.

2. The analyst should ensure that pro forma financial statements are internally consistent. For example, assumptions about sales and various expenses must articulate with the levels of accounts receivable, inventories, and other assets. Amounts projected on the statement of cash flows must articulate with changes in balance sheet accounts and with related income statement amounts.

APPENDIX 10.1

DESIGNING A COMPUTER SPREADSHEET FOR PRO FORMA FINANCIAL STATEMENTS

This appendix describes a procedure for designing a Microsoft Excel spreadsheet to use in preparing pro forma financial statements. The description is relatively detailed and assumes little background in spreadsheet preparation, so students who have previous experience with spreadsheets can skip over or skim this material.

Some general principles should be observed in preparing spreadsheets.

1. Design the spreadsheet to permit the maximum flexibility to change assumptions. One of the benefits of using computer spreadsheets to prepare pro forma financial statements is that assumptions can be changed in order to see right away the effect of the change on the projected financial statements. If the analyst has to change many cells on the spreadsheet or change the formulas underlying these cells, one of the primary benefits of spreadsheets is lost.

2. Design the spreadsheet so that the assumptions made are clearly evident on the spreadsheet, instead of embedded in the formulas in the cells.

The analyst can preserve the desirable attributes of spreadsheets by creating a section of each spreadsheet for any assumptions made. The formula for each financial statement item is then designed so that it feeds directly or indirectly off the assumptions. We illustrate this design for the spreadsheets for Coke's pro forma financial statements.

GETTING STARTED

Begin by opening the Excel program. Click on File/New to create a new file. Click next on File/Save As to save the new file. A box at the bottom of the screen will ask for the name of the file. Type in Coke.Proforma, and click on Enter. Next, name each of the four spreadsheets to use for the pro forma financial statements. At the bottom of the screen will appear Sheet 1, Sheet 2, and Sheet 3. Place the arrow on Sheet 1. Then go to the menu at the top of the screen, and click on Format/Worksheet/Rename. Here type in Income Statement to name the first worksheet. Follow the same procedure to name Sheet 2 as Balance Sheet, Sheet 3 as Statement of Cash Flows, and Sheet 4 as Financial Ratios. Click on File/Save periodically to ensure that your work is not lost.

INCOME STATEMENT SPREADSHEET

Exhibit 10.7 presents the income statement spreadsheet for Coke. Type in the row and column headings as shown in that exhibit. Be sure to place the items in the rows and columns shown to ensure that the formulas we deal with next are correctly specified. The A (first) column will need to be widened to permit the row labels to appear. Click on Format/Column/Width, and type in 31 (any number will do, but 31 allows for all rows in the spreadsheet to appear on the screen and to be printed on a single sheet of paper). Next, type in the actual amounts for Coke for Year 7.

When formulas for future years use actual amounts for the most recent year as a base, it is useful to have these amounts in the spreadsheet. For example, we assume that sales for Coke will increase 6 percent each year. Sales for Year 8 will therefore equal 106 percent of sales for Year 7. Under the column for Year 8 in Exhibit 10.7, we show the formulas for each of the items for Coke *for Year 8*. We generally insert formulas for an entire column to be sure that the mathematics work correctly (that is, revenues minus expenses equal net income, net income minus dividends equals the increase in retained earnings).

Note that there are alternative ways to specify most formulas. If the formula is specified incorrectly, Excel will indicate that an error exists, and either suggest a change to correct it or describe common types of errors and ways to deal with them.

You can see that most of the formulas use information in the assumptions section of the spreadsheet. When we want to change any of the assumptions, we can do so in the assumptions section without needing to adjust the formulas in the cells above.

With the exception of interest expense, all amounts in the income statement spreadsheet use amounts that appear on this spreadsheet. Thus, there is no need to specify the name of another spreadsheet in the formulas. Interest expense, however, uses interest rates that appear on the income statement spreadsheet and notes payable and long-term debt that appear on the balance sheet spreadsheet (discussed later). In this case, the formula for interest expense must specify that the amounts for these liabilities appear on another spreadsheet.

Whenever a formula draws amounts from another spreadsheet, the formula must include a single quotation mark immediately before and after the name of the spreadsheet. The second single quotation mark must then be followed by an explanation mark before specifying the cell number on that spreadsheet. If we were designing a spreadsheet from scratch, we would not yet know the row numbers for

EXHIBIT 10.7

Pro Forma Income Statement Spreadsheet for Coke

A	B	C	D	E	F	G
1 INCOME STATEMENT						
2 COKE	YEAR 7	YEAR 8	YEAR 9	YEAR 10	YEAR 11	YEAR 12
3 REVENUES						
4 Sales	18546	=B4*(1+C19)				
5 Other Revenues	967	=C4*C20				
6 Total Revenues	19513	=C4+C5				
7 EXPENSES						
8 Cost of Goods Sold	6738	=C4*C21				
9 Selling and Administrative	7893	=C4*C22				
10 Interest Expense	286	See Below				
11 Total Expenses	14917	=C8+C9+C10				
12 Income Before Taxes	4596	=C6−C11				
13 Income Tax Expense	−1104	=-C25*C12				
14 NET INCOME	3492	=C12+C13				
15 Dividends	−1247	=B15*(1+C26)				
16 Increase in Retained Earnings	2245	=C14+C15				
18 ASSUMPTIONS		YEAR 8	YEAR 9	YEAR 10	YEAR 11	YEAR 12
19 Sales Growth		0.06	0.06	0.06	0.06	0.06
20 Other Revenues Percentage of Sales		0.03	0.03	0.03	0.03	0.03
21 Cost of Goods Sold/Sales Percentage		0.36	0.36	0.36	0.36	0.36
22 Selling & Admin./Sales Percentage		0.4	0.4	0.4	0.4	0.4
23 Interest Rate on Notes Payable		0.06	0.06	0.06	0.06	0.06
24 Interest Rate on Long-Term Debt		0.08	0.08	0.08	0.08	0.08
25 Income Tax Rate		0.31	0.31	0.31	0.31	0.31
26 Growth Rate in Dividends		0.12	0.12	0.12	0.12	0.12

Interest Expense Formula for Cell C10
=SUM((C23*0.5*('Balance Sheet'!B20+'Balance Sheet'!C20))+(C24*.05*('Balance Sheet'!B21+'Balance Sheet'!C21+'Balance Sheet'!B24+'Balance Sheet'!C24)))

notes payable and long-term debt. Therefore, the analyst should create each of the spreadsheets with appropriate row and column labels before entering any formulas.

Once the analyst enters the appropriate formulas in column C for Year 8, they can be copied to columns D through G for subsequent years. Begin by moving the arrow to cell C4. Then click on Edit/Copy. A box will appear around cell C4. Use the right directional arrow key to move directly to cell D4 and then click on Enter. Excel automatically enters the appropriate formula in cell D4. Repeat this process for the remaining cells for sales (row 4), copying the formula in cell D4 to E4, copying the formula in cell E4 to F4, and so on. Repeat this process for the remaining rows 5 through 16.

The analyst makes various assumptions in preparing pro forma financial statements, and enters them in the assumptions section of the income statement spreadsheet. The amounts shown in Exhibit 10.7 are the assumptions we use in the chapter to prepare pro forma financial statements for Coke.

BALANCE SHEET SPREADSHEET

Exhibit 10.8 presents the balance sheet spreadsheet for Coke. Note again that the financial statement appears at the top of the spreadsheet, and the assumptions appear at the bottom. As with the income statement spreadsheet, the formulas for balance sheet amounts use information in the assumptions section of the spreadsheet. The formulas compute the amounts for Year 8.

When a particular term in a formula uses information from the balance sheet spreadsheet only, there is again no need to specify the name of the spreadsheet. If a formula uses information from another spreadsheet, the formula must specify the name of the other spreadsheet, as we described earlier.

The formulas for cash and marketable securities require elaboration. Excel does not allow formulas to be circular. We assume that cash equals 9 percent of total assets. Yet cash is a component of total assets. If we were to define the formula for the cash cell as 0.09*C16, Excel would indicate that the formula includes an error.

To deal with the circularity problem, we sum all balance sheet amounts other than cash and marketable securities. We know that this sum must equal 90 percent of total assets. Dividing this sum by 90 percent yields total assets. We can then multiply this total assets amount by 9 percent to obtain cash and 1 percent to obtain marketable securities.

The use of turnovers to project any accounts on the balance sheet may produce the "sawtooth" pattern discussed in the chapter. The analyst can either smooth the changes in the balance sheet accounts manually and enter the smoothed amounts in the cells, or write a formula on the spreadsheet to accomplish the smoothing.

STATEMENT OF CASH FLOWS SPREADSHEET

Exhibit 10.9 presents the statement of cash flows spreadsheet for Coke. The analyst derives this financial statement from the pro forma income statement and pro forma balance sheet. Thus, no assumptions section appears.

To ensure that the changes in cash on the statement of cash flows spreadsheet reconcile with the change in cash on the balance sheet spreadsheet, a mathematical check appears in the last three lines in Exhibit 10.9. If a difference in the cash balances occurs, the analyst must search for the source of the difference and correct the spreadsheet accordingly.

FINANCIAL RATIOS SPREADSHEET

Exhibit 10.10 presents the financial ratios spreadsheet for Coke. The financial statement ratios use amounts from all three of the other spreadsheets. Thus, each term in the formulas must specify the spreadsheet in which the amount for that term appears.

<table>
<tr><td colspan="7" align="center">EXHIBIT 10.8</td></tr>
<tr><td colspan="7" align="center">Pro Forma Balance Sheet Spreadsheet for Coke</td></tr>
</table>

A	B	C	D	E	F	G
1 BALANCE SHEET						
2 COKE	**YEAR 7**	**YEAR 8**	**YEAR 9**	**YEAR 10**	**YEAR 11**	**YEAR 12**
3 ASSETS						
4 Cash	1433	=.09*((C6+C7+C8+C10+C14+C15)/.9)				
5 Marketable Securities	225	=.01*((C6+C7+C8+C10+C14+C15)/.9)				
6 Accounts Receivable	1641	=(2*C39)−B6				
7 Inventories	952	=(2*C41)−B7				
8 Other Current Assets	1659	=B8*(1+'Income Statement'!C19)				
9 Total Current Assets	5910	=SUM(C4:C8)				
10 Investments in Securities	5948	=B10*(1+C42)				
11 Property, Plant, and Equipment:						
12 Cost	5581	=B12*(C14/B14)				
13 Accumulated Depreciation	-2031	=B13*(C14/B14)				
14 Net	3550	=(2*C44)−B14				
15 Other Assets	753	=B15*(1+'Income Statement'!C19)				
16 Total Assets	16161	=SUM(C9+C10+C14+C15)				
18 LIABILITIES AND SHARE. EQUITY						
19 Accounts Payable	2972	=(2*C47)−B19				
20 Notes Payable	3388	=C16−C19−C21−C22−C24−C25−C26−C32				
21 Current Maturities-Long-Term Debt	9	(Amount is inputted from note to financial statements)				
22 Other Current Liabilities	1037	=B22*(1+'Income Statement'!C19)				
23 Total Current Liabilities	7406	=SUM(C19:C22)				
24 Long-Term Debt	1116	=C49*C16				
25 Deferred Income Taxes	301	=B25*(1+'Income Statement'!C19)				
26 Other Liabilities	1182	=B26*(1+'Income Statement'!C19)				
27 Total Liabilities	10005	=SUM(C23:C26)				
28 Contributed Capital	1916	=B28*(1+C50)				
29 Retained Earnings	15127	=B29+'Income Statement'!C16				
30 Other Equity Adjustments	−567	=B30*(1+'Income Statement'!C19)				
31 Treasury Stock	−10320	=B31*(1+C51)				
32 Total Shareholders' Equity	6156	=SUM(C28:C31)				
33 Total Liabilities and Share. Equity	16161	=C27+C32				
35 ASSUMPTIONS		**YEAR 8**	**YEAR 9**	**YEAR 10**	**YEAR 11**	**YEAR 12**
36 Cash/Assets		0.09	0.09	0.09	0.09	0.09
37 Marketable Securities/Assets		0.01	0.01	0.01	0.01	0.01
38 Accounts Receivable Turnover		11.1	11.1	11.1	11.1	11.1
39 Average Accounts Receivable		1771	1877	1990	2109	2236
40 Inventory Turnover		6.5	6.5	6.5	6.5	6.5
41 Average Inventory		1089	1154	1223	1297	1375
42 Growth Rate in Investments		0.10	0.10	0.10	0.10	0.10
43 Fixed Assets Turnover		4.7	4.7	4.7	4.7	4.7
44 Average Fixed Assets		4183	4434	4700	4982	5281
45 Purchases		7351	7359	8233	8294	9225
46 Accounts Payable Turnover		2.4	2.4	2.4	2.4	2.4
47 Average Accounts Payable		3063	3066	3431	3456	3844
48 Notes Payable		Plug	Plug	Plug	Plug	Plug
49 Long-Term Debt/Assets		0.07	0.07	0.07	0.07	0.07
50 Growth Rate in Contributed Capital		0.15	0.15	0.15	0.15	0.15
51 Growth Rate in Treasury Stock		0.21	0.19	0.17	0.15	0.13

EXHIBIT 10.9

Pro Forma Statement of Cash Flows Spreadsheet for Coke

A	B	C	D	E	F	G
1 STATEMENT OF CASH FLOWS						
2 COKE	YEAR 7	YEAR 8	YEAR 9	YEAR 10	YEAR 11	YEAR 12
3 OPERATIONS						
4 Net Income		3492	='Income Statement'!C14			
5 Depreciation		479	='Balance Sheet'!B13 − 'Balance Sheet'!C13			
6 Addbacks and Subtractions		−544	='Balance Sheet'!C25 − 'Balance Sheet'!B25 + 'Balance Sheet'!C26 − 'Balance Sheet'!B26 + 'Balance Sheet'!C30 − 'Balance Sheet'!B30			
7 (Increase)Decrease in Accounts Receivable		−230	='Balance Sheet'!B6 − 'Balance Sheet'!C6			
8 (Increase)Decrease in Inventories		−33	='Balance Sheet'!B7 − 'Balance Sheet'!C7			
9 (Increase)Decrease in Other Current Assets		−65	='Balance Sheet'!B8 − 'Balance Sheet'!C8			
10 Increase(Decrease) in Accounts Payable		361	='Balance Sheet'!C19 − 'Balance Sheet'!B19			
11 Increase(Decrease) in Other Current Liabilities		3	='Balance Sheet'!C22 − 'Balance Sheet'!B22			
12 Cash Flow from Operations		3463	=SUM(C4:C11)			
14 INVESTING						
15 Sale (Purchase) of Fixed Assets—Net		−909	='Balance Sheet'!B12 − 'Balance Sheet'!C12			
16 Sale (Purchase) of Investments—Net		34	='Balance Sheet'!B5 + 'Balance Sheet'!B10 − 'Balance Sheet'!C5 − 'Balance Sheet'!C10			
17 Other Investing Activities		−175	='Balance Sheet'!B15 − 'Balance Sheet'!C15			
18 Cash Flow from Investing		−1050	=SUM(C15:C17)			
20 FINANCING						
21 Increase(Decrease) in Notes Payable—Net		1017	='Balance Sheet'!C20 − 'Balance Sheet'!B20			
22 Increase(Decrease) in Long-Term Debt—Net		−475	='Balance Sheet'!C21 + 'Balance Sheet'!C24 − 'Balance Sheet'!B21 − 'Balance Sheet'!B24			
23 Increase(Decrease) in Common Stock—Net		−1397	='Balance Sheet'!C28 − 'Balance Sheet'!B28 + 'Balance Sheet'!C31 − 'Balance Sheet'!B31			
24 Dividends Paid		−1247	='Income Statement'!C15			
25 Other Financing Transactions		−45	=NONE			
26 Cash Flow from Financing		−2147	=SUM(C21:C25)			
27 Change in Cash		266	=SUM(C12+C18+C26)			
28 Cash—Beginning of Year		1167	='Balance Sheet'!B4			
29 Cash—End of Year		1433	=C27+C28			
30 Cash on Balance Sheet		1433	='Balance Sheet'!C4			
31 Difference		0	=C29−C30			

EXHIBIT 10.10

Pro Forma Financial Statement Ratios Spreadsheet for Coke

	A	B	C	D	E	F
1	**FINANCIAL RATIOS**					
2	**COKE**	**YEAR 8**	**YEAR 9**	**YEAR 10**	**YEAR 11**	**YEAR 12**
3	Profit Margin for ROA	=('Income Statement'!C14+(.65*'Income Statement'!C10))/ 'Income Statement'!C4				
4	Total Assets Turnover	='Income Statement'!C4/(.5('Balance Sheet'!B16+'Balance Sheet'!C16))				
5	Rate of Return on Assets	=('Income Statement'!C14+(.65*'Income Statement'!C10))/ (.5*('Balance Sheet'!B16+'Balance Sheet'!C16))				
6	Common Earnings Leverage	='Income Statement'!C14/('Income Statement'!C14+ (.65*'IncomeStatement'!C10))				
7	Capital Structure Leverage	=(.5*('Balance Sheet'!B16+'Balance Sheet'!C16))/ (.5*('Balance Sheet'!B32+'Balance Sheet'!C32))				
8	Rate of Return on Common Equity	='Income Statement'!C14/(.5('Balance Sheet'!B32+'Balance Sheet'!C32))				
9	Cost of Goods Sold/Sales	='Income Statement'!C8/'Income Statement'!C4				
10	Selling & Admin. Expense/Sales	='Income Statement'!C9/'Income Statement'!C4				
11	Interest Expense/Sales	='Income Statement'!C10/'Income Statement'!C4				
12	Income Tax Expense/Sales	='Income Statement'!C13/'Income Statement'!C4				
13	Accounts Receivable Turnover	='Income Statement'!C4/(.5*('Balance Sheet'!B6+'Balance Sheet'!C6))				
14	Inventory Turnover	='Income Statement'!C8/(.5*('Balance Sheet'!B7+'Balance Sheet'!C7))				
15	Fixed Asset Turnover	='Income Statement'!C4/(.5*('Balance Sheet'!B14+'Balance Sheet'!C14))				
16	Current Ratio	='Balance Sheet'!C9/'Balance Sheet'!C23				
17	Quick Ratio	=('Balance Sheet'!C4+'Balance Sheet'!C5+'Balance Sheet'!C6)/ 'Balance Sheet'!C23				
18	CFO/Average Current Liabilities	='Statement of Cash Flows'!C12/(.5*('Balance Sheet'!B23+ 'Balance Sheet'!C23))				
19	Days Accounts Payable Outstanding	=365/'Balance Sheet'!C46				
20	Liabilities/Assets	='Balance Sheet'!C27/'Balance Sheet'!C16				
21	Long-Term Debt Ratio	='Balance Sheet'!C24/('Balance Sheet'!C24+'Balance Sheet'!C32)				
22	Debt Equity Ratio	='Balance Sheet'!C24/'Balance Sheet'!C32				
23	CFO/Average Total Liabilities	='Statement of Cash Flows'!C12/(.5*('Balance Sheet'!B27+ 'Balance Sheet'!C27))				
24	Interest Coverage Ratio	=('Income Statement'!C12+'Income Statement'!C10)/ 'Income Statement'!C10				
25	CFO/Capital Expenditures	='Statement of Cash Flows'!C12/−'Statement of Cash Flows'!C15				

PROBLEMS AND CASES

10.1 PROJECTING GROSS MARGINS FOR CAPITAL-INTENSIVE CYCLICAL BUSINESSES.
AK Steel is an integrated manufacturer of high-quality steel and steel products in capital-intensive steel mills. Its sales for Year 9 totaled $2,307 million, and cost of goods sold totaled $1,852 million. AK's manufacturing cost structure is $670 million fixed cost plus $0.5125 variable cost as a percentage of sales. Nucor manufactures more commodity-level steel at the lower end of the market in less capital-intensive mini-mills. Nucor's sales for Year 9 totaled $3,647 million, and cost of goods sold totaled $3,139 million. Its manufacturing cost structure is $78 million fixed cost and $0.8392 variable cost as a percentage of sales.

Industry analysts anticipate annual changes as follows in steel industry sales for the next five years: Year 10, 4 percent increase; Year 11, 6 percent decrease; Year 12, 8 percent decrease; Year 13, 10 percent increase; Year 14, 6 percent increase.

Required

a. Discuss the structure of manufacturing costs (that is, fixed versus variable) for each firm in light of the manufacturing process and type of steel produced.
b. Using the analysts' forecasts of sales changes, compute the projected sales, cost of goods sold, and gross margin of each firm for Year 10 through Year 14.
c. Compute the gross margin percentage for each firm for Year 10 through Year 14.
d. Why do the levels and variability of the gross margin percentages differ for these two firms?

10.2 IDENTIFYING THE COST STRUCTURE. Sony Corporation manufactures and markets consumer electronics products. Selected income statement data for Year 7 and Year 8 appear below (in billions of yen):

	Year 7	Year 8
Sales	¥ 4,571	¥ 5,636
Cost of Goods Sold	(3,439)	(4,161)
Selling and Administrative Expenses	(918)	(1,132)
Operating Income Before Income Taxes	¥ 214	¥ 343

Required

a. Analysts can sometimes estimate the variable cost as a percentage of sales for a particular cost (such as cost of goods sold) by dividing the yen amount of the change in the cost item between two years by the yen amount of the change in sales for those two years. The analyst can then multiply the variable cost percentage times sales to determine the total variable cost. Subtracting the variable cost from the total cost yields the fixed cost for that particular cost item. Follow this procedure to determine the cost structure (fixed cost plus variable cost as a percentage of sales) for cost of goods sold for Sony.

b. Repeat part a for selling and administrative expenses.

c. Sony Corporation projects sales to grow at these percentages in future years: Year 9, 12 percent; Year 10, 10 percent; Year 11, 8 percent; Year 12, 6 percent. Project sales, cost of goods sold, selling and administrative expenses, and operating income before income taxes for Sony for Year 9 through Year 12, using the cost structure amounts derived in part a.

d. Compute the ratio of operating income before income taxes to sales for Year 9 through Year 12.

e. Interpret the changes in the ratio computed in part d in light of the expected changes in sales.

10.3　SMOOTHING CHANGES IN ACCOUNTS RECEIVABLE. Hasbro manufactures and markets toys and games for children and adults. Sales during Year 5 totaled $3,002 million. Accounts receivable totaled $791 million at the beginning of Year 5 and $807 million at the end of Year 5.

Required

a. Compute the accounts receivable turnover ratio for Hasbro for Year 5.

b. Hasbro anticipates that sales will grow at a compound annual rate of 6 percent each year between Year 5 and Year 10, and that the accounts receivable turnover each year will equal that computed in part a for Year 5. Compute the projected amount of accounts receivable at the ends of Year 6 through Year 10. Also compute the percentage change in accounts receivable between each of the year-ends between Year 5 and Year 10.

c. The changes in accounts receivable computed in part b display the "sawtooth" pattern depicted in Exhibit 10.3 in the text. Smooth the changes in accounts receivable between the end of Year 5 and the end of Year 10 from part b using the compound annual growth rate in accounts receivable between Year 5 and Year 10.

d. Smooth the changes in accounts receivable from part b using the compound annual growth rate in accounts receivable between the end of Year 5 and the end of *Year 9*. Apply this growth rate to compute accounts receivable at the ends of Year 6 through Year 10. Why do the amounts for ending accounts receivable using the growth rate from part c differ from those using the growth rate from this part?

e. Compute the accounts receivable turnover for Year 5 by dividing sales by the balance in accounts receivable at the end of Year 5 (instead of using average accounts receivable as in part a).

f. Using the measure and amount of the accounts receivable turnover determined in part e, compute the projected balance in accounts receivable at the ends of Year 6 through Year 10. Also compute the percentage change in accounts receivable between the year-ends for Year 5 and Year 10.

10.4　SMOOTHING CHANGES IN INVENTORIES. Lands' End sells men's, women's, and children's clothing through catalogs. Sales totaled $1,118,743 thousand and cost of goods sold totaled $609,913 thousand during Year 7. Inventories totaled $164,816 thousand at the end of Year 6 and $142,445 thousand at the end of Year 7.

Required

a. Compute the inventory turnover ratio for Lands' End for Year 7.

b. Lands' End projects that sales will grow at a compound annual rate of 4 percent between Year 7 and Year 12, and that the cost of goods sold to sales percentage will equal that realized in Year 7. Compute the projected amount of inventory at the ends of Year 8 through Year 12, using the inventory turnover ratio computed in part a. Also compute the percentage change in inventories between each of the year-ends between Year 7 and Year 12.

c. The changes in inventories in part b display the "sawtooth" pattern depicted in Exhibit 10.3 in the text. Smooth the changes in inventories between the end of Year 7 and the end of Year 12 using the compound annual growth rate in inventories between Year 7 and Year 12.

d. Smooth the changes in inventories using the compound annual growth rate between Year 7 and *Year 11.* Apply this growth rate to determine the amount of inventories at the end of Year 8 through the end of Year 12. Why do the amounts for ending inventories using the growth rate in part c differ from those using the growth rate in this part?

e. Compute the inventory turnover for Year 7 using the balance in inventories at the end of Year 7 (instead of using average inventories as in part a).

f. Using the measure and the amount of inventory turnover determined in part e, compute the amount of inventories at the ends of Year 8 through Year 12. Also compute the percentage change in inventories between the year-ends of Year 8 through Year 12.

10.5   IDENTIFYING PRO FORMA FINANCIAL STATEMENT RELATIONSHIPS. Partial pro forma financial statements for Watson Corporation appear in Exhibit 10.11 (income statement), Exhibit 10.12 (balance sheet), and Exhibit 10.13 (statement of cash flows). Selected items have been omitted, as well as all totals (indicated by $XXXX).

EXHIBIT 10.11

Partial Pro Forma Income Statement for Watson Corporation
(Problem 10.5)

	Year 10 Actual	Year 11 Projected	Year 12 Projected	Year 13 Projected	Year 14 Projected
Sales	$ 46,000	$ 50,600	$ 56,672	$64,606	$ 74,943
Cost of Goods Sold	(29,900)	(32,890)	XXXX	(40,702)	(46,465)
Selling and Administrative	(10,580)	(11,638)	(12,468)	(13,567)	(14,989)
Interest	(3,907)	(4,298)	d.	(3,866)	(5,227)
Income Taxes	(565)	(621)	(1,372)	(2,265)	(2,892)
Net Income	$ XXXX	$ XXXX	$ XXXX	$ XXXX	$ XXXX

EXHIBIT 10.12

Partial Pro Forma Balance Sheet for Watson Corporation
(Problem 10.5)

	Year 10 Actual	Year 11 Projected	Year 12 Projected	Year 13 Projected	Year 14 Projected
Assets					
Cash	$ 1,200	$ 664	$ 206	$ 416	$ 1,262
Accounts Receivable	8,000	8,433	8,855	10,420	12,286
Inventories	7,500	8,223	c.	10,711	11,333
Fixed Assets:					
Cost	110,400	120,445	126,467	f.	169,895
Accumulated Depreciation	(33,100)	(36,112)	(37,917)	(45,352)	(50,938)
Total Assets	$ XXXX	$ XXXX	$ XXXX	$ XXXX	$ XXXX
Liabilities and Shareholders' Equity					
Accounts Payable	$ 2,500	$ 2,801	$ 3,107	$ 3,376	$ 3,828
Notes Payable	6,500	6,852	7,195	8,467	9,982
Other Current Liabilities	3,300	3,630	e.	4,635	5,376
Long-Term Debt	45,000	49,094	51,549	h.	69,251
Total Liabilities	$ XXXX	$ XXXX	$ XXXX	$ XXXX	$ XXXX
Common Stock	$ 15,000	$ 17,233	$ 17,539	$ 22,434	$ 24,319
Retained Earnings	21,700	22,043	23,700	g.	31,082
Total Shareholders' Equity	$ XXXX	$ XXXX	$ XXXX	$ XXXX	$ XXXX
Total Liabilities and Shareholders' Equity	$ XXXX	$ XXXX	$ XXXX	$ XXXX	$ XXXX

Required
Determine the amount of each of the items following:

a. Dividends declared and paid during Year 11.
b. Depreciation expense for Year 11, assuming Watson Corporation neither sold nor retired depreciable assets during Year 11.
c. Inventories at the end of Year 12.
d. Interest expense on borrowing during Year 12. The interest rate is 7 percent.
e. Other current liabilities at the end of Year 12.
f. Property, plant, and equipment at the end of Year 13, assuming Watson Corporation neither sold nor retired depreciable assets during Year 13.
g. Retained earnings at the end of Year 13.
h. Long-term debt at the end of Year 13.
i. The income tax rate for Year 14.
j. Purchases of inventories during Year 14.

EXHIBIT 10.13

Pro Forma Statement of Cash Flows for Watson Corporation
(Problem 10.5)

	Year 10 Actual	Year 11 Projected	Year 12 Projected	Year 13 Projected	Year 14 Projected
Operations					
Net Income	$ 1,048	$ 1,153	$ XXXX	$ 4,206	$ 5,370
Depreciation	2,378	b.	1,805	7,435	5,586
Change in Accounts Receivable	(394)	(433)	(422)	(1,565)	(1,866)
Change in Inventories	(657)	(723)	(1,322)	(1,166)	(622)
Change in Accounts Payable	274	301	306	269	452
Change in Other Current Liabilities	300	330	436	569	741
Cash Flow from Operations	$ XXXX	$ XXXX	$ XXXX	$ XXXX	$ XXXX
Investing					
Acquisition of Fixed Assets	$ (9,130)	$ (10,045)	$ (6,022)	$ (24,796)	$ (18,632)
Financing					
Change in Notes Payable	$ 320	$ 352	$ 343	$ 1,272	$ 1,515
Change in Long-Term Debt	3,721	4,094	2,455	10,107	7,595
Change in Common Stock	2,029	2,233	306	4,895	1,885
Dividends	(750)	a.	(891)	(1,016)	(1,178)
Cash Flow from Financing	$ XXXX	$ XXXX	$ XXXX	$ XXXX	$ XXXX
Change in Cash	$ XXXX	$ XXXX	$ XXXX	$ XXXX	$ XXXX

10.6 PREPARING AND INTERPRETING PRO FORMA FINANCIAL STATEMENTS. Wal-Mart Stores is the largest retailing firm in the world. Building on a base of discount stores, Wal-Mart has expanded into warehouse clubs and more recently into superstores. Its superstores combine traditional discount store items with grocery products.

Exhibits 3.35 through 3.37 in Chapter 3 (Case 3.1) present the financial statements of Wal-Mart for Year 5, Year 6, and Year 7. Exhibit 3.38 presents selected financial statement ratios.

Required

a. Design a spreadsheet and prepare a set of pro forma financial statements for Wal-Mart for Year 8 through Year 11, following the assumptions set forth below. Project the amounts in the order presented (unless indicated otherwise), beginning with the income statement, next the balance sheet, and then the statement of cash flows.

INCOME STATEMENT

Sales The growth rate in sales was 23.8 percent in Year 5, 13.6 percent in Year 6, and 12.0 percent in Year 7. The decreasing growth reflects increasing saturation of the discount store market. Assume that sales will increase 12 percent each year for Year 8 to Year 11.

This growth rate reflects the offsetting effects of increased market saturation of discount stores and the growth of warehouse clubs and superstores.

Cost of Goods Sold The increasing proportion of warehouse clubs and food products in the sales mix should result in an increase in the cost of goods sold percentage. Assume a cost of goods sold to sales ratio of 79 percent for Year 8 to Year 11.

Marketing and Administrative Expenses The increasing representation of warehouse clubs and superstores in the sales mix should reduce the selling and administrative expense percentage. Assume a marketing and administrative expense to sales ratio of 15.5 percent for Year 8 to Year 11.

Interest Expense Interest expense as a percentage of average interest-bearing debt (notes payable and long-term debt) was 5.9 percent in Year 6 and 5.8 percent in Year 7. Assume that interest rate expense as a percentage of average borrowing will increase to 7 percent for Year 8 through Year 11 because of a higher proportion of long-term debt, as opposed to short-term borrowing, in the capital structure. Delay projecting interest expense until after projecting the amount of interest-bearing debt in the capital structure.

Income Tax Expense Income tax expense averaged 37 percent of income before income taxes during the last three years. Assume a continuation of this average tax rate during the next four years. Delay projecting income tax expense until after projecting interest expense.

BALANCE SHEET

Cash Cash is the plug that equates projected assets with projected liabilities and shareholders' equities. Delay projecting cash until after projecting all other assets and liabilities and shareholders' equity.

Accounts Receivable Wal-Mart's accounts receivable turnover increased from 104.9 to 125.0 during the last three years. This rapid turnover represents a holding period of only three days. Assume that accounts receivable will increase at the growth rate in sales.

Inventories The inventory turnover ratio based on average inventories varied between 5.0 and 5.2 during the last three years. For projection purposes, assume an inventory turnover based on *ending* inventories (to deal with the "sawtooth" problem) of 4.9 for Year 8 to Year 11.

Prepayments Assume that prepayments relate to operating costs and will increase at the growth rate in sales.

Property, Plant, and Equipment (net) Assume that property, plant, and equipment (net) will grow in an amount equal to acquisitions of property, plant, and equipment (net of depreciation) on the statements of cash flows.

Other Assets Assume that other assets relate to operating activities (for example, deposits on facilities) and will increase at the growth rate in sales.

Accounts Payable   The days accounts payable outstanding increased from 27 days to 31 days during the last three years. Assume an accounts payable turnover ratio based on *ending* accounts payable (to deal with the "sawtooth" problem) of 11 times for Year 8 through Year 11.

Notes Payable   Assume that during Year 8 Wal-Mart pays its notes payable outstanding at the end of Year 7, and does not take on additional short-term borrowing during Year 8 through Year 11.

Other Current Liabilities   Other current liabilities relate to various operating costs. Assume that this account will increase at the growth rate in sales.

Long-Term Debt   Wal-Mart uses long-term debt to finance its acquisitions of property, plant, and equipment. Assume that long-term debt will increase in an amount equal to 40 percent of expenditures on property, plant, and equipment each year.

Other Noncurrent Liabilities   Assume that other noncurrent liabilities will increase at the growth rate in sales.
   Note: Project the amount of interest expense on average notes payable and long-term debt, income tax expense, and net income at this point.

Common Stock   Assume that common stock will not change during Year 8 through Year 11.

Retained Earnings   The increase in retained earnings equals net income minus dividends. Dividends increased by 17.1 percent in Year 6 and 5.0 percent in Year 7. Assume that dividends will increase 8 percent each year for Year 8 through Year 11.
   Note: Project the amount of cash on the balance sheet at this point.

STATEMENT OF CASH FLOWS

Depreciation Addback   Increase at a rate of 14 percent each year.

Other Addbacks   Set equal to the increase in other noncurrent liabilities.

Fixed Assets Acquired   Increase at a rate of 16 percent each year.

Other Investing Transactions   Set equal to the increase in other assets.

FINANCIAL STATEMENT RATIOS

   b. Compute the values of the ratios in Exhibit 3.38 for Year 8 through Year 11.
   c. Assess the projected changes in the profitability and risk of Wal-Mart during Year 8 through Year 11.
   d. Wal-Mart is concerned about the decreasing rate of return on common shareholders' equity projected for Year 8 through Year 11. The firm asks you to recompute the projected rate of return on common shareholders' equity for Year 8 through Year 11 under each of three independent alternatives:

1. Dividends grow at 20 percent per year, instead of the 8 percent rate initially assumed.
2. Long-term debt increases in an amount equal to 60 percent of expenditures on property, plant, and equipment, instead of the 40 percent rate initially assumed.
3. The firm repurchases its own common stock in an amount equal to 10 percent of the book value of total shareholders' equity at the end of each year (that is, the balance in the treasury stock account will equal 10 percent of total shareholders' equity before the repurchase of stock). Dividends will grow 7 percent each year instead of the 8 percent initially assumed, to reflect the smaller number of shares outstanding.

e. Evaluate the effects of each of the alternatives in part c.

10.7 **Preparing Pro Forma Financial Statements.** The Gap and The Limited operate specialty retail chains featuring clothing and personal care items. Case 3.2 in Chapter 3 presents financial statements and financial statement ratios for these two firms for Year 5, Year 6, and Year 7.

Required

a. Design spreadsheets and prepare pro forma financial statements for The Gap and The Limited for Year 8 through Year 12. Exhibit 10.14 presents the assumptions to be made. Also calculate the values of the profitability and risk ratios presented in Case 3.2 for each firm for Year 8 through Year 12. Note that the pro forma amounts for accounts receivable, inventories, fixed assets, and accounts payable use turnovers based on year-end values for these balance sheet items to avoid the "sawtooth" problem. Adjust the amount in the treasury stock account to maintain the desired long-term debt to shareholders' equity ratios.

b. The managers of The Limited are disturbed that the pro forma amounts indicate that The Gap will continue to dominate The Limited in terms of both profitability and risk. They are contemplating several strategic changes to enhance The Limited's profitability, and they want to examine the impact of these changes on these financial ratios for Year 9: (1) profit margin for rate of return on assets; (2) total assets turnover; (3) rate of return on assets; (4) common earnings leverage; (5) capital structure leverage; and (6) rate of return on common shareholders' equity. Indicate the pro forma amounts of these six ratios for The Gap and The Limited from part a and the revised amounts for The Limited for each of three independent strategic actions:

Scenario 1: Reduce prices significantly in order to increase volume. This action will lead to a 13 percent increase in sales in total (that is, the 13 percent increase incorporates sales increases previously anticipated in part a as well as the impact of the strategic shift). Selling and administrative expenses will equal 20 percent of sales. The fixed asset turnover (based on year-end values) will equal 1.7. Assume that these are the only changes from this strategic action.

Scenario 2: Eliminate lower-margin products, and place more emphasis on higher-margin products. This action will lead to a 6 percent sales increase in total. Cost of goods sold will equal 62 percent of sales. Selling and administrative expenses will equal 20.7 percent of sales. The inventory turnover will be 5.6, and the fixed asset turnover will be 1.45. Both asset turnover amounts use asset amounts at the end of the year.

Scenario 3: Centralize all purchasing, storage, credit, and other administrative activities. Selling and administrative expenses will equal 17 percent of sales. The cost

EXHIBIT 10.14

Pro Forma Assumptions for The GAP and The Limited
(Problem 10.7)

	The GAP	The Limited
Sales Growth	16%	8%
Other Revenues/Sales	.004%	.004%
Cost of Goods Sold/Sales	59%	67%
Selling and Administrative/Sales	23%	21%
Interest Rate on Notes Payable and		
Long-Term Debt	9%	10%
Effective Tax Rate	38%	38%
Minority Interest in Earnings	Not Applicable	12.3% of Net Income Before Minority Int.
Growth in Dividends	Growth Rate in Net Income	
Cash	Plug	Plug
Marketable Securities	0	0
Sales/Ending Accounts Receivable	220.0	125.0
Cost of Goods Sold/Ending Inventory ...	5.3	5.7
Sales/Ending Net Fixed Assets	1.6	1.5
Growth in Fixed Assets at Cost	Growth in Fixed Assets—Net	
Growth in Accumulated Depreciation ..	Growth in Fixed Assets—Net	
Growth in Other Assets	Growth Rate in Sales	
Purchases/Ending Accounts Payable ...	9.0	18.8
Notes Payable	0	0
Growth Rate in Other Current Liabilities	Growth Rate in Sales	
Growth in Long-Term Debt	Growth Rate in Fixed Assets at Cost	
Growth Rate in Other		
Noncurrent Liabilities	Growth Rate in Sales	
Increase in Minority Interest in	Not Applicable	60% of Minority Interest in Earnings
Net Assets		
Long-Term Debt/Shareholders' Equity ..	1.36	2.43

of goods sold to sales percentage will equal 65 percent. The inventory turnover will equal 5.9 (based on year-end asset amounts).

  c. Evaluate the three alternative scenarios in light of the analysis in part b.

10.8 ASSESSING THE PRO FORMA ASSUMPTIONS IN A BANK LENDING DECISION. Refer to the information about the Massachusetts Stove Company in Case 9.1. You are the bank lending officer at Massachusetts Regional Bank, and have received the pro forma financial statements and related information presented in support of its loan by Massachusetts Stove Company. You want to assess which of management's assumptions are most critical to the firm's ability to generate the necessary cash to remain viable and to repay the loan.

Required

  a. Design a spreadsheet for Massachusetts Stove Company that will permit you to perform a sensitivity analysis of management's assumptions. Label the columns for the income statement and the statement of cash flows: Year 5 Actual, Year 6 Projected, and Year 7 Projected. Label the columns for the balance sheet: Year 5 Actual, Year 5 Actual After Loan, Year 6 Projected, Year 7 Projected before Repayment, and Year 7 Projected after Repayment. Assume that the loan will be made as of January 1, Year 5, instead of January 15, Year 5, as stated in the case.

Depreciation expense each year equals 8 percent of the balance in property, plant, and equipment at the beginning of the year. This assumption means that the firm recognizes no depreciation in the year of the acquisition of fixed assets. Other assets include intangibles that are amortized in the amount of $588 each year. The amounts on your pro forma spreadsheets for Year 6 and Year 7 should agree with the pro forma amounts presented in Case 9.1.

b. Determine the projected balance in cash at the end of Year 6; at the end of Year 7 before repayment of the loan; and at the end of Year 7 after repayment of the loan under each of ten independent scenarios.

1. Sales increase by 21.9 percent each year, the growth rate in Year 5, instead of the 25 percent assumed.
2. Sales increase by 15 percent each year instead of the 25 percent assumed.
3. Sales increase by 10 percent each year instead of the 25 percent assumed.
4. Sales increase by 21.9 percent each year; cost of goods sold to sales remains at the Year 5 level of 53.9 percent; and the selling and administrative expense to sales percentage remains at the Year 5 level of 39.6 percent.
5. Sales increase by 25 percent each year, and cost of goods sold is 53 percent in Year 6 and 52 percent in Year 7.
6. Sales increase by 25 percent each year, and cost of goods sold is 52 percent in Year 6 and 51 percent in Year 7.
7. Accounts payable do not grow.
8. Accounts payable decline by 10 percent each year.
9. Legal costs in Year 6 total $60,000 instead of $45,000.
10. Expenditures on Tile Stove II total $77,500 during Year 6 instead of $62,500.

c. Discuss the sensitivity of management's projections to the assumptions made. Which aspects of the firm's operations would you as a loan officer monitor most closely to ensure repayment of the loan?

CASE 10.1

McDonald's Corporation— A Franchising Experience

McDonald's Corporation maintains a leading market share in the fast food industry. It both owns its own restaurants and franchises them to others. McDonald's charges franchisees an initial franchise fee at the time of awarding a franchise and an ongoing franchise fee based on sales and other performance measures. McDonald's includes franchise fees in its revenues. Neither the sales, expenses, assets, nor liabilities of franchisees generally appear in the financial statements of McDonald's. McDonald's has increased the proportion of restaurants operated through franchising arrangements in recent years.

Exhibits 10.15 through 10.17 present the financial statements for McDonald's for Year 2, Year 3, and Year 4. Exhibit 10.18 presents selected financial statement ratios.

EXHIBIT 10.15

McDonald's Corporation
Income Statements
(amounts in millions)
(Case 10.1)

	Year Ended January 31		
	Year 2	Year 3	Year 4
Revenues	$6,695	$7,133	$7,408
Cost of Goods Sold	(4,336)	(4,475)	(4,545)
Selling and Administrative Expenses ...	(669)	(837)	(872)
Interest Expenses	(391)	(374)	(316)
Income Tax Expense	(440)	(489)	(593)
Net Income	$ 859	$ 958	$1,082

EXHIBIT 10.16

McDonald's Corporation
Balance Sheets
(amounts in millions)
(Case 10.1)

	January 31			
	Year 1	Year 2	Year 3	Year 4
Assets				
Cash	$ 143	$ 226	$ 436	$ 186
Accounts Receivable	255	274	280	315
Inventories	43	43	44	43
Prepayments	108	104	105	119
Total Current Assets	$ 549	$ 647	$ 865	$ 663
Investments	335	374	400	447
Property, Plant, and Equipment				
(at cost)	11,535	12,368	12,658	13,459
Accumulated Depreciation	(2,488)	(2,801)	(3,061)	(3,378)
Other Assets	736	761	819	844
Total Assets	$10,667	$11,349	$11,681	$12,035
Liabilities and Shareholders' Equity				
Accounts Payable	$ 356	$ 314	$ 343	$ 396
Notes Payable	299	278	411	193
Current Portion of Long-Term				
Debt	65	69	269	30
Other Current Liabilities	477	627	522	483
Total Current Liabilities	$ 1,197	$ 1,288	$ 1,545	$ 1,102
Long-Term Debt	4,429	4,267	3,176	3,489
Deferred Income Taxes	695	734	749	835
Other Noncurrent Liabilities	163	225	319	335
Total Liabilities	$ 6,484	$ 6,514	$ 5,789	$ 5,761

Exh. 10.16—Continued	January 31			
	Year 1	Year 2	Year 3	Year 4
Liabilities and Shareholders' Equity				
Preferred Stock	$ 3	$ 10	$ 409	$ 423
Common Stock	220	249	306	349
Retained Earnings	5,215	5,925	6,727	7,613
Cumulative Translation				
Adjustment	47	33	(127)	(192)
Treasury Stock	(1,302)	(1,382)	(1,423)	(1,919)
Total Shareholders' Equity	$ 4,183	$ 4,835	$ 5,892	$ 6,274
Total Liabilities and				
Shareholders' Equity	$10,667	$11,349	$11,681	$12,035

EXHIBIT 10.17

McDonald's Corporation
Statements of Cash Flows
(amounts in millions)
(Case 10.1)

	Year Ended January 31		
	Year 2	Year 3	Year 4
Operations			
Net Income	$ 859	$ 958	$ 1,082
Depreciation	514	555	569
Other Addbacks (Subtractions)	65	22	52
(Increase) Decrease in AccountsReceivable	(41)	(29)	(48)
(Increase) Decrease in Inventories	—	1	—
(Increase) Decrease in Prepayments	—	1	(9)
Increase (Decrease) in Accounts Payable	(23)	1	45
Increase (Decrease) in Other Current Liabilities . . .	49	(83)	(11)
Cash Flow from Operations	$1,423	$1,426	$ 1,680
Investing			
Fixed Assets Acquired (net)	$ (941)	$ (974)	$(1,205)
Other Investing Transactions	1	(25)	(13)
Cash Flow from Investing	$ (940)	$ (999)	$(1,218)
Financing			
Increase (Decrease) in Short-Term Borrowing	$ (677)	$ 17	$ (9)
Increase (Decrease) in Long-Term Borrowing	397	(532)	55
Issue of Common Stock	100	485	—
Acquisition of Treasury Stock	(109)	(80)	(620)
Dividends on Preferred Stock	(19)	(15)	(47)
Dividends on Common Stock	(129)	(146)	(154)
Other Financing Transactions	37	54	63
Cash Flow form Financing	$ (400)	$ (217)	$ (712)
Change in Cash	$ 83	$ 210	$ (250)
Cash—Beginning of Year	143	226	436
Cash—End of Year	$ 226	$ 436	$ 186

> ### EXHIBIT 10.18
>
> ## McDonald's Corporation
> ## Financial Statement Ratios
> ## (Case 10.1)

	Year 2	Year 3	Year 4
Profit Margin	16.6%	16.8%	17.4%
Total Assets Turnover	.6	.6	.6
Rate of Return on Assets	10.1%	10.4%	10.9%
Common Earnings Leverage	75.5%	78.5%	80.4%
Capital Structure Leverage	2.4	2.2	2.1
Rate of Return on Common Shareholders' Equity	18.7%	18.3%	18.3%
Cost of Goods Sold ÷ Revenues	64.8%	62.7%	61.4%
Selling and Administrative Expenses ÷ Revenues	10.0%	11.7%	11.8%
Interest Expense ÷ Revenues	5.8%	5.2%	4.3%
Income Tax Expense ÷ Revenues	10.6%	10.5%	11.0%
Accounts Receivable Turnover	25.3	25.8	24.9
Inventory Turnover	100.8	102.9	104.5
Fixed Asset Turnover	.7	.7	.8
Current Ratio	.5	.6	.6
Quick Ratio	.4	.5	.5
Days Accounts Payable	28	27	30
Cash Flow from Operations ÷ Current Liabilities	114.5%	100.7%	126.9%
Total Liabilities to Total Assets	57.4%	49.6%	47.9%
Long-Term Debt to Total Assets	37.6%	27.2%	29.0%
Long-Term Debt to Shareholders' Equity	88.3%	53.9%	55.6%
Cash Flow from Operations to Total Liabilities	21.9%	23.2%	29.1%
Interest Coverage Ratio	4.3	4.9	6.3
Cash Flow from Operations to Capital Expenditures ...	1.3	1.3	1.3

Required

a. What evidence do you see in Exhibit 10.18 of the increasing proportion of franchise-owned McDonald's restaurants?

b. Prepare a set of pro forma financial statements for Year 5 and Year 6 under two strategic scenarios:

Scenario 1: An increasing proportion of franchised restaurants in the sales mix.

Scenario 2: A decreasing proportion of franchised restaurants in the sales mix.

Follow the assumptions set forth below to implement each of these strategies.

INCOME STATEMENT

Revenues   Scenario 1: Increase 3 percent in Year 5 and 2 percent in Year 6.

Scenario 2: Increase 5 percent in Year 5 and 6 percent in Year 6.

Cost of Goods Sold   Scenario 1: 60.0 percent of sales in Year 5 and 58.6 percent of revenues in Year 6.

Scenario 2: 62.8 percent of revenues in Year 5 and 64.2 percent of revenues in Year 6.

Selling and Administrative Expenses   Scenario 1: 12.0 percent of revenues in Year 5 and 12.3 percent in Year 6.

Scenario 2: 11.6 percent of revenues in Year 5 and 11.3 percent in Year 6.

Interest Expense   Scenario 1: 8.2 percent of interest-bearing debt in Year 5 and 8.1 percent of interest-bearing debt in Year 6.

Scenario 2: 8.5 percent of interest-bearing debt in Year 5 and 8.6 percent of interest-bearing debt in Year 6.

EXHIBIT 10.19

McDonald's Corporation
Pro Forma Common Size Balance Sheet Percentages
(Case 10.1)

	Scenario 1		Scenario 2	
	Year 5	Year 6	Year 5	Year 6
Assets				
Cash	1.5%	1.8%	1.5%	1.8%
Accounts Receivable	2.7	2.8	2.5	2.4
Inventories	.4	.4	.4	.4
Prepayments	1.0	1.0	1.0	1.0
Total Current Assets	5.6%	6.0%	5.5%	5.7%
Investments	3.9	4.1	3.6	3.4
Property, Plant, and Equipment (at cost)	114.5	117.7	115.3	118.0
Accumulated Depreciation	(31.8)	(35.6)	(31.3)	(34.0)
Other Assets	7.8	7.8	7.0	7.0
Total Assets	100.0%	100.0%	100.0%	100.0%
Liabilities and Shareholders' Equity				
Accounts Payable	3.3%	3.3%	3.4%	3.4%
Notes Payable	1.9	2.8	1.3	1.4
Current Portion of Long-Term Debt	.3	.3	.3	.3
Other Current Liabilities	3.8	3.6	4.2	4.4
Total Current Liabilities	9.3%	10.0%	9.2%	9.5%
Long-Term Debt	28.0	27.0	30.0	31.0
Deferred Income Taxes	6.9	6.9	6.9	6.9
Other Noncurrent Liabilities	2.9	3.0	2.9	3.0
Total Liabilities	47.1%	46.9%	49.0%	50.4%
Preferred Stock	3.5%	3.5%	3.5%	3.5%
Common Stock	2.9	2.9	2.9	2.9
Retained Earnings	?	?	?	?
Cumulative Translation Adjustment	(1.1)	.3	(1.1)	.3
Treasury Stock	?	?	?	?
Total Shareholders' Equity	52.9%	53.1%	51.0%	49.6%
Total Liabilities and Shareholders' Equity	100.0%	100.0%	100.0%	100.0%

Note: Delay calculating interest expense until after computing interest-bearing debt on the balance sheet.

Income Tax Expense   Scenarios 1 and 2: 35 percent of net income before income taxes.

Note: Delay computing income tax expense until after computing interest expense and net income before taxes.

BALANCE SHEET

Scenarios 1 and 2: Total assets will grow at the growth rates in sales. Use the common size balance sheet percentages in Exhibit 10.19 to allocate the total asset amounts to individual assets and liabilities and shareholders' equity accounts. Leave the amounts for retained earnings and treasury stock blank at this point.

Note: You can now compute interest expense on interest-bearing debt, income tax expense, and net income.

Retained Earnings   The change in retained earnings equals net income minus preferred and common dividends. Assume that preferred dividends each year will increase at the growth rate in preferred stock. Assume that common dividends will increase at the growth rate in net income available to common.

Treasury Stock   The amount for treasury stock is the amount necessary to equate total assets with total liabilities plus shareholders' equity.

STATEMENT OF CASH FLOWS

The amounts for the statement of cash flows reflect the changes in various balance sheet accounts. Assume that changes in deferred income taxes and other noncurrent liabilities are operating items, the changes in other assets are investing transactions, and the changes in the cumulative translation adjustment account are financing transactions.

c. Assess the changes in the profitability and risk of McDonald's under the two strategic scenarios.

CASE 10.2

MASSACHUSETTS STOVE COMPANY: ANALYZING STRATEGIC OPTIONS

THE WOOD STOVE MARKET

Since the early 1980s, wood stove sales have declined from 1.2 million units per year to approximately 100,000 units per year. The decline has occurred for several reasons, including (1) stringent new federal EPA regulations, which set maximum limits on stove emissions beginning in 1992; (2) stable energy prices, which reduce the incentive to switch to wood heating for cost reasons; and (3) changes in consumers' lifestyles, particularly the growth of two-wage earner families.

During this period of decline in industry sales, the market was flooded with wood stoves at distress sale prices as companies closed their doors or liquidated inventory made obsolete by the new EPA regulations. Downward pricing pressure forced surviving companies to cut either prices or output (or both). Years of contraction and pricing pressure left many of the surviving manufacturers in a precarious position financially, with excess inventory, high debt, little cash, uncollectible receivables, and low margins.

The resulting shakeout and consolidation among wood stove manufacturers and, to a lesser extent among wood stove specialty retailers, has been dramatic. The number of manufacturers selling over 2,000 units a year (characterized within the industry as "large manufacturers") has declined from approximately 90 to 35 in the last ten years. The number of manufacturers selling fewer than 2,000 units per year (characterized as "small manufacturers") has declined from approximately 130 to six.

Because the current wood stove market is not large enough to support all the surviving producers, manufacturers have attempted to diversify in order to stay in business. Seeking relief, virtually all the survivors have turned to the manufacture of gas appliances.

THE GAS APPLIANCE MARKET

The gas appliance market includes three segments: (1) gas log sets, (2) gas fireplaces, and (3) gas stoves. Gas log sets are artificial burning logs that can be installed in a preexisting fireplace. They are primarily decorative, and have little heating value. Gas fireplaces are fully assembled fireboxes that can be installed in new construction or in renovated buildings and houses by a builder or contractor. They also are mainly decorative, and are less expensive and easier to maintain than a masonry or brick fireplace. Gas stoves are freestanding appliances with a decorative appearance but also efficient heating characteristics.

The first two segments of the gas appliance market (log sets and fireplaces) are large, established, and stable markets. Established manufacturers control these markets, and distribution is primarily through mass merchandisers. The third segment (gas stoves) is less than five years old. Although it is growing steadily, it has an annual volume of only about 100,000 units (almost identical to the annual volume of the wood stove market). This is the market to which wood stove manufacturers have turned for relief.

The gas stove market is not as heavily regulated as the wood stove market, and there are currently no EPA regulations governing the emissions of gas heating appliances. Gas stoves are perceived as more appropriate to an aging population because they provide heat and ambiance but require no effort. They can be operated with a wall switch, thermostat, or by remote control. Actual fuel cost (or cost savings) is not an issue for many buyers, so a big advantage of heating with wood is no longer a consideration for many consumers. Gas stoves are sold and distributed through mass merchandisers or natural gas or propane dealers. The gas industry has the financial, promotional, organizational, and lobbying clout to support the development of the gas stove market, attributes that the tiny wood stove industry lacks.

Unfortunately, life has not been rosy for all the wood stove companies entering this new market. Development costs and selling costs for new products using a different fuel and sold through a different distribution system have been substantial. Compared to wood stove designs, which are fairly stable and slow to change, gas logs and gas burners have required rapid changes in product design. Competition for market share has renewed pricing pressure on gas stove producers. Companies trying to maintain their wood stove sales while introducing gas products must carry large inventories to service both product lines. Failure to forecast demand accurately has left many companies with inventory shortages during the selling season, or large inventories of unsold product at the end of the season.

Many surviving manufacturers who looked to gas stoves for salvation are now quietly looking for suitors to acquire them. High debt and inventory levels, together with high development and distribution costs, have made financial success highly uncertain. There will be continued consolidation in this difficult market during the next five years.

MASSACHUSETTS STOVE COMPANY

Massachusetts Stove Company (MSC) is one of the six small manufacturers to survive the EPA regulation and industry meltdown. It has just completed its sixth consecutive year of slow but steady growth in revenue and profit since complying with the EPA regulations. Exhibits 10.20 through 10.22 present the financial statements of MSC for Year 3 to Year 7. Exhibit 10.23 presents selected financial statement ratios.

MSC's success in recent years is a classic case of a company staying small, marketing in a specific niche, and applying a rigorous "stick to its knitting" policy. MSC is the only wood stove producer that has not developed gas products; 100 percent of its sales currently come from wood stove sales. MSC is the only wood stove producer that sells by mail order directly to consumers. The mail order market has sheltered MSC from some of the pricing pressure that other manufacturers have had to bear. The combination of high entry costs and high risks makes it unlikely that another competitor will enter the mail order niche.

MSC's other competitive advantages are the high efficiency and unique features of its wood stoves. MSC equips its wood stoves with a catalytic combuster, which reburns gases

---

EXHIBIT 10.20

Massachusetts Stove Company
Income Statements
(Case 10.2)

	Year Ended December 31				
	Year 3	**Year 4**	**Year 5**	**Year 6**	**Year 7**
Sales	$1,480,499	$1,637,128	$ 2,225,745	$ 2,376,673	$ 2,734,986
Cost of Goods Sold	(727,259)	(759,156)	(1,063,135)	(1,159,466)	(1,380,820)
Depreciation	(56,557)	(73,416)	(64,320)	(66,829)	(72,321)
Facilities Costs	(59,329)	(47,122)	(66,226)	(48,090)	(45,309)
Facilities Rental Income	25,856	37,727	38,702	42,142	41,004
Selling Expenses	(452,032)	(563,661)	(776,940)	(874,000)	(926,175)
Administrative Expenses	(36,967)	(39,057)	(46,444)	(48,046)	(111,199)
Operating Income	$ 174,211	$ 192,443	$ 247,382	$ 222,384	$ 240,166
Interest Income	712	2,242	9,541	9,209	16,665
Interest Expense	(48,437)	(44,551)	(47,535)	(52,633)	(42,108)
Net Income Before Income Taxes	$ 126,486	$ 150,134	$ 209,388	$ 178,960	$ 214,723
Income Taxes Expense	(35,416)	(42,259)	(64,142)	(45,794)	(60,122)
Net Income	$ 91,070	$ 107,875	$ 145,246	$ 133,166	$ 154,601

· EXHIBIT 10.21

Massachusetts Stove Company
Balance Sheets
(Case 10.2)

	December 31					
	Year 2	**Year 3**	**Year 4**	**Year 5**	**Year 6**	**Year 7**
Assets						
Cash	$ 50,794	$ 19,687	$ 145,930	$ 104,383	$ 258,148	$ 351,588
Accounts Receivable	12,571	56,706	30,934	41,748	30,989	5,997
Inventories	251,112	327,627	347,883	375,258	409,673	452,709
Other Current Assets ...	1,368	—	—	—	—	—
Total Current Assets ..	$ 315,845	$ 404,020	$ 524,747	$ 521,389	$ 698,810	$ 810,294
Property, Plant, and Equipment:						
At Cost	1,056,157	1,148,806	1,164,884	1,184,132	1,234,752	1,257,673
Accumulated Depreciation	(296,683)	(353,240)	(426,656)	(490,975)	(557,804)	(630,125)
Other Assets	121,483	94,000	61,500	12,200	—	—
Total Assets	$1,196,802	$1,293,586	$1,324,475	$1,226,746	$1,375,758	$1,437,842
Liabilities and Shareholders' Equity						
Accounts Payable	$ 137,104	$ 112,815	$ 43,229	$ 60,036	$ 39,170	$ 47,809
Notes Payable	25,000	12,000	—	—	—	—
Current Portion of Long-Term Debt	27,600	29,000	21,570	113,257	115,076	27,036
Other Current Liabilities	39,530	100,088	184,194	189,732	244,241	257,252
Total Current Liabilities	$ 229,234	$ 253,903	$ 248,993	$ 363,025	$ 398,487	$ 332,097
Long-Term Debt	972,446	953,491	881,415	599,408	574,332	547,296
Deferred Income Taxes ..	—	—	—	—	5,460	6,369
Total Liabilities	$1,201,680	$1,207,394	$1,130,408	$ 962,433	$ 978,279	$ 885,762
Common Stock	2,000	2,000	2,000	2,000	2,000	2,000
Additional Paid-in Capital	435,630	435,630	435,630	435,630	435,630	435,630
Retained Earnings (Deficit)	(442,508)	(351,438)	(243,563)	(98,317)	34,849	189,450
Treasury Stock	—	—	—	(75,000)	(75,000)	(75,000)
Total Shareholders' Equity	$ (4,878)	$ 86,192	$ 194,067	$ 264,313	$ 397,479	$ 552,080
Total Liabilities and Shareholders' Equity	$1,196,802	$1,293,586	$1,324,475	$1,226,746	$1,375,758	$1,437,842

Massachusetts Stove Company
Statements of Cash Flows
(Case 10.2)

		Year Ended December 31			
	Year 3	**Year 4**	**Year 5**	**Year 6**	**Year 7**
Operations					
Net Income	$ 91,070	$107,875	$ 145,246	$133,166	$ 154,601
Depreciation and Amortization	56,557	73,416	64,320	66,829	72,321
Other Addbacks	27,483	32,500	49,300	17,660	909
(Increase) Decrease in Receivables	(44,135)	27,772	(10,814)	10,759	24,992
(Increase) Decrease in Inventories	(76,515)	(20,256)	(27,375)	(34,415)	(43,036)
Decrease in Other Current Assets	1,368	—	—	—	—
Increase (Decrease) in Payables	(24,289)	(69,586)	16,807	(20,866)	8,639
Increase in Other Current Liabilities	60,558	84,106	5,538	54,509	13,011
Cash Flow from Operations	$ 92,097	$233,827	$ 243,022	$227,642	$ 231,437
Investing					
Capital Expenditures	$(92,649)	$ (16,078)	$ (19,249)	$ (50,620)	$ (22,921)
Cash Flow from Investing	$(92,649)	$ (16,078)	$ (19,249)	$ (50,620)	$ (22,921)
Financing					
Increase in Long-Term Debt	$ 10,000	—	—	—	—
Decrease in Short-Term Debt	(13,000)	$ (12,000)	—	—	—
Decrease in Long- Term Debt	(27,555)	(79,506)	$(190,320)	$ (23,257)	$(115,076)
Acquisition of Common Stock	—	—	(75,000)	—	—
Cash Flow from Financing	$(30,555)	$ (91,506)	$(265,320)	$ (23,257)	$(115,076)
Change in Cash	$(31,107)	$126,243	$ (51,547)	$153,765	$ 93,440
Cash—Beginning of Year	50,794	19,687	145,930	104,383	258,148
Cash—End of year	$ 19,687	$145,930	$ 104,383	$258,148	$ 351,588

emitted from burning wood. This reburning not only increases the heat generated by the stoves but also reduces pollutants in the air. MSC offers a wood stove with inlaid ceramic tile. The tile heats up and provides warmth even after the fire has dwindled in the stove. The inlaid tile also adds to the attractiveness of the stove, which is a selling point for those who use stoves in their living areas. MSC's customer base includes many middle- and upper-income buyers.

MSC's management feels that profitable growth of wood stove sales beyond gross revenues of $3 million a year in the mail order niche is unlikely. There is no manufacturer selling gas appliances by mail order, however, and many of MSC's customers and prospects have asked whether MSC plans to produce a gas stove.

MSC managers are contemplating the development of several gas appliances to sell by mail order. While there are compelling reasons for MSC to do this, there are also some good reasons to be cautious.

EXHIBIT 10.23

Massachusetts Stove Company
Financial Statement Ratios
(Case 10.2)

	Year 3	Year 4	Year 5	Year 6	Year 7
Profit Margin for Return on Assets	8.5%	8.5%	8.1%	7.2%	6.8%
Total Assets Turnover	1.2	1.3	1.7	1.8	1.9
Rate of Return on Assets	10.1%	10.7%	14.1%	13.1%	13.1%
Common Earnings Leverage Ratio	72.3%	77.1%	80.9%	77.8%	83.6%
Capital Structure Leverage Ratio	30.6	9.3	5.6	3.9	3.0
Rate of Return on Common Equity	224.0%	77.0%	63.4%	40.2%	32.6%
Cost of Goods Sold/ Sales	49.1%	46.5%	47.8%	48.8%	50.5%
Depreciation Expense/ Sales	3.8%	4.5%	2.9%	2.8%	2.6%
Facilities Costs Net of Rental Income/Sales	2.3%	.6%	1.2%	.3%	.2%
Selling Expense/Sales	30.5%	34.4%	34.9%	36.8%	33.9%
Administrative Expenses/Sales	2.5%	2.4%	2.1%	2.0%	4.1%
Interest Income/Sales	—	.1%	.4%	.4%	.6%
Interest Expense/Sales	3.3%	2.7%	2.1%	2.2%	1.5%
Income Tax Expense/Income Before Taxes	28.0%	28.1%	30.6%	25.6%	28.0%
Accounts Receivable Turnover	42.7	37.4	61.2	65.3	147.9
Inventory Turnover	2.5	2.2	2.9	3.0	3.2
Fixed Asset Turnover	1.9	2.1	3.1	3.5	4.2
Current Ratio	1.59	2.11	1.44	1.75	2.44
Quick Ratio	.30	.71	.40	.73	1.08
Days Accounts Payable	51	33	16	14	11
Cash Flow from Operations/ Average Current Liabilities	38.1%	93.0%	79.4%	59.8%	63.4%
Debt-Equity Ratio	1,106.2%	454.2%	226.8%	144.5%	99.1%
Cash Flow from Operations/ Average Total Liabilities	7.6%	20.0%	23.2%	23.5%	24.8%
Interest Coverage Ratio	3.6	4.4	5.4	4.4	6.1
Cash Flow from Operations/ Capital Expenditures	1.0	14.5	12.6	4.5	10.1

AVAILABILITY OF SPACE

MSC owns a 25,000 square foot building, but occupies only 15,000 square feet. MSC leases the remaining 10,000 square feet to two tenants. The tenants pay rent plus their share of insurance, property taxes, and maintenance costs. The addition of gas appliances to the product line would require MSC to use 5,000 square feet of the space currently rented to tenants. MSC would have to give the tenants six months notice to cancel its lease.

AVAILABILITY OF CAPITAL

MSC has its own internal funds for product development and inventory, as well as an unused line of credit. But it will lose interest income (or incur interest expense) as it invests these funds in development and increased inventory.

EXISTING DEMAND

MSC receives approximately 50,000 requests for catalogs each year, and has a mailing list of approximately 220,000 active prospects and 15,000 recent owners of wood stoves. There is anecdotal evidence of sufficient demand that MSC could introduce its gas stoves with little or no additional marketing expense other than the cost of printing some additional catalog pages each year. MSC's management worries about the risk that gas stove sales might cannibalize its existing wood stove sales. Also, if the current base of wood stove sales is eroded through mismanagement, inattention, or cannibalization, then attempts to grow the business through expansion into gas appliances will be self-defeating.

VACANT MARKET NICHE

No other manufacturer is selling gas stoves by mail order. The entry costs are high, and the unit volume is small, so it is unlikely that another producer will enter the niche. MSC has had the mail order market for wood stoves to itself for approximately seven years. MSC feels that the absence of existing competition will give it additional time to develop new products, although a timely entry will help to solidify its position in this niche.

SUPPLIERS

MSC has existing relationships with many of the suppliers necessary to manufacture new gas products. The foundry that casts MSC's wood stove parts is one of the largest suppliers of gas heating appliances in central Europe. Yet MSC will be a small new customer for the vendors that provide the ceramic gas logs and gas burners. This could lead to problems with price, delivery, or service for these parts.

SYNERGIES IN MARKETING AND MANUFACTURING

MSC would sell gas appliances through its existing direct mail marketing efforts. It will incur additional marketing expenses for photography, printing, and customer service. MSC's existing plant is capable of manufacturing the shell of the gas units. It will require additional expertise to assemble fireboxes for the gas units (valves, burners, and log sets). MSC will have to add both space and employees to process and paint the metal parts of the new gas stoves. The gross margin for the gas products should be similar to that of the wood stoves.

LACK OF MANAGEMENT EXPERIENCE

Managing new product development, larger production runs and inventories, and a more complex business will require MSC to hire more management expertise. MSC will also have to institute a new organization structure for its more complex business and define responsibilities and accountability more carefully. Until now, MSC has operated with a fairly loose organizational philosophy.

Required
a. Identify clues from the financial statements and financial statement ratios for Year 3 through Year 7 that might suggest that Massachusetts Stove Company is in a maturing business.
b. Design a spreadsheet for the preparation of pro forma income statements, balance sheets, and statements of cash flows for MSC for Year 8 through Year 12, and prepare pro forma financial statements for each of these years under three scenarios: (1) best case; (2) most likely; and (3) worst case. The sections below describe the assumptions to be made.

Development Costs. MSC plans to develop two gas stove models, but not concurrently. It will develop the first gas model during Year 8, and begin selling it during Year 9. It will develop the second gas model during Year 9, and begin selling it during Year 10. MSC will capitalize the development costs in the year incurred (Year 8 and Year 9) and amortize them straight-line over five years, beginning with the year the particular stove is initially sold (that is, Year 9 and Year 10). Estimated development costs for each stove are:

Best Case: $100,000.

Most Likely: $120,000.

Worst Case: $160,000.

Capital Expenditures. Capital expenditures, other than development costs, will be: Year 8, $20,000; Year 9, $30,000; Year 10, $30,000; Year 11, $25,000; Year 12, $25,000. Assume a six-year depreciable life, straight-line depreciation, and a full year of depreciation in the year of acquisition.

Sales Growth. Changes in total sales relative to total sales of the preceding year are as follows:

	Best Case			Most Likely Case			Worst Case		
Year	Wood Stoves	Gas Stoves	Total	Wood Stoves	Gas Stoves	Total	Wood Stoves	Gas Stoves	Total
8	+2%	—	+2%	−2%	—	−2%	−4%	—	−4%
9	+2%	+6%	+8%	−2%	+4%	+2%	−4%	+2%	−2%
10	+2%	+12%	+14%	−2%	+8%	+6%	−4%	+4%	+0%
11	+2%	+12%	+14%	−2%	+8%	+6%	−4%	+4%	+0%
12	+2%	+12%	+14%	−2%	+8%	+6%	−4%	+4%	+0%

Because sales of gas stoves will start at zero, the projections of sales should *use the growth rates in total sales above.* The growth rates shown for wood stove sales and gas stove sales simply indicate the components of the total sales increase.

Cost of Goods Sold. Manufacturing costs of the gas stoves will equal 50 percent of sales, the same as for wood stoves.

Depreciation. Depreciation will increase for amortization of the product development costs on the gas stoves and depreciation of additional capital expenditures.

Facilities Rental Income and Facilities Costs. Facilities rental income will decrease by 50 percent beginning in Year 9 when MSC takes over 5,000 square feet of its building now rented to others, and remain at that reduced level for Year 10 through Year 12. Facilities costs will increase by $30,000 beginning in Year 9 for facilities costs now paid by the tenants and for additional facilities costs required by gas stove manufacturing. These costs will remain at that increased level for Year 10 through Year 12.

Selling Expenses. Selling expenses as a percentage of sales are as follows:

Year	Best Case	Most Likely Case	Worst Case
8	34%	34.0%	34%
9	33%	33.5%	35%
10	32%	33.0%	36%
11	31%	32.5%	37%
12	30%	32.0%	38%

Administrative Expenses. Administrative expenses will increase by $30,000 in Year 8, $30,000 in Year 9, and $20,000 in Year 10, and then remain at the Year 10 level in Year 11 and Year 12.

Interest Income. MSC will earn 5 percent interest on the average balance in cash each year.

Interest Expense. The interest rate on long-term debt will be 6.8 percent on the average amount of debt outstanding each year. Debt repayments are as follows: Year 8, $27,036; Year 9, $29,200; Year 10, $31,400; Year 11, $33,900; Year 12, $36,600; Year 13, $39,500.

Income Tax Expense. MSC is subject to an income tax rate of 28 percent.

Accounts Receivable and Inventories. Accounts receivable and inventories will increase at the growth rate in sales.

Property, Plant, and Equipment. Property, plant, and equipment at cost will increase each year by the amounts of capital expenditures and expenditures on development costs. Accumulated depreciation will increase each year by the amount of depreciation and amortization expense.

Accounts Payable and Other Current Liabilities. Accounts payable will increase with the growth rate in inventories. Other current liabilities primarily include advances by customers for stoves manufactured soon after the year-end. Other current liabilities will increase with the growth rate in sales.

Deferred Income Taxes. Deferred income taxes relate to the use of accelerated depreciation for tax purposes and the straight-line method for financial reporting. Assume that deferred income taxes will not change.

Shareholders' Equity. Assume that there will be no changes in the contributed capital of MSC. Retained earnings will change each year in the amount of net income.

    c. Calculate the financial statements ratios listed in Exhibit 10.23 for MSC under each of the three scenarios for Year 8 to Year 12. Note: You should create a fourth spreadsheet as part of your preparation of the pro forma financial statements that will compute the financial ratios.

    d. What advice would you give the management of MSC regarding its decision to enter the gas stove market? Your recommendation should consider the profitability and risks of this action as well as other factors you deem relevant.

CHAPTER 11

VALUATION: CASH FLOW-
BASED APPROACHES

Much of the work of security analysts and investment bankers involves valuation. Typical questions include: Should I make a buy, sell, or hold recommendation on a particular firm's common shares? What is the right price for an initial public offering of common stock? What is a reasonable price for a seller to accept or a buyer to pay for a firm that is the target of a corporate acquisition?

Economic theory teaches that the value of any resource equals the present value of the returns expected from the resource, discounted at a rate that reflects the risk inherent in those expected returns. Thus:

$$\text{Value}_t = \sum_{t=1}^{n} \frac{\text{Returns}_t}{(1 + \text{Discount Rate})^t}$$

This chapter discusses valuation approaches that use *expected cash flows* as the measure of returns. Chapter 12 discusses valuation methods that use accrual accounting *earnings* as the measure of returns.

There is considerable theoretical and empirical research on the questions as to whether cash flows or earnings are the more highly correlated with stock returns, and the conditions when one or the other (or neither) is likely to be more correlated. We consider some of the important issues and summarize the results of recent research in this debate in the latter part of Chapter 12. Our intention in this chapter (and the first part of Chapter 12) is to present alternative valuation approaches. Our experience indicates that the analyst can gain better insights about the value of a firm using several valuation approaches instead of relying on one approach in all cases.

RATIONALE FOR CASH FLOW-BASED VALUATION

The rationale for using expected cash flows in valuation is two-fold:

1. Cash is the ultimate source of value. When individuals and firms invest in any given resource, they delay current consumption in favor of future consumption. Cash is the medium of exchange that will permit the consumption of various goods and services in the future. A resource has value because of its ability to provide future cash flows.
2. Cash serves as a measurable common denominator for comparing the future benefits of alternative investment opportunities. A machine used in a factory provides benefits in the form of production services. An office building leased to others provides benefits in the form of office space available for rent. An airplane or automobile provides transportation services. To compare these investment alternatives we need a common measuring unit of their future benefits. The future cash flows derived from their future services serve such a function. The factory machine produces a product that the firm can sell for cash. The office building provides monthly rental fees. An airplane owned by an airline provides cash from ticket sales. The automobile saves cash that an individual or a firm would otherwise have to pay to lease transportation services from others.

When they address the cash flows versus earnings issue, economists argue that (1) investors cannot spend earnings for future consumption; (2) accrual earnings are subject to numerous questionable accounting methods (such as acquisition cost valuations of assets, immediate expensing of research and development costs); and (3) earnings are subject to purposeful management by a firm. Thus, earnings are not as reliable or meaningful as a common denominator for comparing investment alternatives as cash. A dollar of earnings by one firm is not necessarily equal to a dollar of earnings by another firm. A dollar of cash is a dollar of cash.[1]

---

[1]Chapter 12 addresses these concerns and raises questions about the meaningfulness of cash flows as a measure of benefits received.

Overview of Cash Flow-Based Valuation

The valuation of any resource using cash flows involves identifying three elements:

1. The expected periodic cash flows.
2. The expected cash flow at the end of the forecast horizon, referred to as the residual, or terminal, value.
3. The discount rate used to compute the present value of the future cash flows.

We discuss each of these elements in turn.

Periodic Cash Flows

Cash Flow to the Investor versus Cash Flows to the Firm. Most of the valuation settings considered in this chapter involve valuing the common stock equity of a firm. Cash flows to the investor in the stock and cash flows generated by a firm each period will differ to the extent that the firm reinvests a portion (or all) of the cash flows generated during the period. Should the analyst use as the measure of periodic cash flows dividends expected to be paid to the investor or cash flows expected to be generated by the firm from using assets?

If the firm generates a rate of return on retained cash flows equal to the discount rate used by the investor (that is, the cost of equity capital), then either set of cash flows will yield the same valuation of a firm's shares at a particular time. Consider several different scenarios.

Example 1. A firm expects to generate cash flows of 15 percent annually on invested equity capital. Equity investors in this firm want a return of 15 percent each year. Assume that the firm pays out 100 percent of these operating cash flows each year as a dividend. Thus, the cash flows generated by the firm equal the cash received by the investor. Each dollar of capital committed by the investor has a present value of future cash flows equal to one dollar. That is:

$$\$1 = \sum_{t=1}^{n} \frac{\$0.15}{(1.15)^t}$$

Example 2. Assume the same facts as in Example 1, except that the firm pays out none of the cash flows generated by operations as a dividend. The firm retains the $0.15 cash inflow on each dollar of capital committed and reinvests it at 15 percent. In this case, the investor receives cash only when the common stock is sold or the firm liquidates. Define this terminal date as n. In this case also, each dollar of capital committed by the investor has a present value of future cash flows equal to one dollar. That is:

$$\$1 = \frac{(1.15)^n}{(1.15)^n}$$

Example 3.   Assume the same facts as Example 1, except that the firm pays out 25 percent of the cash flow from operations as a dividend and retains the other 75 percent. The retained cash flows generate a return of 15 percent. In this case also, each dollar of capital committed by the investor has a present value of future cash flows equal to one dollar. Thus:

$$\$1 = \sum_{t=1}^{n} \frac{(0.25)(0.15)}{(1.15)^t} + \frac{(0.75)(1.15)^n}{(1.15)^n}$$

These three examples simply illustrate the irrelevance of dividend policy in the valuation of a firm.[2] The same valuation should result whether the analyst discounts (1) the expected periodic and liquidating dividend to the investor, or (2) the expected cash flows to the firm. Because liquidating dividends are seldom observable, most empirical research involving valuation discounts the firm's expected cash flows. We follow this approach as well in this chapter.

Relevant Firm-Level Cash Flows.   A second issue is which cash flow amounts from the projected statement of cash flows the analyst should discount to a present value when valuing a firm. Economists distinguish between *unleveraged free cash flows* and *leveraged free cash flows*. Exhibit 11.1 shows the computation of each of these two measures of free cash flows.

The unleveraged free cash flows described in Exhibit 11.1 are the cash flows that a firm generates before considering the particular mix of debt versus equity financing. Thus, no subtraction is made for interest costs in computing unleveraged cash flow from operations. Procedurally, the analyst adds back to reported cash flow from operations the cash outflow for interest (typically reported as additional information at the bottom of the statement of cash flows), net of income tax savings from deducting interest expense for income tax purposes. From unleveraged cash flow from operations the analyst subtracts cash flows related to acquisitions of property, plant, and equipment, investments in securities, and other investing activities to obtain unleveraged free cash flow. This pool of cash flows is then the amount available to service debt, pay dividends to shareholders, and provide funds (through retained earnings) to finance future earnings.

The leveraged free cash flows described in Exhibit 11.1 are the cash flows available to the common shareholders after making all debt service payments to lenders and paying dividends to preferred shareholders. Cash flow from operations in published statements of cash flows already includes a subtraction for interest costs and related tax savings. From this leveraged cash flow from operations the analyst subtracts cash flows for investing activities. The analyst also adds or subtracts cash

[2]Merton Miller and Franco Modigliani, "Dividend Policy, Growth and the Valuation of Shares," *Journal of Business* (October 1961), pp. 411–433. Two other researchers empirically test the replacement property of dividends for future earnings and find support for the irrelevance of dividend policy in valuation. See Stephen H. Penman and Theodore Sougiannis, "The Dividend Displacement Property and the Substitution of Anticipated Earnings for Dividends in Equity Valuation," *The Accounting Review* (January 1997), pp. 1–21.

EXHIBIT 11.1	
Measurement of Unleveraged and Leveraged Free Cash Flows	
Unleveraged Free Cash Flows	**Leveraged Free Cash Flows**
Cash Flow from Operations before Subtracting Cash Outflows for Interest Costs (net of tax savings)	Cash Flow from Operations before Subtracting Cash Outflows for Interest Costs (net of tax savings)
	Minus Cash Outflows for Interest Costs (net of tax savings)
Equals Unleveraged Cash Flow from Operations	Equals Leveraged Cash Flow from Operations
Plus or Minus Cash Flow for Investing Activities	Plus or Minus Cash Flow for Investing Activities
	Plus/Minus Cash Flows for Changes in Short- and Long-Term Borrowing
	Plus/Minus Cash Flows for Changes in and Dividends on Preferred Stock
Equals Unleveraged Free Cash Flow to All Providers of Capital	Equals Leveraged Free Cash Flow to Common Shareholders

flows related to the net change in short- and long-term borrowing and preferred stock, and subtracts dividends paid on preferred stock to obtain leveraged free cash flows.[3] Leveraged free cash flows are the cash flows available to the common shareholders either for common share dividends or to be reinvested in the firm to fund future operations.

The appropriate cash flow measure depends on the resource to be valued.

1. If the objective is to value the *assets* of a firm, then the unleveraged free cash flow is the appropriate cash flow. A later section of this chapter indicates that the appropriate discount rate is the weighted average cost of capital.[4]
2. If the objective is to value the *common shareholders' equity* of a firm, then the leveraged free cash flow is the appropriate cash flow. A later section indicates that the appropriate discount rate is the cost of equity capital.

---

[3]It might appear inappropriate to include changes in debt and preferred stock financing, which appear in the financing section of the statement of cash flows, in the valuation of a firm. Economic theory suggests that the capital structure (that is, the proportion of debt versus equity) should not affect the value. Changes in debt and preferred stock, however, affect the amount of cash available to the common shareholders. The analyst includes cash flows related to debt and preferred stock financing in leveraged free cash flows, but adjusts the cost of equity capital to reflect the amounts of such senior financing in the capital structure.

[4]In most valuation settings in which the analyst uses unleveraged free cash flows, the valuation is of total assets net of liabilities related to operations (for example, accounts payable, income taxes payable, deferred tax liability, employee retirement liabilities).

The difference between these two valuations is, of course, the value of total interest-bearing liabilities and preferred stock. One could always value interest-bearing liabilities by discounting debt service costs (including repayments of principal) at the after-tax cost of debt capital and preferred stock dividends at the cost of preferred equity. Subtracting the value of interest-bearing liabilities and preferred stock from the value of total assets will yield the value of common equity. The approach followed depends on the valuation setting.

Example 4. Suppose one firm wants to acquire the operating assets of a division of another firm. The acquiring firm will replace the current financing structure of the division with a financing structure of its own. The relevant cash flows for deciding on the price to pay for the division's assets are the operating cash flows that those assets are expected to generate (before subtracting financing costs) minus the net cash outflow for investing (that is, the unleveraged free cash flows). Subtracting the net cash outflow for investing provides for the needed replacement or enhancement of fixed assets to sustain or increase future operating cash flows. The acquiring firm would then discount these projected cash flows at the weighted average cost of capital of the new division (which, in theory, should be the weighted average cost of capital of the acquiring firm because the acquisition of the division, like all investments, should cover the total financing costs of the firm).

Example 5. Suppose an investor wants to value a potential common stock equity investment in a firm. The relevant cash flows are the leveraged free cash flows. Cash flow from operations includes the returns generated from using debt capital as well as the cash required to service the debt. Thus, cash flow from operations (plus or minus changes in debt in the financing section of the statement of cash flows) captures the beneficial (or detrimental) effects of financial leverage on the value of the common equity. The investor should discount these projected cash flows at the desired return on equity capital.

Example 6. The managers of a firm intend to engage in a leveraged buyout (LBO) of a firm. A typical LBO works as follows:

1. The managers offer to purchase the outstanding common shares of the target firm at a particular price if current shareholders will tender them.
2. The managers invest their own funds for a portion of the purchase price (usually 20 percent to 25 percent), and borrow the remainder from various lenders. The borrowing is generally contingent on having a certain proportion of the outstanding shares tendered (at least 51 percent but usually a higher percentage). The tendered shares serve as collateral for the loan (called a *bridge loan* for the reason explained below).
3. The managers use the equity and debt capital raised to purchase the tendered shares.
4. After gaining voting control of the firm, the managers direct the firm to engage in sufficient new borrowing to repay the bridge loan obtained to execute the

LBO. In this way, the lenders have a direct claim on the assets of the firm. Also, the managers shift any personal guarantees they may have made on the bridge loan to the firm itself on the new borrowing.

Estimation of the price to pay for the tendered common shares can follow the usual procedure for an equity investment (see Example 5). This price should equal the present value of leveraged free cash flows discounted at the cost of common equity capital. The projected debt service costs after the LBO will differ significantly from their historical levels. The valuation of the equity must reflect the new capital structure and the related debt service costs. Also, the cost of equity capital will likely increase as a result of the higher level of debt in the capital structure (that is, the common shareholders bear more risk as residual claimants on the assets of the firm). The valuation must reflect this new cost of equity capital.

An alternative approach that produces the same value for the common equity is to treat an LBO as a purchase of assets (similar to the approach followed in Example 4). That is, the analyst computes the present value of the unleveraged free cash flows using the weighted average cost of debt and equity capital. This amount represents the value of total assets. Then subtract from total assets the market value of debt raised to execute the LBO (the debt to assets percentage used here should be the same as the weight for debt in the weighted average cost of capital). The result is the market value of the common equity.[5]

Nominal Versus Real Cash Flows.   Changes in general price levels (inflation or deflation) cause the purchasing power of a monetary unit to vary over time. Even after adjusting for the time value of money, a dollar expected to be received one year from today does not necessarily have the same purchasing power as a dollar in the hand. Should the projected cash flows to be used in valuing a resource reflect *nominal amounts*, which include inflationary or deflationary components, or *real amounts*, which filter out the effect of changes in general purchasing power?[6]

The valuation of a resource should be the same whether one uses nominal cash flow amounts or real cash flow amounts, as long as the discount rate used is consistent with the cash flows. That is, if projected cash flows ignore changes in the general purchasing power of the monetary unit, then the discount rate should incorporate an inflation component. If projected cash flows filter out the effects of general price changes, then the discount rate should exclude the inflation component.

---

[5]It is irrelevant whether any debt on the books of the target firm remains outstanding after the LBO or whether the firm engages in additional borrowing to repay existing debt, as long as the weighted average cost of capital properly reflects the costs of each financing arrangement.

[6]Note that the issue here is not with specific price changes of a firm's particular assets, liabilities, revenues, and expenses. These specific price changes affect cash flows and should enter into the valuation of the firm. The issue is whether some portion, or all, or more than all of the specific price changes represent simply a change in the purchasing power of the monetary unit, which should not affect the value of a firm.

Example 7.   A firm owns a tract of land that it expects to sell one year from today for $115 million. This selling price reflects a 15 percent increase in the selling price of the land during the coming year. The general price level is expected to increase 10 percent during this period. The real interest rate is 2 percent.

The value of the land today to the firm is $102.5 million, as shown below:[7]

Nominal Cash Flow	×	Discount Rate Including Expected Inflation	=	Value
$115 million	×	1/(1.02)(1.10)	=	$102.5 million

Real Cash Flow	×	Discount Rate Excluding Expected Inflation	=	Value
$115 million/1.10	×	1/(1.02)	=	$102.5 million

The discounting of nominal cash flows using nominal discount rates is usually easier in practical settings than discounting real cash flows using real interest rates. The latter approach requires the identification of expected inflation rates for many future periods, a procedure likely to introduce considerable measurement error.

PreTax Versus After-Tax Cash Flows.   Extending the discussion in the preceding section, will the same valuation arise if the analyst discounts pretax cash flows at a pretax cost of capital and after-tax cash flows at an after-tax cost of capital? The answer to this question is no.

Example 8.   Consider a calculation of the cost of capital for a firm as follows:

	Proportion in Capital Structure	Pre-Tax Cost	Tax Effect	After-Tax Cost	Weighted Average Cost of Capital	
					Pre-Tax	After-Tax
Debt	0.33	10%	0.4	6%	3.33%	2.00%
Equity	0.67	18%	—	18%	12.00	12.00
	1.00				15.33%	14.00%

---

[7]A 15 percent specific price increase for the land suggests that the market value today is $100 million, not $102.5 million. Perhaps the firm expects a higher rate of specific price change (15 percent) than the market in general anticipates.

Assume that this firm expects to generate $90 million of pretax unleveraged free cash flows and $54 million of after-tax unleveraged free cash flows [= (1 − 0.4)($90 million)] one year from today. The valuation of this firm using pretax and after-tax amounts (assuming a one-year horizon) is as follows:

Pretax:	$90 million × 1/1.1533 = $78.04 million
After-tax:	$54 million × 1/1.14 = $47.37 million

The difference in valuation occurs because cash inflows from assets are taxed at 40 percent, and cash outflows to service debt give rise to a tax savings of 40 percent. The cost of equity capital, however, does not provide a tax benefit. The appropriate valuation in this case is $47.37 million. Thus, the analyst should use after-tax cash flows and the after-tax cost of capital.

Selecting a Forecast Horizon. For how many future years should the analyst project periodic cash flows? The correct answer theoretically is for the expected life of the resource to be valued. This life is a finite number of years for a machine, a building, or a similar resource with limits to its physical existence. In many valuation contexts, however, the resource to be valued is an equity claim on the portfolio of net assets of a firm, a resource that has not a finite but an infinite life (except in the event of bankruptcy). The analyst must project future periodic cash flows for some number of years, and then estimate the likely residual, or terminal, value at the end of this forecast horizon.

Chapter 10 demonstrates that the prediction of future periodic cash flows requires assumptions regarding each item in the income statement and balance sheet and then deriving the related cash flow effects. As we discuss next, estimation of the residual value generally involves short-cut procedures that do not require the analyst to project individual financial statement items for too many years into the future.

Selecting a forecast horizon involves trade-offs. Using a relatively short forecast horizon, such as three to five years, enhances the likely accuracy of the projected periodic cash flows, since the near term is often an extrapolation of the recent past. These near-term periodic cash flows also have the heaviest weight in the present value computations. Using a relatively short forecast horizon, however, causes a large portion of the total present value to be related to the residual value. The valuation process is particularly difficult when near-term cash flows are projected to be negative, as is common for a rapidly growing firm that finances its growth by issuing common stock. In this case, all of the firm's value relates to the less detailed estimation of the residual value.

Selecting a longer period in the forecast of periodic cash flows, such as ten to fifteen years, reduces the influence of the estimated residual value on the total present value. Again, however, the predictive accuracy of detailed cash flow forecasts this far into the future is likely to be questionable.

It is best to select as a forecast horizon the point at which a firm's cash flow pattern has settled into an equilibrium. This equilibrium position could be either no growth in future cash flows or growth at a stable rate. Security analysts typically select a forecast horizon in the range of four to seven years.

RESIDUAL VALUE

When a firm's cash flow pattern has settled into an equilibrium at the end of the forecast horizon, the analyst can estimate the residual value at that time using a valuation model as follows:[8]

$$\text{Residual Value at End of Forecast Horizon}_n = \text{Periodic Cash Flow}_{n-1} \times \frac{1 + g}{r - g}$$

where:

n = forecast horizon;

g = annual growth rate in periodic cash flows after the forecast horizon; and

r = discount rate.

Example 9. An analyst forecasts that the leveraged free cash flow of a firm in Year 5 is $30 million. This is a mature firm that expects zero growth in future cash flows; that is, the operating cash inflows from investments made in previous years exactly equal the cash outflow for investments each year. The residual value of the cash flow at the end of the forecast period, assuming a 15 percent cost of equity capital, is computed as follows:

$$\text{Residual Value at End of Forecast Period} = \$30 \text{ million} \times \frac{1 + 0.00}{0.15 - 0.00} = \frac{\$30 \text{ million}}{0.15} = \$200 \text{ million}$$

The present value at the beginning of Year 1 of this estimated residual value is $99.4 million [= $200 million $\times 1/(1.15)^5$].

Example 10. Assume the same facts as in Example 9, except that the analyst expects the cash flow after Year 5 to grow at 6 percent each year. The computation of the residual value is as follows:

$$\text{Residual Value at End of Forecast Period} = \$30 \text{ million} \times \frac{1 + 0.06}{0.15 - 0.06} = \$30 \text{ million} \times \frac{1.06}{0.09} = \$353.3 \text{ million}$$

The present value of the residual value at the beginning of Year 1 is $175.7 million.

---

[8]This formula is simply the algebraic simplification of the present value of a growing perpetuity.

Example 11. Assume the same facts as in Example 9, except that the analyst expects the cash flow after Year 5 to decline 6 percent each year. The computation of the residual value is as follows:

$$\begin{array}{l} \text{Residual Value} \\ \quad \text{at End of} \\ \text{Forecast Period} \end{array} = \$30 \text{ million} \times \frac{1 - 0.06}{0.15 - (-0.06)} = \$30 \text{ million} \times \frac{0.94}{0.21} = \$134.3 \text{ million}$$

The present value of the residual value at the beginning of Year 1 is $66.8 million. The cash flows of a firm in decline will eventually reach zero (or the firm will become bankrupt). As long as this point occurs many years in the future, it does not have much influence on the present value.

Analysts frequently estimate a residual value using multiples of six to eight times leveraged free cash flow in the last year of the forecast horizon to value the common stock of a firm. The table below shows the cash flow multiples using $(1 + g)/(r - g)$ for various costs of equity capital and growth rates.

Cash Flow Multiples

	Growth Rate		
	2%	4%	6%
Cost of Equity Capital			
15%	7.8	9.5	11.8
18%	6.4	7.4	8.8
20%	5.7	6.5	7.6

Thus, multiples of six to eight times leveraged free cash flow fall within the range of common levels for the cost of equity capital and growth rates.

The residual valuation model illustrated above does not work well when the discount rate and the growth rate are approximately equal. The denominator approaches zero, and the multiple becomes exceedingly large. The model also does not work when the growth rate exceeds the discount rate. The denominator becomes negative, and the resulting multiple is meaningless.

These difficulties in using the residual valuation model arise because the growth rate that is assumed in applying the model is too high. The model assumes that the growth rate will continue in perpetuity. In fact, competition, technological change, new entrants into an industry, and similar factors eventually reduce growth rates. In applying the model, therefore, the analyst must attempt to estimate the long-term sustainable growth rate in cash flows (see the discussion of sustainable earnings in Chapter 4).

An alternative approach to estimate residual value is to use the free cash flow multiples for comparable firms that currently trade in the market. This approach provides a degree of market validation for the theoretical model that we have discussed above. The analyst identifies comparable companies by studying growth rates in free cash flows, profitability levels, risk characteristics, and similar factors. These same inputs are also needed to apply the theoretical model.

Analysts also frequently use earnings-based models, such as price-earnings ratios or market to book value ratios, to estimate a residual value. We discuss earnings-based valuation models in Chapter 12.

COST OF CAPITAL

The third valuation variable in the present value of cash flows model is the discount rate. The analyst uses the discount rate to compute the present value of the projected cash flows. The discount rate equals the rate of return that lenders and investors require the firm to generate to induce them to commit capital, given the level of risk involved. The costs of capital equals the after-tax cost of each type of capital provided to a firm.

Cost of Debt Capital. The common practice in computing the cost of debt capital is to exclude accounts payable and other operating liability accounts (such as accounts payable, deferred income tax liability, retirement benefit liabilities) from the calculation of the weighted average cost of capital. Instead, analysts typically treat these items as negative operating investments. The present value of unleveraged free cash flows is the value of total assets net of operating liabilities, which equals debt plus shareholders' equity.

For purposes of computing the weighted average cost of capital (used when valuing the assets of a firm), the cost of debt capital equals one minus the marginal tax rate appropriate to interest deductions times the yield to maturity of debt. The yield to maturity is the rate that discounts the contractual cash flows on the debt to the debt's current market value. The yield to maturity will equal the coupon rate on the debt only if the debt sells on the market at par value, or face value.

Capitalized lease obligations have a cost equal to the current interest rate on collateralized borrowing with equivalent risk. The analyst should include the present value of significant operating lease commitments in the calculation of the weighted average cost of capital. The lessor bears more risk in an operating lease than in a capital lease, so the cost of capital represented by operating leases is higher than for capital leases. If the analyst treats operating leases as part of debt financing, then the cash outflow for rent should be reclassified as interest and repayment of debt in the computation of leveraged and unleveraged free cash flows.

Cost of Preferred Equity Capital. The cost of any preferred stock capital depends on the preference conditions. Preferred stock, which comes before common stock in the payment of dividends and its priority in liquidation, generally sells near its par value. Its cost is therefore the dividend rate on the preferred stock. Depending on the attributes of the preferred stock, dividends on preferred stock may or may not give rise to a tax deduction. Thus, its pretax and after-tax cost may or may not be the same. Preferred stock that is convertible into common stock has both preferred and common equity attributes. Its cost is a blending of the cost of nonconvertible preferred stock and common equity.

Cost of Common Equity Capital. The approach most commonly encountered to measure the cost of equity capital uses the theory underlying the capital asset pricing model (CAPM). In equilibrium, the cost of common equity capital equals the market rate of return earned by common equity capital. The market rate of return is a function of the level of systematic risk inherent in a particular firm's common stock.[9] Systematic risk relates to the covariability of a firm's stock price with stock prices of all firms in the market. As Chapter 9 discusses, the CAPM measures systematic risk using the market beta for a firm's common stock. The cost of common equity capital is as follows:

$$
\begin{array}{c} \text{Cost of} \\ \text{Common} \\ \text{Equity Capital} \end{array} = \begin{array}{c} \text{Interest Rate} \\ \text{on Risk-Free} \\ \text{Securities} \end{array} + \begin{array}{c} \text{Market} \\ \text{Beta} \end{array} \left[\begin{array}{c} \text{Average} \\ \text{Return on} \\ \text{the Market} \\ \text{Portofolio} \end{array} - \begin{array}{c} \text{Interest} \\ \text{Rate on} \\ \text{Risk-Free} \\ \text{Securities} \end{array} \right]
$$

All common equity securities have a cost at least equal to the interest rate on risk-free securities. Equity securities are not risk-free, of course. The term in brackets in the equation represents the *average* excess return over the risk-free rate that the market provides to investors for assuming more systematic risk as equity investors. An equity security with the average amount of systematic risk of all equity securities in the market has a market beta of 1.0. The cost of common equity capital for such a firm is the average return on the market portfolio. Firms with a market beta higher than 1.0 have greater systematic risk than average; their cost of capital is commensurately higher. Firms with market betas lower than 1.0 have less systematic risk than average, and thereby have a lower cost of equity capital. Exhibit 11.2 sets out the relations graphically.

The objective in selecting a risk-free interest rate is to use securities that have zero systematic risk, or correlation with market rates of return, and zero default risk. It might seem appropriate to use the yield on long-term U.S. government securities. This is not a good choice, however, because the longer the term to maturity, the greater the sensitivity of the yields on U.S. government securities to changes in inflation and interest rates, and therefore the greater the systematic risk (although the systematic risk is still quite low). It is common practice to use the yield on either short- or intermediate-term U.S. government securities as the risk-free rate. This rate has historically averaged around 6 percent.

The average return on the market portfolio depends on the period studied as well as whether the analyst uses a geometric mean or arithmetic mean to measure

---

[9]Note that this model views nonsystematic risk as diversifiable by the investor. The market, according to the CAPM, does not provide a return for a firm's nonsystematic risk.

EXHIBIT 11.2

EXHIBIT 11.2

Relation Between Cost of Equity Capital and Systematic Risk

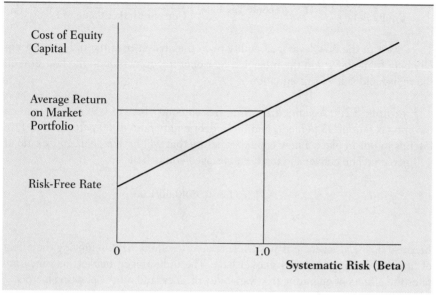

market returns. Historically, the market rate of return has varied between 9 and 13 percent. Thus, the excess return over the risk-free rate has varied between 3 and 7 percentage points.

A variety of financial reference sources regularly publish market equity betas for publicly traded firms, including Standard & Poor's *Stock Reports*. It is not uncommon to find considerable variation in the published amounts for market beta among different sources. This occurs in part because of variations in the period used to calculate the betas.

Adjusting Market Equity Beta to Reflect a New Capital Structure. Recall from the discussion in Chapter 9 that market equity beta reflects operating leverage, financial leverage, and variability of sales. In some settings, such as a leveraged buyout, firms plan to make significant changes in the capital structure of the firm. The market equity beta computed using past market price data reflects the capital structure in place at a particular time. The analyst can adjust this equity beta to approximate what it is likely to be after a change in the capital structure. The approach is to unleverage the current beta, and then releverage it to reflect the new capital structure.

The formula to unleverage the current market equity beta to obtain an unleveraged equity beta (sometimes referred to as an *asset beta*) is as follows:

Current Leveraged
Equity Beta

$$= \frac{\text{Unleveraged}}{\text{Equity Beta}} \left[1 + (1 - \text{Income Tax Rate}) \left(\frac{\text{Current Market Value of Debt}}{\text{Current Market Value of Equity}} \right) \right]$$

To convert to the new leveraged equity beta, the analyst uses the unleveraged equity beta from above and the projected new debt to equity ratio in the last term on the right-hand side of this equation.

Example 12.   Assume that a firm has an equity beta of 0.9, is subject to an income tax rate of 35 percent, and has a debt/equity ratio of 60 percent. The firm intends to put in place a new capital structure that will have a debt/equity ratio of 140 percent. The conversion to an unleveraged equity beta is:

$$0.9 = X [1 + (1 - 0.35)(0.60/1.00)]$$

$$X = 0.65$$

Because financial leverage is positively related to equity beta, removing the effect of financial leverage reduces market beta. The unleveraged market beta incorporates the effects of operating risk, variability of sales, and other operating factors.

The releveraging of market beta is as follows:

$$Y = 0.65 [1 + (1 - 0.35)(1.40/1.00)]$$

$$Y = 1.24$$

Evaluating the Use of CAPM to Measure the Cost of Equity Capital.   Using the CAPM to calculate the cost of equity capital has been subject to various criticisms:

1. Market betas do not appear to be stable over time and are sensitive to the time period used in their computation.
2. The excess market rate of return is not stable over time and is likewise sensitive to the time period used in its calculation.
3. Research by Fama and French suggests that during the 1980s size was a better proxy for risk than market beta.[10]

Weights Used to Compute Weighted Average Cost of Capital.
The weights used to compute the weighted average cost of capital should be the market values of each type of capital. Firms are required to disclose the market value of their debt securities in notes to the financial statements each year. Market price quotations for equity securities provide the amounts for determining the market value of equity.

---

[10]Eugene F. Fama and Kenneth R. French, "The Cross Section of Expected Stock Returns," *Journal of Finance* (June 1992), pp. 427–465.

Example 13. A firm's capital structure on its balance sheet is as follows:

Long-Term Debt, 10 percent annual coupon, issued at par	$20,000,000
Preferred Stock, 4 percent dividend, issued at par	5,000,000
Common Stock	10,000,000
Retained Earnings	15,000,000
Total	$50,000,000

The market values of the securities are as follows: long-term debt $22,000,000; preferred stock $5,000,000; common stock $33,000,000. The debt is priced on the market to yield 8 percent. At an income tax rate of 35 percent, the after-tax cost of debt is 5.2 percent (= 0.65×8.0 percent). Note that this rate differs from the coupon rate of 10 percent. The market value of the debt also differs from its par value. Because the yield to maturity of debt is inversely related to its market value, analysts often use the coupon rate and the book value of debt when computing the weighted average cost of capital. The use of coupon rates and book values in this case results in a higher cost of debt capital (6.5 percent = 0.65×10.0 percent) but a smaller weight in the weighted average. Assuming that the dividend on the preferred stock is not tax-deductible, its cost is the dividend rate of 4 percent, because it is selling at par value. The market equity beta is 0.9. Assuming a risk-free interest rate of 6 percent and a market premium of 7 percent, the cost of equity capital is 12.3 percent [= 6.0 percent + (0.9(7.0 percent))].

The calculation of the weighted average cost of capital is as follows:

Security	Amount	Proportion	Cost	Weighted Average
Long-Term Debt	$22,000,000	37%	5.2%	1.92%
Preferred Equity	5,000,000	8	4.0%	0.32
Common Equity	33,000,000	55	12.3%	6.77
Total	$60,000,000	100%		9.01%

ILLUSTRATIONS OF CASH FLOW-BASED VALUATION

We illustrate cash flow-based valuation methods, first, with a simple example involving the valuation of single project, and then with a more complex example involving the valuation of Coke.

VALUATION OF A SINGLE PROJECT

Assume that a firm is considering an investment that costs $10 million and is expected to generate unleveraged earnings and unleveraged cash flows from operations of $2 million a year forever.[11] The firm will finance the investment with $6 million of debt and $4 million of common equity. The debt bears interest at 10 percent each year, payable at the end of each year. The income tax rate is 40 percent. The cost of equity capital is 25.625 percent.

Example 14. Value of Common Equity.   We can determine the value of just the common equity investment. The leveraged free cash flow to the common equity each year is as follows:

Unleveraged Free Cash Flow	$2,000,000
Interest Paid on Debt: 0.10 × $6,000,000	(600,000)
Income Tax Savings on Interest: 0.40 × $600,000	240,000
Leveraged Free Cash Flow	$1,640,000

The value of the project to the common equity is $6,400,000 (= $1,640,000/ 0.25625). Dividing by the discount rate is appropriate, because we assume that the $1,640,000 annual leveraged free cash flow will last forever (that is, the factor for the present value of an annuity that lasts forever when the discount rate is 0.25625 is 0.25625). The present value to the common equity shareholders in excess of their initial investment is $2,400,000 (= $6,400,000 − $4,000,000).

This valuation approach works well when the analyst wants to assess the reasonableness of the current market price of a firm's common stock. Taking the existing capital structure as given, the analyst can project leveraged free cash flows from the statement of cash flows. Published equity betas provide the basis of determining the cost of equity capital.

Example 15. Value of Debt Plus Equity.   Alternatively, we can determine the value of the debt plus the common equity by discounting the unleveraged free cash flow at the weighted average cost of capital. The debt carries an after-tax cost of 6 percent [= (1 − 0.40)(0.10)]. The common equity carries a cost of 25.625 percent (see Example 14).

The weights to compute the weighted average cost of capital are the relative market values of the debt and the equity. There is circular reasoning in this example, because we need to know the market values to determine the weights, but we need to know the weights to determine the weighted average cost of capital used in measuring the market values. We can avoid this circularity if we assume that a firm targets a particular debt/equity ratio. We assume for purposes of illustration that the firm issues the $6 million of debt at par, so that its market value is $6 mil-

---

[11]The equality of unleveraged earnings and unleveraged cash flows implies a no-growth scenario; the firm experiences no changes in operating working capital over time. We simplify the example by not specifying limited time periods or residual values.

lion. The common equity has a market value of $6,400,000 (see Example 14). The weighted average cost of capital is:

Type of Capital	Amount	Weight	Cost	Weighted Average
Debt	$ 6,000,000	0.48387	0.06000	0.02903
Common Equity	6,400,000	0.51613	0.25625	0.13226
Total	$12,400,000	1.00000		0.16129

The present value of debt plus equity is $12,400,000 (= $2,000,000/0.16129).[12] Subtracting the $6 million value of the debt yields a $6,400,000 value for the common equity, the same as in the previous example.

This valuation approach works well when the analyst wants to determine the value of a firm after taking into consideration major changes in its capital structure. In a leveraged buyout, for example, the proportion of debt typically increases, and the proportion of equity decreases. The analyst can revalue the total debt plus equity (or total assets), given the new capital structure, by discounting the unleveraged free cash flows at the weighted cost of capital.

Example 16. Adjusted Present Value Approach.   An alternative approach to valuing the debt plus the equity appears in finance texts characterized as the *adjusted present value* approach. This approach values the debt and equity (or total assets) in two steps:

1. Value the unleveraged free cash flows at the unleveraged cost of equity.
2. Add the present value of the tax savings from deducting interest expense on debt using the cost of debt capital.

The first component requires the calculation of an unleveraged cost of equity capital. Conceptually, this is the rate of return required by equity investors on a project with no debt financing. Because equityholders assume less risk when there is no debt in the capital structure, the unleveraged cost of equity capital will be less than the leveraged cost of equity capital. We have assumed above that the leveraged cost of equity capital is 25.625 percent. To unlever this cost of equity capital, we solve the equation:

$$\begin{aligned}
\text{Unleveraged Cost} \atop \text{of Equity Capital} &= {\text{Leveraged Cost} \atop \text{of Equity Capital}} \\
&\quad - \left[\left(\frac{\text{Debt}}{\text{Equity}}\right)(1 - \text{Income Tax Rate})\left({\text{Unleveraged Cost} \atop \text{of Equity}} - {\text{Cost of} \atop \text{Debt Capital}}\right)\right]
\end{aligned}$$

$$X = 0.25625 - [\$6,000/\$6,400)(1 - 0.40)(X - 0.10)]$$

Solving for X yields an unleveraged cost of equity capital of 20 percent.

---

[12]There is a small difference from $12,400,000 because of rounding various calculations.

The second component requires the cost of debt capital. We have assumed above that the firm issues the debt at par, so its pretax cost is 10 percent.

The valuation of the debt plus equity is as follows:

1. Value of Unleveraged Free Cash Flows at Unleveraged Cost of Equity: $2,000,000/0.20	$10,000,000
2. Value of Tax Savings on Interest at Cost of Debt: (0.40 × 0.10 × $6,000,000)/0.10	2,400,000
Total Value of Debt Plus Equity	$12,400,000

This total is the same as in Example 15. We can subtract the value of the debt of $6 million to obtain the $6,400,000 value of the equity, the same as in Example 14. Note that in order to use the adjusted present value approach we need to know the amount of debt that will be outstanding that will give rise to interest deductions. This approach works well when the analyst wants to value the equity in a firm, given that the firm has or will have a specific amount of debt.

VALUATION OF COKE

We illustrate the valuation of Coke using amounts from the pro forma statements of cash flows for Coke in Exhibit 10.3. Suppose the analyst concludes that the projected cash flows reliably reflect Coke's expected cash flows for Year 8 through Year 12. The net cash flows available to common shareholders are as follows:

	Year 8	Year 9	Year 10	Year 11	Year 12
Cash Flow from Operations . .	$3,610	$3,788	$3,974	$4,166	$4,366
Cash Flow from Investing	(1,198)	(1,390)	(1,534)	(1,691)	(1,866)
Cash Flow from Debt Financing	1,017	1,355	1,619	1,835	1,988
Leveraged Free Cash Flow . . .	$3,429	$3,753	$4,059	$4,310	$4,488

The cash flows from debt financing include the change in notes payable and long-term debt but exclude changes in common stock and common stock dividends.

The analyst must make some assumption about net cash flows after Year 12. The average compound growth rate in leveraged free cash flows between Year 8 and Year 12 is approximately 7 percent. We assume that this growth rate will continue after Year 12.

The analyst must discount these cash flows to their present value. The discount rate should reflect the investors' desired rate of return, adjusted to reflect the risk inherent in investing in Coke. Coke's market beta at the end of Year 7 is 0.97. Assuming a 6 percent risk-free rate as an excess of market return over the risk-free rate of 7 percent, the cost of equity capital is 12.8 percent [= 6.0 percent + 0.97(7.0 percent)].

Coke's valuation using the present value of projected cash flows is $59,318 million, as shown below (in millions):

Year	Cash Flow	Present Value Factor at 12.8 Percent	Present Value
8	$ 3,429	0.88652	$ 3,040
9	$ 3,753	0.79719	2,992
10	$ 4,059	0.69674	2,828
11	$ 4,310	0.61768	2,662
12	$ 4,488	0.54759	2,458
After Year 12	$82,796*	0.54759	45,338
Total Present Value			$59,318

$$*\$4,488 \times \frac{1.070}{0.128 - 0.070} = \$82,796.$$

Based on the 2,481 million shares outstanding at the end of Year 7, the market price should be $23.91 (= $59,318/2,481) to yield a return of 12.8 percent. Coke's actual market price at the end of Year 7 was $52.63. The difference between these two prices might result from (1) inaccurate projections of future cash flows, (2) errors in measuring the cost of equity capital, and (3) market inefficiencies in the pricing of Coke.

One way to evaluate the difference between the actual and computed market value is to rethink the growth rate used. We can solve for the value of g in the residual value calculation implied by the current market price of $52.63. The aggregate current market value is $130,575 (= 2,481 outstanding common shares × $52.63). Given the cash flows projected for Year 8 through Year 12, the current market price of $52.63 implies a growth rate in projected leveraged free cash flows of approximately 10.47 percent after Year 12 when the cost of equity capital is 12.8 percent.

The calculations are as follows:

Year	Cash Flow	Present Value Factor at 12.8 Percent	Present Value
8	$ 3,429	0.88652	$ 3,040
9	$ 3,753	0.79719	2,992
10	$ 4,059	0.69674	2,828
11	$ 4,310	0.61768	2,662
12	$ 4,488	0.54759	2,458
After Year 12	$212,924*	0.54759	116,595
Total Present Value			$130,575

$$*\$4,488 \times \frac{1.1047}{0.128 - 0.1047} = \$212,924$$

The growth rate in actual leveraged free cash flows for Coke between Year 2 and Year 7 was 13.8 percent. Our pro forma financial statements assume that Coke will not grow nearly as fast in the future as it has in the past. The market appears to be pricing Coke as if the decline in growth rate will not be as large as we assumed.

Another means by which to assess the disparity between our computed value for the common equity of Coke and its current market value is to rethink the cost of equity capital used. Perhaps 12.8 percent is too high a cost of equity capital for Coke. In this case, however, the projected *undiscounted* leveraged free cash flows are less than the current market value of Coke. Thus, given our projections of cash flows and growth rates, there is no positive discount rate that will yield an aggregate market value of $130,575. Of course, some combination of revised growth rates and cost of equity capital would yield such a value.

EVALUATION OF PRESENT VALUE OF CASH FLOWS VALUATION METHOD

The principal advantages of the present value of future cash flows valuation method include the following:

1. This valuation method focuses on cash flows, a base that economists would argue has more economic meaning than earnings.
2. Projected amounts of cash flows result from projecting likely amounts of revenues, expenses, assets, liabilities, and shareholders' equities, which requires the analyst to think through many future operating, investing, and financing decisions of a firm.

The principal disadvantages of the present value of future cash flows valuation method include the following:

1. The residual or terminal value tends to dominate the total value in many cases. This residual value is sensitive to assumptions made about growth rates after the forecast horizon.
2. The projection of cash flows can be time-consuming for the analyst, making it costly when the analyst follows many companies and must regularly identify under- and overvalued firms.

SUMMARY

This chapter illustrates valuation using the present value of future cash flows. As with the preparation of pro forma financial statements in Chapter 10, the reasonableness of the valuations depends on the reasonableness of the assumptions. The analyst should assess the sensitivity of the valuation to alternative assumptions regarding growth and discount rates.

Because we use only a five-year horizon for projecting Coke's cash flows, the residual or terminal value dominates the valuation. This terminal value is heavily influenced by the assumed growth rate in cash flows. The analyst should also calculate the value of firms using other approaches, such as the earnings-based approaches to be discussed in Chapter 12, to validate the cash-based approach.

PROBLEMS AND CASES

11.1 EFFECT OF RESIDUAL VALUE ON COMMON EQUITY VALUATION. Problem 10.6 projects cash flows as follows for Wal-Mart for Year 8 through Year 11 (in millions):

	Year 8	Year 9	Year 10	Year 11
Cash Flow from Operations	$3,487	$4,912	$5,672	$6,403
Cash Flow for Investing	(3,220)	(3,729)	(4,319)	(5,002)
Cash Flow from Debt Financing	608	1,423	1,650	1,914
Leveraged Free Cash Flow	$ 875	$2,606	$3,003	$3,315

The market equity beta for Wal-Mart at the end of Year 7 is 0.83. Assume that the risk-free interest rate is 6 percent and the market premium is 7 percent.

Required
    a. Valuing the common equity of Wal-Mart requires some assumption about the leveraged free cash flows after Year 11. One approach applies a multiple to the leveraged

free cash flows of Year 11. The multiple equals $(1 + g)/(r - g)$, where g is the assumed growth rate in leveraged free cash flows after Year 11, and r is the cost of equity capital. Leveraged free cash flows are projected to grow 10.4 percent [$= (\$3,315/\$3,003) - 1$] between Year 10 and Year 11. Why doesn't this residual value valuation model work with an assumed growth rate of 10.4 percent in perpetuity?

b. Assume that the growth rate in leveraged free cash flows will decline 1 percentage point each year between Year 11 and Year 14 (that is, growth will be 9.4 percent for Year 12, 8.4 percent for Year 13, and 7.4 for Year 14). The growth rate will stabilize at 7.4 percent after Year 14. Compute the value of the common equity of Wal-Mart as of the end of Year 7.

c. Repeat part b, but assume that the growth rate will equal 6.4 percent after Year 14.

d. What do the results of parts b and c suggest about the role of the growth rate in valuation?

e. The actual market value of Wal-Mart at the end of Year 7 was $54,084 million. One approach to dealing with a growth rate that approximately equals or exceeds the cost of equity capital is to solve for the growth rate implicit in the actual market price. Assume that the analyst is confident about the projected leveraged free cash flows for Year 8 through Year 11, and wants to solve for the growth in leveraged free cash flows after Year 11 implicit in the total market value of $54,084 at the end of Year 7. Compute the value of this growth rate.

f. A drawback of the present value of projected cash flows as a valuation method is that the residual value tends to dominate the value. One suggestion for dealing with this criticism is to extend the number of years in the forecast horizon before computing the residual value. Compare the effect of the residual value on the total value when the analyst computes the residual value at the end of Year 11 in part e and at the end of Year 14 in part b. How well does extending the forecast horizon deal with this residual value concern?

11.2 EFFECT OF RESIDUAL VALUE ON COMMON EQUITY VALUES. Problem 10.7 projects leveraged free cash flows for The Gap and The Limited for Year 8 through Year 12 as follows (in millions):

	Year 8	Year 9	Year 10	Year 11	Year 12
The Gap	$517	$462	$536	$622	$722
The Limited	$279	$289	$310	$337	$363

At the end of Year 7, the market equity beta of The Gap is 0.82; The Limited beta is 0.40. Assume a risk-free interest rate of 6 percent and a market premium of 7 percent.

Required

a. What difficulty does the analyst encounter in applying the residual value model, $(1 + g)/(r - g)$, to The Gap and The Limited at the end of Year 12?

b. At the end of Year 7, the total market value of The Gap is $9,787 million; market value of The Limited is $4,751 million. Assuming that the analyst is confident of the projected leveraged free cash flows for Year 8 through Year 12, compute the growth rate in leveraged free cash flows after Year 12 implicitly assumed by the market in arriving at the market values above at the end of Year 7.

c. Evaluate the reasonableness of the implied growth rates computed in part b.

d. The Limited has considerably more debt in its capital structure than The Gap, which would suggest a higher market beta for The Limited. The Limited, however, has a more diversified product line than The Gap which might reduce the variability of its sales and thereby its market beta. Assume for this part that the market equity beta of The Limited is 0.82, the same as The Gap's. Compute the growth rate in leveraged free cash flows after Year 12 for The Limited, assuming a total market value of $4,751 million and a revised cost of equity capital reflecting a market equity beta of 0.82.

e. What does the analysis in part d suggest about the reasonableness of a market equity beta of 0.40 for The Limited?

11.3 CALCULATING THE COST OF EQUITY CAPITAL. Crown Cork & Seal Co. manufactures aluminum, steel, and plastic containers. Dun & Bradstreet provides credit reports and other financial information for businesses. KinderCare operates a chain of childcare centers. Selected data for these companies appear below (in millions):

	Crown Cork & Seal Co.	Dun & Bradstreet	KinderCare
Total Assets	$5,051.7	$3,723.1	$589.3
Interest-Bearing Debt	$2,098.2	$ 407.1	$220.2
Average Pretax Borrowing Cost	9.75%	8.0%	7.4%
Common Equity:			
Book Value	$1,579.8	$1,182.5	$262.5
Market Value	$3,185.8	$4,136.2	$325.3
Income Tax Rate	35.0%	35.0%	35.0%
Market Equity Beta	1.09	0.67	0.50

Required

a. One issue in computing the cost of equity capital is whether the analyst should use short-horizon, intermediate-horizon, or long-horizon riskless rates and market premiums. Appropriate rates for each of these time horizons have recently been as follows:

Time Horizon	Riskless Rate	Market Premium
Short	4.6%	8.8%
Intermediate	5.4%	7.8%
Long	6.0%	7.4%

Compute the cost of equity capital for each of these three companies using (1) short-, (2) intermediate-, and (3) long-horizon riskless rates and market premiums. Under what conditions will the cost of equity capital differ little versus considerably with respect to the time horizon selected?

b. For the remaining parts of this problem, use the intermediate-horizon riskless rate and risk premium from part a. Compute the weighted average cost of capital for each of the three companies.

c. Compute the asset beta for each of the three companies. Assume that the market value of the debt equals its book value.

d. Assume for this part that each company is a potential leveraged buyout candidate. The buyers intend to put in place a capital structure that has 75 percent debt with a pretax borrowing cost of 12 percent and 25 percent common equity. Compute the weighted average cost of capital for each company based on this new capital structure. Why do these revised weighted average costs of capital differ so little from those computed in part b?

11.4 VALUING A LEVERAGED BUYOUT CANDIDATE. Mead Corporation processes wood pulp into various paper products in its capital-intensive plants. Sales of paper products rise and fall with conditions in the economy. At the end of Year 6, Mead reports assets of $4,372.8 million, debt of $853.9 million, and common shareholders' equity at book value of $2,160.2 million. The market value of its common stock is $2,891.9, and its market equity beta is 0.98.

An equity buyout group is considering a leveraged buyout of Mead as of the beginning of Year 7. The group intends to finance the buyout with 75 percent debt carrying an interest rate of 12 percent and 25 percent common equity. It projects that the unleveraged free cash flows of Mead will be as follows: Year 7, $387 million; Year 8, $426 million; Year 9, $468 million; Year 10, $515 million; and Year 11, $567 million.

This problem sets forth the steps that the analyst might follow in deciding to acquire Mead and assessing a value for the firm.

Required

a. Given the information provided, identify the characteristics of Mead that make it an attractive and an unattractive leveraged buyout candidate.

b. Determine the unleveraged equity beta of Mead before consideration of the leveraged buyout. Assume that the book value of the debt equals its market value. The income tax rate is 35 percent.

c. Determine the cost of equity capital with the new capital structure that results from the leveraged buyout. Assume a risk-free rate of 6 percent and a market premium of 7 percent.

d. Determine the weighted average cost of capital of the new capital structure.

e. Although this is an unrealistic premise for a company with cyclical sales, analysts at the buyout group project that unleveraged free cash flows will increase 10 percent per year between Year 6 and Year 11 as shown above. Assume that unleveraged free cash flows will continue to increase 10 percent each year after Year 11. Compute the present value of the projected unleveraged free cash flows at the weighted average cost of capital.

f. Assume that the buyout group acquires Mead for the value determined in part e. Will Mead generate sufficient cash flow each year to service the debt, assuming that the realized unleveraged free cash flows match the projections?

11.5 VALUING A LEVERAGED BUYOUT CANDIDATE. Experian Information Systems is a wholly owned subsidiary of TRW, a publicly traded company. The subsidiary has total assets of $555,443 thousand, debt of $1,839 thousand, and common equity at book value of $402,759 thousand.

An equity buyout group is planning to acquire Experian from TRW in a leveraged buyout as of the beginning of Year 6. The group plans to finance the buyout with 60 percent debt that has an interest cost of 10 percent per year and 40 percent common equity. Analysts for the buyout group project unleveraged free cash flows as follows (in thousands): Year 6, $52,300; Year 7, $56,484; Year 8, $61,003; Year 9, $65,883; and Year 10, $71,154. Because Experian is not a publicly traded firm, it does not have an equity beta. The company most comparable to Experian is Equifax, with an equity beta of 0.86. The market value of Equifax's debt is $366.5 thousand; the value of its common equity is $4,436.8 thousand. Assume an income tax rate of 35 percent throughout this problem.

This problem sets forth the steps that the analyst might follow in deciding to acquire Experian and assessing a value to put on the firm.

Required

a. Determine the unleveraged equity beta of Equifax.

b. Assuming that the unleveraged equity beta of Equifax is appropriate for Experian, determine the leveraged equity beta of Experian after the buyout with its new capital structure.

c. Determine the weighted average cost of capital of Experian after the buyout. Assume a risk-free interest rate of 6 percent and a market premium of 7 percent.

d. The analysts at the buyout firm project that unleveraged free cash flows of Experian will increase 8 percent each year after Year 10. Compute the present value of the unleveraged free cash flows at the weighted average cost of capital.

e. Assume that the buyout group acquires Experian for the value determined in part d. Will Experian generate sufficient cash flow each year to service the debt, assuming that actual unleveraged free cash flows match the projections?

11.6 APPLYING VARIOUS PRESENT VALUE APPROACHES TO VALUATION. An equity buyout group intends to acquire Wedgewood Products as of the beginning of Year 8. The buyout group intends to finance 40 percent of the acquisition price with 10 percent annual coupon debt and 60 percent with common equity. The income tax rate is 40 percent. The cost of equity capital is 14 percent. Analysts at the buyout firm project unleveraged free cash flows for Wedgewood as follows (in millions): Year 8, $2,100; Year 9, $2,268; Year 10, $2,449; Year 11, $2,645; and Year 12, $2,857. The analysts project that unleveraged free cash flows will continue to increase 8 percent each year after Year 12.

Required

a. Compute the weighted average cost of capital for Wedgewood based on the proposed capital structure.

b. Compute the total purchase price of Wedgewood (debt plus common equity). To do this, discount the unleveraged free cash flows at the weighted average cost of capital.

c. Given the purchase price determined in part b, compute the total amount of debt, the annual interest cost, and the leveraged free cash flows for Year 8 through Year 12.

d. The present value of the leveraged free cash flows when discounted at the 14 percent cost of equity capital should equal the common equity portion of the total purchase price computed in part b. Determine the growth rate in leveraged free cash flows after Year 12 that will result in a present value of leveraged free cash flows equal to 60 percent of the purchase price computed in part b.

e. Why does the implied growth rate in leveraged free cash flows determined in part d differ from the 8 percent assumed growth rate in unleveraged free cash flows?

f. The adjusted present value valuation approach separates the total value of the firm into the value of an all-equity firm and the value of the tax savings from interest deductions. Assume that that cost of unleveraged equity is 11.33 percent. Compute the present value of the unleveraged free cash flows at this unleveraged equity cost. Compute the present value of the tax savings from interest expense deductions using the pretax cost of debt as the discount rate. Compare the total of these two present values to the purchase price determined in part b.

CASE 11.1

HOLMES CORPORATION: LBO VALUATION

Holmes Corporation is a leading designer and manufacturer of materials handling and process equipment for heavy industry in the U.S. and abroad. Its sales have more than doubled, and its earnings have increased more than sixfold, in the past five years. In materials handling, Holmes is a major producer of electric overhead and gantry cranes, ranging from 5 tons in capacity to 600-ton giants; the latter are used primarily in nuclear and conventional power generating plants. Holmes also builds underhung cranes and monorail systems that can carry loads up to 40 tons for general industrial use; railcar movers; railroad and mass transit shop maintenance equipment; and a broad line of advanced package conveyers. Holmes is a world leader in evaporation and crystallization systems and furnishes dryers, heat exchangers, and filters to complete its line of chemical processing equipment sold internationally to the chemical, fertilizer, food, drug, and paper industries. For the metallurgical industry, it designs and manufactures electric arc and induction furnaces, cupolas, ladles, and hot metal distribution equipment.

The information on the following pages appears in the Year 15 annual report of Holmes Corporation.

HIGHLIGHTS

	Year 15	Year 14
Net Sales	$102,698,836	$109,372,718
Net Earnings	6,601,908	6,583,360
Net Earnings per Share	3.62*	3.61*
Cash Dividends Paid	2,241,892	1,426,502
Cash Dividends per Share	1.22*	0.78*
Shareholders' Equity	29,333,803	24,659,214
Shareholders' Equity per Share	16.07*	13.51*
Working Capital	23,100,863	19,029,626
Orders Received	95,436,103	80,707,576
Unfilled Orders at End of Period	77,455,900	84,718,633
Average Number of Common Shares Outstanding During Period	1,824,853*	1,824,754*

*Adjusted for June, Year 15, and June, Year 14, five-for-four stock distributions.

Net Sales, Net Earnings, and Net Earnings per Share by Quarter (adjusted for five-for-four stock distribution in June, Year 15, and June, Year 14)

	Year 15			Year 14		
	Net Sales	Net Earnings	Per Share	Net Sales	Net Earnings	Per Share
First Quarter	$25,931,457	$ 1,602,837	$ 0.88	$ 21,768,077	$ 1,126,470	$ 0.62
Second Quarter	24,390,079	1,727,112	0.95	28,514,298	1,716,910	0.94
Third Quarter	25,327,226	1,505,118	0.82	28,798,564	1,510,958	0.82
Fourth Quarter	27,050,074	1,766,841	0.97	30,291,779	2,229,022	1.23
	$102,698,836	$ 6,601,908	$ 3.62	$109,372,718	$ 6,583,360	$ 3.61

Common Stock Prices and Cash Dividends Paid per Common Share by Quarter (adjusted for five-for-four stock distribution in June, Year 15, and June, Year 14)

	Year 15			Year 14		
	Stock Prices High	Low	Cash Dividends Per Share	Stock Prices High	Low	Cash Dividends Per Share
First Quarter	22½	18½	$0.26	11¼	9½	$0.16
Second Quarter	25¼	19½	0.26	12⅜	8⅞	0.16
Third Quarter	26¼	19¾	0.325	15⅞	11⅝	0.20
Fourth Quarter	28⅛	23¼	0.375	20⅞	15⅞	0.26
			$1.22			$0.78

MANAGEMENT'S REPORT TO SHAREHOLDERS

Year 15 was a pleasant surprise for all of us at Holmes Corporation. When the year started, it looked as though Year 15 would be a good year but not up to the record performance of Year 14. As a result of the excellent performance of our employees and the benefit of a favorable acquisition, however, Year 15 produced both record earnings and the largest cash dividend outlay in the company's 93-year history.

There is no doubt that some of the attractive orders received in late Year 12 and early Year 13 contributed to Year 15 profit. But of major significance was our organization's favorable response to several new management policies instituted to emphasize higher corporate profitability. Year 15 showed a net profit on net sales of 6.4 percent, which not only exceeds the 6.0 percent of last year but also represents the highest net margin in several decades.

Net sales for the year were $102,698,836, down 6 percent from the $109,372,718 of a year ago, but still the second-highest volume in our history. Net earnings, however, set a new record at $6,601,908, or $3.62 per common share, which slightly exceeds the $6,583,360, or $3.61 per common share earned last year.

Cash dividends paid in Year 15 of $2,241,892 were 57 percent above the $1,426,502 paid a year ago. The record total results from your Board's approval of two increases during the year. When we implemented the five-for-four stock distribution in June, Year 15, we maintained the quarterly dividend rate of $0.325 on the increased number of shares for the January payment. Then in December, Year 15, we increased the quarterly rate to $0.375 per share.

Year 15 certainly was not the most exuberant year in the capital equipment markets. Fortunately, our heavy involvement in ecology improvement, power generation, and international markets continues to serve us well, with the result that new orders of $95,436,103 were 18 percent over the $80,707,576 of Year 14.

Economists have predicted a substantial capital spending upturn for well over a year, but so far our customers have displayed stubborn reluctance to place new orders amid uncertainty concerning the economy. Confidence is the answer. As soon as potential buyers can clearly see the future direction of the economy, we expect a large latent demand for capital goods to be unleashed, producing a much-expanded market for Holmes products.

Fortunately, the accelerating pace of international markets continues to yield new business. Year 15 was an excellent year on the international front, as our foreign customers continue to recognize our technological leadership in several product lines. Net sales of Holmes products shipped overseas and fees from foreign licensees amounted to $30,495,041, which represents a 31 percent increase over the $23,351,980 of a year ago.

Management fully recognizes and intends to take maximum advantage of our technological leadership in foreign lands. The latest manifestation of this policy is the acquisition of a controlling interest in Société Française Holmes Fermont, our Swenson process equipment licensee located in Paris. Holmes and a partner started this firm 14 years ago as a sales and engineering organization to function in the Common Market. The company currently operates in the same mode. It owns no physical manufacturing assets, subcontracting all production. Its markets have expanded to include Spain and the East European countries.

Holmes Fermont is experiencing strong demand in Europe. For example, in early May a $5.5 million order for a large potash crystallization system was received from a French engineering company representing a Russian client. Management estimates that Holmes Fermont will contribute approximately $6 to $8 million of net sales in Year 16.

Holmes's other wholly owned subsidiaries—Holmes Equipment Limited in Canada, Ermanco Incorporated in Michigan, and Holmes International, Inc., our FSC (Foreign Sales Corporation)—again contributed substantially to the success of Year 15. Holmes Equipment Limited registered its second-best year, although capital equipment markets in Canada have virtually come to a standstill in the past two quarters. Ermanco achieved the best year in its history, while Holmes International, Inc., had a truly exceptional year because of the very high level of activity in our international markets.

The financial condition of the company has shown further improvement and is now unusually strong as a result of very stringent financial controls. Working capital increased to $23,100,863 from $19,029,626, a 21 percent improvement. Inventories decreased 6 percent from $18,559,231 to $17,491,741. The company currently has no long-term or short-term debt and has considerable cash in short-term instruments. Much of our cash position, however, results from customers' advance payments, which we will absorb as we make shipments on the contracts. Shareholders' equity increased 19 percent to $29,393,803 from $24,690,214 a year ago.

Plant equipment expenditures for the year were $1,172,057, down 18 percent from $1,426,347 of Year 14. Several appropriations approved during the year did not require expenditures because of delayed deliveries beyond Year 15. The major emphasis again has been on our continuing program of improving capacity and efficiency through the purchase of numerically controlled machine tools. We expanded the Ermanco plant by 50 percent, but since this is a leasehold arrangement, we made only minor direct investment. We also improved the Canadian operation by adding more manufacturing space and installing energy-saving insulation.

Labor relations were excellent throughout the year. The Harvey plant continues to be a nonunion operation. We negotiated a new labor contract at the Canadian plant that extends to March 1, Year 17. The Pioneer Division in Alabama has a labor contract that does not expire until April, Year 16. While the union contract at Ermanco expired June 1, Year 15, work continues while negotiation proceeds on a new contract. We anticipate no difficulty in reaching a new agreement.

We exerted considerable effort during the year to improve Holmes's image in the investment community. Management held several informative meetings with security analyst groups to enhance the awareness of our activities and corporate performance.

The outlook for Year 16, while generally favorable, depends in part on the course of capital spending over the next several months. If the spending rate accelerates, the quickening pace of new orders, coupled with present backlogs, will provide the conditions for another fine year. If general industry continues the reluctant spending pattern of the last two years, however, Year 16 could be a year of maintaining market positions while awaiting better market conditions. Management takes an optimistic view and thus looks for a successful Year 16.

The achievement of record earnings and the highest profit margin in decades demonstrates the capability and the dedication of our employees. Management is most grateful for their efforts throughout the excellent year.

T.R. Varnum
President

T.L. Fuller
Chairman

March 15, Year 16

REVIEW OF OPERATIONS

Year 15 was a very active year, although the pace was not at the hectic tempo of Year 14. It was a year that showed continued strong demand in some product areas but a dampened rate in others. Product areas in which some special economic circumstances enhanced demand fared well. For example, a continuing focus on ecological improvement fostered excellent activity in Swenson process equipment. Similarly, energy concerns and a need for more electrical power generation capacity were positive factors for large overhead cranes. On the other hand, Holmes's products that relate to general industry and depend on the overall capital spending rate for new equipment experienced slower demand, resulting in fewer new orders and reduced backlogs. The affected products were small cranes, underhung cranes, railcar movers, and metallurgical equipment.

Year 15 was the first full year of operations under some major policy changes instituted to improve Holmes's profitability. The two primary changes include the restructuring of our marketing effort along product division lines and the conversion of the product division incentive plans to a profit-based formula. The corporate organization adapted extremely well to the new policies. The improved profit margin in Year 15, in substantial part, is a result of these changes.

International activity increased markedly during the year. Surging foreign business and the expressed objective to capitalize on Holmes's technological leadership overseas resulted in the elevation of Mr. R.E. Foster to officer status as Vice President-International. The year involved heavy commitments of the product division staffs, engineering groups, and the manufacturing organization to such important contracts as the $14 million Swenson order for Poland, the $8 million Swenson project for Mexico, a $2 million crane order for Venezuela, and several millions of dollars of railcar movers for all areas of the world.

The acquisition of control and commencement of operating responsibility of Société Française Holmes Fermont, the Swenson licensee in Paris, was a major milestone in our international strategy plans. This organization has the potential of becoming a very substantial contributor in the years immediately ahead. Its long-range market opportunities in Europe and Asia are excellent.

MATERIALS HANDLING PRODUCTS

Materials handling equipment activities portrayed conflicting trends. During a year when total backlog decreased, the crane division backlog increased. This is a result of several multimillion dollar contracts for power plant cranes. The small crane market, on the other hand, experienced depressed conditions during most of the year, as general industry declined to make appropriations for new plant and equipment. The underhung crane market experienced similar conditions. As Congressional attitudes and policies on investment unfold, however, we expect capital spending to show a substantial upturn.

The Transportation Equipment Division secured the second order for orbital service bridges, a new product for the containment vessels of nuclear power plants. This is a unique design that allows considerable cost savings in erecting and maintaining containment shells.

The Ermanco Conveyor Division completed its best year with the growing acceptance of the unique XenoROL design. We expanded the Grand Haven plant by 50 percent to effect further cost reduction and new concepts of marketing.

The railcar moving line continued to produce more business from international markets. We installed the new 11TM unit in six domestic locations, a product showing signs of exceptional performance. We shipped the first foreign 11TM machine to Sweden.

PROCESS EQUIPMENT PRODUCTS

Process equipment again accounted for slightly more than half of the year's business.

Swenson activity reached an all-time high, with much of the division's effort going into international projects. The large number of foreign orders required considerable additional work to cover the necessary documentation, metrification when required, and general liaison.

We engaged in considerably more subcontracting during the year to accommodate one-piece shipment of the huge vessels pioneered by Swenson to effect greater equipment economies. The division continued to expand the use of computerization for design work and contract administration. We developed more capability during the year to handle the many additional tasks associated with turnkey projects. Swenson research and development efforts accelerated in search of better technology and new products. We conducted pilot plant test work at our facilities and in the field to convert several sales prospects into new contracts.

The metallurgical business proceeded at a slower pace in Year 15. With construction activity showing early signs of improvement, however, and automotive and farm machinery manufacturers increasing their operating rates, we see intensified interest in metallurgical equipment.

FINANCIAL STATEMENTS

The financial statements of Holmes Corporation and related notes appear in Exhibits 11.3 through 11.5. Exhibit 11.6 presents five-year summary operating information for Holmes.

NOTES TO CONSOLIDATED FINANCIAL STATEMENTS
YEAR 15 AND YEAR 14

Note A—Summary of Significant Accounting Policies   Significant accounting policies consistently applied appear below to assist the reader in reviewing the company's consolidated financial statements in this report.

Consolidation—The consolidated financial statements include the accounts of the company and its subsidiaries after eliminating all intercompany transactions and balances.

Inventories—Inventories generally appear at the lower of cost or market, with cost determined principally on a first-in, first-out basis.

Property, plant, and equipment—Property, plant, and equipment appear at acquisition cost less accumulated depreciation. When the company retires or disposes of properties, it removes the related costs and accumulated depreciation from the respective accounts, and credits or charges any gain or loss to earnings. The company expenses maintenance and repairs as incurred. It capitalizes major betterments and renewals. Depreciation results from applying the straight-line method over the estimated useful lives of the assets as follows:

Buildings	30 to 45 years
Machinery and equipment	4 to 20 years
Furniture and fixtures	10 years

Intangible assets—The company amortizes the unallocated excess of cost of a subsidiary over net assets acquired over a seventeen-year period.

Research and development costs—The company charges research and development costs to operations as incurred ($479,410 in Year 15 and $467,733 in Year 14).

Pension plans—The company and its subsidiaries have noncontributory pension plans covering substantially all employees. The company's policy is to fund accrued pension

EXHIBIT 11.3

Holmes Corporation
Balance Sheet
(amounts in thousands)
(Case 11.1)

	Year 10	Year 11	Year 12	Year 13	Year 14	Year 15
Cash	$ 955	$ 962	$ 865	$ 1,247	$ 1,540	$ 3,857
Marketable Securities	0	0	0	0	0	2,990
Accounts/Notes Receivable	6,545	7,295	9,718	13,307	18,759	14,303
Inventories	7,298	8,685	12,797	20,426	18,559	17,492
Current Assets	$14,798	$16,942	$23,380	$34,980	$38,858	$38,642
Investments	0	0	0	0	0	422
Property, Plant, and Equipment	12,216	12,445	13,126	13,792	14,903	15,876
Less: Accum. Depreciation	7,846	8,236	8,558	8,988	9,258	9,703
Other Assets	470	420	400	299	343	276
Total Assets	$19,638	$21,571	$28,348	$40,083	$44,846	$45,513
Accounts Payable—Trade	$ 2,894	$ 4,122	$ 6,496	$ 7,889	$ 6,779	$ 4,400
Notes Payable—Non-Trade	0	0	700	3,500	0	0
Current Part Long-Term Debt	170	170	170	170	170	0
Other Current Liabilities	550	1,022	3,888	8,624	12,879	11,142
Current Liabilities	$ 3,614	$ 5,314	$11,254	$20,183	$19,828	$15,542
Long-Term Debt	680	510	340	170	0	0
Deferred Tax (NCL)	0	0	0	216	328	577
Other Non-Current Liabilities	0	0	0	0	0	0
Total Liabilities	$ 4,294	$ 5,824	$11,594	$20,569	$20,156	$16,119
Common Stock	$ 2,927	$ 2,927	$ 2,927	$ 5,855	$ 7,303	$ 9,214
Additional Paid-in Capital	5,075	5,075	5,075	5,075	5,061	5,286
Retained Earnings	7,342	7,772	8,774	8,599	12,297	14,834
Cumulative Translation Adjustment ..	0	0	5	12	29	60
Treasury Stock	0	(27)	(27)	(27)	0	0
Shareholders' Equity	$15,344	$15,747	$16,754	$19,514	$24,690	$29,394
Total Equities	$19,638	$21,571	$28,348	$40,083	$44,846	$45,513

costs as determined by independent actuaries. Pension costs amount to $471,826 in Year 15 and $366,802 in Year 14.

Revenue recognition—The company generally recognizes income on a percentage-of-completion basis. It records advance payments as received and reports them as a deduction from billings when earned. The company recognizes royalties, included in net sales, as income when received. Royalties total $656,043 in Year 15 and $723,930 in Year 14.

Income taxes—The company provides no income taxes on unremitted earnings of foreign subsidiaries because it anticipates no significant tax liabilities should foreign units remit such earnings. The company makes provision for deferred income taxes applicable to timing

EXHIBIT 11.4

Holmes Corporation
Income Statement
(amounts in thousands)
(Case 11.1)

	Year 11	Year 12	Year 13	Year 14	Year 15
Sales	$41,428	$53,541	$76,328	$109,373	$102,699
Other Revenues and Gains	0	41	0	0	211
Cost of Goods Sold	(33,269)	(43,142)	(60,000)	(85,364)	(80,260)
Selling and Administrative Expense	(6,175)	(7,215)	(9,325)	(13,416)	(12,090)
Other Expenses and Losses	(2)	0	(11)	(31)	(1)
EBIT	$ 1,982	$ 3,225	$ 6,992	$ 10,562	$ 10,559
Interest Expense	(43)	(21)	(284)	(276)	(13)
Income Tax Expense	(894)	(1,471)	(2,992)	(3,703)	(3,944)
Net Income	$ 1,045	$ 1,733	$ 3,716	$ 6,583	$ 6,602

differences between financial statement and income tax accounting, principally on the earnings of a foreign sales subsidiary, which existing statutes defer in part from current taxation.

Note B—Foreign Operations The consolidated financial statements include net assets of $2,120,648 ($1,847,534 in Year 14); undistributed earnings of $2,061,441 ($1,808,752 in Year 14); sales of $7,287,566 ($8,603,225 in Year 14); and net income of $454,999 ($641,454 in Year 14) applicable to the Canadian subsidiary.

The company translates balance sheet accounts of the Canadian subsidiary into U.S. dollars at the exchange rates at the end of the year, and translates operating results at the average of exchange rates for the year.

Note C—Inventories Inventories used in determining cost of sales appear below:

	Year 15	Year 14	Year 13
Raw materials and supplies	$ 8,889,147	$ 9,720,581	$ 8,900,911
Work in process	8,602,594	8,838,650	11,524,805
	$17,491,741	$18,559,231	$20,425,716

Note D—Short-Term Borrowing The company has short-term credit agreements that principally provide for loans of 90-day periods at varying interest rates. There were no borrowings in Year 15. In Year 14, the maximum borrowing at the end of any calendar month was $4,500,000, and the approximate average loan balance and weighted average interest rate, computed by using the days' outstanding method, were $3,435,000 and 7.6 percent. There were no restrictions upon the company during the period of the loans and no compensating bank balance arrangements required by the lending institutions.

Holmes Corporation
Statement of Cash Flow
(amounts in thousands)
(Case 11.1)

	Year 11	Year 12	Year 13	Year 14	Year 15
Operations					
Net Income	$1,045	$1,733	$3,716	$ 6,583	$ 6,602
Depreciation and Amortization	491	490	513	586	643
Other Addbacks	20	25	243	151	299
Other Subtractions	0	0	0	0	(97)
WC Provided by Operations	$1,556	$2,248	$4,472	$ 7,320	$ 7,447
(Increase) Decrease in Receivables	(750)	(2,424)	(3,589)	(5,452)	4,456
(Increase) Decrease in Inventories	(1,387)	(4,111)	(7,629)	1,867	1,068
Increase (Decrease) Accounts					
Payable—Trade	1,228	2,374	1,393	1,496	(2,608)
Increase (Decrease) in Other					
Current Liabilities	473	2,865	4,737	1,649	(1,508)
Cash from Operations	$1,120	$ 952	$ (616)	$ 6,880	$ 8,855
Investing					
Fixed assets Acquired (net)	$ (347)	$ (849)	$ (749)	$(1,426)	$(1,172)
Investments Acquired	0	0	0	0	(3,306)
Other Investment Transactions	45	0	81	(64)	39
Cash Flow from Investing	$ (302)	$ (849)	$ (668)	$(1,490)	$(4,439)
Financing					
Increase in Short-Term Borrowing	$ 0	$ 700	$2,800	$ 0	$ 0
Increase in Long-Term Borrowing	0	0	0	0	0
Issue of Capital Stock	0	0	0	0	315
Decrease in Short-Term Borrowing	0	0	0	(3500)	0
Decrease in Long-Term Borrowing	(170)	(170)	(170)	(170)	(170)
Acquisition of Capital Stock	(27)	0	0	0	0
Dividends	(614)	(730)	(964)	(1,427)	(2,243)
Other Financing Transactions	0	0	0	0	0
Cash Flow from Financing	$ (811)	$ (200)	$1,666	$(5,097)	$(2,098)
Net Change in Cash	$ 7	$ (97)	$ 382	$ 293	$ 2,318

EXHIBIT 11.6

Five-Year Summary of Operations for Holmes Corporation
(Case 11.1)

	Year 11	Year 12	Year 13	Year 14	Year 15
Orders Received	$55,454,188	$89,466,793	$121,445,731	$ 80,707,576	$ 95,436,103
Net Sales	41,427,702	53,540,699	76,327,664	109,372,718	102,698,836
Backlog of Unfilled Orders	32,339,614	68,265,708	113,383,775	84,718,633	77,455,900
Earnings before Taxes					
on Income	1,939,414	3,203,835	6,708,072	10,285,943	10,546,213
Taxes on Income	894,257	1,470,489	2,991,947	3,702,583	3,944,305
Net Earnings	1,045,157	1,733,346	3,716,125	6,583,360	6,601,908
Net Property, Plant					
and Equipment	4,209,396	4,568,372	4,803,978	5,644,590	6,173,416
Net Additions to Property	346,549	848,685	748,791	1,426,347	1,172,057
Depreciation and Amortization ..	491,217	490,133	513,402	585,735	643,231
Cash Dividends Paid	614,378	730,254	963,935	1,426,502	2,242,892
Working Capital	11,627,875	12,126,491	14,796,931	19,029,626	23,100,463
Shareholders' Equity	15,747,116	15,754,166	19,514,358	24,690,214	29,393,803
Earnings per Share of					
Common (1)	.57	.96	2.03	3.61	3.62
Dividends per Share of					
Common (1)	.34	.40	.53	.78	1.22
Book Value per Share of					
Common (1)	8.62	9.18	10.68	13.51	16.07
Number of Shareholders					
December 31	1,787	1,792	1,834	2,024	2,157
Number of Employees					
December 31	1,303	1,425	1,551	1,550	1,549
Shares of Common Outstanding					
December 31 (1)	1,827,515	1,824,941	1,824,754	1,824,754	1,824,853
% Net Sales by Product Line					
Material Handling Equipment ...	63.0%	54.4%	51.3%	43.6%	46.1%
Processing Equipment	37.0%	45.6%	48.7%	56.4%	53.9%

NOTE: (1) Based on number of shares outstanding on December 31 adjusted for the 5-for-4 stock distributions in June, Year 13, Year 14, and Year 15.

Note E—Income Taxes   Provision for income taxes consists of:

	Year 15	Year 14
Current		
Federal	$2,931,152	$2,633,663
State	466,113	483,240
Canadian	260,306	472,450
	$3,657,571	$3,589,353
Deferred		
Federal	263,797	91,524
Canadian	22,937	21,706
	286,734	113,230
	$3,944,305	$3,702,583

Reconciliation of the total provision for income taxes to the current federal statutory rate of 35 percent is as follows:

	Year 15		Year 14	
	Amount	%	Amount	%
Tax at statutory rate	$3,691,100	35.0%	$3,600,100	35.0%
State taxes, net of U.S. tax credit ..	302,973	2.9	314,106	3.1
All other items	(49,668)	(0.5)	(211,623)	(2.1)
	$3,944,305	37.4%	$3,702,583	36.0%

Note F—Pensions   The components of pension expense appear below:

	Year 15	Year 14
Service Cost	$476,490	$429,700
Interest Cost	567,159	446,605
Actual Return on Pension Investments	(614,210)	(592,900)
Amount Deferred	55,837	98,817
Amortization of Actuarial Gains and Losses	(13,450)	(15,420)
Pension Expense	$471,826	$366,802

The funded status of the pension plan appears below.

	December 31	
	Year 15	**Year 14**
Accumulated Benefit Obligation	**$5,763,450**	$5,325,291
Effect of Salary Increases	**1,031,970**	976,480
Projected Benefit Obligation	**6,795,420**	6,301,771
Pension Fund Assets	**6,247,940**	5,583,730
Excess Pension Obligation	**$ 547,480**	$ 718,041

Assumptions used in accounting for pensions appear below:

	Year 15	**Year 14**
Expected Return on Pension Assets	**10%**	10%
Discount Rate for Projected Benefit Obligation	**9%**	8%
Salary Increases	**5%**	5%

Note G—Common Stock   As of March 20, Year 15, the company increased the authorized number of shares of common stock from 1,800,000 shares to 5,000,000 shares.

On December 29, Year 15, the company increased its equity interest (from 45 percent to 85 percent) in Société Française Holmes Fermont, a French affiliate, in exchange for 18,040 of its common shares in a transaction accounted for as a purchase. The company credited the excess of the fair value ($224,373) of the company's shares issued over par value ($90,200) to additional contributed capital. The excess of the purchase cost over the underlying value of the assets acquired is insignificant.

The company made a 25 percent common stock distribution on June 15, Year 14, and on June 19, Year 15, resulting in increases of 291,915 shares in Year 14 and 364,433 shares in Year 15. We capitalized the par value of these additional shares by a transfer of $1,457,575 in Year 14 and $1,822,165 in Year 15 from retained earnings to the common stock account. In Year 14 and Year 15, we paid cash of $2,611 and $15,340, respectively, in lieu of fractional share interests.

In addition, the company retired 2,570 shares of treasury stock in June, Year 14. The earnings and dividends per share for Year 14 and Year 15 in the accompanying consolidated financial statements reflect the 25 percent stock distributions.

Note H—Contingent Liabilities   The company has certain contingent liabilities with respect to litigation and claims arising in the ordinary course of business. The company cannot determine the ultimate disposition of these contingent liabilities, but, in the opinion of management, they will not result in any material effect upon the company's consolidated financial position or results of operations.

Note I—Quarterly Data (unaudited) Quarterly sales, gross profit, net earnings, and earnings per share for Year 15 are as follows:

	Net Sales	Gross Profit	Net Earnings	Earnings per Share
First	$ 25,931,457	$ 5,606,013	$1,602,837	$0.88
Second	24,390,079	6,148,725	1,727,112	0.95
Third	25,327,226	5,706,407	1,505,118	0.82
Fourth	27,050,074	4,977,774	1,766,841	0.97
Year	$102,698,836	$22,438,919	$6,601,908	$3.62

The first quarterly results are restated for the 25 percent stock distribution on June 19, Year 15.

AUDITORS' REPORT

Board of Directors and Stockholders
Holmes Corporation

We have examined the consolidated balance sheets of Holmes Corporation and Subsidiaries as of December 31, Year 15 and Year 14, and the related consolidated statements of earnings and cash flows for the years then ended. Our examination was made in accordance with generally accepted auditing standards, and accordingly include such tests of the accounting records and such other auditing procedures as we consider necessary in the circumstances.

In our opinion, the financial statements referred to above present fairly the consolidated financial position of Holmes Corporation and Subsidiaries at December 31, Year 15 and Year 14, and the consolidated results of their operations and changes in cash flows for the years then ended, in conformity with generally accepted accounting principles applied on a consistent basis.

Chicago, Illinois
March 15, Year 16

Required
A group of investors is interested in acquiring Holmes in a leveraged buyout.
   a. Describe briefly the factors that make Holmes an attractive leveraged buyout candidate and the factors that make it an unattractive leveraged buyout candidate.
   b. (This question requires you to have read Chapter 10.) Prepare pro forma financial statements for Holmes Corporation for Year 16 through Year 20, excluding all fi-

nancing (that is, project the amount of operating income after taxes, assets, and cash flows from operating and investing activities). State the underlying assumptions made.

c. (This question requires you to have read Chapter 11.) Ascertain the value of Holmes's common shareholders' equity using the present value of its future cash flows valuation approach. Assume a risk-free interest rate of 6 percent and a market premium of 7 percent. Note that information in part d below may be helpful in this valuation. Assume a financing structure for the leveraged buyout as follows:

Type	Proportion	Interest Rate	Term
Term Debt	50%	8%	7-Year Amortization*
Subordinated Debt	25	12%	10-Year Amortization*
Shareholders' Equity	25		
	100%		

*Holmes must repay principal and interest in equal annual payments.

d. (This question requires you to have read Chapter 12.) Ascertain the value of Holmes's common shareholders' equity using the price-earnings ratio and market value to book value valuation approaches. Selected data for similar companies for Year 15 appear below (amounts in millions):

	Agee Robotics	GI Handling Systems	LJG Industries	Gelas Corp.
Industry:	Conveyor Systems	Conveyor Systems	Cranes	Industrial Furnaces
Sales	$4,214	$28,998	$123,034	$75,830
Net Income	$ 309	$ 2,020	$ 9,872	$ 5,117
Assets	$2,634	$15,197	$ 72,518	$41,665
Long-Term Debt	$ 736	$ 5,098	$ 23,745	$ 8,869
Common Shareholders' Equity	$1,551	$ 7,473	$ 38,939	$26,884
Market Value of Common Equity	$6,915	$20,000	$102,667	$41,962
Market Beta	1.12	0.88	0.99	0.93

e. Would you attempt to acquire Holmes Corporation after completing the analyses in parts a through d? If not, how would you change the analyses to make this an attractive leveraged buyout?

CASE 11.2

RODRIGUEZ HOME CENTER, INC.: EQUITY BUYOUT VALUATION*

Rodriguez Home Center, Inc. (RHC) operates a specialty retail store in Los Angeles, offering (fiscal Year 15 sales mix in parentheses) furniture (27 percent); appliances (15 percent); audio and video electronics products (47 percent); selected jewelry (4 percent); and related products and services (7 percent). The company is known for its low and competitive prices, a liberal return-of-merchandise policy, and a willingness to offer first-time credit to its customers. The company's bilingual sales staff and liberal credit terms have supported the development of a substantial customer base that is mostly Hispanic. RHC operates out of one department store and uses one warehouse, both of which it leases.

The company is wholly owned by José Rodriguez, who is 62 years old. His father founded RHC many years ago. The company's competitive advantage is the goodwill generated among the Hispanic community over the years. Although its product offerings are not unique, its competitively low prices for brand-name merchandise and its credit extension policies have garnered an active customer list of 60,000. Two of its top three corporate officers are Hispanic, as are 14 of its 15 line managers. U.S. Census data indicate that the Hispanic community now constitutes 25 percent of the state of California's total population.

EXHIBIT 11.7

Rodriguez Home Center, Inc.
Comparative Income Statements
(amounts in thousands)
(Case 11.2)

| | January 31 | | | | |
	Year 11	Year 12	Year 13	Year 14	Year 15
Sales	$56,058	$69,670	$86,382	$98,534	$110,500
Cost of Goods Sold	(37,404)	(46,214)	(56,892)	(68,054)	(75,774)
Gross Margin	$18,654	$23,456	$29,490	$30,480	$34,726
Selling and Administrative Expenses	(20,149)	(23,566)	(29,262)	(34,161)	(36,184)
Finance Income	6,026	7,007	8,498	10,045	11,109
Credit Insurance Income	1,060	1,312	1,698	2,022	2,210
Interest Expense	(1,871)	(2,269)	(2,492)	(2,366)	(2,707)
Income Before Income Taxes	$ 3,720	$ 5,940	$ 7,932	$ 6,020	$ 9,154
Income Tax Expense	(1,914)	(2,822)	(3,184)	(2,796)	(4,119)
Net Income	$ 1,806	$ 3,118	$ 4,748	$ 3,224	$ 5,035

---

*The authors acknowledge the assistance of Gary M. Cypres in the preparation of this case.

José Rodriguez is interested in selling his ownership in RHC, and has approached his bank to assist in finding a buyer. The bank approached you as a partner in Southern California Investment Partners to see if your investment group might have an interest. The bank provides you with the financial statements and notes for the most recent five fiscal years (Exhibits 11.7, 11.8, and 11.9). The bank indicates its willingness to maintain the working capital loan facility with the company on essentially the same terms as now.

EXHIBIT 11.8

Rodriguez Home Center, Inc.
Comparative Balance Sheets
(amounts in thousands)
(Case 11.2)

	January 31					
	Year 10	Year 11	Year 12	Year 13	Year 14	Year 15
Assets						
Cash	$ 243	$ 436	$ 786	$ 500	$ 802	$ 1,152
Accounts Receivable:						
Gross	30,216	34,976	46,330	59,512	71,360	83,896
Deferred Interest	(2,288)	(2,648)	(4,904)	(5,520)	(7,174)	(9,224)
Allowance for Uncollectible						
Accounts	(578)	(670)	(1,116)	(1,600)	(2,000)	(2,400)
Net	$27,350	$31,658	$40,310	$52,392	$62,186	$72,272
Merchandise Inventories	7,562	10,250	11,294	16,612	16,392	15,646
Prepayments	36	56	106	2,362	3,618	3,004
Total Current Assets	$35,191	$42,400	$52,496	$71,866	$82,998	$92,074
Fixtures and Equipment (net)	3,038	2,906	2,454	2,338	3,116	2,870
Deposits	38	68	192	192	176	178
Total Assets	$38,267	$45,374	$55,142	$74,396	$86,290	$95,122
Liabilities and Shareholders' Equity						
Notes Payable to Bank	$16,410	$18,995	$24,186	$31,435	$37,312	$43,363
Current Portion of Long-Term Debt ..	—	—	—	—	218	268
Accounts and Notes Payable—Trade ..	9,869	11,646	11,154	13,514	16,764	14,305
Other Current Liabilities	2,486	3,425	5,376	10,273	8,794	9,165
Total Current Liabilities	$28,765	$34,066	$40,716	$55,222	$63,088	$67,101
Long-Term Debt	—	—	—	—	804	588
Total Liabilities	$28,765	$34,066	$40,716	$55,222	$63,892	$67,689
Common Stock	$ 36	$ 36	$ 36	$ 36	$ 36	$ 36
Retained Earnings	9,466	11,272	14,390	19,138	22,362	27,397
Total Stockholders' Equity	$ 9,502	$11,308	$14,426	$19,174	$22,398	$27,433
Total Liabilities and						
Stockholders' Equity	$38,267	$45,374	$55,142	$74,396	$86,290	$95,122

EXHIBIT 11.9

Rodriguez Home Center, Inc.
Comparative Statement of Cash Flows
(amounts in thousands)
(Case 11.2)

	For the Year Ended Janaury 31				
	Year 11	Year 12	Year 13	Year 14	Year 15
Operations					
Net Income	$ 1,806	$3,118	$ 4,748	$ 3,224	$ 5,035
Depreciation	512	558	608	730	714
(Increase) Decrease in Receivables	(4,308)	(8,652)	(12,082)	(9,794)	(10,086)
(Increase) Decrease in Inventories	(2,688)	(1,044)	(5,318)	220	746
(Increase) Decrease in Prepayments	(20)	(50)	(2,256)	(1,256)	614
Increase (Decrease) in Accounts Payable ...	1,777	(492)	2,360	3,250	(2,459)
Increase (Decrease) in Other					
Current Liabilities	939	1,951	4,897	(1,479)	371
Cash Flow from Operations	$(1,982)	$(4,611)	$ (7,043)	$(5,105)	$ (5,065)
Investing					
Acquisition of Fixtures and Equipment	(380)	(106)	(492)	(1,508)	(468)
Other Investing Transactions	(30)	(124)	—	16	(2)
Cash Flow from Investing	$ (410)	$ (230)	$ (492)	$(1,492)	$ (470)
Financing					
Increase (Decrease) in Short-Term Debt	$ 2,585	$5,191	$ 7,249	$ 5,877	$ 6,051
Increase (Decrease) in Long-Term Debt	—	—	—	1,022	(166)
Cash Flow from Financing	$ 2,585	$5,191	$ 7,249	$ 6,899	$ 5,885
Net Change in Cash	$ 193	$ 350	$ (286)	$ 2	$ 350

Required

You are asked to ascertain a reasonable purchase price for the equity ownership of José Rodriguez as of January 31, Year 15. You should derive this valuation following three separate approaches:

a. Present value of future cash flows of RHC.

b. Multiples of earnings, using both theoretical models and multiples of comparable companies.

c. Multiples of book values of shareholders' equity, using both theoretical models and multiples for comparable companies.

The most comparable publicly traded companies in terms of product line are Second Family Group, Inc. (traded over-the-counter) and Best Choice Co., Inc. (traded on the New York Stock Exchange). Neither of these two companies offers in-store credit like Rodriguez. Daytona Houston and C.J. Nickel offer in-store credit but also a much broader product line than Rodriguez. Exhibit 11.10 presents selected data for these four companies.

EXHIBIT 11.10

Selected Data for Certain Retailers
For Year 15 Fiscal Year
(Case 11.2)

	Second Family Group	Best Choice Company	Daytona Houston	C.J. Nickel
Sales (000s)	$78,222	$512,850	$14,739,000	$16,736,000
Assets (000s)	$32,779	$156,787	$ 8,524,000	$12,325,000
Net Income (000s)	$ 1,252	$ 5,683	$ 410,000	$ 577,000
Profit Margin for ROA	2.1%	1.6%	4.2%	4.6%
Assets Turnover	2.5	3.5	1.9	1.3
Rate of Return on Assets	5.1%	5.5%	8.2%	6.2%
Common Earnings Leverage	68.4%	70.1%	65.7%	74.4%
Capital Structure Leverage	2.5	2.3	5.0	3.4
Rate of Return on Common Shareholders' Equity	8.7%	9.0%	26.7%	15.7%
Cost of Goods Sold/Sales	72.5%	76.5%	72.3%	65.5%
Selling and Administrative Expense/Sales	24.7%	20.9%	18.6%	31.7%
Accounts Receivable Turnover ...	107.2	74.3	11.6	4.9
Inventory Turnover	4.3	4.0	5.5	4.2
Accounts Payable Turnover	4.8	6.2	8.9	6.4
Current Ratio	1.2:1	1.6:1	1.5:1	2.6:1
Total Liabilities/Total Assets	58.6%	57.8%	75.7%	64.4%
Long-Term Debt/Total Assets	22.9%	22.4%	43.2%	25.4%
Interest Leverage Ratio	2.6	3.6	3.0	3.8
Five-Year Growth Rate:				
Sales	10.4%	24.9%	12.3%	2.3%
Net Income	8.7%	15.7%	7.3%	4.8%
Market Value/Earnings	14.2	16.8	11.8	10.3
Market Value/ Book Value of Equity	1.31	1.44	2.86	1.61
Market Beta	1.18	1.15	1.30	1.22

NOTES TO FINANCIAL STATEMENTS

1. SUMMARY OF SIGNIFICANT ACCOUNTING POLICIES

Revenue Recognition The company recognizes revenue from the sale of merchandise at the time of sale. It typically provides customers with financing for their purchases. The company adds interest at rates varying between 11 percent and 21 percent to the face amount of the receivable (gross amount) at the time of sale, and recognizes this amount as revenue over the term of the installment contract using the interest method. The installment contracts provide for monthly payments and mature at dates from 1 to 24 months after the time of the sale. The company's balance sheet uses 24 months as the operating cycle in accordance with the terms of the installment contracts.

Merchandise Inventories   The company states its inventories at lower of cost (first-in, first-out) or market.

Store Fixtures and Equipment   Store fixtures and equipment appear at acquisition cost. The company computes depreciation and amortization using the straight-line method over the estimated lives of assets as follows:

Automobiles and Trucks	3–5 years
Furniture and Equipment	5–7 years
Leasehold Improvements	Life of lease

Income Taxes   The company provides deferred taxes for timing differences between book and taxable income.

2. Accounts Receivable

An aging of the accounts receivable on January 31, Year 15, reveals the following (dollar amounts in thousands):

Days Past Due	Number of Accounts	Gross Amount Outstanding
31–60 Days	2,996	$2,061
61–90 Days	1,594	1,025
91–120 Days	840	549
121–150 Days	414	304
More than 150 Days	638	393
	6,482	$4,332

The allowance for uncollectible accounts has changed as follows (amounts in thousands):

	Fiscal Year Ending January 31				
	Year 11	Year 12	Year 13	Year 14	Year 15
Balance, Beginning of Fiscal Year	$ 578	$ 670	$1,116	$1,600	$2,000
Plus Bad Debt Expense	1,682	2,160	2,764	3,416	3,868
Minus Accounts Written Off . .	(1,590)	(1,714)	(2,280)	(3,016)	(3,468)
Balance, End of Fiscal Year . . .	$ 670	$1,116	$1,600	$2,000	$2,400

3. INVENTORIES

The book value of inventories exceeded their market value by $800,000 on January 31, Year 15, and the company recorded a writedown to reflect a lower of cost or market valuation. The company took its first complete physical inventory on January 31, Year 14, and discovered that the book inventory exceeded the physical inventory by $2.6 million. The company wrote down the book inventory to reflect this overstatement, but did not restate inventory and cost of goods sold amounts for prior fiscal years.

4. STORE FIXTURES AND EQUIPMENT

Store fixtures and equipment consist of the following (amounts in thousands):

	January 31				
	Year 11	Year 12	Year 13	Year 14	Year 15
Automobiles and Trucks	$ 486	$ 544	$ 609	$ 683	$ 765
Furniture and Equipment	2,809	2,320	2,457	3,021	2,622
Leasehold Improvements	1,210	1,546	1,604	2,099	1,886
Software Development Costs ..	210	360	440	507	698
Gross	$4,715	$4,770	$5,110	$6,310	$5,971
Less Accumulated Depreciation :...........	(1,809)	(2,316)	(2,772)	(3,194)	(3,101)
Net	$2,906	$2,454	$2,338	$3,116	$2,870

Software development costs are capitalized and amortized in accordance with a reporting standard of the Financial Accounting Standards Board.

5. NOTES PAYABLE TO BANK

The company has a revolving line of credit agreement with a bank that provides for borrowings not to exceed the lower of $60 million or 65 percent of eligible receivables. The amounts outstanding on this line bear interest at 0.5 percent over the bank's prime rate. Accounts receivable and inventories not otherwise secured by the company's trade notes (Note 6) collateralize this line of credit. The bank may withdraw the line of credit facility at any time, with any unpaid notes then repayable over a maximum period of 12 months. The line of credit agreement includes restrictive covenants with regard to the maintenance of financial ratios.

At January 31, Year 15, the company's borrowings under the line of credit facility total $43,363,000. These borrowings bear interest at rates ranging from 6.46 percent to 7.01 percent, and have maturities from February 13, Year 15, to July 22, Year 15. The amount of unused credit under this line was $2,446,000 on January 31, Year 15.

6. TRADE NOTES PAYABLE

Trade notes payable finance inventory purchases made through a flooring arrangement with a finance company. The repayment terms typically require payment within 30 days. The flooring company has a first-priority security interest in certain inventories. The supplier of the merchandise pays all finance charges.

7. LONG-TERM DEBT

Long-term debt consists of the following (amounts in thousands):

	January 31	
	Year 14	Year 15
Various equipment notes at interest rates ranging from 8.75% to 9.25%, secured by assets, maturing from Year 15 to Year 18	$ 808	$687
Obligations under capital leases	214	168
Total	$1,022	$855
Less Current Portion	218	267
	$ 804	$588

Maturities of the equipment notes and obligations under capital leases at January 31, Year 15, are as follows (amounts in thousands):

Fiscal Year	Equipment Notes	Capital Leases
Year 16	$217	$ 67
Year 17	162	67
Year 18	176	66
Year 19	132	—
	$687	$ 200
Less Amount Representing Interest . . .	—	31
	$687	$ 169

8. INCOME TAXES

The provision for income taxes consists of the following (amounts in thousands):

	For the Year Ended January 31				
	Year 11	Year 12	Year 13	Year 14	Year 15
Current Taxes					
Federal	$ 599	$1,144	$1,222	$2,286	$1,581
State	186	372	595	798	590
Deferred Taxes					
Federal	$ 868	$ 966	$1,010	$ (213)	$1,440
State	261	340	357	(75)	508
Total Provision	$1,914	$2,822	$3,184	$2,796	$4,119

Deferred taxes arise from timing differences related to revenue recognition and depreciation.

9. COMMITMENTS

The company leases its warehouse and certain computer equipment under five-year non-cancelable operating leases expiring in fiscal Year 18. The warehouse lease provides for a minimum 4 percent rent escalation per year from fiscal Year 15 onward, and has two five-year options to extend. The company also leases its retail showroom under a noncancelable lease expiring in fiscal Year 20. The lease provides for cost-of-living rent escalation plus payment of certain executory costs, excluding property taxes, and has two five-year options to extend.

Aggregate minimum lease payments are as follows (amounts in thousands):

Fiscal Year	Total
Year 16	$ 2,995
Year 17	3,037
Year 18	2,344
Year 19	1,526
Year 20	1,526
Thereafter	1,272
	$12,700

Rent expense for fiscal years Year 14 and Year 15 was $2,389,566 and $2,424,826, respectively.

CHAPTER 12

VALUATION: EARNINGS-BASED APPROACHES

1. Study the theoretical model that relates market prices to earnings (P-E ratio).
2. Study the theoretical model that relates market prices to the book value of common shareholders' equity (P-BV ratio).
3. Apply the theoretical models of the P-E ratio and the P-BV ratio to data of actual companies.
4. Understand the role of the variables, or factors, that explain why actual P-E and P-BV ratios may deviate from those suggested by the theoretical models: (a) cost of equity capital; (b) growth rates; (c) differences between current and expected future earnings; and (d) alternative accounting principles.
5. Gain an appreciation of the relevance of academic research to the work of the practicing financial analyst.

This chapter extends the discussion in the previous chapter by considering the relation between value (in the form of market prices) and certain constructs of the accrual basis of accounting. Specifically:

1. What is the relationship between the market price of a firm's common stock and its earnings for the current period; that is, what is the valuation significance of the *price-earnings ratio*?
2. What is the relationship between the market price of a firm's common stock and the book value of its common shareholders' equity; that is, what is the valuation significance of the *price to book value ratio*?

This chapter explores these relationships at a theoretical level, and summarizes recent research examining the relationships at an empirical level. It also illustrates the use of the P-E and the P-BV ratio in the valuation of firms.

PRICE-EARNINGS (P-E) RATIOS

Analysts' reports and the financial press make frequent references to P-E ratios. Statements such as the following appear frequently:

- General Motors is selling for 15 times earnings.
- A P-E ratio of 18 for Apple Computer is much too high. It should be selling for no more than 12 to 14 times earnings.
- Biotechnology firms are growing rapidly, and should sell for 20 to 25 times earnings.

These statements suggest that there is a "correct" level for the P-E ratio of each firm, or that there is a well-accepted underlying model that determines appropriate levels of P-E ratios. We start the discussion of P-E ratios by exploring the theoretical relation between market prices and earnings. We then demonstrate the difficulties often encountered in reconciling actual P-E ratios with those indicated by the theoretical model.

DEVELOPMENT OF THEORETICAL MODEL

An understanding of the theoretical model requires a step-by-step development.

Cash Flows to the Investor. The theoretical relation between market prices and earnings is based on the classic dividend capitalization model.[1] The market price of an equity security equals the present value of the expected dividend stream discounted at a risk-adjusted discount rate (r). Thus:[2]

$$P_0 = \sum_{t=1}^{n} \frac{\text{Expected Dividend}_t}{(1 + r)^t}$$

One of these dividends is the expected liquidating dividend upon dissolution of the firm. Thus:

$$P_0 = \sum_{t=1}^{n-1} \frac{\text{Expected Dividend}_t}{(1 + r)^t} + \frac{\text{Expected Liquidating Dividend}_n}{(1 + r)^n}$$

---

[1]John Burr Williams, *The Theory of Investment and Value*, Cambridge: Harvard University Press, 1938.

[2]Throughout this chapter, t refers to an accounting period. The period t = 1 refers to the first accounting period after the valuation. The valuation is at the beginning of this first accounting period (for example, January 1), denoted at P_0. Period n is the period of the final projected, or liquidating, dividend.

A liquidating dividend occurs because a firm generates cash flows each period that it does not fully distribute to shareholders as a dividend. These retained cash flows plus returns generated on the retained cash flows constitute the liquidating dividend. As long as a firm generates a return on the retained cash flows equal to the discount rate, or the cost of equity capital, the firm's dividend policy has no effect on the market price of the common stock. This is the Miller and Modigliani dividend irrelevance proposition.[3]

Cash Flows to the Firm.   The source of the cash flows for dividends is the cash flows generated by the firm. Cash flows received by the firm represent the generation of economic value; dividends represent merely the periodic distribution of this economic value to shareholders. Thus:

$$P_0 = \sum_{t=1}^{n} \frac{\text{Expected Cash Flows}_t}{(1 + r)^t}$$

When a firm's expected leveraged free cash flows are projected to remain constant into perpetuity (a non-growth scenario), then the preceding expression for market price simplifies to:[4]

$$P_0 = \frac{\text{Expected Cash Flow}_{t=1}}{r}$$

When leveraged free cash flows are projected to grow at a constant rate equal to g, then

$$P_0 = \text{Expected Cash Flow}_{t=1} \times \frac{1}{r - g}$$

Expected Earnings.   The next step in the theoretical formulation of the P-E ratio substitutes a firm's expected earnings for its expected leveraged free cash flows in the formulation of market price above. This substitution of earnings for cash flows rests on three foundations:

---

[3]Merton H. Miller and Franco Modigliani, "Dividend Policy, Growth, and Valuation of Shares," *Journal of Business* (1961), pp. 411–432. Firms do, however, often generate returns that differ from the cost of equity capital, at least for a period of time. The excess or deficient returns may result from one-time (temporary) events or relate to longer-term earnings advantages or disadvantages. Later sections of this chapter discuss the valuation significance of these temporary and permanent dimensions of returns.

[4]Chapter 11 defines leveraged free cash flows as cash flows available to common shareholders. Operationally, leveraged free cash flows equal cash flow from operations plus or minus cash flow for investing plus or minus changes in borrowing.

1. Over sufficiently long time periods, net income equals leveraged free cash flows. The effect of year-end accruals to convert cash flows to net income lessens as the measurement period lengthens.[5]

2. For a no-growth firm, net income equals leveraged free cash flows. That is, net income before depreciation equals cash flow from operations (including a cash outflow for interest expense on debt); depreciation expense equals capital expenditures; and debt issuances equal debt redemptions. For a firm experiencing a constant rate of growth, net income is a constant multiple of leveraged free cash flows.

3. Accrual-based earnings reflect changes in economic values more accurately than do free cash flows. One objective of generally accepted accounting principles (GAAP) is to reflect the economic consequences of transactions and events without regard to the timing of their related cash flows. Thus, firms recognize revenues when they have provided substantially all of the required goods or services and have received cash or a right to receive cash in the future. The delivery of the goods or the rendering of services is viewed as the critical wealth-generating event, not the receipt of cash. Likewise, firms recognize expenses when they consume goods and services in operations, not when they expend cash. Another objective of GAAP is to measure the economic effects of transactions and events in as objective a manner as possible. Standards setters sometimes must trade off economic relevance and objectivity; an example is in reporting most assets at acquisition cost (instead of market values). Thus, accrual-based amounts might represent biased measures of economic values. The empirical issue is whether these biases are sufficiently similar across firms that the capital market can incorporate them into valuations (for example, the immediate expensing of research and development costs by technology-intensive firms or the use of acquisition cost valuations for fixed assets by capital-intensive firms).

If one accepts the substitution of expected earnings for expected cash flows based on any, or all, of the above foundations, then market price equals:

$$P_0 = \sum_{t=1}^{n} \frac{\text{Expected Earnings}_t}{(1 + r)^t}$$

It is not intuitively obvious that one can "discount" earnings in the same sense that one discounts cash flows to a present value.[6] The discount rate must be re-expressed in terms of a capitalization rate (discussed on the following page).

---

[5]The correlation between earnings and stock prices across firms increases as the earnings measurement interval increases. The values of R^2 for various intervals are: one year, 5 percent; two years, 15 percent; five years, 33 percent; and 10 years, 63 percent. See Peter D. Easton, Trevor S. Harris, and James A. Ohlson, "Aggregate Accounting Earnings Can Explain Most of Security Returns," *Journal of Accounting and Economics* (July/September, 1992), pp. 119–142.

[6]If one accepts the argument above that accrual earnings reflect the wealth-generating effects of operations more accurately than cash flows, and the firm could borrow based on that wealth creation, then discounting in the traditional sense is intuitively appealing.

When a firm's earnings are expected to remain constant into perpetuity, then:[7]

$$P_0 = \frac{\text{Expected Earnings}_{t=1}}{r}$$

The constancy of earnings presumes an equilibrium state in which a firm generates a *permanent* level of earnings. When a firm's earnings are projected to grow at a constant rate, g, the expression for market price is

$$P_0 = \text{Expected Earnings}_{t=1} \times \frac{1}{r - g}$$

Actual Earnings. The final link in the chain relating market prices to earnings substitutes actual earnings of the most recent period for expected permanent earnings. For the no-growth state:[8]

$$P_0 = \frac{\text{Actual Earnings}_{t-1}}{r}$$

For the steady-growth rate case:

$$P_0 = \text{Actual Earnings}_{t-1} \times \frac{1 + g}{r - g}$$

Two possible justifications for using actual earnings in period $t - 1$ as a surrogate for expected earnings in period t are (1) that actual earnings represent the permanent earnings level for the firm, or (2) that earnings follow a random walk, so the actual earnings of the current period are the best predictor of future earnings.

---

[7]An alternative formulation of P_0 expresses expected earnings in terms of certainty equivalents, using the probabilities of various outcomes, and then uses the risk-free rate to capitalize these earnings. The P-E ratio in this alternative setting reflects only the time value of delayed returns and not risk. We do not use this alternative formulation in this chapter.

[8]The formula relating market price at time zero to actual earnings of the most recent period (that is, period $t-1$) assumes that the firm retains all of the earnings, reinvesting the assets generated by those earnings in various projects. Theoretical precision requires that we adjust the formula relating market price to earnings for any dividends paid during the most recent period, since the payment of dividends should reduce the market price of the stock. Thus, the market price at time zero is:

$$P_0 = \frac{\text{Actual Earnings}_{t-1}}{r} - \text{Dividends}_{t-1}$$

Most P-E ratios reported in the financial press ignore this dividends adjustment. Precision would further dictate the restatement of dividends paid during the most recent period (most firms pay dividends quarterly) to their year-end equivalent amount, assuming reinvestment of intraperiod dividends by shareholders. See Stephen H. Penman, "Return to Fundamentals," *Journal of Accounting, Auditing & Finance* (Fall 1992), pp. 465–483.

The diagram below depicts the chain relating market prices to dividends, cash flows, and earnings as we have discussed:

Market Price = Present Value of Future Dividends to Shareholders

$$\downarrow$$

= Present Value of Future Leveraged Free Cash Flows of the Firm

$$\downarrow$$

= Capitalized Value of Future Earnings of the Firm

$$\downarrow$$

= Capitalized Value of Current Earnings of the Firm

Synthesis of the Theoretical Model. We can now express the formulations for market price in terms of the price-earnings (P-E) ratio.

No-Growth Firm. For the no-growth firm:

$$\frac{P_0}{\text{Actual Earnings}_{t-1}} = \frac{1}{r}$$

where $1/r$ is the P-E ratio.

To illustrate this theoretical model with a simple example, suppose that a firm generates earnings during the current period of $700 and has a cost of equity capital of 14 percent. If the firm is expected to generate earnings of $700 next period, the total market value of the firm at the beginning of the next period should be $5,000 (= $700/0.14). Note that a discount rate of 14 percent translates into a P-E ratio of 7.14 (= 1/0.14). Thus, $700 times 7.14 equals $5,000. The P-E ratio is the multiple for capitalizing future earnings, a process analogous to discounting expected cash flows to their present value.[9] The P-E ratio in this formulation reflects the required rate of return by common equity investors.

Given the relationship between expected return and risk, the P-E ratio should reflect in part differences in risk. Higher risk levels should translate into lower P-E ratios, and vice versa. That is, investors will not pay as much for a higher-risk security as for a lower-risk security with identical expected earnings.

Consider the data in Exhibit 12.1 for three segments of the financial services industry. The exhibit shows the mean of the annual industry medians for market beta and the P-E ratio for the years 1992 through 1996.

Commercial banks were highly regulated during this period, with the federal government providing insurance against bankruptcy losses on deposits up to certain levels. Commercial banks display the lowest market beta of the three industry segments. Insurance companies were also regulated but not to the extent of

---

[9]The present value of an annuity of $1 approaches $1/r$ as the number of periods increases. For example, the present value after 40 periods at 14 percent is 7.11; after 50 periods it is 7.13.

EXHIBIT 12.1

Mean of the Industry Median Market Beta and Price-Earnings Ratio for Three Segments of the Financial Services Industry—1992 to 1996

Industry Segment	Market Beta	Price-Earnings Ratio
Commercial Banks	.70	11.76
Insurance Companies	.84	10.86
Securities	1.20	9.32

---

commercial banks; they show a somewhat higher market beta. The securities industry segment (investment banks and securities brokerage firms) is subject to cyclical swings in the economy as investors' interest in purchasing and selling securities changes; it has the highest market beta.

The P-E ratios are in the reverse order of the market betas. The commercial banks, which have the lowest risk, have the highest P-E ratio. The insurance companies fall in the middle, and the securities firms have the lowest P-E ratio. Differences in growth rates may also explain differences in these P-E ratios.

Constant-Growth Firm. The P-E ratio for the constant-growth setting is

$$\frac{P_0}{\text{Actual Earnings}_{t-1}} = \frac{1+g}{r-g}$$

In addition to risk, the P-E ratio reflects the value of earnings growth. The growth occurs because additional investments generate future earnings. To continue the simple example from above, assume that the earnings of this firm are expected to grow 5 percent each year. The theoretical model suggests a P-E ratio of 11.67 [= 1.05/(0.14 − 0.05)] and a market value of $8,167 (= $700 × 11.67). The present value of the growth in earnings adds $3,167 (= $8,167 − $5,000) to the value of the firm.

The theoretical P-E model is particularly sensitive to the growth rate. If the growth rate is 6 percent instead of 5 percent, the P-E ratio is 13.25 [= 1.06/(0.14 − 0.06], and the market value is $9,275 (= $700 × 13.25). The sensitivity occurs because the model assumes that the firm will grow at the specified growth rate forever. Competition, new discoveries or technologies, or other factors eventually erode rapid growth rates in an industry. The objective in using a constant-growth version of the P-E ratio is to select a long-run equilibrium growth rate in earnings.

THEORETICAL VERSUS ACTUAL P-E RATIOS

The theoretical models indicate that the P-E ratio is related to r, the cost of equity capital, and g, the growth rate in future earnings. Several empirical studies have examined the relation between P-E ratios and risk and growth. Most studies use market beta as the measure of risk, according to the notion that the market prices only systematic risk. Growth is measured using realized growth rates of prior periods or analysts' forecasts of future growth. These studies have found that approximately 50 percent to 70 percent of the variability in P-E ratios relates to risk and growth.[10]

Actual P-E ratios of firms are often different from the amounts suggested by the theoretical model. Before making a buy recommendation on firms with actual P-E ratios that are lower than the theoretical model suggests and sell recommendations on firms with actual P-E ratios that exceed those suggested by the theoretical model, the analyst should consider possible reasons for the differences. Besides possible errors in measuring the cost of equity capital and the growth rate, the analyst should consider several earnings-related issues.

Earnings Persistence. Actual P-E ratios will deviate from those suggested by the theoretical models if actual earnings of the current period are a poor predictor of expected future (permanent) earnings. If the current period's earnings are lower than the expected permanent level of earnings (perhaps because the current period's earnings include an unusual or nonrecurring loss), then the P-E ratio will be higher than normal.[11]

Continuing the simple example discussed earlier, assume that the firm generated earnings for the current period of $650 instead of $700 because the firm recognized a $50 restructuring change. If the market views this charge as nonrecurring (that is, not a permanent change in earnings), the market price should remain approximately the same at $5,000 in the no-growth scenario, and the P-E ratio for the period will be 7.69 (= $5,000/$650), instead of the theoretical value of 7.14. If the current period's earnings exceed their expected permanent level, then the P-E ratio will be lower than normal.

The task for the analyst is to assess whether the lower or the higher level of earnings for the current period (and therefore higher or lower P-E ratio) represents a transitory phenomenon or instead a change to a new lower or new higher level of permanent earnings. Transitory changes in earnings should result in a change in the actual P-E ratio, but a reversion to its theoretical level once earnings no longer include the transitory component. A change in earnings that the market views as a permanent change should result in little or no change in the P-E ratio.

For example, if the decrease in earnings from $700 to $650 results from increased competition that the market considers to be permanent, then the market price (assuming no change in risk or growth) should decrease to $4,643 (= $650/0.14). Thus, the P-E ratio remains the same at 7.14 (= 1/0.14).

Penman studied the relationship between P-E ratios and changes in earnings per share for all firms on the Compustat data base for the years 1968 through

---

[10]William Beaver and Dale Morse, "What Determines Price-Earnings Ratios?" *Financial Analysts Journal* (July–August 1978), pp. 65–76; and Paul Zarowin, "What Determines Earnings-Price Ratios: Revisited," *Journal of Accounting, Auditing and Finance* (Summer 1990), pp. 439–454.

[11]"Normal" means 1/r in the no-growth setting and (1 + g)/(r − g) in the growth setting.

EXHIBIT 12.2

Median Percentage Changes in Earnings Per Share for Portfolios Formed on Observed P-E Ratios for Formation Year and Subsequent Years

P-E Portfolio	Median Percentage Change in Earnings Per Share				
	Formation Year 0	Year 1	Year 2	Year 3	Year 4
4 (High)	.039	.522	.175	.178	.150
10 (Medium)	.140	.118	.116	.137	.158
18 (Low)	.184	.048	.102	.123	.131

1985.[12] For each year Penman grouped firms into 20 portfolios on the basis of the level of their P-E ratios. He then computed the percentage change in earnings per share for the formation year and for each of the nine subsequent years, and aggregated the results across years. Exhibit 12.2 presents a subset of the results.

The results for the formation year are consistent with transitory components in earnings. Firms with high P-E ratios experienced low percentage changes in earnings during the formation year relative to the preceding year. Firms with low P-E ratios experienced high percentage changes in earnings during the formation year.

The results for Year 1 after the formation year suggest a counterbalancing effect of the earnings change in the formation year (a low percentage earnings change followed by a high percentage earnings change, and vice versa, for portfolios 4 and 18, respectively).

The results for subsequent years reflect the tendency toward mean reversion in percentage earnings changes to a level in the mid-teens. This result is consistent with the data presented for ROCE in Chapter 8, where Penman observed a mean reversion in ROCE toward the mid-teens. The mean reversion suggests systematic directional changes in earnings growth over time (that is, serial autocorrelation), but the reversion takes several years to occur.

McGee and Stickney study the mean reversion characteristics of P-E ratios for the period 1976 to 1995, and find that mean reversion generally takes five to seven years.[13] Thus, firms on average do not experience just a single year of transitory earnings change. Their earnings tend to include transitory elements for several additional years before settling back to an equilibrium.

Thus, P-E ratios based on reported earnings incorporate the effects of both transitory earnings components and longer-term shifts in permanent earnings. The *ex post* observance of a market price change, or absence of such a change, will signal the transitory or permanent nature of the earnings change. The analyst, who

---

[12]Stephen H. Penman, "The Articulation of Price-Earnings Ratios and Market-to-Book Ratios and the Evaluation of Growth," *Journal of Accounting Research* (Autumn 1996), pp. 235–259.

[13]Victor E. McGee and Clyde P. Stickney, "Mean Reversion in Accounting/Market-Based Financial Ratios," Dartmouth College, 1998.

must make buy, hold, or sell recommendations on particular equity securities, wants to anticipate this change in market prices before it occurs. The observation of a low or a high P-E ratio for the current period by itself is not a sufficient basis on which to differentiate transitory and permanent earnings changes.

Impact of Accounting Principles.   One additional factor that might explain the divergence between actual and theoretical P-E ratios, particularly when comparing companies, is the effect of alternative accounting principles. Industries subject to particularly conservative accounting principles, such as technology-oriented industries that must expense research and development costs in the year the costs are incurred, will report lower earnings and higher P-E ratios than industries that can capitalize and amortize critical cost inputs, as is true for the cost of depreciable assets in the case of capital-intensive firms. Firms that select conservative accounting principles (such as LIFO for inventories during periods of rising prices, and accelerated depreciation of fixed assets) will have lower earnings and higher P-E ratios than firms that select less conservative accounting principles.

APPLICATION OF THEORETICAL P-E MODEL

Let us now apply the theoretical P-E model (growth version) to Coke. Consider the data as follows:

	Coke
Market Price Per Share (December 31, Year 7)	$52.63
Earnings Per Share (Year 7)	$ 1.40
Market Beta	0.97
Cost of Equity Capital	12.8%[*]
Five-Year Compound Annual Growth Rate in Earnings	16.7%
Risk-Free Interest Rate	6.0%
Market Risk Premium	7.0%

[*]12.8% = 6.0% + 0.97(7%)

The historical growth rate in earnings for Coke of 16.7 percent exceeds the cost of equity capital. The theoretical model of the P-E ratio therefore does not work, because the denominator is negative. The theoretical model assumes that the growth rate in earnings will continue in perpetuity. A firm experiencing a growth in earnings in excess of the cost of equity capital will find that other firms will enter the industry and compete away the excess earning power. Fortunately for Coke, only Pepsi has provided much competition in recent years.

   The actual P-E ratio for Coke at the end of Year 7 is 37.6 (= $52.63/$1.40). To assess the reasonableness of the current market price for Coke, we might solve the theoretical model for either the cost of equity capital or the growth rate implied by a P-E ratio of 37.6. In the first approach, the theoretical model suggests a cost of equity capital of 19.8 percent when the growth rate in earnings is 16.7 percent.

That is, $37.6 = 1.167/(x - 0.167)$; $X = 0.198$. Given the performance of the stock market during the mid-1990s, an expected return, or cost of equity capital, of 19.8 percent does not appear unreasonable in the short term. Historical data suggest that long-term returns on equity capital have averaged around 13 percent, so it is unlikely that either Coke or the overall market can sustain returns around 20 percent for any length of time.

In the second approach, we can solve the theoretical model for the growth rate in earnings implied by a P-E ratio of 37.6 and a cost of equity capital of 12.8 percent. The implied growth rate in earnings is 9.9 percent. That is, $37.6 = (1 + g)/(0.128 - g)$; $g = 0.099$ (rounded). This growth rate is considerably lower than the growth rate Coke has experienced in the past, and may reflect the market's assessment that increasingly saturated markets worldwide will inhibit Coke's future growth.

Neither the implied cost of equity capital nor the implied growth rate in a P-E ratio of 37.6 seem unreasonable for Coke in the short term.

SUMMARY OF P-E RATIO

Summarizing, the P-E ratio appears to be related to:

1. Risk.
2. Growth.
3. Differences between current and expected future (permanent) earnings.
4. Alternative accounting principles.

The analyst must assess each of these elements when evaluating reported P-E ratios and using P-E ratios to value nontraded firms. The theoretical model indicates the factors affecting the P-E ratios, but does not provide an unambiguous signal of the "correct" P-E ratio for a particular firm. The analyst should be sensitive to a number of considerations when using P-E ratios:

1. The theoretical P-E ratio is particularly sensitive to the growth rate used, because the model assumes a firm can grow earnings at that rate forever. The analyst should select a sustainable growth rate when applying the theoretical P-E model.
2. The theoretical P-E model does not work when the growth rate in earnings exceeds the cost of equity capital. Firms are unlikely to grow earnings at rates exceeding the cost of equity capital forever. Competition will eventually force growth rates to decrease.
3. The theoretical P-E model does not work well when the cost of equity capital and the growth rate in earnings are similar in amount. The denominator of the theoretical model approaches zero, and the theoretical P-E ratio becomes very large.
4. The analyst can judge the reasonableness of the assumptions about the values of r and g used in computing the theoretical P-E ratio by assuming that the actual P-E ratio is appropriate, and then solving for either the r or the g implied in that actual P-E ratio.

5. Before concluding that the market is undervaluing or overvaluing a firm because the actual P-E ratio differs from the theoretical P-E ratio, the analyst should assess whether earnings of the period include transitory elements. The analyst should cleanse the current period's earnings of unusual, nonrecurring income items before measuring the actual P-E ratio for the period.

6. The analyst comparing actual P-E ratios of firms should consider the impact of firms' use of different accounting principles.

PRICE TO BOOK VALUE (P-BV) RATIOS

The P-E ratio relates a stock measure (a market value at a particular time) to a flow measure (earnings over a period of time). The price to book value ratio relates a stock measure (market value) to a stock measure (book value) of common shareholders' equity. The book value of shareholders' equity reflects capital contributions plus accumulated earnings in excess of dividends.

Here we explore the theoretical and empirical relation between market prices and book values.

DEVELOPMENT OF THEORETICAL MODEL[14]

In the previous section, we developed the relation between market price and expected, or permanent, earnings as follows:

$$P_0 = \sum_{t=1}^{n} \frac{\text{Expected Earnings}_t}{(1 + r)^t}$$

We might expand the numerator as follows:[15]

$$P_0 = \sum_{t=1}^{n} \frac{\text{Expected ROCE}_t \times \text{BV}_t}{(1 + r)^t}$$

---

[14]The ideas underlying the P-BV ratio trace to early work by G. A. D. Preinreich, "Annual Survey of Economic Theory: The Theory of Depreciation," *Econometrica* (1938), pp. 219–241, and E. Edwards and P. W. Bell, *The Theory and Measurement of Business Income* (Berkeley: University of California Press), 1961. Recent valuation practice applying the concepts is found in G. B. Stewart, *The Quest for Value* (New York: Harper Collins), 1991, and in the expanding literature on EVA ®. Credit for the rigorous development of the model goes to Feltham and Ohlson in: J. A. Ohlson, "A Synthesis of Security Valuation Theory and the Role of Dividends, Cash Flows, and Earnings," *Contemporary Accounting Research* (Spring 1990), pp. 648–676; J. A. Ohlson, "Earnings, Book Values, and Dividends in Equity Valuation," *Contemporary Accounting Research* (Spring 1995), pp. 661–687; and G. A. Feltham and J. A. Ohlson, "Valuation and Clean Surplus Accounting for Operating and Financial Activities," *Contemporary Accounting Research* (Spring 1995), pp. 216–230.

[15]Theoretical and empirical research on the P-BV ratio typically defines return on common equity (ROCE) as net income to common shareholders for a period divided by common shareholders' equity at the *beginning* of the period. We, however, use *average* common shareholders' equity in the denominator of ROCE throughout this book. The theoretical development and application of the P-BV model in this section use shareholders' equity at the beginning of the period, although the bias in using average shareholders' equity should not be particularly significant.

where expected ROCE is the expected rate of return on common shareholders' equity for all future periods t, and BV_t is the book value of common shareholders' equity at the beginning of each period t. The numerator in the second equation captures the same as the first equation, expected earnings. In equilibrium, a firm should earn a rate of return on capital (that is, ROCE) equal to the rate of return required by the market for its particular risk level (that is, its cost of equity capital). Thus, in equilibrium, ROCE = r, and P = BV. A P-BV ratio of 1.0 should therefore indicate a firm generating earnings at the cost of equity capital.

We can rewrite the formulation for price as follows:

$$P_0 = BV_0 + \sum_{t=1}^{n} \left[\frac{(\text{Expected ROCE}_t - r)(BV_t)}{(1 + r)^t} \right]$$

This formulation expresses price in terms of a firm's book value of shareholders' equity today (BV_0) and the present (capitalized) value of its expected excess or deficient earning power in the future. When the expected ROCE equals the cost of equity capital (r), there is no excess earning power, and price equals book value.

If the expected ROCE exceeds r (that is, the firm is expected to invest in positive net present value projects for some period of time in the future), then the market price should exceed book value. To illustrate, we can return to the illustration of a firm with a cost of equity capital of 14 percent and expected earning for period t = 1 of $700. Assume that the book value of shareholders' equity today (t_0) is $4,375. The expected ROCE for period t = 1 is 16 percent (= $700/$4,375). Assume that the expected ROCE for period t = 2 is 15 percent and for all remaining periods is 14 percent, the same as the cost of equity capital. The market price of the common stock is $4,490.80, computed as follows:

$$P_0 = \$4,375.00 + \frac{(.16 - .14)(\$4,375)}{(1.14)^1}$$

$$+ \frac{(.15 - .14)(\$4,375 + \$700)}{(1.14)^2}$$

$$\$4,490.80 = \$4,375.00 + \$76.75 + \$39.05$$

The excess of market value over book value represents positive goodwill, the ability to generate higher returns than the market requires, given the firm's risk level. Because accounting does not record this goodwill on the balance sheet under GAAP (except for purchase method corporate acquisitions), the book values of assets and shareholders' equity are lower than their market values. Likewise, a firm experiencing an ROCE less than r should have negative goodwill and a market price lower than book value. If GAAP recognized the positive and negative goodwill, then in theory market price should equal book value. Over time, competition should eliminate the excess earning power of firms with positive goodwill, and improved earnings performance or bankruptcy should eliminate the deficient earnings power of firms with negative goodwill. Thus, P-BV ratios should mean-revert toward 1.0.

Price is also a function of growth in book value. As the book value of shareholders' equity grows through the retention of earnings, the net assets available on which the firm generates the excess returns increase, thereby increasing market price. Note that expected future increases in the book value of shareholders' equity should not add to current market price if the firm earns an ROCE equal to the cost of equity capital (that is, expected growth *per se* should not add value).

We can express the formula for price in terms of the P-BV ratio by dividing all terms by BV_0 as follows:

$$\frac{P_0}{BV_0} = 1 + \left[\sum_{t=1}^{n} \left(\frac{(\text{Expected ROCE}_t - r)(BV_t)}{(1 + r)^t} \right) / BV_0 \right]$$

Continuing the example, the P-BV ratio at t_0 is:

$$\frac{P_0}{BV_0} = 1 + \left[\frac{(\$76.75 + \$39.05)}{\$4,375.00} \right]$$

$$1.0265 = 1 + 0.0265$$

If a firm can generate an excess return over its cost of equity capital for only a limited number of years, then n is the future period when ROCE = r. If a firm can earn an excess return forever, then n becomes infinity, and the equation above for the P-BV ratio becomes:

$$\frac{P_0}{BV_0} = 1 + \frac{\text{Expected ROCE}_{t=1} - r}{r - g}$$

Summarizing, the P-BV ratio is a function of (1) the expected level of profitability relative to the required rate of return, and (2) growth in the book value of common shareholders' equity. This growth in book value is a function of the earnings generated each period in excess of dividends paid plus additional capital contributions by shareholders.

Several empirical studies have found that ROCE of the current period is a reliable predictor of expected future ROCE (implying either that ROCE follows a random walk or that it mean-reverts slowly).[16] McGee and Stickney find that differences in P-BV ratio in any particular period mean-revert slowly, with as much as 30 percent of the difference remaining ten years after the initial year.[17]

---

[16]Jane A. Ou and Stephen H. Penman, "Financial Statement Analysis and the Evaluation of Market-to-Book Ratios," University of California-Berkeley, 1993; Victor L. Bernard, "Accounting-Based Valuation Methods, Determinants of Market-to-Book Ratios and Implications for Financial Statement Analysis," University of Michigan, 1993; William H. Beaver and Stephen G. Ryan, "Differences in the Ability of the Book-to-Market Ratio to Predict Security Return and Book Return on Equity," Stanford University, 1994.

[17]McGee and Stickney, *op. cit.*

Application of Theoretical Model

Consider these data for Coke:

	Coke
Market Value of Shareholders' Equity on December 31, Year 7 (in millions)	$130,575
Book Value of Shareholders' Equity on December 31, Year 7 (in millions)	$ 6,156
Cost of Equity Capital	12.8%
ROCE for Year 7	60.5%
Dividends as a Percentage of Net Income	35.7%

Assume that Coke is expected to generate an ROCE of 60.5 percent for five years, and then the ROCE reverts to 12.8 percent. The assumption of immediate reversion of ROCE to the cost of equity capital after five years is unrealistic, but it simplifies the illustration. The P-BV ratio of 4.437 is as follows:

$$
\frac{P}{BV} = 1 + \left[\left(\frac{(.605 - .128)(\$6,156)}{(1.128)^1} + \frac{(.605 - .128)(\$8,551)}{(1.128)^2} \right. \right.
$$
$$
+ \frac{(.605 - .128)(\$11,877)}{(1.128)^3} + \frac{(.605 - .128)(\$16,498)}{(1.128)^4}
$$
$$
\left. \left. + \frac{(.605 - .128)(\$25,042)}{(1.128)^5} \right) \middle/ \$6,156 \right]
$$

$$4.437 = 1 + [(\$2,603 + \$3,206 + \$3,947 + \$4,861 + \$5,989)/\$6,156]$$

Shareholders' equity grows each year by the amount of earnings and decreases by the amount of dividends. For example, the calculation of shareholders' equity at the end of Year 8 is as follows:

Shareholders' Equity, December 31, Year 7	$ 6,156
Net Income for Year 8: 0.605 × $6,156	3,724
Less Dividends: 0.357 × $3,724	(1,329)
Shareholders' Equity, December 31, Year 8	$ 8,551

The actual P-BV ratio for Coke is 21.2 (= $130,575/$6,156). Differences between actual and theoretical levels of P-BV ratios may relate to (1) errors in estimating the level or sustainability of ROCE; (2) errors in measuring the cost of equity capital; (3) errors in measuring the growth in common shareholders' equity; (4) using an actual ROCE that includes transitory earnings (that is, it does not reflect the expected permanent level of ROCE); or (5) using an actual ROCE that incorporates biases caused by alternative accounting principles.[18]

One might argue that alternative accounting principles should not impact the P-BV ratio because the accelerated writeoff of assets reduces the book value of shareholders' equity at t_0, but, because of lower expenses, increases ROCE of future periods. The P-BV ratios of firms in certain industries, however, suggest that alternative accounting principles do have an impact.

Consider the data in Exhibit 12.3, which shows the mean of the industry median P-BV ratios for eight industries for the years 1992 through 1996. Although the differences in P-BV ratios likely relate in part to an excess of ROCE over the cost of equity capital, alternative accounting principles appear to have an impact as well. Food processors expense advertising expenditures in the year incurred, and therefore do not recognize the value of brand names on their balance sheets. The chemical industry includes pharmaceutical firms, which expense research and development expenditures in the year they are incurred. The personal services and business services industries expense compensation costs in the year incurred and do not recognize the value of their employees on the balance sheet. The balance sheet understates the economic value of key resources in each of these industries, and they have P-BV ratios considerably in excess of 1.0. Inventories by contrast dominate the balance sheets of wholesalers and retailers. Although the use of LIFO will cause the market value of these inventories to exceed their book values, the understatement of assets is not nearly as significant as for the food processing, chemicals, and personal and business services industries, with their higher P-BV ratios. Likewise, the assets of securities firms and insurance companies are dominated by investments in securities, which appear on the balance sheet at market value. The P-BV ratios in this case are thus closer to 1.0.

EXHIBIT 12.3	
Mean of Industry Median P-BV Ratios for Selected Industries—1992 to 1996	
Industry	**Price-Book Value Ratio**
Food Processors	2.14
Chemicals	3.24
Personal Services	2.47
Business Services	2.96
Wholesalers-Durables	1.72
Retailers-General Merchandise	1.42
Securities Firms	1.52
Insurance Companies	1.35

[18]Ryan finds that book value changes lag market value changes because of GAAP's use of historical cost valuations for assets. The lag varies, depending in part on the degree of capital intensity of firms. See Stephen Ryan, "A Model of Accrual Measurement and Implications for the Evolution of the Book-to-Market Ratio," *Journal of Accounting Research* (Spring 1995), pp. 96–112.

EXHIBIT 12.4

**Median ROCEs for Portfolios Formed on Observed
P-BV Ratios for Formation Year and Subsequent Years**

P/BV Portfolio	Median ROCE				
	Formation Year 0	Year 1	Year 2	Year 3	Year 4
4 (High)	.187	.186	.175	.164	.156
10 (Medium)	.135	.132	.129	.130	.133
18 (Low)	.077	.077	.090	.099	.107

The calculation of the P-BV ratio for Coke suggests that several of these explanations might account for the divergence between the actual and theoretical ratio. The value of Coke's brand name does not appear on the balance sheet. Its actual ROCE of 60.5 percent for Year 7 is higher than in previous years, and probably not sustainable. The market, however, appears to price Coke at the end of Year 7 as if it could sustain such a high ROCE for many years.

Empirical research on the P-BV ratio is of relatively recent origin. Penman, using the same data base as in Exhibit 12.2, formed firms into 20 portfolios each year based on their P-BV ratios.[19] He then computed the median ROCE for each portfolio in the formation year and for each of the nine subsequent years. Exhibit 12.4 presents a portion of Penman's results.

The data in Exhibit 12.4 indicate that firms with the highest P-BV ratios have the highest ROCEs in the formation year, and firms with the lowest P-BV ratios have the lowest ROCEs in the formation year. Firms in the median P-BV category display ROCEs similar to the long-term rate of return on common shares. These results are consistent with the idea that the P-BV ratio reflects the presence or absence of positive or negative earning power relative to the cost of equity capital. Note also the slow but steady mean reversion in ROCEs over time, consistent with movement toward equilibrium.

USING P-E RATIOS AND P-BV RATIOS OF COMPARABLE FIRMS

The analyst can use the P-E and P-BV ratios of comparable firms to assess the corresponding ratios of publicly traded firms. The analyst can also value firms whose common shares are not publicly traded by using P-E ratios and P-BV rates of comparable firms that are publicly traded. The theoretical models assist in this valuation task by identifying the variables that the analyst should use in selecting comparable firms.

---

[19]Stephen H. Penman, "The Articulation of Price-Earnings Ratios and Market-to-Book Ratios and the Evaluation of Growth," *op. cit.*

Alford examines the accuracy of the P-E valuation models using industry, risk, ROCE, and earnings growth as the bases for selecting comparable firms.[20] The results indicate that industry membership, particularly at a three-digit SIC code level, provides the most effective comparisons. Firms in the same industry usually experience similar profitability, face similar risks, and grow at similar rates. Thus, industry membership serves as an effective proxy for the variables in the P-E valuation model. Alford observes some improvement in valuation accuracy by adding total assets (as a measure of risk) and ROCE to industry membership.[21] He finds that adding growth to industry membership does not increase valuation accuracy.

SUMMARY COMMENTS ON VALUATION

Chapters 11 and 12 have described multiple approaches to valuation:

1. Present value of projected cash flows.
2. Price-earnings ratios using both theoretical models and multiples for comparable companies.
3. Price-to-book value ratios using both theoretical models and multiples for comparable companies.

Considerable research interest has been directed to an examination of whether cash flows or earnings are more closely associated with stock prices.[22] This research indicates that both earnings and cash flows are similarly correlated with stock returns as the length of the period increases (that is, annual periods versus quarterly periods, five-year periods versus annual periods). For shorter periods, however, earnings show more of an association with stock returns than do cash flows. Even among proponents of the earnings association, debate centers on the importance of current earnings, as reflected in P-E ratios, versus accumulated earnings, which form a part of P-BV ratios.

Recent work addresses whether current earnings may have higher valuation significance in some circumstances, and accumulated earnings have higher valuation significance in other circumstances.[23] The research to date suggests that current

---

[20]Andrew W. Alford, "The Effect of the Set of Comparable Firms on the Accuracy of the Price-Earnings Valuation Method," *Journal of Accounting Research* (Spring 1992), pp. 94–108.

[21]Recent research suggests that size (measured by total assets or market value of shareholders' equity) is a more accurate measure of risk than market beta in explaining market rates of return. See Eugene F. Fama and Kenneth R. French, "The Cross Section of Expected Stock Returns," *Journal of Finance* (June 1992), pp. 427–465.

[22]See Patricia M. Dechow, "Accounting Earnings and Cash Flows as Measures of Firm Performance: The Role of Accounting Accruals," *Journal of Accounting and Economics* (1994), pp. 3–42; C. S. Cheng, Chao-Shin Liu, and Thomas F. Schaefer, "Earnings Permanence and the Incremental Information Content of Cash Flow from Operations," *Journal of Accounting Research* (Spring 1996), pp. 173–181; and Richard G. Sloan, "Do Stock Prices Fully Reflect Information in Accruals and Cash Flows about Future Earnings," *The Accounting Review* (July 1996), pp. 289–315.

[23]See David C. Burgstahler and Ilia D. Dichev, "Earnings, Adaptation and Equity Value," *The Accounting Review* (April 1997), pp. 187–215; Stephen H. Penman, "Combining Earnings and Book Value in Valuation," Working Paper, University of California, Berkeley, 1996.

earnings may play a more dominant role in valuation when ROCE is high and when current earnings include few transitory elements. Accumulated earnings may play a more dominant role when earnings prospects are poor and the firm needs to move into other businesses.

Our experience with valuation suggests that using multiple valuation approaches yields more useful insights than using just one method in all circumstances. The hope is that the various approaches will yield valuations that fall within a relatively narrow range. When one method yields a value that differs materially from the others, the analyst should attempt to understand why the value is so different. For example, one common explanation for an unusually large valuation when using the theoretical P-E ratio is that the assumed growth rate in earnings is not sustainable in perpetuity.

RECONCILING ACADEMIC RESEARCH WITH THE WORK OF THE SECURITY ANALYST[24]

Academic accounting research attempts to develop and test models of the relationship between accounting information and stock prices. The research usually models this relation analytically, and then tests the models empirically on large sets of data involving many firms for many years. The results of this research often show general relationships that do seem to hold.

For example, research has shown that unexpected changes in earnings correlate with unexpected changes in stock prices.[25] The coefficients on the independent variables in this research (such as unexpected changes in earnings) are often significantly different from zero, indicating that a relationship exists. The correlations from the regressions (that is, the R^2s), however, typically fall in the neighborhood of 10 percent. Thus, the independent variables explain only a small portion of the total variance in prices across the firms studied.

The natural question for the security analyst is: How relevant are the models and empirical findings of academic research to my task of making buy, sell, and hold recommendations on individual firms? We conclude our valuation discussion by offering some thoughts on this important question.

LEVEL OF AGGREGATION ISSUE

First, both the academic and the professional analyst communities must recognize that their interest is at a different level of aggregation. The academician is interested in the relationship between accounting information and stock prices for the *average* firm. Is there a statistically significant relation, for example, between invest-

---

[24]This section draws heavily on Clyde P. Stickney, "The Academic's Approach to Securities Research: Is It Relevant to the Analyst?" *Journal of Financial Statement Analysis* (Summer 1997), pp. 52–60.

[25]Raymond Ball and Philip Brown, "An Empirical Evaluation of Accounting Income Numbers," *Journal of Accounting Research* (Autumn 1968), pp. 159–178.

ments in research and development and stock market returns? Does this relation differ across industries? The analyst, however, is more concerned with whether investment in research and development by a *particular* firm, such as Sun Microsystems or Netscape, is likely to enhance the firm's profitability and stock returns.

Academic research indicates general tendencies that might at least provide a basis for an analyst to assess the significance of deviation from the average for an individual firm. Acting on the deviations is the value-added by the professional analysts. Buying underpriced securities and selling overpriced securities is the mechanism through which deviations for actual firms revert to the average over time. Academics should not expect immediate application of their research findings to the work of the professional analyst. Professional analysts should not expect the results of academic research to be immediately applicable to their day-to-day responsibilities.

THEORY DEVELOPMENT AND PRACTICE FEED ONE ANOTHER

There is in fact a common meeting place between the academic and professional analyst communities. Both communities share the desire to understand better how accounting information relates to stock prices. The activities of each community do influence the other. Consider, for example, the usefulness of the academic research on bankruptcy prediction and market beta in the work of the securities analyst during the last several decades. Consider also the attempts by the academic community to explain market pricing "anomalies," such as why the market, when pricing securities, does not fully incorporate information about past earnings changes into earnings predictions.

DOES THE THEORY OF CAPITAL MARKET EFFICIENCY GET IN THE WAY?

For most of the last several decades, academic research has presumed the efficiency of capital markets. Capital markets may be described as "efficient" if market participants react correctly and quickly to available information in the pricing of securities. "Correctly" means that market participants identify the economic implications of available information so that market prices reflect economic values. For example, a change in accounting principles that increases reported earnings but has no cash flow consequences should not cause market prices to change.

"Quickly" means that market participants can earn abnormal returns using the information for only a very short period of time (hours or perhaps days). That is, market prices rapidly capture any valuation-relevant signals in the information. This second dimension of an efficient capital market implies there is little or no role for financial statement analysis; analysts cannot study accounting information to find under- or overvalued securities. Note that market efficiency allows for random valuation errors at the level of the individual firm, but these random inefficiencies cancel out at an aggregated market level.[26]

---

[26]For a discussion of these issues, see Ray Ball, "The Earnings-Price Anomaly," *Journal of Accounting and Economics* (1992), pp. 319–345.

Relying on the efficiency of capital markets, academic research during most of the last several decades has attempted to identify the types of accounting information most highly correlated with stock prices, an approach referred to as the "information perspective."[27] A principal drawback of this approach is that it is difficult to assess whether in fact markets are efficient. A weak association between earnings and stock prices, for example, might suggest that the market does not respond appropriately to earnings information (that is, the market is inefficient). A weak association may also indicate that earnings are not relevant to security pricing, or that the posited relationship between earnings and stock prices is misspecified (fails to consider lags between earnings and stock prices, for example), or something else entirely. A strong association may indicate the relevance of earnings to market pricing but not necessarily that the market responds wisely. For example, a strong association between reported earnings and stock prices may not indicate market efficiency if firms have managed earnings to such an extent that earnings are a misleading indicator of economic values.

An overreliance on the assumption of market efficiency has probably to some extent hindered the conversation between academics and professional analysts. In academic circles, attention has recently shifted toward attempts to explain what have been termed "market anomalies"—circumstances in which the market has not fully used publicly available information in the pricing of securities. These seemingly tarnished spots in the armor of capital market efficiency (some would say "chinks") have led some researchers to shift to a "valuation model perspective." This approach attempts to model the way accounting information should translate into security prices.

The theoretical P-E and P-BV models discussed in this chapter are two models that use the valuation model perspective. The output of these models should indicate the intrinsic value of a security, against which the analyst can compare the actual market price to identify under- or overvalued securities.

The advantage of the valuation model approach is that it provides a means for testing the efficiency of capital markets, particularly in the pricing of individual securities. Inferences about capital market efficiency rely, however, on the ability of the researcher to identify both the appropriate valuation model and the accounting inputs to that model. A finding that intrinsic values differ from market prices might suggest either market mispricing (that is, inefficiencies) or inappropriate identification or application of the valuation model.

The recent emphasis on the valuation perspective in academic research provides a possible bridge between academicians and professional analysts. If much has been learned from the information perspective about the relation between various types of accounting information and stock prices, now might be the appropriate time to incorporate this learning into the development of valuation models.

---

[27]For an elaboration of this view, and the valuation model view discussed next, see Stephen H. Penman, "Return to Fundamentals," *Journal of Accounting, Auditing, and Finance* (Fall 1992), pp. 465–483.

SUMMARY

This chapter develops the theoretical rationale for relating market prices to earnings and to the book value of shareholders' equity. Relating market prices to earnings using the P-E ratio has been a standard for analysts for decades. In more recent years, however, it has been recognized that transitory elements in the earnings of a particular period can make the P-E ratio a problematical indicator of value. Emphasis has shifted, particularly in academic research, to the P-BV ratio. This ratio is affected less by transitory earnings elements of a particular period.

Four variables, or factors, affect the P-E ratio and the P-BV ratio: (1) the cost of equity capital; (2) the growth rate in earnings or common shareholders' equity; (3) the presence of transitory components in the earnings or ROCEs of a particular year; and (4) biases in earnings or common shareholders' equity related to alternative accounting principles. Ongoing empirical research is endeavoring to identify the effects of each of these variables on reported P-E ratios and P-BV ratios. While this research is evolving, the analyst should view the output of theoretical models as directional guides in valuing firms rather than unambiguous indicators of value.

PROBLEMS AND CASES

12.1 COMPARING THEORETICAL AND ACTUAL P-E RATIOS. The grocery store industry is mature. Its defining characteristics are extensive competition, market saturation, and thin margins on commodity products. Exhibit 12.5 presents selected data for five leading grocery store chains for a recent year. Kroger and Safeway experienced major recapitalizations during the late 1980s and added considerable debt to their balance sheets.

EXHIBIT 12.5

Selected Data for Five Grocery Store Chains
(Problem 12.1)

Company	Market Price Per Share	Earnings Per Share	Five-Year Growth Rate in Earnings	Market Beta
American Stores	$22.25	$ .99	2.7%	.60
Great Atlantic and Pacific	$25.00	$1.91	.6%	1.22
Kroger	$26.00	$1.34	6.6%	.50
Safeway	$43.00	$1.93	29.8%	.49
Winn-Dixie	$36.00	$1.36	4.4%	.53

Required

Assume that the risk-free interest rate is 6 percent, and that the excess market return over the risk-free rate is 7 percentage points.

    a. Compute theoretical and actual P-E ratios for each firm.

    b. Compute the growth rate in earnings implied by the actual P-E ratio for each firm, assuming that the costs of equity capital are correct.

    c. Compute the cost of equity capital implied by the actual P-E ratio for each firm, assuming that the historical growth rates in earnings are correct and sustainable.

    d. Given your analyses above, discuss whether each company appears to be undervalued, overvalued, or fairly valued by the market.

12.2 COMPARING THEORETICAL AND ACTUAL P-E RATIOS. Exhibit 12.6 presents selected data for six consumer products companies for a recent year. Assume that the risk-free interest rate is 6 percent, and that the excess market return over the risk-free rate is 7 percentage points.

Required

    a. Compute the theoretical and actual P-E ratios for each firm.

    b. Compute the growth rate in earnings implied by the actual P-E ratio for each firm, assuming that the costs of equity capital are correct.

    c. Compute the cost of equity capital implied by the actual P-E ratio, assuming that the historical growth rates in earnings are correct and sustainable.

    d. Given your analyses above, discuss whether each company appears to be undervalued, overvalued, or fairly valued by the market.

12.3 VALUATION USING P-E AND P-BV RATIOS. Selected data for Wal-Mart Stores for Year 7 appear in Exhibit 12.7.

EXHIBIT 12.6

Selected Data for Consumer Products Companies
(Problem 12.2)

Company	Market Price Per Share	Earnings Per Share	Five-Year Growth Rate in Earnings	Market Beta
Alberto-Culver	$28.25	$1.32	17.9%	.54
Avon	$57.25	$2.38	10.3%	.97
Colgate-Palmolive	$52.00	$2.09	9.4%	1.27
Gillette	$79.50	$1.71	12.0%	1.02
International Flavors				
And Fragrances	$45.00	$1.71	3.0%	.71
Procter & Gamble	$68.00	$2.43	12.8%	1.13

EXHIBIT 12.7

Selected Data for Wal-Mart Stores
(Problem 12.3)

Net Income for Year 7 (in millions)	$ 3,056
Earnings per Share for Year 7	$ 1.33
Dividends/Net Income for Year 7	21%
Historical Annual Growth Rate in Earnings	6.6%
Shareholders' Equity at Beginning of Year 7 (in millions)	$14,756
Shareholders' Equity at End of Year 7 (in millions)	$17,143
Market Equity Beta	.83
Market Price per Share at End of Year 7	$ 23.50
Number of Shares Outstanding at End of Year 7 (in millions)	2,298

Required

a. Compute the theoretical and actual P-E ratios for Wal-Mart at the end of Year 7. Assume that the risk-free interest rate is 6 percent and that the market equity premium over the risk-free interest rate is 7 percentage points.

b. Compute the growth rate in earnings implied by the actual P-E ratio, assuming that the cost of equity capital is correct.

c. Compute the cost of equity capital implied by the actual P-E ratio, assuming that the historical growth rate in earnings is correct and sustainable.

d. Compute the theoretical and actual P-BV ratios at the end of Year 7. Assume that Wal-Mart will maintain a dividend payout rate of 21 percent, and that the rates of return on shareholders' equity will be as follows:

Year 8: 20.5%	Year 11: 18.3%	Year 14: 15.3%	Year 17: 12.3%
Year 9: 19.7%	Year 12: 17.3%	Year 15: 14.3%	
Year 10: 18.9%	Year 13: 16.3%	Year 16: 13.3%	

The rate of return on shareholders' equity will equal the cost of equity capital after Year 17.

e. Given your analyses above, discuss whether you think that Wal-Mart is undervalued, overvalued, or fairly valued by the market.

12.4 INTERPRETING P-BV RATIOS. Exhibit 12.8 presents selected data for seven pharmaceutical companies for a recent year. The growth rate in earnings and the dividend payout rates are five-year averages. The excess earnings years represent the number of years that each firm would need to earn a rate of return on common shareholders' equity (ROCE) equal to that in Exhibit 12.8 in order to produce the P-BV shown. For example, Bristol-Myers Squibb would need to earn an ROCE of 48.9 percent for 58.3 years in order for the present value of the excess earnings over the cost of equity capital to produce a P-BV ratio of 13.9 when applying the theoretical model. For several years just prior to the

---

EXHIBIT 12.8

Selected Data for Pharmaceutical Companies
(Problem 12.4)

Company	P-BV	ROCE	Cost of Equity	Dividend Payout Percentage	P-E	Growth in Earnings	Excess Earnings Years
Bristol-Myers Squibb	13.9	.489	.134	.77	32.4	.068	58.3
Warner Lambert	13.0	.350	.133	.48	42.7	.051	32.2
Eli Lilly	12.4	.281	.155	.42	49.3	.110	89.8
Pfizer	11.2	.350	.143	.43	40.4	.152	27.8
Abbott Laboratories	10.4	.428	.113	.39	26.9	.116	13.5
Merck	10.3	.331	.154	.46	31.8	.130	41.9
American Home Products	6.9	.340	.138	.51	25.0	.065	24.6

most recent year, Bristol-Myers Squibb recognized significant estimated losses related to breast implant claims.

Required

Considering the variables in the theoretical P-BV ratio, discuss the likely reasons for the ordering of these seven companies on their P-BV ratios.

12.5 SENSITIVITY OF P-E AND P-BV THEORETICAL MODELS TO CHANGES IN ASSUMPTIONS. This problem explores the sensitivity of the P-E and P-BV theoretical models to changes in underlying assumptions. We recommend that you design a computer spreadsheet in order to perform the calculations, particularly for the P-BV ratio.

a. Compute the value of the P-E ratio under each of the assumptions A through I below:

Scenario	Cost of Equity Capital	Growth Rate in Earnings
A	0.15	0.06
B	0.15	0.08
C	0.15	0.10
D	0.13	0.06
E	0.13	0.08
F	0.13	0.10
G	0.11	0.06
H	0.11	0.08
I	0.11	0.10

b. Assess the sensitivity of the P-E ratio to changes in the cost of equity capital and changes in the growth rate.

c. Compute the value of the P-BV ratio under each of the assumptions A through I below:

Scenario	ROCE	Cost of Equity Capital	Dividend Payout Percentage	Years of Excess Earnings
A	0.20	0.13	0.30	10
B	0.18	0.13	0.30	10
C	0.14	0.13	0.30	10
D	0.18	0.15	0.30	10
E	0.18	0.11	0.30	10
F	0.18	0.13	0.40	10
G	0.18	0.13	0.20	10
H	0.18	0.13	0.30	15
I	0.18	0.13	0.30	20

d. Assess the sensitivity of the P-BV ratio to changes in the assumptions made about the various underlying variables.

CASE 12.1*

REVCO D.S., INC.

Investors in a firm's debt securities issued to finance a leveraged buyout (LBO) are increasingly using the legal argument of fraudulent conveyance in efforts to obtain financial restitution for losses they incur when the issuing firm is unable to service its debt adequately after the LBO. An understanding of the use of the fraudulent conveyance claim requires an understanding of the financing of an LBO. The sponsoring equity participants in an LBO use the assets of the target firm as collateral for substantial borrowing. The proceeds of the debt issues plus a relatively small amount of funds contributed by the sponsoring equity participants finance the buyout of the shares of the pre-LBO shareholders.

A presumption on the part of the new debtholders, of course, is that the firm is solvent after the LBO. That is, the value of the firm's assets exceeds the claims of creditors. A subsequent finding that a firm is unable to service the LBO debt may suggest (1) that the value of liabilities exceeded the value of assets just after the LBO (either because lenders overstated the perceived value of the assets or because more corporate assets were used to buy out the pre-LBO shareholders than was appropriate), or (2) subsequent management decisions or operating conditions led to a deterioration of asset values or an increase in liability values. Claimants use the fraudulent conveyance claim in the first instance above, arguing that the sponsoring equity participants overpaid to buy out the existing shareholders, and leaving insufficient assets in the firm to service the debt.

Revco D.S., Inc., the largest retail drugstore chain in the U.S., engaged in an LBO transaction totaling $1.45 billion on December 29, 1986. Revco subsequently filed for bankruptcy

*The authors gratefully acknowledge the assistance of Dusty Philip in the preparation of this case.

on July 28, 1988, causing substantial losses for debt and equity participants in the LBO. This case examines whether the value of Revco's net assets at the time of the LBO justified the buyout price.

ECONOMIC CHARACTERISTICS AND CONDITIONS IN THE DRUGSTORE INDUSTRY

Between 1970 and 1985, the drugstore industry experienced a 15 percent annual growth rate in sales. Most of this growth occurred because of the increasingly dominant position of large retail drugstore chains (Revco, Rite Aid, Eckerd, Walgreen). By 1985, these chains commanded a 60 percent market share, with independent drugstores, pharmacies, hospitals, variety stores, and supermarkets representing the remainder. Drugstores compete on the basis of price, convenience, quality, reliability, and delivery. The drugstore chains increased their market share at the expense of the smaller players for the following reasons:

1. Lower prices due to volume purchasing.
2. Greater convenience due to the larger number of locations.
3. Greater diversity of merchandise beyond pharmaceuticals.
4. Improving professional image.

By the mid-1980s, however, the drugstore industry began approaching maturity. The number of retail outlets nationwide reached a saturation point. In 1986, drugstores reported their smallest sales gains in a decade. Competition intensified among drugstores for a larger share of the more slowly growing market. Among the more important industry trends were the following:

1. Frequent Price Wars—Firms began to trade off reduced profit margin for increased assets turnover.
2. Increased Focus on Cost Cutting—Firms trimmed costs to offset the required price reductions. Many drugstores installed computer systems to improve productivity and service.
3. Recentralization—Firms began to reverse the trend of the preceding decade toward autonomous profit centers in an effort to eliminate overhead costs and increase coordination among drugstores.
4. Consolidation—Firms attempted to maintain their historical growth rates and increase their market share by acquiring existing drugstore chains. In addition, supermarket chains attempted to diversify into drugstores by participating in these acquisitions. Some of the major acquisitions included:

Acquiror/Acquiree
Pantry Pride/Adams Drugs
Kroger Co./Hook Drugs
K-Mart/Pay Less Drug Stores
Imasco/People's Drug Stores

5. Diversification—Drugstore chains diversified into higher-growth, higher-profit margin businesses, including auto parts, food distribution, children's toys, and books.
6. Changed Product Mix—Drugstores expanded their product lines to include video cassette rentals and film processing.

Several positive signs appeared on the horizon for the drugstore industry in the mid-1980s.

1. Aging of the Population—Demographers were expecting the number of the population over 65 years of age to increase 30 percent between 1986 and 1990 and of those over 75 to increase by 74 percent. These age groups typically require substantially more prescription drugs than the general population.
2. Increased Health Consciousness—People were placing increased emphasis on exercise, diet, and health monitoring beginning in the early 1980s, a trend expected to continue for the foreseeable future. Drugstores added products to satisfy consumer needs in these areas.
3. Rising Hospital Costs—Rising hospital costs were expected to lead to shorter hospital stays and increased emphasis on outpatient and at-home care, increasing the likelihood that patients would purchase drugs from drugstore chains rather than in-hospital pharmacies.
4. New Tax Legislation—Drugstores were expected to benefit from the drop in the statutory income tax rate from 46 percent to 34 percent.

HISTORICAL BACKGROUND OF REVCO

Exhibit 12.9 presents selected operating data for Revco for the fiscal years ending May 1982 through 1986. At the end of fiscal 1986, Revco operated more than 2,000 drugstores in geographic markets as follows:

Southeast	52.5%
Middle Atlantic	8.5
Midwest	19.9
Southwest	19.1
Total	100.0%

Revco's sales grew at a 15.2 percent compound annual rate during the five years preceding the LBO. Revco increased its number of drugstores at a 6.3 percent annual rate, using both internal growth and acquisitions. Prescription revenues remained a steady 30 percent of drugstore sales, and drugstore revenues remained a steady 95 percent of total revenues. Revco employed an "everyday-low-price" strategy during this period rather than opting for periodic sales.

Exhibit 12.10 presents comparative income statements; Exhibit 12.11 presents comparative balance sheets; and Exhibit 12.12 presents comparative statements of cash flows for the

---

EXHIBIT 12.9

Operating Data for Revco
(Case 12.1)

	Fiscal Year Ended May:					Compound Annual Growth Rate
	1982	1983	1984	1985	1986	
Sales (in millions)	$ 1,555	$ 1,793	$ 2,227	$ 2,396	$ 2,743	15.2%
Number of Drugstores	1,593	1,661	1,778	1,898	2,031	6.3%
Drugstore Retail Square Footage (in thousands)	12,227	12,849	13,909	15,148	16,694	8.1%
Drugstore Sales as Percentage of Total Sales ..	94.5%	94.9%	95.3%	95.1%	95.4%	—
Drugstore Sales Per Square Foot	$ 120	$ 132	$ 153	$ 150	$ 157	6.9%
Like-Drugstore Percentage Sales Growth	8.4%	12.3%	12.3%	5.8%	8.5%	—
Prescription Revenue as Percentage of Drugstore Sales	28.0%	29.6%	29.4%	30.5%	31.1%	—

EXHIBIT 12.10

Revco D.S., Inc.
Income Statement
(amounts in millions)
(Case 12.1)

	1982	1983	1984	1985	1986
Sales Revenue	$1,555	$1,793	$2,227	$2,396	$2,743
Interest Revenue	2	2	3	2	3
Total Revenues	$1,557	$1,795	$2,230	$2,398	$2,746
Cost of Goods Sold	(1,135)	(1,307)	(1,602)	(1,795)	(2,022)
Selling and Administrative Expenses	(321)	(360)	(448)	(520)	(596)
Interest Expense	(11)	(6)	(6)	(15)	(29)
Unusual Items	—	—	—	—	3
Income Before Taxes	$ 90	$ 122	$ 174	$ 68	$ 102
Income Taxes	(40)	(56)	(81)	(29)	(45)
Net Income	$ 50	$ 66	$ 93	$ 39	$ 57

EXHIBIT 12.11

Revco D.S., Inc.
Balance Sheet
(amounts in millions)
(Case 12.1)

	1981	1982	1983	1984	1985	1986
Assets						
Cash	$ 18	$ 27	$ 51	$ 18	$ 8	$ 45
Accounts Receivable	31	31	41	54	75	69
Inventories	258	276	317	472	492	502
Prepayments	11	11	16	19	26	24
Total Current Assets	$318	$345	$425	$563	$601	$640
Property, Plant, and Equipment:						
Gross	$164	$199	$218	$271	$345	$428
Accumulated Depreciation	(46)	(58)	(69)	(84)	(102)	(127)
Net	$118	$141	$149	$187	$243	$301
Other Assets	11	15	24	27	31	46
Total Assets	$447	$501	$598	$777	875	$987
Liabilities and Shareholders' Equity						
Accounts Payable	$ 78	$ 90	$100	$142	$145	$155
Notes Payable	—	—	—	51	121	—
Current Portion of Long-Term Debt	3	3	4	4	4	5
Other Current Liabilities	47	49	66	72	75	94
Total Current Liabilities	$128	$142	$170	$269	$345	$254
Long-Term Debt	66	66	43	39	45	305
Deferred Income Taxes	4	8	13	22	28	36
Total Liabilities	$198	$216	$226	$330	$418	$595
Common Stock	$ 14	$ 20	$ 32	$ 36	$ 36	$ 36
Additional Paid-in Capital	20	15	41	39	39	42
Retained Earnings	215	250	299	372	382	412
Treasury Stock	—	—	—	—	—	(98)
Total Shareholders' Equity	$249	$285	$372	$447	$457	$392
Total Liabilities and Shareholders' Equity	$447	$501	$598	$777	$875	$987

EXHIBIT 12.12

Revco D.S., Inc.
Statement of Cash Flows
(amounts in millions)
(Case 12.1)

	1982	1983	1984	1985	1986
Operations					
Net Income	$ 50	$ 66	$ 93	$ 39	$ 57
Depreciation	17	19	23	28	34
Other Addbacks	4	6	10	6	2
Working Capital from Operations	$ 71	$ 91	$126	$ 73	$ 93
(Increase) Decrease in Accounts Receivable	1	(11)	(7)	(22)	9
(Increase) Decrease in Inventories	(18)	(41)	(142)	(20)	(10)
(Increase) Decrease in Prepayments	—	(4)	(2)	(7)	2
Increase (Decrease) in Accounts Payable	13	11	33	7	11
Increase (Decrease) in Other Current Liabilities	1	17	(2)	(1)	18
Cash Flow from Operations	$ 68	$ 63	$ 6	$ 30	$123
Investing					
Sale of Property, Plant, and Equipment	$ 2	$ 2	$ 1	$ 6	$ 2
Acquisition of Property, Plant and Equipment	(42)	(29)	(58)	(90)	(82)
Other	—	—	—	—	(16)
Cash Flow from Investing	$(40)	$(27)	$ (57)	$(84)	$ (96)
Financing					
Increase in Short-Term Borrowing	—	—	$ 49	$ 70	—
Increase in Long-Term Borrowing	$ 3	—	—	11	$261
Increase in Common Stock	1	$ 38	1	1	2
Decrease in Short-Term Borrowing	—	—	—	—	(121)
Decrease in Long-Term Borrowing	(3)	(24)	(7)	(5)	(5)
Decrease in Common Stock	—	—	—	—	(99)
Dividends	(15)	(17)	(22)	(29)	(27)
Other	(5)	(9)	(3)	(4)	(1)
Cash Flow from Financing	$(19)	$(12)	$ 18	$ 44	$ 10
Net Change in Cash	$ 9	$ 24	$ (33)	$(10)	$ 37

1982 through 1986 fiscal years. Additional information pertaining to these financial statements includes:

1. Revco leases drugstore and warehouse facilities using operating leases. The present values of its lease commitments when discounted at 10 percent are:

May 31:	Present Value of Operating Leases (in millions)
1981	$212
1982	$249
1983	$283
1984	$343
1985	$409
1986	$456

2. Revco uses a last-in, first-out (LIFO) cost flow assumption for inventories and cost of goods sold. The excess of current cost over LIFO inventories at each year-end is as follows:

May 31:	Excess of Current Cost (in millions) over LIFO Inventories
1982	$82
1983	$94
1984	$103
1985	$118
1986	$128

3. Selected per share data are as follows:

	Fiscal Year:				
	1982	1983	1984	1985	1986
Earnings Per Share	$1.39	$ 1.91	$ 2.54	$ 1.06	$ 1.72
Book Value Per Share	$8.12	$10.24	$12.22	$12.48	$12.11

4. On May 24, 1984, Revco acquired the outstanding common shares of Odd Lot Trading Co. by issuing 4.4 million Revco common shares valued at $113 million. Revco treated the acquisition as a pooling of interests, recording the shares issued at the book value of Odd Lot Trading Co.'s common shareholders' equity of $925 thousand. Odd Lot Trading Co.

purchases closed-out merchandise and manufacturers' overruns from various vendors for resale at discount prices through 153 stores located in nine states. Sales and earnings of Odd Lot Trading Co. generally constitute less than 5 percent of Revco's total sales each year. Prior to the acquisition, Revco sold certain merchandise to Odd Lot Trading Co. At the time of the acquisition, Revco was considered a target for an unfriendly takeover. The shares exchanged placed 4.4 million shares (12.0 percent) in what Revco considered friendly hands. Soon after the acquisition, the former owners and managers of Odd Lot Trading Co. made numerous suggestions to improve the operations and profitability of Revco's drugstore operations, suggestions that Sidney Dworkin, long-time chairman and CEO of Revco, did not appreciate. Revco fired these former owners in February 1985, and on July 9, 1985, repurchased the 4.4 million shares held by them for $98.2 million in cash. Revco financed the stock repurchase using the proceeds from $95 million of long-term borrowing.

5. For the year ending May 1985, Revco recognized a pretax loss of $35 million from writing down inventories of Odd Lot Trading Co. Odd Lot operated at a net loss of $9.5 million in fiscal 1985 and at a net loss of $8.6 million in fiscal 1986.

6. On July 1, 1985, Revco acquired the Carls Drug Store chain for $35 million in cash.

7. The income statement for the fiscal year ending May 1986 includes unusual items as follows (amounts shown are pretax in millions):

Gain from Sale of Computer Subsidiary	$ 6.6
Gain on Sale of Alarm Service Division	2.3
Premium for Short-Term Insurance Coverage Following Bankruptcy of Former Carrier	(5.0)
Expenses of Board of Directors to Examine Proposed LBO	(1.1)
Total Unusual Items	$ 2.8

The after-tax effect of the unusual items is $1.5 million.

8. Revco's market price per share was $27.50 in early 1986 just before rumors of the LBO hit the market.

9. An independent appraisal of Revco's net assets as of September 1986 revealed assets (excluding any goodwill) of $1.433 billion and liabilities of .611 billion.

LBO TRANSACTION

The sponsoring equity participants in the LBO included the following:

Transcontinental Services Group	51.0%
Current Management	28.9
Salomon Brothers	13.1
Golenberg & Co.	1.4
Holders of Exchangeable Preferred Stock	5.6
Total	100.0%

These entities obtained financing totaling $1.45 billion, and used the proceeds to purchase Revco's outstanding shares for $38.50 per share and to retire $117.5 million of existing debt. The new Revco entity also assumed $175.0 million of existing Revco debt.

Exhibit 12.13 presents a cash flow analysis relating to the LBO. Revco planned to sell seven nondrugstore subsidiaries soon after the LBO for their independently appraised value of $225 million and use the proceeds to repay a portion of existing debt.

Required

Your task is to assess the reasonableness of the $38.50 buyout price for Revco's common shares. Your analysis should proceed as follows:

    a. Prepare a set of pro forma financial statements for Revco for the fiscal years 1987 through 1991, ignoring the financing for the LBO. That is, project (1) operating income after taxes but before interest expense and related tax effects; (2) assets and current liabilities excluding term debt and the current portion of long-term debt; and (3) cash flow from operations (excluding interest and related taxes) net of cash flow from investing activities. Discount the net cash flow from operating and investing

---

EXHIBIT 12.13

Sources and Uses of Cash Relating to Revco LBO
(amounts in thousands)
(Case 12.1)

Sources

Term Bank Loan, priced at prime plus 1.75% or LIBOR + 2.75%, repayable over five years	$ 455,000
Senior Subordinated Debentures, 13.125%, due in December, 1993 and 1994	400,000
Subordinated Debentures, 13.30%, due in December, 1995 and 1996	210,000
Junior Subordinated Debentures, 13.30%, due in December, 1997 to 2001	93,750
Convertible Preferred Stock, 850,000 shares with $12 per share dividend, convertible into 2.56 common shares each	85,000
Exchangeable Preferred Stock, 7,880,000 shares with $3.8125 per share dividend on liquidation preference ($25) exchangeable for $25 notes yielding 15.25%	130,020
Junior Preferred Stock, 1,203,875 shares with $4.40 per share dividend	30,098
Common Stock	34,381
Revco Cash	9,155
Total Sources	$1,447,404

Uses

Acquisition of Revco Common Stock, 32,433 shares at $38.50	$1,248,674
Repayment of Existing Debt	117,484
Cancellation of Revco Employee Stock Options	3,246
Fees and Commissions	78,000
Total Uses	$1,447,404

activities, including any residual value at the end of fiscal 1991, using a weighted average cost of capital from the LBO. Assume a 40 percent income tax rate for fiscal 1987 and a 34 percent tax rate thereafter. The prime interest rate at the time of the transaction was 10 percent. The debentures were issued for their face value.

b. Assess the reasonableness of the buyout price by examining the valuation of other drugstore chains. Exhibits 12.14 through 12.17 present historical ratio analyses

EXHIBIT 12.14

Fay's Drug Company
Ratio Analysis
(Case 12.1)

	1982	1983	1984	1985	1986
Profitability Analysis					
Return on Assets					
Profit Margin	1.8%	2.4%	3.1%	2.7%	1.3%
× Asset Turnover	2.9	3.0	2.7	2.3	2.2
= Return on Assets	5.3%	7.3%	8.1%	6.2%	2.9%
Return on Common Equity					
Return on Assets	5.3%	7.3%	8.1%	6.2%	2.9%
× Common Earnings Leverage	72.5%	84.3%	85.0%	86.1%	47.0%
× Capital Structure Leverage	4.1	3.8	3.0	2.9	3.4
= Return on Common Equity	15.5%	23.4%	20.7%	15.5%	4.6%
Operating Performance					
Gross Margin/Sales	25.1%	24.9%	25.6%	25.5%	23.7%
Operating Profit Before Tax/Revenues	3.2%	4.6%	5.6%	4.5%	1.9%
Net Income—Continued Operations/Revenues	1.3%	2.0%	2.6%	2.4%	0.6%
Asset Turnover					
Sales/Average Accounts Receivable	61.8	63.1	76.1	68.3	58.0
COGS/Average Inventory	5.9	7.0	6.3	5.5	5.5
Sales/Average Fixed Assets	11.4	12.7	11.5	10.7	10.4
Risk Analysis					
Liquidity					
Current Ratio	1.78	1.98	1.74	1.81	2.56
Quick Ratio	0.52	0.76	0.49	0.52	0.68
Days Payables Held	38	30	33	38	32
Days Receivable Held	6	6	5	5	6
Days Inventory Held	62	52	58	67	66
Operating Cash Flow to Current Liabilities	44.4%	40.5%	30.9%	16.6%	−20.5%
Solvency					
Total Liabilities/Total Assets	73.8%	73.8%	61.8%	67.9%	72.2%
Long-Term Debt/Total Assets	46.0%	46.8%	35.3%	41.5%	53.5%
Long-Term Debt/Owner's Equity	175.6%	178.5%	92.5%	129.2%	192.6%
Operating Cash Flow to Total Liabilities	17.2%	15.0%	12.2%	6.5%	−6.2%
Interest Coverage Ratio	3.51	6.52	6.62	6.32	1.47
Operating Cash Flow to Capital Expense	2.16	1.42	0.80	0.68	−0.40

(assuming the capitalization of all operating leases) for four drugstore chains as follows:

Fay's Drug Company: This firm operated 150 drugstores throughout the Northeast in 1986. The average store size was approximately 15,000 square feet. Drugstore sales constitute the vast majority of revenues. Fay's also operated several auto parts and paper supplies outlets.

EXHIBIT 12.15

Perry Drugstores
Ratio Analysis
(Case 12.1)

	1982	1983	1984	1985	1986
Profitability Analysis					
Return on Assets					
Profit Margin	1.8%	2.1%	2.4%	2.5%	1.7%
× Asset Turnover	2.2	2.0	1.8	1.8	1.7
= Return on Assets	4.0%	4.2%	4.4%	4.4%	2.9%
Return on Common Equity					
Return on Assets	4.0%	4.2%	4.4%	4.4%	2.9%
× Common Earnings Leverage	65.1%	75.0%	87.2%	73.9%	51.9%
× Capital Structure Leverage	4.5	3.6	3.3	4.1	4.9
= Return on Common Equity	11.7%	11.5%	12.7%	13.3%	7.4%
Operating Performance					
Gross Margin/Sales	29.8%	29.9%	31.1%	30.4%	31.1%
Operating Profit Before Tax/Revenues	3.0%	3.7%	3.9%	3.9%	2.9%
Net Income-Continued Operations/Revenues	1.2%	1.6%	2.1%	1.8%	0.9%
Asset Turnover					
Sales/Average Accounts Receivable	65.3	72.2	59.5	38.4	33.2
COGS/Average Inventory	3.9	3.8	3.5	3.3	3.2
Sales/Average Fixed Assets	11.8	12.2	11.3	9.6	8.4
Risk Analysis					
Liquidity					
Current Ratio	1.93	2.24	1.46	1.99	2.24
Quick Ratio	0.18	0.40	0.19	0.32	0.33
Days Payables Held	54	48	51	55	54
Days Receivable Held	6	5	6	10	11
Days Inventory Held	93	96	104	109	113
Operating Cash Flow to Current Liabilities	−12.8%	4.0%	31.4%	−36.9%	−5.3%
Solvency					
Total Liabilities/Total Assets	77.8%	68.4%	71.2%	78.8%	80.6%
Long-Term Debt/Total Assets	51.1%	47.2%	38.7%	54.2%	58.7%
Long-Term Debt/Owner's Equity	229.7%	149.5%	134.2%	255.8%	302.4%
Operating Cash Flow to Total Liabilities	−4.6%	1.2%	11.7%	−12.6%	−1.4%
Interest Coverage Ratio	2.55	3.73	6.90	3.23	1.86
Operating Cash Flow to Capital Expense	−0.83	0.21	0.69	−0.54	−0.15

Perry Drugstores: This firm operated 139 drugstores, primarily in Michigan, in 1986. Perry was involved in drugstores, auto parts, and health care, with drugstores the dominant segment by far.

Rite Aid Corporation: Rite Aid operated 1,403 drugstores throughout 20 states in 1986 (third-largest in the industry behind Revco and Eckerd). The firm's average

EXHIBIT 12.16

Rite Aid Corporation
Ratio Analysis
(Case 12.1)

	1982	1983	1984	1985	1986
Profitability Analysis					
Return on Assets					
Profit Margin	4.5%	4.7%	5.0%	5.2%	4.8%
× Asset Turnover	2.1	2.1	2.0	1.9	1.8
= Return on Assets	9.5%	9.6%	10.1%	9.9%	8.4%
Return on Common Equity					
Return on Assets	9.5%	9.6%	10.1%	9.9%	8.4%
× Common Earnings Leverage	100.5%	101.6%	102.4%	98.0%	90.9%
× Capital Structure Leverage	2.0	2.1	2.1	2.2	2.5
= Return on Common Equity	19.6%	20.8%	21.3%	21.6%	19.1%
Operating Performance					
Gross Margin/Sales	26.2%	27.1%	28.2%	28.9%	28.7%
Operating Profit Before Tax/Revenues	8.8%	9.1%	9.7%	10.1%	9.2%
Net Income—Continued Operations/Revenues	4.6%	5.2%	6.1%	5.1%	4.3%
Asset Turnover					
Sales/Average Accounts Receivable	31.4	34.8	38.9	35.5	25.2
COGS/Average Inventory	3.9	4.0	4.0	3.9	3.7
Sales/Average Fixed Assets	9.2	8.8	8.5	7.7	7.0
Risk Analysis					
Liquidity					
Current Ratio	1.90	1.77	2.26	1.74	2.09
Quick Ratio	0.31	0.36	0.34	0.30	0.45
Days Payables Held	32	29	30	30	27
Days Receivable Held	12	10	9	10	14
Days Inventory held	94	90	91	93	98
Operating Cash Flow to Current Liabilities	25.5%	40.6%	65.0%	32.6%	0.8%
Solvency					
Total Liabilities/Total Assets	51.7%	54.1%	49.2%	60.1%	59.9%
Long-Term Debt/Total Assets	26.5%	26.3%	26.8%	32.7%	34.9%
Long-Term Debt/Owner's Equity	54.8%	57.4%	52.7%	82.0%	87.0%
Operating Cash Flow to Total Liabilities	12.5%	19.6%	28.5%	12.8%	0.3%
Interest Coverage Ratio	11.58	13.61	18.95	12.08	7.23
Operating Cash Flow to Capital Expense	0.70	1.10	1.59	0.35	0.28

drugstore totaled 6,500 square feet. Rite Aid also operated auto part, toy store, and book chains.

Walgreen Company: Walgreen operated 1,273 drugstores in 1986. Although Walgreen ranked fourth in number of stores, it ranked first in sales. The firm also operated a chain of restaurants.

EXHIBIT 12.17

Walgreen Company
Ratio Analysis
(Case 12.1)

	1982	1983	1984	1985	1986
Profitability Analysis					
Return on Assets					
Profit Margin	2.5%	2.9%	3.1%	3.1%	3.0%
× Asset Turnover	2.4	2.3	2.3	2.2	2.1
= Return on Assets	6.1%	6.8%	7.0%	6.8%	6.3%
Return on Common Equity					
Return on Assets	6.1%	6.8%	7.0%	6.8%	6.3%
× Common Earnings Leverage	108.2%	99.7%	97.7%	96.7%	94.6%
× Capital Structure Leverage	3.1	3.1	3.1	3.2	3.3
= Return on Common Equity	20.4%	21.1%	21.4%	21.0%	19.9%
Operating Performance					
Gross Margin/Sales	30.5%	30.6%	30.7%	30.7%	30.3%
Operating Profit Before Tax/Revenues	4.5%	5.3%	5.7%	5.7%	5.4%
Net Income—Continued Operations/Revenues	2.7%	3.0%	3.1%	3.0%	2.8%
Asset Turnover					
Sales/Average Accounts Receivable	139.7	148.0	83.2	79.3	100.8
COGS/Average Inventory	5.3	5.3	5.2	5.1	5.0
Sales/Average Fixed Assets	9.3	9.3	9.5	9.4	8.7
Risk Analysis					
Liquidity					
Current Ratio	1.52	1.55	1.66	1.76	1.85
Quick Ratio	0.25	0.30	0.33	0.33	0.36
Days Payables Held	27	29	28	27	27
Days Receivable Held	3	2	4	5	4
Days Inventory Held	69	69	70	72	72
Operating Cash Flow to Current Liabilities	37.4%	38.9%	28.9%	29.6%	29.8%
Solvency					
Total Liabilities/Total Assets	67.4%	68.5%	67.9%	69.2%	70.5%
Long-Term Debt/Total Assets	38.7%	40.6%	39.0%	43.0%	44.9%
Long-Term Debt/Owner's Equity	118.5%	129.1%	121.4%	139.7%	152.3%
Operating Cash Flow to Total Liabilities	13.7%	14.3%	10.5%	9.9%	9.0%
Interest Coverage Ratio	14.92	20.45	26.73	30.33	18.33
Operating Cash Flow to Capital Expense	1.11	1.39	1.26	1.00	0.69

The market price information as of the end of fiscal 1986 for each firm may assist in your valuation:

	Fay's	Perry	Rite Aid	Walgreen
Price-Earnings Ratio	17	19	19	22
Price to Book Value per Share	2.44	3.81	4.52	4.60

c. Examine acquisitions of other drugstore chains around the time of the Revco LBO in a third approach to assessing the reasonableness of the buyout price. Exhibit 12.18 presents data relating to five such acquisitions. The transaction involving Jack Eckerd Corp. was a management-led LBO, while the Pay Less Drug, Hook Drug, and Thrifty Corp. transactions involved acquisitions by other operating corporations.

EXHIBIT 12.18

Valuation Data on Five Drugstore Acquisitions
(Case 12.1)

Date	Company Acquired	Purchase Price of Common Stock as a Multiple of	Sales	EBIT[a]	EBIDT[b]
Jan., 1985	Pay Less Drug Stores (144 store chain)	One-Year Prior	.58	8.3	6.9
		Five-Year Average	.69	11.0	9.0
Feb., 1985	Hook Drug Inc. (300 store chain)	One-Year Prior	.46	9.5	7.7
		Five-Year Average	.56	10.6	8.7
Oct., 1985	Jack Eckerd Corp. (drugstores, optical centers, clothing stores)	One-Year Prior	.47	9.0	6.9
		Five-Year Average	.53	8.2	6.8
May, 1986	Thrifty Corp. (555 drugstores plus book, auto, and sporting goods stores)	One-Year Prior	.57	10.9	8.7
		Five-Year Average	.62	13.8	10.9
Dec., 1986	Revco (2,000 drugstores)	One-Year Prior	.44	9.2	7.4
		Five-Year Average	.57	9.8	8.2

[a]EBIT is earnings before interest and taxes.

[b]EBIDT is earnings before interest, depreciation and taxes.

SOURCE: Amounts adapted from: Karen H. Wruck, "What Really Went Wrong with Revco?" *Journal of Applied Corporate Finance* (Summer, 1991), pp. 79–92.

KLEEN CLEANING SERVICES: PRICING AN INITIAL PUBLIC OFFERING

Larry Starr, founder and Chief Executive Officer of Kleen Cleaning Services, describes how his young and rapidly growing firm got its start.

> I worked in my parents' residential and commercial cleaning business during high school. Our most challenging task was cleaning drapes. Most drapes require dry cleaning. Drapes, however, are heavy and bulky. Taking drapes down and transporting them to another location for dry cleaning was costly. What we needed was a machine that would perform the dry cleaning while the drapes stayed hanging. The drawback of equipment available at the time was that it left too much dry cleaning fluid in the drapes, weighing them down and causing the hanging apparatus to pull loose from the wall or ceiling. While an engineering student at New York Institute of Technology, I created a cleaning machine that adjusted the amount of cleaning fluids applied in relation to the humidity in the room on the day of application. The machine also has a powerful blower for drying. These two functions reduce the weight problem of existing equipment. After graduation (in Year 10) I started Kleen Cleaning Services, specializing in the cleaning of drapes for residential and commercial customers (like office buildings and movie theaters).

Kleen Cleaning Services maintained a single office in New York City from Year 10 through Year 13. It used telemarketing to obtain customers. Telemarketers called potential customers at random, offering various low-priced packages of drapery cleaning services. The average price per job booked was $90. While performing the work, however, technicians were usually able to get customers to add additional draperies to the job so that the average job completed amounted to $150.

Larry Starr was a key asset of the company during these early years. His energy and enthusiasm were contagious. He had an ability to relate quickly to all types of people (both employees and customers). He was sold on Kleen, and quickly convinced others as well. As one employee said: "Larry could charm the socks off an Eskimo."

The success of the New York City office led Kleen to expand beginning in Year 14. It opened three new offices in fiscal Year 14 and another three offices in fiscal Year 15, all located in the New York City area. Kleen also added restoration services beginning in fiscal Year 15.

Owners of commercial buildings damaged by fire or water typically hire contractors to repair electrical, plumbing, and drywall damage and to clean carpets, draperies, and furniture. Kleen completes such services by subcontracting the repair work and performing the cleaning services itself.

Kleen obtains restoration jobs from a single insurance consultant located in New York City. These jobs require upfront capital, since Kleen must purchase repair materials and cleaning supplies before receiving progress payments from insurance companies. Kleen engaged in short- and long-term borrowing and issued common stock to selected people during fiscal Year 15 to finance restoration work. It also formed joint ventures with others in order to obtain the needed capital, but it must share the profits of this work with the joint venture partners.

During fiscal Year 15, Kleen obtained 55 percent of its revenues from restoration services and 45 percent from residential and commercial drapery cleaning. It has 291 employees, including 86 trained technicians, 86 technician trainees, 88 telemarketers, and 31 administrative personnel.

Exhibits 12.19, 12.20, and 12.21 present the financial statements of Kleen for fiscal Year 13 through fiscal Year 15. The reports of the independent accountants follow these financial statements. Exhibit 12.22 presents selected financial statement ratios. Kleen was taxed as a sole proprietorship prior to January 31, Year 14.

EXHIBIT 12.19

Kleen Cleaning Services
Income Statement
(amounts in thousands)
(Case 12.2)

	For the Year Ending January 31			For the Three Months April 30 (unaudited)	
	Year 13	Year 14	Year 15	Year 14	Year 15
Sales	$ 575	$1,241	$4,845	$ 638	$5,497
Other Revenue	—	—	187	—	—
Cost of Goods Sold	(284)	(577)	(2,051)	(320)	(2,976)
Selling and Administrative	(139)	(306)	(1,125)	(91)	(623)
Interest	—	—	(43)	—	(64)
Income Taxes	—	(36)	(867)	(96)	(938)
Net Income	$ 152	$ 322	$ 946	$ 131	$ 896
Earnings per Share	$ .03	$ .06	$ .12	$ .02	$ .11
Common Shares Outstanding	5,500	5,500	7,700	7,700	7,700

EXHIBIT 12.20

Kleen Cleaning Services
Balance Sheet
(amounts in thousands)
(Case 12.2)

	January 31				(unaudited) April 30
	Year 12	Year 13	Year 14	Year 15	Year 15
Cash	$ 14	$ 4	$ 30	$ 87	$ 10
Accounts Receivable	—	30	—	691	2,461
Inventories	—	—	—	429	336
Prepayments	22	36	77	518	1,436
Total Current Assets	$ 36	$ 70	$107	$1,728	$4,243

Exh. 12.20—Continued

	January 31				(unaudited) April 30
	Year 12	Year 13	Year 14	Year 15	Year 15
Property, Plant, and Equipment:					
Cost	$ 92	$126	$126	$3,223	$3,967
Accumulated Depreciation	(8)	(30)	(68)	(163)	(269)
Net	$ 84	$ 96	$ 58	$3,060	$3,698
Other Assets	13	13	13	258	259
Total Assets	$133	$179	$178	$5,046	$8,200
Accounts Payable	—	$ 2	$ 3	$ 237	$ 363
Notes Payable	—	—	—	1,356	1,972
Current Portion of Long-Term Debt	—	—	—	147	198
Other Current Liabilities	—	—	—	28	1,572
Total Current Liabilities	—	$ 2	$ 3	$1,768	$4,105
Long-Term Debt	—	—	—	429	933
Deferred Income Taxes	—	—	—	819	236
Total Liabilities	—	$ 2	$ 3	$3,016	$5,274
Common Stock ($.01 par value)	$ 55	$ 55	$ 55	$ 77	$ 77
Additional Paid-in Capital	55	55	55	942	942
Retained Earnings	23	67	65	1,011	1,907
Total Shareholders' Equity	$133	$177	$175	$2,030	$2,926
Total Equities	$133	$179	$178	$5,046	$8,200

EXHIBIT 12.21

Kleen Cleaning Services
Statement of Cash Flows
(amounts in thousands)
(Case 12.2)

	For the Year Ended January 31			Three Months Ended April 30 (unaudited)	
	Year 13	Year 14	Year 15	Year 14	Year 15
Operations					
Net Income	$ 152	$ 322	$ 946	$131	$ 896
Depreciation	22	38	97	6	106
Deferred Taxes	—	—	819	90	(583)
(Increase) Decrease in Accounts					
Receivable	(30)	30	(694)	(49)	(1,767)
(Increase) Decrease in Inventories	—	—	(429)	(31)	(220)
(Increase) Decrease in Prepayments	(14)	(41)	(441)	(67)	(605)
Increase (Decrease) in Accounts Payable . .	2	1	234	2	126
Increase (Decrease) in Other					
Current Liabilities	—	—	28	6	1,546
Cash Flow from Operations	$ 132	$ 350	$ 560	$ 88	$ (501)

(continued)

Exh. 12.21—Continued

	For the Year Ended January 31			Three Months Ended April 30 (unaudited)	
	Year 13	Year 14	Year 15	Year 14	Year 15
Investing					
Acquisition of Fixed Assets	$ (34)	—	$(3,097)	—	$ (744)
Other Investing Transactions	—	—	(247)	—	(2)
Cash Flow for Investing	$ (34)	—	$(3,344)	—	$ (746)
Financing					
Increase in Short-Term Borrowing	—	—	$ 1,356	$ (2)	$ 616
Increase in Long-Term Borrowing	—	—	576	—	555
Issue of Common Stock	—	—	909	—	—
Dividends	$(108)	$(324)	—	—	—
Cash Flow for Financing	$(108)	$(324)	$ 2,841	$ (2)	$1,170
Change in Cash	$ (10)	$ 26	$ 57	$ 86	$ (77)
Cash at Beginning of Year	14	4	30	30	87
Cash at End of Year	$ 4	$ 30	$ 87	$116	$ 10

EXHIBIT 12.22

**Financial Statement Ratios for Kleen Cleaning Services,
Business Services Industry, and Personal Services Industry
(Case 12.2)**

				Average, Year 13 to Year 15	
	Year 13	Year 14	Year 15	Business Services	Personal Services
Profit Margin for ROA	26.4%	25.9%	20.1%	6.8%	5.7%
Total Assets Turnover	3.7	7.0	1.9	1.2	1.4
Rate of Return on Assets	97.4%	180.4%	37.3%	8.4%	8.8%
Common Earnings Leverage	1.00	1.00	.97	.89	.88
Capital Structure Leverage	1.0	1.0	2.4	1.9	1.8
Rate of Return on Common Shareholders' Equity	98.1%	183.0%	85.8%	15.3%	15.0%
Cost of Goods Sold/Sales	49.4%	46.5%	42.3%	—	—
Selling & Administrative Expense/Sales	24.2%	24.7%	23.2%	—	—
Income Tax Expense on Operating Income/Sales	—	2.9%	18.2%	—	—
Fixed Asset Turnover	6.4	16.1	3.1	—	—
Price-Earnings Ratio	—	—	—	19.3	15.1
Market Value to Book Value Ratio	—	—	—	2.4	2.1

Kleen intends to make an initial public offering of its common stock on July 1, Year 15. The stock ownership before and after the offering is as follows:

	Before		After	
	Shares	**Percentage**	**Shares**	**Percentage**
Larry Starr	5,500,000	71%	5,500,000	55%
Other Individuals	2,200,000	29	2,150,000	22
Public Owners	—	—	2,350,000	23
	7,700,000	100%	10,000,000	100%

Kleen plans to use its share of the proceeds from the offering to open new offices (four new offices scheduled for opening in fiscal Year 16 and ten in fiscal Year 17) and to finance its growing restoration business without having to enter joint ventures. Kleen estimates that 80 percent of fiscal Year 16 revenues will come from restoration work.

Required

At what price should the 2,350,000 Kleen common shares be issued on the market? Summarize the valuation process that you use.

REPORTS OF INDEPENDENT ACCOUNTANTS

Board of Directors
Kleen Cleaning Services
New York, NY

We have examined the consolidated balance sheet of Kleen Cleaning Services as of January 31, Year 12, Year 13, Year 14, and Year 15, and the respective related statements of income and cash flows for the years ended January 31, Year 13, Year 14, and Year 15. Our examination was made in accordance with generally accepted accounting standards and accordingly includes such tests of the accounting records and such other auditing procedures as we consider necessary in the circumstances.

In our opinion, the accompanying statements together with the related notes present fairly the consolidated financial position of Kleen Cleaning Services at January 31, Year 13, Year 14, and Year 15 and the results of operations and changes in cash flows for the year then ended in conformity with generally accepted accounting principles applied on a consistent basis.

Whitespan & Company
(local CPA firm)

Brunswick, New Jersey
June 1, Year 15

Board of Directors
Kleen Cleaning Services
New York, NY

We have made a review of the consolidated balance sheet of Kleen Cleaning Services, Inc., and subsidiaries as of April 30, Year 15, and the related consolidated statements of income, shareholders' equity, and cash flows for the three-month period ended April 30, Year 15, in accordance with standards established by the American Institute of Certified Public Accountants. A review of the consolidated financial statements for the comparative period of the prior year was not made.

A review of interim financial information consists principally of obtaining an understanding of the system for the preparation of interim financial information, applying analytical review procedures to financial data, and making inquiries of persons responsible for financial and accounting matters. It is substantially narrower in scope than an examination in accordance with generally accepted auditing standards, which will be performed for the full year with the objective of expressing an opinion regarding the financial statements taken as a whole. Accordingly, we do not express such an opinion.

From our review, we are not aware of any material modifications that should be made to the consolidated interim financial statements referred to above for the statements to be in conformity with generally accepted accounting principles.

Andersenhouse & Mitchell
(Big 5 CPA firm)

New York, NY
June 1, Year 15

FINANCIAL STATEMENTS FOR THE COCA-COLA COMPANY AND SUBSIDIARIES

The Coca-Cola Company and Subsidiaries
Consolidated Statements of Income
(*in millions except per share data*)

Year Ended December 31,	Year 5	Year 6	Year 7
Net Operating Revenues	$16,181	$18,018	$18,546
Cost of goods sold	6,168	6,940	6,738
Gross Profit	10,013	11,078	11,808
Selling, administrative, and general expenses	6,376	7,052	7,893
Operating Income	3,637	4,026	3,915
Interest income	181	245	238
Interest expense	199	272	286
Equity income	134	169	211
Other income (deductions)—net	(25)	86	87
Gain on issuance of stock by equity investees	—	74	431
Income before Income Taxes	3,728	4,328	4,596
Income taxes	1,174	1,342	1,104
Net Income	$ 2,554	$ 2,986	$ 3,492
Net Income per Share	$ .99	$ 1.18	$ 1.40
Average Shares Outstanding	2,580	2,525	2,494

See Notes to Consolidated Financial Statements.

The Coca-Cola Company and Subsidiaries
Consolidated Balance Sheets
(*in millions except share data*)

December 31,	Year 6	Year 7
Assets		
Current		
Cash and cash equivalents	$ 1,167	$ 1,433
Marketable securities	148	225
	1,315	1,658
Trade accounts receivable, less allowances of $34 in Year 6 and $30 in Year 7	1,695	1,641
Inventories	1,117	952
Prepaid expenses and other assets	1,323	1,659
Total Current Assets	5,450	5,910
Investments and Other Assets		
Equity method investments		
Coca-Cola Enterprises Inc.	556	547
Coca-Cola Amatil Limited	682	881
Other, principally bottling companies	1,157	2,004
Cost method investments, principally bottling companies	319	737
Marketable securities and other assets	1,597	1,779
	4,311	5,948
Property, Plant, and Equipment		
Land	233	204
Buildings and improvements	1,944	1,528
Machinery and equipment	4,135	3,649
Containers	345	200
	6,657	5,581
Less allowances for depreciation	2,321	2,031
	4,336	3,550
Goodwill and Other Intangible Assets	944	753
	$ 15,041	$ 16,161

December 31,	Year 6	Year 7
Liabilities and Shareowners' Equity		
Current		
Accounts payable and accrued expenses	$ 3,103	$ 2,972
Loans and notes payable	2,371	3,388
Current maturities of long-term debt	552	9
Accrued income taxes	1,322	1,037
Total Current Liabilities	7,348	7,406
Long-Term Debt	1,141	1,116
Other Liabilities	966	1,182
Deferred Income Taxes	194	301
Shareowners' Equity		
Common stock, $0.25 par value—		
Authorized: 5,600,000,000 shares;		
Issued: 3,423,678,994 shares in Year 6;		
3,432,956,518 shares in Year 7	856	858
Capital surplus	863	1,058
Reinvested earnings	12,882	15,127
Unearned compensation related to outstanding		
restricted stock	(68)	(61)
Foreign currency translation adjustment	(424)	(662)
Unrealized gain on securities available for sale	82	156
	14,191	16,476
Less·treasury stock, at cost (919,081,326 shares in		
Year 6; 951,963,574 common shares in Year 7)	8,799	10,320
....	5,392	6,156
....$	15,041	$16,161

See Notes to Consolidated Financial Statements.

The Coca-Cola Company and Subsidiaries
Consolidated Statements of Cash Flows
(in millions)

Year Ended December 31,	Year 5	Year 6	Year 7
Operating Activities			
Net income	$2,554	$2,986	$3,492
Depreciation and amortization	411	454	479
Deferred income taxes	58	157	(145)
Equity income, net of dividends	(4)	(25)	(89)
Foreign currency adjustments	(6)	(23)	(60)
Gains on issuances of stock by equity investees	—	(74)	(431)
Other noncash items	41	45	181
Net change in operating assets and liabilities	307	(192)	36
Net cash provided by operating activities	3,361	3,328	3,463
Investing Activities			
Acquisitions and investments, principally bottling companies	(311)	(338)	(645)
Purchases of investments and other assets	(379)	(403)	(623)
Proceeds from disposals of investments and other assets	299	580	1,302
Purchases of property, plant, and equipment	(878)	(937)	(990)
Proceeds from disposals of property, plant, and equipment	109	44	81
Other investing activities	(55)	(172)	(175)
Net cash used in investing activities	(1,215)	(1,226)	(1,050)
Net cash provided by operations after reinvestment	2,146	2,102	2,413
Financing Activities			
Issuances of debt	491	754	1,122
Payments of debt	(154)	(212)	(580)
Issuances of stock	69	86	124
Purchases of stock for treasury	(1,192)	(1,796)	(1,521)
Dividends	(1,006)	(1,110)	(1,247)
Net cash used in financing activities	(1,792)	(2,278)	(2,102)
Effect of Exchange Rate Changes on Cash and Cash-Equivalents	34	(43)	(45)
Cash and Cash-Equivalents			
Net increase (decrease) during the year	388	(219)	266
Balance at beginning of year	998	1,386	1,167
Balance at end of year	$1,386	$1,167	$1,433

See Notes to Consolidated Financial Statements.

The Coca-Cola Company and Subsidiaries
Consolidated Statements of Shareowners' Equity

Three Years Ended December 31, Year 7	Number of Common Shares Outstanding[1]	Common Stock[1]	Capital Surplus[1]	Reinvested Earnings	Outstanding Restricted Stock	Foreign Currency Translation	Unrealized Gain on Securities	Treasury Stock
(In millions except per share data[1])								
Balance December 31, Year 4	2,595	$852	$ 660	$ 9,458	$(85)	$(420)	$ —	$ (5,881)
Transition effect of change in accounting for certain debt and marketable equity securities, net of deferred taxes	—	—	—	—	—	—	60	—
Stock issued to employees exercising stock options	8	2	67	—	—	—	—	—
Tax benefit from employees' stock option and restricted stock plans	—	—	17	—	—	—	—	—
Stock issued under restricted stock plans, less amortization of $13 .	—	—	2	—	11	—	—	—
Translation adjustments	—	—	—	—	—	148	—	—
Net change in unrealized gain on securities, net of deferred taxes .	—	—	—	—	—	—	(12)	—
Purchases of stock for treasury ...	(51)[2]	—	—	—	—	—	—	(1,192)
Net income	—	—	—	2,554	—	—	—	—
Dividends (per share—$.39)	—	—	—	(1,006)	—	—	—	—
Balance December 31, Year 5	2,552	854	746	11,006	(74)	(272)	48	(7,073)
Stock issued to employees exercising stock options	8	2	84	—	—	—	—	—
Tax benefit from employees' stock option and restricted stock plans	—	—	26	—	—	—	—	—
Stock issued under restricted stock plans, less amortization of $12 .	—	—	7	—	6	—	—	—
Translation adjustments	—	—	—	—	—	(152)	—	—
Net change in unrealized gain on securities, net of deferred taxes .	—	—	—	—	—	—	34	—
Purchases of stock for treasury ...	(58)[2]	—	—	—	—	—	—	(1,796)
Treasury stock issued in connection with an acquisition .	3	—	—	—	—	—	—	70
Net income	—	—	—	2,986	—	—	—	—
Dividends (per share—$.44)	—	—	—	(1,110)	—	—	—	—
Balance December 31, Year 6	2,505	856	863	12,882	(68)	(424)	82	(8,799)
Stock issued to employees exercising stock options	9	2	122	—	—	—	—	—
Tax benefit from employees' stock option and restricted stock plans	—	—	63	—	—	—	—	—
Stock issued under restricted stock plans, less amortization of $15 .	—	—	10	—	7	—	—	—
Translation adjustments	—	—	—	—	—	(238)	—	—
Net change in unrealized gain on securities, net of deferred taxes .	—	—	—	—	—	—	74	—
Purchases of stock for treasury ...	(33)[2]	—	—	—	—	—	—	(1,521)
Net income	—	—	—	3,492	—	—	—	—
Dividends (per share—$.50)	—	—	—	(1,247)	—	—	—	—
Balance December 31, Year 7	2,481	$858	$1,058	$15,127	$(61)	$(662)	$156	$(10,320)

[1]Adjusted for a two-for-one stock split in Year 7.

[2]Common stock purchased from employees exercising stock options numbered 416 thousand, 561 thousand and 881 thousand shares for the years ending December 31, Year 5, Year 6, and Year 7, respectively.

See Notes to Consolidated Financial Statements.

NOTES TO CONSOLIDATED FINANCIAL STATEMENTS

1. ORGANIZATION AND SUMMARY OF SIGNIFICANT ACCOUNTING POLICIES

Organization.   The Coca-Cola Company and subsidiaries (our Company) is predominantly a manufacturer, marketer, and distributor of soft drink and noncarbonated beverage concentrates and syrups. Operating in nearly 200 countries worldwide, we primarily sell our concentrates and syrups to bottling and canning operations, fountain wholesalers, and fountain retailers. We have significant markets for our products in all of the world's geographic regions. We record revenue when title passes to our customers.

Basis of Presentation.   Certain amounts in the prior years' financial statements have been reclassified to conform to the current year presentation.

Consolidation.   Our consolidated financial statements include the accounts of The Coca-Cola Company and all subsidiaries except where control is temporary or does not rest with our Company. Our investments in companies in which we have the ability to exercise significant influence over operating and financial policies are accounted for by the equity method. Accordingly, our Company's share of the net earnings of these companies is included in consolidated net income. Our investments in other companies are carried at cost or fair value, as appropriate. All significant intercompany accounts and transactions are eliminated upon consolidation.

Issuances of Stock by Equity Investees.   When one of our equity investees sells additional shares to third parties, our percentage ownership interest in the investee decreases. In the event the selling price per share is more or less than our average carrying amount per share, we recognize a noncash gain or loss on the issuance. This noncash gain or loss, net of any deferred taxes, is recognized in our net income in the period the change of ownership interest occurs.

Advertising Costs.   Our Company generally expenses production costs of print, radio, and television advertisements as of the first date the advertisements take place. Advertising expenses included in selling, administrative, and general expenses were $1,114 million in Year 5, $1,292 million in Year 6, and $1,437 million in Year 7. As of December 31, Year 6 and Year 7, advertising costs of approximately $299 million and $247 million, respectively, were recorded primarily in prepaid expenses and other assets in our accompanying balance sheets.

Net Income per Share.   Net income per share is computed by dividing net income by the weighted average number of shares outstanding.
   On April 17, Year 7, our share owners approved an increase in the authorized common stock of our Company from 2.8 billion to 5.6 million shares and a

two-for-one stock split. The stated par value of each share remained at $0.25 per share. Our financial statements have been restated to reflect these changes.

Cash Equivalents.   Marketable securities that are highly liquid and have maturities of three months or less at the date of purchase are classified as cash equivalents.

Inventories.   Inventories consist primarily of raw materials and supplies and are valued at the lower of cost or market. In general, cost is determined on the basis of average cost or first-in, first-out methods.

Property, Plant, and Equipment.   Property, plant, and equipment are stated at cost and are depreciated principally by the straight-line method over the estimated useful lives of the assets.

Goodwill and Other Intangible Assets.   Goodwill and other intangible assets are stated on the basis of cost and are amortized, principally on a straight-line basis, over the estimated future periods to be benefited (not exceeding 40 years). Goodwill and other intangible assets are periodically reviewed for impairment based on an assessment of future operations to ensure that they are appropriately valued. Accumulated amortization was approximately $117 million and $86 million on December 31, Year 6 and Year 7, respectively.

Use of Estimates.   In conformity with generally accepted accounting principles, the preparation of our financial statements requires our management to make estimates and assumptions that affect the amounts reported in our financial statements and accompanying notes. Although these estimates are based on our knowledge of current events and actions we may undertake in the future, they may ultimately differ from actual results.

New Accounting Standards.   We adopted Statement of Financial Accounting Standards No. 123, "Accounting for Stock-Based Compensation" (SFAS 123), in Year 7. Under the provisions of SFAS 123, companies can elect to account for stock-based compensation plans using a fair value-based method or continue measuring compensation expense for those plans using the intrinsic value method prescribed in Accounting Principles Board Opinion No. 25, "Accounting for Stock Issued to Employees" (APB 25), and related Interpretations. We have elected to continue using the intrinsic value method to account for our stock-based compensation plans. SFAS 123 requires companies electing to continue using the intrinsic value method to make certain pro forma disclosures (see Note 11).

Statement of Financial Accounting Standards No. 121, "Accounting for the Impairment of Long-Lived Assets and for Long-Lived Assets to be Disposed Of" (SFAS 121), was adopted as of January 1, Year 7. SFAS 121 standardized the accounting practices for the recognition and measurement of impairment losses on certain long-lived assets. The adoption of SFAS 121 was not material to our results of operations or financial position. However, the provisions of SFAS 121 required certain charges, historically recorded by our Company in other income (deductions)-net, to be included in operating income.

2. BOTTLING INVESTMENTS

Coca-Cola Enterprises Inc..   Coca-Cola Enterprises is the largest soft drink bottler in the world. Our Company owns approximately 45 percent of the outstanding common stock of Coca-Cola Enterprises, and, accordingly, we account for our investment by the equity method of accounting. On December 31, Year 7, the excess of our equity in the underlying net assets of Coca-Cola Enterprises over our investment was approximately $150 million, which is primarily being amortized on a straight-line basis over 40 years. A summary of financial information for Coca-Cola Enterprises is as follows (in millions):

December 31,	Year 6	Year 7
Current assets	$ 982	$ 1,319
Noncurrent assets	8,082	9,915
Total assets	$9,064	$11,234
Current liabilities	$ 859	$ 1,390
Noncurrent liabilities	6,770	8,294
Total liabilities	$7,629	$ 9,684
Shareowners' equity	$1,435	$ 1,550
Company equity investment	$ 556	$ 547

Year ended December 31,	Year 5	Year 6	Year 7
Net operating revenues	$6,011	$6,773	$7,921
Cost of goods sold	3,703	4,267	4,896
Gross profit	$2,308	$2,506	$3,025
Operating income	$ 440	$ 468	$ 545
Cash operating profit[1]	$ 901	$ 997	$1,172
Net income	$ 69	$ 82	$ 114
Net income available to common shareowners ...	$ 67	$ 80	$ 106
Company equity income	$ 30	$ 35	$ 53

[1]Cash operating profit is defined as operating income plus depreciation expense, amortization expense, and other noncash operating expenses.

Our net concentrate/syrup sales to Coca-Cola Enterprises were $1.2 billion in Year 5, $1.3 billion in Year 6, and $1.6 billion in Year 7. Coca-Cola Enterprises purchases sweeteners through our Company; however, related collections from Coca-Cola Enterprises and payments to suppliers are not included in our consolidated statements of income. These transactions amounted to $254 million in Year 5, $242 million in Year 6, and $247 million in Year 7. We also provide certain administrative and other services to Coca-Cola Enterprises under negotiated fee arrangements.

Our direct support for certain marketing activities of Coca-Cola Enterprises and participation with them in cooperative advertising and other marketing programs amounted to approximately $319 million in Year 5, $343 million in Year 6, and $448 million in Year 7. Additionally, in Year 6 and Year 7, we committed approximately $55 million and $120 million, respectively, to Coca-Cola Enterprises under a Company program that encourages bottlers to invest in building and supporting beverage infrastructure.

If valued at the December 31, Year 7, quoted closing price of publicly traded Coca-Cola Enterprises shares, the calculated value of our investment in Coca-Cola Enterprises would have exceeded its carrying value by approximately $2.2 billion.

Coca-Cola Amatil Limited.   We own approximately 36 percent of Coca-Cola Amatil, an Australian-based bottler of our products that operates in 17 countries. Accordingly, we account for our investment in Coca-Cola Amatil by the equity method. On December 31, Year 7, the excess of our investment over our equity in the underlying net assets of Coca-Cola Amatil was approximately $137 million, which we are amortizing on a straight-line basis over 40 years. A summary of financial information for Coca-Cola Amatil is as follows (in millions):

December 31,	Year 6	Year 7
Current assets	$1,129	$1,847
Noncurrent assets	2,310	2,913
Total assets	$3,439	$4,760
Current liabilities	$1,077	$1,247
Noncurrent liabilities	881	1,445
Total liabilities	$1,958	$2,692
Shareowners' equity	$1,481	$2,068
Company equity investment	$ 682	$ 881

Year ended December 31,	Year 5	Year 6	Year 7
Net operating revenues	$1,670	$2,193	$2,905
Cost of goods sold	981	1,311	1,737
Gross profit	$ 689	$ 882	$1,168
Operating income	$ 156	$ 214	$ 215
Cash operating profit[1]	$ 247	$ 329	$ 384
Net income	$ 68	$ 75	$ 80
Company equity income	$ 28	$ 28	$ 27

[1]Cash operating profit is defined as operating income plus depreciation expense, amortization expense, and other noncash operating expenses.

Our net concentrate sales to Coca-Cola Amatil were approximately $270 million in Year 5, $340 million in Year 6, and $450 million in Year 7. We also participate in various marketing, promotional, and other activities with Coca-Cola Amatil.

If valued at the December 31, Year 7, quoted closing price of publicly traded Coca-Cola Amatil shares, the calculated value of our investments in Coca-Cola Amatil would have exceeded its carrying value by approximately $1.2 billion.

Other Equity Investments.   Operating results include our proportionate share of income from our equity investments since the respective dates of those investments. A summary of financial information for our equity investments in the aggregate, other than Coca-Cola Enterprises and Coca-Cola Amatil, is as follows (in millions):

December 31,	Year 6	Year 7
Current assets	$1,889	$ 2,792
Noncurrent assets	5,006	8,783
Total assets	$6,895	$11,575
Current liabilities	$1,933	$ 2,758
Noncurrent liabilities	2,555	4,849
Total liabilities	$4,488	$ 7,607
Shareowners' equity	$2,407	$ 3,968
Company equity investment	$1,157	$ 2,004

Year ended December 31,	Year 5	Year 6	Year 7
Net operating revenues	$7,998	$9,370	$11,640
Cost of goods sold	5,416	6,335	8,028
Gross profit	$2,582	$3,035	$ 3,612
Operating income	$ 633	$ 632	$ 835
Cash operating profit[1]	$ 875	$1,079	$ 1,268
Net income	$ 255	$ 280	$ 366
Company equity income	$ 76	$ 106	$ 131

Equity investments include certain non-bottling investees.

[1]Cash operating profit is defined as operating income plus depreciation expense, amortization expense, and other noncash operating expenses.

Net sales to equity investees other than Coca-Cola Enterprises and Coca-Cola Amatil were $1.0 billion in Year 5, $1.2 billion in Year 6, and $1.5 billion in Year 7. Our Company also participates in various marketing, promotional, and other activities with these investees, the majority of which are located outside the United States.

In July, Year 7, we sold our interests in our French and Belgian bottling and canning operations to Coca-Cola Enterprises in return for cash consideration of approximately $936 million. Also in Year 7, we contributed cash and our Venezuelan bottling interests to a new joint venture, Embotelladora Coca-Cola y Hit de Venezuela, S.A., in exchange for a 50 percent ownership interest. Accordingly, we account for our investment by the equity method.

During Year 6, our finance subsidiary invested $160 million in The Coca-Cola Bottling Company of New York, Inc. (CCNY), in return for redeemable preferred stock. As of December 31, Year 7, we held a 49 percent voting and economic interest in CCNY. Accordingly, we account for our investment in CCNY by the equity method.

If valued at the December 31, Year 7, quoted closing prices of shares actively traded on stock markets, the calculated value of our equity investments in publicly traded bottlers other than Coca-Cola Enterprises and Coca-Cola Amatil would have exceeded our carrying value by approximately $574 million.

3. ISSUANCES OF STOCK BY EQUITY INVESTEES

In the third quarter of Year 7, our previously wholly owned subsidiary, Coca-Cola Erfrischungsgertränke Gmb.H. (CCEG), issued approximately 24.4 million shares of common stock as part of a merger with three independent German bottlers of our products. The shares were valued at approximately $925 million, based upon the fair values of the assets of the three acquired bottling companies. In connection with CCEG's issuance of shares, a new corporation was established, Coca-Cola Erfrischungsgertränke AG (CCEAG), and our ownership was reduced to 45 percent of the resulting corporation. As a result, we will account for our related investment by the equity method of accounting, prospectively from the transaction date. This transaction resulted in a noncash pretax gain of $283 million to our Company. Our German subsidiary has provided deferred taxes of approximately $171 million related to this gain.

Also in the third quarter of Year 7, Coca-Cola Amatil issued approximately 46 million shares in exchange for approximately $522 million. This issuance reduced our Company's ownership percentage in Coca-Cola Amatil from approximately 39 percent to approximately 36 percent. This transaction resulted in a noncash pretax gain of $130 million to our Company. We have provided deferred taxes of approximately $47 million on this gain.

In Year 7, Coca-Cola FEMSA de Buenos Aires, S.A., issued approximately 19 million shares to Coca-Cola FEMSA, S.A. de C.V. This issuance reduced our ownership in Coca-Cola FEMSA de Buenos Aires, S.A., from 49 percent to approximately 32 percent. We recognized a noncash pretax gain of approximately $18 million as a result of this transaction. In a subsequent transaction, our ownership in Coca-Cola FEMSA de Buenos Aires, S.A. was reduced to 25 percent.

In the third quarter of Year 6, Coca-Cola Amatil completed a public offering in Australia of approximately 97 million shares of common stock. In connection with the offering, our ownership interest in Coca-Cola Amatil was diluted to approximately 40 percent. This transaction resulted in a noncash pretax gain of $74 million. We provided deferred taxes of approximately $27 million on this gain.

4. ACCOUNTS PAYABLE AND ACCRUED EXPENSES

Accounts payable and accrued expenses consist of the following (in millions):

December 31,	Year 6	Year 7
Accrued marketing	$ 492	$ 510
Container deposits	130	64
Accrued compensation	198	169
Sales, payroll, and other taxes	209	174
Accounts payable and other accrued expenses	2,074	2,055
	$3,103	$2,972

5. SHORT-TERM BORROWINGS AND CREDIT ARRANGEMENTS

Loans and notes payable consist primarily of commercial paper issued in the United States. On December 31, Year 7, we had $3.2 billion outstanding in commercial paper borrowings. In addition, we had $1.1 billion in lines of credit and other short-term credit facilities available, under which $0.2 billion was outstanding. Our weighted average interest rates for commercial paper were approximately 5.7 and 5.6 percent on December 31, Year 6 and Year 7, respectively.

These facilities are subject to normal banking terms and conditions. Some of the financial arrangements require compensating balances, none of which are pres-ently significant to our Company.

6. LONG-TERM DEBT

Long-term debt consists of the following (in millions):

December 31,	Year 6	Year 7
7¾% U.S. dollar notes due Year 7	$ 250	$ —
5¾% Japanese yen notes due Year 7	292	—
5¾% German mark notes due Year 9[1]	175	161
7⅛% U.S. dollar notes due Year 9	250	250
6% U.S. dollar notes due Year 11	252	251
6⅝% U.S. dollar notes due Year 13	149	150
6% U.S. dollar notes due Year 14	150	150
7⅜% U.S. dollar notes due Year 114	116	116
Other, due Year 8 to Year 24	59	47
	1,693	1,125
Less current portion	552	9
	$1,141	$1,116

[1]Portions of these notes have been swapped for liabilities denominated in other currencies.

After giving effect to interest rate management instruments (see Note 8), the principal amount of our long-term debt that had fixed and variable interest rates, respectively, was $1,107 million and $676 million on December 31, Year 6, and $261 million and $864 million on December 31, Year 7. The weighted average interest rate on our Company's long-term debt was 6.5 and 5.9 percent on December 31, Year 6 and Year 7, respectively. Interest paid was approximately $197 million, $275 million, and $315 million in Year 5, Year 6, and Year 7, respectively.

Maturities of long-term debt for the five years succeeding December 31, Year 7, are as follows (in millions):

Year 8	Year 9	Year 10	Year 11	Year 12
$9	$422	$16	$257	$2

The above notes include various restrictions, none of which is presently significant to our Company.

7. FINANCIAL INSTRUMENTS

Fair Value of Financial Instruments. The carrying amounts reflected in our consolidated balance sheets for cash, cash equivalents, marketable equity securities, investments, receivables, loans and notes payable, and long-term debt approximate their respective fair values. Fair values are based primarily on quoted prices for those or similar instruments. A comparison of the carrying value and fair value of our hedging instruments is included in Note 8.

Certain Debt and Marketable Equity Securities. Investments in debt and marketable equity securities, other than investments accounted for by the equity method, are categorized as either trading, available-for-sale, or held-to-maturity. On December 31, Year 6 and Year 7, we had no trading securities. Securities categorized as available-for-sale are stated at fair value, with unrealized gains and losses, net of deferred income taxes, reported in shareowners' equity. Debt securities categorized as held-to-maturity are stated at amortized cost.

On December 31, Year 6 and Year 7, available-for-sale and held-to-maturity securities consisted of the following (in millions):

December 31,	Cost	Gross Unrealized Gains	Gross Unrealized Losses	Estimated Fair Value
Year 6				
Available-for-sale securities				
Equity securities	$ 128	$151	$(2)	$ 277
Collateralized mortgage obligations	147	—	(5)	142
Other debt securities	26	—	—	26
	$ 301	$151	$(7)	$ 445
Held-to-maturity securities				
Bank and corporate debt	$1,333	$ —	$—	$1,333
Other debt securities	40	—	—	40
	$1,373	$ —	$—	$1,373

December 31,	Cost	Gross Unrealized Gains	Gross Unrealized Losses	Estimated Fair Value
Year 7				
Available-for-sale securities				
Equity securities	$ 377	$259	$(2)	$ 634
Collateralized mortgage obligations	145	—	(5)	140
Other debt securities	24	—	(1)	23
	$ 546	$259	$(8)	$ 797
Held-to-maturity securities				
Bank and corporate debt	$1,550	$ —	$(9)	$1,541
Other debt securities	58	—	—	58
	$1,608	$ —	$(9)	$1,599

On December 31, Year 6 and Year 7, these investments were included in the following captions on our consolidated balance sheets (in millions):

December 31,	Available-for-Sale Securities	Held-to-Maturity Securities
Year 6		
Cash and cash-equivalents	$—	$ 900
Current marketable securities	74	74
Cost method investments, principally bottling companies	222	—
Marketable securities and other assets	149	399
	$445	$1,373
Year 7		
Cash and cash-equivalents	$—	$1,208
Current marketable securities	68	157
Cost method investments, principally bottling companies	584	—
Marketable securities and other assets	145	243
	$797	$1,608

The contractual maturities of these investments as of December 31, Year 7, were as follows (in millions):

December 31,	Available-for-Sale Securities		Held-to-Maturity Securities	
	Cost	Fair Value	Amortized Cost	Fair Value
Year 8	$ 21	$ 20	$1,365	$1,365
Year 9–Year 12	3	3	223	214
After Year 12	—	—	20	20
Collateralized mortgage obligations ..	145	140	—	—
Equity securities	377	634	—	—
	$546	$797	$1,608	$1,599

For the years ended December 31, Year 6 and Year 7, gross realized gains and losses on sales of available-for-sale securities were not material. The cost of securities sold is based on the specific identification method.

8. HEDGING TRANSACTIONS AND DERIVATIVE FINANCIAL INSTRUMENTS

Our Company employs derivative financial instruments primarily to reduce our exposure to adverse fluctuations in interest rates, foreign exchange rates, commodity prices, and other market risks. These financial instruments, when entered into, are designated as hedges of underlying exposures. Because of the high correlation between the hedging instrument and the underlying exposure being hedged, fluctuations in the value of the instruments are generally offset by changes in the value of the underlying exposures. We effectively monitor the use of these derivative financial instruments through the use of objective measurement systems, well-defined market and credit risk limits, and timely reports to senior management according to prescribed guidelines. Virtually all of our derivates are "over-the-counter" instruments.

The estimated fair values of derivatives used to hedge or modify our risks fluctuate over time. These fair value amounts should not be viewed in isolation, but rather in relation to the fair values of the underlying hedged transactions and investments, and the overall reduction in our exposure to adverse fluctuations in interest rates, foreign exchange rates, commodity prices, and other market risks.

The notional amounts of the derivative financial instruments do not necessarily represent amounts exchanged by the parties and, therefore, are not a direct measure of our exposure through our use of derivatives. The amounts exchanged are calculated by reference to the notional amounts and by other terms of the derivatives, such as interest rates, exchange rates or other financial indices.

We have established strict counterparty credit guidelines and enter into transactions only with financial institutions of investment grade or better. Counterparty exposures are monitored daily, and any downgrade in credit rating receives immediate review. If a downgrade in the credit rating of a counterparty were to occur, we have provisions requiring collateral in the form of U.S. government securities for transactions with maturities in excess of three years. To mitigate presettlement risk, minimum credit standards become more stringent as the duration of the derivative financial instrument increases. To minimize the concentration of credit risk, we enter into derivative transactions with a portfolio of financial institutions. As a result, we consider the risk of counterparty default to be minimal.

Interest Rate Management.　Our management has implemented a policy to maintain our percentage of fixed- and variable-rate debt within certain parameters. We enter into interest rate swap agreements that maintain the fixed/variable mix within these defined parameters. These contracts had maturities ranging from one to seven years on December 31, Year 7. Variable rates are predominantly linked to LIBOR (London Interbank Offered Rate). Any differences paid or received on interest rate swap agreements are recognized as adjustments to interest expense over the life of each swap, thereby adjusting the effective interest rate on the underlying obligation.

Additionally, our company enters into interest rate cap agreements that entitle us to receive from a financial institution the amount, if any, by which our interest payments on our variable-rate debt exceed prespecified interest rates through Year 8. Premiums paid for interest rate cap agreements are included in prepaid expenses and other assets, and are amortized to interest expense over the terms of the respective agreements. Payments received pursuant to the interest rate cap agreements, if any, are recognized as an adjustment to the interest expense on the underlying debt instruments.

Foreign Currency Management.　The purpose of our foreign currency hedging activities is to reduce the risk that our eventual dollar net cash inflows resulting from sales outside the United States will be adversely affected by changes in exchange rates.

We enter into forward exchange contracts and purchase currency options (principally European currencies and Japanese yen) to hedge firm sale commitments denominated in foreign currencies. We also purchase currency options (principally European currencies and Japanese yen) to hedge certain anticipated sales. Premiums paid and realized gains and losses, including those on terminated contracts, if any, are included in prepaid expenses and other assets. These are recognized in income along with unrealized gains and losses, in the same period the hedged transactions are realized. Approximately $27 million and $17 million of realized losses on settled contracts entered into as hedges of firmly committed transactions that have not yet occurred were deferred on December 31, Year 6 and Year 7, respectively. Deferred gains/losses from hedging anticipated transactions were not material on December 31, Year 6 or Year 7. In the unlikely event that the underlying transaction terminates or becomes improbable, the deferred gains or losses on the associated derivative will be recorded in our income statement.

Gains and losses on derivative financial instruments that are designated and effective as hedges of net investments in international operations are included in shareowners' equity as a foreign currency translation adjustment.

The following table presents the aggregate notional principal amounts, carrying values, fair values, and maturities of our derivative financial instruments outstanding on December 31, Year 6 and Year 7 (in millions):

December 31,	Notional Principal Amounts	Carrying Values	Fair Values	Maturity
Year 6				
Interest rate management				
Swap agreements				
Assets	$ 705	$ 4	$ 30	Year 8–14
Liabilities	62	—	(2)	Year 11–13
Interest rate caps				
Assets	400	2	—	Year 8
Foreign currency management				
Forward contracts				
Assets	1,927	25	36	Year 7
Liabilities	554	(17)	(15)	Year 7–8
Swap agreements				
Assets	390	17	11	Year 7–11
Liabilities	1,686	(46)	(262)	Year 7–13
Purchased options				
Assets	1,823	62	90	Year 7
Other				
Assets	327	7	5	Year 7
	$7,874	$ 54	$(107)	

December 31,	Notional Principal Amounts	Carrying Values	Fair Values	Maturity
Year 7				
Interest rate management				
Swap agreements				
Assets	$ 893	$ 5	$ 13	Year 8–14
Liabilities	25	—	1	Year 13
Interest rate caps				
Assets	400	1	—	Year 8
Foreign currency management				
Forward contracts				
Assets	5	1	(2)	Year 8
Liabilities	2,541	(53)	(42)	Year 8–9
Swap agreements				
Assets	398	18	12	Year 8–9
Liabilities	1,086	(12)	(114)	Year 8–13
Purchased options				
Assets	1,873	42	89	Year 8
Other				
Assets	537	67	33	Year 8
	$7,758	$ 69	$ (10)	

Maturities of derivative financial instruments held on December 31, Year 7, are as follows (in millions):

Year 8	Year 9	Year 10	Year 11–14
$6,037	$622	$204	$895

9. COMMITMENTS AND CONTINGENCIES

On December 31, Year 7, we were contingently liable for guarantees of indebtedness owed by third parties in the amount of $274 million, of which $34 million related to independent bottling licenses.

The Mitsubishi Bank Limited has provided a yen-denominated guarantee for the equivalent of $269 million in support of a suspension of enforcement of a tax assessment levied by the Japanese tax authorities. We have agreed to indemnify Mitsubishi if amounts are paid pursuant to this guarantee. This matter is being reviewed by the tax authorities of the United States and Japan under the tax treaty signed by the two nations to prevent double taxation. Any additional income tax payable to Japan should be offset by income tax credits in the United States and would not adversely affect earnings.

Through our financial subsidiary, we have agreed to issue up to $50 million in letters of credit on CCNY's behalf, of which $21 million was committed on December 31, Year 7.

We do not consider it probable that we will be required to satisfy these guarantees or indemnification agreements. The fair value of these contingent liabilities is immaterial to our consolidated financial statements.

We believe our exposure to concentrations of credit risk is limited, due to the diverse geographic areas covered by our operations.

Additionally, under certain circumstances, we have committed to make future investments in bottling companies. However, we do not consider any of these commitments to be individually significant.

10. NET CHANGE IN OPERATING ASSETS AND LIABILITIES

The changes in operating assets and liabilities, net of effects of acquisitions and divestitures of businesses and unrealized exchange gains/losses, are as follows (in millions):

Year ended December 31,	Year 5	Year 6	Year 7
Increase in trade accounts receivable	$(169)	$(255)	$(230)
(Increase) decrease in inventories	43	(80)	(33)

(continued)

Year ended December 31,	Year 5	Year 6	Year 7
Increase in prepaid expenses and other assets ...	(95)	(160)	(65)
Increase in accounts payable and accrued expenses	197	214	361
Increase (decrease) in accrued taxes	200	26	(208)
Increase in other liabilities	131	63	211
	$ 307	$(192)	$ 36

11. RESTRICTED STOCK, STOCK OPTIONS, AND OTHER STOCK PLANS

Our Company sponsors restricted stock award plans, stock option plans, Incentive Unit Agreements, and Performance Unit Agreements. Our Company applies APB Opinion No. 25 and related Interpretations in accounting for our plans. Accordingly, for our stock option plans, no compensation cost has been recognized. The compensation cost that has been charged against income for our restricted stock award plans was $45 million in Year 6 and $63 million in Year 7. For our Incentive Unit Agreements and Performance Unit Agreements, the charge against income was $64 million in Year 6 and $90 million in Year 7. Had compensation cost for the stock option plans been determined based on the fair value at the grant dates for awards under the plans, consistent with the alternative method set forth under SFAS 123, our Company's net income per share would have been reduced.

The pro forma amounts are indicated below (in millions, except per share amounts):

Year Ended December 31,	Year 6	Year 7
Net income		
As reported	$2,986	$3,492
Pro forma	$2,933	$3,412
Net income per share		
As reported	$1.18	$1.40
Pro forma	$1.16	$1.37

Under the amended Restricted Stock Award Plan A and the amended Restricted Stock Award Plan B (the Restricted Stock Award Plans), 40 million and 24 million shares of restricted common stock, respectively, may be granted to certain officers and key employees of our Company.

On December 31, Year 7, 34 million shares were available for grant under the Restricted Stock Award Plans. In Year 6 and Year 7, 190,000 and 210,000 shares of restricted stock were granted at $35.63 and $48.88, respectively. Participants are entitled to vote and receive dividends on the shares, and under the Restricted Stock Award Plan B, participants are reimbursed by our Company for income taxes imposed on the award, but not for taxes generated by the reimbursement payments. The shares are subject to certain transfer restrictions and may be forfeited if a participant leaves our Company for reasons other than retirement, disability, or death, absent a change in control of our Company.

Under our Year 2 Stock Option Plan (the Option Plan), a maximum of 120 million shares of our common stock was approved to be issued or transferred to certain officers and employees pursuant to stock options and stock appreciation rights granted under the Option Plan. The stock appreciation rights permit the holder, upon surrendering all or part of the related stock option, to receive cash, common stock, or a combination thereof, in an amount up to 100 percent of the difference between the market price and the option price. Options to purchase common stock under the Option Plan have been granted to Company employees at fair market value at the date of grant. Generally, stock options become exercisable over a three-year vesting period and expire ten years from the date of grant.

The fair value of each option grant is estimated on the date of grant using the Black-Scholes option pricing model with the following weighted average assumptions used for grants in Year 6 and Year 7, respectively: dividend yields of 1.3 and 1.0 percent; expected volatility of 20.1 and 18.3 percent; risk-free interest rates of 5.9 and 6.2 percent; and expected lives of four years for both years. The weighted average fair value of options granted was $8.13 and $11.43 for the years ended December 31, Year 6 and Year 7, respectively.

A summary of stock option activity under all plans is as follows (shares in millions):

	Year 5		Year 6		Year 7	
	Shares	**Weighted-Average Exercise Price**	**Shares**	**Weighted-Average Exercise Price**	**Shares**	**Weighted-Average Exercise Price**
Outstanding on January 1, ...	60	$12.38	65	$15.53	74	$20.74
Granted	14	25.35	18	34.88	14	48.86
Exercised	(8)	7.81	(8)	10.63	(9)	13.72
Forfeited/Expired	(1)	20.95	(1)	24.84	(1)	31.62
Outstanding on December 31, ...	65	$15.53	74	$20.74	78	$26.50
Exercisable on December 31, ...	43	$11.31	45	$14.22	51	$18.69
Shares Available on December 31, for options that may be granted	46		59		76	

The following table summarizes information about stock options at December 31, Year 7 (shares in millions):

| Range of Exercise Prices | Outstanding Stock Options | | | Exercisable Stock Options | |
	Shares	Weighted-Average Remaining Contractual Life	Weighted-Average Exercise Price	Shares	Weighted-Average Exercise Price
$3.00 to $10.00	16	2.2 years	$ 6.74	16	$ 6.74
$10.01 to $20.00	5	4.5 years	$14.44	5	$14.44
$20.01 to $30.00	28	7.1 years	$23.60	24	$23.16
$30.01 to $40.00	15	8.8 years	$35.63	6	$35.63
$40.01 to $50.00	14	9.8 years	$48.86	—	—
$3.00 to $50.00	78	6.8 years	$26.50	51	$18.69

In an earlier year, our Company entered into Incentive Unit Agreements whereby, subject to certain conditions, certain officers were given the right to receive cash awards based on the market value of 2.4 million shares of our common stock at the measurement dates. Under the Incentive Unit Agreements, the employee is reimbursed by our Company for income taxes imposed when the value of the units is paid, but not for taxes generated by the reimbursement payment. At December 31, Year 6 and Year 7, approximately 1.6 million units were outstanding.

Also in an earlier year, we entered into Performance Unit Agreements, whereby certain officers were given the right to receive cash awards based on the difference in the market value of approximately 4.4 million shares of our common stock at the measurement dates and the base price of $2.58, the market value as of January 2 of the year the Performance Unit Agreement was instituted. At December 31, Year 6 and Year 7, approximately 2.9 million units were outstanding.

12. PENSION AND OTHER POSTRETIREMENT BENEFITS

Our Company sponsors and/or contributes to pension plans covering substantially all U.S. employees and certain employees in international locations. The benefits are primarily based on years of service and the employees' compensation for certain periods during the last years of employment. We generally fund pension costs currently, subject to regulatory funding limitations. We also sponsor nonqualified, unfunded defined benefit plans for certain officers and other employees. In addition, our Company and its subsidiaries have various pension plans and other forms of postretirement arrangements outside the United States.

Total pension expense for all benefit plans, including defined benefit plans, amounted to approximately $73 million in Year 5, $81 million in Year 6, and $85 million in Year 7. Net periodic pension cost for our defined benefit plans consists of the following (in millions):

Year ended December 31,	Year 5	Year 6	Year 7
Service cost-benefits earned during the period	$ 46	$ 43	$ 48
Interest cost on projected benefit obligation	78	89	91
Actual return on plan assets	(25)	(211)	(169)
Net amortization and deferral	(39)	145	103
Net periodic pension cost	$ 60	$ 66	$ 73

The funded status for our defined benefit plans is as follows (in millions):

December 31,	Assets Exceed Accumulated Benefits		Accumulated Benefits Exceed Assets	
	Year 6	Year 7	Year 6	Year 7
Actuarial present value of benefit obligations				
Vested benefit obligation	$ 731	$ 704	$ 286	$ 343
Accumulated benefit obligation	$ 790	$ 768	$ 316	$ 384
Projected benefit obligation	$ 919	$ 890	$ 394	$ 485
Plan assets at fair value[1]	1,044	1,126	112	156
Plan assets in excess of (less than) projected benefit obligation	125	236	(282)	(329)
Unrecognized net (asset) liability at transition	(44)	(39)	41	36
Unrecognized prior service cost	38	33	25	16
Unrecognized net (gain) loss	(84)	(191)	54	104
Adjustment required to recognize minimum liability	—	—	(60)	(66)
Accrued pension asset (liability) included in the consolidated balance sheet	$ 35	$ 39	$(222)	$(239)

[1]Primarily listed stocks, bonds, and government securities.

The assumptions used in computing the preceding information are as follows:

Year ended December 31,	Year 5	Year 6	Year 7
Discount rates	7½%	7%	7¼%
Rates of increase in compensation levels	5%	4¾%	4¾%
Expected long-term rates of return on assets	8¼%	8½%	8½%

Our Company has plans providing postretirement health care and life insurance benefits to substantially all U.S. employees and certain employees in international locations who retire with a minimum of five years of service. Net periodic cost for our postretirement health care and life insurance benefits consists of the following (in millions):

Year ended December 31,	Year 5	Year 6	Year 7
Service cost	$12	$ 12	$12
Interest cost	21	23	20
Other	(1)	(2)	(3)
	$32	$ 33	$29

In addition, we contribute to a Voluntary Employees' Beneficiary Association trust that will be used to partially fund health care benefits for future retirees. Generally, we fund benefits to the extent contributions are tax-deductible, which under current legislation is limited. In general, retiree health benefits are paid as covered expenses are incurred.

The funded status of our postretirement health care and life insurance plans is as follows (in millions):

December 31,	Year 6	Year 7
Accumulated postretirement benefit obligations:		
Retirees	$ 122	$ 114
Fully eligible active plan participants	40	35
Other active plan participants	141	130
Total benefit obligation	303	279
Plan assets at fair value[1]	42	41

December 31,	Year 6	Year 7
Plan assets less than benefit obligation	(261)	(238)
Unrecognized prior service cost	(3)	5
Unrecognized net gain	(9)	(57)
Accrued postretirement benefit liability included in the consolidated balance sheet	$ (273)	$(290)

[1]Consists of corporate bonds, government securities, and short-term investments.

The assumptions used in computing the preceding information are as follows:

Year Ended December 31,	Year 5	Year 6	Year 7
Discount Rate	8¼%	7¼%	7¾%
Rate of increase in compensation levels	5¼%	4¾%	5%

The rate of increase in the per capita costs of covered health care benefits is assumed to be 7¾ percent in Year 8, decreasing gradually to 5¼ percent by Year 14. Increasing the assumed health care cost trend rate by one percentage point would increase the accumulated postretirement benefit obligation as of December 31, Year 7, by approximately $33 million and increase the net periodic post-retirement benefit cost by approximately $5 million in Year 7.

13. INCOME TAXES

Income before income taxes consists of the following (in millions):

Year Ended December 31,	Year 5	Year 6	Year 7
United States	$1,214	$1,270	$1,168
International	2,514	3,058	3,428
	$3,728	$4,328	$4,596

Income tax expense (benefit) consists of the following (in millions):

Year Ended December 31,	United States	State & Local	International	Total
Year 5				
Current	$299	$38	$779	$1,116
Deferred	24	5	29	58
Year 6				
Current	$204	$41	$940	$1,185
Deferred	80	10	67	157
Year 7				
Current	$256	$79	$914	$1,249
Deferred	(264)	(29)	148	(145)

We made income tax payments of approximately $785 million, $1,000 million, and $1,242 million in Year 5, Year 6, and Year 7, respectively.

A reconciliation of the statutory U.S. federal rate and effective rates is as follows:

Year Ended December 31,	Year 5	Year 6	Year 7
Statutory U.S. federal rate	35.0%	35.0%	35.0%
State income taxes—net of federal benefit	1.0	1.0	1.0
Earnings in jurisdictions taxed at rates different from the statutory U.S. federal rate	(4.3)	(3.9)	(3.3)
Equity income	(1.1)	(1.7)	(1.7)
Tax settlement	—	—	(7.0)
Other—net	.9	.6	—
	31.5%	31.0%	24.0%

In Year 7, we reached an agreement in principle with the U.S. Internal Revenue Service (IRS) settling certain U.S.-related income tax matters. The agreement included issues in litigation involving our operations in Puerto Rico through Year 6. This agreement resulted in a one-time reduction of $320 million to our Year 7 income tax expense as a result of reversing previously accrued contingent income tax liabilities.

Our effective tax rate reflects the favorable U.S. tax treatment of manufacturing facilities in Puerto Rico that operate under a negotiated exemption grant that expires December 31, Year 20. Changes to U.S. tax law enacted in Year 4 limit the utilization of the favorable tax treatment of operations in Puerto Rico. Our effective tax rate also reflects the tax benefit derived from having significant operations outside the United States that are taxed at rates lower than the U.S. statutory rate of 35 percent. Our Year 7 effective tax rate would have been 31 percent, excluding the favorable impact of the settlement with the IRS.

Appropriate U.S. and international taxes have been provided for earnings of subsidiary companies that are expected to be remitted to the parent company. Exclusive of amounts that would result in little or no tax if remitted, the cumulative amount of unremitted earnings from our international subsidiaries that is expected to be indefinitely reinvested is approximately $542 million on December 31, Year 7. The taxes that would be paid upon remittance of these indefinitely reinvested earnings are approximately $190 million, based on current tax laws.

The tax effects of temporary differences and carryforwards that give rise to significant portion of deferred tax assets and liabilities consist of the following (in millions):

December 31,	Year 6	Year 7
Deferred tax assets:		
Benefit plans	$ 369	$414
Liabilities and reserves	178	164
Net operating loss carryforwards	97	130
Other	151	88
Gross deferred tax assets	795	796
Valuation allowance	(42)	(18)
	$ 753	$778
Deferred tax liabilities:		
Property, plant, and equipment	$ 414	$200
Equity investments	170	369
Intangible assets	89	74
Other	205	33
	$ 878	$676
Net deferred tax asset (liability)[1]	$ (125)	$102

[1]Deferred tax assets of $69 million and $403 million have been included in the consolidated balance sheet caption "marketable securities and other assets" at December 31, Year 6 and Year 7, respectively.

On December 31, Year 7, we had $261 million of operating loss carryforwards available to reduce future taxable income of certain international subsidiaries. Loss carryforwards of $17 million must be utilized within the next five years; $244 million can be utilized over an indefinite period. A valuation allowance has been provided for a portion of the deferred tax assets related to these loss carryforwards.

14. NONRECURRING ITEMS

In the third quarter of Year 7, we made a series of decisions that resulted in provisions of approximately $276 million in selling, administrative, and general expenses related to our plans for strengthening our worldwide system. Of this $276 million, approximately $130 million related to the streamlining of our operations, primarily in Greater Europe and Latin America. Our management has taken actions to consolidate certain manufacturing operations and, as a result, recorded charges to recognize the impairment of certain manufacturing assets and to recognize the estimated losses on the disposal of other assets. The remainder of this $276 million provision related to actions taken by The Minute Maid Company (formerly known as Coca-Cola Foods). During the third quarter of Year 7, The Minute Maid Company entered into two significant agreements with independent parties: (a) a strategic supply alliance with Sucocitrico Cutrale Ltda., the world's largest grower and processor of oranges, and (b) a joint venture agreement with Groupe Danone to produce, distribute, and sell premium refrigerated juices outside the United States and Canada. With these agreements, we intend to increase the Minute Maid Company's focus on managing its brands while seeking arrangements to lower its overall manufacturing costs. In connection with these actions, we recorded $146 million in third quarter provisions, representing primarily impairment charges to certain production facilities and reserves for losses on the disposal of other production facilities.

Also in the third quarter of Year 7, we launched a strategic initiative, Project Infinity, to redesign and enhance our information systems and communications capabilities. In connection with this initiative, we recorded an $80 million impairment charge in administrative and general expenses to recognize Project Infinity's impact on existing information systems.

Based upon management's commitment to certain strategic actions during the third quarter of Year 7, these impairment charges were recorded to reduce the carrying value of identified assets to fair value. Fair values were derived using a variety of methodologies, including cash flow analysis, estimates of sales proceeds, and independent appraisals.

Also in the third quarter of Year 7, we recorded a charge in administrative and general expenses as a result of our decision to contribute $28.5 million to the corpus of The Coca-Cola Foundation, a not-for-profit charitable organization.

During Year 6, selling, administrative, and general expenses included provisions of $86 million to increase efficiencies in our operations in North America and Europe.

15. SUBSEQUENT EVENT

In Year 7, we executed an agreement to sell our 49 percent interest in Coca-Cola & Schweppes Beverages Ltd. to Coca-Cola Enterprises. This transaction closed in early Year 8 and resulted in gross proceeds to our Company of approximately U.S. $1 billion, and an after-tax gain of approximately $.08 per share.

16. OPERATIONS IN GEOGRAPHIC AREAS

Information about the Company's operations by geographic area is as follows (in millions):

	North America	Africa	Greater Europe	Latin America	Middle & Far East	Corporate	Consolidated
Year 5							
Net operating revenues	$5,327	$522	$5,029	$1,928	$3,333	$42	$16,181
Operating income	915	174	1,129	710	1,150	(441)	3,637
Identifiable operating assets	3,085	356	3,959	1,164	1,343	1,456[1]	11,363
Equity income						134	134
Investments (principally bottling companies)						2,510	2,510
Capital expenditures ...	253	27	330	129	50	89	878
Depreciation and amortization	130	6	160	36	19	60	411

	North America	Africa	Greater Europe	Latin America	Middle & Far East	Corporate	Consolidated
Year 6							
Net operating revenues	$5,513	$595	$5,999	$1,920	$3,936	$55	$18,018
Operating income	856[2]	205	1,256[2]	798	1,394	(483)	4,026
Identifiable operating assets	3,478	348	4,301	1,294	1,445	1,461[1]	12,327
Equity income						169	169
Investments (principally bottling companies)						2,714	2,714
Capital expenditures ...	286	19	383	87	85	77	937
Depreciation and amortization	148	8	180	31	21	66	454

	North America	Africa	Greater Europe	Latin America	Middle & Far East	Corporate	Consolidated
Year 7							
Net operating revenues	$6,050	$476	$5,947	$1,991	$4,035	$47	$18,546
Operating income	949[3]	118[3]	1,277[3]	815[3]	1,358[3]	(602)[3]	3,915
Identifiable operating assets	3,814	326	2,896	1,405	1,463	2,088[1]	11,992
Equity income						211	211
Investments (principally bottling companies)						4,169	4,169

(continued)

	North America	Africa	Greater Europe	Latin America	Middle & Far East	Corporate	Consolidated
Capital expenditures ..	261	32	379	79	121	118	990
Depreciation and amortization	157	8	176	37	25	76	479

Intercompany transfers between geographic areas are not material.

North America includes only the United States and Canada.

Prior year amounts have been reclassified to conform to the current year presentation.

[1]Corporate identifiable operating assets are composed principally of marketable securities, finance subsidiary receivables, and fixed assets.

[2]Operating income for North America and Greater Europe was reduced by $61 million and $25 million, respectively, for provisions to increase efficiencies.

[3]Operating income for North America, Africa, Greater Europe, Latin America, and the Middle and Far East was reduced by $153 million, $7 million, $66 million, $32 million ,and $18 million, respectively, for provisions related to management's strategic plans to strengthen our worldwide system. Corporate operating income was reduced by $80 million for Project Infinity's impairment impact to existing systems and by $28.5 million for our decision to contribute to the corpus of The Coca-Cola Foundation.

Compound Average Growth Rates Ending Year 7	North America	Africa	Greater Europe	Latin America	Middle & Far East	Consolidated
Net operating revenues						
5 years	6%	18%	10%	13%	14%	10%
10 years	6%	11%	15%	14%	11%	10%
Operating income						
5 years	9%	2%	8%	15%	13%	11%
10 years	12%	19%	15%	19%	15%	16%

REPORT OF INDEPENDENT AUDITORS

BOARD OF DIRECTORS AND SHARE OWNERS

THE COCA-COLA COMPANY

We have audited the accompanying consolidated balance sheets of The Coca-Cola Company and subsidiaries as of December 31, Year 6 and Year 7, and the related consolidated statements of income, shareowners' equity, and cash flows for each of the three years in the period ended December 31, Year 7. These financial statements are the responsibility of the Company's management. Our responsibility is to express an opinion on these financial statements based on our audits.

We conducted our audits in accordance with generally accepted auditing standards. Those standards require that we plan and perform the audit to obtain reasonable assurance about whether the financial statements are free of material misstatement. An audit includes examining, on a test basis, evidence supporting the amounts and disclosures in the financial statements. An audit also includes as-sessing the accounting principles used and significant estimates made by manage-ment, as well as evaluating the overall financial statement presentation. We believe that our audits provide a reasonable basis for our opinion.

In our opinion, the financial statements referred to above present fairly, in all material respects, the consolidated financial position of The Coca-Cola Company and subsidiaries at December 31, Year 6 and Year 7, and the consolidated results of their operations and their cash flows for each of the three years in the period ended December 31, Year 7, in conformity with generally accepted accounting principles.

Ernst & Young LLP
Atlanta, Georgia

January 24, Year 8

REPORT OF MANAGEMENT

We are responsible for the preparation and integrity of the consolidated financial statements appearing in our Annual Report. The financial statements were pre-pared in conformity with generally accepted accounting principles appropriate in the circumstances and, accordingly, include certain amounts based on our best judgments and estimates. Financial information in this Annual Report is consis-tent with that in the financial statements.

We are responsible for maintaining a system of internal accounting controls and procedures to provide reasonable assurance, at an appropriate cost/benefit rela-tionship, that assets are safeguarded and that transactions are authorized, recorded, and reported properly. The internal accounting control system is aug-mented by a program of internal audits and appropriate reviews by management, written policies and guidelines, careful selecting and training of qualified person-nel, and a written Code of Business Conduct adopted by our Company's Board of Directors, applicable to all employees of our Company and our subsidiaries. In our opinion, our Company's internal accounting controls provide reasonable assurance that assets are safeguarded against material loss from unauthorized use or disposi-tion and that the financial records are reliable for preparing financial statements and other data and for maintaining accountability of assets.

The Audit Committee of our Company's Board of directors, composed solely of Directors who are not officers of our Company, meets with the independent audi-tors, management, and internal auditors periodically to discuss internal accounting controls and auditing and financial reporting matters. The committee reviews with the independent auditors the scope and results of the audit effort. The Committee also meets with the independent auditors and the chief internal auditor without management present to ensure that the independent auditors and the chief inter-nal auditor have free access to the Committee.

The independent auditors, Ernst & Young LLP, are recommended by the Audit Committee of the Board of Directors, selected by the Board of Directors, and ratified by our Company's shareowners. Ernst & Young LLP is engaged to audit the consolidated financial statements of The Coca-Cola Company and subsidiaries and conduct such tests and related procedures as it deems necessary in conformity with generally accepted auditing standards. The opinion of the independent auditors, based upon their audits of the consolidated financial statements, is contained in this Annual Report.

M. Douglas Ivestor
Chairman, Board of Directors,
and Chief Executive Officer

James E. Chestnut
Senior Vice President
and Chief Financial Officer

Gary P. Fayard
Vice President
and Controller

January 24, Year 8

FINANCIAL REVIEW FOR THE COCA-COLA COMPANY AND SUBSIDIARIES INCORPORATING MANAGEMENT'S DISCUSSION AND ANALYSIS

We exist for one reason: to maximize shareowner value over time. To fulfill this mission, The Coca-Cola Company and its subsidiaries (our Company) have developed a comprehensive business strategy focused on four key objectives: (1) increasing volume; (2) expanding our share of beverage sales worldwide; (3) maximizing our long-term cash flows; and (4) improving economic profit and creating economic value-added. We achieve these objectives by strategically investing in the high-return beverages business and by optimizing our cost of capital through appropriate financial policies.

INVESTMENTS

With a global business system that operates in nearly 200 countries and generates superior cash flows, our Company is uniquely positioned to capitalize on profitable new investment opportunities. Our criterion for investment is simple: We seek to invest in opportunities that enhance our existing operations and offer cash returns that exceed our long-term after-tax weighted average cost of capital, estimated to be approximately 11 percent.

Because it consistently generates high returns on capital, our business is a particularly attractive investment for us. In developing and emerging markets, where increasing the penetration of our beverage products is our primary goal, we dedicate the bulk of our investments to infrastructure enhancements: production facilities, distribution networks, sales equipment, and technology. We make these investments by acquiring or forming strategic business alliances with local bottlers and by matching local expertise with our experience and focus. In highly

871

developed markets, where our primary goal is to make our products the beverages consumers prefer, we dedicate the bulk of our expenditures to marketing activities.

Currently, 55 percent of the world's population lives in markets where the average person consumes fewer than ten servings of our beverages per year, offering high-potential growth opportunities for our Company and our bottlers. In fact, the emerging markets of China, India, Indonesia, and Russia combined represent approximately 44 percent of the world's population but, on a combined basis, the average per capita consumption of our products in these markets is approximately 1 percent of the United States' level. As a result, we are investing aggressively to ensure our products are *pervasive* and *preferred*, and offer the best *price* relative to value.

Our investment strategy focuses primarily on the four fundamental drivers of our business: bottling operations, capital expenditures, marketing activities, and people.

BOTTLING OPERATIONS

We continue our well-established strategy of strengthening our distribution system by investing in, and subsequently reselling, ownership positions in bottling operations. This strategy provides our Company with yet another value stream resulting from the gains on the sale of these investments. The other value streams from which we benefit are those provided by our core concentrate business and our consolidated bottling operations, as well as our participation in the earnings of bottlers in which we remain an equity investor.

We have business relationships with three types of bottlers—independently owned bottlers, bottlers in which we have a noncontrolling ownership interest, and bottlers in which we have a controlling ownership interest. Independently owned bottlers are bottlers in which we have no ownership interest. These bottlers produced and distributed approximately 40 percent of our Year 7 worldwide unit case volume.

The other bottlers represent businesses in which we have invested. In Year 7, bottlers in which we own a noncontrolling ownership interest produced and distributed an additional 45 percent of our total worldwide unit case volume. Controlled and consolidated bottling and fountain operations produced and distributed approximately 15 percent of total worldwide unit case volume for Company products.

We invest heavily in certain bottling operations to maximize the strength and efficiency of our production, distribution, and marketing systems around the world. These investments often result in increases in unit case volume, net revenues, and profits at the bottler level, which in turn generate increased gallon shipments for our concentrate business. As a result, both our Company and the bottlers benefit from long-term growth in volume, cash flows, and shareowner value.

The level of our investment generally depends on the bottler's capital structure and its available resources at the time of our investment. In certain situations, it can be advantageous to acquire a controlling interest in a bottling operation. Although it is not our primary long-term business strategy, owning a controlling interest allows us to compensate for limited local resources or facilitate improvements in customer relationships while building or restructuring the bottling operations. Bottling businesses typically generate lower margins on revenue than our concentrate business. However, the acquisition and consolidation of a bottler increases revenues and generally increases operating profits on a per gallon basis.

APPENDIX C

OUTPUT OF FINANCIAL STATEMENT ANALYSIS PACKAGE (FSAP) FOR THE COCA-COLA COMPANY AND SUBSIDIARIES

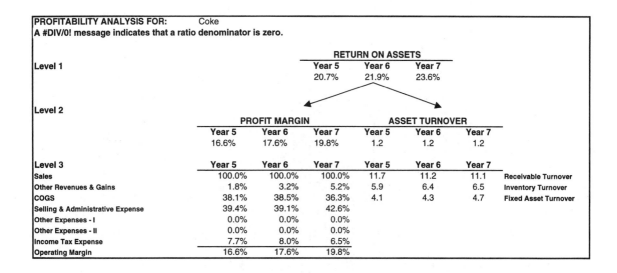

PROFITABILITY ANALYSIS FOR: Coke
A #DIV/0! message indicates that a ratio denominator is zero.

Level 1

	RETURN ON ASSETS		
	Year 5	Year 6	Year 7
	20.7%	21.9%	23.6%

Level 2

	PROFIT MARGIN			ASSET TURNOVER		
	Year 5	Year 6	Year 7	Year 5	Year 6	Year 7
	16.6%	17.6%	19.8%	1.2	1.2	1.2

Level 3	Year 5	Year 6	Year 7	Year 5	Year 6	Year 7	
Sales	100.0%	100.0%	100.0%	11.7	11.2	11.1	Receivable Turnover
Other Revenues & Gains	1.8%	3.2%	5.2%	5.9	6.4	6.5	Inventory Turnover
COGS	38.1%	38.5%	36.3%	4.1	4.3	4.7	Fixed Asset Turnover
Selling & Administrative Expense	39.4%	39.1%	42.6%				
Other Expenses - I	0.0%	0.0%	0.0%				
Other Expenses - II	0.0%	0.0%	0.0%				
Income Tax Expense	7.7%	8.0%	6.5%				
Operating Margin	16.6%	17.6%	19.8%				

COMPANY NAME:	Coke					
YEAR	Year 3	Year 4	Year 5	Year 6	Year 7	
PROFITABILITY FACTORS:						
A #DIV/0! message indicates that a ratio denominator is zero.						
RETURN ON ASSETS:						
Profit Margin	15.3%	16.5%	16.6%	17.6%	19.8%	
x Asset Turnover	1.2	1.2	1.2	1.2	1.2	
= Return on Assets	18.7%	19.8%	20.7%	21.9%	23.6%	
RETURN ON COMMON EQUITY:						
Return on Assets	18.7%	19.8%	20.7%	21.9%	23.6%	
x Common Earnings Leverage	94.4%	95.2%	95.2%	94.4%	94.9%	
x Capital Structure Leverage	2.7	2.7	2.6	2.7	2.7	
= Return on Common Equity	47.4%	51.8%	52.0%	56.2%	60.5%	
OPERATING PERFORMANCE:						
Gross Margin / Sales	61.3%	63.0%	61.9%	61.5%	63.7%	
Operating Profit Before Taxes / Revenues	22.1%	23.6%	23.8%	24.7%	25.0%	
Net Income - Continuous Ops / Revenues	14.2%	15.4%	15.5%	16.1%	17.9%	
Comprehensive Income / Revenues	12.2%	14.4%	16.4%	15.2%	16.7%	
ASSET TURNOVER:						
Sales / Avg. Accounts Receivable	12.7	12.0	11.7	11.2	11.1	
COGS / Average Inventory	5.0	5.0	5.9	6.4	6.5	
Sales / Average Fixed Assets	4.1	3.8	4.1	4.3	4.7	

COMPANY NAME:	Coke					
YEAR	Year 3	Year 4	Year 5	Year 6	Year 7	
RISK FACTORS:						
A #DIV/0! message indicates that a ratio denominator is zero.						
LIQUIDITY:						
Current Ratio	0.80	0.86	0.84	0.74	0.80	
Quick Ratio	0.41	0.45	0.49	0.41	0.45	
Days Payables Held	150	157	142	148	169	
Days Receivables Held	29	30	31	33	33	
Days Inventory Held	72	73	62	57	56	
Operating Cash Flow to Current Liabilities	47.4%	47.9%	56.1%	49.2%	46.9%	
SOLVENCY:						
Total Liabilities / Total Assets	65.4%	61.9%	62.3%	64.2%	61.9%	
LT Debt / (LT Debt + Share Equity)	22.5%	23.8%	21.4%	17.5%	15.3%	
LT Debt / Share Equity	29.0%	31.2%	27.2%	21.2%	18.1%	
Operating Cash Flow to Total Liabilities	33.4%	34.1%	39.6%	36.4%	35.2%	
Interest Coverage Ratio	17.06	19.96	19.73	16.91	17.07	
Operating Cash Flow to Cap. Exp.	2.06	3.14	3.63	3.55	3.50	
Altman's Z Score	2.9	3.1	3.1	3.3	3.4	

COMPANY NAME: Coke

INCOME STATEMENT ITEMS AS % OF SALES:

A #DIV/0! message indicates that a ratio denominator is zero.

YEAR	Year 3	Year 4	Year 5	Year 6	Year 7
Sales	100.0%	100.0%	100.0%	100.0%	100.0%
Cost of Goods Sold	38.7%	37.0%	38.1%	38.5%	36.3%
GROSS MARGIN	61.3%	63.0%	61.9%	61.5%	63.7%
Other Revenues & Gains	1.1%	1.8%	1.8%	3.2%	5.2%
Selling & Admin. Expense	40.1%	40.8%	39.4%	39.1%	42.6%
Other Expenses & Losses - I	0.0%	0.0%	0.0%	0.0%	0.0%
Other Expenses & Losses - II	0.0%	0.0%	0.0%	0.0%	0.0%
Income Tax Expense	7.1%	7.6%	7.7%	8.0%	6.5%
OPERATING MARGIN	15.3%	16.5%	16.6%	17.6%	19.8%
Interest Expense	1.3%	1.2%	1.2%	1.5%	1.5%
Income Tax Savings on Interest	0.5%	0.4%	0.4%	0.5%	0.5%
Minority Interest in Earnings	0.0%	0.0%	0.0%	0.0%	0.0%
Income from Continuing Ops	14.4%	15.7%	15.8%	16.6%	18.8%
Income from Discontinued Ops	0.0%	0.0%	0.0%	0.0%	0.0%
Extraordinary Gains (Losses)	0.0%	0.0%	0.0%	0.0%	0.0%
Changes in Actg. Principles	0.0%	0.0%	0.0%	0.0%	0.0%
NET INCOME	14.4%	15.7%	15.8%	16.6%	18.8%
Other Equity Adjustments	-2.0%	-1.1%	0.9%	-0.8%	-1.3%
COMPREHENSIVE INCOME	12.4%	14.6%	16.7%	15.7%	17.5%

COMPANY NAME:	Coke					COMPOUND GROWTH RATE
YEAR	Year 3	Year 4	Year 5	Year 6	Year 7	
INCOME STATEMENT ITEMS--INTERPERIOD % CHANGES:						
A #DIV/0! message indicates that a ratio denominator is zero.						
	INTERPERIOD % CHANGES					
Sales	13.0%	6.8%	15.9%	11.4%	2.9%	9.1%
Cost of Goods Sold	8.7%	2.1%	19.5%	12.5%	-2.9%	7.4%
GROSS MARGIN	15.8%	9.7%	13.8%	10.6%	6.6%	10.2%
Selling & Admin. Expense	14.0%	8.5%	12.0%	10.6%	11.9%	10.7%
Income Tax Expense	10.9%	14.4%	17.8%	15.6%	-16.2%	6.4%
OPERATING MARGIN	14.4%	15.2%	16.8%	17.9%	16.3%	16.5%
Interest Expense	-10.9%	-1.8%	18.5%	36.7%	5.1%	13.7%
Income Tax Savings on Interest	-10.9%	-1.8%	18.5%	36.7%	5.1%	13.7%
Minority Interest in Earnings	#DIV/0!	#DIV/0!	#DIV/0!	#DIV/0!	#DIV/0!	#DIV/0!
Income from Continuing Ops	16.4%	16.2%	16.7%	16.9%	16.9%	16.7%
Income from Discontinued Ops	#DIV/0!	#DIV/0!	#DIV/0!	#DIV/0!	#DIV/0!	#DIV/0!
Extraordinary Gains (Losses)	#DIV/0!	#DIV/0!	#DIV/0!	#DIV/0!	#DIV/0!	#DIV/0!
Changes in Actg. Principles	#DIV/0!	#DIV/0!	#DIV/0!	#DIV/0!	#DIV/0!	#DIV/0!
NET INCOME	16.4%	16.2%	16.7%	16.9%	16.9%	16.7%
Other Equity Adjustments	#DIV/0!	-44.2%	-199.3%	-202.7%	56.6%	-2.8%
COMPREHENSIVE INCOME	-0.1%	26.2%	32.5%	4.9%	14.8%	19.1%

COMPANY NAME: Coke

BALANCE SHEET COMMON SIZE STATEMENT:
A #DIV/0! message indicates that a ratio denominator is zero.

YEAR	Year 3	Year 4	Year 5	Year 6	Year 7
ASSETS:					
Cash and Marketable. Securities	9.5%	9.0%	11.0%	8.7%	10.3%
Accounts / Notes Receivable	9.7%	10.3%	11.0%	11.3%	10.2%
Inventories (EOP)	9.1%	8.7%	7.5%	7.4%	5.9%
Other Current Assets	9.7%	8.9%	7.9%	8.8%	10.3%
CURRENT ASSETS	38.1%	36.9%	37.5%	36.2%	36.6%
Investments	26.0%	27.5%	28.3%	28.7%	36.8%
Property, Plant & Equipment	47.0%	46.6%	44.4%	44.3%	34.5%
less: Accumulated Depreciation	15.4%	15.5%	15.0%	15.4%	12.6%
Other Assets	4.3%	4.6%	4.8%	6.3%	4.7%
TOTAL ASSETS	100.0%	100.0%	100.0%	100.0%	100.0%
LIABILITIES:					
Accounts Payable - Trade	20.2%	18.4%	18.5%	20.6%	18.4%
Notes Payable	18.6%	13.8%	14.8%	15.8%	21.0%
Current Portion of LT Debt	0.1%	0.2%	0.3%	3.7%	0.1%
Other Current Liabilities	8.6%	10.7%	11.0%	8.8%	6.4%
CURRENT LIABILITIES	47.6%	43.0%	44.5%	48.9%	45.8%
Long Term Debt	10.0%	11.9%	10.3%	7.6%	6.9%
Deferred Tax (NCL)	1.5%	0.9%	1.3%	1.3%	1.9%
Other Non-Current Liabilities	6.3%	6.0%	6.2%	6.4%	7.3%
NON-CURRENT LIABILITIES	17.8%	18.9%	17.7%	15.3%	16.1%
TOTAL LIABILITIES	65.4%	61.9%	62.3%	64.2%	61.9%
STOCKHOLDERS' EQUITY					
Minority Interest in Subsidiaries	0.0%	0.0%	0.0%	0.0%	0.0%
Preferred Stock	0.0%	0.0%	0.0%	0.0%	0.0%
Common Stock	3.8%	3.5%	3.1%	5.7%	5.3%
Additional Paid-in Capital	6.9%	8.3%	7.9%	5.7%	6.5%
Retained Earnings	73.0%	78.7%	79.7%	85.7%	94.2%
Treasury Stock	46.6%	48.9%	51.0%	58.5%	63.9%
Other Equity Adjustments	-2.4%	-3.5%	-2.0%	-2.8%	-4.1%
SHAREHOLDERS' EQUITY	34.6%	38.1%	37.7%	35.8%	38.1%
TOTAL EQUITIES	100.0%	100.0%	100.0%	100.0%	100.0%

COMPANY NAME:	Coke						COMPOUND GROWTH RATE
YEAR	Year 3	Year 4	Year 5	Year 6	Year 7		
BALANCE SHEET - INTERPERIOD % CHANGES:							
A #DIV/0! message indicates that a ratio denominator is zero.							
ASSETS:	INTERPERIOD % CHANGES						
Cash and Mkt. Securities	-4.8%	1.4%	42.0%	-14.1%	26.1%		8.2%
Accounts / Notes Receivable	12.0%	14.5%	22.7%	11.1%	-3.2%		11.1%
Inventories (EOP)	3.1%	2.9%	-0.2%	6.7%	-14.8%		-0.7%
Other Current Assets	1.0%	-1.5%	3.6%	20.1%	25.4%		9.2%
CURRENT ASSETS	2.5%	4.4%	17.4%	4.7%	8.4%		7.4%
Investments	5.7%	14.3%	18.7%	9.8%	38.0%		16.8%
Property, Plant & Equipment	18.0%	6.7%	10.0%	8.1%	-16.2%		4.7%
less: Accumulated Depreciation	10.4%	8.7%	11.2%	11.7%	-12.5%		5.5%
Other Assets	22.0%	13.7%	20.2%	43.0%	-20.2%		13.7%
TOTAL ASSETS	9.7%	7.8%	15.4%	8.4%	7.4%		9.7%
LIABILITIES:							
Accounts Payable - Trade	17.7%	-1.6%	15.7%	21.0%	-4.2%		9.2%
Notes Payable	73.7%	-20.2%	23.9%	15.8%	42.8%		23.2%
Current Portion of LT Debt	-86.4%	26.7%	84.2%	1477.1%	-98.4%		-39.4%
Other Current Liabilities	6.9%	33.1%	19.3%	-13.6%	-21.6%		2.9%
CURRENT LIABILITIES	28.8%	-2.5%	19.5%	19.0%	0.8%		12.4%
Long Term Debt	13.7%	27.5%	-0.1%	-20.0%	-2.2%		2.5%
Deferred Tax (NCL)	53.7%	-31.9%	59.3%	7.8%	55.2%		22.8%
Other Non-Current Liabilities	-20.4%	3.7%	17.9%	13.0%	22.4%		6.1%
NON-CURRENT LIABILITIES	0.7%	14.2%	8.6%	-6.5%	13.0%		5.7%
TOTAL LIABILITIES	19.7%	2.0%	16.1%	11.7%	3.7%		10.4%
STOCKHOLDERS' EQUITY							
Minority Interest in Subsidiaries	#DIV/0!	#DIV/0!	#DIV/0!	#DIV/0!	#DIV/0!		#DIV/0!
Preferred Stock	#DIV/0!	#DIV/0!	#DIV/0!	#DIV/0!	#DIV/0!		#DIV/0!
Common Stock	0.5%	0.5%	0.2%	100.5%	0.2%		15.2%
Additional Paid-in Capital	46.9%	29.8%	9.8%	-21.5%	22.6%		15.0%
Retained Earnings	15.0%	16.2%	16.9%	16.7%	18.0%		16.5%
Treasury Stock	31.9%	13.1%	20.3%	24.4%	17.3%		21.2%
Other Equity Adjustments	5320.0%	55.0%	-35.2%	55.9%	56.1%		165.7%
SHAREHOLDERS' EQUITY	-5.3%	18.6%	14.2%	3.0%	14.2%		8.6%
TOTAL EQUITIES	9.7%	7.8%	15.4%	8.4%	7.4%		9.7%

SUMMARY OF KEY FINANCIAL STATEMENT RATIOS

Profitability Ratios

$$\text{Profit Margin for ROA} = \frac{[\text{Net Income} + (1 - \text{Tax Rate})(\text{Interest Expense}) + \text{Minority Interest in Earnings}]}{\text{Sales}}$$

$$\text{Total Assets Turnover} = \frac{\text{Sales}}{\text{Average Total Assets}}$$

$$\text{Return on Assets (ROA)} = \frac{[\text{Net Income} + (1 - \text{Tax Rate})(\text{Interest Expense}) + \text{Minority Interest in Earnings}]}{\text{Average Total Assets}}$$

$$\frac{\text{Common Earnings}}{\text{Leverage Ratio}} = \frac{(\text{Net Income} - \text{Preferred Dividends})}{[\text{Net Income} + (1 - \text{Tax Rate})(\text{Interest Expense}) + \text{Minority Interest in Earnings}]}$$

$$\text{Capital Structure Leverage Ratio} = \frac{\text{Average Total Assets}}{\text{Average Common Shareholders' Equity}}$$

$$\text{Return on Common Equity (ROCE)} = \frac{(\text{Net Income} - \text{Preferred Dividends})}{\text{Average Common Shareholders' Equity}}$$

$$\text{Cost of Goods Sold Percentage} = \frac{\text{Cost of Goods Sold}}{\text{Sales}}$$

$$\text{Selling and Administrative Expense Percentage} = \frac{\text{Selling and Administrative Expense}}{\text{Sales}}$$

$$\text{Income Tax Expense Percentage (on operating income)} = \frac{[\text{Income Tax Expense} + (\text{Tax Rate})(\text{Interest Expense})]}{\text{Sales}}$$

$$\text{Accounts Receivable Turnover} = \frac{\text{Sales}}{\text{Average Accounts Receivable}}$$

$$\text{Inventory Turnover} = \frac{\text{Cost of Goods Sold}}{\text{Average Inventories}}$$

$$\text{Fixed Asset Turnover} = \frac{\text{Sales}}{\text{Average Fixed Assets}}$$